THE BLACKWELL COMPANION TO
JEWISH CULTURE

THE BLACKWELL COMPANION TO

JEWISH CULTURE

From the Eighteenth Century to the Present

Edited by GLENDA ABRAMSON

Advisory Editors
DOVID KATZ
NICHOLAS DE LANGE
CHAIM RABIN
EZRA SPICEHANDLER

Blackwell Reference

Copyright © Basil Blackwell Ltd 1989
Editorial organization © Glenda Abramson 1989

First published 1989   .

Basil Blackwell Ltd
108 Cowley Road, Oxford, OX4 1JF, UK

Basil Blackwell, Inc.
3 Cambridge Center
Cambridge, Massachusetts 02142, USA

British Library Cataloguing in Publication Data
A CIP catalog record for this book is available from the
British Library.

Library of Congress Cataloging in Publication Data
The Blackwell companion to Jewish culture : from the
eighteenth century to the present / edited by Glenda
Abramson ; advisory editors, Dovid Katz. . . [et al.].
    p. cm.
Bibliography: p.
Includes index.
ISBN 0–631–15111–7
1. Jews—Dictionaries and encyclopedias.
2. Jews—Civilization—Dictionaries. 3. Civilization,
Modern—Jewish influences—Dictionaries. I. Abramson,
Glenda. II. Katz, Dovid.
DS102.8.B46   1989
909′.04924—dc19   89–1008 CIP

Typeset in 10½/12pt Baskerville by Graphicraft, Hong Kong
Printed in Great Britain by Butler and Tanner Ltd, Frome

Contents

Preface

Context and background

The past two centuries have seen an almost unprecedented explosion of talent and scholarship within international Jewish communities. During this time the Jews have found themselves with varying degrees of liberty throughout western Europe, they have migrated from the Pale of Settlement in the east to the USA, Britain, and the British colonies; they have vigorously revived their culture after its having been marked for extinction by the Nazis; they founded the State of Israel in 1948, which has both consolidated and disseminated some of the best and most significant elements of this culture. These major, often cataclysmic, events and their effects on modern Jewish life emerge clearly from the many penetrating reviews and analyses by contributors to this volume.

In 1939 Cecil Roth published *The Jewish Contribution to Civilization* in which he aimed "to assemble and set down . . . a representative selection (at least) of the contribution made to the civilization, culture and the amenities of the western world by persons of Jewish lineage." Roth codified what had already long been established: the fruitful interrelationship between western culture and Jewish creative activity that has grown and developed since the Hebrew Enlightenment (*Haskalah*) in the eighteenth century. Other encyclopedias have, with more or less success than Roth, listed the activities of notable Jews but few have used these lists as the basis of cultural interpretation. *The Blackwell Companion to Jewish Culture* provides such an analytical overview, according to its own

definition of modern Jewish culture. The *Companion* covers wide geographical, intellectual, and artistic areas, and offers material for every kind of reader, from the scholar to the casual browser; although the book is not encyclopedic, its detailed bibliographies provide the means of probing more deeply into the topics and figures treated here. The *Companion* has intentionally avoided the same ground already carefully covered by larger and more comprehensive works, but attempts to provide different viewpoints. Above all, it represents the state of Jewish culture (as it has defined it) in the present, the late twentieth century, 200 years after the massive watershed of Jewish emancipation in Europe.

Definitions

General

"Jewish culture" is one culture among many, growing within its people's social, moral, intellectual, and spiritual history, as distinct from other civilizations as one person is from another. The scrutiny of this singular history, and a careful examination of cultural differences, constitutes an act of explanation, of understanding relationships among Jews themselves, and between Jews and the non-Jewish world. Yet the elusive entity called "Jewish culture" has not developed in isolation; while its growth has been conditioned by the transcendental needs of Jewish communities, it has taken place within and alongside a variety of other cultures, some developed, some developing. The interchange has benefited the cultural thinking of all concerned, and never more so than during the past 200 years.

There have been few geographical or linguistic boundaries to Jewish creative activity. Throughout their history the Jews in all parts of the world have been active in almost every cultural field, and particularly accomplished in the creation of exegetical literature and hermeneutics, philosophy, and liturgical poetry. Since the beginning of the *Haskalah* western Jews have played a constantly growing role in the cultural life of their societies, broadening the cultural range and contributing their knowledge and creativity to the added fields of secular literature, art, and music, the social sciences, natural science, and medicine. There is a substantial Jewish contribution to every endeavor that defines modern society.

"Modern"

The subtitle of the *Companion*, "From the Eighteenth Century to the Present", points to modern culture. The word "modern" is comparatively easy to define. Although there is no one signal point by which the "modern" period of Jewish culture can be deemed to have begun, we could take it to be the English and European Enlightenment movements, particularly the eighteenth-century German *Aufklärung*, and the Hebrew Enlightenment, the *Haskalah*. The *Aufklärung* rapidly changed social and economic patterns and demonstrated a libertarian idea of social and political organization in which human rights were prominent. Around the mid-eighteenth century the movement of many Jews away from their traditional exclusivity echoed the *Aufklärung*'s call for tolerance and an end to obscurantism. Under the influence of Moses Mendelssohn (1729–1786) a school of adherents to the *Haskalah*, called, in Hebrew, *maskilim* (enlighteners), urged the Jews toward western acculturation and also the reappropriation of those traditions within Judaism – for example, rationalist philosophy, ideas of tolerance, an interest in science – that could lead to cultural exchange.

Like its German counterpart, the *Haskalah* was a movement powered by rationalist beliefs and defined by a revolutionary approach to the nature of Judaism and Jewish life. Mendelssohn is generally considered to be its founder but, like many innovative personalities, he crystallized a tendency that had already been evident for some time; Benedict (Baruch) Spinoza (1632–1677) or even Leone Ebreo (Judah Abravanel, *c.* 1460–1535) might both have a claim to being the ideological progenitors of a mode of Judaic thought that anticipates cultural modernism (see PHILOSOPHY, NINETEENTH-CENTURY JEWISH). Yet it was undoubtedly Mendelssohn and his followers who not only eased the way for the giant intellectual and artistic steps taken by the newly enlightened European Jews, but also created the cultural climate that generated many of the problems underlying contemporary Jewish life in the Diaspora.

The *Haskalah* was aided by Jewish political emancipation in western Europe from the 1790s. The emancipation of the Jews, that is, their achievement of civil liberties in the late eighteenth and nineteenth centuries, was the result of a changed, post-Enlightenment, Jewish self-image combined with the ideological and political liberalism that followed the French Revolution and the Napoleonic Wars. Emancipation came close on the heels of the Revolution as the French armies penetrated into western Europe, and the first ghetto walls fell in Holland, Belgium, Westphalia, Frankfurt, and Italy. For some Jews emancipation was a two-edged sword, for it meant the end not only of their civil disabilities but also of their privilege of communal autonomy. In addition, it brought about religious reform, in accordance with the spirit of the time. For most, it meant the culmination, if not also the radicalization, of *Haskalah* ideals, the end of Jewish segregation, and the resulting access to the wealth of European culture with its opportunities for Europeanization. However, despite the new mood of egalitarianism, emancipation was not granted to the Jews in a single libertarian moment: between the French Revolution (1789) and the constitutional changes of the 1870s, European Jews experienced the pendulum-like effects of the granting of civil rights during times of revolution, and their revocation during the waves of reaction. By the end of the First World War, however, Jewish equality had been established as a basic constitutional principle throughout much of western Europe.

The opening up of the cultural world to Jewish artists and intellectuals through enlightenment and emancipation led them to an exciting encounter with modernity. Yet this implied a series of fundamental changes that had to be faced at an individual level, without the old and trusted religious and ideological guidelines. The watershed of the European Enlightenment had brought about changes in Jewish self-perception and in Jewish expectations. For the first time the Jews were confronted by existential choices that did not necessarily mean betrayal of their Jewish identity, for the choices were presented to them *within* a newly diversified Judaism. Even so, they were not easily made: as William Cutter observes (see EDUCATIONAL CULTURAL, JEWISH), the Jews "have stood in tension between an impulse to preserve the Jewish heritage, and the need to adopt social and cultural mores of new host cultures and modern times." The availability of choice led to the cultural clash (*Kulturkampf*) between the traditional Jewish norms of life and those of the non-Jewish world the Jews were entering. The "clash" defined itself through the phenomena of assimilation and modernization; these, in turn, resolved themselves into a number of specific ideological streams, including Reform Judaism, Zionism, and Modern Orthodoxy. The philosophies of Marxist socialism and Freudian psychoanalysis also pointed to – and evaluated – the liberation from a traditional world-view which the Jewish intelligentsia considered to be outdated and irrelevant. These philosophies seemed to declare the need to reorganize Jewish experience to fit the structures of modernity.

The Jewish encounter with modernity was from the start an uneasy one. Once the Jews moved out of the ghettos at the time of the emancipation and entered the multifaceted modernity of western Europe, they came to experience not only outer social conflict with non-Jewish society but also, for the first time, an *inner* conflict which was generated by the historical Christian view of the nature of Jews and Judaism. The external anxiety was accompanied by a growing internal one, which resulted, in the case of some prominent figures, in the Jewish self-hatred defined by Theodore Lessing and to conversion. With their entrance into modernity, the Jews in eighteenth-century Europe began to "question their cultural and spiritual destination" (see PHILOSOPHY, NINETEENTH-CENTURY JEWISH). In the next century the question "Whither?" crystallized into a further series of ideologies, and became the watchword of the Hebrew cultural movement into which the *Haskalah* had evolved during its spread from western to eastern Europe. The answer to the question was not easy to find: for some it was to lie in the proposals of Theodor Herzl and the Zionist movement, migration (*aliyah*) to the Land of Israel, and the revival of a different cultural branch of the strong trunk of Jewish life.

"Jewish"

The second of our nominal definitions for the *Companion*, "Jewish", is more complex, particularly bearing in mind the interminable debate over the definition of a Jew. It is difficult, if not impossible, to determine the nature of Jewish culture when we do not have a clear notion of what is a Jew. There is a further question: whether it is possible to speak of the culture of a people who were for generations scattered and dispersed, and who did not possess either a common language or a land. The gaining of the land and the establishment of the State of Israel, far from answering this question, has led to the contemporary Israeli/Jewish cultural paradox.

The *Encyclopaedia Judaica* ends its long essay on Jewish identity with this comment: "In the broadest sense, significant elements of world Jewry in the modern era have defined, and are defining, Jewish identity as a community of history and destiny of those who still feel their involvement in this community, or about whom others feel strongly that these people belong to Jewry." Unlike Cecil Roth, and unlike many encyclopedic volumes that list Jewish personalities by virtue of Jewish birth or descent alone, the *Companion* does more, attempting to exemplify the *Judaica*'s definition by delving more deeply into the meaning of the term "Jewish" – "those who still feel their involvement in this community" – in relation to cultural and creative activity. Represented in the book are, therefore, those personalities whose Jewishness is, in some way, overtly or covertly, brought to bear on their work, those whose work shows internal evidence of it and in some way refers to or reflects it. There is a great number of prominent Jews who, for various reasons, have remained aloof from any Jewish affiliation, and these, despite their Jewish birth, are of no interest to the *Companion*. On the other hand, self-awareness of Jewishness may not always express itself positively, and there are Jewish personalities whose conflict with their own Jewishness affects their work as it has done their lives. For example, Simone Weil resented her Jewish birth and flirted with conversion to Catholicism all her life, but never went as far as to realize it; Albert Einstein transcended his Jewish identity by participating in a neutral, rational system which worked against any confinement to a single culture. Heinrich Heine regretted his conversion to Lutheranism. Like him, many Austro- and Franco-Jewish intellectuals at the turn of the century became converts for the sake of social or professional advancement, but remained in conflict with their Jewishness nonetheless.

The definition of a *Jewish* creative artist or scholar, even according to the restricted criteria of the *Companion*, is bewilderingly elusive. As Mark Shechner once pointed out, the Jewish imagination is not defined by geography, lifestyle, images, expressive modes, or "merely circumstantial properties" (such as chicken soup). Any of these factors may take precedence at certain times, but changing circumstances within the Jewish communities modify their importance. There is no artistic means that exclusively expresses Jewish experience or Jewish fate (see ART, MODERN JEWISH). Even suffering, which is so tightly bound to the historical perception of Jewishness, finds its most moving popular expression in other, non-Jewish cultural forms, such as the negro spiritual or the blues.

Only questions are able to focus attention on the magnitude, and perhaps impossibility, of this task of definition. Oversimplifying the complicated ideological question "Who is a Jew?" does not help in defining the Jewish cultural sensibility. Does "Jewish" indicate only descent from Jewish parents or grandparents? Or an artist who paints rabbis, or seven-branched candelabra, or the *seder* night? Or people at war with their perception of their own Jewishness in the spirit of the post-emancipation intellectuals? Other and related questions are as difficult to answer: Who are the target consumers of modern Jewish creativity? Exclusively the Jews themselves? The non-Jewish world? Are Jewish authors writing as Jews for Jews, or for non-Jews? Is there a recognition of "Jewish" creativity? Alexander Knapp (see MUSIC, JEWISH) tells us that the ethnomusicologist Curt Sachs defined Jewish music as "that music which is made by Jews, for Jews, as Jews". The questions raised by this uncompromising declaration have vital implications for all branches of Jewish creativity regarding the fulfilment of each of the three conditions, "*by* Jews, *for* Jews, *as* Jews", and the relationship between them. The exact definition of "Jewish literature", for example, is equally difficult: the most logical assumption is that it is literature written by Jews in any language and in any country, but not *for* Jews or *as* Jews. Literature of Jewish authorship is not always "Jewish" in the sense of cultural or spiritual identification, or reference; the audience it aims at is rarely targeted as exclusively Jewish; even works in translation from "Jewish" languages are sent into the world for a non-specific readership.

I believe the *Companion* as a whole goes some way toward focusing on these questions, and points toward answers to them. For example, its many entries and essays develop a view of the Jewish artist, writer, or scholar as a person who represents concerns and convictions which are not overtly Judaic but which have come to be most closely associated with Judaism or Jewishness – among them ideas concerning liberalism, oppression, nationalism, alienation, self-criticism, survival, and morality. More than 200 contributors have written thousands of words on the evidence of Jewishness even in the least candidly Jewish works, and have demonstrated that Jewishness does not necessarily rest in obvious iconography or imagery, but in patterns of thinking and seeing, in certain distinct and repeated themes and topics, and even in an aggressive *absence* of acknowledgement of Jewishness. Diaspora creativity conceals the reality of

Jewish communication in a kind of code which can be deciphered by those with the appropriate historical and cultural tools. The code incorporates the internal Jewish attitudes to non-Jewish society, to non-Jews, to social systems, to religion, to Jews themselves, which are rarely explicitly articulated, but are displaced into other themes and ideologies.

We have to ask whether the "hidden language" of Diaspora culture applies as well to the cultural products of Israel. Here the boundaries are blurred since so many Israeli creators have their roots in the Diaspora, and their Diaspora experience and cultural preconceptions are reflected in the Israeli phase of their creativity. At the same time they identify wholly with the land and language of Israel, they are not fundamentally concerned with the current dilemmas and problems of Diaspora Jewish life, and they do not have a part in "the Jewish problem". Is Israel, then, the trunk upon which the Diaspora branches have grown, or is it the other way round? Whether or not Israeli culture can be termed "Jewish" in the designation of post-Enlightenment sensibility is open to question. One Israeli scholar, when approached for a contribution to this book, declined on the grounds that he was not concerned with "Jewish" culture, being a Hebrew literary critic and an Israeli. It is uncertain whether the Israeli cultural sensibility is comparable with that of Jews in the Diaspora whose ideologies remain the legacy of Emancipation and whose responses to non-Jewish society renew themselves with each generation. The answer is, perhaps, in shared interests derived from the past. Some Israeli writers are not particularly concerned with any kind of Jewish reality; and yet the Hebrew language, bearing the heavy weight of Jewish tradition, enforces this reality upon them. Israelis and Diaspora Jews create from shared cultural sources.

All this has been explored in order to be recognized, and the composite result offered by the *Companion* is the revelation of what can only be called a semiotics of Jewishness. One of the most rewarding results of a compilation such as the *Companion* is the recognition of these shared signs among Jewish artists and scholars through different genres and in entirely different national cultures, and of traits common to diverse Jewish communities.

Of the many features cutting across national boundaries, one of the most significant is the secular Jewish reinterpretation of messianism through nineteenth- and twentieth-century sociopolitical movements, of which Zionism is a primary example. Another is Marxism: the Jewish will for social justice, which strongly revealed itself in art and literature, culminated, for many twentieth-century Jews, in Marxism. Another feature emerging from the *Companion* is the disparity of cultural integration in various societies, most notably the USA and the United Kingdom. Jewish influence can be gauged by examining the extent to which characteristics of Jewish life, language, and popular culture have been permitted to enter the mainstream of the majority society's culture. For example, despite Britain's magnificent record of civil liberties its culture, unlike that of the American "melting-pot", does not acknowledge the Jewish presence within it. A third feature examined by the *Companion* is the change in Jewish self-definition after the Second World War, again revealed in art and literature, and the influence of the Holocaust in the redetermination of Jewish self-identity.

Part of the *Encyclopaedia Judaica*'s definition relates to those figures "about whom others feel strongly that these people belong to Jewry". Personalities such as Karl Marx and perhaps Felix Mendelssohn, both baptized, may appear to have no proper claim to inclusion in a book with strict criteria for the definition of "Jewish", but these, and a few others, are perceived by the world at large as Jews, and it is this perception, and the attitudes deriving from it, that are important when deciding on the function, significance, and effect of these personalities within western society.

Despite the codes and the semiotics, which are an undeniable element of Jewish creativity, and despite the interpretive tools required to understand them, the most valuable, enduring, and vital contribution to what this book has termed "modern Jewish culture" has been made by overt, stated, and exposed Jewishness: by the writers who take issue with it and who, like Philip Roth, may even break the tribal taboos and reveal the codes; by the scholars who prod and poke at it; by the artists who illuminate its traditional features; by the social scientists who demythify it; and by those who, as a group, distrust and therefore challenge the temptations of what Jean-Paul Sartre termed "those totalities which the Christian mind sometimes produces." In short, the Jews who resist taking the easy way out.

"Culture"

Of the three ideas that define this book (or, in the fashionable language of structuralism, of the three signifiers for which the signified is always elusive) – "modern", "Jewish", and "culture" – "culture" is perhaps the most difficult. Herder wrote: "Nothing is more indeterminate than this word, and nothing more deceptive than its application to all nations and periods." Raymond Williams suggests that "'culture' is one of the two or three most complicated words in the English language". Its use and sense have changed in changing social systems, from its being a synonym for "civilization" (to which definition Cecil Roth adheres) to its evolution as a term of modern anthropology. For the purposes of the *Companion*, "culture" retains its Renaissance definition, *cultura bonarum artium* and *cultura litterarum humaniorum* – roughly, the cultivation of fine arts and the humanities. It is defined in a similar way by Williams as "the independent and abstract noun which describes the works and practices of intellectual and especially artistic activity . . . : 'culture' is music, literature, painting and sculpture, theatre and films." According to these definitions, literature, language, music, the performing and visual arts, philosophy, and scholarship in the humanities constitute the traditional core of cultural activity and they have been adopted as the core of this book.

The visual arts and music were perhaps the least exploited by Jews until the late nineteenth century. The reason is commonly accepted to be the second Commandment, which prohibits the making of graven images or likenesses. Another reason, often overlooked, is the exclusion of Jews from the strictly Christian artist-guilds. As far as music is concerned, composers were employed by the church or the royal courts, from which Jews were excluded. Rabbinic restrictions limited – yet did not eliminate – the development of music among Jewish communities, for musical innovation was almost exclusively reserved for religious services. However, the major reason for the pre-Enlightenment circumscription of these activities was the isolation of Judaism, its separation from secular art and music, and the lack of cultural interchange. After Emancipation, and especially in the nineteenth and twentieth centuries, Jewish artists, as equal participants in modern esthetic movements, have taken their place among the great pantheon of graphic artists and sculptors, composers and performers. Jewish image-making skills, so long suppressed, seem to have found a particularly happy outlet in the international motion picture industry, one of the few cultural genres in which Jews have participated, even formed, from its very origins.

Define "culture" how we may, when it is preceded by the word "Jewish" it again changes its meaning. Modern Jewish culture is a synthesis of two contradictory tendencies which can be rendered as "continuity and innovation", or as "continuity and change". This means that Jewish culture is in part a continuation of traditional Jewish intellectual activity. In this sense it is the uninterrupted study of the Word by scholars whose methodology, while building on models of the past, incorporates modernist approaches. The other tendency, that of innovation or change, reveals new Jewish religious and secular responses to the historical and political events which have followed each other from the eighteenth century with the breathless rapidity brilliantly described in the Book of Job: "While he was yet speaking, there came also another . . . ." Modern Jewish culture, then, becomes the confrontation between Jewishness – itself redefined and changing as a result of historical processes – and the world external to it. The forms taken to express this confrontation are the traditional ones, poetry, philosophy, commentary, together with those adopted and adapted from the external culture when they suddenly became available to Jewish creators: fiction, secular music and art, science and technology. Modern Jewish culture is therefore a matter of integrating those themes which appear to be most closely associated with modern Jewish thinking (as suggested earlier) with established forms, those which have signified "culture" for generations.

The character of the *Companion*

The Jewish culture represented in the *Companion* is Ashkenazi; those individual writers, scholars, and artists of Sephardi origin who are included are those who have entered the mainstream of Ashkenazi–western culture. A fitting companion to this *Companion* would be one addressing the richness and variety of Sephardi Jewish culture. While the cultural focus must necessarily be on areas of historical Jewish gathering and activity, most notably Europe and later the USA, the younger colonial and ex-colonial communities have not been neglected. Jewish cultural activity in Australia and South Africa, which has been relatively neglected by global overviews, reveals the Jewish response to those two societies.

A close examination of individuals through their biographies and creative works is an examination as well of their interaction with their cultural environment. Living personalities are widely represented in the book, many of them the most eminent, and others young and promising. It is impossible, and would be irresponsible, to represent the wealth of contemporary Jewish creative accomplishment without including those personalities whose vital activities are in the process of contributing to its growth and richness. Many Jewish scholars are at their peak of creativity; artists, musicians, and writers are representing the modern Jewish experience as we live it. We are as indebted to them as to the great figures of the past.

In the case of many living personalities, published biographical information is scanty and the entries on them have depended upon responses to a questionnaire, with the inevitable result that the coverage is, in places, less extensive than we would have wished. Some important figures do not appear at all, as a result either of their own wishes or their lack of response to requests for information about themselves.

The contributors to this book are renowned experts in their fields: it would not be possible otherwise to remain faithful to the *Companion*'s criteria, or its intention to explore the intricacies, often subtle and concealed, of Jewish self-awareness. They form a multinational scholarly assembly, from Argentina, Australia, Brazil, Canada, Denmark, France, Greece, Holland, Hungary, Israel, Italy, Poland, South Africa, the Soviet Union, Spain, the United Kingdom, and the United States.

The composite "culture" (or the delineation of Jewish culture) is broken down throughout the book by means of three types of entry: biographies, which offer factual details about the subjects, together with brief evaluations of their work; essays on topics relating to Jewish culture as we have defined it, which contextualize the biographies and the works mentioned in them; and survey articles, which cover the areas considered to be peripheral according to our definition of culture. The surveys allow the reader some insight into the general scope of Jewish activity and development even in areas that do not fall within the *Companion*'s definition of culture. A comprehensive picture of "Jewish popular culture" may, for example, be gained through reading the entries on Jewish humour, Jewish folklore, Jewish cooking, Jewish costume, Jewish comedy, Jewish languages, and Yiddish theater, in addition to the biographies of relevant individuals.

The *Companion* has clearly proved the truism of modern Jewish culture: its resilience. It began in Europe and was set to end in Europe, yet in the few postwar decades it has demonstrated its legendary tenacity, and rerooted itself in the fertile soil of Israel and the United States. Whether these two countries will ultimately produce two divergent cultures remains to be seen, for the Ashkenazi European influence still largely dominates Israeli cultural thinking. Meanwhile Israel and the USA, together with smaller and with more remotely situated Jewish communities, continue to confirm the vitality of Jewish cultural responses to the challenges of modernity.

Glenda Abramson
Oxford, 1989

Acknowledgements

A book of this size involves many different kinds of contribution but it is to the writers that my warmest thanks must go, those people whose entries have created the *Companion*, and whose enthusiasm, encouragement, and advice have been of immeasurable help. I am particularly grateful to those who undertook entire sections and provided large numbers of entries: Samuel Adler, Steven Beller, Henriette Boas, Monica Bohm-Duchen, Bryan Cheyette, Alan Crown, Mark Gelber, Barbara Gilbert, George Gömöri, Kevin Gough-Yates, Jocelyn Hellig, Jehoash Hirshberg, John Matthew, Gabriella Moscati-Steindler, Deborah Schechterman, Claude Singer, and Nelly Wilson.

My sincere thanks go to the four Advisory Editors: Dovid Katz (Yiddish), Nicholas de Lange (Jewish Studies), Chaim Rabin (Language and Linguistics), and Ezra Spicehandler (Literature), for their endless patience, their unstinting and invaluable advice, and, as if this were not enough, their own entries and essays.

Other colleagues have generously given time and effort and to them, too, I extend my gratitude: David Sorkin and George Mandel (Oxford), who served as readers, among many other tasks; Yoram Bronowski (London), Dan Cohn-Sherbok (Canterbury), Alexander Knapp (Cambridge), and Jonathan Sarna (Jerusalem), who compiled useful lists of names for inclusion, and made many suggestions. I am very much indebted to Ora Ra'anan (Ramat Gan) for her valuable advice, and to Daniel Walden (Pennsylvania), who gathered together a team of gifted writers and supplied comprehensive lists. Not to be forgotten are the translators, Anthea Bell (French), Jenny Condie (Italian), Grazyna Cooper (Polish), and Brian Harvey (Russian).

It has been a special pleasure to work with the Basil Blackwell Reference department, whose spirited team has nursed me and the book through to the end: Alyn Shipton, Carol Le Duc, Mary Starkey, Rosemary Roberts, and Jo Hadley.

I am eternally grateful to my husband and sons for their practical help and encouragement. To Gill Pink, for her sympathy and succor, and to all those throughout the world who have offered constructive advice, assistance, and support, I express my warmest gratitude.

During the preparation of the *Companion* our picture editor, Patricia Mandel, died after a long illness. Her very discerning eye and her sensitivity and skill have illustrated this volume and contributed greatly to its interest. Her energy and enthusiasm, even through difficult times, will not be forgotten.

We also mourn the death of Dr Ann Duncan, who contributed many of the entries on Latin-American writers, and whose advice and suggestions were invaluable.

Glenda Abramson
Oxford, 1989

Illustration Acknowledgements

The publisher and editor gratefully acknowledge the following for supplying illustrations and granting permission for their use. The titles of articles in which the photographs appear are listed following each source.

Every effort has been made to trace all copyright holders of the illustrations that appear in this book; should anyone inadvertently have been overlooked we shall be pleased to make proper acknowledgement in future editions.

ADAGP, Paris: *Chagall, Marc* (© 1988); *Mané-Katz* (© 1988); *Paris, Jewish School of* (© 1988)

Bibliothèque de l'Alliance Israélite Universelle, Paris: *Alliance Israélite Universelle*

American Jewish Historical Society, Waltham, MA: *Lazarus, Emma*

Leo Baeck Institute, New York: *Holocaust art*

Jerry Bauer: *Levi, Primo*

Beit Lohamei Haghetaot (Ghetto Fighters House), Tel Aviv: *Hasidism*

Alfred Bernheim, Jerusalem: *mysticism, modern Jewish*

Bettmann/Hulton, Hulton Picture Company, London: *Bellow, Saul*; *Eisenstein, Sergei Mikhailovich*; *films, US, Jews in*; *Gershwin, George*; *Kafka, Franz*; *Koestler, Arthur*; *Reinhardt, Max*; *Schoenberg, Arnold*; *Simon, Neil*; *theater, Yiddish*; *Tin Pan Alley*; *Wesker, Arnold*

Bodleian Library, Oxford, Heb.Per.e.11/1868–69: *Haskalah*

Britain/Israel Public Affairs Centre (BIPAC), London: *Agnon, Shmuel Yosef*; *humor, Jewish*

Syndics of the Cambridge University Library: *Schechter, Solomon*

Camera Press, London: *Buber, Martin*

Jonathan Cape Ltd, London: *Roth, Philip*; *Singer, Isaac Bashevis*

Chatto and Windus, London: *Oz, Amos*

Central Zionist Archives, Jerusalem: *Ben-Yehuda, Eliezer*; *Brandeis, Louis*; *Herzl, Theodor*; *Kalischer, Zevi Hirsch*; *Nordau, Max*; *Pinsker, Leon*

Citadel Press, Secaucus, NJ: *Einstein, Albert*

Courtauld Institute of Art, London: *Kramer, Jacob*

Nancy Crampton: *Roth, Philip*

DACS, London: *Chagall, Marc* (© 1988); *Mané-Katz* (© 1988); *Paris, Jewish School of* (© 1988); *Soutine, Chaim* (© 1989)

Deutsche Grammophon: *Bernstein, Leonard*

B. Emanuel, Salford: *Hirsch, Samuel Raphael*

Paul Ehrlich Institute, Frankfurt am Main: *biomedical research, Jews in*

Mary Evans Picture Library, London: *Bergson, Henri*; *Freud, Sigmund* (Mary Evans/Sigmund Freud Copyrights); *psychoanalysis, Jews in*; *Rank, Otto*

Mike Evans: *Bernstein, Leonard*

John Fairfax and Sons Ltd, Sydney: *Waten, Judah*

Lynn Garon Management: *Steve Reich*

Genazim, Tel Aviv: *Kahanowitz, Pinye*; *Tschernichowski, Saul*; *Yehoshua, Avraham B.*

Luke Gertler, London: *Gertler, Mark*

Kariel Gardosh, Tel Aviv (© Dosh): *Gardosh, Kariel*

Judy Goldhill, London: *cooking, Jewish*; *Orthodox Judaism*

David Harris, Jerusalem: *archaeology, modern Israeli*

Contributors

This list names all authors of articles in the *Companion* together with the institution to which they are affiliated or their place of residence.

David Aberbach (McGill University)

Hannah Abrahamson (Bar-Ilan University, Ramat Gan)

Glenda Abramson (Oxford Centre for Postgraduate Hebrew Studies)

Samuel H. Adler (University of Rochester)

Philip S. Alexander (University of Manchester)

Evelyn Avery (Towson State University, Maryland)

Shlomo Avineri (The Hebrew University, Jerusalem)

Joelle Bahloul (Indiana University)

Arnold J. Band (University of California, Los Angeles)

Dan Barag (The Hebrew University, Jerusalem)

David Barnouw (Rijksinstituut voor Oorlogsdocumentatie, Amsterdam)

Andrea Baron (Wallington, Surrey)

Randall Beebe (Pennsylvania State University)

Nitza Behrouzi (Eretz Israel Museum, Tel Aviv)

Ella Belfer (Bar-Ilan University, Ramat Gan)

Steven Beller (Peterhouse, Cambridge)

Isaac Benabu (The Hebrew University, Jerusalem)

Albert Bensoussan (Université de Haute-Bretagne, Rennes)

Chaim Bermant (London)

R. W. Bethlehem (Johannesburg)

David Biale (Graduate Theological Union, Berkeley, California)

David Bloch (Tel Aviv University)

Alexander Bloom (Wheaton College, Norton, Massachusetts)

Shoshana Blum-Kulka (The Hebrew University, Jerusalem)

Henriette Boas (Badhoevedorp, Holland)

Monica Bohm-Duchen (London)

Lavinia Braun (Brasenose College, Oxford)

Rachel Feldhay Brenner (York University, Toronto)

Seth L. Brody (University of Pennsylvania)

Yoram Bronowski (London)

Nedira Yakir Bunyard (Exeter)

Julius Carlebach (Heidelberg)

Calum Carmichael (Cornell University)

Joseph Chetrit (University of Haifa)

Bryan Cheyette (University of Leeds)

Stanley F. Chyet (Hebrew Union College, Los Angeles)

Dafna Clifford (Oxford)

Joseph Cohen (Tulane University, New Orleans)

Shimon Cohen (London)

Stephen Cohen (Jewish Federation Council of Greater Los Angeles)

Dan Cohn-Sherbok (University of Kent at Canterbury)

Vera Coleman (Westfield College, London)

Mel Cooper (Oxford)

Alan D. Crown (University of Sydney)

William Cutter (Hebrew Union College, Los Angeles)

Rachel Dalven (Ladycliff College, New York)

Joseph Dan (The Hebrew University, Jerusalem)

Cathy Davidson (Michigan State University)

Nicholas de Lange (University of Cambridge)

Sergio DellaPergola (The Hebrew University, Jerusalem)

David Desser (University of Illinois at Urbana-Champaign)

Ann Duncan (Newnham College, Cambridge)

Veronica Hayden Eastabrooks (Vienna, Virginia)

Muriel Emanuel (London)

Raphael Emanuel (University of Bath)

Sidra DeKoven Ezrahi (The Hebrew University, Jerusalem)

Ben-Ami Feingold (Tel Aviv University)

Paul B. Fenton (Université de Lyon III)

Sylvia Fishman (Brandeis University)

Sydney Fixman (London)

Ruth Foppema-Wolf (Oegstgeest, Holland)

Michael Freedland (Elstree, Hertfordshire)

Albert H. Friedlander (Westminster Synagogue, London)

Marian Fuks (Warsaw)

Mark H. Gelber (Ben Gurion University of the Negev, Beer Sheva)

Ludy Giebels (Amsterdam)

Barbara Gilbert (Skirball Museum, Hebrew Union College, Los Angeles)

Menucha Gilboa (Tel Aviv University)

Neil Gillman (Jewish Theological Seminary of America, New York)

Harvey Goldberg (The Hebrew University, Jerusalem)

Ellen Golub (Marblehead, Massachusetts)

George Gömöri (University of Cambridge)

Martin Goodman (Oxford Centre for Postgraduate Hebrew Studies)

Zilla Jane Goodman (Ohio State University, Columbus)

Jack S. Gottlieb (New York)

Alfred Gottschalk (Hebrew Union College, Cincinnati)

Kevin Gough-Yates (Open University)

Gershon Greenberg (The American University, Washington DC)

Ilan Greilsammer (Bar-Ilan University, Ramat Gan)

Richard Grunberger (London)

Joseph Gutmann (Wayne State University, Detroit)

Sarah Hacker (University of Haifa)

Ethan Haimo (University of Notre Dame, Indiana)

Nelson Hathcock (St Xavier College, Chicago)

Roger N. Hausheer (University of Bradford)

Jocelyn Hellig (University of the Witwatersrand)

Deborah Hertz (State University of New York at Binghamton)

Susannah Heschel (Southern Methodist University, Dallas)

Patricia Hidiroglou (Université de Paris I, Panthéon-Sorbonne)

Milton Hindus (Brandeis University)

Jehoash Hirshberg (The Hebrew University, Jerusalem)

Eric Homberger (University of East Anglia)

Simon Hopkins (The Hebrew University, Jerusalem)

Allison Huton (Pennsylvania State University)

Christopher Hutton (University of Texas at Austin)

Louis Jacobs (London)

Laura Jacobus (Birbeck Centre for Extramural Studies, University of London)

Kristie A. Jayne (The Jewish Museum, New York)

Anthony Joseph (The Jewish Historical Society of England)

Jacob Kabakoff (White Plains, New York)

Ahuvia Kahane (Balliol College, Oxford)

Edward Kaplan (Brandeis University)

Dovid Katz (Oxford Centre for Postgraduate Hebrew Studies)

Menke Katz (Spring Glen, New York)

Devra Kay (St Cross College, Oxford)

David F. Kessler (Stoke Hammond, Buckinghamshire)

Dennis B. Klein (International Center for Holocaust Studies, New York)

Elizabeth Klein (Champaign, Illinois)

Alexander Knapp (Wolfson College, Cambridge)

Bettina L. Knapp (Hunter College, New York)

Baruch Knei-Paz (The Hebrew University, Jerusalem)

Lionel Kochan (Oxford)

Miriam Kochan (Oxford)

Leandro Konder (Rio de Janeiro)

Orly Leah Krasner (City University of New York)

Oliver Leaman (Liverpool Polytechnic)

Baruch A. Levine (Hebrew Union College, New York)

Esther Levinger (University of Haifa)
Sharona Levy (New York)
David Lewis (Christ Church, Oxford)
Elinor Lieber (Oxford)
Marco Livingstone (London)
Michael Löwy (Centre National de la Recherche Scientifique, Paris)
Noah Lucas (Oxford Centre for Postgraduate Hebrew Studies)
Bonnie Lyons (University of Texas at San Antonio)
George Mandel (Oxford Centre for Postgraduate Hebrew Studies)
Rivka Maoz (The Hebrew University, Jerusalem)
Judith Marcus (New York)
Shimon Markish (University of Geneva)
John Matthew (London School of Economics)
Paul Mendes-Flohr (The Hebrew University, Jerusalem)
Michael A. Meyer (Hebrew Union College, Cincinnati)
David Neal Miller (Ohio State University)
Gabriel Miller (State University of New Jersey, Rutgers)
Maria Modena Mayer (State University of Milan)
Brian Moloney (University of Wollongong, Australia)
Debra Morris (Pennsylvania State University)
Paul M. Morris (University of Lancaster)
Gabriella Moscati-Steindler (Istituto Universitario Orientale, Naples)
Jody Elizabeth Myers (California State University, Northridge)
Pamela Nadell (The American University, Washington DC)
Alice Nakhimovsky (Colgate University, Hamilton, New York)
Stanley Nash (Hebrew Union College, New York)
Ronald Nettler (Oxford Centre for Postgraduate Hebrew Studies)
Albert Neuberger (Charing Cross and Westminster Medical School)
Maren Niehoff (Wolfson College, Oxford)
Michal Oron (Tel Aviv University)
Mortimer Ostow (Jewish Theological Seminary of America, New York)
Herbert Paper (Hebrew Union College, Cincinnati)

Tudor Parfitt (School of Oriental and African Studies, University of London)
David Patterson (Oxford Centre for Postgraduate Hebrew Studies)
Margarita Pazi (Tel Aviv University)
Catherine Phillips (Leningrad)
Sanford Pinsker (Franklin and Marshall College, Lancaster, Pennsylvania)
W. Gunther Plaut (Holy Blossom Temple, Toronto)
Leonard Prager (University of Haifa)
Batya Rabin (Jerusalem)
Chaim Rabin (The Hebrew University, Jerusalem)
Herman Rapaport (University of Iowa)
David Resnick (Bar-Ilan University, Ramat Gan)
Ritchie Robertson (Downing College, Cambridge)
Carole Rosen (London)
Debra Jane Rosen (Oxford)
Ruth Rosenberg (Kingsborough Community College, New York)
David G. Roskies (Jewish Theological Seminary of America, New York)
Jonathan Sacks (Jews' College, London)
Liana Sakelliou-Schultz (University of Athens)
Jeffrey L. Sammons (Yale University)
Jonathan D. Sarna (Hebrew Union College, Cincinnati)
Deborah Schechterman (Cambridge, Massachusetts)
Ellen Schiff (North Adams State College, Massachusetts)
David Schneider (Exeter College, Oxford)
George J. Searles (Mohawk Valley Community College, Utica, New York.
J. B. Segal (London)
Leonardo Senkman (The Hebrew University, Jerusalem)
Beth Shamgar (Bar-Ilan University, Ramat Gan)
Jane Shapiro (Evanston, Illinois)
Michael Shapiro (University of Illinois at Urbana-Champaign)
Uzi Shavit (Tel Aviv University)
Mark Shechner (State University of New York at Buffalo)
Elaine Shefer (University of Haifa)
Judith Shen-Dar (Janco-Dada Museum, Haifa)
Carolyn Shields (Pennsylvania State University)

Harold Shukman (St Antony's College, Oxford)

Simon Sibelman (The Spiro Institute for the Study of Jewish History and Culture, London)

Efraim Sicher (Ben Gurion University of the Negev, Beer Sheva)

Neil Silberman (Branford, Connecticut)

Jon Silkin (Newcastle upon Tyne)

Perrine Simon-Nahum (Raymond Aron Institute, École des Hautes Études en Sciences Sociales, Paris)

Clive Sinclair (St Albans, Hertfordshire)

Daniel B. Sinclair (Tel Aviv University)

Claude Singer (Université de Paris I, Panthéon-Sorbonne)

Robert Skloot (University of Wisconsin, Madison)

K. A. D. Smelik (Rijksuniversiteit, Utrecht)

Norman Solomon (Centre for the Study of Judaism and Jewish/Christian Relations, Birmingham)

Ruth Sonntag (London)

Adam J. Sorkin (Pennsylvania State University)

David Sorkin (Oxford Centre for Postgraduate Hebrew Studies)

Saúl Sosnowski (University of Maryland)

Dora Sowden (Jerusalem)

S. David Sperling (Hebrew Union College, New York)

Ezra Spicehandler (Hebrew Union College, Cincinnati)

John Stachel (Boston University)

Michael C. Steinlauf (Harvard University)

Lance J. Sussman (State University of New York at Binghamton)

Zoltan Tar (New York)

Sefton D. Temkin (State University of New York at Albany)

Patricia Touton-Victor (Paris)

Richard Tuerk (East Texas State University)

Alan Unterman (Gatley, Cheshire)

Melvin I. Urofsky (Virginia Commonwealth University, Richmond)

Edward Van Voolen (Joods Historisch Museum, Amsterdam)

Pamela Vermes (Oxford)

Daniel Walden (Pennsylvania State University)

Cheryl Wanko (Pennsylvania State University)

Mark Washofsky (Hebrew Union College, Cincinnati)

Asher Weill (Jerusalem)

Barry Weinberg (The Spiro Institute for the Study of Jewish History and Culture, London)

Abner Weiss (Beth Jacob Congregation, Beverly Hills, California)

Maxwell Whiteman (Willow Grove, Pennsylvania)

Nelly Wilson (University of Bristol)

Judith Winther (University of Copenhagen)

Gad Yair (The Hebrew University, Jerusalem)

Eli Yassif (Ben Gurion University of the Negev, Beer Sheva)

Roderick Young (London)

Leon I. Yudkin (University of Manchester)

Ruth Zernova (Jerusalem)

Harry Zohn (Brandeis University)

Note on the Use of the Book

Headwords

Entries are ordered alphabetically according to the bold headword, excluding material in parentheses.

Individuals are entered under the preferred form of their names. Parts of a person's given name which he or she did not normally use appear in bold type in parentheses; alternative names (including nicknames, pseudonyms, given names where the subject is better known by a name adopted later in life, etc.) appear in roman type in brackets.

In a few cases articles on individuals who pursued careers in different spheres of activity are in two parts, written by different contributors; each part has its own signature and may have its own bibliography and reading list (see below), but only the first has a bold headword.

Cross-references

When the reader may find elsewhere in the book information pertinent to the subject or individual first looked up, the headwords of such other entries are printed in large and small capitals.

Titles of works

In the texts of entries, titles of books, works of art, and musical compositions are printed in italic type; the titles of poems, short stories, essays, and articles appear in roman type in quotation marks.

Wherever possible (and necessary), a literal English translation is given for any foreign-language title of a literary work, whether or not the work has been translated. Where the translated title appears in italic type, with a date of its own, the work itself has been translated and published.

Bibliographies and Further Reading lists

Works by the subject of an entry are listed under the heading "Bibliography". Works on the subject or containing material relevant to a study of the subject are listed under the heading "Further Reading". Both kinds of list are selective. Generally the works cited in bibliographies are selected from those that have appeared in English translation.

Two important sources of information on Yiddish writers and scholars, which pertain to many articles in the *Companion* and which, because of space limitations, are not always cited in Further Reading lists are:

Zalmen Reyzen, *Leksikon fun der yidisher literatur, prese un filologye*, 4 vols (Vilna: B. Kletskin, 1926–9)

Leksikon fun der nayer yidisher literatur, various editors, 8 vols (New York: Congress for Jewish Culture, 1956–81); supplement by Berl Kagan, *Leksikon fun yidish-shraybers* (New York: Rayah Ilman-Kagan, 1986)

Editorial style

American spelling and punctuation are used throughout.

A

Abrahams, Israel (1858–1924) English scholar. Abrahams was Reader in Rabbinic and Talmudic Literature at Cambridge University (where he succeeded Solomon SCHECHTER) from 1902 until his death; he also taught at Jews' College, the London rabbinical seminary. He did a great deal to promote Jewish studies in England: he was one of the founders of the Jewish Historical Society of England (1893), he edited the *Jewish Quarterly Review*, together with Claude MONTEFIORE, from its creation in 1888 until 1908, and he published a number of scholarly books. However, it is as a popular author on Jewish subjects that he is best remembered, and he set new standards in the Anglo-Jewish tradition of presenting Jewish history and literature to a wider public. His most enduring book of this type was *Jewish Life in the Middle Ages*, first published in 1896 and reissued in a revised edition by Cecil ROTH in 1932. His *Notes to the Authorized Daily Prayer Book* (the so-called "Singer's Prayer Book", edited by his father-in-law, Simeon Singer), published in 1914, also became a firm favorite with English Jews.

Abrahams did not write much on theological subjects, but he had his own clear views on Jewish religion (not necessarily those one might expect from a lecturer in an Orthodox rabbinical seminary). He made an important intellectual contribution to the Jewish Religious Union, founded by Montefiore and Lily Montagu, which later developed into the Liberal Jewish Synagogue. Unsympathetic to Zionism, he preferred his own vision of a well-integrated and articulate English Judaism.

Abrahams was succeeded as Reader in Rabbinics at Cambridge by Herbert Loewe, another fine scholar with a gift for writing for the wider public, although a firm adherent of English Orthodoxy.

FURTHER READING
Jewish Studies in Memory of Israel Abrahams (London, 1927) [includes bibliography]
Hyamson, A. M.: *Israel Abrahams. A Memoir* (London: Jewish Religious Union for the Advancement of Liberal Judaism, 1940)

NICHOLAS DE LANGE

Abramovitz, Shalom Jacob See MENDELE MOKHER SEFARIM.

Abrams, Lionel (b.1931) South African artist. Born in Johannesburg, he was educated at the Jeppe High School and the Johannesburg Technical College's art department. He subsequently trained at the Central School of Art, London. He held his first exhibition in Johannesburg in 1957. Adopting an abstract approach for many years, he prefers landscapes and still lifes as his subjects. In the mid-1970s he developed the technique of photo-pastel, in which the photographic image is etched away chemically and replaced by pastel. The photographic image is a useful tool in his art. His first exhibition of photo-pastel took place in 1975 in Johannesburg.

He tends to work on themes based on works of artists he admires. Sometimes they are based on fact and at other times they are fictitious "gags"

1

allowing him scope for his creative imagination, such as Camille Pissarro meeting Paul Cézanne in a garden, or Dreyfus visiting Edouard Manet in his studio. He painted a series on Manet's *Le Déjeuner sur l'Herbe*, and another on Claude Monet in his studio surrounded by his water lilies. His later style is highly personal and is no longer abstract, nor is it characterized by photographic realism.

His interest in the South African Lubavich movement in the early 1970s led to a four-year phase in which he worked on Jewish themes. He produced a series of pastel portraits of five generations of Lubavicher rebbes. These were later translated into silk screen in an edition of 500. He painted a number of traditional Jewish themes.

He has represented South Africa at a number of international exhibitions. He has works in most galleries and museums in South Africa, and some abroad.

JOCELYN HELLIG

Abse, Dannie (b.1923) Welsh poet and playwright. Born in Cardiff, Abse was educated at St Illtyd's College and the University of South Wales and Monmouthshire. He was trained in medicine at King's College, London, and Westminster Hospital. Assigned to a military chest clinic in London while a squadron leader in the RAF (1951–5), Abse has since continued to practise medicine as a civilian at the same clinic. In 1951 he married Joan Mercer, an art historian. They have three children.

While still a medical student, he published his first volume of poetry, *After Every Green Thing* (1948). It is lushly romantic, unrestrained, and heavily influenced by Dylan Thomas and Rainer Rilke. In the decades following, Abse disciplined himself, found his own voice, and in more than a dozen subsequent volumes he has gone from strength to strength. His most accomplished works are *Poems: Golders Green* (1962) in which Abse's concern with Jewishness emerges; *A Small Desperation* (1968) in which he first utilized his medical experiences; and *Funland and Other Poems* (1973) in which he articulated his anxiety and compassion for a world gone mad. His *Collected Poems 1948–1976* (1977) richly weld together his

Dannie Abse

various roles as Jew, Welshman, British poet, doctor, bourgeois family man, bohemian observer (his clinic is in Soho), pragmatist, and mystic.

In his *Collected Poems* and two volumes published thereafter, *Way Out in the Centre* (1981) and *Ask the Bloody Horse* (1986), Abse displayed a sophisticated, productive affinity with midrashic, hasidic, and kabbalistic legends. Opposed to religiosity and restrictive orthodoxies, Abse's Jewishness manifests itself in his modernized, ironic, and witty, yet profound, adaptations of the parables and mysteries of Jewish mysticism.

A prolific writer, Abse has written 14 stage and radio plays, the two best known being *The Dogs of Pavlov* (1973) and *Pythagoras* (1979). He is the author of three novels. His first one, *Ash on a Young Man's Sleeve* (1954), a charming fictional account of his growing up in Wales, has become a modern classic and is required reading in British schools. A book on modern medicine, an autobiography – *A Poet in the Family* (1974) – and two collections of essays, along with other miscellaneous works, both written and edited, make up Abse's impressive oeuvre.

BIBLIOGRAPHY
Three Questor Plays (Lowestoft: Scorpion Press, 1967); *A Strong Dose of Myself* (London: Hutchinson, 1983)

FURTHER READING

Cohen, J. ed.: *The Poetry of Dannie Abse* (London: Robson Books, 1983)

Curtis, T.: *Dannie Abse* (Cardiff: University of Wales Press, 1984)

JOSEPH COHEN

Adler, Cyrus (1863–1940) Jewish scholar and communal leader. Born in Van Buren, Arkansas, he later moved to Philadelphia where he was raised in the circle of the prominent Sulzberger family. He was the first to be awarded a PhD in Semitics by Johns Hopkins University (1887), and taught Semitics there. In 1893 he was appointed librarian of the Smithsonian Institution, and he served also as curator of historical archaeology at the US National Museum.

Adler was a prominent figure in the American Jewish community and played a leading role in various organizations and cultural bodies. He was one of the founders of the JEWISH PUBLICATION SOCIETY in 1888. In 1892 he was among the organizers of the American Jewish Historical Society and served as its president for more than 20 years. A founder of the American Jewish Committee (1906), he succeeded Louis Marshall as president in 1929. As an advocate of quiet diplomacy, he opposed the formation of the American Jewish Congress. Although a non-Zionist, he participated in the work of the Jewish Agency for Palestine and served as co-chairman of its council.

Adler was an acknowledged leader of Conservative Judaism, with which he was associated from its early days. His close relations with philanthropic Jews enabled him to obtain support for the reorganization of the Jewish Theological Seminary under Solomon SCHECHTER. Upon Schechter's death (1915), he succeeded him as president. At the same time, he continued as president of Dropsie College, a post he had assumed in 1908.

Adler was the author of various studies and books, including an autobiography, *I Have Considered the Days* (1941), and *Lectures, Selected Papers, Addresses*, with a bibliography (1933).

BIBLIOGRAPHY

Robinson, I. ed.: *Cyrus Adler: Selected Letters*, 2 vols (Philadelphia: The Jewish Publication Society, 1985) [with preface by Louis Finkelstein and an introduction by Naomi W. Cohen]

FURTHER READING

Neuman, A. A.: *Cyrus Adler – A Biographical Sketch* (Philadelphia: The Jewish Publication Society, 1941)

Parzen, H.: The Adler administration. In *Architects of Conservative Judaism* (New York: Jonathan David, 1964) 79–127

JACOB KABAKOFF

Adler, Friedrich (1879–1960) Austrian philosopher and socialist politician and theorist. Born in Vienna, Adler was the son of Victor ADLER. He was educated at the Mariahilfergymnasium, and studied chemistry and physics at Zurich. There he spent several years attempting to make a career as a philosopher of science, writing on the epistemological implications of the empiriocriticism of Ernst Mach and Avenarius. For a short period Albert EINSTEIN was one of his colleagues. From 1911 Adler was again in Vienna, as a socialist party official. He achieved notoriety in 1916 by assassinating the Austrian prime minister Stürgkh. Pardoned at the end of the war, Adler continued as a socialist politician, becoming secretary of the Socialist International 1923–39. He lived in Switzerland until his death.

Adler was baptized Protestant at the age of seven, and claimed that religion as such was not an issue for him as a youth. Socialism was his surrogate for religion. Adler, like his father, had a very negative attitude to his Jewish past, regarding Judaism as a barbaric religious tradition. Ironically his wife, Kathia, came from an Orthodox Jewish family, and Adler had to go through a form of Jewish marriage ceremony, which perturbed him greatly. It has been strongly argued, however, that this negative approach in itself played a large role in forming Adler's view of the world, and thus makes him a typical representative of the Jewish side to the culture of Vienna 1900 (Ardelt, 1984).

FURTHER READING

Ardelt, R. G.: *Friedrich Adler* (Vienna: Bundesverlag, 1984)

Braunthal, J.: *Victor und Friedrich Adler* (Wiener Neustadt, 1965)

STEVEN BELLER

Adler, Guido (1855–1941) Austrian musicologist. Born in Eibenschitz, Moravia, Adler attended the Conservatorium of Music in Vienna, and subsequently lectured in music history at Vienna and Prague. In 1898 he was appointed professor of music history at Vienna, a post which he held until 1927. He was further founder and editor-in-chief of *Denkmäler der Tonkunst in Österreich* from 1894 until his dismissal in 1938.

Adler was one of the pioneers of modern musicology. In his early career he took an internal approach to the development of musical form, which endeared him to Eduard Hanslick, who was a great supporter of Adler, despite the latter's passion for Richard Wagner's music. Adler's mature method was to see music history in terms of epochal musical styles, as exemplified in his *Der Stil in der Musik* (1911). This approach, paralleled in England by the work of Hubert Parry, has many similarities with the concept of *Kunstwollen* developed at the time by the Austrian art historian Alois Riegl. Adler was an important advocate of modern musicians in Vienna, especially of his friend Gustav MAHLER. He also defended the work of the SCHOENBERG circle, many of whom were his pupils, although in the *Handbuch der Musikgeschichte* (1924) which he edited, he expressed serious doubts about the new music.

In his autobiography, *Wollen und Wirken* (1935), Adler devoted the first pages to a description of his "religion". This religion is not specifically Jewish (although Adler did not convert), but rather a statement of belief in a form of universal humanism. Adler's experience of Austria provides an interesting, alternative picture of a tolerant, humane society, where the church authorities are liberal, where the priest cooperates with the rabbi. Adler himself carried on this tradition by involving himself with both Jewish and Christian choirs.

STEVEN BELLER

Adler, Hugo Chaim (1894–1955) American cantor and composer. Adler was born in Antwerp, Belgium, and died in Worcester, Massachusetts. He attended the Jewish Teachers' Seminary in Cologne, Germany, graduating in 1917, and the Conservatories of Cologne in 1917, and Frankfurt in 1915–16, besides private compositional studies with Ernst TOCH 1924–6. In 1922 he became cantor of the chief synagogue in Mannheim, Germany, where he remained until his emigration to the USA in January 1939. From 1927 to 1939 he was extremely active in the Kulturbund movement in Germany and wrote many works for performances all over Europe and in Palestine. Some of the most successful of these were: *Licht und Volk* (1928), revised later in the United States under the new title *Bearers of Light* (1954); *To Zion* (1930); *Job* (1932); *Balak and Balaam* (1934, revised 1948); *Shirah Chadasha* (1936); *Akedah* (1938); *Ten German Songs* (1936).

After his arrival in the United States, Adler became cantor and music director of Temple Emanuel in Worcester, Massachusetts, where he continued to write music for the synagogue. In 1942 he was awarded first prize by the CCAR for his *Music for the Synagogue*, settings of liturgical texts for the 1940 *Union Prayer Book*. Besides many other liturgical settings, he wrote larger cantatas: *Jonah* (1944); *Behold the Jew* (1945); *A Parable Against Persecution* (1947); and two complete services: *Avodath Habonim* (1943) and *Nachlath Israel* (1952). Adler also had a great interest in preserving the musical heritage of the Jews of southern Germany and arranged quite a few of their traditional tunes for use in the American synagogue.

SAMUEL H. ADLER

Adler, Jankel [Jacob] (1895–1949) Polish painter. Born in Tuszyn near Lodz into a pious hasidic family, Adler moved to Germany in 1913, and in 1916 began studying at the Barmen School of Applied Arts. Returning to Lodz in 1918, he helped found the *Yung Yiddisch* group of artists and writers. In 1920 he was back in Germany, where, consolidating his earlier links with the left-wing avant-garde while also exploring his own Jewish identity, Adler moved away from the Expressionist tendencies of his earliest works towards a greater linearity and clarity of form often put to the service of Jewish subject matter. Figures from the world of his childhood are endowed with a monumental dignity and mysterious gravity.

By the early 1930s Adler was a highly respected figure and influential teacher at the Düsseldorf Academy of Arts. As a Socialist and a Jew, however, Adler wisely left Germany in 1933, living in Paris and then in Poland (between 1935 and 1937), before returning to France. The year 1937 saw the removal from German museums of all works by Adler and their inclusion in the notorious "Degenerate Art" Exhibition.

In 1940–41 Adler fought with the Free Polish Army before being evacuated to Scotland and demobilized for health reasons. Remaining in Scotland, he played an active role in Glasgow's flourishing artistic immigrant community and influenced a number of young Scottish painters. Moving to London in 1943 he again mixed primarily in émigré circles. His paintings of the early 1940s are generally more readily legible than those of the previous decade, many of which had tended to an organic abstraction; full of a profound empathy for human suffering, they are clearly a response to the rumors circulating about the fate of European Jewry. Although Adler, a lifelong friend of Martin BUBER, did not remain strictly observant, his knowledge of, and pride in, Jewish traditional practices was considerable. While formally he owed much to his contact with the Western European avant-garde, his most distinctive contribution comes in the works in which he marries those influences with an explicit confrontation with his Jewish roots.

FURTHER READING

Jankel Adler (Dusseldorf: Städtische Kunsthalle; Tel-Aviv Museum; Lodz: Muzeum Sztuki, 1985) [exhibition catalog]

Themerson, Stefan: *Jankel Adler* (London: Gabberbocchus Press, 1948)

MONICA BOHM-DUCHEN

Adler, Samuel H. (b.1928)   American composer, conductor, and educator. Born in Mannheim, Germany, Adler went to the USA in 1939, where he settled in Worcester, Massachusetts. He became BM at Boston University in 1948, and MA at Howard University in 1950, studying with Walter Piston, Randall Thompson, Irving Fine, Paul Hindemith, and A. T. Davison; he also studied with Aaron COPLAND, conducting with Serge Koussevitsky, and privately with Herbert Fromm. Adler received honorary doctorates from Southern Methodist University (1969), Wake Forest University (1983), St Mary's College of Notre Dame (1986) and the St Louis Conservatory (1986). He joined the US Army in 1950, and in 1952 founded the Seventh Army Symphony Orchestra. Because of this organization's great impact on the European cultural scene, Adler was awarded the Army Medal of Honor (1953). He has held a professorship at North Texas State University (1956–66), was music director at Temple Emanu-El, Dallas, Texas (1953–66), and since 1966 has been Professor of composition at the Eastman School of Music in Rochester, New York, and department chairman since 1974. He also holds an honorary professorial fellowship at the University of Wales at Cardiff. Among his honors and commissions are the Charles Ives Award, the Lillian Fairchild Award, a Guggenheim Fellowship, and the Koussevitsky commission, as well as four National Endowment grants, ASCAP grants, and grants from the Ford, Rockefeller, and Barlow Foundations.

Adler's many works have been performed by leading orchestras, chamber and choral organizations in the USA, Canada, Europe, South America, the Far East, and Israel. He has over 275 published works including four operas, six symphonies, five concerti, chamber and instrumental music. He has written a great deal of choral music, including five large cantatas, *The Vision of Isaiah* (1963), *The Binding* (1968), *A Whole Bunch of Fun* (1969), *From Out of Bondage* (1969), *Choose Life* (1986); three complete services for the synagogue besides many shorter choral works, both secular and sacred, seven song cycles, and many arrangements of folk songs. Also published are Adler's editions and adaptations of works by Bach, Handel, Salamone Rossi, Felix MENDELSSOHN, and Gottschalk. Adler has written three books: *Choral Conducting* (1971; 1985); *Sight Singing* (1979); and *The Study of Orchestration* (1982), which was awarded the Deems Taylor Award for excellence in 1983.

SAMUEL H. ADLER

Adler, Victor (1852–1918)

Adler, Victor (1852–1918) Austrian socialist politician. Born in Prague, the son of a merchant (and later wealthy land speculator), Adler was taken as a child to Vienna. He attended the Schottengymnasium, and then studied medicine at Vienna. He started a career as a physician, but his political interests soon took over. Although Adler started from a German nationalist standpoint, the anti-Semitic turn in that movement, combined with Adler's great social conscience, pointed him towards socialism. At the Hainfeld Congress in 1888–9 Adler succeeded in reuniting the socialist movement in Austria, and became its leader. As such he played a large role in the achievement of universal suffrage in Austria 1905–6. He became Austria's foreign minister in 1918, shortly before his death.

As a student, Adler was at the center of a group attracted to the political and cultural ideas of the German irrationalists (Arthur Schopenhauer, Richard Wagner, and Friedrich Wilhelm Nietzsche). As a result he was acquainted with many of the major figures of Vienna's *fin-de-siècle* culture, including Siegfried LIPINER and Gustav MAHLER.

Adler converted to Protestantism in 1886; although his wife, Emma, was Jewish, he did his best from early on to complete the process of assimilation started by his father. His wish to leave his Jewish identity behind led him to adopt a very ambiguous attitude to anti-Semitism. In many respects, however, the very strength of Adler's wish not to be Jewish had a large effect on his political aims, and his identification with the workers can be seen as a way of losing his identity as the son of a Jewish money man.

FURTHER READING
Ardelt, R. G.: *Friedrich Adler* (Vienna: Bundesverlag, 1984)

McGrath, W. J.: *Dionysian Art and Populist Politics in Austria* (New Haven: Yale University Press, 1974)

Wistrich, R.: *Socialism and the Jews* (London: Associated University Presses, 1982)

STEVEN BELLER

Adorno, Theodor Wiesengrund (1903–1969)

Adorno, Theodor Wiesengrund (1903–1969) German philosopher and sociologist. He was born in Frankfurt am Main of a German Jewish father and an Italian Catholic mother. He studied philosophy, psychology, and musicology at the university there and received his PhD in 1924. He studied composition under Alban Berg in Vienna from 1925 to 1926. After a *Habilitationsschrift* on Kierkegaard in 1931 he began teaching at the University of Frankfurt where he became closely associated with the Institute for Social Research. After Hitler came to power Adorno moved to England and, in 1938, to New York where he joined the Institute. During the years 1941–9 he lived in California, where he wrote with Max HORKHEIMER the *Dialectic of Enlightenment* (1947; 1972). He returned to West Germany and took part in the reconstruction of the Institute in Frankfurt. He became its director in 1959 and professor of sociology and philosophy at the University of Frankfurt. Adorno died on 6 August 1969, while vacationing in Switzerland.

Adorno's lifework was a one-man multidisciplinary enterprise: he wrote on philosophy, sociology, musicology, social psychology, esthetics, and literature. His oeuvre amounts to over 20 volumes published in German and translated into many languages. His best-known philosophical treatises deal with Søren Kierkegaard, Edmund Husserl, and Martin Heidegger. In the middle phase of his career, Adorno is mainly known as the co-author of the *Dialectic of Enlightenment* and *The Authoritarian Personality* (1950). Almost no Jewish influence can be traced in his pre-1940 work but this changed after the commencement of the final solution to the "Jewish Question" in Nazi Germany, which proved to be the catalyzing event for Adorno. In the *Dialectic*...the authors set out to explain "why mankind...is sinking into a new kind of barbarism." The chapter on "Elements of Anti-

Semitism" proposes that the enlightenment paranoia culminates in anti-Semitism. During the war years Adorno wrote a series of aphorisms that were later published under the title, *Minima Moralia* (1974). The volume consists of "reflections from a damaged life", as the subtitle indicates. It deals with the problem of an intellectual deprived of his native language while in exile and pleads for a new moral philosophy. He concludes the book with an exclamation steeped in Judaic thought: "The only philosophy which can be responsibly practiced in the face of despair is the attempt to contemplate all things as they would present themselves from the standpoint of redemption".

Adorno was the first author of the research project sponsored by the American Jewish Committee, *The Authoritarian Personality* (1950), for which he also wrote the theoretical chapters. The study tried to establish the correlation between "deep-rooted personality traits and overt prejudice", and to measure these traits by means of an interdisciplinary approach. It is considered one of the key works of modern empirical social science, the union of German theory and American empiricism – a union that proved quite productive. In the later phase Adorno's theoretical interests and attitude were determined by the following historical events: the Auschwitz experience, summed up in his famous dictum, "No poetry after Auschwitz"; the bureaucratization and ossification of Soviet-type societies under Stalinist regimes; and the commodification of culture in Western capitalist–industrial societies. Distinctly contradictory to traditional academic sociology, Adorno's sociology advocates the inseparability of philosophy and sociology, a fusion of scientific and artistic cognition. Adorno's "theory of society" is an amalgamation of the theories of Friedrich Hegel, Karl MARX, and Sigmund FREUD; it measures societal reality against what it pretends to be, explores its contradictions, and formulates problems from within the perspective of a just and true society. The summation of his lifework is found in *Negative Dialectics*, and the posthumously published *Aesthetic Theory*. *Negative Dialectics* contains some of the most tortured reflections of the author on his experience as a survivor: "It may have been wrong to say that after Auschwitz you could no longer write poems. But it is not wrong to raise the less cultural question of whether after Auschwitz you can go on living – especially for one who escaped by accident".

Aesthetic Theory is Adorno's major statement on the philosophy of art. He insisted on the autonomy of artistic works and developed a theory of the correlation between the esthetic and social sphere. Authentic works of art represent "the whole", he declared. Adorno assigned to the authentic work of art the task of defending truth, of being oppositional and emancipatory in this age of "culture industry".

BIBLIOGRAPHY

Aesthetic Theory (London: Routledge & Kegan Paul and New York: Methuen Inc., 1986); *Negative Dialectics*, trans. E. B. Ashton (London: Routledge & Kegan Paul, 1973)

FURTHER READING

Tar, Z.: *The Frankfurt School. The Critical Theories of Max Horkheimer and Theodor W. Adorno* (New York: Schocken, 1985)

Marcus, J., and Tar, Z., eds: *Foundations of the Frankfurt School of Social Research* (New Brunswick and London: Transaction, 1984)

JUDITH MARCUS AND ZOLTAN TAR

Agam [Gipstein], **Ya'akov** (b.1928) Israeli painter and sculptor, pioneer of optic and kinetic art. Born in Rishon Letzion, Agam studied at the BEZALEL SCHOOL OF ARTS AND CRAFTS in Jerusalem with Mordechai ARDON, in 1949 at the Johannes Itten School in Zurich, and in 1951 at the Academy of Abstract Art in Paris. Before leaving he had already introduced geometrical abstraction to the Israeli art scene. His *Transformable Painting* and *Transformes Musicales* of 1951–2 mark the beginning of his pictorial research into the third dimension which won him the first international prize in the São Paolo Biennale in 1963.

In 1955 Agam participated in the first international showing dedicated to "Movement in Art" at the Denise René Gallery in Paris, where kinetic art was made public. In the years 1956–7 he produced films about his own work and the effects of movement in painting. In 1958 he developed the process of "simultaneous writing", consisting of superimposed words and inviting the reader to grasp several ideas at once. Several experimental works followed: in 1959–62 *Multiple Stages*, where four scenes surrounding the audience were acted simultaneously; in 1961–7, *Transformes Musicales*, constructions of radio receivers creating an environment with objects and exploring the relationship between sound and light.

Agam's originality lies in the changeability of the abstract image through time and space and in his exploration of the composition which changes through the viewer's movement. His work is relief-like, his sculpture often painted in saturated colors. The unfolding of the multiple views and compositions depends on the viewer's investment of time and motion around the work. His early works were static, and based on a screen created through regularly fan-folded metal sheets. Each facet was painted in an abstract pattern, linking with the next parallel fold into a continuous image, through bright colors, tonal contrasts or through the juxtaposition of "barriers and gaps" where the panel's face is perforated. For example, one moves from black and white abstract compositions on one side of the panel, to colorful abstracts on the other side. In later works he installed electrical motors for the activation of changing compositional views, and added light and sound. At times traditional symbols unfold: the *menorah* or Star of David. Abstract forms, Agam claims, represent the abstraction of religious Jewish concepts.

Agam's work hangs in many public buildings, including the President's mansion in Jerusalem, the Lincoln Center, New York, the Elysée Palace, Paris, and the Defense quarter of Paris.

FURTHER READING

Gamzu, H.: *Agam: Pictures and Sculptures* (Tel Aviv Museum, 1973) [exhibition catalog]

NEDIRA YAKIR BUNYARD

Agnon, Shmuel Yosef [S. Y. Czaczkes] (1887–1970) Hebrew fiction writer. Universally acclaimed as one of the masters of modern Hebrew prose fiction, Agnon set standards for sophisticated fictional composition and addressed the problem of Jewish existence in the modern world. Born and reared in a traditional Jewish environment in Buczacz, Eastern Galicia, then part of the Austro-Hungarian Empire, he first settled in Palestine (Jaffa and Jerusalem) in 1908, during the second *aliyah*. To expand his intellectual horizons, he moved to Germany in 1913 where he cultivated his art, married, and raised a family. In 1924 he returned to Jerusalem where he resided permanently until his death.

Agnon's distinctive Hebrew style, an amalgam of late rabbinic and hasidic diction fused with a Yiddish sub-stratum, provided him with a versatile narrative voice necessary for the ironic stance he adopted towards his material. His prodigious erudition in Hebrew literature of all periods enabled him to evoke maximum effects from the linguistic sources alluded to without obtrusive citation. From the appearance of his first major story, *Agunot*, in 1908, until the publication of the first edition of his collected works in 1931, Agnon was primarily known as a modern version of the hasidic storyteller. The popularity of such stories as *Vehaya he'akov lemishor* (1911; And the crooked shall be made straight) and *Aggadat hasofer* (1921; The tale of the scribe) in both the Hebrew original and in German translation, contributed to this reputation. Most of the stories of that period, particularly his comic novel, *Hakhnasat kallah* (1931; The bridal canopy), take place among the pious Jews of Eastern Galicia. Though his experiences in Jaffa and Jerusalem are also reflected in some of the stories of the 1931 edition, the characteristic Agnonic style invokes echoes of rabbinic texts – even in the stories with secular, even erotic, situations.

The image of pious storyteller was somewhat dispelled in the early 1930s as Agnon began to publish stories focusing on the world and language of the unconscious (the stories of *Sefer hama'asim*, 1932–53; The book of deeds), the problems of marriage and sexuality (*Panim 'aherot*, 1932; A different face), and a novel-length study of madness, its causes and its cure (*Sippur pashut*, 1935; A simple story). During this same period, however, he wrote *Bilvav yamim* (1934; In the heart of seas), the tale of the *aliyah* of a group of Hasidim to Palestine in the pre-modern period, and *Yamim nora'im* (1938; The days of awe), a compilation of customs, homilies, and anecdotes

Shmuel Yosef Agnon with his wife Esther

regarding the Jewish High Holy days. In addition to this sharp contrast between the pious and the modern, one begins to notice in these stories signs of the author's confrontation with the writings of Sigmund FREUD and Franz KAFKA. The complexity of Agnon's fictive world was impressed upon his readers even more by his two major novels, *Oreah nata lalun* (1938–9; A guest for the night) and *Temol shilshom* (1945; Only yesterday). In the former, the narrator, an anonymous writer from Jerusalem, recounts a long sojourn in his native town in Galicia called Shibush, a thinly disguised Buczacz, Agnon's home town. The novel, ostensibly drawing upon Agnon's brief visit to Galicia in the summer of 1930, is both a devastating description of the decline of the typical east European *shtetl* and a subtle exposition of the narrator's inability to cope with the realization that the world of his youth is no longer able to sustain his spiritual life or his imagination. Against the background of this portrait of disintegration, the return of the narrator to his home in Jerusalem at the end of the novel suggests the possible reconstruction of spiritual life.

Temol shilshom, set in the period of the second *aliyah*, tells of the failure of its hero, Yitzhak Kummer, a paradigmatic pioneer, to root himself either in the new society of pioneers being shaped in Jaffa or in the traditional, pious community in Jerusalem. As such, the novel is a critique or a satire of the ideals of both secular Zionism and religious Judaism. The specific nature of the hero's tragic end, bound like the biblical Isaac, suggests a powerful response to the news of the destruction of European Jewry. Similar concerns with the problems of Jewish existence in this century can be found in such stories as *Ido ve'inam* (1950) and *Ad 'olam* (1952), and the novel *Shira* (chapters published in 1948–53). In these late works we find an exploration of questions of faith or the essence of language, and a critique of the entire enterprise of modern Judaic scholarship.

9

The first seven volumes of the revised second edition of Agnon's collected works appeared in 1953. The publication of this edition was followed by widespread recognition. Serious critics devoted many studies to his works; he was awarded the Israel Prize twice, in 1954 and 1958; Festschriften were compiled in celebration of his 70th birthday in 1958; his stories became part of the literature curricula in the *gymnasia* and universities in Israel. He was awarded the Nobel Prize in 1966.

After Agnon's death his daughter, Emunah Yaron, undertook to publish those works which the author had never submitted for publication or had never collected in book form, among them the novel *Shira*. These posthumously published works, together with the eight volumes of the second edition of his collected stories (1953–62), comprise one of the most varied and challenging bodies of prose works in the history of Hebrew literature. Agnon's strength lies not so much in his portrayal of characters or inventiveness of plot, as in his conducting a finely nuanced and subtly varied dialogue with his reader who is constantly challenged to participate in the reading of the text by comprehending its controlling ironies and embedded allusions.

ARNOLD J. BAND

Aguilar, Grace (1816–1847)   British novelist. Born of Portuguese Marrano extraction in Hackney, London, Aguilar was educated at home. She published her first book, *The Magic Wreath*, an anonymous collection of poems, in 1835, and also helped her mother run a preparatory school which specialized in religion and the English and Hebrew languages. Aguilar was unwell for most of her short life, but was nevertheless a prolific writer and first became widely known with the publication of *The Spirit of Judaism: In Defence of her Faith and its Professors* (1842) which was written in 1837. This work demonstrates what has been described as Aguilar's "Jewish Protestantism" or her belief in the accommodation of Judaism and Protestantism in England. In an era when British Jews remained unemancipated, Aguilar's declaration in *Chambers' Miscellany* (1847) that Jews were "in fact Jews only in their religion – Englishmen in

everything else", was a popular message for the supporters of Jewish political emancipation. Her *Records of Israel: Two Tales* (1844) and her *Women of Israel* (1845) idealized Jewish life in Spain and women in the Bible in a further bid, often explicit in the text, to gain sympathy for British Jewry. Aguilar's own spiritual beliefs can be found in her epistolic *The Jewish Faith: its Spiritual Consolation, Moral Guidance and Immortal Hope* (1846).

Aguilar's most popular novels were in fact edited by her mother, Sarah Aguilar, and published after her death. *The Vale of Cedars: Or the Martyr* (1850) was an immediate success and was reprinted many times throughout the nineteenth century. It was, however, a highly sentimentalized account of the Marranos in Spain, based on her family's oral testimony. Sarah Aguilar also edited a collection of previously published short stories, *Home Scenes and Heart Studies* (1853), which is one of the first works of Anglo-Jewish fiction to describe middle-class Jewish homes in England to a wide audience. In this collection, Aguilar's apologetic aim of representing Jews in terms of the values of respectable Englishmen is most apparent. *Sabbath Thoughts and Sacred Communings* (1853) concludes Aguilar's earlier reflections on the Bible and religious matters in general.

As well as being the most important apologetic Anglo-Jewish novelist of the nineteenth century, Aguilar also wrote three extremely popular "domestic" novels for Victorian women, and, perhaps her best-known work, *The Days of Bruce: A Story of Scottish History* (1852). She also translated *Israel Defended* (1838), the apologetic work of the Marrano Don Isaac Orobio de Castro. One of the last pieces completed before her death was a short *History of the Jews in England* published in *Chambers' Miscellany* (1847).

FURTHER READING
Grace Aguilar: A centenary tribute. In *Transactions of the Jewish Historical Society of England* 16 (1945–51)

BRYAN CHEYETTE

Ahad Ha'am ["One of the People"; Asher Ginsberg] (1858–1927)   Hebrew thinker and writer. Born in the Ukraine, he settled in Odessa, where he became involved in the

Ahad Ha'am

Hebrew HASKALAH and later in the *Hibbat Zion* movement. In 1907 he moved to London and in 1922 to Palestine. Through his numerous writings – mainly short and succinct essays – he became one of the most revered intellectuals of the Zionist movement, although he never held any public position in it. Influenced by positivism as well as by idealist philosophy, he introduced into Hebrew letters a cool, analytical style, very distinct from the conventional pathos and self-righteousness sometimes characteristic of both *Haskalah* literature and Zionist propaganda.

Within the Zionist movement, Ahad Ha'am became known both for his advocacy of "cultural", as against merely "political" Zionism, as well as for his insistence on the necessity for an ethical content for Zionism if it were to succeed in becoming a central focus of renewed Jewish life. In his first essay, *Lo zeh haderekh* (1899; This is not the way), he called for a cultural renaissance in the Diaspora prior to *aliyah*, and in his famous 1891 essay, *Emet me'eretz yisra'el* (Truth from the Land of Israel), written after his first visit to Palestine, he voiced serious criticism of the cultural and economic deficiences of the first Jewish settlements in the country. He also drew attention to the need to recognize the existence of a sizable Arab population in the Jewish homeland, and warned against outraging it by thoughtless acts and supremacist policies and attitudes.

Ahad Ha'am gained prominence in his polemics against the purely political approach of Theodor HERZL to Zionism: he warned against the dangers inherent in such an approach, and maintained that a Jewish revival in the Land of Israel could not be reached by political means alone. He argued that a nation can be revived only if its culture is living. In his attempt to foster such a cultural Zionism as a precondition for a political revival, Ahad Ha'am developed his complex and extremely influential thinking about the place of culture, language, and literature in the Jewish renaissance.

As a positivist, Ahad Ha'am saw traditional, Orthodox Judaism as basically archaic, yet his call for a secular, modern Jewish culture was nevertheless built on the historical heritage of the Jewish tradition. In the Uganda plan Ahad Ha'am saw a logical corollary to Herzl's cultural and historical uprootedness, and such an historically alienated Zionism was, according to him, doomed to failure. He further contended that the settlement of Palestine would not achieve immediate personal results for most of the immigrants: only a culture of sacrifice, embedded in national values, would sustain the first settlers in what would, of necessity, be difficult years. In this endeavor, Jewish values should be paramount, and the new society should be a "Jewish state", and not only a " state of Jews", in order to become a cultural center for the many Jews who would remain in the Diaspora.

In his combination of positivism and ethics, Ahad Ha'am became a major inspiration within many later debates in the Zionist movement and in Israel. His lucid prose is still considered as a model language for public discourse.

BIBLIOGRAPHY

Selected Essays, trans. L. Simon (Philadelphia: The Jewish Publication Society of America, 1912);

Nationalism and the Jewish Ethic, Kohn, H. ed.: (New York: Schocken, 1962)

FURTHER READING

Simon, L.: *Ahad Ha'am – Asher Ginzberg: A Biography* (Philadelphia and London: East & West Library, 1960)

Avineri, S.: *The Making of Modern Zionism* (New York: Basic Books, 1981) chapter 12

SHLOMO AVINERI

Aizman, David (1869–1922) Russian–Jewish prose writer and dramatist. Aizman spent his childhood and school years in Nikolaev; subsequently he studied painting in Odessa, while working on local newspapers. During the period 1896–1902 he lived in France; relevant to this time are his first stories and publications in Russian magazines. For the most part Aizman's hero is the assimilated Jewish intellectual, having lost touch with his people, enamored of Russia but alienated by it. Hence there occurs the leitmotif of the Russian Jew in exile, suffering from nostalgia and dreaming of returning. The other motif is the relationship between Russians and Jews and their mutual perceptions (in part connected with the pogroms of the years 1905–6 and set against their background). Aizman's psychological prose – politically and ideologically neutral – is probably the best Russian–Jewish literature produced before 1917. The style of his writing changed, from the purely realistic to modernistic (symbolist). In terms of the remarkable and authentic artistic reproduction of the Russian speech of the uneducated Jew, Aizman is a direct predecessor of Isaac BABEL. His significant works include a collection of short stories entitled *Chernye dni* (1906; Black days, 2nd rev. edn); the narrative tales *Krovavyi razliv* (1908; Bloody flood), *Redaktor Solntsev* (Editor Solntsev, published posthumously); and the play *Ternovyi kust* (1907; Thorny bush).

FURTHER READING

Lvov-Rogachevsky, V.: *A History of Russian Jewish Literature* (Ann Arbor: Ardis, 1979)

Nakhimovsky-Stone, A.: Encounters: Russians and Jews in the short stories of David Aizman. *Cahiers du Monde Russe et Soviétique* (1985), Vol. xxvi (2)

SHIMON MARKISH

Alexander, Haim [Heinz] (b.1915) Israeli composer, pianist, and teacher. Born in Berlin, Alexander emigrated to Palestine in 1936 where he completed his professional training under the composer Stefan WOLPE who resided there from 1934 to 1938, and who represented for him the individual, European attitude of the SCHOENBERG school. Later he studied with Joseph TAL. He was also a fine professional pianist, and in order to make a living during the difficult war years he worked as a jazz pianist in hotels and coffee houses in Jerusalem. He taught piano, harpsichord, and composition at the Academy of Music in Jerusalem, and specialized in improvisation, on which he published a manual in German (in collaboration with the pianist David Dolan). His early works, such as the orchestral overture *Artzah* and the motet *Vekibatzti etkhem* were folkloristic in their light, popular harmony and their optimistic expression, while also reflecting his full mastery of traditional counterpoint and orchestration. In the late 1950s Alexander studied the avant-garde style of the Darmstadt composers and turned to strict serial writing, as in his two intense piano works *Sound Patterns* (1965) and *Bnot Kol*. His works of the 1970s and 1980s represent a synthesis of advanced, dodecaphonic tendencies with traditional harmony (in his piano concerto), and delicate jazzy humor as in the song cycle *Ba'olam* to poems by Nathan ZACH. In addition to many choral, chamber, and orchestral works he also made a series of arrangements of traditional Jewish melodies, written for various instrumental combinations and pedagogically graded, as in the case of Béla Bartók's *Microcosmos*.

JEHOASH HIRSHBERG

Alkan [Morhange], **Charles Henri-Valentin** (1813–1888) French pianist and composer. Born in the Jewish quarter in Paris, he was outstanding in a family of musical prodigies and was a student at the Paris Conservatoire at the age of six, and a double prizewinner by the age of ten.

Alkan was a friend of Frédéric Chopin, George Sand, and Franz Liszt and was poised to enjoy a dazzling career as a virtuoso pianist. However, in 1848, owing to a combination of bad luck and personal intrigue, he was passed over as head of the piano department at the Paris Conservatoire, in favor of an inferior candidate. As a result of this humiliation he became an eccentric recluse, devoting himself to religious studies and to compositions, some of which have religious or mystical themes.

Partly because of its technical demands, his music has remained largely unplayed and therefore unappreciated until recently. Moreover, his affinity with classical, rather than Romantic, ideals of composition and playing alienated some of his contemporaries, who considered his music too dry and academic.

His works for piano are on an epic scale, compressing music of orchestral grandeur into the limitations of the keyboard. They often suggest a mysterious inner world, and typically enigmatic titles include *Storm at Sea* and *The Dying Man*; his *Grande Sonate* (Opus 33) has four movements: "Twenty", "Thirty", "Forty", and "Fifty", each describing different ages of man. Other examples of his originality are his extraordinary satirical piece *Funeral March for a Dead Parrot*, and his Opus 27, *The Railroad*, which contains naturalistic figures which anticipate the work of later composers.

Alkan is said to have died by pulling a heavy bookcase onto himself while lifting down the Talmud from a high shelf, but this story remains unverified.

FURTHER READING

Smith, R.: *Alkan, The Enigma* (London: Kahn & Averill, 1976)

ANDREA BARON

Allen, Woody [Allen Stewart Konigsberg] (b.1935) American film director, screenwriter, playwright, and actor. Woody Allen was born in Brooklyn, New York. He attended Midwood High School, and then New York University and the City College of New York, without attaining a degree. He began his career in show business as a gag writer, submitting jokes to newspaper and television personalities. He wrote for television shows such as *The Tonight Show* and *Your Show of Shows* starring Sid Caesar. He became a stand-up comic in the early 1960s and created the persona of the little loser, the schlemiel, who is in awe of women and unable to succeed with them. This persona was carried over into his early films.

He made his directorial debut with *Take the Money and Run* (1969), a parody of the documentary form, which features Allen as an incompetent outlaw. Filmic parody, the schlemiel persona, and the insertion of ethnic gags typify his major comic strategy in his early films. Through parodying directors such as Ingmar Bergman and Federico Fellini, Allen perfected his craft as a filmmaker, while the choice of comic plots reveals many tensions of Jewish–American life. *Sleeper* (1973), for instance, features Allen as an alien in a futuristic dystopia, which encapsulates the Jewish experience of living as an outsider in a dominant culture.

Annie Hall (1977) marked a turning point in his career and his establishment as a filmmaker of international stature. The film is also a virtual compendium of Jewish–American issues – the Jewish male and the shiksa; the ambivalent attitude toward WASP (white Anglo-Saxon Protestant) society and the phenomenon of Jewish self-hatred; paranoia, psychoanalysis, and self-deprecation. Allen's character is unable to feel happy about his life and searches for some kind of ultimate meaning.

His willingness to confront his own feelings and situation led to the making of *Stardust Memories* (1980), a thinly disguised self-analysis in which Allen agonizes over his role as a comic filmmaker, and *Zelig* (1983), a technically stunning story of a fictionalized celebrity of the 1920s who was a "chameleon man". The latter film is another expression of Jewish fear and paranoia and reveals the desperate desire to fit in, to achieve total assimilation with mainstream society.

Allen has been accused of anti-Semitism for his portrayals of Judaism which, though rare,

are consistently negative. In *Hannah and Her Sisters* (1986), Allen's own character, a Jewish TV writer–producer, stricken with metaphysical paralysis, tries Catholicism and other religions before finding solace in movies and romance. Similarly, it is questionable if the cinematic visions of his Jewish childhood are really affectionate. Nevertheless, his films may be taken as paradigms of the Jewish experience in the USA as Allen's semi–autobiographical characters move up the economic ladder, as his own film career progresses, and attain more than a degree of confidence, competence, worldly success, and status.

FURTHER READING

Benayoun, R.: *The Films of Woody Allen*, trans. Alexander Walker (New York: Harmony Books, 1986)

Brode, D.: *Woody Allen: His Films and Career* (Secaucus: Citadel Press, 1985)

DAVID DESSER

Alliance Israélite Universelle A multinational Jewish cultural organization, founded in May 1860 and based in Paris. Its aims are to work for the emancipation and development of Jews all over the world, to aid Jews suffering from anti-Semitism and to encourage publications which promote these goals. The founder members were Isidor Cahen (1826–1902), Jules Carvallo (1820–93), Narcisse Leven (1833–1915), Aristide Astruc (1831–1905), Professor Eugène Manuel, and Charles Netter.

The foundation of the Alliance marked the culmination of the revival of Jewish unity in the mid-nineteenth century, stimulated by contemporary events and attitudes. The massacre of Jews in Damascus in 1840 and the Mortara case, when a Jewish child was forcibly abducted and baptised in 1858, underlined the need for such an organization. Emancipated Jews in the West felt it was their duty to intervene on behalf of oppressed Jews and the political atmosphere in France at the time made Paris the natural base.

The Alliance works in three ways – through diplomatic channels, helping Jews who wish to emigrate, and educating young Jews – although each approach has altered as the political situation has changed internationally and within each country where the Alliance operates.

In the nineteenth century the Alliance intervened on behalf of the rights of Jews in Belgium, Russia, Switzerland, the Balkans, Serbia, and Romania, and of those in French colonies and protectorates. After about 1880 most of its activities were concentrated in Africa and the Near East. After the First World War it fought on behalf of Jews in Poland, Hungary, and Romania, but it opposed the creation of an independent Jewish homeland, which brought it into conflict with other Jewish organizations. In 1945 however, its policies and aims were redefined to fit the current situation and the Alliance supported the creation of Israel. More recently, the Alliance has worked mainly through the Consultative Council of Jewish Organizations in New York.

The Alliance was very involved in aiding Jewish refugees: mass emigration from Romania and from Russia in the early 1880s led to a conference of Jewish organizations in 1882; Netter was sent to explore the possibility of Jews settling in Europe, as the USA had already accommodated many emigrés, who continued to arrive in large numbers, but by 1891 the problem was so severe that it was decided to discourage further emigration and even persuade emigrés to return to Russia. By 1904 the Alliance had lost face over this issue and it was not included in the conference held in Frankfurt to discuss the problem. In the years before the Second World War the Alliance hesitated to take a stand on the potentially explosive issue of Jewish refugees in Europe.

Education, the third and, in the twentieth century, most important sphere of the Alliance's activities, is seen as a means of increasing the social and legal status of Jews. The first Alliance school was founded in Tétouan in Morocco in 1862 and the network of French-orientated institutions grew rapidly; by 1899 there were schools in over 50 towns and cities around the world. Schools in Bulgaria, Serbia, and Romania were relatively short-lived, and for some time the Alliance's efforts were concentrated in North Africa and the Near East, where there was no state education system. There were, at different times, schools in Beirut, Syria, Iraq, Iran,

Alliance Israélite Universelle École de garçons in Hamadan, Iran, 1909

Tunisia (dealing with nearly 3000 pupils in 1960), Israel, and Egypt. Problems arose with the independence of many of the countries in which the Alliance had its schools and with the 1947–8 Arab–Israeli war, which led to Jewish persecution; many of the schools closed down or were taken over by the new governments, as in Tunisia and Morocco.

With the change in status of Jews throughout the world, the emphasis of the education offered by the Alliance has turned to combatting the assimilation of the Jewish people and indifference amongst Jews. In 1987 there were 41 educational establishments run by or affiliated to the Alliance in Belgium, Canada, France, Iran, Israel, Morocco, the Netherlands, Spain, and Syria. It continues to set up new institutions such as the Section Normale Supérieure d'Études Juives, established in Paris in 1980, which prepares students to teach in Jewish schools, and Beit Hamidrash, an institute offering evening classes in Paris, which had its first full year in 1986–7. The Alliance also runs special schools, such as that for the deaf in Jerusalem and the Mikveh Israel Agricultural school, founded in 1870 on the initiative of Charles Netter and now a joint venture with the Israeli government.

BIBLIOGRAPHY
Periodical publications of the Alliance
Bulletin de L'Alliance Israélite Universelle 1860–1913; *Paix et Droit* 1920–39; *Cahiers de l'Alliance Israélite Universelle* 1946–64; *Les Nouveaux Cahiers* 1965 – present

FURTHER READING
Chouraqui, A.: *L'Alliance Israélite Universelle et la Renaissance Juive Contemporaine* (Paris: Presses Universitaires de France, 1965)
Malino, F., and Wasserstein, B., eds: *The Jews in Modern France* (Hanover: University Press of New England, 1985)
Weill, G.: Emancipation et humanisme: le discours idéologique de l'Alliance Israélite Universelle au XIXe siècle. *Nouveaux Cahiers* 52 (1978) 1–20

CATHERINE PHILLIPS

Aloni, Nissim (b.1926) Israeli playwright and short-story writer. Aloni, who was born in Tel Aviv, was the first playwright to break away from the Israeli preoccupation with social realism and dramatic reportage. However, his first play, *Akhzar mikol hamelekh* (1953; The king is the cruelest of all), still utilized a known Hebrew literary convention: the use of a biblical story as a contemporary allegory. In this case the biblical conflict between Jeroboam and Rehoboam was the basis for an examination of the present Israeli political scene.

In 1956, after having studied French and History at the Hebrew University, Aloni went to Paris and was much influenced by the Theater of the Absurd. Thereafter his plays abandoned any reference to realism or contemporary events. In 1963 he established his own theater, Te'atron ha'onot in Tel Aviv, serving as director and manager. Perhaps the most enigmatic of the Israeli playwrights, Aloni is unique in his creation of an original world with its basic components drawn – after his earlier exercise in biblical allegory – from non-Judaic mythology, folktales, masques, literature, and history. The titles of his plays indicate one of his abiding interests: *Bigdei hamelekh hahadashim* (1961; The king's new clothes), an allegory of corruption, based on Hans Christian Andersen's story; *Hanesikhah ha'amerika'it*, (1963; The American princess), which employs the play-within-a-play device; *Napoleon – hai 'o met* (1970; Napoleon, alive or dead); *Eddie King* (1975), a parable of gangsterism and the American underworld, based on *Oedipus Rex*. The "king" in these plays is the father or ruler who is destroyed by a son-figure. The theme of fathers and sons, which is central to Israeli literature, is also found in other plays such as *Dodah Liza* (Aunt Liza) and *Hatzo'anim miyafo* (1971; The gypsies of Jaffa).

From the start Aloni's drama met with mixed critical success. His plays, the first in Israel to be composed directly for the stage, were highly theatrical exercises in virtuosity, flamboyance, and brilliant language, employing techono-logical aids such as tape recorders, and were often misunderstood by critics and public alike. However, in their synthesis of Israeli consciousness and European cultural sources, they constitute a milestone in Hebrew literature.

Aloni wrote a number of equally brilliant short stories, set in his childhood milieu of the Sephardi working-class quarter of Tel Aviv. Many of these stories are imaginative reconstructions of childhood, utilizing similar mythological and imaginative sources to those of the plays.

GLENDA ABRAMSON

Alotin, Yardena Israeli composer. Yardena Alotin was born in Tel Aviv. She studied piano with Ilona Vincze at the Israel Academy in Tel Aviv, and composition with Oeden PARTOS. In 1976 she held the position of composer-in-residence at Bar-Ilan University.

Much of Yardena Alotin's work has an essentially Hebraic flavor. *Yefeh Nof*, written for choir a cappella, is set to the text of Psalm 48, which speaks of the beauty of Jerusalem, the Holy City. This was rewritten for solo flute at the request of the flautist James Galway in 1978 and received its new York premiere in 1987. *Song of the Stream* was written in 1954 and set to poetry by the Hebrew poet Leah GOLDBERG.

Alotin's music has met with international acclaim, and has been performed all over the world at venues which include the Mann Auditorium, Tel Aviv, the Royal Festival Hall, London, the Jordan Hall, Boston, and NHK TV, Japan. She received a special commission from the Tel Aviv Foundation for Literature and the Arts to mark Tel Aviv's 75th anniversary in 1984. For the occasion she wrote *Shir Hag* for choir a cappella, which was performed by the Israel Philharmonic Choir.

She has also written a trio for violin, cello, and piano at the request of the Vicom Trio, which was premiered in Jerusalem in 1980 and in the USA in 1987.

JOHN MATTHEW

Altenberg, Peter [Richard Engländer] (1859–1919) Austrian poet. Born in Vienna, he was the son of a wealthy merchant, who was a great admirer of contemporary French literature. Altenberg half-heartedly studied law and medicine at Vienna, and for a time worked in the book trade, before becoming a professional bohemian. He started writing in the early 1890s, when he was "discovered" by the literary set of Young Vienna. His first book was *Wie ich es sehe* (1896; As I see it). This was followed by many other collections. Altenberg became the coffee-house poet par excellence, a central figure in the literary world of Vienna. His admirers included Karl KRAUS, Alfred Polgar, Egon FRIEDELL, and Arthur SCHNITZLER.

Altenberg developed an extreme form of literary impressionism, which cut across contemporary literary fashions, appealing both to the "impressionists" of Young Vienna, and the proto-expressionists around Kraus. He was, however, perhaps best known as "P.A.", the subject of many of the cabaret sketches and jokes of Friedell and Polgar.

Altenberg converted to Roman Catholicism in 1900, and hated to be reminded of his Jewish descent, attacking Jews for being too "greedy for life". He seems particularly to have admired the antimaterialistic tenor of Christian teaching. In this he resembled the other Jews and Jewish converts who comprised most of his entourage. Ironically, two of its members, Grossmann and Albert EHRENSTEIN, saw Altenberg as being typically Jewish in his prophet-like pronouncements and his rootlessness.

BIBLIOGRAPHY

Vita Ipsa (1918); *Leben und Werk* ed. H.C. Kosler (Munich: Matthes & Seitz, 1981)

STEVEN BELLER

Alter, Robert (b.1935) American literary critic and Hebrew scholar. Alter was born in New York City. Soon after commencing his studies in literature, he developed an interest in Hebrew literature that was to fuel a lifelong devotion to the subject. In 1967 he accepted the post of Professor of Hebrew and Comparative Literature at the University of California, Berkeley. In 1985 he was made a Doctor of Humane Letters by Hebrew Union College, Los Angeles.

Alter has published widely in scholarly and literary journals on his studies of Hebrew literature. Among his subjects are the life and works of S. Y. AGNON, H. N. BIALIK, and Saul TSCHERNICHOWSKI, as well as analyses of modern Israeli poetry and prose. He has also examined the works of other Jewish writers such as Bernard MALAMUD, Leah GOLDBERG, and Saul BELLOW. His articles have appeared widely in such publications as *Hadoar*, *Commentary*, and the *New York Times Book Review*.

Aside from Hebrew and Jewish literature, Alter has studied general literary forms. His first book, entitled *Rogue's Progress: Studies in the Picaresque Novel* led him to produce *Fielding and the Nature of the Novel* and *Partial Magic: The Novel as a Self-Conscious Genre*. He received a nomination for the National Book Critics' Circle Award for Criticism for *A Lion for Love: A Critical Biography of Stendhal*.

During the 1980s Alter carefully considered the literary form and content of the Bible. He wrote *The Art of Biblical Narrative* in 1981, a book that was translated into Hebrew in 1987, and for which he received the 1982 National Jewish Book Award for Jewish thought. Alter is also the author of *The Art of Biblical Poetry* (1985), a work which was awarded the Present Tense Award for Religious Thought, and which was selected by *Choice* as one of the seven outstanding scholarly books of 1985–6. He also co-edited and co-wrote *The Literary Guide to the Bible* with Frank Kermode (1987).

Alter's primary gift to contemporary Hebrew literary criticism is his rejection of the concessional evaluative approach of earlier critics, in favor of an objective methodological approach. He has also taken issue with the notion of Hebrew literature as no more than a tool in the creation of a national identity. He is one of few critics to have considered Hebrew literature in the framework of world literature, and to have promoted a serious critical awareness of it among the English-language readership.

BIBLIOGRAPHY

After the Tradition. Essays on Modern Jewish Writing (New York: Dutton & Co, 1969); *The Invention of Hebrew Prose* (Seattle and London: University of Washington Press, 1988)

JOHN MATTHEW

Alterman, Natan (1910–1970)

Hebrew poet, dramatist, translator, and essayist. His father, Yitzhak Alterman, was one of the pioneers of the Hebrew kindergarten in Warsaw, where Alterman's mother was a teacher and where Natan Alterman was born. Alterman received a Hebrew education from an early age. After leaving Warsaw for Moscow at the outbreak of the First World War, the family moved to Kiev, later to Kishinev, and finally settled in Tel Aviv in 1925, where Alterman completed his schooling at the *Gymnasia Herzlia*. He later studied agronomy in Paris and Nancy and in 1932 graduated as an agricultural engineer. In 1934, after his return to Palestine, Alterman joined the staff of the Hebrew daily *Ha'aretz* and worked there until 1943 when he joined the rival newspaper *Davar*. Later he also published in the evening paper *Ma'ariv*. In 1935 Alterman married the actress Rachel Markus and their only child, Tirzah, was born in 1941.

Alterman was awarded four literary prizes. In 1947 he received the Tschernichowski Prize for Translation for his rendition of Shakespeare's *The Merry Wives of Windsor* and Racine's *Phaedre*, and in 1967 his translation of Molière's plays won him this prize a second time. In 1957 he was given the Bialik Prize for *belles-lettres* for the cycle of poems *Ir hayonah*, and in 1968 his work as a whole was accorded the prestigious Israel Prize for Literature.

Alterman was an energetic writer. His newspaper columns – *Moments* in *Ha'aretz* and *The Seventh Column* (*Hatur hashevi'i*) in *Davar* – afforded his poetry an unusually wide audience. These popular poems, which he called "Poems of the Time and the Tabloid", focus on the political arena and current events and are, essentially, an extension of his public involvement which ranged from opposition to the acceptance of German Reparations to the founding of the Movement for the Greater Israel. In the last two years of the official British Mandate (1946–7) Alterman's columns were often censored by the authorities as subversive. The *Seventh Column* poems were later collected in two volumes.

Although Alterman's first published volume of poetry *Kokhavim bahutz* (1938; Stars outside) comprises poems written between 1935 and 1938, it is unified into a cycle by common elements which run its length. Its archetypal, somewhat atemporal, alocative setting almost renders this work a *fabula*, though the contemporary is clearly embedded in its lines. The second collection, *Simhat 'aniyim* (1941; Joy of the poor), deals with the torments of love in apposition with the tension between life and death. These themes may derive from a sense of the destruction wrought by the Holocaust. The poem *Shirei makot mizrayim* (1944; Poems of the plagues of Egypt), uses the biblical narrative to illustrate the repetitive nature and historical cyclicality of sin and punishment/judgement. *Ir hayona* (1957; Wailing city) addresses major recent historical events – the Holocaust, the establishment of the State of Israel, mass immigration to Israel. A later collection, *Hagigat hakayitz* (1965; Summer festival), is anchored by a plot set in an urban landscape reminiscent of south Tel Aviv, and one of the characters is an aging writer. Prosody in this cycle departs from Alterman's earlier verse style; it is much looser and the verse often changes into prose. In 1958 Alterman published an anthology of children's verse and in 1969 he wrote a prose narrative *Hamasikhah ha'aharonah* which is a satire aimed at the ideological failure of the State and Zionism.

Alterman wrote five plays, four of which were staged in Israel in the 1960s. He also reworked his translation of Samuel GRONEMANN's *Shlomo hamelekh veshalmai hasandlar* into rhyme form and set it to music. This version was produced a number of times in the 1960s to great popular acclaim.

The complete edition of Alterman's work – the original in 16 volumes, the translations in 13 volumes – was started in 1971, a year after his death and includes works that were not published in his lifetime.

BIBLIOGRAPHY

Individual poems are published in a number of periodicals such as *Israel Argosy, Ariel, Orot*, and others, as well as in English and bilingual anthologies of Hebrew poetry such as *The Penguin Book of Hebrew Verse* (ed. and trans. T. Carmi, 1981); S. Penueli and A. Ukhmani, eds, *Anthology of Modern Hebrew Poetry* (Jerusalem, 1966); Burnshaw, Carmi and Spicehandler, eds, *The Modern Hebrew Poem Itself* (New York, 1965); R. F. Mintz, ed., *Modern Hebrew Poetry* (Berkeley and Los Angeles, 1966)

ZILLA JANE GOODMAN

Altman, Nathan (1889–1970) Russian painter, sculptor, and designer. Born in the Ukraine, Altman studied in Odessa and Paris, and settled in St Petersburg, where he was the first Head of the Department of Fine Arts. He illustrated the Bible in 1914, and in 1923 participated in the "Jewish Graphic Art" exhibition in Berlin. Between 1918 and 1922 he worked in the Constructivist style, the Russian version of modified Cubism, in geometrical abstraction. After 1929 he exhibited with Moshe Kisling and Marc CHAGALL in France. In 1931 he returned to the USSR, and conformed by illustrating *Aesop's Fables* in the style of Socialist Realism.

His stage settings include *The Dybbuk* (Habimah, Moscow), *Uriel Acosta*, and *The Tenth Commandment*. The set for *Uriel Acosta* is in contemporary Constructivist style: suggestive abstract forms are arranged on steps at different levels, where abstract upright structures serve as focal locations for the stage, reminiscent of Gabo and Lissitzky. In Altman's portraits, such as *Head of Lenin* and *Head of a Young Jew* (1916), the realistic, representational element is stronger, faces are depicted in Cubo-Futuristic facets, without loss of either the facial features or the individual's identity. *Head of a Young Jew*, a self-portrait of 1916 made with mixed materials, bronze, copper, and wood, is simplified but representational, and accompanied by a non-referential, abstract form at the back.

NEDIRA YAKIR BUNYARD

Altmann, Alexander (1906–1987) Rabbi, thinker, and scholar of Jewish philosophy. Altmann was born in Hungary but received his higher education at the Rabbinical Seminary in Berlin, where he later served as an Orthodox rabbi until 1938, when he was appointed Communal Rabbi of Manchester, England. Here Altmann established the Institute of Jewish Studies (later moved to London). In 1959 Altmann was appointed Professor of Jewish Philosophy at Brandeis University in the USA and Director of the Lown Institute of Advanced Judaic Studies.

Among Altmann's significant contributions to the history of Jewish thought are: *Saadya Gaon: The Book of Doctrines and Beliefs* (1946), *Studies in Religions, Philosophy and Mysticism* (1969), and numerous articles on Jewish philosophy in learned journals. Altmann edited the successive volumes in German of Moses MENDELSSOHN'S writings and wrote the definitive biography of him: *Moses Mendelssohn: A Biographical Study* (1973).

Altmann was a highly gifted speaker and preacher, in great demand in these roles during his term in the pulpit rabbinate. But on his appointment to Brandeis he devoted himself almost exclusively to academic work.

FURTHER READING

Stein, S., and Loewe, R. (eds): *Studies in Jewish Religion and Intellectual History Presented to Alexander Altmann on the Occasion of his 70th Birthday* (University: University of Alabama Press, 1979) Preface, bibliography, vii and 1–12

LOUIS JACOBS

American–Jewish music Even in nineteenth-century Europe after the French Revolution and following the upheavals of 1848, Jews were generally tolerated in the field of music. However, they were always reminded of their volatile position by nationalists and bigots such as Richard Wagner, Franz Liszt and D'Indy, to name only a few. The unlimited freedom and unrestricted citizenship which the USA offered led the Jews in unprecedented numbers to seek haven there. It afforded them opportunities to contribute immensely to the general culture of the USA, especially during the twentieth century when the bulk of Jewish immigrants had settled in, and assimilated into, the society at large. It must be remembered that the Jewish population of the USA was extremely small from 1776 to around 1880–90 but, after the large wave of immigration from eastern Europe, activities in the arts, and the general entertainment field especially, began to be dominated by Jews. By the early 1930s two of the most "American" composers were prominent on the Broadway as well as the concert stage: George GERSHWIN and Aaron COPLAND, both of Jewish origin.

To skip over the nineteenth century would eliminate two of the most talented American musicians of Jewish descent. Daniel Schlesinger, born in Hamburg in 1799, came to New York in 1836, and wrote both orchestral and chamber music. Unfortunately he died at the age of 40. A memorial service held for him in the Broadway Tabernacle featuring three of his orchestral works made history, for it marked the foundation of the first permanent orchestra in New York City. The other and better-known composer is Louis Moreau Gottschalk. Born in New Orleans, he was the son of a Jewish physician, Edward Gottschalk, and a Creole woman, Aimée Marie de Basle. At 13 Gottschalk was sent to Paris to study with Hector Berlioz, who was so impressed with the young boy that he introduced him to Chopin, who called him "king of pianists". He was a fascinating person, amiable and attractive and became a favorite in the salons of Europe and North and South America. His compositions were mostly based on "native" American folk material, which he collected whenever he traveled in the New World. Gottschalk died in Rio de Janeiro in 1869. Most of Gottschalk's works are for piano and written in elegant, virtuosic parlor-music style. Some of his compositions are heard frequently, even during the latter part of the twentieth century, in arrangements and orchestrations, mainly because of pianist Eugene List's interest in them.

The next significant group of composers was the one that gained prominence just before the emergence of Aaron Copland. Among them were Leopold Damrosch (1832–85) and his son Walter Damrosch (1862–1950). Both father and son were primarily opera composers and both were conductors. Walter Damrosch was better known as the conductor of the New York Philharmonic than as a composer. However, the Metropolitan Opera produced several of his works including *The Man Without a Country* and *Cyrano de Bergerac*.

Another early twentieth-century American composer of Jewish origin famous for his operas was Louis Gruenberg (1884–1964). His great-

est success was his opera *Emperor Jones*, based on the play by Eugene O'Neill, premiered at the Metropolitan Opera and often repeated throughout the country.

The first truly successful composition teacher in America was Ruben Goldmark (1872–1936), nephew of Karl GOLDMARK. Though educated in Europe, he went to the USA and studied there with Antonin Dvořák. Goldmark became a teacher at the Juilliard School and, in addition to composing a large number of works such as a *Requiem*, inspired by Lincoln's Gettysburg Address, a symphonic poem, *Samson*, and the *Negro Rhapsody*, he is best remembered for having taught George Gershwin, Aaron Copland, Vittoria Giannini, and Frederick Jacobi. Frederick Jacobi (1891–1952) became a prolific composer who affirmed his Jewish faith by writing a *Sabbath Evening Service, Three Excerpts from the Prophet Nehemiah*, and *Hagiographa*.

Before Jews were able to "break in" to the American musical stage, they wrote many scores for the Yiddish stage, which was very active during the years of the large immigration from Eastern Europe. The most popular musical figures writing for this theater were Joseph Rumshinsky, Peretz Sandler, Abraham Ellstein, and Sholom Sekunda.

Considerably befor they made their mark on the concert stage, Jewish composers dominated the Broadway musical theater. George Gershwin, Sigmund Romberg (1887–1951), Jerome Kern (1885–1945), Irving Berlin (b.1888), and Richard Rodgers (1902–80) were largely instrumental in shaping the American musical-theater idiom from the mid-1920s to the mid-1960s. They were followed by the German immigrant Kurt WEILL (1900–50) and Leonard BERNSTEIN, Charles Strouse, and Stephen Sondheim. Several of these composers are "crossovers"; they also write music for the concert hall. The most notable of these are Gershwin, Kurt Weill, and Leonard Bernstein.

Jews also found their niche in the field of popular music and jazz. Benny Goodman, Harold Arlen, Frank Loesser, Frederick Loewe, Allen Jay Lerner, Lorenz Hart, Simon and Garfunkel, Burt Bacharach, Barbara Streisand, and Bette Midler are only a few of those who immediately come to mind in this huge area of music. Very few Jews are to be found in the world of rock and country music, although there are exceptions, especially in the field of arranging for these media.

Hollywood and the television industry have also attracted a great number of composers. Many of the older ones, those who composed film music in the 1920s, 1930s, and 1940s, were transplants from Europe as well as native Americans. Such men as Max Steiner, Alfred Neuman, Franz Waxman, Mario CASTELNUOVO–TEDESCO, Alex North, and even Aaron Copland were attracted to this medium. During the latter part of the twentieth century the film industry expanded into television and a new set of men and women began to provide the music for these productions. Because of the sheer production volume and the great number of people employed in creating the music, their names are not as well known as others in the past, but many among the composers writing for film and television are of Jewish origin.

In the USA the composer of "serious" or concert music has found a patron in the university or the conservatory. Because of some built-in prejudices, and even quotas, the academic environment opened late to the Jew. When in the middle of the 1930s many of the outstanding musicians from central Europe fled the Nazi menace, they settled in the USA and taught in major American music schools. Before this time, only a few composers of Jewish origin had been prominent in the field of concert music and involved in the educational process. The group around Aaron Copland included such composers as Israel Citkowitz, Leo ORNSTEIN, and Marc BLITZSTEIN. The first active composers to enter the field of music included many of the refugees from Europe, native-born Americans, and some who had come to the USA before the Hitler era. Ernest BLOCH taught at the Cleveland Institute, Bernard ROGERS at the Eastman School, Arnold SCHOENBERG at the University of California at Los Angeles, Ernst TOCH at the University of Southern California, Darius MILHAUD at Mills College, Henry Brant at Bennington College, Bernhard Heiden at Indiana University. William Schuman headed the Juilliard School, and Efrem Zimbalist founded the Curtis Institute; Richard Franco Goldman became the director of the Peabody Conservatory. After the Second World War, the role of the American Jewish composer proliferated in the concert hall as well as in academia.

Just as American literature became dominated by the American–Jewish novelists, so did the field of American music become greatly enlivened by Jewish composers: Milton Babbit, George Perle, David DIAMOND, Arthur Berger, Irving Fine, Harold SHAPERO, Leonard Bernstein, and Lukas Foss. These composers were followed by a younger generation: Jacob Druckman, Seymour Shifrin, Robert STARER, Samuel ADLER, Karl Kohn, Martin Boykan, Claudio Spies, Ralph SHAPEY, Richard Wernick, Ezra Laderman, Lloyd Ultan, Edward London, Jack GOTTLIEB, and a host of others. Prominent in the 1980s are Philip Glass and Steve REICH, who have emerged as the leading exponents of the minimalist school of composition, as well as Stephen Albert and Jay Reise, who belong to the school often referred to as "the new romanticism". In addition to these men are a significant number of women composers, most of whom have written both sacred and secular works: Miriam GIDEON, Marian Bauer, Vivian Fine, Judith Zaimont, Fay-Ellen Silverman, Susan Blaustein, Deborah Drattell, Laura Karpman, and Ruth Meyer, to name only the few that are most often performed.

Jews have also made great contribution to American musical scholarship, beginning with the musicologists and theorists who settled in the USA during the 1930s and 1940s: Karl Geiringer, Paul Pisk, Curt Sachs, Alfred Einstein, Hugo Leichtentritt, Paul Bekker, Max Graf, Paul Stefan, Willy Apel, and Paul Nettl, followed by another great proliferation of scholars who were their disciples, such as Manfred Bukofzer, Gustav Reese, Bruno Nettl, Alexander Ringer, Leonard Meyer, Carl Schachter, Barry Brook, Leo Kraft, George Perle, Joseph Kerman, and Mark Slobin. This list, as that for composers, could be much more extensive, as these fields are continuing to attract many younger Jewish men and women.

The area of musical performance needs special attention for here, in every category beginning with conductors as well as solo, orchestra, opera, recital, and chamber-music performers, the contribution of Jews to the American musical scene has been, and continues to be, substantial. Even the field of the music presenter and of music publishing has for many years been dominated by Jews in the USA. All these persons have labored diligently to spread music throughout that country so that, contrary to some European situations, music in the USA is not concentrated in a few large centers but, through civic music concerts and the existence of over 1,000 metropolitan and community orchestras, great music can be heard everywhere.

FURTHER READING

Holde, A.: *Jews in Music* (New York: Philosophical Library, 1959)

Rabinovitch, I.: *Of Jewish Music* (Montreal: The Book Center, 1952)

Rothmüller, A. M.: *The Music of the Jews* (New York: Thomas Yoseloff, 1967)

Werner, E.: *From Generation To Generation* (New York: The American Conference of Cantors, 1962)

Werner, E.: *The Sacred Bridge*, 2 vols. Volume 1 (New York: Schocken Books Inc., 1970); Volume 2 (New York: KTAV Publishing House, 1984)

SAMUEL H. ADLER

Amichai, Yehuda (b.1924) Hebrew poet, novelist and playwright. Born in Würzburg, Bavaria, to an Orthodox family, Amichai arrived in Palestine in 1936 and settled in Jerusalem with his parents. He was educated in religious schools both in Germany and in Jerusalem, a fact that bears on the nature of his poetry. During the Second World War he served in the Jewish Brigade and then in the *Palmah* (the elite corps of the Israel Defence Force) in the War of Independence in 1948. At this time he began to read modern English poetry, particularly the works of Dylan Thomas, W. H. Auden and T. S. Eliot, which were to remain a major influence on his own writing. These works led to his exploration of the Hebrew language, stripped of nineteenth-century flourishes, as a vehicle for expressing the post-war mood. The appearance of his first volume, *Akhshav uveyamim ha'aherim* (1955; Now and in other days), marked the emergence of a new style of Hebrew poetry, reflecting changes that had taken place in the

Hebrew language during the previous two decades. Amichai incorporated into his imagery the most common elements of the vernacular, technological and military terms, popular lyrics, proverbs and idioms. At the same time his poetic language revealed a richness of references to biblical, rabbinic and liturgical texts which he manipulated into ironic discourse with the problems of the present.

His second collection, *Bemerhak shtei tikvot* (1958; Two hopes apart), set the tone for poetry that distilled the disillusionment of an entire generation and introduced the themes that were to characterize the remainder of his work: love, war, the passage of time, his memories of his father.

In 1961 he published a collection of short stories, *Baruah hanora'ah hazot* (1961, 1975; some of which appear in *The World is a Room and Other Stories*, 1984), in which he recounted, among other topics, his wartime experiences and demonstrated his ability to write prose. His first novel, *Lo me'akhshav, lo mikan* (1962; *Not of This Time, Not of This Place*, 1973) refers to the dislocation of Jewish life after the Holocaust and the dilemma of response on the part of young Israelis. The novel and the short stories are written in a confessional prose style, embellished with the lavish figuration that characterizes his verse. Amichai had some success as a playwright, with *Masa' leninveh* (1962; Journey to Nineveh), a parable of the prophet Jonah in the twentieth century, staged by Habimah in 1964. He has also written a one-act play and a number of radio plays.

After the Six Day War in 1967 Amichai published *Akhshav bara'ash* (1968; Now in the noise) which contains two long poetic works, *Yerushalayim 1967* (Jerusalem 1967) and the quasi-autobiographical *Mas'ot binyamin ha'aharon mitudela*) (The travels of the last Benjamin of Tudela), a confessional review of his life from the time of his departure from Germany in 1936, and a reflection on the human condition in the twentieth century. In his later volumes of poetry Amichai abandons the careful structure of his earlier verse, the couplet, quatrain and sonnet, and creates a more liberally constructed, less figured open verse which is elegiac and nostalgic in tone.

Amichai conveys a portrait of life in modern Israel fraught with war and insecurity and summarizes and reflects all the major pre-occupations of his generation in Israel. At the same time he is able to explore the human problems specific to life in any modern Western society which has strayed from defined cultural and spiritual roots into urban cosmopolitanism. Unlike most of his contemporary Hebrew poets he explores the alteration of Jewish perspectives, the loss of religious Orthodoxy and the nature of Jewish identity in the middle and late twentieth century. Like the so-called "metaphysical" poets of the seventeenth century, Amichai's writing reveals a tussle between physical love and spirituality, and its tension lies in his failure to synthesize both in religious faith.

Amichai is one of the few Israeli poets who is well known abroad. He has been Visiting Professor of Poetry and poet-in-residence at major American universities and has participated widely in poetry festivals and readings in England, France and the USA. He has received many prestigious prizes, among them the Bialik Prize (1975) and the Israel Prize (1981). His works have been translated into English and other languages, and appear regularly in general anthologies of modern poetry in translation.

BIBLIOGRAPHY

Amen. trans. Y. Amichai and T. Hughes (New York and London: Oxford University Press, 1978); *Love Poems* (New York: Schocken Books, 1981) [bilingual edition]; *Selected Poetry* (Harmondsworth: Penguin Books, 1986) [including *Jerusalem 1967* and *The Travels of the Last Benjamin of Tudela*] trans. C. Bloch and S. Mitchell

FURTHER READING

Alexander, E.: *The Resonance of Dust: Essays on Holocaust Literature and Jewish Fate* (Columbus: Ohio State University Press, 1979)

Abramson, G.: *The Writing of Yehuda Amichai* (Albany: State University of New York, 1989)

Fuchs, E.: *Encounters with Israeli Authors* (Massachusetts: Micah Publications, 1982) 86–92

GLENDA ABRAMSON

An-ski, Sh. [Shloyme Zanvil Rapaport] (1863–1920) Yiddish writer and folklorist. He was born in Vitebsk, White Russia. His mother's name, Hannah or Anna, was probably the source of the pseudonym An-ski. Throughout his life An-ski was a devoted socialist with an intense interest in folklore. Attracted by the ideas of the *Haskalah* and the Russian populist movement *Narodniki*, he left home at the age of 16 to live amongst the Russian workers and peasants, working as a blacksmith, bookbinder, teacher, and factory hand. His increasing involvement in socialist revolutionary politics forced him to flee Russia for Paris in 1892, returning in 1905.

It was only around 1904 that An-ski, who until then had written mainly in Russian, began to turn his attention to the particular condition of the Jewish people. He began to write in Yiddish on Jewish themes and composed *Di shvue* (The oath), the anthem of the Jewish socialist *Bund*. As a result of his increasing expertise and fascination with Jewish folklore, he was chosen to lead Baron Ginzburg's Jewish ethnographical expedition of 1911–14 to Volhynia and Podolia. After the First World War, during which An-ski organized relief for Jewish war victims, he helped rebuild the Jewish community in Vilna. He died in poverty in Warsaw.

The 15 volumes of An-ski's collected works (1920–26) boast a wealth of raw material for the folklorist, as well as poems, stories, re-workings of hasidic legends, and accounts of the destruction of the Jewish communities in Galicia, Poland, and Bukovina during the First World War. An-ski's interest in folklore pervades almost all his literary output. Nowhere is this clearer than in his one completed play *The Dybbuk* (1919; translations 1966, 1974). The play tells the story of a couple, Khonen and Leah, whose predestined marriage is prevented by the material greed of the bride's father. Khonen dies when, in desperation, he turns to the *kabbalah* for help, and he enters Leah's body as a wandering soul, a *dybbuk*. Although the rabbi succeeds in driving him out of Leah's body, she dies and the souls of the couple are united. An-ski, who began writing the play in Russian in 1911, tried in vain during the last years of his life to get it staged. Both Konstantin Stanislavsky (who advised him to include the mysterious figure of the messenger) and Dovid Herman of the Vilna troupe, the

Sh. An-ski with Samuel Niger, Vilna, c.1919

leading Yiddish theater company at the time, decided against putting on *The Dybbuk*. However, when An-ski died, Herman's troupe quickly prepared the play and it was given its première immediately after the 30 days of mourning for its author had elapsed. The production was an enormous success and many others followed, most notably, in 1922, that of the Hebrew-speaking Habimah company, based at that time in Moscow. *The Dybbuk* has been frequently revived on both the Yiddish and non-Yiddish stage, often in the expressionist style which characterized these two influential productions. It has also prompted three films (Warsaw, 1938; Israel, 1968; BBC TV, 1979) as well as operas and musicals.

FURTHER READING

Lifson, D. S.: *A History of the Yiddish Theater in America* (New York and London: Thomas Yoseloff, 1965)

Sandrow, N.: *Vagabond Stars: A World History of Yiddish Theater* (New York: Limelight, 1986)

DAVID SCHNEIDER

Anglo-Jewish Association [AJA] The AJA was founded in 1871 to represent all English-speaking Jews and to help the underprivileged Jews of east Europe, North Africa, and Asia by means of education and diplomacy. Its objectives were modeled upon those of the ALLIANCE ISRAÉLITE UNIVERSELLE of France, with whom it still has close ties today. The Association was begun in response to fears that the work of the Alliance would be interrupted by the Franco-Prussian war. The first council included Jacob Waley, Professor of Political Economy at London University, as its president, and five Jewish members of parliament as vice-presidents.

Through its government contacts the Association sought to put pressure on any country that was persecuting its Jewish communities. It was instrumental in ensuring that the Berlin congress of 1878 would try to safeguard the rights of the Jews in Romania. The Association also tried to help the persecuted Jewish communities of Russia and Morocco. The role of the Association in foreign affairs was at first resented by the Board of Deputies, but in 1878 the two organizations decided to cooperate and established the Joint-Foreign Committee. This faltered briefly in 1917 when Claude MONTEFIORE, as president of the Association, opposed the Balfour declaration, and it was dissolved in 1943 when the Board of Deputies became overwhelmingly Zionist in outlook and the Association did not.

The Association supported schools in many parts of the East. Most famous was the Evelina de Rothschild school in Jerusalem which it ran from 1894 until 1972, and with which it is still closely linked.

In the late 1980s the Association continued its involvement in international affairs by active membership of various United Nations Committees. However its major task is the promotion of Jewish education. It organizes loans and scholarships for Jewish students, in particular to help Israelis study in Britain.

FURTHER READING

AJA Review (London: Anglo-Jewish Association) [the organ of the association]

Hyamson, A. H.: *A History of the Jews in England* (London: Methuen & Co., 1928)

RODERICK YOUNG

Angoff, Charles (1902–1979)

Angoff, Charles (1902–1979) American novelist, editor, poet, teacher, and essayist. Born in Russia, Angoff moved with his parents to the USA while he was still a child. He grew up in Boston and graduated from Harvard College. In 1925, shortly after graduating, he became assistant editor to H. L. Mencken on *The American Mercury*, where he began an editing career devoted largely to discovering new literary talent. In 1934 he succeeded Mencken as editor. In 1954 he became a professor of English at Fairleigh Dickinson University in Rutherford, New Jersey, where, in 1967, he helped found, and became chief editor of, the Fairleigh Dickinson University Press.

He was the author and editor of some 45 volumes, including his two-volume *Literary History of the American People* (1931), two books on musicians, a book-length memoir of Mencken, a handbook on libel, three volumes of short stories, and three volumes of poetry.

He began writing a series of short stories inspired by his own life during the 1940s. Eventually he conceived the idea of writing a trilogy of novels about the Polonsky family, centering on David Polonsky, a figure based loosely on Angoff himself. Gradually the scope of this undertaking grew until, at the time of his death, he had published 11 volumes in the still unfinished saga. Angoff is best known for this work. Although critics disagree about its literary merit, it is universally praised for its authentic treatment of Jewish–American immigrant life.

Two of the novels in the Polonsky saga are *Journey to the Dawn* (1951) and *The Bitter Spring* (1961).

FURTHER READING

Rosa, A. ed.: *The Old Century and the New: Essays in Honor of Charles Angoff* (Rutherford: Fairleigh Dickinson University Press, 1978)

Sherman, B.: *The Invention of the Jew* (New York: Thomas Yoseloff, 1969)

RICHARD TUERK

anthropology, modern Jewish approaches to

anthropology, modern Jewish approaches to Anthropological descriptions of Jewish communities may be found in travelers' reports and travel literature, although these did not purport to contribute to a discipline. Samuel Romanelli's *Massa bearav* (1792) illuminates both internal Jewish life in Morocco and links between the Jews and the wider society. The writings of rabbinic emissaries from Palestine were not aimed at providing descriptions of Jewish communities, but often did so incidentally. Travel literature that emerged in the nineteenth century could look to the medieval account of Benjamin of Tudela. Examples are the visit of David d'Beth Hillel of Vilna to the Middle East and India (1832), and the travels in Asia and Africa of I. J. Benjamin (1856).

Later in the nineteenth century Jews living in the Middle East were enlisted in the exploration of these lands by Europeans. One of these was Mordecai Aby-Serour (1830–86) of Morocco, who served as a guide to Charles de Foucauld, known for his study of the Berbers. Hayyim Habshush assisted the orientalist Joseph Halevi in the 1870s in his search for Sabaean inscriptions, and eventually provided a picture of Jewish life in Yemen (1941). Mordecai Hacohen of Tripoli accompanied Nahum Slouschz in discovering the Jewish communities of Libya in the beginning of the twentieth century, but was also a scholar in his own right (1980).

The anthropology of folklore

Towards the end of the nineteenth century there emerged a concern with Jewish FOLKLORE. This was correlated with a developing sense of Jewish peoplehood, prompting Western European Jews to document traditional Jewish culture in Eastern Europe and in Muslim countries. Max Grünwald founded a folklore society, *Gesellschaft für jüdische Volkskunde*, in 1897 and edited its journal. In the years before the First World War Sh. AN-SKI headed an ethnographic expedition in Volhynia and Podolia, but only a portion of the results of this work is currently available.

Folklore initially was conceived of as the traditions of "simpler people" within literate societies, while anthropology focused on tribal societies which had no written culture. Eventually anthropology came to encompass the full range of social and cultural phenomena, overlapping with both folklore and sociology, and meshing with history. These general trends are reflected in the development of anthropology in Palestine and Israel.

The theme of the return to Zion was linked to a consciousness of Jewish nationhood, and a concern to codify and perpetuate traditions of the past. Hayyim Nahman BIALIK, best known for his role in the development of modern Hebrew poetry, was also active in the preparation of folklore anthologies. He was one of the editors of *Reshumot*, an annual established in 1925 for the publication of "memoirs, ethnography, and folklore in Israel".

Middle Eastern Jewry and modern anthropology

In ethnologic work, both the Jews living in the Middle East and the Arabs of Palestine took on significance. It is said that Eliezer BEN-YEHUDA, one of the main figures in the revival of spoken Hebrew, was inspired by the Hebrew pronunciation of the Jews of Algiers. The Jews of Yemen were perceived as representatives of an authentic Jewish culture. Their music, dance steps, and embroidery were consciously incorporated by European Jews into the developing art forms of the Jewish community. In addition, archaeologists from many different countries found that the names of biblical towns were often preserved in current Arabic place names. The Finnish ethnologist Hilma Granqvist carefully scrutinized customs in a village near Bethlehem with an eye to biblical parallels (1931).

Major works of the Mandate period were Brauer's *Ethnologie der jemenitischen Juden* (1934) and his study of the Jews of Kurdistan (1947). The latter was edited by Raphael Patai, who directed the activities of the Palestine Institute of Folklore and Ethnology in the years before the establishment of the state. Martin BUBER taught courses on the "sociology of culture" at the

Hebrew University. Several of his students came into contact with British social anthropology in the late 1940s and this influence was especially important in the case of Yonina Talmon in her book on the kibbutz (1972).

Mass immigration raised questions about the best way to conceptualize and study the processes of absorption and integration. One approach argued that the immigrants had little attachment to their traditional cultures and that their main orientation was acceptance in the European-derived nucleus of the Jewish population. Consequently it was not necessary to gather detailed background information concerning these groups, whose absorption could be best understood in terms of the institutional development of the country. This may be seen in the literature on the *moshav*, which attracted Israeli social scientists together with anthropologists from abroad. While all researchers appreciated that much of what happened in these villages must be seen in terms of their relationship to centralized bureaux – and national policies–anthropological field studies showed that the history and culture of the immigrant groups continued to be important in the new situation.

Anthropological research also has demonstrated that in contemporary Israel ethnicity often receives situational expression. In some contexts, such as synagogue and family life, it is expected that received customs will be maintained, while in public spheres the official norms have played down marks of ethnic distinctiveness. Gradually people from Middle Eastern lands have become more assertive in portraying aspects of their traditions in general social life. Anthropologists have helped interpret these trends as a natural concomitant of social integration, as opposed to viewing them as signs of cultural regression. These developments have enhanced a sense of equality between Middle Eastern and eastern European expressions of Jewish culture.

In the 1950s planners saw the continuity of ethnic traditions as threatening the emergence of a national Israeli culture. Most immigrants initially committed their energies to making a place for themselves in the new society. By the late 1960s however, mobility had been achieved by many, and there began to appear signs of cultural renewal expressed in ethnic celebrations such as the post-Passover *mimuna* festival among Moroccan Jews, or pilgrimages to the tombs of sainted rabbis. These reworked traditions have formed a central theme of anthropological research. At the same time, anthropologists researched modern social structures and trends such as links between development towns and bureaucracies, aspects of labor organization, or the evaluation of programs such as "project renewal".

A number of governmental and quasi-governmental agencies have recognized the contribution of anthropological study in the fields of health and education. For example, studies indicated how traditional beliefs and practices in the realm of curing and medicine coexisted with the use of Western medical services. Recently the Israeli Ministry of Absorption has utilized anthropologists in connection with immigrants from Ethiopia.

Some anthropologists have turned to historically oriented studies, utilizing cultural insights gained through work with Middle Eastern Jews to illuminate aspects of their past. This research is now encouraged by the Israeli Ministry of Education, to help enrich the curriculum of the schools by incorporating materials relating to the range of Jewish ethnic communities.

The Arab population of Israel has also received considerable attention, focusing, at first, on villages and Bedouin. Later, work has been done on urbanization processes and Arab–Jewish relationships. The kibbutz has been a strong attraction for anthropologists, together with many other social scientists. It has been studied both as a special feature of Israeli life, and as a testing ground for general social issues, such as the effect of early involvement in peer culture on adult behavior, or the limits of gender equality.

Archaeology and physical anthropology

Archaeologists dealing with prehistory have addressed general problems of cultural evolution. Israel's geographic setting links it to paleolithic and neolithic developments in Europe, Africa, and Asia. Findings in this region have enriched the fossil record of early man. Physical anthropologists have also examined the genetic characteristics of contemporary Jewish ethnic groups and long time local populations such as the Samaritans.

Anthropological research has also enriched the understanding of contemporary Jewish communities outside Israel. Middle Eastern Jews in Iran and in Morocco, and Algerian Jews in France, have come under anthropological scrutiny, in studies which explore topics such as Jewish–Muslim relations, the economic role of Jews, and the social significance of customary food practices. Other investigations have dealt with Hasidim in Antwerp and *landsmanschaft* organizations in Paris. Most of the recent research activity has been carried out in the USA, fired by both a reinvigorated ethnic consciousness and the growth of Jewish studies within American universities.

The project of the Language and Culture Atlas of Ashkenazic Jewry, undertaken at Columbia University and YIVO in the 1960s, showed the possibility of linking the anthropological study of Jews with central theoretical concerns. Since then other studies have demonstrated how aspects of shtetl culture are reworked, or how practices such as Talmud study groups are maintained, in the context of American social realities. Patterns of Jewish life which emerged in modern times, such as reform congregations or *havurot* (prayer and study circles), also are subjects of contemporary field research.

Jewish anthropologists

There have been a number of Jews who were central in the development of anthropology as a discipline, while for the most part they did not concern themselves explicitly with their Jewish background or the study of Jewish groups. Historical research may show this to be an oversimplified statement, and the question is obviously open to varied interpretations. Anthropology was established as a discipline within American universities, at Columbia, by Franz Boas (1868–1942), whose choice to emigrate to the USA was motivated, in part, by limitations on the professional advancement of Jews in Germany. Boas appears to have consistently maintained a position that played down

Jewish distinctiveness. Nevertheless his researches, many of which are collected in *Race, Language and Culture* (1940), challenged pseudo-scientific racist theories and were widely appreciated in Jewishly committed intellectual circles. Boas, together with his student and later colleague Edward Sapir (1884–1939), shaped the field of linguistics in the USA, through their studies of American Indian languages. Sapir's father was a cantor. In the last decade of his life, while at Yale, Sapir became increasingly disturbed by the growth of Nazism in Europe, and affiliated with other Jewish scholars in publications giving expression to Jewish issues.

There were also major figures in British social anthropology who were Jewish. Three notable individuals, Isaac Schapera (b.1905), Meyer Fortes (1906–82), and Max Gluckman (1911–75), were from South Africa, while S. Nadel (1903–56) came from Austria. Fortes, Professor of Anthropology at Cambridge, was one of the central figures in forging the sociological analysis of tribal societies and lineage structures. His interest in Jewish tradition, within a comparative framework, is reflected in a study of Tallensi religion entitled *Oedipus and Job in West African Religion* (1959). Similarly, Schapera, in a Frazer lecture, applied insights gained in the study of African societies to the biblical story of Cain. Gluckman, Professor at Manchester University, headed a research project in Israel which put 10 anthropologists into the field there. This had a formative influence on Israeli anthropology, bolstered by his visits to Israel on a number of occasions.

Both general social anthropology, and French ethnology ("anthropology" usually refers to physical anthropology on the continent), are indebted to the work of Émile DURKHEIM (1858–1917), who is also considered one of the founders of sociology. Durkheim came from an Alsace–Lorraine Jewish family. While he stressed his rootedness in French intellectual thought, there were occasions in his life when he was identified by those who opposed his views as a "German Jew". Some have speculated about Jewish influence on his seminal work in the study of religion, although none has explored in detail the nature of his upbringing and the content of the Jewish education he received. When citing

examples of biblical society he shows no indication of insights stemming from Jewish tradition. Perhaps greater Jewish influence can be detected in the work of Marcel MAUSS, Durkheim's student and collaborator, as well as his nephew. It is clear that Mauss's training gave him a knowledge of Hebrew. Mauss devoted much of his energies, after the First World War, to publishing the works of close colleagues in the *Année Sociologique* group who had died during the war, among whom were other Jews.

The influence of Durkheim and Mauss is prominent in the writings of Claude LÉVI-STRAUSS, the most prominent contemporary anthropologist. Lévi-Strauss's "structuralism" first stemmed from an analysis of societies in the Amazon basin and has affected work in both the social sciences and humanities. His intellectual autobiography, *Tristes Tropiques* (1955), points out that his grandfather was the Rabbi of Versailles, but he claims that the Jewish worship he knew did not create any emotional response in him. Because his insights have proved so productive in the study of religions and cosmologies, the question of the influences shaping his work will undoubtedly continue to be debated.

Anthropology and the Bible

A number of anthropologists have attempted to apply anthropological analysis to the Bible. The classic work is Sir James Frazer's *Folklore in the Old Testament* (1918), which focuses on the topics of marriage, residence, and inheritance. More recently, structuralism's successes have tempted many anthropologists to try their hand at biblical scholarship, a trend that was initiated by Edmund Leach. His *Genesis as Myth, and Other Essays* (1969) brings together several papers in this direction. This trend continues today, although papers in this genre are usually written by anthropologists who do not know Hebrew or ancient Near Eastern languages. At the same time, aspects of structuralist-inspired thought have now been incorporated into the work of some biblical scholars.

There has been less of an effect of anthropological thinking upon other branches of Jewish studies. Mary Douglas's study of the "abominations of Leviticus", in her *Purity and Danger* (1966), has stimulated some writers to analyze *kashrut* with reference to rabbinic rules, as well as the biblical text. A few other applications have been made with regard to the rabbinic period, and to a limited extent in connection with work on medieval Jewry as well. While anthropology was initially rejected by scholars of Judaica as bearing no relevance to their investigations, it now has begun to make a mark in different realms of Jewish studies.

FURTHER READING

Cohen, A.: *Arab Border Villages in Israel* (Manchester: Manchester University Press, 1965)

Deshen, S., and Shokeid, M.: *The Predicament of Homecoming: Cultural and Social Life of North African Immigrants in Israel* (Ithaca: Cornell University Press, 1974)

Deshen, S., and Zenner, W., eds: *Jewish Societies in the Middle East: Community, Culture and Authority* (Washington DC: University Press of America, 1982)

Goldberg, H., ed.: *Judaism Viewed from Within and from Without; Anthropological Studies* (Albany: State University of New York Press, 1987)

Kugelmass, J.: *The Miracle of Intervale Avenue: The Story of a Jewish Congregation in the South Bronx* (New York: Schocken, 1986)

Patai, R.: *Tents of Jacob; The Diaspora, Yesterday and Today* (Englewood Cliffs: Prentice-Hall, 1971)

Spiro, M.: *Gender and Culture: Kibbutz Women Revisited* (Durham: Duke University Press, 1979)

HARVEY GOLDBERG

Antin, Mary [Ashe] (1881–1949) American author. Born in Polotzk, Lithuania, Mary Antin emigrated to the USA in 1894. Educated in public schools in Boston and at the Girls' Latin School, she also attended Columbia University's Teachers' College and Barnard College. Publication of her teenage poems and essays in educational journals and Boston papers made her a local celebrity. Her first full-length work, *From Plotzk* [*sic*] *to Boston* (1899), grew out of her letters describing her journey to the USA in 1894. It remains a classic account of the immigrant's voyage.

In Antin's best-known work, *The Promised Land* (1912), the thirty-year-old author described her life in Polotzk and Boston. But more than an autobiography, *The Promised Land* espoused the myth of the American dream, showing how the idea of the USA ran counter to the economic, political, and cultural oppression that she had known in Europe. She pointed to her own adolescent literary success as proof of the abundant opportunities held out to immigrants who abandoned the old to embrace wholeheartedly the new. *The Promised Land* sold nearly 85,000 copies before Antin's death and brought her nationwide fame. Her success once again confirmed what Antin had for so long asserted – that nothing stood in the way of the immigrant in the USA.

She continued to write short stories of the immigrant experience for the *Atlantic*, and opinion pieces for *The Outlook*. Her last full-length work, *They Who Knock at Our Gates* (1914), was a polemic against the movement to restrict immigration. Fatigue and estrangement from her husband, William Amadeus Grabau, over his pro-German stance during the First World War, helped bring on an attack of neurasthenia. Although Antin wrote occasional essays after that, her work had lost much of its former power.

FURTHER READING

Nadell, P. S.: Introduction to *From Plotzk to Boston* (1899; repr. New York: Markus Wiener, 1986)

Handlin, O.: Mary Antin. In *Notable American Women, 1607–1950: A Biographical Dictionary* (Cambridge: Bellknap, 1971)

——: Introduction to *The Promised Land* (1912, repr. Boston: Houghton Mifflin Co., 1969)

PAMELA NADELL

Appelfeld, Aharon (b.1932) Israeli fiction writer. Appelfeld is widely recognized as the most effective writer in Hebrew prose fiction attempting to give expression to the experiences of individuals who were victims of the Nazis during the Holocaust. Though artfully wrought, these stories draw upon Appelfeld's own experience during and after the Second World War. Born near Czernowitz, then in Romania, to a middle-class German-speaking family, Appelfeld saw his secure life abruptly disrupted by the German invasion in the summer of 1941. His mother murdered and his father imprisoned, he was forced to fend for himself. Escaping from the labor camp at Transnistria, he lived among Ukrainian peasants until the area was liberated by Soviet forces in 1944. Appelfeld then worked at odd jobs and finally joined a group of other orphaned youngsters on their way to Italy and, in Appelfeld's case, finally to Palestine, where he was brought in 1946. After several years in a variety of schools for refugee children where he learned Hebrew, he studied at the Hebrew University, settled in Jerusalem, and dedicated himself to his writing. His mastery of his craft was, in effect, part of the process of rehabilitation.

Appelfeld's first volume of stories, *Ashan* (1962; Ashes), was of particular moment since it was the first artistically effective portrayal in Hebrew literature of individuals whose lives had been radically affected by the ravages of the Holocaust. Fiction about the Holocaust was by no means the norm in Hebrew literature of the late 1950s and early 1960s when Appelfeld began to publish; his relentless pursuit of means to find expressive form for the horrors of the period firmly established the viability and legitimacy of the genre in Hebrew literature.

Shrewdly avoiding any attempt to speak about the unspeakable atrocities, Appelfeld never describes life in the ghettos or death camps. His strategy is to focus upon what happened after the camps and before the outbreak of the war in 1939. He assumes that his reader knows only too well what happened between 1939 and 1945; by his choice of materials he implies that any description of what happened in the ghettos and camps would be both impossibly grotesque and obscene. Thus, in most of his stories published in the 1960s (12 volumes were published between 1962 and 1968) we find survivors either resettled in Israel or in the transit camps in Europe trying to cope with the task of living their ordinary, daily lives after the long period of pain, deprivation, and humiliation. In the 1970s Appelfeld began to examine the deceptively tranquil lives these victims lived in central Europe before the war. The technique is one of allusion and indirection, never direct confrontation. The same is true of Appelfeld's style which never depicts either human behavior or nature directly.

Even when the focus moves close to the eye of the storm as in *Kitty* (1963), the story of a young

girl hidden in a convent during the days of deportations and death squads, we are shown the heroine's dim awareness of what was soon to befall her, never the act itself. The reader both knows more than the hero/victim and realizes that the distorted and inadequate comprehension of reality is one of the inescapable marks of the victim. Frequently the survivors are portrayed in a meaningless state of limbo, waiting for something or somebody.

Badenheim 1939 (1974) is the cardinal Appelfeld story presenting the false tranquillity of European Jewry before the Second World War. Set in a central European resort town with all its traditional entertainments for the guests, the story moves slowly but inexorably from a vague feeling of malaise, to bizarre activities of the town's civil servants, to the grotesque reactions of the vacationers, and finally to their orderly deportation in box cars. An extension of this preoccupation can be found in *Tor hapela'ot* (1978; *The Age of Wonders*, 1981). The novel is divided into two halves: the "before", a description of the complicated personal life of a middle-class, professional family; the "after", the return after the war of the son to the town the family had inhabited before the war. Between the two parts we find the eloquent blank page.

ARNOLD J. BAND

Apple, Raymond (b.1935)   Australian rabbi and educator. Apple was born in Melbourne and is one of the first native-born Jews to have entered the Orthodox Rabbinate in Australia. He was educated at the University of Melbourne (Arts/Law) and Jews' College, London. While still an undergraduate he foreshadowed his subsequent career as an educator by inaugurating and administering correspondence courses in Hebrew and Judaism for Jewish children in remote parts of Australia and New Zealand who could not be served by the normal educational institutions. After his ordination in England he served as the religious director for the Association for Jewish Youth before holding pulpits at Bayswater and then Hampstead. In London he was chairman of the Jewish Marriage Council and an office bearer for the Council of Christians and Jews. Since returning to Australia to take the pulpit of the Great Synagogue, Sydney, (the Australian "mother" pulpit), he has been committed to both of these activities: the current friendly relations between the churches (especially the Roman Catholic Church) and the Jewish community owe much to his initiatives. In particular he founded and runs the Christian-Jewish study centre which was established in Sydney in 1973.

Apple's work gained him the Queen's Silver Jubilee Medal (1977) and the Order of Australia (1979). He is the author of several pamphlets, scholarly articles and books, including *The Jews* (1981) and *The Hampstead Synagogue, 1892–1967* (1967).

ALAN D. CROWN

archaeology, modern Israeli The major archaeological sites of the Land of Israel were never completely lost or forgotten, even after the destruction of Jerusalem in 70 CE. The tradition of Jewish pilgrimage to sites of biblical importance continued, and with the acceptance of Christianity as the official religion of the Roman Empire in the fourth century CE, Christian pilgrimage to biblical sites in the Holy Land was encouraged on a truly massive scale. With the advent of Islam, the Quranic versions of biblical traditions encouraged Muslim interest in many of the ancient sites of the country, and through the subsequent centuries of early Islamic, Crusader, and Ottoman rule, the tradition of pilgrimage helped to keep a memory of the country's ancient landmarks alive.

While the object of traditional Holy Land pilgrimage remained primarily religious, a new motivation was added to the study and veneration of biblical antiquities in the eighteenth century. The rise of antiquarianism in Europe sparked a new, secular interest in the monuments and geography of ancient civilizations, and in the course of wide-ranging explorations of the eastern Mediterranean, prominent European scholars such as Carsten Niebuhr and Constantin-François Volney came to the Land of the Bible and undertook the first scientific observation and classification of the country's flora, fauna, and archaeological remains.

During the first half of the nineteenth century, important archaeological discoveries also came from Egypt and Mesopotamia, countries whose ancient civilizations had an obvious bearing on biblical archaeology. Great public acclaim greeted the decipherment of Egyptian hieroglyphics by François Champollion in 1822 and the decipherment of the cuneiform script of Mesopotamia by Henry Rawlinson in 1835, for these archaeological advances provided the first non-biblical references to some of the episodes of biblical history. Equally important, the discovery of the impressive ruins of the temples and palaces of ancient Israel's neighbors provided vivid visual images of biblical peoples and their cultures to a European public becoming accustomed to the visual imagery of the printed engraving and photograph.

Near Eastern archaeological discoveries were soon used in defense of the Bible's historical reliability in the face of attacks by the adherents of German "Higher Criticism". One of the first scholars to use archaeological material in a systematic attempt to disprove the accusations of the biblical critics was the American, Dr Edward Robinson. His extensive explorations of the Palestinian provinces of the Ottoman Empire in 1838 and 1852 led to the identification of dozens of previously forgotten or overlooked biblical localities. After Robinson many scholars – both critics and defenders – came increasingly to rely on archaeological data in support of their historical claims.

As the western powers grew increasingly involved in the affairs of the Ottoman Empire, archaeology, like mission, education, and commercial activity in the region, became increasingly institutionalized. By the late nineteenth century, the academic communities of Great Britain, France, Germany, and the USA had established archaeological organizations devoted to the study, excavation, and display of biblical antiquities. The most important of these, the British-sponsored Palestine Exploration Fund, carried out extensive excavations in Jerusalem (1867–70) and sponsored the first systematic archaeological, ethnographical, and topographical survey of western Palestine (1871–82). An enormous volume of new data was thereby added to the study of the Land of the Bible, but its scholarly application continued to be primarily biblical illustration rather than independent historical research.

This archaeological orientation underwent a sudden and dramatic transformation after the pioneering work of Heinrich Schliemann at Troy and of Flinders Petrie in Egypt. Archaeology now came to be seen as a tool to understand the progressive development of ancient civilization, not merely as an aid to the collection of relics and the discovery of isolated monuments. In the superimposed levels of the *tells*, or ancient city mounds of the Land of the Bible, the entire span of the country's history could be examined, as was demonstrated for the first time by Petrie himself in his 1890 excavations at Tell el-Hesy in southern Judea. The trend toward the long range perspective was also apparent in the large-scale excavations conducted at the biblical cities of Gezer (1902–09), Megiddo (1902–05), Ta'anach (1902–10), and Jericho (1910–14). In their finds and interpretations, archaeologists began to integrate social evolutionary notions of technological progress and racial competition into the country's history.

Archaeological activity in the Land of the Bible expanded significantly with the defeat of the Ottoman Empire in the First World War and the establishment of a British administration in Palestine. Under the supervision of the efficient Palestine Department of Antiquities, expeditions from Europe and the USA conducted excavations at the sites of some of the most important biblical cities such as Ashkelon, Beth Shean, Samaria, Lachish, and Megiddo. As the techniques of excavation were gradually refined, changing styles of pottery and architecture came to be regarded as the primary indicators of evolutionary development and ethnic identity. Yet the religious motivation remained an important part of the archaeological message; among the most prominent academic figures in this period were W. F. Albright of Johns Hopkins University and Père Hughes Vincent of the École Biblique et Archéologique in Jerusalem who stressed their faith in the basic compatibility of biblical history and archaeological evidence.

Until the British Mandate period, however, the Jewish community in Palestine showed little interest in archaeology. Those segments of the *yishuv* whose orientation was primarily religious needed no material confirmation of the Bible. Those whose orientation was toward Labor Zionism were far more concerned with the country's future than with its past. Yet a number of Jewish immigrants to the country, who had been trained in European universities recognized the importance of stressing a national, Jewish dimension to the country's ancient history. To this end, the Jewish Palestine Exploration Society was established in 1914. The organization's first excavation was undertaken in 1920 at the site of a Roman–Byzantine synagogue of Hammath Tiberias – a site which demonstrated the continuity of Jewish life in Palestine long after the destruction of the Temple in Jerusalem.

The establishment of the Hebrew University in 1925 provided an additional incentive to local archaeological activity. Eliezer SUKENIK, director of the university's museum of Jewish antiquities, and his assistant, Nahman Avigad, carried out a number of excavations in Jerusalem and along the coast. A turning point in the public attitude toward archaeology came with the unexpected discovery of an elaborate Byzantine synagogue mosaic by the members of Kibbutz Beit Alpha in 1928. Its ancient Hebrew inscriptions, still legible, aroused great excitement in the Jewish community as a national treasure and symbolic validation for modern settlement. At a time when the Jewish and Arab populations in Palestine were engaged in a struggle for the recognition of their historical rights in the country, every biblical site, every ancient Hebrew inscription uncovered at or near the site of modern Jewish settlement possessed clear modern political significance.

Both foreign and local archaeological work in the country was interrupted during the Second World War and by the increasing violence of the late British Mandate period. Yet in 1948, with the establishment of the State of Israel, archaeological work resumed with a new organizational identity. In July 1948 the Israel Department of Antiquities and Museums was established to oversee the excavation and preservation of the country's archaeological heritage. In the areas of the country that came under the jurisdiction of the Hashemite Kingdom of Jordan, a new antiquities department was also founded, headed by Lancaster Harding, formerly of the mandatary Palestine Department of Antiquities. From this period on, a stress on the nationalistic significance of archaeological remains – rather than on the more universal biblical perspectives – became a primary focus of archaeological work.

The most spectacular discovery in the history of biblical archaeology was made in this period: the 1947 discovery of ancient Hebrew manuscripts in caves near the northwestern shore of the Dead Sea. Sukenik of the Hebrew University was the first to recognize the value of the Dead Sea Scrolls as the oldest surviving manuscripts of the Bible, and as the religio-literary compositions of the ancient Jewish sect of the Essenes. Differing religious perspectives subsequently characterized the study of the Dead Sea Scrolls. While many European and American Christian scholars distinguished the theological roots of Christianity in the Essene literature, the primary interest of most Israeli scholars was on the evolution of the biblical text and on specific issues of Second Temple-period history.

Among the Israeli scholars who rose to prominence in this period was Yigael YADIN, son of Professor Eliezer Sukenik. After service in the *Haganah* and as chief-of-operations of the Israel Defense Forces in the Independence War, Yadin declined continued participation in public life, preferring to complete his archaeological studies and to embark on an academic career. His first major achievement was a continuation of the work of his father, in the acquisition of the Dead Sea Scrolls for the State of Israel and in his publication of the *Scroll of the War of the Sons of Light Against the Sons of Darkness.*

Yadin was deeply interested in the archaeological investigation of Israel's ancient military history and questions about the nature of the Israelite conquest of Canaan were among the main motivations for his large-scale excavations at Hazor (1955–60). His subsequent work continued the theme of unified military action, as it occurred in later periods of Jewish history. Yadin's 1960 discovery in the Judean desert of second-century-CE military communications

from the headquarters of the Jewish rebel leader, Shimon Bar Kochba, confirmed the historical existence of a legendary figure, and Yadin's highly publicized excavations at Masada (1963–65), which uncovered the remains of the last Jewish stronghold to hold out against the Romans, struck a responsive chord among the modern Israeli public.

Also prominent in this formative period of Israeli archaeology were three other scholars, each of whom established a particular field of study within the larger discipline. Michael AVI-YONAH, whose excavations and studies dealt primarily with the remains of the Roman and Byzantine periods, highlighted the continuity of Jewish religious and artistic traditions in the post-biblical periods. Benjamin MAZAR was among the first Israeli scholars to use archaeological data to reconstruct the historical geography of the country. Also important was Yochanan Aharoni, who served as the first director of the Tel Aviv University Institute of Archaeology after its founding in 1968. Largely due to the influence of Aharoni, the archaeological orientation of the Tel Aviv Institute differed from that of Hebrew University, often leaning more toward questions of historical geography than to questions of religious or military history.

While Israeli archaeologists continued their work within the borders of the State of Israel, several foreign expeditions undertook large-scale excavations on the Jordanian-controlled West Bank. Among the most important of these projects were the digs of Kathleen Kenyon at Jericho (1952–58) and Jerusalem (1961–67), of Ernest Wright at ancient Shechem (1956–64), and of Père Roland DeVaux at Tell el-Farah, site of the ancient Israelite capital of Tirzah (1946–60). Although these projects helped to refine the field methodology of ceramic and stratigraphic analysis and shed new light on the pre-biblical cultures of the country, their main impact remained largely a matter of scriptural illustration to a religiously receptive audience in Europe and the USA.

In the aftermath of the 1967 Six Day War, modern political realities once again changed the character of archaeological work in Israel. With the Sinai and the West Bank now under Israeli

Excavations in the Nahal Hever caves, where many of the Bar Kokhba objects were discovered

administration, and with increasing contacts between the foreign and local schools of archaeology, differences in technique and approach began to dissolve. While some large excavations continued, increasing emphasis was placed on extensive archaeological surveys and on joint research projects. The basic philosophical differences between Israeli archaeologists, in their elaboration of national history, and the foreign archaeologists, in their interest in the material illustration of the biblical text, were seldom explicitly discussed. Sharing a nearly identical methodology of digging, recording, and publication, the practitioners of biblical archaeology formed a self-contained discipline that, at the same time, gradually became isolated from archaeological developments in other parts of the world.

Under the influence of the Americanist "New Archaeology" of the 1960s, a number of American scholars, the most outspoken of whom was William Dever, eventually criticized their colleagues' implicit religious orientation and intellectual isolation. Speaking in favor of a more anthropologically oriented approach to archaeology in the Lands of the Bible, they even suggested that the term "Biblical Archaeology" should be replaced by the more neutral "Syro-Palestinian Archaeology". Dever and his supporters argued for a re-examination of such basic concepts as the nature of "cultures", social change, and ethnic identity. Initially, however, this appeal went largely unnoticed or was only superficially accepted, for sacred history, not ancient environmental interaction or the stability of ancient social systems, was the factor that drew explorers and scholars – and before them, the religious pilgrims – to the ancient sites of the Holy Land.

Throughout the 1970s and 1980s, the extent of archaeological work in Israel continued to expand. Three additional academic departments of archaeology were established: at Haifa, Ben Gurion, and Bar Ilan Universities. Foreign expeditions initiated major excavations in close coordination with, and in many cases with the participation of, Israeli colleagues. The remains of the biblical periods continued to exert a special fascination both for scholars and for the general public. Yet with growing interest in prehistoric sites and a growing awareness of the role of the environment in human culture, the archaeologists working in Israel – both Israeli and foreign – were gradually making the final break with the tradition of pilgrimage and sacred relics. Archaeology in Israel was beginning to turn its attention toward the analytical study of social and cultural change.

The archaeology of the Land of the Bible, once preoccupied with a defense of the historical veracity of the biblical traditions, had by the end of the twentieth century undergone a dramatic transformation. Although its social motivation was still based largely on religious identification or on a feeling of national heritage, the modern approaches to archaeological work in the Land of the Bible were gradually orienting themselves toward the social sciences and away from the illustration of a particular religious or national history.

FURTHER READING

Ben-Arieh, Y.: *The Rediscovery of the Holy Land in the Nineteenth Century* (Jerusalem: Israel Exploration Society, 1979)

Pearlman, M.: *Digging Up the Bible* (New York: Morrow, 1980)

Shepherd, N.: *The Zealous Intruders* (San Francisco: Harper & Row, 1987)

Silberman, N. A.: *Digging for God and Country* (New York: Knopf, 1982)

NEIL SILBERMAN

architecture, modern synagogue The only type of building that can be called intrinsi-cally Jewish is the synagogue. There is no such thing as a Jewish style, even though the contemporary British classical architect, Quinlan Terry, in his talk to the Royal Institute of British Architects, as reported in Robin Kent's article "The Tabernacle" (RIBA Journal, May 1985) maintains that the Aeolic or proto-Ionic order was Jewish and based on the curving horns of sacrificial rams.

In the eighteenth century all buildings were constructed in the style of their time, be they church, non-conformist chapel (in the UK), or synagogue, except that a church would be set apart by its tower. There was little to distinguish the interior of the Spanish and Portuguese synagogue in Bevis Marks in the City of London (1701) from a city church except for its internal arrangement, and if today one wishes to savor the atmosphere of an unaltered Wren city church a visit to Bevis Marks is essential, because its interior has survived intact.

Resulting from the precarious nature of Jewish existence, synagogues were more reticent than churches in their external architecture. Bevis Marks and other eighteenth and early nineteenth-century London synagogues (the Hambro Synagogue and the New Synagogue, Great St. Helens), and provincial ones such as Bristol, were approached through courtyards, not directly from a street. Where there were more wealthy or confident communities, as in Amsterdam, the synagogues were very prominent from the street. Even in German towns and villages in which Jews were sufficiently numerous and confident, such as Ichenhausen in Bavaria, the baroque synagogue of 1781 made a contribution to the street scene.

During the later eighteenth century, with the dawn of the Enlightenment, certain German rulers created parks and palaces in the English style. At Wörlitz, Prince Franz of Anhalt-Dessau (1740–1817) built a palace in the Palladian manner and from 1764 onwards laid out the park in the English landscape style as a demonstration of his enlightenment. Such rulers attracted Jews to their states and among the exotic garden buildings at Wörlitz was a neo-Classical synagogue built in 1789 and designed by F. W. von Erdmannsdorff.

Early in the nineteenth century, with the

growth of Romanticism, the style of a building became a matter of great importance. The Germans mistakenly claimed that the Gothic style had originated in their lands and, once the Prussians had acquired Cologne in the settlement after the Napoleonic Wars, they made it a matter of national policy to complete the unfinished medieval cathedral. In nineteenth-century England the established church also adopted the Gothic style, while non-conformist chapels tended to favor the more classically derived styles. Synagogues, such as those in Hope Place, Liverpool (1856), Birmingham (1857), and Manchester (1857) definitely belong to the second category.

The search for a style appropriate for a synagogue started with the Egyptian. Late eighteenth and early nineteenth-century reconstructions of Solomon's Temple in Jerusalem, such as that of C. L. Stieglitz in 1834, were shown in that style and this is reflected in the synagogue built in Karlsruhe as early as 1797–8 designed by F. Weinbrenner. The pointed arch through which the complex was entered was placed between Egyptian temple pylons. The synagogue building itself, not visible from the street, was in a classical style. Most synagogue architects favored the *Rundbogenstil* or round arched style championed by Friedrich von Schinkel (1781–1841), the Prussian state architect, which was derived from an amalgam of Romanesque and Byzantine sources. Significantly it tended to be the style adopted for Catholic churches in Prussia and Protestant churches in Bavaria, therefore a non-comformist style.

The search for a distinctly historical Jewish building mode led to the adoption of the Moorish style of the Alhambra in Granada, the style of the period of the high point of Jewish culture and of the surviving but alienated medieval synagogues of Cordoba and Toledo. The earliest was at Ingenheim in the Palatinate, built 1828–32 and designed by F. von Gärtner. Examples exist as far afield as in the USA where Rabbi Isaac M. Wise, the champion of Reform Judaism described his synagogue of 1866 in Plumb Street, Cincinnati as an "Alhambra Temple with slender pillars and thirteen domes". It also had two minarets. Major British examples are to be found in Princess Road,

Liverpool (1874), the New West End Synagogue in St Petersburg Place, London (1877–79), both with minarets, and the Garnet Hill Synagogue in Glasgow, all three with surprisingly similar interiors. The most influential example of this style was the mammoth synagogue in the Oranienburgerstrasse in Berlin, designed by E. Knoblauch between 1859–66, with a bulbous cupola over a circular entrance hall. It was spared by the Nazis as its destruction would have endangered the buildings on either side between which it was embedded, only to fall victim to war-time bombing. Its crudity of design was perhaps compensated for by the highly sophisticated three domed Romanesque-Byzantine synagogue on the Fasanenstrasse, also in Berlin, designed by E. Hessel, of 1912. The number of synagogues all over Europe and the USA in this style are too numerous to mention.

The greatest endeavor of Jews throughout western Europe in the early nineteenth century was to regain (or attain in Great Britain) the short lived political emancipation they had enjoyed under Napoleon's rule, a goal that was not generally achieved until well within the second half of the century. It was with the help of the architecture of their synagogues that they tried to convince their gentile neighbours of their respectability and worthiness of being treated as social and political equals. The architectural style of the synagogue therefore became a dilemma, especially in Germany. The adoption of the Moorish style had defeated one of the main objects intended by its architects, to build synagogues which not only demonstrated the newly found status of the congregants, but more importantly, their social respectability. The exotic Moorish style picked out the worshippers as foreigners, not as equal citizens worthy of the political emancipation to which they aspired or had only recently attained. Many congregations were even willing to alter their worship in this endeavor, to make it seem less foreign and more akin to church services. To this end, Hebrew was abandoned for much of the service, the organ adopted for synagogue worship and the traditional plan modified by moving the *bimah* or central platform to a position in front of the ark, an arrangement more like that of the church. So the search for an appropriate style continued. This even led to the adoption of the Gothic style for a number of synagogues, one of the first being the Moorish-Gothic, Reform Hauptsynagoge in Frankfurt, designed by J. G. Kayser in 1860, on the site of the city's ancient synagogue in the Judengasse. Even orthodox congregations such as that at Lübeck adopted the style (1880) though modified by a dome over the vestibule. Vienna had three synagogues in the style, but the prize for the most church-like Gothic synagogue must be awarded to the Reform Synagogue in Budweis, Austria, designed in 1888 by M. Fleischer, complete with two western towers with spires, flying-buttresses, aisles, and cross vaulting.

A compromise had to be reached, a style was needed appropriate to religious buildings and the Romanesque seemed to be the answer. It seemed less exclusively Christian than the Gothic, though synagogues had been built in both styles in the Middle Ages. The architect who pioneered this style was Albert Rosengarten (1809–93). His first synagogue at Kassel, built in 1836–39 on a plan strangely like that of St Martin's in the Fields, London, was nearer to the *Rundbogenstil*. In 1857 he published his *Die Architektonischen Stilarten* or "The Diversity of Architectural Styles" in which he argued the case of the superiority of the Romanesque against the Moorish on historical and esthetic grounds. It was in Hamburg where he settled that he made his mark, and, among other buildings, designed three synagogues, establishing the Romanesque as a synagogue style. His most important building was the city's Great Synagogue on the Kohlhöfen built in 1857. On plan it is an enlarged version of the dome within a square, a formula used by Wren in a number of London's city churches. The central cupola is, however, saucer-shaped, hidden from exterior view beneath the roof. The by now almost mandatory external dome which addressed the city was purely decorative, placed as it was above the western gallery. Whether this synagogue should be a free-standing monument or hidden from public view, as had been traditional, was hotly debated at the time. The compromise of withdrawing the building from the street-line, visible but protected behind iron railings, was adopted. None of Rosengarten's synagogues survive; his only remaining religious building is the chapel of the Schröder-Stift

Hanover Synagogue

almshouses which now serves as the church of the local Greek community.

More and more Romanesque synagogues were built, the finest by the architect, E. Oppler, in Hanover, 1864 and Breslau, 1865. Both had high central domes, turrets and rose-windows (a Gothic feature), and could almost have been taken for churches. An added benefit in using the Romanesque style became apparent at the end of the century when it became the preferred style of the newly founded German Empire. The Kaiser Wilhelm Gedächniskirche on the Kurfürstendamm in Berlin of 1890–95 by F. Schwechten could almost be taken for a synagogue. This fact no doubt accounts for the use of the style as late as 1898, for L. Levy's Reform Synagogue in Strasbourg, as its most opulent example, and in 1906 in Hamburg for E. Friedheim's Great Synagogue on the Bornplatz which supplanted Rosengarten's. It was the last major Romanesque synagogue in Germany and Hamburg's first monumental free-standing one, on a public square.

The picture presented in Germany after the 1914–18 war was totally changed. That modern-

37

ism was embraced wholeheartedly was shown in the almost Corbusian synagogue of 1930 at Plauen by F. Landauer. The final farewell to pre-Nazi Germany synagogue architecture was also in Hamburg, the Reform Temple of 1931 on the Oberstrasse by R. Friedmann and F. Ascher. This superb building survives as a broadcasting studio, as fresh looking today as when it was built. The synagogue at Lübeck, shorn of its dome, is the only German synagogue mentioned in this account that has been restored to its original use.

Just as nineteenth-century Jewish architecture was dominated by Germany, in the twentieth, the USA takes on the leading role. The Reform Temple Emanu-El on Fifth Avenue, New York, by R. B. Kohn, C. Butler and C. B. Stein, consecrated in 1930 and of cathedral proportions, is still Romanesque albeit in a streamlined fashion. But this was to change with the migration to the USA of such leading German-Jewish architects as Erich Mendelsohn (1887–1953). He was responsible for a number of synagogues and community centers, as in St Louis, Missouri, Cleveland, Ohio (1946–52), Grand Rapids, Michigan, and St Paul's, Minnesota. Unfortunately his work was never to regain the inspiration shown in his German buildings. Frank Lloyd Wright, the most famous American architect, used his very personal style for the synagogue (1959) of the Beth Shalom Congregation at Elkin's Park near Philadelphia.

Israeli architects, despite their desperate attempts to create expressive synagogue buildings, have, to date, sadly failed to produce one of distinction and still have to make their contribution to this central Jewish building type.

FURTHER READING

Brunner, A. W.: *The Synagogue: A Dictionary of Architecture and Building* (London: A. Sturgis), columns 704–710

De Breffny, B.: *The Synagogue*, (London: Weidenfeld & Nicholson, 1978)

Levy, I.: *The Synagogue. Its History and Function* (London: Vallentine, Mitchell 1963)

RAPHAEL EMANUEL

Ardon, Mordechai [Max Bronstein] (b.1896) Israeli artist. Ardon was born to religious parents in Tuchow, Poland. The eldest of 12 children, he rebelled early against his father's plan that he join him in the watchmaking trade. A precocious student, he was invited to learn Greek and Latin at the Tuchow monastery, to which his hasidic father assented on condition that he continue studying at the *Beth Hamidrash*. He ran away from home at 13, graduating at 17 from the *Gymnasium* in Krakow. By 1919 he was in Berlin, where he studied acting and performed with a traveling theater. However, in 1921 he enrolled at the Bauhaus, studying for five years at its centers in Weimar and Dessau, and with Johannes Itten in Herrliberg (near Zurich) after Itten broke with the Bauhaus over his mystical approach. By 1926, sensing the need to acquire training in the procedures of the old masters, a subject neglected in the experimental ambience of the Bauhaus, Ardon moved to Munich to study with Max Doerner at the Akademie der bildenden Künste. An exhibition of 18 paintings in the Juryfrei Kunstschau in Berlin in 1930 brought an invitation from Johannes Itten to teach at his school in Berlin. Ardon taught there for three years, and, becoming an engagé socialist, was forced into hiding. He managed to flee Nazi Germany in 1933, intending to make his way to Paris, but went instead to Jerusalem. Working on a kibbutz, Ardon was discovered by a Ministry of Education official and in 1935 was appointed to the BEZALEL SCHOOL OF ARTS AND CRAFTS. Ardon has held many distinguished posts, serving from 1940 through 1952 as director of the Bezalel Academy of Art in Jerusalem, and from 1952 as artistic adviser to the Ministry of Education and Culture. From 1949, he lectured at the Hebrew University of Jerusalem retiring simultaneously in 1958 from the University and the Ministry of Education and Culture. Among his students are the leading Israeli artists Avigdor Arikha and Naftali BEZEM. He has won many national and international awards and is represented in the major museums.

Ardon's complex art is nourished by many sources. The formal innovations of the Bauhaus, and in particular the example of Lionel Feininger, Johannes Itten, Paul Klee, and Vasily Kandinsky serve as the ground for his own inventions of color, texture, and symbolic form. His content, profoundly dualistic, reflects his manifold background, Judaic themes conflating with material from Christian and ancient Mediterranean traditions; political references with allusions to religious, philosophic or mystical experience. Ardon's landscapes, a genre he did not practice until his arrival in Palestine, reveal a deeply sensed recognition of the ancestral terrain. In the late 1940s and early 1950s, following two visits to New York, and encounters with the work of Adolph GOTTLIEB, Mark ROTHKO, and Barnett NEWMAN, Ardon's painting became progressively more hermetic, and more metaphysical in content, its expression dependent on signs, iconic devices, and textual quotation. Too difficult at first to cope with, the war, and the Holocaust remain subjects in uneasy gestation, emerging as disguised content – hence the seemingly cryptic inscriptions in *O Nana*, 1955. The text, an ancient Sumerian dirge on the destruction of the city of Ur, becomes a metaphor for his lament on the annihilation of European Jewry. Ardon's mourning for the Holocaust achieves its monumental expression towards the close of the decade in *Missa Dura* (1958–60; London, Tate Gallery). In the central panel, *Kristallnacht*, the act of creation, a paraphrase from Michelangelo's Sistine ceiling, is juxtaposed surrealistically against the order for destruction, Hitler's bellowing mouth caught iconically in triple exposure. The symbol of failed aspirations – Jacob's fallen ladder – conflates with the ladder of the descent from Christian iconography. Above, in the cosmic space, the tribulations of the afflicted (Psalm 62) are inscribed on torn parchment. Mourning for the dead, the individual and collective, Ardon's work, from the 1960s onward, treats the theme of mortality. The once-rejected ambience of the paternal workshop serves as the figuration for time, with clockwork and signs of the hours surging and fading into landscapes of infinity. His pessimistic dualism at the unreconciled conflict within Judaism between the hasidic (mystic) interpreters of the sacred texts and the halakhic (legalistic) – finds expression in the triptych *Homage to Jerusalem* (1965; New York, Israel Discount Bank), as does his perception of Christianity's disillusion with its unconsummated vision. In 1967, Ardon celebrated the reunification of the city in the *Gates of Jerusalem* triptych (Jerusalem, Israel Museum).

FURTHER READING

Kampf, A.: Ardon, the Bauhaus, and the quest for transcendence. In *Ardon, A Retrospective* (Tel Aviv: Tel Aviv Museum, 1985)

Katz, K.: Ardon. *Ariel* 5 (Summer 1963) 4–28

Maisels, Z. A.: Where past meets present: The art of Ardon. In *Ardon, A Retrospective* (Tel Aviv: Tel Aviv Museum, 1985)

Vishny, M.: *Mordechai Ardon* (New York: Harry N. Abrams, 1973)

HANNAH ABRAHAMSON

Arendt, Hannah (1906–75) German–American philosopher. Born in Hanover, Arendt was educated at the universities of Koenigsberg, Marburg and Heidelberg, where she came under the influence of Karl Jaspers. She was also a student of Martin Heidegger and was personally devoted to him at the time. She graduated in 1928 with a thesis on the concept of love in St Augustine. Her first book, published in German in 1931, dealt with the renowned literary hostess of the early nineteenth century, the Jewess Rahel Varnhagen, with whom Arendt clearly identified (English translation: *Rahel Varnhagen: the Life of a Jewish Woman*, 1974). With the rise of Hitler, Arendt moved to Paris, where she remained until 1940 working for several Jewish institutions. In 1940 she emigrated to the USA where she worked initially as an editor for Schocken Publishing. Her book, *The Origins of Totalitarianism*, was published in 1951, establishing her position as one of the leading figures in the group of so-called "New York intellectuals", left-oriented but anti-Communist. Indeed, her book was one of the first to point out the basic similarities between Nazism and Soviet Communism. It was, however, a later book which brought her wide acclaim, or rather, notoriety: *Eichmann in Jerusalem* (1963), which originated in the reports of the Eichmann trial which Arendt wrote for the *New Yorker* magazine. In this book she introduced the idea of the "banality of evil" characteristic of such war-criminals as Eichmann, and also the notion of Jewish cooperation with the Nazi program of extermination of the Jews. This idea produced much controversy and even censure from a great many Jewish leaders and scholars, including Gershom SCHOLEM, and her anti-Zionist bias was widely discussed. In 1963 Arendt produced an essay "On revolution", followed by a sequel "On violence" in 1970. Both essays reflected her views on the war in Vietnam. For many years she worked on a philosophical summa, published posthumously in three parts as *The Life of a Mind* (1978).

FURTHER READING

Botstein, L.: Liberating the pariah: politics, the Jews and Hannah Arendt. *Salmagundi* 60 (1983) 78–81

Young-Breuhl, E.: *Arendt, The Love of the World* (New Haven: Yale University Press, 1982)

YORAM BRONOWSKI

Arnshteyn, Mark [Mark Arnstein, Andrzej Marek] (c.1879–1943)

Yiddish and Polish playwright and theater director. A disciple of Stanisław Przybyszewski, high priest of Polish romantic modernism, Arnshteyn launched his theater career by writing Polish plays on Jewish themes for the Warsaw stage. Among them: *Wieczna bajka* (1901; The eternal story), a drama about working-class life; and *Pieśniarze* (1903; Singers), based on the legendary life of a nineteenth-century Vilna cantor said to have been destroyed by his success on the Warsaw opera stage. Arnshteyn also translated these plays into Yiddish, and as, respectively, *Dos eybike lid* (The eternal song) and *Der vilner balebesl* (The little Vilna householder), they were frequently staged by Yiddish companies throughout the world.

Beginning in 1905, inspired by a group of theater reformers centered around the Yiddish writer I. L. PERETZ, Arnshteyn pioneered as the first modern stage director in the history of Yiddish theater. He worked with the Ester Rokhl Kaminska Troupe in its early efforts at "literary" theater, and with groups of young amateurs who laid the foundations for the development of Yiddish dramatic theater in the interwar period.

Between 1912 and 1924 Arnshteyn directed and wrote for Yiddish theater in Russia, England, and North and South America. Returning to Poland, Arnshteyn translated and directed a number of popular Yiddish plays for the Polish stage, among them, S. AN–SKI's *The Dybbuk* (1925), H. Leivick's *The Golem* (1928), and Jacob GORDIN's *Mirele Efros* (1929). These productions inspired considerable controversy, including accusations in the Yiddish press that they undermined Yiddish theater and encouraged Jewish assimilation.

Incarcerated in the Warsaw Ghetto, Arnshteyn founded and directed a Polish-language Jewish theater, the Nowy Teatr Kameralny (New Chamber Theater). He perished in the Ghetto, or possibly at Treblinka.

Arnshteyn's career, unique among Polish–Jewish creative artists in that it was devoted to work in both Yiddish and Polish, was dedicated, in his own words, to the dream of "building a bridge between Polish and Jewish societies" on the basis of dramatic art.

BIBLIOGRAPHY

The Eternal Song. In *Fifty One-Act Plays*, ed. Constance Martin (London: 1934)

FURTHER READING

M. C. Steinlauf: Mark Arnshteyn and Polish-Jewish theater. In *The Jews of Poland Between Two World Wars*, ed. Y. Gutman, E. Mendelsohn, J. Reinharz and C. Shmeruk (Hanover and London: University Press of New England, 1989)

MICHAEL C. STEINLAUF

Aron, Raymond (1905–83)

French philosopher and writer. Born into a family of the intellectual Parisian bourgeoisie (his father was a professor of law), Raymond Aron may be regarded not so much as being in line of descent from the great Jewish intellectuals of the nineteenth century, such as Émile DURKHEIM and Marcel MAUSS, but rather as one of the first examples, along with Léon BLUM and Pierre MENDÈS-FRANCE, of a new Jewish intellectual, people whose relationship to Judaism was conditioned by the experience of war and the creation of the State of Israel.

Aron liked to describe himself as a "de-judaized Jew", but his own career retained traces of the cultural ambitions of that middle class which in the early years of the century translated the traditional virtues into scholarly achievements and Republican sympathies. Entering the École Normale Supérieure in 1924, Aron came first in the *agrégation* examination in philosophy in 1928. As assistant to Leo Spitzer at the University of Cologne, he discovered German sociology and witnessed the rise of

Nazism. During his time at Cologne, Aron not only decided on the subject of his thesis, the limits of historical knowledge, but also determined the principles which were to run through his subsequent work.

Despite its apparently wide range of forms and styles, Aron's thought – including his attitude to Judaism – is organized around two recurrent themes: the denial of any kind of transcendence, leading to the denunciation of secular religions from 1942, and the rejection of all determinism, with the idea of a fragmented historical rationality in which chance and necessity combine.

Appointed professor at Toulouse in 1939 and called up in 1940, he went to England where, as editor of *France Libre*, he wrote under the name of René Avord before reverting to his own name in August 1943 with his *Chroniques de France*, which already portrayed the institutional and political framework of the post-war period. He continued with this journalistic activity after 1945, when he became leader-writer of *Figaro* in 1947 and of *L'Express* in 1977. Though he might be ignored as an intellectual by the Communist intelligentsia, Aron was still recognized by his peers as a teacher, succeeding Gurvitch as professor of sociology at the Sorbonne in 1955.

As a philosopher turned historian and journalist, he never forgot his original project of a critique of historical reason. Whether writing on international relations (*Le Grand Schisme*, 1948; *Paix et Guerre entre les Nations*, 1962), or on industrial society (*Les 18 Leçons sur la Société Industrielle*, 1963); *La Lutte de Classes*, 1964; and (*Démocratie et Totalitarisme*, 1965), the works of this period affirm the autonomy of politics and the denial of a moralist position through development of the concept of the inter-state situation as characterized by relations of power and ideology, and of the concept of social class. The realism characteristic of Aron's view of events led him to speak out in favor of the independence of Algeria in 1957 (*La Tragédie Algérienne*, 1957; *L'Algérie et la République*, 1958), to examine the paradoxes of democracy (*Les Désillusions du Progrès*, 1969) and the evolution of international relationships.

The success of Aron's *Mémoires*, published in 1983, marked the rallying of younger generations to the teaching of a man who, since holding the chair in the 6th Department of the Écoles des Hautes Études en Sciences Sociales, and teaching at the Collège de France from 1970 to 1979, had developed a pedagogy of severity and ethics. Constantly denying transcendence and rejecting all determinism, Raymond Aron adopted the attitude to Judaism of an atheist rationalist. Having never known religious uncertainties, he saw Judaism only as a moral category involving the singular and the universal, or, since the creation of the State of Israel, as an entity in international law. In the speech he made in Jerusalem in 1973, accepting an honorary doctorate, Aron affirmed a double loyalty to Judaism and to France, to truth and peace. He said nothing of this loyalty during the "time of suspicion" – Aron's pre-war writings, for moral reasons, show no trace of any denunciation of anti-Semitism, nor do those written during the Resistance period refer to the genocide of the Jews – but rationalized it at the time of the creation of the State of Israel, which he analyzed in classic political terms. His definition of its identity took up the nationalist terms of the nineteenth century, posing the problem of double nationality. It is not, therefore, surprising that he underwent a crisis after the Six Day War and de Gaulle's diatribe. On the occasion of the publication of *Israël, de Gaulle et les Juifs*, 1969, he explained his own vehemence by the impossibility of choosing between the language of confession and the language of analysis in his distress, and in the awareness of contradictions which he could not overcome.

FURTHER READING

Mesure, S.: *Raymond Aron et la Raison Historique* (Paris: Vrin, 1984)

PERRINE SIMON-NAHUM

art, modern Jewish Few people nowadays would deny the existence of a long and often rich tradition of Jewish ritual art and architecture, although one should remember that its "discovery" is a relatively recent phenomenon (the magnificent third century CE synagogue of Dura Europos with its collection of figural wall paintings, for example, was excavated as late as 1932). However, whether we consider these wall paintings, a medieval illuminated manuscript, or an eighteenth-century embroidered Torah wrap, one thing is clear: this was an art of largely anonymous craftsmen, intended to form an integral part of Jewish life and worship, in which the talent of the individual was subsumed under the desire to make art serve God – an art akin to that of the Christian Middle Ages and to much Eastern religious art, past and present.

With the loosening of religious Orthodoxy and the political, economic, and social emancipation of the Jews from the later eighteenth century onwards, all this changed dramatically. Only now could the Jewish artist, in the postmedieval sense of the word, emerge to make his mark. That he first appeared in Germany, cradle of the *Haskalah*, is hardly surprising. Only then did the issue of Jewish identity in art – as, indeed, in anything else – become problematic.

The ethnic origins of the earliest purportedly Jewish artists in the modern period (notably, Anton Raphael Mengs and Johann Zoffany) remain shrouded in mystery; while figures of undisputed Jewish origin like Philipp Veit or Eduard BENDEMANN chose to convert to Christianity. Denial of their Jewishness, in other words, was seen as a prerequisite for artistic success.

Soon, however, it became possible for Jewish painters such as Moritz OPPENHEIM in Germany, Isidor KAUFMANN in Vienna, Maurycy GOTTLIEB in Poland, Geskel Salomon in Sweden, Jozef Israëls in Holland and Solomon Alexander HART in England to express their Jewishness directly by providing the burgeoning Jewish middle class with idealized and nostalgic renderings of traditional Jewish life and worship. This romanticized genre painting flourished throughout the nineteenth century, and has its exponents to this day. On the whole, though, emancipation led to assimilation, and even the above-mentioned painters also produced works on non-Jewish themes. Camille PISSARRO, probably the greatest of all late nineteenth-century artists of Jewish birth, barely considered himself a Jew at all, and painted not a single Jewish subject; Max LIEBERMANN, who in his lifestyle represented an almost perfect synthesis of German–Jewish and gentile culture, painted only a handful.

Panel from Ben Shahn's mural at the Community Center, Jersey Homesteads, Roosevelt, NJ

Mass emigration of Jews to the USA and Great Britain led to the emergence in those countries of large numbers of Jewish artists. New York's Lower East Side and London's East End may have provided these artists with similar social backgrounds, and this milieu frequently features in the early part of their oeuvre. But integration into the capitals' artistic life in most cases meant a growing away from their roots (although a number were to return to them in later life). Whereas most of the artists who emerged in Britain and the USA were the children of immigrants from Russia and eastern Europe, Paris (see JEWISH SCHOOL OF PARIS) became the mecca for those young Jews already aspiring to become artists. Although attempts have been made to impose an artistic homogeneity on these artists' output, the primary significance of such groupings remains a sociological one.

The early twentieth century did see a number of collective attempts to forge a specifically Jewish art form. In Poland, Germany, and

Russia, as in England, the USA, and France, Yiddish-language journals (such as *Jung Jiddisch* in Lodz, *Albatross* in Berlin, *Schtrom* in Moscow, *Schriften* in New York, *Renaissance* in London, and *Machmadim* in Paris) were published in which the question of Jewish artistic identity was hotly debated, and links between the artists and intellectuals involved crossed international boundaries. The two most coherent and concerted attempts, however, took place in Revolutionary Russia (see SOVIET-JEWISH CULTURE and RUSSIAN–JEWISH ART) and in Palestine in the early part of the century. Fired by a profound utopianism, both were doomed in their different ways to be short-lived.

In 1902 Martin BUBER (himself originally trained as an art historian) stated categorically that "a national art needs a soil from which to spring and a sky towards which to rise…a national style needs a homogeneous society from which it grows and for whom it exists", and Bulgarian-born sculptor Boris Schatz, founder in 1906 of the BEZALEL SCHOOL OF ARTS AND CRAFTS in Jerusalem, clearly agreed with him. In fact, the early productions of the School were dominated by a kind of orientalized Art Nouveau, a European style grafted onto biblical and Zionist subject matter. The whole history of Israeli art has revolved around the need to reconcile an awareness of European and American artistic developments with an assertion of national identity. Ironically, the very process of normalization in Israeli society has itself proved inimical to the notion of a specifically Jewish art: if Israeli artists are troubled by identity problems (which many of them undoubtedly are), their response has tended to be to stress their identity as Israelis at the expense of their Jewishness.

And yet the question of Jewish identity in modern art continues to raise its head. Anti-Semitism can fuel an interest in the subject just as effectively as Jewish pride; again and again, writers on art, Jews and non-Jews alike, have felt it necessary to attempt a definition of Jewish art in the modern period. Some claim that all art made by Jews deserves the name Jewish art, irrespective of subject matter. This seems too sweeping a claim to be useful, although an investigation into the specific context in which modern Jewish artists have worked can yield important insights into the possibility of historically recurring problems and preoccupations faced by a Jewish artist which are specific to that Jewishness.

Other writers have suggested that it is subject matter and/or intention which alone qualifies art to be considered Jewish. Applied to the pre-*Haskalah* period, this view poses few problems, and even in the modern period ritual artefacts continue to be produced (by Gentile as well as Jewish craftsmen, as has always been the case) which neatly meet these specifications. In the case of paintings and sculptures which are Jewish in subject matter but without functional purpose, the issue becomes more complex. What of the many paintings on Old Testament themes produced over the centuries by Christian artists? (Rembrandt, much beloved by Jewish artists, is a case in point here.) Non-Jews, too, have responded to the major strands of Jewish experience in the modern world, above all, the Holocaust. Conversely, there are Jewish artists who painted not a single Jewish subject, but whose oeuvre is nonetheless perceived in terms of its Jewishness. (Chaim SOUTINE, whose work is often considered the very embodiment of Jewish angst, is a notable example here.) And what of Jewish artists such as the Russian–American painter Max WEBER or the Anglo-Jewish painters Mark GERTLER and Alfred Wolmark – to name just three – who have depicted aspects of Jewish experience in one phase of their careers or in some of their works, but not in others?

Jewish artists and craftsmen of the last two centuries have, as always, shown themselves to be profoundly influenced by the art and culture of their "host" environment. A final line of thought, however, suggests the persistence throughout the history of art of certain characteristics which can be seen as quintessentially Jewish. Conspicuous amongst these qualities as manifested in modern art would appear to be the following: an emphasis on spiritual, rather than material values; a nervously expressionistic handling of paint and line indicative of "disrespect" for an alien academic tradition; a strong social conscience and moral seriousness, and a reluctance, if not inability, to accept the notion of "art for art's sake" – the modern equivalent, perhaps, of the biblical fear of idolatry. Also singled out have been a distinct tendency to melancholy (often expressed through the prominence given to the eyes) and an empathy for human suffering in all its forms; a suspicion of hedonistic sensuousness, especially when it comes to the depiction of the female nude; and finally, a predisposition to abstraction as the purest possible expression of the divine principle. Dangerously ahistorical as such claims are, the frequency with which all or some of these characteristics appear in art produced by Jews, practicing or not, in quite disparate environments, should at least make us pause for thought. As long as the definition of Jewishness in modern culture remains problematic, such speculations offer reassuring constants.

FURTHER READING

Kampf, A.: *Jewish Experience in the Art of the Twentieth Century* (Massachusetts: Bergin & Garvey, 1984)

Pincus-Witten, R.: Six propositions on Jewish art. *Arts Magazine*, December (1975)

Rosenberg, H.: Is there a Jewish art? *Commentary*, July (1966)

Roth, C., ed.: *Jewish Art: An Illustrated History* (London: Vallentine, Mitchell, 1971)

Saul, G.: Is there a Jewish art? *Jewish Affairs*, September (1982)

MONICA BOHM-DUCHEN

art, Russian–Jewish Individual Jews such as Isaac Levitan and Léon Bakst (né Rosenberg) had made their mark on the Russian visual arts well before the 1917 Revolution. These, however, had tended to be affluent and assimilated Jews whose Jewishness found little direct expression in their work. A notable exception is the realist sculptor Mark Antokolsky, who in the 1870s responded to the outbreak of anti-Semitic violence by depicting Jesus as a Jew, amid considerable controversy. CHAGALL may well have adopted the name Marc in homage to this man. Although the groundwork had been laid earlier by the advocacy of influential critic Vladimir Stassof, in the late nineteenth century, of an art based on ethnic loyalties, and the interest in Jewish folk art fostered by the Jewish Academy in St Petersburg and the Jewish

Ethnographic Society, only the utopian mood of the Revolutionary period could inspire a collective attempt to create a specifically Russian–Jewish art form.

Sharing the fascination with the "primitive" prevalent in all early twentieth-century avant-garde circles, Jewish artists such as El Lissitzky, Issachar RYBACK, Joseph Tchaikov, David Sterenberg, Boris Aronson, and Nathan ALTMAN took their cue from Russian–Jewish folk art. Marc Chagall too, although he sheered away from movements and refused to theorize, needs to be seen in this context: sharing the others' enthusiasm for the decorated wooden synagogues along the River Dneiper, and the eighteenth-century synagogue of Mohilev in particular, he went so far as to adopt "Haim the son of Isaac Segal of Sluzk", who painted its walls, as his fictitious grandfather. The unsophisticated forms of these decorated synagogues and of the Jewish *lubok* or woodblock print were seen by Lissitsky to partake of "an abstract spiritual quality", and thus to express the essence of Judaism. Hebrew calligraphy, too, played an important part in their conception of a truly Jewish art form, as did the notion of deep, velvety tones as characteristically Jewish.

Until the early 1920s a synthesis of these ideas and influences did indeed produce an art of overtly Jewish content. Seemingly naive images of synagogues, picturesque old Jews and traditional customs, illustrated Haggadot, designs for the Yiddish and Hebrew theater, were created amid considerable enthusiasm. Nearly all these artists, moreover, had been given positions of some authority in the new artistic institutions set up by Lunacharsky. In 1920, however, the running of Jewish communal affairs was handed over to the Yevsektsiya, the Jewish section of the Communist Party, which, aiming at the Bolshevization of the Jewish masses, promptly instigated the systematic eradication of all nationalist aspirations. Only Chagall, who left Russia in 1922, continued to celebrate traditional Jewish culture; the others turned to the creation of a geometric, abstract, and supposedly universal art, claiming (probably by way of justification) that, as Ryback and Aronson put it, "it is the emphasis on formal aspects of painting rather than the subject matter which reveals the true racial identity of the artist". By the mid-1920s this kind of art too was under attack, and many members of the avant-garde, Jews and non-Jews alike, left the country. Ironically, one of the chief proponents of the Socialist Realist art that finally won the day in Soviet Russia – Isaak Izraelevich Brodsky – was also a Jew.

FURTHER READING

Kampf, A.: In quest of the Jewish style in the era of the Russian Revolution. *Journal of Jewish Art* 5 (1978) 48–75
Golomstok, I.: Jews in Soviet art – the early years. *Soviet Jewish Affairs* (1983)

MONICA BOHM-DUCHEN

Ascher, Saul (1767–1822)   German political and religious thinker. Born in Berlin, Ascher received limited early training in Hebrew and Talmud. In 1810 he received his doctorate in philosophy from the University of Halle, on the basis of various philosophical writings. His first work of Jewish concern, *Bemerkungen über die bürgerliche Verbesserung der Juden* (1788) criticizes Austria's attempt to recruit Jews for the army before granting them civil rights. *Leviathan, oder über Religion im Rücksicht des Judenthums* (1792) analyzes the nature and history of religion and its culmination in Judaism. In *Eisenmenger der Zweite* (1794) Ascher attacked philosopher Johann Gottfried Fichte as a medieval anti-Semite. In *Ideen zur natürliche Geschichte der politischen Revolutionen* (1799) he analyzed historical progress from the sensual stage to the rational and moral. He avered that revolution is history's inherent means of ameliorating social conflict, and that Napoleon's served to release reason to help Christianity spread Judaism's moral monotheism. *Napoleon, oder über den Fortschritt der Regierung* (1808) describes Napoleon as an incarnation of revolutionary spirit which bursts the "seed" to produce the "fruit" of new social order.

Although Ascher was jailed briefly in 1810 for lampooning the economic and bureaucratic elite, he went on to attack the notables of the Christian–German *Tischgesellschaft*, such as

dramatist Heinrich von Kleist (1811). In *Die Germanomanie* he identified the dichotomy between Germanic nationalistic paroxysms and French enlightenment, and attacked the German messianic nationalists who wanted to make Jews into the first "twig" in the "fire" built to burn everything foreign. After the book was burned publicly at Wartburg, Ascher proceeded to contrast Jews cooperating with enlightenment governments, with German mystical anti-Semitism and myths of supremacy.

To Ascher Judaism is the pre-eminent religion of revelation. It combines rational religion's metaphysical God with its ethical implications, and natural religion's community organization. Following Immanuel Kant's terminology, he separated the "regulative" aspect of Judaism which is in harmony with human and national needs of the Israelites, the "essence" of Judaism or Judaism's "thing-in-itself" identified by 14 declared beliefs, from the "constitutive" aspect responding to threats against Judaism's mission to universalize moral monotheism, the "form", consisting of laws, ordinances, and rules. Ascher wished to relinquish the constitutive aspect. Since form and essence have long settled into coincidence, the change must be revolutionary. The tool is scientific study.

Ascher revolted against German anti-Semitism on the one side, and withdrew from traditional observance and legislation on the other. He produced a Judaism which is rooted in belief, and formed by Kantian reason to become the leading force in the post-Napoleonic universe.

FURTHER READING

Littmann, E.: Shaul Ascher, first theorist of progressive Judaism. *Yearbook of the Leo Baeck Institute* (1960)
Pinkuss, F.: Saul Ascher, a theoretician of the emancipation of the Jews from the generation after Moses Mendelssohn. *Zeitschrift für die Geschichte der Juden in Deutschland* (1935)

GERSHON GREENBERG

Ascoli,   Graziadio   Isaia   (1829–1907) Italian linguistician. His native town of Gorizia, a city in which both German and Slavic were spoken, was an important factor in his formation. His education was erratic but he came under the cultural influence of Samuel David LUZZATTO.

His work can be divided into two periods. In the first he studied non-Indo-European and non-Semitic languages, such as Turkish, Chinese, and the Dravidian languages. In the second period he concentrated his attention on the study of Indo-European, Romance, and Celtic languages. He carried out important research on Indo-European and his work on Italian dialects was particularly innovative.

The first volume of *Studi critici* (1861) clearly illustrates the breadth of his learning. The enormous range of his interests is revealed in his research on the language of gypsies, published in German in 1865, and in an article entitled "Studi ario-semitici" (in *Memorie Istituto Lombardo*, 1865), in which he aimed to demonstrate the common origin of Indo-European and Semitic.

The *Archivio glottologico italiano* was founded by Ascoli in 1873, and he continued to direct this prestigious journal until 1901. His main contribution to the phonology of Indo-European is contained in the second volume of *Studi critici* (1877). His *Iscrizioni inedite o mal note greche, latine, ebraiche di antichi sepolcri giudaici del Napolitano* (1880) filled a gap of many centuries' standing in Hebrew epigraphy. Ascoli taught in Milan from 1860 to 1907 and was considered the greatest Italian linguistician; recognition and honors were accorded him both at home and abroad.

FURTHER READING

Dardano, M.: *G. I. Ascoli e la questione della lingua* (Rome: Istituto della Enciclopedia Italiana, 1974)

GABRIELLA MOSCATI-STEINDLER

Ash [Asch], **Sholem** (1880–1957) Novelist, dramatist, essayist and story writer. Ash, who was born in Kutno, Poland, began writing in Hebrew, but turned to Yiddish, under the influence of I. L. PERETZ by the time he was 20. Compared to SHOLEM ALEICHEM's brilliantly skilful and imaginative use of the Yiddish language, Ash's Yiddish is decidedly clumsy and laced with much Germanized Yiddish, far removed from everyday language. However, he

Sholem Ash (left) with I. L. Peretz, Lucjan Peretz, and Hersh Dovid Nornberg (reclining)

became a very popular and prolific writer. He attended the Chernovitz Language Conference in 1908 where he strongly defended Yiddish as the Jewish national language. His works include *Moyshele* (1900), *Dos shtetl* (1904; The village), *Motke ganev* (1971; Motke the thief), later adapted for the Yiddish theater, and *Kidesh hashem* (1920; Martyrdom). His plays such as *Got fun nekome* (1907; God of vengeance) drew large audiences. His later works about Jesus, the merciful Jewish rabbi from Nazareth, which tried to reconcile Jesus with the Jewish faith, were *The Nazarene* (1939), *The Apostle* (1943), and *Mary* (1949), which drew him into deep controversy with his Jewish readers and alienated many of them. However, he drew large non-Jewish audiences because all these books appeared in English translation before the Yiddish originals were printed. They were also translated into other languages. Ash settled in Israel in 1954 where the controversy gradually subsided and he wrote *Der novi* (The prophet). His main achievement was to remove Yiddish literature from an all-Jewish readership and popularize it internationally. Ash's work was popular in his own day but has failed to stand the test of time.

DEVRA KAY

Assaf, Simha (1889–1953) Judaic scholar, historian, and jurist. Assaf received rabbinic ordination at the Telz *yeshivah* and studied at universities in western Europe before emigrating to Palestine in 1921. He joined the faculty of the Hebrew University in Jerusalem at its opening in 1925, serving as lecturer and administrator until shortly before his death. His interests in Jewish studies were wide-ranging. He published numerous articles and books on the history of the Jewish community in medieval times and in Palestine; his four-volume collection, *Mekorot letoledot hahinnukh beyisra'el* (1935–43), is an invaluable sourcebook on the history of Jewish education and of the Jewish community. Assaf's most notable achievements in Jewish studies were his researches on the Geonic period in Babylonia and Palestine. Through publication of materials from the Cairo Genizah, and in the painstaking work of supplying footnotes, cross-references, commentary, and learned emendations to these texts, Assaf made inestimable contributions to our knowledge of the history of rabbinic law in this crucial period of its development. Among his works: four volumes of Geonic responsa from manuscript; *Sefer hashetarot lerav hai ga'on*; and *Seder rav sa'adyah ga'on* (with I. Davidson and I. Joel, 1941). His student, Mordekhai Margoliot, edited a collection of Assaf's university lectures and articles on geonic history and literature; the book, *Tekufat hage'onim vesifrutah* (1955), remains to this day the most comprehensive introductory survey of the period.

Assaf's interest in the history of Jewish law led to some of his earliest publications: histories of the post-talmudic development of penal law (1922), and of court procedure (1924). Appointed in 1948 as one of the first Justices of the Israel Supreme Court, he advocated the reception of Jewish law into the Israeli legal system and peppered his opinions with frequent references from Jewish legal sources.

MARK WASHOFSKY

Asscher-Pinkhof, Clara (1896–1984) Dutch writer. She was the fourth child and eldest daughter of Dr Herman Pinkhof and Adèle de Beer, a family that was both cultured and Orthodox Zionist. Her five brothers – who perished as a result of the German occupation – and two sisters were gifted intellectually and artistically. Her father was a general practitioner who also occupied public office both in the general and the Jewish field.

She became an elementary school teacher, first in a small village and then in Amsterdam where she met her husband, Rabbi Abraham Asscher. On his appointment as Chief Rabbi of the province of Groningen they married and set up home in Groningen where they had six children. After some years her husband contracted tuberculosis, and died in May 1926. She chose to continue living in Groningen and began writing in her spare time, first general novels for girls and then, at the invitation of a Dutch–Jewish weekly, a book in instalments about a Jewish girl, *Rozijntje*, and Jewish children's songs for which she also composed the music. Both *Rozijntje* and the song booklets were reprinted around 1980. Her first novel for adults was *De Weg alleen* (1935; The road by oneself), followed by *Roep deze Sunamitische* (1938; Call this Shunamite woman).

After the German occupation Asscher-Pinkhof moved to Amsterdam, where she became a teacher at a trade school for Jewish girls. In May 1943, she was taken to Westerbork transit camp and then to Bergen-Belsen. She was one of the 222 fortunate Jews from Holland who, due to a complicated exchange with German citizens in Allied hands, arrived in Palestine in July 1944. She remained in Israel, which one of her two daughters had managed to reach in 1939, and where her three other surviving children later moved as well.

Her novels published after 1945 are *Sterrekinden* (1946; Children with [yellow] stars), about Jewish children she had met during the German occupation in Amsterdam, Westerbork and Bergen-Belsen; it was later translated into German and received a West German literary prize in 1960. *Tirza* (1952) is about an Israeli girl on a kibbutz. Her other novels, for example *De Koopbrief* (1955; The purchase-deed), are situated in pre-war Holland, and contain auto-biographical elements. Her last full-length novel *Danseres zonder Benen* (Dancer without legs) is her autobiography.

Several of her novels have been reprinted more than once. Yet, partly due to the fact that from 1944 to her death she did not live in the Netherlands, and visited it only rarely, she has remained outside the circle of well-known Dutch literary figures.

HENRIETTE BOAS

Atlan, Jean-Michel (1913–1960) French–Algerian painter and poet.

Born in Constantine, Algeria, Atlan traveled to Paris at the age of 17 to study philosophy at the Sorbonne, and remained in France thereafter. He survived the war in a lunatic asylum, having feigned insanity when arrested for Resistance activities. He published several collections of poems (including *Le Sang profond*), but from 1946 until his death worked almost exclusively as a painter. Jewish patronage was important in sustaining Atlan's work, which suffered from the vagaries of artistic fashion during his own lifetime. Atlan wrote of his painting that it "is neither abstract nor figurative...it has a barbaric force, a magic power, evoking a sense of the intensity of life itself". In these works dark forms flail against shattered backgrounds of vivid color, anthropomorphic yet inhuman in their suggestion of limbs, teeth, and claws.

The extent to which Jewish experience is reflected in Atlan's work is debatable. The obsession with savagery is overpowering, but it is cruelty rather than suffering which is presented to us. Some works have titles which suggest biblical inspiration (*The Magic Mirrors of King Solomon, The Lion of Judah*), but this cannot itself be taken as evidence of a concern with Jewish themes; many of his titles are drawn from the mythologies and rituals of distant cultures, and are intended to evoke a world of primordial violence and ecstasy. This cult of mystic primitivism is reflected in biographies by the artist's friends Ragon and Verdet, which exoticized his origins and stressed his "Judeo-Berber" descent. They treat the atavistic quality of his work as authentic racial expression, and it is likely that Atlan himself saw the Jewishness of his art in similar terms.

FURTHER READING

Ragon, M., and Verdet, A.: *Jean Atlan*, trans. J. T. Piageman (Geneva; Plageman, 1961)
Atlan: Oeuvres des Collections publiques françaises (Paris: Centre Georges Pompidou, 1980) [exhibition catalog]

LAURA JACOBUS

Atlan, Liliane (b.1932) French dramatist and poet.

She was born in Montpellier. Because they were Jews, Liliane and her sister were kept hidden in their home, and in the homes of non-Jewish families, during the Second World War. It was at an early age that she began writing poetry that seemed to cry out from her very depths. After the war, as a student of philosophy and literature, she and some of her Jewish friends, feeling at an impasse, began searching for an answer to metaphysical problems, to questions concerning identity, the belief in God, the reason for evil. Atlan had found her answer in the Bible, the Midrash, the *kabbalah*. It was in the wisdom as enunciated by the Jewish sages that she discovered her own path, not through escape in some hyperemotional fad, but via her own roots.

Atlan expressed her feelings of outrage and love for the human and the divine in a poetic theater, the power of which brands and sears. *Mister Fugue, or Earth Sick*, performed in 1967 by the Comédie Saint-Etienne, and in the fall of that same year by the Théâtre National Populaire in Paris (as well as in other Western countries and in Israel), dramatizes the fantasies of children as they are being led to the crematorium. Despite the excruciating nature of their situation, these children are not morbid. They live out the few hours remaining to them in their fantasy world – with verve, humor, and irony. *The Messiahs* was first performed in Avignon in 1969. It affirms a faith the author cannot shed, one that enables her to live out her earthly destiny and to experience her pain and guilt not as destructive forces, but rather as creative instruments. *The Carriage of Flames and Voices,* staged in Avignon in 1971, takes audiences into the double world of a woman split in two, attempting to find an answer to her torment through eroticism, drugs, knowledge, and revolt.

Writing enables Atlan "to express a whole network of lives lived out simultaneously", as attested to in her other works: plays, such as *The Emigrants, The Musicians* (1976); in a new brand of video-cassette theater, *Lessons in Happiness* (1980); and *Even Birds Cannot Always Get High* (1980); in brief texts, *Lapsus* (1971); poems, *Hand-Cutters of Memory* (1969); autobiographical imagistic writings, *The Dream of the Rodents* (1985); *The Passers By* (1988). Her most revolutionary theatrical work, *An Opera for Tcrezín* (1988), takes the Terezin experience and links it to the Passover feast.

Atlan's theater is cosmic in dimension though inhabiting the earthly plane; hallucinatory in its phantasms yet rooted in actuality. Embedded in history, in the event of the moment, it likewise transcends these limitations.

BIBLIOGRAPHY

Theatre Pieces: An Anthology (Greenwood: Penkevill Publishing Co. 1985); An interview with Liliane Atlan. *Yale Theatre* (1980); Mister Fugue or Earthsick. In *Plays of the Holocaust, an Informational Anthology* ed. E. Fuchs (New York: Theater Communication Group, 1987)

FURTHER READING

Knapp, B. L.: *Liliane Atlan* (The Hague: Rodopi Publications, 1988)

BETTINA L. KNAPP

Auerbach, Berthold (1812–1882)

German novelist. Born in Nordstetten, a small town in the Black Forest, Auerbach patched together an education despite his poverty, and launched a career as a free-lance writer that brought him to national and international fame, though his reputation began to decline in his own lifetime and is now purely historical. Gregarious and peripatetic, he was an ubiquitous figure in nineteenth-century German literary life who wrote about, corresponded with, and knew personally many writers of the time. He owed his fame primarily to a series of novels and novellas collectively known as the *Schwarzwälder Dorfge-*schichten (from 1843; *Black Forest Village Tales*, [selections] 1869, 1969), pioneering examples of realistic regional literature, and to several social novels. Jewish themes and characters are absent from these works, but he began his career with two distinctly Jewish novels: *Spinoza:* (1837; *Spinoza*, 1882) and *Dichter und Kaufmann* (1840; *Poet and Merchant*, 1877). The first presents Spinoza as a model figure, emancipated from Orthodoxy, and achieving equanimity of spirit. Auerbach, who profoundly admired Spinoza, translated his works into German, and published a five-volume edition along with a biography in 1841. The second, a cautionary case, is a fictional biography of the eighteenth-century Jewish epigrammist Ephraim Kuh (1731–90), contemporary of Lessing and Moses MENDELSSOHN, whose chaotic life, trapped in the perplexities of a still unachieved emancipation, ends in isolation and mental deterioration.

Despite the absence of Jewish themes in his best-known works, Auerbach held strongly and publicly to a modern Jewish allegiance. He was a partisan of Reform and an intensely committed assimilationist who insisted that there was no incompatibility between his Jewish and German identities. He came to be seriously shaken in his convictions by the rise of political anti-Semitism toward the end of his life, but his fundamentally optimistic disposition was never wholly undermined. He died in Cannes, France.

Many of Auerbach's works were translated into English in the nineteenth century, and may be found in older libraries. Twentieth-century translations are: *Black Forest Village Tales* (1969) and *Little Barefoot* (1914).

FURTHER READING

Sammons, J. L.: *Imagination and History: Selected Papers on Nineteenth-Century German Literature* (New York, Bern, Frankfurt am Main, and Paris: Peter Lang, 1988) 177–192

Sorkin, D.: The invisible community: emancipation, secular culture, and Jewish identity in the writings of Berthold Auerbach. In *The Jewish Response to German Culture from the Enlightenment to the Second World War*, ed. J. Reinharz and W. Schatzberg (Hanover and London: Clark University Press, 1985) 100–119

JEFFREY L. SAMMONS

Auerbach, Frank (b.1931) British painter. Born into a prosperous and assimilated Berlin Jewish family, Auerbach was sent to England in 1939; he was never to see his family again. After abandoning his original intention of becoming an actor, he attended various art classes in London (including the one at the Borough Polytechnic run by David BOMBERG, an important influence), before studying at St Martin's School of Art (1948–52) and the Royal College of Art (1952–5). Although he was given his first one-man show as early as 1956, he continued to teach in art schools until the late 1960s; fame has come to him only relatively recently.

Auerbach paints only those motifs he knows intimately: the buildings and parks in the vicinity of his studio in Primrose Hill, London (to which he has remained faithful since 1954), and portraits of people close to him. His work has always been characterized by a heavily impastoed, almost encrusted surface, although the somber earth colors of his early paintings have gradually been replaced by brighter and more vibrant ones. Auerbach is acutely aware of painting as "a cultured activity"; the artists he admires most – Albrecht Dürer, Titian, Frans Hals, and Rembrandt – share with him a strong sense of the dignity but also the pathos of mankind. Stephen Spender, among others, has perceived Auerbach's human subjects as "people who themselves seem burdened with perhaps terrible experience...like refugees conscious of concentration camps", and sought to explain his lifelong preoccupation with construction sites as partial compensation for the destruction of the world of his childhood.

FURTHER READING

Auerbach, Frank (London: Arts Council, 1978) [exhibition catalog]

Hughes, R.: *Frank Auerbach* (London: Thames & Hudson, 1988)

MONICA BOHM-DUCHEN

Avi-Yonah, Michael [Jonah Buchstab] (1904–1974) Israeli archaeologist and art historian. He was born in Lemberg, Galicia (then in the Austro-Hungarian empire), and brought up in a German-oriented, middle-class, assimilated Jewish home. He emigrated in 1919, with his parents, to Palestine, and settled in Jerusalem in 1921. From 1925 to 1928 he studied classical archaeology and history at the University of London. From 1931 to 1948 he served in the Palestine Department of Antiquities, and 1948–53 in the Israel Department of Antiquities. In 1953 he joined the Hebrew University where he was Professor of Classical and Byzantine Archaeology from 1963 to 1974.

Avi-Yonah was a prominent member of the first generation of Jewish scholars in Mandatary Palestine and later Israel, who combined deep roots in western culture with a belief in the role and contribution to be made by Israeli scholars in many fields. His main contributions are in the study of ancient art where he focused his attention on the re-emergence of the oriental civilizations in the late Hellenistic, Roman, and Byzantine periods discussed in his *Oriental Elements in the Art of Palestine* (1944–50) and *Oriental Art in Roman Palestine* (1961). Other studies concentrated on the mosaic pavements of Palestine from the fourth to the seventh centuries CE, lead coffins of Palestine and southern Phoenicia in the Roman period, and he wrote numerous articles on related subjects. Avi-Yonah published a general survey on the historical geography of Palestine during the Hellenistic–Byzantine periods, *The Holy Land* (1966), and numerous important studies in that field as well as a history, *The Jews of Palestine* (1976).

His broad field of studies also included the topography of Jerusalem (he supervised the construction of a model of Jerusalem in the first century CE), and Greek and Roman epigraphy.

FURTHER READING

Cassuto Salzmann, M.: Bibliography of M. Avi-Yonah. *Israel Exploration Journal* 24 (1974) 287–315; 34 (1984) 183–6

Barag, D.: *Israel Exploration Journal* 24 (1974) 1–3 [obituary]

DAN BARAG

Avidan, David (b.1934) Israeli poet. Avidan was born in Tel Aviv, and is one of the first writers belonging to "The generation of the State" (*Dor hamedina*), the first generation of writers to be born in Israel, having Hebrew as their first language.

From the outset Avidan established himself as the *enfant terrible* of modern Hebrew poetry, and as a "militant" modernist. He gained high critical acclaim, but was also often misunderstood and severely criticized, "Avidan is something of an Israeli Baudelaire. No other writer of his generation had the courage to write as he did, nor is qualified to do so" (Aharon Shabtai, *Ha'aretz* 17–8–1973). Though highly individualistic, Avidan's poetry influenced the generation of younger poets who started publishing in the 1980s.

Avidan's first book, *Berazim 'arufei sefatayim* (literally: Faucets with cut-off lips), was published in 1954. Although incorporating some traditional forms, rhythms, and imagery, the poems in this book already possessed many of Avidan's characteristic features. The general surface tone is aggressive, blatantly sexual, self-satisfied, and often almost inhumanly cynical. This, however, is very often a thin disguise for feelings of alienation, despondency, and frustration. Technology and the modern world often feature in Avidan's work. He was one of the first writers to incorporate colloquial syntax and vocabulary, including slang, in poetry, often claiming to have composed his poems direct and un-edited on a dictating machine.

Avidan has experimented widely with composite words (a rare phenomenon in standard Hebrew), loan-words and neologisms. He has played an important role in Israeli poetry's shift toward a more modern, current diction. This, however, often appears alongside traditional forms and meter, as well as usage of biblical linguistic features.

Among Avidan's other books in Hebrew are *Shirei lahat* (1962), *Mashehu bishvil mishehu* (1964), and *Sefer ha'efsharuyot* (1985).

BIBLIOGRAPHY

Megaovertone (London and Tel-Aviv: The Thirtieth Century, 1966); *Cryptograms from a Telestar, Poems, Translations, Documents* (Tel Aviv: 1980)

AHUVIA KAHANE

Avidom, Menahem [Menachem Mahler-Kalkstein] (b.1908) Israeli composer. Born in Poland, he emigrated to Palestine in 1925. In the 1930s he studied at the American University in Beirut. From 1945 to 1952 he was the General Secretary of the Israel Philharmonic Orchestra, then consultant for the Ministry of Tourism, and, from 1955 until his retirement, he has been the General Director of ACUM, the Israeli Performing Rights Society. Avidom was one of the spokesmen for a national folkloristic style, representing the national revival in the Land of Israel. His predilection for the modern French style encouraged him to write in clear, neo-classical forms and with coloristic, transparent orchestration. His stylistic tendencies are reflected in the titles of his symphonies: *Mediterranean Sinfonietta* (1951), *Folk Symphony* (1945), and by the frequent use of *hora* rhythms, and the incorporation of vocal movements. Yet, Avidom has also adapted advanced dodecaphonic techniques, as in his piano work *Dodecaphonic Episodes*.

JEHOASH HIRSHBERG

Avni, Aharon (1906–1951) Israeli painter and art educationist Avni was born in Yekaterinoslav in the Ukraine. Between 1923 and 1925 he studied at the Academy of Arts in Moscow, and in Palestine, at the BEZALEL SCHOOL OF ARTS AND CRAFTS. He traveled extensively before settling in Tel Aviv in 1929, where he participated in the *Massad* group exhibition.

During the 1930s Avni painted in the French Intimist style, but during the 1940s he became an Expressionist. He belongs to the second generation of Israeli artists in that he freed himself from romantic attitudes and opened up Israeli art to pure painting. In Modernism the intrinsic painterly qualities are stressed and in Avni's work they are apparent within traditional subjects: interiors and portraits. These are painted mainly in blue-green and orange harmonies, with obvious brush-strokes, but are controlled and internalized in their expression. Avni became the leading figure in Israeli Modernist painting.

Avni's activities in the area of art education was wide, novel in Israel, and influential mainly on artistic developments in Tel Aviv. In 1936, with the sculptor Sternhuss, he opened a studio, and in 1939 he founded the Histadrut Seminary for Painting and Sculpture, which he directed for 15 years and which after his death was renamed for him. Avni was also active in encouraging art education within the *kibbutzim*. He set a precedent by being the first teacher to take his art students on a trip to Italy. Before the War of Independence in 1948 he served in the *Haganah* (later the Israeli Defense Force) where he painted his comrades, as he later painted soldiers in the War of Independence.

FURTHER READING
Gazit 26 (1969) 156–7
Beit ha'omanim (Tel Aviv: Yonah Fisher) [exhibition catalog]

NEDIRA YAKIR BUNYARD

Avni, Zvi (b.1927)   Israeli composer. Born in Germany, he emigrated with his parents to Palestine in 1935. He studied with Abel Ehrlich, Paul BEN-HAIM, and Mordechai SETER, and later in the USA with Aaron COPLAND, Lukas Foss, and Vladimir Ussachevsky. His early works reflect the influence of the Mediterranean School. After his studies in the USA Avni incorporated contemporary ideas of harmony, serial technique, and aleatoric techniques into his style. He was the founder of the studio for electronic music at the Rubin Academy of Music in Jerusalem, where he became a professor of composition.

Avni is a prolific composer, and his works include powerful orchestral works such as *Meditation on a Drama* (1966), chamber works such as the string quartet *Summer Strings* (1962), and electronic elaboration of the human voice such as his *Vocalise* (1973).

JEHOASH HIRSHBERG

B

Ba'al Shem Tov [Israel ben Eliezer; BeShT; the Besht] (*c.*1700–1760) eastern European mystic and founder of HASIDISM. Little first-hand information is preserved about Israel's life, the earliest published source being *Shivhei habesht*, a biography which appeared in 1815. Despite its hagiographic nature, it reflects the fundamental outlines of Israel's life and the milieu in which he operated.

An orphan, Israel preferred the natural world to school and evaded attempts to provide him with a talmudic education. During his youth he served as a teacher's assistant, an elementary school instructor, and a ritual slaughterer, the lowest levels of the intelligentsia. Nonetheless, he developed a profound spiritual bent, practicing contemplation while living in the Carpathian mountains. His later teachings reveal that he gained a deep and insightful knowledge of the mystical tradition. Afterwards he served as a *ba'al shem*, an itinerant healer who used folk remedies and the names of God (*shemot*) in amulets to effects cures. Thus he gained his title, Israel Ba'al Shem Tov, which means Israel, the Master of the Good Name.

More than a healer and amulet writer, Israel achieved a profound level of spiritual illumination. A visionary who claimed access to a heavenly teacher, the biblical prophet Ahijah the Shilonite, Israel had a charisma and insight which inspired scholars with far superior academic credentials to accept him as their master. Israel did not write. His teachings, in the forms of epigrams and scriptural interpretations, are instead transmitted in the writings of his chief disciples, Jacob Joseph of Polonnoye

(d.1782) and Dov Baer of Mezhirech (d.1772). The heart of Israel's teaching is the ecstatic experience of the presence of God in all things. Egocentrism and ignorance prevent the mind from perceiving the divine sparks animating all reality. Equally injurious to spiritual health are depression and an overwhelming sense of sinfulness, which sidetrack the seeker. As He is always present, God is to be served with joy, and extreme asceticism eschewed. This powerful sense of divine immanence leads to the radical claim that God can be served through all aspects of daily existence – eating, drinking, conversation, as well as the spiritual activities of prayer and study. Constant communion and centering of the mind upon God (*devekut temidit*) is a religious duty incumbent upon every Jew.

While affirming the service of God through material actions, Israel placed prayer at the center of the religious life. Each word of prayer must be pronounced with total concentration and fervor. The words and letters of the liturgy are themselves worlds filled with divine light with which the Jew can commune. Torah study is not denigrated but prayer becomes the center of spiritual quest. The goal of study becomes communion with light residing in the divine word.

Jewish mysticism had been an elite, learned tradition. Israel daringly took his message to the masses, revealing God's closeness to all Jews. He taught that all should embark upon the path of communion and that the rabbinate serve the common people, speaking to them in the comprehensible language of parable and raising their spiritual level. Striving to reinvigorate

Judaism, Israel trained a coterie of disciples who created a mass mystical movement which in a generation conquered much of eastern European Jewry.

FURTHER READING

Ben-Amos, D., and Mintz, J. trans.: *In Praise of the Baal Shem Tov*: (*Shivhei haBesht*): *The Earliest Collection of Legends about the Founder of Hasidism.* (Bloomington and London: Indiana University Press, 1970)

Green, A., and Holtz, B. W., eds and trans.: *Your Word is Fire – The Hasidic Masters on Contemplative Prayer* (New York, Ramsey and Toronto: Paulist Press, 1977)

Jacobs, L.: *Hasidic Prayer* (New York: Schocken, 1973)

SETH L. BRODY

Babel, Isaac Emmanuilovich (1894–1941)

Soviet Jewish short-story writer and dramatist. Born in the Black Sea port of Odessa, Babel grew up in Nikolaev, then returned to the cosmopolitan atmosphere of Odessa, a thriving center of Hebrew and Yiddish literature. The family was fairly well assimilated but insisted on a Jewish education at home. The *numerus clausus* barred Babel from university in Odessa and from 1911 he studied economics and commercial studies in Kiev. There in 1913 he published his first short story *Old Shloime*, which tells of an old man's suicide against the background of expulsion of Jews and pressure to convert. All Babel's work bears the mark of his intense Jewish sensibility and the impressions of Russian anti-Semitism, tinged with his ironic sense of humor.

After the outbreak of the First World War Babel continued his studies in Saratov before moving, in late 1915, to Petrograd where he enrolled in the Law Faculty of the Psychoneurological Institute, known for its revolutionary activity and tolerance of Jews. A number of sketches and short stories appeared under the name Bab-El in *Zhurnal zhurnalov* on esthetic themes, among them the programatic *Odessa* (1916). Maksim Gorky published two stories in his important periodical *Letopis* and after the Bolshevik takeover Babel contributed horrifying accounts of brutality and corruption in starving Petrograd to Gorky's newspaper, *Novaya zhizn*,

closed down in July 1918 for its virulent attacks on the new regime. The enigma of human love attracted Babel's voyeuristic approach to sex and prostitution in several of the stories in the unfinished books, *Peterburg 1918* and *Oforty* (Etchings), and a similarly disturbing curiosity characterizes the observer of scenes of violence and sensuality in later works.

This is particularly true of the masterpiece which brought Babel to fame, *Konarmiya* (1926; *Red Cavalry*, 1929). Based on Babel's experiences as a war correspondent on the Soviet–Polish front in 1920, these harrowing stories portray Kirill Lyutov, a Jewish intellectual among Cossack warriors. He is caught between his faith in the Communist future and the bloody destruction of the revolutionary war, between the epic, sensual Cossacks and his identity as a Jew with spectacles, unable to sever his nostalgic roots in the dying Jewish past. The stories first appeared in Odessa in 1923 and their publication in Moscow literary journals in 1923–5 caused a sensation. Budenny, commander of the First Red Cavalry, issued a wrathful denunciation, but Gorky later defended Babel from attacks on the ideological position of the author.

Odesskie rasskazy (Odessa tales, 1921–32; first edition 1926), are a hilarious series of short stories about Odessa Jewish gangsters before the Revolution and during the first years of Soviet rule. The antics of Benya "The King" reflect an unashamed Jewish pride and joie de vivre, as well as a delight in action that contrasts with the stammering bespectacled intellectual.

The autobiographical narration of Babel's series of stories *Istoriya moei golubyatni* (Story of my dovecot, 1925–37; first edition 1926) mixes fact and fiction to evoke the haunting maturation of a Jewish boy through pogroms and his initiation into the mysteries of art.

Babel's foray into the theater was not successful. His adaptation of the Odessa stories in his play *Zakat* (Moscow première and first edition 1928; *Sunset*, 1931) is symbolic of the sunset of Russian Jewry and the Odessa Jewish ethos, but suggestive in its biblical motifs of the cyclical nature of historical and generational change. Another play, *Mariya* (1935), is part of an unrealized trilogy on the Civil War.

His success as a writer did not satisfy Babel

and he was sickened by the increasingly repressive climate of ideological debate in the second half of the 1920s. His mother, sister, and wife had left for the West and he visited them abroad. He could not reconcile himself to emigration and he returned to the USSR. Financial straits forced Babel to take on hack-work in the Soviet film industry. He worked with Sergei EISENSTEIN and wrote a film version of his stories *Benya Krik* (1926; English translation 1935), as well as of SHOLEM ALEICHEM's *Wandering Stars* (1926).

Babel's love of Yiddish is evident in the word play in his Russian prose, his reworking of a Hershele Ostropoler story *Shabos Nakhamu* (1918) and his translations from Sholem Aleichem (1926–7), Dovid BERGELSON (1957), and MENDELE MOKHER SEFARIM (unpublished).

Evidence that Babel was trying to master the novel form is found in a fragment, *Evreika* (1969; The Jewess). A widow leaves the shtetl, now in its final death throes, and goes to live in Moscow with her Red Army officer son, Boris. He has none of Lyutov's crippling complexes about war and poetry, but it is unclear how successful is the transition to the new life.

At the 1934 First Soviet Writers' Congress Babel declared himself a "master of silence", but the collectivization epic *Velikaya Krinitsa* (1930), the lost novella *Kolya Topuz*, and other stories of Soviet life suggest Babel was writing intensively.

As the purges of the 1930s reached their climax, Babel found it increasingly hard to publish, and collections of his earlier writings were censored. In 1939 he was arrested and disappeared. Officially rehabilitated in the post-Stalin "thaw", Babel was readmitted into Soviet literature with the republication in the 1950s and 1960s, largely under pressure from Ilya EHRENBURG, of his expurgated stories, correspondence, and some newly discovered material. Gorbachev's *glasnost* policy has raised the possibility of publication (1989) in the USSR of Babel's collected works, hitherto published in uncensored form only outside the USSR, *Detstvo i drugie rasskazy* (*Childhood and Other Stories*, 1979) and *Peterburg 1918* (1988).

BIBLIOGRAPHY

Benya Krik trans. I. Montagu and S. Nolbandov (London: Collett's, 1935); *Collected Stories* (London: Methuen, 1957); *Lyubka the Cossack and Other Stories* (New York: New American Library, 1963)

FURTHER READING

Ehre, M.: *Isaac Babel* (Boston: Twayne, 1986)
Sicher, E.: *Style and Structure in the Prose of Isaac Babel* (Columbus: Slavica, 1986)

EFRAIM SICHER

Bacher, Wilhelm (1850–1913) Hungarian Semitic scholar. Born in what is now Czechoslovakia, he was the son of the Hebrew poet Simon Bacher. In 1876 he was ordained Rabbi of Szeged (Hungary). A year later he became professor at the newly founded Rabbinical Seminar at Budapest, where he taught biblical exegesis, Midrash, Hebrew poetry and grammar. He was the head of that seminar in 1907–13. In 1884 he founded the Hungarian–Jewish monthly *Magyar Zsidó Szemle*. In 1894 Bacher was involved in establishing a Hungarian Literary Society which, among other activities, instituted the publication of a Hungarian Bible translation.

His scholarship ranged widely over a number of fields, some of which he was the first to explore. His most momentous research was on the Midrash and Talmud, to which he applied systematically critical methods for the first time. His *Die Agada der Babylonischen und Palestinischen Amoräer* and his *Die Agada der Tannaiten* remain the standard collections and analysis of rabbinic sayings.

He also devoted several works to the history of biblical exegesis. Believing that the Bible was the source of inspiration providing the essential framework of reference for all cultural experiences, he aimed to discover the broader views of each generation of Bible exegetes. His investigations of medieval Bible interpretation were particularly valuable because he was singularly able to assess the Jewish and the Arabic background of the works in question.

In addition, Bacher initiated the study of both Yemenite and Persian Judaism. His work on the Judeo-Persian poets Schahin and Imran is especially acknowledged for its profound analysis of their diverse source-materials.

FURTHER READING
Finkelstein, L.: *The Jews, Their History, Culture and Religion* (New York: Harper & Bros., 1949)

MAREN NIEHOFF

Baeck, Leo (1873–1956) German theologian. Born in Lissa (now Leszno, Poland), Baeck studied at the Breslau rabbinical seminary and the Hochschule für die Wissenschaft des Judentums in Berlin, and concurrently at the universities of Breslau and Berlin. He served as rabbi at Oppeln, at Düsseldorf, and from 1912 at Berlin where he also taught at the Hochschule. In 1943 he was deported to the Theresienstadt concentration camp, and after the war he settled in London.

Baeck was the author of a number of influential books. *Das Wesen des Judentums* (1905; *The Essence of Judaism*, 1936, 3rd edn, revised by Irving Howe, 1948), was originally written in response to the Christian theologian Adolf von Harnack's *Wesen des Christentums*. *Dieses Volk* (2 vols 1955–7; *This People Israel*, 1965) and is the fullest expression of his theological understanding of the Jewish identity and mission. The English volume *Judaism and Christianity* sets out his famous contrast between the "classical" religion (Judaism), rooted in the world and striving for its perfection, and the "romantic" religion (Christianity), yearning for an abstract salvation.

But Leo Baeck's fame rests not so much on his writings and teachings as on the power of his personality, and the destiny that called him to be the spiritual supporter and guide of German Jewry during the nightmare years of the Nazi ordeal. As president of the *Reichsvertretung* (the representative body of German Jewry) from 1933, when the Nazis came to power, he determined to remain in Germany, devoting himself to defending the rights of the Jews, to preserving their dignity and moral integrity, and to giving them the courage to face up to their destiny.

Two famous institutions bear his name: the Leo Baeck Institute, founded in 1954 for the study of the history of German-speaking Jewry, and Leo Baeck College, founded in London in 1956 for the training of Reform (subsequently also Liberal) rabbis.

FURTHER READING
Friedlander, A. H.: *Leo Baeck, Teacher of Theresienstadt* (London, 1968)

NICHOLAS DE LANGE

Baer, Werner (b.1914) German composer, arranger, and conductor. Baer studied piano, composition and conducting at the Hochschule für Musik, Berlin, and was a student of Artur Schnabel. Before the First World War Baer was the organist at the Church of St Thomas, Leipzig, and was choirmaster and organist for the Liberal synagogue group in Berlin. He toured as an organist and as accompanist to Richard Tauber.

Baer left Nazi Germany in 1938 and settled in Singapore where he became instructor in piano and lecturer in music at the Raffles College.

At the outbreak of war he emigrated to Australia and joined the army. Since the end of the war he has been a mainstay of the music scene in Australia and was awarded the MBE (Member of the British Empire) and the Queen's Jubilee Medal for service to music. He has written numerous compositions for varying branches of music. He has also held the post of organist and choirmaster at the Liberal Synagogue in Sydney and that of choirmaster of the Great Synagogue, Sydney. His settings for the prayers *Adon Olam* and *Mah Tovu* are the more frequently used of his liturgical compositions. Among the posts he has occupied are conductor of the Sydney Male Voice Choir, program director, assistant director of music and music editor for the Australian Broadcasting Commission, and director and chairman of the music board of Opera Australia. In recent years he has become musical director of the Sydney Jewish Choral Society. Of his many songs and compositions the most frequently played are *Test of Strength, Life of the Insects, Harvester's Song,* and *Psalm 8.*

ALAN D. CROWN

Bajgielman, Dawid (1887–1944) Violinist, conductor, and composer. Born in Ostrowiec (Radom region), one of nine children in a musical family, he was taught music by his father. At the age of 8 he could play the violin, and at 12 he had already played with an orchestra. He began his career as a conductor in Lodz and settled there. In 1912 he worked for the National Theatre in Lodz from which he moved to Zandberg's Jewish Theatre, also in Lodz, where he composed music for the plays. He was known as an excellent arranger and conductor of operettas not only in Lodz but also in Warsaw and other Polish cities. In 1926 he toured with a Lvov company, Gimpel's Theatre, in South America and some African countries. He became known as a composer of songs and orchestral compositions based on Jewish themes. During the German occupation he lived in the Lodz ghetto where he ran a small theater company, (*Kleinkunst-Gruppe*), for which he wrote many songs, for instance, *Dos Shnaderl* (The tailor), *Nisht Kajn Rozynkes, Nisht Kajn Mandlen* (Neither currants nor almonds), *A jidish Lidl* (A Jewish song). His compositions, inspired by traditional Jewish themes, were performed by an orchestra active in the ghetto, and he continued working with the Jewish choir, Hazomir. During the dismantling of the ghetto he was sent to Auschwitz and was never seen again.

MARIAN FUKS

Bal-Makhshoves [Isidor Elyashev] (1873–1924) Yiddish literary critic and historian. Born in Kovna, Lithuania, Bal-Makhshoves studied in a *musar*-inspired *yeshivah* in Courland, from which he "escaped" to study medicine in Heidelberg and Berlin. He became active in Jewish student circles and read his first piece in Yiddish before a group of students *c*.1895. His first critical writings on Yiddish literature, *c*.1899, made him well known. He qualified as a physician in Russia in 1905 and began to practice medicine alongside his literary endeavors, which included editing a short-lived daily Yiddish newspaper in Riga in 1910. He settled in Warsaw in 1912 and later moved to Russia. He returned to Kovna in 1920 and settled in Berlin in 1921.

Although there had previously been Yiddish literary criticism on individual works, it was Bal-Makhshoves who became the first critical master of modern Yiddish literature. He always viewed writers in the context of the new litera-

ture which they were helping to establish. By setting standards based on west European models, Bal-Makhshoves effectively inspired the new young literature to meet those standards. His five volume *Geklibene shriftn* (1910–15; Collected writings) first appeared in Vilna. Bal-Makhshoves was one of those responsible for effecting the intelligentsia's recognition that there was a Yiddish literature and not just individual Yiddish writers. By the time of his death, his role as the "king" of Yiddish literary criticism had largely passed to the young Shmuel NIGER.

DOVID KATZ

Balázs, Béla [Herbert Bauer] (1884–1949) Hungarian poet, dramatist, critic and writer. Born into a Jewish middle-class family, he completed his secondary education at Szeged and then studied philology at the University of Budapest. He made his debut as a poet with philosophical and meditative verse in the spirit of Symbolism. His first collection of verse, *A vándor énekel* (1910; The song of the wanderer), was followed by a long poem and a story both used as libretti by Béla Bartók, for the opera *A kékszakállú herceg vára* (1911; Duke Bluebeard's castle) and the ballet *A fából faragott királyfi* (1917; The wooden prince).

Though Balázs wrote for *Nyugat* he never belonged to the inner circle of this influential review; on the other hand, he frequented meetings of the left-elitist group *Vasárnapi Kör* (Sunday circle) and became friends with György LUKÁCS who later published a collection of essays – *Balázs Béla és akiknek nem kell* (1918; Béla Balázs and those who won't accept him) – extolling Balázs's artistic merits. Balázs also tried his hand at drama, tackling the problem of modern career-women torn between their vocation and their womanhood in *Doktor Szélpá Margit* (1909). An army officer during the First World War, Balázs nevertheless had Socialist leanings, and during the Hungarian Soviet Republic of 1919 he was a member of the literary Directorate.

After Béla Kun's fall Balázs emigrated to Vienna. Although he continued to write poetry with strong political undertones, his attention gradually turned towards the new medium of the film and he wrote the earliest systematic theory of the cinema: *Der sichtbare Mensch* (1924; The visible man). In 1926 he moved to Berlin where he directed films and wrote film scenarios until 1931, when he left for Moscow. There he taught at the Academy of Cinematography but also continued to write poetry in Hungarian. Balázs returned to Hungary in 1945 and for some time was Professor at the Budapest Academy of Theatrical and Cinematographic Arts and was awarded the Kossuth Prize. He also wrote the scenario of the first important Hungarian film after the war, *Valahol Európában* (1946; Somewhere in Europe).

Balázs's career was, in many ways, typical of Hungarian–Jewish intellectuals with left-wing sympathies. His early interest in mysticism and the cult of art for art's sake did not prevent him from shifting to a radical position during the First World War and collaborating with Soviet Communism for the rest of his life. Although he had little interest in Judaism, Balázs was influenced by his liberal Jewish upbringing, the metropolitan artistic milieu, and the anti-Semitic campaign that followed the collapse of the Hungarian Soviet Republic. It was to a large extent this last which influenced his political course in exile. The emotional and intellectual development of Balázs's youth is described in *Álmodó ifjúság* (1946; Dreaming youth), while the atmosphere of Hungarian intellectual society before 1914 appears in the loosely constructed novel, *Unmögliche Menschen* (1930; Impossible people). Some of his stories, for example *Az igazi égszínkék* (1946; The Real Sky Blue, 1936), have been translated into English, as have his writings on the cinema: *Theory of the Film: Character and Growth of a New Art* (1952).

BIBLIOGRAPHY
The Real Sky Blue (London: John Lane, 1936)

FURTHER READING
Czigány, L.: *The Oxford History of Hungarian Literature* (Oxford: Clarendon Press, 1984) 269–270

GEORGE GÖMÖRI

Balcon, Michael (1896–1977) English film producer. Balcon, one of the most important British-born film producers, was sometimes seen as exhibiting a "suburban" imagination. Yet his parochialism turned out to be a major component of his creative strength. It enabled him to establish the "Ealing comedy", the comedy–drama most closely associated with the British cinema.

Balcon entered the film business as a salesman, went into production in 1923, and formed Gainsborough Pictures in 1924, remaining its managing director for 12 years. In 1932 he became head of film production at Gaumont British and Gainsborough Pictures, in charge of two studios, and produced some of the most important British films of the period, including the Hitchcock films: *The Man Who Knew Too Much* (1934), *The Thirty-Nine Steps* (1935), and *The Secret Agent* (1936). He was associated with the director and producer, Victor Saville, and Berthold VIERTEL made three films for his companies before leaving for America in 1940.

Cautious though he was, he nevertheless took some commercial risks, backing *Man of Aran* (1934, directed by Robert Flaherty) and the expensive financial disaster *Jew Süss* (1934, directed by Lothar Mendes; see BRITISH CINEMA INDUSTRY, JEWISH PRESENCE IN).

In 1937 Balcon joined Ealing Studios as head of production and produced many successful films. When Ealing Studios closed in 1955 he transferred the company to Rank at Pinewood, but he soon left, and in 1959 became Chairman of a consortium which included Bryanston Films.

Jew Süss was something of a personal commitment and Balcon was instrumental in getting Conrad Veidt (who had a Jewish wife) out of Germany, where the Nazis had been determined to keep him. Balcon was the producer behind many of the spy films of the 1930s in which the enemy could be inferred as Germany. His feelings, however, can be seen in the postwar *Frieda* (1947), which examines a darker side of little England.

Other films associated with Balcon include: *The Foreman Went to France* (1942), *Went the Day Well?* (1943), *Dead of Night* (1945), *Hue and Cry* (1947), *Kind Hearts and Coronets* (1949), *The Man in the White Suit*, (1951), and *The Ladykillers* (1955).

BIBLIOGRAPHY

with E. Lindgren, F. Hardy, and R. Manvell: *Twenty Years of British Films, 1925–45* (London: Falcon Press, 1947); *Michael Balcon Presents...A Lifetime of Films* (London: Hutchinson, 1969)

KEVIN GOUGH-YATES

Band, Arnold J. (b.1929)   American literary scholar. Born in Boston, Massachusetts, Band was educated at the Boston Latin School. He earned his AB and MA at Harvard University and received his Ph.D. from Harvard in Classics and Comparative Literature. He studied at Hebrew College, the Hebrew University in Jerusalem, and the Sorbonne. He was on the faculty of the University of California at Los Angeles from 1959, as Professor of Hebrew Literature, and in 1969 he founded the department of Comparative Literature, serving as its Chair for ten years. Band's distinguished career has included appointments at Harvard, Brandeis, and Hebrew College, numerous visiting professorships and three honorary doctorates. Among his numerous awards are those from the National Endowment for the Humanities, the Guggenheim Foundation, and the American Council of Learned Societies.

A classical scholar as well as consummate modernist, Band is renowned for his critical eclecticism. Equally at home in European and American literatures as he is in classical and modern Hebrew literature, he has brought a profound knowledge and understanding of modern and post-modernist critical theory to his evaluation of literary texts. His seminal work on S. Y. AGNON is a major scholarly contribution to the field of literary criticism generally, and of inestimable value to English-language scholars for whom Hebrew literary criticism is inaccessible. His work on Agnon unites accepted views with elements of contemporary critical thought and of Agnon's own intellectual experience which was not previously explored. Although part of the Hebrew critical hierarchy Band is not identified with any of its prevailing philosophies, applying international critical models rather than the doctrinaire traditionalist approaches which avoid objective evaluation of Hebrew literature.

In addition to his work on Agnon, Band has published a book on NAHMAN OF BRATSLAV and numerous articles on Hebrew literature.

BIBLIOGRAPHY

Nostalgia and Nightmare: A Study in the Fiction of S. Y. Agnon (Berkeley and Los Angeles: University of California Press, 1968).

GLENDA ABRAMSON

Baron, Salo Wittmayer [Shalom] (b.1895) American historian and teacher. Born in Tarnow, Galicia, Baron took doctorates at the University of Vienna in philosophy (1917), political science (1922) and jurisprudence (1923). He also received a rabbinical degree from the Jewish Theological Seminary in Vienna (1920). He began his teaching career at the Jüdisches Paedagogium, Vienna, where he taught history (1920–26). From 1927 he taught in the USA, where he emigrated at the invitation of Steven S. WISE, first at the Jewish Institute of Religion in New York (where he later became professor of history), at the Jewish Theological Seminary as visiting professor, and at the Graduate School for Jewish Social Work in New York. But his most important teaching position was at Columbia University where he was the first incumbent of the Miller Chair of Jewish History, Literature, and Institutions (1930–63). This was the first such position in American academia and set the pattern for many similar chairs, particularly in the post-war years.

Baron has also been active in Jewish extra-curricular scholastic and academic bodies (American Academy for Jewish Research, American Jewish Historical Society, Conference on Jewish Social Studies). His first important work was a study of the Jewish question at the Congress of Vienna (*Die Judenfrage auf dem Wiener Kongress*, 1920), valuable for its use of much archival material. Amongst other notable works are *The Jewish Community: its History and Structure to the American Revolution*, 3 vols (1942), in which Baron made able use of a combined sociological and historical technique; and *The Jews of the United States 1790–1840: A Documentary History*, 3 vols (1963) which Baron edited with J. L. Blau.

His outstanding contribution to Jewish historiography is the monumental *Social and Religious History of the Jews*, 3 vols (1937; 2nd ed. vols I–XVIII 1952–1983; in progress). Baron rejects what he calls "the lachrymose conception of Jewish history" in favor of a view that stresses national Jewish self-assertion both in the Diaspora and Palestine. Thus Baron gives relatively less attention to the role of individuals and more to that of the people as a whole. He largely eschews narrative but presents his material in the form of detailed analytic set-pieces. The work is particularly rich in demographic and occupational material. It is also notable for Baron's ability to synthesize a vast amount of secondary material drawn from the most diverse sources. In some volumes the notes and references amount to between one-quarter and one-third of the text. The whole seems destined to become one of the most significant historiographical achievements of the twentieth century.

FURTHER READING

Blau, J. L., Friedman, P. L., Hertzberg, A., and Mendelsohn, I. eds *Essays on Jewish Life and Thought Presented in Honour of Salo Wittmayer Baron* (New York: Columbia University Press, 1959)

Liberman, S., ed.: *S. W. Baron – Jubilee Volume on the Occasion of his Eightieth Birthday* (Jerusalem: 1974) 1–37 [with bibliography of his work to 1973: English Section 1]

LIONEL KOCHAN

Bartov, Hanokh (b.1926) Israeli author. Bartov was born in Petah-Tikvah. From the start of his career as a novelist, Bartov devoted himself to a description of the emergent Israel, its natural and human landscapes. More specifically, he has concentrated on its social problems, from a standpoint sympathetic to the Israeli polity.

Shesh kenafayim le'ehad (1954, 1973; Six wings to each), deals with immigrant absorption in the first years of statehood. Are the immigrants getting a fair deal? The veterans are patronizing to them, whilst keen to have the weight of their physical presence. The difficulties, such as grinding poverty, Arab emnity awaiting its opportunity, and inter-communal strife, are formidable.

By its nature, Bartov's fiction acts as a chronicle of modern Israeli history. Israel in its formative period is set against the background of the War of Independence just fought. There is also the war in Europe as recorded in *Pitz'ei bagrut* (1965; Adolescent pimples), seen through the eyes of one of the "Palestinian Regiment" (which Bartov joined himself in 1913). He also records the background of his own colony in *Shel mi 'attah yeled* (1970; Whose child are you?), this time through the omniscient narrator.

However, the author has also moved out of the immediate range of his own autobiography in such novels as *The Dissembler* (1975), an exciting mystery story and *Ba'emtza haroman* (1984; In the middle of it all), an attempt to chart the final dissolution of the archetypal Israeli now living in the USA and his breach with the motherland.

BIBLIOGRAPHY

The Brigade (Philadelphia: The Jewish Publication Society of America, 1967)

FURTHER READING

Yudkin, L. I.: *Escape into Siege* (London: Routledge & Kegan Paul, 1974)

LEON I. YUDKIN

Basch, Victor Guillaume (1863–1944) French philosopher. Born in Budapest, he studied German at the Sorbonne but switched to philosophy, with a special interest in esthetics, which he taught at the Universities of Rennes and, from 1918, Paris. He was active in the Dreyfus Affair and the League for the Rights of Man of which he became president in 1926. A libertarian socialist, he supported left-wing movements, including the Popular Front. His wartime underground activities led to his and his wife's execution by a French Fascist group.

NELLY WILSON

Baskin, Leonard (b.1922) American sculptor and graphic artist. Born in New Brunswick, New Jersey, the son of a rabbi of Lithuanian origin, Baskin attended a *yeshivah* in Brooklyn until the age of 16. Although he later rejected Orthodox Judaism, he has acknowledged that his brain remains "serried with an infinity of memory-traces that recall the sound and smell of *shul*, of home, of *yeshivah*, of the nearly all-Jewish street". Determined from the age of 14 to become an artist, he started attending life drawing classes at the Educational Alliance on New York's Lower East Side, and went on to study at Yale University, the New School for Social Research in New York, the Académie de la Grande Chaumière in Paris, and the Accademia in Florence. Baskin taught art at various American institutions, as well as establishing his own Gehenna Press.

Unswervingly figurative, Baskin believes that "the human figure...contains all and can express all". Drawing widely on mythological and biblical themes, his protagonists – whether carved in wood, cast into bronze, or delineated in prints – tend to be vulnerable and unglamorous, a powerful comment on the post-Holocaust, nuclear age. This tendency to expressionist angst is tempered, however, by the artist's belief that man, in spite of all, is "collectively redemptible", that "the forging of works of art is one of man's remaining semblances to divinity".

FURTHER READING

Fenn, A., and O'Sullivan, J.: *The Complete Prints of Leonard Baskin, and Catalogue Raisonńe, 1948–1983* (New York: New York Graphic Society, 1984)

Jaffe, I. B.: *The Sculpture of Leonard Baskin* (New York: Viking Press, 1981)

Leonard Baskin: Graphics, Drawings, Sculptures (London: The Cottage Gallery, 1981) [exhibition catalog]

MONICA BOHM-DUCHEN

Leonard Baskin Man of Peace *1952. Museum of Modern Art, New York*

Bassani, Giorgio (b.1916) Italian novelist and poet. He was born in Bologna but brought up in Ferrara (with its large, and generally right-wing, Jewish community) where most of his fiction is set. Although he was able to take his degree in Italian literature at Bologna University in 1939, the anti-Semitic legislation of 1938 cut him off from the society of which he had felt a part. He taught at the segregated Jewish school in Ferrara, and took part in anti-Fascist activities for which he was arrested, and released only when Mussolini fell. He then moved to Rome. His first volume of tales and poems, *Una città di pianura* (1942; A city on the plain), was published under the pseudonym of Giacomo Marchi. Bassani excelled at the depiction of the sense of isolation created by Fascist racial policy (*Gli occhiali d'oro*, 1958; *The Gold-Rimmed Spectacles*, 1960), and of the sense of disillusionment experienced by Jews who had until 1938 felt integrated into Italian society (*Il giardino dei Finzi Contini*, 1962; *The Garden of the Finzi Contini*, 1965). After *L'airone* (1968; *The Heron*, 1970), he published little new fiction, but revised all his previous narrative works, ordering them in a cycle with the general title of *Il Romanzo di Ferrara* (1974) in such a way as to suggest that anti-Semitism is the norm from which "liberal" society only temporarily deviates. Bassani's collected poems are in *In rima e senza* (1982).

FURTHER READING

Hughes, H. S.: *Prisoners of Hope. The Silver Age of Italian Jews* (Cambridge, MA: Harvard University Press, 1983)

Radcliff-Umstead, D.: *The Exile into Eternity. A Study of the Narrative Writings of G. Bassani* (London and Toronto: Associated University Presses, 1987)

BRIAN MOLONEY

Bauer, Otto (1881–1938) Austrian socialist leader and political theorist. Born in Reichenberg, Bohemia, Bauer was the son of an industrialist. After attending the local *Gymnasium*, he studied law at Vienna, where he was a prominent member of the Böhm-Bawerk seminar, with Otto NEURATH and Ludwig von MISES. In 1907 he was a co-founder of the socialist journal *Der Kampf* (The struggle). On the death of Victor ADLER in 1918 Bauer succeeded to the leadership of the socialist party, and the post of foreign minister. He resigned the latter after a brief tenure, but retained the former until the civil war of 1934 forced him to flee. He died in Paris.

Bauer was one of the foremost theorists of what has come to be known as Austromarxism. His best known work is *Die Nationalitätenfrage und die Sozialdemokratie* (1907; Nationalism and social democracy), and he also wrote copiously on the inter-war problems facing socialism. His *Nationalitätenfrage* deals in detail with the question of Jewish identity. His attitude was very ambivalent, praising the Jewish role in history, but denying Jews full national status. Bauer argued that Jews in the West were being absorbed by society, and in the East, even if this was not happening, it should be, for the sake of progress. This was an expression of the common bias of a German Jew against the *Ostjuden*. However,

Bauer ends his discussion by praising Jewish racial traits and hinting that a form of eugenics is the answer to the Jewish problem.

FURTHER READING

Leichter, O.: *Otto Bauer: Tragödie oder Triumph?* (Vienna, 1970)

Wistrich, R.: *Socialism and the Jews* (London: Associated University Press, 1982)

STEVEN BELLER

Baum, Oscar (1883–1941) Czech–German writer. Born in Plzen, Baum lost his sight as a boy and trained as a pianist and organist at the Vienna Institute for the Blind. Later he worked as a music critic and became a member of the Prague Circle, making the acquaintance of Franz KAFKA and Max BROD. The latter took down Baum's first stories in shorthand and persuaded him to get them published.

He made his literary debut in 1908 with *Uferdasein* (Life on the shore), and the autobiographical *Das Leben im Dunkeln* (Life in darkness). These two, together with *Nacht ist umher* (1929; Night is all around), were hailed by Stefan ZWEIG as "the most moving documents, in the German language, of the lightless world taken from the life of the blind". The burden of Baum's writings on his handicap was opposition to the compassion society extended to the blind. In its stead he called for the creation of equality of opportunity for the handicapped – a call which influenced modern educational practice in this area.

Baum's other chief topic was the situation of the Jews. His novel *Die böse Unschuld* (1913; Malign innocence), depicted Jewish pre-war life in Bohemia against the background of the German–Czech nationality struggle. His last published work, *Das Volk des harten Schlafes* (1937; The people of the hard sleep), purported to take place in the medieval Jewish kingdom of the Khazars, but actually dealt with the problems of Jews in the first years of Nazi rule. Baum also wrote a play, *Das Wunder* (1920; The miracle). He died in Prague shortly before deportations to the death camps began.

RICHARD GRUNBERGER

Be'er, Haim (b.1945) Israeli poet and novelist. An eighth generation Jerusalemite on his mother's side, whose family roots date back to the pilgrim Ashkenazi immigration to Palestine at the beginning of the nineteenth century, Be'er was educated in religious schools. He served in the chaplaincy corps in the army, and began publishing poems and short stories at the age of 18.

Be'er's collection of poems *Sha'ashu'im yom-yom* (1970; Day to day delights), tries to recapture a lost childhood in religious Jerusalem at the end of the British Mandate and the first years of the State. The poems have strong autobiographical elements. In a language rich with associations and symbols, deeply rooted in religious literature, Be'er patiently reconstructs in minute detail a typical Jerusalemite experience as seen in retrospect.

In 1980 he published his first novel, *Notzot* (Feathers), which immediately became a bestseller and was subsequently dramatized. It describes the haunting memories of a boy from one of Jerusalem's Orthodox neighborhoods, who has become a soldier serving in a burial unit at the Suez Canal. Be'er paints a rich canvas of Jerusalem's eccentric characters in the distant and recent past. As in David SHAHAR's writing, the marginal characters are of considerable importance. Be'er's second novel, *Et hazamir* (1987; The time of trimming), is a political satire which follows the emergence and rise of the right-wing religious nationalist movement, *Gush Emunim*.

Be'er's work in English translation: *Feathers* (Chapter one), *Ariel* 51 (1982), pp.5–23.

FURTHER READING

Shaked, G.: Between utopia and apocalypse: on Haim Be'er's *Feathers*. *Modern Hebrew Literature* 6 (1980) 14–18

Sharoni, E.: Day to day delights. *Hebrew Book Review* 11 (1971) 20–23

RIVKA MAOZ

Beer-Hofmann, Richard (1886–1945) Austrian dramatist, novelist, essayist, and poet. He was born in Vienna but raised in Brno. He took his law degree at the University of Vienna, but an inheritance made him financially independent, and he became a respected member of the "Young Vienna" circle of writers, and the only *homo judaicus* in that largely Jewish group. In the 1920s he collaborated with Max REINHARDT on various theatrical projects. Having visited Palestine in 1936, he had to emigrate three years later. Via Switzerland he went to the United States, where he spent the rest of his life, living in New York with his daughters Miriam and Naëmah. His son, Gabriel, became a writer in England, using the pseudonym G. S. Marlowe.

Beer-Hofmann's literary output was relatively small; his *Gesammelte Werke*, edited by Martin BUBER in 1963, fill only one volume. The poet achieved early fame with his philosophical lullaby *Schlaflied für Miriam*, written in 1897 at the cradle of his first-born. While it does express the *fin-de-siècle* feeling of isolation and evanescence, he also derived solace from the Jewish tradition and continuity of existence. A notable figure in Beer-Hofmann's first play, *Der Graf von Charolais* (1905), is the misanthropic Roter Itzig, who is reminiscent of the Wandering Jew and of Shylock.

Beer-Hofmann's *magnum opus* is a grandly conceived cycle of poetic plays about King David, who is viewed as the symbolic embodiment of the Jewish psyche in all its ambivalence. Of these, only *Jaakobs Traum* (1918; *Jacob's Dream*, 1946), *Der junge David* (1933), and *Vorspiel auf dem Theater zu "König David"* (1936) were completed. Beer-Hofmann's writings in exile center largely about the beloved figure of his wife Paula, a convert to Judaism, who died in Switzerland in 1939. *Paula, ein Fragment*, a poignant memoir, appeared in 1949. A collection of *Verse*, issued in 1941, contains Beer-Hofmann's lyrical output of a scant dozen poems.

FURTHER READING

Elstun, E. N.: *Richard Beer-Hofmann: His Life and Work* (University Park: Pennsylvania State University Press, 1983)

Liptzin, S.: *Richard Beer-Hofmann* (New York: Bloch, 1936)

Oberholzer, O.: *Richard Beer-Hofmann* (Berne: Francke 1947)

HARRY ZOHN

Saul Bellow

Bellow, Saul (b.1915) American Jewish writer. Winner of a Nobel Prize, the Pulitzer Prize and several National Book Awards, Bellow is the most celebrated American Jewish writer of the twentieth century and his career has spanned more than four decades. As a writer Bellow is a stylist who is a post-Modernist, perhaps an anti-Modernist. He has time and again asked: "How does a good man (a mensch) live" in a complex, technologized urban world? Like all great writers he has no answer.

Bellow was born in Lachine, Quebec, a suburb of Montreal. Raised in a religiously Jewish house, where he spoke Yiddish as well as French, and also learned Hebrew and English, he grew up in a rather unsettled atmosphere. His father was unsuccessful but his mother hoped Saul would become a rabbi. In 1924 when the family moved to Chicago, Bellow chose to roam the streets and play baseball. After leaving Tuley High School he went to the University of Chicago and then Northwestern University from which he graduated in 1937 with honors in sociology and anthropology. In 1937 he decided

to become a writer. He worked briefly for the Works Progress Administration, then went to Mexico in 1940. In 1943 he worked for Mortimer Adler's "Great Books" and then joined the Merchant Marines.

In 1944 *Dangling Man* was published. Taking on T. S. Eliot's *The Waste Land* and Ernest Hemingway's "Hardboileddom", he detailed the problems of waiting to be called up by his draft board and the increasing loss of self-control. At the end, like Dostoevsky's Underground man, he gives in, crying "Long live regimentation". To some the book was lightweight, but Edmund Wilson, Diana Trilling, and Delmore SCHWARTZ saw it as one of the most honest testimonies on the psychology of a whole generation. His second novel, *The Victim*, was published in 1947.

The Adventures of Augie March (1953), Bellow's third book, was written while traveling on a Guggenheim Fellowship through Paris and Rome, in New York City, and at Princeton University. It was his "fantasy holiday", for it created Augie as an energetic devotee of adventure, sex, and people, oppressed by the world. In *Seize the Day* (1956), a tightly elegiac novella begun in the 1940s, Tommy Wilhelm's penchant for success without hard work, his willingness to depend on his father, and Dr Tamkin's cure-all advice to "seize the day", result in defeat. Though Tommy is a sloppy sentimentalist, a schlemiel, he is a worthwhile and likeable man whose breakdown can be seen as a portent of a new beginning.

Henderson the Rain King (1959) is both a very funny and a very imaginative novel. Set in a mythical Africa, Eugene Henderson's quest reflected Bellow's desire to develop a fiction that can accommodate the full tumult of modern experience, as well as seek a remedy for the anxiety over death. After marrying for the third time in 1961, and teaching in Puerto Rico and the University of Chicago, Bellow decided to return to the anonymity of Chicago to avoid New York's politicized intellectuals.

After writing *The Last Analysis*, a play that failed, he published *Herzog* (1964), his best known and most celebrated novel. Moses Herzog, an intellectual professor rendered almost impotent literarily and generally, searches his memory for solutions even as he writes large numbers of imaginary letters. Only when he is able to free himself from his fantasy life, in prose that is rich and full of the impressions that reflect the 1960s, can he relax, reject fashionable existentialism, and move from an emotionally charged and unstable life, to a more rational and moderate one. In *Mr Sammler's Planet* (1970), a 70-year-old Polish Jew who has survived the Holocaust is surrounded by young people, mostly relatives, who test his ability to live moderately, wisely, and to do his duty, in the late 1960s.

In the early 1970s Bellow published *Humboldt's Gift* (1975), and was divorced for the third time, only to marry again the following year. *To Jerusalem and Back* (1976) is Bellow's coverage of the Arab-Israeli wars. *The Dean's December* (1982), a didactic novel about Chicago's evils, is an indictment of American urban society. *More Die of Heartbreak* (1987) is an attempt to point out the differences between our fears of what might be – nuclear holocaust, for example – and the reality of what is.

As Bellow's friend Richard Stern has written, it is hard to name many other American writers (Henry James and William Faulkner are possible examples) who have published first-rate imaginative books over four decades. As John Updike put it in the *New Yorker*, Bellow is one of the rare writers who, when we read them, make us feel he is taking mimesis a layer or two deeper than it has gone before. Through ten novels, two collections of short stories, several plays, and many essays and articles, he has maintained his standing as one of the greatest American Jewish writers.

FURTHER READING

Clayton, J. J.: *Saul Bellow: In Defense of Man* (Bloomington: Indiana University Press, 1968)

Malin, I.: *Saul Bellow and the Critics* (New York: New York University Press, 1967)

Opdahl, K.: *The Novels of Saul Bellow* (University Park: Pennsylvania State University Press, 1967)

Tanner, T.: *Saul Bellow* (Edinburgh and London: Oliver & Boyd, 1965)

Walden, D., ed.: *Twentieth Century American Jewish Writers* (Detroit: Gale, 1984)

DANIEL WALDEN

Ben-Ami (Rabinovich, Mordekhai-Mark) (1854–1932) Russian–Jewish prose writer and publicist. During the pogroms of the years 1881–2 he was a student at Novorossiisk University (Odessa) and one of the organizers of Jewish self-defense. In 1882 he went abroad in order to arrange assistance for those fleeing from the pogroms and until 1886 he resided in Geneva. During the period 1887–1905, back in Odessa, he actively participated in the Zionist movement. In 1905 he emigrated, remaining in Geneva until 1923, and spent his last 10 years in Tel Aviv. He was the first to emerge in Russian–Jewish literature as an apologist of tradition (religious, spiritual, domestic). He revealed the elevated, poetic side of the commonplace life of the "old Jews" and for the first time not the *maskil* intellectual but the "dark" mass, the common person became the protagonist.

He was the first Russian–Jewish writer to be guided, at last, exclusively by Jewish readers, attempting to inspire them with love for their own people, and not by the surrounding majority, as those of the previous literary generation (for example Osip RABINOVICH or Grigorii BOGROV). Ben-Ami's primary material is of the 1860s, the time of his childhood and youth; his basic literary form is the autobiographical (or pseudo-autobiographical) narrative. His main fictional works include the cycle of short stories and narrative tales *Vospominaniia detstva* (1882–93; Reminiscences of childhood); the cycle *Rasskazy moim detiam* (1902–5; Stories to my children); and the unfinished novel *Detstvo* (1902–6; Childhood). His most significant publicistic cycle is *Glas iz pustyni* (1900–4; Voice from the wilderness). Ben-Ami also wrote in Yiddish *A Nakht in a Klein Shtetl* the narrative tale (1909; Night in a small town).

SHIMON MARKISH

Ben-Gurion, David (1886–1973) Israeli statesman and labor leader, first Prime Minister of Israel. Born David Gruen in Plonsk (then Russian Poland), he joined the *Po'alei Zion* movement in 1903 and came to Palestine in 1906. After working for some time as an agricultural laborer, he emerged as one of the leaders

David Ben-Gurion (standing), with his family, c.1910

of *Po'alei Zion*. From 1911 to 1914 his writings, while generally following the Marxist-Zionism of BER BOROKHOV, are already distinguished for the stress they place on the centrality of the nation-building processes in Palestine for the future of Zionism. This contrasts with the more conventional view which still saw Zionist activity in the Diaspora as determining the course of events. In line with this view he advocated, on the outbreak of the First World War, active support for the Turkish war effort on the part of Palestinian Jewish youth, but his ideas were rejected by the Ottoman authorities and he was deported to Egypt. After the Balfour Declaration of 1917, which supported the establishment of a Jewish state in Palestine, he helped recruit American Jews to fight on the side of the British. He joined the British army in Canada and arrived in its ranks in Palestine towards the end of the war.

In 1919 he was among the founders of the *Ahdut ha'avodah* party, which tried to broaden the base of *Po'alei Zion* in Palestine. In 1921 he became secretary of the newly-founded Histadrut (General Federation of Jewish Labour) and for 14 years he used this position to cement the political power of the organized labor movement in Palestine and made it into the most powerful economic and political organization in the *yishuv*. In 1930 he was instrumental in the unification of *Ahdut ha'avodah* with *Hapo'el Hatza'ir* into the new labor party, Mapai, which he headed until the mid-1960s.

Ben-Gurion succeeded in making Mapai into the main party in the *yishuv* and, since the 18th Zionist Congress in 1933, also into the major party in the World Zionist Organization. In 1935 he became Chairman of the Jewish Agency for Palestine and, as such, the *de facto* leader of the *yishuv* and the second ranking leader in the Zionist movement after Chaim WEIZMANN.

His tenure as Chairman of the Jewish Agency was characterized by a policy combining activism with pragmatism: in this he sought a middle course between the more pro-British diplomatic orientation of Weizmann, and the extremist militancy of the Revisionists under Vladimir JABOTINSKY. He turned the *Haganah* into an effective paramilitary organization and forged the alliance with the American Jewish community which facilitated the diplomatic moves leading after 1945 to the establishment of the State of Israel (the Biltmore Program). During the Second World War he developed the two-track strategy of "fighting against Hitler as if there were no British White Paper, and fighting against the White Paper as if there were no war against Hitler".

After the war his activities, aimed at achieving independence even at the price of partition, combined limited military activities against the British with highly publicized attempts to bring masses of illegal immigrants into the country. These helped to lead towards the 1947 United Nations partition plan and the eventual Declaration of Independence on 14 May 1948. Ben-Gurion emerged as Prime Minister and Minister of Defense in the provisional government, and led his party to win the first parliamentary elections of 1949. Under his leadership the *Haganah* (later the Israel Defense Force) was able to defend Israel against attempts, first by Palestinian Arabs, and later by invading Arab armies from neighboring countries, to prevent the establishment of a Jewish state. After the 1948–49 war he led the country's process of rapid population growth through mass immigration, mainly of Holocaust survivors from eastern Europe and refugees from Arab countries. During this period he emerged as the unchallenged leader of Israel, despite the fact that his party never achieved a parliamentary majority and he had to rely on often fragile coalition governments. He left the premiership for a short while during 1953–5, but returned to lead the government and the country into the Sinai–Suez War of 1956.

In 1963 Ben-Gurion resigned and turned over the leadership of his party and the government to Levi Eshkol. After a complex and sometimes confusing series of events he was expelled from his own party. He headed the breakaway Rafi party (together with Moshe Dayan and Shimon Peres), but did not succeed in dislodging Eshkol and Mapai from power, and his life ended in the political wilderness. After 1967 he called for an Israeli withdrawal from all conquered territory except Jerusalem, in return for peace.

Ben-Gurion was a complex and contradictory person, whose verbal aggression and rhetorical combativeness sometimes masked a cautious pragmatism and an uncanny ability to build political coalitions. A socialist agnostic, he nonetheless based all his cabinets on alliances with some of the religious parties, and his former radical, almost Marxist, socialism eventually mellowed to the conclusion that Israel's place is within the Western democratic camp.

As the architect of Israel's military might, he always knew the limits of power. The institutional and intellectual underpinnings of his long period of leadership have, in their achievements and limitations alike, left an indelible stamp on Israel.

BIBLIOGRAPHY

Rebirth and Destiny of Israel (London: Thomas Yoseloff, 1959); *Israel: Years of Challenge* (London: Anthony Blond, 1964); Bransten, T. R., ed: *Recollections* (London: Macdonald & Co., 1970)

FURTHER READING

Edelman, M.: *Ben-Gurion. A Political Biography* (London: Hodder & Stoughton, 1964)
Tevet, S.: *The Burning Ground* (London: Robert Hale, 1988)

SHLOMO AVINERI

Ben-Haim, Paul [Paul Frankenburger] (1897–1984) Israeli composer. Ben-Haim was born in Munich, the son of a professor of law. From 1915 to 1920 he studied piano, conducting and composition at the Munich Academy of Music, primarily with Friedrich Klose and Ludwig Thuille. Between 1920 and 1924 Ben-Haim served as assistant to Bruno Walter and Hans Knappertsbusch, among others. In 1924 he was appointed conductor of the Augsburg

Opera and Symphony Orchestra. In 1931 he returned to Munich where he built up a significant reputation as a composer.

The works written during his years in Germany show, naturally enough, the influence of early twentieth-century composers in the European mainstream. His orchestral idiom relates to the late Romanticism of Jean Sibelius and William Walton, whereas his songs reveal a close affinity with Claude Debussy. But the special role of biblical texts and subjects, which were to become such an important factor in his later music, is evident even among his earliest compositions.

With the rise of Nazism in 1933, Ben-Haim emigrated to Palestine, settling in Tel Aviv. He immediately became active as a conductor, pianist, and accompanist, and joined the teaching staffs of the Tel Aviv and Jerusalem Conservatoires. In 1939 he met Brachah ZEPHIRA, a Yemenite singer and folklorist, and for nine years he accompanied her in concert, bringing to life chants and songs that had hitherto been familiar to him only through the somewhat theoretical research publications of the ethnomusicologist, Abraham Zvi IDELSOHN.

Ben-Haim published his arrangements of Sephardi, Persian, Bukharan, and Yemenite Jewish melodies, sacred and secular, and composed original songs in the Levantine style, typical features of which were melodic ornamentation, intricate rhythms and oriental tone-colours. These characteristics also began to permeate his instrumental works. By the mid 1940s he was acknowledged as the founder and leader of the "East Mediterranean School" of composition.

The music he composed during the second part of his life was conceived for every medium: from large-scale orchestral works, through choral, vocal, instrumental chamber music, to solo pieces, such as the three-movement Sonata for Solo Violin, composed for Yehudi Menuhin in 1952 and premiered by this artist the following year. All these compositions express different aspects of the Holy Land in sound: dance, meditation, elegy, each blending the traditions of the ancient past with the vitality of the present.

Recognition came to Ben-Haim in the form of frequent broadcasts on Israeli radio and television, as well as numerous national awards. He was chosen to represent Israel at many international gatherings. He died in 1984 at the age of 86.

BIBLIOGRAPHY
Short Biography and Work List with Explanations (Tel Aviv, 1967)

ALEXANDER KNAPP

Ben-Ner, Yitzhak (b.1937) Israeli writer. Ben-Ner was born in Kfar Yehoshua. His career as a novelist had two beginnings as his first novel, *Ha'ish misham* (1967; From over there), appeared long before the rest of his stories and novels, which were published from the mid 1970s.

His prose is stark and emotional, and he associates his characters, their careers and memories, with death and the thought of death. The title story of *Sheki'ah kafrit* (1976; Rustic sunset), tells of the narrator's preparation for death through his constant association with it in the village. The writing seems to be at the one time both very immediate and imbued with distance. Although the narrator is in the village, he continues to long for it, for its past, for its future, and for its present in a purified form. Even the title of a later volume *Eretz rehokah* (1981; A distant land), projects an ideal of distance, although here the ideal is one of place rather than time, with an idyllic New Zealand contrasted to a troubled, cramped, noisy Israel.

Although Ben-Ner has specialized in the novella genre, both his first novel and his massive *Protokol* (1983) deal with larger themes, where the main character has to make his personal path through the large fields of history. His confessional tone imparts a fervent involvement to the politics; indeed, politics are incorporated into the personality of the character.

BIBLIOGRAPHY
Cinema. In *Meetings With the Angel* eds L. Yudkin and B. Tammuz (London: André Deutsch, 1973)

LEON I. YUDKIN

Ben-Yehuda, Eliezer [Eliezer Yizhak Perelman] (1858–1922) Hebrew writer and lexicographer. He was the founder and leader of the movement to revive Hebrew as a spoken language. Born in Luzhky, Lithuania, Ben-Yehuda received an exclusively Jewish-Orthodox education until, in his teens, he was attracted by the Jewish Enlightenment (*Haskalah*), especially by the Hebrew literature being produced as part of that movement. In search of a wider education he entered the state secondary school in Dünaburg (today, Daugavpils, Latvia) where he became a sympathizer with the Russian revolutionary movement and grew detached from Jewish concerns. The outbreak of war between Russia and Turkey in 1877 led to an abrupt change. The struggle for the liberation of Bulgaria from Turkish rule gave Ben-Yehuda the idea that the Jews, too, should strive for a national revival. His resolve to do so himself was strengthened when he read George Eliot's novel *Daniel Deronda*, and he went to Paris to study medicine, intending to settle in Palestine thereafter. In 1879 he wrote an article for the Hebrew press advocating Jewish immigration to Palestine. Ben-Yehuda argued that only in a country with a Jewish majority could a living Hebrew literature and a distinct Jewish nationality survive; elsewhere, the pressure to assimilate to the language of the majority would cause Hebrew to die out. Shortly afterwards he reached the conclusion that the active use of Hebrew as a literary language could not be sustained, notwithstanding the hoped-for concentration of Jews in Palestine, unless Hebrew also became the everyday spoken language there.

Ben-Yehuda settled in Jerusalem in 1881 (without completing his medical studies) and devoted himself to the task of reviving spoken Hebrew. He insisted on making Hebrew the language of his own household, so that his children learned it as their mother-tongue, and he made a pioneer effort to use Hebrew as the language of instruction in the classroom (the "natural" or "direct" method) during a brief spell as a schoolteacher. He was one of the founders and foremost members of the Hebrew Language Council, the forerunner of the Academy of the Hebrew Language. He edited a newspaper which helped to spread a popular

Eliezer Ben-Yehuda, 1910

style of Hebrew and through which he introduced many neologisms of his own invention into the language, and he founded the world's first Hebrew newspaper for children. For nearly 40 years Ben-Yehuda worked on his great *Dictionary of Ancient and Modern Hebrew*, much of which appeared only after his death, having been completed by others. He founded the Zionist and Israeli tradition of exchanging European surnames for Hebrew ones when he officially registered his surname as Ben-Yehuda ("Son of Judea") instead of his previous Russian name, having already used Ben-Yehuda as his penname.

The attempt to revive Hebrew succeeded, though the important breakthrough was made not in Jerusalem, where the conservative influence of a highly traditionalist Jewish community proved too strong, but in the scattered and rather isolated farming villages newly set up in other parts of Palestine by nationalist-minded Jews. The instrument of the revival was the exclusive use of Hebrew in the schools of these settlements, whose pupils grew accustomed to speaking Hebrew among themselves even outside school so that, later, they were able to bring their own children up in Hebrew-speaking households. By the time of Ben-Yehuda's death a Hebrew-speaking generation had arisen in these villages, and the British, who had conquered Palestine from the Turks during the First World War, had recognized Hebrew as one of the country's official languages.

For much of his life Ben-Yehuda was at war with the Orthodox Jewish community of Jerusalem. In the 1890s they denounced him to the Turkish authorities and he was imprisoned for sedition before an appeal led to his release. Ben-Yehuda was an enthusiastic supporter of the scheme for Jewish settlement in East Africa which seriously divided the Zionist Congress of 1903. This, and his support for the administration of the Jewish agricultural colonies by Baron Rothschild's officials, made him unpopular with the members of the second *aliyah*, who were the dominant group in the *yishuv* for many decades. During the First World War, when Zionism was outlawed by the Turkish military administration, Ben-Yehuda lived in the United States.

BIBLIOGRAPHY

A weighty question, trans. D. Patterson. In E. Silberschlag, ed: *Eliezer Ben-Yehuda. A Symposium in Oxford* (Oxford: Oxford Centre for Postgraduate Hebrew Studies, 1981)

A Dream Come True trans. T. Muraoka (forthcoming) [autobiography]

FURTHER READING

Fellman, J.: *The Revival of a Classical Tongue. Eliezer Ben Yehuda and the Modern Hebrew Language* (The Hague and Paris: Mouton, 1973)

GEORGE MANDEL

Ben-Zvi, Yitzhak [Yishak Shimshelevitz] (1884–1963)   Israeli statesman. He was a modest but influential man whose life was once characterized by Kadish Luz, speaker of the Knesset, in three words: "Labor, politics and scholarship".

Ben-Zvi was the scion of a Zionist house. His father, Zvi Shimshelevitz was a *Hovev Zion* and a member of the order of the Benei Moshe who visited Palestine in 1891. Ben-Zvi studied Hebrew firstly in a traditional and then in a modern *heder* under the guidance of A. M. Borochov with whose son, Ber, he struck up a strong friendship. He spent one year in the science faculty of the University of Kiev.

His first visit to Palestine was in 1904. En route he visited a number of Sephardi communities in the Levant and Turkey. He then spent two months wandering through the young Jewish villages of the *yishuv*, and this period left its impress in a love of the natural history and historical geography of Palestine which is reflected in his subsequent writings on the *yishuv*. Clearly this period laid the foundation for his interest in and his activities on behalf of oriental and Karaite Jews which was to culminate in the years after the founding of the State in a conscious policy of bringing Jews from Yemen, North Africa, and Persia, and Karaite Jews from Europe, into the new State.

In 1906 his father was sentenced to permanent exile in Siberia for housing an arms cache of the self-defense movement and the rest of the household was sentenced to various terms of imprisonment. Ben-Zvi escaped to Vilna where he continued working for the *Po'alei Zion* movement, spending two short periods in jail for his activities. He left for Palestine in 1907 and settled in Jaffa with a Samaritan family. His life-long ties with the Samaritans began with that period. It is probable that he influenced the Samaritans to start a rapprochement with the Jews – the resulting series of Jewish–Samaritan marriages which brought new blood to the group certainly saved the sect from extinction.

A study of his subsequent career, as Levi Eshkol observed in a eulogy, is tantamount to recounting the history of Israel's struggle for independence. Throughout his life Ben-Zvi worked closely with BEN-GURION. In 1908 Ben-Zvi participated in the establishment of the Hebrew *Gymnasium* in Jerusalem and became one of its first teachers. He was active in inspiring the Jews of Turkey to take a pro-Zionist stance. With Ben-Gurion he went to Constantinople to study law, so that he would be better equipped to handle the political work of the *Po'alei Zion* movement. After his return to Palestine in 1915 he organized a Jewish militia in Jerusalem, with David Ben-Gurion and both he and Ben-Gurion were expelled from the *yishuv* for Zionist activity. They went first to Egypt and thence to the USA where they were active in setting up the *Hehalutz* movement. He also collaborated with Ben-Gurion in writing *The Land of Israel: Past and Present* in Yiddish.

He returned to Palestine in 1918 as a soldier in the Jewish Legion. In the following year he was actively involved in the unification of the Labor parties and was elected to the central committee of the *Ahdut ha'avodah* movement. He was also elected a member of the forerunner of the Knesset, the *Asefat hanivharim*.

Herbert Samuel, the first British High Commissioner for Palestine, appointed Ben-Zvi to the Government Advisory Council but he resigned in protest after the Arab riots of 1921 were followed by a ban on Jewish migration. In that year he participated in the formation of the Histadrut and founded an Arab paper, *Ittihad-el-amal*.

From 1925 to 1929 he became a Histadrut representative at a number of workers' conventions and conferences throughout the world and attended all the Zionist congresses. During this active period he found the time to publish his *Sefer hashomeronim*. His standing was such that he attended the coronation of George VI in 1937 as the representative of the Jews of Palestine.

In 1948, during the war of Independence (in which he lost his son), he established the Institute for Research on Jewish Communities in the Middle East, which was to become his memorial in the form of the Yad Ben-Zvi (the Ben-Zvi Institute, founded 1953) which was affiliated with the Hebrew University. This Institute now houses a very valuable ethnic archive. The following year he was elected to the first Knesset.

His years of activity on behalf of the *yishuv*, and his close association with Ben-Gurion were rewarded in 1952 by his election to the Presidency of Israel, a post to which he was re-elected in 1957 and 1962. As President he set the tone for the scholarly involvement of his successors in Jewish studies. He brought together the various ethnic groups in Israel through studying their history and customs and by inviting their leaders to monthly meetings in the Presidential home. These resulted in a number of published symposia on aspects of Jewish history.

ALAN D. CROWN

Benda, Julien (1867–1956)   French writer and critic. Born into an assimilated, wealthy Parisian family, he had a good education and studied history at the Sorbonne. He seemed all set to lead the leisurely life of a young man of independent means when the Dreyfus Affair brought home to him what he later ceaselessly denounced as "Byzantine France". This was the anti-rationalist climate fostered by writers (from the symbolists to the surrealists, to nationalist, racialist, religious, and political literati) and philosophers (notably Henri BERGSON, initially Benda's favorite target of attack, and later existentialists, Marxists, and neo-rationalists). He believed poets and philosophers had betrayed their mission of upholding rational and universal values. And since in modern times the intellectual increasingly assumed the function of the priest, his word heeded by half-educated masses with the right to vote but still ruled by instinct and passion, the intelligentsia's desertion of its role was a calamity. This is the underlying theme of Benda's prolific writings – literary, historical, philosophical, and journalistic. They remain controversial, a passionate crusade for rationality whose virulence, dogmatic judgments, wholesale dismissal of modern literature and philosophy are often disconcerting. On the other hand, few people nowadays will quarrel with the grave political and moral implications of the anti-rationalism or pseudo-rationalism he so vigorously denounced. Fascism shocked but did not surprise Benda. His commitment to fighting it in alliance with communists and socialists, previously almost as much attacked as right-wing propagandists, has been diversely interpreted as a contradiction and a logical translation into action of his earlier insistence that the lucid intellectual's place is above the mêlée. His Jewishness, too, in turn denied and assumed, remains a matter of debate.

FURTHER READING

Niess, R. J.: *Julien Benda* (Ann Arbor: University of Michigan Press, 1956)

NELLY WILSON

Bendemann, Eduard Julius Friedrich

(1811–1880) German painter. Bendemann was possibly the most successful Jewish artist working in Germany during the nineteenth century, although it is doubtful whether he would have achieved the honors heaped upon him had he not converted to Christianity early in his career. Born in Berlin, he received a conventional training at the Düsseldorf Academy before traveling to Rome, where he stayed from 1829 to 1831. There his style was formed, not so much by the work of Raphael and Michelangelo as by the work of the Nazarenes, a group of German painters whose aims included the conscious imitation of Renaissance art.

On his return to Germany, Bendemann painted *The Mourning Jews in the Babylonian Exile*, an accomplished pastiche of Michelangelesque and Raphaelesque figures in the highly-colored, detailed style of his teacher Gottfried von Schadow. The painting was well received, Bendemann's conversion to Christianity followed, and the door was open to a meteoric career. In 1839 he became a professor at the Dresden Academy and in 1859 succeeded von Schadow (now his brother-in-law) as Director of the Düsseldorf Academy. He received prestigious patronage; major commissions included the decorations of the King of Saxony's palace at Dresden and the ancient Roemersaal in Dresden Town Hall. Bendemann was a good portraitist but a mediocre painter of large historical compositions; it is his misfortune that his reputation rests on the latter.

FURTHER READING

Roth, C.: *Jewish Art: An Illustrated History* (London: Vallentine, Mitchell & Co., 1971)
The Dusseldorf Academy and the Americans (Atlanta: The High Museum of Art, 1972) [exhibition catalog]

LAURA JACOBUS

Bender, Alfred Philipp (1863–1937)

South African minister. Bender was born in Dublin and was the first Jewish minister to be educated at St John's College, Cambridge, where he obtained his Master of Arts degree. He was well versed in Semitic languages and English literature.

He became the recognized leader of Cape Town Jewry from 1895 until his death. As minister of the Cape Town Hebrew congregation, he was an eloquent and persuasive preacher and a committed philanthropist. He was responsible for the initiation of several educational, social, and cultural services, such as special services for children and Sunday morning classes for women. He was sympathetic to assisting east European Jewish immigrants when they settled in South Africa although he was very English in orientation and the Anglo-Jews tended to regard their east European co-religionists as "foreign" and "unmannerly".

He had wide-ranging influence, relating easily to both the Jewish and Gentile population. Representing the Jewish community in its dealings with the wider world, he was opposed to the formation of the (Cape) Jewish Board of Deputies (1904) as he opposed lay representation of South African Jewry. As a result, his congregation did not affiliate with the Board until 1919. He was also opposed to Zionism, only supporting it after the Balfour Declaration of 1917, which gave it British government support.

He was a competent teacher of Hebrew; with the endowment of a chair of Hebrew studies at the South African College (now the University of Cape Town), he was appointed its first professor of Hebrew.

FURTHER READING

Saron, G. and Hotz, L., eds: *The Jews in South Africa: A History* (Cape Town: Oxford University Press, 1955)

JOCELYN HELLIG

Benjamin, Walter (1892–1940)

German writer. Born in Berlin, Benjamin became involved in the student movement during the reign of Kaiser Wilhelm II. His speech, "On student life" (1914), contains some of his future preoccupations, like cultural criticism of "progress", knowledge conceived as "alien to the state, frequently hostile to the state" and utopian images considered as elements of a "permanent spiritual revolution". He studied philosophy and gained a PhD at Bern University with a thesis entitled *The Concept of Art Criticism in German Romanticism* (1919). In 1925, however, he was deprived of the possibility of making a career as a professor, because the Frankfurt University refused his thesis to allow him to teach, *Ursprung des deutschen Trauerspiels* (The origin of German baroque drama), where he first developed one of his key concepts, that of allegory as the cipher message of a repressed truth, the voice of betrayed men, the expression of his stubborn hope of redemption.

Through his lifelong friend, Gershom Scholem, Benjamin became acquainted with Jewish theological writings about the Messiah; he established a bond between anarchism and Messianism. After 1924 Marxism became an increasingly important ingredient of his worldview. He traveled to the Soviet Union and wrote an entry on Johann Goethe for the *Great Soviet Encyclopaedia*, but when it was printed in 1929 only about one eighth of the original text had survived. Benjamin was attracted by communism; however, he felt a certain mistrust towards the Soviet Union and never joined the communist party. *Einbahnstrasse* (1928; *One-way Street*, 1978), is a book whose form is that of a street, a sequence of houses and shops, a literary montage of images and ideas; Ernst Bloch called it "surrealistic thought".

When the Nazis came to power, Benjamin moved to Paris and there he continued to work. He wrote essays on his friend, Bertolt Brecht, on the French poet, Charles Baudelaire, on the German historian, Eduard Fuchs, on the Czech storyteller, Franz Kafka, and many others. His main work throughout this period remained unfinished: a large collection of fragments on Paris, seen as the "capital of the nineteenth century", placed under the growing influence of commodity fetishism (its title, *Passagenwerk*, refers to the architectonic arcades of the city). In

The Work of Art in the Age of Mechanical Reproduction (1935), he made an analysis of the new relationship between capitalist society and artworks whose "aura" vanishes.

The Nazi–Soviet pact of 1939, the beginning of the war, and the fall of France changed Benjamin's life: he was arrested, and after two months in a concentration camp (Clos St Joseph, Nevers) he was released, and prepared his last work, the *Theses on the Philosophy of History*, where he describes revolution as a "redemptive interruption" of the continuum of history and attacks those who feel time as empty or homogeneous. The Jews learn that "every second of the future bears within it that little door through which Messiah may enter".

In September 1940 Benjamin tried to leave France, was caught by the police on the Spanish border, and committed suicide.

BIBLIOGRAPHY

Illuminations (London: Fontana, 1973); *One-Way Street and Other Writings* (London: NLB, 1979); *Reflections: Essays, Aphorisms, Autobiographical Writings* (New York: Harcourt Brace, 1979)

FURTHER READING

Roberts, J.: *Walter Benjamin* (London: Macmillan, 1982)

Wolin, R.: *Walter Benjamin, an Aesthetic of Redemption* (New York: Columbia University Press, 1982)

LEANDRO KONDER

Berdyczewski [Bin-Gorion]**, Micha Yosef** (1865–1921) Hebrew writer. Born in Miedzyborz (Medzibezh), Ukraine, to a rabbinic family, Berdyczewski typifies the modern Hebraist conflict between prodigious talmudic learning and the passion for European scholarship. His Hebrew stories reflect the tensions of an orphaned childhood, an early first marriage and a stagnant society where tragic lives, grotesque portraiture, and latent volatility are intermingled. His stories, particularly *Mahanayim* and *Orva parah* (1900), are seen (by Dan Miron) as marking the transition from nineteenth-century narrative to a new mode of Hebrew fiction. Berdyczewski's Yiddish stories, such as *Yidishe* *kesavim fun a veit'n qorov* (1912), by contrast, depict this small-town society with nostalgia.

Berdyczewski's first article in 1887 on the history of the Volozhin *yeshivah*, where he studied for two years, began a writing career equally prolific in publicistics, in a unique approach to Jewish lore and in belles lettres. His studies in philosophy in Breslau, Berlin, and Berne culminated in a doctorate in 1896 on "The connection between ethics and esthetics". The impact of Nietzsche and Schopenhauer led to a series of influential pamphlets advocating a change of values in the Jews' overly bookish and spiritual life orientation. As the leader of a group of young rebels (*tze'irim*), his approach contrasted with that of AHAD HA'AM. Berdyczewski argued for broader, more European, emphases in Hebrew literature as well as for a more heterodox conception of the nascent nationalist ideology. His article *Ahad Ha'am vede'otav* (Ahad Ha'am and his views) is representative of these views.

As folklorist and scholar Berdyczewski's output was prodigious in both German and Hebrew. His belletristic embellishments on Jewish myth and lore are in evidence in the collection *Sefunot ve'aggadot* (1924, 1956).

BIBLIOGRAPHY

Mimekor Yisra'el, 3 vols ed. E. Bin-Gorion; trans. I. M. Lask (Bloomington: Indiana University Press, 1976)

FURTHER READING

Spiegel, S.: *Hebrew Reborn* (Philadephia: Jewish Publication Society, 1962) 327–370

STANLEY NASH

Bergelson, Dovid (1884–1952) Yiddish

novelist, short-story writer, and journalist. Born near Uman, Ukraine, Bergelson received a traditional Jewish education, and also studied non-Jewish subjects with a local teacher, read Hebrew *Haskalah* literature, and started learning Russian at the age of 12. At 13 he began writing two novels in Hebrew, and tried his hand at writing in Russian. With N. Meisel, in 1910, he co-edited the journal *Der yidisher almanakh*, in which his story *Der toyber* (The deaf one) was printed. His novel *Nokh alemen* (1913) was acclaimed as a major event in Yiddish literature when it appeared. In 1919 *Arum vokzal* (*Around the depot*, 1973) was published in Warsaw, partly at his own expense, and was received enthusiastically by Yiddish literary critics. A Hebrew translation of some chapters of *Nokh alemen* was printed in the same year in the Odessan weekly *Ha'olam*, under the title *Kikhlot hakol* suggested by H. N. BIALIK.

In 1912 Bergelson was invited to Vilna by the publisher B. A. Kletzkin, to edit the literary section of the journal *Di yidishe velt*. The novella *Yosef Shur* (*Joseph Shur, Ashes Out of Hope*, 1977), dates from the end of Bergelson's period of greatest creativity, in which his themes are taken from Jewish small-town life in the years prior to the Revolution. In an impressionistic style and with minimal plot Bergelson records the states of mind of his characters through frequent monologues in which they give vent to their dissatisfactions.

In 1920 Bergelson left Russia to settle in Berlin, where he began to write for the newspaper *Forverts*. In 1926 he transferred his allegiance from *Forverts* to the pro-Soviet *Frayhayt*, and in 1933 he returned permanently to the Soviet Union.

In the collection of stories *Shturemteg* (1927; Storm days), and the novel *Mides hadin* (1929; Divine justice), Bergelson describes the effects of the chaotic conditions of the early post-Revolutionary years on the Jewish communities in his native Ukraine. His major work of the 1930s, the partially autobiographical, two-volume novel *Bam Dnyeper* (On the Dniepr), displays the strain of writing during the Stalinist terror. Dovid Bergelson was arrested in 1949 and murdered on 12 August 1952. In 1961 his reputation was rehabilitated in the USSR.

BIBLIOGRAPHY

A Shtetl and Other Yiddish Novellas, trans. R. Wisse (New York: Library of Jewish Studies, 1973); Howe, I., and Greenberg, E., eds: *A Treasury of Yiddish Stories* (New York: Schocken, 1973); Howe, I., and Greenberg, E., eds: *Joseph Shur, Ashes Out of Hope* (New York: Schocken, 1977)

FURTHER READING

Madison, C.: *Yiddish Literature. Its Scope and Major Writers* (New York: Schocken, 1971)

Waxman, M.: *A History of Jewish Literature* vol. 4 (New York: Thomas Yoseloff, 1971)

DAFNA CLIFFORD

Bergman, George (1900–1979)

Australian Jewish historian, writer, and biographer. Bergman was born in Germany and studied economics, history, and law, graduating with a Ph.D. in economics, but practising as a lawyer. Bergman escaped to France from Nazi Germany in 1933 and served in the French Foreign Legion during the Second World War. In North Africa he enlisted with the Allies, emigrating to Australia in 1947 where he entered the public service.

In the first part of his writing career (1922–66), he wrote almost exclusively on his passion, mountaineering. In Australia he devoted his time to writing on Australian Jewish history, co-writing a most successful study of the origins of the Australian Jewish community, *Australian Genesis: Jewish Convicts and Settlers, 1788–1850* (1974). He wrote numerous articles on Australian Jewish history, including 11 items for the *Dictionary of Australian Biography* and articles on Australian Jews for the *New Australian Encyclopaedia*. Until his death he contributed a monthly historical feature page to the *Australian Jewish Times*.

A diligent researcher, Bergman is regarded by many as having set new standards for the writing of Australian Jewish history, despite his success as a popularizer in this field.

FURTHER READING

Forbes, M. Z.: George Bergman, 1900–1979: A tribute. *Australian Jewish Historical Society* 8 (1979)

ALAN D. CROWN

Bergman, Samuel Hugo (b.1883)

Czech Jewish philosopher. In the world of twentieth-century European Jewish thought Bergman was a leading philosophical figure. From his student days in Prague, he was influenced by both Zionism as a political ideology and the religious ideas of Martin BUBER. From 1907 to 1919 he served as a librarian at the University Library in Prague (though he served in the Austrian army during the First World War). In 1920 he emigrated to Palestine where he worked as the director of the National and University Library, a post he held until 1935. In 1928 he was appointed a lecturer in philosophy at the Hebrew University; subsequently he became a professor, and rector from 1935 to 1938. One of his major editorial tasks was to serve as editor of general philosophy for the *Encyclopaedia Hebraica*. He was also an editor of the philosophy periodical journal *Iyyun*. In addition he was a member of *Hapo'el hatza'ir* and later *Berit shalom*.

Bergman's philosophical development can be divided into two periods. Initially he was influenced by the views of Brentano and attempted to analyze the phenomena of perception and evidence. The second period was dominated by neo-Kantianism especially as interpreted by Hermann COHEN and Ernst Cassirer Among his philosophical writings were studies of Immanuel Kant and Solomon MAIMON as well as epistemological investigations. In 1954 he was awarded the Israel Prize for Humanities for his study of logic, *Introduction to Logic* (1953). Regarding religion, Bergman's views were influenced by such writers as Rudolph Steiner, Martin Buber, and Franz ROSENZWEIG as well as Christian and Indian philosophers. According to Bergman, faith involves a direct experience of God – a dialogical meeting involving prayer. His religious writings include such classic studies as *Faith and Reason: An Introduction to Modern Jewish Thought* (1961) and *Philosophy of Solomon Maimon* (1967).

DAN COHN-SHERBOK

Bergner, Herz (1907–1969)

Australian Yiddish novelist. Bergner is the most important Australian Yiddish writer of the post-GOLDHAR generation and an important Australian writer *per se*. The younger brother of Melekh RAVITSH, Bergner emigrated from Poland to Melbourne in 1938. He immediately resumed a literary career begun in Poland, where he had published a book of short stories, *Shtubn un gasn* (1935; Houses and streets), with a continued output of short stories in Yiddish published in periodicals in Israel, the USA, and Australia. His first novel, *Dos naye hoyz* (1941; The new house), fuses his Polish background with Australian scenes. His second novel, *Tsvishn himl un vaser* (1947; Between sea and sky) was awarded the gold medal of the Australian Literary Society for the best book of the year. The story of a boatload of refugees, mostly Jewish, at sea after the Nazi invasion of Greece, was described as a literary *tour de force*, and put Bergner into the first rank of Australian authors. His largest novel, almost a sociological work, *A shtot un Poyln* (1950; A town in Poland), was a literary monument to Polish Jewry. In 1955 he published another collection of short stories, *Dos hoyz fun Jacob Isaacs* (The house of Jacob Isaacs), which presents the theme of Jewish alienation in the Australian environment, a theme which he was to take up at greater length in his *Likht un shotn* (1960; *Light and Shadow*, 1963). This novel highlighted the problems of integration into an alien environment and the consequences for different members of the family. Bergner's later short stories continued to focus on Jewish migrant life in postwar Australia, especially the life of the Yiddish speakers.

BIBLIOGRAPHY

Between Sea and Sky (Melbourne, 1941); *Light and Shadow* (Melbourne: Angus & Robertson, 1963)

FURTHER READING

Kahan, I.: Three Australian Yiddish writers. *Australian Jewish Historical Society* 7 (1973) 286–290

ALAN D. CROWN

Bergner, Yosl (b.1920) Israeli painter. Bergner was born in Vienna, son of the Yiddish poet Melekh RAVITSH who, in 1921, took his family to Warsaw where they remained until 1937, after which they moved to Australia. Bergner had his first formal art tuition at the Melbourne Academy of Art and later he traveled extensively, painting and exhibiting in different countries. During the 1930s he painted in Melbourne, and his socialist–realist style had an influence on the development of a strain of social criticism in Australian art. In 1950 Bergner and his artist wife emigrated to Israel and settled in Safed. His early expressionistic style soon gave way to surrealism: in his painting of the Safed period he depicts the façades of stone houses, their high walls perforated by windows in which figures are seen engaged in dramatic actions and gestures. Bergner's people are painted in simplified geometrical shapes and in precise linear style. Heads are usually depicted in stark frontality, shaped in a perfect oval and with extremely large gazing eyes fixed at the viewer or at infinity. These, together with eerie, ominous landscapes overhung with heavy skies, are all painted in careful brushstrokes and a limited range of colors, predominantly cold blues and stone greys. His later work, in emotive surrealism, depicts the emotional world of the early Russian settlers in Palestine, through extensive representation of people dressed in nineteenth-century clothes, set stiffly in Middle Eastern surroundings. After 1957 Bergner's themes frequently reflected the trauma of the Holocaust. His paintings of the 1960s and 1970s depict daily household objects; chairs, pots, and irons, at times animated to singing and dancing in vast landscapes. These objects, the meager belongings of the refugees who fled to Israel, have a life of their own and bear memories of destroyed communities. Later images of trauma combined with the historical memory of horror appear in Bergner's paintings of the medieval synagogue of Toledo, now a church. In these works he links the nightmares of the Spanish Inquisition and the Holocaust. In the 1970s he became concerned with the disintegration of the Israeli pioneering myth. Throughout his work he remains a linear monochromist, with an obsession for repeated themes always of tragic proportions, exemplified through symbols of ill-omen such as butterflies, birds, and halved apples, all bearing the sense of humanity abused, and painted in vast landscapes and heavy, looming skies.

Bergner was active as a book illustrator, illustrating Kafka and others, and in stage design. He has exhibited extensively in Melbourne, Paris, and New York, among other cities. In 1955 he exhibited at the BEZALEL SCHOOL OF ARTS AND CRAFTS in Jerusalem, and in 1957 in Tel Aviv. In 1956, 1958, and 1962 he contributed to the Venice Biennale, and in 1957 to the São Paolo Biennale. In 1982 and 1986 exhibitions of his work were held (respectively) at the Tel Aviv Museum and in Melbourne.

FURTHER READING
Fisher, Y.: *Ariel* 11 (1965) 16

NEDIRA YAKIR BUNYARD

Bergson, Henri (1859–1941)   French philosopher. Son of a Polish Jew who emigrated to France and married an English Jewess, Bergson was born in Paris where he lived until his death during the German Occupation. Bergson studied at the École Normale and taught philosophy in several provincial towns before returning to Paris in 1888, and devoting himself to a life of reflection and writing. His first book, *Essai sur les Données Immédiates de la Conscience* (1889; *Time and Free Will*, 1910), was followed by his great work, *Matière et Mémoire* (1896; *Matter and Memory*, 1911). Bergson rapidly achieved wide acclaim, notwithstanding his failure to secure a post at the Sorbonne. He was, however, awarded a Chair at the Collège de France where his lectures attracted wide audiences. *Le Rire* (1900; *Laughter: An Essay on the Meaning of the Comic*, 1910) was followed, in 1907, by *L'Evolution Créative* (*The Creative Evolution*, 1911) which became his most popular work. In 1914 he was elected to the Académie Française and in 1927 he received the Nobel Prize for Literature.

Bergson was always admired for his fine French style; in fact he was frequently described as more of a poet than a philosopher. His greatness as a stylist explains, in part, his influence which was more apparent in the literary and artistic world than among philosophers, although his influence on Marcel PROUST, who attended his lectures at the Collège de France, was primarily philosophical. Bergson's central notion was that of the life-drive, the great power permeating all the living, creating its constant movement and its energy. This notion was set against the mechanistic worldview predominant in the nineteenth century, with its belief in progress and science. Bergson's views were often seen as anti-rationalistic and even mystical. He was undoubtedly interested in

Henri Bergson

mysticism, as well as in religiosity in general. He dedicated his last book almost entirely to a discussion of the validity of, and even necessity for, religion. Drawn to Catholicism, he considered conversion during the last years of his life, but remained a Jew. His will in 1937 indicated that he chose to identify with persecuted European Jewry. His death was said to have been caused by his having to queue for hours to be registered as a Jew by the Nazi authorities in Paris.

BIBLIOGRAPHY
Two Sources of Morality and Religion (New York: Anchor Books, 1956); *Time and Free Will* (London: Swan Sonnenschein & Co., 1910); *Laughter: An Essay on the Meaning of the Comic* (London: Macmillan & Co., 1910); *The Creative Evolution* (London: Swan Sonnenschein & Co., 1911); *Matter and Memory* (London: Swan Sonnenschein, 1911)

FURTHER READING
Kolakowski, L.: *Bergson* (Oxford: Oxford University Press, 1985)

YORAM BRONOWSKI

Berkovits, Eliezer (b.1900) Rabbi and theologian. Berkovits was born in Oradea, Transylvania and ordained in 1934 at the Hildesheimer Rabbinical Seminary. First serving as a rabbi in Berlin, he officiated in Sydney, Australia and then served as a rabbi in Boston, Massachusetts, until 1958. He later became chairman of the department of Jewish philosophy of the Hebrew Theological College in Chicago. His early writing was concerned with the tension between secular Jewish nationalism and the Jewish religious tradition. This was the subject of his *Towards a Historic Judaism* published in 1943. Subsequently he wrote *God Man and History* (1959); *Jewish Critique of the Philsophy of Martin Buber* (1962); and *Judaism: Fossil or Ferment* (1956). His later works deal with the theological implications of the Holocaust: *Faith After the Holocaust* (1973); *Crisis and Faith* (1976); *With God in Hell* (1979). According to Berkovits, the modern Jewish response to the destruction of six million Jews should be modeled on Job's example. Jews must believe in God because Job believed. At Auschwitz God was hidden, yet in his hiddenness he was actually present. As hidden God, he is savior; in the apparent void he is the redeemer of Israel.

FURTHER READING
Katz, S.: *Post-Holocaust Dialogues: Critical Studies in Modern Jewish Thought* (New York: New York University Press, 1983)

DAN COHN-SHERBOK

Berkowitz, Yitzhak Dov (1885–1967) Hebrew and Yiddish writer and translator. Born in Slutsk, Belorussia, Berkowitz received a *heder* education. In 1905 he became literary editor of *Hazeman*, and his articles and stories appeared in most of the Hebrew and Yiddish journals of his day. In 1906 he married SHOLEM ALEICHEM's daughter and in 1913 went to the USA where he continued his editorship of Hebrew journals, *Hatoren* and *Miklat*. He settled in Palestine in 1928 and became one of the first editors of *Moznayim*.

Berkowitz's short stories are realistic and humorous and notable for their precise style. He wrote about east European Jewish life in the late 19th century, influenced mainly by MENDELE MOKHER SEFARIM and later by Sholem Aleichem. His stories considered the general crisis of Jewish life at that time, and the problems of emigration. Later stories dealt with the Jewish immigrants in America and in Palestine. His work of the 1930s includes two novels, *Menakhem Mendel be'eretz yisra'el* (1936; Menakhem Mendel in Palestine), which is a satirical epistolary novel discussing the life of the immigrants to Palestine. In *Yemot hamashiah* (1938; The days of the Messiah) Berkowitz presents the evolution into a Zionist of an Americanized Russian–Jewish intellectual who identifies himself with the new life in the Land of Israel. Berkowitz was also the author of several plays, one of which, *Oto ve'et beno* (He and his son) was produced by the Habimah Theater in 1934. Berkowitz translated into Hebrew the collected writings of Sholem Aleichem, and wrote a five-volume memoir in which Sholem Aleichem and his generation constitute the central elements: *Harishonim kivenei 'adam* (1933–48; The first as they were).

Berkowitz has fallen into some obscurity, but his work was much admired during his lifetime as a true portrait of the dilemmas of the period.

GLENDA ABRAMSON

Berl, Emmanuel (1892–1976) French journalist and man of letters. Born into a middle-class Parisian family which hardly practised Judaism, ritual observances being passed on by the women, Berl was related on his mother's side to Henri BERGSON, Marcel PROUST, and the poet Henri FRANCK. Through the poet Anna de Noailles, a leading figure in the Paris Salons, he was to become acquainted with Jean Cocteau, Gabriele d'Annunzio, Edmond Rostand, and Maurice Barrès. In the same period he moved in pro-Dreyfus circles.

After the war, Berl became deeply interested in mysticism, and in 1923, on Bergson's advice, he published the first volume of his thesis *Recherches sur la nature de l'amour* at his own expense. In the same year he became literary critic of *L'Europe Nouvelle*. The failure of his first book did not discourage him, and his *Méditation sur un Amour Défunt* was published by Grasset in 1925, in a series edited by Daniel HALÉVY. He was consistently successful from then on. Both a literary critic and a writer, Berl continued to publish books up to the time of his death, including novels in autobiographical vein, essays, and pamphlets. His works express an anti-conformist attitude preoccupied with the idea of decadence.

The attitude which marked his whole career and his friendships between the wars was adherence to a deeply felt pacificism. He was the author of *Mort de la Pensée Bourgeoisie* (1929) and of *Mort de la Morale Bourgeoisie* (1930), and critic on *Le Monde*, (the paper founded in 1928 by Henri Barbusse), in which he defended the policies of the Soviet Union and supported the struggle against Fascism. He left the French Communist Party in 1931. He became editor of the important journal founded by *Nouvelle Revue Française* at the beginning of the 1930s, *Marianne*, leaving it in 1937. A pro-Munich supporter, in 1938, of the 1938 Munich Agreement, Berl was to be closely involved with those around Paul Reynaud, going so far as to rewrite Pétain's speeches in June 1940. In 1941 he became anxious for his own safety, and hid in the south of France. After the war, he was to write a series of essays about the reflections of a French Jew on his relations with the State of Israel. At this time he also discovered the *kabbalah*, through the works of Gershom SCHOLEM, and took up his pre-war works on mysticism again.

Emmanuel Berl is undoubtedly one of those Jewish intellectuals who have left us, if not very comprehensive, at least very personal evidence of the way in which the position of Jewish intellectuals evolved after the Holocaust, a position he himself describes as similar to that of Edmond FLEG. His Judaism was no longer a basic religious factor, but the result of a sudden awareness, and of reflection on the Diaspora and the existence of Israel.

BIBLIOGRAPHY
Les Derniers Jours (Paris, 1927); *Sylvia* (Paris, 1952)

FURTHER READING
Berl, E.: *Essais* (Paris: Julliard, 1986)

PERRINE SIMON-NAHUM

Berlin, Isaiah (b.1909) British philosopher and historian of ideas. Born in Riga, Latvia (now USSR), Berlin was educated at St Paul's School, London, and Corpus Christi College, Oxford. After holding Fellowships at All Souls College and New College, Oxford, he did war service at the Ministry of Information in New York from 1941 to 1942, at the British Embassy in Washington from 1942 to 1946, and spent a period at the British Embassy in Moscow from September 1945 to January 1946. Berlin was Chichele Professor of Social and Political Theory in Oxford from 1957 to 1967; the first President of Wolfson College, Oxford, from 1966 to 1975; and President of the British Academy from 1974 to 1978. He became a Knight in 1957, and was awarded the Order of Merit in 1971. He is the recipient of several prizes, including the Jerusalem Peace Prize, 1979, and holds some score of honorary doctorates, including those of the Universities of Jerusalem, Tel Aviv, and Ben-Gurion in Beersheba.

After his classic biography *Karl Marx: His Life and Environment* (1939), Berlin's principal contribution as a historian of ideas has been to show, particularly in his work on *Vico and Herder* (1976), and the essays collected together in *Against the Current* (1979), how the emergence since the eighteenth century of a cluster of seminal general ideas has transformed thought and feeling in the West. The 2,000-year-old universalist belief in a single objective structure of timeless truth concerning all questions of theory and practice has increasingly made way for a bewildering variety of subjectivist and irrationalist currents of thought. Berlin's investigations have thrown a brilliant light on the origins of historicism, nationalism, romanticism, voluntarism, relativism, and that central strand of modern liberalism, pluralism. The fact that men, as individuals and communities, pursue a vast variety of values, some of which are conceptually guaranteed to conflict, confers supreme value on the largest possible degree of freedom of choice. This conception of freedom as consisting in the maximum number of open doors and the minimum of interference has been a central concern of all Berlin's writings, and his celebrated distinction of it, in his essay "Two Concepts of Liberty" (1958; contained in

Four Essays on Liberty, 1969), as "negative" liberty as opposed to "positive" liberty, which prescribes a single path to freedom, has set the framework for serious discussion of liberty ever since. This essay, taken together with "Historical Inevitability" (1954), which is also contained in the same volume, and which is a trenchant comprehensive critique of determinist theories of human affairs, contains the core of Berlin's political thought. It is summed up to some degree in his Premio Senatore Giovanni Agnelli lecture (1988).

Throughout his life Berlin has been an unswerving supporter of Zionism, chronicling some of its most crucial and least known moments as an inside observer, as well as drawing memorable portraits of some of its central actors. Through his wide contacts, both formal and informal, he has performed many acts of beneficence towards the State of Israel. Its birth against all the historical odds is for him one of the living refutations of determinist conceptions of history, and, to the degree that it is a secular, democratic state, an unparalleled triumph of free, unrelenting moral effort. It exists, moreover, to fulfill that deep need of people for links with a particular territory and membership of a continuous historical community and culture, identification of which Berlin has shown to have been one of Herder's major achievements. Berlin sees the creation of Israel as helping to "normalize" the condition of Jews the world over, making them more nearly a people like any other. His writings combine expression of a positive outlook with a good deal of criticism. While some of his essays on Jewish subjects, principally Moses HESS and Chaim WEIZMANN, whose general position and views he steadfastly shares, have been incorporated in his volumes of essays, many are scattered widely

ROGER N. HAUSHEER

Berlinski, Herman (b.1910) American composer, conductor, and organist. Born in Leipzig, Berlinski began his musical studies at the Leipzig Conservatory but left Germany in 1933 when the Nazis took power. He continued his studies in Paris with Alfred Cortot in piano

and Nadia Boulanger in composition. During the Second World War, he joined the French Foreign Legion, eventually emigrating to the United States in 1946.

Berlinski earned a doctorate in composition from the Jewish Theological Seminary. Very active as an organist, he held positions at Temple Emanu-El in New York City, and the Washington Hebrew Congregation from 1963 to 1975. He also served as visiting professor of Comparative History of Sacred Music at the Catholic University of America and is artistic director of the Shir Chadash Chorale in Washington, DC. In 1964 Berlinski was the recipient of the Marjorie Peabody Waite Award from the American Academy and Institute of Arts and Letters.

Herman Berlinski is best known for his organ works and is one of few Jewish organ recitalists. During these recitals he often features his own compositions. His music shows a deep involvement with the Bible and Jewish liturgy and tries to reflect the rhapsodic elements of Hebrew cantillation, combining it with contemporary harmonic and contrapuntal procedures, sometimes even dodecaphonic devices. He is also influenced by French music, especially of the impressionistic era.

Among his compositions are *Eleven Sinfonias* (organ), *Avodat Shabbat* (1958), *Job* (1971), song cycles, and chamber music. One of his organ works, *The Burning Bush* has become standard repertory for organ, and his *Glass Bead Game* was premiered on the occasion of the dedication of the new organ in Carnegie Hall.

SAMUEL H. ADLER

Berman, Hannah (1883–1955) English novelist and translator. Born in Lithuania into a family with a background of Hebrew scholarship, Hannah Berman translated novels by SHOLEM ALEICHEM and I. A. Lisky, as well as short stories from the Yiddish for the *Jewish Guardian*, the short-lived *Jewish Woman* and other periodicals. A rare female voice in *shtetl* literature, her two novels in English depict life in her native Lithuania under the despotic rule of Nicholas I (1825–55), when many Jews strove to loosen the bonds of rigid religious laws and customs as the *Haskalah* started to bring new ideas into their culture.

Melutovna (1913) particularly highlights the tragic plight of Jewish boys snatched in childhood, cruelly ill-treated, and discharged after 25 years of military service. Most were left to wander through towns and villages, ignorant by then of their families and origins, and with no means of support. The fate of Daniel, the returning soldier, is linked with Simson, enlightened head of the community of Melutovna, and the intolerant fundamentalist Jeremiah, to whom the slightest whiff of independent thought is designated Epicureanism. Simson's young second wife, Zelda, is vigorous in her efforts to oppose the hidebound traditions of the village, but the forces of reaction and formalism ultimately triumph over even the pitiful advances to which she, and a very few others, aspire. Similarly in *Ant Hills* (1927) the happiness of a young couple is crushed by a relentlessly pious grandfather, because the boy has dared to express an interest in *Haskalah*. In these books, life in the Pale of Settlement is faithfully and movingly recorded, although the dialogue, in English intended to represent Yiddish phrases, rhythms and curses, sometimes falls awkwardly.

VERA COLEMAN

Bermant, Chaim (b.1929) British writer. Bermant was born in Poland. After his family emigrated to the United Kingdom he was educated at Glasgow *yeshivah*, Glasgow University, and the London School of Economics from which he graduated with a Master of Science degree in economics. He was at various times a schoolteacher, economist, television writer, and journalist, but devoted himself fulltime to writing from 1966. His first book, *Jericho Sleep Alone*, was published in London in 1964, followed by *Diary of an Old Man* (1966) and *Israel* (1969), an account of the modern Jewish State.

He has described his characters as "hapless but not helpless, beset by many small calamities which somehow never amount to an irreversible disaster and which certainly do not diminish their hope that even if the worst is not over, the best is yet to come". His early novels, in

particular, demonstrate that Bermant is one of the most successful authors of Anglo-Jewish family sagas.

Bermant published 17 novels up to 1988, and some important works of popular history such as *Troubled Eden: An Anatomy of British Jewry* (1969), *The Cousinhood: The Anglo-Jewish Gentry* 1961 and *Point of Arrival: A Study of London's East End* (1975); *Coming Home* (1976), his autobiography, won the *Jewish Chronicle* Wingate Book Award. He has also published *The Jews* (1978) and edited, with Murray Mindlin, *Explorations: An Annual on Jewish Themes* (1967).

JOHN MATTHEW

Bernard-Lazare [Lazare Marcus Manassé Bernard] (1865–1903) French writer, critic, and journalist. Bernard-Lazare was born in Nîmes into a prosperous family of traders with deep roots in that part of France and a vague emotional attachment to Jewish traditions which did not go beyond the observance of certain festivals and a twice yearly attendance at the "Temple". There, as in the State school, the French Revolution and Republic were honored as the eleventh commandment. Rebelling against the education he received, Bernard-Lazare settled in Paris in 1886 and quickly gained notoriety as a formidable critic of the establishment. He sought refuge from shallow rationalism and unheroic materialism first in heroic legends and esoteric cults, the inspiration of his symbolist stories (*Le Miroir des Légendes*, 1892), and before long in anarchism whose humanitarian gospel he expounded in numerous articles and illustrated in social fables (*Les Porteurs de Torches*, 1897). Anarchist thought played an unusually positive role in his Jewish journey from anti-Jewish Israelite, calling for assimilation to be completed by severing all ties with a religion ossified and spiritually insignificant but still capable of arousing atavistic solidarity, to Jewish nationalist, urging emancipation *from* assimilation, from a form of cultural totalitarianism. If the anarchist belief in enriching diversity, in maintaining the uniqueness of each individual or ethnic group, brought him to Zionism (he was the star of the Second

Zionist Congress, 1898), libertarian misgivings about autocratic leaders and power politics drove him from the official movement led by Theodor HERZL. However, to his dying day, he remained concerned with the fate and role of the Jewish people, especially the ghetto masses, source of his despair and hope.

His Jewish journey is recalled in the uncompleted epic *Le Fumier de Job* (posthumously published in 1928). It is also reflected, unintentionally, in the inconsistencies found in his controversial history of anti-Semitism, composed over a lengthy period and hastily published in 1894 with a promise, unfortunately unfulfilled, of subsequent revision and completion. The work has been exploited by anti-Semites ever since. Bernard-Lazare's most outstanding achievement is his work on the Dreyfus Affair. His tireless efforts, three years before Zola's *J'Accuse*, not only prepared the ground for re-opening the case but transformed it into a moral issue. At stake, for him, was no simple miscarriage of justice but an illegality consciously committed by some and condoned by many more of the Republic's military and political leaders too frightened to stand up to anti-Semitic pressures, ready to sacrifice the individual, a mere Jew, to reasons of state. He made it his mission to prove Dreyfus's innocence and thereby deprive modern anti-Semitism of a replacement symbol for Judas. Bernard-Lazare died (aged 38) before Dreyfus's rehabilitation in 1906.

BIBLIOGRAPHY

L'Antisémitisme, son Histoire et ses Causes (1894; Paris: Editions de la Différence, 1982); *Une Erreur Judiciaire: la Vérité sur l'Affaire Dreyfus* (Brussels: Monnom, 1896)

FURTHER READING

Wilson, N.: *Bernard-Lazare: Antisemitism and the Problem of Jewish Identity in Late Nineteenth-Century France* (Cambridge: Cambridge University Press, 1978)

NELLY WILSON

Bernstein, Leonard (b.1918) American composer, conductor, pianist, author, lecturer, and teacher. One of the most versatile musicians of the twentieth century, Bernstein's eclecticism is a kind of migration through various lands of musical endeavor in pursuit of an artistic homeland. Such preoccupations have been typical of twentieth-century Jewish composers, those who have crossed over from the rigors of concert music to populist expressions: Kurt WEILL, Gould, Marc BLITZSTEIN, Erich KORNGOLD, and Aaron COPLAND, or George GERSHWIN, in the other direction. Arnold SCHOENBERG, in his search for a new system of musical language (resulting in dodecaphonism) is yet another sort of Jewish wanderer.

In Bernstein's case, the most potent musical example of such global peregrinations, paralleled both by geography and national styles, is his operetta *Candide* (originally 1956, but reworked several times, most recently in 1988 for Scottish Opera). Among its variegated jokes, there is a parody on *shofar* calls. His *Mass* (1971), richly interwoven by strands of Catholic ritual and Jewish thought, demonstrates a pandemic religious sensibility. Bernstein's commitment to tonality has impelled him to demonstrate, in his unmatched television work, the unchanging laws of the musical universe. This is informed by a strong overlay of Torah exegesis. His father, Samuel, inculcated Jewish values in him, but the elder Bernstein was also opposed to his son's musical career ambitions. The resulting tension was probably beneficial. Moreover, the sermons of Rabbi H. H. Rubenowitz (Temple Mishkan Tefila, Boston) enthralled the youngster, foreshadowing his clear expository style as an author.

Elsewhere this writer has demonstrated how the second of Bernstein's three symphonies, based on W. H. Auden's *The Age of Anxiety* (1949), reflects the poem's declaration of Jewish monotheism. Auden's invocation of *Shema Yisrael* is mirrored by Bernstein's musical pun on the tetragrammaton in the symphony's Epilogue. His first symphony, *Jeremiah* (1942), develops various aspects of synagogue chant: the cadence for the Ashkenazi intonation of the festival *Amidah* and cantillations of both Prophets and Lamentations. His third symphony, *Kaddish* (1963), while less concerned with liturgical quotations, is, of course, a profoundly Jewish work, particularly in its confrontational aspects

Leonard Bernstein

between man and God (Martin BUBER's "I and Thou").

Although his meditative *Opening Prayer* (1986; written for the reopening of Carnegie Hall) concludes with the three-fold priestly benediction of *Yevarekhekha*, Bernstein has written only one work directly for the synagogue: *Hashkiveinu* (1945) for cantor, choir, and organ. This has been a cause for regret in Jewish music circles. Nevertheless, Bernstein has always maintained a strong Jewish identity in his works, ranging from the early spirited settings of Palestinian folk songs (*Simchu Na* and *Reena*, 1947) to the more recent and adventurous *Jubilee Games* (1986, reworked as *Concerto for Orchestra*, 1989). The latter was written (on the occasion of its fiftieth anniversary) for the Israel Philharmonic Orchestra, closely linked with Bernstein's extraordinary career as a conductor. Another IPO premiere, the 1981 *Halil* for solo flute and small

orchestra, is Bernstein's memorial tribute to soldiers who died in Israeli wars. (Some listeners have detected a depiction of battle in the cadenza section.)

In his 1974 ballet *Dybbuk*, the composer utilized *Kabbalah* manipulations, assigning "secret" numerical relationships, in conjunction with Hebrew letters, to intervals. The result was a stringent but apt musical counterpart to the famous drama by AN-SKI.

FURTHER READING

Gottlieb, J.: A Jewish Mass or a Catholic Mitzvah? *Journal of Synagogue Music* (New York: Cantors Assembly, Vol. III, No. 4, December 1971) 3–7
——: Symbols of faith in the music of Leonard Bernstein. *The Musical Quarterly* (April 1980) 287–295

JACK S. GOTTLIEB

BeShT See BA'AL SHEM TOV.

Bettelheim, Bruno (b.1903) American psychologist. Born in Vienna, Bettelheim received his doctorate from the University of Vienna in 1938. He was arrested by the Nazis and imprisoned at Dachau and Buchenwald until released in 1939. Bettelheim then settled in the United States and joined the faculty of the University of Chicago as a researcher in progressive education, psychology, and psychiatry. He directed the Sonia Shankman Orthogenic School for Autistic Children.

While in the camps, Bettelheim surreptitiously interviewed more than 1,500 fellow prisoners. His observation of personality changes in people in extreme situations provided him with new insight into the nature of human psychosis. His findings, published in *Individual and Mass Behavior in Extreme Situations* (1943) and *The Informed Heart: Autonomy in a Mass Age* (1960) defined the course of all subsequent discussion on Holocaust victims and survivors. It is Bettelheim's contention that the victims were not martyrs dying for their convictions, but rather suicides who saw death as the only way to put an end to hopeless conditions no longer compatible with life as human beings.

These experiences provided the framework for

Bettelheim's understanding of childhood autism. He feels that children become schizophrenic when they perceive their lives to be dominated by random and irrational forces, totally out of their control. When deprived of hope, autonomy, and meaningful human relationships, personality develops abnormally. Treatment at the Orthogenic School, designed to counter these forces, helps the autistic child satisfy unmet needs and develop competence to master future developmental tasks. The school's program is further described in *The Empty Fortress: Infantile Autism and the Birth of the Self* (1967).

Bettelheim's interests extend to educational and sociological issues: how children make sense of the world, and how society should be structured to encourage the best possible psychological development of individuals. In 1964 Bettelheim studied the structure and child-rearing practices of the Israeli kibbutz. By providing an attentive peer group, few demands, and meaningful work from an early age, the kibbutz strives to prevent the alienation of its individual members by educating children to expect a low level of personal autonomy. In *Children of the Dream* (1967) Bettelheim poses this model as an alternative to the Western model of increased demands on a child's autonomy coupled with more societal alienation. In *On Learning to Read: the Child's Fascination with Meaning* (1982), Bettelheim criticized denatured reading primers which restrict thought and discourage children from finding value in reading. These readers are contrasted with classic fairy tales, studied by Bettelheim in *The Uses of Enchantment: The Meaning and Importance of Fairy Tales* (1976), which describe children's deepest fears and fantasies, while expressing hope for their resolution. Bettelheim continues to write on child-rearing, stressing the importance of dealing with children empathetically.

BIBLIOGRAPHY

Surviving and Other Essays (New York: Knopf, 1979)

JANE SHAPIRO

Bezalel School of Arts and Crafts

The first art institute in Palestine, which established an early Israeli–Jewish artistic style. It was founded in 1906 (following a decision made at the Seventh Zionist Congress at Baz), on the windswept Judean mountains, by the visionary artist, Boris Schatz (1866–1932) with Ephraim Moshe LILIEN who accompanied him to Palestine and eventually gave the first art class at the school. Lilien illustrated biblical books in a late Art Nouveau style and was instrumental in establishing the style usually associated with the Bezalel School: biblical narratives, depicted on a Middle Eastern backcloth, with visionary Zionistic overtones and messages, and usually with hyperbolic pathos and drama. That style prevailed for the first two decades after the foundation of the Bezalel School, and still survives in some crafts in contemporary Israel. Boris Schatz believed in the unity of arts and crafts, and hoped to turn Jerusalem into an international art center, where true Jewish art would be created. In addition to these romantic ideas there was also the practical one of providing a livelihood both for native artists and for newcomers to Palestine, fullfiling the call of national revival. Most of Boris Schatz's sculptures were done before his arrival but his indefatigable energy was crucial for the realization of the arts school. Shortly after the opening of Bezalel he founded the Bezalel Museum, which housed a collection of Jewish art, and later exhibited international contemporary artists. In 1908 the school moved to new premises and studios for carving and silverwork were opened.

Zeev Raban (1890–1970) joined the school in 1912 and was responsible for the formulation of a craft style by combining Western designs with local patterns, as in his illustrations of the "Song of Songs" and metal- or wood-work. In his lithographs and paintings Abel Pan depicted biblical heroes with obvious Palestinian–Semitic features, in tattered Middle Eastern rags, against the local desert or mountain background. He used a narrow range of colors, almost monochromatic, favoring the warm earth tints. In a broad sense Abel Pan can be seen as related to European Orientalism, but without the interest in the decorative and idyllic moods those painters explored. His art was surprisingly non-idealistic, but rather dramatic and chthonian. Abraham, the patriarch to whom the promise of a nation was given, features largely in Pan's works, and he made several representations of the *Akedah* (The binding of Isaac). A lithograph of the 1920s depicting the *Akedah* reacts to the pogroms in Kishinev; in 1942, a pastel *Akedah* responds to the Holocaust; and a later *Akedah* reflects the victims of the War of Independence in which Pan's son was killed at Gush Etzion a day before the Declaration of Independence. In several of these depictions both the angel and the sacrificial ram are omitted, the father increasingly resembling, and thus replacing the ram.

Mordechai ARDON, the director of The New Bezalel, established in his painting a new, non-sentimental abstract style attempting to create a graphic equivalent of abstract Jewish mystical thought. Under his tutelage the school became the focus of the so-called Jerusalemite painting, heavily based on expressionism mingled with Jewish–Israeli themes and symbols. These were usually in figurative works with strong local interest, promoting a regional approach contrary to the international approach which stemmed from Yosef ZARITSKY's painting, and eventually evolved into the style associated with the Avni Institute in Tel Aviv. In 1965 the Bezalel Museum was absorbed into the much larger Israeli Museum, with one section dedicated to Judaica, and the other to contemporary Israeli artists. There has recently been a revived interest and reevaluation of the achievements of the old Bezalel, and an exhibition in Jerusalem, accompanied by a comprehensive catalog.

NEDIRA YAKIR BUNYARD

Bezem, Naftali (b.1924)

Israeli figurative painter and draughtsman. Born in Essen, Germany, Bezem went to Palestine in 1939 with the youth *Aliyah*. Between 1943 and 1946 he studied at the BEZALEL SCHOOL OF ART AND CRAFTS, Jerusalem, mainly under Mordechai ARDON. In 1947 he became a teacher of painting in the detention camp in Cyprus. His subject matter as well as his compositional arrangements express a fascination with ritual and traditional symbols turned into the personal landmarks of a sensitive imagination, as indicated by the titles of his paintings: *Benediction of the Candles*, *The Great Atonement*, *Rachel and Leah*,

Creation of Man, and *The Return*, with childlike simplified forms arranged on the flat plane of the picture, not unlike Paul Klee's forms and compositions. In 1968 he painted an *Akedah* – (the binding of Isaac) – as a personal reaction to the Six Day War, in which Isaac is winged, with a cactus (*tzabar*, the nickname of a native-born Israeli) growing out of one of his wings. During this period Bezem's style had affinities with that of Fernand Léger. Forms are heavily outlined, painted in flat, two-dimensional, strong, saturated colors, arranged in contrasting proximity. In the late 1970s Bezem's son was killed by a booby trap in central Jerusalem. After this personal tragedy Bezem worked for a while in Paris, where he painted a series of *Akedah* paintings, devoid of optimism and with nothing growing out of the wings; figures lie on the altar, a lion – the symbol of Judea – falls from the sky; a couple – the parents – are lying in a boat; candles are extinguished, and all symbols of national or religious salvation seem to be participating in the mourning.

NEDIRA YAKIR BUNYARD

Bialik, H(ayyim) N(ahman) (1873–1934)

Hebrew writer. Born in Radi, Russia, Bialik is universally acknowledged as the greatest Hebrew writer of the modern period. He was foremost a poet but was also a writer of fiction, an essayist and translator. Bialik's father died when he was seven and he was raised by his grandfather, a stern, scholarly Hasid. The separation from his widowed mother at an early age deeply affected the sensitive, highly gifted child: the themes of poverty, orphanhood, and widowhood pervade much of his writing. He was able to transform his personal suffering into symbols of the suffering artist, his oppressed people and struggling humanity.

At 16, Bialik was sent to the *yeshivah* of Volozhin, the great talmudic academy in Lithuania where he spent several months steeping himself in talmudic studies, recounted in his poem, *Hamatmid* (The diligent student). Soon he was drawn to secular ideas and began questioning the beliefs and dogmas of traditional Judaism.

In 1890 he left for Odessa, the literary center

H. N. Bialik (right) with Sholem Ash (left) and Mordkhe Specktor, a Yiddish writer and editor

of South Russia, and came into contact with AHAD HA'AM's circle. Y. H. Ravnitsky, the editor of their periodical, *Hapardes*, agreed to publish Bialik's *El hatzipor* (To the bird), a Zionist poem. Unable to support himself in Odessa, Bialik returned to Zhitomir where he married Manya Auerbach in 1893. Unsuccessful as a supervisor in his father-in-law's lumber business, he taught Hebrew in several Jewish community schools between 1896 and 1900.

El hatzipor was well-received and Bialik became a frequent contributor to *Hapardes*. His verse also appeared in *Hashiloah*, the prestigious magazine founded by Ahad Ha'am, and in other Hebrew periodicals. He wrote love and nature poetry but especially poems on Jewish themes, in keeping with Ahad Ha'amist cultural Zionist views. In 1900 he moved to Odessa, the center of Hebrew literature. This move marked a new, maturer phase in Bialik's literary career. Although he never abandoned national themes, his poems became more subjective and less parochial. In collaboration with Y. H. Ravnitsky and S. Ben Zion, Bialik founded *Moriah*, a publishing house which specialized in the printing of textbooks. Together with Ravnitsky he edited *Sefer ha'aggadah* (The book of legends), to this day a classic omnibus of rabbinic legends and aphorisms. In 1903 the notorious Kishinev pogrom occurred and Bialik was sent to that city by the Odessa Relief Committee to investigate the tragedy. The encounter with the victims of the pogrom resulted in the publication of two poems *Be'ir haharegah* (In the city of slaughter) and *Al hashehitah* (On the slaughter). The former poem, written in biblical cadences, had a powerful impact on Russian Jewry. Bialik himself translated it into Yiddish, and Zeev Jabotinsky into Russian.

In 1902 Bialik wrote *Metei midbar* (The dead of the desert), an allegorical poem, in epic form, based on a talmudic legend that the Exodus generation did not really die but lies dormant in the desert awaiting rebirth in messianic times. To Bialik they not only symbolized the somnolent Jewish people awaiting redemption and rebirth, but also man's promethean struggle against mortality.

From 1904 to 1909 Bialik served as literary editor of *Hashiloah*. His stewardship opened the doors of Hebrew letters to a host of younger writers, including Joseph Hayyim BRENNER and Yitzhak Dov BERKOWITZ. After moving to Warsaw, the location of *Hashiloah*'s editorial office, Bialik formed personal friendships with such Polish Hebrew writers as I. L. PERETZ and David FRISCHMANN whose neo-romantic views and impressionist style differed from the more realistic, linear style of the Odessans. His exposure to the Warsaw school resulted in a series of "folk poems", and in the experimental prose poem *Megilat ha'esh* (1905; Scroll of fire). In 1907 he attended the Zionist Congress in The Hague; a second journey was undertaken in 1916 to Palestine, where he was hailed as the national poet by its Jewish community. Bialik's literary output declined after 1916, but the few poems he wrote until his death in 1934 were, on the whole, masterfully wrought. During this period he published *Safiah* (Aftergrowth) fragments of which may have been planned as a novel and which were often quasi-biographical. Some of his poems reflected his growing doubt about the future of the Ahad Ha'amist hope of creating a synthesis between Judaism and Western culture.

During this "silent" period Bialik also wrote several essays. *Halakhah ve'aggadah*, ostensibly an argument in favor of Jewish legalism, is really a defense of classicism as superior to romanticism. His essays on Hebrew literature and on the Hebrew language were important milestones in the development of modern Hebrew literature. In 1921, with the aid of Maksim Gorky, who had befriended him, Bialik succeeded in obtaining permission from the Soviet government for himself and a group of Hebrew writers to emigrate to the Land of Israel. After leaving Russia, he first moved to Berlin where he established *Dvir*, a new publishing house. In 1924 he finally settled in Tel Aviv where he founded the Hebrew Writers' Association and its periodical, *Moznayim*.

Bialik's literary output after 1924 was scant. However, his prose poem *Aggadat shlosha ve-'arba'ah* (The legend of three and four) published in 1930 is one of his major works. He visited the United States and Great Britain in 1926. He died in Vienna in 1934, soon after undergoing surgery.

BIBLIOGRAPHY

Carmi, T., ed.: *The Penguin Book of Hebrew Verse* (Harmondsworth: Penguin, 1981) 509–515

Efros, I., ed.: *Bialik, Hayyim, Complete Poetic Works* (New York: Histadruth Ivrith, 1948)

Nevo, R.: *Bialik, Hayyim Nahman, Selected Poems* (Jerusalem, Dvir, 1981)

FURTHER READING

Aberbach, D.: *Bialik* (New York, Grove Press, 1958)

Carmi, T., Spicehandler, E., and Burnshaw, S., eds: *The Modern Hebrew Poem Itself* (New York: Holt Rinehart Winston, 1965)

Kabakoff, J.: Bialik's work in English translation. *The Jewish Book Annual* 17 (1959–60)

EZRA SPICEHANDLER

Bible, place of, in modern Judaism

The study of the Bible (*Tanakh*) was once a highly valued discipline among Jews, but by the sixteenth century had become neglected in favor of Talmud and *kabbalah*. Only with the onset of Emancipation and the publication of Moses MENDELSSOHN's *Bi'ur* did biblical studies experience a vigorous revival which continues to this day. Today, *Tanakh* is the basic textbook of Israeli Jews and is widely studied in the Diaspora, though it is viewed very differently by different segments of the people. For while in pre-modern times all Jews had shared a belief in the direct revelation of the Torah by God and in the divine inspiration of the rest of the *Tanakh*, this belief is no longer their common ground of faith.

The Orthodox view

Orthodox Jews continue to hold the traditional belief. In their view, while the two faces of Torah – the Written and the Oral Law – were revealed together and both have authority as expressions of God's will, it is the latter which determines the meaning of the former. In this understanding there is no historical development of Torah and tradition. Each generation merely attempts to uncover God's original will, and while in each age rabbis have a different vantage point from which they arrive at its understanding, it is the past and its teachings which remain regnant. Even today, therefore, Orthodoxy will not ask what the original meaning of the biblical text was, for the Written Law cannot be understood without the Oral, and it is the latter which provides us with the original sense. Archaeology and a knowledge of cognate languages and cultures are therefore rarely relevant to its understanding.

In Orthodoxy, while the biblical text is not a subject for specialized study in depth, the Talmud is, as are the writings of later generations which explore the Talmud. To be sure, for the observant, large portions of the Bible will be thoroughly familar, for tradition commands that one reads the weekly Torah portion both in the original Hebrew and its Aramaic translation, and that one listens to its public reading in the synagogue along with the *haftarah* and *megilah*. In addition, the prayer services for weekdays, Sabbaths, and festivals are filled with biblical quotations, especially from Psalms, and these services ensure, therefore, a wide acquaintance with biblical texts (although these will not usually be studied separately, except by children in their early years).

Non-Orthodox attitudes

Non-Orthodox Jews, who form the majority, hold different views of the nature of the biblical canon. These will range from considering the Torah a document created through Israel's experience with God, to a purely human view of the process, which sees traditions of successive ages setting down what they believed God wanted of his people.

What becomes important to those who take this view is less the theology involved than the result: Torah is the end product which Israel adopted as its law. Conservative Jews will place their emphasis on the need to continue the observance of tradition, regardless of its origin, and therefore consider themselves as "*halakhic* Jews" – an ascription denied them by the Orthodox to whom the acceptance of Torah as the will of God remains the *conditio sine qua non* of authentic Judaism. Conservatism in its various shadings speaks of historical Judaism and, along with its belief that *halakhah* needs a more vigorous development, makes the Jewish people (and especially the Jewish State) the focus of its concern. Reconstructionist Jews will generally follow this view, though they display a greater willingness to accept changes in the *halakhah* and adhere to a theology which is far more radical.

Conservatism and RECONSTRUCTIONISM are, historically considered, outgrowths of the Reform movement which arose in Germany in the early part of the nineteenth century. Although at first its rabbis professed continued adherence to the Written Law as God's revelation at Sinai, they considered the Oral Law as a purely human creation and therefore felt free to change it when modern conditions seemed to demand it. In time, however, the Written Law also came to be viewed as a human document, albeit of a higher spiritual order, and therefore biblical laws were subjected to contemporary scrutiny. Only the ethical demands were considered to be eternally relevant and especially so the Prophets, with their emphasis on social justice. Reform theology spoke of prophetic Judaism which challenged

modern Jews to be aware of the needs of society; it directed itself to pervasive poverty and the dangers of war, to racial inequality, and women's rights. The moral precepts of Torah and the Prophets became the core of REFORM JUDAISM. Even though during the last decades of the twentieth century Reform has become much more traditional in its observances and worship modes, the status of the *Tanakh* as the repository of moral demands has not changed, and biblical studies occupy the center of Reform education.

We observe, therefore, a striking paradox: in Orthodoxy, where Torah is absolutely commanding, it is its *halakhic* consequences (through Talmud and its ancillaries) which are primarily studied; in non-Orthodoxy, and Reform in particular, Talmud lacks the same compelling force, and the focus is once again on biblical texts and their religious, literary, historical, legal, and ethical aspects.

Therefore, even though the commanding force of the Bible has greatly lessened for the majority of today's Jews, it continues to have a sacred place among them, and is studied widely once again, and particularly so in Israel.

FURTHER READING

Hertz, J. H., ed.: *The Pentateuch and Haftorahs* (Oxford: Oxford University Press, 1929–36; repr. America 1941) [Orthodox]

Plaut, W. G., ed.: *The Torah – A Modern Commentary* (New York: Union of American Hebrew Congregations, 1987, 5th rev. edn 1987) [non-Orthodox]

W. GUNTHER PLAUT

biblical scholarship, modern Premodern Bible scholarship concentrated on exegesis, that is, text-explication. Modern scholarship is concerned, in addition, with text, source, form, tradition and redaction criticism, and comparative philology. Archaeology, art history, anthropology, and comparative religion are employed to evaluate the Bible's historicity, and to understand the environment in which the books were produced. Jewish scholars are active in all of these areas, with Israelis prominent in archaeological and historical researches.

The first Jewish scholar to offer a systematic

critical approach to the Bible was Baruch [Benedict] Spinoza (1632–1677), who in *Tractatus Theologico-politicus* attempted to identify the authors of biblical books and their dates of composition. But Spinoza, an excommunicate who wrote in Latin, did not influence Jewish Bible scholars of his day. Indeed, although Jews acquired the disciplines involved in biblical scholarship when they began to attend universities in Europe and North America in the nineteenth century, Jewish Bible research lagged behind Christian by about 50 years. No small part was played by the traditional East European Jewish school curriculum, which placed a low value on the Bible by prescribing it solely for the youngest students not yet ready for the study of Talmud. At the same time, study of the Bible unmediated by authorized interpretations was construed by pietists as heterodoxy. Needless to say, critical study, which questioned the accuracy of the received text, challenged hallowed attributions of authorship and discovered disparate sources where tradition asserted unity of composition, was unacceptable to Orthodox Jews. But even among the practitioners of WISSENSCHAFT DES JUDENTUMS little attention was paid to the Bible. Because the Wissenschaft scholars sought rights of European citizenship, the reconstruction of the history of the Jews in the Gentile world was personally relevant. In contrast, the study of historic ancient Israel in its own land had overtones that were embarrassingly nationalistic. Jewish scholars were deterred as well by the tenor of such biblicists as Julius Wellhausen (1844–1918), whose work was sometimes described as higher anti-Semitism. In the USA Isaac Mayer WISE opposed the study of biblical criticism at his Reform seminary, Hebrew Union College, as did Solomon SCHECHTER at the Conservative Jewish Theological Seminary.

Nonetheless, between the late nineteenth century and the First World War, Jewish Bible scholarship made significant strides. We may mention the commentaries of the Italian S. D. LUZZATTO and the work of the American Rabbi Benjamin Szold (1829–1902). Szold's *The Book of Job with a New Commentary* (1886), written in Hebrew, remains an important work of conservative criticism, drawing on the Jewish exegetical tradition as well as on nineteenth-century Christian scholarship.

Arnold EHRLICH was a unique figure. Born in Polish Russia, Ehrlich, a convert to Christianity and an associate of Franz Delitzsch (1813–90) at the missionary Institutum Judaicum, returned to Judaism in the United States. Ehrlich wrote his three-volume *Mikra kifeshuto* (1899–1901; repr. New York, 1969) for Jewish readers, and the seven-volume *Randglossen zur hebräischen Bibel* (Leipzig, 1908–14) for a larger audience. Both works demonstrate Ehrlich's mastery of philology and biblical style. Their lasting influence on Jewish scholarship may be seen in the Bible translations sponsored by the JEWISH PUBLICATION SOCIETY, as well as in the work of Harry TORCZYNER and Harold L. GINSBERG.

The most influential Jewish Bible scholar before the First World War was Max MARGOLIS, editor-in-chief of the 1917 Jewish Publication Society translation. Margolis's interests were in text-criticism, masoretic studies, and ancient versions, primarily the Greek Septuagint. With regard to higher criticism, Margolis was extremely conservative. He was the first professor of Biblical Philology at Philadelphia's Dropsie College, a non-sectarian, non-theological graduate school under Jewish auspices, where he trained, among others, E. A. Speiser. Margolis served as editor of the *Journal of Biblical Literature* and the *Journal of the American Oriental Society*.

Two early Jewish scholars firmly committed to systematic higher criticism were Morris Jastrow (1861–1921) and Julian Morgenstern (1881–1976). Jastrow, primarily an Assyriologist, was professor of Semitics at the University of Pennsylvania, and published prolifically in biblical studies. Morgenstern was the first American–Jewish scholar with a primary interest in Bible, who practised higher criticism systematically. As professor, and later president, at Hebrew Union College, Morgenstern emphasized the relevance of biblical criticism to the ideology of REFORM JUDAISM. Morgenstern began as a strict literary critic whose interests broadened into anthropology and comparative religion.

A noteworthy achievement of early scholarship was the Hebrew series *The Bible with a Critical Commentary* edited by A. Kahana (1874–1946), begun in 1903 but never completed.

The volumes made use of the ancient versions, ancient near eastern sources, comparative Semitics, and the documentary hypothesis. Among Kahana's collaborators were Samuel Krauss, H. P. Chajes, F. Perles, M. Z. SEGAL, and Max Margolis. Events between the world wars were extremely significant for Jewish Bible scholarship. The Hebrew University of Jerusalem opened in 1925, inaugurating an academic tradition in a native Hebraic culture in ancient Israel's native land. At the same time, the deterioration of the European Jewish communities as the Nazis rose to power encouraged immigration to Palestine. European Jews, notably, Harry Torczyner, Umberto CASSUTO, and Yehezkel KAUFMANN laid the foundations of Israeli Bible scholarship.

The same period witnessed the expansion of middle eastern archaeology. Some Jewish scholars followed the lead of W. F. Albright (1891–1971) and combined their field researches with biblical text study. Of special importance is the work of the dean of Israeli archaeology, Benjamin MAZAR. Bold syntheses of biblical text and near eastern discoveries were essayed by E. A. Speiser (1902–1965) of the University of Pennsylvania, who served on the translation committee of the Jewish Publication Society, and wrote the influential *Genesis* (1964) of the Anchor Bible series. Speiser argued that analyses of literary sources or of history of traditions were insufficient for biblical study. Instead, it was imperative to go beyond the biblical texts to the ancient realities that underlay them. Indeed, repetitions and contradictions in the sources of the Pentateuch were due to the great antiquity of the traditions with which the compilers worked. Speiser's line of argument was warmly received in quasi-Orthodox circles where the antiquity of a tradition bolstered its historicity, which in turn supported its religious claims. The current senior figures of American Bible scholarship, Harold L. Ginsberg and Harry M. ORLINSKY, were also trained in the period between the wars.

Jewish biblical scholarship has become increasingly international since the Second World War. Movement has generally been from the Diaspora to Israel, a notable exception being the Israeli Moshe Held (1924–1984), a professor at Columbia University, specializing in comparative Semitics who trained many current younger biblicists. Some 40 North American Jewish scholars contributed to the Bible articles in the Israeli *Encyclopaedia Judaica*, 1972. Bible scholarship has also become increasingly interconfessional. Many more Jewish scholars contributed to the *Supplementary Volume* (1976) of *Interpreter's Dictionary of the Bible* than to its original edition, 1962. The polemics that characterized the work of writers such as David HOFFMANN, Umberto Cassuto, Yehezkel Kaufmann and B. Jacob (1862–1945) have abated. In interconfessional settings the work of Jewish scholars on the Pentateuch is becoming increasingly prominent. In the Anchor Bible four commentaries on the Torah books have been, or are being, written by American–Jewish scholars: *Genesis* by Speiser; *Leviticus* by J. Milgrom; and *Numbers* by B. Levine. An Israeli, M. Weinfeld, is responsible for *Deuteronomy*. A multi-volume Jewish Publication Society Commentary is under way in the United States.

The 1970s and 1980s witnessed two significant cultural changes in Bible studies. First, women have entered Jewish biblical scholarship. We may mention the Israeli, Sarah Japhet, former chairman of the Bible department at Hebrew University, and the Americans, A. Berlin, C. Meyers, S. Niditch and T. Frymer Kensky. Second, an Orthodox institution, the Israeli Rabbi Kook Institute, is well established with a multi-volume Bible commentary that makes use of "corroborative" modern scholarship, especially archaeology.

A number of Jewish scholars whose major interests are extra-biblical have made significant contributions to biblical scholarship. Of the older generation, Cyrus Gordon (b.1908) has attempted to demonstrate the interrelatedness of biblical, near eastern, and Aegean cultures. Undoubtedly the widest-ranging comparatist is British-born Theodor H. Gaster, (b.1906). The preface to Gaster's monumental *Myth, Legend, and Custom in the Old Testament*, 1969, describes his "attempt to gather...all that that can be derived from comparative folklore and mythology for the interpretation of the Old Testament". Among recent writers whose comparative work has significantly influenced biblical studies are the American Sumerologist W. Hallo (Yale) and the Israeli Assyriologist H. Tadmor.

FURTHER READING

Levine, B.: A decade of Jewish Bible scholarship in North America. *Jewish Book Annual* 39 (1981)

Orlinsky, H.: Jewish Bible scholarship in America. In Orlinsky, H.: *Essays in Biblical Culture and Bible Translation* (New York: Ktav, 1974)

Sperling, S. D.: Judaism and modern biblical research. In *Biblical Studies: Meeting Ground of Jews and Christians*, ed. L. Boadt and others. (New York: Paulist Press, 1980)

BARUCH A. LEVINE AND S. DAVID SPERLING

Bickerman, [Bickermann; Bikerman]**, Elias** (1897–1981) American historian. Born in the Ukraine, the son of a journalist who was politically active for Jewish rights but had broken away from purely traditional Jewish learning, he studied first at St Petersburg, then from 1921 in Berlin. After 1933 he fled to Paris and in 1942 or 1943 to the United States, where he taught at Columbia University (1952–67), and was a research fellow at the Jewish Theological Seminary. He wrote voluminously in three languages, varying the spelling of his name to suit the language of composition. Much of his work dealt with problems of general Greco-Roman history (especially chronology) and religion, but from 1923 he began a series of articles on Jews and Christians. Those on Jews mostly discussed the dating and interpretation of specific texts from the Second Temple period; a collection of these articles was published as *Studies in Jewish and Christian History* (1976–86), and a general idea of the originality of his approach may be gleaned from his survey *From Ezra to the Last of the Maccabees* (1962). His work was characterized by his great knowledge of documentary formulae and legal institutions, and it was his mastery of such issues in the study of the Seleucid kingdom which led him in 1937 to his novel and highly influential interpretation of the Maccabean revolt, republished in English as *The God of the Maccabees* (1979). He claimed that all his research into the Jewish past was an accidental by-product of his studies into more general history, but it is hard to know how seriously to take such a denial of personal interest since he believed that the vicissitudes of his own life were irrelevant to his scholarship and he preferred to be reticent about himself.

BIBLIOGRAPHY

The God of the Maccabees (Leiden: E. J. Brill, 1979)

FURTHER READING

Smith, M.: Elias J. Bickerman. In Bickerman, E.: *Studies in Jewish and Christian History* (Leiden: E. J. Brill, 1986) Part 3, xi–xiii

Momigliano, A.: L'assenza del terzo Bickerman. In Momigliano, A.: *Settimo contributo alla storia degli studi classici e del mondo antico* (Rome: Edizioni di Storia e Letteratura, 1984) 371–375

MARTIN GOODMAN

Binder, Abraham W. (1895–1966) American composer and conductor. He was born in New York City, the son of Cantor Sholem Binder, and received his first musical education from Cantor Frachtenberg, in whose choir he was an alto. At the age of seven, he had already begun to compose short pieces for the synagogue, and some of his youthful works were published before he entered college. Binder received his higher education at the New York College of Music and Columbia University, where he received a Bachelor of Music degree in 1926. From 1919 until his death, he was the music director of the Young Men's Hebrew Association of New York, where he conducted a choir and a symphony orchestra, and ran a music school. He was also a professor at the Sacred School of Music of the Hebrew Union College in New York City.

Binder was one of the first highly trained musicians well versed in the music of the synagogue to be engaged as a musical director at a Reform temple when Rabbi Stephen WISE appointed him in 1923. To familiarize himself with the songs of the *halutzim* and other folk music of Israel, he went to Palestine in 1925. This resulted in his publishing a collection of songs, and also a large orchestral work, *Holy Land Impressions*. The song collections appeared under the titles of *Songs of Palestine I, II, Pioneer Songs of Palestine*, and *Palestine in Song*. Binder's life was devoted to raising the standard of the music of the Reform and Conservative synagogue, and his contribution to the 1940 Union Hymnal, as well as that to various anthologies for Holydays, was invaluable. Furthermore he wrote a book called *Biblical Chant* which contains all six systems of cantillation applied to the books of the Bible.

SAMUEL H. ADLER

biomedical research, Jews in   The French Revolution of 1789, followed by the reign of Napoleon and his conquests of a large part of Europe, made Emancipation of the Jews a political possibility. The disappearance of the ghetto walls soon led to the entry of Jews into all the liberal professions, and the number of Jews who achieved distinction in various branches of science and learning, particularly medicine, is quite astonishing. At that time Jews made up about 1 percent of the population of the various countries in middle or western Europe. An important factor in this connection was that, at a time when literacy was not widespread, practically all Jewish males were literate, because of the old traditions of learning. It is impossible to give an adequate account of individual achievements, but certain general points can usefully be made. Emancipation was closely linked with a partial or complete loss of the cultural or social autonomy which had existed up to that time. Moreover, since the time of Voltaire, traditional beliefs of Christianity had been questioned and, amongst a wide section of the educated public, traditional religion was being replaced by rationalistic deism; religious forms and ceremonies appeared irrelevant, and seemed to be associated with outmoded philosophical attitudes. Thus, a large proportion of the Jews leaving the ghetto were attracted by the new universalism, and believed in "natural" as opposed to "revealed" religion. This accounts for the fact that the majority of Jews who were entering the new intellectual life of western Europe were indifferent to their traditions or actively embraced Christianity.

Thus, Julius Cohnheim, who was born in 1839 and who might be considered the founder of experimental pathology and did pioneering work on inflammation and circulatory diseases, was,

so far as we know, completely indifferent to his Jewish background. Jacob Henle, born in 1809 and, like Karl MARX, the grandson of a rabbi, was baptized by his parents at the age of 11. Henle discovered the tubules in the kidney which bear his name and made many outstanding contributions to anatomy, physiology, and pathology. Rudolph Heidenhaim, who was also a convert to Christianity, was one of the great physiologists of the nineteenth century. This movement away from Judaism was, of course, greatly helped by the fact that, while full civil rights had been granted, this did not imply in fact equality of treatment. In Germany, with very few exceptions, Jews were not eligible to be appointed to full professorships or to be made officers in the Army. But such promotion was on the whole easily achieved once the link to Judaism was severed.

However, there were remarkable exceptions. Paul Ehrlich, who was born in 1854, was one of the greatest scientists working in medicine during the period under discussion. He was the main founder of haematology, had a tremendous influence on the development of immunology, and provided, in fact, the basis of chemotherapy. Above all, he was responsible for introducing chemical concepts into biology, and he is the father of modern molecular biology. Ehrlich's influence on modern biological science is similar to that of Louis Pasteur or Charles Darwin. Ehrlich remained a Jew, and throughout his life was actively associated with a Jewish charitable institution. He took a close interest and was involved in starting moves to create The Hebrew University of Jerusalem. Although he never had a university post, he became director of a large and important research institution and was greatly honored in Germany.

Another similar case was that of August von Wassermann. Amongst his many achievements he devised the Wassermann reaction, was director of a large research institute, and was ennobled in 1910. Wassermann remained an active Jew throughout his life.

A third case which might be quoted in this category is that of W. M. W. Haffkine, who was born in Odessa, became an assistant at the Pasteur Institute, went from there to India to introduce prophylactic inoculation against

Paul Ehrlich in his study

cholera and plague, and founded the research institute which is named after him, greatly influencing medical research in that country. Apart from his medical interests, he was respected as a Jewish scholar and was, at least for the latter part of his life, an Orthodox Jew.

At the end of the First World War discrimination on racial and religious grounds in the western world and the United States largely disappeared. This led to a very marked increase in Jewish activities in the fields of medical research and practice. It is impossible to describe further developments in detail, but a few highlights might be mentioned. Thus, penicillin, which had been discovered by Alexander Fleming in 1929, was purified and put to clinical use by the combined efforts of Chain and Howard Florey. Ernst Chain was a colorful person and, particularly in the latter part of his life, was actively involved in many Jewish activities.

Further developments in antibiotics owe much to the efforts of Selman Waksman. The successful eradication of poliomyelitis in the western world resulted largely from the activities of Albert Sabin. There is hardly any field in medical research and practice to which Jews have not contributed, very much out of proportion to their relative numbers in populations of the western world. This could be considered a continuation of the long tradition of Jewish involvement in medicine, which goes back to the early Middle Ages, and is exemplified by Maimonides, who combined greatness as a codifier of Jewish law with philosophy and the practice of medicine.

ALBERT NEUBERGER

Birnbaum, Nathan [Mathias Archer] (1864–1937) Philosopher and publisher of journals.

Born in Vienna, Birnbaum began study as a law student at Vienna University in 1882, and immediately became involved in Jewish Zionist activities. "Zionism", in fact, is a term he coined. Birnbaum realized, however, that there was a strong need to combat assimilation, and, together with two other students, Ruben Bierer and Moritz Schnirer, founded the first Jewish nationalist students' organization named *Kadimah* (eastward or forward). The name symbolized the purpose of the organization which was to fight for recognition of a Jewish national settlement in Palestine. In 1884, as a founder of *Kadimah*, Birnbaum published his first public pamphlet, *Die Assimilationssucht: ein Wort an die sogenannten Deutschen, Slawen, Magyaren, mosaischer Confession von einem Studenten juedischer Nationalitaet.* A year later, in 1885, he founded the first Jewish nationalist journal in German, *Selbstemancipation.* By then he had become the spiritual leader of *Kadimah*, and continued to publish pamphlets, edit and write for his journal, and give lectures.

From 1885 to 1895, while continuing his writing and publishing on Zionism, Birnbaum faced very hard times. Students collected money for the journal and supplied him with food; his mother sold her china shop to support his journal. At last, in 1896, due to his financial situation, he accepted the position of editor of the Berlin monthly *Zion.*

By this time Birnbaum's concepts had altered. He, who had been a chief secretary of the central Zionist office run by Theodor HERZL, became the first General Secretary of the ultra-Orthodox anti-Zionist movement *Agudat yisra'el* in 1919. He explained in his memoirs that Herzl appeared to be an impostor and he could not unquestioningly accept his decisions. Birnbaum therefore began to publish works opposing the Zionist movement in general and Herzl in particular. In 1906 and 1907 he wrote, mainly in *Neue Zeitung*, about Yiddish as a national language, which he followed by a conference in Czernowitz in 1908, in favour of Yiddish. Between the years 1908 and 1911, while Birnbaum was publishing the newspapers *Dos Folk* and *Vokhen-Blat*, his concern about religious problems caused him to embrace Orthodoxy. Between 1934 and 1937 he published yet another journal, *Der Ruf*, in The Hague, his refuge after having left Berlin in 1933.

A selection of his works, *The Bridge* (1956), was edited by his son, Solomon BIRNBAUM.

FURTHER READING

Fraenkel, J.: *Mathias Archer's Fight for the "Crown of Zion"* (New York: Conference on Jewish Relations, 1954)
Fishman, J. A.: *Ideology, Society and Language: The Odyssey of Nathan Birnbaum* (Michigan: Karma, 1987)

DEBORAH SCHECHTERMAN

Birnbaum, Solomon [Salomo; Shloyme] **A.** (b.1891) Yiddish scholar. The eldest son of Nathan BIRNBAUM, Solomon Birnbaum was born in Vienna, and emigrated with his family to Czernowitz in 1908. In his youth he was immersed in Jewish studies and went on to study architecture from 1910 to 1912. He served with the Austrian Army in the First World War, and was wounded. When the war ended he pursued Semitic studies at the Universities of Vienna, Zurich, Berlin, and Würzburg where he earned his doctorate in 1921. In 1922 he became the first twentieth-century university lecturer in Yiddish at the University of Hamburg. He emigrated to London in 1933 and lectured on Hebrew paleography at the School of Oriental and African Studies. In 1988 he was still writing and was living in Toronto.

Birnbaum's many accomplishments include the first sophisticated grammar of modern Yiddish, his *Praktische Grammatik der Jiddischen Sprache für den Selbstunterricht*, written while recovering from his war wound in hospital and published around 1918 as part of the *Die Kunst der Polyglottie* series; the first modern study of the Semitic elements in Yiddish (his doctoral thesis) published in 1922; the first sophisticated systematization of the vowel sounds of the Yiddish dialects (1923); discovery of the then oldest-known dated Yiddish manuscript (published in 1932); and the first major breakthrough in reconstructing the sound system of older Yiddish via structural interpretation of spelling (1932). His work on Hebrew paleography is indispensable, and his ability to pinpont the date of an Old Yiddish document, usually to the correct decade, is legendary. His major contribution to Hebrew paleography is his two-volume *The Hebrew Scripts* (1954–71).

Birnbaum, uniquely among modern Yiddish scholars, worked in a framework of traditionalist Jewish Orthodoxy, and his Yiddishism was deeply rooted in the inherent religiosity of traditional speakers of the language. He rejected the standard spelling and pronunciation adopted by twentieth-century secular Yiddish scholars. Ideologically he rejected modern forms of Orthodoxy which discard Yiddish. He considered Yiddish to be the unique language of the religious Ashkenazi Jew and the southern dialects to be the model for its standard pronunciation.

BIBLIOGRAPHY

Yiddish. A Survey and a Grammar (Manchester: Manchester University and Toronto: University of Toronto, 1979); Two methods. In *Origins of the Yiddish Language* ed. D. Katz (Oxford: Pergamon, 1987) 7–14

FURTHER READING

Katz, D.: *Journal of Semitic Studies* 26 (1981) 171–176

DOVID KATZ

Blankfort, (Seymour) Michael (1907–1982)

American novelist, playwright, and screenwriter. Born in New York, Blankfort grew up in what was then Jewish Harlem. He received his BA from the University of Pennsylvania and his MA from Princeton. After teaching psychology at Bowdoin College and at Princeton he worked briefly as a clinical psychologist before embarking on a career as freelance novelist and dramatist and, after 1939, as a screenwriter for Hollywood studios. Blankfort served as president of the Writers Guild of America and, for more than ten years, on the board of governors of the American Academy of Arts and Sciences from which he had received an Academy Award nomination for his film script *Broken Arrow*, recipient of the 1951 Screen Writers Award for Best Script. The author of six plays, the last, *Monique* (1955), written with his second wife, Dorothy V. Stiles, he also wrote more than 15 movie scripts, including *The Caine Mutiny* (1954), from Herman WOUK's well-known novel. Blank-

fort's adaptation of his own novel, *The Juggler* (1952), was the first American movie to be shot in Israel.

The Juggler, one of Blankfort's 12 novels, traces the disturbance, flight, and eventual recovery of Hans Muller, a Holocaust survivor, in the new State of Israel. It explores the two great historical events of twentieth-century Jewish life, both the trauma of the first and the redemptive power of the second. Blankfort received the Daroff Award for this work. *Behold the Fire* (1965), winner of the Commonwealth Club Gold Medal in 1965, is set during the First World War and deals with the NILI, a secret group of Palestinian Jews acting as spies for the British forces under General Allenby. Salem Malberg, an artist, the protagonist of *I Didn't Know I Would Live So Long* (1973), is a Jew whose personal and artistic development is intimately intertwined with the historical force of Jewish experience.

In 1978 Blankfort won the S. Y. Agnon Award from the Hebrew University.

FURTHER READING

New York Times (July 16, 1982) [Obituary]
LA Times (July 19, 1982) [Obituary]

ELIZABETH KLEIN

Blitzstein, Marc (1905–1964)

American composer. He was born in Philadelphia and died from internal injuries after being severely beaten by three sailors in Fort-de-France, Martinique. Upon graduation from high school, he received a scholarship to the University of Pennsylvania, where he stayed only three semesters, entering the Curtis Institute of Music in 1924. In 1926 Blitzstein went to Europe to study with Nadia Boulanger in Paris and Arnold SCHOENBERG in Berlin, returning home the following year. In Berlin Blitzstein wrote the score to an experimental film called *Hands*. He composed in a dissonant style then considered ultramodern; his works were performed mostly at the COPLAND–Sessions concerts and those of the League of Composers in New York and Yaddo.

Until 1935 Blitzstein traveled frequently between the USA and Europe, making his living by writing critical articles and lecturing at educational institutions and to women's clubs. After

1935 he became a musical spokesman for the political left and devoted himself to theatrical works of social consciousness along the lines of Bertolt Brecht and Kurt WEILL. The most significant work in his new populist style was *The Cradle Will Rock* (1937), followed by *I've Got the Tune* (1937), *No for an Answer* (1941), and the film score to *Native Land* (1942). In 1940 and 1941 he received Guggenheim Fellowships.

During the Second World War Blitzstein was stationed in London. In 1949 he returned to the Broadway stage with a musical adaptation of Lillian HELLMAN's play, *The Little Foxes*, entitled *Regina*. Many critics regard this opera as his most enduring work. Later efforts for Broadway included *Reuben Reuben* (1955) and *Juno* (1959), a musical based on O'Casey's *Juno and the Paycock*. In 1960 he was commissioned by the Ford Foundation to compose *Sacco and Vanzetti* for the Metropolitan Opera, but he died before it could be completed. A one-act opera, *Idiots First*, based on the short story by Bernard MALAMUD, was almost finished at the time of his death. Completed by Leonard Lehrman, it received a New York production in 1978.

Besides his stage works, Blitzstein wrote some chamber music, piano music, songs, and choral works, and made a new adaptation of Brecht's libretto for *The Threepenny Opera*.

SAMUEL H. ADLER

Bloch, Ernest (1880–1959) Swiss–American composer, conductor, and teacher. Bloch was the third child of Sophie (née Braunschweig) and Maurice Bloch. Records dating back to 1732 confirm a continuous line of Bloch's ancestors in western Europe. His grandfather Isaak, president of the Jewish community of Lengnau (Canton Aargau), was a celebrated lay cantor. His father had at one time considered entering the Rabbinate; he regularly intoned traditional Sabbath and festival chants in the home.

Ernest was born in Geneva and began full-time music studies at the Conservatoire at the age of 14. Between 1896 and 1904 he traveled to Brussels, Frankfurt, Munich, and Paris where he developed his style and technique as composer and violinist with several prominent teachers,

as well as from the music of Richard Wagner, Strauss, Gustav MAHLER, and Claude Debussy. In 1904 he returned to Geneva. In 1901 Bloch had met Edmond FLEG who wrote the libretto for his opera *Macbeth*, and furthermore inspired his Jewish "awakening" around 1906. This culminated in the mainly orchestral *Jewish Cycle* (1911–18) comprising: *Trois Poèmes Juifs*, *Prélude et Deux Psaumes 137 et 114, Psaume 22, Schelomo, Israel Symphony, String Quartet no. 1*, and *Jézabel* (an unfinished opera). Typical of these works are melodies constructed from short phrases, some containing *shofar* calls or quartertones; exotic scales and modes; "Scotch snap" rhythms; dramatic pauses; changes of tempo and meter; rhapsodic improvisation; extremes of pitch and dynamics; colorful orchestration; poignant moods tempered, however, by a thoroughly western conception of form and counterpoint.

Anti-Semitic experiences caused Bloch to emigrate. In 1916 he sailed to New York where, for the first time, his music received general acclaim. Gradually his ambivalence toward Judaism and Jewishness, evident even before his *bar mitzvah*, came to the fore once again and his search for a wider musical vocabulary encompassed idioms as diverse as neo-classicism and neo-romanticism; influences of Gregorian Chant, Renaissance styles, and Far Eastern pentatonicism; use of Swiss, American Indian, and Black folk musics. Nevertheless, *Ba'al Shem Suite, From Jewish Life, Méditation Hébraïque*, and *Abodah* were all written during this period.

From 1930 to 1938 Bloch lived in Europe where he composed *Avodath hakodesh* (Sacred service), and *Voice in the Wilderness* (abbreviated into *Visions and Prophecies*). From 1939 until his death, Bloch stayed mainly on the West Coast of the USA where, after the Second World War, a steady stream of works flowed from his pen. These were, on the whole, simpler, smaller in scale, and more objective in mood; some flirted with serialism. The few overtly Jewish compositions were *Six Organ Preludes for the Synagogue, Four Wedding Marches, Suite Hébraïque*, and *Meditation and Processional*.

Of Bloch's total production of about 100 works, the first 30 were designated *oeuvres de jeunesse*: none of these has been published and

Ernest Bloch

FURTHER READING
Bloch, S. and Heskes, I.: *Ernest Bloch: Creative Spirit* (New York: National Jewish Welfare Board, 1976)
Knapp, A.: *Ernest Bloch: The Early Years* (London: Kahn & Averill, forthcoming)
Kushner, D.: *Ernest Bloch: A Guide to Research* (New York and London: Garland Publishing, 1988)
Strassburg, R.: *Ernest Bloch: Voice in the Wilderness* (Los Angeles: California State University, 1977)

ALEXANDER KNAPP

only one (*Fantaisie*) recorded. About a quarter of the remainder are specifically Jewish, and of these about a half contain direct quotations from traditional cantillations, prayer modes, fixed chants, or folksongs. His non-Jewish compositions include symphonies, symphonic poems, concertos, suites, shorter works for orchestra and for chamber orchestra, piano quintets, string quartets, a trio, numerous pieces for piano, violin, viola, cello, and two groups of songs. Many have common features with Jewish works written contemporaneously; this suggests that his cultural heritage and environment were both integral to his art, varying in proportion according only to the circumstances of his life. An individualist, influential in his day, who preached the brotherhood of mankind in words and music, Bloch never truly found his "promised land". He remains one of the enigmatic figures of the twentieth century.

Bloch, Ernst (1885–1977) German Marxist philosopher. Born in Ludwigshafen, West Germany, Bloch studied philosophy in Munich and Berlin. In 1910 he met Gyorgy Lukács, starting a life-long, though occasionally stormy, friendship. During the First World War Bloch went into exile in Switzerland, where he wrote his first work, *Geist der Utopie* (1918; The spirit of utopia), a unique blend of Jewish mysticism and Christian heresy, German romanticism and Marxist utopia, expressionist literature and revolutionary politics. The chapter called *Symbol: the Jews* is one of the few essays Bloch ever wrote on Jewish matters. Refusing both the assimilationist attitude of the German-Jewish bourgeoisie and the traditionalist conservatism of the east European Ghetto, he hoped for a renewal of Judaism. "The pride of being Jewish awakes again": the Jews are the people of the Psalms and of the prophets and they have a messianic task in changing the world. However, Bloch rejected Zionism which would, in his opinion, "make of Judaea an Asiatic Balkan state".

References to Jewish motives – the Lurianic *kabbalah* and its messianic expectation of the *Olam hatikkun* – appear also in Bloch's next work, *Thomas Münzer: Theologian of Revolution* (1921) but his main focus is on the Christian heretical movements of the sixteenth century, interpreted as anticipations of the modern revolutionary utopias.

As an anti-Fascist and a Jew, Bloch left Germany in 1933 and emigrated to the USA in 1938. During the next ten years, living in difficult conditions, he wrote his major opus, *Das Prinzip Hoffnung* (1954–1959; The principle of hope), a monumental excursion through two thousand years of utopian thinking (in social systems, art, religion, music, technology, etc.), and a Marxist philosophical legitimation of the anticipatory consciousness. Some sections of the book – such as the chapter, "Moses or the utopia in religion, the religion in utopia" – refer to the Jewish religious heritage, but only as one among many other spiritual sources.

In 1948 Bloch was invited to teach philosophy at the University of Leipzig in East Germany. However, after growing conflicts with the authorities, he left for West Germany in 1961 and became professor at Tübingen. He remained a convinced Marxist and celebrated the spirit of utopia to his last day.

FURTHER READING

Habermas, J.: Ernst Bloch: a speculative materialist. *Talos* 33 (1977)
Hudson, W.: *The Marxist Philosophy of Ernst Bloch* (New York: St Martin's Press, 1982)

MICHAEL LÖWY

Bloch, Jean-Richard (1884–1947) French writer. Born into a family of the new bourgeoisie, the son of an École Polytechnique graduate, Bloch belonged to a generation too young to have taken any active part in the Dreyfus Affair, but upon which the anti-Semitism that accompanied it had left its mark. He failed the entrance examination for the École Normale Supérieure in 1901, and also failed to get his arts degree in 1902. He then turned to history but soon abandoned the teaching profession to devote himself to literature. In the same year, he married Marguerite Herzog, sister of the writer André Maurois.

His literary vocation was marked from the first by echoes of the Dreyfus Affair and by his Socialist commitment. Jean-Richard Bloch is part of the massive movement of committed writers that arose in the literary climate engendered by the Affair, upon which the three major works which punctuate Bloch's considerable body of writing are reflections made at different periods of his life. *Lévy*, his first work, published in 1911, describes the world of Jewish tradesmen at the time of the wave of anti-Semitism arising from the Zola trial. In subsequent works, references to the Affair are fewer, while the theme of a social consensus expands. *Et Cie* ... (1918), his best-known novel, takes up the theme of social and cultural exclusion again. A prolific and committed writer, he continued to publish didactic novels, including *Locomotives* (1924), *Le Dernier Empereur* (1927), and *Sybilla* (1931). But it is his work for the theater and his criticism which best illustrate the committed and internationalist character of his writing. The articles on the popular theater which appeared in *L'Effort*, a journal he began in 1910, brought him together with Romain Rolland. Their friendship led, in 1924, to the founding of *Europe*, one of the most important magazines committed to socialism of the period between the wars. A Socialist since 1903, Bloch was to be one of the leading figures of the internationalist and anti-Fascist movement in the 1930s. At the time of the Socialist split of 1920, he founded the first Communist Section in Poitiers, and joined the Communist Party the next year. His Communist commitment enabled him to play a central part in the anti-Fascist struggle. Seeing Hitler's intentions more clearly than he saw Stalinist policies, he founded the great pre-war Communist daily paper, *Ce Soir*, in 1937, together with Louis Aragon, to oppose the policies of Munich. A witness at the 1940 trial of the Communist deputies instituted by the Vichy authorities, he left the country in 1941 for the Soviet Union, where he broadcast for the Resistance. Once back in France, he returned to his post as editor of *Ce Soir*. He was elected a Councillor of the Republic in 1946. But he had been deeply affected by the tribulations of the war – his daughter France and his son-in-law had been deported and died – and he himself died in 1947.

As his international commitment grew, Bloch saw his Judaism in a different light. Though he was present at the inauguration of the Hebrew University of Jerusalem in 1925, his last works on the subject of Judaism, *Quels Services les Juifs Peuvent-ils Rendre au Monde?* (1927); *Destin du Siècle* (1931) took on an ambiguous tone in view of his internationalism.

FURTHER READING

Europe 135–6 (1957) [issue devoted to Jean-Richard Bloch]

PERRINE SIMON-NAHUM

Bloch, Marc (1886–1944) French social and economic historian. In addition to teaching medieval history at Strasbourg University (1919–36) and becoming an eminent authority on the subject, notably on feudalism (*La Société Féodale*, 1939–40), Bloch's general concern for what and how history was taught found expression in the *Annales d'Histoire Économique et Sociale*, founded by him and Lucien Febre. This review made an important contribution to socio-economic historiography. Bloch's lifelong aloofness from politics and from Jewish affairs abruptly ended with the Second World War. Refusing both exile and the isolation imposed on French Jews by Vichy legislation, he decided to live and fight in France as a citizen of that country. Under various assumed names (e.g. Blanchard, Narbonne) he played a leading role in the Resistance until his execution by the Gestapo near his home-town of Lyon. In the posthumously published account of his wartime experiences, *L'Étrange Défaite* (1946), he proclaimed his unshaken faith in France, cherished by his Alsatian family for generations, and his respect for, but detachment from, Jewish traditions.

NELLY WILSON

Bloom, Harold (b. 1930) American literary critic and editor. Born in New York, Bloom has taught at Yale since receiving his doctorate there (1955). His career as a critic has been intertwined with prolific and ambitious work as an editor. In 1961 he edited *English Romantic Poetry*; in 1965 he produced editions of work by John Ruskin and William Blake, as well as a *Festschrift* for Frederick A. Pottle, editor of Yale's Boswell papers. He has also edited the poems of Percy Bysshe Shelley (1966), and Walter Pater, and compiled *Essays in Criticism* (both 1970), followed by a selection from Samuel Taylor Coleridge's poetry (1972). The same year a 33-volume anthology (*The Romantic Tradition in American Literature*) appeared under his editorship. In 1973, for Oxford University Press, he edited *Romantic Prose and Poetry; Victorian Prose and Poetry*, as well as the *Oxford Anthology of English Literature*.

In the late 1980s he was editing and writing introductions for five series of critical anthologies which will result in 800 separate volumes covering the whole of literature. While still teaching at Yale, he produced three 12-page introductions a week. His reading rate – 1,000 pages in an hour – is legendary.

Bloom's critical career has had Jewish subtexts in each of its three phases. Martin BUBER contributed the notion of transforming an I-it relationship into an I–thou relationship to Bloom's explanation of the mythopoeic mode of the Romantic poets. Bloom's earliest books of criticism showed that these Romantics sought to transform nature from an object to a subject through their "mythmaking". The first trio of Bloom's critical interpretations were *Shelley's Mythmaking* (1959), *The Visionary Company* (1961), and *Blake's Apocalypse* (1963).

The *kabbalah* became the subtext for Bloom's exegeses in the seventies. *Yeats* (1970), *The Anxiety of Influence* (1973), *A Map of Misreading* (1975), *Kabbalah and Criticism* (1975), and *Poetry and Repression* (1976) employed metaphors from Gnosticism such as *tzimtzum* and "the breaking of the vessels" as analogies for the creation of poetry. The predominant image for Bloom, which recurs throughout *Agon: Towards a Theory of Revisionism*, is Jacob's wrestling the angel to win his name. Thus an antithetical or revisionist rereading of one's forebears permits a "strong" voice a place in the canon. Bloom interpolated the Freudian defenses as "moves" a newcomer might make against ancestral figures. The apprentice-poet, whom he called an "ephebe", undertook the agonistic struggle for a place in the canon through a series of six defensive postures which ended in his totally subsuming his father-figure, as John Milton absorbed all his predecessors. Bloom called these defense mechanisms "tropes" and gave them the Greek terms: *clinamen, tessera, kenosis, daemonization, askesis*, and *apophrades*. He also refers to them as "revisionary ratios". These are associated with the six active phases or *behinot* of the kabbalistic emanations or *sefirot*.

In *Wallace Stevens: Poems of our Climate* (1977) a further layer of complexity was interwoven with the theory, which he calls "crossings" or "crisis points": election, solipsism, and identification. Bloom based these upon the doctrine of Isaac Luria in whose descriptions of creation he saw parallels to revisionist poetics.

In 1982 Bloom won the Morton Dauwen Zabel Award of the American Academy of Arts and Letters. In 1985 he was given a MacArthur Award.

FURTHER READING

Riley, C., ed.: *Contemporary Literary Criticism* (Detroit: Gale Research Co., 1974–86)
Kinsman, C. D., ed.: *Contemporary Authors* (Detroit: Gale Research Co., 1976)

RUTH ROSENBERG

Bloom, Hyman (b.1913)   American painter of the Boston School of Figurative Expressionism. Born in Bounoviski, Lithuania, Bloom emigrated to the United States in 1920 with his parents. The family settled in the West End of Boston, then the favored neighborhood of Eastern European immigrants. Bloom's talent was recognized early, and he was sent to Boston school system's High School of Art Classes that were under the auspices of the Boston Museum of Fine Arts. Like many immigrant artists, Bloom concurrently received art instruction at an Educational Alliance School established to acculturate Eastern European immigrants. In 1927 Denman Ross of the Art Department of Harvard invited Bloom along with Jack LEVINE to study at Harvard free of charge. During the Depression, following his training at Harvard, Bloom was employed by the Federal Arts Project (WPA) in Boston.

Throughout his career, Bloom has consistently adhered to an emotional, highly charged figurative style of painting. The reasons for this preference were the generally conservative nature of early twentieth-century art in Boston that denigrated abstract art, the influence of the German Expressionist artist, Karl Zerbe, who worked in Boston, and Bloom's emotional and

stylistic allegiance to expressive figurative artists of the past from Michelangelo and Matthias Grünewald to the more recent examples of Georges Rouault and Chaim SOUTINE. His method is the antithesis of the expressionist temperament. Slow working and methodical, Bloom is known to rework his paintings heavily.

Early in his career Bloom painted some works dealing with the Eastern European Jewish experience. But it was in the 1940s, partly in reaction to the Holocaust, that Bloom returned to themes of the synagogue and Jewish observance. These were painted in a highly feverish pitch. Becoming interested in cantorial music at the time, he listened to records, attended synagogue, and painted about his emotional response to the experience. The most famous of these works is *The Synagogue* (*c*.1940) in the Museum of Modern Art, New York.

FURTHER READING

Freedberg, S.: Hyman Bloom. *Perspectives USA* 6 (1954)
Hyman Bloom Retrospective (Boston: Institute of Contemporary Arts, 1954) [exhibition catalog]

BARBARA GILBERT

Blum, Léon (1872–1950)   French statesman. Although born in a family belonging to the commercial bourgeoisie of Paris, Léon Blum was chairman of the Council of the Popular Front, itself a legend of the French left. He did not enter politics until he was 47, but became the first Jew to become a head of government without repudiating any of his Jewish allegiance. He thus occupies a special position in French politics.

Actively pro-Dreyfus, Blum was a Frenchman of secular interests impelled by two passions: the love of justice and the struggle against anti-Semitism. In 1891 Blum, Pierre Louys, and Paul Valéry founded a literary journal, *La Conque*. An anarchist, he shared the aspirations and literary affiliations of the symbolist generation, which he encountered in connection with the *Revue Blanche*, of which he was literary critic. A pro-Dreyfus stance was the rule in this literary avant-garde. Blum wrote about the Zola trial, and took part more actively by working with Maître Labori.

Obliged to leave the École Normale Supérieure for disciplinary reasons in 1891, he graduated in law at the École Libre des Sciences Politiques, and entered the Council of State in 1895 as an auditor, becoming master of audit in 1907. His connection with politics began in 1898 when he joined the "Socialist Unity" Party and became literary critic of *L'Humanité*. In 1907 he published *Du Mariage*, and in 1914, *Stendhal et le Beylisme*, which marked the end of his literary career.

Blum's rise to head the French section of the Workers' International occurred in three stages between 1919 and 1920, hinging on the discussion of "the old régime" at the Congress of Tours, where there was a split over membership of the Third Communist International. By formulating the distinction between conquest, the exercise of power, and participation in a bourgeois government, he tried during the 1920s to demonstrate that, although opposed to the Second Communist International and while remaining a parliamentary force, the French Section of the Workers' International was not a bourgeois party. Blum favored nonparticipation and was faithful to the tactics of the Congress of Amsterdam. Convinced that 6 February 1934 had been an attempted nationalist coup d'état, and disturbed by Hitler's rise to power, he was led to develop the idea of occupation of power. His election as premier of the first Popular Front government in May 1936 unleashed the anti-Semitic virulence of both the right and the left against him as France's first Jewish and Socialist Prime Minister, signatory of the Matignon agreement, and the man who brought in paid holidays. Present at Vichy on 10 July 1940, to vote against the granting of full powers, Léon Blum was tried by the High Court of Riom and deported in March 1943 to Buchenwald and then Dachau. At the time of the trial he had again become leader of a party reconstituted in secret, and wrote his political testament *À l'Échelle Humaine*. On his return to France in May 1945, his political authority was restored to him. From December 1946 to January 1947 he formed the first homogeneous government of the Fourth Republic, in which he also held the portfolio of Foreign Affairs. In 1948, after having failed to form a new government, he retired from political activity, leaving the French section of the Work-

Léon Blum

ers' International to the federations run by Guy Mollet.

The devout regard for justice which impregnated his socialism made him particularly sensitive to anti-Semitic attacks on him. His description of the Dreyfus Affair in the *Souvenirs sur l'Affaire* (1935) calls on Jews to remain clear-minded in the face of anti-Semitism, which cannot be dismissed as a simple denial of justice. Hence his vigorous opposition to anti-Semitism in 1938, and his denunciation of the ostracism of Jewish immigrants by French Jews who thought they could thus protect themselves against anti-Semitism.

FURTHER READING

Lacouture, J.: *Léon Blum* (Paris: Seuil, 1977)
Rémond, R., and Renouvin, P., eds: *Léon Blum, chef de gouvernement (1936–1937)* (Paris: Presses de la Fondation National des Sciences Politiques, 1981)

PERRINE SIMON-NAHUM

101

Blume, Peter (b.1906) American painter. Peter Blume's family emigrated to the USA from Russia in 1911, settling in Brooklyn, New York. In 1921 he studied briefly at the Beaux-Arts Institute of Design and at the Art Students League, both in New York. His paintings of the late 1920s already contained the odd, Surrealist juxtaposition of recognizable, yet seemingly unrelated objects which characterizes his entire oeuvre. His emphasis on precisely rendered forms and smooth paint surfaces was closely related to the style of the Precisionist artists then associated with the Charles Daniel Gallery, where he had his first one-man exhibition in 1930, as well as to his love of fifteenth- and sixteenth-century Flemish and Italian masters.

The artist's precocious debut on the international art scene took place in 1934 when his decidedly Surrealist *South of Scranton* (1931) won First Prize at the Carnegie International Exhibition of Paintings in Pittsburgh. On a Guggenheim Fellowship in Italy in 1932, Blume was offended by the vulgarity of Mussolini's new order and his reaction provided the theme for his best known painting *The Eternal City* (1937), a savage portrayal of the dictator and his Fascist regime.

Blume traveled extensively in Mexico, Italy, and the South Pacific. References to the art and architecture, political events, and landscape of these areas appear repeatedly in his paintings. Certain motifs, such as crumbling architecture and the excavation of the earth, which occur with some frequency, suggest a concern with the decay and regeneration of civilization. In 1976 Chicago's Museum of Contemporary Art held a retrospective of his paintings and sculpture.

FURTHER READING

Buckley, Charles E.: *Peter Blume: Paintings and Drawings in Retrospect, 1925 to 1964* (Manchester: The Currier Gallery of Art, 1964) [exhibition catalog]

KRISTIE A. JAYNE

Blumenfeld, Simon (b.1907) English novelist, journalist, and playwright. After a few early pieces published in *Left Review* (of which he was later on the editorial board), Blumenfeld first attracted wider attention with his provocatively titled *Jew Boy* (1935), an autobiographical story of youth in London's East End, and the first Anglo-Jewish proletarian novel. Hailed by Charles LANDSTONE in the *Jewish Chronicle* as "a ferocious first novel", it is tough in tone, a counterbalance to novels by Jewish writers which Alec, the hero, condemns as sentimental and unreal. Sensitive to music and literature but trapped in a sweatshop, bitterly rejecting Zionism as a capitalist stunt, and victimized for his political views, Alec, like many of his contemporaries, sees Communism as the answer to his frustrations. Here is East End life as it really was lived, with the atrocious working conditions, the unwanted pregnancy and abortion, the occasional solace of the Worker's Circle in Alie Street, the Saturday night dance, and the Sunday ramble in the Chilterns. Above all Blumenfeld conveys a sense of frustration, a conflict between background and aspirations which is not really resolved by a dream of Communism.

His next novel, *Phineas Kahn* (1937) opens in Russia and moves via Vienna to London, with a brief episode in the USA. The background of immigrant life from the turn of the century to the 1930s is movingly depicted, with telling descriptions of economic hardship but without the overt propaganda of *Jew Boy*. After *Doctor of the Lost* (1938), a fictionalized account of Dr Barnado's early life, Blumenfeld returned in his last novel, *They Won't Let You Live* (1939), to the immediate pre-war years, at a time when the small shopkeeper was facing the onslaught of multiple stores. Two families, one Jewish and one Gentile, are faced with ruin and suicide, victims of big business and the banks.

Blumenfeld later turned to journalism and drama, writing several plays, and associated with the forerunner of the Unity Theatre and the Workers' Theatre Movement. After the war he held various editorial jobs before joining *Stage*, the theatrical magazine, for which he was still working in 1988. In 1987 his play *The Battle of Cable Street* was performed at the Edinburgh Festival. Blumenfeld was, in 1988, working on his autobiography.

BIBLIOGRAPHY

Jew Boy (London: Jonathan Cape, 1935; repr. London: Lawrence & Wishart, 1987) [introduction by K. Worpole]

VERA COLEMAN

Blumenkranz, Bernhard (b.1913) French historian and researcher. He was born in Vienna, where he went to school and college. He began studying at the Sorbonne in Paris in 1937, was interned as an "enemy alien" when war was declared in 1939, subsequently joined the French Army as an "enlisted foreigner", and was then detained again in various camps in France. He fled to Switzerland in 1942, where he resumed his studies at Basel in 1943. The publication of his thesis *Die Judenpredigt Augustins* (1946) established him as a historian of Judeo-Christian relations. On returning to France in 1945 he continued his research from 1947 within the framework of the Centre National de la Recherche Scientifique, and published more than a hundred works on the history of the Jews in the Middle Ages, among them *Juifs et Chrétiens dans le Monde Occidental, 430–1096* (1960), *Les Auteurs Chrétiens Latins du Moyen Âge sur les Juifs et le Judaïsme* (1963), and about three hundred short pieces in the *Encyclopedia Judaica*. As chairman of the Commission Française des Archives Juives, of which he was one of the founders, and editor of the *Archives Juives* (1964), he encouraged research into French Judaism, and the drawing up of inventories and safe-keeping of material relevant to it: epigraphic material, documents, sacred and secular objects, and monuments. He took an interest in a project for a museum of Jewish art which would bring together the frequently inaccessible collections of public museums with items dispersed throughout France. In *Le Juif Médiéval au Miroir de l'Art Chrétien* (1966) he opened up the field of the investigation of Jewish history through art and archaeology, a hitherto neglected sphere of study. In teaching the economic and social history of the Jews (at the École Pratique des Hautes Études, 1953 and 1959–68, and the Sorbonne, Paris III, 1971–78), he extended his research to modern history, and also edited the series of joint works entitled *Franco-Judaïca*, among which were *Les Juifs et la Révolution Française* (1976), *Documents Modernes sur les Juifs* (1979), *Art et Archéologie des Juifs en France Médiévale* (1980), and *Les Juifs devant le Droit Français* (1984).

BIBLIOGRAPHY
Germany (843–1096) and The Roman Church and the Jews. In *The Dark Ages. Jews in Christian Europe, 711–1096* (London: W. H. Allen, 1966)

PATRICIA HIDIROGLOU

Bogrov, Grigorii (1825–1885) Russian–Jewish prose writer. He is best known for his autobiographical novel *Zapiski evreia* (Memoirs of a Jew) of approximately 1,000 printed pages, published during the years 1871–3 in *Otechestvennye zapiski* (The Fatherland's notes), the most prestigous Russian magazine of that period. For the first time the Russian reader was presented with a detailed panorama of Jewish life in Russia, with numerous interpretations both in the text itself and in abundant annotations. This panorama, however, is distorted by a fanatic abhorrence of traditional Jewish life and customs, leading Jews to accuse the author of slander, while anti-Semites referred to him with sympathy. Ten years later, however, in the novel *Nakip veka* (1879–81; Scum of the century), a Jewish version of the Russian anti-nihilist novel, Bogrov speaks respectfully and sympathetically of traditional Jewish values and ridicules the abnormality of superficial assimilation. Nevertheless, Bogrov's own assimilationist convictions were not affected even by the pogroms of 1881–2: the narrative tale *Maniak* (1884; Maniac) was an extremely ascerbic and crude satire of the *Hibbat Zion* (Love of Zion) movement.

During the 1880s Bogrov participated actively in Russian–Jewish journalism and was one of the chief editors of the St Petersburg weekly *Rassvet* (Dawn).

FURTHER READING
Lvov-Rogachevsky, V.: *A History of Russian Jewish Literature* (Ann Arbor: Ardis, 1979)

SHIMON MARKISH

Bomberg, David (1890–1957) British painter. Born in Birmingham, the son of a Polish–Jewish immigrant leather-worker, Bomberg moved with his family to the East End of London in 1895, where he was to live until the age of 23. As a youth he belonged to a tightly-knit group of young Jewish intellectuals resident in Whitechapel, which included Joseph Leftwich and fellow aspiring artists Mark GERTLER and Isaac ROSENBERG. Apprenticed as a teenager to a commercial lithographer, he attended various art classes in the evenings. On the recommendation of the well-known Anglo-Jewish portraitist Solomon J. Solomon, the Jewish Educational Aid Society enabled Bomberg in 1911 to enter the Slade School of Art. In 1913, the year he left the Slade and traveled to Paris in the company of Jacob EPSTEIN, Bomberg began exhibiting radically geometricized figure compositions which had marked affinities with the work of the Vorticist Group and met with considerable acclaim. A number of these were inspired by Whitechapel scenes, such as Schevzik's steam baths and the local Yiddish theater. In 1914 he organized the Jewish section of the Twentieth Century Art exhibition at the Whitechapel Art Gallery.

The First World War destroyed his faith in the beauty of the machine age, and Bomberg retired from active participation in British artistic life. Between 1923 and 1927 he was living in Palestine, as the result of a commission from the Zionist Organization to record the life of the pioneers. Bomberg soon broke his side of the arrangement, but did go on to paint numerous landscapes, some of them meticulously detailed, others much more freely handled, in a style that anticipates his work of the next three decades.

He traveled widely thereafter (above all in Spain, where he lived between 1934 and 1935), producing thickly painted, richly colored, expressionistic landscape images, as well as portraits and flower pieces. Between 1945 and 1953 he taught on a part-time basis at the Borough Polytechnic in London, where he proved to be an inspiring teacher. On the whole, though, the last 30 years of Bomberg's life were marked by bitterness and neglect. Jewish subject-matter resurfaces in *The Talmudist* of 1953 and, most powerfully, in one of Bomberg's last canvases, a tragic and moving self portrait entitled *Hear O Israel*.

David Bomberg Ghetto Theatre *1920. Ben Uri Art Society, London*

FURTHER READING

Cork, R.: *David Bomberg* (New Haven and London: Yale University Press, 1987)

David Bomberg in Palestine 1923–1927 (Jerusalem: Israel Museum, 1983) [exhibition catalog]

MONICA BOHM-DUCHEN

Börne, Ludwig [Löb Baruch] (1786–1837) German writer, editor, and critic. Born in Frankfurt am Main into a wealthy banker's family, Börne studied medicine in Giessen and Berlin. He associated with Marcus Herz, the eminent Jewish physician and Kantian philosopher, and frequented one of the premier intellectual centers of the Prussian capital, the salon of the latter's wife, Henriette Herz, with whom Börne fell hopelessly in love. Later, he studied law, political science, and administration in Heidelberg, receiving his doctorate in 1809 and dabbling early on in journalism. Owing to the new opportunities afforded Jews in the wake of the French Revolution, and the propagation of its ideals following the French conquest of German lands, Börne received an important post as police actuary in Frankfurt, only to lose this position after the defeat of Napoleon and the onset of the reactionary restoration. His writings in opposition to the post-Napoleonic repression and the particular oppression of Jews were censored by the local government. Magazines he edited were suppressed; also, he was fined and imprisoned for a time. In 1818 he converted to Protestantism (Lutheran), but continued to express himself politically by means of trenchant theater criticism. Drawn to Paris after the July Revolution in 1830, he continued his journalistic and literary activities and became recognized subsequently, together with Heinrich HEINE, as the (co-)initiator of the German feuilleton.

Börne is best known as a publicist, for his lucid prose in support of the French revolutionary ideals of human liberty and equality, and for his sustained attack on all forms of Germanic philistinism. His volumes of *Briefe aus Paris* (Letters from Paris), the first number of which appeared in 1832, contained radical political, literary, and social reflections, and ensured his place as the leading spokesman for thousands of German émigrés for democratic, revolutionary ideas. Börne's political vision informed his literary criticism. His writings in favor of Jewish emancipation and equality (*Für die Juden*, In favor of the Jews, and *Der ewige Jude*, The eternal [wandering] Jew) tend to place the particular Jewish struggle within the larger universal, human emancipation movement. Börne viewed contemporary anti-Semitism as a phenomenon that was primarily economically motivated. As an assimilationist, he rejected the notion that Jews would desire to maintain a separate identity, after the struggle for emancipation had been won. Late in his career, Börne despaired that a speedy structural assimilation was even possible. Attacked bitterly during his lifetime by German reactionaries and chauvinists, his works were censored and banned, but he was not included in the famous decree of the German federal diet in 1835 which proscribed the literary oppositional group, Young Germany, with which he was usually associated. Also, he was posthumously denounced by Heine (*Ludwig Börne. Eine Denkschrift*, 1840; Ludwig Börne. A memoir) as a misguided, intellectual revolutionary, among

other defamations, in view of Heine's conception of his own greater literary and poetic achievement. Karl Gutzkow, the young German novelist and critic, as well as Richard Wagner (*Das Judentum in der Musik*, 1848), came to Börne's defense and praised him unstintingly.

BIBLIOGRAPHY

Because I am a Jew I Love Freedom. In *The Jew in the Modern World* ed. P. R. Mendes-Flohr and J. Reinharz (New York and Oxford: Oxford University Press, 1980) 224–225

FURTHER READING

Liptzin, S.: *Germany's Stepchildren* (Philadelphia: The Jewish Publication Society of America, 1944) 27–44

MARK H. GELBER

Borokhov, Ber (1881–1917)

Yiddish scholar. Born in the Ukraine, Borokhov became the theoretician of Jewish socialism. He joined the Russian Social Democratic Party, but later became a Zionist. He was the founder of *Po'alei Zion*, the workers' Zionist movement, in 1906, and he served as the secretary of its world union for many years until his death in 1917. He left Russia in 1907 and from 1914 continued his political activity in the USA where his analysis of Jewish strike activity was important to the labor movement. He died in Russia, after having returned to participate in the Congress of Minorities convened by the Kerensky regime. Using Marxist principles, Borokhov analyzed the economic and social structures of the Jewish people, maintaining that only in Palestine could the Jewish laborer achieve normalization and create a proper socialist State.

GLENDA ABRAMSON

Best known for his leadership of the *Po'alei Zion* (Labor Zionists) and his economic and political writings, Borokhov was also the founder of modern Yiddish Studies. Much of the last decade of his short life was spent combing the libraries of western Europe for the sources necessary to understand and reconstruct the history of Yiddish language and literature. In addition to scholarly discoveries and analyses, Borokhov consciously erected the new academic discipline which he called *Di yidishe filologye* (Yiddish philology). He perceived the field as a new branch of the social sciences, with linguistics as its principal discipline, that would center around Yiddish language and culture. This was in sharp contrast to the preceding centuries of multifarious interest in Yiddish for a variety of extraneous motives (see YIDDISH STUDIES).

Borokhov's two brilliant works, which took east European Jewish intelligentsia by surprise (few knew of his passion for Yiddish), both appeared in the *Pinkes*, the first modern anthology of works on Yiddish linguistics and literary history, which was edited by literary critic Sh. NIGER (1913). The first, with which the *Pinkes* started, was *Di ufgabn fun der yidisher filologye* (The tasks of Yiddish philology) which established the justification and the need for a self-centered discipline of Yiddish and which set out its actual goals, including the preparation of an academic grammar and dictionary, history of the language, history of the literature, standardization of orthography, and the establishment of an authoritative language academy, a dream that was realized after his death with the founding of Yivo in 1925.

The second, with which the *Pinkes* concluded, was his *Biblyotek funem yidishn filolog: Fir hundert yor yidishe shprakh-forshung* (Library of the Yiddish philologist: four hundred years of Yiddish linguistics). It is an annotated bibliography, comprising 499 items, starting in 1514, date of the first known work on Yiddish. Most of Borokhov's brief and incisive annotations have come to represent authoritative reflections on the state of the art. Borokhov demonstrated a startling ambiguity by way of his *Biblyotek*. On the one hand, Yiddish had been researched more and for longer than anyone knew. On the other, all the work had been carried out by scholars using Yiddish for some extraneous motive and frequently negatively disposed toward the language. Hence, Borokhov argued, the need for a new and autonomous Yiddish Studies. Borokhov's Yiddish Studies was conceived of as the "scientific component" in the cultural renaissance of Eastern European Jewry. His love for Yiddish, and his active campaign for the

rights of the language within the Zionist movement went hand in hand with his philological work. He concluded his *Biblyotek* with the words: "If the Jewish reader will come to appreciate that Yiddish...is not a free-for-all open to dilettantes, then the key goal of this project will have been achieved – that we might have respect for our language".

On his deathbed in Kiev, Borokhov lamented the seizure by the authorities in Petrograd of his suitcases, upon his return to revolutionary Russia in 1917. They were filled with his unpublished work on Yiddish. Some have since been recovered and still await publication.

FURTHER READING

Katz, D.: Ber Borokhov, pioneer of Yiddish linguistics. *Jewish Frontier* 47 (1980) 10–20

DOVID KATZ

Boscovitch, Alexander Uriah (1907–1964)

Israeli composer. Boscovitch was born in Cluj, Transylvania, to an Orthodox family, and grew up subject to the mixed influences of Hungarian, Romanian, German, and Jewish culture. He studied piano, conducting, and composition in Vienna and Paris, where he was greatly influenced by the modern French style. Returning to Cluj he conducted the Jewish Goldmark orchestra, but the anti-Semitism of the government prevented him from finding a suitable position. In 1938 he visited Palestine for a performance of his Golden Chain Suite based on Jewish folk songs of Eastern Europe, and decided to settle there. Boscovitch soon became a spokesman and polemicist, advocating a new national school in which the composer would be the representative of a large collective, suppressing his personal, subjective expression, and reflecting the new reality of life in Palestine, which he regarded as a bridge between East and West. Boscovitch's theory was based on the evolutionary dialectics of time and place, claiming that music is part of life, representing landscape and human qualities, such as language, speech, and behavior. He opposed the direct quotation of folk songs, and instead strove to perfect a style in which all elements reach a full synthesis. His most important work in this direction was the *Semitic Suite* (1946). Boscovitch's early works are an attempt to reject tonal harmony in favor of oriental rhythmic and melodic patterns, with harmony resulting from doublings of fifths in organum and heterophony. During his later years he turned to a complex synthesis of Eastern patterns and rhythms derived from the Hebrew language and a very advanced serial technique, as in his *Concerto da Camera* and *Ornaments*. He also became a music critic for the daily *Ha'aretz*, an outlet he used for the advancement of his bold national ideology.

JEHOASH HIRSHBERG

Braham [probably Abraham], **John** (1774–1856) English tenor and composer. Braham received his earliest musical training in the Great Synagogue in London where his father, Abraham of Posnitz, was a chorister. John's musical talents were discovered by the cantor and opera singer Meyer Leoni, who introduced Braham as a boy soprano at Covent Garden in 1787. When John's voice broke shortly thereafter, he became a piano teacher with the backing of the financier Abraham Goldsmid.

Several years later Braham, now a tenor, went to Bath to study with Venanzio Rauzzini. A contemporary observer writing in *The Harmonicon* (1 January 1832) characterized Braham's voice as a magnificent, flexible, tenor instrument with a large range and well integrated falsetto. His diction, too, elicited praise. His operatic roles included Max in the first English adaptation of Carl Weber's *Der Freischütz* and later in his career the baritone title roles William Tell and Don Giovanni.

As a composer he won popular esteem for his ballads, duets, and patriotic songs. Although his early Jewish training seems to have had little influence on his professional life, in 1815 Braham collaborated with Isaac NATHAN on a work called *Hebrew Melodies* for which Lord Byron wrote the text.

ORLY LEAH KRASNER

Brandeis, Louis Dembitz (1856–1941) American reformer and lawyer. Born in Louisville, Kentucky, Brandeis was educated in the Louisville public schools, spent a year at the Annen-Realschule in Dresden, and then entered the Harvard Law School, where he graduated first in his class. By the mid-1890s, Brandeis had become one of the most successful lawyers in the United States.

Like many progressives, Brandeis began his reform work on the local level, fighting for good government and the control of public utilities, and then moved to the state level. He gained national attention because of his then unusual practice of refusing to accept compensation for the legal work he did for reform groups. In his fight against efforts to create a monopoly of New England railroads, he actually paid his own firm $25,000 out of his pocket for services he had asked of it.

In 1908 Brandeis submitted a brief to the United States Supreme Court in defense of an Oregon statute regulating working hours for women. The "Brandeis brief", which contained over 100 pages of supporting facts, paved the way for the introduction of sociological data in defense of public policy before the courts. Over the next few years Brandeis's reputation as the "people's attorney" grew, and he became one of the leading progressive reformers in the nation and a close adviser to president Woodrow Wilson. Brandeis's philosophy of a small-unit, highly competitive economy provided the intellectual underpinnings for Wilson's New Freedom.

In 1910 Brandeis was asked to mediate the great New York garment strike, and he later claimed that his exposure to Jewish workers led him to explore his own Jewish roots. A few years later Jacob de Haas introduced Brandeis to Zionism and, at the outbreak of war in 1914, Brandeis agreed to head an emergency Zionist committee to raise funds for the *yishuv* and for Jewish war victims.

He soon emerged as the leader of American Zionism, and by applying the organizational techniques he had developed as a reformer, built American Zionism into a powerful force in American Jewish life. He expounded what has come to be known as the "Brandeisian synthesis", which combined the Zionist desire to re-establish a homeland in Palestine with American democratic ideals. This made it possible for American Jews to support Zionism without fear

Louis Brandeis

of engaging in "dual loyalties". Brandeis and his associates resigned in 1921 from leadership of the Zionist Organization of America (which they had built up from 12,000 to nearly 200,000 members) after a bitter fight with Chaim WEIZMANN over the goals and methods of the World Zionist Organization. In the two decades remaining of his life, Brandeis continued to play an influential part in American Zionist affairs.

In 1916 Wilson nominated Brandeis to the Supreme Court and, after a bitter four-month confirmation fight (led by opponents to his economic and reform ideas), he became the first Jew to sit on the nation's highest court. In the 23 years he served as an associate justice, he earned a reputation as one of the greatest legal craftsmen in the court's history. Brandeis advocated "judicial restraint", the idea that courts should not second-guess the legislative branch on the wisdom of policy; but in one area he believed that courts had a special role to play – the protection of civil liberties. His arguments laid the basis for the doctrine of incorporation,

by which the guarantees of the Bill of Rights have been applied to the states as well as to the national government. Brandeis lived long enough to see many of his views, first articulated in dissent, adopted as the law of the land.

FURTHER READING

Gal, A.: *Brandeis of Boston* (Cambridge: Harvard University Press, 1980)
Strum, P.: *Louis D. Brandeis: Justice for the People* (Cambridge: Harvard University Press, 1984)
Urofsky, M. I.: *American Zionism from Herzl to the Holocaust* (Garden City: Anchor Press/Doubleday, 1975)

MELVIN I. UROFSKY

Brandes, Georg Morris Cohen (1842–1927) Danish literary critic and essayist. Brandes was born in Copenhagen to fairly affluent parents who, although religiously indifferent, were members of the Mosaic congregation.

During his studies at Copenhagen University Brandes was influenced by Søren Kierkegaard's philosophy and views of Christianity, and he spent several years enduring a religious crisis of a chiefly Christian orientation, resulting in the total denunciation of all manner of faiths, including Judaism. Judaism, whose basic philosophy he found personally oppressive, for him became identical with political reaction. Nevertheless, he was, for a couple of decades, mainly during his German exile, engaged in the study of Jewish political radicals who, in his almost propagandist delivery, became his partners in the struggle for human freedom.

During his first stay abroad, in Paris in 1866–7, Brandes moved away from his Feuerbachian atheist idealism and Hegelian speculative estheticism towards a more psychologically oriented literary criticism. This was due to the influence of Hippolyte Taine, then professor at the Sorbonne, Charles Sainte-Beuve, and John Stuart Mill. Brandes' first major work, a doctoral thesis, is a critique of Taine and contemporary French esthetics (1871).

After he returned from his next trip abroad, (1870–71), charged with radical philosophical and literary ideas, he embarked on a series of lectures entitled *Hovedstrømninger i det nittende Århundredes Litteratur* (*Main Currents in Nineteenth-century Literature*, 1901–05). His ambitious aim was to arrest the prevalent Danish cultural stagnation. His call was for a literature in which the problems of real life are debated. These lectures continued until 1887, and were published in six volumes from 1872 to 1890. In the final volume he described the revolutionary movement – in both a literary and a political sense – known as Young Germany, whose leading personality was Heinrich HEINE. Ludwig BÖRNE also features prominently, as do several others of Jewish extraction.

Brandes' lectures met with immense interest but also with such national, moral, and religious disapproval that he failed to obtain the post of professor of esthetics that he aspired to. Not until the political "systems shift" of 1902 did he become a full professor.

The herald of libertarian ideas, he attracted the enquiring young minds of his time. But he was so opposed by the élite, non-progressive circles that he went to live in Germany from 1877 to 1882.

In the 1870s Brandes published a number of biographical studies, among them the pioneering *Søren Kierkegaard* (1877) and *Ferdinand Lassalle* (1877; 1911, 1925, 1968). Finally, in 1895–96, he produced his main work, *William Shakespeare*, which marks his entrance into the English-speaking world (14 English editions appeared between 1889 and 1963). In 1883 he published *Det moderne Gennembruds Mænd* (The men of the modern breakthrough), a review of the key figures in the new literary movement generated by his own activity, among them the Norwegian writer Henrik Ibsen. Brandes was himself moving towards a new theory, that of the Great Man as the source, as well as the goal, of culture. This forms the background to his innovative lectures on Friedrich Nietzsche which appeared in book form as *Aristokratisk radikalisme* (*An Essay on the Aristocratic Radicalism of Friedrich Nietzsche*, 1909).

His major work as an old man was his autobiography, *Levned* (1905–8; Life), and his single hero studies, such as *Wolfgang Goethe* (1914–15; 1924).

His loathing of religion remained. In his last and very personal books, he engaged in a fierce battle against the religious revival of the 1920s. He was unable to define himself as Jewish but was defined as such by those Gentile groups who refused to accept him as Danish, which is what he aspired to be. In fact he never solved his identity problem. He wrote passionately about the cruel suppression of East European Jewry, protesting against the pogroms, and he often defended oppressed minorities and peoples. He refused to see Jewishness as race or nationality. When Theodor HERZL sent him *Der Judenstaat* he responded with a rejection of the book's premises. After the First World War and the Balfour Declaration, however, he stated in an article in Martin BUBER's journal *Der Jude* that Zionism had his personal sympathy, and a brilliant future perspective, but only if seen from the point of view of East European Jewry, and until his death he vacillated between acceptance and rejection of Zionism.

BIBLIOGRAPHY

Main Currents in 19th Century Literature (London and New York, 1901–1905)

FURTHER READING

Borum, P.: *Danish Literature* (Copenhagen: Det Danske Selskab, 1979) 47–49
Mitchell, P. M.: *A History of Danish Literature* (New York, 1971)
Nolin, B.: *George Brandes* (Boston: Twayne, 1976)

JUDITH WINTHER

Brasch, Rudolph (b.1912) Australian rabbi, broadcaster, and author. Brasch was born in Berlin and was educated at the University of Berlin, and the Jewish Theological Seminary, Würzburg, graduating (Ph.D.) in 1936, and being ordained in 1938. In 1959 he received an honorary DD degree from the HUC – Institute of Religion, Los Angeles.

Brasch emigrated to Australia in 1949 after holding pulpits in England, Eire and South Africa, and occupied the pulpit of the Liberal Synagogue in Sydney – Temple Emanuel – until his retirement in 1979. Rabbi Brasch has been involved in numerous community activities and, in consequence of his book *How Did it Begin: Customs and Superstitions and their Romantic Origins,* became a regular telecaster, answering questions on the *Today* show.

He has written 24 books some of which have enjoyed considerable popularity. They include: *Midrash Shir Hashirim Zuta* (1936), *The Renegade in Rabbinic Literature* (1937); *The Irish and the Jews* (1947); *The Star of David* (1955), *The Eternal Flame* (1958); *The Judaic Heritage* (1969); *Australian Jews of Today and the Part They Have Played* (1977); and *Thank God I'm an Atheist* (1987).

Brasch was awarded the Order of the British Empire in 1967 for services to the community; in 1977 he was awarded the Silver Jubilee Medal, and in 1979 he became a Member of the Order of Australia.

ALAN D. CROWN

Braudes, Reuben Asher (1851–1902) Hebrew novelist, editor, and advocate of social and religious reform. Born in Vilna and a brilliant talmudic student, he early became influenced by *Haskalah* and the critical attitude towards traditional Judaism dominating contemporary Hebrew literature. A life of wandering led him to Zhitomir and thence to Odessa, Vilna, St Petersburg, Bucharest, Lemberg, Krakow, and finally Vienna. After the pogroms of 1881 he joined *Hibbat Zion*, edited the nationalist Yiddish periodical *Yehudit* and later became editor of the Yiddish edition of Theodor HERZL's Zionist weekly *Die Welt*. He was a regular contributor to Hebrew periodicals, in which his novels were first published. Of these the best known is the unfinished *Hadat vehahayyim* (1885; Religion and life), which portrays the struggle for religious reform within Lithuanian Jewry between 1869 and 1871, and its hero is modeled on M. H. LILIENBLUM. A second novel, *Shetei haketzavot* (1888; The two extremes), reflects the clash of contemporary and traditional modes of Jewish life in and about Odessa. Another unfinished novel *Me'ayin ule'an* (Whence, and whither) was published in 1891, while the completed version of a long autobiographical novel *Shirim 'attikim* (Ancient songs) appeared posthumously in 1903. Braudes's narratives are clear, concise and interesting, with carefully constructed and powerful plots which avoid the melodrama and crude devices of

his contemporaries. Both characterization and dialogue are competent within the linguistic limitations of the period, while even the strong didactic elements do not grate upon the reader's susceptibilities. In *Shetei haketzavot* the author's advocacy of social reform is introduced with such consummate skill that the novel achieves an artistic unity unrivalled in the Hebrew literature of the period. Braudes succeeded in depicting the spiritual conflicts in the Jewish community of his time with uncanny accuracy.

DAVID PATTERSON

Brauer, Erich (b.1929) Austrian painter, performer, and set designer. Born in Vienna, Brauer spent his childhood in circumstances marked by extreme poverty. As an intern in a forced labor camp from 1938 until 1945, he experienced first-hand the cruelties of anti-Semitic persecution. For eight years following the war he studied at the Academy of Fine Arts in Vienna; during part of this period he studied singing at the Vienna City Conservatory. During the 1950s Brauer traveled extensively in Europe, Africa, and Israel. He lived for five years in Paris before building a house in 1964 in Ein Hod, Israel; since that time he has lived in both Austria and Israel.

Brauer's artistic career has been remarkable for its diversity. While in Paris he performed as a lute player, folksinger, and dancer. He designed the set and costumes for the opera *Bomarzo* at the Zurich Opera House (1970), for the opera *Medea* at the Vienna State Opera House (1972), and for the ballet *The Seven Mortal Sins* at the Theater an der Wien in Vienna (1972). In 1973 his multi-media work, *All that has Wings Takes Flight*, consisting of paintings, sculptures, a television production, and a record, was shown on television in Austria, West Germany, and Switzerland.

Best known as a painter, Brauer drew upon such sixteenth-century masters as Hieronymus Bosch and Pieter Breughel, and the modern Surrealists, Salvador Dali and Max Ernst, to develop a personal, yet readily communicative style of surrealism with which to render historical scenes and biblical subjects. He is especially preoccupied with depicting historical crimes against Jews, such as pogroms, and the Holocaust. He typically distorts reality or fashions a fantastical reality anew, replete with fine detail and bright color. Brauer has exhibited his paintings, drawings, and prints widely in Germany, Austria, Israel, and the USA. In 1979 the Jewish Museum, New York, organized an important retrospective of his work.

FURTHER READING

Restany, P.: *Brauer Retrospective* (New York: The Jewish Museum, 1979) [exhibition catalog]

Brauer New York (New York and Glarus: Goldregen AG, 1975) [exhibition catalog]

DAVID PATTERSON

Bréal, Michel (1832–1915)   French linguist. Of Alsatian origin, educated in Paris, Bréal quickly rose to eminence in the then relatively new discipline of comparative linguistics, with special interests in the study of semantics, which he pioneered (*Essai de Sémantique*, 1897). His scholarly works, which include studies of Greek language and mythology, and an etymological Latin dictionary, earned him prestigious awards (Legion of Honour and membership of the French Academy) and posts (Professorship at the Collège de France and Inspector General for secondary schools).

NELLY WILSON

Brenner, Joseph Hayyim (1881–1921) Hebrew novelist, publicist, editor, and literary critic. Brenner was born in Novi Mlini in the Ukraine into a pious but poverty-stricken home. Estranged from family and religion at an early age, although a brilliant talmudic student, Brenner faced the harsh reality of life without God. In turn a Bundist and a Zionist, he espoused justice and morality above ideology and became the conscience of his generation. After two years in the Russian army, he fled to London in 1904 where he lived in the Jewish East End until 1908. After some months in Lemberg he emigrated to Palestine in 1909 where, after suffering the deprivations of the First World War, he died a martyr's death in Arab riots in 1921.

A prolific writer and editor, his stories and novels reflect the grim realities of Jewish life in Russia, England, and Palestine. His writings mirror his own experience in graphic and distressing detail. His principal characters are anti-heroes, uprooted and despairing intellectuals, trapped in the poverty and physical degradation of Diaspora life, which Brenner regarded as a morass both in Europe and in traditional Jerusalem. Six novels, a play, many short stories, translations, and countless articles written in a powerful, distinctive, and groundbreaking prose, together with wide-ranging and penetrating literary criticism, combined to make him a major and influential force in modern Hebrew literature. His literary techniques included stream-of-consciousness, fragmentation, shifting perspective, emotive punctuation, and the direct infusion of vocabulary from Yiddish, Russian, German, and English with startling effect. In addition Brenner was a passionate and devoted founder-editor of a number of important journals. He was also a formative and highly respected figure in the Jewish labor movement in Palestine. Incapable of moral compromise, Brenner portrayed society with shattering honesty, preaching the simple but powerful message of responsibility for everyone at all times, and, above all, compassion.

BIBLIOGRAPHY

Breakdown and Bereavement, trans. Hillel Halkin (Philadelphia: Jewish Publication Society, 1971)

DAVID PATTERSON

Broch, Hermann (1886–1951)   Austrian writer. Born in Vienna, the son of a textile manufacturer, Broch went to Realschule and was subsequently given a vocational training with a view to inheriting his father's business. In 1909 he married, converted to Catholicism, and began studying at the University of Vienna, while director of the family factory. Heavily influenced by Arthur Schopenhauer and Otto WEININGER, Broch began writing on philosophical themes. In 1927 he began his trilogy, *Die Schlafwandler* (1931–2; *The Sleepwalkers*, 1932). He then worked on a religious novel, until being forced to flee Austria in 1938. His most acclaimed work is *Der Tod des Vergil* (1945;

The Death of Virgil, 1945), written in American exile. He died in the USA.

Broch is regarded as one of the great figures of modern German literature. *The Sleepwalkers* and *The Death of Virgil* introduced many innovations, paralleling James Joyce's impact on English literature. Broch was centrally concerned with what he saw as the breaking up of the Catholic–Christian world picture under the onslaught of modernity. The theory of the "decay of values" is an important part of the third part of *Sleepwalkers*, and is paralleled there by the story of the Salvation Army girl, which is mostly about Jews. In this work the Jews are seen as an extreme form of Protestantism, having a completely abstract idea of God, and thus without the claims on this world which Catholicism requires. Broch's attitude here is ambiguous, for he sees the Jews as capable both of the highest spirituality and the worst materialism. He does see in them, though, the symbol of the coming world.

By 1938 Broch was identifying the Jew as the religious man per se, and by 1945 had come to see being Jewish as the most effective way of building character. When he came to write his essay on Vienna, *Hofmannsthal und seine Zeit* (1953; *Hugo von Hofmannsthal and His Times*, 1984) he approached Hofmannsthal from the perspective of Jewish assimilation.

BIBLIOGRAPHY

The Death of Virgil, trans. J. S. Untermeyer (Oxford: Oxford University Press, 1983); *Hugo von Hofmannsthal and His Times*, trans. M. Steinberg (Chicago: University of Chicago Press, 1984); *The Sleepwalkers*, trans. E. Muir and W. Muir (London: Quartet, 1986)

FURTHER READING

Durzak, M.: *Hermann Broch* (Stuttgart: W. Kohlhammer Verlag, 1968)

Kahler, E.: *Die Philosophie von Hermann Broch* (Tübingen: Schriftenreihe wissenschaftlicher Abhandlungen des Leo Baeck Instituts, 1962)

Lützeler, P. M.: *Hermann Broch*, trans. J. Furness (London: Quartet, 1987)

STEVEN BELLER

Brod, Max (1884–1968) Austrian novelist, biographer, essayist, dramatist, poet, and composer. Born into a middle-class Jewish family that had lived in Prague for many generations, Brod graduated in law from the University of Prague (where he met his friend Franz KAFKA) in 1907. He became a postal official, continued his government service as an art critic, and then worked as an editor. In 1918 he helped form the National Council for Czech Jews. In 1939 Brod emigrated to Palestine, where he lived in Tel Aviv as dramatic adviser to the Habimah Theater and was active as a writer, music critic, composer, lecturer, and cultural mediator. After the end of the Second World War he extended these activities to German-speaking Europe.

Having come under the influence of the Jewish and Zionist thought of Hugo Bergmann and Martin BUBER at an early age, Brod, a German-speaking Jew in a Czech environment, came to the conclusion that he was a *homo judaicus* with a "*Distanzliebe*" (a love characterized by detachment) for German culture and the German people. From the "indifferentism" of his early novels Brod increasingly turned to Jewish themes (*Jüdinnen*, 1911; *Arnold Beer*, 1912; *Eine Königin Esther*, 1918). His *magnum opus* as a storyteller is a Renaissance trilogy collectively entitled *The Fight for Truth*, consisting of *Tycho Brahes Weg zu Gott* (1916; *The Redemption of Tycho Brahe*, 1928); *Rëubeni, Fürst der Juden* (1925; *Rëubeni: Prince of the Jews*, 1928); and *Galilei in Gefangenschaft* (1948; Galileo imprisoned).

The major work of Brod the thinker is *Heidentum, Christentum, Judentum* (1921; *Paganism, Christianity, Judaism*, 1968), with its doctrine of "noble misfortune" (the inescapable limitations of the human condition, such as illness and death) and "ignoble misfortune" (the kind that man has brought upon himself and must strive to alleviate, such as injustice, strife, and war). Brod's later works include editions of Kafka and several books about him; novels, *Der Meister* (1951; The master), on Jesus; *Unambo* (1949, a novel of the war in Israel, translated 1952); a monograph on Johannes Reuchlin (1965); several volumes of essays (*Das Unzerstörbare*, 1968; *Von der Unsterblichkeit der Seele*, 1969); and two autobiographical works (*Streitbares Leben*, 1960; *Der Prager Kreis*, 1966).

FURTHER READING

Gold, H., ed.: *Max Brod: Ein Gedenkbuch* (Tel Aviv: Olamenu, 1969)

Pazi, M.: *Max Brod: Werk und Persönlichkeit* (Bonn: Bouvier, 1970)

Wessling, B. W.: *Max Brod* (Gerlingen: Bleicher, 1984)

HARRY ZOHN

Brod started composing at about the turn of the century and, in 1924, he joined the *Prager Tagblatt* as its music and theater editor, having written biographies of Leoš Janáček and Weinberger, and made German translations of *Jenufa* and *Schwanda the Bagpiper*. Among his musical writings are a Hebrew libretto for Marc LAVRY's opera *Dan Hashomer* (Dan the guard), and the book *Die Musik Israels* which deals with the early development of Israeli music, as well as the Jewish elements he sensed in the music of Felix MENDELSSOHN and Gustav MAHLER (but not Ernest BLOCH).

Among Brod's 38 compositions with opus numbers there are piano pieces, songs, Israeli dances, chamber music (including a piano quintet), and a *Requiem Hebraïcum* which utilizes traditional cantillation. Whereas the European works show a clear Czech influence, those written in Israel blend Oriental and Western traditions in keeping with the precepts of the "East Mediterranean School", of which he was one of the founders.

BIBLIOGRAPHY

Israel's Music trans. T. Volcani (Tel Aviv: Sefer Press, 1951)

ALEXANDER KNAPP

Brodski, Iosif Aleksandrovich [Joseph]

(b.1940) Russian poet. A leading modernist. Arrested several times, Brodski was effectively expelled from the USSR in 1972. His long poem *Isaak i Avraam* (Isaac and Abraham) is an interesting treatment of the *Akedah*. Brodski does not generally deal with Jewish subjects, but *Evreiskoe kladbishche okolo Leningrada* (The Jewish cemetery near Leningrad) is considered one of the finest contributions to Soviet Jewish poetry. Brodski lives in the USA. His stature as an original and leading poet was recognized by the award of the Nobel Prize for Literature in 1987.

BIBLIOGRAPHY

As Brodsky, J.: *A Part of Speech* (Oxford: Oxford University Press, 1980); *Less than One: Selected Essays* (London: Viking, 1986)

EFRAIM SICHER

Bródy, Sándor

(1863–1924) Hungarian writer and playwright. Born in Eger into a Jewish merchant family who moved to Budapest in the 1870s, Bródy became a colorful chronicler of metropolitan life. He was established as a writer with the naturalistic collection of short stories *Nyomor* (1884; Misery). In the following years he earned his living as a journalist, mainly in Budapest, writing for dailies and the best literary review of the period, *A Hét* (The Week). In 1900 he founded and filled the periodical, *Fehér könyv* which closed after two years. Brody's early work was influenced by Émile Zola but his style was a blend of naturalism and romanticism. His prose, which drew, amongst other things, on contemporary urban slang, was regarded by some as "literary journalism" of a higher order. The thematic innovation of both *Nyomor* and such later cycles of stories as *Erzsébet dajka* (1900–01; Nursemaid Elisabeth) was the discovery of the life of the urban poor; its outspoken description shocked conservative opinion. Among his novels *Az ezüst kecske* (1898; The silver goat), and *A nap lovagja* (1902; The champion of the day), are considered the most accomplished: both are satirical career-stories in which the youthful hero has either to compromise his principles in order to succeed, or become a tragicomic victim of his blind ambition. *Az ezüst kecske*, the main protagonist of which is non-Jewish, is also critical of the ways in which Jewish capital shores up the political fortunes of the ostensibly liberal, but in reality corrupts an autocratic State administration.

Bródy is regarded as the father of the Hungarian naturalistic theater – especially his *A dada* (1902; The nurse) and *A tanítónö* (1908; The schoolmistress), which are daring attempts to stage real social conflicts which could be interpreted as an indictment of the then prevailing social structure in Hungary. Another of Bródy's themes which caused controversy was his recognition of female sexual appetite and of the suppression of those sexual desires.

113

Bródy's personal life was filled with unresolved conflicts. In 1905 he attempted suicide; after 1919 the role he had played in the literary life of the Soviet Republic and the anti-Semitic wave of the counter-revolution forced him into exile. In Vienna he wrote *Rembrandt* (1925; *Rembrandt: A Romance of Divine Love and Art*, 1928), a cycle of stories on the life and career of the great Dutch artist, which, to some extent, represents Bródy's confessions about his own career. In spite of the decline in the last decade of his life, Bródy was a seminal influence on an entire generation of Hungarian writers.

BIBLIOGRAPHY

Rembrandt: A Romance of Divine Love and Art (New York, 1928)

FURTHER READING

Földes, A.: *Bródy Sándor* (Budapest: Gondolat, 1964)
Czigány, L.: *The Oxford History of Hungarian Literature* (Oxford: Clarendon Press, 1984) 280–281

GEORGE GÖMÖRI

Broner, E(sther) M(asserman) (b.1930)

American novelist, playwright, and essayist. Born in Detroit, Michigan, Broner received BA and MFA degrees from Wayne State University and a PhD from the Union Graduate School. She taught for many years at Wayne State University in Detroit and is now guest writer at Sarah Lawrence College, living in New York and writing. A recipient of many awards, including an O. Henry Award and two National Endowment for the Arts fellowships, Broner is acclaimed for combining experimental narrative techniques with absorbing plots, soaring lyricism with earthy humor, and profound spirituality with political activism.

Her first novel, *Her Mothers* (1975) charts Beatrix Palmer's search for her runaway daughter, Lena. While looking for her daughter, Beatrix continues to research a rich lineage of women writers and activists for a book entitled *Unafraid Women*. *Her Mothers* culminates in a stunning symbolic confrontation scene, the mother and daughter swimming and struggling together in the ocean.

Similar themes are developed in *A Weave of Women* (1978), a novel inspired by the year Broner taught creative writing and women's studies at the University of Haifa. In this novel, an international community of women and "wayward girls" lives together in the Old City in Jerusalem. Their small stone house is the novel's center, a scene of love and violence, a place where traditional religious rituals are rewritten and a women's utopia is envisioned.

Creating a female tradition is one of Broner's major preoccupations, as seen also in *A Woman's Passover Haggadah* (with Naomi Nimrod, 1977), published in *Ms*, a magazine to which Broner is a regular contributor.

Her other work includes: *Journal Nocturnal and Seven Stories* (1968); the plays *Summer is a Foreign Land* (1966), *Colonel Higginson* (1968), and *The Body Parts of Margaret Fuller* (1976); and a collection of essays, *The Lost Tradition: Mothers and Daughters in Literature* (co-edited with Cathy N. Davidson, 1980).

FURTHER READING

French, M.: Introduction *Her Mothers* (1975, repr. Bloomington: Indiana University Press, 1985)
——: Introduction *A Weave of Women* (1978, repr. Bloomington: Indiana University Press, 1985)

CATHY N. DAVIDSON

Brooks, Mel [Melvin Kaminsky] (b.1926)

American film director, writer, and actor. Born in New York, Brooks has a background in most phases of American show business. He found a niche as a comedian shortly after the Second World War in the "Borscht Belt" of New York's Catskill Mountain resorts which catered to largely Jewish audiences. He was one of a team of comedy writers on *The Sid Caesar Show* and *Your Show of Shows*, and was also a co-creator of the television series *Get Smart*. He achieved public recognition as the 2,000-year-old man on television and records.

He wrote and directed his first film, *The Producers*, in 1968, which revealed what became some of Brooks's major preoccupations, especially Hitler and the Nazi era. While Brooks wanted originally to title the film *Springtime for Hitler* the distributor thought the title would be too offensive and misunderstood. Nevertheless, the film's most memorable sequence is the show produced by the title characters, a musical comedy about Hitler and the Nazi party.

His major commercial successes were achieved in 1974 with *Blazing Saddles* and *Young Frankenstein*. Both films are comic parodies of Hollywood genres and through this strategy Brooks is able to present a number of serious critiques of American values. In particular, *Blazing Saddles*, a spoof of the Western, condemns racism, provincialism, political corruption, and the myth of the West as the repository of true Americanism. Brooks has called this film "a Yiddish Western with a Black hero", and he demonstrates solidarity and sympathy with American Blacks and Indians.

Parody remains his most comfortable film form and he has targeted the films of Alfred Hitchcock with *High Anxiety* (1977), the biblical and historical epic with *History of the World, Part 1* (1981), and *Star Wars* and other science fiction films with *Spaceballs* (1987). His most serious film to date has been *To Be or Not To Be* (1983), in which he tries to confront Nazism directly, with overt allusions to the Holocaust and Hitler's war against the Jews.

Brooks is part of a long line of comic writers who recognize that humor has been a traditional Jewish response to adversity as well as a way of effacing one's anger. However, his near-obsession with Nazism is coupled with what might be called an aggressive Jewishness, a constant reminder to the mainstream audience that he is Jewish and that although history has witnessed many crimes against the Jews, he will not hide his identity or be silent.

FURTHER READING

Yacowar, M.: *Method in Madness: the Comic Art of Mel Brooks* (New York: St Martin's Press, 1979)

DAVID DESSER

Bruggen, Carry van [Carolina Lea de Haan] (1881–1932) Dutch novelist and philosopher. Born into the large and very poor family of a cantor and teacher, Carolina Lea de Haan grew up in a small country town near Amsterdam. Her younger brother, Jacob Israel DE HAAN, achieved some fame as "the poet of the Jewish

song". As a lively, intelligent and freedom-loving girl of 18, Carolina went to teach children in the Amsterdam slums. In the early 1900s she met and married the non-Jewish journalist Kees van Bruggen, by whom she had two children. She went with him to the East Indies, where she began her literary career by making various contributions to local newspapers.

After their return to Holland the van Bruggens settled in Amsterdam, where their home soon became the center of an artistic and intellectual set. Being a typical autodidact, Carolina studied hard to keep up with her new friends and eventually started publishing novels in a naturalistic vein. Most of her tales had an autobiographical background; one of them, *De Verlatene* (1910; Forsaken), about the disintegration of a devout Jewish family, attracted much notice. During these years, roughly before and during the First World War, she prepared, by assiduous reading, her comprehensive essay on the struggle between individualism and collectivism which appeared under the title *Prometheus* in 1919. She considered this to be her life's work was deeply disappointed when it received only scant attention.

During the First World War she was divorced by Kees van Bruggen and in 1920 she married an elderly art historian. In the tranquil years that followed she revived the ever-present memories of her youth.

In 1928 van Bruggen published what was to be her last work, the novel, *Eva*, a fictionalized account of her emotional and spiritual pilgrimage, especially her detachment from the bonds of Judaism and the resulting inner loneliness. The writing of this book, however, proved too great a strain; shortly after publication she broke down in body and mind, never fully to recover, and in 1932 she died, probably by her own hand.

Carry van Bruggen's work has several points of interest. First, she is a born story-teller, especially in her colorful, warm and intimate accounts of Jewish small-town life in Holland during the 1890s. Second, she depicts with characteristic honesty her tribulations as a housewife and mother who wishes to write and meditate on philosophical problems, but who has no "room of her own". Third, she is an exceptionally gifted thinker, who, without regard to her physical and mental health, continued her search for what she considered ultimate truth: that the individual must strive to restore the broken unity between the self and the world, be it at the peril of his or her own annihilation. In this respect van Bruggen is unique among Dutch Jewish authors, but her achievement came to be recognized only after her untimely death.

FURTHER READING

Wolf, Ruth: *Van alles het middelpunt. Over leven en werk van Carry van Bruggen* (Amsterdam, 1980)

RUTH FOPPEMA-WOLF

Brunschvicg, Léon (1869–1944) French philosopher. Remembered by many generations of French students for his critical edition of Blaise Pascal's *Pensées* (1897), which established his reputation, Brunschvicg became professor of philosophy at the Sorbonne, member of the *Académie des Sciences Morales et Politiques*, and editor for many years of the *Revue de Métaphysique et de Morale*. He played a leading part in the idealistic or neo-rationalist movement prevalent in French academic circles during the first decades of the twentieth century. Rejecting both positivist rationalism and metaphysical idealism, this school was more concerned with philosophies of mind than the philosophy of science. On this common theme several rationalist variations emerged. Unlike Emile MEYERSON, Brunschvicg remained a firm rationalist, speculating more on consciousness than on the unconscious. His views on religion led to the charge of atheism, which he denied. However that may be, he regarded the Old and New Testaments as destined to be surpassed in spiritual purity by a "third covenant", a philosophical religion which would emerge once the development of consciousness had attained its highest level. A socialist, he contributed to various left-wing ventures (the Popular University movement, *Pages Libres*). His wife Cécile served in the first Blum cabinet (1936) of the Popular Front.

BIBLIOGRAPHY

Introduction à la Vie de l'Esprit (Paris: Alcan, 1900); *Le Progrès de la Conscience dans la Philosophie Occidentale* (Paris: Alcan, 1927); *La Raison et la Religion* (Paris: Alcan, 1939)

NELLY WILSON

Buber, Martin (Mordecai) (1878–1965) Austrian religious thinker, philosopher, and Zionist leader. Born in Vienna, he was brought up, on the breakdown of his parents' marriage, by his grandparents, Solomon BUBER and his wife, in Lvov (Lemberg). At 18 he enrolled as a student of philosophy at the University of Vienna, traveling also to Leipzig, Zurich, and Berlin, where he attended the lectures of Wilhelm Dilthey and Georg Simmel. In 1898 Buber embraced Zionism and thus renewed his ties with Judaism, which he had abandoned in adolescence. He was, however, mainly interested in it from the point of view of the renaissance of Hebrew and of Jewish and Yiddish culture. At 21 he married Paula Winkler, a Gentile girl from Munich. Buber's dedication to his own idea of Zionism led him to oppose Theodor HERZL's leadership, and at the 5th Zionist Congress he resigned his editorship of the weekly organ, *Die Welt*, and joined the Zionist Democratic Faction. In 1904 Buber discovered Hasidism and with it at last an understanding of the religiousness of Judaism. For the next five years he devoted himself to the study of Hasidism, withdrawing from all his Zionist activities. Among his earliest books are adaptations of hasidic works such as *Die Geschichten des Rabbi Nachman*, (1906; *The Tales of Rabbi Nachman*, 1956) and *Die Legende des Baalschem* (1908; *The Legend of the Ba'al-Shem*, 1955). Of Buber's later books on this subject the following are prominent: *Gog umagog* (1944; *For the Sake of Heaven*, 1946), and *Or haganuz – sippurei hasidim*, i–ii (1946–7; *Tales of the Hasidim: Early Masters – Later Masters*, 1947–8).

His concern with Hasidism went at first hand in hand with an involvement with mysticism in general. In 1903 he was already planning an anthology of Sufi, Chinese, Christian, Hindu, and Jewish mystical writings, but these did not appear until six years later under the title *Ekstatische Konfessionen* (1909).

In 1909 Buber returned to public life and for the next few years traveled annually to Prague to address a Jewish student society there, the *Bar*

Kochba Verein. In 1916 he founded and began to edit the monthly *Der Jude*, which became the leading organ of central European Jewry. During the years immediately following the war, he was concerned with what he called Hebrew humanism. On the political front he was already stressing in Zionist circles, and in particular at the Zionist Congress of 1921, his belief that Jews and Arabs should collaborate in building a common homeland in Palestine.

In 1923 *Ich und Du* (*I and Thou*, 1937), Buber's masterpiece, appeared. With this book he arrived at maturity. Into it went the teachings of the BA'AL SHEM TOV, the founder of Hasidism, themselves drawn from the Bible and *kabbalah*, and out of it flowed the notions of relation, encounter, meaning, and unity, and in particular a new form of the Deity for today and a new complete man shaped in his image. This is Buber's "new answer to everything", his outline of the life of dialogue.

Prior to this event, a major turning-point in Buber's career had been the renewal of his acquaintance with Franz ROSENZWEIG, who persuaded him in 1921 to join the *Freies Jüdisches Lehrhaus* in Frankfurt. From 1925 he also taught Jewish religion and ethics, and in 1930 was made professor of religion at the University of Frankfurt. In the early 1920s Buber and Rosenzweig embarked on a new German translation of the Bible for the publisher Lambert Schneider. The first volumes of *Die Schrift* began to appear in 1925, though the whole was not completed until 1961, the collaboration with Rosenzweig having ended with the latter's death in 1929. Buber's initial exegetical work was *Königtum Gottes* (1932; *Kingship of God*, 1967). It presents the first explanation of the Buber–Rosenzweig rendering of Exodus iii.14 as "I will be there such as I will be there" instead of "I am that I am". With Hitler's accession, Buber lost his university chair in Frankfurt, but in 1936 Hugo Bergmann, Rector of the Hebrew University, offered him a professorship in social philosophy, an earlier attempt to appoint him to a post in general religious studies having failed because of Orthodox opposition. The Bubers moved to Jerusalem in 1938.

Buber's political position continued to be one of passionate hope for the co-operation of Jews and Arabs in the development of a bi-national commonwealth. To this end, he founded in 1942, with Judah Magnes, Ernst SIMON, Leon ROTH, and others, the movement *Ichud*.

After the Second World War Buber traveled extensively in Europe and the USA but continued to be publicly active and to write. In 1947 he published *Netivot be'utopiah* (*Paths in Utopia*, 1949), on the theme of the historical development of utopian socialism. Other books followed, chief among them *Zwei Glaubensweisen* (1950; *Two Types of Faith*, 1951) and *Eclipse of God* (1953). The first contrasts the faith, *emunah*, typical of Judaism with *pistis*, characteristic of Christianity, associating the former with Jesus and the latter with Paul. The message of *Eclipse of God*, Buber's last major work, continues the notes sounded in so much of his later writings that God is not dead but has become temporarily hidden from sight.

Buber's popularity in the State of Israel was at that time not great. He antagonized religious Orthodoxy by his idiosyncratic attitude towards Jewish tradition, and aroused political hostility because of his stand on the Arab–Jewish dispute. He nevertheless became in 1960 the first president of the Israel Academy of Sciences and Humanities, and his international standing was high. Among the principal distinctions awarded him were the Hanseatic Goethe Prize in Hamburg in 1951, the Peace Prize of the German Book Trade in Frankfurt in 1953, the Dutch Erasmus Prize in 1963, and the Albert Schweitzer Medal in 1964 for "having exemplified the spirit of reverence for life and other tenets of the philosophy of Albert Schweitzer". In 1961 he was elected a fellow of the American Academy of Arts and Sciences. Buber died after a fall at the age of 87 in Jerusalem on 13 June 1965.

BIBLIOGRAPHY

I and Thou (Edinburgh: T. & T. (Clark, 1937); *The Legend of the Ba'al-Shem* (New York: Harper, 1955); *For the Sake of Heaven* (Philadelphia: The Jewish Publication Society of America, 1946); *Tales of the Hasidim: Early Masters–Later Masters* (New York: Schocken, 1947–1948); *Kingship of God* (New York: Harper & Row, 1967)

FURTHER READING

Friedman, M.: *Martin Buber's Life and Work*, vols 1–3 (New York: Dutton, 1982–1983)

Martin Buber

Schaeder, G.: *The Hebrew Humanism of Martin Buber* (Detroit: Wayne State University Press, 1973)

Vermes, P.: *Buber on God and the Perfect Man* (Atlanta: Scholars Press, 1980)

———: *Buber* (London: Peter Halban/Weidenfeld & Nicolson; New York: Grove Press, 1988)

PAMELA VERMES

Buber, Solomon (1827–1906) Galician scholar and editor of rabbinic literature. Born in Lemberg, Galicia, Buber was educated in the religious Jewish tradition by his father, Isaiah Abraham Buber, who was his teacher of Jewish philosophy, and by selected professional teachers in biblical and talmudic studies. At the age of 20 he entered the commercial world, and became active in public life. He was one of the governors of the Austro-Hungarian Bank, the National Bank and the Galician Savings Bank. He was also one of the directors of the Lemberg congregation, and took a leading part in various philanthropic associations. He was consequently able to finance his scholarly research. One of his main activities as a scholar was to produce critical editions of *midrashim*, based on manuscripts and compared with printed texts. His personal fortune enabled him to send people to copy manuscripts in various places.

Buber's first scholarly work was an edition of *Pesikta de-Rav Kahana* (1868) based on a manuscript written in Egypt in 1565. The book gained immediate scholarly attention both for Buber's elaborate commentary and his introduction, which was devoted to discussions of the history of the collection of homilies by Rav Kahana. By a similar method Buber edited an enormous number of *midrashim*, including *Likkutim mimidrash avkir* on Genesis and Exodus (1883); *Midrash lekah tov* or *Pesikta zutra* by Tobias ben Eliezer on Pentateuch (1884); an older and different version of the *tanhuma* on the Pentateuch (1885); and, in the same year, *Likkutim mimidrash zuta* on Deuteronomy. His editions (1886–1902) covered the Books of Psalms, Proverbs, and Lamentations, and the Five Scrolls, in addition to various other editions of *midrashim* on the Pentateuch. These critical editions reveal Buber's unique power to create a combination of scientific West European systems and traditional rabbinic East European knowledge.

He also edited a great number of medieval and historical writings, and wrote hundreds of articles for various periodicals. Other writings include research on the Jews in Poland, among them two biographical treatises.

Solomon Buber was the grandfather of Martin BUBER, who spent the years between the ages of three and fourteen in his home.

DEBORAH SCHECHTERMAN

Büchler, Adolph (1867–1939) Rabbi and historian. Born in Slovakia within an impoverished rabbinic family, but nephew of the Oxford Hebraist and librarian Adolph Neubauer, Büchler studied at the rabbinical seminary and university at Budapest and at Leipzig. He taught Jewish history at the Vienna Jewish Theological Seminary until 1906, when he moved to Jews' College in London, acting as Principal from 1909 to his death. Equally at home in rabbinic and in classical sources, he devoted himself to study of the last part of the Second Temple period and its immediate aftermath. He used the critical tools of nineteenth-century Jewish learning but made his special trait a claim that the rabbinic material contains more reliable historical evidence than other scholars (particularly non-Jews) had been prepared to admit. Among the theses he argued with great learning and ingenuity, two of the most influential were his investigation of the divisions of the Law in public recitations in the synagogues before 70 CE ("The reading of the Law and Prophets in a triennial cycle", *Jewish Quarterly Review*, (1893), pp. 420–68; (1894), 1–73), and his theory that there were two, not one, Sanhedrins in Jerusalem at that period (*Das Synedrion in Jerusalem*, 1902). His work was of as much interest to students of New Testament as to students of Judaism, and some of his later publications, such as *Der galiläische Am-ha'Ares* (1906), *Types of Jewish–Palestinian Piety* (1922), and his main theological work, *Studies in Sin and Atonement in the Rabbinic Literature of the First Century* (1928), were partly addressed to them.

His scholarly range on Jewish matters within his chosen field was vast but his influence is less clear. The Jewish community in England did not greatly appreciate his learning and at the end of his life he was under pressure to allow the training of rabbis at Jews' College to be less academic.

FURTHER READING

Epstein, I.: Adolph Büchler: The man and the scholar. In Büchler, A.: *Studies in Jewish History* (Oxford: Oxford University Press, 1956) xiii–xxii

MARTIN GOODMAN

Burnshaw, Stanley (b.1906) American poet, publisher, translator. At the time of his son's birth, Ludwig Burnshaw, teacher of Greek and Latin, had become director of an orphanage, and later, in 1912, of a boarding school in Westchester with a Renaissance curriculum. Burnshaw's career was to exemplify the benefits of these educational experiments. He attended Columbia University, and received his BA from the University of Pittsburgh (1925). While working as an advertising apprentice for a steel mill, he founded *Poetry Folio* (1926–29) setting press by hand, and published the first five sections of a book-length poem. He continued his education in France, first at the University of Poitiers (1927), then at the University of Paris (1928).

André Spire and his Poetry: Two Essays and Forty Translations (1933), on which Burnshaw worked while serving as advertising manager for the Hecht Company in New York (1928–1932), resulted from an encounter with the poet at the Sorbonne. He earned his MA in 1933 from Cornell, then became drama critic, from 1934 to 1936 for *The New Masses*. The poem begun at the steel mill, *The Iron Land*, an indictment of industrialism, was published in 1936. For the next 20 years he designed and ed8ted books for the Dryden Press which he founded in 1939, while he also taught literature at New York University.

Four later volumes of poetry won critical acclaim for their integrity and their courageous confrontation of the atomic threat *Early and Late Testament* (1952), *Caged in an Animal's Mind* (1963), *In the Terrified Radiance* (1972), and *Mirages: Travel Notes in the Promised Land: A Public Poem* (1977). An interdisciplinary study of poetic creativity was published in 1970, *The Seamless Web: Language-Thinking, Creature-Knowledge, Art-Experience*, showing how poems could ensure man's survival.

He was founder and editor of an important educational periodical, *Adult Leadership*, and recipient, in 1971, of the National Institute of Arts and Letters Award. His most singular achievement was to make poems in foreign languages accessible by means of two collaborative projects. *The Poem Itself: 45 Modern Poets in a New Presentation* (1960) printed side-by-side versions of the original text and its literal translation, followed by explicatiⁱns. *The Modern Hebrew Poem Itself: From the Beginnings to the Present:* was co-edited by T. CARMI and Ezra SPICEHANDLER (1960).

RUTH ROSENBERG

C

Cahan, Abraham (1860–1951) Russian–American editor, journalist, novelist, and socialist leader. Born near Vilna, Cahan attended *heder* and *yeshivah* before studying at the Vilna Teachers' Institute, where he became secular, radical, and russified. In 1882, to avoid arrest for associating with revolutionaries, he emigrated to the USA, settling in New York. During his first years there, he taught English to immigrants in evening schools and wrote for Russian, English-language, and Yiddish periodicals. In 1897 he helped found the *Forverts* (Jewish Daily Forward), with which his name is indissolubly linked, and which he ran from 1903 until 1946.

Cahan took greater pains in English than in Yiddish. *Yekl: a Tale of the New York Ghetto* (1896), the first short novel by an immigrant about an immigrant, received glowing praise from the influential realist critic William Dean Howells, who encouraged Cahan to write in English. The hero of this tale loses his old-world values without gaining a satisfactory set of new ones. Unfortunately the author's attempt at direct representation of his characters' broken English renders them outlandish. While not a literary success, *The White Terror and the Red: a Novel of Revolutionary Russia* (1905) is immensely instructive about Czarist Russia in the 1880s and especially about the contradictions faced by young Jewish revolutionaries. Cahan's *The Rise of David Levinsky* (1917), however, enjoys the status of a minor classic. In this partly autobiographical work, Cahan details the urban immigrant experience and the ironies of success that brings no joy.

Cahan was a central figure in Jewish political and cultural life. Largely because of him, the American Jewish labor movement began to support Jewish labor in Palestine. An increasingly pragmatic socialist, Cahan came to see Franklin D. Roosevelt as fulfilling socialist objectives and helped him win popularity among Jews. He was also a leading opponent of communist influence in the labor movement. In the cultural sphere he disliked those who dared to differ from him, waging bitter feuds with Jacob GORDIN, Sholem ASH, and others.

Cahan's single greatest achievement was the *Jewish Daily Forward*, which in the mid-1920s reached a circulation of around 200,000. It brought serious writers like SHOLEM ALEICHEM, Israel Joshua SINGER and Isaac Bashevis SINGER, as well as *shund* (trash), to an audience who loved its paper, which was school, library, and social club all in one.

BIBLIOGRAPHY

Rischin, M. ed.: *Grandma Never Lived in America: The New Journalism of Abraham Cahan* (Bloomington: Indiana University Press, 1985); *The Education of Abraham Cahan*, trans. L. Stein. A. P. Conan, and L. Davison. Introduction by Leon Stein. (Philadelphia: Jewish Publication Society of America, 1969)

FURTHER READING

Chametzky, J.: *From the Ghetto: The Fiction of Abraham Cahan* (Amherst: University of Massachusetts Press, 1977)

Howe, I.: *World of Our Fathers* (New York and London: Harcourt Brace Jovanovich, 1976)

LEONARD PRAGER

Calisher, Hortense (b.1911) American short story writer and novelist. Calisher was born in New York to an Ashkenazi mother and a Sephardi father. A precocious child, she began, at the age of seven, to write stories about her German and Southern relatives. When, in the 1940s, she began publishing in the *New Yorker*, she was still seeking reconciliation of these disparate traditions through an autobiographical persona, Hester Elkin. Her short story collection, *In the Absence of Angels* (1951) marked the emergence of a unique voice. Although her 11 novels have had mixed critical receptions, her short fiction has won her world-wide acclaim, including four O. Henry Prize story awards and a National Book Award nomination for *The Collected Stories of Hortense Calisher* (1975). The high esteem in which she is held by fellow writers is marked by her PEN presidency (1986 and 1987), and by her having been elected president of the American Institute of Arts and Letters for the term from 1987 to 1990.

The novel *False Entry* (1961) was followed by a novella and 12 short stories, *Tales for the Mirror* (1962). The setting of the title story – an old Hudson River estate – is her own home whose descriptions figure often in her fiction. The novel *Textures of Life* (1963) sensitively explores intergenerational conflicts. The short stories in *Extreme Magic* (1964) include the notable *The Rabbi's Daughter*. A Utopian novel about a woman anthropologist, *Journal from Ellipsia* (1965), has occasioned much feminist commentary. Two controversial novellas followed in 1966. In 1969 Calisher returned to her first novel, and let Ruth Mannix, who had listened to the narrator in that work, now tell her version in *The New Yorkers*. Her next two books were comic meditations on the excesses of the 1960s, *Queenie* (1971) and *Eagle Eye* (1973); the novel *Standard Dreaming* (1972) assumes the guise of a medical report about a mysterious disease afflicting rejected parents. *On Keeping Women* (1977) explores the dilemma of Lexie, a 37-year-old mother of four children, searching for some basis of self-worth. A novel of space flight, *Mysteries of Motion* (1983) showed a group of people attempting to escape the polluted earth and being forced to orbit it forever. *The Bobby–Soxer* (1986) plays with American notions of gender identification.

Among Calisher's many honors were Guggenheim fellowships (1951 and 1953) and a National Council of the Arts Award (1967).

BIBLIOGRAPHY

Herself: An Autobiographical Work (New York: Arbor House, 1972)

FURTHER READING

Riley C., ed.: *Contemporary Literary Criticism* vols 2, 4, 8, 38 (Detroit: Gale Research Co., 1974–86)

RUTH ROSENBERG

Canetti, Elias (b.1905) Austrian novelist, essayist, and dramatist. A native of Ruse, Bulgaria, Canetti had a multicultural and polyglot upbringing. His writings are in German, the fourth language he acquired – after Ladino, Bulgarian, and English. After taking a degree in chemistry at the University of Vienna in 1929, Canetti became a freelance writer and translator. In 1938 he emigrated and lived in London from early 1939, with periods of residence in Zurich, the home of his second wife and daughter.

Canetti originally intended to produce an eight-volume "human comedy of madmen", a fictional typology of the insanity of our age, with each novel presenting a different kind of monomaniac. *Die Blendung* (1935; *Auto da Fé*, 1946) is the only novel to have appeared. It is the complex, grotesque, and richly symbolic story of an erudite and reclusive scholar whose descent to the lower depths of society after his expulsion from the paradise of his enormous library ends with his apocalyptic act of self-immolation.

The *magnum opus* of Canetti the thinker is *Masse und Macht* (1960; *Crowds and Power*, 1962), an unorthodox essay in social psychology in which the author presents a typology of the mass mind and searches for the wellsprings of human behavior generally and the root causes of Fascism in particular. Through the "accoustical masks", the unmistakable speech patterns of their characters, Canetti's three plays (*Hochzeit*, 1932; *Komödie der Eitelkeit*, 1950; and *Die Befristeten*, 1956 – variously translated as *The Numbered*, *The Deadlined*, and *Life Terms*) betray the influence of the author's onetime mentor Karl KRAUS. In addition to several volumes of essays and aphorisms, Canetti published a three-volume intellectual autobiography: *Die gerettete Zunge* (1977; *The Tongue Set Free*, 1979); *Die Fackel im Ohr* (1980; *The Torch in My Ear*, 1982), and *Das Augenspiel* (1985; *The Play of the Eyes*, 1986).

Despite his long residence in England, Canetti's literary heritage is Austrian, in the tradition of Nestroy and Kraus. His stature as one of the most original writers and thinkers of our time was recognized by the award of the Nobel Prize for Literature in 1981.

BIBLIOGRAPHY

Auto da Fé (London: Jonathan Cape, 1946); *Crowds and Power* (London: Victor Gollancz, 1962); *The Tongue Set Free* (New York: Seabury Press, 1979); *The Torch in My Ear* (New York: Farrar Straus Giroux, 1982)

FURTHER READING

Barnouw, D.: *Elias Canetti* (Stuttgart: Metzler, 1979)
Daviau, D., ed.: Special Elias Canetti issue. *Modern Austrian Literature* 16 (1983)

HARRY ZOHN

cantorial song, influences on   The many processes of acculturation are reflected, to a greater or lesser degree, in the music of all ethnic groups, except those that have remained isolated from the outside world. But the Jewish people has been a "nation among the nations" for the best part of two millennia, and so it is hardly surprising that Jewish music should be so highly prone to acculturation that its very existence has sometimes been brought into question.

Of the five main categories of music in society – liturgical, semi-religious, folk, popular/commercial, and art – it is the first that has generally resisted acculturation most successfully. The reason for this is that most communities regard their religion and its appurtenances as their most precious corporate possession, and are therefore keen to preserve this sacred component in their tradition against external intrusion. Consequently, the least acculturated of all forms of Jewish music are derivatives of Temple chant as performed by the Levites, and prayer modes and fixed chants as developed by the *Hazzan* in the synagogue after the destruction of the Second Temple. Indeed, it is universally accepted that

the public declamation of the prose books of the Bible known as "cantillation" which is said to have been initiated by Ezra in the 5th century BCE in order to educate the ignorant populace, is the oldest and most authentic type of Jewish liturgical music in existence today. This is supported by remarkable similarities among interpretations of the *ta'amei hamikra* (accents of biblical recitation) of the numerous Ashkenazi, Sephardi, and Oriental communities of the Diaspora, as recorded by Abraham Zvi IDELSOHN, the "father of Jewish musicology", during the early decades of the twentieth century.

But although these affinities suggest a common origin in Temple times, not a single wonder of modern science has yet enabled contemporary scholars to reproduce the music as it would definitely have sounded two thousand years ago. Our ancestors did not leave any theoretical treatises such as those of Pythagoras or Aristoxenos in Ancient Greece. The Bible, Talmud, and writings of early Jewish historians, such as Josephus and Philo, do contain certain descriptions concerned largely with statistics, instrumental measurements, and musical textures; and archaeologists have unearthed some fascinating relics. Nevertheless, we still know frustratingly little about melodic intervals, rhythm, and harmony (if it existed); so the problem of determining the degree to which synagogue music of today has deviated from the Temple prototype is almost insurmountable.

Not completely so, however. The Bedouin of the East Egyptian desert have remained comparatively isolated. Their day-to-day life is reflected in their simple folksong, whose melodies are limited to a range of a few notes, and usually accompanied by rhythmic hand-clapping. It is possible that Bedouin songs may have been handed down from generation to generation, virtually unchanged over the centuries, and that, as such, they may be the nearest approach we have to ancient Palestinian folksong upon which Temple chant was originally founded.

Oriental influences

The Jewish music tradition was born from and influenced, in the first instance, by the musics of ancient East Mediterranean nations: the Egyptians in the south-west, the Mesopotamians in the east and north-east, the Phoenicians in the north, and the Greeks in the north-west; and later, after the destruction of Jerusalem, by those of various oriental peoples such as the Arabs, Turks, and the Tartarian tribes, according to political or military ascendancy. Since these oriental musics constitute the first significant influence on Jewish liturgical music in the Diaspora, it is worth taking a brief look at their overall characteristics, and noting how closely they are paralleled in traditional cantorial song.

Oriental music is based on modal form, comprising a number of short musical figures or groups of notes within a certain scale. These motifs have different functions such as beginning or concluding, joining or separating; and it is these that the composer/performer manipulates in his individual fashion. Most tunes consist of an accumulation of short phrases, and these form the basis for improvisation – one of the distinctive characteristics of oriental music.

The microtonal division of the octave affords a large variety of scales. Among the most frequently heard are four which correspond in many ways to the Jewish *Hashem malakh*, *Magen avot*, *Ahava rabba*, and *Av harahamim* modes. The first two resemble the Ecclesiastical Mixolydian and Aeolia scales respectively, and are found in traditional cantillation. The *Ahava rabba*, analogous to the Phrygian scale – hence the term *Freigish*, and the *Av Harahamim*, based on the Ukrainian–Dorian scale, are much later developments; indeed they are almost unknown in some long-established north– and west–European Jewish communities.

This music is chiefly non-rhythmical, though there is a genre of rhythmical music reserved for dance (considered an inferior form).

There is marked emphasis upon melodic ornamentation. The *Krechts*, or Yiddish-style "Italian sob", far from being an emotive affectation, is a genuine feature of oriental voice production, as also is nasality.

A solo voice may be accompanied by one or more instruments, not in harmony – which, strictly speaking, does not exist in the orient – but according to the principle of heterophony. This occurs when the accompaniment anticipates or follows the melody with some variation

(a situation not uncommon in congregational participation in most Orthodox synagogues), creating a somewhat "unrehearsed" impression to Western ears.

Women are excluded from direct participation in religious music.

The music is not written down, but transmitted orally from father to son, teacher to pupil.

Western influences

Those who settled further west, however, shed much of their oriental character and adopted the significantly different traits of Western music such as, for example, a preference for major and minor scales and keys, stricter rhythms, and more regular phrase lengths. This may be exemplified in *Abodah*, a setting of the fixed chant *Vehakohanim* as conceived for violin and piano by Ernest BLOCH in 1929 where the most westernized aspects are the absence of microtones and the use of "classical" harmonic progressions.

As long as the Jews of the Diaspora were forcibly crowded behind ghetto walls, the opportunity for influences from the outside arose comparatively rarely. Even then, the most unlikely melodies sometimes managed to seep through, for example *Ma'oz Tzur*. Abraham Idelsohn has shown that the Ashkenazi tune for *Ma'oz Tzur* originates in two sixteenth-century Germany melodies: the first half is based on a Lutheran chorale which had earlier been a drinking song and the second half is based on a battle song (1504)). After Emancipation many kinds of musical activity and entertainment became accessible on a large scale; and as a consequence the opera house and concert hall entered into the consciousness of even the most pious and traditionally minded cantors. Popular arias whistled in the street would become molded into the overall framework of *nusah* (cantorial style), or accepted as fixed chants in their own right but – as it were – "Judaized" and "spiritualized", according to the celebrated hasidic principle of "saving secular tunes from the devil".

It was against the excesses of the "extreme" Reformers (who had dispensed with cantorial song altogether and introduced hymn tunes in the Church tradition, set to words in the vernacular) that the "moderate" Reformers reacted. Their musical champions, Solomon SULZER, Lewandowski and many others, appreciated the value of the modes and melodies of traditional song, despite their intensive education in the art music of the European mainstream. The interpretation of the Yom Kippur *Abodah* referred to earlier is but an extension of this procedure.

The ever-growing musical literacy among cantors over the past two centuries has brought about increasing diversity of styles, especially among the Ashkenazim, whose cantorial music has developed at the fastest rate. But whereas enterprising exploration of untapped resources as suitable vehicles for modern *hazzanut* is to be applauded, indiscriminate novelty can lead to bewildering lapses in taste. A typical example of this is the currently popular *Sheheheyanu* which one cantor of repute has dubbed "a Jewish Knees-Up-Mother-Brown"; indeed, parts of this particular setting sound remarkably like the "patter-song" idiom of W. S. Gilbert and Arthur Sullivan – ideal for secular entertainment, but perhaps less than appropriate for a sacred text.

This leads directly to consideration of the regrettable tendency toward virtuosity for its own sake, which has often goaded even the greatest cantors of the past and present into concluding almost every recitative "fortissimo, prestissimo, in altissimo" regardless of meaning or context. Whether this results from an oriental urge to unbridled embellishment or from an occidental aspiration toward the glory of the operatic stage, is surely immaterial; for only by allowing and encouraging cantorial song to be itself – that is, a uniquely expressive and delicate blend of east and west – will it fulfill its rightful role among the vocal art forms of the world.

FURTHER READING

Idelsohn, A. Z.: *Jewish Music in its Historical Development* (New York: Shocken, 1967)

—: *Thesaurus of Hebrew-Oriental melodies*, 10 vols (Leipzig: 1914–32)

Spector, J.: On Jewish music. *Conservative Judaism* 21 (i) (New York: J.T.S.A./R.A.A., 1966) 57–72

ALEXANDER KNAPP

Carmi, T(charney) (b.1925) Hebrew poet and literary historian. He was born in New York City to one of a few Hebrew-speaking families. As a small child he lived for a while in Palestine. He graduated from Yeshiva University and studied at Columbia University before leaving for France in 1946, where he worked with Jewish war orphans. This experience was the topic of his collection *Ein perahim shehorim* (1953; There are no black flowers). He moved to Israel in 1947 and later fought in the War of Independence. Since that time he has lectured widely on Hebrew and other literature and has published more than ten volumes of poetry, a number of which have been translated into English.

Carmi's poetic language, like that of many of his contemporaries, draws heavily on traditional texts while incorporating the lively idiom of modern Hebrew, a synthesis which greatly distinguishes much contemporary Hebrew verse. His poetry, marked both by its irony and by its sophisticated lyricism, deals primarily with love and the Israeli landscape. He has also written about contemporary experience and Israel's social reality (*Sheleg biyrushalayim*, 1956; Snow in Jerusalem), but the majority of his verse is more concerned with the lyrical exploration of feeling and personal reaction, charted through his own "responsive and resilient sensibility". He is preoccupied with the conversion of external reality into symbols of internal response, as in one of his most famous and frequently anthologized poems, *El harimon* (To the pomegranate). His love poems, for example in the collection *Leyad 'even hato'im* (1981; *At the Stone of Losses*, 1983), depend for their intensity on a sense of loss and guilt, and are noted for their transpositions of sacred images into erotic experience: words and phrases familiar to the reader from religious texts are transmuted (sometimes with some irony) into expressions of secular love.

As editor of *The Penguin Book of Hebrew Verse* (1981), Carmi charted the development of Hebrew poetry from the Bible to the most contemporary Israeli verse. It includes many poems that had not previously been anthologized and a comprehensive introduction which in itself is a course in Hebrew literary history. Carmi co-edited *The Modern Hebrew Poem Itself* (1965), with Ezra SPICEHANDLER and Stanley BURNSHAW and has translated into Hebrew works by Wallace

Stevens, Dom Moraes, Nazim Hikmet, Sophocles, and Shakespeare's *A Midsummer Night's Dream*, *Hamlet*, and *Measure for Measure*.

BIBLIOGRAPHY

Somebody Like You, trans. Stephen Mitchell (London: André Deutsch, 1971); *T. Carmi and Dan Pagis*, trans. Stephen Mitchell (Harmondsworth: Penguin Books, 1976); *At the Stone of Losses*, trans. Grace Schulman (Manchester: Carcanet New Press, 1983)

GLENDA ABRAMSON

Caro, Anthony (b.1924)

English sculptor. Anthony Caro was born in the London suburb of New Malden into a Jewish family which can be traced back to the sixteenth-century talmudic scholar, Rabbi Joseph Caro. In 1944 he was awarded an MA in engineering from Christ's College in Cambridge. Between 1947 and 1952 he attended the Royal Academy Schools in London, where he received a strict academic training.

Between 1951 and 1953 Caro worked as an assistant to Henry Moore, whose work, along with Picasso's expressionistic animal images, inspired Caro to model a series of massive expressionistic pieces in which the figure is distorted and the surface roughly rendered. On visits to the United States in 1959, and again in 1963 when he taught at Bennington College in Vermont, Caro was impressed by the work of Abstract Expressionists, in particular the sculpture of David Smith. His mature Abstract Expressionist works are typically large-scale, low, and horizontal. They often incorporate "found" steel pieces, such as airplane propellers, I-beams, girders, and tank ends, and are painted with household or industrial paints. Comprising several parts which are bolted or welded together, his works emphasize the relations between parts, in contrast to the minimalist focus on the whole.

Since his first one-man exhibition in 1957 in London, Caro has exhibited widely in Europe and the United States. His sculpture is included in many distinguished European and American public and private collections.

FURTHER READING

Rubin, W.: *Anthony Caro* (New York: The Museum of Modern Art, 1975) [exhibition catalog]

Whelan, R.: *Anthony Caro* (Harmondsworth: Penguin, 1974) [with texts by Michael Fried, Clement Greenberg, John Russell, and Phyllis Tuchman]

KRISTIE A. JAYNE

Cassin, René (1887–1976)

French lawyer and Nobel Peace Prize Laureate (1968). Cassin was born into a Jewish family in Bayonne. After a brilliant student career, he specialized in private and international law, which he taught as a university professor at Lille and then in Paris. Severely wounded in the First World War (in which he was awarded the Croix de Guerre), he campaigned actively for the welfare of former soldiers. He and André Maginot drew up the French law of 1923 on employment reserved for veterans and their families. He attended the International Labor Office from its first meetings, and represented France at the League of Nations (1924–38). An anti-Fascist and a patriot, he strongly opposed the policy of appeasement pursued in 1938–9. After the fall of France in May and June of 1940, he went to London, where he immediately placed himself at the disposal of General de Gaulle's Fighting France. At de Gaulle's request, he drew up the Charter of the Free French Forces which was co-signed by Churchill in August 1940. He was the only civilian to be on the *Conseil de Défense de l'Empire français*. Between 1941 and 1943 he was the Free French national commissioner for justice and education. A republican humanist of secular inclinations himself, Cassin was in touch with English and Zionist Jewish circles in London, and after 1942 he set to work to reorganize the ALLIANCE ISRAÉLITE UNIVERSELLE, of which he was also president until his death. He was vice-president of the *Conseil d'Etat* in France after the war (in which 27 members of his family had perished), and was one of the founders of UNESCO. The Universal Declaration of Human Rights, which he drew up in 1948, his courage, and his staunch and determined defense of human dignity everywhere earned him the Nobel Prize. The award, with the prestige it carries, enabled him to found the International Institution of Human Rights in Strasbourg.

BIBLIOGRAPHY

La Pensée et l'Action (Paris: Lalou, 1972); *Les Hommes partis de rien: le Réveil de la France abattue (1940–1941)* (Paris: Plon, 1974)

CLAUDE SINGER

Cassuto, Umberto Moshe David (1885–

1951) Italian historian, biblical exegete, and Semitic scholar. He was born in Florence and studied there at the university and at the Collegio Rabbinico. After graduating in the Humanities in 1906 and taking his diploma as a rabbi, he took up teaching posts in both institutions.

During this time he carried out research into the literature and the history of the Jews in Italy, producing, among other works, an article on the Italian element in Immanuel Romano's *Mahbarot* (published in *Rivista Israelitica* 1905–6), and *Gli ebrei a Firenze nell'eta del Rinascimento* (1918; republished 1965). This was an important work which was the result of 10 years of research into archival sources and Jewish documents, many of which were unpublished, and it won him the prize of the Accademia dei Lincei. On the death of his teacher, Rav Margulies, Cassuto succeeded him as the Chief Rabbi of Florence from 1914 to 1925. In 1925 he became Professor of Hebrew Language and Literature at the University of Florence and this was followed by his appointment to the chair of Hebrew and Comparative Semitic Hebrew Language at the University of Rome.

Cassuto's interest focused on biblical exegesis, and in his *La Questione della Genesi* (1934; *The Documentary Hypothesis*, 1961), he tackled the complex question of the redaction of sacred texts. Cassuto contested the validity of Julius Wellhausen's documentary theory on the origin of the Pentateuch and attributes its composition to a "teacher" or a school, both active around the 10th century BCE. In Rome Cassuto began to catalog the manuscripts in the Vatican Library but was not able to complete this work before his departure for Palestine. Forced by the racial laws to leave university teaching in Italy, he continued his academic career at the Hebrew University of Jerusalem. Cassuto made an important contribution to the field of Ugaritic studies, particularly with his work on the epic poem *Ha'elah Anat* (1951; *The Goddess Anath*, 1970). He was still active in teaching and research until his death in Jerusalem.

BIBLIOGRAPHY

A Commentary on the Book of Genesis, trans. I. Abrahams (Jerusalem: The Magnes Press, 1961–1964); *The Documentary Hypothesis*, trans. I. Abrahams (Jerusalem: The Magnes Press, 1961); *A Commentary on the Book of Exodus*, trans. I. Abrahams (Jerusalem: The Magnes Press, 1967); *The Goddess Anath* (Jerusalem: The Magnes Press, 1970)

GABRIELLA MOSCATI-STEINDLER

Castel, Moshe (b.1909) Israeli painter.

Born in Jerusalem, to a fifth-generation Israeli family, he studied at the BEZALEL SCHOOL OF ARTS AND CRAFTS, Jerusalem in 1922–5. From 1927 to 1940 he lived in Paris, where he studied at the Julien Academy, and in 1951–3 he lived in the USA. Unlike many other Israeli painters he is emotionally embedded in the country, and the titles of his paintings of the 1930s reveal an interest in reinterpreting European artistic milestones: *The Mona Lisa of Jerusalem*, and *Dejeuner sur l'Herbe*, painted in saturated colors, with fluid oil paint and brush strokes, depicting a group of local people having a meal in the open sunny landscape. In 1940 Castel returned to Palestine and thereafter divided his time between Safed and Paris. A painting of this period, *Shabbat in Safed* (1940; Tel Aviv Museum), is representative of his style and ideas at the time. It is painted with thick impasto and deep colors, a combination reminiscent of Rouault's style, but is related thematically to the kabbalistic atmosphere of Safed. He was intent on creating a style that was authentic and intrinsic to Israel, and painted several works including altars, supernatural and sacrificial themes which incorporated formal elements of ancient local art, such as the *Beit Alfa* floor mosaics. In an *Akedah* (1942) he inscribed the names of the protagonists above their heads, in a primitivism derived from the mosaics.

Castel's style has changed drastically during his prolific life, but his interest in Judaism and

Israel was permanent. Until the Second World War he was an Expressionist, afterwards painting in abstract forms. In 1960 he began using thick sand-like textures from which he made reliefs, with ancient script-like abstract forms, resembling archeological tablets or stelae.

His works appear in the collections of the Museum of Fine Art, Boston; the Fogg Art Museum, Cambridge, Mass.; the Georgia Museum, USA; the Jewish Museum, New York City, and Le Musée d'Art Moderne de São Paolo, Brazil. He has exhibited widely in London, Paris, Venice, and throughout the USA. In 1959 he represented Israel in the São Paolo, Biennale. He created a mural in the Accadia Hotel in Israel, and a vast painting for the El Al offices at the Rockefeller Center in New York, as well as monumental panels in the Knesset building in Jerusalem.

NEDIRA YAKIR BUNYARD

Castelnuovo-Tedesco, Mario (1895–1968)
Italian composer and pianist. Mario Castelnuovo-Tedesco exhibited his musical promise early. By his early teens he was attending the Florence Conservatory, earning a diploma in piano in 1914 and one for composition four years later. His early compositions, among his finest, are short piano pieces and songs reflecting the influence of Pizzetti, his teacher at the Conservatory, and Maurice Ravel.

Not until the mid-1920s did Castelnuovo-Tedesco incorporate his Jewish identity into his musical style. The turning point came with the composer's discovery of a slim notebook containing prayers in three-part harmony composed by his recently deceased grandfather. The immediate result was a piano suite based on themes he remembered hearing from his grandfather in childhood, the *Danze del re David*, opus 37 (1925). Throughout the rest of his life, Castelnuovo-Tedesco continued to draw on his Jewish heritage for musical ideas.

Castelnuovo-Tedesco's rise to fame was precipitated by the attention of Alfredo Casella. Thus encouraged he remained in Florence during the inter-war years as a freelance composer and pianist. By 1939, however, he chose to leave Italy for the United States, settling first in Larchmont, New York, and later in Beverly Hills, California. Here he was active as a film composer, and from 1946, the year he became an American citizen, he also taught at the Los Angeles Conservatory. After the war he would often spend the summer in Italy, his property having been restored to him.

Much of Mario Castelnuovo-Tedesco's music still remains unpublished, making a complete assessment difficult. His best works are in miniature genres, especially piano pieces and songs such as his *Thirty-Three Shakespeare Songs*, opus 24. His choral works in particular rely on Jewish themes, such as the oratorios *Il libro di Ruth* and *The Book of Esther*, cantatas *Naomi and Ruth* and *The Queen of Sheba*. In addition, his output includes guitar pieces and dramatic works, as well as chamber and orchestral music. Mario Castelnuovo-Tedesco also left an unpublished autobiography, *Una vita di musica* (A life of music).

ORLY LEAH KRASNER

Celan, Paul [Paul Anczel] (1920–1970)
German–Jewish poet. He was born into a German-speaking Orthodox Jewish family in the city of Czernowitz, which on the dissolution of the Austrian Empire had passed to Romania. In 1942 his parents were deported by the Germans to a labor camp, where they died. Celan survived by luck, but spent two years doing forced labor. After the war he lived in Bucharest, translating from Russian into Romanian, until he escaped in 1947. He went first to Vienna, then, in 1948, to Paris, where he lived as a translator and language-teacher until his suicide. He was married to the artist Gisèle Lestrange; they had one son.

Early influences on Celan's poetry included Rainer M. Rilke and French Surrealism. The long, surging, dactylic lines of his early poems soon became compressed into concise, emotionally restrained, mostly rhymeless verse, fragmentary in syntax, tentative and questioning in tone. He exploited the German language's potential for word-formation by continually coining new words or splitting familiar words into their components. Many poems sketch surreal landscapes whose components (stone, sand, pool, glacier) acquire multiple and precise symbolic connotations. Their imagery often draws on Celan's thorough knowledge of botany and geology. From 1967, with the collection *Atemwende* (Turn of the breath), the poems become even more elliptical and obscure.

"The poem today tends towards silence", Celan said in 1960; "the poem survives on the edge of itself". He called the poem a "crystal" from which all clichés, "the garish talk of rubbed-off experience", have been "etched away". But he also described his poems as "messages in bottles, dispatched in the hope that they will be washed up on land, somewhere and some time", and many are addressed to a "you", a role for the patient reader to assume. Reading Celan is like learning a new, difficult language which slowly becomes intelligible, though never fully so. He is unquestionably one of the two or three outstanding poets to have written in German in this century.

Several of Celan's poems, including his famous "Todesfuge" (Fugue of death), commemorate the victims of the Holocaust. Some address Job-like reproaches to an absent or indifferent God. Jewish themes and allusions are most numerous in the 1963 collection *Die Niemandsrose* (The no-man's-rose), dedicated to Osip MANDELSTAM, in which Celan expresses allegiance to an annihilated tradition that survives only in memory.

Celan also translated Shakespeare's sonnets and much modern French, Italian, and Russian poetry into German. Of his few prose writings, the most important are *Das Gespräch im Gebirg* (Conversation in the mountains) and the speech he delivered on receiving the Büchner Prize, the chief West German literary award, in 1960. His works have been collected as *Gesammelte Werke* in 5 volumes (1983).

BIBLIOGRAPHY

Poems, trans. M. Hamburger (Manchester: Carcanet New Press; New York: Persea Books, 1980)

FURTHER READING

Glenn, J.: *Paul Celan* (New York: Twayne, 1973)

RITCHIE ROBERTSON

Paul Celan

Chagall, Marc [Moshe] (1887–1985) Russian–French painter. Marc Chagall was born into a large, poor, and pious hasidic family living in Vitebsk. Leaving school in 1906, he studied with a local Jewish painter, Yehuda Pen, and in 1907 moved to St Petersburg, attending the School of the Imperial Society for the Protection of the Arts, then a private school run by Saidenburg, and finally the Svanseva School, to study under the famous Jewish artist Léon Bakst.

In 1910, a subsidy from Maxim Vinaver, the Jewish liberal lawyer and politician, enabled him to move to Paris, where he sporadically attended the art schools of La Palette and La Grande Chaumière and soon moved to La Ruche (see JEWISH SCHOOL OF PARIS). As the dark tones and relative naturalism of his earlier work were replaced by the bright colors of Fauvism and the faceted planes of Cubism, the artistic, social, and religious freedom of Paris enabled him to draw on childhood experiences in a richly imaginative and allusive fashion denied to him in Russia.

Marc Chagall De Violist *1912/13. Stedelijk Museum, Amsterdam*

In 1914 Chagall traveled to Berlin for the opening of his first one-man exhibition, and from there to his native Vitebsk, where he was stranded by the outbreak of war. In 1915 he married Bella Rosenfeld, a constant inspiration to him until – and beyond – her untimely death in 1944. His works of this period are generally more accessible than those he produced in Paris, probably as a response to his re-immersion in the visually unsophisticated Jewish community. Swept up by revolutionary fervor, Chagall was appointed Commissar for Arts in Vitebsk in 1918, but soon became disillusioned; in 1920 he moved with his wife and daughter to Moscow, where he produced murals and stage designs for the Kamerny State Jewish and the *Habimah* Theaters.

Chagall left the Soviet Union for good in 1922, spending a year in Berlin, where he was taught printmaking by the Jewish artist Herman Struck, before returning to Paris. Although he traveled widely (he paid the first of many visits to Palestine in 1931) and spent the years 1941–48 in the safety of the United States,

France remained his home. His work of the 1920s and early 1930s is generally light-hearted, lyrical, and often sensuous in mood. In the later 1930s the mood darkened, largely in response to world events; it lightened again only in the early 1950s. From this time until his death at the age of 97, his repertory of motifs and media widened, although the Bible, as mediated by the world of his childhood, remained his primary inspiration.

Chagall's relationship to Judaism was a complex and ambivalent one. While he never denied the centrality of Russian–Jewish culture to his artistic psyche, he soon ceased to be a practicing Jew, and tended increasingly to stress the universality of his subject-matter (to non-Jewish audiences at least). His frequent use from the 1930s of Christian motifs, notably the Crucifixion (primarily as a metaphor for modern – Jewish – suffering), has been controversial among Jews and non-Jews alike. While he produced numerous stained glass images for Christian churches, his preference for figurative subjects meant that he received only one commission to decorate a synagogue (at the Hadassah Hospital in Jerusalem). All this notwithstanding, Chagall's reputation as the greatest celebrator in paint of a culture lost forever is almost certain to persist.

BIBLIOGRAPHY
My Life (London: Peter Owen, 1985)

FURTHER READING
Alexander, S.: *Marc Chagall, a Biography* (London: Cassell, 1978)
Meyer, F.: *Marc Chagall* (London: Thames & Hudson, 1964)

MONICA BOHM-DUCHEN

Charles, Gerda [Edna Lipson] (b.1915) English novelist. Born in Liverpool, Charles left school at 15 and worked with her mother as a hotelier in the north of England. After this she moved to London and began writing short stories in the 1950s. Her first story, "The Staircase", was published in *Vanity Fair* in 1956, and her first novel, *The True Voice*, was published in 1959. Charles is an unusual British–Jewish novelist as she has throughout her life remained

Orthodox Jew at the center of Jewish communal life in England. Her novels reflect this commitment – especially in their moralizing – and her central concern is accurately described in *The Slanting Light* (1963), as "the region of everyday hurt". In fact, this is the subject matter of Charles's fourth novel, *A Logical Girl* (1967), which points to life's "everyday hurt" as the moral equivalent to historic evils such as Nazism.

Although *The True Voice* contrasts the aridity of Jewish suburban life with Charles's talented heroine, it was not until *The Crossing Point* (1961) that Charles was comprehensively to examine this theme. In this, her second novel, she was to paint a convincing portrait of an ambivalent Anglo-Jewish rabbi who is alienated from "hollow" bourgeois Jewry but who also wants to remain true to the "perfect fusion" of Judaism. Utilizing the rabbi's search for a marriage partner, this novel successfully examines common Anglo-Jewish themes concerning the question of intermarriage, hypocritical conformity to Judaism, and the modern revolt from Jewish spiritual values.

With the publication of her fifth novel, *The Destiny Waltz* (1971), Charles was the recipient of the prestigious Whitbread Prize. This novel concerns the contemporary resurrection on television of a famous Jewish poet from the East End of London who died in the 1920s. A Jewish couple who knew the poet are called in to help make the television documentary, and are able to juxtapose the world of the poet with the modern vulgarity which tries to reclaim him. It is the contrast between the world of talent and sensitivity and its moral opposites that is Charles's major concern.

BIBLIOGRAPHY

Modern Jewish Stories (London: Faber, 1963; Englewood Cliffs: Prentice Hall, 1965)

BRYAN CHEYETTE

Chayefsky, Paddy [Sidney] (1923–1981) American playwright and screenwriter. Born in New York City to Russian émigré parents, Paddy Chayefsky graduated from DeWitt Clinton High School in the Bronx, and received his bachelor's degree in 1943 from City College of New York. While in the army he received his nickname of Paddy, along with a Purple Heart for wounds sustained in Germany during the Second World War.

He began his career writing scripts for the *Theater Guild of the Air*, a radio show which adapted plays. He made the transition to live television in 1953 with the *Philco Television Playhouse*, thus becoming an integral part of the so-called "Golden Age of Television". Chayefsky's teleplays were realistic character studies of "little people", drawn from the milieu he knew best: working- and lower middle-class New York. Many of these hour-long plays had a specifically Jewish dimension to them. *Holiday Song*, his first play for television, concerned a cantor who has a crisis of faith until he miraculously reunites two Holocaust survivors, while *The Reluctant Citizen* (1953) has a Holocaust survivor as its focus.

His most famous teleplay of this period is *Marty* (1953), which Chayefsky adapted for film in 1954. The first of Chayefsky's Broadway plays, *Middle of the Night* (1956), focuses on a middle-aged Jewish widowed garment manufacturer who falls in love with a much younger non-Jewish woman who works for him. Like *Marty*, the focus is on loneliness amidst the urban crowds, and the redemptive, if imperfect, power of love.

The Tenth Man (1959) is Chayefsky's most successful theatrical encapsulation of major themes which draw on specifically Jewish dimensions: chosenness, Jewish ritual, folklore, transplantation from the *shtetl* to America, faith, and disbelief (as Leslie Field has pointed out). The play is loosely based on Sh. AN-SKI's Yiddish classic *The Dybbuk*. *Gideon* (1961) also draws on a classic Jewish text, this time the biblical Book of Judges. Again Chayefsky deals with the question of faith, and he makes his Gideon a very modern man who must find meaning within himself.

Chayefsky's greatest popular successes were achieved in film. His most important works are the original screenplays for *The Hospital* (1971), and *Network* (1976). Both films draw heavily on American–Jewish milieux, but are more concerned with how contemporary institutions have failed the individual. These may be seen as cinematic counterparts to Chayefsky's political activism of the 1970s, as a delegate to the International Conference on Soviet Jewry in 1971, and as a co-founder of Writers and Artists for Peace in the Middle East.

FURTHER READING

Clum, J. M.: *Paddy Chayefsky* (Boston: Twayne, 1976)

Field, L.: Paddy Chayefsky's Jews and Jewish dialogues. In *From Hester Street to Hollywood: the Jewish-American Stage and Screen*, ed. S. B. Cohen (Bloomington: Indiana University Press, 1983) 137–151

DAVID DESSER

Chocrón, Isaac (b.1932) Latin American dramatist and novelist. Born in Venezuela and educated partly in the USA, Chocrón is one of the most significant contemporary dramatists in Venezuela. He has also written three novels, including *Rómpase en caso de incendio* (*Break in Case of Fire*, 1975), an epistolary novel about a Sephardi Jew recovering from the traumatic loss of his family in an earthquake, who attempts to discover his roots in Spain and Tangier.

The marginality of the emigrant or immigrant, and the difficulty of putting down roots in a new country, is central to Chocrón's work. His first play, *El quinto infierno* (1961; The fifth circle of hell), dramatizes the clash between North and South American values, and the difficulty of cultural assimilation felt by a returned expatriate. The second, *Animales feroces* (1963; Wild animals) is a probing psychological drama centering on the relationships of an extended Sephardi family in Caracas, on the repressed antagonisms and guilt which surface after one of the sons has killed himself. "No Jew in our community has ever killed himself. Jews do not kill themselves", declares Benlevi, the only member of the family to attend the synagogue regularly and to insist on the Jewishness the others are trying to ignore. The central character, the dead boy's mother, can be seen as exemplifying the possessive, destructive love portrayed so expertly by Philip ROTH in *Portnoy's Complaint*; yet she is far from being the homely figure of the *Yidishe mame*. Her narcissism and mythomania are not meant to illustrate specifi-

cally Jewish traits. The play presents certain Jewish problems and Jewish types, yet goes far beyond that in its psychological and social scope.

This work initiates the innovations of Chocrón's later theater characterized by open endings, variety of meaning, and experimental techniques.

ANN DUNCAN

Chouraqui, André (b.1917) Israeli lawyer and writer. Born in Aïn–Timouchet, Algeria, Chouraqui studied political economy and Muslim law at the University of Paris and later pursued advanced research at the Institut de France. At the outbreak of the Second World War, Chouraqui joined the French Resistance and saw active service. With the creation of the State of Israel, he was among the few North African Jewish intellectuals who decided to make *aliyah*. Chouraqui has served as personal advisor to David BEN-GURION on the problems of the integration of various ethnic communities into greater Israeli society (1959–63), as a counsellor of the Jerusalem Municipal government (1965–73), and as Deputy Mayor of Jerusalem. He has received numerous honors, among them the Légion d'Honneur and the Ordre Nationale de la Côte d'Ivoire. The Institut de France awarded him the Louis Marin Prize in 1952, and in 1970 he won the coveted Prix Sévigné.

Chouraqui's literary activities have produced numerous scholarly monographs, notably those on biblical topics, as well as considerations of medieval Jewish, Arabic, and Christian philosophies. His history of the North African Jewish Community, *Between East and West: A History of the Jews of North Africa* (1968), is considered a masterpiece of analytical historical writing on that subject. In that study, Chouraqui demonstrated his awareness of the necessity for Jews to understand their roots as well as their interrelations with host cultures in the Diaspora, and the need for the positive assimilation of elements from host cultures into Jewish life and thought. Chouraqui's fundamental desire is to establish an awareness of the uniqueness of Jewish existence. Chouraqui likewise desires to ensure the Jewishness of his roots. This influenced him to offer a new translation of the Old Testament from Hebrew into French. In recent years, Chouraqui has similarly sought to restore the New Testament to its Jewish origins.

BIBLIOGRAPHY
A Man Alone. The Life of Theodor Herzl, trans. Y. Guiladi (Jerusalem: Keter Books, 1970)

SIMON SIBELMAN

Christianity, modern Judaism and

The discriminatory legislation which, from the time of Constantine, governed relations between Jews and Christians throughout Christendom was gradually if incompletely removed in most western countries during the eighteenth and nineteenth centuries, and in the Soviet Union in 1917. Political and social emancipation did not necessarily ameliorate religious tensions between Jews and Christians, but it made it possible for Jews to relate to the surrounding population as co-citizens under the secular government.

Moses MENDELSSOHN, following Manasseh ben Israel, formulated a Jewish apologetic which defused ongoing Christian attempts to convert Jews. Mendelssohn, drawing heavily on Enlightenment and deist ideas, argued that Judaism was in essence a religion of reason, with no "dogma" demanding an act of faith, hence it did not need to proselytize Christians; by implication, no enlightened Christian should seek to proselytize Jews. As Lavater's challenge demonstrates, political emancipation had not freed Mendelssohn from Christian pressure to religious conformity. Claude MONTEFIORE, one of the first Jews to take a serious interest in New Testament studies, moved from apologetics to genuine dialogue, a step made possible towards the end of the nineteenth century by the rise of liberal theologies amongst Jews and Anglicans. This move towards cooperation between Jews and Christians in the intellectual and moral fields gained social expression by the foundation in 1927 of the London Society of Jews and Christians. Meanwhile, in the United States, in response to anti-Semitism fomented by the Ku Klux Klan and others, in 1923 the Federal Council of Churches of Christ in America set up a Committee on Good Will between Jews and Christians.

These early attempts to encourage Christian–Jewish understanding achieved a broader organizational base in 1928 when Protestants, Catholics, and Jews, with the aim of promoting "justice, unity, and understanding" and of eliminating "intergroup prejudices which disfigure and distort religious, business, social, and political relations", set up the National Conference of Christians and Jews, which engaged in educational work, such as the Brotherhood Week inaugurated in 1934, and which was ready to speak out about Nazism when the time came.

Despite the participation of some Roman Catholics in the National Conference, the Vatican was not, until Second Vatican Council (1965), ready for dialogue. Typical was the attitude of Pope Pius X when, in 1904, he sent Theodor HERZL away with the words "The Jews have not recognized our Lord so we cannot recognize the Jewish people. If you come and settle your people there, we shall have churches and priests ready to baptize all of you".

If Emancipation, Enlightenment, the secularization of government, the historical study of the New Testament, and the weakening of traditional religious ties all made it easier for Jews and Christians to talk to one another, it was Nazi racism and the Holocaust which forced Christians to recognize their historic responsibility for vilification of Jews, and actively to seek dialogue and reconcilation. In 1942 William Temple, Archbishop of Canterbury (one of the few churchmen to speak out boldly against Nazi atrocities), and Chief Rabbi HERTZ had set up the Council of Christians and Jews, and after the war the National Conference of Christians and Jews in the United States mooted the question of holding an international conference to redefine attitudes to Jews and Judaism in the light of the terrible events which had taken place. The conference was held at Oxford in August 1946, and marks the initiation of that serious Christian reappraisal which has resulted in growth of Jewish–Christian dialogue in the post-Holocaust period. It promulgated a statement on "the fundamental postulates of Christianity and Judaism in relation to human order", and put forward two practical proposals. The first of these was that a smaller conference should be held the following year, at which the problem of anti-Semitism should be addressed. The second was to set up an International Council of Christians and Jews. The former was achieved in August 1947 in Seelisberg, a Swiss village, from where the "Ten points of Seelisberg", the first of a long series of Christian documents attempting to shape attitudes to Jews and Judaism, was sent forth. The International Council of Christians and Jews began life soon afterwards in Fribourg, Switzerland, and in 1987 celebrated its fortieth anniversary with a Colloquium in that very town.

The newly created World Council of Churches held its very first Assembly in Amsterdam in 1948. "We cannot forget that we meet in a land from which 110,000 Jews were taken to be murdered. Nor can we forget that we meet only five years after the extermination of six million Jews", runs the report, *The Christian Approach to the Jews*, which the Assembly received and commended to the churches for serious consideration and action (Croner, 1977, pp. 67–92). There is nothing ambivalent about the forthright condemnation of anti-Semitism articulated in this document, nor about the acknowledgment of the failure of the Churches to "manifest Christian love towards our Jewish neighbors", and the way this has contributed to anti-Semitism. The emergence of the State of Israel is acknowledged, though the attitude expressed towards it is ambivalent; "On the political aspects of the Palestine problem...we do not undertake to express a judgment." The sting in the tail is a theological one. It appears that the way that Christians should atone for their past animosity to Jews is by "redoubling evangelistic efforts towards them" – after all, how better to show your Christian love for anyone than by bringing them to Christ?

In the years since Amsterdam the World Council of Churches has consistently condemned anti-Semitism, but attitudes to Israel remain ambivalent, especially as the World Council is anxious to give voice to Eastern Christians. Jews are no longer targeted for mission, though there is a difference of opinion as to whether they should be excluded from it.

The World Council of Churches' work on Jewish–Christian dialogue has both fed into and been fed by the work of its constituent Churches, many of whom have produced their own guidelines of value and importance. In Britain the 1980s have seen the United Reformed Church engaging in regular discussions with Jews, and the Church of Scotland produced its own excellent guidelines both on anti-Semitism and on Jewish–Christian relations generally. The Church of England held its first high-level consultation with Jews in 1980, and the second at Shallowford House, Stafford, in April 1987. Following on these developments, a major step forward was taken in 1988 when the worldwide Anglican Conference, which meets at Lambeth once every 10 years, commended for study and action its first ever document on Christian–Jewish relations. On a broader scale the Lutheran World Federation has been especially active in this field, and recently there has been a growth of interest behind the Iron Curtain, in Hungary, Poland, and East Germany. Third World countries are involved also, and in November 1986 a major consultation was held in Nairobi with delegates from the non-Roman Catholic African Churches and the International Jewish Committee on Interreligious Consultations.

Only in the mid 1960s, during the pontificate of John XXIII, did the Roman Catholic Church, through the medium of the Second Vatican Council, address itself to people of other faiths. The Roman Catholic Church did not relinquish at Vatican II, nor has it subsequently relinquished, its exclusive claim to the full truth in matters of "salvation"; its recognition of others is polite, even friendly, but ultimately condescending. However, thanks to the strenuous efforts of exceptional Catholics such as Cardinals Bea and Willebrands, and with the encouragement and assistance of a galaxy of inspired Jews, including Jules Isaac and Abraham HESCHEL, the Vatican published on 28 October 1965 a short document, *Nostra Aetate* (In our age), on relationships with non-Christians, and about one third of its length is about Jews and Judaism. The final text, unlike earlier drafts, contained no explicit mention of the Holocaust, and not even an implicit mention of the State of

Israel. It was strong in its condemnation of anti-Semitism, and this was something new for Jews to hear spoken with the full authority of the Church. It also laid down that Jews collectively, even those of the time of Jesus, should not be held responsible for the crucifixion of Jesus; nevertheless it maintained that "the Jewish authorities and those who followed their lead pressed for the death of Christ". *Nostra Aetate* stresses the "common spiritual heritage" of Jews and Christians, and calls for special love of Jews by Christians.

The Vatican has shown itself anxious to implement *Nostra Aetate*, and on 22 October 1974 Pope Paul VI set up a Commission for Religious Relations with the Jews and asked them to recommend ways of doing this. It was thus that in January 1975 the second major Roman Catholic document on Christian–Jewish Relations was published, under the title *Guidelines and Suggestions for Implementing the Conciliar Declaration Nostra Aetate (n.4)*, by the Vatican Commission for Religious Relations with the Jews. It says: "Such relations as there have been between Jews and Christian have scarcely ever risen above the level of monologue. From now on, real dialogue must be established"; and the document shows itself sensitive to Jewish suspicion of Catholic motives and missionizing. There is a call to exercise great care in liturgy and homiletics in order to avoid portraying Jews and Judaism in a false light, and recommendations on teaching and education "at all levels of Christian instruction", with a recognition that "the history of Judaism did not end with the destruction of Jerusalem, but rather went on to develop a religious tradition". Catholic–Jewish collaboration in joint social action is urged. Once again, neither the Holocaust nor the State of Israel is mentioned.

A third Vatican document on Christian–Jewish Relations appeared in November 1985 under the title: *The Common Bond: Christians and Jews; Notes for Preaching and Teaching*, and its production and publication were instigated and encouraged by Pope John-Paul II. It stressed that "Jews and Judaism should not occupy an occasional and marginal place in catechesis; their purpose there is essential and should be organically integrated". This time the Holocaust

and the State of Israel were mentioned – both for the first time explicitly in an official Vatican document. Catholics, moreover, were to recognize and teach the profound spiritual significance of both these events to Jews. Jews will regard the treatment of the Holocaust in particular as somewhat cavalier; its spiritual significance surely touches Catholics as well as Jews, and some element of acknowledgment of the Church's tacit complicity and "preparing of the way" would have been opportune. The document offers precise suggestions on such delicate subjects as how to handle Gospel reference to Jews or to Pharisees. Unfortunately it does not entirely escape supersessionism, and actually advocates a typological approach to the interpretation of Scripture – something which is shunned by many leading Catholic theologians today.

Jewish participation in dialogue

Joint social endeavors involving Jewish and Christian religious leadership have been commonplace for much of the twentieth century; perhaps the most noteworthy examples were the collaboration of Jewish and Christian chaplains in the pastoral care of allied soldiers in the Second World War, and the leadership of the American Civil Rights campaign in the 1960s by such men as Martin Luther King and Abraham Joshua Heschel. From 1962 Jewish leaders took an active interest in maintaining dialogue with the World Council of Churches and, after Vatican II, the Roman Catholic Church. But how could a denominationally, as well as geographically, wide Jewish representation be secured? Jews are after all "not only a religious group or 'denomination', but a people in a concrete historical sense". In Autumn 1969 the World Jewish Congress and the Synagogue Council of America established the Jewish Committee on Interreligious Consultations, and this became the *International Jewish Committee on Interreligious Consultations* (IJCIC) when, soon afterwards, it was joined by the American Jewish Committee, the Anti-Defamation League of B'nai B'rith, and the Jewish Council in Israel for Interreligious Relations. Since the mid 1970s IJCIC has met approximately annually with both the World Council of Churches and the

Roman Catholic Church, and keeps a watching brief on developments in the field.

FURTHER READING

Brockway, A., *et alia* ed.: *The Theology of the Churches and the Jewish People* (Geneva: World Council of Churches, 1988)

Croner, H., ed.: *Stepping Stones to Further Jewish-Christian Relations* (New York: Paulist Press 1977)

——: *More Stepping Stones to Jewish-Christian Relations* (New York: Paulist Press, 1985)

Davies, A. T. ed.: *Anti-Semitism and the Foundations of Christianity* (New York: Paulist Press, 1979)

Eckardt, A. R.: *Jews and Christians: The Contemporary Meeting* (Bloomington: Indiana University Press, 1986)

Flannery, A. ed.: *Vatican Council II: The Conciliar and Post Conciliar Documents* (Dublin: Costello Publishing Co., 1975)

International Catholic–Jewish Liaison Committee: *Fifteen Years of Catholic–Jewish Dialogue 1970–1985* (Rome: Libreria Editrice Vaticana and Libreria Editrice Lateranense, 1988)

Oesterreicher, J. M.: *The New Encounter Between Christians and Jews* (New York: Philosophical Library, 1986)

Wigoder, G.: *Jewish–Christian Relations since the Second World War* (Manchester: Manchester University Press, 1988)

NORMAN SOLOMON

cinema industry, British, Jewish presence in

In 1934 the film critic of the *Observer* newspaper, C. A. Lejeune, wrote a short article, "Judaism on the Screen", in which she argued that the "Jews are at last using their own medium as a racial manifesto to the world". This timely piece argued that the "epics...of Jewry have begun. They are not blatant or controversial. Nobody has yet made the real saga of the latter-day exodus". *Jew Süss*, (directed by Lothar Mendes), she felt, escaped from being "mere ghetto drama". She looked forward to the studio's version of Louis Golding's *Magnolia Street*, which Victor Saville was about to direct.

Lejeune makes another point, a more telling one. "The odd and particularly characteristic quality of this new Jewish movement in the cinema is its diffidence". In fact, *Magnolia Street* was not made and Jewish themes and concerns have rarely appeared in the British cinema. The "domestic comedies" to which she refers have not existed in Britain, although it could be argued the later adaptations of Wolf MANKOWITZ novels were just that: *Make Me an Offer* (1954) and *A Kid for Two Farthings* (1955) have a clutch of Jewish actors in stock situations. Few films from Britain have shown any interest in what can loosely be considered as Jewish subjects. There is no British equivalent to Paul Wegener's *Der Golem* (1920), to E. A. Dupont's *Das alte Gesetz* (1923), or to some of the recent films that have been made in the USA.

Jewish participation in the British film was, initially, strongest in distribution and in exhibition, although by the early 1920s it was to be found also in production. The film careers of Michael Balcon, Isidore Ostrer, and Victor Saville began at this time. Many British films of the early 1930s – the early days of sound – were made in more than one language version. They attracted technicians, designers, and screenwriters, many of whom were Jews, from Europe and the number increased after 1933 when Jewish filmmakers were prevented from working in Germany. Therefore, while British cinema has never contained a Jewish cinema, it always had an important Jewish presence working in it. The émigré artists and technicians who introduced an esthetic and artistic component to British cinema were also responsible for much of the training of the next generation of filmmakers.

Some refugees, the actors Fritz Kortner and Peter Lorre and the directors Hans Brahm and Richard Oswald, for example, were simply en route to America. For them, England was, as Thomas Elsaesser might express it, a bus station where they waited for the contract to arrive from America. Many, however, had successful careers in Britain.

Even at the peak of Fascism in Europe and Britain, there is barely a sense of a Jewish subject from any studio. Unquestionably, this is due to the homogeneity of British society in which there is no separation of Jewish and national issues. In the early 1930s an anti-Semitic newspaper, *The Fascist*, attempted to isolate the Jews it considered as controlling the film business. It listed names, and was dutifully ignored. At the height of the refugee crisis, in

1940, a letter to the Prime Minister from Colonel Charles Ponsonby MP, which requested curbs on Jewish refugees, was treated derisively. Ponsonby had noticed "evidence of a most unhealthy symptom in the body politic" and feared the "Jewish vote". The dismissive reply made it clear that it had never been the policy of His Majesty's government to consider racial origin or religious faith in deciding whether or not an applicant should be granted British nationality (PRO. HO 213/4). Similarly, Jews have not seen themselves, or been seen as, a distinct group within the industry, and its Jewish producers, Alexander KORDA, Michael BALCON, the Italian born Filippo del Giudice, and Lew Grade, for example, have simply worked closely with the best talent available to them.

In 1932 Alexander Korda and his brothers, Vincent and Zoltan, established London Film Productions. He had always been aware of the dangers of German Fascism and his company offices in Europe were used as centers for intelligence gathering. He was closely associated with Sir Robert Vansittart and Winston Churchill throughout the 1930s, both of whom were on the payroll of his company. When war came, Korda helped establish intelligence operations in the USA and was soon knighted, the first knight of the British film industry. The films which were produced at Korda's studio were generally patriotic and historical or Empire and Colonial: *The Private Life of Henry VIII* (1933), *The Scarlet Pimpernel* (1934), *Fire Over England* (1937), *The Four Feathers* (1939). His brother Vincent, an excellent painter before Alexander brought him into the film business, was generally the designer and the composers Miklós Rózsa or Mischa SPOLIANSKY provided the music, although Ernst TOCH wrote it for *Catherine the Great* (1934), and Arthur Benjamin did the same for the *Scarlet Pimpernel*. Korda also experimented with effects and with color. Ned Mann, the American special effects expert, and Vincent Korda trained and encouraged many who were later to come to the forefront of the industry. Ken Adam, who Vincent Korda advised to study architecture, was later to become the designer for *The Trials of Oscar Wilde* (1960) and the Bond films, but during the war he was still a young German national, the only one to

fly fighter planes. The writers Lajos Biro and Emeric PRESSBURGER, the composers Allan Gray and Benjamin Frankel, the actors Elisabeth Bergner and Anton Walbrook, the directors Ludwig Berger and Alexander Esway are among the many artists who were associated with Korda.

If Korda had the highest profile, the more cautious Michael Balcon at Gaumont British and later at Ealing, was equally important. He saw himself as a Gladstonian Liberal. He had forced the Nazis to allow Conrad Veidt to leave Germany to join his wife in England. Veidt was contracted to act in an adaptation of the Lion FEUCHTWANGER novel, *Jew Süss* (1934). This expensive film was a labor of love and a financial disaster, something which must have been feared from the beginning. Although Paul Grätz appeared as Landauer, the quality of the supporting cast had to be reduced, and the film ran heavily over budget. It was superbly designed, but the stage was too small for the crowd scenes, much of the acting lacked conviction, and the exteriors were noticeably cramped. Balcon, although he was proud to have made it, recognized it as an artistic failure.

Veidt, who was not Jewish, had also played the lead in Maurice Elvey's second attempt at converting *The Wandering Jew* to the screen for Julius Hagen's company, Twickenham, which went on to produce an interesting reworking of *Broken Blossoms* (1936), perhaps the film which comes closest to considering the anti-Semitism of the period. It was made by the refugee Hans Brahm (who as John Brahm was to have a successful Hollywood career) and starred his then wife Dolly Haas. Although it lacked the visual spendor of D. W. Griffith's earlier version, its topicality makes it a fascinating work of the time. The theme of Jewish persecution lies only a shade beneath the surface, displaced onto the story of an immigrant Chinese in the East End of London.

Hagen's companies collapsed in 1937 and he died before the end of the decade. Ludwig Blattner, who committed suicide in the early 1930s, was another of the interesting failures of the period. He owned the non-American rights to an early and, in the end unsuccessful, lenticular color process, the Keller–Dorian system, which created color by the use of filters, but it had problems, especially in the making of copies. He also developed the Blattnerphone, a pre-tape system for recording sound, which incorporated some German patents. The Blattnerphone found favor with the BBC, but proved too cumbersome for the cinema. The funds from his color and sound systems were intended to supplement film production but, as they led to nothing, Blattner became a broken man. The studio was taken over by an American producer, Joe Rock; Blattner's son, Louis, became its manager.

Another important producer of the time was Max Schach, described as "a slick Jew" in the diaries of Sir Robert Bruce Lockhart. He had arrived in England in 1934. In spite of some barbs from *World Film News*, whose editor, Hans Feld, had known of Schach in Germany, he had managed to borrow substantial sums of money for a string of companies within the Capitol Film Corporation. He was ambitious but wasteful and, as the film historian Rachel Low notes, invested none of the money in the industry. *Abdul the Damned* (1935) was directed by his close associate Karl Grune, starred Fritz Kortner, and was photographed spectacularly by the Czechoslovakian Otto Kanturek, with music by Hanns Eisler. In the cast was another refugee actor, Walter Rilla, whose son, Wolf, was to become a leading post-war British film director. Schach and Grune's careers were virtually finished by 1938, when financial reality caught up with the industry, for Schach was not the only one living on borrowed money. Even Korda lost his studio at Denham.

Balcon and Saville took a more staid course. Throughout the 1930s films such as *I Was a Spy* (1933), *The Man Who Knew Too Much* (1934), *The Thirty Nine Steps* (1935), *Secret Agent* (1936), and *Dark Journey* (1937) all hint, obliquely, at a possible war with Germany. It is a moot point whether or not they were intended to raise public sensitivity or whether commercial astuteness directed producers to use spy themes and the actors Peter Lorre and Lucie Mannheim, with their foreign accents. Balcon, later, certainly felt that he had failed to confront the political issues of the time. Just before the war Emeric Pressburger began his series of screen stories which

play with the difficulties of the English language which many refugees were experiencing. *The Spy in Black* (1939) subtly casts Veidt so that he is given a lesson in English pronunciation. Others, too, used this device: Anton Walbrook in *Victoria the Great* (1937), as well as in *The Life and Death of Colonel Blimp* (1943), and Richard Tauber in *Heart's Desire* (1935) all receive instruction in English conversation.

Pressburger wrote and produced, though did not direct as the credits claim, a series of outstanding films with Michael Powell, whom he had met in 1938 through Korda. Even when he was assisted by native English writers, his screenplays indicate only a slowly developing confidence with the language. By the middle of the war he was coming to terms with it and was able to displace the characterization which he normally saved for a German on to an American GI in *A Canterbury Tale* (1944) or, in his next film, *I Know Where I'm Going* (1945) on to an English girl. Another writer, Fritz Gotfurt, who had edited a literary journal and produced cabaret in Berlin in the 1920s also came to Britain without a word of the language, and rose, albeit with meticulous self-taught written English, to become the head of the scenario department at Associated British after the war. Even later he adapted *The Brothers Karamazov* for television.

Many non-English Jews found themselves interned in 1940, at least for a period, Allan Gray, Lilly Kahn, Filippo del Giudice, and Emeric Pressburger amongst them. Others – Mischa Spoliansky, Lucie Mannheim, Walter Rilla, for example – worked for the BBC's European service. Filippo del Giudice had arrived in England from Italy in December 1932, threatened with political imprisonment. Subsequent anti-Semitic legislation would, anyway, have caused him difficulties, and his company, Two Cities, was later refused permission to film in Italy because its board was considered to be controlled by Jews. Del Giudice, too, struggled with English; he had taught himself, poorly by all accounts, whilst giving lessons to the children of Italian waiters in Soho. As another extravagant, flamboyant producer – but one who confessed to knowing nothing about filmmaking – del Giudice was responsible for a series of excellent British films: *French Without Tears* (1939), *In Which We Serve* (1942),

This Happy Breed (1944), *The Way to the Stars* (1945), and *Odd Man Out* (1946) amongst them. He used no capital of his own and relied solely on distributors' money. When the production cost of *Henry V* (1945) escalated, he lost his independence to J. Arthur Rank, a Methodist who had entered the film business to promote religious ideas and finally owned the major production and exhibition outlets for films in Britain. Del Giudice was skillful at acquiring the friendship of politicians: Sir Stafford Cripps, Ernest Bevin, and Hugh Gaitskell were to be seen at his table.

Del Giudice had also been responsible for *Mr Emmanuel* (1944), the only film of the war with a Jewish subject. Set in 1935, it tells the story of an elderly Jew (Felix Aylmer) who returns to Germany in order to find the mother of a young boy. His British passport helps him little and he returns without her. The cast included Eric Freund, Irene Handl, and Walter Rilla. Mischa Spoliansky wrote the music and the photography was by Otto Heller. Although some reviewers found it honest and perceptive, others considered it mawkish and contrived.

British cinema after the war involved Korda, Balcon, and del Giudice, but only for a while. In the 1970s Lew Grade, the son of a cinema-owner and once a "speciality dancer", appeared. Many brilliant technicians and artists continued in the cinema but the majority of British films took on a parochial air or were obsessed by war-heroism.

An exception was *Frieda* (1947) from Balcon's Ealing. It is the only British feature film to make direct visual reference to the concentration camps. A wounded airman (David Farrar) is assisted by a German nurse (Mai Zetterling) to escape to England at the end of the war. The English are suspicious and frigid towards her. The film is rich in metaphors and raises a number of issues about responsibility and forgiveness. The way in which the British should look to reconstruction in Europe lies at the back of many scenes. The couple, who intend to marry, postpone their wedding and in a key sequence Farrar, perhaps deliberately, confronts his fiancée with the cinema newsreel footage from the concentration camps. By rushing her out of the cinema, he associates her, personally, with it. The community where they live has a Vansittart attitude to the war and to the concept of responsibility. It only comes to recognize its own capacity for cruelty when the young heroine feels driven to attempt suicide. *Frieda* is an unusual attempt at self-examination and raises a number of important issues.

The British film industry has always kept one eye, and sometimes two, on the American market. Its directors seek the "main chance" in Hollywood. Exceptions are Jack Gold and John SCHLESINGER. Gold, like Schlesinger, worked on *Tonight* for the BBC before entering the feature industry with *The Bofors Gun* (1969), but his most assured work is for television, *The Naked Civil Servant* (1976), especially. When John Schlesinger returned from feature films to television to direct a play based on the life of the spy Guy Burgess, in Moscow, *An Englishman Abroad* (1984), he was able to draw on inner resources and produce a piece of fine comic observation.

FURTHER READING

Durgnat, R.: *A Mirror for England: British Movies from Austerity to Affluence* (London: Faber & Faber, 1970)

Elsaesser, T.: Pathos and leave taking: the German émigrés in Paris during the 1930s. *Sight and Sound* (Autumn 1984)

Lejeune, C. [CAL]: Judaism on the screen. *Observer* (7 January 1934)

Low, R.: *Film Making in 1930s Britain* (London: Allen & Unwin, 1985)

Perry, G.: *The Great British Picture Show* (London: Hart-Davis, MacGibbon, 1974)

Walker, A.: *Hollywood England: The British Film Industry in the Sixties* (London: Michael Joseph, 1974)

——: *National Heroes: British Cinema in the Seventies and Eighties* (London: Harrap, 1985)

KEVIN GOUGH-YATES

Cohen, Albert (1895–1981)   French novelist. Born in Corfu, Cohen spent his early childhood in the Jewish quarter he later described in his novels, and which inspired his creation of picturesque and lively characters. In 1900 the family emigrated to Marseilles and lived there in poverty. As a schoolboy there Cohen became acquainted with Marcel Pagnol. He later returned to Corfu for his *bar mitzvah* and this visit remained fixed in his imagination. After his baccalaureat he settled in Geneva, where he studied law until 1917, together with literature.

Meanwhile, he had several stormy love-affairs and became involved in politics. He also attended the Zionist Congress in Basle. In 1919 he married the daughter of a Protestant minister and for her wrote the poems entitled *Paroles Juives* (1921). His next move was to Egypt where he practiced as a lawyer, and discovered Marcel PROUST's *Remembrance of Things Past*, the literary reference of Cohen's own work. He returned to Switzerland on account of his asthma. In 1930 he published *Solal*, which met at once with great success in Europe. In the same year he published a play, *Ezechiel*, which was staged by the Comédie Française in 1933. After the death of his wife in 1924, he engaged in tumultuous love affairs until he met his last wife, Bella, in 1943. He published *Mangeclous* in 1938, *Le Livre de ma Mère* in 1954, *Belle du Seigneur* in 1968, which was awarded the highest distinction of the French Academy, *Les Valeureux* in 1969, *O Vous Frères Humains* in 1972, and *Carnets 1978* in 1979. Affected by the Second World War, he devoted much time to the fate of refugees at the *Bureau International du Travail*, part of the League of Nations. He then retired to Geneva to complete his literary work, and led a peaceful life there, a sick, withdrawn man, busy with his work, until his death in 1981.

The world of Albert Cohen is a dichotomy: it opposes the brilliant, beautiful, alluring world of western Christianity, passionate but evil, to the miserable, ugly, frightened world of the Jewish ghetto, dirty but immensely good. His caricature of bourgeois society is without concession, his vision of the world sarcastic and cruel, pessimistic and tender. He opposed to the people of nature, advocated by Nazi ideology, the followers of the Mosaic law of anti-nature. His mother, the repository of stories, and of goodness, is the model and the reference of his work. Cohen's writing, through its themes, its historical testimony (genocide, Zionism), and its morality, is the most Jewish of twentieth-century French literature.

FURTHER READING

Bensoussan, A.: L'image du Sépharade dans l'Oeuvre d'Albert Cohen. *Les Temps Modernes* 394 (1979) 396–409

Goitein-Galperin, D.: *Visage de mon Peuple, Essai sur Albert Cohen* (Paris: Nizet, 1982)

ALBERT BENSOUSSAN

Cohen, Hermann (1842–1918) German philosopher. Cohen was born in Coswig. While studying in a talmudic school in Breslau, with the intention of becoming a rabbi, Cohen encountered a volume of Immanuel Kant's writings. He then decided to break his ties with rabbinical Judaism and to become a student, and possibly a teacher, of philosophy. He eventually settled in Marburg where he remained until the end of his life. He published his first book, *Kant's Theory of Experience* in 1871. With this work, an almost talmudic commentary on Kant's *Critique of Pure Reason*, Cohen became one of the propagators of the movement which called for a renaissance of Kantian thought as a remedy for the decline of German idealism in the second half of the nineteenth century. Cohen was soon to become the leader of this neo-Kantian movement, otherwise known as the Marburg School. His attempt to provide a commentary to Kant's theory of knowledge in his first book was followed by *Kantian Foundation of Ethics* (1877), and *Kantian Foundation of Aesthetics* (1899). While Cohen revered Kant and the entire scope of his thought, he did not follow him slavishly, not even during his early phase when he appeared to be retracing accurately the path of Kant's three great "critiques". Even then he began to formulate his own system, different in many respects from Kant's, although always faithful to the essential spirit of Kantianism as humanism. Cohen's own system emerged with *Die Logik der Reinen Erkenntnis* (The logic of pure knowledge) in 1902, the first volume of an intended trilogy; *Die Ethik des reinen Willens* (The ethics of pure will) and *Die Aesthetik des reinen Gefühls* (The esthetics of pure emotion) followed, to constitute together Cohen's main philosophical work. In it he constructed his system of "philosophical psychology", the last great system of German classical thought, which at the same time was a critique of the entire course of this thought, from Kant to Hegel and Schopenhauer.

It was in his approach to Judaism that Cohen differed from Kant. Whereas Kant was deeply antagonistic to Judaism, considering it an obsolete religion, Cohen attempted to present it as a religion of reason, or rather as the source of the religion of reason. To this he devoted his last great work, published posthumously, *Die Religion der Vernunft aus den Quellen des Judentums* (1919; *Religion of Reason out of Sources of Judaism*, 1972). Even before this Cohen had devoted a number of essays to Judaism, expounding its essential humanism, one example being *Neighbourly Love in the Talmud* (1888). He was also at pains to demonstrate the profound affinity between German and Jewish spirituality, the title of his 1916 essay. Yet Cohen was an ardent German patriot and many anti-Zionist remarks are to be found in his later articles and letters.

BIBLIOGRAPHY

Religion of Reason Out of the Sources of Judaism, trans. S. Kaplan (Frederick Ungar Publishing, 1972) [introductory essay by Leo Strauss]; *Reason and Hope*, trans. E. Jospe (New York: 1971)

FURTHER READING

Rotenstreich, N.: *Jewish Philosophy in Modern Times: From Mendelssohn to Rosenzweig* (New York: Holt, Rinehart & Winston, 1968)

YORAM BRONOWSKI

Cohen, Leonard (b.1934) Canadian poet, novelist, and composer–singer. Born in Montreal, Cohen graduated from McGill University. He has lived in Greece, on the island of Hydra, in England, and in the United States in California and New York. By the late 1980s he was again living in Montreal. In the 1960s Cohen's popularity as a singer, his unconventional lifestyle, and controversial public statements earned him the reputation of a social rebel.

As a poet and novelist, Cohen focuses on the innovative and experimental. His best known novel, *Beautiful Losers* (1966), deals with the martyrdom of a Mohawk girl, who died in Quebec in 1680, in the context of today's emotional and moral alienation suggested by the anonymity and unrelatedness of the novel's characters. The tendency to nihilistic and often cynical repudiation of moral responsibility surfaces in Cohen's view of his Jewish heritage.

Three books of poetry – *Let Us Compare Mythologies* (1956), *The Spice-Box of Earth* (1961), and *Flowers for Hitler* (1964) – mark Cohen's attempts to adopt an impartial view of mankind's irredeemable corruption. Speaking of Judaism as "a tradition composed of the *excuviae* of visions", Cohen disclaimed any religious identification. His vision of evil inherent in all mankind surfaced in his treatment of the Holocaust. As one of Cohen's critics observes, Cohen's notion of evil communicates that "we all carry our own private Hitlers".

The universality of evil, however, can hardly offer a satisfying answer to the recent loss inflicted upon the Jewish people. In one of his finest prose poems, *Lines from My Grandfather's Journal*, Cohen admits, albeit reluctantly, that Israel's military power provides the best deterrent to yet another outburst of anti-Jewish hatred.

Other works include poetry collections *Parasites of Heaven* (1966), *Selected Poems* (1968) for which he declined a Governor General's Award, *The Energy of Slaves* (1972), *Death of a Lady's Man* (1978), and *Book of Mercy* (1984).

FURTHER READING

Ondaatje, M.: *Leonard Cohen* (Toronto: McClelland & Stewart, 1979)
Scobie, S.: *Leonard Cohen* (Vancouver: Douglas & McIntyre, 1978)

RACHEL FELDHAY BRENNER

comedy, Jewish In the USA the roll call of Jewish comics who have made their mark on stage and screen, or in nightclubs, vaudeville, radio and television, spans the alphabet from A to Y, from Allen to Youngman, and if we looked hard enough we could find a Z – perhaps a dozen Zs – among the hundreds of Jewish comedians who came and went in vaudeville or on the Borscht circuit from Second Avenue to the Catskills. American comedy has sometimes appeared to be a Jewish invention, and according to a survey reported in *Time* magazine, while Jews constitute some three per cent of the American population, about eighty per cent of its professional comedians are Jewish (*Time*, 2 October, 1978, 76).

So dominant have Jews been in comic theater that in the period between about 1920, when they joined the mainstream of American entertainment, and the 1980s, they revolutionized American comedy. The earthiness of their wit, the tautness of their one-liners – uttered as if in preparation for flight – the extravagance of their routines, and the brio and agility of their deliveries constituted a new comic style – comic modernism – that simply outpaced the droll and folksy humor associated with the likes of Mark Twain and Will Rogers, and in more recent times, Garrison Keillor. "Indeed it is difficult", observe William Novak and Moshe Waldocks in *The Big Book of Jewish Humor* (1981), "to imagine what would remain of American humor in the twentieth century without its Jewish component". Woody ALLEN, Morey Amsterdam, Jack Benny (Benjamin Kubelsky), Milton Berle (Milton Berlinger), Shelly Berman, Mel BROOKS, Lenny Bruce (Leonard Schneider), Myron Cohen, Rodney Dangerfield (Jacob Cohen), Buddy Hackett (Leonard Hacker), Danny Kaye (David Daniel Kaminsky), Jack E. Leonard (Leonard Lebitsky), Sam Levenson, the Marx Brothers, Jackie Mason (Yacov Moshe Maza), the Ritz Brothers, Joan Rivers, Smith and Dale (Joe Sultzer and Charlie Marks), Sophie Tucker, and Henny Youngman are names extracted from a list so long that an encyclopedia entry could be composed out of names alone. (For a fuller list, see Novak and Waldocks).

The roots of Jewish comedy

This astonishing fact demands an explanation, and there has been no shortage of these. Those most commonly adduced are variants on the "laughter through tears" thesis, that humor arose among the Ashkenazi Jews of Eastern Europe and Russia during times of poverty and persecution as a way of maintaining community morale in the face of oppression. A recent translator of SHOLEM ALEICHEM praises the "therapeutic force" of his humor, which left the Jews of his time "feeling immeasurably better about themselves and their fate as Jews". The "therapeutic" explanation has much to recommend it, for it does seem that humor and comedy flourish among the downtrodden, who cultivate laughter as a balm for their wounds. The rich traditions of comedy in Ireland and Black America seem to give independent confirmation to the thesis that laughter is a universal human device for coping with pain.

But while that says something about the social functions of Jewish humor and comedy, it says nothing about their unique forms – the trenchant social observation, the nervous patter, the mayhem – or about how it was that Jews should flourish as comics in America, where the tears of the past were staunched by opportunities on a scale unparalleled in the history of *galut* (exile). It also leaves us unenlightened about how one ethnic group's comedy of anguish gained such eager applause from the non-anguished and the non-Jewish. For although Jewish comedy underscored the uniqueness of Jewish culture and history, it also served to ease assimilation by bringing Jewish voices into the center of American life and demonstrating that, for all their differences, Jews could express the suffering, and also the resiliency, of people everywhere.

It is one of the paradoxes of this comedy that the universal language of the Jewish comics was English, and an English, moreover, steeped in the turbulence, the irony, and the clear-eyed realism of Yiddish. Jewish humor and comedy – and the two should be distinguished – arrived in the New World intact, embodied in a tradition of story-telling, a lore of anecdotes, and a biting wit that needed only the opportunity and the media of dissemination to become staples of American entertainment. Despite the dire circumstances of Jewish history and the unremitting sobriety of the Jewish holy books the propensity for humor has been a defining feature of Ashkenazi Jewish culture. Not only did laughter in the face of woe mark the life of that culture, but humor, no less than piety, lay at the very root of its identity.

The sources of this comic spirit are little understood, however, as they are buried in the unrecorded folk life of the Yiddish-speaking Jews of Poland and Galicia. Humor, we know, had little place in the Jewish holy books and played virtually no role in rabbinic Judaism, and as for the theater, it was disdained by the rabbis of the Middle Ages as the "seat of the scornful". The one significant point of contact between rabbinic Judaism and the Yiddish comic spirit was in the festival of Purim. Purim, which celebrates the rescue of the Persian Jews from Haman, lieutenant of King Ahasuerus, by Queen Esther and Mordecai (see the Book of Esther), was traditionally celebrated by the Ashkenazim as a festival of license in which common restraints were abandoned and conventional pieties mocked.

The heart of the Purim festivity was the Purim *shpil*, the recitation by a "Purim rabbi" of a ludicrous "Purim Torah" which parodied some familiar liturgical text and ridiculed the subtleties of Midrash. The Purim *shpil* was sometimes accompanied by a comic play performed by clowns and fools, and there was even, according to Nahman Sandrow, historian of the Yiddish theater, a typology of such clowns: "the *lets, nar, marshelik, badkhen,* and *payets*". *Lets* and *nar* were simple clowns who did slapstick and pratfalls, while the *marshelik* was a master of ceremonies who specialized in talmudic wordplay and disputation. The *badkhen*, also a master of wordplay, traditionally performed at weddings, where he recited long rhymed sermons. The *payets* was the narrator and stage director of the Purim play.

While such festivities are now out of fashion in most Jewish communities, their spirit remains alive in secular forms; as comic types, the fool (Ed Wynn, Rodney Dangerfield, Gene Wilder), the master of ceremonies (Jack Benny, Sid Caesar, Milton Berle), the trickster (Marx Brothers, Ritz Brothers, Mel Brooks), adapted ancient social roles to new times and new media.

It is significant that the Jewish comic spirit should intersect the religious in that ceremony in which Jews were licensed to feign irreverence and act out impieties that are elsewhere proscribed. This normalization of the comic spirit under the umbrella of the Purim festivity suggests a way in which the religious life accommodated the comic and turned its anarchic tendencies to the service of religion itself: binding the restless Yiddish folk humor by giving it the limited sanction of a festival all its own. For except in the oral tradition of joke and storytelling, the Jewish comic impulse had no other public outlet until the rise of Yiddish theater in the nineteenth century.

The influence of Yiddish humor

If the Purim *shpil* and the Yiddish theater are the close ancestors of modern Jewish comedy, then comedy inherited something of the rebelliousness of those institutions, inherited, indeed, the tension between rabbinic Judaism and cultural Yiddishism that reached a pitch in the nineteenth century, when Yiddish asserted itself as a language of art and culture. Jewish humor is contiguous with the folk life of the Ashkenazi Jews, touching with affection all things, sacred and secular, that constituted that life, but Jewish comedy dispenses with that affection; it is mutinous and discordant. If we think of Jewish humor as it crystallized in the writing of Sholem Aleichem and was transferred to the stage by performers such as Myron Cohen and Sam Levenson; and if by comedy we mean the low farce and mad antics of the Marx Brothers, Sid Caesar, or Mel Brooks, or the insult comedy of Don Rickles, Jack E. Leonard, and Joan Rivers, then it is plain that we are dealing with different forms of the comic spirit and very different refractions of Jewish life. The humorists are sentimental, *gemutlich*, and warm; the comics agitated, theatrical, and cold.

Few comics are pure practitioners of either humor or comedy, which are ideal categories, unevenly blended in most of their work. Woody Allen is a prime example of the comic-cum-humorist who embodies qualities that Judaism has traditionally held dear – modesty, wit, verbal agility – but turns those qualities into a performance in which modesty becomes a boast and verbal agility is continuous with verbal aggression. The ambiguity of his later films – *Zelig, Broadway Danny Rose, The Purple Rose of Cairo, Radio Days* – is the ambiguity of a comedian in search of humor, who desires to merge with a community and nourish it from within but can find none to merge with. The buoyancy and invention of his comedy is darkened by the pathos of his ambition to transcend it and cut deeper into the human condition.

Comedy, then, is to humor as theater is to community; it stands in dialectical and uneasy relation to the culture from which it has emerged. That tells us something about the broad appeal of Jewish comedy in America, where its anarchism spoke to the anarchic instincts of a nation of immigrants let loose from the chains of Old World servitude. A classic image of this in American films was the Marx Brothers' use of Margaret Dumont as a constant

The Marx Brothers Animal Crackers *(1930)*

foil, in the films *The Cocoanuts, Animal Crackers, Duck Soup, A Night at the Opera* and *A Day at the Races*. Proper, quintessentially Anglo-Saxon, and the very caricature of a "lady", she was the perfect straight-woman for the Marx Brother's comedy of immigrant *ressentiment*, and what Irishman, what Italian, what Pole, what Black could resist a comedy in which Yankee propriety was vexed time and time again by immigrant cunning?

Finally, no word on Jewish comedy is complete without some remarks on the place of Yiddish in its formation. Jewish comedy's entire repertoire of mannerisms originates in the Yiddish language, whose earthiness and realism made it the perfect vehicle for comic deflation. Some of those qualities that fitted Yiddish for comedy reflect its subordination, as a homely

jargon, to the *loshen ha-kodesh* of the Jews: Hebrew. The Ashkenazim of Eastern Europe inhabited two sharply divided worlds. One was the world of labor and trade, money, politics, love, marriage, family, trouble, death. Its domain was the six days from Saturday night through to Friday, and its language was Yiddish. The other was the world of the Sabbath, of prayer and study, Torah and Talmud, faith and prophecy. Exalted and transcendent, its language was Hebrew. In daily life the languages tended to fuse, as Yiddish penetrated the language of prayer and Hebrew formed a sacred canopy over common speech.

It was this juxtaposition of higher and lower worlds within the mental economy of the Jewish people that established the terms for a comedy of deflation, whose basic trope was a sudden

143

thrusting downward from the exalted to the workaday. From Sholem Aleichem to Woody Allen, this comedy of internal juxtaposition has been fundamental. In Sholem Aleichem's *The Adventures of Menaham-Mendl*, for example, the ritual openings of all the letters between the wandering Menaham-Mendl and his long-suffering wife, Sheineh-Sheindl, are Hebrew/Yiddish mélanges, in which the exalted sentiments of the Hebrew salutation are brought low by plain truths uttered in Yiddish.

> To my dear, esteemed, renowned, and honored husband, the wise and learned Menaham-Mendl, may his light shine forever.
> In the first place, I want to let you know that we are all, praise the Lord, perfectly well, and may we hear the same from you, please God, and never anything worse.
> In the second place, I am writing to say, my dearest husband, my darling, my sweet one – may an epidemic sweep all enemies away! You villain, you monster, you scoundrel, you know very well that your wife is on her deathbed after the reparation which that wonderful doctor made on me – I wish it on all your Yehupetz ladies! The result is I can hardly drag my feet.

Even in translation the comedy of the elevated and formal (and false) being sabotaged by the plain and vernacular (and honest) comes across unambiguously. Woody Allen's humor too is an almost ritual yoking of the exalted and the worldly, which sometimes produces explosive punchlines. In *God*, a one-act play on the death of God, a modern rendition of a Greek tragedy goes haywire and gets away from both cast and playwright, until Zeus is lowered from on high to put things in order and is accidentally strangled by the machinery. "God is dead", announces an actor. "Is he covered by anything?" responds a physician who has rushed up from the audience.

Indeed, the taste for parody, which has been a staple of Jewish comedy, also profits from this genius for deflation, and there is no better representative of that than S. J. Perelman, who built a career on doing parodic sendups of other writers, great and small. His *Waiting for Santy*, a Depression-era parody of Clifford ODETS's play *Waiting for Lefty*, was a stunning x-ray of "proletarian" rhetoric; the revolt in Santa's workshop, led by revolutionary Marxist elves,

was not the least among the causes of the proletarian literary movement's quick demise.

It is this ready availability of formal devices that are also ancient properties of the Jewish mind in exile, rather than the specific details of Jewish history, that gave rise to these special brands of humor and comedy. And it is this slant on life – earthy, blunt, rebellious – that promises a continued vitality for Jewish comedy even as the culture that gave birth to it is being transformed – in America, in Israel, in Russia – into something quite different from what it had been.

FURTHER READING

Cohen, S. B., ed.: *From Hester Street to Hollywood: The Jewish–American Stage and Screen* (Bloomington: Indiana University Press, 1986)

——: *Jewish Wry: Essays on Jewish Humor* (Bloomington: Indiana University Press, 1987)

Novak, W., and Waldocks, M., eds: *The Big Book of Jewish Humor* (New York: Harper & Row, 1981)

Smith, R. L.: *The Stars of Stand-up Comedy: A Biographical Encyclopedia* (New York and London: Garland Publishing, 1986)

Weinreich, M.: Internal bilingualism in Ashkenaz. In *voices from the Yiddish: Essays, Memoirs, Diaries*, ed. I. Howe and E. Greenberg (Ann Arbor: University of Michigan Press, 1972)

MARK SHECHNER

Conservative Judaism Conservative Judaism is a movement in contemporary Jewish religious life, which occupies the religious middle ground between Orthodox and Reform Judaism. It is centered in the USA, but is also represented in Canada, South America, Europe, and Israel. Institutionally the movement is composed of the Jewish Theological Seminary of America, an academy for higher Jewish studies which primarily trains rabbis, cantors, educators, and academicians; the Rabbinical Assembly, with a membership of some 1200 rabbis; and the United Synagogue of America, an association of over 800 congregations. The World Council of Synagogues extends movement affiliation to congregations outside North America, and the *Masorti* (or "traditionalist") Movement coordinates its activities in Israel.

The first formal articulation of the principles

which distinguish the Conservative movement from alternative readings of Judaism was published in 1988 in a pamphlet entitled *Emet Ve-emunah*, written by a Commission of Seminary professors, rabbis, and lay people. This statement emphasizes the movement's commitment to a modern, historical, and critical approach to the study of Judaism, to the ongoing role of the living community in shaping the content of the tradition, and to the observance of Jewish law as the classical, authentic form of Jewish religious expression. The movement recognizes that Jewish law has always evolved in response to changing cultural conditions, and it seeks to define the criteria and limits for such development in our day. In general, its programatic approach to such development is more gradualist and evolutionary than that of Reform.

The historical antecedents of this reading of Judaism can be traced to Rabbi Zacharias FRANKEL who broke with the emerging European Reform movement (1845) by insisting on the indispensability of Hebrew as the language of the liturgy, and later became the first head of the Jewish Theological Seminary of Breslau (1854). In the USA a parallel "conservative" reaction to the increasing radicalization of American Reform, as embodied in Reform's Pittsburgh Platform (1885), was led by Rabbi Sabato Morais (1823–97) who became the first President of the Jewish Theological Seminary of America in 1886.

The movement's initial period of expansion began under the aegis of Solomon SCHECHTER who became President of the Seminary in 1902. Schechter assembled the faculty of renowned scholars that established the Seminary's reputation as the fountainhead of modern Jewish scholarship; his many addresses and scholarly papers spelled out the ideology of the Conservative movement; and in 1913 he founded the United Synagogue as its congregational arm.

Conservative Judaism's most notable accomplishments include the establishment of a distinctive style of synagogue worship which aims to synthesize traditional Jewish forms (for example, the traditional liturgy in Hebrew) along with a measure of accommodation to modern American tastes (for example, family seating in the synagogue). They include also the popu-

lating of departments of Jewish Studies in American universities with professors trained at the Seminary and in western, critical canons of scholarship; and the creation of innovative educational programs, most notably Camp Ramah, a network of Hebrew-speaking camps that integrate formal and informal Jewish education with a summer camping experience.

In two recent policy decisions of note, the Seminary Faculty voted (1983) to admit women to training for the Rabbinate, climaxing an extended process whereby women have been gradually accorded an equal role in the ritual of most Conservative synagogues. However, in its 1987 convention, the Rabbinical Assembly explicitly reaffirmed its commitment to the principle of matrilineal descent as the sole determinant (apart from conversion) of halakhic Jewish identity, in contrast to the position of Reform Judaism.

FURTHER READING

Emet Ve-emunah: Statement of Principles of Conservative Judaism (The Jewish Theological Seminary of America, The Rabbinical Assembly and The United Synagogue of America, 1988)

Dorff, E. N.: *Conservative Judaism: Our Ancestors to Our Descendants* (New York: Youth Commission, United Synagogue of America, 1977)

Sklare, M.: *Conservative Judaism: An American Religious Movement* (New York: Schocken Books, 1972)

NEIL GILLMAN

cooking, Jewish Cooking and table manners are daily practices that visibly and concretely distinguish the Jews from their Gentile neighbors. Cooking has always been a cultural emblem throughout the centuries of Jewish history. Jewish culture is thus obviously present in Jewish cooking, as well as the history of the Jews and their religious code. In a similar perspective, Jewish cookbooks appeared at the beginning of the nineteenth century as a literary genre whereby the authors expressed their wish to safeguard popular traditions and customs, and to integrate them into the prestigious scholarly culture. But what is most characteristic of the cultural meaning of Jewish cooking and table manners is the religious codification of diet which is found in the Pentateuch, and especially in the eleventh chapter of Leviticus. One might ask: what is Jewish about this cuisine? What distinguishes a Jewish *kugel* from a Gentile Alsatian *kugel*? Are there specific cooking techniques and items which are only used by the Jews? Is there a Jewish version of each local cuisine? The answer is obviously its religious codification. Biblical, talmudic, and rabbinic literatures seem to be mostly concerned with the consumption of meat and of other animal ingredients, while the consumption of vegetable food essentially prohibits hybrid species. According to Hebrew dietary laws, or *kashrut*, edible – or kosher – meat is the flesh of the following animals:

1   Animals living on the earth must be quadruped mammals that chew their cud and are cloven-footed (Leviticus xi. 2–3); in this category, the swine, the camel, the hare and the rock-badger are strictly prohibited – or *taref* – because they fulfill only one of the two requirements for edibility (Leviticus xi. 4–8)
2   Animals living in the waters (sea and rivers) must possess scales and fins (Leviticus xi. 12)
3   Among animals living in the air, only those not mentioned in a prohibited list of birds are permitted (Leviticus xi. 13–22); this list is mainly composed of carnivorous and hybrid species.

The absence of hybrid species in the Jewish diet is one of its major principles. To belong to two categories is to be in no category or to be unclassifiable. The Hebrew dietary laws do not like disorder. They classify edible animals according to the order of the divine creation, as it is described in the first verses of Genesis. According to recent anthropological and biblical studies, Hebrew dietary laws are imbued with the Jewish idea of God; they convey major principles of holiness. One can thus consider the Jewish diet as a form of expression of the holy concept of sacrifice according to which edible animals have to be slaughtered before consumption. One should interpret in a similar perspective the Hebrew prohibition of the consumption of blood (Deuteronomy xii. 23), and the forbidden association of meat and dairy ingredients in cooking techniques (Exodus xxiii. 19). Cook-

ing meat and dairy food in the same pot would be a sort of symbolic confusion of sacrifical death (meat) and beneficient life (milk). In other words, no Jewish dish should display death, or death with life, in the same culinary combination. For the same reason, kosher meat has to be cleared of its blood, through salting procedures, before selling it in the butcher's shop, and before cooking it at home. That is why Jewish cuisine and especially meat dishes are generally overcooked: meat should not display any semblance of blood. The perfect example of this culinary pattern is epitomized by the various recipes for sabbath meals. They all describe heavy and rich stews, generally cooked on a slow and lasting fire. They combine several varieties of meat, vegetable, and cereal ingredients. Their names generally contain the principle of overcooking and overwarmth. The word *tshulent* which designates the Yiddish version of this sabbatical cooking pattern, is supposed to be the combination of two French words, *chaud* (warm) and *lent* (slow). But this is a hypothetical explanation. The Judeo-Arabic designation of these dishes is more significant. In Morocco and Algeria, the sabbath stew is called *dafina* or *t'fina* which means "burial". It may also be called *s'hina* or *hamin* (literally "the warm dish") in other Mediterranean communities. These terminologies suggest a technique of cooking which may have consisted of burying a pot under burning charcoal or of any slow and long cooking. In fact, this technique is the strict application of a sabbatical rule which requires that the fire be lit just *before* the beginning of the seventh day and not *during* it. All the dishes scheduled for Saturday meals are thus to be cooked from Friday evening and during the entire night. Sabbath cooking is the gastronomic suggestion of the domestic warmth that wraps the Jewish hearth on this day.

Jewish cooking is therefore specifically governed by the organization of the religious calendar. It is the emphatic and gustative way of pacing domestic Jewish time: every religious celebration has its own menu, its own "taste". The *tshulent* is the *ta'am*, the taste of Sabbath. Passover is another ritual, having its specific food techniques and recipes, because of the temporary prohibition of leavened aliments.

Kosher kitchen in East London

Most breads and leavened pastries are thus absent in Passover traditional recipes. In the Mediterranean communities, some families would also avoid the consumption of rice dishes, although *hametz* – the prohibited leavened food – mainly refers to wheat ingredients. The Passover *seder*, which relates a major event in the Hebrew sacred history, the Exodus from Egypt, is a spectacular table dramatization of the biblical tale. It is as if each sequence of this story had to be physically memorized through the tasting of symbolic foods like *matzah* (the unleavened bread), *maror* (the bitter herb), and *pesah* (the lamb bone), these three items being the central trilogy of a variety of suggestive tastings.

Because cooking is so important in the perpetuation of the Jewish religious system, it has imposed a complex communal organization for the distribution of kosher food. The training of the *shohatim* (ritual slaughterers) and the network of kosher stores are thoroughly controlled by rabbinic institutions in most contemporary communities. In the medieval Jewish ghetto, the communal oven was generally located in a central position, for the baking of the Sabbath bread, the *hallah* and for the meticulous preparation of *matzot* (Passover unleavened breads).

Jewish cooking has not been impervious to Gentile local gastronomies. Jews have always cooked ingredients of the local market and have very often "borrowed" specialities of the surrounding cultures. From this point of view, the Jewish *kugel* is somehow similar to the Alsatian *kugel*, and the Yiddish *blintzes* to the Russian *blini*. But Jews have usually prepared these dishes in compliance with the laws of *kashrut*. In other words, they have judaized Gentile cuisines. An example of this cultural appropriation is found in the celebration of *Rosh Hashanah*, the Jewish new year ritual. According to the *Shulhan arukh* (lit. "set table", the code of Jewish law compiled by Rabbi Joseph Caro, published in 1565), this reunion has to be a happy and "sweet" table festivity displaying fruits and vegetables that are considered beneficent in the language spoken by each local community.

North African Jewish families would therefore eat Swiss chard or spinach dishes, two vegetables that local Arab beliefs treat as bearers of *baraka*, or "good fate". Moreover, these beneficient vegetables, called *selq* in Arabic, are eaten while the family recites the Hebrew benediction containing the sacred word *yistalku* (eradication of the enemies). The phonetic similarity between the Arabic name of the vegetable (root: s−l−q) and the Hebrew term in the benediction (root s−l−k) provides the symbolic principle of the ritual: when eating spinach (*selq*), the taster recites *yistalku*, and finally "eats" the word of the benediction. Through this process, a familiar Arabic word is integrated into the ritual Hebrew terminology. It is as if the Jewish cooking intended to appropriate the surrounding culture through Hebrew religious values. It suggests that Jewish cuisine is nothing but a Jewish interpretation of Gentile gastronomies.

FURTHER READING

Douglas, M.: The abominations of Leviticus. In *Purity and Danger, an Analysis of Concepts of Pollution and Taboo* (London: Routledge & Kegan Paul, 1966) 41–57

Fredman-Gruber, R.: *The Passover Seder: Afikoman in Exile* (Philadelphia: University of Pennsylvania Press, 1981)

Kirshenblatt-Gimblett, B.: The kosher gourmet in the nineteenth century kitchen: Three Jewish cookbooks in historical perspective. *Journal of Gastronomy* 2 (1986/7) 51–89

Milgrom, J.: The biblical diet laws as an ethical system. *Interpretation* 17 (1963) 288–301

Soler, J.: The semiotics of food in the Bible. In *Food and Drink in History*, ed. R. Forster and O. Ranum (Baltimore: Johns Hopkins University Press, 1979) 126–138

JOELLE BAHLOUL

Copland, Aaron (b.1900) American composer, author, and conductor. A national treasure of the USA, his influence on at least two generations of composers has been incalculable. The family (originally named Kaplan) belonged to a Brooklyn synagogue whose Rabbi, Israel Goldfarb, composed a world-famous melody for SHOLEM ALEICHEM. Copland became *bar mitzvah* at this congregation, although religious observance was for him "more of a convention than a deep commitment". Nevertheless, at the age of 19 he wrote a *Lament* (cello/piano) that incorporated a traditional *Rosh Hashanah* melody for *Adon Olam*. The latter probably was sung at Goldfarb's services.

In the first of *Four Motets*, psalm paraphrases of 1921, the composer, subconsciously, also paraphrased motives of Yiddish folksong. He again drew upon the Bible for his 1947 cantata *In the Beginning* (Genesis i:1–ii:7), a work evocative of *davening* (Hebrew prayer-song). But whereas the biblical account of creation culminates in an abstraction, the Sabbath, Copland chose the creation of man for his conclusion. Back in 1929, however, he was partial to other-worldly matters. His trio *Vitebsk* (violin/cello/piano) was based on a hasidic tune used in Sh. AN-SKI's mystical drama *The Dybbuk*. Called *Mipne mah*, the song asks "why does the soul descend from on high and then ascend?", mirroring *The Dybbuk*'s plot. Although the printed score of *Vitebsk* is subtitled "Study on a Jewish theme", the original manuscript is titled "Trio On Yiddish Themes", suggesting that Copland's original impulse was to adapt more than one Jewish musical source. Indeed, heretofore unnoticed by commentators, there is another quotation, played by the violin shortly before the middle fast section. It is the familiar cantillation motive of *etnachtah* in the mode of Prophets, chanted by *bar mitzvah* boys. The quotation is marked "liberamente (recitativo)", implying that it was a deliberate reference.

Copland arranged *Banu*, a Palestinian hora in 1937 (words by Natan ALTERMAN, music by Joel Valbe). Its leftist slant: "We came with nothing ...yesterday/Fate has given us tomorrow's millions", must have appealed to the composer, since much of his work in the mid-1930s was designed for the working classes. Several composer-colleagues of Copland (Roger Sessions, Lazare SAMINSKY, Leonard BERNSTEIN) have written about his "Jewish temperament". As early as 1932 Virgil Thomson went so far as to call him "a prophet", his music "an evocation of the fury of God". After other such pronouncements, Thomson stated: "All this I write is bunk, naturally". When the essay was reprinted in 1981, this was altered to: "All this I

Aaron Copland (center) on his eightieth birthday with Isaac Stern (left) and Leonard Bernstein

write is overstated". Fifty years later Thomson's hyperbole was regarded in retrospect as more actual than exaggerated.

Arthur Berger has perceptively noted Copland's special type of synagogical declamation, citing a repeated-note phrase in Copland's *Short Symphony* and *Quiet City*, both of which suggest "a cantor's lament". In fact, Hebraic eloquence and starkness is characteristic of other non-Jewish Copland works. The finale of the *Piano Sonata* is a case in point. *Fanfare for the Common Man* might well be retitled *Isaiah's Prophecy*, and the New England psalmody in the Suite from *Our Town* resembles a Torah chant. The first section of *The Promise of Living* quintet, from the opera *The Tender Land*, would not be out of place as a congregational hymn in a Reform synagogue.

BIBLIOGRAPHY

With Perlis, V.: *Copland, 1900–1942* (New York: St Martin's Press/Marek, 1984)

FURTHER READING

Berger, A.: *Aaron Copland* (New York: Oxford University Press, 1953)
Idelsohn, A.: The Kol Nidre tune. *Journal of Synagogue Music* (New York: Cantors Assembly, Vol. III, No. 1, September 1970)

JACK S. GOTTLIEB

Costa, Isaac Da (1798–1860) Dutch author and poet. His parents belonged to the upper layer of the Amsterdam Sephardi congregation and could afford to send their son to the University of Leyden. There he first took his

149

degree in Law and, in 1821, in the Humanities. In the same year he married his first cousin, Hanna Belmonte. As early as the age of 15, while still at college, he had come into contact with the Dutch non-Jewish author and poet Willem Bilderdijk (1756–1831), who was to influence him and his views, as was the Leyden professor D. J. van Lennep. Partly under Bilderdijk's influence he, together with his wife and his Sephardi friend Abraham Capadose, converted to Protestantism in 1822, out of conviction. As a protestant Da Costa played a prominent part in the introduction of the *Réveil* movement in the Netherlands. Also, like Bilderdijk, he was a fervent opponent of liberalism, both political and theological, and of revolutionary movements, and a strong defender of the House of Orange as an institution deriving its authority from the Lord. He can be considered one of the spiritual fathers of the neo-Calvinist political Anti-Revolutionary Party, though it was established only after his death. He first gave evidence of his political convictions in his *Bezwaren tegen den geest der eeuw* (1823; Objections to the present political–theological climate) which became a classic. This was followed by many other similar polemical works.

Despite his baptism Da Costa remained strongly attached to his Jewish, and in particular to his Sephardi, roots. As a result of this interest he wrote a comprehensive history of Judaism from the earliest times to his day, *Israel onder de volken* (1848), which was translated into English in 1850 as *Israel and the Gentiles*, with additional chapters by Bertrand Brewster and Cecil ROTH in the 1936 edition.

He also wrote some romantic tragedies with the history of the Jews in Spain as their theme, such as *Alfonsus* and *Inez de Castro*; and *Hagar* (1847), a biblical epic. Several studies have been published about him, both by Dutch Calvinists on his importance for neo-Calvinism, and by Jaap Meijer on his Jewish aspects.

HENRIETTE BOAS

costume, Jewish   Jewish costume during the past 200 years cannot be evaluated as one homogeneous entity since many diverse forms evolved with the dispersion of Jews throughout the world. Each country left its own imprint on Jewish culture, while the Jewish religion itself influenced everyday life.

The objects which form the tangible expression of culture (costume and jewelry on the one hand, ceremonial objects on the other) were generally made according to local style yet it is possible to discern styles and decorations unique to Jews, especially in their mode of dress. The components of costume, including fabric, style, adornment, and even quality of workmanship, are age-old stylized forms, carefully preserved by tradition as a function of place and time. Status differences between the Jews and the local population often obliged them to adopt forms of dress that would distinguish them from their neighbors.

Thematic categories of costume
Costume can be studied according to either geographic dimensions, or to cross-sectional and thematic categories, of which there are three: function, magic symbols, and esthetics.

Function   This category is derived from the Bible and rabbinical Law. The first mention of dress is as a cover for the naked body: "They knew that they were naked; and they sewed fig leaves together, and made themselves girdles" (Genesis iii.7). The first description of dress is also found in Genesis: "The Lord God made for Adam and for his wife garments of skins, and clothed them" (iii.21). Dress also distinguishes role and status: "Thou hast a mantle, be thou our ruler" (Isaiah iii.6). The rabbinical dictum that Gentile dress should not be imitated also derives from the Bible: "And ye shall not walk in the customs of the nation" (Leviticus xx.23). This restriction led to the evolution of many unique attributes that eventually became a hallmark of Jewish costume in the Diaspora.

Over the last 200 years, role and function aspects of costume have become well-defined: secular dress for everyday wear, formal dress for Sabbath and Festivals, and ceremonial costume connected to man's life cycle (circumcision, *bar mitzvah*, marriage, and mourning). Ensembles of costume, including jewelry, signified the socio-economic class of the wearer, often serving as the repository of family wealth and property. Costumes were therefore kept within the family and served their owners for many years, until they could no longer be worn. They then became symbols of prosperity and success.

Magic symbols Dress serves not only to cover nakedness or to signify status and role. The symbolic and magical functions of costume are intrinsically connected with the evolution of national and local beliefs. Fabric, colors, decorative patterns, and the cut of the garment played an important role in the embodiment of folk beliefs amongst the local population and Jews alike. In many cultures, customs, objects, and talismans are used to protect the leading participants from evil spirits in ritual celebrations. Many of these have become symbolically incorporated into specific ceremonial garments for special occasions.

Uniquely Jewish decorative components proliferated in those countries with many craftsmen, such as Yemen and Morocco. In countries where Jews engaged primarily in commerce, for example Bukhara, there were fewer peculiarly Jewish features, and Jewish costume resembled that of the local population. Costume decorations always included an element of symbolism, most of which was drawn from nature. The most popular animals used were the fish – symbol of fertility; birds – depicted both for their song and as a symbol of the innermost soul (prosperity and a long life); doves – marital harmony. The rooster symbolized masculinity and power, the cock's crow at dawn represented light driving out dark spirits.

The most popular plant in decorative patterns was the vine: both grapes and tendrils, which represented rejoicing, prosperity, and fertility. Wheat and barley denoted abundance and fertility. The paisley (mango) design, usually connected with sweetness, made its way from India to Persia and Turkey, eventually settling in Europe. Another common image was the bote (shrub, pine, almond), which signified eternity and majesty, found in India, Persia, and Turkey. The rose was one of many flowers used, either embroidered or woven into the fabrics; it also originated in the Far East and drifted to Europe, Asia and Africa. Many other typical designs evolved in each community.

Esthetics It is customary in Judaism to treat the

bride and bridegroom on their wedding day as queen and king and this is reflected in the most lavish dress possible. In Yemen, to prevent embarrassment to the needy bride, a bridal outfitter ensured that her traditional bridal costume included even the most valuable items.

Artistic trends and styles which have influenced costume design since the eighteenth century can also be identified. In Europe contemporary fashions had a greater effect on dress than traditional elements. In Africa and Asia these factors began to make inroads only towards the end of the nineteenth century. Artistic motifs migrated in the wake of the Wandering Jew: itinerant pedlars who made their living on the road, and those who had no alternative, for example, following the expulsion from Spain under the Inquisition in the late fifteenth century. Various regional motifs merged with those from remote communities. Silk was brought to the Near East and Europe from China, India, Persia, and Afghanistan via the Silk Road by Jews and Gentiles alike. Spanish brocade, interwoven with gold thread, moved through Flanders and the Mediterranean Basin to the shores of Asia and Africa.

Jewish costume of the western world

Emancipation and assimilation into the Gentile world left its imprint on Jewish costume. Contemporary elements of fashion from each period were incorporated into Jewish dress, reflecting the prevailing spirit of European thought from the French Revolution at the end of the eighteenth century onwards.

Eastern Europe Jewish dress differed from Gentile dress until the middle of the eighteenth century. The decisions made by the Lithuanian Jewish Council (1732–62) directly affected the nature of dress. By the eighteenth century. Polish Jews had adopted typically upper class attire, basically the *caftan* and fur hat, with regional variations. The skullcap (*yarmulke*) and fur hat (*spodek*) became part of hasidic costume. A special hat – the *streimel* – was worn on the Sabbath, in Galicia and other places. Grander clothes were worn on the Sabbath: especially by women, but constraints of modesty shielded them from strangers: "All glorious is the king's daughter within the palace" (Psalms xlv.14).

The Jewish woman's dress was a chaste version of contemporary fashion. Yet even in the nineteenth century there were some uniquely Jewish items of dress: a beaded vestal trimmed with lace, worn over the dress; a *brusttukh* (breastplate) made of a rectangular strip of velvet or brocade, decorated with silk threads and precious stones; the apron, decorated with embroidery and ribbons, was worn typically by religious women.

The eighteenth-century Jewish woman wore a lace and silver decorated headdress on the Sabbath. In Lithuania and Russia she wore a lace shawl on her head, held down with colored ribbons, glass, and beads. Diamonds and pearls gradually ousted these commonplace decorations. The strictly observant woman ensured that her veil was made out of seven pieces, an allusion to the seven species. A tiara of diamonds, pearls, and gold on a velvet base was worn on the Sabbath. This tiara was in use until the nineteenth century when it was replaced by an intricate pearl and diamond headdress on a cloth base, which had to be made by a master craftsman. This too gradually fell into disuse. One pearl or one link in the decoration was always omitted as a reminder that while the Temple is destroyed there cannot be total happiness. By the twentieth century, a typical hat would be made of pleated brown or white satin trimmed with organdy ribbons and colored flowers.

Men wore a robe (*kapote*) made of expensive fabric such as velvet or shiny heavy silk, with a skullcap or a fur hat. Decrees by Czar Nicholas I in 1852 led to the disappearance of most of these traditional costumes. Natural wear and tear of cloth and organic materials, as well as the Holocaust at a later date, destroyed almost all remnants of the glorious costumes worn by Eastern European Jews.

Central and Western Europe In the mid-eighteenth century, rigid laws were enacted in places like Hamburg and Ancona (1766), imposing many restrictions on Jewish dress. Men were prohibited from wearing the minor *tallit*, so it became reserved for weddings only.

The costumes of Germany, Austria, Hungary, Switzerland, and Alsace-Lorraine had many similar features. The historian Johann Caspar Ulrich documented German–Jewish apparel as being predominantly black for men, while women were allowed to wear colors. Leaders of the community were recognized by a rounded white linen collar decorated with pleats. The trend towards assimilation in dress gained impetus in the eighteenth century. In 1781 the Emperor Josef II abolished all distinctions in dress, such as yellow cuffs worn by the Jews of Prague and yellow stripes worn by unmarried women. In Germany and Austria the custom of wearing Jewish costume was confined to the Sabbath. The artist Moritz OPPENHEIM left a wonderful record of traditional costumes of that period. Typical items of dress seen in his pictures were the three-cornered hat, three-quarter length breeches, tight at the knees, and buckled shoes. He even depicts the gift belt (*sivlonot*) worn by the bridegroom. In Hungary in the mid-nineteenth century, the Jews wore white or black silk stockings, silver-heeled shoes, colored waistcoats, and a tailed coat with silver buttons. The Rabbi wore his *streimel* on the Sabbath, and a boat-shaped hat during the week.

Oriental Jewish costume: China

The evolution of this costume goes hand in hand with the development and spread of the silk industry. Large numbers of people, including Jewish merchants, were attracted to China. Chinese Jews originally came from Persia, Turkestan and even Bukhara. Pottery figurines from the T'ang dynasty found at Kaifeng (618–907CE) display similarities in dress to ancient Persian and Semitic designs, suggesting that they were of Jews. Uniquely Jewish features gradually disappeared apparently because Jewish men married local women. An etching done by a Christian visitor to China in 1723 shows religious figures reading from the Torah, their costume unmistakably Chinese.

Jewish costume in Islamic countries: the Ottoman Empire

Jews prospered throughout the Empire. This led to the evolution of many geographic variations. Restrictions on the use of decorative elements for their own sake increased concomitantly with the distance between the Jewish settlement and the center of government, as in North Africa and Yemen. These restrictions were rapidly perceived by the Jews as being based on religion; for instance, a combination of dark colors (blue or black) signified mourning for the destruction of the Temple.

Documentation on costume from this period is found in an annotated album of etchings published by the French Ambassador in Turkey, M de Ferriol, in 1814. He describes Jewish men wearing black robes, and a violet-colored turban with a checkered border. This head covering (*kaveze*) was typical to the Jews of the Ottoman empire until the end of the nineteenth century. Typical Jewish costumes with their own unique style flourished in Smyrna and Salonika. Although Jewish and Gentile dress was dissimilar, Jewish women followed the customs of their Muslim counterparts regarding different dress at home and outside it. They wore somber and modest robes when they left the privacy of home. In Salonika the woman wore a dark cape over her dress, with a scarf (*yashmak*) over her head reaching to her chest and down her back. At home she would perhaps wear a wide-sleeved floral dress trimmed with fur, with a thick scarf totally covering her hair, the edges tucked in. The festive headdress in Salonika was trimmed with pearls, making it one of the most opulent items of attire. The *entari*, a long garment which distinguished married from unmarried women, formed the basis of their costume. Jewish women favored a style which was gathered at the waist with a wide opening at the breast, worn over a shirt. At a later date Jewish women adopted a long straight-cut robe, without gathers or folds, the Muslim *caftan*.

Bukharan Jewish costume (Uzbekistan)

Men wore a luxurious velvet cape with floral and geometric motifs embroidered with silk and gold threads. The coat opened down the front, revealing an ikat-dyed silk fabric cravat. These were made by Jewish artisans and hence enjoyed wide popularity. Ikat designs were based on brilliantly-hued flame (or paisley) patterns. A white shirt was worn under the coat, high leather boots and a colored brocade band on the head completed the costume. The woman's costume consisted of an overcoat made of local fabric cut along traditional lines. When she left her home she would wrap herself in an overcoat which covered her completely from neck to ankles. Dresses were straight and loose, made of embroidered velvet or brocade. Everyday dresses were made of soft, tie-dyed silk, also a typical creation of Bukharan Jewish craftsmen. The headdress consisted of a shawl topped with a gold embroidered domed cap, the latter being typical to both men and women. Women's boots were often made of pieces of colored leather sewn together with silk thread. Jewish men could be recognized by two identifying signs: a rope belt and a fur hat. The bride wore a special headdress of sequined white cotton tulle, with a *parchona* (a large jeweled gold ornament) on her forehead. This was sometimes the Star of David, as opposed to the Muslim *hamsa* design (the hand with five outstretched fingers). The bride wore her scarf spread over her head and back, while married and older women wore it tucked in around the edges.

Caucasian Jewish costume

For many generations the typical costume of these mountain Jews was a long coat with a tall fur hat. A sword was belted at the waist, a pistol at the shoulder, and cartridge belts around the chest, suggesting a reputation of bravery to match their fierce appearance.

North African Jewish costume

Several distinct forms of costume were discerned in Morocco. Town dress was typical of the north and west, along the Atlantic Ocean coast; rural costumes were found in the south, towards the Atlas mountains and the Sahara Desert. The attire of city Jews can be seen in paintings of the French Romantic School and the Orientalists of the nineteenth century, and the connection with the style of dress brought to Morocco after the expulsion from Spain is clearly visible. The "great dress" (*keswa el kbira*) was worn at weddings and other special family occasions, but after the mass Moroccan immigration to Israel in the mid twentieth century it assumed the role of typical Moroccan costume, and is usually worn at the *henna* (nuptials). The ensemble consists of a wrap-around skirt, a shirt with wide triangular sleeves, and a richly embroidered bodice and waistcoat, usually of green, blue, or purple velvet. The needlework is done on a cardboard cutout. A tiara of pearls and precious stones, worn with a long veil draped down the back, holds in place a fringe and two plaits of imitation hair. When the French came into power at the beginning of the twentieth century the *caftan* – a robe made of expensive fabric, heavily embroidered in gold, which was also popular amongst the Muslims – gained in popularity. This costume is frequently worn at family celebrations and the Mamouna festival.

In Tafilalet, near the Atlas Mountains, Jewish and Muslim dress differed in many respects. Jewish women favored red since it signified abundance and prosperity. The headdress consisted of a small embroidered cap with heavy woollen coils forming horns on either side of the head – tying the ribbons was often a ritual in itself – with a wide muslin veil. Dark colors played an important part in more formal wear, originally signifying Jewish servitude, but becoming over the years a symbol of the destruction of the Temple. Men wore a blue and white spotted scarf tied in front, while rabbis and important people were distinguished by a long black veil.

Diverse styles of head covering in various regions of Morocco denoted both Jewish identity and district of origin.

The style of women's clothing in Algeria drew its inspiration from Andalusia and Turkey. Men's clothing consisted of a shirt plus a long black or white overcoat worn over a *burnous* (cloak), and slippers. Jews wore a red skullcap edged with a light-colored fabric stripe. Women also wore black slippers; and in the street they covered their faces almost completely, as was the Muslim custom, with white tulle. The bride wore an abundance of jewelry. A characteristic headdress worn by the married woman in the nineteenth century was a tall coneshaped hat constructed with a metal framework. Typical of women's dress in the same period was a short-sleeved, low-cut tunic reaching down to the ankles, worn under a sleeveless robe which was open at the sides. Men wore a tasseled turban, with a long jacket reaching down to the hemline fastened with a row of buttons, and embroidered sleeves. Trousers were loose and gathered at the knees; shoes were backless mules.

Tunisian women wore white pants over white stockings, a short-sleeved embroidered jacket over a sleeveless tunic, a gold-embroidered pointed hat tied with red or gold silk ribbons, and slippers.

Libyan costume resembled that of the other North African countries. Men wore a long white robe with a linen or silk bodice fastened with huge buttons, a coat, and trousers. Women covered their heads with a large head square held in place with ribbons.

The cave-dwellers of Libya could be identified by their distinctive costumes. A striped fabric was draped around the body and head, and adorned with heavy jewelry. The robe was fastened with a crescent-shaped brooch.

In Djerba checkered fabric in primary colors (blue and yellow, red and blue) was worn for the *henna*. It was draped around the body like a toga over a floral or plaid shirt with one large sleeve decorated with brocade or silk, while the other sleeve (hidden from view) was made of a simple fabric. The Djerban woman wore a small hat tied flat over her forehead, trimmed with coins and tiny golden fish (symbolizing abundance and prosperity).

Kurdestan Jewish costume

The Jews wore clothing similar to that of their neighbors, often made from hand-woven sheep wool or goat hair. Very elegant suits made from this cloth were worn at weddings and other important occasions. The woman wore a wide underdress at home and at work in the fields; plus a bodice and a long coat. The man's suit consisted of two parts: a short jacket and loose trousers. A special cotton-padded overcoat was worn in the colder regions. Green and purple were especially popular colors. Older women took care to incorporate black into some items of their clothing. Town clothes were characterized by their bright colors, as opposed to predominant greys and browns of the village. Silk or brocade cloaks draped over the whole body and head were worn by many women, while an embroidered skullcap attached to a black and white head square was worn by men.

Jewish costume of Yemen

The Jews of South Arabia were always famous for their expertise as gold- and silversmiths. The wealth of motifs that abound testify to a long continuous tradition that predates the spread of Islam. Each item of dress and jewelry worn by the Jews of San'a has its own well-defined patterns and time-honored significance. The craft was passed down from father to son, thereby keeping it in the family. There are considerable differences in dress and jewelry between the San'a community and other districts, town–country differences being the most obvious. The rural work was usually much heavier and more crudely made than urban work.

The most opulent costume, used for the *henna* ceremony, was called the *teshbuch-lulu*. It consisted of an upper section (*antari*) often made of gold-threaded brocade and leggings, a magnificent headdress decorated with filligree and pearls, and many strands of neck and chest jewelry. Every single item had its own name and magical or historical significance. Embroidery, too, denoted status and even place of origin. It also served to distinguish ceremonial robes from everyday clothes and to denote marital status of the woman. It was customary in Yemen to cover the heads of their children (both girls and boys) with a special hood-like hat (*gargush*) with its own special embroidery and jewelry. After marriage it was replaced by a different sort of *gargush*. The *gargush* worn at festivals was especially grand.

On the whole, the costume of Yemenite Jews was dark colored, except for the brocade cloak worn for the *henna*. Inroads into age-old traditions began to be felt after the first wave of emigration to Palestine in 1882, and especially after the largest wave in the early 1950s – "Operation Magic Carpet". On the other hand, Yemenite needlework and jewelry have become an integral part of the local Israeli scene. In recent years renewed interest in the past and a return to the roots has prevented the disappearance of traditional motifs.

FURTHER READING

Cohen Grossman, G., ed.: *Jews of Yemen* (Chicago: Spertus College of Judaica Press, 1976)

Hacohen, D., and Hacohen, M.: *One People: The Story of Eastern Jews*, trans. I. I. Taslitt (New York: Sabra Books Funk & Wagnall, 1969)

Rubens, A.: *A History of Jewish Costume* (London: Vallentine & Mitchell, 1967)

Tchernowitz, N.: Marriage customs of Jews in north and east Yemen. *Israel – People and Land: Haaretz Museum Yearbook, vol. 1* (1983–84) 19

NITZA BEHROUZI

Cowen, Zelman (b.1919) Australian jurist, legal scholar, and administrator. Born and educated in Melbourne, Cowen was only 32 when he was appointed Professor of Public Law and Dean of the Law Faculty of the University of Melbourne, a position he held for 15 years. From 1970 to 1977 he served as Vice-Chancellor of Queensland University, and from 1967 to 1970, as Vice-Chancellor of the New England University in New South Wales. In 1977 he was appointed Governor-General of Australia. The institution of Governor-General was in considerable disrepute after the dismissal of the Whitlam government by Sir John Kerr, then Governor-General. Cowen restored its dignity and reinstated it as an acceptable institution of government. He was awarded four orders of knighthood, in 1976, 1977, and 1980.

Cowen fulfilled his early promise by following a career of extraordinary distinction, incorporating 14 honorary doctorates, numerous Fellowships, including that of the Royal Society of Arts, and the chairmanship of significant public bodies in Australia and abroad, including the Press Council of Great Britain. He was appointed Provost of Oriel College, Oxford, in 1982.

Cowen has served Jewish interests as ably. His lifelong interest in the Hebrew language was awakened when he excelled in its study as a student. Later he was the Victorian member of the Jewish Quarterly Foundation which published *The Bridge*, an Australian–Jewish quarterly journal. He has been an active fundraiser for Jewish causes, and one of the most successful international scholarly interchange schemes is the one founded in his name, the Sir Zelman Cowen Fund for the exchange of scholars between the Hebrew University in Jerusalem and the University of Sydney. He is a governor of the Hebrew University and chairman of the Van Leer Foundation in Jerusalem.

Cowen has published widely on legal topics, and has written a study of Sir Isaac Isaacs, the first Jewish Governor-General of Australia and also the first Australian to serve in that capacity.

ALAN D. CROWN

Crémieux, Adolphe (1796–1880) French statesman. After a brilliant legal career first in his native Nîmes and then in Paris, Crémieux entered political life in 1842 as deputy for Chinon. He participated in the 1848 revolution and became Minister of Justice in the provisional government which abolished the death penalty in France and slavery in the French colonies. After the Second Empire he returned to active political life in 1870 as member of the Government of National Defense and Minister of Justice. He was elected senator for life in 1875. Ardent in his allegiance to the ideals of the French Revolution, Crémieux was outspoken and fearless in his defense of Jewish rights both in France and abroad. He battled for 20 years for the abolition of the *more-judaico* oath (abolished in 1846). In 1840 he fought energetically and successfully, together with Sir Moses Montefiore, for the withdrawal of the ritual murder charge brought against a member of the Damascus Jewish community. Less successfully but no less vigorously he intervened on behalf of Russian and Romanian Jewry. His crowning success was the Crémieux law (1870) which accorded French citizenship to Algerian Jews. He became the first president of the ALLIANCE ISRAÉLITE UNIVERSELLE (1863) and remained one of its most active collaborators.

NELLY WILSON

D

Dahlberg, Edward (1900–1977) American novelist. Dahlberg, the illegitimate son of an itinerant hairdresser, was born in Boston. He was to spend a lifetime rewriting his autobiography. Before he was six his immigrant mother, Elizabeth, took him from city to city looking for work. Eventually they settled in Kansas City, Missouri, where she opened a ladies' barber shop. The local politicians, ranchers, and railroad men who frequented the shop reappeared in Dahlberg's first novel, *Bottom Dogs*, which was published in London in 1929, with a long introduction by D. H. Lawrence.

Dahlberg lived in a Cleveland orphanage from the time he was 12 until the age of 17. His memories of the Jewish Orphan Asylum figured in his second novel, *From Flushing to Calvary* (1932). For the next two years he held a variety of temporary jobs, from clerk to dishwasher. His hobo existence is retold in *Because I was Flesh: The Autobiography of Edward Dahlberg* (1964). From 1925 to 1928 Dahlberg traveled throughout Europe. He saw the rise of Nazism in Germany. *Those Who Perish* (1934), dealt with the impact of Hitler on a small American–Jewish community, reworking what he had witnessed. Dahlberg's poetry was later collected in *Cipango's Hinder Door* (1965), published by the University of Texas at Austin.

Dahlberg's brief involvement with the Communist Party is recounted in *The Confessions of Edward Dahlberg* (1971). His long friendship with Sir Herbert Read resulted in the eventual publication of their correspondence, *Truth is More Sacred: A Critical Exchange on Modern Literature by Edward Dahlberg and Herbert Read* (1961).

Read wrote the preface for *Do These Bones Live?* when it was reprinted in London in 1947, the introduction to the London edition of *The Flea of Sodom* (1950), printed by Peter Nevill, and the foreward for *Alms for Oblivion* (1964).

FURTHER READING

DeFanti, C. L., Jr.: *The Wages of Expectation: A Biography of Edward Dahlberg* (New York: New York University Press, 1979)

Moramarco, F.: *Edward Dahlberg* (New York: Twayne, 1972)

RUTH ROSENBERG

Daiches, David (b.1912) Scottish literary scholar and critic. Daiches, the son of an Orthodox rabbi, was born in Sunderland and grew up in Edinburgh. Educated at the Universities of Edinburgh and Oxford, he taught English literature at the Universities of Chicago, Cornell, Cambridge, and Sussex and before retiring he was the director of the Institute for Advanced Studies in the Humanities at Edinburgh University.

A wide-ranging and prolific author, Daiches has written more than 40 books. His critical studies of modern literature, such as, *The Novel and the Modern World* (1939), *Poetry and the Modern World* (1940), *Virginia Woolf* (1942), *Critical Approaches to Literature* (1956) *A Critical History of English Literature* (1960), *English Literature* (1965), did much to establish the academic place of the study of contemporary literature.

In 1956 he published his first autobiographical volume, *Two Worlds: An Edinburgh*

Jewish Childhood, in which he presents the view that these two very different "worlds" were not in conflict as he was growing up. This study offers a moving portrait of his father whilst tracing the stages in his own rejection of Judaism. These two "worlds" have been the subject of much of his writing. Drawing on his background and knowledge of Hebrew, from his doctoral thesis, *The King James Bible: a Study of its Sources and Development* (1941), via *Moses* (1975) to *God and the Poets* (1984), he has written essays on: contemporary Judaism; the translation of the Hebrew Bible; Jewish liturgy and the major role of the Bible in literature; and religion and the Bible. These have all been persistent and dominant themes in his writings.

Scotland, the other "world", has been his other main scholarly concern, and his work in this field has led him to be considered a major figure in the study of Scottish literature and culture. His early studies of *Robert Louis Stevenson* (1947), and Walter Scott (1951), were significant factors in the revival of scholarly interest in these two neglected authors. He has also published, on matters Scottish, studies ranging from, *Robert Burns* (1950), *Sir Walter Scott and his World* (1971), *Robert Louis Stevenson and his World* (1973), *Robert Furgusson* (1982), *The Paradox of Scottish Culture* (1964), *Scotland and the Union* (1977), *Literature and Gentility in Scotland* (1982), to *Charles Edward Stuart: the Life and Times of Bonnie Prince Charlie* (1982), and *Scotch Whisky: Its Past and Present* (1969).

Other works include two further volumes of autobiography, *A Third World* (1971) and *Was: A Pastime from Time Past* (1975).

PAUL M. MORRIS

Dan, Joseph (b.1935)   Scholar of Jewish mysticism. Dan was born in Bratislava, Czechoslovakia. His family emigrated to Palestine in 1938. Dan studied at the Hebrew University, Jerusalem, and accepted a teaching post there in 1959, becoming associate professor and more recently, professor of *kabbalah*. In 1983 he was appointed the Gershom Scholem Professor of *kabbalah* in the Department of Jewish Thought.

Early in his academic career, Dan directed his studies towards the ideology of Judaism, with particular reference to Hasidism. His Ph.D. thesis, supervised by Gershom SCHOLEM and Ephraim URBACH, dealt with the theological basis of the ethical thought of Ashkenazi Hasidism. He subsequently published extensively on hasidic literature, history, and thought.

Dan broadened his range of Jewish study, producing his 5-volume work *Ideological Movements and Conflicts in Jewish History* in 1978. The research for this work led him into deeper analysis of Jewish mysticism, and especially the origins and history of kabbalistic tradition. He has concentrated on the development of the *kabbalah*, isolating individual themes such as the concept of evil and the paradox of nothingness. Dan is a leading scholar of the *kabbalah* and has contributed extensively to international symposia and scholarly journals on the subject in Hebrew, German, and English. He is the author of "Jewish Studies after Gershom Scholem" in the *Encyclopaedia Judaica Year Book 1983/85*, as well as "Jewish Ethical Literature" and "Hasidism: Overview" in *The Encyclopaedia of Religion*, vol. viii, published in 1987.

Aside from academic research, Dan was a member of the Council of Higher Education of the State of Israel from 1981 to 1986 and has sat on the Board of Directors of the World Union of Jewish Studies since 1979. He is also the editor of *Jerusalem Studies in Jewish Thought*.

JOHN MATTHEW

dance, Israeli   Besides the many folk-dance groups, some of which travel abroad so often as to be almost professional, Israel has six professional art dance companies, with a seventh making its debut in Jerusalem in 1988. Most of the companies have subscription series – members running into several thousands in the case of the Bat-Dor company – and all of them frequently tour abroad. All of them, except Kol Demama, have guest choreographers from abroad, as well as Israelis.

The oldest company is the Inbal Dance Theater, launched in 1949, when the State had hardly progressed beyond its Declaration of Independence, and was still struggling against hostile forces. There were antecedents: a migra-

A traditional Moroccan dance at the Mimouna (Maimouna) celebrations in Jerusalem

tion of Yemenites even before the "Magic Carpet" (1948–50) had prompted Rina Nikova, a dancer from the USSR, to form a "Yemenite Singing Ballet" in the 1930s. It closed down but a decade later Sara Levi-Tanai, born in Jerusalem of Yemenite parents, revived the idea. She gathered the dances as well as dancers from the Yemenite Jewish community, but the word "Yemenite" was later dropped from the name when she saw the wisdom of introducing other ethnic Jewish material into her choreography. In 1985 the Inbal Dance Theater was invited to Spain to participate in the 850th anniversary of the birth of Maimonides in Cordoba. Sara Levi-Tanai is still its artistic director/choreographer.

There were attempts at forming modern dance companies in the 1950s, such as the Lyric Theater of American choreographer, Anna Sokolow, but it was not until 1964 that anything

permanent was achieved. Baroness Bethsabee (Batsheva) de Rothschild, who settled in Israel in 1958, decided to found a modern company. Martha Graham, a close friend, as artistic adviser gave permission for some of her works to be staged, and most of the dancers went to New York to train in her studios.

When the Batsheva Dance Company celebrated its tenth anniversary in 1974 Graham herself came to create a work, *The Dream*, based on the story of Jacob. However, in 1975, when de Rothschild proposed that to reduce costs the Batsheva company should merge with the Bat-Dor she had founded in 1968, the Batsheva company refused and "went public". It has since had a series of exceptional artistic directors – Paul Sanasardo, Brian Macdonald, Jane Dudley, William Louther, among others – who altered its style, especially as Graham had withdrawn her works.

The Bat-Dor [Contemporary] Dance Company, founded in 1968, has had Jeannette Ordman as principal dancer and artistic director from its inception, also as director of the Bat-Dor Studios founded the previous year. Ordman's aim was to create a blend of classical and modern techniques, then rare, that has given the company a distinctive character. Ordman herself has appeared in many roles, some in works by Israeli choreographer Domy Reiter-Soffer.

The Israel Ballet was founded by two Israeli classical dancers, Berta Yampolsky and Hillel Markman, who had been members of French companies and the Ballet Russe de Monte Carlo, but returned to Israel and opened a studio. By 1967 they had formed a company which they were still directing in 1988, first called Classical Ballet, now capable of staging full-length ballets like *Cinderella*. Yampolsky herself has made notable contributions to the repertory.

The Kibbutz Dance Company, founded at Ga'aton in the Galilee by Yehudit Arnon, a survivor of Auschwitz, celebrated its 20th anniversary in 1986. All the dancers of this company are members of kibbutzim, with Arnon still in charge. One fine young choreographer, Rami Be'er, born at Ga'aton, has emerged from the company.

Moshe Efrati has added something unique to the Israel dance scene: in 1965 he began to train deaf young dancers by devising a system of floor vibrations and other signals. His deaf group, called *Demama*, was amalgamated in 1975 with his hearing group, the new group being called *Kol Demama* (sound and silence or the sound of silence). His choreography makes no concessions and during performance it is impossible to distinguish the deaf dancers.

Apart from *Kol Demama*, all the Israeli companies have guest choreographers both Israeli and from abroad. Most widely known is Domy Reiter-Soffer who has created many works for the Bat-Dor Company and has worked extensively for the Irish National Ballet. His works are also performed in the USA (by several Companies), Australia, and Yugoslavia. Choreographers who returned to work with companies in Israel include Igal Perry (New York), Ohad Naharin (New York), Ya'acov Sharir (Austin, Texas), Margalit Oved (California), Ze'eva Cohen (New York) and Mirali Sharon (New York).

The seventh company, called Tamar Jerusalem Dance Company, consists of Israeli dancers, most of them returning from abroad. They will also teach at the Tamar school, and will be officially under the auspices of the Jerusalem Foundation.

The only institution in Israel where a degree in dance is obtainable is the Jerusalem Rubin Academy Dance Department, linked to the Hebrew University.

FURTHER READING

Sowden, D.: The Bat-Dor Company. *Ariel* 52 (1982)
——: The Israel Ballet. *Ariel* 62 (1985)
——: Inbal Dance Theatre. *Ariel* 70 (1987)

DORA SOWDEN

dance, Jewish contribution to Jews have always danced, as biblical references make plain. Jewish dancers appeared in Classical Rome and in medieval Europe. In the fifteenth century a dancer-teacher, Guglielmo Ebreo of Pesaro, wrote a treatise on dance; in the sixteenth century Jacchino Massarano danced in Rome. Curiously, Jewish participation in dance was less conspicuous in the early days of the Emancipation. Later, in 1775, the Pope granted permission to at least two notable personalities, Grescian Azziz and Emanuel de Rabbi Jalomoacis, to teach dancing and singing.

The eighteenth century

The Jewish contribution to dance in the eighteenth century was remarkable, through hasidic dance. In the ghettos and Pales of Settlement in Eastern Europe, the Ba'al shem tov's approval of dance in the expression of joy and faith encouraged hasidic dance with developed stylized steps that have passed not only into Israeli folk dance but have filtered into art dance in Israel and elsewhere.

The nineteenth century

The first Jewish dancer–choreographer of note in the nineteenth century was Arthur Saint-Léon (1821–70), choreographer of the famous ballet *Coppélia*. In his *Stenochoreographia* (1862) he advocated the addition of a line to the music staff where markings would indicate dance movements: this was one of the first systems of dance notation. Today, one of the three major notation systems in use was created in Israel by Noa Eshkol and Avraham Wachman (the Eshkol–Wachman system), and the first International Movement Notation Conference was held in Israel in 1983. As the nineteenth century advanced, Jews became more conspicuously involved in theater dance and, by the twentieth century, even more: Diaghilev's star ballerinas included Ida Rubinstein (1883–1960) and Anna Pavlova (1881–1931), the latter variously said to have been christened, to have had a Jewish mother, and to have confided to impresario Sol Hurok that her father was Jewish.

Modern times

Prominent Jewish dancers in the USSR include Asaf Messerer (now a Bolshoi teacher), his sister Sulamith (teaching in London), their niece Maya Plisetskaya (Bolshoi prima ballerina), her brother Azari Plisetsky, and Mikhail, Sulamith's son. Among those who left the USSR to enrich the West are Valery Panov and his wife Galina (who carry Israeli passports), Alexander Livschitz and his wife Emma (to teach in Jerusalem), Leonid and Valentina Koslov (to dance in Australia) and David Shur (to teach at the Bat-Dor studios in Tel Aviv).

Hasidic dance from Fiddler on the Roof *(1971)*

In Britain, two Jewish ballerinas received the DBE (Dame of the British Empire) – Marie Rambert in 1962, and Alicia Markova in 1968. London-born Markova (Lillian Alicia Marks) danced principal roles in the first British productions of the classics. Regarded as a great Giselle, she entitled her autobiography *Giselle and I* (1960).

Among the numerous Jewish dancers of the USA few are innovators – except perhaps Meredith Monk – but most show individuality as dancers, choreographers, directors, and founders of companies. Writer Lincoln Kirstein brought Balanchine to New York, and founded the School of American Ballet and the New York City Ballet (NYCB). Jerome Robbins, now co-director of the NYCB, is famous as the choreographer of *West Side Story*. Anna Sokolow, a dancer in Martha Graham's company, became a choreographer of social comment. Star dancer Nora Kaye (1920–87) formed a company with her husband, Herbert Ross, and choreographed *The Dybbuk* (1960) based on Sh. An-Ski's play. Other prominent Americans, many of whom formed companies, include Melissa Hayden, Pauline Koner, Bella Lewitzky, Laura Dean, Martha Clarke, Lar Lubovitch, Matthew Diamond, and, among an increasing number who have introduced Jewish themes into their choreography, are Sophie Maslow, Pearl Lang, Helen Tamaris, and Eliot Field. After leaving Graham's company, Robert Cohan became

161

director of the London Contemporary Dance School and company – thus establishing modern dance firmly in Britain.

The works of the most renowned Israeli choreographer, Domy Reiter-Soffer, are performed in the USA, Ireland, Australia, and Yugoslavia. The Dance Theatre of Harlem (New York) staged his *Equus* and *La Mer* at the 1987 Salzburg Festival. He has created many works for the Bat-Dor company, several with Jewish content. Yemen-born Margalit Oved, Inbal dancer in Israel, has introduced a new form of ethnic theater dance in California.

Ivan Marko is founder–director of the Gyori Ballet, Hungary, and is guest choreographer for the Kibbutz Company. Mauricio Wainrot, dancer–director–choreographer from Buenos Aires, is choreographing in Canada, Germany, and Israel. South African-born John Cranko (1927–73) developed as choreographer in London and, as director–choreographer, gave the Stuttgart Ballet world status. He created *Song of My People – Forest People – Sea* for the Batsheva company.

There are six professional companies in Israel, two of which (both modern) were founded by Baroness Bethsabee (Batsheva) de Rothschild when she settled in Israel: the Batsheva Dance Company (1964) and the Bat-Dor Dance Company (1968). The others are the Inbal Dance Theater (ethnic, 1949), The Kibbutz Dance Company (modern, 1965), the Israel Ballet (classical, 1967), and the *Kol Demama* (deaf and hearing dancers, modern, 1978). The Tamar Jerusalem Dance Theater is the latest addition (1988). All the existing companies tour abroad frequently.

One of Israel's greatest achievements is the creation of its folk dance. While elsewhere folk dance develops over centuries, in Israel it was an almost instant phenomenon. Out of the dances that pioneers brought with them and the dances of people already in the land – Arabs as well as Jews – a new dance form, distinctly Israeli, was born. Its arrival was signaled at the first Dalia Festivals in 1944 and 1947. Israeli folk dance is now studied and taught in many countries, including the USA, where Fred Berk (1911–80) was a dominant figure in its promotion.

See also DANCE, ISRAELI.

FURTHER READING

de Mille, A.: *Dance to the Piper* (New York: Bantam, 1953)

Rosen, S.: The Middle Ages. In Besk, F.: *Mahol ha'am* (American Zionist Youth Foundation, 1978)

DORA SOWDEN

Danziger, Itzhak (1916–1978) Israeli artist. Danziger was born in Berlin of intellectual, artistic, and Zionist parents who emigrated to Jerusalem in 1923. From the start, Danziger's art had one aim: to create unity with his environment. His work thus defies such characterization as sculpture, painting, or architecture, and goes beyond the accepted patterns of the plastic arts. Danziger's art is interdisciplinary, and anything is used to serve his means: ecology, geography, anthropology, and archaeology.

His art continuously integrates contradictory forces: the unyielding desert with life and fruitfulness, the pagan with the religious. By combining these varied elements into one, time ceases to exist as a limiting factor and is replaced by the idea of endless cycles and their relationship to nature. This concept is reflected in such works as *The Rehabilitation of the Nesher Quarry* (1971) and *The Golan Tree-Planting Ceremony* (1977).

Jerusalem provided Danziger with many early childhood experiences that would find their way into his art: the sight of the Moslem Quarter within the Old City, the sheep that flooded the Arab market on Friday, the closeness between himself and other young Jewish and Arab students who attended the Calvin Private School, the archaeological discoveries in Jerusalem of that period, and the inspiration of his father, who was both a pianist and an artist. It was not, however, until 1934, when he was attending The Slade School of Art at London University, that these influences merged in Danziger's art under the tutelage of A. H. Gerrard, who was then head of the sculpture department. Gerrard's emphasis on the value of primitive art, both its style and use of material, caused Danziger to turn his attention to the ancient cultures of Sumer, Egypt, India, and Africa. The influence of these cultures on the artist can be seen in his early works; indeed, his now-famous *Nimrod*, in combining the idea of the old and the new, created a revolution in Israeli sculpture.

Danziger returned to Israel in 1955 and began teaching three-dimensional design at the Technion–Israel Institute of Technology in Haifa (a position he maintained until his untimely death in an automobile accident in 1978). In 1958, he completed a large stone relief (3.5 × 70 m) for the outside wall of the Givat Ram campus of The Hebrew University in Jerusalem. In 1965, in collaboration with Shamai Haber, he completed the largest statue ever erected in Israel: a 1,000-meter square "graphic stain" on the slopes facing the Valley of the Cross, at the entrance to the Israel Museum in Jerusalem. Danziger was represented at the Olympic Games in Mexico City in 1968 through his contribution of a massive concrete sculpture entitled *Brotherhood*. From 1968 until his death, Danziger continued to develop his art and environment ideas through highway sculpture, war memorials, and landscape architecture.

ELAINE SHEFER

Darmesteter, James [Y. D. Lefrançais] (1849–1895) French orientalist. He was born in Lorraine to which his paternal ancestors had emigrated in the eighteenth century from the Darmstadt ghetto. Both on the paternal and maternal sides (his mother descended from the Brandeis family) there had been distinguished Jewish scholars and rabbis. The family moved to Paris in the 1850s where James and his brother Arsène were educated. Sons of a poor bookbinder barely able to feed his family (James's ill-health is often attributed to the early poverty), the boys won various scholarships which took them to the most prestigious establishments where they both distinguished themselves. Arsène (1846–88), who originally trained to be a rabbi at the Jewish seminary, specialized in philology and medieval French in which he was later professor at the Sorbonne. He is the co-author (with Hatzfeld) of a dictionary of the French language. James then went to the *lycées* Charlemagne and Condorcet, followed by the École Normale Supérieure. He taught at the Collège de France and the École des Hautes Études. Intellectually brilliant and versatile, he eventually made his reputation in ancient Persian language and literature. Together with Renan, his admired teacher, he was one of France's brightest stars, honored in his life-time and mourned by the academic community when he died at the age of 45. He was married to the English writer Mary Robinson. Although his ardent republicanism did not lead to any direct political involvement, it made him sensitive to the turmoil threatening the stability of the young, strife-torn Third Republic. Under the name of Y. D. Lefrançais he wrote a popular history for schoolchildren, *Lectures Patriotiques sur l'Histoire de France à l'Usage de l'Enseignement Primaire* (1882), and in 1893 he assumed the political editorship of the *Revue de Paris*. His most popular work, *Les Prophètes d'Israël* (1892), represents an attempt to reconcile the two major warring intellectual factions: materialists/atheists/modernists, given to transforming science into a religion, and traditionalists rejecting modern science. The Jewish prophetic tradition is proposed as a reconciling force, capable of revitalizing a dying, outmoded Catholicism and of bringing a moral and spiritual dimension to science. Though evidently indebted to Renan and to Joseph SALVADOR (to whom the last chapter is devoted), the reconciliation here advocated owes most to Darmesteter's personal search, following his mother's tragic death in 1880, for a religion which would harmonize the different phases of his life and strands in his personality: Jewish childhood – atheist scholar; ironic intellectual – messianic dreamer; modernity – love of the past. The return to religious roots, albeit in the form of a Judaism both highly personal and entirely divorced from the Jewish community, posed no problem for the patriotic Frenchman. Jewish prophetic traditions were seen to fuse perfectly with the ideals of the French Revolution and with the Republic's efforts to put these ideals into practice. Republican France had assimilated and was in the process of institutionalizing Jewish values and aspirations: unity, justice, equality, and a paradise on earth. This was the first systematic formulation of Franco-Jewish symbiosis. It was to inspire French Jewry and anti-Semitism alike for years to come. If the "Israelites of France" did not always fully appreciate the judaization postulated here, that is that Jerusalem had emancipated Paris, it was not lost on conservative anti-Semites delighted to discover such authoritative confirmation of their view of Judaism as a subversive force, a threat to traditional Christian and French values.

FURTHER READING

Spire, A.: *Quelques Juifs et Demi-Juifs* (Paris: Grasset, 1928)

Marrus, M. R.: *The Politics of Assimilation* (Oxford: Oxford University Press, 1971) 100–110

NELLY WILSON

Daube, David (b.1909)   British legal scholar. A product of German Jewry, Daube achieved early mastery in the classics and in Talmud along with his brother Benjamin, whose work in Greek law and literature was soon to exert profound influence. He began to study music and literature in Paris, and later studied Roman law under Otto Lenel in his native Freiburg and then under Wolfgang Kunkel in Göttingen, where he was also introduced to Old Testament criticism by Johannes Hempel.

Sent from Nazi oppression to Cambridge by Lenel, Daube pursued his work in Roman law under W. W. Buckland and joined C. H. Dodd's seminar on the New Testament. He maintained for many years an Orthodox religious stance as well as an attachment to his South German background. Latterly his sense that religious systems claimed to know too much loosened his adherence to a strictly observant Jewish life. His interest, however, in the questions that religions raise was intense and, like Ludwig WITTGENSTEIN, he would claim that the most important matters are beyond human comprehension and that only the fringes can be explored.

In academic circles his reputation has been that of the foremost humanist of the law. The reputation was founded on his erudition in many areas of knowledge and the unique manner in which he communicated it both orally and in a great range of publications. Although striking, the erudition is not the key to his uniqueness. From his absorption in the intricacies of different legal traditions he was alert to those elements in the law that also find expression in the world of literature, Greek, Roman, Jewish, and Christian.

His illumination of literary and religious texts that require an appreciation of some legal matter has given his scholarship a distinctive stamp. His originality, however, is difficult to characterize because, rather than any systematic discussion of a topic or theme, it is invariably his way of looking at a text that is memorable and gives his work the mark of true novelty. He exemplifies Goethe's remark that to think is more interesting than to know but less interesting than to see.

During an active teaching career, Daube's unbounded intellectual energy has become a well-recognized force in the diverse cultures of Cambridge, Aberdeen, Oxford, Berkeley (California), and Constanz. At all times and places he has fastened onto current issues, looked at the way in which they were handled in the past, sought to say something new about our understanding of that past, and tried to show that its perspective may have some relevance for modern life. He has devoted equal energy to training a select number of pupils (now in important academic positions throughout the world) in the many different areas of his own interest – Greek, Roman, and Jewish law, Greek, Latin, rabbinic, Old and New Testament literature. Honorary degrees (Cambridge, Edinburgh, Göttingen, Hebrew Union College, Leicester, Munich, Paris) and honorary lectureships (for example, Gifford, Edinburgh, in philosophy and theology; Gray, Cambridge, in classics; Jordan, London in comparative religion; Lord Cohen, Jerusalem, in medical ethics; Messenger, Cornell, in the humanities; Petrie, Uppsala, in law and theology) give some measure of his standing in the international world of scholarship.

BIBLIOGRAPHY

Studies in Biblical Law (Cambridge: Cambridge University Press, 1947); *The New Testament and Rabbinic Judaism* (London; Athlone Press, 1956); *Roman Law* (Edinburgh: Edinburgh University Press, 1969)

CALUM CARMICHAEL

Davidson, Israel [David Ze'ev Movshovitz] (1870–1939)   American rabbinic scholar. Born in Yonava in Lithuania, Davidson lost his father when he was two years old and his mother when he was six. Adopted by his uncle, Rabbi Isaac

Klebansky in Grodno, Davidson was educated at the *yeshivah* of Grodno and Slobodka. In 1888 he escaped to the USA, and at that time changed his name to Davidson, not wanting to choose between the family names of his father and uncle. As he had arrived with neither money nor a word of English, he began selling matches and shoelaces on the street. He then became an assistant in a grocery store and, after being dismissed from the job, he began to teach Hebrew. At the same time he studied English and in 1902 he received his Ph.D. from Columbia University. He then became a chaplain of the prisons of Dannemora and Sing Sing.

In 1905 Davidson began teaching at the Jewish Theological Seminary of America, but due to his financial situation, he was obliged to hold three other positions, including that of Principal of the Hebrew Orphan Asylum, which he held until 1917. In spite of all this he found time to publish his first book, *Parody in Jewish Literature* (1907). The preface was written in English and in the book Davidson defined parody in general and characterized Jewish parody. The peak of his creativity is the *Otzar hashirah vehapiyyut* (Thesaurus of medieval Hebrew poetry) in four volumes, the first of which appeared in 1924. This became a basic reference book for scholars. It is a work of identification, classification, and description of 35,000 poems, and for it Davidson received the first Bialik Prize in 1936.

By opening medieval Hebrew literature to the non-Hebraist scholar, Davidson's work marked a turning point in Jewish studies. His books enable even the non-specialist student to gain access to a field which was always highly specialized. The books he published in this system include *Joseph ibn Zabara's Sefer Sha'ashu'im*, 1914, with an English introduction (1925, with a Hebrew introduction), and *Saadia's Polemic against Hiwi al Balkhi* (1915). He also published English translations by Israel Zangwill of Ibn Gabirol's poetry, poems from *Ginzei Schechter*, and the Cairo Genizah.

Before his death, Davidson left his daughters a list of his unfinished works together with precise instructions for their completion. The most important of these was *Otzar hameshalim vehapitgamim misifrut yemei habeinayim* (A treasury of proverbs from medieval literature), which was published 18 years after his death.

DEBORAH SCHECHTERMAN

De Haan, Jacob Israel (1881–1924)

Dutch author, journalist, and lawyer, brother of the novelist and essayist Carry van BRUGGEN. De Haan was born into an Orthodox family, his father being a cantor. In 1904 he published the novel, *Pijpelijntjes*, in which he described quite openly the homosexual relationship between two students living in an Amsterdam working-class quarter. De Haan, at that time a teacher in an elementary school, was dismissed because of the scandal his novel had created; it also cost him his job as editor of the children's page of a socialist newspaper. Because of the resulting emotional crisis and in spite of having married a non-Jewish woman, De Haan found his way back to the Orthodoxy of his youth. From this time on his poems acquired a strong Jewish religious and national character and he designated himself "the poet of the Jewish song". It was at this time that he began his legal studies.

In 1912 De Haan had joined the *Mizrahi*, the Orthodox party of the Zionist Organization, and in 1919 he emigrated to Palestine. He was provided with a moderate salary as Palestine correspondent of the *Algemeen Handelsblad*, a leading Dutch newspaper. The serials he wrote mostly for this journal ran to more than 400 parts, and they achieved great popularity because of the witty and poetic style in which daily life in Palestine was pictured. In 1920 he was appointed lecturer in commercial and criminal law at the Law School in Jerusalem established by the Mandate government. During the years in Palestine, however, his views on the moral and practical implications of Zionism underwent a deep change. He became affiliated with the *Agudah*, the Orthodox party opposed to the claims of Zionism. He criticized the manner in which Zionism ignored the interests of this Orthodoxy, as well as those of the Arab population, and he became spokesman for the *Agudah* to the British authorities. This, and the fact that his criticism was expressed in non-Jewish newspapers, among them the *Daily Express*, led to the antagonism of the Palestinian *halutzim* who suspected him of having secret dealings not only with the Mandate government, but also with Arab nationalists to harm the Zionist cause. However, historical research has not so far revealed grounds for this last accusation, although De Haan had contacts with many Arabs. De Haan's tragedy was his utter intransigency. In 1924 he was shot by a Zionist terrorist group, the first political murder in the Jewish National Home. After his death De Haan's *Kwatrijnen* were published, poems which revealed the full extent of the torture of repressed homosexuality, the utter loneliness of his Palestinian life, and the longing for a religiousness he could never attain.

His poems were much admired by contemporary as well as later critics, and all were collected in two volumes in 1952.

LUDY GIEBELS

De Haan, Meyer I. (1852–1895) Dutch painter. He studied with the painter P. F. Greive in Amsterdam, where he spent most of his career, though he also lived for some years in France. Chiefly a painter of portraits, both of individuals and groups, he executed a number of works on Jewish themes, including *Portrait of an Old Jewish Woman* and *A Difficult Place in the Talmud*, which shows three scholars at a table with a copy of the Talmud. This picture was reproduced in 1880 by the Protestant theologian Hendrik Oort of Leiden University in a pamphlet attacking the Talmud, which gave rise to retaliatory publications by the rabbis Tobias Tal, Lion Wagenaar and Jacob Vreedenburg in a controversy that lasted for more than a decade. Among De Haan's Jewish pupils were painters such as L. J. Hartz, B. López de Leao Lagua, and C. Pothuis.

HENRIETTE BOAS

Deinard, Ephraim (1846–1930) Hebrew author, bibliographer, and bookseller. Born in Sasmakken, Latvia, he was young when he began his travels, which he described in a number of books. On his many trips through Europe and the Near East he collected rare books and manuscripts, which he later sold to libraries.

Deinard's long career was divided between Russia and the USA. In Russia he published his first book, *Toledot Even Rashaf* (1875; The biography of Even Rashaf), an attack upon the Karaite scholar, Abraham FIRKOVITCH, whom he accused of various forgeries. Other works, such as *Sefer massa' krim* (1878; A journey to Crimea), and *Sefer massa' bahatzi ha'i krim* (A journey through the Crimean peninsula), presented historical and demographic data on these areas. In Odessa, where Deinard opened a bookstore in 1880, he continued to engage in literary and publishing activity. Following a visit to Palestine in 1881, he advocated emigration to Palestine and opposed the efforts of the ALLIANCE ISRAÉLITE UNIVERSELLE to settle Jews in the USA.

Despite Deinard's enthusiastic support of the early Zionist movement, he was led by deteriorating conditions to emigrate to the USA in 1888. Except for the years 1913–16, during which he lived in Palestine, he spent the rest of his life in the USA. While he continued to agitate for Zion, he also stressed the importance of agricultural work and helped found an agricultural colony in Nevada in 1897.

Deinard's main preoccupation, however, was as a bookseller. Convinced that America was to become a center of Jewish scholarship, he sought to place his collections in libraries. Among the libraries that acquired Hebrew books and manuscripts through his efforts were the Jewish Theological Seminary, the Library of Congress, Columbia University, and Harvard University. As a veteran bibliophile, Deinard prepared a number of bibliographies. In 1896 he issued *Or Mayer* which listed the holdings of Judge Mayer Sulzberger of Philadelphia. His *Kohelet America* (1926) contains a comprehensive listing of the Hebrew books printed in the USA from 1735 to 1926.

Throughout his life Deinard was a stormy petrel, engaging in sharp polemics. A prolific writer, he was the author of more than fifty books and pamphlets.

FURTHER READING

Berkowitz, S. B.: Ephraim Deinard: bibliophile and

bookman. *Studies in Bibliography and Booklore* 9 (1971) 137–142

Schapiro, I.: Ephraim Deinard. *Proceedings of the American Jewish Historical Society* 34 (1947) 149–163

JACOB KABAKOFF

Della Torre, Lelio Hillel (1805–1871)

Italian teacher, exegete and poet. He was born into a family of modest means in Cuneo, Piedmont but, after being orphaned at a young age, he was brought up by his maternal uncle, the Rabbi of Asti, Piedmont.

He began studying Hebrew while little more than an infant, and by the age of six he was already able to translate complex passages of the Bible into Italian. He learnt Latin and Greek only at grave cost, since their study was held to be sacrilegious by the cultural milieu which surrounded him. On his uncle's transferral to Turin, Della Torre followed him, and began his teaching career at the Collegio Colonna e Finzi where he worked from 1823 to 1829. In Turin he was able to deepen his knowledge of the classical languages and Italian literature.

The lack of prestige enjoyed by rabbis in the smaller Italian communities decided Della Torre against ever accepting such a post. In 1829 the Collegio Rabbinico Italiano was founded in Padua. It was the first school of Jewish theology in Europe, and aimed to provide its students with, among other things, an adequate literary foundation. Della Torre was appointed to teach the Talmud and theology, and retained this post from 1829 until his death.

Della Torre's thought is representative of the religious Italian Jew on the path to emancipation: he was against any type of Reform since, in his opinion, this had had such negative results in Germany. He felt a deep attachment to Italy, which he considered as a benevolent country of adoption. He was learned in the fields of philology, exegetics, and theology, and left numerous works in Hebrew, French, and German, as well as Italian. In his poetry, collected in two volumes entitled *Tal yaldut* (The dew of youth), and *Eglei tal* (1869; Dewdrops), he describes the city of his birth, and his life. He also wrote a satire on the times called *Olam hafukh* (1866; The world upside down). He translated the Psalms into Italian (1845) and produced a commentary, only the first volume of which was published (1854). He also, for pleasure, worked on Hebrew translations of the poetry of Petrarch and Metastasio.

Della Torre's death was mourned by Jews and Gentiles alike; in his native city of Cuneo he was commemorated on a memorial stone alongside other illustrious citizens.

FURTHER READING

Della Torre, M., and Delle Torre, E., eds: *Scritti Sparsi, Preceduti da uno Studio Biografico Intorno all'Autore*, 2 vols (Padua, 1908)

GABRIELLA MOSCATI-STEINDLER

demography, Jewish

1700 to 1939

The size and structure of world Jewish population during the Middle Ages and early modern period cannot be accurately assessed, but fragmentary evidence points to a range between one and two million persons. While population size tended to be stable in the long term, major fluctuations reflected occasional catastrophic events. These included epidemics, often the outcome of famine and wars, and usually shared by Jews and non-Jews; but Jewish population also declined following massacres, mass expulsions, and forced conversions that repeatedly occurred in different countries. After the second half of the seventeenth century, a diminished incidence of these negative factors, and modest improvements in general standards of living, allowed for Jewish population growth to build up. World Jewry rose from an estimated million around 1700 to 2.5 million around 1800, and 10.6 million around 1900. Jewish population growth rates during this period were higher than among most other national populations in Europe, Asia, and Africa. Most of the increase, reaching maximum momentum after 1850, occurred in eastern Europe. The new demographic trend effected a rapid shift in the global ethnocultural composition of Jews from the earlier quite balanced split between Ashkenazi, and Sephardi and oriental communities, to an overwhelming numerical predominance of Eastern European Jewry. Population growth also accrued socioeconomic pressure among impoverished Eastern European Jewry, thus decisively stimulating the mass westward migration starting in the 1880s.

The main determinant for the onset of Jewish population growth was the comparatively early start of declines in mortality levels, and of low infant mortality rates in particular, in the context of Jewish family patterns characterized by a predominance of nearly universal, relatively young, and homogamous marriages, and high fertility levels. These demographic features to a considerable extent reflected the influence of traditional Jewish norms, institutions and behaviors in the daily life of Jewish individuals and communities before the start of modernization. Eventually, however, cultural and social structural transformations of Jewish society – especially the widespread geographical and occupational mobility processes set into motion since the Emancipation – led to a diminished impact of religious norms in the life of the Jewish Diaspora. As Jews had anticipated the surrounding population in the transition from high to lower mortality levels, they also precurred the transition from high to low fertility levels. Jewish immigrants to the western countries, who initially had imported the demographic models of their communities of origin, rapidly adapted to the modern environments of western societies. Rates of natural increase declined, though in absolute terms Jewish population growth was still substantial. At the end of the 1930s the Jewish population was estimated at 16,500,000.

1939 to present

The Holocaust of six million Jews during the Second World War signified the destruction of 36 percent of pre-war world Jewry, of over 60 percent of European Jewry, and the virtual annihilation of large central–eastern European Jewish communities. World Jewry has not yet recovered its pre-war size. Long-lasting structural imbalances in Jewish population were determined by high child mortality and low birth rates during the persecution. Of the 11,000,000 Jews left in 1945, 600,000 lived in Palestine. This section of the Jewish people was to grow rapidly since the independence of the State of Israel, to

717,000 by November 1948, 1,982,000 in 1961, 2,959,000 in 1975, and 3,562,000 in 1986. Mass immigration was the major determinant of growth until the 1960s; later natural increase predominated. The aggregate size of Diaspora Jewry declined from 10,800,000 in 1948 to 10,250,000 in 1961, 10,000,000 in 1975, and 9,401,000 in 1986. After the initial effect of mass *aliyah* to Israel, a negative internal balance of demographic variables was emerging. World Jewish population, after some increase during the post-war years, by the 1970s was approaching a stage of zero-population-growth. Natural increase in Israel was compensated by natural decrease in the Diaspora. Waves of international migration of declining intensity affected the geographical distribution of Jewish population. During the 1950s and 1960s over 500,000 Jews left North Africa and the Middle East; since the late 1960s, over 250,000 have left the USSR. Overall a majority of these emigrants went to Israel. In 1986, of a world total of 12,964,000 Jews, 95 percent lived in nine countries each with 100,000 Jews or more: the USA (5,700,000), Israel (3,562,000), the USSR (1,515,000), France (530,000), the United Kingdom (326,000), Canada (310,000), Argentina (224,000), South Africa (115,000), and Brazil (100,000). At least 100 Jews – up to 77,000 in Australia – were found in each of 65 further countries. In spite of some local differences, similar sociodemographic trends prevailed across the Diaspora: intense concentration in major metropolitan areas, movement to suburbs, high levels of educational attainment, occupational specialization in tertiary activities – trade, and more recently, especially managerial and liberal professions. Recent international migrants were rapidly absorbed and acculturated. Demographic patterns, too, followed similar courses in the Diaspora. Fertility, after a temporary post-war increase, declined to very low levels. Since the mid 1970s the Total Fertility Rate converged to 1.5 children per Jewish woman in the Diaspora, also reflecting a growing diffusion of postponed marriages, permanent celibacy, and divorce. Low birth rates were the major determinant of a steady process of population aging. While these features were common to all industrialized countries, Jewish populations were more intensively affected. The other major feature of Jewish demography was the rapid growth in the extent of mixed marriage. Already widespread in western–central Europe since the early twentieth century, mixed marriage had not been significant in North America until the late 1960s; by the 1980s, an estimated 30 percent of new Jewish spouses in the USA, and higher percentages in Latin America and Continental Europe, were marrying non-Jewish-born partners who did not convert to Judaism. According to the available evidence, the majority of children of mixed marriages were not raised as Jews. The combined effect of low Jewish birth rates, growing proportions of Jewish elderly, frequent mixed marriages, and other forms of assimilation determined increasing demographic attrition among the Jews in the Diaspora, namely a negative balance between Jewish births and deaths. By contrast, the Jewish population in Israel continued featuring relatively frequent marriages, a Total Fertility Rate of 2.8 children per Jewish woman, virtually no assimilatory losses, a comparatively young age structure, and a moderate but persisting rate of natural increase. Differentials in demographic behaviors that had previously characterized immigrants during the early statehood years sharply declined, through a general process of internal convergence among Jewish origin groups in Israel.

Prospect

Continuation of the demographic trends observed during the 1970s and 1980s in Israel and in the Diaspora were expected to produce significant changes in the total size and geographical distribution of world Jewry – in spite of the reduced impact of international migrations – namely a net balance of migrations to and from Israel close to nil. By the year 2000, according to the medium version among a wider range of projections, the Jewish population in Israel would reach 4.2 million – an increase of 640,000, or 18 percent, over the 1986 total; the aggregate Jewish population of the Diaspora would decline to 8.2 million – a loss of 1,200,000, or 13 percent; the world total of 12.4 million Jews would be lower by nearly 600,000, or 5 percent, than the 1986 estimate. The proportion of Jews in Israel out of the world total would

increase from 23 percent in 1975 and 27.5 percent in 1986 to 34 percent in the year 2000. Because of differences in fertility levels and age composition, the proportion living in Israel out of all Jews in the world aged 15 or less could approach 50 percent; on the other hand, Jewish Diaspora communities would become increasingly overaged, and therefore even more exposed to continuing population decline. World Jewish population tends toward polarization between the two major centers in Israel and the USA, while the aggregate weight of other communities is diminishing.

FURTHER READING

Bachi, R.: *Population Trends of World Jewry* (Jerusalem: The Hebrew University, 1976)

——: *The Population of Israel* (Jerusalem: The Hebrew University and Israel's Prime Minister's Office, 1977)

Schmelz, U. O.: *World Jewish Population: Regional Estimates and Projections* (Jerusalem: The Hebrew University, 1981)

Schmelz, U. O. and DellaPergola, S.: World Jewish population, 1986. *American Jewish Year Book* 88 (1988)

SERGIO DELLAPERGOLA

Der Nister See KAHANOWITZ, PINYE.

Derrida, Jacques (b.1930) French philosopher. Born in Algiers, Derrida came to Paris in his late teens. He has taught at the École Normale Supérieure and in 1988 teaches at the École des Hautes Études en Sciences Sociales in Paris. He has also been affiliated in the USA with Yale University, Cornell University, and, most recently, the University of California at Irvine. In addition, Derrida has been an active leader in educational reform in France and has been involved in establishing a new university in Paris.

In 1967, at the age of 37, Derrida published three extraordinary works which have altered the course of contemporary philosophy: *Speech and Phenomena*, *Writing and Difference*, and *Of Grammatology*. The most polemical and influential of these studies has been *Of Grammatology* wherein theocentric notions of writing, inherited from the Patristic Fathers, were challenged and confronted with an alternate conception of writing that conforms with a Jewish understanding of writing opposed to those features which typify a metaphysics of presence. Derrida's essay on the Jewish writer Edmond JABÈS in *Writing and Difference* discloses Derrida's Jewish perspective: to rethink the question of "being" outside the Western concept of the book, and to think of scripture as something other than a site wherein "being" takes residence in the word. In "Violence and Metaphysics", from *Writing and Difference*, an essay on the Jewish philosopher, Emmanuel LEVINAS, Derrida recollected Levinas's critiques of the guiding terms of Western ontology in order to consider the destiny of the correspondence between metaphysics and what is disruptive within or to it. Like Levinas, Derrida is not interested in the dialectics of metaphysics versus violence, but in the very subtle ways in which they are bound together within concepts like eschatology, totality, and infinity. In fact, metaphysics depends for its cohesion on the threat of external disruption. And this threat is historically attributed to the Jews. Derrida's attempt is to challenge the "integrity" of this difference in order to dismantle the metaphysics of anti-Semitism.

In the books *Margins of Philosophy* (1970), and *Dissemination* (1972), Derrida develops essays of enormous originality and power which concentrate on literary structures that subvert the very aims they are being used to establish. These studies touch on concepts such as metaphor, the preface, mimesis, and semantic drift. In *Glas* (1974) Derrida embarks on a very ambitious project wherein he writes a text in two columns, the left column on the philosopher George Friedrich Hegel, and the right column on the novelist Jean Genet. These columns counterpoint Hegel's writings on the family as heterosexual unit to Genet's writings on homosexual love. Embedded in this text is a very complex consideration of the author as Jew suspended between two anti-Semitic formations (German and French), each articulated through a notion of *Geschlecht* (sexuality, race, genealogy). A strong suggestion in *Glas* (the death knell) is that, although the Jew remains, it is anti-Semitism which survives.

In the late 1970s Derrida published *Truth in Painting*, which takes issue with Kantian esthetics. And in 1980 Derrida published *The Post Card* which has an autobiographical text, "Envois", followed by texts on Sigmund FREUD and Freudian psychoanalysis. Part of the "Envois" touches on a reading of the Book of Esther from the Old Testament. In *Of an Apocalyptic Tone Recently Adopted in Philosophy* (1982), *Shibboleth* (1986), *Feu la Cendre* (1987), *Ulysse Gramophone* (1987), and *Geschlecht I/II*, Derrida touches more and more on the Holocaust and the relationship between language and Diaspora. In fact, these essays can be read as a gloss on the much earlier "Violence and Metaphysics" from *Writing and Difference*. Recently Derrida has lectured in Jerusalem on negative theology and, at Irvine, on the writings of Baruch Spinoza, Franz ROSENZWEIG, and Hermann COHEN.

FURTHER READING

Culler, J.: *On Deconstruction* (Ithaca: Cornell University Press, 1981)

Handelman, S.: Jacques Derrida and the heretic hermeneutic. In *Displacement*, ed. M. Krupnick (Bloomington: Indiana University Press, 1983)

Rapaport, H.: *Heidegger and Derrida* (Lincoln: Nebraska University Press, 1989)

HERMAN RAPAPORT

Déry, Tibor (1894–1977) Hungarian novelist and playwright. Déry was born into a well-to-do family of assimilated Hungarian Jews. At an early age he became involved in radical politics and made his début as a writer with the short novel *Lia* in the review *Nyugat* in 1917. Apart from prose conceived in the spirit of "romantic naturalism" the young Déry also wrote Surrealistic and Expressionistic poetry. Having joined the Hungarian Communist Party in 1919, Déry left Hungary in 1920 and spent the next six years in Czechoslovakia, Vienna, Paris, and Italy. In 1926 he returned to Hungary where he took part in co-editing the activist review *Dokumentum*, but within a few years he once again resumed his journeys abroad. It was in Vienna in 1933 that he started his first long novel, *A befejezetlen mondat* (1947; The unfinished sentence), which highlighted the deep class divisions in Hungarian society.

In 1938 Déry translated André Gide's *Retour de l'URSS* into Hungarian, a feat which earned him both Communist hostility and a short prison sentence for the propagation of "subversive literature". When the Germans occupied Hungary in March 1944 Déry went into hiding and survived on false papers. After the war he rejoined the Hungarian Communist Party and published a new cycle of stories *Alvilági játékok* (1946; "Games of the Underworld", in the selection *The Portuguese Princess*, 1966). In 1948 he was awarded the Kossuth Prize. Although he supported the Communist regime that assumed power in 1948, Déry once again clashed with the official party line when he published his two-volume novel *Felelet* (1950–52; The answer), which was strongly attacked by Hungary's cultural "overseer" for its alleged minimization of the role of the illegal pre-war Communist Party. Between 1953 and 1956 Déry wrote some excellent short stories, critical of corruption and the abuse of power in Hungary, collected first in *Vidám temetés* (1960; Merry funeral), together with the short novel *Niki* (1955; *Niki: the Story of a Dog*, 1958). Through the life of a fox-terrier *Niki* shows the vicissitudes of a family (and indirectly of the whole country) during the years of Stalinist oppression. For his activities during and after the revolution of 1956 Déry was sentenced to nine years' imprisonment in 1957, but he was released in 1960. It was in jail that he wrote *G. A. úr X.-ben* (Mr A. G. in X.) published in 1964, an anti-utopia depicting the anarchistic regression of human society to the level of pure vegetation.

Déry's most important work after 1956 is his loosely constructed autobiography *Ítélet nincs* (1968; No verdict) in which he evokes the spirits of the dead and confronts them with his own thoughts and confessions. Some of his short novels written in the 1970s are attempts to grapple with the problems of the technotronic age with its mass cults and terrorism.

Jewishness does not appear as a specific problem or tradition in Déry's work, although one of his themes in *Alvilági játékok* is the persecution of Jews in Budapest during the last months of 1944. In the rarely-performed play *Tanuk* (1948; Witnesses), Déry strongly condemned the indifference of the Hungarian middle classes in the face of the mounting persecution of Jews; for him this is proof of the final degradation of "bourgeois" values.

BIBLIOGRAPHY

Niki, the Story of a Dog, trans. E. Hyams (London: Secker & Warburg, 1958); Games of the Underworld. In *The Portuguese Princess*, trans. K. Szasz (London: Calder & Boyars, 1966)

FURTHER READING

Fehér, F.: There is a verdict. *New Hungarian Quarterly* 10 (1969)

Sanders, I.: Tibor Déry at eighty. *Books Abroad* 49 (1975) 12–18

GEORGE GÖMÖRI

Desnos, Robert (1900–1945) French poet and journalist. Desnos was born into a fairly assimilated Parisian–Jewish bourgeois family. He "lived in poetry", believing his mission in life was to write. Though never fully identifying with the Jewish people until the Nazi Occupation of France, his search for poetic inspiration and the Platonic ideal ironically follows a methodical path akin to that employed by medieval Kabbalists. He adhered literally to the surrealist poetic doctrine of investigating all aspects of the word by submitting the inner self to a "rêve vigilant", a somnambulant trance in which the poet and his inspiration engaged in mystical dialogue. This dialogue eventually evolved into the poem, a concrete conception which, for Desnos, was a poor representation of the higher, universal truth he had encountered while in his poetic trance. Like other avant-garde artists and poets of the era, he did use drugs in an attempt to facilitate his elevation to his own poetic nirvana. Despite the highly mystical nature of his early poetry, his works remain among some of the most simple and comprehensible of the first Surrealist Group. This "accessibility" led to an inevitable break with other adherents of the Surrealist movement.

Desnos created a public literary scandal with the publication of two works: his essays *De L'Erotisme Considéré dans ses Manifestations Écrites* and *La Liberté ou l'Amour* (1927). These works, along with another, *The Night of Loveless Nights* (1930), were condemned and consequently severely censored by the Paris law courts.

In 1930, following the publication of a collection of his poetry, *Corps et Bien*, Desnos broke with the Surrealists and pursued a career in journalism and radio broadcasting. His journalistic writings demonstrate an awareness of the growing threat which Fascism posed to liberal democracies and, most particularly, to the Jewish people. With the Nazi Occupation in 1940, Desnos entered into active service with the Resistance. During this period, he published an autobiographical novel, *Le Vin est Tiré* (1943). Shortly afterwards, on 22 February 1944, he was arrested and was then deported to Terezín in Czechoslovakia where he died of typhus in 1945.

His vast poetic output was published posthumously in *Domaine Public* (1953).

SIMON SIBELMAN

Dessau, Paul (1894–1979) German composer. Born in Hamburg, the grandson of a cantor, he began as a violinist but soon turned to conducting and composing and, helped by such supporters as Otto Klemperer and Bruno Walter, was appointed to a number of posts in various German opera houses. During the 1920s he also wrote music for the cinema. However he was chiefly known for such concert works as his Symphony No. 1 (1927).

Between 1933 and 1938 he lived in Paris and there absorbed the political ideas which were later to dominate his music. In 1939 he emigrated to New York, and in 1942 he met the poet and playwright Bertolt Brecht. Before this, Dessau had written a number of works with Jewish themes, including a dramatic oratorio, *Haggadah* (1936), with words by Max BROD, which was based on the *Haggadah*, Midrash, and the Bible and used Jewish folk melodies. He also wrote several psalm settings and two choral works in Hebrew, *Zwei Gebete* (1939), and *Jeworechecho* (1941).

However, after his meeting with Brecht and his subsequent move to Hollywood to further their collaboration, which resulted most notably in his music for *Mutter Courage und Ihre Kinder* (1946), his musical aims became more overtly political and in 1948 Brecht and Dessau, both refugees from Macarthyism, emigrated to East Berlin. There they found the recognition and opportunities previously denied to them.

After initial difficulties Dessau's relationship with the authorities seems to have improved. In 1952 he was appointed to the German Academy of Arts and in 1959 he became Vice President and professor. During this time he received many awards and prizes and expressed his gratitude to the German Democratic Republic, when asked to contribute music to celebrate its 10th anniversary, with the following words: "All these works are dedicated to the DDR, for without her they would have been quite unthinkable. It is a mutal gift".

FURTHER READING
Esslin, M.: *Brecht, a Choice of Evils* (London: Methuen, 1984)

ANDREA BARON

Deutsch, Babette (1895–1982) American poet, translator, critic, author of children's books, and novelist. Born in New York of German–Jewish parents, Deutsch began writing poems at the age of five. Educated at the Ethical Cultural School and Barnard College, from which she graduated in 1917, she already had several publications before receiving her BA. *Banners* (1919) celebrated the Russian Revolution. She collaborated with Avraham Yarmolinsky, later her husband, on the translation of Blok's *The Twelve* (1920), and *Modern Russian Poetry* (1921). *Potable Gold: Some Notes on Poetry and This Age* (1929) contained five critical essays on the impact of technology upon poetry. *Poetry in Our Time* (1952) commented on the work of 226 poets writing in English throughout the world. *Poetry Handbook: a Dictionary of Terms* (1957) was considered the definitive work on prosody for its time.

Deutsch's classical scholarship culminated in a philosophical poem, *Epistle to Prometheus* (1931), and a novel about Socrates, *Mask of Silenus* (1933). *One Part Love* (1939) collected 53 poems previously printed in periodicals. From 1933 to 1935 Deutsch taught at the New School for Social Research, at Queens College in 1942, and from 1944 to 1971 she taught at Columbia, which accorded her an honorary doctorate in 1946. From 1960 to 1966 she served as Honorary Consultant to the Library of Congress.

Her biography, *Walt Whitman* (1941), won the Ford Foundation Award for children's literature. For younger readers, Deutsch told the story of Ernst, a Jewish refugee from Germany, in *The Welcome* (1942). Also, two folklore anthologies, *Tales of Faraway Folk* (1952), and *More Tales* (1963), were written in collaboration with her husband. When he retired as director of the Slavonic Division of the New York Public Library in 1955, they worked on *Two Centuries of Russian Verse* (1966). In 1976 Barnard College established a scholarship in the name of one of its most distinguished alumna.

FURTHER READING

Gould, J.: *American Women Poets: Pioneers of Modern Poetry* (New York: Dodd, Mead, 1980)

Kinsman, C. D., ed.: *Contemporary Authors*, vol. 4 (Detroit: Gale Research Co., 1976)

RUTH ROSENBERG

Deutscher, Isaac (1907–1967) Polish Marxist thinker, interpreter, and chronicler of modern Russia. Born near Krakow Deutscher received a traditional Jewish education, later supplemented by studies at Krakow University. In 1926 he joined the outlawed Polish Communist Party but after advocating united Communist–Socialist action against the threat of rising Nazism, a view opposing the Stalinist position, he was expelled from the party in 1932. In 1939, as correspondent for a Warsaw Jewish newspaper, he came to London, which was to remain his permanent home.

Deutscher's reputation as an authority on Soviet affairs was established in 1949 with the publication of *Stalin: a Political Biography*. His wholesale condemnation of Joseph Stalin and his ideology, tracing Stalin's deviations from Karl MARX and Vladimir Ilyich Lenin, and offering an appreciation and understanding of Stalin's political maneuvers, is matched by an equally certain conviction that the revolution could be purged of Stalinism, in the same way that the French revolution was purged of Robespierre. His reputation grew with the publication of his major work, a massive three-part biography of Leon Trotsky – *The Prophet Armed: 1879–1921* (1954), *The Prophet Unarmed: 1921–1929* (1959),

and *The Prophet Outcast, 1929–1940* (1963). This sympathetic portrait of Trotsky does not conceal the author's admiration for this tragic revolutionary leader whilst acknowledging Trotsky's major tactical errors. His condemnation of Stalin is here even harsher and Trotsky emerges as the true voice or prophet of international Marxist revolution. The most comprehensive statement of Deutscher's position on the revolution appeared under the title, *The Unfinished Revolution: 1917–1967* (1967), and at the time of his death he was working on a biography of Lenin.

Deutscher consistently argued, before and after his first trip to Israel in 1953, that a Jewish nation-state in an age of growing internationalism was a dangerous, anachronistic, and retrograde step for Jewry. He considered anti-Semitism and Jewish survival to have the same cause – "that Jews represented the market economy amidst people living in a natural economy". In his 1958 essay, *The non-Jewish Jew*, he argued that Baruch Spinoza, Heinrich HEINE, Karl MARX, Rosa Luxemburg, Leon Trotsky, and Sigmund FREUD were Jews who went beyond the boundaries of a constricting Judaism to a universalistic international vision of the "ultimate solidarity of man", a tendency that he felt was a natural product of Jewish life and thought, which he contrasted with the narrowness of Orthodoxy and nationalistic Zionism.

Deutscher remained throughout his life committed to the truth of Marxist doctrine and was optimistically convinced of the eventual success of the revolutionary movement. He retained his position as an independent Marxist theoretician and activist.

Other works include: *Heretics and Renegades* (1955), *The Great Contest; Russia and the West* (1960), *Ironies of History; Essays on Contemporary Communism* (1966), and *The Non-Jewish Jew and Other Essays* (1968).

FURTHER READING

Horowitz, D.: *The Study of Isaac Deutscher* (London: Macdonald, 1971)

Steiner, G.: Trotsky and tragic imagination. In *Language and Silence* (London: Faber, 1967)

PAUL M. MORRIS

Diamond, David (b.1915) American composer. Born in Rochester, New York, he began his violin studies at the age of seven, and began composing in his early teens. He studied with Bernard Rogers at the Eastman School of Music (1930–4), moved to New York to take courses with Roger Sessions, and in 1936 went to Paris to work with Nadia Boulanger and there was associated with such men as André Gide, Albert Roussel, Maurice Ravel, Charles Despian, and Charles Munch. It was in Paris that he wrote *Psalm* for orchestra, the work that brought him to national attention. Returning to New York in 1940 he was able to devote himself entirely to composition, due to the fact that he received a number of large grants and awards. During 1953 to 1965 he made his home in Florence, and when he returned to the USA he became chairman of the composition department of the Manhattan School of Music (1965–7). In 1973 he joined the faculty of the Juilliard School.

Diamond's early music shows him as a classicist whose music is marked by a great melodic sweep, complex harmonic and contrapuntal writing, and a strong sense of rhythmic flow. These traits are retained throughout his very extensive output, and even though in later works he experiments with serial techniques, the works never lose their basic tonal structure and feeling. His list of works is enormous and includes: nine symphonies, a symphony for organ, ten string quartets, and other chamber music, and concertos. In 1951 he wrote a sacred service called *Mizmor LeDavid*. He has also written many songs including the highly successful cycle, *Hebrew Melodies*, for voice and piano on texts by Byron (1967). His latest works include *A Song of Hope*, text by Elie WIESEL for eight solo voices and small orchestra; and an opera, *The Noblest Game* (1971–5).

In 1986 David Diamond was awarded the second William Schuman Lifetime Achievement Award by Columbia University.

SAMUEL H. ADLER

DIGB (Deutsch-Israelitischer Gemeindebund) [German Israelite community league] The DIGB was the first organization which attempted to represent all the German–Jewish communities. Although in its heyday two-thirds of Germany's Jewish community were affiliated to it, it was never an official representative of German Jewry, owing to internal dissent and government opposition to its existence. Its links with the Reform movement alienated it from many of the Orthodox communities. It was founded in 1869 by members of the Leipzig community but, because of its unpopularity with the government of Saxony, it moved in 1882 to Berlin, where its president was Samuel Kristeller. He was followed in 1896 by the historian Martin Philippson during whose presidency, in 1898, the DIGB was given legal status. Salomon Kalischer was the next president, from 1912 to 1924, but after his death the post remained unfilled and the DIGB was undermined by the creation of separate organizations in different states of the Weimar Republic.

The first task of the DIGB was to try to fight anti-Semitism by distributing pamphlets written by Christians and Jews, intended to educate the Christian community about Judaism. Later, in 1885, it set up the Historical Commission for Investigating the History of the Jews in Germany, which produced three important volumes. The DIGB did much charitable and educational work. In response to the number of immigrants from Russia, funds were established to give welfare to itinerants, and to help Jews who wished to learn a trade. The DIGB also ran two homes for neglected children, a home for the mentally retarded, and a working men's colony for the unemployed. It provided pensions for Jewish civil servants and helped poor communities by funding buildings and teachers, and it was instrumental in the creation of the Jewish Teachers' Association. Much of the DIGB's work was stopped by the inflation of the 1920s.

FURTHER READING

Schorsch, I.: *Jewish Reactions to German Anti-Semitism 1870–1914* (New York: Columbia University Press, 1972)

RODERICK YOUNG

Dilon [Zhuravitski], **Avrom-Moyshe** (1883–1934) Yiddish poet. Avrom-Moyshe Dilon was born in Zhetl, near Grodna, and emigrated to

New York in 1904. He began writing poetry very young, and made his debut in the anthology *Literatur*. He joined the young group of poets known as the *Yunge*, who rebelled against the forms, styles, and contents of accepted forms of poetry, and against the abstract romanticists. However, Dilon was not a rebel. His style was influenced by the Russian poets Pushkin and Lermentov who belonged to the Romantic period at the beginning of the nineteenth century. He gloried his mystical poems with strong as well as light iambic rhythms. At times one hears in his poems the falling step of the iambic foot, at times rising, elevated by his moods. In his first book, *Gele bleter* (1919; Yellow leaves), a wondrous poet carries a beggar-bag with yellow leaves which frighten everyone around him. A mysterious someone behind him asks: "Why and where do you carry the yellow leaves?" The poet answers: "Ask God, people, the world".

Before he died, he whispered his last poem to the poet Menke KATZ. His second book, *Di lider* (1935; The poems), was published a year after his death. He was a bachelor crowned with romantic chivalry, and was always in love with real or imaginary women.

MENKE KATZ

Doctorow, E(dgar) L(aurence) (b.1931)

American novelist. Born in New York City, Doctorow received his AB degree in 1952 from Kenyon College, where he studied with John Crowe Ransom. Married to Helen Setzer, he has three children. After working for some years as an editor, he became writer-in-residence at the University of California at Irvine soon after the publication of his second book, *Big As Life* (1966), and has since taught at Sarah Lawrence College, Yale University, and New York University.

As author of seven novels, a collection of stories, and a play, he is one of the USA's most successful and controversial writers, unusual in both his commercial success and literary acclaim. Three of his novels – *Welcome to Hard Times* (1960) published in England as *Bad Man from Brodie* (1961) *The Book of Daniel* (1971), and *Ragtime* (1975) – have been made into movies. *Ragtime*, written while he held a 1972 Gug-

genheim fellowship, won the National Book Circle Critics Award in 1976, sold more than 200,000 copies in hardback, and received a then record-breaking contract for paperback rights. *World's Fair* (1985), his recreation of a Jewish boy's New York childhood in the 1930s, had an initial printing of 100,000 copies. The chief narrator of *World's Fair* is the boy, Edgar. Living in the Bronx with his parents and an older brother, he discovers himself against a background of Depression economy and events leading to the Second World War. His self-conscious account of personal growth set in the historical moment, and his gradual awakening to tensions in the family – members of whom narrate their own reflections – culminates in his visit to the World's Fair, and his startling recognition of the future. Although Edgar's life resembles his own youth, Doctorow describes this work as "the illusion of a memoir", "an invention" despite the factual material. This curious mixture of historical reality and fiction characterizes most of Doctorow's work. The title character of *Billy Bathgate* (1989) shadows Thomas E. Dewey, special public prosecutor in New York during the 1930s. Historical figures like Houdini, Sigmund FREUD, and Emma GOLDMAN pervade the pages of *Ragtime*, a book set in the early twentieth century, in decidedly unhistorical encounters with fictional characters. *The Book of Daniel*, Doctorow's most overtly Jewish work, presents the character of Daniel Isaacson, whose parents, modeled on Ethel and Julius Rosenberg, were Jewish immigrants convicted and executed for treason during the early 1950s. Doctorow often plays with narrative strategy with the same experimental energy that he does history. In much of his work he creates a character who tells the story for him.

Although sometimes thought to be ideologically left-wing, and a political writer, Doctorow sees himself as an ethical writer, calling the Ten Commandments "very left dogma". He dismisses efforts to categorize his work, declaring that "writing is an exploration" and that he is just "a novelist".

FURTHER READING

Trenner, R. ed.: *E. L. Doctorow: Essays and Conversations* (Princeton: Ontario Review Press, 1983)

Weber, B.: The myth maker. *New York Times Magazine* (October 20 1985)

ELIZABETH KLEIN

Doniach, Nakdimon S. (b.1907) Judaic scholar and lexicographer. Born in London, Doniach began a composite course at London University in 1923, the main subjects at King's College being Hebrew, Greek, and Latin, with Rabbinic Hebrew at Jews' College. He studied Arabic at the School of Oriental Studies and at the end of two academic years at London University he became the Holy Scholar (for Hebrew) at Wadham College, Oxford.

Gaining the Boden Scholarship in Sanskrit in 1926 enabled him to go to Palestine to visit his mother who was then the organizing secretary of WIZO. On his return to London in 1929 he became a freelance scholar, spending the mornings in teaching and the afternoons in research, including the study of Jewish scholars of the nineteenth century. His studies resulted in the publication of his first academic article, a conjecture on some missing words in the Moabite Stone, which appeared in 1932 in the Journal of the Palestine Exploration Fund. He also made several contributions to the *Revue des Études Juives* and other journals, and published a book, *Purim on the Feast of Esther*, in 1933.

At the outbreak of war Doniach volunteered and was accepted into the RAF. After the war he became a Civil Servant with duties concerning technical terms, and language training in many languages. He retired from the Civil Service in 1960 with the award of an OBE. In 1972 his *Oxford English–Arabic Dictionary of Current Usage* was published, followed, in 1982, by *The Concise Oxford English–Arabic Dictionary of Current Usage*.

It was at this time that the idea of an *Oxford English–Hebrew Dictionary of Current Usage* was mooted. Due to the efforts of David PATTERSON the project was able to begin under Doniach's editorship. This dictionary incorporates the constant and ongoing changes in both English and modern Hebrew.

Apart from his lexicographical activities, Doniach has taught Hebrew at Oxford University for many years. A warm, witty and engaging teacher, his teaching reflects not only his encyclopedic knowledge and mastery of a variety of languages both ancient and modern, but also the profound insight into language which greatly distinguishes his dictionaries.

Doniach is a permanent Member of the Senior Common Room of Wadham College, Oxford, and he was elected Honorary Member of the Faculty of Oriental Studies on his eightieth birthday.

BIBLIOGRAPHY

Purim on the Feast of Esther (Philadelphia: The Jewish Publication Society of America, 1933)
Oxford English–Arabic Dictionary of Current Usage (Oxford: Oxford University Press, 1972)

GLENDA ABRAMSON

Doubrovsky, Serge (b.1928) French critic and novelist. Serge Doubrovsky described himself as a secular and assimilated Jew. His name was originally associated with the late 1960s debate about literary criticism, when, in an article entitled *Pourquoi la nouvelle critique? Critique et objectivité*, he sided with Roland Barthes against the conventional literary views of Raymond Picard and initiated a new mode of textual interpretation partly involving structuralism and psychoanalysis. His first published work, *Corneille et la dialectique du héros*, (1963), was a monograph in which he offered an existentialist reading of classical drama.

More recently, Doubrovsky wrote a number of works of fiction, notably *Fils* (1977), *Un Amour de soi*, (1980), and *La Vie l'instant*, (1985), where he has turned towards his Jewish past and origins, the Second World War, and, more specifically, the treatment of Jews in France during the German occupation. This was a period which abruptly confronted him, as a young boy, with a Jewish identity previously kept in the background, and led him, like many of his fellow countrymen, to realize the precariousness of his attachment to the French state.

His Jewishness played an important part in his creative writing, which is a combination of genuine autobiography and fiction. In the late 1980s, Serge Doubrovsky was living between two cultures as a professor of French in New York, paying frequent visits to France. His writing tends to gravitate largely around the themes of displacement and identity.

Cynical, self-critical, sharp, and displaying a phenomenal virtuosity in the handling of language, his novels are often written in a witty combination of French and English in complex interaction.

PATRICIA TOUTON-VICTOR

drama, Hebrew At the beginning of the eighteenth century Hebrew drama had almost no tradition of its own, there being no Hebrew-speaking professional theater, and very little dramatic literature in the Hebrew language. Only one Hebrew play, in fact, had been published before 1700, although a number of important plays had been written earlier, such as Judah Leone Sommo's *Zahut bedihuta dekidushin* (An eloquent marriage farce: written 1555, published 1946 actually considered to be the first Hebrew play). The turning point came in 1743 with the publication of the allegorical drama *Layesharim tehillah* (Praise to the upright), a play by Moses Hayyim LUZZATTO which was widely imitated until almost the end of the nineteenth century. Hebrew allegorical drama was generally not concerned only with the moralistic and the theological but was highly contemporary as well. Indeed, the various dramatic conflicts depicted between "Good" and "Evil" often symbolized the rivalry between the Enlightenment movement and its adversaries, the "opponents of light". A typical example is *Emet ve'emunah* (1867; Truth and faith) by Abraham Dov LEBENSOHN, behind whose allegorical trappings hide the influential forces in Jewish affairs of the period: the Orthodox, the hasidic zealots, and the followers of the Enlightenment.

The second characteristic type of Hebrew drama of the eighteenth and nineteenth centuries was the biblical play. Some 15 biblical plays were published, dealing with a variety of subjects, from the patriarchs to the kings and prophets, most of them written from a traditional canonic point of view. The most important of these plays was *Melukhat Sha'ul* (1794; Saul's kingdom) by Joseph Haefrati. By the end of the nineteenth century there was a growing tendency to write historical plays with national and Zionist themes, a development which was con-nected to the birth of national and Zionist movements. The most prominent playwright of this period was Judah Loeb LANDAU whose plays, such as *Bar Kokhba* (1884), *Aharit yerusha-layim* (1886; The last days of Jerusalem), and *Hordos* (1886; Herod), among others, dealt mainly with historical characters who had led the Jewish people in their struggle for survival in times of crisis and revolt. The fact that Hebrew drama of the eighteenth and nineteenth centuries had developed without a Hebrew theater meant that the majority of plays were never performed, and were written in a flowery, over-literary style of non-colloquial Hebrew. The plays were clearly out of touch with the important developments in contemporary world drama. Luzzatto, for instance, imitated Guarini of the sixteenth century rather than his contemporaries Goldoni or Maffei. Similarly the Hebrew playwrights of the nineteenth century were totally unaffected by the important Russian and Scandinavian drama that was developing at the time. The period was unmarked by any major forays into realistic writing in the modern sense. Signs of modernity and social realism were to be found only in certain allegorical or symbolic devices or, very marginally, in a few satires and comedies.

The end of the nineteenth century saw an almost revolutionary transformation in Hebrew drama, resulting from a number of factors: first, the development and institutionalization of a professional Yiddish theater in eastern Europe proved to be an indirect impetus for the development of Hebrew drama; second, Hebrew became a natural spoken language; third, amateur theaters were established in the settlements and towns of Palestine as a preliminary step towards an eventual professional local theater; fourth, the development of modern Hebrew literature, especially poetry and prose, encouraged writers to try their hand at creating Hebrew drama of comparable quality. When a new generation of writers arose, soon followed by actors and directors, the foundations were laid for a new era in Hebrew theater which was launched in 1918 by the founding of the Habimah Theater in Moscow, today the National Theater of Israel. The birth of a professional Hebrew theater, as part of the general Hebrew renaissance, also raised fundamental questions concerning the nature of Hebrew drama, which remain unresolved to this day: is it to be a didactic or prophetic drama, as the poet Hayyim Nahman BIALIK claimed, for example, or should it aim only to reflect realistically the context, style, and personalities of renewed Jewish life in modern Israel?

While early in the twentieth century Hebrew theater continued to follow the traditional historical–biblical trend, the plays became more sophisticatedly modern. Among the notable examples were the original biblical plays of Matityahu Shoham – *Yeriho* (1924; *Jericho*, 1974), *Bilam* (1925–9; Balaam), *Tzor viyerushalayim* (1933; Tyre and Jerusalem), and *Elohei barzel lo ta'aseh lakh* (1937; Thou shalt not make iron gods) – whose representation of the historical conflict between prophetic Judaism and the various forms of paganism is conveyed through intensive yet poetic rhetorical style. Another important instance is *Beketz hayamim* (1934, 1950; At the end of days) by Hayyim HAZAZ, an expressionistic and theatrical play whose depiction of the struggle between anarchic messianism and rational conservatism within the Jewish community at the time of Shabetai Zevi had clear implications for the ideological conflicts and dilemmas of modern Judaism and Zionism.

Another development in Hebrew drama of the early twentieth century was the search for new patterns of dramatic expression that would reflect the contemporary reality of the modern Jewish world in both Palestine and the Diaspora – a world marked by upheaval and the disruption of traditional Jewish family life, by great migrations and ideological ferment, affecting not only the younger generation of Jews but their more traditional elders as well. Two outstanding examples were, *Oto ve'et beno* (1928; Him and his son) by Yitzhak Dov BERKOWITZ, a well-made realistic drama about the struggle between assimilation and awakening nationalism in a non-traditional Jewish family, and *Me'ever lagevulin* (1907; Beyond the borders) by Joseph Hayyim BRENNER, which depicted the daily life of rootless and aimless Jewish immigrants on the outskirts of London. Both these plays are particularly notable for their lively dialogue, psychological insight, flowing tempo, and exciting theatricality.

The pre-State period saw the appearance of dozens of plays. Most were sentimental and didactic melodramas, some were mere reportage-like slices of contemporary life, others, historical treatments of the early days of Jewish settlement in Palestine, the life of the pioneers, the traditional Jewish community life in the "holy cities", and, in rare cases, of relations between Jews and Arabs. In all, however, the search continued for the best forms of linguistic and theatrical expression to enhance the thematics of the new situation in Palestine. One of the most significant of these plays, and one which also had a successful run on the stage, was *Ha'adamah hazot* (1942; This land) by Aharon Ashman, a didactic play about a young settlement's battle with malaria and its internal emotional struggles. The parallel development of local satire and humor on the stage in Palestine during this period eventually led to the creation of a satirical theater. The most outstanding contribution to this new genre of Hebrew drama was made by Natan ALTERMAN whose satirical Hebrew "chanson" successfully combined elements of local color, folklore, and witty language with the European cabaret musical style.

Once the State of Israel had come into existence after 1948, new characters began appearing on the Hebrew stage, especially the young Israeli Palmach soldier and *kibbutznik*, who spoke colloquial Hebrew mixed with slang. Indeed, Hebrew writing in general became less stylized and elevated, almost journalistic in style, yet authentic and relevant to the spirit of the times. The play that most embodied this change was *Hu halakh basadot* (1948; He walked in the fields), by Moshe SHAMIR, which became a model for many subsequent playwrights. The range of subjects and themes dealt with in Israeli drama soon expanded to include war, mass immigration, the ethnic melting pot and the Holocaust. It was not long before the "sobering up" after the heady days of Independence, and the politicization of Israeli society created a need for serious social criticism. In *Kera li Syomka* (1950; Call me Syomka), for instance, Natan SHAHAM satirizes the weakening of Zionist pioneering ideals, while in *Tura* (1963), a ritualistic play of great psychological power, Josef Bar-Josef portrays the tragic clash of

Habimah Theater production of The Orange Grove *by Josef Bar-Josef*

moral values which oriental Jewish immigrants faced when they were forced to confront modern Israel's permissive and westernized society. The theme of the Holocaust was articulated in a particularly interesting way by Leah GOLDBERG in *Ba'alat ha'armon* (1955; The lady of the castle), which dramatizes the major dilemmas raised as the old confronts the new after the Holocaust, when efforts were being made to find Jewish children who had survived the war.

Israeli drama has nonetheless attempted to break out of its local and contemporary context by returning, with a fresh viewpoint, to more traditional historical and biblical thematics, and by incorporating universal themes and traditions. The most important writer of this sort of play is Nissim ALONI whose *Bigdei hamelekh* (1961; The king's clothes), an allegorical fantasy about government, revolt and conformism, based on Hans Christian Andersen's story, mixed with elements of absurdist theater, was a

milestone in the history of Israeli theater. This was not only from the point of view of genre and theme, but also because of Aloni's unique, almost revolutionary, contribution to the development of a highly literate yet theatrical style of stage Hebrew. A variation of this same development was *Pundak haruhot* (1963; Inn of ghosts) by Natan Alterman, a poetic *Künstler-*drama, much influenced by *Faust* and *Peer Gynt*, which focuses on the universal theme of the artist who must choose between two conflicting possibilities: loyalty to his wife and home or striving for creativity and self-fulfillment.

Another historical event, the Six Day War in 1967 and its aftermath, brought about a somewhat reactionary development: Israeli drama reverted once again to its local, contemporary context, and to sociopolitical satire. In an attempt to question, even criticize harshly, the fundamental principles underlying Israeli society, the latest generation of playwrights no longer takes traditional Zionist ideology for granted.

179

This outlook has not only been influenced by the social and moral dilemmas Israel has had to face since the Six Day War, but has also been an outcome of changes in post-1967 Israeli politics. The most notable representatives of this shift in Israeli drama are Hanoch LEVIN and Yehoshua SOBOL. In *Malkat ha'ambatyah* (1970; Queen of the bathtub), written in the style of traditional satirical cabaret, Levin's aggressive attack on the myths of heroism and patriotism paved the way for a provocatively new and controversial view of the Zionist ethos which, until then, had been the almost unquestioned ideological basis of early Israeli drama. Later Levin wrote a number of black comedies about the misery of the human condition, several of which exemplify a conscious intention to deflate classical and mythical motifs. Sobol, a playwright of great technical skill in a range of styles, has attempted to focus such plays as *Nefesh yehudi: halaylah ha'aharon shel Otto Weininger* (1982; The soul of a Jew: Otto Weininger's last night), *Ghetto* (1985), or *Hapalestina'it* (1985; The Palestinian girl), on various aspects of individual and collective Jewish identity in times of crisis and transition, and on Israel's newly emerging political polarization.

As the 1990s approached, Israeli drama, still greatly influenced by the changes which began in 1967, continued to develop amidst a growing number of creative projects which enjoyed the support not only of various fringe organizations but of the cultural and theatrical establishment as well. Nevertheless, despite a few international successes, Israeli drama was still characterized by a single-minded affinity for contemporary local themes, and oriented on Israeli rather than on Jewish issues. It is as yet too early to speak of firmly established patterns and traditions in Israeli drama. Its overall achievement has still not equalled that of Hebrew prose and poetry, nor of world drama. Indeed, Israeli drama remains very much a work in progress; its major challenge, to develop a canon of original national drama whose intellectual and esthetic value is nevertheless universal, still lies ahead.

FURTHER READING

Abramson, G.: *Modern Hebrew Drama* (London: Weidenfeld & Nicolson, 1979)

Citron, S. J.: Yiddish and Hebrew Drama. In *A History of Modern Drama*, ed. B. H. Clark and G. Freedley (New York and London: Appleton-Century, 1947) 601–638

Kantum Blum, R.: *From Tyre to Jerusalem* (Berkeley and Los Angeles: University of California Press, 1969)

Kohansky, M.: *The Hebrew Theatre: Its First Years* (Jerusalem: Weidenfeld and Nicolson, 1969)

BEN-AMI FEINGOLD

Dreyfus, George (b.1928) Australian composer and arranger. Dreyfus, who is regarded as one of Australia's finest contemporary composers, specializing in film music, was born in Wuppertal, Germany, and emigrated to Australia in 1939. After a basic education at an Orthodox Jewish school and Melbourne High School he entered the Melbourne Conservatorium where he studied clarinet, cor anglais, and bassoon. His first arrangements, which are said to reflect both his culture shock and his Jewish background, were written at this time. In 1947 he wrote his *Wind Quintet* for two oboes, horns, and bassoons. The next eight years were spent touring with theater orchestras, one year with the Victorian Symphony orchestra after which he went to Vienna to study the bassoon.

He received public notice in 1963 for his *From Within Looking Out*, a setting of a street song from Amman, for soprano, flute, celesta, vibraphone, and viola, and was commissioned to write the scores for two films and a television series on *Australian Painters*. Eight more film scores followed and from several of these he developed successful full-length orchestral works.

After spending some time overseas on a UNESCO scholarship Dreyfus returned to a music fellowship at the Australian National University where he continued to compose. His output has been about one major work per year, including some memorable film music, two symphonies, choral and operatic works, and chamber music. While in Israel, as Composer in Residence in the *Mishkenot Sha'ananim*, Jerusalem (1980), he wrote the music for a Yiddish musical (unfinished 1988).

His 16 awards and prizes include a Prix de Rome (1976), and the APRA Serious Music Award (1986).

BIBLIOGRAPHY

The Last Frivolous Book (Sydney, 1984)

ALAN D. CROWN

Dubnow, Simon (1860–1941) Russian historian. Born in Mstislavl, White Russia, Dubnow received a traditional Jewish education but was otherwise self-taught. Between 1880 and 1906, when he settled permanently in St Petersburg, he lived variously in Odessa, Mstislavl, and Vilna. He supported himself by journalism (*Rassvet, Voskhod*) and teaching (from 1908 at the Institute for Jewish Studies). Dubnow helped to found the Jewish Historico-Ethnographic Society in 1908 with Maxim Vinaver and Baron David Gunzburg, and until 1918 edited its quarterly journal *Yevreyskaya Starina*. Apart from journalism, teaching and historical research, Dubnow took an active part in current Jewish politics, particularly in relation to self-defense policy against pogroms and in the struggle for equality of Jewish rights in Czarist Russia. In 1906, in the ferment generated by the abortive

Simon Dubnow (6th from left) visiting a summer colony for children in Poland. Also in the group is Marc Chagall (5th from left)

revolution of 1905, he founded the Jewish People's Party to campaign for Jewish autonomy in Russia, but it never had much success. This brought him into opposition to both the Zionists and the Bundists. Dubnow welcomed the February revolution of 1917 but condemned the Bolshevik coup in October and left the USSR in 1922. He settled in Berlin, but in 1933, on the Nazi seizure of power, he moved to Riga. He refused all offers to emigrate, either to Palestine or the USA, and was killed in Riga in December 1941.

Dubnow's life work was his ten-volume *World History of the Jewish People* (Berlin 1925–9), translated into German by Dr A Steinberg from the Russian manuscript. Other important works of the Berlin period were Dubnow's edition of the Lithuanian *Pinkas 1623–1761* (1922) together with an introduction, and a *History of Hasidism* (in Hebrew; 1930–32). With the *World History* Dubnow became the successor to Heinrich GRAETZ as the Jewish "national" historian. But he set out from markedly different presuppositions. Dubnow was a secularist, influenced by John Stuart Mill and Auguste Comte, and, although deeply appreciative of the role of Judaism in preserving the Jewish people, he early rebelled against all religious attachment. In his own mature work he rejected what he termed the spiritual conception of a Leopold ZUNZ or a Graetz in favor of a sociological conception which saw the Jews as a nation, not merely as a religious community – and, moreover, a nation that had always asserted its autonomy. Thus he visualized Jewish history as a succession of changing autonomous centers, each dominant at a particular period. He saw an overriding connection linking the Sanhedrin at Yavneh, the Gaonate in Babylon, the *aljama* in Spain, the rabbinical assemblies in medieval France and Germany, and the Councils of Poland and Lithuania in the sixteenth and seventeenth centuries. In his own day Dubnow hoped to see the synagogal communities of Germany turn themselves into peoples' communities, that is, secular national autonomous bodies; and since he was writing in the era of mass emigration to the USA he hoped to see a Jewish corporate existence emerge there also. It followed from this that the Diaspora was not an anomaly, as the Zionists claimed, but the scene of what Dubnow called "substitutes for state-forms", that is, autonomous communities controlling not only religious life but also social relations, with their own educational and charitable institutions, enjoying powers of taxation and judicial administration. Dubnow's theory of what may be termed "the chosen people" grew out of this situation. He esteemed Israel as a unique nation that had emancipated itself from land and territory and yet preserved its nationhood. This was the highest type of nation to emerge hitherto.

BIBLIOGRAPHY

Pinson, K. S., ed. and trans.: *Nationalism and History: Essays on Old and New Judaism* (Philadelphia: Jewish Publication Society of America, 1958)

FURTHER READING

Steinberg, A. S., ed.: *Simon Dubnow, the Man and his Work* (Paris: Congrès Juif Mondial, 1963)
Rawidowicz, S. ed.: *Simon Dubnow in Memoriam* (London, Jerusalem, Waltham, 1954)

LIONEL KOCHAN

Dujovne, Leon (1899–1983) Argentine philosopher, lawyer, and writer. Dujovne was born in Russia and emigrated to Argentina as a child, settling with his family in one of the Jewish farmers' colonies in the province of Entre Rios. He belonged to the same generation of Russian-born Jewish immigrants who grew up in these colonies, like Alberto GERCHUNOFF, Samuel EICHELBAUM, and Nicolas Rapoport whose childhood was nurtured by the life and social environment of the Jewish pioneers in the JCA's settlements. Graduating very young as a lawyer at the University of Buenos Aires, Dujovne continued studying at the Faculty of Philosophy and Letters, and received his Ph.D. He taught for several decades and became one of the most prestigious professors of that faculty.

He published many books on the history of European philosophy, the most important of which is *Baruj Spinoza: su vida, su epoca, su obra e influencias* (1941–4, 4 vols; Baruch Spinoza: his life, his times, his works and influences). Among his other books *Teoria de los valores y filosofia de la*

Historia (1959; Theory of the values and philosophy of history), was awarded the first National Prize for philosophy in Argentina.

Dujovne was an original commentator on Jewish thinkers and a disseminator of Jewish philosophy. His main essays on the subject are: *Introduccion a la historia de la filosofia judia* (1949; Introduction to the history of Jewish philosophy), and *Martin Buber: sus ideas religiosas, filosoficas y sociales* (1966; Martin Buber: his religious, philosophic, and social ideas). Thanks to his stubborn endeavour to provide relevant works of Judaica in Spanish, Dujovne became the editor, translator (with collaborators) of the following, to which he provided the introduction: *Historia Universal del Pueblo Judio* (1950–51, 10 vols, by Simon DUBNOW; Universal history of the Jewish people); *Guida de los Descarriados* (1955; 3 vols, by Moses ben Maimon, Maimonides: Guide of the perplexed); works by B. Ibn Pakuda, Saadya Gaon, Shomo Ibn Gabirol; and Moses HESS's *Roma y Jerusalem* (1962; Rome and Jerusalem).

Dujovne also translated the Bible (1961, 2 vols) with the collaboration of Manases and Moshe Konstantynovsky, and the first books of *Sefer hazohar* (1978). As publicist and promoter of Jewish thought, Dujovne wrote short monographs published in the series *Great Individuals in Jewish History*, edited by the World Jewish Congress, Latin American branch; among the subjects were Heinrich GRAETZ, Salomon Ben-Maimon, and David BEN-GURION.

Dujovne's last book, *El Judaismo como cultura*, (1980; Judaism as culture), represents his attempt to interpret the Jewish heritage in terms of culture. Dujovne refers to a cultural model of explanation in order to create an interpretative Jewish framework for such concepts as man, nature, God, society, world, people, nation, exile, and redemption, by tracing them to the biblical source. His approach led him to a humanist, not religious, but national conception of the spiritual development of the Jewish people during the Diaspora experience until the birth of the State of Israel.

Dujovne lived in Israel for some years, and taught at the Hebrew University. He was editor of the weekly *Mundo Israelita*, Buenos Aires, and was appointed president of the Sociedad Hebraica Argentina and of the other central community institutions of Argentine Jewry.

LEONARDO SENKMAN

Dukas, Paul (1865–1935)

French composer, critic, and teacher. Born in Paris, Dukas entered the Paris Conservatoire in 1882, and came second in the Prix de Rome competition for his Cantata *Velléda* (1888). Further study produced many diverse works, all unpublished. Leaving the Conservatoire in 1889, he spent over a year in military service, returning to composing in 1891 when he completed his first major work, an overture to Pierre Corneille's *Polyeucte* (first performance 1892). This work showed the influence of two of his idols, Richard Wagner and César Franck. In 1895 Dukas started work on his three movement *Symphony in C Major* (first performance 1897). In the same year his most famous work, the symphonic scherzo *L'Apprenti Sorcier* also received its première. 1901 and 1903 saw the first performances of two important works in the repertory of French piano music, *Sonata in E Flat Minor* and *Rameau Variations*. His opera, *Ariane et Barbe-Bleue*, received its first performance in 1907, the ballet, *La Péri*, in 1912. He taught orchestration at the Paris Conservatoire from 1910 to 1913 and composition from 1928. He was elected to the Académie des Beaux Arts in 1934.

FURTHER READING
Favre, G.: *L'Oeuvre de Paul Dukas* (Paris, 1969)

SYDNEY FIXMAN

Dukes, Leopold Judah Loeb (1810–91)

Rabbinic scholar. Born in Pressburg, Hungary, Dukes received an Orthodox education, and was sent to the school of Moses Sofer. At the age of 23 he published the first volume of his book *Raschi zum pentateuch* (1883), which was a German translation of Rashi's commentary on the Pentateuch (*Hamishah humshei Torah 'im ha'atakah ashkenazit al perush Rashi*, 5 vols, 1933–38). He continued to publish books in various areas of Hebrew literature. Nevertheless, his scholarly work did not gain the unequivocal appreciation of the academic world, for he was not systematic and more than once made errors. Yet he was one of those scholars who devoted himself exclusively to study and, in spite of his poverty, visited European libraries, and discovered and published Hebrew manuscripts. In this way he contributed an enormous number of books and texts to Hebrew literature, including poetry by Ibn Gabirol and Moses ibn Ezra.

FURTHER READING

Davidson, I.: The study of mediaeval Hebrew poetry in the XIX century. *Proceedings of the American Academy* 1 (1928) 42–43

DEBORAH SCHECHTERMAN

Durkheim, Émile (1858–1917) French sociologist. Descended from an Alsatian rabbinical family, Durkheim began by teaching philosophy and before long specialized in sociology. His courses at the universities of Bordeaux (1887–1902) and Paris (from 1902), where he held the chair of education, his enquiries into issues of public concern (*The Division of Labour*, 1893; *Suicide*, 1897), and the foundation in 1898 of *L'Année Sociologique*, to which he was an assiduous contributor, did much to establish sociology as an academic discipline and a social science with practical aims. He had numerous followers, though not all of them sociologists; among them were several Jewish scholars: Halbwachs, Marcel MAUSS, Ernst BLOCH, Lucien LÉVY-BRUHL and his son Henri. In spite of Durkheim's self-proclaimed atheism, it is tempting to see his social philosophy – with its emphasis on the collective, group solidarity, and the fusion between morality and law – as having been inspired to some extent by his evident familiarity with Jewish law and ethics.

BIBLIOGRAPHY

Essays on Morals and Education (London: Routledge & Kegan Paul, 1979)
The Rules of Sociological Method (New York: Macmillan, 1982)

FURTHER READING

Fenton, S.: *Durkheim and Modern Sociology* (Cambridge: Cambridge University Press, 1984)

NELLY WILSON

Dutch–Jewish writing The 1880s were a watershed in the history of Dutch literature with the rise of the movement of the so-called "Eightiers", influenced by the English poets John Keats, Percy Bysshe Shelley, and Algernon Charles Swinburne, and authors such as Emile Zola, who were concerned with naturalism and social engagement.

Estella Hijmans (née Hertzveld, 1837–81), was the well-educated granddaughter of a Chief Rabbi of Zwolle. From the age of 15 she wrote numerous poems in the style of her time, often on a biblical theme, such as *Saul's Death* and *Esther*, in which she attempted to show in a lofty style the beauty of Judaism and the happiness it can bring even to the poorest Jews. Quite popular in her own day, she is now almost forgotten. Herman van den Bergh (1897–1967) is considered the founder of expressionist poetry in the Netherlands, through the literary journal *Het Getij* (1916–24). He published many volumes of poetry between 1917 and 1925, and again from 1954 to 1965.

Arnold Aletrino (1858–1916), born of a Sephardi family, became a medical doctor. As a hospital doctor he became familiar with the miserable life of many prostitutes and also of nurses whose working conditions he sought to improve. His naturalistic and pessimistic novels, such as *Zuster Bertha* (1891) and *Martha* (1895), give expression to this, and *Uit de Dood* (Out of death) to his obsession with death.

Herman de Man (1898–1946) was the son of poor Jewish parents but as an adult, together with his wife, converted to Roman Catholicism. His numerous powerfully written novels deal neither with his Jewish origins nor with his Roman Catholic faith but with the life of Calvinist peasants in the flat countryside between Utrecht and Gouda, an area he had got to know well as a pedlar when still a boy. He happened to be outside Holland at the time of the German invasion but his wife and most of his children were deported. Many of his twenty or more full length novels written between 1922 and 1940 deal with the struggle of man against the elements of water and wind.

Marianne Philips (1886–1951) was, in addition to writing novels, active as a socialist and was a Socialist Municipal Councillor in Bussum, east of Amsterdam. She began writing novels only after the age of 40. Some, such as *Henri van de overkant* (1936), contain autobiographical elements. After her death an annual literary prize was established in her name.

The post-war period

The five years of German occupation served as a watershed for Jewish authors in Holland. Several died in concentration camps such as Sally Pinkhof whose poems written in Bergen–Belsen were published posthumously as *Belsenbergen*, and Joseph Gompers, both of whom were closely connected with the Jewish community.

During the first two years following the German occupation several Jews who had survived either in hiding or in concentration camps published their experiences, for example S. van den Bergh (b.1912) in *Deportaties*. However the general public soon lost interest in these accounts; *The Diary of Anne Frank* could not at first find a publisher and even after its publication it gained little attention until its translation into English and German. The short novel by Marga Minco (b.1920) about her experiences during the German occupation, *Het Bittere Kruid* (The bitter herb), was published only in 1957. It was followed by several other short novels by her on the same theme, some of which have been translated. In 1958 she received the Vijverberg Prize.

Diaries of Dutch Jews who perished were published posthumously much later, for example those of David Koker (1914–1943) and the journalist Philip Mechanicus (d.1944). His *In Depot* (1978) had already been published in English translation in 1968 as *Year of Fear: A Jewish Prisoner Waits for Auschwitz*. *The Diaries of Etty Hillesum*, first published in 1983, translated into English as *An Interrupted Life*, were reprinted many times and translated into several languages, and were followed by two publications of later discovered manuscripts by her.

Interest in the wartime experiences of the Jews of Holland had first been aroused again by the historical survey, *Ondergang* by Jacob PRESSER, published in 1965, 20 years after the end of the German occupation. The three-volume *Collaboratie en Verzet* (1969/70; Collaboration and resistance) by Friedrich Weinreb (1910–88) was a controversial account by a highly controversial Jew.

Dr Eli A. Cohen, a psychiatrist who survived Auschwitz took his Ph.D. degree in 1953 with a thesis on human behavior in concentration camps (translated into English) and in 1979 published *The 19 Trains to Sobibor*.

During the past few years, and in particular on the occasion of the 40th anniversary of the liberation of The Netherlands in 1985, there have been numerous published personal accounts of Jewish survivors and of local Jewish communities in The Netherlands between 1940 and 45.

Memories of pre-war Dutch Jewry, and in particular of the poorer section of the Amsterdam Jewish quarter, where he himself was born, were recounted in the first place by Meyer Sluyser (1902–72), originally in sketches in the daily *Het Parool*, and then in five different volumes, beginning with *Die-en-die is er nog* (So-and-so is still there). These volumes of often humorous stories describe the Amsterdam Jewish quarter of Sluyser's childhood, soon after the turn of the century. They achieved enormous success among the Jewish and non-Jewish public, and were reprinted in one Omnibus volume in 1961. Sluyser was a Labor journalist who for many years worked for the Dutch Labor daily and the Dutch Labor broadcasting station.

Poets of Jewish origin are Maurits Mok and Leo Vroman. Mok (1907–89) published many volumes of poetry, both before and after the Second World War, including *Aan de vermoorden van Israel* (1950; To the murdered Jews). He has received several literary prizes.

Leo Vroman (b.1915), a biologist, has been living in New York since 1946, after escaping from Holland during the German invasion, and having been a prisoner of the Japanese during the Japanese occupation of the Dutch East Indies. Although he has been away from Holland for over forty years he writes his poetry in Dutch. He is highly regarded in Holland and in 1965 received the P. C. Hooft Prize. His poetry has no Jewish content.

Although there are many journalists of Jewish origin in Holland today, few, if any, novels or even short novels have been written on present-day Jewish life in The Netherlands, except for the impact on it of war-time traumata.

HENRIETTE BOAS

E

economics, Jews and Any discussion of "Jews and economics" has to confront two questions: "What is a Jew?" and "What is an economist?" These, however, are questions which invite controversy. To limit the present discussion to a manageable size, it is necessary, right at the start, to specify a particular approach which will confine consideration only to economists of eminence and yet will allow also for the inclusion of individuals, such as Ricardo and Marx, whose identification as Jews might be challenged on strict religious grounds.

It is evident that the Jewish contribution to economics and economic thought has been considerable. Of the 24 winners of the Nobel Prize in Economics from its institution from 1969 until 1986, eight, Paul Samuelson (1970), Kuznets (1971), Kenneth Arrow (1972), Leonid Kantorovich (1975), Milton Friedman (1976), Herbert Simon (1978), Lawrence Klein (1980), and Modigliani (1985), have been Jewish or of Jewish origin. Such a fact is interesting in itself but the researcher must probe further, despite the difficulties presented by the frequent non-availability of confirmation of Jewish identity in standard biographical texts. A Jewish name can be no assurance of pedigree; nor is the fact that a person was born in Israel or was a professor at the Hebrew University. One way out in identifying economists of eminence has been to follow Blaug (1985) in his identification of 100 great economists since Keynes (1883–1946). Investigation reveals that of these, 22 have a confirmed Jewish connection and five more, one strongly suspects, are or were Jewish. Of the approximately 1,070 leading world economists between the years 1700 and 1981, listed by Blaug and Sturges (1983) in their *Who's Who in Economics*, Jewish representation can be confidently estimated at being not less than ninety. These are the most prominent only. There have been hundreds more. Even the Blaug and Sturges directory has serious omissions as far as important Jewish economists are concerned.

What has been the reason for this extraordinary Jewish involvement in economics? Has it simply to do with socioeconomic factors and the high incidence of Jews generally in academic and professional pursuits, or is a reason possibly to be found in similarities between Judaism and economic philosophy? Certainly such similarities exist. Most importantly, both are concerned with the place of man in a wider context. Where the scope of Judaism is universal, that of economics is social, but both endeavor to provide perspective and guidance for behavior and action. There is also in both an interesting symbiotic connection between the prophetic and existential. In Judaism determinism is linked to God's concern for man and his consequent intervention in history. In economics, determinism has its origins in causality and is directed towards predicting economic and social processes. The existential in Judaism is linked to the continuing presence of an unchanging morality, and the unalterable value of the individual consciousness. The existential in economics is linked to the need to suspend time and ignorance for the purpose of analysis in the building of models which may be of help in understanding a more complex reality. Epistemologically both Judaism and economics embrace similar issues.

But further explanation of Jewish interest in economics no doubt is also to be found in the Jewish involvement with business and finance. In both Jewish experience and in economic experience, there has been a need to reconcile or integrate material concerns with those more transcending.

The story of eminent Jewish participation in economics must begin with David Ricardo, the London stockbroker who rose to prominence in the early nineteenth century, first as a member of Parliament and then as an expert in taxation and wider economic problems. It was Ricardo who developed further the labor theory of value of Adam Smith (*The Wealth of Nations*, 1776) which was later used by Karl MARX in the exposition of dialectical materialism and the Marxian theory of history and capitalist exploitation. Interestingly, both Ricardo and Marx rejected the Jewish faith, but their contribution to economic thought was such as to change everything thereafter. Even in our own time it has not been rivalled although individuals such as R. F. Kahn, Milton Friedman, Kenneth Arrow, and Harry Markowitz have participated in major turning-points in the direction of economic inquiry. Kahn's involvement was with John Maynard Keynes in his writing of *The General Theory of Employment, Interest, and Money* (1936), Friedman's with the revival of monetarism, Arrow's with the application of mathematics to the solution of economic problems and Markowitz's with the development of portfolio theory. A central idea in *The General Theory*, probably the most important work in economics this century, is that of the multiplier effect. Keynes borrowed this directly from Kahn. Friedman's revival of the quantity theory of money has been central to the contemporary emphasis in economic policy formulation on the causal link between monetary growth and inflation. The strong empirical emphasis in Friedman, and his reliance on statistical analysis, finds its quantitative theoretical counterpart in the works of both Arrow and Markowitz. Arrow's application of symbolic logic has transformed the nature of quantitative analysis while Markowitz's system of portfolio selection has transformed both the theory and practice of finance.

From the point of view of this note, however, perhaps the most interesting development has been the Jewish contribution to the contemporary revival of the Austrian school, and to subjectivism in economic methodology. Here the names of von Mises, Lachmann, and Kirzner must be mentioned. While sharing common origins with modern neo-classical thought, subjectivism has raised important objections to the whole notion of general equilibrium upon which much of such thought rests. Essentially, the subjectivist contention is that general equilibrium is flawed because it postulates a state of knowledge, a harmony of plans and expectations, and a simultaneity in adjustment which are totally at odds with the real world. The direction of neo-classical economics has been greatly influenced, since Isaac Newton, by the development of the physical sciences. Subjectivism has taken issue with attempts at quantification in economics, as if the latter could be likened to classical mechanics, because of the critical role in economics of the indeterminate expectations of economic agents, and, hence, of uncertainty. Subjectivism, therefore, changes the entire focus of economics as an intellectual discipline and would drive its progress along a totally new course. If this proves to be so, a Jewish presence will once again have made itself felt.

FURTHER READING

Blaug, M.: *Economic Theory in Retrospect* (London: Heinemann Educational Books, 1977)
——: *Great Economists since Keynes: An Introduction to the Lives and Works of One Hundred Modern Economists* (Brighton: Wheatsheaf Books, 1985)
Schumpeter, J. A.: *History of Economic Analysis* (London: George Allen & Unwin, 1954)

R. W. BETHLEHEM

education, modern Jewish The development and dilemmas of modern Jewish education reflect the profound challenges which Jewry faced with its acceptance into general culture, and as it confronted unprecedented historical events. The condition of Jewish education is an especially important indicator, both of the Jews' various modes of adaptation to their surroundings and, as a prime Jewish value, of the vitality of the culture itself.

Eighteenth century

While traditional pre-modern Jewish education had occasionally included instruction in secular sciences and languages, the norm (particularly in Eastern Europe) was an emphasis on traditional texts for the majority of boys through *bar mitzvah* age. The main institution was the *heder* (literally, "room"). Communally supervised, it was financed by the family of each student, with a separate *heder* for the poor, financed by the community. Among the weaknesses of the *heder* was the generally unprofessional, under-educated background of the teachers, and their total reliance on the goodwill of the parents. Advanced Talmud study – the educational ideal – was reserved for a small minority of students in *yeshivot*. Girls generally did not receive more than a rudimentary formal education at home. In Sephardi communities (Middle East and North Africa), there was a greater emphasis on Bible, though economic pressures reduced enrollment.

The beginnings of the Emancipation brought new ideas in the realm of education, too. Naphtali Herz WESSELY's essay "Words of peace and truth" (Berlin, 1782), is important both for its new conception of education and for the reaction it provoked. Wessely asserted that Jews should first learn "human knowledge" (etiquette, natural and social sciences, and German) before undertaking the study of God's Torah. The explicit goal was to prepare Jews to become productive participants in general society. Traditionalists attacked Wessely, seeing in his proposals not an accommodation to modernity, but the total undermining of traditional life.

Nineteenth century

Several key education issues arose from the Emancipation. The first was the balance between Jewish and secular studies. With the desire to become integrated into western life, instruction in Jewish subjects took second place to secular studies. Indeed, the issue of the control of the schools reflects the struggle over whether Jews were to be educated by the local Jewish community as was traditional, or in government schools, with Jewish education either a private affair for each family or as a supplementary endeavor sponsored by the community. The languages to be learned, and the language of instruction, are another barometer of the adaptations to modernity. Use of Yiddish as a language of instruction has, to this day, betokened a rejection of modernity among religious groups. Towards the end of the century, use of Hebrew indicated the acceptance of a new Jewish nationalism.

The content of religious studies themselves underwent a transformation, from the study of classical texts with a uniquely Jewish message (Talmud and codes), to the study of a more universalized Jewish religion and ethics, often modeled on Christian forms, in terms of content (for example catechisms), ceremonies (for example confirmation), and educational settings (the first Jewish Sunday school in the US was founded by Rebecca Gratz in 1838 in Philadelphia). The forces of change were so great that in western Europe the *heder* and *yeshivah* almost totally disappeared by mid-century, though they persisted in eastern Europe.

A prime example of governmental intervention to acculturate Jews was the network of schools sponsored by the Russian government, established by Max Lilienthal in 1841. They functioned for more than a generation, educating thousands of pupils and, equally important, gave their faculty the security and status which helped them to become the leadership of the Russian Jewish Enlightenment.

The response of the traditionalists was twofold: first, new forms of the traditional *yeshivah* (for example Rabbi Haim's founding of the *yeshivah* in Volozhin, Lithuania, in 1803, which was independent of the local community), which have persisted to this day, despite the death blow dealt by the Holocaust; and also the founding of modern seminaries and universities within the framework of traditional observance (for example Azriel HILDESHEIMER's rabbinic seminary in Berlin, 1873, and Yeshiva University in the USA, 1886). The ultra-Orthodox also founded new institutions, for example the Hatam Sofer's *yeshivah* in Pressburg (1806), the largest since the talmudic age.

Neo-Orthodoxy had its educational innovators at the elementary and secondary levels, too. Samson Raphael HIRSCH opened a school in

Frankfurt in 1855, noteworthy for its being coeducational and for combining an intensive program of Jewish studies with a secular studies program modeled on German private schools.

Judaism's new religious movements also founded institutions of higher learning, primarily for the training of rabbis: Zacharias FRANKEL's Jewish Theological Seminary (Breslau, 1854) was the spiritual forerunner of the Conservative Jewish Theological Seminary of America (New York, 1886); and the Reform Hebrew Union College (Cincinnati, 1875).

In North Africa and the Middle East, the major innovation was the school system established by the ALLIANCE ISRAÉLITE UNIVERSELLE, beginning in the 1860s. While French language and culture were emphasized, Jewish subjects were taught as well. Traditional schools were often influenced by the neighboring AIU school.

Before the First World War

The waves of mass migration from east to west which preceded the war led to profound changes in Jewish education. The mass of new immigration overwhelmed local school systems. The initial reaction was the opening of private *hadarim*. Communal responses to the new situation soon developed, often with the goal of acculturating the new immigrants and of counteracting missionary activity. In the USA, community *talmudei torah* were founded, their success often due to well-educated teachers from Europe and an ideological fervor linked to rising Jewish nationalism. The first Bureau of Jewish Education was founded in New York in 1910 with Samson Benderly as director. Patterned after the board of education in the public schools, the BJEs did much to organize and standardize Jewish education, especially in terms of teacher training and licensing, publishing textbooks, and so on. In the following decades, every major US city was to have a BJE in one form or another. In London, the Talmud Torah Trust was founded in 1905, which supplemented the various "free [all day] schools", many of which dated from the early part of the nineteenth century.

A second major innovation came in the area of Jewish education for women. In 1917 Sarah Schenirer founded the Bais Ya'akov schools, primarily to strengthen the commitment to Judaism of girls from very observant homes, who were allowed exposure to secular culture forbidden to their brothers. The schools also included a vocational training component, absent from most traditionalist boys' schools.

The positive stance of S. R. Hirsch towards women's education has already been noted (as early as 1855) and, in general, the Enlightenment in western (though not eastern) Europe and USA resulted in increased Jewish education for women.

The World Wars

The main positive development of this period was the national rebirth in Israel, especially after the Balfour Declaration (1917). It enhanced Zionist and Hebrew school systems among both the religious and non-religious, especially in eastern Europe. There was a counter-reaction among the ultra-religious, as well as increasing linkage of a variety of Jewish political parties with school systems. Yiddish education reached its zenith.

There were numerous negative developments. The revolution in Russia isolated its Jewry and ended most Jewish education, except for some activity in Yiddish. The war destroyed or disrupted many of the leading *yeshivot*. These disruptions – together with flight from Nazism – did yield the transfer of some traditional scholarship to western Europe (for example, Gateshead *yeshivah* was founded in England in 1927) and the USA. Many of the scholars found their way to the rabbinical seminaries and to the newly formed Hebrew teachers' colleges in nearly a dozen USA cities.

The Holocaust ended half a millennium of Jewish scholarship in eastern and central Europe. Gone, too, was comprehensive Jewish communal living which was the social base for effective education. No Diaspora community has been able to reconstruct those achievements on a large scale. In the Nazi-occupied territories of North Africa and Italy, education was suppressed, though not destroyed.

Post-war developments

Following the destruction of European Jewry, the centers of Jewish education shifted to North America and the new State of Israel, with important individual educational institutions in Latin America, the English-speaking world (Australia and South Africa) and western Europe. In the US, synagogue-based supplementary schools gradually displaced the communal *talmudei torah*, with increasing enrollment but much less intensive programs of study. All-day Jewish schools (pioneered by the Orthodox) increased in popularity, attaining nearly one-quarter of total enrollment. In many other parts of the world, all-day Jewish education is the norm, reaching over 90 percent in some Latin American and Moslem countries. Jewish education in the US is highly decentralized, with most decisions made autonomously by each of the approximately 2,500 schools. Other countries tend towards more centralization, with about 1,000 schools outside the USA.

Total enrollment in Jewish schools in the Diaspora in 1982 was about half a million, two-thirds of that amount in the US. About 40 percent of eligible Jewish students (age 3–17) are enrolled in Jewish schools at any one time, ranging from about 25 percent in France, to about 40 percent in the US, to about 70 percent in the small countries of Latin America. Enrollment beyond *bar mitzvah* age is problematic. In the USA, pre-*bar mitzvah* enrollment includes about two-thirds of Jewish youth, while enrollment of 13 to 15 year olds is only half that and continues to drop throughout the high school years. The burgeoning of Jewish studies programs at hundreds of universities and, at the other extreme, early childhood programs has been a very positive development.

Israel plays an important role in world-wide Jewish education, both for the materials and personnel it provides to Diaspora schools (schools in some small and mid-sized communities could not function without them), as well as being the site for the thousands of young people who each year take part in educational trips to Israel, some of them lasting from several months to a year.

Informal education

A. P. Schoolman founded the Cejwin camps in 1919 and, since then, summer camping has been recognized as a powerful educational force. Various youth groups and movements have also been effective, though maintaining educational, in addition to purely social, activities has been a challenge. Similarly, Jewish community centers have been important social magnets, and there is a recent trend to upgrade the Jewish content of their programs.

Some current issues

Perhaps the critical issue world-wide is the shortage of Jewish education personnel (paralleling the shortage in general education). While Jewish teaching has always been a high status function, it was almost always a low status position. In earlier times, an enriched Jewish community (family and neighborhood) compensated somewhat for the weak instructional staff. New educational materials and technology only partially offset the current shortage of effective teachers.

Adult education has always been a Jewish ideal, and new forms of adult and family education make this a promising area. The outstanding modern example was the "Free Jewish House of Learning" (*Lehrhaus*) established by Franz ROSENZWEIG and others in Frankfurt in 1920.

FURTHER READING

Fishman, I.: *History of Jewish Education in Central Europe (from the End of the Sixteenth to the End of the Eighteenth Century)* (London: Edward Goldston, 1944)

Kurzweil, Z.: *Modern Trends in Jewish Education* (New York: Thomas Yoseloff, 1964)

Ozer, C.: *Jewish Education in the Transition from Ghetto to Emancipation* (Historia Judaica, 1947)

Pilch, J.: *History of Jewish Education in America* (New York: American Association for Jewish Education, 1969)

DAVID RESNICK

educational culture, Jewish The demands of Jewish learning begin with two well known passages in the Torah: "You shall teach them diligently to your children", and "You shall tell your child (about the Exodus) on that day, saying...". The first of these passages follows the charge "Hear, O Israel", the declaration of faith, as it has come to be called, and refers to the obligation to teach the basic religious principles in every time and venue. The second refers to the obligation of a parent to instruct children about the liberation from Egypt. These obligations are carried forth into the post-biblical period with the same intensity as is suggested by Scripture, and the Talmud dwells at length on the variety of ways to carry it out; on the nature of the students and the prescriptions for teachers and parents. Learning is a basic obligation which rests upon the family. The notion of family as an instrument of teaching has been propelled – vaguely at times, more vigorously at other times – into modern and post-modern life. But once the biblical period concluded, two revolutions turned Jewish learning inside out. First was the emerging discipline of exegesis, and the second was the emergence of formal institutions of learning. The two are related.

Jewish schooling must be said to begin at a later date than the biblical charge to teach. It begins, really, at the time when the Temple cult was disrupted by Greek domination in the Middle East, and more definitively by the hostile Roman government. This political condition developed simultaneously with the decline of the institution of the Priesthood. The Jewish response to this cataclysm was to develop something that was as close to schooling as we can find in the ancient world. Along with that schooling arose the quintessential Jewish activity of textual interpretation. In this period the talmudic and midrashic literatures came to develop new kinds of reference: to the study house of Moses; to a mythic learning in which the righteous engage in the eternal life after their death; and to the sound of children's voices emanating from one or another house of study. Such metaphors represent the beginning of a new esthetic in Jewish literature which has dominated thinking about culture and education for nearly two millennia. Through these metaphors, one can see that leadership of the Jewish community has shifted to a class of scholars who developed the consolation that the destruction of the Temple is, at one and the same time, a punishment for Jewish suffering, and an opportunity for the development of learning as a substitution for the old Temple cult. As Alan Mintz has noted in his work *Hurban*, "Israel is never alone...if they lack God, they possess the text which...can be their solace". Thus texts abound which promise that studying about the sacrifical cult is a substitute for the performance of the cultic obligations. To be sure, the establishment of a scholarly class is a kind of consolation – for those who are part of it, obviously, and even for those who only identified with it. In this way, the endurance of Torah as an institution was viewed by some as the natural outgrowth of the loss of the previous institution, the Temple. One Midrash notes that the Temple was destroyed because the Children of Israel had forsaken study of the Torah (implying the reverse, as well, namely that study of Torah will now be rewarded). Rabbinic literature began to develop not only themes about the importance of study, but methods of reading and communication which became the early prototypes of instruction: repetition and rote learning, mnemonic devices, rules for textual exegesis, the use of story and parable, intertextual allusion, and rhetorical argument for proper religious and moral practice.

The scholarly leadership was more democratic than the previously dominant mode of leadership, the priesthood. This elite became a meritocracy. The teachings of both Jews and many early Christians were conducted with forms which grew up during this "rabbinic period"; and they were aimed at the broad public. Yet some of those forms re-instituted an elitism of interpreters, cadres of men who were initiated, for example, into the special reference of allegory and parable. The parable on parables which we find in Mark and Matthew reflects a tension between populism and elitism (Mark iv and Matthew xiii). For here one view of parable is that, by way of the device, the uninitiated come to understand mystery; whereas, the second view is that parables may only be penetrated by the initiated. The history of education and interpretation is a kind of paradigm for the constant swings between the maintenance of a tradition in the hands of the proper interpreters, and the sharing of that tradition with the population at large. In any event, Torah became the norm for Jewish behavior, and the word "Torah" developed into the signification that was to dominate Jewish value systems for the next 2,000 years.

Torah means "study" generically, but the reading of "The Torah", the sacred book itself, is perpetuated through weekly readings, or lections, which became one of the dominant instructional modes of Jewish life. As if anticipating some contemporary literary theory, repetition became one of the ways of finding something new in the ancient literature. For only recently have scholars given theoretical justification to the persistent re-reading of the same text. And as if anticipating the modern struggle to privilege, translation, the Aramaic rendering of Torah, became one of the profound topics of rabbinic conversation. The translation of the Torah into that vernacular may be seen as an early model for what all instruction of an ancient tradition comes to be: the teaching of a sacred notion in a "language" that people in a different time will understand. And with Targum, Jewish culture is introduced into yet another area in which teaching and esthetic development come together: the imaginative potential in translation. For every time we translate we are using language to do what the good educator tries to do: to find words in the contemporary vernacular to capture an essence from another vernacular.

Torah came to be viewed as the native activity of the Jew; and in a surprising way, interpretation became equally native. The *perush*, as Simon Rawidowicz has pointed out, is essential to Jewish continuity. The Islamic ascription of the term "people of the book" changed meaning, from its intended sense that Jews were the people whose story is told in the Torah, to the signification that Jewish destiny is dependent upon a life of reading and learning. The "people of the book" retain that label within American culture because so many book store customers are Jewish.

Under the dominion of the Romans, Jews may have studied at their peril. A popular legend developed about Rabbi Akiba, whose disciples asked one day if he were not afraid for his life since the Romans had interdicted Torah study. He answered with a parable comparing Torah to water: A fox sees that the fish in a stream are struggling to escape the nets of their tormentors. He therefore invites the fish to come onto land safely out of the reach of their enemies. The fish answer the fox with the confident notion that they would rather remain swimming in their native territory than try to survive in some presumably safer but foreign atmosphere. But the parable of the fox and the fish is more important than the singular allegorical notion of the fish out of water. It points out as well that the study of the Jewish tradition may be carried out at the expense of relations with the dominant social power. Sometimes that strain is characterized by out and out prohibition, as in ancient Rome, or the contemporary USSR. Sometimes it has been more subtle, and has included the voluntary relinquishing by Jews in the face of a more popular host culture, as may be said to have been the case in Russia early in this century and in North America to which Jews have emigrated for the past century and a half. Its legendary example was Germany in the pre-Hitler period. As the notion of host culture becomes more global, it is even true in contemporary Israel, where secular universalism grows from the nation's very Jewish particularity.

Indeed, one of the characteristic descriptions of Jewish educational experience in the West has included the realization that Jews have stood in tension between an impulse to preserve the Jewish heritage, and the need to adopt social and cultural mores of new host cultures and modern times. The genius of Judaism has been an inspired use of adaptation motifs combined with a commitment to preservation of tradition. Jewish educational experience has, to some extent, become a paradigm for efforts to retain culture, to establish traditions, and to canonize a proper literature for the maintenance of culture. The Jewish educational problem is much at home in the discourse of literary critics who have written of the struggle to retain tradition (such as Kermode and Eliot). And Jewish educational institutions share the efforts of the western university tradition to preserve learning while insisting that humanistic culture can penetrate a technologically biased future. But, lofty as these notions are, there is a pragmatic aspect to this thinking about learning and teaching. In the contemporary Jewish world, schools have replaced the home as the locus of learning. As schools have assumed their task, a more technologically oriented world outside of schools meets a more institutional attitude within the life of schools. Jewish education loses some of its natural and organic relationship to the environment of the child. On a practical level, Jewish educators must think first of both teaching Jewish facts to children, and bringing them into some comfortable relationship with the living aspects of the culture. For them, the tasks of high culture and its analogies must be secondary.

Yet there is a relationship between what drives an educational history and what sustains an intellectual tradition and cultural heritage. The struggle reflected within the history of Jewish education, whether around method or around content, is part of what is evident in the broader fields of literature and art; and the search for pluralistic approaches to meaning is evidenced in Jewish literature and art. Many cultures are struggling to identify the basic immutable principles in a world of constant change, and to retain a sense of the classic within the dynamic present. Jewish educational history is a natural paradigm for understanding culture in general, committed as that history has been to interpreting an original text (sometimes thought to be pure) for an impure and constantly evolving nation. The cultural behavior of the human family draws heavily from that tension.

In the effort to promote the Jewish future, every generation has created houses of study, and organizational networks for the production of teachers, materials, and places for the teachers to present the material to the learner. At the level of advanced study, universities in America and western Europe support the vast scholarly resources of contemporary Israel; and the major religious movements continue to nurture seminaries of advanced research and professional training. At the more popular levels, there are huge numbers of Jewish schools, representing both different instructional strategies and varied philosophical attitudes. With millions of Jewish citizens committed to particular settings of philosophical and instructional design, the current scene in Jewish education carries the promise of a future. And while ideological battles continue between the Orthodox and non-Orthodox communities, most Jews have developed a prior agenda of Jewish survival, the continuation of Jewish schooling, and an enhancement of affiliation with both the universal values of Jewish tradition and the centralization of the national dream in Israel. To that end Jewish young people are served by thousands of schools, tens of thousands of teachers, publishing houses, and instructional networks, and the classic aspirations for the future. Much of this growth seems to spite the ruthless program of Nazism, but much of it is, as well, part of the inner energy of Jewish educational tradition. The weakening knowledge among modern enlightened adult communities may, however, be the very stimulus for the assurance of a future.

This basic pattern of Jewish educational history, the pattern of adapting while retaining through interpretation, counter reading and innovation, will continue into the twenty-first century with its newest instances of struggle to associate with the past.

FURTHER READING

Mintz, A.: *Hurban: Responses to Catastrophe in Hebrew Literature* (New York: Columbia University Press, 1984)
Rawidowicz, S.: *Studies in Jewish Thought* (Philadelphia: Jewish Publication Society, 1974)

WILLIAM CUTTER

Ehrenburg, Ilya Grigorevich (1891–1967)

Russian writer. Born in Kiev, Ehrenburg moved with his family to Moscow at the age of five. His father was a well-to-do brewery owner and the family were assimilated, but Ehrenburg's schooldays were not free from anti-Semitic insults. During the 1905 revolution Ehrenburg joined the Social Democrats and became close to Nikolai Bukharin. After his arrest, his parents managed to get him abroad to Paris. Around 1911 he turned to Catholicism. Francis Jammes and Léon Bloy influenced the Christian mysticism of the early verse of these years and Ehrenburg's prose of the 1920s speaks in not dissimilar terms of Jewish suffering in the pogroms as part of a Divine plan of redemption through evil. Ever the chameleon, Ehrenburg nevertheless consistently declared his identification with the Jewish people whenever anti-

Semitism threatened, despite his distance from a Jewish way of life.

Ehrenburg's journalism of the First World War declares his pacifism, though by the Second World War he was being criticized for his aggressive anti-German stand. After the February Revolution Ehrenburg returned to Russia, but in 1918 he decided to join the White retreat southwards. Caught up in a pogrom in Kiev, Ehrenburg traveled to the Crimea. He then returned to Bolshevik Moscow, rejecting religious faith and collaborating with "History". Following a brief incarceration by the Cheka secret police, Ehrenburg emigrated from the USSR in 1921.

Works on Jewish themes include *Neobychaynye pokhozhdeniya Khulio Khurenito i ego uchenikov...* (1922; *The Extraordinary Adventures of Julio Jurenito and his Disciples*, 1958), which features representatives of various nations, including Ehrenburg himself, who discuss the Jewish Question and criticize the modern world. An apocalyptic pogrom is depicted in the story, "Shifs-Karta" (1922; The steamship ticket), illustrated by El Lissitsky, with whom Ehrenburg collaborated in Berlin. *Burnaya zhizn Lazika Roytshvanetsa* (1928; *The Stormy Life of Lazik Roitshvants*, 1960), tells of a luckless Jewish tailor from Gomel, a Švejk type who finds himself in trouble in the USSR, the West, and Palestine. The novel is critical of both Bolshevism and Zionism, and it has never been published in the USSR.

During the years of emigration, Ehrenburg alternated between west European cosmopolitanism and Russian patriotism, provoking much hostility from fellow émigrés for the presumptuousness of such a stand by a Jew. Ehrenburg championed the cause of Russian culture even in accounts of hasidic life in Poland, which he saw as corrupted and decaying, apart from the joy he discerned among followers of NAHMAN OF BRATSLAV.

The destruction of east European Jewry in the Holocaust affected Ehrenburg deeply. He was active in the wartime Soviet–Jewish anti-Fascist Committee and, after the liberation of the concentration camps, compiled, together with Vasilii GROSSMAN, witness accounts of Nazi crimes, *Chernaya kniga* (The black book; repressed by the Soviet authorities, but published in

the West). Ehrenburg also protested at the anti-Semitic treatment of Jewish war heroes and campaigned for the full recognition of their contribution to the Soviet war effort. The USSR recognized the State of Israel in 1948, but in a *Pravda* article Ehrenburg warned Soviet Jews that the USSR was their homeland and that they should not put their hopes in Zionism. There are differing views on Ehrenburg's position during the "anticosmopolitan" campaign and the repression of Jewish culture in the last years of Stalin's life; however, in 1953, at the time of the "Doctors' plot", he wrote a letter to the Soviet leader, refusing to sign an anti-Jewish petition.

The post-Stalin "thaw" was signalled by Ehrenburg's novel called *Ottepel* (1954; *The Thaw*, 1954), which characterizes the petty tyranny and inhumanity of a factory manager and other bureaucrats under Stalinism. The Jewish physician, Vera Sherer, stands out as a figure of unusual human warmth, who is treated sympathetically as a victim saved by Stalin's death from the trumped-up charges of the "Doctors' plot" affair.

Between 1960 and 1965 there appeared Ehrenburg's multi-volume memoirs, *Lyudi, gody, zhizn* (*People and Life*, 1962; *Memoirs*, 1964), which describe many of Ehrenburg's contemporaries, including such figures as Marc CHAGALL, Isaac BABEL, Solomon Mikhoels, Itzik FEFER, Peretz MARKISH, and Dovid BERGELSON, but which evade the question of Ehrenburg's own survival.

Enfant terrible and party mouthpiece, anti-Zionist and proud defender of Jews against Nazism and anti-Semitism, poet, essayist, journalist, and novelist, Ehrenburg remains one of the most controversial personalities in Soviet Jewish culture.

BIBLIOGRAPHY

The Thaw, trans. M. Harari (London: Harvill, 1954); *Julio Jurenito*, trans. A. Bostok (London: Macgibbon & Kee, 1958); *The Stormy Life of Lazik Roitshvants*, trans. A. Brown (London: Elek Books, 1960); *People and Life*, 6 vols (London: Macgibbon & Kee, 1961–66)

FURTHER READING

Goldberg, A.: *Ilya Ehrenburg: Writing, Politics and the Art of Survival* (London: Weidenfeld, 1984)

Redllich, S.: *Propaganda and Nationalism in Wartime Russia: The Jewish Antifascist Committee in the USSR, 1941–1948* (Boulder: East European Monographs, 1982)

EFRAIM SICHER

Ehrenpreis, Marcus (Mordecai) (1869–1951)

Swedish rabbi and writer. Ehrenpreis was born in Lemberg (Lvov), son of a printer. After his examination in Rabbinics at Berlin, Ehrenpreis completed his Ph.D. thesis, *Kabbalistische Studien*, in Erlangen (1895). He served as a rabbi in Djakovo and Esseg, Slovenia (1896–1900), and was Chief Rabbi of Bulgaria (1900–14), and of Stockholm (1914–41). He sought to improve the conditions of Jews in the Balkans during his period there, and organized humanitarian aid for Jewish refugees during both World Wars.

He was prominent among the initiators of the first Zionist congress in Basel, and at subsequent congresses acted as adviser on cultural matters.

Ehrenpreis took up writing in Hebrew in 1884 for *Hamaggid*, and later for the journal, *Hashiloah*. His stimulating criticism and scholarly essays had a formative influence on modern Hebrew literature. He became one of the leading figures among those late nineteenth-century writers, *Hatze'irim*, whose goals were the formation of a Judaism with European cultural elements, combined with emancipation from Orthodox traditionalism. Opposing the cultural politics propagated by AHAD HA'AM, Ehrenpreis demanded a thoroughly secularized Hebrew literature.

During the First World War his theoretical as well as his practical perspective moved away from Zionism. He now became the advocate of a spiritual nationalism, the dispersal of the Jewish people, accepting their historic and religious mission among the nations.

As Chief Rabbi of the Stockholm congregation he established several Jewish cultural institutions, for example, the journal *Judisk tidsskrift*, founded in 1928. He attempted to increase people's knowledge of Judaism, both among Jews and non-Jews. His importance for Swedish Jewish life is immense.

His Swedish writings, the larger part of which have been translated into several European languages, consist of a great many books, a large number of pamphlets, and translations from Yiddish and modern Hebrew. Among his books are *De som byggt Israel*, (1929–43; The builders of Israel), a collection of essays containing a number of soulful characterizations of biblical prophets.

He won recognition as an outstanding Swedish stylist with his pensive books on travels to the East and to Spain, one of them *Österlandets själ* (1926; The soul of the East), the other *Landet mellan öster och väster* (1927; The country between East and West). In 1946 his autobiography *Mitt liv mellan öst och väst* (My life between East and West) appeared, also in Hebrew translation.

FURTHER READING

Waxman, M.: *A History of Jewish Literature* (New York: Thomas Yoseloff, 1960) vol. 4, 408–409

JUDITH WINTHER

Ehrenstein, Albert (1886–1950)

Austrian writer. Born in Vienna, Ehrenstein spent most of his life in Berlin. In 1933 he emigrated to Switzerland, and in 1941 to the USA. He died in New York. He was one of the foremost German Expressionist writers. His first work was *Tubutsch* (1911), followed by *Selbstmord eines Katers* (1912; Suicide of a cat), both prose works. Poetry collections include *Die rote Zeit* (1917; The red age), and *Briefe an Gott* (1922; Letters to God).

Ehrenstein had a generally pessimistic view of modern Western society, and became engrossed in the culture of the Orient, especially China. His style has been likened (Weiss) to that of an Old Testament prophet. In his youth Ehrenstein was heavily critical of Jews, as shown in his *Begräbnis* (1912; Burial), but his views changed. In the collection of essays *Menschen und Affen* (1925; Men and apes), he elaborated on many aspects of the Jewish question. In "Zionismus" Ehrenstein criticized assimilants for aping their environment, but saw Zionism as, in turn, merely creating a "Jewish national park", which, through separation, would neutralize the Jews, who constituted one of the few vibrant elements in European civilization. In the same volume Ehrenstein attacked the Jews for inventing monotheism, in his view unnatural, but, on the other hand, praised Jews for their contribution to modern culture. He further attacked as cowards those who denied their Jewish identity. He explained the large Jewish role as being due to the religious tradition of the Word, and stressed the ethical component of this Jewish contribution. In 1930 Ehrenstein visited Palestine.

FURTHER READING

Weiss, E.: Albert Ehrenstein. In *Juden in der deutschen Literatur*, ed. G. Krojanker (Berlin: Welt-Verlag, 1922)

STEVEN BELLER

Ehrlich, Arnold Bogomil (1848–1919)
American biblical exegete and philologist. Born in Wlodawa, Russian Poland, where he received a traditional Jewish education, he left for Germany in 1865 in order to pursue general studies. In Leipzig he was befriended by Franz Delitzsch whom he assisted in translating the New Testament into Hebrew (1877). He converted to Christianity in order to enter the world of scholarship in Germany, but upon settling in the USA in 1876 he returned to the Jewish fold. Ehrlich remained an admirer of Delitzsch and in 1888–9 published his autobiographical recollections in *Saat auf Hoffnung* (Seed for hope), a missionary journal edited by Delitzsch. In his struggle to made a living in America, he took up various occupations. He opened an artist's studio and offered lessons in calligraphy and stenography. For some years he taught at the Hebrew Preparatory School of Temple Emanu-El in New York. His chrestomathy of rabbinic literature, *Rashei perakim* (Outlines), appeared in 1884.

Ehrlich was a pioneering contributor to the American Yiddish press. He made his debut in 1879 in *Di Yudishe Gazetn* with a poem. During the 1880s he contributed novels and articles to this publication. In 1886 his novel *Tray biz in der tod* (True unto death) appeared as a separate publication.

Ehrlich soon forsook Yiddish writing for biblical scholarship, which was to be his main preoccupation for the rest of his life. His biblical works include: *Mikra kifeshuto* 3 vols, (1889–1901; The Bible according to its plain meaning), *Die Psalmen* (1905; The Psalms), a new translation and commentary; and *Randglossen zur hebraeischen Bibel* 7 vols., (1908–14; Marginal notes to the Hebrew Bible).

Because of his originality and linguistic expertise Ehrlich has been ranked with the leading Bible scholars of the nineteenth century. While he was taken to task for an independence of spirit, which led him to reject previous Hebrew exegetes and to deride Christian scholarship, his many insights into the biblical text, and his remarkable feeling for biblical Hebrew have rendered his work among the most important contributions to biblical scholarship made in the USA.

FURTHER READING

Gottheil, R.: Arnold B. Ehrlich. In *The Life of Gustav Gottheil* (Williamsport, 1936) 75–81
Kabakoff, J.: New light on Arnold Bogomil Ehrlich. *American Jewish Archives* 36 (1984) 202–224
Orlinsky, H. M.: Prolegomenon. In *Mikra kifeshuto*, vol. 1 (repr. New York, 1969) ix–xxxiii

JACOB KABAKOFF

Ehrlich, Joseph R. (1842–1899)
Austrian writer. Born in Brody, Galicia, Ehrlich grew up in the hasidic community there. Educated at the German Jewish school, more or less against his guardian's will, he eventually broke with the Hasidim and made his way to Vienna where he studied philosophy at the university and subsequently made a career as a poet and journalist. He was described by Heinrich GOMPERZ as a successful example of Jewish "self-overcoming," and by the young Theodor HERZL as "a shabby little Jew."

Ehrlich's autobiography, *Der Weg meines Lebens* (1874; My life's way), provides a fascinating view of life in the Jewish community of Brody in the 1840s and 1850s. The hasidic community is seen as a hive of reaction and superstition. The tradition of learning has become hollow, the teaching methods irrational and cruel. The richer *maskilic* community is seen as performing a true mission of civilization in opening a German Jewish school, where Ehrlich learns of a new world, of Nature, and virtue (mainly through reading Moses MENDELSSOHN's *Phaedon*). Germany is seen by the young Ehrlich as an ideal country; his great act of rebellion against the Hasidim is to put up a map of the world in the synagogue. Ehrlich emerges as a remarkable mixture of the two strands of Judaism, transferring Hasidism's high spirituality to the natural world, experiencing God in Nature. His vision of himself as being "part of the ordered universe" provides parallels with figures from a similar background, such as Siegfried LIPINER and Wilhelm NEURATH.

BIBLIOGRAPHY

Gomperz, H., and Kann, R. A. eds: *Briefe an, von und um Josephine von Wertheimstein* (Vienna: Österreichischen Akademie der Wissenschaften, 1981)

FURTHER READING

Stewart, D.: *Theodore Herzl* (London: Hamilton, 1974)

STEVEN BELLER

Eichelbaum, Samuel (1894–1967) Argentine playwright. Born in Dominguez, Entre Rios Province, Argentina, and raised in an area dotted by Jewish agricultural colonies – a bucolic remembrance that he evoked in several plays – Eichelbaum showed an early inclination for the theater, although he was also to publish several volumes of prose fiction. Upon arriving in Buenos Aires, he promptly began a career as a journalist by contributing to major cultural magazines (for example *Caras y caretas*), but also to ephemeral literary publications. His theatrical debut took place in 1919 with the staging of *En la quietud del pueblo*; some critics contend, however, that his first major work is *La mala sed* (1920). From that time Eichelbaum's plays became regular features of the capital's theatrical season.

Eichelbaum received numerous awards, notably Argentina's National and Municipal Prizes for *Un guapo del 900* (1940). This play, considered by some as a watershed in his production, captures the climate and the profile of the "guapo", an individual who "cultivates courage", and whose self-styled sense of honor prescribes obedience solely to his own legal code. While some scenes are built on local color ("costumbrista"), the play centers, as most of Eichelbaum's other plays, on individual motivations rather than on societal forces. With recognizable echoes from Henrik Ibsen and August Strindberg, and without diminishing his international appeal, he developed a thematical treatment that portrays his theater as unequivocally Argentine. His works, moreover, served to redirect the national theater away from strictly realistic scenarios.

In 1928 Eichelbaum defined himself as "a maniac of introspection". His probing of human behavior and the obsessive analysis of the hidden motives behind even the most insignificant acts, were to remain defining features of his work. Forever closer to intellectual curiosity rather than to a setting steeped in movement, Eichelbaum's dramas are meticulously crafted to elicit the uniqueness of each of his characters – frequently focusing on the inner strength of women – even as they portray identifiable social groupings and everyday conflicts. Among his more than thirty plays, the following merit particular attention for they cover a broad spectrum of dramatic motifs: *Un hogar* (1922), *El judio Aarón* (1926), *Nadie la conoció nunca* (1926), *Tejido de madre* (1936), *Pájaro de barro* (1940), *Un tal Servando Gómez* (1942), and *Dos brasas* (1955).

SAÚL SOSNOWSKI

Einhorn, David (1809–1879) German–American reform rabbi and religious philosopher. Born in Diespeck, Bavaraia, Einhorn attended the Fuerth *yeshivah* where his teachers included the Orthodox scholar Wolf Hamburger. He studied philology, philosophy and theology at the universities of Wûrzburg, Munich, and Erlangen. Einhorn was recommended to the Wellhausen pulpit in 1838 but the Bavarian government withheld approval. In 1842 he became Rabbi of Birkenfeld and in 1847 succeeded radical Reform Rabbi Samuel Holdheim in Mecklenburg-Schwerin. He left in 1851, oppressed by the conservative atmosphere, and went to Pesth in Hungary. He served as rabbi for nine months after which the synagogue was closed, and then dedicated himself to writing the first part of *Das Prinzip des Mosaismus* (1854). He left amidst political oppression generated by the War of Independence, antagonisms with the Orthodox, and a sense that his own destiny was tied to the historical movement from the past in Europe to the future in the USA. He arrived at Baltimore's Har Sinai Congregation in 1855, and remained until 1859 when he left on account of personality disputes for Philadelphia's Knesset Israel. In 1866 he went to Adath Jeshurun in New York and remained, through its merger with Anshe Chesed to become Beth El (later Temple Emanuel), until his death.

Einhorn founded and edited *Sinai* (1856–64), in which he published his essays on the differences between old and new Judaism, modern Judaism's view of the Talmud, and Judaism and Christianity compared. He wrote a catechism, *Ner tamid (bestaendige Leuchte) die Lehre des Judenthums* (1854). His sermons have been published under many titles including *David Einhorn Memorial Volume* (1911).

In *Das Prinzip des Mosaismus* Einhorn defines the principle of Judaism, identified with "Mosaism", as a dialectical centralization of polarities without injury to their original identities. He is touched by a spark of creation through the fiery letters of Torah. The new awareness brings him to understand God as a synthesis between transcendental YHWH, and *Elohim* who epitomizes cyclical nature. Man is the synthesis of divine spirit and microcosm of the physical world. Spirit and body are centralized in the *nefesh* (soul) residing in his blood. The centralizing process activates freedom and reason to explicate revealed truths available in nature and history. History offers time for reason to carry out the explication, until rational history culminates inevitably in universal light. The world, including human history, is already reconciled with God as *Elohim* on an essential level, and the harmony will be manifest existentially as reason carries out its task. The history of Israel leads the way.

Beginning with Sinai, Israel increasingly crystallizes the apprehension of revealed content.

Her distinctive ceremonies express and reinforce rational accomplishments and prevent relapse into paganism. The symbolic forms should change according to contemporary needs, and will be totally dispensable when the essential truths become universal. Einhorn's overwhelming sense of the messianic end to history brings him to regard the USA as Zion, despite personal alienation and his contempt for American materialism. Having invested his hopes in Germany, when it failed him he was forced by his conception of history to see the USA as the new threshold to messianic fulfillment.

FURTHER READING

Greenberg, G.: The significance of America in David Einhorn's conception of history. *American Jewish Historical Quarterly* (1973)
——: Mendelssohn in America: David Einhorn's radical reform Judaism. *Yearbook of the Leo Baeck Institute* 27

GERSHON GREENBERG

Einstein, Albert (1879–1955) The most renowned physicist of the twentieth century. The child of non-religious German–Jewish parents, he was born in Ulm, but spent his early years (1881–95) in Munich. A period of intense religiosity as a child was followed by a free-thinking adolescence, and belief in an impersonal, Spinozistic cosmic reason, manifested in nature, as an adult. He attended primary school, where he first encountered anti-Semitism among his fellow pupils, and *gymnasium* in Munich. After his parents moved to Italy, he completed his secondary education in Switzerland, attended the Swiss Federal Institute of Technology (ETH) from 1896 to 1900, and became a Swiss citizen in 1901. Unable to obtain an academic position, he worked in the Swiss Patent Office from 1902 to 1909. In 1903 he married Mileva Marić, a fellow ETH physics student of Serbian descent, with whom he had a daughter and two sons.

His scientific work, notably on the special theory of relativity, the quantum hypothesis, and Brownian motion, brought him increasing prominence after 1905 in the physics community, of which he became an acknowledged leader by

Albert Einstein

the end of the decade. His work in physics is characterized by concern for fundamental problems and profound conceptual innovations. In 1909 he got his first academic position at the University of Zurich, moving to the German University in Prague (1911–12), then to the ETH in Zurich (1912–14). In 1914 he accepted a specially-created research position in Berlin, then the world center of theoretical physics, where he stayed until 1933. He separated from his wife immediately after moving to Berlin, and in 1919 married his cousin Elsa Einstein.

He worked on a relativistic theory of gravitation for eight years, publishing his general theory of relativity in 1915, which introduced further changes in current concepts of space, time, force, and matter. In 1919 verification of the predicted gravitational deflection of light rays by two British solar eclipse expeditions brought him international celebrity. He won the 1921 Nobel Prize in physics. Recruited to the Zionist cause, he accompanied Chaim WEIZMANN on a trip to the USA in 1921 to help raise money for the Hebrew University, and in 1923 spoke at the ceremony of its inauguration in Jerusalem. He

refused to join the Jewish religious community, but identified himself with innumerable Jewish causes, Zionist and non-Zionist, for the rest of his life. He favored a binational state in Palestine before the Second World War, but after the Holocaust hailed the establishment of the State of Israel, while advocating full equality for its Arab citizens, and reconciliation with the Arab states. Active in the pacifist movement in Germany during the First World War, he was one of its leading world figures during the 1920s, and was generally identified with the internationalist left. An anti-relativity campaign, often with overtly nationalistic and anti-Semitic overtones, developed in post-war Germany; at moments of political tension there were threats against Einstein's life. Visiting the USA when Hitler came to power, he resigned his position in Berlin and settled permanently in Princeton, New Jersey, taking US citizenship in 1940, and working at the Institute for Advanced Study until his death.

The grave deterioration in the international situation in the 1930s led Einstein to devote more time to politics. Holding pacifism useless as a tactic against Fascism, he called for rearmament and alliance of the anti-Fascist states in order to resist aggression, and supported the allied efforts in the Second World War. He aided numerous refugees, Jewish and non-Jewish, forced to flee Europe. Frequently credited – or blamed – for his role in suggesting the US atomic bomb project, after the war he warned incessantly against the dangers of nuclear weapons, favoring universal disarmament under the aegis of a world government. He staunchly defended civil liberties in the USA during the anti-communist witch-hunts accompanying the cold war. While condemning Soviet totalitarianism, he advocated a socialist economic order that embraced individual liberties. Offered the presidency of Israel in 1952, he refused on grounds of age and lack of aptitude. Working on his scientific ideas and political projects, he awaited the impending end calmly. In death, as in the later years of his life, he has become a mythic figure, whose popular image often has little to do with the complexities of the real human being.

JOHN STACHEL

Sergei Eisenstein's film October *(1928)*

Eisenstein, Sergei Mikhailovich (1898–1948) Russian film director and theorist. One of the first directors to exploit the formal expressive possibilities of the film medium, he had a major and lasting influence on the art of cinematography.

Eisenstein was born in Riga of an assimilated Jewish father and Russian mother. By joining the Red Army after the Revolution, he broke with his father who left for Berlin with the White Russians. He remained throughout his life a dedicated Communist, though he suffered considerably in the 1930s, when Soviet policy parted company with experimental art.

In 1924 Eisenstein produced his first film, *Strike*, using techniques typical of his early work: the downplaying of plot, concentration on mass action, and the use of "type" characters rather than professional actors. Most significant was his experimentation with montage, the juxtaposition of seemingly unrelated material for a symbolic or emotionally expressive end. Eisenstein achieved international renown after the 1926 release of *Potemkin*, with its famous sequence depicting a massacre on the Odessa harbor steps. *Potemkin* was followed by *October* (*Ten Days that Shook the World*, 1928), the story of the 1917 revolution that recreated the storming of the Winter Palace.

In 1930 Eisenstein went on contract to Hollywood, but was forced out after wide publicity labeled him a Bolshevik and Jew. He began his next film in Mexico, financed by the American socialist writer Upton Sinclair. With its religious and anthropological bent, *Que Viva Mexico* would have been a major statement for Eisenstein. But

Sinclair, fearful for his investment and fortified by a telegram from Joseph Stalin, never permitted Eisenstein to edit it.

Back in Moscow Eisenstein found his projects rejected, although he continued to teach. Public attacks seemed to portend arrest, but he recanted in print and was set to work on *Alexander Nevsky* – this time with collaborators to insure artistic orthodoxy. *Alexander Nevsky* (1938) proved a masterpiece of dramatic spectacle and was followed in 1944 by *Ivan the Terrible* Part I. But if Part I fitted in with Stalin's nationalist revival, Part II, with its concentration on Ivan's psychological disintegration, was withheld from the public until 1958.

Eisenstein was an early, outspoken opponent of Nazi Germany. But after the Nazi–Soviet pact of 1939 he was used by Stalin to initiate a program of German–Russian cultural relations. Later, in a move that was undoubtedly more sympathetic to him despite his remote ties to his Jewish heritage, he appeared in an appeal to world Jewry together with Ilya EHRENBURG and Mikhoels.

BIBLIOGRAPHY
Immoral Memories trans. H. Marshall (Boston, 1983)

FURTHER READING
Barna, I.: *Eisenstein* (London: Secker & Warburg, 1973)
ALICE NAKHIMOVSKY

Elbogen, Ismar [Yitzhak Moshe] (1874–1943) German scholar. Born in Schildberg, Posen province, Elbogen was educated in Breslau by his uncle, Jacob Levy (1819–92), a lexicographer. His scholarly foundation was laid later at the Theological Seminary in Breslau, and he received his doctor's degree from the Breslau University for his thesis on Spinoza. In 1899 he received his rabbinical diploma, and shortly after was appointed lecturer on biblical exegesis and Jewish history at the Collegio Rabbinico Italiano in Florence. Three years later, in 1902, he was called to Berlin, where he became privat-docent at the *Lehranstalt für die Wissenschaft des Judentums*, and remained there almost until the last moment when, in 1938, like many German scholars who escaped from Hitler to the USA, he emigrated to New York. He was

honored there by Jewish institutions, and was appointed a research professor by several of them, including the Jewish Theological Seminary, and the Hebrew Union College.

Although Elbogen produced numerous publications on Jewish history and Hebrew literature, his major contribution to Jewish scholarship was in the study of the Jewish liturgy. He came to this subject by accident, attracted by a prize which was offered in 1898 for research into the Eighteen Benedictions. Winning the prize enabled him to publish his *Geschichte des Achtzehngebetes* (1902), followed by his book *Der Jüdische Gottesdienst in seiner historischen Entwicklung* (1912), on the history of Jewish prayers and worship.

In the contemporary academic world, however, his work is considered to be written in too popular a style, and some of his studies have lost their value, such as, for instance, his references to the *kabbalah* and the *Shabta'ut*, written before Gershom SCHOLEM's research in those fields. Nevertheless, no similar work on this subject exists, and his book is fundamental reading for every scholar and reader in this field.

Elbogen's last work, completed a few days before his death, was *A Century of Jewish Life* (1944). The posthumously published book was a supplement to Heinrich GRAETZ's history. Elbogen was also an editor of periodicals and encyclopedias, as well as one of their contributors, and he reviewed almost every book which appeared in his field. A bibliography of his writings is to be found in *Historia Judaica*, viii (1946), pp.69–94.

FURTHER READING
Marx, A.: Ismar Elbogen: an appreciation. In Elbogen, I.: *A Century of Jewish Life* trans. Moses Hades (Philadelphia: The Jewish Publication Society of America, 1960)

DEBORAH SCHECHTERMAN

Elias, Brian (b.1948) English composer. Elias was born in Bombay and lived there until the age of 13, when he went to school in England. He began composing when he was only seven and, upon leaving school in 1966, he entered the Royal College of Music where he studied composition with Humphrey Searle and Bernard Stevens. His principal studies, however, were with Elizabeth Lutyens whom he met at the Dartington Summer School of Music. His first acknowledged work, *La Chevelure* for soprano and orchestra, was written at this time. Based on a text by Charles Pierre Baudelaire, it was selected in 1968 by the Society for the Promotion of New Music for a public orchestral rehearsal.

Upon leaving the Royal College of Music, Elias traveled to the USA and spent some time at the Juilliard School of Music in New York, continuing his composition studies in an extra-mural workshop. He then returned to England, and in 1977 his *Proverbs of Hell* (text by William Blake) won joint second prize in the prestigious Radcliffe Music Award. Never a prolific compos-er, he gained increasing respect with each new piece and produced large-scale works such as *At The Edge Of Time*, a song cycle composed to a commission from Sir William Glock and Brian Burrows. Also notable is his *L'Eylah* which was performed at the 1984 Promenade Concerts to great critical acclaim. He composed *Song* (1986), for soprano and hurdy-gurdy, in re-sponse to a commission by the B'nai B'rith Festival. This work was first performed by Andrea Baron at the Wigmore Hall, London, in July 1986.

A composer of true originality, Brian Elias continues to excite eager anticipation with each new composition. In 1988 he completed an extensive set of variations for piano, and began a large work for soprano and orchestra.

JOHN MATTHEW

Elijah ben Solomon, Zalman

[the Vilna Gaon; Elijah Gaon; Ha-Gra] (1720–1797) The foremost scholar–sage of eighteenth-century Lithuanian Jewry, Elijah was a pro-ponent of a Torah-centered spirituality, and a fierce opponent of Hasidism.

Born to a distinguished rabbinic family, Elijah revealed his intellectual prowess at an early age. His restless curiosity led him far beyond the normative talmudic curriculum to a mastery of astronomy, mathematics and music, as well as Scripture and Hebrew grammar. His talmudic studies reflect a keen sensitivity to problems of historical and textual criticism. Where his contemporaries generally limited themselves to the Babylonian Talmud and the medieval law codes, and strove to reconcile the contradictory opinions of the earlier commentators, Elijah mastered the entirety of the rabbinic literary tradition. He strove to uncover the original meaning of the rabbinic sources, often obscured by corrupt texts and scholastic exegesis. An independent legal thinker, he would reject the decisions of prior jurists if they proved to be based upon faulty readings of the Talmud.

Elijah's attempt to comprehend the entirety of the tradition through intensive rational analysis is founded upon a vision of Torah as Divine Wisdom. The link between divinity and human-ity is reason. Reason is to be focused upon Torah for it is the primary manifestation of God's Will, and students who study it think divine thoughts. Furthermore, the process of learning transforms the consciousness and emotions of the student, leading him to holiness and moral integrity. Underlying this intellectualistic spirituality is a profound commitment to the autonomy of human reason and volition.

This commitment results in a deep suspicion of pneumatic illumination. Elijah was a mystic, a commentator on the Zohar, the central text of the *kabbalah*, and a visionary who experi-enced dream ascents to the heavenly academies. Although these revelatory dream visions were accepted as rewards for his waking labors, Elijah treated much of his pneumatic experience with suspicion. Fearful of self-delusion, he rejected appearances of heavenly teachers, offering to reveal "mysteries of the Torah" without prior analytical labor, as a threat to the centrality of rational analysis in religious life.

Elijah's emphasis upon learning as the heart of Jewish spirituality led to profound opposition to Hasidism. Playing a major role in the excommunications of 1772 and 1781, he rejected Hasidism's teachings concerning the ubiquity of God in the world, arguing instead that only His providential power was omnipresent. He feared that Hasidism's emphasis upon contemplative prayer and ecstasy would supplant the centrality of Torah, and objected strenuously to the claims that religious illuminati possessed miraculous powers.

Elijah gathered around him a disciplic circle

of mature scholars who were ordered to spread his teachings among the masses. His disciple Haim founded in 1803 the great Volozhin *yeshivah*, which played a pivotal role in the life of eastern European Orthodoxy. Elijah's vision continues to flourish in the spirituality of learning espoused in contemporary *yeshivot*, and the writings of Orthodox thinkers such as Joseph SOLOVEITCHIK.

FURTHER READING

Ginzberg, L.: The Gaon, R. Elijah Vilna. In *Students, Scholars and Saints* (Philadelphia: The Jewish Publication Society, 1928)

Lamm, N.: Scholarship and piety In *Faith and Doubt* (New York: Ktav, 1972)

Weinryb, B. D.: *The Jews of Poland* (Philadelphia: The Jewish Publication Society, 1972)

SETH L. BRODY

Eliyia, Joseph (1901–1931) Greek lyric poet, scholar, Hebrew and French translator. He was born in Janina, Greece, and educated at the ALLIANCE ISRAÉLITE UNIVERSELLE where he studied French, Hebrew, and Greek; he graduated in 1918 and was appointed the following year to teach French at his alma mater. He was conscripted into the Greek army (1920–21) then returned to his teaching at the Alliance where he remained for the next four years, devoting all his spare time to the study of talmudic and post-talmudic philosophy and poetry, and Hebrew literature. Inspired by his Hebraic and Hellenic heritage, he wrote original poems that were revolutionary in tone. These were published in the Janina progressive newspaper *Epiritikon Agon* (*Epirus Struggle*). On 5 January 1925 the police, as well as Jewish notables who looked upon Eliyia as a revolutionary, persuaded the principal of the Alliance to expel the poet from his teaching post. To add further to his humiliation and insecurity, an article he had written the year before, severely criticizing one of the government officials, put him behind bars for a month. Upon his release, he severed all relations with Janina and settled in Athens.

During his first years there, Eliyia taught Hebrew and French in the community Hebrew school, and gave private lessons in Hebrew and French to support himself and his widowed mother. However, in Athens he enjoyed the companionship of leading demotic writers and poets such as Varnalis, Palamas, Xenopoulos, who recognized his worth as a poet. All his demotic poems were published in various Athenian newspapers and periodicals, including *Noumas Vigla, Nea Estia*.

Eliyia's greatest ambition was to translate the whole of the Old Testament into vernacular Greek. In this way he aspired to familiarize his coreligionists with their Hebrew heritage, since many of them did not understand Hebrew, and make known the Old Testament to his Christian compatriots in a language they could understand. In Athens he translated into vernacular Greek the books of Isaiah, Job, Ruth, Jonah, and the Song of Songs. He also translated the poems of Judah Halevi, Solomon Ibn Gabirol and the works of such writers as H. N. BIALIK, Y. L. PERETZ, and Saul TSCHERNICHOWSKI.

In 1927 Eliyia entered the École Française d'Athènes, graduated in 1928, and in 1930 received his appointment to teach French in State high schools. He selected Kilkis, a remote town in northern Greece, as it was near Salonika, and Eliyia could spend his weekends at the Hebrew library there. In July 1931 he became ill after drinking polluted water. He returned to Athens and died there three months before his thirtieth birthday.

At the time of his death Eliyia had written 209 articles on Hebrew subjects, all of which appeared in the *Large Greek Encyclopedia*, and 257 original poems, a large part of which are found in the *Literary Supplement of the Large Encyclopedia*. Eliyia is regarded not only as a Greek–Jewish poet of Janina, but also as the only Greek–Jewish poet of stature in all of Greece.

BIBLIOGRAPHY

Eliyia, J.: *Poems* (Thessaloniki: B'nai Brith, 1938) [In Greek]

Eliyia, J.: *Poetry, Translations from the Hebrew*. Introduction by G. Zographaki. (Athens. 1967) [In Greek]

Schwartz, H. and Rudolf, A. (eds): *Voices within the Ark*. Trans. R. Dalven. (New York, 1980)

FURTHER READING

Dalven, R.: *Poems* (New York, 1944) [biography of Eliyia and 90 verse translations of original poems]

RACHEL DALVEN

Elkin, Stanley (b.1930) American short-story writer and novelist. Elkin is distinguished by stories which tend to be episodic rather than coherently plotted narratives, and by his exuberant and inventive comic style.

Elkin's stories often focus on unheroic characters in outlandish situations. Many of his characters feel victimized by life, as noted by the protagonist in his most recent novel, *The Magic Man*: "Like the poet said, most blokes lead lives of quiet desperation, but the poet was wrong. Most blokes shouted it from the rooftops". Bullies and charlatans abound: their stories most unabashedly demonstrate the irrepressible demands of selfhood, which Elkin shows to define human character. His stories often illustrate the relentless democratization of the human experience, regardless of man's purported values.

While only about half his protagonists are Jewish – and secular Jews at that – Elkin's use of language ties him to the tradition of Jewish humor. Elkin often utilizes clichés and plebian speech in startling, original formulations. Commonplace utterance is heightened by keen and unusual juxtapositions of language, which ultimately convey the message in a mode characteristic of poetic expression.

BIBLIOGRAPHY
Boswell: A Modern Comedy (London: Hamish Hamilton, 1964); *Criers and Kibitzers, Kibitzers and Criers* (London: Anthony Blond, 1967); *Alex and the Gypsy* (Harmondsworth: Penguin, 1977); *The Living End* (London: Cape, 1979)

SYLVIA FISHMAN

Elon, Amos (b.1926) Israeli journalist and writer. Elon was born in Vienna and emigrated to Palestine as a child, later settling in Jerusalem. He began his career as a journalist for the Israeli daily, *Ha'aretz*, and in 1956 he became the newspaper's correspondent in Washington, DC, a post he retained until 1961. He spent the next four years as a correspondent in Paris and then in Bonn. He remained an editorial writer and columnist for *Ha'aretz* until 1984.

Elon published his first full length work, *In einem heimgesuchten Land* (*Journey Through a Haunted Land*), in 1966; his next work was the bestselling *The Israelis, Founders and Sons* (1971), a portrayal of the rise of the Zionist movement and the events leading to the foundation of the State of Israel, including descriptions of the Hebrew fiction and poetry that reflected these events. This book was followed by *Between Enemies*, written with Sana Hassan in 1974. He completed his major biography of Theodor HERZL in 1978. This led to a theatrical collaboration with Dore Schary – *Herzl* – which was produced at the Palace Theater on Broadway in 1976.

Elon has contributed occasional pieces to the *New Yorker*, the *New York Times Magazine*, and the *New York Review of Books*, including an analysis of the uprising in Gaza (*NYRB*, 14 April 1988). Elon has also contributed to the journals, *Commentary* and *Encounter*. His book, *A Certain Panic*, was published in Tel Aviv.

BIBLIOGRAPHY
Journey Through a Haunted Land: The New Germany, trans. M. Roloff (London: André Deutsch, 1967)

JOHN MATTHEW

Engel, Yoel (1868–1927) Composer, critic, folk song collector, pioneer of Jewish national music. Born in Berdiansk, Southern Russia, he studied at the Moscow conservatory under Tanejew and Ippolitov-Ivanov. He was active for 20 years as a music critic and was the editor of the Russian edition of Riemann's *Musik-Lexikon* and of an opera handbook. He was also active in the field of music education and was one of the founders of the Moscow Popular Conservatory. In 1900 he organized the first concert of Jewish folk songs at the Society for Anthropology and Ethnology in Moscow. The interest generated in such concerts led to the formation of the Society for Jewish Folk Music in St Petersburg in 1908, with a chapter in Moscow opened in 1914. The society followed the lines established by the Russian "Mighty Five" in collecting and publishing folk songs and encouraging composition in Jewish vein. Engel composed the incidental music for the epoch-making production in Hebrew of Sh. AN-SKI's *The Dybbuk* by the Habimah Theater, produced all over the world and finally becoming a classic of the repertory of Habimah in Palestine. In 1922 Engel moved to Berlin where he founded the *Yuval* publishing house, in cooperation with *Yibneh*, *Ever*, and the *Jüdische Verlag*. *Yuval* published numerous songs and short works for violin and piano and for piano solo, mostly with bilingual titles in German and in Hebrew. In 1924 Engel consented to invitations by musicians in Palestine to move his activities there as a step towards fulfilling the Zionist ideology of making Palestine a center of Jewish art and culture. In 1925 he transferred most of the activities of *Yuval* to Tel Aviv, where he also made significant contributions to the field of elementary and kindergarten music education. His warm personality attracted much love and admiration in the small community of Tel Aviv, and his sudden death in 1927 caused a national day of mourning. His activities were continued by his friends Rosenstein and Shlomo ROSOWSKY. The city of Tel Aviv grants a yearly composition prize named after Engel.

FURTHER READING

Weisser, A.: *The Modern Renaissance of Jewish Music* (New York: Bloch Co., 1954)

JEHOASH HIRSHBERG

Enlightenment, Hebrew   See HASKALAH.

Epstein, Jacob (1880–1959)   British sculptor. Born in New York's Lower East Side to Orthodox Polish–Jewish immigrant parents, Epstein won an art competition in his early teens which enabled him to attend the Art Students' League for the next eight years. In 1901 the non-Jewish writer Hutchins Hapgood commissioned him to illustrate his pioneering study of Lower East Side life, *The Spirit of the Ghetto*: the sensitive drawings that Epstein produced, both of eminent intellectuals and artists, and of everyday life in the ghetto, were a logical extension of the sketches he had been working on for several years.

The proceeds from this commission enabled him in 1902 to become an art student in Paris. In 1905 he settled in London, where he soon acquired a reputation as one of the most subversive members of the avant-garde. Just prior to the First World War Epstein was briefly

Jacob Epstein working on the TUC War Memorial, 1956–7

associated with the Vorticist movement, sharing its enthusiam for the dynamism of the machine age.

Inspired to a large extent by the example of ancient and "primitive" sculpture, Epstein became a pioneering advocate of the concept of direct carving, and exercised an important influence on contemporaries such as Eric Gill, Henri Gaudier-Brzeska, and the young Henry Moore. All the public commissions he received met with controversy, if not hostility; the elemental quality, rough primitivism, frank sexuality, and Jewish–American vitality of his carved sculptures continued to shock the polite British art world well into the 1920s. Responses to his work were often marked by xenophobia, tinged with anti-Semitism.

Partly for financial reasons, Epstein devoted much of his energy from the 1920s onwards to the modeling of naturalistic portrait busts to be cast into bronze. His sitters included the rich and famous, among them George Bernard Shaw, Joseph Conrad and Albert EINSTEIN. Although these works lack the originality of the carved sculptures, Epstein achieved unusual psychological insights and a strong sense of interior life through expressive exaggeration of form and fluidity of surface textures.

In later years Epstein received a number of important commissions from the Christian Church (notably, for Llandaff and Coventry Cathedrals). Had the Synagogue been in a position to use his talent, he would undoubtedly have been delighted. As it was, he produced only a handful of Old Testament motifs (*Genesis*, 1929–30 and *Jacob and the Angel*, 1940–41, for example), which are nevertheless among his most powerful and memorable sculptures. Jewish themes feature more prominently in his graphic output, above all in the series of watercolors inspired by the Old Testament that he produced in the early 1930s, and in his 1933 illustrations to Moysheh Oyved's *Book of Affinity*.

BIBLIOGRAPHY

Epstein: an Autobiography (London: Hulton Press, 1955)

FURTHER READING

Jacob Epstein: Sculpture & Drawings (Leeds: City Art Gallery, 1987) [exhibition catalog]

Silber, E.: *The Sculpture of Epstein* (Oxford: Phaidon, 1986)

MONICA BOHM-DUCHEN

Espinoza, Enrique [Samuel Glusberg] (1898–1987) Argentine writer, editor, and literary journalist. Born in Kishinev, he was taken to Argentina at the age of seven. In the early 1920s he became an editor of monthly literary reviews: *Trapalanda*, *La Vida Literaria*, and the most famous, *Babel*, which continued to be published almost without interruption for 30 years (1921–51).

Espinoza published many books by important Argentine writers. In 1928 he helped found the Argentine Writers' Association, of which he was elected first secretary. He was involved, too, in the creation of the vanguardist literary movement in Argentina called *Martín Fierro* (1919).

As a writer he published a collection of short stories, *La Levita Gris* (1924; The gray frock coat)

about Jewish life in Buenos Aires, one of which, "Mate Amargo" ("Bitter Herb", 1928) is an account of the first pogrom to strike the Jewish community of Buenos Aires in January 1919.

Ruth y Noemi (1934), his second book, contains a play inspired by elements of the traditional Passover *seder* with reference to Buenos Aires' Jews of the time. Espinoza has also published *Chicos de España* (1935; Children of Spain) and *Companeros de Viaje* (1937; Fellow voyagers) about the circumstances before and during the Spanish Civil War, after visiting Spain in solidarity with the Republicans' cause.

Espinoza lived in Chile for many years from 1935, and was closely in touch with the local liberal writers. During his long residence in Santiago, he wrote and published his finest critical works about Latin American culture, literary criticism, and social polemics, and his essays on leading Argentine, Chilean, Peruvian, and Cuban writers. He also wrote an essay on the fascination which Henrich HEINE held for his generation of Argentine Jewish writers, *El Angel y el Leon* (The angel and the lion) devoted to analyzing the plight of those Jewish intellectuals who lived at the edge of two spiritual worlds, the Argentine, and the Jewish.

The topic of the transculturation of identities and spiritual heritages in Latin America pervades most of Espinoza's critical works. He himself was fully integrated and, like other Jewish writers of his generation, succeeded in being acculturated to Latin American spiritual values, but he was concerned about the paradoxes and strains of developing a national consciousness out of the various collectives abounding in a multi-ethnic society such as Argentina's. He supported assimilation through education and the making of a national culture which allowed each immigrant writer to incorporate diverse ethnic and social patterns, including the Jewish component (*El Castellano y Babel*, 1974, a polemic response to the intolerant nationalist book of Arturo Capdevilla, *Babel y el Castellano*).

Other writings include a two-volume collection that Espinoza edited on behalf of the Argentine Friends of The Hebrew University of Jerusalem (*Cuadernos de Oriente y Occidente*, 1929), and memoirs, the most comprehensive of which is *Gajes del oficio* (1976; Tricks of art). He also published collections of poems.

FURTHER READING

Senkman, L.: *La Identidad Judia en la Literatura Argentina* (Buenos Aires: Pardes, 1983) 263–9

LEONARDO SENKMAN

Esther [Malke Lifshits; Esther Frumkin] (*c.*1880–1939?) Russian editor, political writer and Yiddishist leader. Esther was born in Minsk as Malke Lifshits. Her father was a follower of the Berlin Englightenment. She remains for modern scholarship a woman of mystery, about whom conflicting views abound. On her first marriage she took on her husband's name, and became Esther Frumkin. She was, however, for most of her career universally known by the name Esther. She was highly educated in traditional Judaism and studied the sacred texts in their original Hebrew, and later attended the University of Berlin. She became a teacher in a girls' school which specialized in professional subjects. In 1901 she joined the Bund, the Jewish trade union movement, and became a propagandist for them. Esther became St Petersburg correspondent for the daily newspaper *Der veker* which later became *Di folktsaytung*. She participated in the 1908 Chernowitz Language Conference, and as an ardent Yiddishist she caused endless controversy and bitter feeling that lasted beyond her death. Her personal record of the conference was published in *Di naye tsayt, 4* (1909). Her longest published work is *Tsu der frage vegn der yidisher folk-shul* (1917; On the question of the Jewish folk-school). She was arrested many times between 1910 and 1914 and was forced to flee abroad, becoming an important member of the international Bund.

At the beginning of the First World War she returned to Russia and took over the editorship of the main Bund forum, *Der Veker*, and rose to prominence in the Bund movement, and after the Russian revolution she held high rank. However, she became an extreme exponent of Soviet Bolshevik Communism which led the Bund to regard her as a traitor to this day.

Esther was elected a member of the Minsk city council. Inevitably becoming a victim of Stalinist tyranny, she was arrested in 1936, and nothing more was ever heard of her.

DEVRA KAY

ethics, Jewish, in the twentieth century

The fate of Jewish ethics in the last two centuries presents a peculiarly clear illustration of the tensions between Judaism and modernity. What was self-evident to biblical and rabbinic tradition became problematic to the modern Jew. A prolonged debate began about the relation between the Jew and the world, central to which were questions about the place, nature, and task of Jewish ethics.

To the question "What shall I do?" Jewish tradition offered a lucid answer. The Bible contained a series of binding imperatives and absolute values. Their authority lay in the fact that they were the revealed will of God. Their translation into a comprehensively detailed and workable system was the task of the Oral Law, ultimately given literary expression in the landmark works of the rabbinic period, the Mishnah and the Babylonian and Jerusalem Talmuds. Human action is decisive as the locus of religious significance, but ethics as a distinctive concept is the product of a later age. The key words of tradition are *mitzvah* (commandment) and *halakhah* (Jewish law). Its unifying vision is that of the holy life lived in accordance with the Divine will as revealed at Sinai and articulated through tradition. This life is the particular vocation of the Jewish people, the terms of its covenant with God.

Modernity challenged this vision in a succession of ways. The Enlightenment suggested that ethics could be separated from religion and given independent grounding in reason. Emancipation invited Jews to jettison their distinctiveness and enter a common humanity. Could Jewish ethics be shown to have the necessary universality? The direction of these forces was sharply reversed by the Holocaust. This cast doubt on whether a secular morality had the power to prevent the most savage inhumanity, on whether rationality fully accounted for the human condition, and on whether Jews could subscribe to a diminution of their singularity. The subsequent founding of the State of Israel raised questions about the ethical use of power and the creation of a total social order that had long been unasked or merely theoretical. Secularization and technological advance created an ongoing series of dilemmas for traditional values. Jewish ethics became the intellectual battleground on which these challenges were faced.

The first was the cluster of issues raised intellectually by the Enlightenment and socially by the process of Emancipation. The transitional figure is Moses MENDELSSOHN, who argued that tradition and modernity could be equally affirmed without modifying the claims of either. Mendelssohn held that religious truth and moral law were universal and based on reason. The general principles of ethics could be "demonstrated with geometric rigor and force". Within Judaism they were represented by the seven Noahide laws traditionally understood as binding on all mankind. They were revealed but essentially independent of revelation. What was disclosed at Sinai was the "religious legislation" which constituted Israel's particular relationship with God. Jews were distinctive in their ritual, universal in their ethics, and could thus participate fully in the common enterprise of civilization without sacrificing their singular religious vocation. The broad outlines of this synthesis remain influential among Orthodox thinkers and have been restated by such contemporary figures as Joseph SOLOVEITCHIK and Eliezer BERKOVITS.

But the equilibrium proposed by Mendelssohn was not inherently stable. In the nineteenth century Reform thinkers stressed the primacy of ethics and universality over "ceremonial" and particularism. The 1885 "Pittsburgh Platform" stated of the Mosaic Torah that "today we accept as binding only its moral laws, and maintain only such ceremonies as elevate and sanctify our lives". Judaism was identified with "ethical monotheism" whose source was human reason and whose eternal spokesmen were the prophets. Hermann COHEN gave this view its most sophisticated philosophical formulation at the beginning of the twentieth century.

The impact of rationalism and the assault on

revelation and particularism divided European Jewry. Contemporary Jewish ethics still bears the signs of the denominational schisms of the nineteenth century. Reform Judaism tends to see ethics as the core of the Jewish enterprise. It rejects traditional ideas of the verbal revelation of Torah, the immutability of the commands and the authority of *halakhah*. For a representative thinker like Eugene Borowitz, Jewish ethics is marked by a stress on personal autonomy in which the individual makes informed choices in the light of his reading of Jewish tradition.

Conservative thinkers like Robert GORDIS, Louis JACOBS, and Seymour Siegel likewise reject the traditional view of revelation but prefer to think in terms of a more communal ethic embodied in a *halakhah* which they see as the constantly evolving response of the Jewish people to history. Tradition is given weight, not as categorical command but as influential precedent which may have to yield to a changing ethical climate. When Jewish law conflicts with ethics – they argue that it does so in the case of the marital disabilities of the *mamzer* (illegitimate child) and in the role assigned by tradition to women – the law must change (see also CONSERVATIVE JUDAISM).

Orthodoxy is defined by its commitment to traditional belief in the Divine authorship of the Mosaic books and the binding character of *halakhah*. Some authorities, especially those influenced by Moses Sofer, have seen Judaism as incompatible with modernity. Its timeless transcendent norms pass a negative judgement on contemporary morality. Others (Eliezer Berkovits, Emanuel Rackman) see the development of Judaism in terms of a continuing tension between its ideals and their concrete halakhic actualization. Like the Conservatives, they would argue for a liberalization of the law, especially in relation to the rights of women. Unlike the Conservatives, they do so on the basis of internal Jewish values rather than by reference to contemporary secular morality.

Orthodoxy's approach to ethics is diverse. Some schools emphasize the *Musar* tradition, revived in the nineteenth century by Israel Salanter (1810–83). This stresses personal discipline, inner piety, close study of the classic ethical texts and critical self-examination. Hasidic groups such as Lubavitch lay great weight on the collective nature of Jewish ethics, the responsibility of Jews one for another, and the mystical function of religious action in restoring the lost harmony of creation (the idea of *tikkun*, drawn from Lurianic *kabbalah*). Abraham KOOK developed a striking mystical reading of modernity, in which the various Jewish secularisms contributed to an uncovering of long-dormant elements in the Jewish tradition – a sense of peoplehood, social justice, and universal love of humanity. Both the religious and moral impulse are natural to the human soul. Exile had fragmented Jewish sensibility, but a renascent Judaism in the land of Israel would sanctify the secular and renew the prophetic spirit in which ethics and law merge.

The essential optimism of Jewish ethics in the early twentieth century was broken by the Holocaust. The motifs of synthesis and harmony were replaced by a sense of disillusionment with secular and Christian ethics, and a more lonely affirmation of the uniqueness of Judaism. The Reform thinker, Leo BAECK, signaled a retreat from the once-prevalent notion of a common Judaeo-Christian ethical tradition. Pauline Christianity, he argued, was a romantic religion valuing feeling and ecstatic abandonment, thereby devaluing human action and the ethical enterprise. Judaism preserves both mystery and ethics in the commandment, while Christianity contains a tendency to become a "religion of pure egoism" (*Judaism and Christianity*, 1958). The Conservative Robert Gordis delivered a searching critique of secular ethics. The rise of science has both enlarged man's powers and diminished his sense of freedom and significance. What is needed is a return to the vision of the opening chapter of Genesis, a natural law based on man's place within a divinely created order (*Judaic Ethics for a Lawless World*, 1986).

Two philosophers, Emil FACKENHEIM and Michael Wyschogrod, provided a systematic context for a revival of Jewish particularly. For Fackenheim, the radical evil revealed in the Holocaust is an annhilation of the common humanity presupposed by Kantian ethics. The determination to continue Jewish existence after the Holocaust has more than Jewish significance: it helps mend the moral rupture created by an evil philosophers thought impossible (*To Mend the World*, 1982). For Wyschogrod "ethics is the Judaism of the assimilated", and while Judaism cannot be divorced from ethics, Jewish ethics cannot be divorced from cult, land, and the special claims of one's own people. The universalist tendency of nineteenth-century Jewish ethics was an inauthentic flight from the concrete reality of Jewish existence (*The Body of Faith*, 1983).

The "Jewish return into history" signified by the State of Israel is central to these philosophies. Israel has changed the tone and agenda of Jewish ethics from the vocabulary of powerlessness to that of power. The terms of the argument were set in the 1897 debate between Micha BERDYCZEWSKI who argued for a return to pre-rabbinic values of active strength and the "culture of the sword" and AHAD HA'AM who held that a Jewish state could survive only by spiritual, not material, power. Among the most persistent critics of Israeli use of military force has been Yeshayahu LEIBOWITZ. Leibowitz, an Orthodox thinker, noted that exilic existence had spared Jews from confrontation with the ethical dilemmas of power, a "decisive test of moral values". He warned against the moral danger of investing the state with religious terminology. The rise of religious–political messianism since the Six Day War in 1967 has led to a positive evaluation of force, war, and activism in some Orthodox circles, and a renewed defense by others of an ethic of peace, compassion, and responsible restraint.

Yeshayahu Leibowitz was among the first to diagnose another ethical challenge posed by Jewish statehood. In the Diaspora, Jewish law had not had to come to terms with responsibility for maintaining a society as a whole. Sovereignty lay in non-Jewish hands. *Halakhah* lacked the resources for administering a modern pre-messianic state. Religious Zionism was therefore caught in an equivocal position, attaching religious value to the state but lacking any positive program for its religious function. Despite sympathy for Leibowitz's critique in some Orthodox circles, a new macro-economic and social *halakhah* has yet to emerge.

Within narrower parameters, however, Jewish law has been responsive to the dilemmas posed by modernity. Ethics in general has been marked since the 1970s by a move from abstraction to substantive practical issues. This had been the traditional rabbinic orientation, so recent years have witnessed a new interest in the halakhic sources, especially in the Responsa literature in which rabbinic authorities bring Jewish law to bear on individual problems.

The most active field has been Jewish medical ethics. The literature cannot be summarized: rabbinic authorities frequently disagree, in some fields a consensus has yet to emerge, and the halakhic approach is too case-specific to allow easy generalizations. But there are characteristic emphases. Jewish law attaches unique sanctity to human life, each moment of which is precious, and views the relation between the person and his/her life as one of guardianship rather than ownership. It thus sanctions abortion in the case of risk to the mother's life or health, but rejects the argument for abortion on the grounds of a woman's right to her own body. It forbids voluntary or active euthanasia, though it will sometimes permit the withdrawal of treatment from a patient whose death is imminent, and the prescription of analgesics for the terminally ill though they may shorten life.

Jewish authorities have generally steered a middle course between two extremes: unreserved worship of scientific advance, which they see as compromising human sanctity, and refusal to interfere with nature, which they view as contrary to the partnership between God and the physician in the work of healing. Positive concern for the treatment of infertility has led to general approval of artificial insemination and *in vitro* fertilization where the husband's semen is used. Concern for family values lies behind the disapproval of techniques involving a third party: artificial insemination using donated sperm, and surrogacy. A generally conservative attitude is taken towards medical experimentation on human beings, anatomical dissection, autopsies, and genetic engineering. A more liberal attitude is taken where there is a direct and immediate chance of saving a life.

If medicine has challenged Jewish ethics to apply traditional values to new questions, the "sexual revolution" invited it to apply new values to traditional questions. The biblical and rabbinic literature attached great weight to marriage, fidelity, and the raising of children. Within this context sexuality was affirmed, but a sense of the reality of temptation pervades the protective legislation surrounding marriage and modesty. The sexual liberation of the 1960s found some Jewish protagonists, but the primary response was a strong defense of tradition. Not only ethical values were at stake. Images of marriage and family pervade Jewish theological language about the covenantal relation between God and Israel. The stability and fertility of families is crucial to the demographics of Jewish survival. It seems unlikely, therefore, that alternative sexual lifestyles will find a permanent place in even liberal Jewish ethics, though they remain one of the realities of contemporary Jewish life.

Biblical ethics is particularly concerned with the creation of a just society. Many of its commands relate to measures alleviating poverty and mitigating economic dependence. The experience of slavery in Egypt is constitutive, a model of what should not be. The socioeconomic order should promote freedom and militate against oppression and corruption. The theme persists in prophetic critiques of the abuse of power and rabbinic legislation to protect the vulnerable. The key word *tzedakah*, combining as it does the meanings of charity, righteousness, and justice, illustrates the fusion of morality and law in Jewish thought. The problem of Jewish social ethics lies in applying these values to the structures of the modern state. They bring together three realms – theological, social, and interpersonal – so they cannot be translated directly into a secular political program. In general, contemporary Jewish writing on social themes shares a vocabulary of values rather than a common philosophy.

Ethics constituted the meeting-ground of Jewish tradition with modernity. Its development followed the attraction to, and the post-Holocaust disillusionment with, a universal social order. The range of positions held is vast, between those who see ethics as the fruit of reason and those who see it as the content of revelation, those who stress the common ethical enterprise and those who advocate the singular Jewish vocation, those who see ethics as an independent realm and those who think it incomprehensible outside its theological context, between those who see it as defined by personal choice, historical influence, or timelessness. Is there a common factor? Jewish ethics constitutes the search for values and moral guidance using the resources of Judaism – biblical, rabbinic, philosophic, and mystical. It shares a literature, a common task of interpretation, and a faith that contemporary problems are illuminated, if not unequivocally resolved, by the perspective of tradition.

FURTHER READING

Fox, M. ed.: *Modern Jewish Ethics: Theory and Practice* (Columbus: Ohio State University Press, 1975)

Herring, B.: *Jewish Ethics and Halakhah for our Time* (New York: Ktav, 1986)

Kellner, M. M., ed.: *Contemporary Jewish Ethics* (New York: Sanhedrin Press, 1978)

Rosner, F.: *Modern Medicine and Jewish Ethics* (New York: Ktav, 1986)

Spero, S.: *Morality, Halakha and the Jewish Tradition* (New York: Ktav, 1983)

JONATHAN SACKS

Euchel, Isaac Abraham (1756 [or 1758]– 1804) Hebrew author, Yiddish playwright, and activist in the German HASKALAH movement. Born in Copenhagen, Euchel went to Königsberg in 1773, and studied at the University there. Despite his being one of Immanuel Kant's distinguished students, the proposal to appoint him a professor at the University was rejected as he was a Jew. The official reason was, however, that "it is hardly possible [for him] to abstain from [his] rabbinic expositions".

In 1782 he published his first work, *Sefat 'emet* (The language of truth), a pamphlet on the need to establish a school reflecting *Haskalah* concepts. In 1783 he became the first editor of *Hame'assef*, and, with others in Berlin, he founded the *Hevrat doreshei leshon 'ever* (The Society of the Seekers, or Friends, of the Hebrew Language). Furthermore, he was one of the founders of the *Gesellschaft der Freunde* in Berlin (1791 or 1792), of which he served as director (1797–1801).

Euchel's contribution is to be found in a variety of areas. In the biblical field, he trans-

lated Proverbs into German, with a commentary, his contribution to Moses MENDELSSOHN's *Bi'ur*. In the field of Hebrew literature he wrote *Iggerot Meshulam ben Uriyyah ha'eshtemo'i*, which shows the influence of Charles Louis Montesquieu's *Persian Letters*. Euchel is to be recognized as the composer of the first monograph on Mendelssohn and of the first modern Yiddish satire, *R. Henekh oder vos tut men damit*. The latter is a play about a complex set of relationships between Orthodox and non-Orthodox Jews, and Jews and non-Jews. It reveals Euchel's attitude toward Yiddish, which he, like other of his contemporary *maskilim* (Enlighteners), regarded as a corruption of literary German.

FURTHER READING

Pelli, M.: Isaac Euchel: tradition and change in the first generation of *Haskalah* literature in Germany. *Journal of Jewish Studies* 26 (1975) 152–167

DEBORAH SCHECHTERMAN

Eydoux, Emmanuel [Roger Eisinger] (b.1913) French poet and novelist. Born in Marseille of Alsatian Jewish parentage, Eisinger was educated in his native city and entered business there until 1965 when he suddenly abandoned commerce in order to devote himself to the teaching of Jewish history, culture, and thought in the local ORT School. The first steps toward his radical evolution from commercial to cultural figure occurred during the heady, chaotic post-war years when he published some poetry under the *nom-de-plume* of "Catapulte".

Sadly ignored by translators, Eydoux's principal poetic works include *Le Chant de l'Exil* (1945–7), *Abraham l'Hébreu et Samuel le Voyant* (1946), and *Elégies Inachevées* (1959). In these and other works, Eydoux examines the Jewish condition of existence and its creative, although precarious, nature in exile. In 1960 he wrote a moving poetic drama, *Le Ghetto à Varsovie*, whose thematic and emotional content influenced his 1967 play, *Le Dernier Pourimspiel des Orphelins du Docteur Janusz*. Both pieces explore the painful reality of the double tragedy of the Jewish people during the Holocaust: the extermination of European Jewish civilization by the

Nazis, and the murder of one million Jewish children who symbolized the future survival of Jewish life.

SIMON SIBELMAN

Ezekiel, Moses Jacob (1844–1917) American sculptor. Ezekiel was probably the first sculptor of Jewish origin to have gained an international reputation. Born in Richmond, Virginia, to Sephardi Jews of Dutch descent, he was the first Jew to attend the Virginia Military Institute (1862–6). In 1864, as a cadet, he participated in the Civil War Battle of Newmarket. After living in Cincinnati, Ohio, where his family had settled after the Civil War, he sailed for Europe in 1869. There he gained admittance to the Royal Art Academy in Berlin, from which he was graduated in 1871. He remained in Berlin to work in the studios of Rudolf Siemering and Albert Wolff. In 1873 he was awarded the Michael Beer Prix de Rome for his relief, *Israel*, an allegory based on Jewish history, showing Israel in the guise of a crucified Jewish Jesus, the suffering Messiah, who will lead mankind to salvation. He settled in Rome in 1874, living there until his death in 1917.

Ezekiel's first major commission, *Religious Liberty* – a large marble sculptural group – was made for the Centennial Exhibition held in Philadelphia in 1876. Among Ezekiel's best works are his many realistic busts in marble and in bronze, such as those of the composer Franz Liszt, and the Reform rabbi Isaac Mayer WISE. His numerous creations include a series of full-length statues of artists for the niches of the original Corcoran Art Gallery in Washington, DC. Loyal to the Confederate cause, he delighted in commissions to sculpt Civil War heroes, especially General Stonewall Jackson and his beloved General Robert E. Lee, who first advised him to become a sculptor. Around 1910–14, commissioned by the United Daughters of the Confederacy, he produced a large bronze monument entitled *The New South*, which stands in Arlington National Cemetery in Washington, DC. At the foot of the monument Ezekiel lies buried.

Ezekiel's life differs from that of many expatriate American artists, whose company he largely shunned. In spite of his Jewish origins, which he never denied, he felt comfortable with and was accepted in European aristocratic circles. His associations read like a veritable Who's Who of nineteenth-century society. He was knighted by three European monarchs. He worked in the academic–classical style – the prevailing style of the period – with its emphasis on historical, allegorical narrative subject matter, and the emulation of ancient masterpieces, all rendered in an idealized, but realistic fashion.

FURTHER READING

Greenwald, A., ed.: *Ezekiel's Vision. Moses Jacob Ezekiel and the Classical Tradition* (Philadelphia: National Museum of American Jewish History, 1985) [exhibition catalog]
Gutmann, J., and Chyet, S. F.: *Moses Jacob Ezekiel: Memoirs from the Baths of Diocletian* (Detroit: Wayne State University Press, 1975)

JOSEPH GUTMANN

F

Fackenheim, Emil Ludwig (b.1916) Canadian philosopher. Born in Halle, Germany, Fackenheim graduated from the local Stadtgymnasium in 1935. He proceeded to the Hochschule für die Wissenschaft des Judentums in Berlin, from which he received ordination in 1939, and he attended the University of Halle, 1937–8. In the winter of 1938–9 he was detained at Sachsenhausen concentration camp. After release he attended the University of Aberdeen in Scotland and the University of Toronto, and there received the doctorate in philosophy in 1945. He served as rabbi in Hamilton, Ontario and then Professor of Philosophy at the University of Toronto. In 1983 he moved to the Hebrew University of Jerusalem.

Fackenheim liberated Jewish philosophy from the premises of Emancipation: that Jews were anachronistic as Jews and on trial as men; that Jewish faith would be fairly judged, and the humanity of Jews put on trial by the civilization which persecuted them. Instead, the Holocaust placed western civilization on trial. The State of Israel made the image of Jews as a dead people factually absurd. Fackenheim renounced the religious idealism which Americans (Kaufmann KOHLER) inherited from nineteenth-century German–Jewish liberals, where God was replaced by concept and His actions depended upon human conscience, as well as the religious naturalism (M. M. KAPLAN) which was an immanentism that projected human values on to the cosmos. Fackenheim concentrated initially on human existence which led up to God and then awaited divine revelation (Kierkegaard).

Later he turned to Jewish tradition, to find God descending from eternity into time (Martin BUBER), while revelation remained metaphysical and transhistorical, beyond analysis and finity.

The encounter in time with metaphysical revelation became brittle to the point of disappearing when Fackenheim subsequently considered the Holocaust. As theological explanations collapsed, reason could no longer provide a context for the divine order of faith. Moreover, historical reality escaped thought, undermining reason even if it should find a way back to faith. Fackenheim was left only with fragmentary knowledge of God and historical reality. But he also found an environment in which the fragments could be enunciated, possibly even brought together. The Jewish State did not explain the Holocaust, but it was a living response, and it created the possibility for the religious thinker to reassert himself, and delineate choices. To "go up" to the State was to do *teshuvah* (repentance), and to return to an ancient land through modern voluntary decision. To reside in it was to share in the mending of the world, "where the impulse below calls forth an impulse above", and historical wholeness was once again real.

BIBLIOGRAPHY
Paths to Jewish Belief (New York: Behrman House, 1960); *God's Presence in History* (New York: New York University Press, 1970); *Encounters Between Judaism and Modern Philosophy* (New York: Basic Books, 1973); *The Jewish Return into History* (New York: Schocken, 1978)

FURTHER READING

Meyer, M.: *Judaism after Auschwitz; The Religious Thought of Emil L. Fackenheim. Commentary* (1972)

GERSHON GREENBERG

Faludy, György (b.1910) Hungarian poet and translator. Faludy came from a middle-class Jewish background, his father being a science teacher in a secondary school. For some years he studied abroad, mainly in Vienna. He appeared as a poet in the early 1930s but first made his name with two free poetic adaptations: Heine's *Deutschland* as *Németország* (1937), and *Villon balladái* (1938; Villon's ballads). He published his first collection of verse *A pompeji strázsán* (1938; On guard at Pompeii) and left Hungary for France the same year. When Paris fell to the Germans Faludy escaped south, made his way to Casablanca, and eventually to the USA. There he volunteered for the army and served in the Far East, but in 1945 returned to Hungary. For some years after his return he was literary editor of the Social Democratic daily *Népszava*, but in 1950 he was arrested and interned in the notorious forced labor camp at Recsk. Released in 1953, he earned his living through translations but in 1956 some of his poems reappeared in the literary press. After the failure of the 1956 revolution Faludy fled Hungary and settled down in London where he became editor of the re-established *Irodalmi Ujság*. After 1963 Faludy lived in Florence and Malta, and in 1968 he went to live in Toronto. For three years he taught Hungarian literature at Columbia University, New York. For his seventieth birthday his *Összegyújtött versek* (1980; Collected poems) were published in New York. In recent years several selections of his poems were published in English, the latest being *Selected Poems 1933–80* (1985).

Faludy's poetry is characterized by humanitarian idealism and (especially in his earlier work) by strong sensualism. The Brechtian–Villonesque rebelliousness of Faludy's pre-war poetry gave way in later years to a more sparing, somber, but still fairly "Baroque" style. As a rationalist and a libertarian Faludy has opposed totalitarianism all his life: he was first persecuted by the Nazis for his Jewish origins and his radical anti-Fascism, later by the Communists for his "bourgeois liberal" views. Faludy wrote several books in English, including a monograph on Erasmus (1970), and a most entertaining, if not always exact, autobiography (1962).

BIBLIOGRAPHY

My Happy Days in Hell, trans. K. Szász (London: André Deutsch, 1962); Skelton, R.: Introduction. *Faludy: Selected Poems* (Athens 1985)

GEORGE GÖMÖRI

Fefer, Itzik (1900–1952) Yiddish poet, critic, political propagandist, and dramatist. Fefer was born in Shpola, Ukraine. He was one of a new wave of Russian Yiddish poets who updated Yiddish vocabulary and style in Russian Yiddish literature to bring it into line with the new revolutionary changes. He worked in a printing house at the age of 12 and joined the Bund for a time in his youth. In 1919, the year in which his first poem was published in the Kiev newspaper *Komunistishe fon* (Communist flag) he joined the Communist Party. *Dos taybele un andere mayselekh* (The little dove and other stories), a book of short stories, was published in 1931. In *Di yidishe literatur in di kapitalistishe lender* (1933; Yiddish literature in capitalist countries), he describes highly acclaimed non-Communist Yiddish writers such as H. N. BIALIK, Israel Joshua SINGER, Aron TSAYTLIN and the Yiddish scholar, Max WEINREICH, in insulting terms. In 1943 he traveled to the USA and Canada as an official envoy in order to gain support from Jews for the Soviet struggle against Nazi Germany. However, like many Russian Jewish writers, in spite of dedicated patriotism he was arrested in 1948, imprisoned, tortured, and shot by Stalin's régime in 1952.

DEVRA KAY

Feierberg, Mordecai Ze'ev (1874–1899) Hebrew short-story writer. Feierberg was born in Novograd-Volinsk in the Ukraine to a hasidic family. His father was a ritual slaughterer of extreme piety who expected his son to follow in his footsteps. Feierberg studied Talmud, but he also read on his own – midrashic legends, Bible, medieval Jewish philosophy, and mysticism. The Enlightenment, which penetrated religious schools at the time, drew him to secular, contemporary Hebrew literature. Soon he rebelled against the narrow-minded traditional society which in turn persecuted him bitterly. He did not succumb to the physical and mental pressure exerted upon him, and in 1896 he published his first story. Apart from his literary activity, Feierberg also engaged in organizing Hebrew and Zionist discussion groups.

Because of his early death from tuberculosis his literary contribution is quantitatively slight. It consists of several mostly autobiographical sketches, one long story, *Le'an* (1899; *Whither*, 1973), and two articles on Hebrew literature.

Although a keen supporter of the Enlightenment, Feierberg was part of the romantic reaction to its optimistic rationalism. In lyrical–symbolical stories, he pays a loving tribute to the spiritual world of the Orthodox Jews. The main theme of Feierberg's stories is the internal struggle of the Jew of the post-Enlightenment period who stands at the crossroads; he is equally attracted to and repulsed by both the world of tradition and the world of Enlightenment. He portrays the tragedy of a whole generation which undergoes an emotional crisis, looking for a solution for the anomalous existence of the Jewish people, but at the same time unwilling to forsake Jewish spiritual values. This problem is presented fully in *Le'an*. The protagonist – a famous young Talmudist – publicly commits an act of impiety: he extinguishes a candle in the synagogue on the Day of Atonement as a protest against all he considers antiquated in Judaism, but he suffers from the spiritual emptiness of a person who has lost his faith. The protagonist slowly declines until he dies, but not before he outlines a program of a spiritual national revival of Judaism in the East, along the lines of AHAD HA'AM's ideology.

BIBLIOGRAPHY

Whither? and Other Stories, trans. H. Halkin (Philadelphia: The Jewish Publication Society of America, 1973)

FURTHER READING

Waxman, M.: Mordechai Zeev Feierberg. In *History of Jewish Literature* (New York, Thomas Yoseloff, 1960) vol. 4, pt 1, 55–62

RIVKA MAOZ

Feiffer, Jules (b.1929)

American playwright and cartoonist. A Depression child growing up in New York, the art-school-educated Feiffer first came to national attention in the late 1950s as the contributor of political cartoons to the newly founded weekly, the *Village Voice*, which is still his artistic "home". Over the course of a generation, Feiffer has, in both his theatrical and journalistic endeavor, created a mordant vision of modern life, savage in its attack on the self-centeredness of personal relationships, the cheapness in consumer society, and the hypocrisy behind political action. Much of his satire is based on an uneasy Jewish sensibility, revealed in the image of the anxious victim at the mercy of a hostile, degenerate environment, whose fears are expressed as weary resignation or wisecracking complaint. Alternatively, Feiffer turns his attention to the victimizers, loutish opportunists and nasty deceivers who, through pushiness or sleaziness (or both), subdue the objects of their rapacious insensitivity. The humor of Feiffer's work ranges from the sentimental to the vicious while he writes his version (as does Jake, the harried protagonist–journalist of *Grown Ups*) of "a wonderful story – the moral and ethical disintegration of the American Dream, basically".

Little Murders (produced 1967), Feiffer's first full-length play, describes the urban life of the Newquist family before and after young Patsy Newquist is killed by a sniper. In the final scene, in the grip of a justifiable urban paranoia, and after visits from an assortment of bizarre characters from the straight and drug culture, the father and fiancé of the deceased are shown in their barricaded apartment revenging themselves by shooting at the pedestrians below. *The White House Murder Case* (produced 1970), is a "whodunit" dealing with the problem of covering up the assassination of the president's wife, and the incompetence of

A scene from the last act of Jules Feiffer's The White House Murder Case *(Robert Skloot's production at the University Theater, Madison, WI; 1976)*

the Americans at war with the "Chicos" in a Latin jungle. Both venues are shown on stage for greater theatricality and comparison.

Feiffer's best recent plays are both more personal and more Jewish than his two earlier political satires. *Knock, Knock* (produced 1976), whose joke/title announces itself as a more whimsical piece, shows Abe and Cohn in a secluded cabin when their philosophical discussions about reality are interrupted by a visit from Joan of Arc. The upbeat ending (for Feiffer) suggests that suffering for doing something is better than suffering for doing nothing. In *Grown Ups* (produced 1981), the image of modern life is Feiffer's most bitter, showing the anxiety and selfishness in three generations of a family whose members refuse to grow up or allow others to, and whose defense against

unhappiness and loneliness is to hurl joking recriminations at uncomprehending antagonists and a discomfited audience.

ROBERT SKLOOT

Feinstein, Elaine (b.1930)   British poet and novelist. Born in Bootle, Merseyside, Feinstein was educated at Cambridge University and subsequently worked as an editor for Cambridge University Press. She has also lectured in English literature at Bishop's Stortford Training College and the University of Essex. Under the influence of modern American verse, Feinstein began writing poetry in the early 1960s and published *In a Green Eye* (1966), her first volume of poetry. During her period as a university lecturer she edited the *Selected Poems of John Clare* (1968). This was followed by *The Circle* (1970), her first novel, which can be regarded as an extension of her poetry. After this initial breakthrough, Feinstein published three volumes of poetry, *The Magic Apple Tree* (1971), *At the Edge* (1972) and *The Celebrants and Other Poems* (1973), as well as two novels, *The Amberstone Exit* (1972), and *The Glass Alembic* (1973). *The Glass Alembic* was republished as *The Crystal Garden* (1974) in the USA and established Feinstein as one of Britain's leading postwar novelists.

By the mid-1970s Feinstein had moved away from a single narrative voice and her fiction began to explore the wider territory of European history and mythology. This resulted in three novels, *Children of the Rose* (1975), *The Ecstasy of Dr Miriam Garner* (1976), and *The Shadow Master* (1978) the last of which evoked the Jewish false messiah, Shabetai Zevi. All three novels combined the experience of the European Jewish past with Feinstein's personal preoccupations as a wife, mother, and writer. Whilst retaining a tightly controled use of language, she also began in this period to experiment with different prose forms and to take greater risks with language in her lyric poetry.

With the publication of *The Survivors* (1982), *The Border* (1984), *Badlands* (1987), and *Mother's Girl* (1988), Feinstein has confirmed her reputation as an outstanding post-war British writer. Moving from concealed autobiography to history and, finally, mythology, Feinstein is able to generate distilled sparks of emotion and, at the same time, to situate these in contexts which transcend the personal. *The Border* in particular combines a sense of history and individual poignancy which characterizes Feinstein's best work.

Feinstein consciously writes in a central European tradition, drawing on forms of expression and subject matter which are unusual for a Jewish writer in Britain. Her work, in this sense, can be viewed as a progressive widening of focus from her personal experience to European history and mythology. Paradoxically, it was in her work as a translator of modern Russian poets that Feinstein was finally to develop a distinctive voice of her own. She has pub-

lished two works of translation, *The Russian Poets: Margarita Aliger, Yunna Moritz, and Bella Akhmadulina* (1979) and *The Selected Poems of Marina Tsvetayeva* (1971).

Other works by Feinstein include *A Captive Lion: The Life of Marina Tsvetayeva* (1987), *New Stories 4* (1979), and two volumes of short stories, *Matters of Chance* (1980) and *The Silent Areas* (1980). She has also written four radio and four television plays.

FURTHER READING

Hailo, J. L., ed.: *British Novelists Since 1960* (Detroit: Gale Research Co., 1983)

Schmidt, M., and Jones, P., eds: *British Poetry Since 1970* (Manchester: Carcanet New Press, 1980)

BRYAN CHEYETTE

Feiwel, Berthold

Feiwel, Berthold (1875–1937) Austrian–German editor, poet, translator, and Zionist activist. Born in Pohrlitz, Moravia, Feiwel studied in Brünn (Brno) and founded Veritas, the first Jewish nationalist students' organization at the university. He became a Zionist activist, moving to Vienna ostensibly to study law, but in reality to be closer to HERZL and to assist him in organizing the first Zionist Congress in Basel in 1897. In his early polemical writings and speeches Feiwel expressed an enthusiastic Zionist message, thoroughly consistent with that of his mentor, Herzl. In 1901 Feiwel assumed the editorship of *Die Welt*, the weekly newspaper founded by Herzl as the primary journalistic instrument of the nascent Zionist movement.

Soon after, Feiwel gravitated towards the opposition camp within the larger Jewish nationalist–Zionist spectrum, namely the cultural Zionist movement, viewing creative Jewish artistic and educational activity as complementary, if not necessarily more important, for the ultimate realization of Jewish nationalist goals. Distancing himself to a degree from Herzl, Feiwel left his post as editor of *Die Welt*, and helped create the democratic faction of the Zionist organization, which proprounded a decidedly cultural and educational orientation at the Fifth Zionist Congress, and included several young and energetic Zionist personalities such as Martin BUBER, Chaim WEIZMANN, and E. M. LILIEN. Most important, Feiwel moved to Berlin and together with Buber, Lilien, and Davis Trietsch, founded the Jüdischer Verlag (Jewish Publishing Company), which soon became the most dynamic publishing firm in Central Europe, dedicated to a Jewish national program. The broad range of Jewish writing published in German by the Jüdischer Verlag had a far-reaching cultural and political impact through the Nazi period.

Feiwel himself spearheaded and directed a rich literary, poetic, and artistic outpouring, a movement known as the "jungjüdische Bewegung" (young Jewish movement), the modern Jewish Renaissance movement. As editor of the sensational anthologies, *Jüdischer Almanach* (1902, 1904), and *Junge Harfen* (1903), Feiwel brought together modern Hebrew and Yiddish writing (in German translation) with Jewish works in German and other "non-Jewish languages" in an esthetically evocative form. In addition to contributing his own poetry, Feiwel translated many of the Yiddish poems included in these anthologies. He also edited and translated the Yiddish ghetto songs of Morris Rosenfeld (*Lieder des Ghetto*), published by the Jüdischer Verlag in 1902. Feiwel's concern for the deprived and oppressed masses of East European Jewry, evident already in the Rosenfeld collection, is also poignantly expressed in his pseudonymously published *Die Judenmassacres zu Kishinew*, which was based on his on-the-spot reportage of the Kishinev pogrom in 1903–4.

Feiwel later moved to London and worked together with Chaim Weizmann in furthering the Zionist cause. He became managing director of the Keren Hayesod (Jewish National Fund) in London and continued to be a high ranking member of the Zionist organization throughout his life. He emigrated to Jerusalem in 1933.

FURTHER READING

Gelber, M. H.: The jungjüdische Bewegung: an unexplored chapter in German–Jewish literary and cultural history. *Leo Baeck Institute Year Book* 31 (1986) 105–19

MARK H. GELBER

Feldman, Louis [Leibl] (1896–1975) South African Yiddish writer. Born in Lithuania, he emigrated to South Africa in 1910 and was educated at the Jewish Government School, Johannesburg. He later became a successful businessman, pursuing Yiddish writing as recreation. His first work, *Yidn in Dorem Afrike* (Jews in South Africa), printed in Poland in 1937, was the first attempt to describe the socioeconomic and cultural life of the Lithuanian Jews who had settled in South Africa. *Oudtshoorn: Yerusholayim d'Afrike* (1940; Oudtshoorn: the Jerusalem of Africa), describes the distinctive qualities of the colorful Jewish community of Oudtshoorn while the ostrich-feather boom was at its height there, and, although only a slim volume, it is one of his best works.

In 1955 his most ambitious work, *Yidn in Yohanesburg* (Jews in Johannesburg), appeared. Providing a picture of the pioneering years, one of the most complex periods of Johannesburg Jewry's history, he recorded punctiliously an imposing amount of previously inaccessible historical information.

Apart from his enthusiastic chronicles of the history of Jewish life, he was also interested in the history of the South African Indian population and wrote *Hundert yor Indyer in Dorem Afrike* (1961; A hundred years of Indian life in South Africa), and returning from Israel, wrote a book on his impressions, *Yisroel vi ikh ze es* (1965; Israel as I see it).

A founder of the Yiddish Folkschool and of the Yiddish Cultural Federation, in which he played a leading part for several years, he was a regular contributor to the Federation's official organ, *Dorem Afrike* (South Africa). Holding strong political views, he was a deeply compassionate man and fighter for the underprivileged. An ardent champion of Yiddish language and literature, his major contribution was his pioneering work in the field of South African Jewish historiography.

JOCELYN HELLIG

feminism, modern Judaism and Feminism, which has brought marked changes to western society, has not left Jewish life unscathed: in religion, Jewish studies, and communal and voluntary organizations, its force is felt. Books and articles on the subject of Jewish women appear everywhere. Courses on the subject can be found on countless university and adult education curricula. Although contemporary Jewish life has witnessed a major upheaval due to the demands of women, the story starts over a century ago.

Influential Jewish women in modern times

With the Enlightenment and Emancipation, Jewish men extended their influence as legal disabilities in Western European countries were lifted from them. Jewish women reaped the benefits, although they were still subject to the same restrictions as gentile women. Some of them renounced their Judaism, some embraced it, some were indifferent. Salon Jewesses like Rahel Varnhagen (1771–1833) in Berlin and the poet Penina Moïse (1797–1880) in Savannah, Georgia, attracted many writers and influential people. Actresses like the French tragedienne Rachel (1821–58) and the American Adah Isaacs Menken (1835–68) captivated the imagination and hearts of Europe as much with their scandalous lives as with their acting abilities. Rachel MORPURGO wrote Hebrew poetry in Italy, Emma LAZARUS poetry and verse drama in the USA, and Grace AGUILAR novels and Jewish histories in England. Jewish women, like Rebecca Gratz (1781–1869) – the supposed model for Scott's Rebecca in *Ivanhoe* – immersed themselves in community work.

By the end of the nineteenth century, as women gained more rights, Jewish women accordingly took advantage and played their part in improving the lot of people in Jewish and wider society.

In politics Jewish women inflamed, organized, and enraged their compatriots. Emma GOLDMAN espoused anarchy, campaigned for birth control and against the draft, and was subsequently deported from the USA. "Red" Rosa Luxemburg (1871–1919), assassinated for her political activities, championed the cause of Social Democracy and Communism in Germany and Poland, and argued against the First World War. In England the socialist Eleanor Marx (1855–98), through working with the Jewish poor in the East End of London, learned to take pride in her Jewish background, unlike her father, Karl MARX, and her sisters. Rose Schneiderman (1882–1972), unceasingly active in union organizing, worked for the International Ladies' Garment Workers' Union (ILGWU), and rose to the presidency of the Women's Trade Union League in 1918.

Lily Montagu (1873–1963), an English magistrate and social worker, helped to form the Liberal and Progressive Movement in Judaism. She was probably the first woman to preach in a European synagogue. Aletta Jacobs (1854–1929), renowned as the Netherlands' first woman physician and university student, campaigned for women's rights and pacifism, as did "the Susan B. Anthony of France", Louise Weiss (1894–1984) and Hungarian Nobel Peace Prize nominee Rosika Schwimmer (1977–1948).

Within the Orthodox world, Sarah Schnirer (1883–1938) stands out. Alarmed at the growing drift of girls from traditional homes towards a secular society which offered more intellectual gratification, she realized the need to provide them with religious education. In 1917 Schnirer opened a school in Krakow with 30 pupils. By 1929 there were 167 Beis Yaakov schools in existence; 9 years later, in Poland alone, there were 230 schools, responsible for 27,000 girls, as well as summer camps and a teachers' seminary.

While Henrietta Szold (1860–1945), the founder of Haddassah, Lilian Wald (1867–1940), who opened the Henry Street Settlement, and other American–Jewish women became important forces within social and communal work, Bertha Pappenheim (1859–1936), Freud's "Anna O", pioneered international social work in the area of Jewish prostitution, and formed the Jüdischer Frauenbund (Jewish Women's Organization) in 1904.

Though individual Jewish women increasingly made their mark on society, the lot of the average Jewish woman hardly changed, especially in the area of religion. Reform Judaism, which had proclaimed women's religious equality in 1845, had yet to ordain women in its seminaries. (Regina Jonas was privately ordained in Berlin in the 1930s.) In 1922 Judith

Kaplan Eisenstein, eldest daughter of Reconstructionism's founder, had the first recorded *bat mitzvah* ceremony. Of all the religious movements, only Reconstructionism encouraged women's full participation in synagogue life. In other areas of Jewish life women were no better off. With the exception of organizations like Haddassah and the National Council of Jewish Women in America, women occupied volunteer or low-paid and low-prestige positions. Their voices were effectively as silent in the community as in the synagogue.

The 1960s, feminism, and change

In the late 1960s, however, the climate changed. Along with a general critique of the establishment, the Jewish world came in for its fair share of criticism. Alternative and counterculture journals like *Chutzpah*, *Response*, and *Davka* in the USA abounded, calling for the recognition of gays, women, and alternative lifestyles. The Havurah movement, founded on the principle of egalitarianism, inspired young Jews to explore the religion for themselves. And in the general American milieu of Black Power and ethnic pride, Jews, who had rejected their Jewish identity for wider social and political concerns, returned to the fold. Pride in Israel's victory in the Six Day War in 1967 also spurred Jews to search out their "roots".

Concurrently, developments in the Women's Liberation Movement encouraged Jewish women to re-examine their background. Again ethnic pride and "identity politics" – which emphasizes individual ethnic, sexual, and economic identification – helped to erode a traditional liberal, monolithic view of feminism. One immediate consequence was the National Jewish Women's Conference, held in New York City in 1973, which attracted women of diverse backgrounds, ages, and locations. *Lilith* appeared in 1976, the first magazine in the USA for Jewish women since Rosa Sonneschein's *American Jewess*, 1895–9.

But there was a negative impetus to Jewish women's return. As in other radical movements, anti-Semitic and anti-Zionist utterances surfaced in feminist circles. The problem, gaining in intensity throughout the United Nations' Decade of Women (1975–85), peaked in the aftermath of Israel's 1982 invasion of Lebanon. Jewish women, feeling increasingly isolated, began to question whether the general Women's Movement was still a "safe" place for them.

In this climate all the religious denominations felt the pressure to institute changes in women's position. Few responded with alacrity. The Reform movement, not surprisingly, was the quickest. On 3 June 1972 Hebrew Union College made history by ordaining Sally Priesand. Three months earlier the women's study group Ezrat Nashim (literally "help for women" and the name of the women's section in the ancient Temple and Orthodox synagogue) presented its demands to the Rabbinical Assembly of America. They called for the Conservative movement to put "an end to the second-class status of women in Jewish life" (quoted by Lacks, p.171). Many Conservative rabbis were sympathetic, but the majority shied away from major change. The women's issue created a furore unlike that of any other halakhic issue. In 1973 the Conservative movement ruled that women were to be counted towards making up the *minyan* – the 10 "men" needed to form a quorum for the recitation of public prayers – and allowed to read from the Torah. Implementation of the ruling, though, was left to the discretion of each congregation. While agreeing in principle to the ordination of women, the rabbinical program at the Jewish Theological Seminary still refused them admission. In 1985 Amy Eilberg became the first woman ordained by the Jewish Theological Seminary. As a result, a breakaway faction of rabbis and laity calling themselves the Union for Traditional Conservative Judaism was formed. But the Movement could not go back, and in 1987 women were admitted to the cantorial program for certification.

Orthodox Judaism and feminism

The Orthodox movements proved least responsive to women's demands. Obliged to pray behind curtains or on balconies out of sight of the men, unable to take an active role in the public celebration of Judaism, some women felt like vicarious participants. At a time when women had greater responsibilities outside of the home, Orthodox Judaism was telling them that there was no role for them other than the traditional one. Some women left Orthodoxy, some opted out of public worship, but a different solution presented itself to others. If they are forbidden by Jewish law from full participation due to the presence of men, what could stop them if no men were present?

The first women's prayer group met in Baltimore, Maryland, in 1971. Fifteen years later the Women's Tefillah (i.e. "Prayer") Network could claim over 700 members in North America and Israel. For the members, most of whom identify as Orthodox, the groups represent a way for women to lead services, read from the Torah and Haftorah, celebrate *bat mitzvas* and baby namings, without contravening the *halakhah*. Although some groups call themselves *minyanim* and perform all the prayers which appear in a normal service, most of the prayer groups follow a stricter interpretation, refraining from reciting prayers such as the *kaddish* and the *kedushah* which require a quorum.

Most Orthodox women see religious study as the key to greater participation and respect. Opportunities are increasing, such as women's *yeshivot* and study groups, but among the stricter sects of Orthodoxy, women's access to advanced study remains a halakhically sensitive issue, with no clear or immediate resolution.

Some perceive the restrictions upon Orthodox women as degrading and reactionary: for example, rituals such as *halizah*, whereby a childless widow removes her brother-in-law's shoe and spits at him to be freed from the obligation to marry him; the prohibition against women singing in mixed company; a woman's ineligibility to serve as a witness (*'edah*) before the religious court. But of greatest concern to Orthodox women is the problem of the *'agunah* – the "chained" woman. These women cannot remarry, due either to a missing husband for whom there is insufficient proof of his death, or a husband who cannot or will not give her a bill of divorce (*get*). The husband, who can remarry, often refuses to free his wife unless she pays a large sum, gives in to his demands, or out of spite.

While the other denominations have addressed the problem, the Orthodox rabbinate has been unable or unwilling to institute changes in the halakhah to correct flagrant abuses and inequalities in the divorce laws. Forced into the realization that help will not come *ex nihilo*, women have organized themselves at the grassroots level. It is no longer uncommon to see Orthodox women picketing an establishment whose owner has refused to give his wife a *get*. A group of Canadian women came up with a unique solution to one case: they refused to go to the *mikveh* (ritual bath) and resume sexual relations with their husbands until one member of the community, who was demanding $25,000, gave his wife a *get* gratis (Greenberg, p.139). Organizations like GET (Getting Equitable Treatment) and Agunah fight not only for individual cases, but also to bring the issue to the public's attention and to put pressure on the Orthodox rabbinate.

Even the ultra-Orthodox world has felt the force of feminism, if only in its reaction against it. These groups, in stressing the importance of the woman's traditional role as bearer of the spirit of Judaism, have raised the significance of rituals, such as lighting the sabbath candles to almost mystical levels, and increased their emphasis on modest dress and behavior for women. Most importantly, the right-wing of Orthodoxy exercises a conservative pull over the whole movement, making liberalization within groups like the modern Orthodox more difficult. A good example of this has been the reaction of moderate rabbis to women's *tefillah* groups. Though they seem halakhically sound, influential rabbis at New York's Yeshiva University strongly condemned them, and with few exceptions, their pulpit colleagues followed suit. But even here, in the stalwart of traditional Judaism, change has come: for example there is now some acknowledgment of a girl's coming of age in almost every denomination of Judaism, whether it is called a *bat mitzvah*, or disguised as in the British *bat hayil* (lit. "daughter of valor") ceremony.

While some women have concentrated on achieving religious parity with men, or increasing their role in public worship, others pursue a different route. Many feminists are reclaiming traditional women's rituals and holidays, like *mikveh*, and *Rosh hodesh* (new moon). Others totally reject their patriarchal associations.

Some women are investing traditional models with feminist insight and interpretation and writing *midrashim* and Bible commentaries. One can now find feminist and lesbian *seder* services all over the world. In New York a feminist *Tashlikh* service, where women come together to throw their sins into the water, is performed every *Rosh hashanah*. New rituals and blessings, suited to women's life experiences, are being created – for example, menstruation, birth, bringing daughters into the covenant, rape, and menopause. In general, the liturgy is being explored for ways to make it more egalitarian or feminist. New prayer books, like *Vetaher Libenu* (Purify our hearts), speak of "the God of our fathers", and "of our mothers"; they list the matriarchs alongside the patriarchs; and may address God in the feminine as well as the masculine, or in neutral terms.

But for some feminists this is not enough. Labeling God "Queen of the Universe" is hardly an improvement. The problems with Jewish liturgy cannot be rectified merely by redressing the gender imbalance of Hebrew prayers; the matter goes much deeper. Feminism rejects hierarchical and authoritarian models as oppressive. So the concept of "rulership" itself is suspect. Other metaphors and images, such as "bride" and "master", are also seen by some as ultimately unsatisfying, leading many Jewish feminists to seek new ways of expressing their relationship with God.

Feminism has generally transformed Jewish life. In the academic world women are rediscovering their foremothers, and expanding and reinterpreting Jewish history and sociology through studies of women's lives. Feminist concerns have awakened the Jewish world to problems such as battered wives, incest, and child abuse. Women are demanding that the community be more responsive to the needs of one-parent families, working women, single, and homosexual Jews. Exploration of female spirituality continues to change religious life. Feminism's stress on the value of each woman's life experiences has helped Ashkenazi and Sephardi women to learn from each other – to appreciate what they have in common, while respecting their differences. In many places Jewish women are forging similar links with Christian and Muslim women. The perception of women is changing, reflecting their modern social and economic circumstances. This has enabled men to re-examine their place and role. On all fronts, feminism has helped to widen and modernize Jewish life, making it more responsive to the concerns and new reality of the contemporary Jew, both male and female.

FURTHER READING

Biale, R.: *Women and Jewish Law: An Exploration of Women's Issues in Halakhic Sources* (New York: Schocken, 1984)

Greenberg, B.: *On Women and Judaism: A View from Tradition* (Philadelphia: The Jewish Publication Society of America, 1981)

Heschel, S. ed.: *On Being a Jewish Feminist: A Reader* (New York: Schocken, 1983)

Lacks, R.: *Women and Judaism: Myth, History, and Struggle* (Garden City: Doubleday, 1980)

Schneider, S. W.: *Jewish and Female: Choices and Changes in Our Lives Today* (New York: Swan Sonnenschein, 1984)

SHARONA LEVY

Feuchtwanger, Lion (1884–1958) German novelist. Born and raised in an Orthodox family in Munich that also maintained cultural links with German secular culture, Feuchtwanger was exposed from the start to traditional Jewish and modern German secular learning. He studied philology, history, and anthropology, and wrote his doctoral thesis on the genesis of Heine's *The Rabbi of Bacherach*. An academic career seemed possible, but he declined to convert to Christianity in order to realize this goal.

Feuchtwanger turned to drama, and several of his early one-act plays (1905–6) dealt with Jewish subjects: *Joel*, *König Saul* (King Saul), and *Das Weib des Urias* (Uriah's woman). He wrote a play, *Jud Süss* (1917), centering on the life of the eighteenth century South German court financier Joseph Süss Oppenheimer, which dealt with the issues of conversion and anti-Semitism in an historical setting. He utilized this work as the basis of his first historical novel of the same name written in 1921–2. This work brought Feuchtwanger international fame.

Feuchtwanger dealt with Jewish subjects in about half of his 15 major historical novels, the genre in which he distinguished himself above all else. His trilogy *Josephus*, written between 1931 and 1941, began as a testimony to the ideals of reason and progress, but ended as a personal contribution in the war against Fascism by incorporating scarcely veiled allusions to contemporary political figures and developments. The same is true of his *Der Wartesaal* (1927–39; The waiting room), set in contemporary national-socialist Germany. In his last decade he continued in this vein in *Die Jüdin von Toledo* (1952; *Raquel, the Jewess of Toledo*, 1956) and *Jefta und seine Tochter* (1958; Jephta and his daughter), which promoted his belief in the superiority of spiritual values and pacifism over physical force.

Feuchtwanger wrote many literary pieces and essays on Jewish topics. In the short satire, "Gespräche mit dem ewigen Juden", (1920; Conversations with the Wandering Jew), he evidenced optimism about Jewish life in Germany, convinced of the sure success of the German–Jewish symbiosis. In "Die Verjudung der abendländischen Literatur" (1920; The Judaization of Western literature), and in "Der historische Prozess der Juden" (1930; The historical process of the Jews), he argued that Judaism was essentially a spiritual principle or mentality, embedded in tradition and historical consciousness. For Feuchtwanger Judaism was internationally orientated. In fact, he believed that modern Jewry was incapable of forming a nation. In "Nationalismus und Judentum" (1933; Nationalism and Judaism), he argued that the four ideologies required for nation building were missing in modern Jewish life: a common land and climate, a common race, a common history, and a common language. Nevertheless he saw some value in Zionism to the extent it represented for him a pacifist messianic movement.

Feuchtwanger found temporary refuge from Nazism in France and subsequently emigrated to the USA. He collaborated during the period in exile with Arnold ZWEIG and Bertolt Brecht.

MARK H. GELBER

Feuerring, Maximilian (b.1896) Polish–Australian painter, teacher, and lecturer. Feuer-ring was born into an Orthodox Jewish family, in Lvov, Poland and arrived in Australia in 1950. He studied at art school in Berlin (1916), Florence (1922), The Royal Academy of Fine Arts of Rome (1923–7), Paris and Warsaw. In 1926 he gained a diploma with distinction, at the Municipal School of Decorative Art, Rome. He taught at the Academy of Fine Arts, Warsaw, from 1934 to 1939. He survived the war in a prisoner of war camp in Bavaria. From 1947 to 1950 he taught at the Universität International, Munich.

Feuerring's paintings are expressionistic and semi-abstract and yet they reflect a classical artistic education. His work is constantly inventive, and he painted in oils, acrylics, watercolors, and gouache. In his native Poland he was the leader of the movement known as the "New Generation", a revolt against classical and nationalistic concepts in art. Feuerring was the founder-member and President of a society of avant-garde Jewish artists, the rest of whom were murdered by the Nazis.

He arrived in Australia at a time when Australian artistic tastes were changing, and was able to introduce painting loaded with symbolism and making intellectual demands into his new working environment. These contributions were recognized by critics of his contribution at the Contemporary Art Society exhibition in Brazil in 1961 where he was acclaimed "a master of forms in flaming colours".

His awards included 16 major prizes, from Rome, Lvov, Prague, Warsaw, Munich, and Australia, and numerous local prizes. His work is represented in every Australian state gallery, the Merz collections, in the USA, the Israel Museum, the Museum of Modern Art, Lodz, Bnai Brith, Washington, and the Rappersvil collection, Switzerland. He has held 43 solo exhibitions in Rome, Paris, Berlin, Munich, Amsterdam, various Polish and Australian cities, and in Brazil.

ALAN D. CROWN

Fiedler, Leslie (b.1917) American literary critic. Always identified as a member of the

New York intellectual community, Leslie A. Fiedler never actually lived in New York. Born in Newark, New Jersey, Fiedler did commute to New York University, graduating in 1938. He undertook graduate work at the University of Wisconsin and was awarded an MA and a Ph.D. From 1941 to 1964 (with several years off for naval duty during the Second World War) Fiedler taught at Montana State University; in 1964 he moved to the State University of New York at Buffalo. Nonetheless, he has always been thought of as a member of the New York intellectual world.

Fiedler's connection with this milieu derives from his early publication in several journals central to this intellectual group and his interest and contributions on particular subjects. That the designation "New York intellectual" is more a political–cultural description than a regional one, is nowhere better demonstrated than in the career and writings of Leslie Fiedler.

He first came to intellectual attention with his provocative essay, "Come Back to the Raft Ag'in, Huck Honey", published in *Partisan Review*. Moving from a mild radicalism in the 1930s to an interest in psychological and mythical concerns in the postwar years, Fiedler argued the neglected concern in American letters with adult male relationships (especially a white man and a dark companion, such as Huckleberry Finn and the slave Jim), and the "failure of the American fictionist to deal with adult heterosexual love and his consequent obsession with death, incest and innocent homosexuality". This essay later reappeared in his most influential work of criticism, *Love and Death in the American Novel* (1960). While sensational at the time, Fiedler's thesis won acceptance, sometimes with revision, and in the 1960s and 1970s seemed much tamer than when it first appeared.

The second area which brought him notoriety came from his critique of liberalism after the failure of the American left in the 1930s. "The age of innocence is dead", he wrote in *The End to Innocence* (1952). "Liberal principle is not a guarantee against evil".

His own attempts at fiction proved less successful than his criticism and political commentary. His first two novels, *The Second Stone: A Love Story* (1963), and *Back to China* (1965), drew harsh criticism. In 1966 he published to more acclaim three long stories in a book entitled *The Last Jew in America*. His short stories, collected in *Nude Croquet: The Stories of Leslie Fiedler* (1969), included many written throughout the 1950s and 1960s. Interest in popular culture and myths led to works on Indians (*The Return of the Vanishing American*, 1968), Jews in American culture (*To the Gentiles*, 1972), science fiction (*The Messengers Will Come no More*, 1974), and freaks (*Freaks: Myths and Images of the Secret Self*, 1978). Fiedler gained a different kind of public reknown when, in 1967, he was arrested for having "maintained a premise" where marijuana was smoked. Faculty adviser to a student group advocating the legalization of marijuana, Fiedler's conviction and six-month jail sentence were ultimately overturned. His account of all this appeared in *Being Busted* (1969).

FURTHER READING

Bloom, A.: *Prodigal Sons: The New York Intellectuals and Their World* (New York & Oxford: Oxford University Press, 1986–7)

Wald, A.: *The New York Intellectuals* (Chapel Hill: University of North Carolina Press, 1987)

ALEXANDER BLOOM

films, European, Jews in   The cinematic depiction of Jews during the 20 years from 1929 to 1948 might be expected to vary considerably, depending on the country in which a particular film was produced, made, and shown. A study of Jewish characters as presented in films of the time, however, reveals a certain homogeneity in the cinema of this period. Indeed, the image of Jews in fiction films made in European studios varies less from country to country than according to the time when a film was made.

In 1929 talking pictures, which had first appeared in the USA two years previously, won acceptance in almost all European countries. Within a few months, silent films found themselves relegated to outdated, second-class status. With them went a universal language. Charlie, as loved in China, Russia, Brazil, or Australia, was to develop step by step into the more talkative – and inevitably less well understood – Charlie Chaplin. The advent of the talkies, the first signs of the 1929 economic crisis, and stronger competition from Hollywood, all helped to hasten the restructuring of the cinematographic industry. Faced by an invasion of technically superior American films, the *Film Europe* movement, under the aegis of the German producer, Erich Pommer, tried to put up a European resistance. At this point, language might have been a way of restricting the ambitions of American film companies. The first synchronized sound films made in Europe were shot in the latest German and English studios. Elstree Studios, near London, for instance, was equipped with the most modern technology, and provided facilities for shooting *La route est belle* (1929), one of the first French talking pictures, made by Robert Florey (1900–79). Besides the fact that the scriptwriter Pierre Wolff and the producer Pierre Braunberger were Jewish, one may note a short sequence in the film featuring a Jewish shopkeeper, the corpulent Salomon (Léon Bélières), who easily cheats the naive and lanky Tony (the singer André Baugé) over the purchase of his first dinner jacket.

Sound dubbing of films for export came in only gradually. At first, for various reasons, the method preferred was to make several versions of the same film, using the same technical team but different actors, well known in their own countries and speaking their mother tongues. The German–Jewish director, Ewald Andreas Dupont (1891–1956), for instance, shot *Two Worlds* at Elstree Studios in 1930. Besides the English version of this film, a nostalgic re-creation of the life of a small Galician *shtetl* during the Austrian occupation, a French version and a German version were made. At the same time, in France, André Hugon was producing and making a lighter type of comedy, *Lévy et Compagnie* (1930), with Léon Bélières in the part of Salomon Lévy, claimant to the inheritance of an American millionaire of the same name. In the same year, Jaap Speyer made a German version of the film, which was distributed under the title of *Meier und Co* or *Moritz macht sein Glück*. *Dreyfus*, made by the German director Richard Oswald (1880–1963), was probably the original of Milton Rosmer's English film *The Dreyfus Case* (1931), in which

the stage actor Sir Cedric Hardwicke brought talent and feeling to the part of the Jewish captain falsely accused of treason. There was no French version of the film because at the time censorship still prohibited any reference to the *affaire Dreyfus* in France. In 1931 Erkmann-Chatrian's novel *Le Juif polonais*, was brought to the screen by Jean Kemm in France, and by Oscar Wemdorff and Harcourt Templeman in England under the title of *The Bells*. Other examples of co-operation in the industry of the European dream could be cited. The name of ACE, one of the most important film companies of the time, producing works in English, French, Italian, and German, is significant in itself: the initials stood for *L'Alliance Cinématographique Européenne*. Despite the obvious industrial and commercial supremacy of the USA, the European cinema was still able to compete with Hollywood on the artistic level. The sharing of scripts, cameramen, and actors must initially have made the decline of the European cinema seem less obvious.

However, from 1932 the economic crisis ceased to spare the film industry of the Old World. Companies were seen to be drawing in their horns in almost all European countries. The days of cooperation and multiple versions of films were over. Instead, the trend was towards less expensive and safer options, such as the dubbing or subtitling of a film's original version. Films with Jewish subjects or characters were still being made in various countries, but language became a considerable barrier to the foreign distribution of films.

The only films made in Europe which temporarily escaped these problems and appealed to a large, cosmopolitan public were those made in Poland. Yiddish songs and the Yiddish language were still understood by several million people in Central and Eastern Europe, as well as in the USA, Palestine, and all the capitals to which there had been large-scale emigration. It is no coincidence, therefore, that the golden age of the Yiddish cinema falls precisely between 1935 and 1939. There was a truly remarkable burst of filmmaking during this short period, not only in quantity (around ten full-length films were shot in rural Poland, where, it must be remembered, the cinema industry was in its infancy), but most of all in quality. What is more, these films were exported to the USA, where they had considerable success. Among them may be mentioned Joseph Green's cheerful *Yidl mitn Fidl* (1936; Yidl with a fiddle), with the extraordinary Molly Picon; Michael Waszynsky's captivating *The Dybbuk* (1937); and Joseph Green's very moving *A Brivele der Mamen* (1938; A letter to Mother). In Europe, anti-Semitism was spreading even before Hitler came to power. In the face of increasingly numerous and violent street demonstrations, Jewish subjects progressively disappeared from the screen. After 1933 films made by Jewish emigrés were banned in Germany and Austria. To avoid this boycott and limit xenophobia, some producers did not hesitate to take the names of their foreign employees off the credits, or sometimes names of technicians or actors with too obviously Jewish a ring to them were altered. Such camouflage was impossible for those who were already famous. The anti-Nazi German actor Conrad Veidt (1893–1974), living in exile in Britain with his Jewish wife, made no secret of his condemnation of Hitlerian anti-Semitism. His remarkable performances in *Jew Süss* (1934), made by Lothar Mendes (1894–1974) from Lion FEUCHTWANGER's famous novel, and in *The Wandering Jew* (1934), made by Maurice Elvey (1887–1967), did not escape notice. However, films on Jewish subjects like these were not very successful commercially, since politics had become a bar to their distribution in Europe at the time. For similar reasons, films made in the USSR at the same period, such as Herbert Rappaport and Adolf Minkine's *Professor Mamlock* (1938), from the play by the anti-Fascist German writer Friedrich Wolf, and Grigori Roshal's *The Oppenheim Family* (1938), also inspired by a Lion Feuchtwanger novel, did not get very wide distribution. *Professor Mamlock* was banned by the English censor several months before the signing of the German–Soviet pact because the film was considered socially subversive.

With the declaration of war in September 1939, and the military successes of the German armies, the anti-Semitic depiction of Jews in the cinema tightened its grip on almost the whole of Nazi Europe. Its vehicles were German fiction films such as Heinz Helbig's *Leinen aus Irland* (1939), Hans Heinz Zerlett's *Robert und Bertram* (1939), Erich Waschneck's *Die Rothschilds* (1940), and in particular Veit Harlan's appalling version of *Jud Süss* (1940). Shown almost all over Europe, *Jud Süss* was seen by several million spectators who paid for their seats. Commercially, therefore, it was a huge success. It need hardly be said that the image of Jews in these films, where they were presented as vicious and depraved foreigners, had nothing to do with that of the previous decade. Jews were now shown as a race apart, almost entirely consisting of shopkeepers or bankers, frequently lubricious, always shady. After the war and the disclosure of the Holocaust, European films abandoned this kind of stereotype, as they also abandoned the light comedy tone. Jewish characters were now presented almost exclusively as victims confronting a series of terrible trials. Thus, in *Ulica graniczna* (1948; Truth has no frontiers), Aleksander Ford (1908–80) depicts the dramatic fate of the inhabitants of the Warsaw ghetto during the war. The fate of Hungarian Jews falsely accused of ritual murder at the end of the last century was well described in the Austrian film *Der Prozess* (1948), made by Wilhelm Pabst (1885–1967). In France, Henri-Georges Clouzot (1907–77) showed Jewish survivors of the extermination camps making their clandestine way to Palestine in *Manon* (1948). Finally, in the same year and thanks to the Italian Goffredo Alessandrini (1905–78), audiences were able to watch Vittorio Gassmann's agony and redemption in *L'Ebreo errante* (The Wandering Jew), following the Jew from ancient times to our own days.

In 1949 the Cold War was at its height on the European continent; the Council of Europe was set up the same year. The young State of Israel was tentatively laying the foundations of its own film industry. A new cinematic image of the Jew, in Technicolor and on the large screen, was gradually making its mark. It was the image presented in an American super-production made by Cecil B. De Mille (1881–1958): his *Samson and Delilah* (1949). Facing these courageous fighting Hebrews as conceived by Hollywood, European screens, with their small budgets and drab black and white films, could only surrender. Biblical epics extolling the courage of the fighting men of Israel temporarily reigned supreme. Not until the end of the 1960s did a new wave of filmmakers begin depicting less Manichean Jewish characters, first in Europe and then in the USA. Those to be seen on the world's screens at the end of the 1980s have many features in common. The main dividing line today is not between Europe and the USA, nor even between East and West. It has shifted, daily moving the cinematic vision of Israel farther from the remaining Jews of the Diaspora.

FURTHER READING

Balcon, M.: *The Pursuit of British Cinema* (New York: The Museum of Modern Art, 1984)

Chertok, S.: Jewish themes in soviet cinema. *Soviet Jewish Affairs* 16 3 (1986) 29–42

Goldman, E. A.: *Visions, Images, and Dreams: Yiddish Film Past and Present* (Ann Arbor: UMI Research Press, 1983)

Singer, C.: Cent personnages en quête d'habits. *Les Nouveaux Cahiers* 88 (1986) 18–23

CLAUDE SINGER

films, US, Jews in　In the first cinema films made in the USA before 1900, the image of Jews was neither varied nor of any great significance. The cameraman, frequently left to his own devices, was almost always the prisoner of his unsophisticated technical equipment and his own limited notions of Judaism. Usually he simply presented a contemporary character like Captain Dreyfus, the more or less comical adventures of fictional personages with names like Levy and Cohen, or exotic costumes, dances, and customs. At least until the approach of the First World War, film-making was a small-scale workmanlike craft, which did not systematically entail any great financial risk. The declaration of war, which in a way constituted the true moment of birth of the American film industry, brought with it considerable changes. The almost total disappearance of European competition was a gift to the American cinema, which was also rationalizing itself. It now made the optimum use of qualified staff, sunlight, space, and sets built in the big Californian studios. The public wanted longer films with a proper story, and heroes with whom they could easily identify. The man to deal with all these changes was the producer. It was his business to find the considerable sums of money required. Almost all the producers who managed to make their mark in the industry of the American Dream during the 1920s were Jewish. Immigrants or the sons of immigrants from central or eastern Europe, these relatively uneducated self-made men, whose Yiddish accents people sometimes liked to exaggerate, had been working in the rag trade before they became so successful in films. Among them were Wilhelm Fried (William Fox, 1879–1952) and Adolf Zukor (1873–1975). Coming from more-or-less Orthodox backgrounds, these Jewish producers almost always married Jewish women, and formed bonds resembling family alliances with each other.

Paradoxically, these dynamic producers who did not hesitate either to take great risks or to employ a large number of Jewish associates seem to have remained rather conformist in many ways, particularly where the content of their films is concerned. They did not try to shrug off their own Judaism. Moreover, the number of American films containing Jewish characters made between 1920 and 1940 can be put at about two hundred, some ten films per year. Yet it must be admitted that the image of Jews as presented in these films, which were of course intended for a very wide audience, seems no less stereotyped than the characteristics attributed by Hollywood to other ethnic or social groups at this time. One should not forget the parallel existence of a cinema for minority groups – ethnic movies – and in particular the distribution of a considerable number of Yiddish films.

Names to be mentioned from among the American producers and directors of low-budget B films, very marginal compared to the powerful Hollywood industry, are Joseph Seiden, Henry Lynn, and Edgar G. Ulmer; in cinematic history, several of the latter's horror films figure as particularly successful.

The Hollywood cinema of the years between the wars was not intended to promote the

Adolph Zukor (2nd from left) with associates in the Players–Lasky Corporation: (from left) Jesse Lasky, Zukor, Sam Goldwyn, Cecil B. DeMille, A. Kaufman, c.1914

specific character of any minority group. On the contrary: as the ideological melting-pot of America it pointed the way to better and faster integration by depicting individual experience, sometimes through a Jewish character. This fact helps to explain why, unlike the producers themselves, whose legal wives were nearly always Jewish (marriages outside Judaism still being very much in the minority), the protagonists of films made in the big studios were often shown facing the problems of mixed marriage. As right-minded Americans were in favor of integration, the film producers of America could not but extol the benefits of the melting pot. They did so wholeheartedly. Of all the films

made on the subject, three shown in 1928 may be mentioned: *We Americans*, made by Edward Sloman for Universal; *Abie's Irish Rose*, made by Victor Fleming for Paramount; and *The Cohens and the Kellys in Paris*, directed by William Beaudine for Universal.

The two last-named were part of a whole range of light comedies, very popular on screen (and a few years later on the radio), describing the friction between immigrants of different origins. Here, of course, the marriage of the Jewish daughter to the Irish son was to be at the root of trouble between the two families. If rumor was to be believed, the arguments between the German Jew Carl Laemmle and his Irish

Catholic associate, Pat Powers, at Universal were the inspiration behind the famous series of seven full-length films, *The Cohens and the Kellys*.

Most producers dwelt on the courage and patriotism of Jewish characters in their films. Even before 1914 there were several films extolling the heroism of Jewish fighting men, in particular *Cohen Saves the Flag*, made by Frank Powell in 1913 for Keystone. The film was set in the American Civil War. The same year, Fox produced *Bar Kochba: The Hero of a Nation*, in which the Jewish rising against the Romans in 132–5 CE was presented as a desperate struggle for equality and liberty. It may be noted that the messianism of the fighters depicted in this film, as in many others, was perhaps more American that Jewish! However that may be, the fervent patriotism of Jewish producers, at which Scott Fitzgerald poked fun in his novel *The Last Tycoon*, comes across in many films.

Another peculiarity of films produced in the 1920s and 1930s is one of interpretation. While the best film actors of the present day try actually to become the characters they are asked to play, pre-war actors had practically no chance of getting a Jewish part in a film if they themselves were Jewish. Jewish stars like Edward G. Robinson, John Garfield, and Lauren Bacall, who in any case had often adopted stage names with an Anglo-Saxon ring to them, were not generally keen to play stereotyped parts.

One famous anecdote is a perfect illustration of the atmosphere in the big studios of the time. The story goes that a director employed by Columbia once asked his boss, Harry Cohn (1891–1958, known as King Kohn because of his legendary rages), to engage a certain actor for an important part. Cohn categorically refused to have the actor, who, he said, looked "too Jewish". In his studio, he pointed out, Jews only played Indians.

Even the great Paul Muni (Muni Weisenfreund, 1897–1967), already famous for his performance in *Scarface*, made by Hawks in 1932, and who made no secret of either his early career in the Yiddish theater of New York or even his militant Zionism, did not play Jewish parts in films until much later. In the courageous film *The Life of Emile Zola*, made by

William Dieterle for Warner Brothers in 1937, another actor (Joseph Schildkraut) played the part of Captain Dreyfus.

It may be noted that in spite of the Oscars it won, this film had a rather difficult career. It was not shown either in France, because of the strong feeling the *affaire Dreyfus* still aroused, or in Nazi Germany, where anti-Semitism was already rife. The very real danger of losing various markets explains the care Jewish producers took to avoid awkward subjects, and thus Jewish characters. Only about thirty films showing Jewish characters on screen were made between 1934 and 1941, while the number of full-length films made annually has never been so high. Jewish characters reappeared in the cinema after America entered the war. Hollywood then abandoned its isolationism to castigate anti-Semitism openly. Even after the war was won, however, it must be stressed that Jewish producers were cautious.

The 1950s showed a distinct decline in the fortunes of the last film moguls and the big studios, and particularly in the number of films made annually in America. However, there was no actual drop in the number of Jewish characters shown: quite the opposite. A new generation of men and women in show business expresses itself with great freedom. The people it comprises are actors, directors, and producers at the same time. They work both in Los Angeles and on the East Coast. The older generation of major producers – poor actors, who had hardly ever been behind a camera – had never been able to bring themselves to leave Hollywood, a place that in a way constituted a reassuring gilded ghetto for them.

FURTHER READING

Erens, P.: *The Jew in American Cinema* (Bloomington: Indiana University Press, 1984)

Goldman, E. A.: *Visions, Images, and Dreams: Yiddish Films Past and Present* (Ann Arbor: University of Michigan Press, 1983)

CLAUDE SINGER

Finkelstein, Louis [Eliezer Arye Ha-Levi]

(b.1895) American rabbinic scholar, Conservative rabbi, and the leader of the Conservative movement in the USA. Born in Cincinnati, Finkelstein was educated in the Jewish religious tradition by his father, Shim'on Yitzhak Ha-Levi, an Orthodox rabbi. In 1918 he completed his Ph.D. studies at Columbia University, but his closest academic relations were with the Jewish Theological Seminary. In 1919 he received his rabbinical ordination and shortly after became a teacher at the Seminary, a post he held for 50 years (from 1920 as a teacher of Talmud, from 1924 as a teacher of theology, and from 1931 as a professor of theology). He was also president of the Institute for 31 years (from 1940) as well as chancellor for 20 years (from 1951). At the age of 76 he retired from the Seminary administration, explaining that he wanted to allow an opportunity to the younger generation.

Finkelstein, considered to be the leader of the contemporary Conservative movement, was deeply involved in public activities both in the USA and in Israel. In the USA he became one of the representative Jewish personalities: he pronounced the prayers at the inauguration of President Eisenhower, he was sent to the coronation of Pope Paul VI with the delegation appointed by President Kennedy, and he preached special services in the White House at the invitation of President Nixon. His activities in Israel included serious attempts to bridge the gap between Orthodox and Conservative points of *halakhah*, especially regarding cases of *get* (letters of divorce).

Many of Finkelstein's publications aroused wide controversy, for he was often provocative. For example, his *Jewish Self-Government in the Middle Ages* (1924) in which he analyzed the autonomous democratic communities established by Jews, remained an important source for medievalists. In his introduction to the second edition (1964), he related his findings to contemporary Jewish experience in the State of Israel. However fascinating Finkelstein's evidence, his thesis, according to some scholars, is difficult to prove.

In *Haperushim ve'anshei keneset hagedolah* (1950; the Pharisees and the men of the Great Synagogue), Finkelstein re-examined the relevant material regarding the origin and development of the Great Synagogue. In *New Light from the Prophets* (1970) he continued to trace the Pharisaic sayings, as well as the general process of oral transmission. Finkelstein is universally recognized as the prime authority on Pharisaic thought. Furthermore, his contribution to textual studies of classical Judaism is fully appreciated in the current academic world, for his scholarly work is carried out with supreme attention to textual details.

BIBLIOGRAPHY

ed.: *American Spiritual Autobiographies* (New York: Harper & Bros., 1948)

DEBORAH SCHECHTERMAN

Finkielkraut, Alain (b.1949) French philosopher and essayist. Along with Bernard Henri-Levy, Shmuel Trigano and other post-war Jewish intellectuals, Finkielkraut began to probe the essence and nature of the Jewish condition in the late twentieth century. Like his intellectual peers, Finkielkraut has become obsessed with attempting to understand Jewish identity beyond the traditional parameters established by Jean-Paul Sartre and Raymond ARON.

He was born into a family of Holocaust survivors who had emigrated to France from Poland. Jewish life and consciousness were kept to a minimum during his childhood. It was during his education in Paris that he felt himself excluded from authentic Jewish life and his true Jewish self. In his profoundly disturbing study *Le Juif imaginaire* (1980), Finkielkraut addresses the question of how the Holocaust deformed his own Jewish identity. He refers to himself as an "orphan from Judaism", a person who perceives himself only through the eyes of others (that is, non-Jews). The Jew he had believed himself to be had been determined and defined in accordance with those views expressed by Sartre in *Réflexions sur la question juive* (1946; *Anti-Semite and Jew*, 1965). Finkielkraut recognized the necessity of seeking to create an acceptable Jewish identity which happened to be formed from within himself and his tradition. And yet, in forming this image, he sees himself as "an imaginary Jew", one divorced from true

Jewishness. Excluded from the horrors and realities of the Holocaust and denied a Jewish heritage through the silence of his parents, Finkielkraut determines that the only solution to his particular problem as an "imaginary Jew" would lie in a full return to Judaism.

Finkielkraut's intellectual activities have drawn him into the raging debate concerning "revisionist historians" in France. His study, *L'Avenir d'une négation* (1982), examines the claims of certain "revisionists" and sets them into broader historical, philosophical, and critical arguments in which he refutes their assertions.

Finkielkraut's desire for honesty extends beyond the realm of Jewish life and thought. His latest publication, *La Défaite de la pensée* (1988; *The Undoing of Thought*, 1988) is a study which deals with the disorderly habits of thought and philosophy threatening world civilization. "So barbarism has finally taken over culture, in the shadow of which lofty word intolerance grows, along with infantilism". This is Finkielkraut's shocking conclusion to his quest to understand how the universal ideal underlying the foundation of the United Nations have so sadly devolved into the chauvinism that currently characterizes world politics and philosophy.

His other works include: *Le Nouveau désordre amoureux* (1979), written with Pascal Bruckner, *Au Coin de la rue* (1982), *La Réprobation d'Israël* (1983), and *La Mémoire* (1989).

SIMON SIBELMAN

Finn, Ralph (b.1912)   English novelist, poet, and football writer. Born in the East End of London and educated at the Jews' Free School and Davenant Foundation, Ralph Finn was a brilliant scholar who won, against all the odds, a place at Oxford University. After one term there, impoverished and disillusioned, he left to complete his education at London University, and worked as a teacher in one of East London's worst slum areas. During the war he embarked on what was to prove a highly successful career in advertising, but always maintained a steady output of short stories, poems,

novels, and books on football. *Out of the Depths* (1942), comprises stories and vignettes of East End characters gathered nightly in an air-raid shelter during the blitz, and *Return to Earth* (1944), applies a similar format to the later buzz-bomb attacks.

Several of these tales and portraits reappear in his autobiographical *No Tears in Aldgate* (1963), and *Spring in Aldgate* (1968), in which he recalls the teeming, exuberant life of his childhood in the Petticoat Lane area. The heroic widowed mother, struggling to feed and educate a large family; the battles between the "Choots" and the "Polaks" in Broughton Buildings; the local con-men, criminals, and prostitutes, and the many idiosyncratic characters, are all depicted with verisimilitude, albeit overlaid with a film of nostalgia. Unashamedly sentimental, Finn intersperses these recollections with poetry and elegaic apostrophes, but his evocation of an era and area of the Anglo–Jewish past stands as a chronicle of a unique and fast-vanishing world.

No Tears in Aldgate and *Spring in Aldgate* were re-issued in 1985 by Futura, London, as *Time Remembered* and *Grief Forgotten*.

VERA COLEMAN

Firkovitch, Abraham (1786–1874)   Karaite scholar and leader. Born in Luck, Poland, Firkovitch made a noteworthy contribution to scientific research as a book-collector and *maskil*. In 1830 and 1840 he brought back to Europe from visits to the Near East an important collection of Hebrew and Samaritan manuscripts. In the 1840s he engaged in archaeological expeditions to the Crimea and the Caucasus, collecting manuscripts and tombstone inscriptions. He published a description of his travels in *Avnei zikkaron* (1872; Memorial stones).

After a brief stay in Constantinople (1831–2), he settled in Eupatoria, where he served the local Karaite congregation and was responsible for establishing a Hebrew press which published works of the early Karaites. During the Crimean war he stayed in Vilna and Troki (1853–6), caring for the social and religious interests of the local Karaites. His various communal positions as Karaite *hakham*, and his wide travels enabled him to bring together one of the most important private collections of Hebrew, Arabic, and Samaritan manuscripts. His passion for manuscripts brought him, in 1863, to the Cairo genizah, the importance of which he was to realize long before Solomon SCHECHTER. Shortly after returning from a scholarly trip to Austria and Germany, undertaken at the age of 85, Firkovitch died in Chufut-Kale, Crimea, where he had spent the last years of his life.

Firkovitch was a virulent anti-rabbinate polemicist, having given vent particularly to his anti-hasidic feelings, in his vitriolic *Massah umerivah* (1838; Trial and strife). In his determination to prove, for political reasons, the antiquity of the Karaite community in Russia, he resorted even to forgery. Notwithstanding their unreliability, the results of his investigation of ancient manuscripts, though undoubtedly arousing renewed interest in the history of Judaism and Karaism, incited a bitter controversy among the scholars of his time, including Alexander HARKAVY and D. Chwolson. On the other hand, historians of Karaism, such as S. Pinsker and J. Fuerst, based their research on material supplied by Firkovitch. His collections, containing unique and priceless Jewish manuscripts, were subsequently acquired by the Imperial Library, later to become the Leningrad State Public Library.

BIBLIOGRAPHY

Starkova, C.: *REJ* 134 (1975) 101–17

PAUL B. FENTON

Fleg [Flegenheimer], **Edmond** (1874–1963) French writer and poet. Fleg was born in Geneva into a prosperous family attached to Jewish tradition and practices. At the age of 18 he went to Paris, entered University life, and soon ceased all religious practices. At the École Normale Supérieure, where he specialized in German after reading philosophy at the Sorbonne, he had the reputation of a dandy, an esthete in love with music, painting, poetry, and

France. The Dreyfus Affair was a rude awakening. Instead of applying for French citizenship (deferred until 1921), he identified himself with the victims of anti-Semitism, and offered his services to the Zionist cause (he attended the third Zionist Congress in 1899). However, the identity crisis was more acute than profound. It did not make him feel or understand a Jewishness assumed under pressure by way of moral reaction. Spiritually more significant was his reading of ZANGWILL's *Had Gadya* in 1904. The birth of his first son (1908) was decisive in sending him in search of his forefathers. Though he continued to write secular drama, including a French version of *Faust* (1937) and the libretti for Ernest BLOCH's *Macbeth* (1910) and George Enesco's *Oedipus* (1936), Jewish themes henceforth dominated his creative work. The first and most ambitious, *Ecoute Israël*, is a verse epic which in its definitive edition (1954) tells the whole of Jewish history until the rebirth of Israel. Begun in 1906, Fleg worked on it for almost the rest of his life. The poet's own Jewish journey is recalled in the novel – dedicated to ZANGWILL – *L'Enfant Prophète* (1926) and in *Pourquoi je suis Juif* (1928). Once he felt secure in his Jewish roots, he also felt at ease in his beloved France, a rare example of unanguished, conflictless double loyalty which imbues his Jewish writings with unusual calm and hope. Convinced that Israel's voice must not be lost in assimilation, that it had its own distinctive contribution to make to French life and literature, he published in 1923 an anthology of Franco-Jewish writings *Anthologie Juive* (1956). The same belief inspired the clandestine wartime lectures on Judaism he gave to the *Éclaireurs Israélites de France* (the French–Jewish Scouts engaged in the Resistance, whose president Fleg became in 1934), *Le chant nouveau* (1972).

BIBLIOGRAPHY

Elbaz, A. E., ed.: *Correspondance d'Edmond Fleg pendant l'Affaire Dreyfus* (Paris: Nizet, 1976)

FURTHER READING

Revue de la Pensée juive (January 1950) [special number in honor of Edmond Fleg]

NELLY WILSON

Flusser, David (b.1917) Israeli scholar. Flusser was born in Vienna into an assimilated family. Like many of his contemporaries, he came to Judaism accidentally, when a Protestant priest gave him a gift of a Czech translation of the Bible while he was a student of classical philology at Prague University. He arrived in Israel in 1939 and received his doctorate from the Hebrew University in Jerusalem in 1955. He was appointed as a lecturer there and became a professor of religious studies in 1970.

Flusser's output is prolific, written in many languages (Hebrew, English, German, French) and on several subjects, such as the Second Temple period, trends in Judaism, and the Qumran Scrolls. However, it is his research into early Christianity which brought him the status of an international expert in this field. His book, *Jesus in Selbstzeugnissen und Bilddokumenten* (1968; *Jesus*, 1969), reveals Flusser's approach to Jesus, which is quite different from the accepted one. He regarded Jesus as a Jewish figure and analyzed the textual sources within their Jewish context. His observations caused controversy among those Christian and Jewish scholars who rejected his approach. Nevertheless, many of them might agree with Dr Robert Lindsey, a Baptist scholar, who said of Flusser's books and articles that "it is even sadder to report that there is hardly a Christian scholar living today who could intelligently follow the methods Flusser proposes in working with the sources of the life of Jesus."

Among Flusser's other works are his books and articles on Josippon including a critical edition of the text, and on the Qumran community. For his work on the Jewish sources of Christianity as well as for his other scholarly activities he was awarded the Israel Prize for Judaism in 1980.

BIBLIOGRAPHY
Jesus, trans. R. Walls (New York: Herder & Herder, 1969)

DEBORAH SCHECHTERMAN

folklore The cultural and social movement in Europe of the eighteenth and nineteenth centuries, known as "the discovery of the people" created, among other phenomena, the modern study of folklore. This movement had neoromantic, philosophical, social, and nationalistic implications. It created new interest in the "folk" and the diverse forms of its activities. The creations of the people, in literature, art or ritual, began to be considered as the authentic voice of the "spirit of the people". This cultural and social atmosphere was the fertile ground from which the modern study of Jewish folklore arose, although its actual beginning was some time later, in the second half of the nineteenth century.

A second factor that had important implications for the study of Jewish folklore was the beginning of Jewish Studies in Germany in the early nineteenth century. The founders of *Jüdische Wissenschaft* had dedicated their work mainly to the goal of discovering and studying "high" Jewish culture – philosophy, poetry, language, and theology, thus securing the place of Judaism within advanced European culture. The study of folk-tales, superstitions or customs

Josef Herman The Storyteller c.*1940–1943*

233

might therefore have interfered with their main goal, and so was abandoned. However, the second generation of the *Wissenschaft* in Germany demonstrated a new approach. Central figures in Jewish Studies, such as Moritz STEINSCHNEIDER in an important essay published in 1872, and Moritz Güdemann in his major book, *Geschichte des Erziehungwesens und der Cultur der abendländischer Juden Während des Mittelalters* (1880), and in additional studies on Rabbinic *Haggadah*, use folkloristic concepts developed in German *Volkskunde* at the time. The importance of Steinschneider's seminal essay lies in its drawing the lines for the future study of Jewish folklore: the study of sources such as memorial books, chapbooks, and family genealogies, and folklore in the Jewish dialects – YIDDISH, JUDEO-SPANISH, and JUDEO-ARABIC.

As in the study of European folklore in the late nineteenth century, two distinct approaches to Jewish folklore can be observed: the "literary" folklorists who collected, described and analyzed elements of folklore in ancient literary sources (the early name of folklore was "popular antiquities"), and the "ethnographic" approach, which emphasized the importance of field-work, and the observations made on the "living" material. The aforementioned scholars, Steinschneider and Güdemann, clearly took the first, "literary" approach. The second began around 1896, with the questionnaire published by Max Grunwald (1871–1954) in German, and later in Yiddish and Hebrew. He emphasized the importance of Jewish folk traditions, and thus started the trend of collection of Jewish folklore. The questionnaire of S. Ginzburg and P. Marek in Russia, urging the systematic collection of Jewish folklore, was published in the same year. Earlier activities, for example the Wisla Group and the I. L. PERETZ circle in Warsaw, the work of the great folklorist Friedrich Krauss in Vienna and eight years of publication of his *Am Urquell*, the activities in St Petersburg, including an ethnographic expedition in 1892, offer sufficient justification to mark the last decade of the nineteenth century as witnessing the birth of the modern, professional study of Jewish folklore.

The work of Grunwald and the vast amount of material published in the scholarly journal he founded and edited for many years (under the names *Mitteilungen zur jüdischen Volkskunde, Jahrbuch für jüdische Volkskunde*), are the first attempts at a serious collection and description of Jewish folklore. The field-work of many folklorists who responded to Grunwald's appeal, from everywhere in Europe, and the activities in Warsaw and Russia, allowed for the first time, at the beginning of the twentieth century, the drawing of some general outlines of Jewish folklore. The folk literature, customs, life and year cycles, folk beliefs, costumes, food, material culture, games, and children's lore – the basic branches of Jewish folklore – began to be established. The first overviews started to be drawn not on the basis of theoretical generalizations, but on reliable data. Most important was the immense diversity of Jewish folklore: for example great differences between customs and folk-beliefs have been discovered even between neighboring villages. On the other hand, a clear unity among the variety of folklore items collected was obvious, a unity that justified seeing them as units of a larger system, that of "Jewish folklore".

A cornerstone of the second phase of the study of Jewish folklore which used the achievements of earlier scholars was the expedition organized and directed by Sh. AN-SKI to 66 Jewish settlements in Podolia and Volynia between 1911 and 1913. It seems that the main driving force behind this expedition was not its scientific goal but neo-romantic and socialist tendencies. The initiators of the expedition believed that the real esthetic and cultural values lay within the working and peasant Jewish classes and it was these "buried treasures" that the expedition came to explore. The material collected and recorded by the expedition, and the death of An-ski in 1920, advanced the establishment of YIVO in Vilna. The central figure behind its achievements was Y. L. Cahan, who worked to establish YIVO in New York, and thus salvaged a great deal of folklore material collected in Eastern Europe that would otherwise have been lost in the Second World War. The YIVO Institute for the Study of Jewish Folklore in Eastern Europe marks the transition of the study of Jewish folklore, both in time – from its beginning in the late nineteenth and early twentieth centuries to the present; and in space – from Eastern Europe to America.

At the same time that these scholars were studying the folk-culture of east European Jewry, another trend developed among European Jewish scholars; the study of the folklore of oriental Jews. Here the main driving force was the romantic yearning for the Orient that was popular in Europe in the nineteenth century and which had an immense impact on folklore studies. One factor of this attraction to the east was uniquely Jewish: the scholars tended to see the language, customs, folk beliefs, and religious behavior as an authentic reflection of ancient Jewish culture before the dispersal. Through the study of the folklore of those oriental communities they saw a means of recovering ancient Jewish culture, not from documents, but from living evidence. Scholars like Abraham Zvi IDELSON, Shlomo Dov Goitein, Erich BRAUER, and Raphael Patai had been educated in the European schools of ethnography and philology, and emigrated at the beginning of the twentieth century to Palestine. Their encounter with the oriental Jewish communities – predominantly the Yemenites – resulted in some of the most important studies of Jewish folklore. The scholarship and cultural activities of these eminent figures advanced Jewish folklore-studies in two main directions: the nationalistic, which explored the relationship between the folklore of the present and ancient Jewish culture (the Bible and talmudic–midrashic literature); the second, marking the beginning of folklore studies in the State of Israel, being the search for relationships between Jewish folklore and the cultural environment of the Arab Middle East.

In addition to the two branches of the Jewish people – the east European and the Oriental or Arabic-speaking – an important place has been devoted to the folklore of the Judeo-Spanish (or Ladino) speaking communities in the Balkans, Turkey, among Palestinian Sephardim, and large groups of South American Jewish communities. In addition to the common genres of Judeo-Spanish folklore and the other Jewish communities, for example folk-tales, proverbs, folk-beliefs, life and year cycles, this Jewish community developed one outstanding feature – the *romancero*, or ballad peculiar to them. It is not therefore surprising that most studies have concentrated on this genre. One of the interesting discoveries (although by no means the only one) is the connection between Jewish oral ballads and the Spanish ballads of the Middle Ages.

The folklore of the oriental Jewish communities was also a by-product of historical studies of specific Jewish communities and settlements. In almost every historical description of a Jewish community, Yemen, Morocco, Iraq, Syria, India and so on, one chapter at least has been dedicated to a description of the folk-life and traditions, life and year cycles of that community. In many cases accounts were written by amateur folklorists whose love for their subject overshadowed strict and critical ethnographic observation. However, the vast amount of original material recorded and saved while the communities themselves disappeared, is of importance to a comprehensive overview of Jewish folklore.

The establishment of the State of Israel in 1948 and the mass immigrations that followed brought about important developments in the study of folklore. The European–Jewish ethnographers mentioned earlier utilized the research possibilities afforded to the folklorist by the "ingathering of the exiles": the concentration in one place of Occident and Orient, of the multitude of languages and dialects, of old and new traditions. Their studies and memoirs attest to their full appreciation, even then, of the significance of the new situation which had actually begun to develop in Palestine three decades earlier. During the early 1940s two folklore societies were established in Jerusalem and Tel Aviv: *The Palestine Institute of Folklore and Ethnology* (by Y. Y. Rivlin and R. Patai) and *Yeda-Am* in Tel Aviv by Y. T. Lewinsky and N. Slouscz. Each one published a journal (*Edoth* and *Yeda-Am*) while at the same time a new series of *Reshumot*, originally established in 1918 in Odessa under the editorship of H. N. BIALIK, Y. H. Ravnitzki, and A. Druyanow, appeared.

The intensity of folklore studies in Palestine between 1941 and 1946 is the outcome of two major historical and sociological events: the destruction of Jewish culture in Europe, and the establishment of the State of Israel with the subsequent absorption of the Jewish Diaspora into the new state. Folklore scholars in Palestine of that time considered themselves *avant-garde* both in the preservation of the Jewish culture lost in the Holocaust, and in preparing the country for the communities that would come, by studying and understanding their folklore.

The study of folklore in Israel is centered around the work of Dov Noy. He is a direct disciple of the founders of folklore studies in Palestine but also marks the development of the new trend of academic and institutional folklore-study. He was trained both in Jewish Studies at the Hebrew University and in the discipline of folklore-study in its United States center in those years (Indiana University, under Stith Thompson, the leading folklorist of the time). In 1955 Noy founded the Israel Folktale Archives (IFA) in Haifa, the first institution to take upon itself the creation of a network of voluntary informants to collect, classify, publish, and direct studies of the folktales of all the Jewish communities living in Israel. More than 15,000 folktales were recorded from all the communities and classified according to the community-of-origin, narrator, and the scientific classification of motifs and tale-types used throughout the world. The central task of the IFA was to supply the data for the study of Jewish folk-literature and answers to the basic questions of Jewish folklore: what is the relationship between modern Jewish folklore and that of the past? What are the differences between Jewish and international folklore? What change did it undergo during the ages, and what is its social and cultural significance? Many studies – doctoral theses, monographs and scholarly articles – used the material in the IFA as basic data and it is also used as an important means for the education of future Jewish folklorists.

In addition to the folk traditions brought by communities from their lands of origin special attention has been given to Israeli folklore. The question of whether an Israeli folklore already exists, created under the new conditions, intrigues folklorists. Folk-dance and folk-song, new dietary habits and costumes, new customs emerging from specific Israeli rituals (for example Independence Day and Holocaust Day), and folk literature such as the *tchizbat* (tales told by the pre-military troops before the establishment of the State) and jokes, proverbs, and folk-songs created in the Israeli army, especially during the wars, are all clear indications of the creation of a new corpus of Jewish folklore in Israel. A similar approach was used for studying Jewish folklore in the largest Jewish community, that of the USA. The Jewish emigrants of the late nineteenth and early twentieth centuries brought with them their own traditions. However, since then, their social aspirations, political organizations, and personal hopes have expressed themselves through the creation of a specific folklore that reflects the character of that community. Study of the various ways in which Israeli or American Jewish folklore symbolically reflects the struggle for identity by the *sabra* or the American Jew constitutes one of the most important tasks for future folklorists.

Two central attitudes regarding the function of folklore appear to exist in modern Jewish scholarship: the first considers folklore studies as a means toward other, more important goals, and the second is that of the professional folklorists. The first is a continuation of the methods and goals of nineteenth-century Jewish Studies: students of the Bible, of Jewish history, Jewish literature, of anti-Semitism, and Jewish mysticism recognized the benefit their studies gain by their employment of folklore methodology. Biblical scholarship used folkloristic methods and concepts in order to explain the creation and character of large portions of the Hebrew Bible. The study of Jewish history indicated the folkloristic character of Jewish historiography mainly in the Middle Ages and to the importance of the folk-life element in comprehensive historical description; the study of anti-Semitism emphasized the vital role of folklore in the creation and dissemination of anti-Semitic material, for example the blood-libel stories and the legend of the "wandering Jew". The study of Jewish literature, mainly in Hebrew and Yiddish, demonstrated the importance of identifying the folkloric elements in a literary work in understanding its meaning and function. The main importance of these many studies is the emphasis on the functional aspect of Jewish folklore: that it is a vital force behind many phenomena in Jewish life and culture.

The second trend of folklore studies is interested mainly in folklore itself, and not as a means towards other ends. Jewish folklorists of the present generation are disciples of the best folkloristic schools in the West; they are active members of the academic societies of international folkloristics, and succeed in raising the study of Jewish folklore to the same high level of international scholarship. The major approaches – the historic–geographic, structural, functional, psychoanalytical, and semiotic – have been used extensively in the study of Jewish folklore during the past decades. In addition, most scholars accept that the special socio-historical conditions of the Jewish people have created a different entity, that should be treated differently. For example, the fact that the Jewish people was "the people of the book", and that even in the most ignorant ages every Jewish man knew to read and write, is shedding new light on the problem of orality in folklore, different from other cultures, but of vital importance.

The transformation of Jewish folklore-studies into a recognized academic discipline, the activities launched by YIVO in New York and IFA in Haifa, and the growing recognition that Jewish folklore is not a primitive product of a subculture, but the expression of all social layers of the Jewish people, are the contributions of students and scholars of Jewish folklore of the past few generations.

FURTHER READING

Haboucha, R.: The folklore and traditional literature of the Judeo-Spanish speakers: recent scholarship and research. In *The Sephardi and Oriental Heritage*, ed. I. Ben-Ami (Jerusalem: 1982) 571–89

Hasam-Roken, G., and Yassif, E.: The study of Jewish folklore in Israel. In *Continuity and Change in Contemporary Jewish Folklore*, ed. Y. Zerubavel (New York: forthcoming)

Kirshenblatt-Gimblett, B.: Jewish folklore in Europe and the United States: a century in retrospect. In *Continuity and Change in Contemporary Jewish Folklore*, ed. Y. Zerubavel (New York: forthcoming)

Noy, D.: Eighty years of Jewish folkloristics: achievements and tasks. In *Studies in Jewish Folklore*, ed. F. Talmage (Cambridge: 1980) 1–12

——: Collecting folktales in Israel. In *In The Dispersion* 7 (1967) 151–67

Schwarzbam, H.: *Studies in Jewish and World Folklore* (Berlin: 1968)

Tobi, Y.: *The Jews of Yemen, Bibliography* (Jerusalem: 1975) 110–26

Weinreich, U., and Weinreich, B.: *Yiddish Language and Folklore. A Selective Bibliography for Research* (The Hague: Mouton & Co., 1959)

Yassif, E.: *Jewish Folklore. An Annotated Bibliography* (New York and London: Garland, 1986)

ELI YASSIF

Formstecher, Salomon (1805–1889) Religious philosopher and Reform rabbi. Born in Offenbach am Main, Formstecher received a traditional Jewish education locally. He studied philology, theology, and philosophy at the University of Giessen, where he came under the influence of the Hegelian philosopher Joseph Hillebrand (1788–1871). He received his doctorate in 1831 and then returned home to serve as *Prediger* (preacher) of the "Israelite" community. In 1882 he celebrated his fiftieth year with the congregation.

In 1836 Formstecher wrote a guide for expressing early religious feelings, and in 1837 an essay on stability and progress in Judaism (in *la Regeneration*, Paris). He contributed historical studies on the Judaic concept of the soul's immortality and of eschatology to *Wissenschaftliche Zeitschrift für Jüdische Theologie*; on angelology and demonology to *Israelitische Annalen* and on Israelite worship to *Die Synagoge*, all during 1838/39. His major work, *Die Religion des Geistes*, appeared in 1841. His exposition of "Mosaic" religious doctrine for use in Israelite religious schools appeared in 1860 and a popular study of Moses MENDELSSOHN as a philosopher in the Jewish *milieu* in 1863 in *Gedenkblätter an Moses Mendelssohn*. His published sermons include *Zwölf Predigten gehalten in dem Israel. Gotteshaus zu Offenbach* (1833), *Israels Klage und Israels Trost*

(1835) and "Was ist Sünde? Predigt am Ver-soehnungstage" (in *Israelitische Volkslehrer*, 1852).

Formstecher applies Schelling's mythological terminology of the cosmos to Jewish history. God is pure spirit. He bears the attribute of world-soul, of which He is conscious. World-soul, which contains spirit which is subjective and free in equilibrium with nature which is objective and necessary, is expressed pheno-menally as the earth. Man is a power of the world-soul and, like God, self-conscious. Through self-consciousness, itself spiritual, human history uncovers the world-soul placed by God in the earth before history began. Self-consciousness manifests the world-soul in the direction of spirit.

Judaism prevents the equilibrium from being overwhelmed by nature as paganism would have it, and leads history in the direction of spiritualizing nature. Judaism proceeds from an "objective" period of revelation which lasts through the prophets, to the "subjective–objective" period of reflection on revelation which lasts through the Sages, to the "objective–subjective" period which lasts through the *posekim* (textual interpreters) who allowed rationality to be eclipsed, and finally to the "subjective" period which begins with Mendelssohn. In this last phase, to which Formstecher himself contributes, divine tran-scendence and revelation become rationally comprehensible.

FURTHER READING

Bamberger, B.: Formstecher's history of Judaism. *Hebrew Union College Annual* (1950–1)
Maybaum, I.: Samuel [*sic*] Formstecher, a contribu-tion to the history of Jewish religious philosophy in the 19th century. *MGWJ* (1872) [German]

GERSHON GREENBERG

Foss, Lukas (b.1922) American composer, conductor and pianist. He was born in Berlin, Germany and studied piano and theory with Julius Goldstein-Herford. At the onset of the Nazi period the family moved to Paris where Foss continued his musical studies with Lazare Levy in piano, Noel Gallon in composition, and Felix Wolfes in orchestration. In 1937 he emi-grated to the USA and enrolled in the Curtis Institute of Music in Philadelphia. There he studied piano composition, and conducting. During 1940–1, Foss took an advanced course in composition with Paul Hindemith at Yale and in 1945 became the youngest composer ever to be granted a Guggenheim Fellowship. After 1950 Foss lived in Rome for two years under a Fulbright Fellowship. Upon his return home he taught composition at the University of Califor-nia at Los Angeles. There he also established the Improvisation Chamber Ensemble to per-form "music of controlled improvisation". From 1963 to 1970 he was conductor of the Buffalo Philharmonic Orchestra; in 1971 he became principal conductor of the Brooklyn Philharmo-nia and at the same time (1972–5), conductor of the Jerusalem Symphony. In 1980 he ac-quired the music directorship of the Milwaukee Symphony Orchestra.

During all these "conducting years" Foss has remained a most prolific and innovative com-poser. Stylistically his compositions may be di-vided into two idioms: traditional (1940–59) and freely experimental. Throughout his entire compositional career, he demonstates complete technical facility of every idiom he may choose and a spontaneous lyricism which pervades all of his music. He has written for all media, from opera to solo piano works, and many have found their way into the permanent repertory of the major performing organizations.

SAMUEL H. ADLER

Fram, David (b.1903) South African Yid-dish poet. Born in Poniewez, Lithuania, he left at the age of 13 for Russia where he studied at the Russian Gymnasium at Lomanosow. He published his first poem in Russian when only 18. In 1921 he returned to Lithuania where he contributed regularly to Kovno's Yiddish news-papers. It was with his poem *Reb Yoshe in zayn gortn* (Reb Yoshe in his garden) that he entered the world of Yiddish poetry.

The poetry of his Lithuanian period is char-acterized by graceful language, simplicity, pithy realism, and deep lyricism. It was in this lyricism, in which Yiddish poetry flowers, that he demonstrated his original talent.

Emigrating to South Africa in 1927, he changed from the delicate lyrics of his Lithuanian poetry to a depiction of the vibrant, pulsating, and problematic life of Southern Africa. One of his poems, *Poyern* (Farmers), depicts the rural Afrikaner, while others reflect the struggle of some whites to advance the political and social development of blacks. His long epics, *Efsher* (Perhaps) and *Dos letste kapitl* (The last chapter), were considered by the Nobel Prize Committee in 1948. The latter, unquestionably his masterpiece, is a sanctification of the victims of the Holocaust. To commemorate his eightieth birthday in 1983, he published an anthology, *A shvalb afn dakh* (A swallow on the roof). This volume is a mixture of love and nature poems in epic form.

His poetry is especially popular among the Yiddish-speakers of South Africa and is also enjoyed widely by the large Yiddish-speaking community of the USA.

JOCELYN HELLIG

Franck, Adolphe (1809–1893)   French philosopher. Descended from a humble beekeeping family in the province of Alsace-Lorraine, he was brought up in a strictly Orthodox tradition, and quickly distinguished himself by his intellectual gifts. A disciple of Victor Cousin, whose eclecticism reigned supreme in French philosophy of the first half of the nineteenth century, he spent some years teaching in provincial high schools and in 1840 was appointed to an assistant lectureship at the Sorbonne. In 1851 he went to the Collège de France, taking over the chair in Greek and Latin philosophy from Barthélémy Saint-Hilaire before being appointed in 1854 to lecture on "Natural and International Law" and became professor of that department in 1856. In 1886 he retired from a career wholly devoted to the teaching of philosophy.

Franck maintained relations with Judaism both institutionally, as Vice-President of the Central Consistory, and in the field of scholarship, where his chairmanship of the Society for Jewish Studies crowned a long career devoted to Jewish studies. Indeed, Franck belongs to that group of French scholars which developed Semitic studies in France. His first work, which was published in 1843 and on Cousin's recommendation, won him the distinction of being the first Jew elected to the Académie des Sciences Morales et Politiques, is a study of the Kabbalah.

Within the tradition of Cousin, which through its contacts with German philosophy made Franck one of those French scholars influenced by the WISSENSCHAFT DES JUDENTUMS, his work reveals a constant concern with demonstrating the monotheistic character of Judaism. Indeed, reference to the works of Cousin is essential for an understanding of the philosophical presuppositions which guided Franck in Jewish studies. They are set out in the introduction to the *Dictionnaire des Sciences Philosophiques* which he edited from 1844 to 1852, an encyclopaedia which made room for a number of Jewish philosophers such as Rabbi Akiba and Maimonides. It is in the relationship between faith and reason that Frank was to situate his study of the *kabbalah*, excluding all mystery. This interpretation of the *kabbalah* marks the beginning of a campaign in which Franck was to be involved until the year of his death when he became head of a National League Against Atheism, to combat pantheism and paganism. Judaism, a model of pure monotheism even on its kabbalistic fringes, demonstrates the unity of God through the unity of His created works. In making the words of Scripture pass for symbols, the *kabbalah* sets reason in the place of authority, bringing philosophy to birth in the heart of religion. Franck's interpretation of early Jewish mysticism enabled him to establish a link between Judaism and Christianity compatible with the syncretic view of the history of thought as the cumulative progress of the truth. By regarding the *kabbalah* as one of the branches of Pharisaism, which also inspired St Paul's preaching, Franck establishes not only a relationship but also a line of descent.

As an adherent of Cousin's philosophy, which at the time was under attack from Comtean positivism, and in retreat before innovators such as Solomon MUNK, Michel BREAL, and

Derenbourg in the field of Jewish studies, Franck became unpopular after the end of the nineteenth century.

BIBLIOGRAPHY
La Kabbale ou la philosophie religieuse des Hebreux (Paris: 1843)
Philosophie et religion (Paris: 1867)

PERRINE SIMON-NAHUM

Franck, Henri (1888–1912) French poet. Born into a wealthy, assimilated Parisian family, Franck was the great-grandson of Arnaud Aron (1807–90), Chief Rabbi of Strasbourg. Franck was among a group of young Jews who studied with Henri BERGSON. In the aftermath of the Dreyfus Affair, these young intellectuals became aware of their Jewishness and sought to combat the rising tide of French nationalism and anti-Semitism. Their goal was to articulate a metaphysical ideal for the nation which would save France from the destructive forces found in the mounting fanatical xenophobia and materialist individualism. During his own philosophical and intellectual quest, Franck became acutely aware of his own Jewishness and spent the remainder of his short life seeking to integrate this Jewishness with his intense belief in the liberal principles of republican France.

Writer of numerous philosophical essays and literary criticism, Franck's major work was a 2000-line poem, *La Danse devant l'Arche* (1912), which bears evidence of influence of André SPIRE. The poem's almost epic porportions attempt to harmonize the emotional power of Biblical inspiration with the rigid linguistic purity of French Cartesian logic. The poet projects himself into the role of a "modern day King David", dancing ecstatically before the Ark of the Covenant, a symbol of Jewish faith and heritage. At its conclusion, Franck's poem strikes a note of disillusionment as the poet's co-religionists refuse to follow his lead and join in his inspired dance.

In the years following the second Dreyfus Trial, Franck devoted his energies to philosophical musings about identity. His work during this period led him to neglect his health and

contributed to his early death from tuberculosis. His life and passionate beliefs inspired his friend, Jacques de Lacretelle, to create the tragic hero, Silbermann, in the novel by the same name. Franck's attitudes were also influential in Jean-Paul Sartre's considerations about authentic Jewish identity in his study *Réflexions sur la question juive* (1948).

SIMON SIBELMAN

Franco-Mendes, David (1713–1792) Hebrew poet. Born in Amsterdam to a wealthy, enlightened family, Franco-Mendes studied at the esteemed *Etz hayyim Yeshivah* and also received an outstanding secular education. A businessmen by profession, he was active in the Amsterdam Jewish community and in 1769 was appointed honorary secretary of the community. In the same year he also became a member of Amadores das Musas, a Jewish literary society. Some years later he lost his fortune and until his death worked as a copyist. Franco-Mendes began to write Hebrew poetry as a boy and later composed plays and oratorios and translated into Hebrew. Most of this work has never been published and its importance is historical rather than literary. Perhaps his best-known work is the biblical play *Gemul Atalia* (1770; The punishment of Athalia), which is reminiscent of Racine's tragedy *Athalie*. He also wrote many biographies of famous Sephardic Jews for *Hame'assef*. An acquaintance of M. H. LUZZATTO and N. H. WESSELY, Franco-Mendes was regarded as one of the best Hebrew poets of his age.

DAVID ABERBACH

Frank, Anne [Anneliese Marie Frank] (1929–1945) German-born writer. She was born in Frankfurt to a liberal Jewish family and moved to Amsterdam with her parents and her sister Margot after Hitler came to power in 1933. They became friendly with other Jewish immigrants in Amsterdam, and the sisters attended the local Montessori school. After the German invasion in May 1940 their lives did not immediately change. Gradually, however, the Nazis introduced anti-Jewish measures, and after the summer of 1941 Anne and Margot were forced to attend a Jewish school. In May 1942 the Germans ordered the wearing of the yellow star, further widening the gap between Jews and non-Jews. In July of that year, when Margot received a notice calling her to a German labor camp, the Frank family went into hiding in the so-called "Secret Annex" in Frank's office building. They lived there with four other Jews from 6 July 1942 until 4 August 1944, when the families were arrested and transported to concentration camps in Eastern Europe. Of the Frank family, only Anne's father survived; two months before the liberation, Margot and Anne died in Bergen-Belsen.

In her diary Anne wrote about her life in hiding, her friends from school, her family, the others in the Secret Annex, her growing love for one of them, Peter, and her longing for freedom. In March 1944 she began to rewrite her diary in a more mature style: "Just imagine how interesting it would be if I were to publish a romance of the 'Secret Annex'!" She succeeded in giving not only a vivid picture of a family in hiding, but also an uncompromising portrayal of herself, her struggle for independence while living within a group of older people, and her change from the freshness of childhood.

After the war Otto Frank returned to Amsterdam and recovered Anne's diaries from friends, with the intention of publishing them in the rewritten version, as a memorial to his daughter. They were eventually published in 1947, being translated into French and German in 1950, and into English two years later. In the late 1950s a play and film based on the *Diary of Anne Frank* achieved great success and the book remained an international best-seller for many years. Schools have been named after her and the Anne Frank house is one of the most popular museums in Amsterdam. The *Diary* remains one of the most profoundly moving documents of the Second World War.

BIBLIOGRAPHY
Anne Frank. The Diary of a Young Girl, trans. B. M. Mooyaart-Doubleday (London: Vallentine, Mitchell & Co., 1954); *Tales from the House Behind* (London: Pan Books, 1965). *The Diary of Anne Frank: The Critical Edition*, prepared by the Netherlands State Institute for War Documentation, trans. A. J. Pomerans (New York: Doubleday, 1989, and London: Viking 1989)

DAVID BARNOUW

Frankel, Zecharias (1801–1875) Rabbi, historian of the Talmudic period and theologian. Born in Prague, Frankel studied Talmud under Rabbi Bezalel Ronsberg and philosophy, natural science, and philology in Budapest, thus preparing himself for his role as a pioneer in combining traditional Talmudic learning with modern historical methodology. In 1854 Frankel became principal of the Jewish Theological Seminary in Breslau where, in 1871, he founded the learned journal *Monatsschrift für Geschichte und Wissenschaft des Judentums*. In addition to important studies on the Septuagint, Frankel published *Darkhei hamishnah* (1859), and *Mevo hayerushalmi* (1870), important works on the history and development of the Talmudic literature.

In his theological works Frankel (and the Breslau School which he established) sought to demonstrate that there need be no incompatibility between investigation into the origins of Jewish sacred literature and Jewish observances, and strict adherence to these observances in practice. Origins, he maintained, are important to the objective historian but the religious life depends on the institutions adopted by the living community. The dietary laws and the Sabbath, for example, may have had their origin in primitive taboos – that was for the historian to determine – but these became the instruments for a life of holiness through a kind of mystical consensus on the part of the Jewish community. This explains Frankel's departure from both Orthodoxy and Reform. Reform was wrong, according to Frankel, in its readiness to jettison many traditional observances, but Orthodoxy was also wrong in its insistence on a literal understanding of the doctrine "The Torah is from Heaven" so that one had to accept that every detail of the Torah was given directly by God to Moses.

241

FURTHER READING
Ginzberg, L.: Zechariah Frankel. In *Students, Scholars and Saints* (Philadelphia: 1928) 195–216

LOUIS JACOBS

Frankenthaler, Helen (b.1928) American painter. Born in New York City, Helen Frankenthaler studied painting in the late 1940s at Bennington College in Vermont and at the Art Students League in New York. Her early abstract landscapes reveal an absorption of the principles of Picasso's Cubism and the fluid lines and bright-colored organic shapes also suggest the influence of Kandinsky and the American painter Arshile Gorky.

Jackson Pollock's famous exhibition at the Betty Parsons Gallery in New York in 1951 proved to be a decisive influence on the emergence of Frankenthaler's mature abstract style. She took his drip technique and Surrealist-derived automatism one step further, pouring and dripping thinned paint directly onto unprimed canvas. The resulting abstract compositions are built around various zones of different color, which often evoke different emotional states. Often her compositions suggest associations with the landscape. Like many of the Abstract Expressionists, the titles of her paintings suggest she drew inspiration from myth and the Old Testament. Her painting method had an important influence on the Color Field painters Morris Louis and Kenneth Noland. As her career progressed, Frankenthaler intensified her palette. In the 1970s she often produced paintings in which single colors occupied the entire field.

In 1956 Frankenthaler designed ark curtains for Temple of Aaron Congretation in St Paul, Minnesota. After numerous gallery showings throughout the 1950s, Frankenthaler had her first major museum exhibition in 1960 at the Jewish Museum in New York. The Whitney Museum of American Art, New York, together with the Museum of Modern Art, New York, organized a major retrospective of her work in 1969.

FURTHER READING
Goossen, E. C.: *Helen Frankenthaler* (New York: Whitney Museum of American Art, 1969) [exhibition catalog]

O'Hara, F.: *Helen Frankenthaler: Paintings* (New York: The Jewish Museum, 1960) [exhibition catalog]

KRISTIE A. JAYNE

Franzos, Karl Emil (1848–1904) Austrian writer and editor. Franzos was born in Podolia (Russia) and spent his early years in Czortkov in Eastern Galicia. He studied in Czernovitz, Graz, and Vienna and became a journalist, at first as a contributor to the Viennese *Neue Freie Presse*. He later moved to Berlin. From 1882–5 he edited the newspaper *Neue Illustrierte Zeitung* in Vienna. He founded the German literary journal, *Deutsche Dichtung*, in 1886 and was its editor until his death. Inheriting from his "enlightened" father an enthusiastic German–national self-identification and a surprisingly tenacious Jewish religious–ethical affirmation, he argued in much of his work for Jewish cultural assimilation on one hand, and cultural pluralism under the egis of German culture in the entire Austro-Hungarian Empire, on the other.

Franzos was an important contributor to the stream of German literature about provincial Jewish life often called ghetto literature. At the same time, he became an indefatigible opponent of what he saw to be the narrowmindedness and insularity of orthodox or traditional shtetl life, especially of Hasidism, and his fiction is characterized by negative portraits of unassimilated Jewish figures. In his extremely popular *Die Juden von Barnow* (1877; The Jews of Barnow), and in the many vignettes contained in *Aus Halb-Asien* (1876–83; From Half-Asia), he tended to excoriate Jewish superstition, fostered by irrational rituals and customs, and, in his view, false Jewish nationalism. Repeatedly in his stories, the natural and healthy love of young people is thwarted by religious and national prejudices, often destroying the lovers' lives. Franzos was a mediator between East and West, whose pleas for understanding and tolerance of shortcomings in east European life can only be understood in terms of his concomitant championship of the extension of German culture in the border regions of the Austro-Hungarian Empire. Franzos travelled widely in eastern Europe and wrote an extensive travel literature describing in detail the multifarious national and ethnic groups resident in the East and their particular customs and lifestyles.

Franzos edited and published the collected works of the German dramatist Georg Büchner (1879), and wrote many fine literary–critical essays, the most important of which treat the writings of Heinrich HEINE, Berthold AUERBACH, and Conrad Ferdinand Meyer.

BIBLIOGRAPHY
A savior of the people. In J. Leftwich, ed.: *Yisroel. The First Jewish Omnibus* (London and New York: Thomas Yoseloff, 1952) 264–8; Every country has the Jews it deserves. In P. R. M. Flohr and J. Reinharz eds: *The Jew in the Modern World* (New York and Oxford: Oxford University Press, 1980) 218–19

FURTHER READING
Gelber, M. H.: Ethnic pluralism and Germanization in the works of Karl Emil Franzos (1848–1904). *The German Quarterly* 56 (1983) 376–85

MARK H. GELBER

Freed, Isadore (1900–1960) American composer, organist, pianist, and educator. He was born in Brest-Litovsk, Russia and went to the USA at the age of three. He graduated from the University of Pennsylvania with a BM degree in 1918, and subsequently studied with Ernst BLOCH and then with Vincent d'Indy and Nadia Boulanger in Paris. Upon Freed's return to the USA in 1934, he taught at various music schools in both Philadelphia and New York, finally accepting a position at the Hartt School of Music in Hartford, Connecticut, where he taught from 1944 until his death. He was also very active as an organist and choir director in several temples, beginning with Knesset Israel congregation in Philadelphia. His contribution to the music of the American synagogue was most significant and, besides a great deal of service music including three complete settings of the service, he published a practical edition, for use in the American synagogue, of music by Salomone Rossi, many anthems, and a book entitled *Harmonizing the Jewish Modes*. Freed's activities were widespread not only in Jewish music but also in the field of secular music and

he was greatly concerned with introducing young pianists to a twentieth-century repertory. To this end he edited an extensive list of works for young pianists published by Theodore Presser.

The influence of his Jewish background and his French education pervades all of his compositional output, giving especially his synagogue music a unique and most personal flavor. His output is quite considerable and, besides his synagogue music, includes two operas, a ballet, two symphonies, some concerti; a few shorter orchestral works, a number of chamber works, songs, and pieces for piano and organ. One of his final works was an oratorio called *Micah*, which was written in 1958 and dedicated to the tenth anniversary of the State of Israel.

SAMUEL H. ADLER

Freud, Lucian (b.1922) British painter. Born in Berlin into an affluent, cultured and assimilated Jewish family of Austrian origin (his father, Ernst, an architect, was the youngest son of Sigmund FREUD), Lucian Freud grew up in the shadow of Nazism. The family moved to England when he was not quite eleven, and Lucian became a naturalized British subject in 1939. Passionately committed to art from an early age, he studied at the Central School of Art in London and at the East Anglian School of Drawing and Painting.

His work, when first exhibited at the Lefevre Gallery, London in 1944, aroused considerable interest, although critics recognized in its taut linearity, minute attention to detail, and already marked sense of alienation, qualities they deemed more Germanic than British. (Many of Freud's most memorable works of the late 1940s are disturbingly intense portraits of his first wife, Kitty Garman, daughter of the sculptor, Jacob EPSTEIN.) Although since the late 1950s Freud's handling of paint, like his draughtsmanship, has become a great deal freer, the human figure, nude or clothed, in all its unglamorous vulnerability, remains his primary obsession. Created a Companion of Honour in 1983, Freud has been hailed (by American critic Robert Hughes) as "the greatest living realist painter".

Lucian Freud The Refugees *1941. Private collection, UK*

FURTHER READING

Gowing, L.: *Lucian Freud* (London: Thames & Hudson, 1982)

Lucian Freud, paintings (London: The British Council, 1987) [exhibition catalog]

MONICA BOHM-DUCHEN

Freud, Sigmund (1856–1939) Founder of psychoanalysis. Born in Freiberg, Moravia (now Príbor, Czechoslovakia), Freud moved with his family to Vienna in 1859, where he remained until 1938. Freud is widely regarded as one of the most seminal and influential thinkers of the twentieth century. His complete psychological works are embodied in English in 23 volumes, edited by James Strachey and others (1953–66). In 1902, with three others, he formed a "society" to explore the new method of psychoanalytic interpretation. By 1910, the circle grew into an international movement, exerting considerable intellectual force. Though Freud's most direct impact is felt in the fields of psychology and psychotherapy, his imaginative grasp of how the human mind works and affects behavior has influenced, perhaps even more, the fields of art and literature. Not the least reason, by far, for this was the way he used metaphor and intrigue to persuade his readers. For their literary power even more, perhaps, than their theoretical precision, *The Interpretation of Dreams* (1900), *The Psychopathology of Everyday Life* (1904), *Totem and Taboo* (1913), *Civilization and Its Discontents* (1929), and *Moses and Monotheism* (1939), have attracted a broad audience and rank among the great works of modern literature.

It is, of course, open to debate why psychoanalysis has become a basis of modern cultural interpretation, but few would doubt that it offered a compelling method of understanding how irrational impulses and rational restraint interact and conflict. Freud observed the habits individuals and societies formed in order to keep the impulses in check. But, with the rare insight that invigorated his search for knowledge and self-understanding, he posited that reason and self-control are weak and must compromise with implacable, primitive desires. Even if civilized behavior succeeds in domesticating these drives, it is helpless in thwarting their fulfillment by indirect or substitute means. For Freud, civilization was not the conquest of reason over chaos, but a haphazard deflection of unconscious and unruly drives, and ultimately the neurotic fulfillment of repressed wishes.

Few recognized during his lifetime how important a role Freud's Jewishness played in his life and work. Freud was not an observant Jew. Indeed, he was hostile to all religious beliefs and practices. In his published writings (e.g. *Future of an Illusion*, 1927), he regarded belief in God as a helpless clinging to a figure even more powerful than the father. During his adolescence Freud sought to abandon all traces of traditional Judaism and his Jewish heritage in favor of the dominant liberal and humanitarian ideas then in ascendancy during Austria's brief but vivid era of constitutional reform (1861–79). He vigorously disparaged "unassimilated" Jews migrating in increasing numbers to Vienna, and, around 1870, replaced his given name "Sigismund", which his father had conferred in honor of a sixteenth-century Polish monarch who implemented a policy of toleration toward Jews, with the Germanic-sounding "Sigmund." During his engagement to Martha Bernays

(1861–1951) in the early 1880s, he rejected her Jewish orthodoxy, wanting to make a "heathen" of her, and momentarily pondered a conversion to the Protestant faith. Freud insisted on establishing a non-religious home and discouraged his children from acquiring a formal Jewish education or attending worship services. He never supported Zionist ideals, although, tellingly, he once praised Theodor HERZL as "the poet and the fighter for the human rights of our people".

Freud's fascination with the Hebrew prophet, Moses, from the early 1890s to the end of his life, and the fact that his early psychoanalytic followers were all Jews (see PSYCHOANALYSIS, JEWS IN) suggest that his Jewishness was nonetheless important to him. What exactly being Jewish meant seemed to elude him: he knew what, for him, it was not – a religious or political creed. But he was never sure what being Jewish was, except that it somehow generated strong feelings. For someone otherwise able to fathom the hidden and the irrational, it seems strange that he could not better define his Jewishness. Yet he was clear that it was "inaccessible to any analysis so far".

It may be enough to say, however, that his belief in a common "mental construction," and his "irresistible" attraction to other Jews were precisely what was important to him. Time and again Freud felt reassured simply by being with other like-minded Jews. He referred to their "secret sympathy" and "racial kinship". His home, devoid as it apparently was of Jewish observance, was open, virtually without exception, to Jewish guests. His greatest and most productive sense of belonging, however, developed from an unusually strong association he formed with the B'nai B'rith lodge in Vienna. More than just reassurance or consolation, he drew inspiration and self-confidence from that Jewish association. A forum for Freud, especially between 1897, the year he joined and 1902, this circle of Jews became a springboard for the movement he formed in 1902 and which eventually achieved universal acclaim.

Freud's activity in the B'nai B'rith was, for five crucial years, intense. During this time, he attended almost every meeting. He was a member of its judicial committee and chairman of

Sigmund Freud, 1891

the cultural committee. His participation in the society appears also to have become a basis of his search for the new psychology of psychoanalysis. As a member of a committee charged with the responsibility of forming a second Viennese lodge (1901–3), he enlisted at least two members who later joined his psychoanalytic circle – Oskar Rie (1863–1931), a longtime friend, and Eduard Hitschmann (1871–1958). More important, he delivered to the brotherhood eight lectures based on his investigations. Of these eight, he addressed the B'nai B'rith three times before he published the results. On two other occasions Freud explored psychoanalytic topics in greater detail than he did in print. Having abandoned for the time being academic forums, which were unreceptive

to his ideas, Freud found in the B'nai B'rith intellectual as well as social fulfillment. Beyond that, the society effectively encouraged his germinating theories of dreams and parapraxes.

Freud's association with the society must have clarified and reinforced his commitment to fostering ethical or humanitarian ideals, as well. During the period of the brotherhood's growth around the turn of the century (the lodge in Vienna was formed in 1895), many members believed in preserving "the ideal of humanity through the [current] period of moral degeneration." Referring to the strife among nations that fragmented the Austro-Hungarian empire, and the palpable hostility toward Jews, members believed Jews alone could prevent mankind from "totally sinking into perverse hands." Whether or not Freud supported these views completely, the members' urgent appeal to a more tolerant world substantiated his own liberal outlook.

Of course, psychoanalysis is a sovereign set of ideas and may well have flourished in any environment or under any circumstances. But in creating a movement to advance its ideas, Freud acquired from his bond with other Jews a firm basis of confident independence and collective purpose. In this, Freud's Jewishness, even if it was not sufficient as an impetus to his formation of the movement, appears to have been necessary.

FURTHER READING

Bakan, D.: *Sigmund Freud and the Jewish Mystical Tradition* (Princeton: D. van Nostrand, 1958)

Cuddihy, J. M.: *The Ordeal of Civility: Freud, Marx, Levi-Strauss and the Jewish Struggle with Modernity* (New York: Basic Books, 1974)

Gay, P.: *A Godless Jew: Freud, Atheism, and the Making of Psychoanalysis* (New Haven: Yale University Press, 1987)

Grunfeld, F. V.: *Prophets Without Honour: A Background to Freud, Kafka, Einstein and Their World* (London: Hutchinson and Co., 1979)

Jones, E.: *The Life and Work of Sigmund Freud* 3 vols. (New York: Basic Books, 1953–7)

Klein, D. B.: *Jewish Origins of the Psychoanalytic Movement* (Chicago: University of Chicago Press, 1985)

Robert, M.: *From Oedipus to Moses: Freud's Jewish Identity*, trans. R. Manheim (Garden City: Anchor Books, 1976)

DENNIS B. KLEIN

Fried, Erich (1921–1988) Austrian writer and translator. He was a child actor from the age of five, when he began to write poetry. He witnessed the events of the Bloody Friday massacre in Vienna in 1927, and in 1938 his parents were arrested and he fled the Nazis, settling in England, where he had a variety of jobs. He worked for the Jewish Refugee Committee for a time, and helped 73 Jews – including his mother – to escape from occupied Europe. In 1940 his first poem appeared in an exile periodical. He began to contribute to collections of exile writings and in 1944 his first books were published, including a collection of poetry, *Deutschland*. He continued to write exclusively in German.

After the war he worked on periodicals such as *Blick in die Welt* and then as a political commentator for the BBC, broadcasting to Germany. In later works abstract linguistic experiments gave way to political and social concerns. Whilst deeply sympathetic to Communism, and opposed to capitalism, his works reflect no black and white political line. He has always maintained close contacts with both East and West Germany, criticizing and encouraging both sides.

From 1946 he worked on his semi-fictional novel *Ein Soldat und ein Mädchen* (A soldier and a girl), published in 1960. The girl of the title, based on twenty-two-year-old Irma Grazer, is a guard at Belsen, and is now in prison in Nuremburg awaiting execution. Her guard is a German Jew, and the novel revolves around his response when the girl, who has fallen in love with him, asks that he spend her last night with her. Fried argues that one so young cannot be blamed for the crimes of the Nazis, that she too was a victim. The novel was very influential in helping German youth to come to terms with their parents's generation, to see them not as monsters but as human beings.

Fried's volumes of poetry, such as *Warngedichte* (1964; Poems of warning), *Und Vietnam und...* (1966; And Vietnam and...), and *100 Gedichte ohne Vaterland* (*100 Poems Without a Country*, 1978), have appeared regularly. His writings on Vietnam were read with great excitement in Berlin in the 1960s: he drew the parallel between the actions of the Americans in Vietnam and Fascism, which contributed great-

ly to the development of student opposition to the war in Germany. His sympathy for the motives, if not the methods, of the Baader–Meinhof group led to heavy criticism in the press. In works such as *Ist Antizionismus Antisemitismus?* (Is anti-Zionism anti-Semitism?; in *Merkur*, xxx/337, Stuttgart, June 1976, pp.547–55) and *Höre o Israel* (1974; Hear O Israel), he criticized Israel for its persecution of the Palestinians, accusing the state of being guilty of the crimes formerly committed against it. As a Jew and a victim of persecution, he felt it to be his duty to stand up for the rights of the Palestinians.

Fried, with Heinrich Böll and many other writers, was a member of the influential Gruppe 47, which was committed to the prevention of the repetition of the rise of Fascism in Europe in the 1930s.

Other works include *Angst und Trost. Erzählungen und Gedichte über Juden und Nazis* (1983; Fear and consolation. Stories and poems about Jews and Nazis), and *Gegen das Vergessen* (1987; Lest we forget). He wrote the libretto for the opera *Arden muss sterben* (1967; Arden must die; music by Alexander GOEHR), and he translated 26 of Shakespeare's plays, as well as works by, amongst others, Dylan Thomas, e e cummings and Sylvia Plath. He won almost every literary and humanist award in Germany and Austria and remains the best-selling German language poet.

FURTHER READING
World Authors (London: H. W. Wilson, 1975)
Corino, K., ed.: *Autoren im Exil* (Frankfurt-am-Main: Fischer, 1981)

CATHERINE PHILLIPS

Friedell, Egon (1878–1938) Austrian writer. Born in Vienna, Friedell studied there and at Heidelberg. He made his name after 1899 as a cabaret performer, partnered with Alfred Polgar. His two-volume *Kulturgeschichte der Neuzeit* (1927–31; *A Cultural History of the Modern Age*, 1931–2) gave Friedell the reputation of being a serious writer as well as a brilliant dilettante.

In the late 1930s Friedell became an active opponent of the Nazis, and committed suicide when the Gestapo came to his apartment in

March 1938. The image of Jewish martyrdom is, however, deceptive. Friedell converted to Protestantism in 1897, and accepted H. S. Chamberlain's view that Jews should shake off their Jewishness. His *Cultural History* sees Jews as the embodiment of the rationalistic poison which had destroyed faith; he talked of the "Jewish hatred of ideality", and believed that the hope for the future was the spiritual purity of the Germans. It is not surprising, therefore, that Friedell had tried to come to a collaborative arrangement with the Nazis in 1935. It was only after the rejection of his advances that Friedell's eyes were opened to the true situation. His subsequent fate thus has even more poignancy than was once thought.

FURTHER READING

Patterson, G.: Race and antisemitism in the life and work of Egon Friedell. *Jahrbuch des Instituts für deutsche Geschichte* (1981)

STEVEN BELLER

Friedländer, Saül [Paul Friedländer; Paul-Henri Ferland] (b.1932) French writer and professor of contemporary history at Tel Aviv University and also at the Institute Universitaire des Hautes-Études Internationales in Geneva. Friedländer has been a champion of the use of psychological theory in the reading and study of history. His work in this interdisciplinary field has enabled psychohistorical inquiry to lend its potential to incisive explication of historical events and personalities. In his study *L'Histoire et psychanalyse: Essai sur les possibilités et les limites de la psychohistoire* (1975; *History and Psychoanalysis*, 1978), Friedländer cogently explored the theoretical and practical applications of psychoanalysis in historical enquiry. The book's findings set the fundamental methodological matrix for this controversial development. Friedländer employed these very techniques in his moving autobiographical study, *Quand vient le souvenir* (1978; *When Memory Comes*, 1979) which explored his own traumatic childhood in the wake of horrors in Nazi-occupied France.

Born in Prague, his parents decided to flee the growing threat of Hitler's Germany and in 1939 he arrived in Paris, a bewildered child who was soon placed in a Catholic school at Montluçon where his name became Paul-Henri Ferland. His devotion to his Catholic studies convinced the director of the school that Paul-Henri ought to become a priest, a notion which the young boy accepted. When, at the age of 14, he learned of his Jewish origins the revelation had a profound effect on him and in 1948 he left France for Israel. Upon arrival in Israel he changed his name to Shaul or Saul, thus reflecting his own personal rites of passage.

Friedländer's work as an historian and educator has sought to clarify the meaning of Jewish identity in the twentieth century and to attempt to give deeper meaning and psychological insight into those characters who played central rôles in the events of the Third Reich and the Second World War. He has also been a leading intellectual figure in seeking to influence Israeli policy into more moderate modes in the treatment of Arabs.

Other works in English include *Reflections of Nazism* (1986), *Prelude to Downfall: Hitler and the United States, 1939–1941* (1967), and, with Mahmoud Hussein, *Arabs and Israelis: A Dialogue* (1975).

SIMON SIBELMAN

Friedman, Bruce Jay (b.1930) American novelist. Born and raised in the Bronx, New York City, Friedman studied journalism at the University of Missouri, earning his BA in 1951, followed by two years as a US Air Force correspondent. Classified a "black humorist" (a term he invented), Friedman was one of the first to satirize alienated middle-class American Jews excluded from Christian society and ignorant of their own heritage. Bordering on caricatures, they bumble through life, victims of the environment and their own cowardice. Thus the 34-year-old protagonist of *Stern*, Friedman's wacky, surrealistic first novel, dislikes his job, distrusts his wife, disapproves of his son, and fears his anti-Semitic neighbor but resumes his shallow suburban life after a nervous breakdown.

In his second novel, *A Mother's Kisses* (1964),

Meg, oversexed and manipulative, humiliates her adolescent son, Joseph, who, like Stern, remains an outsider. Praised for its vivid style, the novel was also criticized for lampooning Jewish mothers, a charge to be levied against Philip ROTH's *Portnoy's Complaint*, five years later. Friedman's third novel, *The Dick* (1970), centers on another Jewish misfit, whose name change, unfaithful wife, and police work symbolize his divided self.

Recognized primarily for his novels, Friedman has also written two plays, *Scuba Duba: A Tense Comedy* (1968), spoofing mindless liberalism, and *Steambath* (1971), parodying human weakness in purgatory. His story, "A Change of Plans", was popularized in the 1972 film, *The Heartbreak Kid*, burlesquing Jewish men's attraction to Gentile beauties.

Overwhelmed by a decadent environment and depressing outlook, Friedman's satire sometimes fails, as in the novel, *About Harry Towns* (1974), whose gambling, cocaine-snorting antihero destroys himself without evoking any sympathy from the reader. Still, Friedman's early novels have influenced a generation of readers and helped shape Jewish–American satire.

Other works include: *Far from the City of Class and Other Stories* (1963), *Black Angels* (1966), a short story collection and *Black Humor* (1965), edited by Friedman.

FURTHER READING

Lewis, S. A.: Rootlessness and alienation in the novels of Bruce Jay Friedman. *College Language Association Journal* 18 (1975) 422–33

Schulz, M. F.: *Bruce Jay Friedman* (New York: Twayne, 1974)

EVELYN AVERY

Frischmann, David (1859–1922)

Frischmann, David (1859–1922) Hebrew and Yiddish author, editor and critic. Born in Zgierz, Poland, Frischmann received a traditional education together with studies of European culture. His early publications were written in the spirit of the *Haskalah* but his story, *Bayom hakippurim* (1880; On the Day of Atonement), which describes the artistic development of an orthodox Jewish girl at the expense of her tradition and family, set the tone for Frischmann's later exploration of the demands of tradition opposed to individual will and human instinct. His subsequent works included critical essays on modern Hebrew literature – which were distinguished by a biting wit – stories, poetry, and feuilletons. His editorial and journalistic activity was prodigious.

Following the Revolution of 1917 Frischmann was invited to be chairman of the editorial board of the Hebrew publishing house of Stybel in Moscow and subsequently moved with Stybel to Warsaw. He had become deeply disillusioned by the First World War and the Russian Revolution, in which he saw the destruction of his hope of a creative synthesis of the European and Jewish cultures, due not only to growing anti-Semitism but also to the degeneration of postwar European culture. However, Frischmann was very productive during the post-Revolutionary period, publishing many translations from German, English, and French literature, and critical essays. He edited a number of Hebrew periodicals and anthologies. One of his last works was a series of stories, *Bamidbar* (In the wilderness), published posthumously in 1923. While written in biblical style and language, and set in the post-Exodus period, these stories deal with themes relevant to Frischmann's own time, predominantly the conflict between the demands of religion and human instinct. They also express his increasingly pessimistic views on the Judaic–European cultural synthesis.

Frischmann was nevertheless responsible for introducing European literary values into Hebrew literature. He opposed the use of literature for nationalistic ends, believing in its universality and humanism. He attempted to refine Hebrew literature by emphasizing greater attention to form and by advocating the reduction of the artificiality of plot which had come to characterize *Haskalah* writing.

GLENDA ABRAMSON

Fromm, Erich Pinchas (1900–1980)

Fromm, Erich Pinchas (1900–1980) German social psychologist and psychoanalyst.

He was born in Frankfurt–am–Main into an Orthodox Jewish family. While educated at a *Gymnasium* and at Heidelberg University, he also received intensive training in Talmudic studies with famous rabbis (Nobel, Rabinkov). He co-founded, with Franz ROSENZWEIG et al., the *Freies Jüdisches Lehrhaus* in Frankfurt in 1920. This led to a dissertation, *The Jewish Law. A Contribution to the Sociology of Diaspora Jewry* (1925). Deeply troubled by the "irrationality of human mass behaviour" during the First World War and the war itself, Fromm turned to the study and then to the practice of psychoanalysis. He studied with Abraham, Alexander and others at the Berlin Psychoanalytic Institute (1929–32) and co-founded the Frankfurt Psychoanalytic Institute in 1929. His first major publication, *The Dogma of Christ* (1930), was intended to transcend the approach of individual psychology to historical and social phenomena; thus, it analyzed the socio-economic conditions of the social group which embraced Christian teachings. He had joined the Frankfurt Institute of Social Research in 1930, an affiliation that lasted until 1938. In a series of essays published in the Institute's journal, Fromm attempted to lay the foundations of a "materialist psychoanalysis" that was meant to be a synthesis on the basis of the understanding and criticism of FREUD's concepts and MARX's theory. Wishing to explain the rise of Nazi barbarism in Germany, Fromm and other members of the Institute pioneered a social–psychological study that became the *Studies on Authority and the Family* (1936); it explored the "authoritarian character type" that would become a follower of Hitler.

The first major publication of the second phase of Fromm's career was *Escape from Freedom* (1941), a study devoted to the "character structure of modern man and the problems of the interaction between psychological (individual) and sociological factors". In his view, modern man attained freedom at the cost of anxiety and isolation, and while fleeing from this freedom may enter into new dependencies and submission – as is the case under Nazism. "Positive freedom" can be obtained through work and love, through the realization of one's full potential. During his years as a practicing psychoanalyst in New York City, Fromm was said to have entertained friends with "soulful (hasidic) songs". He held visiting professorships at Columbia and Yale universities, and at Bennington College, but moved permanently to Mexico City in 1949, where he built an Institute of Psychoanalysis. He wrote extensively on social psychology, and went on lecture tours in the USA. In the 1960s he became an opponent of the Vietnam War and an advocate of nuclear disarmament. He believed in the possibility of the "choice of good" by way of "duty and obedience to moral commands". Up to the last phase of Fromm's life and career, the Judaic influences remained strong. In his book, *You Shall be as Gods* (1966), he elaborates on the theme that had captured him in his youth: that the "Old Testament is a *revolutionary* book because its theme is the liberation of man". Fromm always emphasized the humanistic content of Judaism, which he attempted to merge with other religious and intellectual currents: Marxism, Christianity, and Zen Buddhism.

In failing health, Fromm, returned to Europe in 1969, and died of a heart attack at his Swiss residence in Muralto on March 18, 1980.

BIBLIOGRAPHY
Escape From Freedom (New York: Avon, 1965)

FURTHER READING
Knapp, G. P.: *Erich Fromm* (Berlin: Colloquium, 1982)

JUDITH MARCUS AND ZOLTAN TAR

Frug, Semyon [Shimon-Shmuel] (1860–1916) Russian–Jewish poet, prose writer, and publicist. He was born in the Jewish agricultural colony Bobrovyi Kut (Kherson province) in Russia, wrote for almost all the organs of the Russian–Jewish periodical press and for some Russian periodical publications, and died in Odessa. He was the most prominent Jewish national poet writing in Russian. He enjoyed the enthusiastic recognition of his readers and gained critical attention, including that of Russian critics. Saul TSCHERNICHOWSKI said of him: "No one writing in Russian for Jews has made use of such popularity...as Frug. A young generation of Jewish writers writing in Hebrew and colloquial Jewish language (i.e. Yiddish) has been raised on the charm of Frug's poetry...". If the thematics and mood of Frug's poetry (a return to national values, a national revival in terms of Zionism) preserved topicality, his means of poetic expression became outdated. His prose remains more interesting today: short stories and essays, publicistic writings and critical articles. He also wrote in Yiddish and he was the first to introduce into Yiddish poetry the landscape, in the contemporary meaning of the word.

FURTHER READING
Lvov-Rogachevsky, V.: *A History of Russian Jewish Literature* (Ann Arbor: Ardis, 1979)

SHIMON MARKISH

Fuchs, Daniel (b.1909) American novelist, short-story writer, and screenwriter. Fuchs's parents came to New York from eastern Europe and settled on the Lower East Side, where he was born. When he was five they moved to the Williamsburg section of Brooklyn. After his graduation from City College in 1930, Fuchs taught elementary school in Brooklyn and wrote his first three novels during summer vacations.

Summer in Williamsburg (1934), mingles humor and compassion as it looks, mainly through the eyes of a fledgling writer, at the squalid lives of several families of Jews too poor to escape from their ghetto slum – except through fantasy, madness, crime or suicide. *Homage to Blenholt* (1936), also set in Williamsburg, abandons naturalism for romantic comedy. As two young men are steered toward marriage by a pair of practical young women, the book gently mocks their childish dreams even as it laments their loss. *Low Company* (1937), set in and around a seaside ice cream parlor, offers neither naturalistic analysis nor melancholy laughter, but rather a bleak and bitter procession of desperate souls seeking consolation in shabby fantasies. These works were reprinted as *Three Novels* (1961).

Fuchs's first three books were critical successes but financial failures. From the late 1930s

onwards, he wrote short stories for popular magazines, many of which are reprinted in *The Apathetic Bookie Joint* (1979), and screenplays for Hollywood studios. His last novel, *West of the Rockies* (1971), transposes the themes of his earlier work to southern California, as do some of his later stories, where the dreams are gaudier but the spiritual poverty no less grim.

FURTHER READING
Howe, I.: Daniel Fuchs: Escape from Williamsburg. *Commentary* 6 (July, 1948) 29–34
Miller, G.: *Daniel Fuchs* (New York: Twayne, 1979)

MICHAEL SHAPIRO

Fuchs, Ernst (b.1930) Austrian painter. Born in Vienna, of a Jewish father and a Catholic mother, Fuchs was taught at the academy in Vienna by Albert Paris Gütersloh, 1946–50. He became one of the major members of the Viennese school of Fantastic Realism, along with Arik Brauer and Friedrich Hundertwasser among others. Based in Vienna, he has exhibited all over Europe; one of his more recent exhibitions being at the Biennale in Venice in 1984.

Fuchs, who, while in Paris, was acquainted with Dali, treats biblical and mystical themes in a Mannerist style reminiscent of Hieronymus Bosch and identifies quite closely with the Jewish tradition. Apart from the obvious Biblical references, he includes allusions to the *Kabbalah* in many of his paintings. He has also used Hebrew lettering in his paintings, such as his portrait, *Eva*.

FURTHER READING
Oxford Companion to Twentieth Century Art ed. H. Osborne (Oxford: Oxford University Press, 1981)

STEVEN BELLER

Füst, Milán (1888–1967) Hungarian poet, novelist and esthetician. His family name was Fürst and he came from a lower middle-class Jewish family in Budapest. He lost his father at the age of eight and had to support himself while still in secondary school. He studied law and for a while taught economics in a commercial school in Budapest. His first work appeared in the review *Nyugat* and by 1913, when he published his first collection of poetry, *Változtatnod nem lehet* (You cannot change it), he was regarded as an established figure of the "modern" movement. In 1920 he lost his teaching job because of his participation in the cultural activities of the shortlived Hungarian Soviet Republic. Between the two wars he traveled abroad a great deal. In 1934 his *Válogatott versei* (Selected poems) was published, and after the war his lectures on esthetics *Látomás és indulat a művészetben* (1948; Vision and impulse in art) came out. He won the Kossuth Prize in 1948 and during the 1950s he taught esthetics at the University of Budapest.

Although the volume of Füst's poetry is relatively small, his achievement is considerable. His main preoccupation was the tragic nature of human fate: according to his fellow-poet, Kassák, an essential feature of Füst's poetry is "the experience of a constant and objectless fear". His poems are archetypal in the sense that he hides behind different rôles and attempts to express "eternal" human situations. His long lines, which have the sonorous weight of Greek tragedies but are often spiced with grotesque humor, have made a considerable impact on the development of modern Hungarian verse.

As a prose writer Füst will be remembered mainly for his novel, *A feleségem története* (1942; The story of my wife), a riveting tale about the growth of jealousy. His plays include *Boldogtalanok* (1923; The unhappy ones) and *IV. Henrik király* (*King Henry IV*), first published in 1940, a historical drama with Shakespearean undertones. A two-volume selection from his diaries (*Napló*) was published in 1976. Two of Füst's poems translated by Edwin Morgan were included in *Modern Hungarian Poetry* (1977).

Although Jewishness is an issue which rarely appears in Füst's work, in the *Diaries* he expresses his pride in belonging to a race which "has created a spiritual culture". Sometimes he connects the experience of "alienness" on earth with Jewish history: "and that which befell Jews so abundantly at all times scorn and loneliness – these two were my patrimony in the world!" (David Copperfield). In the poem *A Magyarokhoz* (To the Hungarians) he asserts his double loyalty: to the Hungarian language ("my only treasure") and to the ancient race which produced him ("I am the descendant of prophets") and gave him the wisdom to wait for better times.

BIBLIOGRAPHY

Vajda, N., ed.: *Modern Hungarian Poetry* (New York: Columbia University Press, 1977) [two poems trans. E. Morgan]

FURTHER READING

Somlyó, G.: Milán Füst. *The New Hungarian Quarterly* (1968)

GEORGE GÖMÖRI

G

Galanté, Abraham (1873–1961) Turkish scholar and historian. Galante was born in Bodrum, Turkey. Soon after completing his schooling he became a teacher and journalist. Due to his political journalism he was forced to leave Turkey and went to Cairo, where he became an editor of and contributor to the French newspaper, *Le Progrès*. In Egypt he founded a new paper, *La Vara* (1905–8), and wrote articles for it about the corruption of the Jewish local leadership under the decadent Ottoman authorities. In 1914 he was called back to Turkey, and appointed Assistant Professor of the Grammar of Semitic Languages at Istanbul University, later Professor of the History of the Ancient Orient, a post he held until 1933. He was also a member of the Portuguese Academy of Science. Beside his scholarly work, Galante was involved in politics and was even a member of the Turkish Parliament (1942–6).

Galante's main scientific contribution was to the study of the history of the Jews in the Near East, especially in Turkey. His first scholarly historical work was *Don Joseph Nassi, Duc de Naxos, d'après de nouveaux documents* (1913), which contained twelve official Turkish documents. He wrote more than fifty works, many of them collections of Jewish-Turkish documents such as *Documents officiels turcs concernant les Juifs de Turquie* (1931–54).

FURTHER READING

Elmaleh, A.: *Le Professeur Abraham Galante* [includes a bibliography of his writings] (1947)

DEBORAH SCHECHTERMAN

Galich [Ginsburg]**, Alexander** (1919–1977) Russian poet, songwriter, and dramatist. Galich was one of the best known of the dissident, guitar-playing "bards" who came to prominence in the 1960s and 1970s. Though he was permitted only one public concert (in Akademgorodok in 1968), homemade tapes of his singing in crowded Moscow flats reached the most varied strata of Soviet society.

Galich was born in Ekatorinoslav. As an adolescent in Moscow, he studied poetry with Bagritsky and acting under Stanislavsky. At the war's end he became a successful dramatist, working in both theater and film. Then, in the early 1960s, his career underwent a precipitous change: he began to compose anti-establishment ballads, many of which showed a stong awareness of his Jewish roots; he was baptized into the Russian Orthodox Church, and, in line with all this, found himself at the forefront of the cultural opposition. In 1971 he was expelled from the Writers' Union. Deprived of a source of income, he left Russia in 1974, but his life abroad was tragically brief. Settling in Munich and later Paris, he worked for Radio Liberty and gave concerts in Europe and Israel. In 1977 returning from a concert, he electrocuted himself on an open wire.

Galich's songs include both comic ballads and songs and poems on the twin themes of the Holocaust and the Stalinist camps. The comic songs are celebrated for their precise reflection of everyday Soviet life, including Soviet anti-Semitism; their cast of characters, befuddled little men who speak in a mixture of slang and bureaucratese, have entered popular mythology.

253

Most notable of his Jewish works are the song "Poezd" (The train), dedicated to the memory of Solomon Mikhoels, and the long poem "Kaddish" (despite the title, the only religious references are Christian). The Jewish experience in the war is the subject of Galich's suppressed play *Matrosskaya tishina* (Sailor's rest). The text of the play, together with Galich's analysis of the anti-Semitic reaction to it, appears in the autobiographical *General'naya repititsia* (1974; Dress rehearsal).

A volume of selected works has appeared in English translation: *Songs and Poems* (1971).

BIBLIOGRAPHY
Songs and Poems, trans. G. S. Smith (Ann Arbor: 1971)

FURTHER READING
Smith, G. S.: *Songs to Seven Strings: Russian Guitar Poetry and Soviet Mass Song* (Bloomington: Indiana University Press, 1981)

ALICE NAKHIMOVSKY

Gardner, Herb (b.1934)   Born in Brooklyn, New York, Herb Gardner attended New York High School of Performing Arts and then Carnegie Tech and Antioch College, where he studied sculpture in addition to drama. His first major play, *A Thousand Clowns* (1962), was based on a short story he wrote in 1956 called "The Man Who Thought He Was Winston Churchill". Set in New York City, the setting for all of Gardner's plays, *A Thousand Clowns* focuses on Murray Burns, an unemployed television writer, and deals with the compromises of modern life and the willingness to make accommodations to middle-class behavior. The play reveals Gardner's strongest asset: the creation of witty characters who use words as weapons against the outside world. The major characters are recognizably Jewish, but save for references to delicatessen cuisine, little in the play is overtly Jewish.

The Goodbye People (1968), Gardner's next Broadway success, also possesses characters who are recognizably Jewish, but this time many of the major motifs encapsulate Jewish issues. The play (which Gardner adapted and directed for film in 1985) deals with two archetypes of male Jewish personalities; Max, with his heavy Eastern European accent and his aggressive and clever way with words, and Arthur, who is shy and self-deprecating. Shirley, with her plastic surgery and name change, is stereotypical of the Jewish woman's attempts to conform to WASP standards.

With *I'm Not Rappaport* (1985) Gardner more directly confronts contemporary American–Jewish issues with his play about the relationship between an elderly Jewish man and an elderly Black man who meet in the park. Gardner reveals that despite differences of race and background, the old men share emotional and physical circumstances which outweigh any differences.

Gardner's primary theme is the importance of an inner life – a fantasy, a dream – which acts as a buffer against reality. This links Gardner with a long line of European–Jewish authors whose characters responded to grim external circumstances with vibrant imaginary stories and dreams. In juxtaposition to the fantasists, Gardner pits the representatives of the forces of ordinary life, who are typically members of the fantasists' families. While Gardner sentimentally sides with the fantasists, he also recognizes the need for compromise with the real world.

Other works include the play *Thieves* (1974; film version 1977) and the original screenplay for *Who Is Harry Kellerman and Why Is He Saying Those Terrible Things About Me?* (1971).

DAVID DESSER

Gardosh, Kariel ["Dosh"] (b.1921)   Israeli cartoonist and satirist. Gardosh was born in Budapest, Hungary and was educated at Szeged University in Hungary and the Sorbonne in Paris. He left Hungary for Israel in 1948 and since 1953 has been a staff member of the Israeli daily newspaper, *Ma'ariv*, published in Tel Aviv.

The cartoons of "Dosh", mainly on political themes, are incisive and cynical, yet always humorous and demonstrative of his affection for Israel. His little *sabra*, "Little Israel", dressed in shorts, shirt and the distinctive Israeli *kova tembel* (a hat or cap), has become an established part of Israel's popular iconography, apart from being a sharp commentator on current affairs. Although he is best known for his daily cartoons in *Ma'ariv*, Gardosh is also a prolific writer of prose. He has used his comic talents to the full in his published books which range from collections of his own cartoons to *Smoker's Book* and *Forty!* He collaborated with Ephraim KISHON on *Selihah shenitzahnu* (1967; Excuse us for winning), an off-beat celebration of Israel, written shortly after the Six Day War.

During his time with *Ma'ariv* Gardosh has also contributed serious articles and essays to the newspaper on a wide range of topics. His *Teshuvah helkit* (1981; A partial answer), is a collection of articles, including a number of autobiographical pieces. Aside from his prose, Gardosh has also written several dramatic works which have been staged in the theater and produced on radio and television. His obvious visual artistic skills and keen observant eye are used to the full in the lively illustration of several Hebrew books.

For his work "Dosh" has received the Herzl, Nordau and Jabotinsky prizes. He has also received a "Fighter for the State" Medal and has been a member of both the Israeli Arts Council and Board of Directors of the Israeli Broadcasting Authority. From 1981–3 he represented the State of Israel as the Cultural Attaché at the Israeli Embassy in London.

JOHN MATTHEW

Gary, Romain [Emil Ajar] (1914–80) French diplomat and novelist. Born in Vilna of mixed parentage which he declared to be "part Cossack and Tartar, part Jew", Gary struggled to sublimate his Jewish heritage for the best part of his life. The family moved to greater Poland in 1921, and in 1926 he emmigrated to Nice, France, where he was educated. At the outbreak of the Second World War he was a fighter pilot in the French Air Force. Following the defeat of the French forces, he joined General DeGaulle and the Free French Forces in London. Following the war, Gary balanced his life

Kariel Gardosh ("Dosh") I Love Israel

between his literary activities and a diplomatic career. His last diplomatic post was as Consul-General in Los Angeles, USA (1956–60).

Gary's early literary creations, *Education européenne* (1945; *A European Education*, 1960) and *La Promesse de l'Aube* (1960) were highly autobiographical. Though these and other works are generously populated with Jewish characters, Gary portrays them from without as they were perceived by the non-Jewish world, rather than from the interiority of the Jewish experience. Gary's literature tended more to urbane wit and social satire, as in his English novel, *Lady L* (1958) and does not seek to address weightier social issues or the complexities of contemporary identity. In 1956, Gary won the prestigious Prix Goncourt for his novel, *Les Racines du ciel*.

In 1967, Gary suffered a traumatic experience while in a Warsaw museum. He became painfully aware of his Jewish heritage and the ramifications of being Jewish. The result was perhaps his most memorable book, *La Danse de Gengis Cohn* (1967; *The Dance of Genghis Cohn*, 1969). It is the sardonic tale of the protagonist's awareness of his Jewishness which is imposed upon him by the advent of the Nazi era. Cohn is a Jewish comedian who is ruthlessly murdered by a Nazi officer. His ghost then relentlessly haunts his executioner. The black comedy and profound irony stand as hallmarks of Gary's own struggle with his Jewish identity and, by extension, the conflicts often faced by assimilated Jews.

In the later years of his life, Gary constructed an alter ego, Emil Ajar. Named for his nephew,

Gary intended Ajar as a literary mystery, but his pleasantry became quite serious when Ajar's first novel, *La Vie devant soi* (1975) won the Prix Goncourt. Ajar's name was afixed to a second novel, *L'Angoisse du roi Salomon* (1979). Both novels examine various sorts of Jewish characters from their fundamental Jewish essence, something Gary seemed unable to achieve under his own name.

Gary committed suicide in 1980 after the death of his wife, Jean Seberg.

BIBLIOGRAPHY

Education Européenne as *Nothing Important Ever Dies*, trans. V. Garvin (London: Cresset, 1944; repr. 1960)

The Dance of Genghis Cohn, trans. R. Gary and C. Sykes (London: Cape, 1969)

SIMON SIBELMAN

Gaster, Moses (1856–1939) Rabbi, Zionist leader, Jewish scholar, and folklorist. In 1873 Gaster received his BA from Bucharest University, and in 1877 his Ph.D. from the University of Leipzig. He also studied at the Rabbinical Seminary in Breslau under Zecharias FRANKEL and Heinrich GRAETZ, and was ordained as rabbi in 1881. Until 1885 he lectured on Romanian language and literature at Bucharest University. In 1883 he published his first book, *Literatura Populara Romănă* (Romanian folk-literature), a pioneering work in the study of Romanian culture. This was followed by his *Chrestomathie Romăně* (1891), in two volumes, still considered one of the most influential contributions to Romanian literature. During the same period Gaster began his lifelong and intensive Zionist activity. He guided Lawrence Oliphant on his visits to Romania, Constantinople, and Palestine, and was among the founders of *Hovevei Zion* in Romania. He was also active in the foundation of the first settlements of Romanian Jews in Palestine: Zikhron Ya'akov and Rosh Pina. Despite his contribution to Romanian scholarship, his activity in Jewish affairs in Romania led to his deportation in 1885. Later he was "rehabilitated", and elected to the Romanian Academy of Sciences in 1929.

REV. Dr M. GASTER

Micrographic portrait of Moses Gaster

The second and most important stage in Gaster's life was in England. He began as Ilchester Lecturer on Slavonic and Byzantine Literature at Oxford University (1886, 1891). From 1887 to 1919 he was *hakham* of the Spanish and Portuguese Jewish Congregation of London. His Zionist activity also increased in this period, and he was elected first chairman of the English Zionist Federation and Vice-President of the second, third, fourth, and seventh Zionist Congresses. His close relationship with Theodor HERZL and the leadership of the Zionist movement in Britain deteriorated after his opposition to the Uganda Program.

During the whole period of his intensive public activity, Gaster continued his scholarly work. Upon arrival in England he was accepted favorably in leading British folklorist circles. He was elected Vice-President of the Royal Asiatic

Society, and President of the Folklore Society – outstanding achievements for a recent Jewish immigrant. Among his many publications on Jewish and international folklore are the three-volume collection of his articles, *Studies and Texts* (1928), and his publication with critical notes of *The Chronicles of Jerahmeel* (1899), *The Exempla of the Rabbis* (1924), and the *Ma'aseh Book* (1934). Gaster's stormy and dynamic character and his occasionally hasty and unfounded conclusions aroused much criticism. However, his immense contribution to both Jewish public life in the late nineteenth and early twentieth centuries, and to the study of Jewish folklore, are still of great importance.

BIBLIOGRAPHY

ed. B. Schindler: *Occident and Orient: Gaster Anniversary Volume* (London: Taylor's Foreign Press, 1936)

FURTHER READING

Newall, V.: The English Folklore Society under the presidency of Haham Dr Moses Gaster. *Folklore Research Center Studies* 5 (1975) 197–225

Yassif, E.: *Jewish Folklore: An Annotated Bibliography* (New York and London: Garland, 1986)

ELI YASSIF

Geber, Hana (b.1910) American sculptor. Geber was born in Prague to an assimilated and cultivated family. In 1939 she left Czechoslovakia to escape the Nazis and after six years of homelessness she arrived in New York City where she settled.

Geber's subject matter centers on the Jewish experience, much of it originating in the Bible. Her sculptural style has been compared to that of Giacometti in its intensity and scale. Apart from small, expressive figures, many of them of biblical archetypes, a great deal of her work is functional: *mezuzot*, spice holders, *kiddush* cups, Hanukkah lamps, created in silver and gold out of sculptural form. She has also accepted commissions from a number of American synagogues.

Geber has exhibited regularly throughout the East Coast of the USA and Los Angeles, Toronto, and Haifa. Her work is included in university collections across the United States, as well as in museums in Tel Aviv, Haifa, and Kyoto, Japan, the State Jewish Museum in Prague, and the Jewish Museum in Amsterdam.

JOHN MATTHEW

Gebirtig, Mordechaj [Bertig] (1877–1942) Folk singer, poet and composer. Gebirtig was born in Crakow to a poor family and was initially educated in a *heder*. Poverty forced his parents to apprentice him to a carpenter and he remained a carpenter all his life. From his earliest years he revealed a considerable gift for music and fondness for poetry, but he received no training in either of these arts. Without any knowledge of score notation he taught himself to play on a home-made pan-pipe. With the help of this instrument he composed melodies with rhythmic patterns akin to those found in old pastoral pipe music.

His poetry describes the lives of simple people which ended tragically with the Holocaust. Although he was self-educated, he eventually developed his own literary style and wrote drama reviews in addition to poetry and songs. He was also active in the Jewish Socialist movement in Galicia and during the First World War he served five years in the Austrian army.

Gebirtig's earliest songs, *A Little Orphan*, *The King is Born*, *Hershele*, became extremely popular, as did his lullabies. Some of his songs, such as *Huliet, Huliet Kinderlech*, became hits. His first collection of songs, *Folksstimlech* (Folk tunes), was published in 1920. His works were performed in such Jewish theatres as the Azazel, the Ararat and the Sambation. The thirtieth anniversary of his debut (1936) was marked by the publication in Vilnius of a collection of 50 of his songs entitled *Majne Lider* (My songs). Gebirtig composed one of the best of his songs in 1938 after the pogrom in Przytyk: *S'Brent, Undzer Shtetl Brent* (Our town is on fire), which later became an anthem sung in the fighting ghettos.

During the Nazi occupation Gebirtig was imprisoned in the Crakow ghetto, and later in a village-ghetto in Lagiewniki. He continued to write songs, some devoted to his daughter Chajele, a popular folk singer (Lola Gebirtig) and some describing his situation and experience, such as *Tog Fun Nekume* (The day of revange). He was murdered on the way to the railway trucks destined for the Belzec concentration camp.

The exact number of Gebirtig's poems and songs is not known, particularly since unpublished manuscripts were lost in the war. Of the remaining works there are 100 published items and 20 in manuscript. Gebirtig was the last of the Jewish folksingers whose songs described life in the ghettos during the Holocaust.

MARIAN FUKS

Geiger, Abraham (1810–1874) German reform rabbi, historian, and publicist. Born in Frankfurt-am-Main, Geiger received a traditional Orthodox Jewish education. He later studied Oriental languages and Greek at Heidelberg and Arabic at Bonn. His first rabbinical post was at Wiesbaden in 1832 where, in 1837, he summoned the first convention of reform rabbis. In 1843 he finally became rabbi at Breslau (though the orthodox minority of the congregation withdrew after prolonged controversy). He later held rabbinical posts at reformed congregations in Frankfurt and Berlin. He was active at the reform assemblies in Frankfurt (1845) and Breslau (1846). Geiger was also prominent in the formation of the Jüdisch-Theologisches Seminar in Breslau and the Hochschule für die Wissenschaft des Judentums in Berlin which he directed until his death.

Geiger wrote widely on a variety of subjects: his doctoral dissertation (Marburg, 1834) was devoted to the study of the influence of Jewish tradition in the Koran, *Was hat Muhammad aus dem Judenthume aufgenommen?* (1833). In later years he not only translated into German a selection of medieval Hebrew poetry, contributed frequently to the *Jüdische Zeitschrift für Wissenschaft und Leben* and the *Zeitschrift der deutschen Morgenländischen Gesellschaft*, but also wrote studies of Maimonides, Ibn Gabirol, Isaac of Troki and Judah Aryeh de Modena, and edited the Diwan of Judah Halevi. Geiger's principal work was his *Urschrift und Übersetzungen der Bibel in ihrer Abhängigkeit von der inneren Entwicklung des Judentums* (1857; The original text and translations of the Bible in their dependence on the internal development of Judaism). Using the Greek and Aramaic translations of the Bible Geiger revealed the development of Jewish religious understanding expressed in the readings of the biblical text, from which the masoretic version was as little exempt from change as any other. Geiger's views had particular relevance to the disputes between Pharisees and Sadducees. He identified this dispute in terms, respectively, of a dispute between populist democratic nationalists and the aristocratic, conservative Saducean element. The Pharisees were seen by Geiger as the bearers of a tradition in evolution.

He placed himself in this tradition and in lectures at the Hochschule in the last years of his life, he distinguished four periods in the history of Judaism: the first was that of revelation which continued after the exile; the second, that of tradition which stretched from the completion of the Bible to the final redaction of the Babylonian Talmud; this was followed by a period of legalism which lasted until the mid-eighteenth century and was marked by casuistry and the fear of innovation; the fourth period was an era of liberation from the fetters of the past, made possible by the use of reason and historical research, and which called for the revitalization of Judaism.

This was the role that Geiger chose for himself as reformer, rabbi, and historian. He aspired to create a form of Judaism consonant with the liberal, universalist, and emancipatory trends of the nineteenth century. Thus in his lectures, *Das Judentum und seine Geschichte* (1864–1871; Judaism and its history), he saw the conception of God gradually freeing itself from the limitations of land and people, and Judaism becoming purely a religion. To this end Geiger sought to remove from Judaism all marks of national differentiation, although he later mellowed somewhat; he opposed prayer in Hebrew and eliminated all references to the return to Zion from his prayer-book of 1854. What would be left of Judaism would be a monotheistic confession of faith.

FURTHER READING

Geiger, L.: *Abraham Geiger – Leben und Lebenswerk* (Berlin: 1910)

Reichmann, E., ed.: *Essays Presented to Leo Baeck* (London: 1954) 75–93

Schechter, S.: *Studies in Judaism* 3 (Philadelphia: The Jewish Publication Society of America, 1924) 47–83

LIONEL KOCHAN

Geiger, Ludwig (1848–1919) German critic and literary hitorian. Born in Breslau, he studied at the College for the Science of Judaism that his father Abraham GEIGER had founded in Berlin. His doctoral dissertation (presented to Leopold von Ranke) analyzed the attitude of Greek and Roman authors to the Jews and Judaism. Appointed Professor of German Literature and Cultural History in 1880, Geiger had three main areas of interest: Renaissance and Reformation Studies, German–Jewish history, and Goethe research. (His reputation as a Renaissance scholar was such that the reputedly anti-Semitically inclined Jakob Burckhardt asked him to edit all subsequent editions of his *Civilisation of the Renaissance in Italy*.)

In Jewish affairs Geiger maintained the traditions of his father by both espousing Reform Judaism and buttressing it with scholarly endeavors. He wrote the two-volume *Geschichte der Juden in Berlin* (1871; History of Berlin Jewry) and *Die Deutsche Literatur und die Juden* (1910; German literature and the Jews) supervised the posthumous publication, in five volumes, of his father's *Nachgelassene Schriften*, and was co-author of *Abraham Geiger – Leben und Lebenswerk* (1910; Abraham Geiger – life and work). He founded and edited a journal of German–Jewish history which appeared for five years, served as editor of the *Allgemeine Zeitung des Judentums*, the communal weekly, and in 1911 sent a birthday letter to Kaiser Wilhelm II, protesting at the social discrimination to which German Jews were subjected. Within the community he combatted political Zionism.

In the area of Renaissance and Reformation studies he published *Johannes Reuchlin, sein Leben und seine Werke* (1871; Johannes Reuchlin, his life and works) and *Renaissance und Humanismus in Italien und Deutschland* (1882; Renaissance and humanism in Italy and Germany).

As a Goethe scholar Geiger wrote about the poet's relationship to Jews and Judaism, and founded (in 1889) the *Goethe Jahrbuch* which he edited until 1913. Six years later he died in Berlin.

RICHARD GRUNBERGER

Gelléri, Endre Andor (1906–1945) Hungarian writer. He came from a lower middle-class background and was brought up in a working-class district of Budapest. His education was completed in a technical school, after which he had a series of manual jobs such as locksmith, dyer and later worked as a factory clerk. His literary talent was discovered at an early age and his first story was printed in 1924. In 1928–9 he visited Germany with financial support from a Budapest newspaper. Gelléri's first novel *Nagymosoda* (1931; Laundry) already displays the characteristic traits of a style which the poet Kosztolányi described as "a fairytale-like realism", a blend of reality and imagination. Most of Gelléri's heroes are people at the fringe of society, atypical, mysterious workers and rebellious artisans; in their lives he found "the poetry of poverty". In 1932 Gelléri received the prestigious Baumgarten Award and from 1933 onwards he published several collections of short stories all of which met with great critical acclaim.

During the war he was conscripted into the forced labour service (established for Jews by the Horthy regime), yet it was during this time that he wrote his posthumously published fragmentary autobiography, *Egy önérzet története* (1957; The story of a self-respect). In this work he describes his youthful conflicts with anti-Semitism and his struggle for a life of self-respect, often against enormous odds. He was deported to Germany towards the end of 1944 and sent first to Mauthausen, then to Günskirchen; he died of typhoid two days after liberation. His collected short stories were published in *Varázsló, segíts* (1959; Help, magician). Several of his stories have been translated into English: "Ház a telepen" as "House on an Empty Lot" in *Twenty-Two Hungarian Short Stories* (1967) and "Részegen" as "Drunk" in *The New Hungarian Quarterly* (1969).

BIBLIOGRAPHY

House on an Empty Lot. In *Twenty-Two Hungarian Short Stories* (London, 1967); Drunk. *The New Hungarian Quarterly* 36 (1969)

GEORGE GÖMÖRI

genealogy, Jewish   A remarkable phenomenon of the post-war era is the immense development of interest in the subject of family trees. However, in Jewish tradition, genealogy is rooted in the very origins of the people itself. In Genesis, the first book of the Bible, much commentary is devoted to the lineage of the patriarchs. The very definition of who is a Jew, while not capable of being rendered down to a single concept, in the case of those born into the faith requires matrilineal proof of identity. A wise insistence on acknowledgment of the mother for basic Judaic inheritance dates from the earliest times and this was skilfully blended with paternal transmission in such matters as the handing on of land and the priesthood. Early Jewish thinking demonstrates a lucid grasp of the nature of some genetic disorders: for example the laws pertaining to ritual circumcision were modified in cases of haemorrhagic illnesses in such a way that all potentially affected males of that family would be spared exposure to risk of bleeding.

"Do-it-yourself" genealogy has been an increasingly popular leisure pursuit and whilst initially Jewish involvement therein was slow to develop, this has now significantly changed. The membership of the London Society of Genealogists numbered about a thousand in 1955; today it has increased some six-fold but the proportion of Jews in the Society remains small. In other parts of the world, notably in the USA and Australasia, there has been an even more dramatic increase in formal membership of genealogical societies. Over the past 10 years numerous Jewish genealogical societies have been formed in the USA, France, Switzerland, and Israel, which hold regular meetings and issue various publications. No Anglo-Jewish genealogical society exists and those who work in this field are loosely affiliated to the Jewish Historical Society of England (JHSE) and Anglo-Jewish Archives. The First International Seminar on Jewish Genealogy took place in Jerusalem in 1984 and the second in 1987 in London.

Modern Jewish genealogical technique researches data from many sources and for the UK, it is the secular records that are logically the first that should be checked. The civil primary records have been centralized in England and Wales since 1 July 1837 and in Scotland since 1 January 1855, from which dates registration of all births, marriages and deaths became compulsory. However, penalties for failure to comply with the law were not imposed until 1872. Recent immigrants, frequently Jews, have a relatively greater proportion of early non-registrations due to unfamiliarity with the requirements. Apparent non-registration may in fact be simply "misplacings" due to spelling variations. Non-registration occurred much more frequently with births than marriages or deaths.

If an exact address for a person is known at a given date the relevant decennial census from 1841 to 1881 should be consulted but the information given in 1841 is more meager and therefore less useful than for those of the later years. All grants of wills and administrations since 1 January 1858 have been centralized to the Principal Probate Registry, but for earlier estates numerous diocesan consistory courts held jurisdiction; the most frequently used are the Prerogative Courts of Canterbury and of York. A list of grants at the former, for Jewish persons deceased prior to 1848 has been published by the JHSE. Jewish newspapers, and especially the London *Jewish Chronicle* (published since 1841), with its family announcements section, are unsurprisingly important but not infrequently the general press, too, contains useful data. The *Gentleman's Magazine* is a particularly rich source and an index to its obituaries of Jewish persons has been published in the Miscellanies of the JHSE. The indexes of naturalized persons in the Public Records Office are worth checking but the actual papers themselves, while often very informative, may only be inspected if they are over a hundred years old.

The records of all individual Jewish congregations, both active and defunct, are logical searching grounds for such matters as synagogue seatholders, relief and charitable organizations, some *brit milah* (ritual circumcision of the male infant usually eight days after birth) registers, marriage authorization records and burial registers. The largest single repositories today for such records are the Office of the Chief Rabbi and that of the Spanish & Portugese Jews' Congregation in London. Cecil Roth's book *The Rise of Provincial Jewry* (1950) includes many references to specific Jews and their families. Several important organizations such as Anglo-Jewish Archives (including the Colyer–Fergusson and D'Arcy Hart pedigrees in the Mocatta Library), the Jewish Museum in London, and the Sternberg Centre for Reform Judaism are also useful genealogical stores. Anglo-Jewish Archives will ultimately contain the Mordy pedigree collections which are already available on microfilm at the Mormon Church, Utah, USA.

Finally, it is worth noting that much other archival material is also on Mormon microfilm and in some Israeli repositories. The information contained there may be all that has survived of the records of those European Jewish communities that were obliterated during the Nazi era.

FURTHER READING

Anglo-Jewish wills and letters of administrations. Jewish Historical Society of England (1949)

Gandy, M.: *My Ancestor was Jewish: How Can I Find Out More About Him* (London: Society of Genealogists, 1982)

Roth, C.: The rise of provincial Jewry *The Jewish Monthly* (1950)

Steel, D. J., and Samuel, E. R.: *National Index of Parish Registers Volume 3: Sources for Roman Catholic and Jewish Genealogy and Family History* (London: Society of Genealogists, 1974)

Transactions and Miscellanies of the Jewish Historical Society of England (published since 1893)

ANTHONY JOSEPH

Gerchunoff, Albert (1889–1950) Argentine writer

Gerchunoff's parents fled from the pogroms in Russia when he was two and settled in Argentina, in the rural community of Entre Rios. He worked as a journalist on the paper *La Nación* and became the first writer to give expression to the aspirations of the Jewish immigrants to South America, particularly in his book *Los gauchos judios* (1910; *The Jewish Gauchos of the Pampas*, 1955). This is a series of sketches of Jewish life in farming communities, showing the integration of the Jews into Argentina in a lyrical celebration of the simplicity of rural life. Folklore and legend, both Russian and Argentine, are mixed with realism. The picture of the gauchos and of life in Argentina is idealized. Violence and prejudice are always resolved in the hope they will disappear as the Jews become known for their honesty, industry and pacifism.

Gerchunoff's writing reflects the initial impulse of the immigrant who seeks a land where he can wipe out the memory of persecution and build a new life. He equated Argentine with Palestine, a promised land of freedom, where Jews would no longer need to live in fear, or follow prescribed trades, but could return to their Biblical rôles as farmers. His gratitude to his new country prevented him from seeing the anti-Semitism in Argentina, and he turned a blind eye to the conflicting loyalties of being a Jew and an Argentine. This did not however limit his defense of the legitimacy of Israel as the homeland for displaced Jews during the Second World War.

BIBLIOGRAPHY

The Jewish Gauchos of the Pampas, trans. P. de Pereda (New York: Abelard–Schuman, 1955)

ANN DUNCAN

Gershwin, George [Jacob Gershvin] (1898–1937) American composer.

He was born in Brooklyn, the son of immigrants from St Petersburg. His father was an unsuccessful small-time businessman and entrepreneur and the family moved house 25 times during George's childhood. He was a poor student, preferring to play and fight in the streets, but he soon developed a passion for music, despite an unmusical family background, and in 1912 he began piano studies with Charles Hambitzer who considered him a genius and introduced him to classical and modern music, theory, harmony and composition.

He first worked as staff pianist for a TIN PAN ALLEY publisher, Remick's, and in 1917 was employed by Max Dreyfuss of Harms publisher as a composer. 1919 saw both the production of *La La Lucille*, his first musical, and the composition of *Swanee* for Al Jolson. In 1923 he accompanied a concert singer, Eva Gauthier, when she sang some of his songs at a recital. This inspired bandleader Paul Whiteman to organise a "serious jazz concert" a year later, at which Gershwin played his *Rhapsody in Blue*, composed for the occasion. Thus began a meteoric rise to social and professional stardom, which included such successes as *Tip Toes* (1925), *Funny Face* (1927), and *Of Thee I Sing* (1931), the first musical to win a Pulitzer Prize, all in collaboration with his lyricist brother, Ira.

In 1929 Gershwin began work on AN-SKI's *The Dybbuk* for the New York Metropolitan, but the project was shelved as was an earlier plan in 1915, for him to collaborate on a piece for Yiddish Theatre with Sholom Sekunda, who, however, refused to work with the young unknown.

Gershwin's distinctive contribution was to blur the boundaries between serious and popular music, and his output included several high-

George Gershwin painting a portrait of Arnold Schoenberg

ly successful concert works, including *Concerto in F* (1924), *Three Piano Preludes* (1926) and *An American in Paris* (1928). However, *Porgy and Bess* (1935) in which he attempted to incorporate negro folk and jazz music into the framework of opera, was unenthusiastically received, although many now consider it his greatest work.

He died suddenly of a brain tumor, at 38. His funeral was held simultaneously at synagogues in Hollywood and Manhattan and silence was observed in Hollywood's studios in his honor.

FURTHER READING

Crawford, R. and Schneider, W.: Gershwin, George. In *The New Grove Dictionary of American Music*, ed. H. W. Hitchcock and S. Sadie (London and New York: Macmillan, 1986)

Kendall, A.: *George Gershwin* (London: Harrap, 1987)

Schwartz, C.: *Gershwin: His Life and Music* (Indianapolis: 1973)

ANDREA BARON

Mark Gertler The Rabbi and his Grandchild *1913. Southampton City Art Gallery*

Gertler, Mark [Max] (1891–1939)   British painter. Gertler was born in Spitalfields, London into a poor Jewish immigrant family from Galicia. After returning briefly to Austria, they settled in England for good in 1896. Ten years later Gertler chanced upon the autobiography of the Victorian painter W. P. Frith and announced his intention of becoming an artist. Although economic necessity forced him to stop attending art classes at the Regent Street Polytechnic and to become an apprentice at a stained glass works, his talent was recognized by the established Anglo-Jewish painter William ROTHENSTEIN who, in 1908, persuaded the Jewish Educational Aid Society to finance Gertler's attendance at the Slade School of Art.

Once there, Gertler won a scholarship and several prizes, and proved a considerable social success: fellow student C. R. W. Nevinson, for example, described him as a "Jewish Botticelli". Contact with established writers and painters after leaving the Slade in 1912, and an introduction to Lady Ottoline Morrell, led to him mixing with the intellectual, social and artistic elite of London society. Gilbert Cannan

based his novel *Mendel* on Gertler, and he provided the inspiration for Loerke in D. H. Lawrence's *Women in Love* and for Gombauld in Aldous Huxley's *Crome Yellow*.

Gertler's earliest extant work is traditional in style, albeit highly skilled, and consists chiefly of portraits and still-lifes. From 1912 onwards, his style became more consciously primitivizing. Many of the works of this period are solemnly hieratic renderings of his family and the Jewish community amongst whom he was still living; they remain his most impressive and distinctive achievement. Socially, however, Gertler was beginning to feel torn in two.

By 1914 Gertler had virtually abandoned overtly Jewish subject matter. In the 1920s he turned almost exclusively to the depiction of the female form, whose rich sensuousness earned him a certain popularity. His personal life, on the other hand, was far from satisfactory. Ill health combined, in the 1930s, with the death of several people close to him and the failure of a number of one-man shows, exacerbated the depression that had plagued him throughout his life. After an earlier unsuccessful attempt, Gertler committed suicide in 1939.

263

FURTHER READING

Carrington, N. ed.: *Selected Letters of Mark Gertler* (London: Rupert Hart-Davis, 1965)

Woodeson, J.: *Gertler: Biography of a Painter, 1891– 1939* (London: Sidgwick & Jackson, 1972)

MONICA BOHM-DUCHEN

Gideon, Miriam (b.1906) American composer and educator. She was born in Greeley, Colorado but was raised and educated in Boston, where she received a BA from Boston University, and in New York, where she was granted an MA in musicology from Columbia and a Doctor of Sacred Music in composition from the Jewish Theological Seminary. Miriam Gideon taught at Brooklyn College, City College of the City University of New York, where she was made Professor Emeritus, and at the Cantors Institute of the Jewish Theological Seminary and the Manhattan School.

In 1975 Gideon became only the second woman composer elected to membership in the American Academy and Institute of Arts and Letters. Among her many other awards and prizes have been the Ernest Bloch Choral Award, a grant from the National Endowment for the Arts and in 1986 an award from Boston University naming her a "Distinguished Alumna."

Her works are performed widely throughout the world and, besides many compositions for orchestra and chamber groups, Gideon has written a complete *Friday Evening Service* (1974), as well as a *Sabbath Morning Service* (1970) and many other compositions for the synagogue which include: *Adon Olam* (1954), *The Habitable Earth* (1965), *Psalm 84, Biblical Masks* (1958) (1960), and *Ayetet Hashahar* (1980), all for solo voice, or chorus, with various instrumental accompaniments.

Gideon's works number well over sixty, with her favorite combination, that of voice and chamber ensemble, constituting a large part of her output. Her fascination with language and her love of the voice have played a great role in her choice of compositional media.

SAMUEL H. ADLER

Gilboa, Amir (1917–1984) Israeli poet. Born in Radzivilov, Ukraine, to a religious family, Gilboa went to Palestine in 1937 as a pioneer. In 1942 he joined the British Army in Egypt which advanced through the desert and north Africa into Holocaust-ridden Europe. A booklet of his first poems appeared in 1942: *La'ot* (For the sign). During the war his poems appeared in various soldiers' publications. After two more books, he published his collected poems: *Kehulim ve'adumim* (1963; Blues and reds) dedicated to his family, all of whom were killed by the Nazis.

In his poetry he fused a nightmarish awareness of the Holocaust with ecstatic, apocalyptic hopes of Israel's national revival. His poetry is deeply rooted in traditional Hebrew literature: in the Bible, talmudic legends, medieval Hebrew poetry in Spain, hasidic stories, and is also influenced by modern Hebrew poetry. Still he strikes a highly individual tone and cannot be categorized in any school or generation of Hebrew poets. In 1968 he published *Ratziti likhtov siftei yeshenim* (I wanted to write the lips of those asleep). In it the original exuberant expressionistic poetry where light was the recurrent motif gave way to a feeling of anguish. It was born out of a feeling of uncertainty and disorientation both on a personal and national level. Poems became fragmentary, disjointed, and punctuation disappeared – a nightmarish surrealistic quality prevailed. This trend continued in his later poems.

BIBLIOGRAPHY

The Light of Lost Suns (New York, 1979)

FURTHER READING

Brown, M.: Biblical myth and contemporary experience: the Akedah in modern Jewish literature. *Judaism* (1982) 99–111

Yudkin, L.: Israeli poetry – Gilboa, Amichai and Zach. In *Escape into Siege* (London: Routledge & Kegan Paul, 1974) 135–149

RIVKA MAOZ

Ginsberg, Allen (b.1926) American poet. With the publication of *Howl* in 1956, one of the most widely read poems of the age, Allen Ginsberg almost single-handedly revolutionized traditionalist American poetic practice. He was born in Newark, New Jersey, to a high school English teacher and lyric poet, Louis Ginsberg, and a dedicated communist, Naomi Levy Ginsberg, whose mental illness powerfully affected Ginsberg. His lamentation at her death, *Kaddish* (1961), confirmed his stature as a major poet, despite much uneven work throughout his prolific career. Ginsberg is particularly important as a literary artist who, rather than adapt his Jewish heritage to mainstream culture, or disguise it, assimilated American eclecticism and idealism to his own vision.

Ginsberg entered Columbia University in 1943 and was temporarily expelled in 1945. In New York, he established formative artistic, drug, and homosexual relationships with William Burroughs and Jack Kerouac, fellow beat movement rebels. Other important influences were Blake, Whitman, Surrealism, William Carlos Williams, who encouraged an American speech prosody, and Buddhism.

Howl, a furious and surrealistic prophetic excoriation and ecstatic sacrament of the self, is Ginsberg's best work. It was granted notoriety by government censorship and made the poet a cultural phenomenon and international celebrity: social critic, political activist, hippy guru, global traveler, and messianic bard continually producing verse. Books of note include *Planet News* (1968), reflecting 1960s countercultural turmoil – for instance, Ginsberg was King of the May in Prague in 1965 and helped organize the 1967 San Francisco Human Be-In – and *The Fall of America* (1972), an ambitious poetic sequence, which won a National Book Award. Still flamboyant but increasingly venerated, in 1974 Ginsberg was inducted into the American Institute of Arts and Letters, and in 1984 his collected poems were published.

BIBLIOGRAPHY

Ball, G., ed.: *Allen Verbatim: Lectures on Poetry, Politics, Consciousness* (New York: McGraw-Hill, 1974); *Collected Poems, 1947–80* (New York and London: Harper & Row, 1984)

FURTHER READING

Kramer, J.: *Allen Ginsberg in America* (New York: Random House, 1969)

Tytell, J.: *Naked Angels: The Lives and Literature of the Beat Generation* (New York: McGraw-Hill, 1976)

ADAM J. SORKIN

Ginsberg, Harold Louis (b.1903) American Bible scholar. Born in Montreal, Ginsberg studied Semitics at the University of London. During the early 1930s in Palestine, Ginsberg concentrated on ancient Semitic, notably Aramaic and Ugaritic. His *Ugaritic Texts* (1936) demonstrated the cultural continuity between the literature of ancient Syria and the Bible.

The writings of Ginsberg's Palestine period make numerous biblical comparisons. Upon coming to Conservative Judaism's Jewish Theological Seminary in New York in 1936, Ginsberg made the Bible the center of his scholarly interests, while continuing his significant contributions to the study of Ugaritic, Aramaic and Phoenician. Ginsberg's presence there for four decades inspired many students to enter biblical scholarship.

Ginsberg's studies have made him one of the outstanding biblicists of the century. Unrivalled as a philologist of ancient Northwest Semitic, Ginsberg has employed his analysis of biblical diction to reconstruct inner-biblical literary development as well as ancient Israelite history and culture. One is always struck by the common sense of Ginsberg's observations. Thus, he accounts for the Aramaisms in Job by the convincing observation that the book's protagonists are "easterners", and as we (and Job's author) know from Genesis, "easterners" speak Aramaic. Ginsberg's numerous articles and monographs are essential for the proper understanding of Isaiah, Hosea, Daniel, Job and Ecclesiastes. In recent years he has concentrated on the Pentateuch, departing from his earlier acceptance of the theories of Yehezkel KAUFMANN, and provocatively reconstructing the ancient Israelite calendar and festivals, notably in *The Israelian Heritage of Judaism* (1982).

The results of many of Ginsberg's researches arc available to a larger public because he served as an editor and translator of the *Torah* (1962) and *Prophets* (1978) of the JEWISH PUBLICATION SOCIETY Bible, and as Bible editor of *Encyclopaedia Judaica* (1971) to which he also contributed original, detailed articles.

FURTHER READING

Tigay, J.: Classified bibliography of H. L. Ginsberg's writings. *Eretz Israel* 14 (1978)

S. DAVID SPERLING

Ginzberg, Louis (1873–1953) Talmudic and midrashic scholar. Born in Kovno, he studied at the *yeshivot* of Telz and Slobodka as well as at several German universities before emigrating to the USA where, in 1900 he was named as Rabbinical Literature editor of the *Jewish Encyclopedia*. In 1903 Ginzberg was appointed professor of Talmud at the Jewish Theological Seminary of America, where he taught until his death. His wide-ranging scholarly interests encompassed classical rabbinic texts and the history of Palestine in the Second Temple period. *Legends of the Jews* (seven volumes, 1909–38), is a running account of the legendary history of biblical Israel which traces the textual history of the legends and uncovers parallels in Hellenistic and early Christian sources. He edited and published numerous fragments discovered in the Cairo Genizah. His *Geonica* (1909) includes an introduction which, though dated, is still the most comprehensive introduction in English to the history and literature of geonic Babylonia. Ginzberg also concentrated heavily on the study of the Palestinian Talmud. In 1909 he published a collection of manuscript fragments to that Talmud from the Genizah (*Seridei yerushalmi*). 1941 marked the appearance of the first three volumes of his massive commentary to that Talmud, *Perushim vehiddushim layerushalmi*. A fourth volume was published posthumously in 1961. The work in fact addresses the entirety of rabbinic literature. His introduction is a valuable survey of the textual state of that Talmud and the history of its study. Ginzberg introduced the lay reader to the world of traditional Jewish learning in works such as *Legends of the Bible* (1956), and his essay collections *Students, Scholars and Saints* (1928), and *On Jewish Law and Lore* (1955).

FURTHER READING

Finkelstein, L.: Louis Ginzberg. *Proceedings of the American Academy for Jewish Research* 23 (1954)

MARK WASHOFSKY

Ginzburg, Natalia Levi (b.1916) Italian writer. As the daughter of Giuseppe Levi, professor of anatomy at Turin University who lost his post as a result of Mussolini's racial legislation, and wife of Leone Ginzburg, Russian-born but resident in Italy since early childhood and who was killed in a Fascist prison, Ginzburg could not be other than conscious of her Jewishness, especially as her husband and several members of her family were actively engaged in anti-Fascist activities.

In a deceptively simple style, which is nevertheless capable of great variety of tone, ranging from pathos to humor, she conveys penetrating psychological analyses of states of anxiety, loneliness and disappointment. In much of her best fiction such as *Le voci della sera* (1961; *Voices in the Evening*, 1963), although partly set in the Fascist period, there are no specifically Jewish characters or themes (although her Jewishness may have accentuated her sense of isolation and alienation): but in *Tutti i nostri ieri* (1952; *Dead Yesterdays*, 1956), which deals with the horrors of war and occupation and is based on her own war-time experiences, there are a number of foreign Jewish refugees, destined to be deported or shot, while in *Sagittario* (1957), in *Cinque romanzi brevi* (1964), Dr Chaim Wesser, a Polish refugee, survives the war. In the autobiographical *Lessico famigliare* (1962; *Family Sayings*, 1967), Ginzburg gives an account which is witty, amusing and also deeply moving, of life in an anti-Fascist family in Turin. The family hid the socialist activist Filippo Turati for over a week before he made his escape to Corsica, smuggled out by Carlo Rosselli, and welcomed Jewish refugees from Nazi Germany.

FURTHER READING

Bullock, A.: Introduction. *Le voci della sera* (Manchester: Manchester University Press, 1982)

Hughes, H. S.: *Prisoners of Hope. The Silver Age of Italian Jews* (Cambridge: Harvard University Press, 1983)

BRIAN MOLONEY

Glatshteyn, Yankev (1896–1971) Yiddish poet. Born in Lublin, Poland, Glatshteyn moved to the USA in 1914. In 1920 with A. Glants-Leyeles and N. Minkoff he founded the introspectivist or *Inzikh* group of poets, which published a journal *In zikh* (1919) and an important anthology *In zikh – a zamlung introspektive lider* (1920). The poetic manifesto of this group involved a rejection of the "artificial" and imprecise lyricism of the *Yunge* poets and the espousal of a realist or even naturalist concept of poetry, where restrictions on poetic form and content were set aside in the name of faithfully and exactly recording the psychology of the poet. This was modernism that sought to break up the false stylized order of traditional lyric forms. In spite of this programme, Glatshteyn became the most playful and inventive experimenter with form in Yiddish poetry, delighting in parody, word-games, neologisms, and narrative tricks. Glatshteyn's poetry is intellectual, playing off different stylistic levels and registers. Glatshteyn's publications include *Yankev Glatshteyn* (1921), *Fraye ferzn* (1926; Free verses) and *Kredos* (1929). Glatshteyn also published two long narrative poems (*Ven yash iz geforn* (1939; When Yash went), and *Ven yash iz gekumen* (1940; When Yash returned), and volumes of criticism and essays. A sense of the tragic nature of Jewish history dominated his later writing.

BIBLIOGRAPHY

Harshav, B., and Harshav, B.: *American Yiddish Poetry* (Berkeley: University of California Press, 1986) 209–385

CHRISTOPHER HUTTON

Glick, Srul Irving (b.1934) Canadian composer, conductor, and music producer. He was born in Toronto where he attended the University of Toronto, receiving a Bachelor of Music and a Master of Music. His composition studies continued in Paris, where he studied with Darius MILHAUD, Louis Saguer, and Max Deutsch. Upon his return to Canada, he became a teacher of theory and composition at the Royal Conservatory of Music in Toronto and at York University. From 1962 to 1986, Srul Glick was a producer of serious music for the CBC, and this involvement with fine performing, recording, and broadcasting has won him four Grand Prix du Disque and a Juna Award.

He has had a lifelong interest in the music of the synagogue and has a prolific output integrating Hebraic elements with lyric and classical compositional techniques. In 1969 Glick assumed the position of choir director of Beth Tickvah synagogue in Toronto. Many of his compositions have been performed by major symphonic and choral organizations throughout North America, Europe and Israel.

Glick has written both large and small liturgical works, including: *Hashirim Asher L'Yisrael* (1982), for cantor and choir; *Kedusha* for cantor and choir (1976); *Sing Unto the Lord a New Song* (1987) for chorus and harp; and over fifty shorter anthems and prayers. Works based on Jewish themes include *Deborah* (1972), for narrator and brass quintet; *Music for Passover* (1963–75), for chorus and string quartet; *Yiddish Suite* (1979), for chorus and cello; six *Suites Hebraique* for various chamber combinations; and a *Sonate Hebraique* for solo cello. Some secular works include: two symphonies (1966, 1967), *Psalm for Orchestra* (1971), and *Sonata for Orchestra "Devequt"* (1982).

SAMUEL H. ADLER

Gluckman, Leon (1923–1978) South African actor and producer. The son of Dr Henry Gluckman, who served as minister of health in the Smuts government and was the only South African Jew to have attained cabinet rank, Leon was educated in Johannesburg and subsequently studied law at Rhodes University, Grahamstown. During the Second World War he served in the Navy, returning to Rhodes where he attained a master's degree in English literature.

He staged T. S. Eliot's *Murder in the Cathedral* in Johannesburg, after which he signed up as an assistant director with the Nottingham Players, England and then moved to the Old Vic Theatre Company where he gained a reputation as a forceful actor in classical and Shakespearian roles.

During the late 1950s he was eclectic, staging classics, modern works, and indigenous theater. His most noteworthy contribution was the promotion of indigenous theater in South Africa. His production of Athol Fugard's deeply moving *The Blood Knot* was the first public viewing of Fugard's work in Johannesburg. Gluckman helped to pioneer black theater in South Africa. His production of the fiery *King Kong* (1959) was the first opportunity afforded to black people to express African talent and through it, Africans made a forceful entry into the field of the musical play.

While not claiming to be political or particularly "Jewish" in his work, he saw historic and social victimization of Africans as analogous to the historic degradation of the Jews. The spirit of compassion which entered into his work should therefore be seen in a Jewish context.

JOCELYN HELLIG

Glueck, Nelson (1900–1971) American archaeologist and educator. Born in Cincinnati, Ohio, Glueck received a Bachelor of Hebrew Literature degree from the Hebrew Union College (HUC) in 1918. He added a Bachelor of Arts degree from the University of Cincinnati in 1920, and ordination as a Reform rabbi from HUC in 1923. Glueck pursued Biblical studies in Germany throughout 1923–4. He gained his Ph.D. at the University of Jena in 1926. In 1927 Glueck studied under Professor William F. Albright, director of the American School of Oriental Research (ASOR) in Jerusalem.

Glueck made significant contributions to the field of Biblical archeology through the 1950s. During his career he surveyed over 1,500 sites in Jordan, Sinai, and the Negev. He was a pioneer in using the technique of pottery identification, which he learned from Albright, to survey large, previously unexamined areas. Glueck's work was also characterized by a novel attitude toward the Bible itself. While never forgetting the distinction between "Bible as history" and "history in the Bible", Glueck insisted upon, and allowed his research to be guided by, the essential correctness of the "historical memory" in the Bible. Glueck served as director of ASOR 1932–3 and 1936–40. In 1960 he established the Hebrew Union College Biblical and Archaeological School in Jerusalem.

Glueck's work as an archaeologist did not overshadow his contribution as an educator. He became professor of Bible and Biblical Archaeology at HUC in 1936, and in 1947 he succeeded Julian Morgenstern as the fourth president of the college. In 1950 he became the first president of the newly combined Hebrew Union College–Jewish Institute of Religion. During his tenure as president, HUC–JIR strengthened its position as a modern institute of Jewish learning of international significance. Branches were established in California and Jerusalem, and the American Jewish Archives was established in Cincinnati. Glueck's personal influence on several generations of Reform rabbis trained at HUC–JIR was inestimable.

BIBLIOGRAPHY
"Hesed" in the Bible, trans. A. Gottschalk (Cincinnati: Hebrew Union College Press, 1967); *Deities and Dolphins* (New York: Farrar, Straus and Giroux, 1965); *The River Jordan* (London and Redhill: Lutterworth Press, 1946); *Rivers in the Desert* London: Weidenfeld & Nicolson, 1959)

ALFRED GOTTSCHALK

Gnessin, Uri Nissan (1879–1913) Hebrew writer. Born in Starodov, Chernigov, Gnessin had a traditional Jewish education, and, at the talmudical academy, formed a friendship with one who was also to be a famous Hebrew writer, J. H. BRENNER. His first volume of stories was called *Tzelalei hahayyim*, 1904 (Shadows of life), and constituted an attempt at a Hebrew, naturalist fiction. His first story, "Genia", revolves around the frustrated love of a young, passionate, but alienated young man. Gnessin was one of the first Hebrew writers to make subjective feeling the primary content of fiction, and to describe it authentically, rather than to treat the national situation didactically.

However, it is in the following years that the author found his distinctive voice, and with *Hatziddah* (1905; Sideways) introduced the stream-of-consciousness technique into Hebrew literature. The language was made to bear the weight of an internal monologue, reflecting on the landscape, individuals, people and ideas in general, and, above all, on the reflective consciousness. A series of stories, bearing titles such as *Beterem* (1909; Before) and *Etzel* (1913; Near) (the titles themselves indicate the author's sense of separation from life's mainstream) testify to an original talent, prematurely cut down.

BIBLIOGRAPHY

Sideways. In *Eight Great Hebrew Short Novels*, eds. A. Lelchuk and G. Shaked (New York: New American Library, 1983)

LEON I. YUDKIN

Goehr, Alexander (b.1932) British composer and scholar of music. Goehr was born in Berlin, the son of a distinguished conductor. The family moved in 1933 to England, where he attended school, and later the Royal Manchester College of Music. In 1955 Goehr completed his musical education in Paris with Olivier Messiaen and Yvonne Loriod. His musical contact with Germany was renewed at this stage by his association with Pierre Boulez and Luigi Nono, who was based in Darmstadt.

Later Goehr settled in London, active as a concert planner for the BBC. From 1968 he spent two years teaching in the USA and during this time studied not only American music and culture but also Japanese and Hebrew musical traditions. He also traveled to Hungary and to China in his pursuit of the understanding of musical cultures other than his own.

Goehr is recognized as one of Britain's leading academic composers and he has accepted music professorships at Leeds and Cambridge universities. Before that he had already established himself as a teacher of composition. His qualities of leadership and his innovative nature led his association with Harrison Birtwistle and Peter Maxwell Davies (who also studied at the Royal Manchester College); the three became known as the "Manchester School".

Goehr's first compositions, written during his years in Manchester, exhibit the shared traits of his contemporaries. His unmistakeable personal style is first revealed in *Little Symphony* (1963), written in memory of his father. During this time Goehr explored various textures and forms, encompassing chamber music, orchestral works, and music-theater pieces.

Notable among these works are *Naboth's Vineyard* Op. 25, a dramatic madrigal with the text in Latin and English adapted from 1 Kings. It was commissioned by the City Arts Trust for the 1968 City of London Festival and first performed on 16 July 1968. His *Romanza* Op. 24 for cello and orchestra was first performed by Jacqueline du Pré, and both *Konzertstuck* Op. 26 and *Concerto for Piano and Orchestra* Op. 33 were premiered by Daniel Barenboim. *Sonata about Jerusalem* Op. 31 is a music-theater piece with text adapted from the autobiography of Obadiah the Proselyte and the Chronicle of Samuel de Yahya ben al Maghribi (twelfth century) by Recha Frier and Alexander Goehr. The work was commissioned by Testimonium Jerusalem and first performed in Tel Aviv in January, 1971.

Since these works, Goehr's output has increased steadily, establishing him as an indispensable contributor to British music.

JOHN MATTHEW

Gold, Herbert (b.1924) American novelist, short story writer, and essayist. Gold was nominated to the American Institute of Arts and Letters in 1957 and he won the Longview Award in 1959. He was also a Fulbright fellow (1950–1), Hudson Review fellow (1956), Guggenheim fellow (1957), and has won an award from the Ford Foundation (1960).

Gold is a prolific and expert chronicler of a broad span of American and American–Jewish character types. He is particularly skillful at rendering the little quicks and habits of people defined by their time and turns a witty and knowing eye on idiosyncracies and inconsistencies of character. His prose style adapts to the mood of each particular piece, with the narrative description taking on the flavor of the dialogue. For example, the prose of *Family* (1981), a memoir-novel describing the generations of a Cleveland Jewish family, patters along, now bitter, now tender, in the cadences of the English-Yiddish hybrid language typical of the semi-assimilated second-generation American Jews who largely populate the piece. On the other hand, *A Girl of Forty* (1986) which describes a thoroughly modern, cheerfully promiscuous California woman, her lovers, and her son, is written in a sophisticated, brittle, zingy style.

BIBLIOGRAPHY

Fathers (London: Secker & Warburg, 1967); *The Great American Jackpot* (London: Weidenfeld & Nicolson, 1971); *My Last Two Thousand Years* (London: Hutchinson, 1973); *Waiting for Cordelia* (London: Hutchinson, 1978); *He/She* (London: Severn House, 1980)

SYLVIA FISHMAN

Gold, Michael [Itzok Isaac Granich] (1893–1967)   American radical author. Born the son of an immigrant housepainter in the lower East Side of New York, he was unable to finish school because his father was poor. Granich's first published works, romantic poems, appeared in Max Eastman's *The Masses*. Never quite at ease with Eastman's Greenwich Village bohemians, Granich played the role of rough proletarian in highbrow circles and carefully hid from the public the fact that he had attended Harvard for part of a semester. With his dark, good looks, Granich soon came to rival his patron Eastman as a major league womanizer. He took a cautious sabbatical in Mexico in 1918–19 to avoid the draft, before returning to New York to edit *The Liberator*. Granich adopted the name "Michael Gold" as a *nom de guerre* during the Palmer Raids on radicals in 1919.

No intellectual, he was often criticized for writing with his heart and not his head; and at heart he was a sentimental, sometimes scathing, but always highly impassioned Communist journalist. As an advocate of "proletarian literature" and a scourge in *The New Masses* of bourgeois writers like Thornton Wilder and

Ernest Hemingway, he was unmatched, and, after the 1930s, largely unfollowed. Gold's memoir-novel, *Jews Without Money* (1930), was his most enduring work. He wrote about his childhood with a charm and wit which was less visible in his polemical journalism collected in *Change the World!* (1935) and the bitter *The Hollow Men* (1941). Included among those doing "passionate and authentic work" in Sinclair Lewis' Nobel Prize address in 1930, nothing Gold wrote after that date had either the passion or authenticity of *Jews Without Money*.

BIBLIOGRAPHY

Folsom, M., ed.: *Mike Gold: A Literary Anthology* (New York: International Publishers, 1972)

ERIC HOMBERGER

Goldberg, Lea (1911–1970)   Hebrew author and literary scholar. Goldberg was born in Koenigsberg, East Prussia and spent her early childhood in Russia but moved with her parents to Kovno where she attended the famous Hebrew *Gymnasium*. She studied at the Universities of Kovno, Bonn and Berlin, receiving her doctorate in Semitics at the latter university (1933). In 1935, she emigrated to Palestine, living in Tel Aviv.

She began writing Russian verse as a child and published her first Hebrew poem in 1928. Her first volume of verse *Tabbe'ot 'ashan* (Smoke rings) appeared in 1935. Avraham SHLONSKI recognized her literary talents and did much to further her early career. She collaborated with him in editing and translating Russian poetry (1942). Eventually, Goldberg became editor of *Al hamishmar*'s literary supplements, served as children's book editor of *Sifriat Poalim* and literary advisor to *Habimah*. In 1952 she was invited to organize the Department of Comparative Literature at the Hebrew University, where she taught until her death.

Primarily a poet, she also wrote a number of popular children's books, translated major Russian and German novels, was the author of a novel and two plays, and wrote critical works on Petrarch (1953), and on prose fiction *Omanut hasippur* (1963; The art of the short story), and Russian literature (1968). Goldberg is associated with the SHLONSKI–ALTERMAN school of the Palestine Mandate. She was a sensitive, erudite writer who, like the Russian acmeists, rejected symbolism and preferred concrete imagery and clear unadorned diction. She eschewed the bombastic expressionism of some of her contemporaries, generally avoided ideological verse and rarely touched on Jewish themes. Only after the Holocaust did she refer to the Jewish world of her girlhood (*Mibeiti hayashan*; 1944, From my old home). She wrote of childhood, the Lithuanian and Jerusalem landscapes, love (especially unrequited love) and, as she grew older, of aging and death, resignation to the tragedy of existence and the solace in discovering beauty in ordinary phenomena. Among her outstanding poems are *Mishirei hanahal* (1948; Songs of the stream), *Beharei yerushalayim* (1956; In the hills of Jerusalem) and the sonnet series *Ahavatah shel Teresa di Mon* (1956; The love of Teresa di Mon).

BIBLIOGRAPHY

[Selections in English translation in:]
Carmi, T., ed.: *The Penguin Book of Hebrew Verse* (Harmondsworth: Penguin Books, 1981) 552–554; Frank, B., ed.: *Modern Hebrew Poetry* (Iowa: University of Iowa Press, 1980) 43–7; Mintz, R. F., ed.: *Modern Hebrew Poetry, a bilingual anthology* (Berkeley and Los Angeles: University of California Press, 1966) 228–48; Spicehandler, E.: *The Modern Hebrew Poem Itself* (Harvard University Press, 1989)

EZRA SPICEHANDLER

Goldemberg, Isaac (b.1945) Peruvian novelist. Goldemberg went to Israel aged 17 and settled two years later in New York, where he wrote his first novel, *The Fragmented Life of Jacobo Lerner*. This is one of the rare Spanish American Jewish novels to be a richly innovative literary creation at the same time as a valuable social document. The narrative alludes to many aspects of Peruvian Jewish life – the problems facing both new and established immigrants, the struggle of poor salesmen as well as the prosperity of successful merchants and professionals, the lives of women as well as men, children and old people, life in Lima and

the provinces, among the educated and the illiterate. The narrative alternates with newspaper cuttings integrating the fiction with issues of wider interest to Jewish life, both spiritual and material. This mixture of genres and styles constitutes its modernity. The fragmented life of Jacobo Lerner is gradually assembled through the voices of the many people who were important to him. Each has his own distinctive style and preoccupations and each brings a new view of Lerner. Jacobo himself scarcely appears; he lies dying and it is the meaning of his death for others which is the focus of interest. Beyond its function as a psychological novel, or a novel of customs, this is a suggestive contemporary text, built up in often contradictory segments without chronological order, with many voices and no omniscient viewpoint.

This is to date the most significant novel on Jewish life to emerge from Peru, which has produced very few Jewish writers of note, as well as being a moving and witty novel in its own right.

BIBLIOGRAPHY

The Fragmented Life of Jacobo Lerner, trans. R. S. Picciotto (New York: Persea Books, 1976); *Play by Play*, trans. H. St Martin (New York: Persea Books, 1985)

ANN DUNCAN

Golden, Harry (1902–1981) American journalist. Golden's father, Leib Goldenhurst, an Austro-Hungarian immigrant, became an editor of the *Jewish Daily Forward*. Golden graduated from the East Side Evening High School (1918) and attended City College (1919–22). He worked in various jobs in New York for the next four years. In 1929 he was imprisoned for selling stocks on margin. After his release, he wrote for the *Post*, the *Mirror*, the Zionists, the New Deal, and the Socialists.

In 1941 he began publishing the *Carolina Israelite*, a 16-page tabloid that came out six times a year. He began with 800 subscribers; by 1958, subscriptions had grown to 16,000. His book, *Only in America* (1958), became a bestseller. His satirical proposals to end segregation brought him fame: for example he proposed the Vertical Negro Plan of standup desks in the public schools, since Southerners only objected to *sitting* next to blacks. Other equally satirical ideas followed.

By 1963, circulation had soared to 45,000 paid subscribers. Subsequent essay collections were also best sellers, including *For 2¢ Plain* (1959), *Enjoy, Enjoy!* (1960), *You're Entitled* (1962), *So, What Else is New?* (1964), *Ess, ess mein kindt* (1966), *Abee gezundt* (1970).

BIBLIOGRAPHY
The Right Time (New York: G. P. Putnam's Sons, 1969)

RUTH ROSENBERG

Goldfaden [Goldfadn], **Avrom** (1840–1908) Yiddish dramatist. Goldfaden, the father of the modern Yiddish theater, was born in Old Constantin, Russia. A medical student and journalist, he turned to writing plays in a conscious effort to develop the Yiddish theater. He was a prolific creator of melodramatic historical and biblical productions filled with songs which themselves became popular successes. His first play was performed in a wine cellar in Jassy, Roumania in 1876. He founded a Yiddish theater, the Marinksy, in Odessa after Alexander II's restrictive laws were lifted. His subsequent eviction forced his company to tour with his own operetta entitled *Shulamis*. Reinstalled in the Marinsky theater he staged his historical musical *Bar Kokhba*. In 1883 the Tsar banned all Yiddish theater in Russia. Goldfaden moved to Bucharest and began again with a new company. His example inspired new Yiddish theater troupes to form and travel all over Eastern Europe. Actors of the time were mainly illiterate, relying on their own ingenuity in improvising dialogue. Goldfaden's theater was aimed at the masses and his plays were particularly suitable for performance rather than written, literary works. He always set his plays around a moral theme. He found great popularity in Europe when in 1889 he founded *Club dramatique Israelite Russe* (Jewish-Russian dramatic club) in Paris. He also presented plays in Lemberg in 1891. He was selected as a Parisian delegate to the Zionist Congress in London in 1900. In

Avrom Goldfaden

1903 he accepted a long-standing invitation to join his brothers in New York. He was by then ill and unable to take an active part in theater but wrote the occasional newspaper article. When Goldfaden died in New York in 1908, his immense reputation and popularity attracted 75,000 mourners to his funeral where 250 policeman were posted to keep the crowds in order. His obituary in *The New York Times* was full of praise.

DEVRA KAY

Goldhar, Pinhas (1901–1947) Australian Yiddish essayist, novelist, translator and editor. Born in Lodz, Poland, Goldhar migrated to Australia in 1928 where he continued a career as a writer begun in Poland. The contrast between the vibrant Jewish life of his home town

272

and the hostility to the newcomers and the Anglo-Jewish snobbery of Melbourne's Jewish "establishment" forms the background to much of his writing.

He wrote mostly in Yiddish and it is for his writings and his contribution to Australian literature in this language that he is most respected, but some of his later essays in the *Australian Jewish Forum* are in English. Some of his earlier work has been translated: in particular his story, "Cafe in Carlton", *Southern Stories*, 1945, was rated the best story of the year by literary critics. A second story, "The Funeral", was published twice in translation in two years, in the prestigious *Meanjin* (1945) and in the annual anthology *Coast to Coast* (1947).

The recurring theme of his essays and short stories is the tensions and trials of migrants trying to adjust themselves to a new life, as he put it, "eating the hard bread of an immigrant". He considered that the Jewish life of Europe could not easily survive the transfer to alien shores. However, he argued, on the basis of his extensive studies of Australian literature, that a new Yiddish literature could be created in Australia and that, by writing this new literature in Yiddish, Australian Jewry could be at one with creative Jewish communities the world over.

Goldhar played a double role. He interpreted for Jews their own lives and, through his excellent translations into Yiddish, he introduced them to Australian literature. He saw many analogies between the nineteenth-century Australians and their creative literature and the Jewish immigrants' need to express themselves. Goldhar is regarded as the pioneer of Yiddish literary expression in Australia. He edited the first Yiddish paper to go into more than one issue, *Oystralyer lebn* (1931), he wrote the first Yiddish literary book to be published in Australia, *Dertseylungen fun Oystralia* (1939) – parts of which were reprinted in his posthumous *Gezamlte shriftn* (1949) Collected works – he was the first Yiddish writer to be published in Australian anthologies and to be acclaimed by Australian literary critics, and the first to translate Yiddish writers into English for Australian audiences. Since his Yiddish translations of Australian literature were reprinted in South America he was an innovator in this respect also. Also in English translation are his stories "His Only Love" *Coast to Coast* (1961), "The Circumcision" and "The Last Minyan" in *Short Stories of Australia* and "Drummond Street", and "Newcomers" in *The Bridge* (1967).

FURTHER READING

Brezniak, H.: *Pinchas Goldhar* (Sydney, 1967)
Waten, J.: Contemporary Jewish literature in Australia, *Australian Jewish Historical Society* (1949)

ALAN D. CROWN

Golding, Louis (1895–1958) English novelist, poet, and travel writer. Born in Manchester to recent immigrants, Golding won scholarships to Manchester Grammar School and to Queen's College, Oxford, for history, but later turned to classics, his love for which is reflected in several of his novels and travel books. He wrote from an early age, but his first published work was a collection of poems *Sorrow of War* (1919) based on his experiences in an ambulance unit in Salonika and France.

Golding's best known books are those set among the immigrant Jewish society of his native Manchester, which he called Doomington. With these writings he assumed the mantle of Zangwill as the foremost Anglo-Jewish litterateur and became, according to *The Times*, "an apt interpreter of British Jewry to its friends and neighbors". His first novel, *Forward from Babylon* (1920) however, raised a storm of protest in the pages of the *Jewish Chronicle*, initiating a correspondence under the heading "Jewish anti-Jewish Writers". Strongly autobiographical, the story of Philip Massel is a rebellion against family and tradition, in this case a deeply religious and harsh father and the tyranny of the "cheder" over which he presides. In *Day of Atonement* (1925) the psychology of race and religion is sensitively analyzed. The story of Philip Massel continues in *Give Up Your Lovers* (1930) which treats of love between Jew and Gentile.

With *Magnolia Street* (1932) Golding became internationally famous. This chronicle of a typical provincial street from 1910 to 1930, with Gentiles living on one side and Jews on the other, was translated into twenty different languages and sold over a million copies. The bitterness and rebellion of the earlier novels is here supplanted by humanity and humor – and a generous measure of sentimentality – as the colorful characters fight, love, hate, and occasionally cross the street towards one another. Several of these characters reappear in later novels. The Silver family saga starts with *Five Silver Daughters* (1934); in which gentle, honest Sam and Hannah rise from poverty to uneasy wealth, ultimately relinquished, while their daughters pursue divergent paths. Susan's adventures in post-revolutionary Russia, and the errant Elsie's in post-war Berlin, provide exciting passages. Elsie is the heroine of *The Glory of Elsie Silver* (1946), set in the Warsaw ghetto at the time of its destruction, and of *The Dangerous Places* (1951) which highlights the plight of refugees after Hitler. *Mr Emmanuel* (1939) relates the experiences of the gentle but resilient pious Jew who ventures into Nazi Germany to find the mother of a refugee boy. It was made into a successful film.

Golding was a wonderful raconteur, a bon viveur with a zest for life and catholic interests, and a dedicated traveler. Often criticized for writing too much and too easily, he never reached the first rank of novelists, but could always hold his readers with a good tale.

BIBLIOGRAPHY
Magnolia Street (repr. London: Victor Gollancz, 1986); *Five Silver Daughters* (repr. London: Victor Gollancz, 1987)

VERA COLEMAN

Goldman, Emma (1869–1940)

American anarchist, political essayist, and autobiographer. Born in Russia, Goldman was introduced to revolutionary ideas while living in St Petersburg before emigrating to the USA in 1886. She was inflamed by events following a labor rally in Chicago's Haymarket Square, at which a bomb had exploded killing seven policemen. A politically motivated trial led to the execution in 1887 of four anarchists whose responsibility for the bombing was never proved. With their deaths, Goldman embraced "a great ideal..., a determination...to make their

cause my own". After a brief marriage she moved from Rochester, New York to New York City among other Jewish immigrants and became active in the anarchist movement. In 1889 she met Alexander Berkman, her sometime lover and lifelong companion whom she supported after his assassination attempt on Henry Clay Frick, a steel-industry executive, in 1892. During the fourteen years of Berkman's subsequent imprisonment, she worked tirelessly for their cause. A mesmerizing speaker, who delivered lectures in German, Russian, Yiddish and English, she was accused of inspiring Leon Czolgosz to assassinate President William McKinley in 1901. Her magazine *Mother Earth*, founded in 1906, continued publication until 1917.

An early feminist, Goldman was deeply committed to improving conditions for women. She wrote, "everything within [a woman] that craves assertion and activity should reach its fullest expression". In 1916 she went to jail for defying the law by giving a speech on birth control.

Despite her reputation as the rabble-rousing speaker Red Emma, she also presented radical views in seemingly innocuous talks on modern drama. Some of her work was collected in *Anarchism and Other Essays* (1910) and her drama lectures appeared in *The Social Significance of the Modern Drama* (1914).

A public outcry rose against her and Berkman during the Red Scare that followed the Bolshevik Revolution, and they were deported to Russia in 1919. Goldman described their disappointment with the new Russian government in *My Disillusionment in Russia* (1922). After two years they left, exiles without a country. A Welsh anarchist married Goldman in 1925 to provide her a British passport and she settled in France to write her vibrant autobiography *Living my Life* (1931). Goldman died in Canada at the age of 70. She was buried in Chicago near her Haymarket "martyrs".

FURTHER READING
Drinnon, R.: *Rebel in Paradise* (Chicago, University of Chicago Press, 1961)
Wexler, A.: *Emma Goldman: An Intimate Life* (New York, Pantheon Books, 1984)

ELIZABETH KLEIN

Goldman, William (b.1911) English novelist. Born in the East End of London to immigrant parents and forced to leave school at 14 to start earning his living, Willy Goldman was, like many of his generation, largely self-educated. His urge to write was always strong, and some early pieces were published in the *Left Review* and John Lehmann's *New Writing*. From his experience of the slums and sweatshops, the degradation of unemployment and his own cultural frustration emerged the most effective contemporary novel of its genre, *East End My Cradle* (1940, republished 1988), an autobiographical tale of Jewish working-class life. While not lacking in sympathy and humor, it expresses above all his passionate indignation at a society which is responsible for the death of a genuinely promising artist and a gentle consumptive girl, and which stifles any artistic or literary aspirations. Against a background of petty criminals, ageing prostitutes ready to initiate young boys into sleazy sex, bug-ridden tenements, the vagaries of seasonal work in the tailoring trade, and estrangement from his family, he struggles to produce his first book and take a step out of the ghetto.

The problems of young writers continued to preoccupy him in three subsequent novels; *Light in the Dust* (1944), claims to be based on notes in the form of a diary of another East End Jewish writer who had committed suicide from a sense of total isolation and despair, but is probably partly autobiographical; *Some Blind Hand* (1946), and *The Forgotten Word* (1948), dwell on the difficulties of novel-writing. With *A Tent of Blue* (1946), Goldman returns to Jewish life of the prewar years, and the forced marriage, through unwanted pregnancy, of a couple far too young to take on domestic responsibilities. *A Start in Life* (1947) depicts a Jewish family ruled by a tyrannical father, a suffering mother dying of sheer exhaustion and the resigned assumption of her role by the daughter, while the elder son schemes for elusive business success and the younger son drifts into billiard halls and gambling, between genuine attempts to better himself. The "slack" and the "busy" dominate their lives as they struggle for economic security. The stories in *A Saint in the Making* (1951), almost all portray the life of the Jewish

East End with which, as a writer, Goldman was most at ease.

VERA COLEMAN

Goldmann, Nahum (1895–1982) international Jewish statesman. Born in Visznevo, Lithuania, Goldmann was reared and educated in Germany, receiving a law degree from Heidelberg in 1920 and a Ph.D. in 1921. Skilled in linguistics and diplomacy, Goldmann devoted his life to lobbying for Jewish causes. With Jacob Klatzkin, Goldmann founded Eshkol Press, which published 10 volumes of the *Encyclopaedia Judaica* in German and two in Hebrew, from 1928–34.

Following the First World War Goldmann was active in the Committee of Jewish Delegations, an umbrella organization of Jewish groups seeking guarantees of minority rights and representing Jewish interests in the disposition of Palestine in the framing of the Versailles Treaty. In 1936 the Committee was succeeded by the World Jewish Congress, which sought to safeguard Jewish rights and promote Jewish culture throughout the world. Goldmann served as president of the Congress until 1977.

As a committed Zionist, Goldmann served on the political committee of the Zionist Congress, and in 1935 came to New York to represent the Jewish Agency at the League of Nations. He lobbied the British and American governments for the partition of Palestine. He served as president of the World Zionist Organization from 1956 until 1968. Goldmann's opinions about the State of Israel were often iconoclastic and controversial. He criticized the failure of Israel to recognize the legitimacy of Diaspora Judaism, on the one hand, and Arab rights on the other. His belief in the ongoing importance of Diaspora Jewry led to the development of the Museum of the Diaspora in Tel Aviv.

Goldmann is best known as the pivotal force in the negotiations for German reparations after the Second World War. After organizing the centralized Conference on Jewish Material Claims, he met with Chancellor Konrad Adenauer in December 1951, to lay out the framework for a settlement, which encompassed payments in cash and goods to the State of Israel, as well as individual Jewish claimants. Goldmann established the Memorial Foundation for Jewish Culture with German funding, to sponsor and support a new generation of Jewish teachers and scholars.

BIBLIOGRAPHY

The Autobiography of Nahum Goldmann: Sixty Years of Jewish Life (New York: Holt, Rinehart & Winston, 1969); *The Jewish Paradox* (New York: Grosset & Dunlap, 1978)

JANE SHAPIRO

Goldmark, Karl (1830–1915) Hungarian composer, teacher, and conductor. Born into a poor Jewish family, one of 20 children, his father was the cantor of a local synagogue. Goldmark received his first basic instruction on the violin in 1841 and started to compose in 1842. In 1844 he went to Vienna for violin studies and in 1847 was accepted as a student at the Vienna Conservatory. He subsequently earned his living as a violinist in the theater orchestras, and taught piano. In 1858 he organized a concert of his own compositions before leaving for Budapest for further study. In 1859 he returned to Vienna and in 1860 became a music critic, championing the works of Richard Wagner. During this period his *String Quartet* Opus 8 gained him recognition as a composer. In 1865 his *Overture Sakuntala* Opus 13 was acknowledged as a work of importance. His first opera *Die Königin von Saba* which took almost ten years to complete, was produced in 1875 at the Vienna Court Opera, receiving much acclaim. Goldmark composed five more operas, two on English subjects *Das Heimchen am Herd*, based on Charles Dickens' *Cricket on the Hearth*, and *Ein Wintermärchen* (1908) based on Shakespeare's *A Winter's Tale*. His *Violin Concerto No 1 in A minor* (1827), has enjoyed much popularity among violinists. His musical language was influenced by many sources including Hungarian folk music and his early memories of the synagogue. He also composed much chamber music.

FURTHER READING

Káldor, M. and Várnai, P.: *Karl Goldmark: Life and Music.* (Budapest, 1956)

SYDNEY FIXMAN

Goldschmidt, Meïr Aron (1819–1887) Danish novelist and journalist. Goldschmidt was born in Vordingborg, Zeeland, where his father ran a grocery store. His parents were assimilated. At the age of seven he lived in Copenhagen for a year in order to improve his school education. There, in his aunt's home he encountered, for the first time, Jewish customs and Jewish festivals. These left an indelible impression on him and nourished his extensive writing. He observed that his "Danish birth and Jewish blood were the two factors determining [his] fate, and contestants for the right of way." Loyalty towards both the Danish and the Jewish attitude to the world became the basic element of thought as well as deed for him.

Not yet 21, in 1840, Goldschmidt launched *Corsaren* (1840–6; The corsair), the first satirical Danish magazine containing literary and political material. Appearing weekly, it was mostly written by himself. At its peak it reached a circulation of 3,000. The journal's basic concept was the devolution of absolute monarchy and the inauguration of the republic. Goldschmidt had no political affiliations, paid no allegiance to any specific powers in the literary establishment, and consequently was able to subvert anything. In the 1840s, *Corsaren* was the most progressive element in Danish public life and came to play a decisive role for Søren Kierkegaard.

Journalism became the breeding ground of Goldschmidt's fiction and he became the most significant forerunner of contemporary Danish realism. While *Corsaren* was still being published running, Goldschmidt published his first full-length work, the novel *En jøde* (1845; *A Jew*, 1852 and 1864). In this book Goldschmidt attempted to illustrate the position of a typical Jewish citizen, explaining his psychological makeup partly as a function of his religious and cultural environment. This novel became something of a sensation, for most Danes knew little or nothing about the life of the Jews in Denmark, or of Jewish culture. It was well written and well received but in Jewish circles it was seen as a kind of treason in that it made an open display of familial Jewish life. In the long run, however, the novel provided a step towards better understanding between Jew and Gentile in Denmark.

Goldschmidt's main *oeuvre*, the *bildungsroman*, *Hjemløs* (*A Poet's Inner Life*, 1861) appeared in instalments in *Nord og Syd* (1853–7). The novel's events confirm the existence of a Supreme Power, a Justice which punishes evil deeds and rewards good ones – combined with the notion that penalties are paid in this life.

Goldschmidt's are the first Danish novels to meet international standards, a fact of which he was himself aware. His stories, novels and dramas dominated Danish literature in the 1860s. 1865 saw his *Arvingen* (*The Heir*, 1865), another developmental novel, and in 1867 came his final novel *Ravnen* (The raven), which is also permeated by the idea of nemesis, this time through the agency of a round-shouldered, raven-like commissioner named Simon Levi. He became one of Goldschmidt's most original and popular characters, and appears again in *Maser* (1869).

Goldschmidt is at his best in his stories, produced over a lengthy period. His first collection of these, *Fortællinger* (Tales), containing, among others, "Erindringer fra min Onkels Hus" (Memories from my uncle's house), appeared in 1846; his own favorite was *Avromche Nattergal* (1871; *Avromche Nightingale*, 1928). His descriptions of Jewish families and groups remain interesting on account of his humorous empathy with his Jewish types.

Goldschmidt engaged in scholarly studies of the nemesis concept during the 1870s. The result appeared in the second volume of his *Livserindringer og Resultater* (1877; Memoirs and results). For Goldschmidt, who never fully embraced either Judaism or Christianity, nemesis became a religion.

FURTHER READING

Borum, P.: *Danish Literature* (Copenhagen: 1979) 44–45

Mitchell, P. M.: *A History of Danish Literature* (New York, 1971)
Ober, K. H.: *Meïr Goldschmidt* (Boston: 1976)

JUDITH WINTHER

Goldziher, Ignaz (1850–1921) Hungarian orientalist. He was born in Hungary and educated in Budapest and Vienna. Despite his outstanding international reputation he found it difficult to find appropriate employment in Hungary until 1904 and his appointment to a professorship at Budapest University. He also taught in the Budapest Rabbinical Seminary. He was in many ways the father of modern Islamic scholarship and established on a sound footing many areas of investigation which hitherto had been dealt with rather haphazardly. He described critically the history of the Islamic traditions (*hadith*) and Islamic sects, pre-Islamic culture, religious and legal history of the Arabs, and their ancient and modern poetry.

His *Beiträge zur Literaturgeschichte der Schi'a un-deder Sunnitischen Polemik* (1874) provides a fascinating analysis of contemporary documents on the nature of disputes between Shi'i and Sunni Islam. In *Die Zāhiriten* (1884) he describes the history of an important Islamic sect. His *Muhammedanische Studien* (1889–90; *Muslim Studies*, 1971) deals with a wide variety of topics concerning medieval Islam and its cultural impact. His work on Islam is important because of its critical orientation and its use of strict historical scholarship to examine the evidence for a particular interpretation of Islamic history.

Goldziher wrote a great deal on Jewish topics, in particular his *Der Mythos bei den Hebräern* (1876) and many other works in which he explored relations between Islam and Judaism, concentrating on Muslim critiques of Jewish theology. A pronounced anti-Zionist, he refused calls to influence his many friends in the Arab world in favour of Zionism after the founding of the Mandate in Palestine.

BIBLIOGRAPHY

Gesammelte Schriften (Hildesheim: Collectanea, 1967–73)

FURTHER READING

Ignace Goldziher Memorial Volume ed. S. Loewinger *et al.* (Budapest: 1948–58)

Patai, R.: *Ignaz Goldziher and his Oriental Diary* (1987)

OLIVER LEAMAN

Goll, Iwan [Issac Lang] (1891–1950) German–French poet and dramatist. Born in St Die, Alsace-Lorraine, Goll studied in Metz and Strassburg, receiving his doctorate in law in 1914. As a committed pacifist, he fled to Switzerland during the First World War, where he met and later married Claire Studer, a writer and poet with whom he subsequently collaborated in poetic ventures. He also associated with like-minded artists and intellectuals during this period, including Jules Romains, Franz WERFEL, James Joyce, and Stefan ZWEIG. Forced into exile during the Nazi period, he wrote resistance poetry and spent time in the USA, principally in Brooklyn, New York, and wrote poetry in English, in addition to German and French. He returned to France after the war.

Goll's career may be divided into three periods. The first phase was decidedly German expressionist. For example, he contributed his expressionist poetry to the early, sensation-arousing collection, *Menschheitsdämmerung* (1922; The twilight of mankind) edited by Kurt Pinthus. The second phase was French surrealist. In fact, he may have been the first person to use the term surrealism in the particular sense of a new "grotesque-satirical" drama form he was developing in the 1920s. He published his work, mostly French poetry, in *Surréalisme* and founded the short-lived journal *Hemisphères*, whose collaborators included André Breton, Saint John Perse, Denis de Rougement and Henry Miller. His late work has been seen to constitute a third phase, his symbolist period, which includes his flirtation with occult and mystical sources, including the *kabbalah*.

Growing up in a traditional Jewish household and in a bi-lingual cultural environment, Goll maneuvered intellectually between German, French, and Jewish tendencies, while cultivating a particular self-image as a cosmopolitan who was nowhere at home. In his dithyrambic *Noemie*, he seems to yearn for a new religion of spirit, in light of the perception of the Jewish heritage as overly fateful and burdensome. The figure of the homeless, wandering outsider, the modern Ahasver, played an important part in his work *Jean sans terre* (Jean without earth), as did the figures of Lilith and Job in *Hiob* and *Hiobs Revolte* (Job, Job's revolt). His works were translated into over twenty languages, but because of their difficult linguistic and formal characteristics, above all else, have never found a wide audience or broad critical acceptance.

BIBLIOGRAPHY

Landless John, trans. L. Abel, W. C. Williams, *et al.* (San Francisco: Crabhorn Press, 1944)

MARK H. GELBER

Gollancz, Victor (1893–1967) British publisher. Born into a prominent Orthodox Jewish family, Victor Gollancz was an exemplary scholar at St Paul's school and Oxford and an influential, experimental teacher on secondment from the armed services at Repton during the First World War. Rebelling against his family, he developed at an early age the interests that were characteristic of him for the rest of his life: a socialist consciousness, political curiosity, and an idiosyncratic intoxication with religion that was quasi-mystical. He considered Jesus's ministry as a culmination of the Jewish tradition to that date.

After making his reputation as a publisher in the 1920s at Ernest Benn Limited, Gollancz founded his own highly successful company in 1927. From the time Hitler took power in Germany in 1933, Gollancz felt compelled to concentrate considerable energy on political publishing, and launched the Left Book Club in 1936 with John Strachey and Harold Laski. His awareness of the Holocaust in Germany precipitated a nervous breakdown. He recovered, confirmed in his ecumenical and idealistic approaches both to religion and to society, and worked as a supporter of the Allies. He worked to save as many people from Hitler as possible throughout the war and was a founding member of the post-war Jewish Society for Human Services. He supported the establishment of the State of Israel after the War but also (more controversially) reconciliation with and reconstruction of Germany. He also caused considerable controversy and dismay by preaching the imperative need for Jews, especially, to help displaced Palestinian Arabs after 1948. He insisted on religious syncretism throughout the rest of his life and when Eichmann was brought to trial in Israel in the early 1960s, Gollancz vocally opposed the death penalty. The eloquence, logic and moving idealism of much of his thought was overlooked because of reactions to the insistently provocative and sometimes headstrong polemic of his writings. He was awarded the Order of Merit by West Germany in 1953 (the first non-German to be so honored) and a knighthood in 1965. An early advocate of nuclear disarmament and of a United Europe, his synthesis of socialism, liberalism, humanism and "Jewish Christianity" created much debate in his lifetime. His publishing house and its list remain as an important contribution to the artistic, political and religious life of the UK.

BIBLIOGRAPHY
"Nowhere to Lay their Heads": The Jewish Tragedy in Europe and its Solution (London: Victor Gollancz, 1945)
My Dear Timothy: An Autobiographical Letter to His Grandson (London: Victor Gollancz, 1952)

FURTHER READING
Edwards, R. D.: *Victor Gollancz, A Biography* (London: Gollancz, 1987)
Hodges, S.: *Gollancz: The Story of a Publishing House, 1928–78* (London: Gollancz, 1978)

MEL COOPER

Gomperz, Heinrich (1873–1942)

Austrian philosopher. Born in Vienna, Gomperz was the son of Theodor GOMPERZ. He studied at Vienna, Freiburg and Berlin. In 1900 he habilitated at Berne, and from 1905 lectured at Vienna. He was professor of philosophy there 1920–34, when he was forced to resign for not joining the Fatherland Front. In 1935 he emigrated to the USA. Gomperz wrote several works of philosophy; his ideas appeared in English in the posthumous volume *Philosophical Studies* (1953). He also edited the correspondence of his father (1974) and his aunt, Josephine von Wertheimstein (1981).

Gomperz is a link figure in Viennese culture. He was a close friend of Sigmund FREUD, whom he greatly admired, and close to the philosophers of the Vienna Circle, especially Carnap and NEURATH. He also knew many of Vienna's socialist leadership.

Gomperz followed his father in many things, moderating the latter's positivism, but maintaining the rationalist tradition. His attitude to his Jewish background was similarly a reflection of his father's assimilationist views. His conversion as a teenager to Catholicism was performed on strictly utilitarian grounds, to do away with "unnecessary" divisions in society. Nevertheless, he agreed with his father that Jewish minds were different from others, were too "bright" to be truly deep thinkers, and in this he seems to have included himself.

BIBLIOGRAPHY
ed. with R. A. Kann: *Theodor Gomperz: ein Gelehrtenleben im Bürgertum der Franz-Josephszeit* (Vienna: Österreichische Akademie der Wissenschaften, 1974)

STEVEN BELLER

Gomperz, Theodor (1832–1912)

Austrian classicist. Born in Brünn, Moravia, Gomperz was the brother of Josephine von Wertheimstein. He studied at Vienna, and from 1873–1901 was professor of classical philology there. Gomperz is best known for his three volume work, *Griechische Denker* (1896–1909; *Greek Thinkers* 1901–12, four vols). He approached Greek thought from a liberal and positivist viewpoint and was regarded by the Vienna Circle of philosophers as a central figure in Austrian positivist thought.

Gomperz's correspondence, published in *Theodor Gomperz: ein Gelehrtenleben im liberalen Bürgertum der Franz-Josephszeit* (1974; Theodor Gomperz: a scholar's life in the liberal bourgeoisie of Franz-Joseph's era) and his memoirs, published in Gomperz, *Essays und Erinnerungen* (1905; Essays and memoirs) give a comprehensive picture of his life and background. Gomperz was true to his family's liberal tradition; at the same time he was very proud of the scholarly tradition of his rabbinical ancestors. He was very sensitive to anything which might endanger assimilation. He had his son baptized in the interests of the new, unified society. He was thus opposed to any form of Jewish nationalism, including HERZL's Zionism, but also to anti-Semitism: he made a point of dining with Captain Dreyfus in 1902.

Gomperz occasionally speculated on the Jewish character, and accepted that it might be true that the Jewish mind was "too bright" to be truly creative. He argued, however, that such differences lay so deep that they were beyond the level of social relations, and, in any case, genius could overcome all limits. In this Gomperz shows the ambiguous faith of liberalism in assimilation.

BIBLIOGRAPHY

Greek Thinkers: A History of Ancient Philosophy, trans. L. Magnus (London: John Murray, 1901–12)

STEVEN BELLER

Goodman, Paul (1911–1972) American poet, social critic, and novelist. Goodman was a man who is remembered now either with fierce, devoted admiration or scorned as a figure who was for the most part popularized not for the originality of his ideas or skill of writing, but for his outrageous musings on anything from Aristotle to "gestalt" therapy. He was born in New York City on 9 September 1911, some months after his failing businessman father had abandoned the family. The youngest of three children, Goodman remembered being raised in an all-female household as his older brother had left the family as a teenager. At the age of nine, Goodman's sister Alice took over the care of the infant Paul and Alice and Paul's troubled relationship continued until her death in 1969. It was to this confusion of mother–sister roles, combined with the lack of a male role model, that Goodman later attributed his avowed bisexuality and hostility toward women.

A bright student, Goodman received a degree in philosophy from City College of New York in 1931 and went on to graduate study at the University of Chicago from 1936–40. Determined to be a writer, he published his first novel, *The Grand Piano*, in 1943 and a collection of short stories, *The Facts of Life* in 1945. Always insecure and isolated, he began to develop anarchist views that led to the book of essays *Art and Social Nature* and the novel *State of Nature* in 1946. In 1947, Goodman collaborated with his brother Percival on what is considered by some to be his finest social criticism, a study of utopian urban planning. In the late 1940s Goodman made his entrance into the marginal bohemian circles of New York society, where he began to experiment with psychoanalytic therapy and developed the theory of "gestalt therapy" along with F. S. Perls and R. Hefferline. During the 1950s, Goodman practised therapy and wrote for various journals, ending the decade with his masterpiece, *The Empire City* (1959).

In 1960 Goodman published *Growing Up Absurd*, a collection of topical social commentary that has been condemned as sexist and shallow, but which nevertheless was immensely popular and launched him into a career as public figure. Throughout the decade Goodman lectured at colleges, wrote poetry, dabbled in art and the theater, and became increasingly visible in social demonstrations protesting against academic intolerance and America's involvement in Vietnam. In 1967 his only son, Mathew, died in a mountaineering accident and Goodman fell into a depression that lasted until he died at his farm in North Stratford, New Hampshire.

FURTHER READING

Parisi, P.: *Artist of the Actual: Essays on Paul Goodman.* (Metuchen and London: The Scarecrow Press, Inc., 1986)
Widmer, K.: *Paul Goodman*, ed. W. French, (Boston: Twayne, 1980)

CAROLYN SHIELDS

Gordin, Jacob (1853–1909) Yiddish dramatist. Gordin was born in Mirgorod, Ukraine into a hasidic family. He moved to New York in 1891 where he lived until his death. The idealistic Gordin transformed the banality of existing Yiddish theater into a didactic forum which attempted to re-educate the cultural tastes of Jewish immigrants in New York. Through his efforts Yiddish theater became a major medium for informing and influencing the Jewish community who had not yet learned English, or had no desire to do so. He introduced themes of social awareness. He adapted or translated works from world literature including those by Goethe, Shakespeare, Ibsen, Hugo and Schiller. Such works include *Der yidisher keynig Lir* (1892; The Jewish King Lear) based on Shakespeare's play, and *Got, mentsh un tayvl*, (1900; God, man and the devil) adapted from Goethe's *Faust*. He built major rôles for his actors, inspiring in them new standards of language and acting skill. He also influenced new writing talent in the theater. Although the old style *Shund* plays continued to be written and performed, Gordin inspired future generations of the Yiddish theater with a striving for artistic excellence.

FURTHER READING

Zalmen Reyzen, *Leksikon fun der yidisher literatur, prese un filologye*, vol. 1, B. A. Kletskin (Vilna 1926), pp. 519–30

Leksikon fun der nayer yidisher literatur, vol. 2, Congress for Jewish Culture (New York 1958), pp. 142–53

DEVRA KAY

Gordis, Robert (b.1908)   Bible scholar and author. Gordis was born in Brooklyn, New York, and studied in New York City, graduating with distinction as a rabbi from the Jewish Theological Seminary in 1932. He then served as Professor of Religion at Columbia University and Temple University. He was Visiting Professor of Old Testament studies at the Union Theological Seminary, the only Jewish scholar to occupy this post at this famous Protestant institution. In 1970 he served as Visiting Professor of Bible at the Hebrew University in Jerusalem. He was awarded a Guggenheim Fellowship in 1973.

Gordis was President of the Synagogue Council of America, the overall body representing all wings of American Judaism, and of the Rabbinical Assembly, the international association of the Conservative rabbinate. He was made Rabbi Emeritus of Temple Beth El of Rockaway

Park, where he served as rabbi for over thirty years. He founded the oldest existing Conservative day school in the USA, the Beth El School in Rockaway Park, now called the Robert Gordis Day School.

Gordis published more than twenty books in the field of biblical scholarship and in the area of religion and its relevance to Jewish and general contemporary life. His biblical scholarship encompasses the Wisdom Literature (for example the Song of Songs, Ecclesiastes and Job); biblical poetry and the *masorah* (the traditional annotations to the biblical text). Gordis has also discussed religion and contemporary problems, in particular the position of Judaism and its role in the modern world. An important work is *A Faith for Moderns* (1960), a presentation of religious values and concepts; *Love and Sex: A Modern Jewish Perspective* (1978), which received the Jewish Welfare Board National Book Award as the outstanding work in the field of Jewish thought.

Gordis contributed to numerous journals in the USA, UK and Israel and held the editorship of *Judaism*, a quarterly journal dedicated to Jewish religion, philosophy and ethics as well as holding the posts of Professor Emeritus of Bible and the Philosophies of Religion at the JTS, and Chairman of the Commission on the Ideology of Conservative Judaism.

BIBLIOGRAPHY

Koheleth: The Man and His World (New York: Schocken, 1951)

JOHN MATTHEW

Gordon, Judah Loeb [YaLaG] (1831–1892) Hebrew poet. Gordon was born in Vilna. An erudite talmudist, possessing a profound knowledge of Hebrew and related languages, he taught himself modern and classical languages, and became one of the first Hebrew writers to be thoroughly acquainted with Russian literature. As a young man he was one of the leading *maskilim* (enlighteners) in Vilna and from 1853 he taught in Jewish government schools. His early poetry showed the influence of the LEBENSOHNS in its romanticism and in his themes borrowed from the Bible, such as *Ahavat David*

281

veMikhal (1857; The love of David and Michal) and *Asenat bat Potipherah* (1868; Asenath, the daughter of Potiphar), or from medieval Jewish history, such as *Bimetzulot yam* (In the depths of the sea) which describes a fearful episode in the expulsion of the Jews from Spain in 1492. He also published a collection of fables, mostly taken from La Fontaine and Krylov, together with aggadic and midrashic fables, *Mishlei Yehudah* (1859; The fables of Judah). Most of his poems, however, are devoted to mirroring Jewish life in Russia in his day, and directed against the conditions of the Jewish communities. His poem, *Hakitzah 'ammi*, (1863; Awake, my people), became the watchword of the Russian *Haskalah*. Gordon later used historical themes as frames for his criticism of the supremacy of religion in Jewish life, and of Jewish communal organization. He painted a severe portrait of the unenlightened life of the Jewish masses which he laid at the feet of the religious leaders. His series of poems, *Korot yameinu* (The events of our days) which includes *Bekotzo shel yod* (1876; On the point of a *yod*) and *Shenei Yosef ben Shimon* (Two Joseph ben Simons), respectively express outrage at the plight of Jewish women and sympathy for other underprivileged sections of the community.

In 1865 Gordon moved to St Petersburg where he became secretary of the Jewish community and director of the Society for the Promotion of Culture among the Jews. In 1879, as a result of an accusation by the hasidim, he was imprisoned for a short while for political conspiracy. On his release, he became editor of *Hamelitz*, but from this time despair and disappointment began to characterize his work.

Like M. L. LILIENBLUM and others, Gordon was destined for disappointment with the outcome of the *Haskalah* which brought the east European Jews no closer to emancipation without the loss of their Jewish identity. His conviction that isolation was the source of the Jewish problem ("Be a Jew at home and a man in the street" is one of his most famous aphoristic lines) changed with the growing intensity of Russian anti-Semitism. Whereas he had urged his people to religious reform, to learn Russian, to adapt to the Gentile environment, first the assimilation of the young Jews and then the

Judah Loeb Gordon

pogroms of 1881 changed his mind. His *Lemi ani 'amel* (For whom do I labor) is a protest against assimilation. Yet he did not see the land of Israel as a solution and advocated emigration to the USA.

Gordon's importance to the *Haskalah* is undisputed; his significance as a social commentator, translator, feuilletonist and linguistic innovator has forged him an honorable place in the history of Hebrew literature. His poetry, admired by H. N. BIALIK, lacks certain elements of liveliness: his descriptions of nature and love, for example, do not attain the quality of M. Y. Lebensohn's, yet Gordon's poetry is superior in style and structure, and it is in his creation of Hebrew realist poetry that his major contribution lies.

FURTHER READING

Raisin, J. S.: *The Haskalah Movement in Russia* (Philadelphia: The Jewish Publication Society of America, 1913)

Waxman, M.: *A History of Jewish Literature* (New York: Bloch, 1960) vol. 3, 233–55

GLENDA ABRAMSON

Gordon, Samuel (1871–1927) British novelist. Born in Buk, Bavaria, Gordon moved to England at the age of 13. He was educated at the City of London School and Cambridge University. In 1894 he began to publish short stories based on his mother's folk-tales about the Russian Pale of Settlement in the eighteenth century. This resulted in his first collection, *A Handful of Exotics: Scenes and Incidents Chiefly of Russo-Jewish life* 1897, followed by a novel, *In Years of Transition* (1898) which was set in Paris, and *Daughters of Shem, and Other Stories* (1898) which was composed mainly of anglicized Yiddish folk-tales about Jewish women in the Pale of Settlement. The title story of this volume, *Daughters of Shem* was rewritten as a stage play and occasionally staged in London until the 1920s.

With the publication of *Sons of the Covenant: A Tale of Anglo-Jewry* (1900) Gordon established himself as a significant British Jewish novelist who was writing in the tradition of Israel ZANGWILL's *Children of the Ghetto* (1892) and who could command a large readership. Gordon was given a dinner by the Maccabaeans in celebration of the publication of this novel and it was highly praised by the London *Jewish Chronicle* in particular. As the novel's main theme was the eventual dissolution of the Jewish East End and the marriage of poor immigrant Jews with the respectable Jewish elite, one can view the promotion of this novel as a reaction to the growing anti-immigrant anti-Semitism in England at the turn of the century. Gordon was to reverse this rather apologetic picture of Anglo-Jewry with a satirical attack on the materialism of Anglo-Jewry's elite in *Unto Each Man his Own* (1904) which also dealt with the thorny question of intermarriage and which caused a prolonged controversy within Anglo-Jewry.

Gordon also wrote a Russian–Jewish novel *The Ferry of Fate* (1905), but his final collection of short stories set in the Pale of Settlement,

God's Remnants: Tales of Israel Among the Nations (1916), is his most interesting work on this theme. Other works published include five romances, a cockney novel *Lesser Destinies* (1899), and a children's story. Gordon was also a brilliant linguist and worked for the Censorship Division of the Foreign Office during the First World War.

BRYAN CHEYETTE

Gottlieb, Adolph (1903–1974) American painter. Gottlieb was born in New York City, where he received most of his formal artistic training. He first enrolled in the Art Students League in 1920. While a two-year stay in Paris and Germany stimulated his interest in modern art, his early work is reminiscent of the realist style of the American Ash-Can painter John Sloan, with whom he had studied at the League.

In the 1930s Gottlieb's work became more expressionistic and abstract and in the 1940s he became associated with Mark ROTHKO and other young artists involved in the emerging group of Abstract Expressionists. Under the concomitant influences of Surrealism, Cubism and primitive art he created his "Pictographic" series of 1941 to 1951. The paintings of his next series, *Grids and Imaginary Landscapes* of 1951–7, present skies filled with disk shapes floating above landscapes or seascapes. His last group of paintings (1957–74), *Bursts*, present the most simplified compositions: uniform color fields containing disk shapes hovering above bundles of thick, black strokes.

Gottlieb had solo exhibitions at the Jewish Museum in New York in 1957 and the Walker Art Center in Minneapolis in 1963. A 1968 retrospective was sponsored jointly in New York by the Solomon R. Guggenheim Museum and the Whitney Museum of American Art. A posthumous traveling retrospective was organized by the Adolph and Esther Gottlieb Foundation in 1981.

FURTHER READING

Doty, R., and Waldman, D.: *Adolph Gottlieb* (New York: Frederick A. Praeger for the Whitney Museum of American Art and The Solomon R.

Guggenheim Museum, 1968) [exhibition catalog]

MacNaughton, M. D., and Alloway, L.: *Adolph Gottlieb: A Retrospective* (New York; The Arts Publisher in association with the Adolph and Esther Gottlieb Foundation, 1981)

KRISTIE A. JAYNE

Gottlieb, Jack (b.1930) American composer and conductor. Gottlieb was educated at Queens College, Brandeis University, and the University of Illinois, where he received a BA, MFA, and DMA, respectively. His major teachers were Irving Fine, Harold SHAPERO, Burrill Phillips and, at Tanglewood, Aaron COPLAND and Boris Blacher. During his formative years, Gottlieb spent his summers at the Brandeis Camp Institute in California, where he was encouraged to express his Judaism in his art by Max Helfman and Robert Strassberg. This influence and love of American show tunes, jazz, art songs, and opera have pervaded his musical output. Although he played the clarinet and piano, he was most active in singing groups during both his high school and college years, even singing in the New York Schola Cantorum under the direction of Hugh Ross.

His love for Jewish music, Jewish subjects, and the Yiddish theater stage is evident in his compositions. He has written a Friday Evening Service called *Love Songs for Sabbath* (1965), a *New Year's Service for Young People* (1970), *Verses from Psalm 118* (1973), and many shorter works for the synagogue.

Gottlieb taught at Loyola University in New Orleans in 1966 at the Institute in Judaic Arts at Warwick, New York from 1966–7; he became music director of Congregation Temple Israel in St Louis in 1970 and in 1973 was named composer-in-residence at the Sacred School of Music at the Hebrew Union College in New York. He has long been associated with Leonard BERNSTEIN, first as his assistant at the New York Philharmonic (1958–66), and in 1979 he joined Bernstein's publishing firm, Amberson Enterprises Inc., forming an outlet for publishing his own works.

Gottlieb's major works include operas,

orchestral works, song cycles and chamber music. In 1972 he devised a multimedia lecture entertainment which he calls *From Shtetl to Stage Door, A Melting Pot-pourri Showing the Jewish Influence on the American Musical Theater*. This has proven to be a most successful presentation and has been given numerous times.

SAMUEL H. ADLER

Gottlieb, Maurycy (1856–79) Polish painter. A brilliant, sensitive artist who died at the age of 23, Gottlieb has become a romantic figure in the history of Jewish art; his role is consequently difficult to assess.

Raised in Galicia, Gottlieb's prococious talent was fostered in the liberal atmosphere of the *Haskalah* movement, and at the age of 16 he was sent to Krakow to study at the Academy. Here he came under the influence of his teacher Jan Matejko (a strong Polish nationalist), and began producing patriotic scenes from Polish history. The allure of assimilation at this time is reflected in the first of Gottlieb's major self-portraits, in which he portrays himself in the costume of a Polish aristocrat, his features modified and refined, his expression profoundly uneasy.

Traveling to Germany and Austria, Gottlieb discovered in the work of Rembrandt a new way of handling paint and – of greater personal significance – a way of painting Jews without descending into the literalness or caricature which marred the Jewish art of his own day. There followed a number of deeply introspective self-portaits, of which the finest is the melancholic *Ahasver, the Wandering Jew*. Gottlieb's struggle for a style and for a role culminates in *Yom Kippur*, the painting for which he is best known. Here in the gloom of the synagogue, the artist stands sorrowing in the midst of his community, surrounded by relatives both living and dead. The nearby Torah mantle is signed "In memory of Moshe Gottlieb, may it be blessed, in the year 5638". He died within a year.

Gottlieb never developed a fully personal style of painting and so his reputation cannot rest on his talent alone. Rather, it is based on the way he transformed himself into an archetype of the emancipated Jew, searching for an identity in the modern world.

FURTHER READING

Narkiss, M.: *Maurycy Gottlieb* (Jerusalem: Bezalel National Museum, 1956) [exhibition catalog]

Roth, C. *Jewish Art: An Illustrated History* (London: Vallentine, Mitchell & Co., 1971)

LAURA JACOBUS

Goudsmit, Samuel ["Sam"] (1884–1954)

Dutch–Jewish author. Goudsmit was born of poor Jewish parents in the provincial town of Kampen, at the mouth of the river IJssel, where in his childhood both the division between the non-Jewish majority and the Jews, and that between the small number of Jewish notables and the Jewish poor, were strong. This filled him with bitterness and as a young man, newly settled in Amsterdam, it alienated him from his Jewish environment and made him join the Communist party. He sought in particular to expose social abuses, and his naturalism was influenced by established authors such as Herman HEIJERMANS and Israel QUERIDO.

Several of his early novels are situated in his native Kampen, although the town is not mentioned by name, and return to memories of a Jewish childhood. Among them are *Dievenschool* (1905), *In de Grote Leerschool* (1913), and much later, *Jankefs Jongste* (1929; Jankef's youngest child) and *Jankefs Oude Sleutel* (1930; Jankef's old key), all of which end tragically.

With the rise of Nazism in Germany Goudsmit threw in his lot with the persecuted Jews and wrote *Simcha, de knaap uit Worms* (1936; Simcha, the boy from Worms), about the persecution of the Jews in the Rhine provinces during the Crusades. He published a sequel to this after the German occupation, the last years of which he spent in hiding, as *De Gouden Kroon van Beieren* (1952; The golden crown of Bavaria).

HENRIETTE BOAS

Grade, Chaim (1910–1982)

Yiddish poet and short-story writer. Grade was born in Vilna, Lithuania, the traditional center of Jewish scholarship and studied at various *yeshivas*. He belonged to the "Young Vilna" writers' group who stood against social injustice. His first poems were published in 1936. His poems are either lyrics or long narratives interlaced with reflective passages. He arrived in New York in 1948 where he lived until his death and firmly established a reputation as a Yiddish poet. His works include: *Musernikes* (1939) about the followers of the *muser* (ethics) movement to which he belonged in his *yeshiva* days; *Yo* (1936; Yes), his first lyrical work; and *Der mames tsavoe* (1949; My mother's will), where he idealized his mother who worked ceaselessly to pay for his education and was killed by the Nazis in 1941. Poems against the Germans' actions in the war include: *Doyres* (1945; Generations) and *Pleytim* (1947; Refugees) and the postwar *Di agune* (1961), *Der mentsh fun fayer* (1962; Man of fire) and *Tsemakh Atlas* (1967). Grade began writing short stories late in life, including "My quarrel with Hersh Rasseyner", a religious–philosophical discussion between a committed Jew and a non-believing narrator, and "Mayn mame's shabosim" (1955; My mother's sabbaths), and three short novels comprising *Der shulhoyf* (1958; The synagogue courtyard) about pre-war Vilna.

DEVRA KAY

Graetz, Heinrich (1817–1891)

German–Jewish historian, founder of modern Jewish historiography. Born in the region of Poznan (Posen), then under Prussian rule, Graetz had a traditional religious education, then studied at Breslau and Jena, and, in 1853, after many vicissitudes became teacher at the newly founded Jewish Seminary in Breslau. His major work is his 11-volume *Geschichte der Juden*, published between 1853 and 1876, which became the major source of knowledge about Jewish history for generations of educated Jews in central and eastern Europe, and was translated into several languages. His systematic approach to Jewish history was published in 1846 as a long essay under the title *Über die Konstruktion der jüdischen Geschichte*.

Graetz's historical opus was influenced greatly by Hegel and Ranke, and was intended to be a rebuttal both to conventional Christian historiography as well as to Jewish Reform attitudes which viewed Judaism mainly in religious terms and hence denied the very possibility of Jewish history as such. Viewing the Jews as a people, and not merely as a community of believers, Graetz argued that the Jews have a distinct history with specific structures and institutions which have undergone considerable changes over the generations, but nevertheless evince a clear continuity representing a number of elements peculiar to the Jewish *Volksgeist* ("national spirit").

According to Graetz, the moment Judaism entered history it appeared as a protest, a revolt against paganism. Paganism is understood by Graetz as the cult of nature and of the material aspects of reality, whereas the Jewish people raised its antithesis, spirit, as an object of worship: this, to Graetz, is the core of Jewish monotheism. Yet this monotheism is to be understood not as a mere abstract idea, but is objectified in an historical entity – the People of Israel.

The Jewish people is, according to Graetz, the only people whose political institutions claim to objectify a divine message, and hence religion and politics are intertwined in Judaism and persist – in the semi-political structures of Jewish communal life – also in the Diaspora. Judaism is further distinct from Christianity in its emphasis on this world and in its communitarian orientation – being a religion aimed at the survival of a social group (the People of Israel) and not the salvation of individual souls. This communitarian nature of Judaism enabled it to survive as a national culture even after the loss of its territorial base and political sovereignty. The concentration of Jewish messianism on the future – a direct outcome of its politico-religious nexus – was equally connected with a vision of redemption connected with a terrestrial *Eretz Israel*. Thus Graetz sees in Reform Judaism, as it developed in nineteenth-century Germany, a travesty of the historical nature of Judaism. Graetz maintained that either of the two modes of Jewish existence – the political and the religious – can appear as dominant in any given period, and his periodization of Jewish history evolves around the relative prominence of these two modes of the Jewish historical experience.

Though Graetz did not explicitly call for a return to Palestine, his communitarian and national reading of Jewish history meant that his approach was relevant to new interpretations of Jewish history in the light of the emergence of Zionism. Moses HESS, one of the precursors of modern Zionism, was greatly influenced by Graetz and also translated some of his writings into French.

BIBLIOGRAPHY
History of the Jews, 6 vols (repr. Philadelphia: The Jewish Publication Society of America, 1967); *The Structure of Jewish History* trans. I. Schorsch, New York, 1975

FURTHER READING
Avineri, S.: *The Making of Modern Zionism* (New York: Basic Books, 1981)
Baron, S.: *History and Jewish Historians* (Philadelphia: The Jewish Publication Society of America 1964) 269–75

SHLOMO AVINERI

Green, Gerald (b.1922)   American novelist. Gerald Green was born in Brooklyn, New York in 1922, son of Samuel Greenburg, a physician, and Anna Ruth Matzkin Greenberg. In 1942 he received an AB from Columbia and an MS in journalism in 1947. Green, a heavily biographical writer, draws on his Brooklyn and Columbia experiences in much of his work.

Dr Samuel Abelman in *The Last Angry Man* (1956), Green's first critical success, and Dr Sol Abrams in *To Brooklyn with Love* (1967) are both modeled after Green's own father. The doctors are honest, concerned men, battling against meaner characters in a decaying area of Brooklyn in the 1930s. *An American Prophet* (1977) is Green's fictional tribute to the late Joseph Wood Krutch, literary critic and professor at Columbia whom Green greatly esteemed. The novel concentrates on Krutch's years of retirement in Arizona.

Green calls himself a writer of "thematic novels". "I hate to sound like a sociologist, but I want to write about important issues" (*Pub-*

lishers *Weekly* 1977); the Holocaust is one of these issues. *The Legion of Noble Christians* (1965), *The Artists of Terezin* (1969), and the teleplay and novel, *Holocaust* (1978), perhaps Green's greatest popular success, each offer a humanized and rounded depiction of the Holocaust.

About his work Green says, "I always approach a new novel, not as some august observer of the human scene, but as someone entering a course of study – what can I learn?" (*Publishers Weekly* 1977). Readers of Green ought to adopt the same approach.

BIBLIOGRAPHY

The Sword and the Sun (1953); *Murfy's Men* (1981)

FURTHER READING

Baker, J. F.: *Publishers Weekly* Interviews Gerald Green. *Publishers Weekly*, 211 (1977) 10–11

Harap, L. In the mainstream: The Jewish presence in twentieth-century American literature, 1950s–1980s. In *Contributions in Ethnic Studies Number 19* (New York: Greenwood Press, 1987)

ALLISON HUTON

Greenberg, Joanne [Hannah Green] (b.1932)

American novelist and short-story writer. Born in Brooklyn, New York, Greenberg received her undergraduate degree from American University. The mother of two, she has been an adjunct professor at the Colorado School of Mines and is a certified medical technician.

Although her first book *The King's Persons* (1963), which deals with the explosive relationship that existed between the Jewish moneylenders and Christian barons in twelfth-century England, was highly praised for its use of historical detail in capturing medieval everyday life, it was *I Never Promised You a Rose Garden*, (1964), her autobiographical novel published under the pseudonym Hannah Green, that captured critical attention. The moving story of Deborah Blau, a sixteen-year-old schizophrenic and her struggle, with the help of a tough-minded, brilliant psychiatrist, to overcome mental illness, received praise from both the literary and psychiatric communities. Deborah's escape into her private kingdom of Yr was an escape from a

private vulnerability sometimes heightened by her awareness of her Jewish vulnerability. As she moves between fantasy and the reality of the mental hospital in which she is undergoing treatment, the reader comes to understand the attraction of madness for this sensitive young woman and to applaud her successful resistance.

Subsequent novels, *The Monday Voices* (1965) and *In This Sign* (1968), are concerned with the problems of the disadvantaged and handicapped, the second about the difficulties faced by a deaf couple. Later novels, *Founders Praise* (1976) and *A Season of Delight* (1981) explore religious themes, the latter about a middle-aged Jewish woman whose children have rejected her loving connection to Jewish life for radical feminism and Hare Krishna.

The recipient of the Daroff and Epstein awards from the National Jewish Welfare Board, Greenberg has also published three collections of short stories: *Summering* (1966), *Rites of Passage* (1971), and *High Crimes and Misdemeanors* (1979). In these, she addresses her recurrent themes of good and evil, her belief in traditional values, and a playful invocation of mystical fantastic powers to right the unfairnesses of life.

FURTHER READING

Kinsman, C. D., ed.: *Contemporary Authors*, vol. 14 (Detroit: Gale Research Co., 1985) 203–5

Riley, C., ed.: *Contemporary Literary Criticism*, vols 7, 30 (Detroit: Gale Research Co., 1977, 1984)

ELIZABETH KLEIN

Greenberg, Uri Zvi (1891–1981)

Hebrew and Yiddish poet. Born in Bilkamin, Galicia, to a line of hasidic rabbis, and educated in Lvov, Greenberg began writing poetry in Hebrew and Yiddish in 1912. As a soldier in the Austrian army during the First World War, he was witness to the horrors of war generally and also to pogroms against the Jews. These left their imprint on his extensive early poetic output in Yiddish, and later emerged as literary archetypes of his Hebrew opus.

Greenberg was among the founders of Yiddish expressionism in Warsaw, writing during

1921 and 1922 in such short-lived journals as *Albatross* and *Khaliastra* (The gang), together with Melekh RAVICH and Peretz MARKISH. His *Mefisto*, a collection of nihilistic, world-weary verse, dates from this period. After some time in Berlin, where he met Franz WERFEL and Else LASKER-SCHÜLER, Greenberg moved – under the impact of the Ukranian pogroms and his personal encounters with anti-Semitism – from universal to intensely nationalistic themes. In December 1923 he left for Palestine, abandoning the Europe he viewed as "kingdom of the cross", and abandoning his "mother tongue", Yiddish, for Hebrew, the "blood language of the Hebrew wanderer". From Palestine he published, prolifically, poems of extraordinary emotional intensity such as *Yerushalayim shel matah* (Earthly Jerusalem). This poem appeared in his collection *Emah gedolah veyare'ah* (1924; A great terror and the moon), and was followed by *Hagavrut ha'olah* (1925; The rising), and *Anacreon 'al kotev ha'itzavon* (1928; Anacreon at the pole of sadness), to mention but a few. His poems of this period reflect the influence of Walt Whitman as well as the Hebrew prophets, as may be seen in his poem "With my God, the blacksmith" (analyzed in S. BURNSHAW, E. SPICEHANDLER, and T. CARMI: *The Modern Hebrew Poem Itself*, 1965).

Greenberg's poems of the 1930s, such as those in *Ezor magen une'um ben hadam* (1930; A shield of defense and the word of the son of blood), and in *Sefer hakitrug veha'emunah* (1937; The book of accusation and faith) reflect his increasing politicization. His active role in the leadership of Revisionist Zionism colored his depiction of life in Palestine, and many poems began to sound like partisan diatribes in verse. From that period on, Greenberg became the object of veneration for extremist factions on the right of the Israeli political spectrum, while others attacked him with such epithets as "racist".

The Holocaust caused Greenberg to produce extraordinary verse, combining profound lament with thunderous affirmations of the Jews' will to survive and of their "manifest destiny" to resurrect the image of Jewish sovereignty. These poems were collected in one of the great classics of Jewish literature, Greenberg's *Rehovot hanahar*

(1946; Streets of the river). Greenberg continued to write until close to the time of his death.

FURTHER READING

Alter, R.: A poet of the Holocaust. *Defenses of the Imagination* (Philadelphia: The Jewish Publication Society of America, 1978) Band, A.: The "rehabilitation" of Uri Zvi Greenberg. *Prooftexts* 1 (1981) 316–26

Arnon, Y., ed.: *Uri Zvi Greenberg: A Bibliography of his Works and of what was Written about him* (Jerusalem: Adi Moses, 1980)

Hever, H., ed.: *Uri Zvi Greenberg on his Eightieth Anniversary* (Jerusalem: Jewish National and University Library, 1977) [exhibition catalog]

Kahn, Shalom J. Uri Zvi Greenberg: Poet of Kingship. *Ariel*, 13, 1966, 35–52

Mintz, A.: *Hurban* (New York: Columbia University Press, 1984)

Nash, S.: The development of some key metaphors in Uri Zvi Greenberg's poetry. *Hebrew Studies* 24 (1983) 121–35

Yudkin, L. The "Mission" of Uri Zvi Greenberg. *Modern Hebrew Literature*, autumn 1976, 3–11

STANLEY NASH

Grinshpan, Yosl (1902–1934) Yiddish poet. Born in Kletsk in the district of Minsk, Grinshpan emigrated to Canada in 1918, and then to New York where he began to publish poetry in 1927 in the journal *Hamer*. His first work was *Tsvishn vent* (Among walls) which comprised half the volume *Erev tsayt* (1931; On the eve of time), published jointly with the poet Leyb Sobrin whose half of the volume is called *Tsvishn mentshn* (Among people). His second book, *Lider un poemes* (1937; Songs and poems) was published after his death.

Grinshpan was a member of the Yiddish writers' organization *Proletpen* but his voice was always heard clearly through the multitudinous crowd of the proletarian poets. He was a stormy poet whose imagery had speed and fire. His poems portray the scornful fists of the jobless poor during the depression years and the struggle of the downtrodden. His shorter love poems sparkle with the grace and charm of his fantastic maiden Santaluria, while his longer poems display great versatility and vision, and use

Utopian metaphors. Most of Grinshpan's poetry is down to earth, intense, vivid and powerful. There is some affinity between his poems and the poetry of Andrew Chenier who influenced the French Romantic movement. Both died at the age of 32. Chenier died on the gallows, Grinshpan, hungry and homeless, of cancer brought on by malnutrition in the 1930s.

MENKE KATZ

Gronemann, Samuel (1875–1952) Lawyer, German satirist, and Zionist activist. Born in Strassburg in a traditional, religious Jewish family, Groneman studied at the Rabbinical Seminary in Halberstadt, before enrolling in the law faculty at the university in Berlin. As a religious Jew, he joined the Zionist organization, attending Zionist Congresses as a delegate from 1901. He was a member of the Zionist Action Committee and later became president of the Zionist Congress Court. He served on the Eastern Front in the First World War, where he encountered east European Jewry and worked as an army translator from Yiddish to German. Later, he turned to journalism, drama, and satiric fiction, and some of his major works deal with east European Jewry, notably his novel *Tohuwabohu* (1920). This novel also makes a strong pro-Zionist, anti-assimilationist argument. His comic, satiric characterizations of traditional eastern European Jews served to lessen deep-seated misunderstandings between Jewish East and West. Also, Gronemann was instrumental in bringing the Vilna Yiddish Theater Company to western Europe, the impact of which among even highly acculturated central European Jews was quite significant.

Gronemann's comedies were adapted for the Hebrew stage, after he settled in Tel Aviv in 1936. In *Jakob und Christian* (1936), he attacked Nazi racial theories. In *Der Weise und der Narr: König Salomo und der Schuster* (1942; The wise man and the fool: King Solomon and the Cobbler), he exercised his comic wit in a biblical setting. A Hebrew version of this comedy was set to music and became the first successful Hebrew musical comedy.

MARK H. GELBER

Gropper, William (1897–1979) American political cartoonist and painter who, throughout his career, identified with the oppressed. Born in New York's Lower East Side of an immigrant family, Gropper's parents were among the many Jews who worked in the garment industry's sweatshops. Leaving school at the age of 14, Gropper worked carrying bolts of cloth, experiencing first-hand the inequities and physical humiliation of the immigrant poor. His first training in art was under Robert Henri and George Bellows at the liberal Ferrer School. He also studied at the New York School of Fine and Applied Art.

In 1920 he was hired as a political and social cartoonist for the *New York Tribune*. It was in this position that he first used his artistic talents in aid of liberal causes. He later worked for a number of liberal publications including *The Rebel Worker, New Masses* and *The Sunday Worker*. In 1924 he began contributing daily to the liberal Yiddish paper, the *Freiheit*. During the 1920s and 1930s he contributed to leading magazines such as the *New Yorker* and *Vanity Fair*.

Gropper began to paint in 1921, adding the subjects of American folklore and regional lifestyles to his repertoire of themes. He always painted in a representational style, borrowing elements of angularity from Cubism that by the 1920s was almost an international style. His experience as a political cartoonist, creating images rapidly and with only those elements necessary for communication, influenced his painting style. As a painter, Gropper was part of New York's circle of Yiddish artists, exhibiting at the Jewish Art Center in the 1920s. During the 1930s, Gropper received commercial and government mural commissions, including a mural for Schenley Distilleries in 1934, a mural on a colonial American theme for Hotel Taft, a mural sponsored by the Works Progress Administration (WPA) for the Post Office in Freeport, Long Island, and a mural in the Department of the Interior building in Detroit.

The tragic events of the Holocaust caused Gropper, as well as a number of other American–Jewish artists, to turn to Jewish themes. His most noted work on the theme is *De Profundis*, 130th Psalm "Out of the Depths have I Called Thee, O Lord" (1943). In 1966 he also painted a work in memory of the victims of the Warsaw Ghetto.

In 1967 Gropper designed a series of stained glass windows for Temple Har Zion in River Forest, Illinois. Late in life, nostalgia for life in eastern Europe that he had experienced only second-hand motivated *The Shtetl*, a portfolio of colored lithographs that Gropper acknowledged as "...looking for my roots...a village and people that no longer exists, but a faint memory" (Introduction to *The Shtetl*.)

FURTHER READING
Freundlich, A. L.: *William Gropper: Retrospective* (Los Angeles: Ward Ritchie Press in conjunction with the Joe and Emily Lowe Art Gallery of the University of Miami, 1968) [exhibition catalog]
Gropper (New York: ACA Gallery Publications; New Masses Editions, 1938) [exhibition catalog]

BARBARA GILBERT

Gross, Chaim (b.1904)

American sculptor and graphic artist. Born in Galicia to a hasidic Jewish family, the joyousness of life consistently influenced his work, regardless of the subject matter. The abundance of wood in the heavily forested Carpathian Mountains where he grew up, and the native skill for woodworking there affected his choice of medium and technique of working. After fleeing from his family home during the 1916 Cossack invasion of the Jews of Galicia, he studied in 1919 at the short-lived National Art School in Budapest founded under the Radical Socialist government of Karolyi. In 1920 following the fall of the Karolyi government, Gross went to Vienna where he studied in the Kunstgewerbeschule. He emigrated to the USA in 1921 with the help of his brother, Naftoli Gross, a Yiddish poet who had preceded him to the USA. Settling in New York, in 1921 he began to study sculpture at the Educational Alliance where he met fellow immigrant artists Raphael, Moses and Isaac SOYER, Philip Evergood, Saul Berman, Louis Ribak, and Peter BLUME. He simultaneously studied modeling at the Beaux Arts Institute of Design where Elie Nadelman was one of his teachers. He also studied at the Art Students League under Robert Laurent.

Adopting a primal, direct method of carving in wood, Gross fashioned sculptures dealing with a broad range of figurative subjects: single and multi-figured acrobats, mother and child figures, genre themes, portraits, and since the 1950s, Judaic and biblical themes. After the 1950s Gross made the transition from carving to modeling, casting his works in bronze.

Biblical and Judaic themes have dominated his work following several trips to Israel. He has received several important commissions for synagogues including cast monumental *menorot* at Temple Sinai in Pittsburgh, Pennsylvania, Congregation Adath Jeshuran in Elkins Park, Pennslyvania and the Menorah Home for the Aged in Brooklyn. He created six nine-and-a-half-feet-high bronze relief panels on the Ten Commandments for the International Synagogue at Kennedy Airport in New York. Commissions in Jerusalem include *Birds of Peace* (1959–1966) for the campus of Hebrew University and *Mother Praying* for the Hadassah Hospital.

Gross' work is represented in some fifty museums, mainly in the United States and Israel, including The Metropolitan Museum of Art, the Newark Museum of Art, The Philadelphia Museum of Fine Art, The Art Institute of Chicago, the Whitney Museum of American Art, The Jewish Museum in New York, the Hebrew Union College Skirball Museum in Los Angeles, the Tel Aviv Museum of Art, and the Billy Rose Garden of the Israel Museum.

BIBLIOGRAPHY
Lombardo, J. V.: *Chaim Gross: Sculptor* (New York: Dalton House Inc., 1949)
Getlein, F.: *Chaim Gross* (New York, 1974)

BARBARA GILBERT

Grossbard, Batia (b.1910)

Israeli artist. Born in Ostrow in Poland, Grossbard emigrated to Palestine in 1938 and served with the British Army in Egypt during the Second World War. Earning a living teaching in the elementary schools, she settled in Haifa. She is married to painter Yehoshua Grossbard. Grossbard trained in Warsaw and in 1954 she studied in Paris at the atelier of André Lhote.

The most distinguished of Batia Grossbard's

oeuvre includes her mountainscape drawings of the post-Six Day War period through the mid 1970s. She found her motifs in Mount Carmel, the Judean Hills, and the vineyards of Zichron Yaakov. The work of this period is characterized by a density of stroke and pattern that endows it with a quality at once abstract and figured. Seen at close range, the drawings induce an awareness of a richly embellished surface, the oft-repeated cursive marks in pencil on roughly textured papers recalling the arts of embroidery and knitting. The stroke is informed by early experience. Knitting and stitching Slavonic folk patterns, Grossbard contributed to the family income from the age of six. Seen from afar, stroke and pattern – now thick, now thin, now frequent, now sparse – evoke form, mass, movement, and such ephemera as light filtered through passing clouds. Hers is a long view of distant hills and slopes, of forests, cultivated orchards, and the bramble of untouched ground. Yet it is one that describes individual shrubs, leaves, blades of grass, and patterns of growth. Grossbard's format is large. Most of the drawings measure about 70 × 100 cms. and encompass a broad vista. Yet the minutiae of detail they embody enlivens the surface with an infinitely sensitive registration of visual stimuli. In the awe they inspire of the natural world, they rank in the tradition of the landscape of the sublime. In the simultaneous focus on the far and the near, they embrace the cherished terrain freshly defended.

From the late 1970s Grossbard's art turned highly abstract, recapitulating styles from abstract expressionism of the 1950s through more recent experiments in color field painting. Her work of the 1980s includes mixed media on paper and oil on canvas, the latter on a monumental scale. Grossbard is the recipient of the Hermann Struck Prize for the Plastic Arts awarded by the Municipality of Haifa in 1971 and 1986. Her work is represented in collections in Israel, Europe, and the USA, notably at the Museum of Modern Art, Haifa, the Albertina Graphische Sammlung, Vienna, and the Eidgenossische Technische Hochschule, Zürich.

FURTHER READING
Batia Grossbard (Ein Harod: Mishkan Lcomanut, 1978) [introduction by G. Silber]

Batia Grossbard (Haifa: Museum of Modern Art, 1970) [introduction by M. Janco]
Batia Grossbard (Haifa: Museum of Modern Art, 1972) [introduction by G. Tadmor]
Abrahamson, H.: *The Master Drawings of Batia Grossbard* (Ramat-Gan: Bar-Ilan University, 1974)

HANNAH ABRAHAMSON

Grossman, David (b.1954) Israeli novelist. Born in Jerusalem, Grossman studied philosophy and drama at the University there and later worked as an editor and broadcaster on the Israeli radio. His first story appeared in 1978, his first book, *Du krav* (1982; A duel) was a children's book. It depicts the world of a group of elderly people in Jerusalem, haunted by their past, through the eyes of a sensitive, lonely child. *Ratz* (1983; Runner) contains two stories about individuals in emotional crisis.

Grossman's first novel, *Hiyukh hagdi* (1983; The smile of the lamb) is a novel about loss of innocence. An Israeli soldier, captivated by the imagination of an old Arab on the West Bank, establishes a unique relationship with him in an impossible situation. It is a story about the moral dilemma of the Israeli soldier, but it is also a story about love, marriage, friendship and betrayal. Reality and fantasy intermingle. Grossman endeavours to present a complex non-stereotypical portrait of Israelis and Arabs caught in conflict, by using of a number of narrators, each providing his subjective, individual point of view. *Hiyukh hagdi* reflects an ever-growing tendency in Israeli writers to produce committed literature of political importance. In 1985 the novel was made into a successful movie.

The novel, *Ayen 'erekh 'ahavah* (1986; See under "love"), is about the repeated efforts of a son of Holocaust survivors to recreate, understand, and cope with the Holocaust phenomenon which will forever remain beyond human comprehension. The book is rich in unprecedented techniques which match unprecedented, fantastic occurrences.

David Grossman's later work, *Hazman hatzahov* (1987; *The Yellow Wind*, 1988), has provoked much controversy. It is the result of the author's month-long research on the West Bank, including interviews with West Bank Palestinians.

BIBLIOGRAPHY
The Yellow Wind (1988)

FURTHER READING
Frankel, G.: Heartbreak at the edges of Israel. *Washington Post Book World* (20 March, 1988)

RIVKA MAOZ

Grossman, Vasilii (1905–1964) Russian prose writer. In his pre-war work there are elements of Jewish thematics, despite Grossman's almost entire lack of participation in Jewish culture. The events of the war and of the post-war years – the loss of his mother in the Berdichev ghetto, the fact that he was the first writer in the world to see a German death camp, Treblinka, and to write about a death factory, and that he fell victim to the anti-Semitic campaign of 1953 – immeasurably intensified his inclination toward and love for Jewry. In his novel *Zhizn i sudba* (Life and fate, written during the period 1950–60 and published in 1980 in Switzerland) and in the narrative tale "Vse techet..." (written in 1955–63 and published in 1970 in Frankfurt-am-Main) an important place is given to the Holocaust and the Soviet anti-Semitism of the Stalinist epoch. No one had written in Russian about this with as much poignancy and emotion. An awakened Jewish consciousness regenerated Grossman as a writer, and made of him one of the most significant Russian prose writers of the second half of the twentieth century.

FURTHER READING
Markish, S.: A Russian writer's Jewish fate. *Commentary* 81 (April, 1986)

SHIMON MARKISH

Group Theater (1931–1941) American theater company. For a decade during the Depression, the Group Theater provided New York audiences with vibrant performances of original plays and an alternative to the commercialism of American theater. Its basic principles grew out of discussions begun in 1925 among its three founders and directors, Harold Clurman, Lee Strasberg, and Cheryl Crawford. These principles are:

1 a permanent company accustomed to working together
2 an approach to acting derived from the ideas of Constantin Stanislavsky
3 a commitment to theater as serious commentary on contemporary life.

How Jewish was the Group? Clurman once denied that the majority of its members were Jews, although many important figures had Jewish backgrounds. Some were influenced by YIDDISH THEATER – Clurman as a child was often taken by his parents, while Luther and Stella Adler were children of Jacob Adler, a leading American Yiddish actor. The Group's collective ethos and its vision of a socially relevant theater may in part have derived from Jewish socialism, although other ideological influences were readily available during the 1920s and 1930s. Finally, some of its plays, particularly the early work of Clifford ODETS, reflect the circumstances and speech rhythms of the children of Jewish immigrants from eastern Europe.

Inspired by the New York productions of the Moscow Art Theater and by courses with one of Stanislavsky's disciples, Richard Boleslavsky, Strasberg began in the mid 1920s to develop "the Method," techniques designed to help actors draw on their own emotional experience to define and delineate the feelings of their characters. In 1928 Clurman and Strasberg worked informally with Morris Carnovsky, Franchot Tone, Sanford Meisner, and others who would later become the nucleus of the Group. Clurman formulated the company's theoretical foundations in the talks he gave in 1930–31 to interested actors. In June of 1931, the three founding directors and twenty-eight young actors went to Connecticut for the summer to work on *The House of Connelly* by Paul Green, which opened in New York in September under Strasberg's direction.

For the next few years, the Group produced two or three plays each season – several designed by Mordecai Gorelik – by such dramatists as Maxwell Anderson, John Howard Lawson, and Sidney Kingsley. The communal spirit of the Group solidified as the company made road tours and spent summers together in the country to rehearse and to work on various aspects of their craft. Few of its early productions were financial successes and critical reponses were divided.

In 1935, however, the Group's fortunes rose abruptly, along with those of Odets, then one of its minor actors. Odets' short play, *Waiting for Lefty*, produced with Group actors but not under its auspices, was an overnight sensation, encouraging the directors to produce his first full-length play, *Awake and Sing*, directed by Clurman and designed by Boris Aronson. Although the Group produced plays by such dramatists as William Saroyan, Robert Ardrey, and Irwin Shaw, Odets' works were its mainstays until its demise, even after Odets himself had moved to Hollywood. If Odets gave the Group its voice, the company inspired him to find his: "Without the Group Theater I doubt that I would have become a playwright" (Brenman-Gibson, p.220). His final dissociation from the Group was costly to him and possibly fatal to the company.

The Group survived for ten years against formidable odds. From the outset, it lacked adequate funding. After the Theater Guild withdrew its sponsorship in 1931, the Group continued to function as an art theater, despite its commercial environment. No foundation or government grants were then available and private funds were scarce. Ticket sales produced limited revenues. To keep a permanent company, it had to pay actors all year round, although wages were meager. In the 1930s many actors accepted such terms, but some went to Hollywood, most notably Tone and John Garfield (né Jules Garfinkle). Backers could be found for individual plays, but what held the Group together was the willingness of its members to make sacrifices to sustain the collective vision.

That vision itself was tested over time. Tensions developed between actors and directors as well as within the triumvirate. Clurman finally assumed sole control of the Group in 1936. Some actors resented casting choices, and some, who disliked Strasberg's stress on psychological introspection, took comfort when Stella Adler returned in 1934 from Paris, where she had studied with Stanislavsky, to offer a competing Method. Indeed, the controversy among members over the value and proper use of "emo-

tional memory" or "affective memory" continued for several decades. Members also differed ideologically: some were apolitical, others felt a generalized sympathy with the victims of economic and social injustice, while others, according to Elia Kazan, belonged to a Communist Party cell. Moreover, the sacrifices required to sustain the Group as well as the Method itself generated self-awareness and contentiousness. Strasberg put it succinctly: "We did a good deal of 'kvetching'" (Chinoy, p.552). Nevertheless, the Group remained more or less stable, produced about two dozen plays, and introduced American audiences to a style of ensemble playing characterized by psychological authenticity.

It also revolutionized the training of American actors, as former members of the Group disseminated Stanislavskian approaches and techniques. Crawford, Strasberg, Kazan, Meisner, and Robert Lewis were involved in the Actors Studio, as well as in other training programs in Hollywood, New York, and Yale Drama School. Stella Adler, Carnovsky, and Phoebe Brand have also influenced the development of young actors, while Kazan, Clurman, and others have utilized the Group's approaches as directors.

FURTHER READING

Brenman-Gibson, Margaret: *Clifford Odets, American Playwright* (New York: Atheneum, 1981)

Chinoy, H. K. ed.: Reunion: a self-portrait of the Group Theatre, The way we were – 1931–1941, and Looking back – 1974–1976. *Educational Theatre Journal* 28 (1976)

Clurman, H.: *The Fervent Years: The Story of the Group Theatre and The Thirties* (repr. New York: Hill & Wang, 1957)

MICHAEL SHAPIRO

Grumberg, Jean-Claude (b.1939) French dramatist. He was born in Paris where his father had moved from his native Romania before the Second World War. Emigration did not save the elder Grumberg; he was deported, never to return. The young Jean-Claude, separated from his mother during the Occupation, left school at 14 and found work in a tailor's shop. These early experiences would ultimately provide the substance of Grumberg's strongest play, *L'Atelier* (1979; The workroom). Grumberg began his theatrical career as assistant stage manager and actor in the Jacques Fabbri company.

His early works include *Chez Pierrot* (1965), *Demain une fénêtre sur rue* (1966; Tomorrow a window on the street), which won the Prix U on its premiere in 1968, and *Rixe* (1967), presented by the Comédie Française in 1969. Another early work is the one-act *Michu* (1965). This Jules Feifferesque one-acter cleverly defuses its eponym, a bigoted, intimidating know-it-all. Michu's oneupmanship backfires when he "accuses" a timid co-worker of being a Jew, which turns out to be exactly the qualification their boss, who really is Jewish, is looking for in the next employee to be promoted.

In 1974 Grumberg scored a hit with *Dreyfus*, which won the "Plaisir du Théâtre" and the Society of Authors and Dramatic Composers Prizes for that year. In *Dreyfus*, an amateur Yiddish theatrical troupe in a Polish *shtetl* in 1930 struggles to rehearse a play its director has written about the ill-fated officer. Try as they may, the actors find both Dreyfus the man and his story incomprehensible and much less compelling than certain personal concerns. Only when the rehearsal is interrupted by hoodlums in what threatens to be the vanguard of a pogrom does the Dreyfus military regalia, which helps ward off the brutes, take on any meaning at all for these Jews. At the play's end they remain as oblivious of the implications of the Affair as they are to the much larger storm about to break over their heads. Adapted and directed by Garson Kanin, the play has been produced in English as *Dreyfus in Rehearsal*.

Grumberg is deservedly best known for *L'Atelier*, a poignant work which has played to critical and popular acclaim both in the original and in Tom Kempinski's English translation. Here Grumberg tells his mother's story in the years that followed her husband's deportation. Simone lives somewhere between fear and hope that the authorities will be able to issue her husband's death certificate, but finds companionship with her co-workers in a tailor shop and consolation in her two small sons, one of whom represents the playwright-to-be.

Other plays include *Amorphe d'Oftenburg* (1970), *En R'venant de l'Expo* (1973; Coming back from the expo), *La Vocation* (1974; The vocation) and *L'Indien sous Babylone* (1985; The Indian under Babylone). In the 1980s, Grumberg has turned to writing for television, where he had made his debut in 1969 with *Un Miel amer* (A bitter honey). For Simone Signoret, he wrote *Therese Humbert* and *Music Hall* (1986). The TV play *Les Lendemains qui chantent* (A Brighter Future) concerns Jewish Communists in the 1950s.

FURTHER READING

Schiff, E.: *From Stereotype to Metaphor: The Jew in Contemporary Drama* (1982)

ELLEN SCHIFF

Grünberg, Carlos (1903–1968) Argentine poet, lawyer, and translator. He was born in Buenos Aires, graduated as a lawyer at the University of Buenos Aires and for many years taught Spanish literature. Throughout the 1920s Grünberg participated, with important writers such as Jorge L. Borges (who became a particular friend of his), in literary gatherings and shared the pages of local vanguardist journals, *Proa* and *Martin Fierro*. Like many other poets and writers of his generation, Grünberg also published his first book, *El Libro del Tiempo*, (1924; The book of time) under the imprint of Manuel Gleizer, a Jewish pioneer of literary publishing in Argentina. Grünberg was among the principal contributors of the Spanish literary and cultural review, *Judaica*.

Grünberg's best known book is *Mester de Juderia* (1940; The art of Jews: the title is a play on the medieval *mester de juglaria*, "the art of minstrels"). Grünberg's verse in this collection, says Borges in his laudatory introduction, gives voice to the "honor and pain of being Jewish in the perverse, unbelievable world of 1940". In fact, it is a lyric protest against anti-Semitism, not only the European variety, but the home-grown, Argentine kind. *Mester de Juderia* marked a new phase in Argentine-Jewish literature because the author overcame the early stage characterized by the insecure and anxious greenhorn Jewish immigrant eager to be accepted by Argentine society. Instead, Grünberg represents a fully fledged citizen unafraid to censure the distortions of the pluralist Argentine tradition of which he was always proud, and who fights the xenophobic atmosphere of the time. Grünberg became the most hispanic of the Argentine poets and writers, together with Alberto GERCHUNOFF. His poetic language is rich in the Spanish vocabulary and idioms he traced to the golden tradition of the medieval Spanish Jewish period, which he manipulates into a lyric discourse dealing with the Jewish problems of the present.

In his other important collection of poems, *Junto a un rio de Babel* (1965; Beside a river of Babylon) Grünberg expresses his Zionist ambivalence: on the one hand he defines himself as an exiled Jew eager to return to the land of his ancestors, and on the other, he refuses to give up his pride in being an Argentine citizen, and love of his birthplace.

Grünberg was enlisted into the local Zionist movement by his friend, Moshe Tov, who became Assistant Legal Adviser of the Jewish Agency Department for Latin America and who appointed Grünberg in August, 1948 as liaison officer between the new State of Israel and the Argentine Government.

His editing and translation into Spanish of the *Haggadah* (1946) aroused great interest because of the author's gift for using language with an old Spanish flavor to express the traditional book of Passover, both in prose and verse.

FURTHER READING

Borges, J. L.: Homenaje a Carlos M. Grünberg. *Davar* 119 (1968) 28–9
Senkman, L.: *La Identidad Judia en la Literatura Argentina* (Buenos Aires: Pardes, 1983) 323–7

LEONARDO SENKMAN

Grune, Karl (1890–1962) British film director and producer. Grune, who left his fortune for the purpose of settling poor immigrant people in Israel, was born in Vienna, a Czechoslovakian citizen. He was a long-term associate of the producer Max Schach and shot to fame with *Die Strasse* (1923). He claimed to have become interested in the cinema watching the faces of Russian soldiers as a prisoner of war, unable to understand the language. He

rose, through acting on the stage, to directing films. He directed and wrote, with Carl Mayer, *Am Rande der Welt* (1927). With Schach, he was forced to resign as head of production from Emelka in 1931. Rather disingenuously, he later claimed to have been driven out by Hitler. He went first to Paris and arrived in England in 1934.

In Britain, Schach's company co-financed *Abdul the Damned* (1935). Grune directed, Fritz Kortner starred and Hanns Eisler wrote the music. The story of the overthrow of the Turkish tyrant, Abdul Hammid, in 1908, it was one of the earliest British films to make, albeit obliquely, a reference to Nazi Germany. The *Daily Telegraph* thanked Schach, Grune, and Adolph Hitler, but for whom it would probably never have been made.

When Schach went out of business in 1938, Grune's career came virtually to an end. Other films include: *Die Nacht ohne Morgen* (1921), *Die Brüder Schellenberg* (1926), *La Maison Jaune*. *The Marriage of Corbal* (1936), *The Silver Darling* (1947, Prod. only).

FURTHER READING

Eisner, L.: *The Haunted Screen* (London: Thames & Hudson, 1969)
Interview with Max Breen. *Picturegoer* 12 (October, 1935)
All Films are Documentary. *Picturegoer* 23 (May 1936) [interview]

KEVIN GOUGH-YATES

Guri, Hayyim (b.1922) Israeli poet, novelist, and journalist. Guri was born in Tel Aviv and educated at Kadoori, a well-known agricultural school that maintained a close relationship with the Labor Party. Guri spent his early years in the Palmach. In 1947 he was sent to Europe as an *aliyah* official. He studied at the Hebrew University in Jerusalem and at the Sorbonne. Guri is one of the prime representatives of what is sometimes referred to as the "generation of the Palmach" (*dor hapalmah*). In 1987 he was the recipient, together with Moshe SHAMIR, of the Israel Prize for literature. Guri writes for the Hebrew daily, *Davar*.

Pirhei 'esh, Guri's first volume of poetry,

appeared in 1949, an outburst of emotion rather than an innovative poetic statement. It is a lyric elegy, the voice of a romantic generation thrown into the harsh reality of war. The poetry is direct, powerful and, some have said, undisciplined. In subsequent volumes of poetry, *Shirei hotam* (1954), and *Shoshanat haruhot* (1960), Guri moves closer to contemporary modernist tones, using simpler, more prosaic language and directing more attention to the self. The voice of the lost generation is still heard, a generation whose youth was spent in heroic struggle and is now trying to adapt to "the grey prose of existence".

Guri's novels are generally regarded as being written in "a poet's prose". *Iskat hashokolada* (1965; *The Chocolate Deal*, 1968), the story of two Holocaust survivors, was well received in the English-speaking world. In *Hasefer hameshuga'* (1972; The crazy book) he presents an "anthology" of memories from his Tel Aviv childhood in an enchanting mixture of dream and reality. The mythical, mythological, fantastic and prophetic are also evident in Guri's later poetry, among which are *Mar'ot gehazi* (1974), *Ayuma* (1979), and *Mahbarot elul* (1984).

Guri writes regularly for the press. His articles covering the Eichmann Trial have been published in collected form as *El mul ta hezehuhit* (1962; The glass cage). He has made several full length documentary films, notably *Hamakah hashemonim va'ahat* (The eighty-first blow), about the Holocaust.

AHUVIA KAHANE

Guston [Goldstein], **Philip** (1913–1980) American painter. Philip Guston was born in Montreal of Russian–Jewish immigrant parents. The family moved to Los Angeles, California in 1919, and Guston's father, who had a difficult time adjusting to life in the USA, committed suicide. Guston's earliest instruction in art was through a correspondence course he took from the Cleveland School of Cartooning. In 1927 he attended Manual Arts High School where he befriended Jackson Pollock – a relationship that continued later in New York during the 1940s and 1950s where both artists were leaders in the Abstract Expressionist Move-

ment. Guston next worked on the backlots of movie studios and appeared as an extra in a few films – the experience undoubtedly influenced his lifelong interest in theatrics and the cinema.

During the 1930s Guston identified with liberal political and social causes and played an active role in the mural movement, receiving mural commissions throughout the USA. He was awarded first prize for his mural *Maintaining America's Skills* for the WPA Building at the New York World's Fair of 1939. *Bombardment*, (1937–8), an easel painting of the period was a statement in opposition to the Fascist bombing of civilians during the Spanish Civil War, foreshadowed later, more abstract works that were commentaries on inhumanity and genocide. He built upon his experience as a muralist in the 1940s, but the subjects changed from recognizable social issues to imagined allegories of conflict and war. From scenes of mock battles of young boys in an urban setting, he turned to more generalized anti-terror and war subjects. Yet, the events of the Holocaust and the post-war release of newsreel footage of gaunt survivors and piles of dead victims are the point of reference for *Porch II* (1947), a tightly packed composition of lifeless, corpse-like figures. Between 1945 and 1947 Guston taught at the St Louis School of Fine Art of Washington University in St Louis, Missouri. The influence of Max Beckmann, who was also in St Louis, is apparent in his figurative works of the 1940s.

In 1950 Guston moved back to New York where he gradually shifted from figuration to total abstraction and was among the vanguard of the Abstract Expressionist Movement. In the late 1960s he returned to the use of figurative imagery, making critical comments about the current state of civilization in a direct, childlike style. This change was not readily accepted by art critics. Although there is little specific Jewish imagery in the late works, Guston's deep concern for the common man is an inherent part of the Jewish tradition. There are parallels that can be drawn between these late works and elements of the Jewish experience. Because of his concern for society and a sense of helplessness as to a means of making any substantial changes, Guston acknowledged a similar sense of alienation to that expressed by Franz KAFKA.

In his late figurative works, Guston felt an affinity with the Jewish legend of the Golem, the human effigy that was said to have been created by the rabbis out of clay. He simultaneously questioned and marveled at the act of creation, feeling a similar contradiction to the lesson intended by the Golem legend.

FURTHER READING

Ashton, D.: *Yes But...: A Critical Study of Philip Guston* (New York: The Viking Press, 1976)

Storr, R.: *Philip Guston* (New York: Abbeville Press, 1986)

BARBARA GILBERT

Gutman, Nahum (1898–1980) Israeli painter, illustrator, and writer. Gutman was born in Bessarabia, son of the Hebrew author, S. Ben-Zion. At the age of seven his family emigrated to Palestine and settled in Tel Aviv. His first art lessons were with Ira Jan, who opened a studio a year after the foundation of the city (1910). In 1912 Gutman studied at the BEZALEL SCHOOL OF ARTS AND CRAFTS, Jerusalem, with Boris Schatz and Abel Pan. In 1920 Gutman went to Vienna and in 1922 to Berlin, where he studied graphics with Herman Struck. There he also met H. N. BIALIK and illustrated his work. Gutman returned to Palestine in 1926, and immediately became active in the artistic life there, exhibiting in Jerusalem and Tel Aviv. In 1929 Gutman participated in the Levant Fair, and in the early 1930s in the Paris exhibition of Jewish artists, with Marc CHAGALL, Moshe Kisling, Chaim SOUTINE, and Jules Pascin.

Gutman's oils and watercolors thematically bear witness to the early days of Tel Aviv; these humorous genre works show an optimistic sense of fulfillment about the return of the nation to its own land. Stylistically his forms and colors are strongly influenced by the esthetic, lyrical branch of French Expressionism. His exuberant, airy forms and colors are akin to those of Chagall and Raul Dufy, in his quick light drawings, loaded with humor and humanistic benevolence. Gutman's landscapes and cityscapes of the 1920s and early 1930s contain a contrast between the light quality in the background, and the depic-

tion of magnified, highly stylized human figures, populating these settings.

Among the famous paintings of that period are *Woman on a Balcony* (1926), colorful pastel square houses by the seashore, with women on their balconies; *Resting at Noon* (1926), depicting massive people resting in a field in the heat of the day, a subject depicted by Camille PISSARO, and Picasso. Other paintings observe indigenous qualities and their encounter with modern technology, as does the oil *Orchard in Jaffa* (1926), where Arab women in their traditional clothes are seen strolling in a deep green orchard, with a train visible on the horizon.

Gutman also painted portraits and designed stage sets, for which he received the Paris Gold medal. Gutman was an author of children's stories and a prolific book illustrator. Among the many he illustrated are: *Esther* (1932); *Passover Haggadah* (1952); Bialik's *Veyehi hayom*. In 1983 a memorial retrospective exhibition of his oeuvre was held in the Tel Aviv Museum.

NEDIRA YAKIR BUNYARD

Gutmann, Jacob (1845–1919) Rabbi and scholar of Jewish philosophy. Gutmann was born in Beuther, Silesia, and received an Orthodox education there, studying at a rabbinical seminary and at the University of Breslau. On the completion of his studies, he became a teacher of religion in Breslau. In 1874 he was appointed rabbi in Hildesheim where he served until 1892, and then in Breslau from 1892. In 1910 he was appointed Chairman of the German Rabbinical Assembly, a post he filled until his death.

Gutmann's academic activity was focused upon the investigation of the origins of Jewish philosophy. A survey of his work reveals a distinction between two methods of writing: the first examines the ideas and concepts of a certain philosophical system and the second clarifies the influence of Jewish philosophy on Christian theology.

In his writings dealing with the examination of a particular doctrine, Gutmann usually dealt with the theories of a single philosopher, mainly from among medieval Jewish thinkers, and carefully investigated his stand on philosophical problems in the areas of physics and metaphysics. Among these writings, three are worthy of mention: *Die Religionsphilosophie des Abraham Ibn Daud aus Toledo* (1879); *Die Religionsphilosophie des Saadja* (1882) and *Die Philosophie des Salomon Ibn Gabirol* (1889).

Gutman's second method had already been revealed in his doctoral work, *De Cartesii Spinozaeque Philisophiis* (1848), an investigation into the reference between western Jewish and Christian philosophers. The most important of his writings on this topic are those dealing with the influence of the works of Maimonides on Thomas Aquinas. In 1891 Gutmann wrote *Das Verhaeltnis des Thomas von Aquino zum Judentum und zur Jüdischen Literatur*, and the essay, "Der Einfluss der Maimonidischen Philosophie auf das Christliche Abenland" (1914) which appeared in a book devoted to Maimonides, a volume of articles of which Gutmann was one of the editors.

Gutmann wrote many more books and articles in German on the topic of the interrelationship between Jewish and Christian thought. An extensive bibliography of his works appeared in a *Festschrift* in honor of his seventieth birthday in 1915.

DEBORAH SCHECHTERMAN

H

Haïm, Victor (b.1935) French playwright. Born in Asnières, he attended the Conservatory in Nantes where his family had moved on the eve of the Second World War. He went to Paris in 1954. Lacking the confidence to pursue an acting career, he supported himself as a journalist, while beginning to write for the theater. His early plays earned him the encouragement of the Minister of Cultural Affairs. 1967 marked his first successes, the most important being a commercial production of *L'Arme blanche* (Cold steel), a study of the Vietnam War. Since, there have been some fifty full-length and one-act works. Some of his thought-provoking comedies integrate Jewish and universal themes, like *Abraham et Samuel* (1973). Here a wily peasant, proud of being a Jewish worker, outsmarts his employer who has tried to mask both his Jewishness and his gender the better to exploit others. In *La Servante* (1976; The maidservant), a Marivaux-like heroine, Judith, is determined to bring to justice a doctor who once tortured prisoners in the name of scientific experimentation. Just as contemporary issues are viewed through the transparent guise of a medieval farce in *Abraham et Samuel*, so the eighteenth-century setting of *La Servante* does not conceal the play's subtext: Judith is modeled on the Nazi hunter Beate Klarsfeld. Another anachronistic treatment of modern Jewish experience occurs in *Isaac et la sage-femme* (1976; Isaac and the midwife), set in biblical Egypt. The despair felt by the fisherman Isaac in a world where Jews are subject to the cruelty of tyrants dissolves in a bittersweet encounter with the life force represented by a midwife, condemned for saving Jewish firstborns.

La Visite (1975; The visit) is a psychological thriller in which the self-assurance of a doctor crumbles before an assailant who she thinks has discovered her guilty secret: relieved to be spared her Jewish father's fate, she has never reproached her Gentile mother for denouncing him to the Nazis. A number of Haïm's plays deal with the vulnerability of creative souls in conflict with their muses or with an unsympathetic world. Of particular importance are *La Baignoire* (1979; The bath tub), *Accordez vos violons* (1982; Tune up your violins), and *Le Grand Invité* (1988; The great guest).

Death frequents the theater of Haïm. A theme in many of his plays, it is dominant in *L'Escalade* (Climbing), where a group of tourists kill their guide; *La Valse du hasard* (1986; The waltz of chance), which deals with the fate in purgatory of the victim of a car accident; and in *Qui a tué le général?* (Who killed the general?). Despite this preoccupation, Haïm knows how to make audiences laugh as well as think. His plays are often humorous and have been translated for performance all over the world. Haïm has received numerous awards, among them the Prix Ibsen of the Syndicat de critique dramatique (1971), the Prix des U (1974), the Prix Lugné-Poe (1977), the Prix Plaisir du théâtre, that of the Société des auteurs dramatiques (1986), and the Prix Jacques Audiberti (1987).

He finally overcame his stage fright to play the lead role in *Isaac et la sage-femme* to critical acclaim. Not content to be only an acclaimed playwright and actor, he made his directorial debut with *Qui a tué le général?* (1983).

FURTHER READING

Schiff, E.: *From Stereotype to Metaphor: The Jew in Contemporary Drama* (Albany: State University of New York Press, 1982)

L'Avant-Scène Théâtre, No. 548 (15 September, 1974) [issue devoted to Victor Haïm]

L'Avant-Scène Théâtre, No. 836 (15 October, 1988)

Riochet, C.: Le Salaire de l'angoisse. *L'Humanité* (29 September, 1987)

ELLEN SCHIFF

halakhah in the twentieth century The development of *halakhah* (Jewish law) in the twentieth century may conveniently be divided into three phases which reflect the influence of wider historical events. They are: the period to the end of the First World War, the period between the two World Wars, and the period from the Second World War to the present day.

Halakhah prior to the First World War

Despite the mass emigration of east European Jews to the west from the 1880s the main center of halakhic creativity until the end of the First World War was among the vast concentration of Jews in Russia, Poland and Lithuania (representing a single cultural complex because of shifting boundaries), and in the eastern lands of the Austro-Hungarian Empire. It was in this area that the most important rabbinical academies, *yeshivot*, were situated, and the majority of traditional Jewish communities were to be found. Since *halakhah* was the lifeblood of these mainly Orthodox Jews the need for halakhic solutions to the problems of modernity was a pressing one. The halakhic productivity of rabbis in Germany and western Europe was far less extensive, since there the newly acquired values of European culture dominated Jewish life.

An example of the subject matter which occupied rabbis in central Europe is found in the work of the outstanding German halakhist Rabbi David Zevi HOFFMANN (1843–1921). His responsa collection *Melammed leho'il* (1926–32) consists of relatively terse answers to questions from all over Germany. A number of Hoffmann's responsa deal with the innovations that Reform Judaism had introduced into Jewish ritual. Thus he argued that organs should not be played in synagogues even on weekdays, and that changes to the length or content of the services were not permitted, although he allowed an Orthodox rabbi to continue serving a congregation which introduced minor changes lest a Reform rabbi be appointed in his place. His general tendency was towards leniency, however, and he was willing to count Jews, who publicly desecrated the Sabbath, as part of the quorum for public prayer. They were not to be regarded as deliberate sinners but as people led astray by the influence of their environment. He also suggested a clause in the marriage document to alleviate the situation of a woman bound by levirate marriage whose brother-in-law would not release her.

Two of the most important examples of the development of halakhic codification in eastern Europe during this period are the major commentary on the *Orah hayyim* section of the most authoritative code, the *Shulhan arukh*, by Rabbi Israel Meir Hakohen Poupko (1838–1933) of Radun, Poland, and the complete scholarly reworking of almost the whole of the *Shulhan arukh* by Rabbi Jehiel Michael Halevi Epstein (1829–1908) of Novogrudok, Lithuania. Rabbi Israel Meir is popularly known as the "Hafetz Hayyim" after the title of his book on the laws of evil speech which he wrote to curb the widespread abuse of gossip. His code commentary, the *Mishnah berurah* (1884–1907), seeks to update the rulings of the *Shulhan arukh* by incorporating the additions of later authorities. The work comprises short halakhic decisions for popular reference and longer, more learned, discussions of why certain decisions seem most appropriate. The "Hafetz Hayyim" had a saintly reputation as a scion of the Musar Movement, and this gave his purely halakhic writings considerable authority so that they came to be widely accepted. His *Mishnah berurah* was a rather conservative work, which did not make any radical breaks with the past. Since he was not himself the rabbi of a community, having spent most of his adult life in study and in helping to run a *yeshivah*, he did not have to deal with the intractable problems inherent in day to day rabbinic leadership.

Epstein, by contrast, was the head of the Jewish community in a large Lithuanian town. His reworking of the *Shulhan arukh*, known as the *Arukh hashulhan* (1884–1907), is a scholarly and innovative attempt to cope with twentieth-century problems. Epstein's method was to analyze in great detail the way the author of the *Shulhan arukh* reached his decisions in the light of the Talmudic and post-Talmudic literature, and then to assess subsequent modifications found in the major commentaries on that code. Because his approach was analytic it enabled him to come to independent conclusions about new issues, and to find lenient rulings. An example of Epstein's practical approach in his code was his decision that prayers may be said in the presence of married women whose hair is uncovered. He argued that since this had become a common occurrence the showing of such hair no longer constituted illicit exposure of the body. He expressed regret that the tradition of married women covering their hair had changed, but found a solution to deal with the problem going back to Talmudic precedent. Epstein was one of the first rabbis to discuss the nature of electricity and its implications for many areas of Jewish life. He published a special document stating that electricity was to be viewed as a light substance flowing through the wires from its source in a power station. Thus on festivals it may be switched on and off because no light is thus created or extinguished. This view has been rejected by most subsequent authorities who have dealt with the subject.

Halakhah between the two World Wars

After the Russian revolution, and the subsequent limitations on Jewish life under Communism, halakhic creativity was centered on those areas of eastern Europe remaining outside Soviet influence, and also on the new center of Jewish life in Palestine. The growing population of the Holy Land, in which Zionist settlers outnumbered the old traditional community, was faced by halakhic problems associated with farming and modern life. One of the most important halakhists who grappled with solutions to these problems was Rabbi Abraham Isaac Hacohen KOOK (1865–1935), first Ashkenazi Chief Rabbi of the land of Israel. Rabbi Kook put forward practical solutions in various responsa to enable Palestinian farmers to continue working their fields during the Sabbatical year, and devoted a special book to the subject *Shabbat ha'aretz* (1937). His leniency in this regard was severely criticized by opponents of Zionism who regarded his halakhic arguments as having been perverted by his love for the land and for the irreligious pioneers who worked it. A colleague of Kook's, Rabbi Ben-Zion Meir Hai Ouziel (1880–1953) who was later to become the first Sefardi Chief Rabbi of Israel, collaborated with him in dealing with problems affecting Jews in the Holy Land. In the responsa collected in his *Mishpetei Ouziel* (1947–64), he permitted milking cows on the Sabbath if done in a different way from normal; he allowed women to vote and put themselves forward for election; he argued that Jewish prisons should have parchment texts, *mezuzot*, on their doors, and that Jews living in distant lands such as Japan should keep the Sabbath according to Israeli time rather than the much earlier time in their own countries.

Halakhah from the Second World War to the present

The Nazi conquest of Europe, and implementation of the "Final Solution to the Jewish Problem", destroyed the nerve centers of talmudic studies in eastern Europe. The *yeshivot* of Poland, Lithuania and Hungary were closed, their teachers and students exterminated or dispersed. Some of the rabbis in the concentration camps continued to guide Jewish inmates on very delicate matters of halakhic policy, although they obviously had no access to learned literature. Orthodox Jews wanted to know to what lengths they could go to save their own lives if this meant putting the lives of others at risk, and how they could maintain Jewish life under the most adverse circumstances. In the immediate post-war period the problems of women whose husbands had disappeared, *agunot*, occupied all the major halakhists in the West. It was decided by a number of leading rabbis that evidence of a husband being selected to go to the gas chambers at a concentration camp should be sufficient proof of his actual death, and his widow could thus remarry. This position was argued by Rabbi Isaac Jacob Weiss in a responsum he wrote immediately after the war while still in Rumania and reprinted in his *Minhat yitzhak* (1955). Weiss was himself a Holocaust survivor who recounts, at the end of the first volume of his responsa, the miraculous manner of his rescue from death at the hands of the Nazis. He escaped after the war from Rumania to Manchester, and eventually was appointed head of the ultra-Orthodox Beth Din in Jerusalem. His volumes of responsa are highly respected by those who favour an uncompromisingly strict interpretation of the *halakhah*.

Jewish life was resurrected in the post-Holocaust era in two major centers: the USA and the newly formed State of Israel. Most of the surviving halakhic authorities found their way from the charnel-house of Europe to these two new havens. They rebuilt their academies and were appointed as rabbis of communities. The new developments in technology, with advances in birth control, test-tube babies, organ transplants, and medical discussion of abortion, euthanasia, and the determination of death through the cessation of brain function, all found their place in halakhic literature. Rabbi Eliezer Judah Waldenberg of Jerusalem, for instance, devoted about 15 per cent of the responsa in his many-volumed *Tzitz Eliezer* (1945–) to medical matters. The many additives used in the mass production of processed food raised problems for the Jewish diet, and the electronic revolution had implications for various branches of religious law.

Until his death in 1986 Rabbi Moshe Feinstein (b.1895) was the leading halakhic figure in North America, best known for his volumes of responsa *Iggerot Mosheh* (1959–82). Feinstein settled in the USA in 1937 as a refugee from Poland and in the course of 50 years there dealt with many of the issues facing American Orthodoxy. His responsa are characterized by his ability to find new solutions to problems, and he showed great courage in putting them forward even when this meant facing the criticism of more traditional colleagues for departing from accepted norms. His authority as a halakhist did not prevent a demonstration by ultra-Orthodox Jews against his lenient ruling on the subject of artificial insemination. He allowed the ordinary bottled milk of New York dairies to be drunk, without any supervision of the milking process, because he held that government inspection was sufficient guarantee that the milk came from a cow and not some non-kosher animal. He also allowed someone who had undergone a Reform marriage ceremony, and could not obtain a religious divorce, to remarry since the first marriage had taken place without any acceptable witnesses – the guests and clergy all having sat down to a shrimp breakfast after the wedding, thus disqualifying themselves. Although advocating a strict conversion procedure Feinstein was inclined to accept the validity of conversions where the convert to Judaism did not practise all of the commandments. His reasoning was that such converts were influenced by the generally lax standards of Jews, and thus they might not actually have rejected parts of Judaism but might be considered ignorant of them. He dealt with the vexed problem in the USA of a separation, *mehitzah*, between men and women in synagogues. Feinstein ruled that such a separation is required by biblical law and should be sufficient to prevent any contact between the sexes although he allowed them to actually see each other.

FURTHER READING

Bleich, J. D.: *Contemporary Halakhic Problems*, 2 vols (New York: Ktav, 1977, 1983)

Freehof, S. B.: *The Responsa Literature* (Philadelphia: The Jewish Publication Society of America, 1959)

——: *A Treasury of Responsa* (Philadelphia: The Jewish Publication Society of America, 1963)

Jacobs, L.: *Theology in the Responsa* (London: Routledge & Kegan Paul, 1975)

ALAN UNTERMAN

Halévy Family of writers, historians, artists, and musicians. Elie Halphen (or Halfon) Levy (1760–1826) was born in Fürth, Bavaria, the son of a rabbi, and himself became a *hazzan* and teacher. He settled in Paris after the French Revolution and thereafter called himself Halévy.

He was the ancestor of several generations of outstanding Parisian artists and scholars. Elie composed religious music and acted as cantor at the main Paris synagogue. Fusing admiration for French culture with a fidelity to his Jewish upbringing, he modernized Hebrew, using it to celebrate contemporary events, as in the poem *Hashalom* commemorating the Lunéville peace treaty of 1801. He is also responsible for one of the first Hebrew–French dictionaries, complete by his younger son, Léon, and for a much appreciated moral code in Hebrew and French, combining traditional Jewish law with the decisions of the Napoleonic Sanhedrin.

NELLY WILSON

Halévy, Daniel (1872–1962)   Historian and critic. Younger son of Ludovic. His decision to study Semitic languages after completing his studies at the *lycée* Condorcet (where he met PROUST and other future writers) would seem to have been motivated more by a desire to assert his independence vis-à-vis his family, who advised against it, than by genuine interest. Immediately upon graduating with a degree in Arabic in 1894, he turned to the eminently more suitable career of "gentleman of letters". "Perpetually lucid and uncertain, beset by doubts and remorse", as Romain Rolland remarked, Halévy recorded the collapse of his class, finding confirmation of his ideas in Nietzsche and looking for new values in the ideas of Proudhon, Sorel, and Péguy. This refined, complex, bored Parisian intellectual yearned for the earthiness of humble peasants and defended the heroic struggle of the proletariat. A streak of anti-Semitism was part and parcel of his rejection of bourgeois values. It produced a curious retrospective interpretation of the Dreyfus Affair and of his regretted participation in it.

NELLY WILSON

Halévy, Elie (1870–1937)   Historian and philosopher. Ludovic's elder son, named after the founder of the "Halévy dynasty". A brilliant student (*lycée* Condorcet, École Normale Supérieure, he became a distinguished neo-rationalist

active in the creation of *La Revue de Métaphysique et de Morale* and *La Société Française de Philosophie*. He is best remembered for his authoritative five-volume *Histoire du peuple anglais au XIX siècle* (1912–32). *L'Ere des tyrannies* (1937), an examination of Fascism and Communism, brings his work to a pessimistic close.

NELLY WILSON

Halévy,   (Jacques-François-)Fromental (-Elias) (1799–1862)   French composer. Born in Paris, Halévy was the elder son of Elie Levy (Halévy). He studied at the Conservatoire from 1809 and in 1819 won the Prix de Rome. Before leaving for Italy, he composed a Funeral March and *De Profundis* in Hebrew on the death of the Duc de Berry, dedicated to his teacher, Cherubini, which was performed at the Synagogue in the Rue St Avoye. His large output of successful operatic works included a version of Shakespeare's *The Tempest* in Italian, premiered at Her Majesty's Theatre in London, and *Le Juif errant* (The Wandering Jew) based on the novel by Eugene Suë. Only his best known work *La Juive* (The Jewess) with libretto by Eugène Scribe (1835), is occasionally revived with its two great roles for Eleazar, the Goldsmith (tenor) and Rachel, his supposed daughter (soprano).

From 1840 Halévy was Professor of Composition at the Paris Conservatoire where his pupils included Gounod and Bizet, who married his daughter. Halévy, as a member of the Consistoire Israélite, endorsed Samuel Naumbourg's proposals for the reorganization of the French synagogue service and contributed various musical settings.

CAROLE ROSEN

Halévy, Léon (1802–1883)   Writer, leading Saint-Simonian. He was the brother of the composer Fromental Halévy. Talented but restless, he abandoned a promising teaching career (Chair of French Literature at the École Polytechnique) to pursue diverse interests ranging from serious scholarship (including a two-volume history of the Jews, 1828) to writing popular light comedies. His major preoccupation came to center on the Saint-Simonian movement. He edited Saint-Simon's unwieldy writings and, after the master's death, the movement's journal, *Le Producteur*. Saint-Simonism, one of several pre-Marxist, "Utopian" socialist groups which flourished during the first half of the nineteenth century, attracted many young Jews of this, the first assimilated generation. Several came from prosperous families and helped to finance the movement. Halévy himself was introduced to Saint-Simon by a relative, Benjamin Olinde Rodrigues, a mathematician and financier, who also recruited the bankers Emile and Isaac Pereire.

Léon was the last of the Halévys to retain an interest, albeit of an historical nature, in his Jewish origins and the first, followed by his son Ludovic, to marry into a well-established Protestant family.

NELLY WILSON

Halévy, Ludovic (1834–1908) French writer. He was the son of Léon Halévy. His name, often coupled with that of his main collaborator, Henri Meilhac, is inseparable from the glittering Second Empire society immortalized – and satirized – by them in words and by Offenbach in music. *La Belle Hélène* (1865), *La Vie Parisienne* (1866), *La Grande Duchesse de Gérolstein* (1867) are among the best known of their operettas. Halévy provided the libretto for many other compositions, notably (with Meilhac) for Bizet's *Carmen* (1875). He wrote much else and in serious vein: novels, parliamentary reports, essays on the Franco-Prussian War and over fifty volumes of *Carnets*, a lively record of daily life between 1862 and 1899. He was elected to the French Academy in 1884. His elegant salon was a lively cultural rendezvous. Seeming indifference to his paternal Jewish origins was somewhat shaken by the Russian pogroms and the Dreyfus Affair. The Halévys' support for Dreyfus led to painful differences, notably with Degas, an old family friend.

NELLY WILSON

Halpern, Moyshe Leyb (1886–1932) Yiddish poet. Born in Zloczow, East Galicia, Halpern was sent at the age of 12 to Vienna to study sign-painting. There he came into contact with German literature and socialist ideas and began to write in German. On his return to Galicia in 1907, under S. IMBER's influence, he began to write in Yiddish. In 1908 Halpern left for New York, where he lived in great poverty. In 1912 he worked for the Montreal newspaper *Di folkstsaytung*, publishing a poem called *Tsum strayk* (To the strike) that became a popular success. The paper collapsed and Halpern returned to New York.

Halpern was associated with the *Yunge* group of poets, but never completely identified with them. In 1919 he married Royzele Baron, and published his most influential work, *In nyu-york*. A close association with the communist *Di frayhayt* was broken in 1924, and in the same year Halpern published a second collection of poetry, *Di goldene pave* (The golden peacock). Halpern was much in demand as a public performer of his poetry, and made several tours in the USA. He died suddenly in 1932, having just returned from two years in Los Angeles. In 1934 two further volumes of poetry were published under the title *Moyshe Leyb Halpern* and much material still remains unpublished.

Halpern was a poet of great psychological complexity, with a tortured, unsentimental and often deeply hostile attitude toward the eastern European *shtetl* he left behind, but he was never able to find the peace and identity he craved in the USA. His poetry involves a search for equilibrium and tranquility and for the reconciliation of the parts of a divided self.

FURTHER READING
Harshav, B. and Harshav, B.: *American Yiddish Poetry* (Berkeley: University of California Press, 1986), 393–505

CHRISTOPHER HUTTON

Halter, Marek (b.1932) French artist, writer and activist. Born in Warsaw, Poland,

Halter's childhood was infused with elements of that city's unique blend of religious and secular Jewish cultures. He escaped from the Warsaw Ghetto and spent the remainder of the War in Soviet Uzbekistan. In 1945 he returned to Poland but found life there intolerable. In 1950 he moved to Paris in order to study art, and remained there.

Halter first achieved notoriety in 1953 when he won the prestigious Grand Prix de la Peinture. In 1969, he was awarded the coveted Prix International de la Biennale d'Ancôme (Venice) for his massive canvas, "Croquis de mai", which attempted to capture the spirit and events associated with the student uprisings in Paris during May, 1968.

Halter's artistic expressions are paralleled by his political activities and writings. He has tirelessly struggled for equal rights and justice for all people, especially racial minorities in France. As senior editor of *Eléments*, a left-wing journal which seeks a negotiated peace settlement to the Middle Eastern situation, he has traveled extensively in the region. His research in Middle Eastern affairs resulted in a book, *Le Fou et les rois* (1977), for which he won the Prix Aujourd'hui. His profound commitment to combatting the rise of racism in France led him to assist in the creation of SOS Racisme in 1984. He is also currently serving as the President of the European Foundation for Science, Art and Culture.

Halter's activities have their roots deep in his Jewish heritage. His positive action on behalf of minorities should be seen in the light of public indifference during the Holocaust. He has actively worked within the Jewish community in France to ensure better race relations. President Mitterrand selected Halter to serve as the first director of the new Centre du Judaisme in Paris, as well as to assist in the organization of the government sponsored programme, "Le Mois du Judaisme" (January, 1986), a one month's celebration of two millenia of French-Jewish life.

Halter achieved international recognition for his epic novel, *Le Mémoire d'Abraham* (1985; *The Book of Abraham*, 1986), a fictional account of Jewish survival as experienced in one family.

The tale spans the 2,000-year history of the Jewish Diaspora.

SIMON SIBELMAN

Hamburger, Michael (b.1924)

British poet and translator. Like Karen GERSHON and other refugees who came to England as children from Nazi Germany, Hamburger has had to contend with his own survival and with exile from a language which has in many senses rejected him. The poet has no homeland ("The search", in *Weather and Season*, 1963). Theodore ADORNO's and George STEINER's remarks on silence and poetry after the Holocaust inform "Treblinka" (in *Ownerless Earth*, 1973), which gives a survivor's impression of the crematoria the first night in an extermination camp. "At Staufen" (in *Real Estate*, 1977) suggests a contiguity with nature, similar to Jon SILKIN's poetry, when Hamburger juxtaposes mass destruction in the insect world with the man-made mass killing in the East.

Hamburger has translated from the German, including the work of Paul CELAN, and written critical studies of German poetry.

BIBLIOGRAPHY
A Mug's Game: Intermittent Memoirs (Manchester: Carcanet, 1973); *Collected Poems 1941–1983* (Manchester: Carcanet, 1984; corrected edn, 1985)

FURTHER READING
Schmidt, M.: *An Introduction to Fifty Modern British Poets* (London: Pan, 1979)
Sicher, E.: *Beyond Marginality: Anglo-Jewish Literature After the Holocaust* (Albany: State University of New York Press, 1985)

EFRAIM SICHER

Harby, Isaac (1788–1828)

Teacher, journalist, and playwright. Harby was born in Charleston, South Carolina, where he was educated and spent the greater part of his life. The city had attained a high reputation for its educational institutions and cultural life. In Harby's youth, a Jewish community was well established in the life of Charleston and had not yet been overtaken by New York. "Culturally, religiously and possibly in other directions as well, the center of gravity in American Jewish life during the first quarter of the nineteenth century was located in Charleston, S.C." (J. R. Marcus, *Memoirs of American Jews*, i, 11).

In this milieu Harby made his name early. At sixteen he became an instructor at Charleston College and a year later wrote the first of a number of plays. While later critics have commented favorably on them (having regard to the standard of American drama at the time), Harby's plays were not well received, and he had to earn his living as a teacher. His talents as a writer found an outlet in journalism, where he was more successful.

Harby was a leader, and perhaps the moving spirit, in the first organized attempt to establish Reform Judaism in the USA. Congregation Beth Elohim was conducted according to the Sefardi ritual; in 1824 47 families petitioned for reforms in the service, and when their request was denied they established a Reformed Society of Israelites in January 1825. The aims of this group were set out in the address (subsequently printed), which Harby delivered on the first anniversary of its establishment. In 1827 Harby became president of the Society.

Financial necessity impelled Harby to move to New York in 1828, where he died suddenly in the same year. His death contributed to the demise of the Society. In 1841 the seeds of Reform germinated when Beth Elohim adopted the reforms which the separatist group had advocated.

FURTHER READING

Kohler, M. J.: Isaac Harby, Jewish religious leader and man of letters. *American Jewish Historical Society* 32 (1931) 35–53

Plaut, W. G.: *Growth of Reform Judaism* (New York: World Union for Progressive Judaism, 1965) 7, 8, 134–7, 172–7

Schappes, M. U.: *A Documentary History of the Jews in the United States* (New York: Schocken, 1971)

SEFTON D. TEMKIN

Harkavy, Alexander (1863–1939) Yiddish lexicographer. Born in Navaredok (Nowogródek), Lithuania, into a family of illustrious rabbinic ancestry, Harkavy migrated to the United States in 1882. He went on to become a pioneer of Yiddishism and modern Yiddish lexicography. In 1885 he produced, while in Paris, a Hebrew study entitled *Sefat yehudit* (The Yiddish language). A parallel Yiddish pamphlet appeared in New York in 1886. In the 1880s these treatments regarding Yiddish were intellectually sensational.

Harkavy became a beloved cultural leader and educator of the Jewish immigrants on the Lower East Side of New York City, publishing dozens of books to help the immigrants master English, American history and other secular subjects. At the same time, he published numerous works designed to disseminate knowledge and appreciation of Yiddish, as well as a number of academic studies. His marriage to Bella Segalowsky, just after she had attempted suicide, endeared him further to the immigrants.

Harkavy's greatest accomplishments are his dictionaries, starting with his 1891 *English–Yiddish Dictionary* and his 1898 *Yiddish–English Dictionary*. His most permanently valuable reference work in his trilingual *Yiddish–English–Hebrew Dictionary*, 1925, which remains indispensable to advanced students of Yiddish. To this day, it remains the best dictionary for readers of the great Yiddish classics of the late nineteenth and early twentieth centuries. At the time of his death, he had completed a Yiddish–Yiddish defining dictionary, which still awaits publication.

FURTHER READING

Katz, D.: Alexander Harkavy and his trilingual dictionary. In *Yiddish–English–Hebrew Dictionary* ed. A. Harkavy (New York: Schocken Books and Yivo Institute for Jewish Research, 1988)

DOVID KATZ

Hart, Solomon Alexander (1806–1881) British painter. Born in Plymouth, Hart was apprenticed at the age of 14 to Samuel Warren, a line-engraver. In 1820, he moved to London with his father, a Jewish goldsmith. Three years later, resolving to devote himself to painting, he entered the Royal Academy in London. At first a miniaturist, he later developed as a portraitist and painter of large-scale historical and biblical genre. He also depicted literary themes drawn from Shakespeare, Milton and Scott. His work is characterized by the precise realism and attention to detail prescribed by nineteenth–century Realism.

Hart's debut in the English art world came in 1830 when his painting *Jewish Synagogue* was purchased at the Society of British Artists. He was elected an Associate of the Royal Academy in 1835 and Academician in 1840. In 1841–2, he visited Italy where he made genre studies of Italian peasants and interior and exterior views of Italian churches. During his lifetime, he received numerous commissions from institutions in London, including synagogues and hospitals, as well as from private residences. The subject matter of his commissioned paintings varied widely, and included both Old and New Testament stories and literary themes. Hart also contributed illustrations to the *Athenaeum*, *Jewish Chronicle*, and other newspapers in London.

Hart was Professor of Painting at the Royal Academy between 1857 and 1863, and Librarian there from 1865 until his death. During his lifetime, he exhibited at both the Royal Society of British Artists and at the British Institution.

BIBLIOGRAPHY

Brodie, A., ed.: *Reminiscences of S. A. Hart, R. A.* (London: privately published, 1882)

KRISTIE A. JAYNE

Hasidism An eastern European mass mystical and revivalist movement, originating with the charismatic teacher and healer Israel BAAL SHEM TOV. Both a mass mystical and social movement, Hasidism commenced with Baal Shem Tov's realization that there was no place free of God's presence. Directed to the masses as well as the elite, this insight was expressed in homilies, stories and song. Israel demanded that even the simplest Jew achieve *devekut* – uninterrupted communion with God. As a social movement, Hasidism sparked a radical reorganization of the Jewish community into a series of collectives centering around charismatic spiritual teachers called *tzaddikim* (righteous ones). This provoked violent clashes with the established community, led by a wealthy aris-

tocracy and a Talmudically educated rabbinate. Around 1736, Israel began a public teaching career, based upon his sense of the immediate presence of God in all things. If God suffuses all reality, all daily tasks and experiences are potential portals to mystical awareness. The Jew should serve God in all of his ways and with ecstatic joy.

Although not a Talmud scholar, Israel's profound insight drew members of the rabbinic class into his circle. Two, Dov Ber and Jacob Joseph, became pivotal theoreticians and organizers of the fledgling community. After Israel's death, Dov Ber established the first permanent hasidic court in the town of Mezritsch, where he attracted a circle of well educated and talented disciples such as Levi Yitshak of Berditchev, Shneur Zalman of Lyady and Elimelech of Lizensk. These would establish flourishing hasidic communities throughout Poland and the Ukraine.

The great theoretician of early hasidic mysticism, Dov Ber taught a sophisticated form of contemplative prayer. All worlds are imbued with Divine Vitality. This vital energy is a manifestation of Divine Consciousness, in which there is no separation between subject and object. In prayer, the devotee is to nullify all sense of self, in order to merge his consciousness with God's and view the world suffused with divine light and energy.

Jacob Joseph turned his attention to the issue of leadership and developed the ideology of the *tzaddik*. His books, such as *Toledot Ya'akov Yosef* (1780; The generations of Jacob Joseph), depicted the traditional rabbinate as an ivory tower elite, unconcerned with the masses, overly beholden to the wealthy leadership who hired and fired them. In contrast, while living a contemplative life, the *tzaddik* was to be a rabbi deeply involved with the common people. A throne for the divine presence, he should connect heaven and earth and transmit God's blessings to his community.

This emphasis upon contemplation and spiritual charisma over Talmudic learning as sources of authority and fierce criticism of the aristocracy, led to a brutal backlash. Starting in 1772, the hasidic community was repeatedly excommunicated, its teachers often run out of

Hasidic Jews after morning prayers in a village in Hungary, c.1920

town and its literature burnt. Such actions did not slow its explosive growth but true peace was not established between the two camps until the appearance of the Enlightenment in eastern Europe around 1830 presented both camps with a common foe. Major hasidic communities continue to flourish, despite the ravages of the Holocaust. Hasidic thought remains a source of inspiration to modern Jewish thinkers, particularly Martin BUBER and the contemporary North American *Havurah* movement.

FURTHER READING

Dan, J., and Milch, R.: *The Teachings of Hasidism* (New York: Behrman House, 1983)

Dresner, S.: *The Zaddik: The Doctrine of the Zaddik According to the Writings of Rabbi Yaakov Yosef of Polnoy* (New York: Schocken Books, 1974)

Jacobs, L.: *Hasidic Prayer* (New York: Schocken Books, 1973)

Weinryb, B.: *The Jews of Poland: A Social and Economic History of the Jewish Community in Poland from 1100 to 1800* (Philadelphia: The Jewish Publication Society of America, 1973)

Weiss, J.: *Studies in Eastern European Jewish Mysticism* (Oxford and London: Oxford University Press, 1985)

SETH L. BRODY

Haskalah [Enlightenment] The term "*Haskalah*" is commonly attributed to the Hebrew social, spiritual and literary movement that developed and spread throughout central and eastern Europe from the last quarter of the eighteenth century up to the 1880s. It proposed the breaching of the ghetto walls, teaching the Jews foreign languages and lucid Hebrew, conceiving new Hebrew poetry and literature, and Jewish integration into European culture. The term *Haskalah* is also widely perceived as equivalent to the German *Aufklärung* and the English Enlightenment. This perception, albeit inaccurate, is to some extent valid. For the Hebrew *Haskalah* emerged in Germany, was influenced by the intellectual fashion of the *Aufklärung* and drew pivotal ideas from it, adapting them to Jewish social and cultural realities. The word *haskalah* itself is midrashic; it was not used in the Middle Ages and reappeared in the eighteenth century, indicating "rational inquiry" (as in N. H. WESSELY's *Halevanon*, 1765). The word was not, however, widely used in the Hebrew *Haskalah* literature of the eighteenth and first half of the nineteenth centuries. It became popular as the common term for the movement and its central idea only as late as the early 1860s, when the periodicals *Hamelitz* and *Hatzefirah* were produced.

The beginning of the *Haskalah* as a social, spiritual and literary movement can be traced to the late 1760s in Germany, particularly in Prussia (Königsberg and Berlin), although earlier signs had already been evident in the middle of the century (M. H. LUZZATTO's *Leyesharim tehillah* (Praise to the upright) in 1743 in Amsterdam, and *Kohelet musar*, the first *maskilic* periodical edited by Moses MENDELSSOHN, in 1755). In the first half of the nineteenth century the *Haskalah*'s center shifted to Galicia, and in the mid nineteenth century to Russia, especially to Lithuania and Volhynia. This moving of the *Haskalah*'s center was not coincidental but was a consequence of the movement's sociohistorical nature. The *Haskalah* grew in a climate of partial openness to European culture, when economic integration and social interaction were already taking place but equal rights had not yet been fully achieved; when the Jewish cultural basis was still intact and before circumstances facilitated complete assimilation. As soon as these circumstances had altered – with the Emancipation – the *Haskalah* gradually lost its sociocultural *raison d'être*; when the process of assimilation and adoption of host languages had commenced the Hebrew *Haskalah* weakened or vanished altogether.

In the second half of the eighteenth century the Jewish community in Prussia was generally non-traditional and consisted largely of "court-Jews". The first *maskilim*, such as teachers, officials and physicians, emerged from the group around them and from within this group there grew, in the late 1770s, a movement that aspired to change Jewish society and culture. Its most noticeable manifestations were in the domains of education and culture. In 1778 the first modern school, whose curriculum included both Hebrew and general topics, was established in Berlin. In 1782, stimulated by the Austrian Kaiser Joseph II's Edict of Tolerance, Wessely published his *Divrei shalom ve'emet*, (Words of peace and truth). In this treatise, which can be seen as the *Haskalah*'s manifesto and the essence of its program, Wessely called for the founding of modern schools in the spirit of the Kaiser's declaration. The treatise stimulated a fierce reaction on the part of the rabbis and a vehement controversy developed, a phenomenon which was to recur later in Galicia and Russia.

At the same time Mendelssohn initiated the great enterprise of *Habi'ur* (The commentary), a translation of the Old Testament into German in Hebrew script and with a modern literary commentary. This translation by Mendelssohn himself, and the commentary, in which prominent *Haskalah* personalities took part, became the main educational device for diffusing esthetic values (for example, the concept of the Bible as literature), teaching lucid German and repelling Yiddish, which was deemed a jargon. Indeed, for a long period *Habi'ur* served as the primary device for spreading the principles of the *Haskalah*.

In 1783 a group of young *maskilim* (enlighteners) came together in Königsberg under the name of *Dorshei leshon 'ever* (Seekers of the Hebrew language) and from 1783 they began to issue the periodical *Hame'assef*, whose purpose was to publish new Hebrew poetry, articles, and biographies, and translate poetry from German. *Hame'assef* appeared continuously until 1790 and continued to appear, with long breaks, until 1812. Despite the fact that it did not publish any literary works of great value, it played a significant role in the development of Hebrew literature and served as a model for the periodicals that followed.

Mendelssohn is considered to be the founding father of the *Haskalah*, a role which stemmed from his highly esteemed status in German philosophy. Another prominent figure in the early stages of the *Haskalah* was Wessely who, in *Divrei shalom ve'emet*, presented not only a practical program for Jewish educational change, but also a new ideological manifesto. The underlying idea of the manifesto is the distinction drawn between "the knowledge of man" (the humanities and sciences), and "the Law of God" (the written and oral law), the former associated with the state's language (German) and the latter with the holy language (Hebrew). Furthermore, Wessely perceived the esthetic experience, poetry first and foremost, to be the pinnacle of the *Haskalah*, a notion that echoed the primacy of esthetics and poetry in eighteenth-century German culture. This perception, which reflected the intellectual mood typical of the German *Aufklärung*, marked a full-scale revolution in the Jewish spiritual world: no longer a world centered on the Talmud and its armor bearers but a new one, based on the harmony of three equivalent elements: the knowledge of man (emphasizing European languages and science), the Law of God (Hebrew and the Bible), and esthetics (poetry). Following many generations throughout which central and east European Jewry had excluded everything but halakhic, moral and kabbalistic literature, the emergence of the *Haskalah* marked the beginning of a secular Hebrew literature.

The underlying concept of *Haskalah* literature, up to the 1850s, was undoubtedly classicist and rationalist, inspired by eighteenth-century German literature and French classicism. Following classicism, *Haskalah* literature drew a sharp distinction between high and low literature, the former being poetry and the latter prose. This dichotomy was both thematic and lingual: poetry was more spiritual and cosmopolitan, and employed biblical language; prose was anchored in concrete Jewish reality, its style less adorned and partly based on mishnaic language (satire) and medieval language (reflective prose). In *Haskalah* literature's first phase in its German center, poetry played a crucial role. The two pivotal works, which became classics of this literature, were M. H. Luzzatto's *Leyesharim tehillah* and Wessely's *Shirei tif'eret* (1789; Poems of splendor). The former is a lyric allegorical drama, inspired by the Italian poetic drama, the latter, a long didactic epic of Moses's life, inspired by Klopstock's *Messias*. Twenty-four Hebrew editions of *Leyesharim tehillah* were printed during the time of the *Haskalah*, and many works followed, the most notable being Shalom Hakohen's *Amel*

vetirtzeh (1812) and Abraham Dov LEBENSOHN's *Emet ve'emunah* (1867).

Other significant genres of *Haskalah* poetry apart from the poetic historical drama, were the long reflective poem, the ode, the elegy and the proverb. The most important dramatic work was Yosef Haefrati's *Melukhat Shaul* (1794; Saul's reign). It gained much popularity and revealed the imprint both of the *Haskalah* and of the French Revolution. As in *Haskalah* poetry in general, many influential sources can be found in this play: those of Luzzatto and Wessely, German poetry (Albrecht von Haler and Schiller), and Shakespeare (Macbeth, King Lear and Hamlet), with whose works Haefrati became familiar via their translations into German. The noticeable work in the field of reflective poetry is Shlomo Pfafenheim's *Agadat arba' kosot* (1790; The legend of the four goblets), which was written in lyric prose, and in which the imprint of Edward Young's *Night Thoughts* (1742–5) is evident. Among the many odes published in the *Haskalah* period, Shlomo Levizon's "Hamelitzah medaberet" is particularly noteworthy. This lyrically accomplished ode opens Levizon's important book on poetry, *Melitzat yeshurun* (The poesy of Jeshurun), which contains elements of Herder, Edmund Burke and Robert Lowth.

The Emancipation and the spread of German language and education among local Jewry reduced the importance of the *Haskalah* in Germany, and in the first half of the 19th century its center moved to Austria, particularly to Galicia. Following Joseph II's Edict of Tolerance, over a hundred German–Jewish schools were founded in Galicia. Their establishment encountered the antagonistic reaction of the rabbis, the *hasidim* in particular, and produced, fierce conflict, which stimulated some of the most outstanding works of *Haskalah* literature in Galicia: Yosef Perl's anti-*hasidic* satire, *Megaleh tmirin* (1819; The revealer of secrets), and Yizhak Erter's *Hatzofeh lebeit yisra'el* (1858).

Although in its Austrian phase, the *Haskalah* drew its strength from the dense Jewish population in Galicia, the bulk of publishing activity took place in Vienna. There the main *Haskalah* periodicals of the first half of the nineteenth century, which succeeded *Hame'assef*, were published: *Bikurei ha'itim* (1821–33), *Kerem hemed* (1833–56) and *Kokhavei Yitzhak* (1845–76). The contribution of the *Haskalah* in Austria and Galicia to the development of Hebrew poetry was minimal, the notable poets being Shalom Hakohen and Meir Halevi Letteris. The former was influenced by Luzzatto and Wessely and the latter dedicated himself chiefly to translation. The Galician writers excelled in prose and developed both narrative satire and literary criticism – one of the chief contributors to the latter being Solomon I. Rappaport. One of the most prominent among *Haskalah* writers in Galicia was Nachman Krochmal, author of *Moreh nevokhei hazman* (Guide to the perplexed of the time), which was published posthumously in 1851. This historiosophic work is undoubtedly the most important treatise of later Hebrew *Haskalah* literature. Its views on history and Jewish distinctiveness exerted a major influence on Jewish thought in the second half of the nineteenth century.

Galicia also served as a stepping-stone for the spread of the *Haskalah* further eastwards, to Russia. The dominant influence then shifted from German culture to Russian. The early development of the *Haskalah* in Russia is usually attributed to Yizhak Baer Levinsohn, who was Perl's disciple. His treatise, *Te'udah beyisra'el* (1828) fulfilled a function in Russia similar to that of Wessely's *Divrei shalom ve'emet* in Germany and Austria. The most important center of the *Haskalah* in Russia was Lithuania which produced a considerable literature. Pre-eminent among the first generation of *Haskalah* writers in Lithuania were Mordekhai Aharon Ginzburg, whose autobiography, *Avi 'ezer*, (1863) served as a model for Moshe LILIENBLUM's autobiography *Hata'ot ne'urim* (1876); and Adam Hakohen Lebensohn, who won fame through his *Shirei sfat kodesh* (1842). From the mid-nineteenth century *Haskalah* literature developed in narrative skill. In 1853 the first Hebrew novel, Abraham MAPU's *Ahavat Zion* (Love of Zion), was published. The success of this romantic adventure novel was vast: within 35 years it was republished in 8 editions. Mapu subsequently wrote two more novels: *Ayit tzavu'a* (1857; The hypocrite) and *Ashmat Shomron* (1865). At the same time *Les Mystères de Paris* by Eugene

Suë was published in Kalman Schulman's Hebrew translation. Its popularity assisted in placing the novel genre at the center of the Hebrew literary arena. Many writers followed Mapu's lead and developed the realistic novel under the influence of Russian positivism. The most noteworthy among these was Peretz SMOLENSKIN whose highly successful novels were printed in several editions within a short period. Other significant contributors to the development of the realistic novel were Shalom Jacob Abramovitz, (MENDELE MOKHER SEFARIM) and Reuven Asher Broides.

Side by side with the flourishing of the novel, *Haskalah* poetry also underwent major transformations. The prominent *Haskalah* poets, Micah Joseph LEBENSOHN (Mikhal) and Judah Loeb GORDON (Yalag), gradually relinquished the classicist tradition of Wessely's poetry. Certain motifs characteristic of the post-*Haskalah* era, such as the loss of belief in divine providence, and the undermining of the ideal of reason as the basis for progress, are identifiable in their poetry. Mikhal's poetry exhibited elements of romanticism and the personal lyric, for the first time in the *Haskalah* poetry. *Haskalah* poetry reached its zenith with Gordon: in reaction to the emergence of the novel he abandoned the didactic epic and developed instead the short narrative poem with lyrical digressions. Russian poetry, both romantic and realistic, served as his model. Through his poems, which were divided into two groups: *Shirei kalilah korot yamim rishonim* and *Shirei kalilah korot yameinu*, Gordon severely criticized his contemporary Jewish community and the dominance of the rabbis. He advocated its changing from rooted Orthodoxy, dominated by the clerical establishment, into a free and enlightened part of European Society. Gordon invigorated both the Hebrew language and Hebrew poetry, and provided a stepping-stone to the Hebrew poetry that developed in the 1890s with BIALIK and TSCHERNICHOWSKI.

A significant factor in the development of the Hebrew *Haskalah* and its literature in the second half of the nineteenth century were the new periodicals: *Hashahar* (1868–85), edited by Smolenskin, was the foremost literary periodical of its time, expressing the innovative national

Front page of the first issue of Hashahar *(Vienna, 1868)*

FURTHER READING

Altman, A.: *Moses Mendelssohn: A Biographical Study* (London, 1973)

Halkin, S.: *Modern Hebrew Literature* (New York, 1970)

Miron, D.: Rediscovering Haskalah Poetry *Prooftexts*, 1 (1981) 292–305

Patterson, D.: *The Hebrew Novel in Czarist Russia* (Edinburgh, 1964)

Pelli, M.: *The Age of Haskalah* (Leiden, 1979)

Raisin, J. S.: *The Haskalah Movement in Russia* (Philadelphia, 1923)

UZI SHAVIT

Hatvany, Lajos (1880–1961) Hungarian writer, critic, patron of the arts. Hatvany came from an upper-class Jewish family of industrialists which was ennobled under Franz Joseph. After studies of classical philology in Germany, Hatvany received his doctorate at the University of Budapest. In 1908 he became the chief financial supporter of the literary review *Nyugat* which played a major role in the development of modern Hungarian letters. In 1917 he edited the daily *Pesti Napló*. He was a member of the National Council set up by the 1918 democratic revolution, but after the Communist takeover in March 1919 he emigrated to Vienna and lived there until 1927. After his return to Hungary he was prosecuted and, for some months, imprisoned for his earlier "revolutionary" activities. In 1938 he emigrated for the second time, lived first in Paris and then (during the Second World War) in Oxford. He returned to Hungary in 1947 and in 1959 was awarded the Kossuth Prize.

Hatvany's criticism earned the adjective "impressionistic"; his literary journalism, while enjoyable and informative, is not particularly important. On the other hand, his knack of recognizing new talents helped him to support the great modern poet Endre Ady: Hatvany's writings on Ady were published in two volumes in 1959. As literary historian Hatvany's main contribution was a day-to-day chronicle of Sándor Petőfi's life in five volumes, *Igy élt Petőfi* (1955–7; This is how Petőfi lived). In the collection of essays and reminiscences *Utak, sorsok, emberek* (1973; Roads, destinies, people) an interview of 1924 is included in which Hatvany

ideas of its editor; *Hehalutz*, edited by Yehoshua Heschel Schorr, was concerned with the controversy with religious Orthodoxy. Weeklies began to appear in the late 1850s and early 1860s, *Hamagid* (1856–86), *Hakarmel* (1860–70), *Hamelitz* (1860–1903) and *Hatzefirah* (1862–1931).

The *Haskalah* movement ended following the atrocities inflicted upon Russian Jewry in 1881–2, when it became evident that enlightenment alone was unable to provide the desired emancipation or a solution to the Jewish problem. New streams and movements emerged from the *Haskalah*'s ruins, drawing from its ideas but seeking new ones. Such was the case with the *Hibbat Zion* movement, Zionism, the Jewish socialist movements and the immense waves of immigration to the USA. Modern Hebrew literature in Russia and Palestine was derived from the modest foundations created by *Haskalah* literature and became its direct continuation.

talks about his Jewish and Hungarian identity. He points out that he has no desire to write in German, for he wants to address himself mainly to Hungarians; he cannot see any contradiction between his roots and his Hungarian cultural loyalty. An aristocrat with democratic tastes, Hatvany remained throughout his life a libertarian liberal and a conscientious philologist.

GEORGE GÖMÖRI

Hazaz, Hayim (1898–1973) Hebrew writer. Born in Siderovitchi in the district of Kiev, Russia, Hazaz spent a good deal of his youth in rural areas of the Ukraine, where his father was a timber agent. His early stories, dealing largely with the tumultuous impact on rural Jews of the Russian Revolution, reflect this environment as well as his prodigious self-instruction in Hebrew and Russian literature. The novel *Daltot nehoshet* (1956; *Gates of Bronze*, 1975) is a reworking of Hazaz's *Revolution Stories* (1924), and representative of his life-long preoccupation with the disenchantment and terror of his experiences in the Ukraine and Crimea. His story "Shmuel Frankfurter" (1925), prefigures Hazaz's fascination with thwarted messianism and the Jesus story, about which he published segments of a projected novel. Hazaz captures the experience of being one of a group of lonely Jewish exiles in Istanbul and then Paris (until leaving for Palestine in 1930) in his fragmentary novel, *Beyishuv shel ya'ar* (1930–1), and in his biblical literary tone-poem, *Hatan damim* (1929; *Bridegroom of Blood*, 1931).

Following Hazaz's settling in Palestine two tendencies become marked in his fiction. One is his penchant for romanticizing the eastern European small town environment in an overt emulation of MENDELE's colorful linguistic virtuosity and flair for the burlesque. The second tendency is Hazaz's emergence as Hebrew literature's "novelist of ideas" par excellence. This can be seen in a large number of stories in which Hazaz pits the cynical life-weary intellectual against simpler, regenerative, life-affirming principles, such as the Yemenite porter in *Rahamim* (1933) and the young kibbutz girl – also Yemenite – in *Ofek natui* (1958; Extended

horizon). The drama of messianism and Zionism in Judaism, European and Oriental, becomes Hazaz's overbearing preoccupation. Hazaz gives equal dramatic thrust to the tendencies which hinder or cast doubt upon the Zionist impulse, as can be seen, typically, in his *Beketz hayamim* (1933–4; *The End of Days*, 1982), *Drabkin* (1939) and *Haderashah* (1943; *The Sermon*, 1952). In the context of Hazaz's long-term ethnographic fascination with the Yemenite community, aspects of the collision between mysticism and twentieth-century reality are most fully realized in his multi-volume work, *Ya'ish* (1947), and, especially, in the masterful novel, *Hayoshevet baganim* (1944; *Mori Sa'id*, 1956).

BIBLIOGRAPHY
Bridegroom of Blood (1931); Canopy and wedding ring, trans. B. Halpern. *Jewish Frontier* 16, no. 9 (1949) 18–28; The wanderer, trans. I. M. Lask. In *Tehilla and Other Israel Tales* (London: Agnon Ltd, 1956); *Gates of Bronze* (1975); *The End of Days* (1982)

FURTHER READING
Band, A.: Between fiction and historiography. *Midstream* 10, no. 2 (1964) 90–5
Bargad, W.: *Ideas in Fiction* (Chico: Scholars Press, 1982)
Nash, S.: Hazaz's "Aristotle". *Modern Hebrew Literature* 10 (1984) 20–3
——: A review of Bargad's *Ideas in Fiction*. *AJS Review* 10, no. 1 (1985) 124–5

STANLEY NASH

Hebrew The language of the Jewish Bible (except for some parts of Daniel) and of most of Jewish literature until the nineteenth century; now the official and cultural language of Israel.

Hebrew belongs to the Semitic language family, which includes also two other languages much used by Jews, Aramaic and Arabic. Its closest known relative is Phoenician, spoken in ancient times in Southern Lebanon, but it is probable that Canaanite, spoken then in Palestine, was even closer. The oldest texts in the Bible originated before 1000 BCE, but the majority of biblical texts are written in classical Biblical Hebrew, standardized with the establishment of the state of David and Solomon, and used in the Kingdom of Judah. There is evidence that the language of the Kingdom of Israel was somewhat different. After the destruction of the First Temple and the Babylonian exile, we find Late Biblical Hebrew, influenced by the spoken language.

Biblical Hebrew is shown by inscriptions to have been written in the same script as Phoenician. This script indicates only consonants, the vowels having to be supplied by the reader. Towards the end of the biblical period, the letters "w" and "y" were inserted, though not consistently, to indicate the vowels "o", and "u" or "i" and "e" respectively. We can reconstruct the full sound of biblical Hebrew only by assumptions based upon Canaanite words written in the Babylonian script in the Tell-Amarna tablets, c.1400 BCE, writing of proper names in Assyrian and Babylonian texts and in the Greek translation (the "Septuagint", third century BCE), as well as in remnants of a complete transliteration into Greek letters about 300 CE. The present Hebrew Bible (Old Testament) indicates the vowels by signs added to the letters, the so-called pointing, which represent the pronunciation used at Tiberias c.900 CE. These signs were read differently in different countries. The way it is read in academic circles is based upon the "Sephardic" pronunciation of Jews of Spanish origin, as is also the Israeli Hebrew of our own day. The Hebrew Bible contains between 7,000 and 8,000 words, according to the manner of counting. This is probably about 10 percent of the words the language had, allowing for changes in the 1,000 years of its existence, and the large number of synonyms. The meaning of a small percentage of the words is still disputed. Some of the Biblical Hebrew words used in Modern Hebrew now have quite different meanings.

From the first century BCE a different type of written Hebrew appears, now called Mishnaic Hebrew. This is now widely acknowledged to be based upon the spoken language of the time, though some scholars still consider it an unsuccessful attempt of Aramaic-speaking Jews to write Hebrew. Mishnaic Hebrew contains a large number of words found in biblical Hebrew, and around 14,000 additional words, many of which are probably inherited from biblical

Hebrew, but did not occur in the Bible. At that time Jews in the Diaspora spoke local languages, and probably a large part of the Jews of Palestine spoke Aramaic or Greek. In the fourth century CE, Mishnaic Hebrew ceased to be spoken, but continued to be used in writing, as was Biblical Hebrew for some purposes. Although the following centuries produced literatures in Greek, Aramaic, and later Arabic, and later still in various Jewish languages (see entry), Hebrew continued to be the principal written language of the Jewish people. There was *diglossia*, a state in which the same community uses one language for formal purposes and another for everyday activities, as we find, for example, in medieval England with Latin and English. Both languages are alive and change, though the "upper" language has stronger links with the past. Hebrew developed considerably during the 16 centuries of this diglossia, and adapted itself to the development both of Jewish thought and of technical and scientific progress.

Scientific and religious prose, as well as private letters, were during the Middle Ages written in a development of Mishnaic Hebrew, the only exception being the Jewish community of Muslim Spain, who used Arabic for prose purposes. On the other hand, prayers and poetry, as well as narrative literature, were from the beginning written in a somewhat more biblical style, and as time went on, in ever purer biblical Hebrew. The need to express in Hebrew not only scientific concepts, but also the complicated argumentation of philosophical Arabic heavily influenced by Greek, created many new words and turns of phrase which ultimately furthered the development of Modern Hebrew as a scientific language.

In the middle of the eighteenth century, purist tendencies in French and German influenced the europeanizing Enlightenment (HASKALAH) movement to employ Biblical Hebrew also in non-narrative prose, such as periodicals and scientific works. In the nineteenth century there began a stream of novels in Biblical Hebrew. From the 1850s "realistic" novels of contemporary life were translated and written, with everything, including dialogue, in purest Biblical Hebrew. This created a crisis, which caused, inter alia, one of the most gifted writers, S. J. Abramowitz, to abandon Hebrew and to write in Yiddish, under the pseudonym MENDELE MOKHER SEFARIM.

In the years around 1880 the growing despair of the Jews in Czarist Russia of obtaining full citizens' status, led to the penetration of the ideas of the national independence movements of central-European and south-European peoples into Russian Jewish circles. One of these was the "revival" of national languages, generally by establishing a written literature in their vernaculars, thus in most cases rejecting existing diglossic situations. Both the idea of establishing a cultural center in Palestine and the revival of Hebrew literature were advocated in 1879 in an article published by Eliezer BEN-YEHUDA, who raised the possibility of speaking Hebrew again as an everyday language. The idea caught on, and while Ben-Yehuda was active in Palestine setting up elementary education in the Hebrew medium, Hebrew Societies started to emerge all over eastern Europe.

It was probably the new spirit of Jewish nationalism which moved Mendele Mokher Sefarim in 1885 to return to writing his novels in Hebrew, and later to translate his Yiddish novels into Hebrew. He did this, however, in Rabbinic Hebrew. When asked about this, 20 years later, he stated that he wanted "to write for the Jews", that is, to be understood by the ordinary reader unaccustomed to neo-biblical purism, but using in his Yiddish thousands of Medieval Hebrew words. Mendele introduced into this popular language devices taken from realistic Russian novel-writing, as he had done already in his Yiddish works. Immediately this technique and language were adopted by an ever-growing number of other Hebrew writers, and in 1890 H. N. BIALIK used Rabbinic Hebrew for the first time in a poem ("*El hatzippor*"). Meanwhile Ben-Yehuda used Medieval Hebrew in Palestine, and in 1908 began to write his monumental *Thesaurus Totius Hebraitatis*, in which for the first time in Hebrew lexicography, medieval word-formations were included. This became the basis for modern written and spoken Hebrew.

Although Modern Hebrew is in fact a natural continuation of Medieval Hebrew, and the re-vival only consists in adding the spoken dimension, this is not generally recognized by Israeli public opinion. The canonic view is that Mendele made a "synthesis" of two dead languages, Biblical and Mishnaic Hebrew. This ignores Medieval Hebrew altogether, and implies that the two components are Biblical Hebrew as in the Bible, and Mishnaic Hebrew as in the writings of 100–600 CE, and that the grammatical and syntactical rules of these two stages of the language are also those applying to Modern Hebrew. In actual fact, school grammars contain rules mainly taken from Biblical Hebrew. The language of Hebrew literature was until the 1950s predominantly the Rabbinic Hebrew as shaped by Mendele, with constant reminders of the Bible and of mishnaic-talmudic literature. The most outstanding writer in this idiom was S. Y. AGNON who also drew upon the eighteenth-century Hasidic stories written in a more popular form of Rabbinic Hebrew.

It seems that already at an early stage spoken Hebrew began to develop grammar, syntax and vocabulary of its own, as well as slang. In the 1930s we find educationalists discussing how schoolchildren could be weaned off what was then considered to be a special children's language, and made to speak standard Hebrew identical to a normal written style. On the other hand, a few writers did use some features of the spoken language in dialogue in novels and plays, to portray the language of the *sabras*, the native-born Israelis. In the War of Independence in 1948, some of the young *sabra* soldiers, such as Moshe SHAMIR, wrote stories in a more colloquial language, but hardly any of them continued in this style after the War. Only in the mid 1960s, due to some extent to translations of foreign literature with colloquial elements, dialogue came to be written in imitation of the actual spoken language in its different local, social, and communal (Occidental and Oriental) varieties.

The distance between the colloquial and the standard written idiom, and the difficulty schoolchildren had in acquiring the use of the standard language, produced a spate of written guides concentrating on inculcation of normative rules in school-teaching rather than systematic grammar and syntax, and non normative admonitions in special broadcasts. In spite of the eagerness of the public to obtain such instruction, the spoken language remained as it was in informal speech, and the "correct" language was used only in formal situations by those who had mastered it. But gradually certain features of the colloquial entered formal speaking and writing, a process which can be observed in newspapers, where such language is still rare in reportage, almost absent in leading articles, but prominent in advertisements.

When Hebrew speaking was revived, the idea was that it would become the home language of all national-minded Jews, including those that did not live in Palestine. In eastern Europe and in North Africa a network of Hebrew schools was set up, where the language of instruction was Hebrew; some such schools also existed in North and South America. Many of the post-First World War Hebrew writers and orators had been trained in such schools. The Second World War destroyed the east European schools, and in Soviet Russia the teaching of Hebrew as a spoken language was forbidden. In western Europe and in the USA the use of Hebrew as classroom language is now mostly restricted to religious teaching. On the other hand, there are intermittent waves of return to Jewish languages, such as Yiddish and Ladino, and Yiddish especially rivals Hebrew as a subject taken up in Universities. The mass of translations of contemporary Hebrew literature reduces the necessity of knowing Hebrew in order to keep in contact with Israel's art and thinking, just as the increasing rate of translation of the source works of Jewish religion and thought make the command of medieval Hebrew unnecessary for learning about Jewish Studies. Yet there is still a large network of institutions specializing in teaching the essentials of Modern Hebrew (see ULPAN), and a constant stream of young people taking Hebrew courses in Israel.

CHAIM RABIN

Hebrew literature Modern Hebrew literature continues one of the world's oldest literatures. Its earliest expressions are found in the Hebrew Bible and have been dated by some scholars as written before the eleventh century BCE. Until the eighteenth century, it was predominantly sacred, although occasional secular poetry and fictional works appear in the Hebrew Bible, in the literature of the Jews of medieval Spain, Provence, and renaissance and early modern Italy. Authors of these works rarely questioned the authority of the Jewish religious tradition, and frequently criticized the "sinful" nature of their secular writings, attributing them to "youthful folly".

The German Haskalah

A salient characteristic of modern Hebrew literature is its general secularity. Originating as a Jewish expression of the *Aufklärung* (Enlightenment) movement in eighteenth-century Germany which, in Hebrew, was called the HASKALAH, its founders sought a synthesis between religion and reason in keeping with the deistic philosophy of their mentor Moses MENDELSSOHN. They strove for the Europeanization of Jewish culture and were devout believers in the "good and the beautiful". Under Mendelssohn's guidance, they founded *Hame'assef* in 1783, the first Hebrew periodical. There they published their learned essays, poetry, satires, and didactic articles. The early *maskilim* (enlighteners) emerged from the rising, educated, German–Jewish bourgeoisie. Although raised in the tradition of and thoroughly at home in Jewish religious literature, they had also acquired a secular education. They wrote in Hebrew, the literary language of the Jewish community, not only to disseminate their doctrines but also to give them esthetic form. They shunned Yiddish, the spoken language of most of their Jewish contemporaries, because they mistakenly considered it to be a debased and ignorant form of German. Hebrew enjoyed the prestige of a classical language, even in enlightened gentile circles whose opinion *maskilim* highly prized. The leading figure of the German *Haskalah* after Mendelssohn was Naftali Hertz (Hartwig) WESSELY (1725–1805) whose *Shirei tif'eret* (Songs of praise) was an epic poem on the life of Moses. Wessely's Moses is an enlightened rationalist hero – the model of the *maskil*, par excellence.

As German Jewry entered the modern world

during the first third of the nineteenth century, adopted German as their mother tongue, and accommodated themselves to the new enlightened society, Hebrew gradually ceased to be their literary language and was replaced by scholarly, literary, and periodical literature written in German.

The *Haskalah* shifted to Galicia, that part of the Polish–Lithuanian Kingdom annexed by Austria–Hungary. The Edict of Toleration of Joseph II encouraged the modernization of Galician Jewry. Coincidental with this policy was the rise of an educated merchant class in Galicia which had commercial and social contacts with their German co-religionists. Unlike German Jewry, Galician Jewry were densely settled in a part of Europe, then hardly touched by modernity. They possessed a far deeper ethnic sense and, while attracted to the German culture of the monarchy, had little regard for the cultures of the various Slavic-language communities among whom they resided. The Galician *Haskalah* established several important Hebrew periodicals. Its authors were most adept in the areas of Jewish philosophy and historiography. Nachman KROCHMAL's important historiographical work *Moreh nevokhei hazman* (A guide to the perplexed of the age) was a serious attempt to reconcile modern thought with the tradition. Krochmal presented a schema for Jewish history, attributing its evolution to manifestation of the Divine Spirit. He was influenced by such European thinkers as Vico and Hegel. In the area of Jewish historiography, Solomon I. Rappaport (1790–1867) and the Italian scholar S. D. LUZZATO (Italy was then part of the Austro-Hungarian Empire) wrote several essays dealing with Talmudic and medieval Jewish literature. Luzzato, in addition, wrote theological essays, urging a romantic rather than a rationalist approach to the tradition. His devotion to ethnic Jewish values marks him as a precursor of the Jewish nationalist movement. Galician authors also opened new vistas in prose writing. Isaac Erter (1791–1851) and Joseph Perl (1773–1839) penned biting satires against the rapidly rising hasidic movement [see HASIDISM] which they viewed as obscurantist and reactionary. Perl's parodying of the Yiddishized Hebrew style of the pietistic

hasidic works unwittingly prepared the way for the reconciliation of the diglossal clash between the basically Indo-European structure and rich folkishness of Yiddish, the spoken language of author and reader, with the more classical, Semitic Hebrew, their literary language. Galicia produced no important Hebrew poet, although in his day Meir Letteris (1804–70) was held in high esteem.

The Russian Haskalah

The majority of European Jewry resided in Czarist Russia. The *Haskalah* penetrated that area moving into Lithuania via Germany and into Southern Russia via Galicia. In Lithuania the rationalist Orthodox tradition advocated by Eliezer, the Gaon of Vilna, permitted limited study of the sciences and mathematics. In South Russia, Isaac Baer Levinsohn (1788–1860), the "Mendelssohn of Russia", argued in *Te'udah beyisra'el* (1828; The Jewish mission) that tradition and modern culture are not contradictory.

The Lithuanian school produced two poets: Adam Hakohen LEBENSOHN, a rationalist, philosophical lyricist, and his son Micah Josef LEBENSOHN, a romantic poet of extraordinary talent who had received a thorough European education. In Vilna Mordecai Aaron Ginzberg (1796–1856) published the first modern Hebrew autobiography (*Aviezer*). Abraham MAPU was the first Hebrew novelist. Written in a superb Biblical Hebrew style, his romantic first novel, *Ahavat Zion* (Love of Zion) recalled the glories of ancient Judah. Its protagonists embody the ideals of the *Haskalah*. Perhaps more significant was Mapu's attempt to write a social novel. In *Ayit tzavu'a* (The hypocrite) he attempted to portray the contemporary social scene. Although the novel is structurally weak and populated by stock-characters, Mapu laid the ground-work for the typology which would be developed by later authors.

The second generation of the Russian *Haskalah* marks the gradual movement from romanticism to realism. Peretz SMOLENSKIN's novels are transitional. His picaresque novel *Hato'eh bedarkhei hahayim* (Wanderer in the paths of life) is a rambling *Erziehungs-Roman*, at times a realistic portrayal of the life and the types of

317

the eastern European Jewish *shtetl*, but at times a concoction of rather incredible coincidences of circumstance.

Moshe Leib LILIENBLUM (1843–1910) began as a staunch advocate of religious reform. Persecuted for his nonconformist views, he abandoned the battle for changes and flirted with the budding Jewish socialist movement, but finally embraced the rising Jewish national movement. His *Hata'ot ne'urim* (1876; Sins of youth) is a moving, realistic autobiography describing the various crises of his life. In his literary criticism, Lilienblum joined critics like Uri Kovner (1842–1909) in advocating the new realism preached by Russian positivist essayists. They attacked the mellifluous, biblical style (*melitzah*) employed by their contemporaries and urged realistic writing dealing with the social problems of the Jewish community.

The period of national revival

The great watershed which led to a complete reordering of values was the anti-Jewish pogroms which struck the Jewish communities of the Czarist empire, following the assassination of Alexander II in 1881. The failure of the Russian intellegentsia, on the whole, to condemn the atrocities and the tendency of many actually to blame the Jews for the plight of Russia's peasantry put into question the *Haskalah*'s thesis that Jews could integrate into Russian society. Many, in despair, began to emigrate to the USA and western Europe. Others turned to the revolutionary movements abandoning any hope of amelioration under the Czarist regime. A sizeable segment, inspired by other romantic nationalist movements, turned to Jewish nationalism and the dream of creating a national home in Israel's ancient homeland. Hebrew authors tended to support this new *Hibbat Zion* (Love of Zion) movement. Peretz Smolenskin had anticipated this trend in several essays which he published in *Hashahar*, a periodical he founded and edited (1868–84). In a book-length essay *Am 'olam* (1872; Eternal people) he argued against the view of western European Jewry that Jews are a religious and not an ethnic community. The Reform movement could not, he believed, preserve Jewish continuity, particularly because it eliminated the

hope for national restoration. The shock of 1881 spread Jewish nationalism into wider circles. From then on auto-emancipation rather than emancipation became the central theme of Hebrew literature. Publicists like Lilienblum and Eliezer BEN-YEHUDA spread the new gospel in the Hebrew press.

Concurrently with the new movement, occurred the maturing of Hebrew literature. By now a century of intensive experimentation in the writing of fiction and poetry gave the revived Hebrew a suppleness which would serve a younger generation of Hebrew writers. The new trend was anticipated by two Hebrew writers, Judah Loeb GORDON and MENDELE MOKHER SEFARIM. Gordon, although committed to the *Haskalah*, moved from writing romantic verse and short stores to a more realistic mode. His mastery of Biblical Hebrew gave his verse an elasticity and fluency which his predecessors lacked. Mendele was from the start committed to realism. His concern for the real led him to conclude that Yiddish rather than Hebrew was the more apt medium by which to portray life in the *shtetl*. He is rightly considered the father of Yiddish literature. In the late 1880s he returned to writing in Hebrew. Here again his achievement was most influential. Wrestling with the problem of describing in Hebrew a society which spoke and thought in Yiddish, he forged a new Hebrew style which welded biblical, rabbinic, and medieval Hebrew into a single pliable prose idiom. Mendele reincorporated into his style Hebrew words and phrases which had been absorbed into Yiddish, words drawn from the Hebrew prayerbook and those portions of the Bible and rabbinical literature which were familiar to most educated Jews.

The ideologue of the more realistic nationalist movement was AHAD HA'AM, father of cultural Zionism. As an essayist and editor, he advocated a national movement which would be primarily concerned with the solution of the problems of Judaism rather than that of the Jews. He criticized the populist Zionist propaganda as being unrealistic in urging mass settlement of Jews in Palestine. Neither the people nor the land were spiritually prepared for such a drastic move. He called for "the preparation of the hearts" for this enterprise through rebirth of Hebrew culture. He proposed Palestine as "a spiritual center for world Jewry" populated by an elitist element of committed men and women. The new Jewish culture, he contended, would be rooted in the older culture but would be modified by a reassessment of the traditional moral and cultural values by the application of positivist rather than theological values. He avoided confronting his Orthodox opponents by insisting that he had no quarrel with them. His message was addressed to Jews who no longer accepted the religious outlook. As founder and editor of *Hashiloah*, he exercised a determining influence on Hebrew literature. A man of impeccable if rather conservative literary tastes, he raised the standards of modern Hebrew literature. Aware that Hebrew was not a spoken language, he urged writers to use Hebrew to express Jewish themes, rather than such universal themes as love or landscape. But Hebrew literature was by then enjoying a remarkable florescence. Micah Josef BERDYCZEWSKI attacked Ahad Ha'am's "rationalist" bias and his attempts to define Jews and Judaism. Writers, he urged, should not be restricted by dogmatic rules but should be free to write on any subject in the revived national language.

In Warsaw, a coterie of writers who looked to I. L. PERETZ as their literary mentor generally opposed Odessa's conservatism and turned to neoromanticism. Peretz himself, like Mendele, wrote both in Yiddish and in Hebrew but while considered a great Yiddish writer, he did not play the central role which Mendele did in the development of Hebrew literature. Another Warsaw figure was David FRISCHMANN (1859–1922) who, although fiercely independent and no admirer of Peretz, both as critic and author of fiction favored neoromanticism, insisting that it was more contemporary and more European than the realism of the Odessans.

Hayyim Nahman BIALIK, the greatest modern Hebrew poet, settled in Odessa in 1900 and viewed himself as a disciple of both Mendele and Ahad Ha'am. From Mendele, Bialik acquired a strong, rich linear Hebrew style in his poetic and prose writings; from Ahad Ha'am, an ideology which sustained him after he lost his faith in traditional Judaism. Bialik's genius,

however, could not be confined merely to "Jewish national" themes. Although hailed as the "national poet", his poetry became increasingly individualist and subjective after 1900, extending to themes of orphanhood, loss of faith, nostalgia for the lost Eden of childhood, and unrequited love. While, on the whole, his language and forms were conservative, and he generally adhered to fixed accented lines (which he was among the first to employ) and to strict rhyming patterns, he experimented with the writing of free verse based on biblical cadences. Bialik emerged as the leading figure in Hebrew letters. After he settled in Palestine in 1924, he became almost the sole arbiter of literary taste. An entire generation of Hebrew poets came under his influence.

The second most important poet of the late Russian period was Saul TSCHERNICHOWSKI. Unlike Bialik, who was a product of the traditional *shtetl*, Tschernichowski received a less traditional upbringing. He attended modern schools in Odessa and took a medical degree at Heidelberg. Tschernichowski was more "European" than Bialik and less burdened by his Jewishness. His poetry, while not eschewing Jewish themes, was more universal, and he introduced many European verse forms into Hebrew literature. While Bialik bemoaned the lost world of religious faith, Tschernichowski viewed the tradition as impeding the natural instincts of Jews and advocated a more individualistic pantheism freed from its bonds.

The Palestinian period (1905–1918)

The *Hibbat Zion* movement led to a gradual growth of the modern Jewish community in Ottoman Palestine. About the time of the first Russian revolution (1905), a new generation of young pioneers began emigrating to Palestine. The pioneers of the Second *Aliyah* (migration) had broken with the orthodoxy of *shtetl* life and were, in the main, influenced by various Socialist–Zionist ideologies. A small literary center rose in Jaffa; it soon moved to Tel Aviv, a new suburb of Jaffa.

The pioneers of the Second *Aliyah* founded *Hapo'el Hatza'ir* as their literary organ. Among its contributors was Josef Hayyim BRENNER, father of the Hebrew psychological novel.

319

Brenner, born in South Russia, came under the influence of writers like Turgenev and especially Dostoievsky. Even in Russia, his main characters were "underground" types, maladjusted young men who rebeled against the traditional ways of their parents' generation and were desperately and vainly looking for a new philosophy that would replace their shattered system of beliefs. Their alienation was not merely intellectual but also affected their social relationships. Brenner had flirted with Russian Socialist ideas, but his deep concern for the Jewish situation led him to Socialist Zionism. His iconoclasm, however, made him question any doctrinaire solutions. He gave expression to the despair of the young pioneers in Palestine who suffered from malnutrition, malaria, unemployment, and loneliness. He preached a dogged doctrine of "holding on", of persisting in the attempt to create a new society, despite the likelihood of failure. He mocked the "Zionists" who sentimentalized about Palestine from afar. Brenner had no patience with Ahad Ha'amists or romantics who believed they could patch up the ancient tradition and restore its relevance. Palestine would, he believed, either produce a new Jew, free from the burdens of the past, or fail. For him there was no other way, no other place. His novel *Shekhol vekishalon* (Breakdown and bereavement) is the novel of his generation. In the circle of the *Hapo'el Hatza'ir's* writers were the young S. Y. AGNON ("discovered" by Brenner) who was to become a key figure after the 1930s, and Devorah Baron (1887–1956), a realistic writer of moving short stories usually set in the Russia of her childhood.

Mandated Palestine (1920–1948)

With the arrival of Bialik in Tel Aviv, its primacy as the center of Hebrew Literature was established. The first World War and the Communist Revolution disrupted Jewish intellectual life in eastern Europe and the great centers of Odessa and Warsaw were all but destroyed. The Bolshevik regime, after a short period of neutrality toward Hebrew letters, outlawed Zionism and Hebrew as counter-revolutionary. Only Yiddish was recognized as the Jewish national language and was supported by the State until the Stalinist purges of Yiddish

writers in the 1950s. Small, struggling Hebrew literary centers emerged in Warsaw, in Vilna and Kovno, lasting until the Holocaust. A minor center also existed in New York during the interbellum period but after Israel's establishment most of its key writers (Simon Halkin, Avraham Regelson, Israel Efros) migrated there.

In Tel Aviv of the 1920s the establishment writers published in *Moznayim*, the organ of the Hebrew Writers' Society, which still appears. Soon the younger writers rose in revolt against the "classicism" of Bialik and his disciples (namely the poets Zalman Schneur (1886–1959), David Shimoni (1886–1956), and Jacob Fichman (1881–1958) and the prose writers Y. D. BERKOWITZ, (1885–1967) Judah Burla (1886–1969), and Asher Barash (1882–1952)). The rebels took over *Ketuvim*, originally founded by the Hebrew Writers' Society, and turned it into an organ of literary revolt. Among its editors was Avraham SHLONSKI who was inspired by Russia's revolutionary expressionist and symbolist writers such as Blok and Yesinin. Shlonsky advocated a new poetry reflecting the youthful enthusiasm of young pioneers and their revolutionary zeal. Hebrew had now become their spoken language and he insisted that its neologisms be legitimized as a source for a more "conversational" idiom. Shlonsky's subjects were *halutziut* (pioneering), a "beat"-like sense of group adventure, and an *ennui* with the dying European landscape. He became the troubadour of the new society.

Natan ALTERMAN arrived in Tel Aviv a few years later. Alterman had no ambitions to be a cult leader. Yet more than Shlonsky, Alterman became the voice of his generation, often using wild expressionist metaphors. Like Shlonsky, despite his avant-gardism he stuck to traditional rhyme and nature patterns. Alterman also wrote humorous and satirical verse for the theater. His political verse, under the title of *Hatur hashvi'i* (The Seventh Column) gave vent to the struggle of Palestine's Jews against Great Britain's anti-Zionist policies and enjoyed enormous popularity during the closing years of the mandate.

Lea GOLDBERG, who began her career in Lithuania, joined the Tel Aviv literary circle in 1935. She was influenced by European modernism and especially Russian Acmeist poetry (Anna Akhmatova, MANDELSTAM, and others). Thoroughly grounded in European literature she wrote finely lyrical poems, using a simple conversational style and adhering to standard verse forms.

While Shlonsky, Alterman, and Goldberg remained committed to Socialist-Zionism, Uri Zvi GREENBERG broke with the movement and identified with the political right. He began as an expressionist Yiddish poet but upon arrival in Palestine turned to Hebrew. A writer of extraordinary power, he wrote mostly in free verse composed of bombastic long lines which pound away with a Whitmanesque vigor. Unlike the socialistic humanistic ideologies of most of his contemporaries, Greenberg's ideology was quasi-racist: the Jews were God's chosen seed in exile who had been corrupted by foreign ideologies which had quelled their messianic zeal. The Christian world, he argued, was only ostensibly Christian. Under the skin, its denizens were a barbarian race committed to murder, drink, and fornication. The Holocaust for him was not a sudden, unanticipated event but the inevitable culmination of the encounter between the holy Jews and the defiled European. Greenberg castigated his contemporaries for abandoning their messianic role for secular ideologies. He viewed the establishment of Israel as the renewal of God's covenant but expressed his fear that Israelis would miss the chance of redemption because of their inability to read the sacred meaning of their history. As a consequence of his right-wing views, Greenberg was denied the recognition he deserved until the last few decades of his life, when ideology no longer played the role it once did during the period of the national struggle.

Two prose writers dominated the fiction of the mandatory period: S. Y. Agnon and Hayyim HAZAZ. Agnon was the first and only Hebrew writer to win a Nobel prize. Born in Galicia, he migrated to Ottoman Palestine in 1909. He attracted the attention of Brenner, who published *Agunot* (Grass widows) in *Hapo'el Hatza'ir* – henceforth he took the name "Agnon". His early writings were in the neo-romantic tradition of such writers as Ibsen and Hamsun, but translated into a Jewish milieu.

He spent the war years and the early 1920s in Germany, returning to Jerusalem in 1924. Agnon's novels and short stories are situated in three geographical locations: The Galician *shtetl* of the eighteenth, nineteenth, and twentieth centuries; central Europe of the 1920s (Germany–Austria); and Palestine and Israel (1905–60). *Tmol shilshom* (Only yesterday) is a novel depicting the Second *Aliyah* and the conflict between Jaffa (representing the new secularism) and Jerusalem (tradition). *Oreah natah lalun* (A guest for the night) is his eulogy for the *shtetl*. In the 1930s, Agnon moved to a type of writing which had middle European overtones. Many of his stories are described by an Israeli critic as meta-realistic. They begin realistically but evolve into a surreal, dream-like tale redolent of symbolism. Agnon exerted a profound influence upon the early works of the authors of the post-State generation.

By contrast, Hazaz continued the realistic or satirical tradition of his European forerunners. His early works are set in revolutionary Russia, but later his main locus is Israel. Hazaz wrote two novels depicting the world of Israel's Yemenite community, a *tour de force* for a Western writer.

The period of the State (1948–1988)

Following the Second World War, Palestine Jewry intensified its struggle for national independence in earnest. Hebrew writers of the period were committed to this effort. The young writers who began publishing in the 1940s were either native speakers of Hebrew or had arrived in the country as children, or as graduates of the better Hebrew schools in eastern Europe. S. YIZHAR (b.1916), whose first story appeared before the Second World War, anticipated the new movement. These writers relished their command of the new Hebrew and their at-home-ness in the middle-eastern landscape. They accepted the socialist, nationalist ideology of their parents but disdained their intellectualizing. They were labeled as "a generation in the land", the "we generation", or the "Palmach [the military strike force of Israel's war of independence] generation". Their main themes were life in Palestine during the Second World War, the struggle against the British and

Israel's War of Independence. The leading poets were Hayyim GURI, Amir GILBOA, and T. CARMI. Since they continued writing long after Israel was established, many were later to write verse in consonance with later trends. Besides Yizhar, Moshe SHAMIR (b.1921) and Aharon MEGGED were the principal writers of fiction.

The most popular novel written during the War of Independence is Shamir's *He Walked in the Fields*. Uri, its main character, a Palmach officer, is committed to the struggle more out of a sense of duty than out of deep ideological convictions. A far profounder work is *Yemei Ziklag* (Days of Ziklag) by Yizhar which graphically depicts the terror of battle and the ruminations of young soldiers under stress. Yizhar's characters at times question the ideology which sent them to war.

In the late 1950s a second generation of native writers emerged. Many were students at the Hebrew University and were influenced by Shimon Halkin a poet and novelist who served as Professor of Hebrew Literature. Halkin was raised in the USA, the world power in whose cultural orbit Israel had now found itself. Through him, the younger writers became exposed to the dominant trends in Anglo-American literature: the poetry of Eliot and his school and the new criticism. The normal ennui which follows a war of liberation, the disillusionment with political radicalism and the encounter with mass immigration of refugees from the survivors camps and the Islamic countries undermined the accepted Zionist and socialist ideals.

Nathan ZACH, a young poet, articulated the new esthetics. He demanded a literature of the individual which eschewed national or socialist ideologies. He criticized the classical metrical and rhyme schemes employed by Alterman and Shlonsky and called for a freer line in which stress patterns are not automatically set but skilfully used to emphasize key words and phrases. He advocated a move from figurative language to a more sophisticated use of metonymy and synecdoche. Above all he insisted on a simple conversational style which masks a subtle ironic statement.

Zach and his associates rediscovered earlier poets whose poetry anticipated the new trend such as David VOGEL and the later Yaacov Steinberg (1887–1947), and also considered Yehudah AMICHAI, Amir Gilboa, and Abba KOVNER of the immediately preceding generation as their precursors. All these poets abandoned the rich and often wild imagery of the Shlonsky–Alterman school as well as their fixed metrics and rhyme schemes. Other leading poets of the new school were Dan PAGIS and David AVIDAN.

Many of the fiction writers of this new generation began their careers under the overwhelming influence of the later Agnon's meta-realism. This was particularly true of A. B. YEHOSHUA who moved from short writing to more realistic novels, without completely abandoning a subtle symbolism. Yehoshua's novels are also fascinating experiments in the shifting of point of view. Amos Oz, a member of a kibbutz, like A. B. Yehoshua deals with the ideological crisis of his generation and, like him, somehow retains his humanist–Zionist ideology. Amalia KAHANA-CARMON's novels and short stories are permeated with a surrealism, somewhat reminiscent of Virginia Woolf. Much of Israeli fiction in recent years is set during the early years of Jewish settlement. This trend has been described as an attempt to recapture the innocence of the early pre-state society, a period in which ideologies were not shaken by the realities of the post-modern age. Nathan Zach has argued that much of recent fiction is either nostalgic or more often permeated by "death wishes" which he asserts is a result of the disillusionment caused by romantic commitments to unrealizeable ideological goals. He singles out the novels of Jacob SHABTAI (1934–1981), Amos Oz, Haim BE'ER, and Benjamin TAMMUZ as characteristic of this trend. To this list one might add the nostalgic but at the same time ironic novels of David SHAHAR.

Aharon APPELFELD, a survivor of the Holocaust, has written movingly about the eerie world occupied by its victims or survivors. He hardly ever writes directly about the actual experience of the horror of the death camps, usually describing the milieu of the victims either before or after the final catastrophe. David GROSSMAN (b.1954), one of the ablest younger novelists, too young to have experienced the Holocaust himself, has written a powerful novel, combining the portrayal of the impact on a child of survivors, with a surrealistic depiction of the world of a Holocaust victim and his relationship to a Nazi intellectual (*Ayen 'erekh 'ahavah*; See under love).

The Holocaust continued to affect many of Israel's poets. Gilboa's first volumes of verse contain some of the most powerful surrealistic poems on the theme: "Yitzhak" (Isaac) and "My Sister's Boy Joshua" are among the best Hebrew poems of this century. Of almost equal merit are Dan Pagis's poem "Katuv ba'iparon, bakaron hehatum" (Words written in pencil in a box car) and many poems in Kovner's *Ahoti ketanah* (My sister is little).

Hebrew writers have not produced many dramas of high quality. Mention should be made, however, of Hazaz's play, *The End of Days*, Nissim ALONI's subtle use of the technique of the theater of the absurd and the rather strident satires of Hanoch LEVIN and Yehoshua SOBOL [see DRAMA, HEBREW].

A noticeable trend has been a return to political poetry following the rise of Israel's right wing to power and the abortive Lebanese war. Poets like Dalia RABIKOVITCH, Nathan Zach, Meir Wieseltier and Dan Laor have composed verse condemning the ultra-nationalism and militarism advocated by the right. Another recent development is the rise of a number of poets and writers of Sephardic (Asian–African Jewish descent). These range from A. B. Yehoshua – perhaps Israel's best novelist – to Erez Biton, a promising younger poet.

Israeli literature, while reflecting the appalling crises of contemporary Israel society – the Arab–Jewish conflict, the inner Jewish communal strife, the loss of faith in Zionist and socialist ideologies, the struggle of immigrants to integrate into a harsh landscape, the normal clash of ideologies of the left and right – is remarkably vibrant. It is enriched by the fact that most authors bring to their work a rich heritage and a multitude of literary traditions drawn from the cultures from which their parents emigrated. Thus they graft their work on a continuous literary tradition which has been constantly growing since biblical times. They enjoy a readership which, although small, is highly responsive and has not yet lost its enthusiasm for the written word.

EZRA SPICEHANDLER

Hecht, Anthony (b.1923) American poet. Hecht was born in New York City, earned his BA at Bard College in 1944, then served as an infantry rifleman in the army. His first academic appointment at Kenyon College in Ohio, in 1947, brought him into contact with John Crowe Ransom, who, as editor of the literary quarterly, the *Kenyon Review*, published Hecht's first poems, responses to his wartime experiences in Germany. In 1949 Hecht taught at New York University and came under the influence of Allen Tate, whom he later described as having taught him about the "richness, toughness and density of some sustaining vision of life."

In 1950 Hecht earned an MA at Columbia University. In 1951, the American Academy of Arts and Letters awarded him its Prix de Rome. There he met George Santayana to whom he dedicated his first book, *A Summoning of Stones* (1954). Its epigraph quotes the philosopher's saying that it is the poet's duty "to call the stones themselves to their ideal places". While in Rome, Hecht also translated Rilke's poetry. These translations were set to music by Lukas Foss as the cantata, *A Parable of Death*. In 1958 two long poems were printed in limited editions by Gehenna Press of Northampton, Massachusetts: *The Seven Deadly Sins: Poems* with woodcuts by Leonard BASKIN, and *Struwelpeter*. In 1954 and in 1959 Hecht won Guggenheim Fellowships. He has received numerous other awards and since 1968 he has been John H. Deane Professor of Poetry at the University of Rochester.

The Hard Hours (1967) is dedicated to his two sons and the title poem warns them of the tragic qualities of life. The book won the Pulitzer Prize and the Loines Award. In England it was a Poetry Book Society selection. *Millions of Strange Shadows* (1977), presented 31 poems including "Exile", dedicated to Joseph BRODSKY whose work Hecht had been translating from Russian. Of particular interest to Jewish readers is his long poem, "Rites and Ceremonies". It commemorates the endurance of the Jews through history, concluding with a prayer.

FURTHER READING
Gerber, P. L., and Gemmetts, R. J.: An interview with Anthony Hecht. *Mediterranean Review* 1 (1971) 3–9

RUTH ROSENBERG

Hecht, Ben (1894–1964) American journalist, novelist, playwright, and screenwriter. He was born on the Lower East Side of New York and his family later moved to Racine, Wisconsin. In 1910 he left home for Chicago, where he began a noted career as a reporter, first for the *Chicago Journal*, and later for the *Chicago Daily News*. In 1918 he was sent by the *Daily News* to Berlin, where he stayed until 1920; here he cemented his interest in literary experimentation and developed a friendship with George Grosz.

In 1921 his first novel, *Eric Dorn*, was published. Based largely on his experiences in Berlin, the novel displays Hecht's absorption of European modernism in his portrait of an alienated intellectual at odds with society. Back in Chicago, Hecht became associated with the "Chicago School" of writers which included Sherwood Anderson and Maxwell Bodenheim. Next Hecht moved to New York, where he began a highly successful collaboration with Charles MacArthur, the play *The Front Page* which opened in 1928 being their most famous work. Among their other successful Broadway collaborations were *Twentieth Century* and *Swan Song*, and they also wrote a number of film scripts.

Hecht gained his greatest fame as a screenwriter, at the height of his success earning one thousand dollars a day. He all but invented the gangster film with his scripts for *Underworld*, (1927) which won the first Academy award for best original story, and *Scarface* – still one of the best gangster films. He won his second Oscar for *Villa Villa*, worked uncredited on *Gone with the Wind*, and scripted Alfred Hitchcock's *Spellbound* and *Notorious*.

While in Hollywood Hecht wrote his notorious *A Jew in Love* (1931), the quintessential novel of Jewish self-hatred; it is a catalog of stereotypes of scheming, conniving, assimilationist Jews. Hecht was never to live down that novel, which he later regretted writing. In the late 1930s, increasingly conscious of his Jewishness, Hecht became a propagandist for Jewish self-defense and nationalism as well as a tireless denouncer of the Nazis and an avid supporter of a free Palestine. Torn between backing the British against the Nazis and opposing their stance on Palestine, he wrote *A Guide for the Bedevilled* (1944). After the war he constantly attacked the British and raised money for the Irgun in their fight against England. Following the War for Independence Hecht became disillusioned with the Irgun and with the policies of David BEN-GURION. Three years before his death his vicious attack on Zionism, in *Perfidy*, only increased Israeli and British disapproval of his work, which was boycotted in those countries. In the last two decades of his life Hecht worked mostly on screenplays and his autobiography, *Child of the Century* (1954).

BIBLIOGRAPHY
The Collected Stories of Ben Hecht (London: Hammond, Hammond & Co., 1950)

GABRIEL MILLER

Heijermans, Herman (1864–1924) Dutch novelist and dramatist. He was the fourth of eleven children, several of whom achieved prominence. His father was a Rotterdam journalist who had abandoned Orthodoxy. After completing secondary school Heijermans would have liked to have become a journalist, but had to go into business where he was not successful. In 1891 he began writing sketches and in 1892, the year he moved to Amsterdam, he devoted himself entirely to writing. In 1895 he joined the young Socialist Democratic Labour Party (SDAP) and in 1897 founded a socialist literary journal, *De Jonge Gids*. From the end of 1894 he published an innumerable number of sketches, often humorous, under the pen-name of Samuel Falkland, in daily newspapers.

Heijermans derived most of his fame as a dramatist. He wrote fifty plays, many of which criticize social abuses, such as *Op Hoop van Zegen* (1900; Hoping for [God's] blessing), about the malpractices of owners of fishing vessels. The play was not only performed many hundreds of times but also led to the adoption of a law in 1909 that ships could put to sea only with a certificate of seaworthiness. In this category also belongs *Glück auf* (1912) about the life of miners. Other plays are situated in a middle-class milieu, such as *De opgaande zon* (1908; The rising sun), about a small shopkeeper who tries in vain to survive against chain-store competition. In many of these plays the idealistic main character is confronted with the narrow-mindedness of his surroundings. Still other plays have a fantastic, romantic character, such as *De Wijze Kater* (1918; The wise tom-cat) which was also performed hundreds of times. In 1912 Heijermans established his own company, the Tooneelvereniging Ltd., which existed until 1922.

A few of Heijermans' novels and plays have Jewish themes. His novel, *Diamantstad* (1904; Diamond city), about the slums in part of the Amsterdam Jewish quarter, contributed to their improvement 12 years later. His play, *Ghetto* (1898), was a protest against Jewish Ortho-doxy. An earlier play, *Ahasverus* (1893), about a pogrom in Czarist Russia, was originally pro-duced under the name of a fictitious Russian author, Ivan Jelakowitch, and achieved some success.

Many of Heijermans' plays were translated and performed abroad: in Berlin, London, Paris, Warsaw, and New York. A granite bust of him by the Amsterdam Jewish sculptor Joseph Mendes da Costa was placed in a public garden near the Amsterdam Municipal Theater in 1929, five years after his death. During the 1930s it was damaged by unknown vandals and in 1940 it was removed on the orders of the Germans. In 1959 after many vicissitudes, it was largely repaired and returned to its original spot.

FURTHER READING

Flaxman, S.: *Herman Heijermans and his Dramas* (The Hague: Martinus Nijhoff, 1954)
Yoder, H. van Neek: *Dramatizations of Social Change:* *Herman Heijermans' plays* (The Hague: Martinus Nijhoff, 1978)

HENRIETTE BOAS

Heine, Heinrich (1797–1856) German poet and essayist. Born in Düsseldorf and educated primarily in a French Catholic *lycée*, Heine was intended by his family for a business career, at which he failed out of boredom, and was then sent to the university to study law, which he detested. After having had himself baptized, despite serious doubts, as a Lutheran, he received his degree in 1825, by which time he had already achieved a considerable reputa-tion with his several cycles of bittersweet love poems. In 1827 they were collected as *Buch der Lieder* (Book of songs), which was to become, largely through hundreds of musical settings, the most widely known book of German poetry in the world. He had also begun his four volumes of *Reisebilder* (1826–31; Travel pic-tures), ingenious mixtures of fiction and essay, some of which were inspired by journeys to England in 1827 and Italy in 1828. During his association as a student in Berlin with the "Society for the science and culture of the Jews", a short-lived effort to raise the level of Jewish history and scholarship, he attempted a Jewish historical novel, *Der Rabbi von Bacherach* (The Rabbi of Bacherach); he published it, with additions but still as a fragment, in 1840 in reaction to the Damascus pogrom of that year. He wished to defend the cause of Jewish eman-cipation, but he remained implacably opposed to all religions.

Unable to find a position in Germany and increasingly threatened owing to his political dissidence, he moved in the spring of 1831 to Paris, where he was to live in exile for the rest of his life. He reported to Germany on post-revolutionary France during 1831–2 in news-paper articles published as *Französische Zustände* (Conditions in France) in 1833, and again in a series from 1840–3, which he revised and pub-lished in 1854 under the title of *Lutezia*, the ancient Roman name of Paris. At the same time he tried to interpret modern Germany in works appearing in both French and German, *Zur Ge-schichte der Religion und Philosophie in Deutschland*

Heinrich Heine

(1834; On the history of religion and philosophy in Germany) and *Die Romantische Schule* (1836; The Romantic school), in which he developed his dichotomy of sensualism versus spiritualism, or Hellenism versus Nazarenism, and in which he placed in opposition the repressive alliance of despotism with religion and a utopia of political liberty, sensual emancipation, and material gratification. Along with a second volume of poetry, *Neue Gedichte* (1844; New poems), including a selection of his aggressive political verse, he composed his longest poems, *Deutschland ein Wintermärchen* (1844; Germany, a winter's tale), a biting satire on conditions in Germany, and *Atta Troll, ein Sommernachtstraum* (1847; Atta Troll, a midsummer night's dream), a burlesque of political poets whom he charged with puritanical repressiveness. During the writing of the *Wintermärchen* he had a brief but warm relationship with the young Karl MARX, whose essay "On the Jewish question" (1843), may owe something to Heine's influence.

During his most radical phase, which peaked in the mid 1840s, Heine was intensely anti-religious and located Judaism along with Christianity on the repressive, spiritualist or Nazarene side of his dichotomy. But gradually he began to shift Judaism to the positive, sensualist side, a symptom of a great change that was to come over him in 1848, the year of the discouraging revolution and also of his collapse into a painful, paralytic illness that was to confine him to his "mattress-grave" for eight years. Thus struck down, he abjured his faith in the divinity of men, repudiated Hegel and Marx, and asserted his belief in a personal God with whom he needed to contend about the unjust governance of the world. He publicly announced this change of attitude in the afterword to his third volume of poems, *Romanzero*, in 1851, which contains a series of poems in the persona of the suffering Lazarus and three "Hebräische Melodien" (Hebrew melodies), expressing simultaneously his reattachment to his Jewish tradition and his skeptical, ironic distance from it.

Heine has had by a considerable margin the most contentious reputation in the history of German literature. Not only was he violently attacked, during his lifetime and long afterward, by nationalists, reactionaries and anti-Semites; he alienated many of his natural allies by his belligerent scorn for the ideal values they endeavored to keep intact, by his intolerance of others, and by the ethical recklessness with which he conducted his career. At first the spokesmen of the German–Jewish community joined the general rejection of him; only in the late nineteenth century did some Jewish scholars and intellectuals begin to acquire a more positive view of him. For a long time his reputation was more secure in foreign countries than in his native land. Since the Second World War he has been vigorously rehabilitated and, in some quarters, turned into a monument of revolutionary virtue. His relationship to Judaism and to his own Jewishness continues to be a topic of lively inquiry and discussion.

BIBLIOGRAPHY

The Complete Poems of Heinrich Heine: A Modern English Version, trans. H. Draper (Oxford: Oxford University Press, 1982); *Poetry and Prose*, ed. J. Hermand and R. C. Holub (New York: Continuum, 1982); *The Poetry and Prose of Heinrich Heine*, ed. F. Ewen (New York: Citadel, 1948)

FURTHER READING

Prawer, S. S.: *Heine's Jewish Comedy: A Study of his Portraits of Jews and Judaism* (Oxford: Clarendon Press, 1983)

Reeves, N.: *Heinrich Heine: Poetry and Politics* (Oxford: Oxford University Press, 1974)

Sammons, J. L.: *Heinrich Heine: The Elusive Poet* (New Haven and London: Yale University Press, 1969)

——: *Heinrich Heine: A Modern Biography* (Princeton: Princeton University Press, 1979)

Tabak, I.: *Judaic Lore in Heine: The Heritage of a Poet* (Baltimore: Johns Hopkins University Press, 1948)

JEFFREY L. SAMMONS

Heller, Bernhart (1871–1943) Arabist and literary scholar, and folklorist. Heller was born in Nagybicse, Hungary. Between 1890 and 1895 he was a student at Budapest University and the Rabbinical Seminary in Budapest. He emerged with a Ph.D. in philosophy and as an ordained rabbi. In both institutions he was influenced by the great Hungarian Jewish scholars, Wilhelm BACHER, David KAUFMANN and Ignaz GOLDZIHER. Until 1919 he taught languages at high schools in Budapest, and was then elected Director of the Jewish High School in Pest. In 1922 Heller was appointed to the Chair of Bible at the Rabbinical Seminary, where he was professor until 1931. He was a member of the Ethnographic and Oriental Societies of Hungary.

Heller's scholarly work is recognized mainly in four areas: the study of ancient Jewish literature (the Bible and its interpretations, the Apocrypha and Pseudepigrapha); Jewish folk literature; the study of Muslim legends (where the great influence of Ignaz Goldziher is obvious: Heller wrote many items on Arabic legends in the *Enzyclopädie des Islam*, and the classic study of the Antar Romance); comparative study of modern literature (the comparison of themes and motifs in European literature: Shakespeare, Schiller, HEINE, and Mann, and modern Hungarian literature).

His main contribution to the humanities and Jewish Studies lies in his studies of Jewish folk literature. His profound knowledge of European, Arabic and Jewish cultures enabled him to study in depth the relations between, and status of, Jewish folklore and the other great cultures in the Middle Ages and modern times. His classical studies on Haggadic literature, the history of Hebrew folk tales (1930), his contributions to GASTER's *Exempla of the Rabbis* (1925), to Louis GINZBERG's *The Legends of the Jews* (1933–5), and many others, are examples of his historical–comparative methodology. Heller was interested in both an overview of Jewish folk literature and its place in international folklore, and in the analysis of the smallest motif.

FURTHER READING

Scheiber, S.: *Bibliographie der Schriften Bernhart Hellers. Jubilee Volume in Honour of Prof. Bernhart Heller on the Occasion of His Seventieth Birthday* (Budapest, 1941) 22–51

Prof. Heller. *Essays on Jewish Folklore and Comparative Literature* (Budapest, 1985) 48–56

Yassif, E.: *Jewish Folklore: An Annotated Bibliography* (New York and London: Garland, 1986)

ELI YASSIF

Heller, Joseph (b.1923) American novelist. Born of immigrant Russian–Jewish parents in Brooklyn, Heller attended New York schools before his enlistment in the US Army Air Force in 1942. Following military service, he married Shirley Held and entered college. He graduated from New York University in 1948, took a master's degree at Columbia University in 1949, and was a Fulbright scholar at Oxford University in 1949–50. After teaching English for two years, he became an advertising copywriter for *Time* (1952–6) and *Look* (1956–8), and promotion manager for *McCall's* (1958–61). Since the publication of *Catch-22* (1961), he has lived largely on his earnings as a novelist.

Heller did two adaptations of *Catch-22* for the theater, *Catch-22 A Dramatization* (1971), and *Clevinger's Trial* (1972). Neither of these plays nor his other two-act drama, *We Bombed in New Haven* (1968), was particularly successful. His stature as a novelist, however, has increased steadily, with the publication of *Something Happened* (1974), *Good As Gold* (1979), and *God Knows* (1984). In 1986 he published *No Laughing Matter* with Speed Vogel, an account of his near fatal bout with Guillain-Barre syndrome and the experience of being nursed back to health by this close friend.

Though his output has been small, Heller has been recognized as a major novelist since the appearance of *Catch-22*. Consistent with the Vietnam anti-war spirit in the USA at the time, the novel's attack upon military idiocy, callousness and corruption, its black humor, and its strong moral imperative – Jewish in tone – arguing that the saving of an individual's life even through desertion, is justified in the face of meaningless destruction, made it widely hailed as a humanistic, pacifist protest against warmongering. Experimental in style, it balances psychological and linear time, juxtaposing Greek epic conventions (its subject is the wrath of Yossarian, a modern-day Achilles) with the realities of combat in Europe in the Second World War.

Where *Catch-22* exposes human weakness and corruption in the military, *Something Happened* exposes it in the corporate world, *Good As Gold* exposes it in government, and *God Knows* exposes it in religion. The latter two novels draw heavily upon the Jewish experience in contemporary USA and in antiquity. Both are hilariously funny but overdone. Nonetheless, Heller's is one of the major talents in the pantheon of American Jewish writers.

FURTHER READING

Gelb, B.: Catching Joseph Heller. *New York Times Magazine* (4 March 1979)

Nagel, J. ed.: *Critical Essays on Catch-22* (Encino: Dickenson, 1974)

JOSEPH COHEN

Hellman, Lillian (1906–1984) American dramatist and screenwriter. Hellman was born in New Orleans but spent half of each year in New York City and later studied at New York and Columbia Universities. Her first play, *The Children's Hour* (1934), in which the lives of two women teaching in an all-girls school are destroyed by the rumor that they are lesbians, was an enormous success on Broadway. *The Little Foxes* (1939), still frequently revived, is a well-crafted melodrama of intrigue in an avaricious family of southern patricians, possibly based on her mother's Jewish family.

None of her plays focus on Jewish characters or explore Jewish issues. *Watch on the Rhine* (1941), a powerful anti-Nazi play, barely glances at the persecution of the Jews. Active in anti-fascist causes before and during the Second World War, she was blacklisted by the Hollywood studios in 1948 and subpoenaed to appear before the House Un-American Activities Committee in 1952.

In contrast with the melodramatic tendencies of most of her plays, *The Autumn Garden* displays a Chekhovian tenderness toward the failed and lonely characters gathered in a southern summer resort. In *Toys in the Attic* (1960), a return to her taut, confrontational style which brought her a second New York Drama Critics Circle Award, a succession of dark secrets explode in the lives of the adult children of a New Orleans family. She also wrote a number of screenplays, the libretto to Leonard BERNSTEIN's *Candide* (1956), and a series of three book-length memoirs published eventually in one volume, *Three* (1979). Her last play, *My Mother, My Father, and Me* (1963), was adapted from *How Much?*, Burt Blechman's satiric novel about the American–Jewish middle class.

FURTHER READING

Dick, B. F.: *Hellman in Hollywood* (Rutherford: Fairleigh Dickinson University Press, 1982)

Lederer, Katherine: *Lillian Hellman* (Boston: Twayne, 1979)

MICHAEL SHAPIRO

Herman, Josef (b.1911) British painter. The son of a Warsaw cobbler, Herman's formal artistic training began in 1929, when he took lessons from a minor academic painter called Slupski; in 1930–1 he studied at the Warsaw School of Art and Decoration, earning his living thereafter as a freelance graphic artist. His first one-man exhibition took place in Warsaw in 1932; in 1935–6 he became a founder-member of a group known as *The Phrygian Cap*, which took the lives of working people as its subject-matter.

Having moved to Brussels in 1938–9, the German invasion of Belgium in 1940 forced him to move again, first to France and then to Glasgow. All too well aware of the mortal danger facing Polish Jewry as a whole and his family in particular (all of whom were indeed to perish), his work of 1938–43 depicts the world of his childhood with an affectionate and nostalgic humor. In 1944 Herman settled in the Welsh village of Ystradgynlais, where involvement with the tightly-knit mining community over the next 11 years helped him come to terms with his loss. After that he traveled widely, although the UK remained his home.

Herman cares little for religious or nationalist dogma. When in 1952–3 he visited Israel for the first (and only) time, it was to the pioneering spirit of those days and above all to the heroism of the workers on the land that he responded with enthusiasm. To him, Jewishness, particularly in a post-Holocaust world, entails certain moral and social responsibilities and "supra-personal dreams", and it is the role of the Jewish artist to express these in his art, irrespective of subject-matter. Whether he paints Jewish cobblers, Welsh miners, Italian peasants, or CND marchers, human dignity is Herman's true subject.

BIBLIOGRAPHY
Related Twilights: Notes from an Artist's Diary (London: Robson Books Ltd., 1975)

FURTHER READING
Mullins, E.: *Josef Herman, Paintings and Drawings* (London: Evelyn, Adams & Mackay, 1967)

MONICA BOHM-DUCHEN

Hermann (Borchardt), Georg (1871–1943) German novelist. Born in Berlin, he worked first as a merchant, before studying philosophy, art history and literature in Berlin with the hope of becoming an art critic. He dabbled early on in prose fiction and art criticism. He wrote a major essay on the German–Jewish artist Max LIEBERMANN for Martin BUBER's cultural Zionist collection, *Jüdische Künstler* (1903; Jewish artists).

He wrote many novels, two of which became major bestsellers: *Jettchen Gebert* (1906), and *Henriette Jacoby* (1908). Set in the Berlin middle-class Jewish milieu of the first half of the nineteenth century, these works are in the tradition of the family or generational novel of Theodor

Fontane and Thomas Mann. These novels established Hermann's career and presented a positive account of aspiring Jewish business families in Germany, within a broad spectrum of Jewish characters. Hermann's Jewish orientation was not religious; rather, he viewed the Jewish people as a racial-ethnic-social group, defined by its common fate. He rejected both German and Jewish nationalist movements and expressions. According to Hermann, the German Jew was an integral part of the German people, whose own particular tradition was thoroughly honorable.

He was a member of the liberal "Central Verein deutscher Staatsbürger jüdischen Glaubens" (Central Organization of German Citizens of Jewish Faith) and criticized German anti-Semitism. Forced into exile with the rise of Nazism, Hermann found temporary refuge in the Netherlands. After the Nazis conquered the Low Countries, he was deported and murdered in Auschwitz.

MARK H. GELBER

Hertz, Henri (1875–1966) French journalist and poet. Born in Nogent-sur-Seine, his father was an army officer from an old Alsatian Jewish family. His education was similar to that of other bourgeois French–Jewish children. Hertz gradually evolved into a bitter, sardonic poet, profoundly influenced by the Surrealist poets Louis Aragon, Max JACOB and Guillaume Apollinaire, as well as by the early writings of Jean Cocteau. His own avant-garde tendencies manifested themselves in the language and content of his early collections of poetry: *Sorties* (1921), *Vers un monde volage* (1924), and *Enlèvement sans amant* (1929).

Hertz's literary reputation was assured by his passionate journalistic pieces. He distinguished himself as a political essayist and his articles on art and literature which appeared in various avant-garde journals championed the new directions in French culture. During the 1920s Hertz began to support Jewish and Zionist causes in the popular press, and in 1925 was elected General Secretary of the France-Palestine Society. During the Second World War he played an active role in the Resistance.

His most Jewish work, *Tragédies des temps*

volages (1955) is an odd assortment of verse and prose pieces on various Jewish topics. One of the selections, "Ceux de Job", stands as an eloquent expression of the aspirations and tragic despair of the Jewish people throughout the ages.

SIMON SIBELMAN

Hertz, Joseph Herman (1872–1946)

South African rabbi, champion of human rights, chief rabbi of the British Empire. Born in Rebrin in present-day Slovakia, he was educated in the USA where he gained his Ph.D. at Columbia University. Studying simultaneously at the Jewish Theological Seminary of New York, he was its first recipient of the rabbinical diploma in 1894, the year in which he became rabbi in Syracuse, New York State.

In 1898 he was appointed rabbi to the Witwatersrand Old Hebrew congregation, Johannesburg, and, with an interruption during the Anglo-Boer war (1899–1901), continued in that office until 1911. Prior to the Anglo-Boer War, in a time of mounting tension, he became a notable figure in Jewish and Gentile circles for his controversial battle against political, civic, and educational disadvantages suffered by Jews and Catholics in the Transvaal Republic. He plunged fearlessly into the prevailing political controversies, vehemently calling for removal of all such disabilities, affirming Jewish patriotism, and publicly criticizing the Kruger regime. He was ordered to leave the Republic and on his way to Cape Town, where he spent the war years ministering to Jewish refugees from the Transvaal, he met the young Winston Churchill in Moçambique. He became an active Zionist, later to become consultant to the British government before the publication of the Balfour Declaration.

Back in Johannesburg (after 1901) he was involved with the post-war rehabilitation of the Jewish community and, involving himself in several spheres of Jewish communal life, was instrumental in the formation of the Jewish Board of Deputies for the Transvaal and Natal, a new organization based on the British model. While in South Africa, he held several other important communal and academic positions. His influence in the post-war development of Jewish life was great and it is in South Africa that his greatest contribution lay.

In 1913 he was appointed chief rabbi of the United Hebrew congregations of the British Empire, an appointment to which his close association with Lord Milner, formed during his ministry in South Africa, undoubtedly contributed. His 33-year tenure in Britain further enhanced his reputation as a forthright controversialist and champion of human rights.

In 1920 he revisited South Africa traveling and preaching extensively throughout the country. On his arrival in Johannesburg, the crowd to meet him had to be restrained by police barricades.

A prolific author, with some sixty publications on a vast variety of topics to his credit, he wrote on South African Jewry and affirmed traditional Judaism against the liberal Judaism to which he was militantly opposed. His major works, which have become classics of Jewish Theological writing in English, include his *Book of Jewish Thoughts* (1917), which was translated into several languages and ran to 25 editions, his widely-used commentaries on the Pentateuch, *The Pentateuch and Haftarahs* (1936), and *The Authorised Daily Prayer Book* (1941, revised 1946).

JOCELYN HELLIG

Herzberg, Abel (b.1893)

Dutch author and lawyer. Herzberg was born in Amsterdam into a Russian family who had emigrated after the pogroms of 1881. He studied law and became established as a lawyer. In the 1930s he was editor of *De Joodsche Wachter*, the journal of the Dutch Zionist Federation of which he was chairman from 1934 until 1937. He influenced the movement deeply because of his moving, almost literary speeches. Although he had already published a play in 1934, his talent as an author was properly developed after the war. The impetus behind this was his desire to explain the Holocaust and Jewish consciousness to the Dutch non-Jewish community. Much of his work was therefore first published as newspaper articles. In *Amor Fati* (1946), he attempted to give a moral and psychological explanation of life in a concentration camp from the point of view of the victims as well as the torturers. This approach, so soon after the war and from an inmate of the camps (he had been deported to Bergen-Belsen in 1944), was much admired by the Dutch public. In his later work Herzberg continued his attempts to analyze the Holocaust and the problem of being Jewish. In 1950 he published his diary from Bergen-Belsen and his articles on the Eichmann Trial were collected in *Eichmann in Jerusalem* (1962).

Another important theme in his work lies in his recollections of the pre-war Jewish world in Amsterdam. In *Brieven aan mijn kleinzoon* (1964) he described the milieu of the Russian immigrants in Amsterdam at the turn of the century. Before the First World War he had visited Russia and his family there and this book accordingly begins in Russia. Finally, Herzberg was inspired by the figure of Herod the Great about whom he wrote fictional memoirs and a play.

Herzberg's work gave the Dutch public not only an insight into the persecution of the Jews and anti-Semitism, but also into the moral and psychological dilemmas of being a Jew. He was awarded most of the important literary prizes in the Netherlands.

LUDY GIEBELS

Herzl, Theodor (1869–1904) Viennese author and journalist, founder of the World Zionist Organization. Born in Budapest, he moved with his comfortable, middle-class family to Vienna when he was 18 years old. He attended German schools in Budapest and in Vienna he studied law. After graduating he did not, however, pursue a legal career but began intensive activity as a playwright and journalist. Some of his plays, like *Das Neue Ghetto* (1895; The new ghetto) were performed to moderate acclaim. He joined the staff of the *Neue Freie Presse* which in many respects was the mouthpiece of the liberal, assimilated Viennese Jewish bourgeoisie. During 1891–5 he served as the newspaper's Paris correspondent.

It was in Paris, during the Dreyfus Affair which he covered for his paper, that Herzl became convinced that emancipation, far from solving the "Jewish question" only exacerbated it through the entry of so many Jews into the middle class and the professions. Herzl had become aware of the problem earlier in Vienna, both when confronting the anti-Semitism of the nationalistic student fraternities, as well as witnessing the emergence of the populist movement of Karl Lueger, which drew his attention to the rise of a modern, socially-oriented anti-Semitism. But his Paris experience convinced him of the universal scope of the problem. For a fleeting moment he toyed with the idea that perhaps a mass conversion of all Jews could do away with the hatred and envy directed towards them; but he quickly abandoned this thought.

During his stay in Paris he began to form his ideas about a political solution to the dilemma posed for Jewish existence in the modern world. He tried to interest Jewish magnates, like Barons Hirsch and Rothschild, in his ideas, but the response was disappointing. In 1895 he returned to Vienna to become literary editor of the *Presse*, and in 1896 he decided to go public with his ideas and published his pamphlet *Der Judenstaat* (The Jewish state). Its main thesis is that the Jews are a nation, not merely a community of believers, and hence neither civil emancipation nor cultural assimilation can be an adequate solution to the question of Jewish identity; nor do such solutions go to the roots of anti-Semitism. In an era of nationalism, he argued, the Jewish problem is a political problem, and a political solution has to be sought for it. Such a solution could be achieved through the establishment of a Jewish commonwealth, to which the unwanted surplus Jewish population could emigrate and which could also normalize the position of those Jews who would remain in the Diaspora. Though Herzl left it open whether Palestine, or some territory in North or South America should be a basis of such a solution, he soon realized that only the historical homeland of the Jewish people could serve as a drawing point to such a revolutionary endeavour.

Reactions to Herzl's pamphlet were enthusiastic on the one hand and extremely hostile on the other. The positive response came mainly from those circles, like the *Hovevei Zion* movement in Russia, where Jews were sensitized, through education as well as external pressures, to their tenuous position as a national minority. Harsh criticism, on the other hand, was leveled against Herzl from both Orthodox and Reform rabbinical circles which viewed his ideas as dangerous in terms of the Judaic tradition, as well as undermining the historical efforts at emancipation and the attainment of complete civic equality. Buoyed by the positive response, which was especially strong in Eastern Europe, Herzl embarked on a campaign to convene an international Jewish congress to promote his ideas. Such a congress did indeed take place in Basel on 29–31 August 1897, as the first Zionist Congress.

This was the first public success of a modern political movement among Jews, transcending European political boundaries. The Congress adopted the Basle Program, established the World Zionist Organization and elected Herzl as the organization's first president. The establishment of a national homeland for the Jews in Palestine, recognized by international law, became the first principle of the Basel program.

The rest of Herzl's life was spent, in a hectic and not always successful manner, as a spokesman for the nascent Zionist organization. He traveled widely, tried to enlist the support of major European rulers and statesmen, and at the same time built up the WZO as an effective political institution. In the latter effort he was more successful than in his diplomatic endeavors: the first Zionist bank was established, as was the Jewish National Fund, aimed at purchasing land for Jewish settlements in Palestine; thus the financial, parliamentary and organizational structures of the WZO were laid.

Herzl sought to gain Turkish support for a "Charter" for the Jewish settlement of Palestine by trying to enlist Jewish financial help for the ailing Ottoman Empire. Yet his negotiations with the Turkish government remained inconclusive, as did attempts to enlist German diplomatic support to influence the Turkish government in that direction.

In the course of his diplomatic negotiations, Herzl received some encouragement in 1903 from the British Colonial Secretary, Joseph Chamberlain, for Jewish settlement in East Africa (the Uganda Plan). Under the impact of

Theodor Herzl with his mother, 1902

the murderous Kishinev pogrom of the same year, Herzl clutched at this idea as a stop-gap measure and submitted it to the Sixth Zionist Congress as a temporary alternative to the Land of Israel. He was, however, defeated in the Congress, and abandoned the idea, reverting to further feverish – but futile – attempts to achieve diplomatic support (and even Papal help) for the idea of a Jewish homeland in Palestine.

In 1902 Herzl's last book, the utopian novel *Altneuland* (1960; Old-new land) was published, in which he envisaged the existence of a co-operative Jewish commonwealth in Palestine, based on ideas of national solidarity and social "mutualism". In its combination of a socially planned, yet mixed economy, based on science and technology, the novel echoes many of the prevalent ideas of other nineteenth-century progressive and socialist utopias.

Having suffered for years from a heart condition, Herzl died in 1904 from complications resulting from his illness. He was buried in the Jewish cemetary in Vienna, but in 1949 his remains were transferred to Jerusalem and reinterred on a mountain on the city's western outskirts, which was named Mount Herzl.

While Herzl's ideas were far from original, and he was preceded by many thinkers from Moses HESS to Leon PINSKER, his flair for public relations, his organizational vision and his willingness to unleash an unprecedented diplomatic campaign based on a mass movement on behalf of his ideas, made him into a symbol for Jews and non-Jews alike, and his name became identified with the emergence of modern, political Zionism.

FURTHER READING
Avineri, S.: *The Making of Modern Zionism* (New York: Basic Books, 1981)
Bein, A.: *Theodor Herzl* (Cleveland, 1962)
Elon, A.: *Herzl* (New York, 1975)

SHLOMO AVINERI

Heschel, Abraham Joshua (1907–1972)

American theologian. Heschel was born into a family of hasidic rabbis in Warsaw. As a teenager, he studied in Vilna and became a member there of a group of Yiddish poets, known as Jung Vilna, publishing his first book, a collection of Yiddish poetry. At the age of 20 he arrived in Berlin for doctoral study in the philosophy faculty at the University, and also enrolled in the *Hochschule für die Wissenschaft des Judentums*, the Reform movement's seminary. After completing his doctorate in February 1933, with a study of prophetic consciousness, he remained in Berlin, publishing a series of articles on technical issues in medieval Jewish philosophy, and two semi-popular biographies of medieval Jewish figures, Maimonides and Abravanel. Replacing Martin BUBER at the Lehrhaus in Frankfurt in 1937, he remained in Nazi Germany until the end of October 1938, when he, like all Polish Jews, was deported back to Poland. Heschel remained in Warsaw until the summer of 1939, when he fled to England where he founded an Adult Institute for Jewish Studies. He arrived in the USA in 1941, thanks to a visa secured for him by the Hebrew Union College in Cincinnati, the head of the Reform movement in the USA. In 1946 he moved to New York City, where he remained as professor of Jewish ethics and mysticism at the Jewish Theological Seminary until his death.

Heschel achieved prominence in three areas: for his theological writings, his social activism, and his scholarship on aspects of Jewish thought, including rabbinics, medieval philosophy, and Hasidism. His major theological writings, which appeared in English during the 1950s, reflect certain key elements of *Kabbalah* and Hasidism, particularly in his understanding of divine pathos (God as the "most moved mover") and of the *mitzvot* as a divine necessity. His theology also contains a critique of major movements in modern liberal theology, both Protestant and Jewish. He argues for the centrality of human subjectivity as a theological category, yet asserts the transcendent otherness of God. Revelation is similarly two-sided: the commandments issued by God at Sinai, and the experience of the event in the consciousness of those present and properly attuned to spiritual experience. The Bible, he wrote, is God's book about human beings, but the beginning of theology must come in cultivating the human experience of wonder, awe, and mystery. Heschel's theological writings have been the subject of conferences and monographs within the Jewish, Protestant and Catholic communities, and have been translated into a dozen languages.

The Civil Rights movement, Second Vatican Council, Soviet Jewry movement, and the anti-Vietnam war movement were all central involvements of Heschel's life. He explained his political activism as derived from his understanding of the Hebrew prophets: they represent, he wrote, a "ceaseless shattering of indifference". Heschel himself became the major Jewish spokesman on issues of social injustice in the USA during the 1960s and until his death.

Heschel's scholarship includes studies of Saadia, Ibn Gabirol, and Maimonides; analyses of manuscripts dealing with the history of Hasidism, particularly the earliest followers around the BA'AL SHEM TOV; a two-volume Yiddish monograph on the life and thought of the Kotzker rebbe; and a three-volume Hebrew study of rabbinic thought, in which he traces conflicting theological tendencies in talmudic, midrashic, and later rabbinic literature.

BIBLIOGRAPHY
God in Search of Man (New York: Farrar, Straus, & Cuddihy, 1955); *The Prophets* (New York: Harper & Row, 1962)

FURTHER READING
Merkle, J. C., ed.: *Abraham Joshua Heschel: Exploring*

his Life and Thought (New York: Macmillan, 1985) contains proceedings of a conference on Heschel held in 1983

Rothschild, F. A., ed.: *Between God and Man: An Interpretation of Judaism from the Writings of Abraham J. Heschel* (New York: Free Press, 1959)

SUSANNAH HESCHEL

Hess, Moses (1812–1875)   German socialist and precursor of Zionism. Born in Bonn into an Orthodox family, Hess received a traditional education and for a while lived with his Orthodox grandfather. However, he demonstrated assimilationist tendencies in his youth and later married a Christian. His early philosophical studies were mainly concerned with Spinoza and Hegel, who influenced his own socialist ideas. He aroused the interest of MARX and Bakunin with his "ethical" socialism and with his initially extreme ideas regarding Jewish capitalism. Marx later rejected Hess's form of socialism which was suffused with biblical ideas of social justice and influenced by prophetic messianism. After the 1848 uprising Hess was forced to leave Germany because of his radical politics, and he spent most of the remainder of his life in Paris, with some periods in Belgium and Switzerland. From 1842 to 1849 he was associated as editor and correspondent with a number of radical journals in Europe, but from the mid-1840s he devoted himself mainly to scientific Jewish studies.

After having promulgated the idea of a United States of Europe in 1841 (*Die Europaeische Triarchie*; The European triarchy), Hess later abandoned his cosmopolitanism and his thinking turned towards a humanitarian Jewish nationalism. The prevailing European nationalist ideologies suggested to Hess that the Jews, too, might be entitled to a homeland and national identity. In 1862 Hess developed these ideas in a volume entitled *Rome and Jerusalem*, which envisaged a Jewish nation in Palestine, founded on socialist principles. It reflected his protracted transition from cosmopolitan socialism to Jewish nationalism, during which he had renounced Marx's concept of dialectical materialism. Hess nonetheless attempted to integrate his socialist idealism with his national idea of a Jewish nucleus on its own homeland.

He strongly believed that anti-Semitism would not be eradicated by Jewish assimilation or conversion. He argued that the Jews should accept that they, too, were a separate nation to be revived in their own land and advocated a Jewish state based on territory and social institutions "in association with Mosaic, that is, socialist principles". Hess, who had been termed by Marx the "Communist rabbi", believed the Jewish religion to be the best means of preserving Jewish nationality until the foundation of a Jewish state. Although Hess had himself suffered from anti-Semitism, and the Damascus Affair (1840) had deeply troubled him, his plea for a Jewish return to Zion was not conceived as a remedy against anti-Semitism, but out of his belief in a national Jewish genius which could grow only on its own soil.

The central idea of *Rome and Jerusalem*, that the Jews would never earn the respect of the nations unless they accepted and respected their own historical memories, incited the assimilated German Jews to a harsh reaction against Hess.

He died in Paris, and was buried at the Jewish cemetery near Cologne. His remains were transferred to Israel in 1961.

FURTHER READING

Cohen, I.: *Moses Hess, Rebel and Prophet* (New York: 1951) [reprinted from *Zionist Quarterly*]

Silberner, E.: *Moses Hess. An Annotated Bibliography* (New York: Burt Franklin, 1951)

GLENDA ABRAMSON

Heymann, Isaac (?1818–1906)   Russian–Dutch cantor and composer of liturgical music. Heymann laid the foundation for the Amsterdam school of cantoral music. He was the son of a famous cantor, Pinchas Heymann-Bialystock, and distinguished himself as a cantorial singer as a boy. After brief periods of service as a cantor with the Jewish congregations of Filehne, Graudenz, and Gnesen he was appointed as Chief Cantor of the Great Synagogue of the Amsterdam Ashkenazi Congregation in May 1856, and remained at this post for fifty years, until his death soon after his golden jubilee. After his appointment in Amsterdam he studied composition at the Cologne Conservatoire with

Ferdinand Hiller, and in 1870 spent some time in New York. In Amsterdam he was usually called "the Gneser chazzan" after his previous post. Many of his compositions are still sung in synagogue services in Amsterdam.

HENRIETTE BOAS

Hildesheimer, Azriel (1820–1899) German leader of Orthodox Jewry. Born in Halberstadt, Hildesheimer was educated in local Jewish schools and at Berlin University where he studied Semitics, philosophy, history and science. He received his doctorate from the University of Halle. Through an advantageous marriage he became financially independent, enabling him to pursue freely his studies and rabbinical career. In 1851 he was appointed rabbi of Eisenstadt where he reorganized the education system and established a *yeshivah* which included secular studies. Despite the success of this school, a number of Orthodox Hungarian rabbis bitterly opposed Hildesheimer's modernism. In the congress of Hungarian Jewry in 1868–9, a debate took place about the establishment of a rabbinical seminary for all of Hungary which split the delegates. Disillusioned with this state of affairs, Hildesheimer became the rabbi of a newly founded Orthodox congregation in Berlin in 1869. In 1873 he founded a *yeshivah* which became the central institution for training Orthodox rabbis in Europe. With Samson HIRSCH, Hildesheimer shared the leadership of the Orthodox Jewish community in Germany. In addition, he was actively involved in assisting the victims of Russian pogroms from 1882 onwards and pleaded that they be directed to Palestine rather than the New World. An enthusiastic Zionist, he collected money for Jerusalem Jewry and attempted to raise their education and vocational standards. His contributions to Jewish scholarship included studies in rabbinics, and Responsa on the first two parts of the *Shulhan Arukh*.

FURTHER READING

Jung, L., ed.: *Jewish Leaders 1750–1940* (Jerusalem: Boys Town Jerusalem Publishers, 1953)

DAN COHN-SHERBOK

Hillesum, Etty (1914–1943) Dutch writer. Born in Middelburg, she was educated in Deventer and gained a Masters degree in Law at Amsterdam University in 1939. Due to the German occupation of the Netherlands in 1940 she was not able to complete her studies in Slavonic Languages.

Etty Hillesum came from an assimilated Dutch–Jewish family, although her mother, Riva Hillesum, born Bernstein (1881–1943), was a Russian–Jewish refugee. Etty's father, Louis Hillesum (1880–1943, Ph.D. in Classical Languages in 1908), was head of the Deventer grammar school and belonged to the cultural elite of this provincial town. Etty had two gifted brothers, the younger, Mischa Hillesum (1920–44), being a promising musician. During the 1930s Etty Hillesum was active in the left-wing anti-Fascist student movement. In 1941 however, she met the German–Jewish refugee Julius Spier (1887–1942), a former banker who maintained that he could analyze people's character by studying the shape of their hands. Due to his influence her interest in political matters diminished and she concentrated on her spiritual development. She drew inspiration mainly from the works of Rilke and from the Bible (including the New Testament). Spier advised her to keep a diary and to record her inner growth. These diaries testify to her great literary skill and strength of mind.

Because of the German occupation she had to endure the anti-Jewish regulations and the threat of deportation. In July 1942, she began work at an office of the *Joodsche Raad* (Jewish Council) in Amsterdam. After two weeks she was transferred to the Dutch transit camp, Westerbork, where she was assigned to take care of the people who were due to leave for the extermination camps. Because of illness she was obliged several times to remain in Amsterdam, but she returned voluntarily and continued her work in the camp. During this period she wrote several letters. All the efforts of friends to persuade her to save herself were in vain. She wanted (in her words) "to share the fate of my people". On 30 November 1943, she was killed in Auschwitz.

At the same time the Dutch Resistance published two letters in which Etty Hillesum gave a penetrating report of life in the camp. More letters survived, as well as her Amsterdam diaries. In 1981 a selection from her diaries appeared in Dutch and, in 1982, a collection of her letters. In 1986 a complete edition of her writings appeared in Dutch.

BIBLIOGRAPHY
Etty: A Diary, 1941–1943 (London: Jonathan Cape, 1983); *Letters from Westerbork* (London: Jonathan Cape, 1986)

K. A. D. SMELIK

Hirsch, Emil Gustave (1851–1923) American Reform rabbi. Born in Luxemburg, where his father, Samuel HIRSCH, was rabbi, he received his early education in Germany. He moved to the USA in 1866. It was from his father that Emil Hirsch gained his introduction to Judaic and philosophical learning. He attended the University of Pennsylvania, and then returned to Germany to study at the universities of Berlin and Leipzig and the *Hochschule für die Wissenschaft des Judentums* (1872–6). He served congregations in Baltimore and Louisville and married a daughter of David EINHORN. In 1880 he succeeded his brother-in-law, Kaufman KOHLER, as rabbi of Sinai Congregation, Chicago, where he remained for the rest of his life.

Hirsch made the pulpit of Sinai famous by his outstanding eloquence and his fearless radicalism in both religious and social matters. Among Reform rabbis he was decidedly of the avant garde, repudiating the traditional ceremonial side of Judaism and going to the length of transferring the sabbath service to Sunday. He used his pulpit to advocate social reforms, and was instrumental in having added to the Pittsburgh Platform (1885) – the widely accepted formulation of the ideas of REFORM JUDAISM – the clause affirming the duty to attack social evils.

Hirsch's eloquence was backed by a considerable fund of scholarship. His contributions to literature were principally in *The Jewish Encyclopedia* (1901–6), where he became editor of the biblical department. In 1891 he established the *Reform Advocate*, a weekly which carried his ideas. In 1892 the University of Chicago appointed him to the Chair of rabbinic literature and philosophy, but he appears to have done little teaching.

Hirsch was very much a solo performer, showing something of a prima donna temperament, and played little part in the affairs of the Central Conference of American Rabbis. He flourished in an age when the pulpit virtuoso was an outstanding figure in society, and there is no doubt that his combination of qualities made him one of the leading luminaries of his day. Except for the continuing interest of the Reform rabbinate in social justice, Hirsch's influence has been limited.

FURTHER READING
Hirsch, D. E.: *Rabbi Emil G. Hirsch: The Reform Advocate*, (Chicago, 1969)
Schwartz, S. D.: *American Jewish Yearbook* 27 (1926–7) 230

S. D. TEMKIN

Hirsch, Samson Raphael (1808–1888) Rabbi, educator, writer. Hirsch was born in Hamburg, Germany. In 1828 he attended the *Yeshivah* of the enlightened Orthodox Rabbi Jakob Ettlinger in Mannheim. Hirsch spent the following year at the University of Bonn where he read classical languages, history and philosophy. Hirsch grew up in a strictly observant home, but one which also encouraged secular learning. His mentor was Hakham Bernays, who included secular studies in the curriculum of the Talmud Torah School in Hamburg, founded by Hirsch's grandfather, Mendel Frankfurter.

In 1830 Hirsch was appointed Rabbi of the principality of Oldenburg where he officiated for 11 years. There he wrote *Neunzehn Briefe ueber das Judentum* (1836; *Nineteen Letters on Judaism*, 1899; *The Nineteen Letters of Ben Uziel*, 1969). It is written as an exchange of letters between Benjamin, who voices the doubts of an intellectual young Jew, and Naphtali, the representative of traditional Judaism. This work came to be widely read and discussed in western Europe. *Choreb, oder Versuche ueber Jisroels Pflichten in der Zerstreuung* (1837, 1921; *Horeb – Essays on Israel's duties in the Diaspora*, 1962, 1982) gives

Hirsch's fundamental views on Judaism. While in Oldenburg he married Johanna Juedel.

In 1841 Hirsch was appointed Rabbi of the Hanoverian District of Aurich and Osnabrueck, and lived in Emden. His new diocese offered him a larger area of activity. Due to the desperate poverty of most of his parishioners Hirsch established an interest-free loan fund, possibly the first in Germany.

Hirsch was appointed District Rabbi of Moravia in 1846 and lived in Nikolsburg (Mikulov). Here he presided over a *Yeshivah* attended by students from many countries. He founded schools and organized social welfare services. The extremists on both sides of his community viewed him with suspicion. For the less committed he was too orthodox, while the extreme faction objected to some of his practices, such as wearing a robe during services, his rejection of casuistic argumentation, and his refusal to neglect the study of the Bible in favor of concentrating solely on the Talmud. During the revolution of 1848 Hirsch fought to obtain emancipation for Austrian and Moravian Jewry.

In Frankfurt-am-Main, as in many other towns, the community leaders favored Reform Judaism, which actively opposed the observance of ritual laws such as the diatary and matrimonial laws and avoided references to the Return to Zion in the prayers. In an attempt to counteract the influence of the Reform Movement, thirteen strictly orthodox families in Frankfurt banded together and decided to appoint their own rabbi. They chose Samson Raphael Hirsch. In 1851 Hirsch left his secure position in Nikolsburg and followed their call to Frankfurt. From these small beginnings he built up a large and flourishing community. The school he founded and directed with 87 children grew into primary and high schools for boys and girls, which became models for many such schools in Germany and abroad. The education they gave was based on the mishnaic saying *Torah im derekh eretz* ("The study of Torah together with a worldly occupation is an excellent thing"). This became Hirsch's slogan and one of his most important contributions to modern Judaism. The underlying values of western civilization were not in opposition to Orthodox

Samson Raphael Hirsch

Judaism; they could be brought into harmony with it. Hirsch realized the need for revision within Judaism, but only of externals which would not affect the principles of Jewish faith and observance of the law. Thus, while he introduced a choir into his synagogue and gave his highly effective sermons in German, he insisted on Hebrew as the sole language for prayer.

Hirsch's importance as a religious spiritual leader, teacher, preacher, writer, and organizer made him a dedicated champion of Orthodoxy in its controversy with Reform–Liberal Judaism. While advocating strict adherence to *halakhah*, Hirsch sought a solution of the political and cultural challenges presented by modern life to Judaism.

BIBLIOGRAPHY

Collected Writings of Rabbi Samson Raphael Hirsch; The Jewish Year by S. R. Hirsch; Hirsch Haggadah; Hirsch Psalms; Hirsch Siddur (New York: Feldheim, 1984–9)

FURTHER READING

Breuer, M.: *The "Torah-im-derekh-eretz" of Samson Raphael Hirsch* (Jerusalem, 1970)

Grunfeld, I.: *Three Generations, The Influence of S. R. Hirsch on Jewish Life and Thought* (London: Jewish Post Publications, 1958)

BATYA RABIN

Hirsch, Samuel (1815–1889) US Reform rabbi. Hirsch was a leader of German and American Reform Judaism. Born in Thalfang, Prussia, he studied at the universities of Berlin, Bonn and Leipzig. He served first in Dessau, then as chief rabbi of Luxembourg (1843–66) before taking a leading role in American Reform Judaism as successor to David EINHORN in Philadelphia (1866–88) where he guided the radical wing of the movement in its Philadelphia and Pittsburgh Conferences. At the age of 27, he published *The Jewish Philosophy of Religion* (1842), a brilliant Hegelian text which nevertheless placed Judaism alongside Christianity as "absolute religion" and gave it equal validity. Hirsch anticipated Franz ROSENZWEIG's teachings in seeing Christianity's task as proclaiming God to the pagan world, viewing it as an "extensive" religiosity, while Judaism was the "intensive" religiosity already living with God in its midst. Hirsch stressed the centrality of human freedom and its choice between good and evil. Against pagan submission to nature and to fate, Abraham's rejection of child sacrifice set a pattern of human experience confirmed by the Sinaitic revelation. Hirsch's messianism was linked with an emphasis upon social justice which became central to the "platform" of American Reform, partly through the dedicated work of his son Emil G. Hirsch in Chicago. His emphasis upon the *Torah* (Law) as *Lehre* (Teaching) also influenced Reform Judaism, alongside his emphasis upon ceremonies as symbols that can and do change. His imprint endures within Reform Judaism today.

ALBERT H. FRIEDLANDER

Hirschfeld, Georg (1873–1942) German author. Born in Berlin, Hirschfeld worked in business and industry for a time, until he turned to a career in writing. Influenced decisively by the work of Henrik Ibsen and Gerhart Hauptmann, the major proponent of German naturalism, he strove to apply naturalist principles of dramatic composition to middle-class Jewish material. His dramas, *Die Mütter* (1896; The mothers) and *Agnes Jordan* (1898), which were received enthusiastically, are good examples of this tendency. Still, Hirschfeld was criticized in some Jewish quarters for his stark, negative dramatic depictions of Berlin Jewish life, precisely at the time of rising anti-Semitism in the last decade of the nineteenth century.

A prolific writer of fiction, poetry, and drama, Hirschfeld's work was sometimes included in Jewish nationalist collections. For example, his poem "Jeremias" (Jeremiah), was reprinted in Berthold FEIWEL's cultural Zionist anthology, *Jüdischer Almanach* (1902, 1904). Nevertheless, Hirschfeld was not attracted to Zionism. After the turn of the century, his work failed to receive critical acclaim. Hirschfeld virtually disappeared from the literary and cultural scene in Berlin, and the later part of his career is obscure.

MARK H. GELBER

Hirshbeyn [Hirshbein], **Peretz** (1880–1948) Yiddish dramatist. Born in the district of Grodne, Hirshbeyn moved to Vilna around 1900. He was a young disciple of Y. L. PERETZ whom he consulted about his early works. His first published work, a poem in Hebrew entitled "Gaaguim" (1901; Yearnings), made him a celebrity in the youthful Jewish literary circles of Vilna. Hirshbeyn was the chief instigator of the revival of Yiddish drama following the 20-year ban on Jewish theatrical productions in Russia. He began by writing plays in Hebrew, such as *Miriam* (1905), a tragedy about a Jewish prostitute, although there was no theater company performing Hebrew plays until 1917 when the Habimah group was founded. In 1906 Hirshbeyn began writing plays in Yiddish, changing from the realism of his Hebrew works to symbolism under the influence of the French symbolists. In 1908 he founded a Yiddish theatrical group in Odessa called the *Hirshbeyn trupe*, which toured the Ukraine and White Russia performing mainly his own plays, but also those of Sholem Asн, Dovid Pinski, Jacob Gordin, and Sholem aleichem. The group broke up in 1910 because of shortage of money and intrigue within contemporary literary circles. He settled in New York in 1911. His works include *Af yener zayt taykh* (1906; On the other side of the river); *Di erd* (The earth) written in Berlin in 1907 with the theme of escape from city life to the countryside and closeness to nature; *Tkies kaf* (1907; The contract) written in Petersburg, a tragic love story later developed in An-ski's *The Dybbuk*, and *Afn sheydveg* (1907; Parting of the ways) which has a feminist theme; *Di puste kretshme* (1912; The empty inn) and *A farvorfn vinkl* (1912; A neglected corner). There was no troupe to stage them until 1918 when the Jewish Art Theater was formed. Later works include *Grine felder* (1916; Green fields) which was made into a film in 1937, and a novel *Di royte felder* (1935; Red fields). He was at his best in his depictions of rural life, preferring to write of Jewish agriculturalists rather than factory workers. His characters are complex and recognizable both as individuals and as universal models. His works are often criticized for being better on paper than on the stage; however, he brought literary quality back to the Yiddish stage of an even higher standard than was established by Avraham Goldfaden.

DEVRA KAY

Hirszenberg, Shmuel (1863–1908) Polish painter. Born in Lodz, Poland, Hirszenberg was initially sent to a local spinning school but went on to study painting in Krakow and Munich. Here he received an academic training which he never abandoned – even though it rendered his work increasingly old-fashioned and acted as a self-imposed straightjacket on his own Expressionistic tendencies. A stay in Paris (1889–91) exposed him to the work of earlier nineteenth-century French painters and older contemporaries. Gericault's dark, Romantic vision was to prove an enduring influence, whilst the grim social Realism of Courbet and Daumier demonstrated the potential power of visual imagery allied to a social or political cause.

Returning to Poland in 1891, Hirszenberg continued to exhibit internationally with considerable success. The degradation and suffering of Polish Jewry under Czarist rule became his subject-matter. In 1899 he painted *The Wandering Jew*, an allegory of Jewish persecution in which a horrified man runs through a forest of crosses, stumbling over the bodies of crucified Jews which strew the path. It is possibly the first time in the history of art that the image of crucifixion had been applied to Jewish experience. The pogroms of the early twentieth century were reflected in several paintings, most notably *The Black Banner* (1905), which comes close to Expressionism in its depiction of a traumatized and threatened hasidic community.

Hirszenberg's work must be understood in the context of his growing commitment to Zionism and his belief that art should engage in this political struggle. In 1901 he had participated in the Exhibition of Jewish Art organised by Martin Buber at the Fifth Zionist Congress in Basel, but he did not share Buber's view that a Jewish art should aspire to spiritual wholeness; rather, he felt it should raise political consciousness. In furtherance of these ideas he went to Palestine in 1908 to teach at the Bezalel School, but died there later the same year.

FURTHER READING

Shilo-Cohen, N., ed.: *Bezalel 1906–1926* (Jerusalem: The Israel Museum, 1983) [exhibition catalog]
Kleeblatt, N., et al., eds: *Treasures of the Jewish Museum* (New York: Universe Books, 1986)

LAURA JACOBUS

historiography, Jewish The branch of Jewish cultural creativity which seeks to render an account of the Jewish past. Its motivations have variously been theological, national, secular, and scholarly. For modern Jews writing about their past has served and still serves to help establish their Jewish self-definition. Beyond the work of recounting and explaining, it seeks continuity between past and present experience, and aims at determining the reasons for Jewish suffering and survival.

The first Jewish historians were the writers and editors of the historical portions of the

Bible. Essentially they were theologians who found evidence of God's will in historical events. Victory over an enemy was a sign of faithfulness, loss an indication of failure to keep the covenant.

Greek historiography, as inquiry rather than the illustration of religious truth, did not penetrate Judaism until long after Alexander the Great's conquest of the Near East. Josephus Flavius (first century CE) broke with biblical tradition when he insisted that his purpose was to present historical truth strictly for its own sake. Yet Josephus found no imitators in succeeding centuries. With the loss of political sovereignty and the destruction of the Temple in the year 70 CE, the Rabbis turned away from empirical investigation, instead embroidering the biblical past with imaginative *midrashim* and dreaming of future restoration. They saw themselves as living within the boundaries of Jewish law rather than inside history; historical time had ceased to be a meaningful category.

It was not until the sixteenth century that there was a major revival of Jewish historiography. In the wake of the Jews' expulsion from Spain in 1492, a number of works attempted to deal with the catastrophe, some seeking mainly to console, others to provide empirical explanation. The critical temper of the Renaissance introduced a new, more secular approach, evident especially in the work of Solomon ibn Verga and Azariah dei Rossi. Following a dearth of Jewish historical writing in the seventeenth and eighteenth centuries, Jewish historiography blossomed in the nineteenth. The Romantic movement, which now displaced the Enlightenment in western Europe, understood truth as lying less in philosophical abstractions than in collective historical experience. Careful empirical investigation of the roots of contemporary phenomena was thought to be the best means for self-understanding and the best resource for organic political and social change. In the endeavor to determine their own identity and relation to the past, young Jewish intellectuals turned to the traditional sources, armed with the new tools of criticism learned in German universities. They established their own area of scholarship termed WISSENSCHAFT DES JUDENTUMS (the scientific study of Judaism).

While the most outstanding early practitioner of the critical study of Jewish sources, Leopold ZUNZ, remained mainly interested in textual analysis rather than historiography, others soon began to write coherent narrative accounts. The first Jew in modern times to attempt a comprehensive history of the Jews was Isaac Marcus JOST, whose multi-volume *History of the Israelites* began to appear in Germany in 1820. His purpose was as much apologetic as scholarly: he wanted to provide a sound basis on which Jews and gentiles could judge who the Jews really were and so decide how they and their religion might fit into modern society. Like the theologian and scholar Abraham GEIGER, Jost understood Jewish identity as essentially religious and its historical continuity as that of ongoing adherence to a religious idea.

Without question the most important Jewish historical work of the nineteenth century is Heinrich GRAETZ's *History of the Jews* (1853–76). Graetz understood his subject to be the folk soul of the Jewish people that expressed itself primarily in religion, but also in a wide range of cultural creativity. Jewish history, to his mind, was a combination of passively endured suffering and actively pursued learning. Though as a historian he was critical in the use of sources, as a religious believer Graetz held that God was actively present in Jewish and world history.

The first major historian strictly secular in his approach was Simon DUBNOW, a Russian Jew with a positivist orientation. His magnum opus, *The World History of the Jewish People* (originally written in Russian in the 1920s), reflects the author's Jewish nationalism in its sharper focus on the autonomous institutions of the people as a whole in preference to the religious writings of individuals. It also shifts the balance away from central and western Europe to the much larger Jewish communities of Russia and Poland with which he was intimately familiar.

Contemporary Jewish historiography can be understood as divided between the Israeli and American approaches. While both show a commitment to impartial scholarship, they tend to differ in their emphases; Israelis stressing the significance of the return to Zion, and the Holocaust as the devastating climax of existence outside the Land, while American Jewish historians dwell more upon the ongoing vitality of a Diaspora Jewish existence shaped by the Enlightenment and Emancipation.

FURTHER READING
Meyer, M. A., ed.: *Ideas of Jewish History* (New York: Behrman House, 1974)
Yerushalmi, Y. H.: *Zakhor: Jewish History and Jewish Memory* (Seattle: University of Washington Press, 1982)

MICHAEL A. MEYER

Hobson, Laura Keane Zametkin (1900–1986)

American author. Hobson's heritage shaped the liberal tone she established in her novels. Her father, Michael Zametkin, was an editor of a Yiddish newspaper and promoted the liberal cause as a labor organizer. She spent her childhood in Long Island, and then went on to Cornell University, earning her BA. During the period of her first marriage, which ended in divorce in 1935 she adopted two sons and began her career in publishing as an advertising copywriter. Her training in the publishing world included work as a consultant and promotion director for journals such as *Time*, *Life*, *Fortune*, *Sports Illustrated*, and the *Saturday Review*.

Laura Hobson typically depicts in her novels those social and religious prejudices which affected her own life. Her first novel, *The Tresspassers* (1943), conveys the liberalness and the quality of tolerance she was consistently to advocate. The novel itself uncovers the cruelties underlying the immigration laws. Her most successful novel, *Gentleman's Agreement* (1947), also examines a controversial issue as it explores the anti-Semitism pervasive among "nice" people after the Second World War and upholds the need for understanding among people. In the novel *The Celebrity* (1951), Hobson briefly moves away from portraying those concerns mirroring her own, and instead observes a lifestyle distant from her. However, with the novel *First Papers* (1964), she resumes the style which brought her success. She writes of her family and through the character Stefan Ivarin pays tribute to her father. Continuing in this vein, Hobson presents those prejudices closer to her own experience when she writes of single motherhood in *The Tenth Month* (1971) and of homosexuality from the parental perspective in *Consenting Adult* (1975).

BIBLIOGRAPHY
Over and Above (Garden City: Doubleday, 1979); *Untold Millions* (New York: Harper & Row, 1982); *Laura Z: A Life* (New York: Donald I. Fine Inc., 1986)

FURTHER READING
Mainiero, L., ed.: *American Women Writers: A Critical Reference Guide from Colonial Times to the Present in Four Volumes* (New York: Frederick Ungar Publishing Co., 1981)

DEBRA MORRIS

Hoffmann, David (Zevi) (1834–1921)

Rabbinic scholar. Born in Slovakia, Hoffmann studied at Hungarian *yeshivot*, at the Hildesheimer Seminary, and at the Universities of Vienna, Berlin and Tubingen. When HILDESHEIMER established a rabbinical seminary in Berlin, he invited Hoffmann to lecture on rabbinics. In 1899, on Hildesheimer's death, Hoffmann became rector of the seminary. At the end of his career he was regarded as the major halakhic authority of German Orthodox Jewry. In 1918 he was awarded the title of professor by the German government. Hoffmann's *Responsa* are characterized by a concern with contemporary conditions and are lenient in character. His biblical studies were directed against biblical criticism; this enterprise he viewed as a holy undertaking. Opposing Wellhausen, Hoffmann rejected the idea that the biblical text is composed of numerous sources. His works on the Talmud, however, were critical in nature, though he was intent not to negate the *halakhah*. Such an approach evoked a hostile response from such Orthodox scholars as Samson Raphael HIRSCH. In his study of the Mishnah he argued that there existed a First Mishnah which was edited before the destruction of the Second Temple on which later *tanna'im* held different views. In his exploration of halakhic *midrashim*, he differentiated between those originating in the school of Rabbi Ishmael and those of the school of Rabbi Akiva. By dividing the *midrashim* in this way, Hoffmann was able to explain differences in terminology, in the names of *tanna'im* mentioned, and in the methods of interpretation found in various *midrashim*.

FURTHER READING

Ginzberg, L.: *Students, Scholars and Saints* (Philadelphia: The Jewish Publication Society of America, 1928)

Jung, L., ed.: *Guardians of Our Heritage* (New York: Bloch Publishing Co., 1958)

DAN COHN-SHERBOK

Hofshteyn, Dovid (1889–1952) Yiddish poet. Hofshteyn was born in Korostishev, Ukraine. Between 1911 and 1919 he wrote an early cycle of lyrical nature poetry concerned with naivety and love, portraying himself as a young branch of an old tree gathering strength from the old trunk. He became an avid socialist during the 1917 Revolution. With the lifting of restrictions on Jews in Russia he became a lecturer in Moscow and head of the Yiddish Cultural League in Kiev. His songs rejoicing in the revolution established his popularity both in Russia and elsewhere in radical Jewish circles. In 1922 he published his elegies illustrated by Marc CHAGALL in which he mourns for the ruined Jewish communities of a shamed Ukraine. In danger himself, he left the USSR in 1923, settling in Palestine via Leipzig and Berlin. He wrote Hebrew songs for the Labor Zionists. In 1924 his biblical dramatic poem *Shol – der letster meylekh fun Yisroel* (Saul – the last King of Israel) was published, and *Moshiekh's tsaytn* (The times of the Messiah) followed in 1925.

Hofshteyn decided to return to the USSR in 1926, as did KVITKO and MARKISH. His *Lider* (1935; Songs) mapped out his road to Marxism via a religious childhood. He wrote prolifically but his poetry declined in quality as it came to be dominated by the Marxist cause. When the USSR supported the foundation of the new state of Israel in 1948 he was free to voice his enthusiasm at the event. However, a few months later, Russia's foreign policy towards Israel changed, and Hofshteyn, together with other Jewish intellectuals from the Kiev Group,

was arrested. He was transported to Moscow for interrogation and exiled to Tomsk, Siberia. He was shot on 12 August 1952 with his cell mate, Dovid BERGELSON.

DEVRA KAY

Holdheim, Samuel (1806–1860) Reform Jewish leader. In the history of nineteenth-century Reform, Samuel Holdheim was one of the most radical reformers. Growing up in Prussian Poland, Holdheim was regarded as a talmudic prodigy. After University, he became rabbi of several German communities. Influenced by Abraham GEIGER and others in the late 1830s, Holdheim published pamphlets and books attacking the validity of talmudic law and the legal functions of the rabbinate. After 1846 he served as rabbi of the Reform temple of Berlin. Under Holdheim's influence the Berlin Reform Temple in 1849 replaced the Sabbath services by Sunday services and also abolished the observance of the second day of festivals. Other reforms instituted in the Berlin congregation were the non-segregation of the sexes, prayers without head cover or prayer shawl, the elimination of Hebrew in the service, and the abolition of the blowing of the *shofar*. According to Holdheim, the Talmud was irrelevant in meeting the needs of contemporary Jewry. Talmudic Judaism, he believed, was only one state in the evolution of Judaism. For Holdheim, the essence of tradition was not conservatism but innovation. Such a view was diametrically opposed to the neo-Orthodoxy of Samson Raphael HIRSCH who believed that traditional rituals could take on symbolic and allegorical meanings. For Holdheim, ceremonial law (including dietary prohibitions, the ritual of circumcision, the sacrificial cult of the biblical Temple) had been valuable in ancient times when Jews were socially isolated from other peoples. But in modern society the Jewish community had no political aims of its own; thus all rituals connected with a specifically Jewish nationality should be regarded as obsolete and ought to be abolished. The universal essence of Judaism, Holdheim believed, was that God is the Creator of the world, that He possesses unity, personality and holiness, and that the messianic age will be marked by universal justice and love.

FURTHER READING
Plaut, G.: *The Rise of Reform Judaism* (New York: World Union for Progressive Judaism, 1963)
Seltzer, R.: *Jewish People, Jewish Thought* (New York: Macmillan; London: Collier Macmillan, 1980)

DAN COHN-SHERBOK

Holocaust and literature With the passage of time, memories of any major historical event diminish, and strategies of recall evolve. Within survivor communities private memories are subsumed into collective memory which in turn becomes the group's epistemological ground and the imagination's battlefield. For students of literature, the distance of nearly half a century from the events themselves invites a critical assessment of the ways in which the Holocaust has been incorporated into and has reshaped prevailing myths. At the heart of each reading of this literature is a set of assumptions about the semantic field and the subversive effect of the historical matter on inherited cultural codes and ways of perceiving the past. To study the codes of memory – private and public – embedded in poetic language is to reveal an ongoing process by which the past is being continually renegotiated into the present.

What has come to be referred to as "Holocaust literature" actually represents less a unique phenomenon and more a culmination or a radicalization of processes of dislodgement of both figurative and representational language that originated in the literature of the First World War, if not earlier. A broad overview of literary responses to catastrophe in the twentieth century would identify a number of major shifts in the literary discourse: linguistic displacement as a primary manifestation of the widespread experience of exile; the anonymization and deritualization of death with its implications for all rites of passage; the massive assault on the integrity of the individual and on his or her place in the fictive space once reserved for the hero; and the shifting role of the reader. In reflecting the struggle of each writer with memory and with language, these processes have redefined cultural options in our century.

We credit Homer with having invented a new language out of formulaic fragments that survived in the oral tradition, both to trace and to imagine the ruination of Troy that had taken place some four to five centuries earlier. Archaeologists of the word draw tentative distinctions between "artifact" and "fiction", between "memory" and "invention". The tension between the accountability and the autonomy of the historical imagination or between the historical and the mythopoeic remains as pronounced and unresolvable after the most recent cataclysm in western civilization as it was in the eighth century BCE.

The principal development in literary responses to catastrophe in the twentieth century, culminating in the literature of the Holocaust, is a two-pronged challenge to poetic or symbolic language on the one hand and to the status of realism as a belief in the possibility of reliable representations of reality, on the other.

The critical discourse on the nature, the parameters, and the direction of literary responses to the Holocaust began to evolve some twenty years after the end of the war. Since the fiction and poetry that had appeared constituted a literature of displaced persons, which for the most part could not be located within any natural cultural boundaries, the discussion which ensued focused on the very nature of poetic language in the face of unprecedented atrocity. From his place of refuge in the USA after the Second World War, the German-Jewish philosopher T. W. ADORNO was one of the first to approach this material in terms of the imagination's debt to history, to seek those poetic forms which would not betray the victims by diminishing, through estheticization, the pain of the reader's encounter with their suffering and the brutality of their death. The poet Csezlaw Miłosz, speaking from the desolation of a Poland dotted with empty Jewish towns and concentration camps and the bleak realities of the post-war Communist regime, went even further in trying to formulate a poetics so stark, so fundamental, that the text could "preserve [its] validity even in the eyes of a man threatened with instant death" (*The Captive Mind*).

George STEINER entered the discussion with an assault on notions of the civilizing pretense of art and the neutrality of metaphor. Recent history demonstrates, he argues, that art proved not only powerless to stem the tide of barbarism washing over Europe – many of the perpetrators of Nazi atrocities were in fact readers of Goethe and aficionados of Bach – but actually *complicitous* in having provided over the centuries the pictorial and literary figures of damnation that had become deeply embedded in the imagination long before they were enacted in reality: "The concentration and death camps of the twentieth century . . . are the transference of Hell from below the earth to its surface. They are the deliberate enactment of a long precise imagining." (*In Bluebeard's Castle*).

While both Adorno and Steiner are addressing, in different terms, the tensions between the autonomy and the latent social functions of art, they highlight the precariousness of the post-Enlightenment separation between esthetics and morality. The images of the Inferno invoked by Steiner have, as it were, been set free from their moorings in both a religious vision of Divine supervision and a promise of beatitude and the humanistic vision of human perfectibility. Critics and philosophers such as J.-P. Sartre and György LUKÁCS who would still enlist art in the crusade for social melioration present their own powerful counter-arguments. An esthetics of evil or extreme suffering thus comes to be viewed by various thinkers as suspect on the grounds that it serves either to temper reality or to legitimate and reinforce it. However one responds to the positions represented here, they are a powerful affirmation of the moral import accorded by many readers to the forms, no less than to the themes, of a literature responding to catastrophe.

A related concern about the place and impact of symbolic language informs the attempts to trace the course of images that originated in the universe of ghettos and death camps. The growing public familiarity with the history of the Holocaust has resulted in the symbolic diffusion of the subject into the culture at large. Because the signs of life under the Swastika are so over-determined, once they are loosed upon

the world they cannot infiltrate other semantic universes unobtrusively – exhibiting in the extreme what Paul de Man has called, in another context, the "proliferating and disruptive power of figural language" ("The Epistemology of Metaphor"). There is, on the one hand, a growing fascination with Nazism in the latter decades of the twentieth century; Saül FRIEDLÄNDER describes the trajectory of certain powerful images which assume a kind of autonomy vis à vis the contexts that seek to domesticate or ironize them, recalling the realm of their origins and evoking the powerful Nazi myths that spawned them (*Reflections of Nazism*). Such phenomena and the quarrying of the camps and ghettos for sensational themes and images in such texts as the late poems of Sylvia Plath, William Styron's *Sophie's Choice*, or D. M. Thomas' *The White Hotel*, tend to evoke a moral response on the part of the reader which deviates from more clinical principles of critical reading. It may not be surprising, then, that whether they are arguing for historical accuracy or esthetic norms, critics often relate to this literature as qualitatively different from other poetic or fictive material and assume the role of guardians of particular versions of collective memory. A moralized reading challenges the detached critical stance of the literary critic and contributes to the rise of self-conscious, engaged criticism as a competing force in the late twentieth century. Of course any art form that addresses historical matter that is so morally loaded will invite criticism as it stakes out the spheres of its autonomy. It is therefore no simple enterprise to keep the subject within the general critical discourse on literature and art, while recognizing that this literature often tests the very limits of that discourse.

History and the imagination: shifting boundaries

The radicalizing effect of the Holocaust on literary conventions can, perhaps, be best highlighted by reference to those forms whose status as fiction is somewhat indeterminate. Autobiography, which was hardly conceived as a construct of the imagination until quite recently, can serve as fertile ground for beginning such an exploration.

The autobiographical narrative of the Holocaust survivor is inevitably an attempt to construct a self from the fragments of a past that lost its coherence not through the normal passage of time, but through cataclysmic disruption. To some extent all autobiographical writing is the creation of a myth of the self – but for the survivor, there is an added intensity, an urgency, that stretches this process to its outer limits and thereby illuminates the entire genre. Even as we recognize that an insistence on factuality characterizes both the autobiographies and most of the autobiographical fiction, there is usually a moment of separation, even in the most confessional forms of this literature, which is generative of all the fiction to come – a gesture of distancing between the experiencing self and the possible fictive selves. The Holocaust autobiography most familiar to western readers is Elie WIESEL's *Night*. Originally written in Yiddish, it was rewritten in French and appeared in English translation in 1960, inaugurating (with the Eichmann trial one year later) a new level of public awareness of the Holocaust – particularly in America and western Europe. The last paragraph of this narrative, in which the 15-year-old inmate just liberated from Buchenwald encounters his emaciated, orphaned reflection in a mirror, provides closure to the autobiography and an opening unto possible fictional worlds; "from the depths of the mirror a corpse gazed back at me. The look in his eyes, as they stared into mine, has never left me." He both leaves his dead self ("corpse") behind, making some sort of an after-life possible, and preserves it for future visits when, reaching through the looking-glass, as it were, he will attempt both to retrieve and reshape the past. In this *literally* "reflexive" or self-reflective moment, fiction becomes the only available manner of return.

As we move from autobiography to the more clearly symbolic realm of fiction, poetry, and drama, the tension between the fictive mode and the testimonial imperative not only does not disappear but continues to contribute to the literary endeavor in complex ways. Irving HOWE in "Writing and the Holocaust" has claimed that the historical matter acts as ballast, disciplining the imagination and ultimately limiting its flight. Here the moral burden of historical accountability and the ambiguous sta-

tus of the esthetic are made explicit. And yet as we explore this literature, we find that the mimetic conventions and authenticating procedures by which fiction is traditionally grounded in history provide no more of a compass for orientation than would a map of the terrain of eastern Poland for the person who was about to board a train for Auschwitz in 1942. An example of the persistent but elusive and even subversive presence of historical evidence in the fictive realm can be found in Avrom SUTSKEVER's poetry. There is a stubborn insistence, particularly in the poems written during the war, while he was still in the Vilna Ghetto, on the documentary validity of the text. As Anita Norich has shown, Sutskever's poems are "historical artifacts"; they are "signed with the place and date of composition – 'Vilna, August 30 1941'; 'Vilna Ghetto, March 5 1943' – underscoring their documentary function, but also pointing to the defiant imagination capable of creating art then and there" ("Yiddish Poetry") What is *historically* significant is not what is related in these poems but the fact that poetry was written at all. The poem "The leaden plates of Romm's printing works" describes a group of partisans melting down the lead plates of a major Jewish press to forge bullets:

By the casting of bullets the lead
illumined thoughts – letter after letter melted.
One molten line from Babylon, another
from Poland, flowed into the same mold.
Jewish bravery once hidden in words
must now strike back with shot!...

(Burnt Pearls)

The dating at the end ("Sept. 12, 1943") seemed to many readers to authenticate the action imitated. How, then, does it affect one's grasp of the relationship between history and the imagination to discover that in all probability this entire event was invented by Sutskever? What may be reproduced in this poetry, as in much of Holocaust literature, are not the arbitrary facts of history but the *logic* of history. Such an event could well have taken place in the Vilna Ghetto; symbolically, it *had* to take place, and the poet's task is to redress historical gaps with symbolic necessities. David Roskies (*Against the Apocalypse*) dates the actual writing of this poem as no earlier than February 1944, and presents a convincing case for a kind of retrospective "self-censorship" by which Sutzkever and other writers actually altered certain facts to create a "myth of destruction and rebellion" that could serve the regenerating spirit of the surviving community in the aftermath of the war.

The historical matter thus becomes molten in the imagination. Constructing certain facts and dismantling or effacing others (the Germans, as Roskies points out, were "consigned to verbal annihilation" through absence in Sutskever's poetry – and this is true of other writers as well), occasionally even editing the story or the poem at a later stage to serve shifting perceptions of the social resonances of the text, the survivor–writer enters into a dynamic relationship with his own memories. Like Sutzkever in poetry, Isaiah Spiegel was engaged after the war in a desperate effort to accommodate his Yiddish fiction to what he saw as the changing exigencies of the hour; whereas a critic such as Yehiel Sheintuch (*Yiddish and Hebrew Literature under the Nazi Rule*) discounts those stories written or revised even one week after liberation as "inauthentic" representations of the poetic voice *in extremis*, we can see that with the passage of time some texts take on the aspect of a palimpsest, preserving, half-exposed, several layers of consciousness. Holocaust narratives are as often engaged in "de-realizing" as in reconstructing history. The Lodz Ghetto can serve as an example of a place and a moment in time that have generated divergent modes of recall, by turns appealing to and denying "factuality": Spiegel's stories written during and following his incarceration; the fiction and drama of outsiders focusing on the enigmatic personality of *Judenrat* chairman, Adam Rumkowski. One novel in particular, written by a survivor of Lodz, defies the historical imperative by raising a barricade of fiction against intolerable reality, and violates esthetic decorum by introducing humor into the narrative. Jurek Becker's *Jacob the Liar* is predicated on the power of the imagination to construct alternate worlds; the characters in this novel inhabit a ghetto that bears circumstantial resemblance to Lodz, while denying its actual status; and even if the survivor–writer must surrender his

characters at the end of the narrative to their historical death (unlike a writer remote from the events like D. M. Thomas, who, in *The White Hotel*, takes the liberty of resurrecting his heroine after her death at Babi Yar), he has succeeded, for a time, in keeping death at bay.

Elie Wiesel demonstrates this dialectic between the impulses of commemoration and denial in one passage in which his narrator describes himself leafing through an album of photographs taken by Nazi officers. One of the pictures captures a group of naked women just before they are to be shot:

> And from Treblinka – or is it Birkenau, Ponar, Majdanek? – this image which one day will burst inside me like a sharp call to madness; Jewish mothers, naked, leading their children, also naked, to the sacrifice.... Look at the women, some still young and beautiful, their frightened children well-behaved.... And you, what are you doing? Go ahead, go on, snatch a flower, offer it to the mothers in exchange for their children – what are you waiting for? Hurry up, quickly, grab a child and run, run as fast as your legs will carry you, faster than the wind, while there's still time, before you are blinded by smoke.... (*One Generation After*)

Exchanging a flower for a child (suspending time at the edge of the pit so that a story can be told) – the bargain that the writer strikes with fate – is an act that, like Sheherazade's, must be repeated daily, because at the end of each fictional day, history arrives as the Angel of Death to claim his due. That dooms some writers to a kind of pathology of repetition – of theme, of character – which readers and critics often note with impatience.

Aharon APPELFELD, who survived the war years as a young child in a labor camp in Transnistria and eventually made his way to Palestine, defines writing as a compensatory act which defies history's successes. Responding to a rhetorical query about the place of imaginative literature "in a sphere which demands either action or silence", he asked

> who will redeem from the darkness the fears, the pain and the suffering, the hidden beliefs, the sense of nothingness, and the sense of eternity? Who will take them out of their obscurity and grant them a bit of warmth and dignity, if not the

imagination [lit. "art"] that is so conscientious in its choice of words, so concerned with each feeling and each nuance of feeling. Art evolves as a kind of continual defiance of the anonymization of man. (*Essays in the First Person*)

On what scale do we weigh such defiance? And, conversely, of what significance is the fact-mindedness of the documentary writer? In staging the proceedings of the trial of twenty-one Auschwitz criminals, German–Jewish playwright Peter WEISS claimed that his "condensation of the evidence" contained "nothing but facts. Personal experience and confrontations must be steeped in anonymity." Emotion and all forms of individualization are excluded from the script as non-factual. Yet any reader's or viewer's quest for information is defeated by the very nature of the material (if you have found out exactly how many calories were consumed by the inmates of the concentration camp per day, and how many grams of Cyklon B were needed to kill a two-year-old child, what do you *know?*)

While the gap between "information" and "knowledge" is never really bridged even as the historical record mounts, the struggle to get closer to the truth often persists in the literary realm as an attack upon fictive forms. "Coal black milk of morning, we drink it at evening/ we drink it at noon and at daybreak. We drink it at night," writes Paul CELAN in the opening lines of what has become the most famous and most controversial of Holocaust poems, *Todesfuge* (Fugue of death). Celan's poem remains at the center of the struggle over poetic language, over the place of esthetic forms and figurative language in the search for linguistic correlatives of the experience of ghettos and death camps. The German playwright Rolf Hochhuth, conceding that Celan's poem, "in which the gassing of the Jews is entirely translated into metaphors", is "masterly", nevertheless contends that it would be "perilous" to employ such an approach on stage:

For despite the tremendous force of suggestion emanating from sound and sense, metaphors still screen the infernal cynicism of what really took place – a reality so enormous and grotesque that even today [1963]...the impression of unreality it produces conspires with our natural strong tendency to treat the matter as a legend, as an incredible apocalyptic fable. (*The Deputy*)

That is, the normal contract between playwright and audience, in which the "willing suspension of disbelief" secures tolerance for even the most far-fetched of human actions, is violated here in favor of an extra-textual appeal to historical authority.

Hochhuth's own method in the drama *The Deputy*, which revolves around Pope Pius XII's muted response to the deportation of the Jews of Italy, not only incorporates documentary material into the fictive space, but appends a 60-page essay on the historicity of the events portrayed and the esthetic principles that can be admitted into such a dense historical moment. Hochhuth thus contributes to the creation of a hybrid genre which later appears in the popular culture as the "docudrama" (the American television series "Holocaust" was the first of many such productions) – a genre that remains ultimately accountable neither to the dictates of history nor to the autonomy and inner coherence of the imagination.

When we return to the dominant image in Celan's poem, we find the documentary imperative clearly subordinated to the shaping hand of the artist – and yet in their glaring starkness, the fragments of historical consciousness often remain recalcitrant and unassimilable, potentially subverting the entire poetic enterprise. Celan registers the enormity of the historical upheaval by straining the poetic language to its limits; through the use of the oxymoron "black milk", the impossible image that defies the laws of contradiction, he both invents a new rhetoric of catastrophe and remains faithful to the historic moment in which ash was the camp inmates' daily ration. The dominant gesture in the poem (a man ordering "his Jews" to "shovel a grave into the ground" and to "strike up and play for the dance") is accompanied in 1947, in its earliest, Rumanian, edition, by a precautionary note that the poem is "based upon data"; that in the Nazi camps "some of the condemned were forced to play music while others dug graves." Yet, as John Felstiner demonstrates in his "Biography of a poem", Celan himself felt, over time, that his poem was "lapsing into a purely esthetic niche" and becoming regarded conveniently as a lyrical exercise divorced from the moral urgency of historical or documentary art. Volumes were written and educational curricula devised, especially in Germany, around the musical structure and the intricate imagery of *Todesfuge*. Finally, in the late 1950s, Celan wrote a long sequel to the poem in which, as Felstiner says, the "night and ashes of 'Todesfuge' [have been] stripped of cadence and metaphor". The ultimate retreat to a kind of esthetic minimalism seems to be a form of insistence on the urgency of the historical matter in the poetics of a writer whose earlier transformational images seemed to constitute a strategy for personal survival.

The ongoing debate focuses on the degree of remove of poetic images from their historical reference and on the artistic sublime as a betrayal of the ground of suffering. Yet what may be more fundamentally at issue is the collapse of the presupposition, underlying all metaphoric activity, of an organic universe in which elements can be provisionally linked in ways that confirm the coherence and benevolence of the natural and the human order.

Ultimately, there is a challenge to historical continuity, mimetic conventions and the order and symmetries of a symbolically organic universe, manifested in the extreme in the poetry of Celan and a few others. In Hebrew poetry, Dan PAGIS reveals an equally fragmented, rudderless universe from which the principle of order, human or divine, has been withdrawn. We may be witnessing here the collapse or recasting not only of certain esthetic and philosophical conventions fundamental to western culture, but also of basic presuppositions of Jewish civilization. The prevailing response to catastrophe in Jewish tradition, which can be traced from the poetry and prose written in the wake of the destruction of the Second Temple through to the modern era, is anti-apocalyptic, affirming, through theological or historical schemes, faith in the regenerative powers of the people and its culture. Whereas this faith is reflected in Israel in the official rhetoric of "rebirth," for writers like Pagis and Celan none of the systems of meaning hold. And yet, even these negations resound within a highly crafted poetry which still presupposes the primacy of communication and

the viability of the imagination in a world that has survived such cataclysm.

Writing may always be a hedge against despair; writing in the wake of the total devastation of a civilization becomes a positive act of defiance. Words function here not as compensation for imperfections in the world, but as a *replacement* for the world. The readers of this literature may discern a tension between the writing act itself, as a gesture of retrieval and communication of lost realities, and the dissolution of continuities of form and content, the radicalization or subversion of cultural conventions that characterizes much of this fiction and poetry.

With the passage of time one can also measure a redefinition of the connection between the historical events and the literary imagination, a diminution of the "testimonial imperative"; particularly as the survivor generation gives way to a generation of writers removed from the events themselves, the subject enters dynamically into the sphere of myths that govern each culture in ways that still recall, but constantly reinterpret, their historical origins.

FURTHER READING

Améry, J.: *At the Mind's Limits* (Indiana University Press, 1980)

Des Pres, T.: *The Survivor: An Anatomy of Life in the Death Camps* (New York: Pocket Books, 1977)

Ezrahi, S. De K.: *By Words Alone: The Holocaust in Literature* (Chicago: The University of Chicago Press, 1980)

History and Anthropology, 1986, vol. 2, part 2

Kahler, E.: *The Tower and the Abyss: An Inquiry into the Transformation of Man* (New York: The Viking Press, 1967)

Langer, L.: *The Holocaust and the Literary Imagination* (New Haven: Yale University Press, 1975)

Mintz, A.: *Hurban* (Columbia University Press, 1984)

Rosenfeld, A.: *A Double Dying: Reflections on Holocaust Literature* (Bloomington: Indiana University Press, 1980)

Steiner, G.: *In Bluebeard's Castle: Some Notes Towards the Redefinition of Culture* (New Haven: Yale University Press, 1971)

White, H.: *Tropics of Discourse* (Baltimore, 1978)

Young, J.: *Writing and Rewriting the Holocaust: Interpreting Holocaust Narrative* (Bloomington: Indiana University Press, 1988)

SIDRA DEKOVEN EZRAHI

Felix Nussbaum Camp *1940. Leo Baeck Institute, New York*

Holocaust art For a long time the art of the Holocaust was considered almost a taboo subject: not only because the memory of those years remained too vivid, but because of a feeling of embarrassment that art produced in such circumstances could evoke an esthetic response or be judged by normal esthetic criteria; others have felt that esthetic merit is unlikely to be compatible with fidelity to historical facts. What, in other words, is the exact status of these images? Clearly, there are no easy answers to such questions, but, as various recent publications and exhibitions testify, the time has come to confront the evidence.

Approximately 30,000 works produced by victims of the Holocaust have survived. Given that works were hidden (and sometimes found), smuggled out (not always successfully), and many of them destroyed by the artists themselves for security reasons, it has been reasonably assumed that this number, large as it is, represents only a small fraction of the victims' actual output. The main repositories of Holocaust art are as follows: research centers on the Holocaust (notably, *Yad Vashem*, Kibbutz *Lochamei Haghettaot*, and the *Centre de Documentation Juive Contemporaine* in Paris); museums

located in former concentration camps (Auschwitz, Buchenwald, Mauthausen, Dachau, and others); museums devoted to the military history and Resistance movements of the Second World War (the *Musée des Deux Guerres Mondiales* in Paris and the *Instituut voor Oorlogsdocumentation* in Amsterdam, the Documentation Archives of the Austrian Resistance Movement in Vienna and the Paris *Chancellerie del'Ordre de la Libération*); Jewish institutions in Europe, America and Israel (such as the State Jewish Museum in Prague and the YIVO Institute for Jewish Research and Leo Baeck Institute in New York) which include the Holocaust among their other collection areas; and, finally, private collections, including those held by the artists themselves or handed down to their families.

Contrary to Nazi propaganda, German Jews had played a relatively inconspicuous part in the pre-war art scene. Ironically, many victims who had never wielded a brush before or had merely been amateurs, became committed artists by force of circumstance. Some of the professional artists (Felix Nussbaum, for example) perished; while some of those who discovered or consolidated their talent during the war (Arnold Daghani, for example) survived to become professionals in the post-war period. Not surprisingly, the styles employed by the victims varied widely.

That conditions were scarcely conducive to artistic creation hardly needs stating. Considerable ingenuity was required merely to obtain materials, although this was obviously easier in the ghettos and transit camps than in the concentration camps. Zoran Music, for example, tinted his paintings with rust taken from the bars of his jail cell in Dachau. How, then, does one account for the huge number of works of art produced against all the odds?

Art, it seems, served three primary and interrelated functions for the inmates of the camps and ghettos. Firstly, it provided a much-needed link with their former identity, acting as a defiant assertion of individuality in the most dehumanizing circumstances. Secondly, it provided a means of transcending the awful present by proving oneself the master of one's medium; and lastly, it acted as a bridge to the future, a means of communicating the horror of their experience to later generations and of perpetuating some small physical remnant of themselves. The artists' own later statements bear this out: Josef Szajna, for example, wrote that "the idea of painting or drawing was to leave a trace of yourself behind you"; Boris Taslitzky drew "for myself, for my comrades, and for the future"; Waldemar Nowakowski "involved himself with art in order to survive"; while Zoran Music, who hid his works in a hollowed out volume of *Mein Kampf* in the library at Dachau, claimed: "For an artist it is not possible to not create...art gave me the force to survive, and the danger of being caught was even more exciting".

Distinctions must be drawn, however, between the different types of art produced. Firstly, there was the art produced to Nazi orders, in the form of portraits, genealogical charts, "sentimental realist" scenes from history or mythology, forgeries of other works of art, landscapes, images of animals, architectural drawings, greeting cards, and party invitations. These at least gave one respite from harsher labor. Secondly, there was the unofficially tolerated art, not done to order but acceptable because deemed unsubversive (this might include some of the categories mentioned above, produced as a means of barter with the Nazis). Both these types of art tend to be bland and lacking in individuality.

Lastly, and most importantly, there were the unofficial "resistance" works, produced at mortal risk. Although some of these works are – justifiably – expressionistically angst-ridden, many of them stress the dignity of life in spite of all, in objectively and naturalistically rendered scenes of everyday occurrences; some of the most poignant depict scenes from happier days. Special mention needs to be made here of the heart-breakingly escapist drawings produced by the children of Terezín. The art produced on the theme of the Holocaust after the event both by survivors (Leo Haas and Lea Grundig, for example) and by Jews who did not experience it (R. B. KITAJ is a notable recent example) tends, not surprisingly, to be more complex and allusive in its imagery. The notion of the Jews as Christ's modern representatives and of Jesus as the original Jewish martyr, explored by Jewish artists both before and during the Holocaust, has exercised a still more powerful attraction in the post-Holocaust period.

FURTHER READING

Blatter, J., and Milton, S.: *Art of the Holocaust* (London: Pan, 1982)

Green, G.: *The Artists of Terezín* (New York: Hawthorn Books, 1978)

Toll, N.: *Without Surrender: Art of the Holocaust* (Philadelphia: Running Press, 1978)

Volavkova, H.: *I Never Saw Another Butterfly...: Children's Drawings & Poems from Terezín Concentration Camp* (New York: McGraw Hill, 1962)

Yad Vashem – Martyrs' & Heroes' Remembrance Authority Art Museum (Jerusalem, 1982) [exhibition catalog]

MONICA BOHM-DUCHEN

Holocaust in American–Jewish philosophy

With the possible exception of Abba Hillel Silver's *Conspiracy of Silence* in 1943, American Jewish theological thought about the Holocaust during the event and during the following two decades is confined to Orthodox Jewish circles. Even such a notable work as Will Her-berg's *Judaism and Modern Man* (1951) does not discuss the Holocaust.

The catastrophe only began to have an impact on Jewish thought in the USA on a broad scale after the 1967 War. By the time the war began, the Jewish State offered enough psychological security for Jews to be able to gaze upon the terror. Enough time had passed to separate the object of thought from the thinker and to produce the freedom to work with the event intellectually. The war itself, where the Jews at first appeared victims then became victors, brought the Holocaust to the front of consciousness. Terrifying questions poured out. At the center was the issue of whether covenantal Jewish history remained alive.

Richard Rubenstein

RUBENSTEIN views history as an inevitable process of increasing secularization, of demystification or disenchantment of the environment. History begins, he explains, with God's commandment to Adam to rule over nature. History climaxes with Nazi technology which demystifies nature, and Nazi bureaucracy which neutralizes human sentiment. This process which God sets into motion, confronts the very being of God's moral relationship to Israel, at the entrance to the death camp. Rubenstein rejects the idea that God uses Hitler as an instrument of punishment or education – as enunciated in the USA by Menachem Mendel Schneersohn (in *emunah umada*, *iggerot kodesh*, 1977) and Isaac Hutner (in *Jewish Observer*, October 1977). Rubenstein sees an apocalyptic battle raging within God. It ends with a shattered covenant, with the covenantal thread uniting God and man, heaven and earth broken. The God of the Jews is reduced to Holy Nothing.

But then, at the very moment God's nothingness is confronted, Rubenstein turns around towards the world to find his perceptions supported from above and below by a divine *plenum*, an "ocean" whose "waves" are mankind. Once impelled by the *plenum*, Rubenstein endeavours to create new vehicles for Jewish expression: the nuclear family and the grander family, *kehillah yehudit*; family-orientated Jewish traditions which, since they are cyclical, avoid

the line of history and its empty results; life with nature which is immune to history; and the will for power instead of passive acceptance of the Lord of history's *dicta*.

Arthur Cohen

FOR COHEN, the Holocaust is unique. The death camp is outside all known normative history and causal connections. The victims may not even be called martyrs, lest it be said their historical due has been paid. The uniqueness paralyzes thought. Yet thought cannot be still, lest the evil become an untethered *mysterium*, free to assume absolute and metaphysical character. Cohen finds a place for thought between the impossibility that it can relate to the event and the impossibility that it can renounce itself. Thought can comprehend the object as a *caesura* on the underside of history, a demonic subscension of the historical. The Holocaust is conceivable as a *tremendum*, bracketed off from historical connection yet bounded by time. The *tremendum* is not reducible to history where it would lose its uniqueness, yet stops the Holocaust from becoming metaphysical or achieving status as an article of faith. Thought can relate to the Holocaust as to an "earthquake", where tremors precede it and shocks continue after it.

The Jewish people are by nature aligned to thinking about the *tremendum*, for they are not only historical as if there were no God, nor solely ontological as if held by God against the movements of history. They are a "bridge," with "pylons" positioned on both sides of the abyss below. God, who is neither in conjunction with history nor in disjunction with it, knows this people. In redemption, this knowledge, the meaning of the people, will be made explicit. This includes the meaning of their *tremendum*.

Eliezer Berkovits

BERKOVITS discovers metahistorical faith, trust and *mitzvah* in the conduct of Orthodox Jews during the Holocaust. The hiddenness of God's "face" (*Hester panim*) becomes an opportunity for a pure faith, where the results of love for and trust in God remain unknowable. The covenant seems broken, but like Abraham who is prepared to sacrifice his son upon God's command (*akedah*) even though the covenant promised that his seed would thrive, there are victims who continue in covenantal faith (*emunah*). Such faith begins atop the highest peak of history, beyond knowing God in reference or relationship to history.

Emunah is also enacted by *mitzvah*. This, even though *mitzvah* makes no sense: the observant are not rewarded, there is no reason to believe that a Jewish community would survive and continue the *mitzvah* or that the community and *mitzvah* would give life to one another. Zelik Kalmanowitz celebrates *simhat torah* in the Vilna ghetto in 1943. He speaks of joining his congregants not only to those still alive but to those who have departed for the holy community of another world. The Jewish people, he believes, would live as long as "the days of the heaven over the death". Moshe Borochowicz of Zelichow writes a *siddur*, while hidden in a bunker and unable to know if any Jews would survive to use it. *Mitzvah* continues through the moment of death, as *kiddush hashem*. Jossel Rackover of Tarnapol, about to burn himself along with his attackers during the last days of the Warsaw ghetto revolt, shouts at God, "Nothing will avail You! You have done everything that I deny You, that I shall not trust You. Yet I died as I lived – with rock-like *emunah* in You." These *mitzvot* are situated where human history ends and divine history begins. After Auschwitz they are suspended, until the moment when history will arise from the lower depths to re-enter God's covenant in time.

Emunah and *mitzvah* represent the stance of the Jew within Torah-being against the being of Satan/Amalek. The Torah realm has its own anchor, it does not react to Amalek or to contemporary history as defined by him. Each day the young hasidim of Lodz declare that the German is Amalek. Therefore one must do the opposite of everything he says, one should not be bewildered by his action, and one should know that he tries to prove that all is lost, there is no escape and that one can only submit. They conclude, "Either our Talmudic group or death" (*O chevrussa o messusa*), exactly as did the Sages. They tell themselves, "As individuals, it is difficult to deal with the satan. But by the strength of the *chevrussa* we will endure him".

Emunah and *mitzvah* remain in suspension until history ascends to its original position through the State of Israel. At Auschwitz God's presence is in His hiddenness. With the State, God's holy presence is proclaimed at the heart of His hiddenness. *Emunah* and *mitzvah* are realigned with history, and God's presence in history is vindicated.

Irving Greenberg

GREENBERG interprets the covenant as a drama of divine self-limitation. In the covenant with the Noahides after the flood, God limits himself to allow man to continue in dignity and freedom, even though this means that evil is possible. God does not force man to be good. But God does retain the principle of human perfection. He rewards and punishes mankind and he establishes a people to act as his partner by anticipating and teaching about perfection. However, the people of Israel fail, first at the time of the exile of 586 BCE and then in 70 CE. With the second exile, God restrains himself even more. He increases his presence (*shekhinah*) to allow for a proportional increase in Israel's responsibility. The responsibility is carried out through building synagogues and enhancing learning. But in time, the Holocaust appears to annul the partnership (*shutafut*). *Shutafut* turns out to require more suffering than could possibly be imagined without any covenant. There are no moral grounds to expect Israel to continue in its special role.

Nevertheless, Israel does assume its role as partner. Israel has a special perspective on history, because it is positioned at the intersection between the universal freedom granted after Noah and the special role as harbinger of human perfection. Israel can observe both the human cause of the Holocaust and the human success in putting an end to Nazi power. This knowledge impels Israel after the Holocaust voluntarily to re-establish the covenant itself. Jewish children are born and educated as Jews, and the State of Israel comes into being. If Auschwitz means Israel is cut off from God and that the covenant may be destroyed, then Jerusalem means that God's promises are faithful and that His people live on.

Thus, Rubenstein abandons history as the stage for Jewish experience. Cohen finds the Jewish people in a realm between the historical and the anti-historical. Berkovits sees history lowering itself during the Holocaust, until the State of Israel returns it to the level where God and Jews can meet again through *emunah* and *mitzvah* in time. Greenberg sees covenantal history suspended during the Holocaust and reasserted by the voluntary action of Jews thereafter.

Emil Ludwig Fackenheim

FACKENHEIM brings the discussion to a conclusion by demonstrating that Jewish history continues during the Holocaust, through extraordinary acts of resistance. These acts mend the world (*tikkunim*). The reader is not told what makes such *tikkunim* possible. But the sounds of Jehudah Halevi's poem *darashti kirvatekha* can be heard around them:

I sought your nearness
With all my heart I called towards You
And when I went out towards You
I found you on your way
Towards me

Until Fackenheim's *To Mend the World* (1982), American Jewish thinkers tapped and explored the range of impulses within the Jewish community. Fackenheim enters as this process reaches completion, to declare that the empirical explanation to God and history has been residing all along within Judaism itself.

Fackenheim defines the Nazi onslaught in terms of a logic-of-destruction, which forces the Jewish victim over the brink of psychological and physical survival into an abyss empty of all understanding of reality and of all possible hope. Some victims discover an inner space into which to retreat, where they gaze upon the Holocaust kingdom and grasp the Nazi endeavour to erase all sanity, all Jewishness, all life, all reason. The victims sense an imperative – it can only be from God – to resist. In morality in general, the "thesis" of evil elicits an anti-thesis. But in the Holocaust kingdom, where evil is absolute, there is no common ground for reaction. Something totally different emerges, a relationship of pure resistance to all connection, even to that of opposition. The resistance begins in awareness:

...They wished to abase us, to destroy our dig-nity, to efface every vestige of humanity...to fill us with horror and contempt toward ourselves and our fellow...From the instant when I grasped this motivating principle...it was as if I had been awakened from a dream...I felt under order to live (Pelagia Lewinska of Auschwitz, *Twenty Months at Auschwitz*, 1968)

Resistance continues in declarations of action:

The moment has come for us to perform the precept of *kiddush hashem* of which we have spoken, to perform it in fact. I beg one thing of you: do not get excited and confused. Accept this judgment calmly and in a worthy manner. (Daniel Movshovitz, rabbi of the Musar movement, "speaking serenely as though he were delivering one of his regular Sabbath sermons in the synagogue" before the Jews of Kelme, Lithuania are shot and thrown into a pit they were forced to dig).

Resistance culminates in revolts, from the small Lachwa ghetto to Warsaw, and in the death camp itself.

The *tikkunim* during the event have an ontological character, making subsequent *tikkunim* possible. In an individual way, they continue in the very act of remaining alive, sane and Jewish; or in the act of bearing children. Should one have children and thereby possibly condemn them to death (for all reality shows that Jews die), or not have children and thereby align oneself with Hitler's logic-of-destruction? The response is that children are born in defiance of the choices established by the Holocaust kingdom.

In a collective respect, *tikkun* is primarily Israel. 100,000 survivors emigrate there, the one place in the world where their very presence means automatic Jewish identity. The power of the State of Israel defies the powerlessness into which the Nazis thrust their Jewish victims. When Tel Aviv is attacked by Egyptians following the Declaration of Independence, it is defended by Kibbutzniks of Yad Mordechai – with its statute of Mordechai Anielewicz, leader of the Warsaw revolt. Following the Six Day War, the newspaper *Panim el panim* carries a picture of a European ghetto Jew in a *tallit* kneeling before a bayonet, alongside one of an Israeli soldier standing in prayer at the Western Wall wearing a *tallit* and carrying a rifle. The *tikkun* continues with the prayer by the Auschwitz survivor, who arises each day while it is still dark to celebrate the *simhah* of *shaharit* at the Wall and then return to his *kibbutz* in time for work. It is in the prayer of the Israeli Chief Rabbinate, that the State is the onset of the dawn of redemption. It is where the *shofar* sounded by Rav Finkler on Yom Kippur in Treblinka to tear up the evil decree can be heard. Outside Israel, collective *tikkun* is possible by rejecting the inclination to universalize the Holocaust and through unconditioned support of the Jewish State.

Reverberations

Michael Wyschogrod says he would not allow the Holocaust to become the theological basis for Jewish survival. What of universal evil? Of the actuality of continuing Jewish life? Attention should rather be drawn to Israel's election where God enters the biological people, the chain of physical descent from Abraham. Wyschogrod does not consider that this may be an assertion of what the Nazis endeavoured to obliterate, namely the special chosenness and corporeality. Or that it is because the *tikkunim* were enunciated by Fackenheim and the tear between *tremendum* and Jewish experience is mending, that he is enough at home in history to deny the centrality of the Nazi Holocaust.

David Hartman's covenant combines God's self-limitation for the sake of man's intellectual assertion, with man's submission to divine transcendent will. The *mitzvah*-community resolves the dialectic empirically, for *mitzvah*-life enacts understanding and incomprehensibility together. The State of Israel, the basis for complete life of covenantal *mitzvah*, preludes redemption. Then, the community will settle into the quiescent root of the combining – and even the fragmentary understanding of the suffering of the pious will be resolved. Hartmann does not consider that it is because *tikkunim* have been enunciated that he is able to bring even the utterly incomprehensible, the Holocaust, within dialectical range.

FURTHER READING

Berkovits, E.: *With God in Hell* (New York, 1979)
Cohen, A.: *The Tremendum* (New York, 1981)
Fackenheim, E. L.: *To Mend the World* (New York, 1982)
Greenberg, I.: Cloud of smoke, pillar of fire; Judaism, Christianity and modernity after the holocaust. In *Auschwitz: Beginning a New Era*, ed. E. Fleischner (New York, 1977)
Hartman, D.: *A Living Covenant: The Innovative Spirit in Traditional Judaism* (New York, 1985)
Rubenstein, R.: *After Auschwitz: Radical Theology and Contemporary Judaism* (Indianapolis, 1966)
Wyschogrod, D.: *The Body of Faith: Judaism as Corporeal Election* (New York, 1983)

GERSHON GREENBERG

Hond, Meyer de (1882–1943) Dutch rabbi and author. The son of poor parents, de Hond studied at the Rabbinical Seminary in Amsterdam, where he obtained his second-class rabbinical degree together with a B.A. in Classical Philology at the University of Amsterdam. He had not obtained the highest rabbinical degree allegedly because his teachers did not consider him sufficiently dignified to be a rabbi. Members of the Society "Touro Our", of which he had become the beloved religious leader, collected funds to enable him to continue his studies in Berlin where he was ordained at the Rabbinical Seminary in 1911; in 1913 he obtained a Ph.D. in Würzburg. However, his German rabbinical degree was not recognized in The Netherlands. He was permitted to work as a religious teacher for young pupils and adults, and as such was enormously successful among those middle-class traditional Jewish youths who were neither attracted to socialism nor to Zionism but wished to remain Jewish. In 1908 de Hond founded a drama circle for the Jewish working-class society "Betsalel" for which he wrote a play nearly every year. He also wrote numerous short stories on life in the Amsterdam Jewish quarter, which were first published in Jewish periodicals and later collected in two volumes of *Kiekjes* (Snapshots) in 1926 and 1930. In these *Kiekjes* his style is exuberant, with a predilection for Amsterdam Yiddish. Very few of his plays ever appeared in print. In the 1920s he established the *Joodse Jeugdkrant* (Jewish Youth Journal), which he filled largely by himself.

He was a fervent anti-Socialist at a time

when Socialism made great progress among the working-class Jews of Amsterdam, in particular among the diamond workers, and also an anti-Zionist and admirer of the Royal House of Orange. In 1943 he and his wife and children were deported by the Nazis and perished in Sobibor.

HENRIETTE BOAS

Horkheimer, Max (1895–1973) German philosopher. Born in Stuttgart, he was educated at the universities of Munich, Freiburg and Frankfurt-am-Main, where he received his Ph.D. in 1922. His *Habilitationsschrift* examined Kant's *Critique of Judgment*. In 1931 he became a full professor at the University of Frankfurt and the director of the Institute for Social Research. Upon Hitler's ascent to power, the Institute moved to Geneva, then Paris, and finally New York. Horkheimer's 1939 essay, "The Jews and Europe" was one of the major attempts of the Frankfurt Institute to come to terms with fascism and anti-Semitism. Horkheimer went to live in California in 1940. In his capacity as director of the Research Division of the American Jewish Committee, he instituted the series "Studies in Prejudice"; the major study to come out of the series was *The Authoritarian Personality* (1950), a work still debated today. He returned to West Germany in 1949, became professor at the University of Frankfurt and the director of the newly established Institute for Social Research until his retirement in 1959 when he went to live in Switzerland. He died at a Nuremberg hospital on 7 July 1973.

Deviating from traditional German scholarship, most of Horkheimer's work consists of essays, ranging from philosophy of history and science to reflections on religion, authority, mass culture and justice. A chronology of his intellectual career would show that the 1920s were years of youthful existentialism, marked by strong Jewish consciousness; the 1930s would show him as an eclectic Marxist, with "subterranean" Jewish influence. The 1940s brought the philosophy of despair under the impact of the Holocaust; the 1960s were characterized by an intensification of Jewish consciousness. Indeed, the Judaic themes of ethical commitment, Messianism and concern with social justice can be traced throughout the writings of his career. He repeatedly asserted the primacy of ethics over epistemological and ontological issues. In the 1937 essay, "Traditional and Critical Theory," Horkheimer developed "Critical Theory", which meant a continuity with the critical philosophy of German idealism and Marx's critique of the political economy of capitalist society – complete with the aim of making society more just and humane. It was the will for social justice, the cornerstone of Judaic thought, that drove young Horkheimer towards Marxism as the only realistic alternative to a totalitarianism of the Right, represented by Hitler's Germany. Ten years later, the brutality of left totalitarianism in Stalin's Russia turned him away from Marxism. These historical shocks are responsible for the pessimistic philosophy of history of *Dialectic of Enlightenment*, (1947; 1972), co-authored with Theodor W. ADORNO. In the chapter "Elements of anti-Semitism," the authors attempted a philosophical explanation of the phenomenon. In the same year (1947), Horkheimer published his philosophy of science, *Eclipse of Reason*, which critically examined all forms of "instrumental reason" such as positivism, pragmatism and scientism. He again evoked the theme of *Mitleid* (compassion) but with a new emphasis when he spoke of the "martyrs of the concentration camps" who are the symbols of a "humanity that is striving to be born. The task of philosophy is to translate what [transpired] into language that will be heard...". This is Horkheimer's ultimate philosophical statement. It was rather symbolic that he delivered his last lecture, a few weeks before his death, in the *Israelitische Cultursgemeinde* in Zurich.

BIBLIOGRAPHY
Critical Theory (New York: Herder & Herder, 1972)

FURTHER READING
Tar, Z.: *The Frankfurt School* (New York: Schocken, 1985)
Marcus, J., and Tar, Z., eds: *Foundations of the Frankfurt School of Social Research* (New Brunswick and London: Transaction, 1984)

JUDITH MARCUS AND ZOLTAN TAR

Horovitz, Bela (1898–1955) Austrian and British publisher. Bela Horovitz, doyen and pioneer of the publishing of fine art books and books of Jewish cultural heritage, was born into a loving home of strict Jewish observance in Budapest. Classically educated in Imperial Vienna, he took a Law degree in 1922. From this background emerged a man of rare warmth and a humanist sensitive to the problems of contemporary Judaism. His passion was a desire to spread knowledge; so together with his friend, Ludwig Goldscheider, he began the Phaidon Verlag in 1923 in Vienna, a city whose traditions of music and culture were flourishing again after the First World War, and where only a few publishers existed. Phaidon's early books were in German, bibliophile editions of poetry, aphorisms and plays (by authors such as Klabund, Hofmannsthal, Arthur SCHNITZLER, and Unamuno) that were hand-set in elegant type, printed on hand-made paper and handsomely bound. In 1937 Horovitz made publishing history and won an international reputation for Phaidon with three large-sized volumes of modern design on Van Gogh, the French Impressionists, and Botticelli, all outstandingly illustrated. The success of the venture exceeded all expectations and Phaidon continued from then on to bring serious books about the fine arts within the reach of a wide, popular market. In 1938 when the Nazis marched into Austria, the Horovitz and Goldscheider families managed, with the active help of their friend, Sir Stanley Unwin, to transfer their activities to England. They continued to publish energetically during and after the war years, having settled permanently in England.

The Jewish tragedy of the Nazi years activated in Bela Horovitz a need to contribute positively to his people. Helping refugees from the Nazi terror, he became convinced of the paramount need to bring Jews back to awareness of their own intellectual heritage, their long history and their world of thought. In 1944 Horovitz founded the East and West Library which he devoted to the publication of books of Jewish interest, all of high spiritual and cultural value. Horovitz commissioned original publications by experts and made available source works of Jewish scholars and thinkers. Among his many important publications were: illustrated editions of Cecil ROTH's *A Short History of the Jewish People*, Chaim WEIZMANN's autobiography, *Trial and Error*, works by Martin BUBER, a biography of Theodore HERZL, the *Philosophia Judaica* series and the *Leo Baeck Institute Year Books*.

Bela Horovitz died suddenly in New York while on a business trip. He had devoted to concerns with Jewish culture, education and heritage the same creative talents and personal care that had brought him to create his famous Phaidon art books. His publishing activities were all characterized by vision, integrity and an instinct for the needs of his readership. For many years his family continued and expanded his work. The Phaidon Press still exists independently; and the East and West Library is now an imprint of the Hebrew Publishing Company in New York.

FURTHER READING

Altmann, A., ed.: *Between East and West, Essays Dedicated to the Memory of Bela Horovitz* (London: East & West Library 1958)

MEL COOPER

Horovitz, Israel (b.1939) American playwright. Born in Wakefield, Massachusetts, he was educated at Harvard University, the Royal Academy of Dramatic Art (London), and the City University of New York. In 1965, he became the first American invited by the Royal Shakespeare Company to serve as playwright-in-residence.

Horovitz found his métier early, writing his first play, *The Comeback*, when he was 17. In 1968, he triumphed in New York with a brilliant first season. Four of his plays were produced in a four-month period: *Line*, *It's Called the Sugar Plum*, *The Indian Wants the Bronx*, and *Rats*. Hailed by critics, Horovitz won the 1968 Obie and Vernon Rice Drama Desk awards. Ellen Stewart's La Mama Troupe took *Line* on a successful European tour. A subsequent production in Greenwich Village established a record for an off-Broadway run, while a production at the Théâtre de Poche in Paris has been going on for eleven years. A study of the struggle for power, the play shows five people jockeying for first place in a line whose purpose is never specified.

The Indian Wants the Bronx, a terrifying portrait of the vulnerability of a foreigner lost in a tough New York neighborhood, also scored hits at the 1968 Spoleto Festival (Italy) and the World Theatre Festival (England). Other outstanding successes include *The Honest-to-God Schnozzola*, which won a 1969 Obie, and *The Primary English Class* (1976), which became Canada's longest-running play. *The Widow's Blind Date* (1983), critically acclaimed in Paris, was filmed for French National Television. Horovitz, who has won the French Critics Prize, has translated Ionesco's *L'Homme aux valises* (1976; Man with suitcases).

Horovitz's productivity demonstrates his confessed compulsion always to "have a new play in the works while an old play is being done". There are presently over thirty plays, translated into more than twenty languages. In *Stage Directions*, one of the seven works composing *The Wakefield Plays*, a brother and two sisters who dislike one another are brought together by the death of their parents. Ruby Cohn has called the play "a parable of the cultural heritage of the Jews". Yet for all that the characters are identifiably Jewish, the kind of anguish and alienation they experience is so endemic to contemporary society, it is difficult to attach any cultural particularity to their story.

By contrast, the 1987 trilogy based on Morley Torgov's book *A Good Place to Come From* (1973) treats in loving detail Jewish life in Sault Ste. Marie, Ontario, in the years between 1941 and 1947. In *Today, I Am a Fountain Pen*, 10-year old Irving Yanover's friendship with the family's Ukranian "live-in" proves mutually helpful as each deals with devoted but overprotective parents. *A Rosen By Any Other Name* picks up the story three years later in the midst of World War II. Irving's arch-rival Stanley Rosen copes imaginatively as his mother plans his *bar mitzvah* extravaganza and his father, fearful that Canadian Jews will suffer the fate of their European brethren, almost succeeds in changing the family name. Stanley's proud assertion of Jewish identity finally dissuades him. In *The Chopin Playoffs*, the competition between the two families comes to a climax as Stanley and Irving vie for a music prize and the affection of Fern Phipps, who can't tell them apart.

In addition to the stage plays, Horovitz has written for film (*Author! Author!* and *The Strawberry Statement*, which won the 1970 Prix de Jury at Cannes), television and radio. He has published a novel, *Cappella*, a novella, *Nobody Loves Me*, and dozens of articles on long-distance running, a favorite sport. He is a founder of the Eugene O'Neill Memorial Theater Foundation and the New York Playwrights Lab, of which he is artistic director. He also founded the Gloucester Stage Company in Massachusetts, for which he has written his most recent plays.

ELLEN SCHIFF

Horovitz, Joseph (b.1926) British composer. Horovitz, the son of Bela HOROVITZ, was born in Vienna and moved with his family to England in 1938. He was educated at New College, Oxford, where he attained a B.Mus., and at the Royal College of Music, London. He studied with Nadia Boulanger in Paris and shortly after that began his career as a composer in London.

Horovitz has composed prolifically and has mastered many genres including ballet scores, concerti, orchestral and chamber music, music for brass band, wind band and other instrumental combinations, vocal and choral music. He has also written scores for many TV and film productions. He was awarded the Commonwealth Medal for composition in 1959, the Leverhulme Music Research Award in 1961 and the Ivor Novello Award of 1976 for Best British Music for children for *Captain Noah and his Floating Zoo*.

Aside from composition, Horovitz has also distinguished himself as a conductor. He spent seasons as the resident conductor of the Festival Gardens Orchestra and Ballet, co-conductor of the *Ballets Russes* for the English season of 1952 and associate conductor of the Glyndebourne Opera in 1956. He has also taught composition and has been professor of composition at the Royal College of Music since 1961, and a Fellow there since 1981.

Horovitz has drawn his musical inspiration as well from Jewish source material: *Ghetto Song*, 1970, for guitar solo, is based on the traditional melody, *Belz*. He wrote the music for the TV productions of *The Dybbuk*, *Bar Kokhba* and for *Modigliani*, a drama-documentary on the artist's life.

JOHN MATTHEW

Horowitz, Leopold (?1837–1917) Hungarian painter. Born in Rozgony, Hungary, and trained at the Vienna Academy, Horowitz persued a highly successful career in the urban centers of the Austro-Hungarian Empire and beyond. Specializing initially in a Rembrandt-esque style of portraiture, he found favor at the Court of Emperor Franz Joseph when he adopted a manner closer to that of Van Dyck. His ability to endow children with an air of aristocratic good breeding, and their mothers with a suggestion of natural elegance, was highly valued by nobility and *haute bourgeoisie* alike.

From the 1870s onwards Horowitz started to produce genre scenes of Jewish *shtetl* life in paintings which fully justify the late nineteenth century's reputation for excessive sentimentality. Such scenes were popular with the Jewish middle classes of Vienna and elsewhere, and accord with the more general taste for domestic genre painting at that time. Horowitz's chief originality consisted of adopting a well-established type of painting, giving it a Yiddish accent, and purveying the hybrid results to an assimilated, urban Jewish market.

FURTHER READING
Roth, C.: *Jewish Art: An Illustrated History* (London: Vallentine, Mitchell & Co., 1971)

LAURA JACOBUS

Howe, Irving (b.1920) Irving Howe has carved out a career in three distinct areas of intellectual endeavor – literature, politics, and cultural history. Born in the Jewish immigrant ghettos of the Bronx, Howe grew up in the mixed world of poverty and intellectualism, urban toughness and immigrant provincialism so characteristic of that life. The Depression brought additional financial hardship on Howe's family.

Howe's interest in radicalism found an outlet during his college years. A member of the famous Alcove No. 1 crowd at New York's City College – other habitués included Irving Kristol, Daniel Bell, Seymour Martin Lipset, and Nathan Glazer – Howe became the Trotskyist intellectual of the alcove and a member of the Young People's Socialist League. The economic situation made employment opportunities appear severely limited. College no longer seemed like preparation for life. "It was taken for granted that one would be unemployed ... You went to college, there was nothing else to do." After graduation, Howe took a job in a factory, from which he was fired six weeks later for attempting to organize the workers. He also began graduate school at Brooklyn College, but left after a year.

The Second World War readjusted the personal and political landscape. Howe spent three and a half years in the Army, and of that eighteen months stationed in Alaska where he read voluminously. After 1945, his political radicalism had lessened (although not as much as many of his contemporaries) and his Jewish consciousness had grown in the wake of the revelations of the Holocaust. The young Jewish intellectual, he wrote in 1946, "is a victim of his own complexity".

His first book, a study of the UAW and Walter Reuther, appeared in 1949, and a steady stream of publications followed. In the early 1950s he brought out critical studies of Sherwood Anderson (1951), William Faulkner (1952), an edited work on Yiddish literature (1954), and helped found the magazine *Dissent*, to promote democratic socialism. Howe had grown uncomfortable with the conformistic trend among post-war intellectuals, which he criticized in a famous article in *Partisan Review*, "This Age of Conformity". *Dissent*, of which Howe has been editor, aimed to move against this trend.

In 1953, he also joined the Brandeis English department, after several visiting academic positions. He remained at Brandeis until 1961, when he moved to Stanford. In 1963, he returned to New York and the City University of New York, with which he is still affiliated. Despite his radical inclinations and interest in modernist literature, Howe stood firmly against the

Bronislaw Huberman

New Left and the counterculture during the 1960s.

His great triumph came in 1976, with the publication of *World of Our Fathers*, his massive social history of the eastern European Jews. He has remained a major force in resurrecting and chronicling Yiddish–American culture (four collections beyond the 1954 volume have been published). His recently published memoirs, *A Margin of Hope* (1982), reveal more of the political nature of this intellectual than the personal motives and dilemmas which he encountered.

FURTHER READING

Bloom, A.: *Prodigal Sons: The New York Intellectuals and Their World* (New York and Oxford: Oxford University Press, 1987)

Pells, R.: *The Liberal Mind in a Conservative Age* (New York, 1985)

ALEXANDER BLOOM

Huberman, Bronislaw (1882–1947) Violonist and founder of the Israel Philharmonic

Orchestra. Born in Poland to a poor Jewish family, his extraordinary talent was discovered early, and he began performing as child prodigy at the age of 10. He studied with Joseph Joachim for a short time, and within a brief period became one of the world's leading violinists, establishing his personal interpretations of the great violin masterpieces. After the First World War he became active in the Pan-European movement, as a humanist fighting for peace and for the improvement of the social status of the working classes. With the advance of Fascism in Europe he turned his energy to Palestine, where his performances were greeted with unprecedented enthusiasm. He conceived of a comprehensive institute for music, at the center of which would be a major symphony orchestra, a professional school of music and additional ensembles. The deteriorating situation in Europe during the early 1930s led Huberman to concentrate on founding an orchestra which would maintain the highest artistic standards and fulfil the dual purpose of making Palestine an international music center while at the same time providing positions for the leading Jewish musicians dismissed from important European orchestras. Almost single-handed, he founded the Palestine Philharmonic Orchestra, raising large sums of money through playing benefit concerts around the world. The orchestra began its performances in 1936. In 1937 Huberman was involved in an aircraft crash. He overcame his severe injuries and resumed his performances during the war years, but his health deteriorated and his untimely death prevented him from meeting the orchestra again after the war.

FURTHER READING

Ibbeken, I., ed.: *An Orchestra is Born (Huberman's Speeches, Letters and Articles)* (Tel Aviv: 1969)

JEHOASH HIRSHBERG

humor, Jewish One speaks of Jewish humor as one speaks of Italian opera or Russian ballet, as if humor itself was a uniquely Jewish speciality, and as a result any comedian of international standing is generally taken to be Jewish (certainly by Jews) unless he can show proof to the contrary. Groucho Marx, Jack Benny, Eddie Cantor, Milton Berle, Sid Ceasar, Shelley Berman, Danny Kaye, Lenny Bruce, Mort Sahl, Phil Silvers, Peter Sellers, Jerry Lewis, Mel Brooks, Bud Flanagan, Woody ALLEN, are names which come immediately to mind, but there are many others, and a clue to the Jewish dominance in this field may lie in the fact that the one thing they have in common (apart from their Jewishness) is their wordiness. There is not one Jewish comedian among the stars of the silent cinema. The Jewish people are not only the people of the Book, they are the people of the word. In the beginning was the word, and the word was made hilarious.

One does not normally associate the Bible with humor, but those who seek it can find in abundance. There are, for example, numerous instances of word-play. The very name of Adam, who was fashioned out of dust, is a play on the word *adamah*, meaning "earth". A few generations later we have the three sons of Lamech: Jabal, Jubal and Tubal-Cain. Jabal was "the father of all such as handled the harp

and the organ", while Tubal is the Hebrew for tumult, and the three taken together sound almost like a pop-group. More amusing still is Laban, Jacob's father-in-law, sly, cunning, and devious, the blackest character in Genesis, whose name, however, means white.

The cynical wit of Proverbs and Ecclesiastes is widely quoted even if the source is not always known: "Better open rebuke than secret love." "Be not wise in thine own eyes." "Be not righteous overmuch." "Better a living dog than a dead lion." One finds wit even in Isaiah: "Woe unto them that are mighty – to drink wine, and men of strength – to mingle strong drink."

If the Bible is spoken of among devout Jews as the written law, the Talmud is part of the oral law (which, to complicate matters further, was likewise committed to writing), but it also contains a wealth of homiletics, legends, ethical teachings, medical and scientific opinions, and, not infrequently, simple diversions, all of which have their moments of humor and wit.

There are, for example, the stories about Rabbi Ishmael Ben Yosi and Rabbi Eleazar Ben Simeon whose bellies were so huge "that when they faced each other a herd of oxen could pass beneath them." A Roman lady told them: "Your children must have been sired by others, for how can men with such bellies beget them?" "Our wives are even fatter than us", they replied. "Which makes it all the more likely", said the lady, "that your children were sired by others." Ben Yosi in particular could have served as the original for Falstaff. He once gulped down a cup of wine in one draught. Isn't it greedy to do so?, he was asked. "Not when the cup is small, the wine is sweet and the stomach is large", he retorted.

There are also some memorable *obiter dicta*:

"Wine elevates the noble and degrades the low."

"Honor evades those who seek it, and seeks those who avoid it."

"Better a meal of herbs and solvency therewith than roast duck and penury therewith."

"Three things should be used in moderation, salt, leavening, and humility."

"If you have to hang, be hanged from a tall tree."

And yet if holy writ is not without humor, humor itself has always been regarded as unholy. Scripture dismisses the laughter-maker as a scorner, than whom none was more scorned: "A scorner seeketh wisdom and findeth it not ...He that winketh with the eye causeth sorrow...Cast out the scorner and contention shall cease...Sorrow is better than laughter, for by the sadness of the countenance the heart is made better...For as the crackling of thorns under a pot, so is the laughter of the fool...', while the Talmud declared that one could only laugh at idols and idol worshippers, otherwise it was forbidden, except on certain licensed occasions like the feast of Purim.

Purim commemorates the deliverance of the Jews of Persia from their enemies some 2,500 years ago, as recorded in the Book of Esther, but it takes place about the time of the spring equinox, so that it may have the same pagan origins as the pre-Lenten carnivals of Christendom. Whatever its origins it is celebrated with great zeal. Merry-making is almost unrestrained and it provided an outlet for people with a talent to amuse. One finds them, for example, in S. Y. AGNON's novel *The Bridal Canopy*: "...in Brod there were many jokers known as Brod singers who used to describe the troubles of their day in rhyming couplets, and made up funny songs. Normally they were regarded with contempt by respectable Brod folk, but on Purim they came into their own..."

One could not establish a humorous tradition on the licence afforded by that one day, and what we now think of as Jewish humor came into its own only after the ghetto walls began to crumble. In Germany, and to a lesser extent in the Habsburg lands, where emancipation was rapid, Jews rushed headlong to drink at the font of Western culture, so that humor of someone like Heinrich HEINE was Teutonic or Gallic rather than Jewish, and what we now think of as Jewish humor is largely a product of the Russian Pale of Settlement, where the process of emancipation was so slow as to be almost imperceptible, and where the Jews existed in such numbers as to evolve a secular culture of their own.

Not that humor was ever absent from Jewish life. It existed in the street wisdom which sometimes hardened into proverbs:

"If God lived on earth His windows would be broken."

CAN JEWISH HUMOR SURVIVE A CONFERENCE ON JEWISH HUMOR?

Cartoon of Sholem Aleichem

"If the rich could pay people to die for them the poor would make a good living."

"All brides are beautiful and all the dead are pious."

"Where there's a quiet wedding, they have something to be quiet about."

"If all pulled in one direction, the world would keel over."

It was inherent in the exuberance, the irreverence and color of Yiddish, the lingua franca of east European Jewry, but its potential was not fully realised until it was caught in the work of the greatest of all Yiddish writers, SHOLEM ALEICHEM (1859–1916).

In reading Sholem Aleichem one can find the wryness, the dryness, the sharpness, the rancor, the irony, the self-deprecation, the world-weary cynicism, and the pathos which characterize Jewish humor. It has a bitter-sweet quality with rather more bitterness than sweetness. There is no hearty joviality or cheerful stoicism, but rather a sort of resigned stoicism; and while there is faith that the Lord will ultimately provide, there is also impatience and one can hear voices murmuring: "Who will provide till the Lord provides?" It also has something of the dialectic of Talmudic debate, only it is pseudo-dialectic, with its own perverted logic, as in the exchange:

361

"Will you close the window, it's cold outside."

"And if I close the window, will it be warm outside?"

Sholem Aleichem gave Jewish humor respectability not only because of the genius which he brought to bear on it, but because of Jewish reverence for the written word, at least as caught in book form. The laughter-maker had to wait until his transition to the New World before he found a milieu where there was a livelihood and even social standing to be had from mere verbal humor. And in the New World too he could indulge in a ribaldry which would have been unacceptable in the old, to a point, almost, where it became his principal stock in trade.

The New World, of course, also offered ample scope for the humorous talents of writers like S. N. Behrman, Paddy CHAYEFSKY, Joseph HELLER, George Kaufman, S. J. Perelman, Mordechai RICHLER, Leo ROSTEN, Philip ROTH, J. D. Salinger and Neil SIMON, and while Woody ALLEN is best known as a comedian, his written work deserves more than passing attention if only because he catches his world as completely and hilariously as Sholem Aleichem caught his. Where Sholem Aleichem dealt with the poor and oppressed, Allen deals with the affluent and depressed. The latter have less ground for their worries than the former, but Allen suggests that being born is worry enough, and they almost confirm the old Jewish adage that an imaginary illness is worse than a real disease. Here too the laughter has a mildly bitter flavor, and one may almost speak of Allen as the Sholem Aleichem of Manhattan.

Jewish humor is pernaps a reaction to the soul-searching, breast-beating expiation and lamentation required by Jewish tradition, and a defence against the humiliations and torments of their own experience so that in laughing at themselves Jews were able to withstand more readily the scorn of others. Laughter, of course, has always been the weapon of the weak against the strong, and the clown, provided he is sufficiently amusing, is forgiven everything, even – where necessary – his Jewishness.

Moreover, living, as they did, in two worlds, or rather in three – for they often invoked the next world to redress the balance of this one – Jews enjoyed a perspective denied to others. Their mixed fortunes and nomadic history also gave them a wider range of experience to draw on, and it is always the improbable, the quaint and comical aspects of a place which first catch the attention of newcomers, and even where they are settled they can draw on an infinite fund of folk memories. They also have well-honed critical faculties which in some instances gives rise to an urge to reform and improve, and in others to laughter.

Jews have been around for a very long time. They have been everywhere, tried everything and have been done by almost everybody, and know the world to be menacing, ridiculous, and full of strange paradoxes – none of them stranger than their own experience of being at once "chosen" and ostracized. And they have found that laughing at it is just about the best way of coming to terms with it.

Jews are now comparatively well established, at least in western society. They are part of it, and perhaps even central to it, so that they no longer have to clown their way into acceptance; but habits of mind acquired over the centuries do not easily change. One is reminded of the Jewish grandmother who was asked if her grandson could walk. "Yes", she said proudly, "but thank God he doesn't have to." Jews can still laugh, but thank God they don't have to.

FURTHER READING
Abrahams, G.: *The Jewish Mind* (London: Constable, 1961)
Bermant, C.: *The Jews* (London: Weidenfeld, 1977)
——: *What's the Joke?* (London: Weidenfeld, 1986)
Rosten, L.: *The Joys of Yiddish* (London: W. H. Allen, 1970)

CHAIM BERMANT

Hurwitz, Saul (Israel) (1861–1922) Hebrew publicist and editor. Born near Homel in White Russia he received an enlightened Talmudic education and early decided to emulate the progressive tendentious scholarship of such authors as M. L. LILIENBLUM in Hebrew and Elijah Orshansky in Russian. After attending some university classes in St Petersburg Hurwitz began his study of Jewish laws concerning women, which culminated in his monograph, *Ha'ivriyah vehayehudiyah* (1892). While primarily engaged in what was to become a flourishing lumber and banking business he also published a study of nationalistic elements in the work of Nachman KROCHMAL, *Tziyun lenefesh Krokhmal* (1887), and a translation of Moses HESS's *Rome and Jerusalem*. He wrote a eulogistic appraisal of the apologist for Hasidism, Eliezer Zvi Zweifel, who was Hurwitz's neighbor in the isolated Ukrainian town of Gluchov where he settled. After a hiatus of ten years Hurwitz emerged as a feisty polemicist and promoter of innovative cultural endeavors. Inspired by figures such as M. Y. BERDYCZEWSKI and Reuven Brainin, Hurwitz often used his engaging Hebrew style to outdo the rhetoric of his mentors. His considerable wealth afforded him the time and means to foster creative enterprises and made him a central figure in Berlin, where he moved in 1905. With Brainin, Ya'akov KAHAN and others he founded the cultural organizations "Ivriyyah" and "Sinai".

Hurwitz's polemics against wide sectors of the Hebraist intelligentsia provide a cross-section of the cultural issues occupying Jewry in the decade 1904 to 1914. Among his causes – which often became miniature scandals – were his rude anti-AHAD HA'AM posture, his non-Zionist agonizing over Jewish survival, his vitriolic assault on neo-Hasidism, and his affirmation of the positive content of Christianity and Sabbateanism. Once engaged in bitter exchanges and a libel suit over some of these issues, Hurwitz made freedom of expression and "extending of the boundaries" central to his rhetoric. As editor of the fine journal *He'atid* (1908–13) he published some excellent papers by DUBNOW and many others and published one of the first surveys of opinions on "Judaism and its Prospects for Survival" (1912). Hurwitz's own articles were republished in his collection *Me'ayin ule'an?* (1914).

The outbreak of the First World War led to Hurwitz's being trapped for seven years, as a Russian national, in Russia away from his family and at the mercy of the Bolsheviks. After teaching for a time in Kharkhov and, with his cousin Simon Dubnow, in St Petersburg, he returned, impoverished, to his family in Berlin. There he managed to do some editorial work and published a study of Bahya Ibn Pakuda before he succumbed to a recurrent malignancy.

FURTHER READING

Nash, S. L.: *In Search of Hebraism: Shai Hurwitz and his Polemics in the Hebrew Press* (Leiden: Brill, 1980)

STANLEY NASH

I

Idelsohn, Abraham Zvi (1882–1938) Latvian-born ethnomusicologist, cantor, and composer. Born in Felixburg, Latvia, he studied with cantor A. M. Rabinowitz in Libau, and received professional music education at the Leipzig conservatorium. Following a brief period of employment as cantor and *shohet* in Regensburg, Germany, he accepted a position in South Africa which he held for only one year. In an autobiographical sketch he claimed that he was deeply disappointed by the South German cantorial singing, and his interest in the origins of ancient Jewish music led him to settle in Jerusalem, where he lived from 1906 (or early 1907) until 1921. During this period he was active in research, education, and the organization of musical life in the small Jewish community in Palestine. He was one of the first scholars to make use of the Edison Phonograph to record representatives of the Oriental Jewish ethnic groups in Jerusalem. His transcriptions, with extensive introductory essays, were published in his major scholarly work, the *Thesaurus of Hebrew Oriental Melodies*, which included five volumes of Oriental Jewish melodies and five of Ashkenazi. The first volume was published in 1914, and the remainder between 1922 and 1932. Idelsohn approached his research with ideological hypotheses in mind, attempting to prove that despite the extreme differences among the numerous Jewish communities there are basic characteristics common to all of them, which not only prove their ancient ancestry but also open the way for the discovery of the old Hebrew chant. He also claimed that the same traits appear in the Gregorian chant, indicating the indebtness of early Catholic music to the Jewish tradition of the Second Temple. Idelsohn tried to found an Institute for Jewish Music but the opposition of orthodox Jewish circles and the hardship of the war years prevented the realization of this project. Idelsohn also tried to carry his research into the realm of modern composition, writing a biblical opera, *Jephtah*, which consisted mostly of quotations of melodies from his transcriptions, arranged for chorus and orchestra. In 1919 he became a teacher at a new music school in Jerusalem, but two years later he decided to leave for Europe where he had a greater opportunity to publish his research. He was invited by the Hebrew Union College in Cincinnati to catalog the Birnbaum collection and to teach. In 1932 he suffered a stroke which impaired his speech and forced him into early retirement.

Idelsohn's pioneering work brought to light the importance of the oral tradition for musicological research and for the study of Jewish subjects, and set a standard of research for future years. His influence was enormous, both on scholars and on composers, such as SETER and TAL who used the Thesaurus as a source of thematic material. Idelsohn's archives, including his recordings and the original phonograph, are kept at the National and University Library in Jerusalem.

FURTHER READING

Adler, I., and Cohen, J.: *A. Z. Idelsohn Archives at the Jewish National and University Library* (Jerusalem: The Magnes Press, 1976)
Adler, I., Bayer, B., and Schleifer, E.: *The A. Z.*

Idelsohn Memorial Volume: Yuval 5 (Jerusalem: The Magnes Press, 1986)

JEHOASH HIRSHBERG

Ignatow, David (b.1914) American poet.

Born in Brooklyn, New York, Ignatow is a product of the New York public schools. His parents, to whom his book *Leaving the Door Open* (1984) is dedicated, were immigrants from Russia. They, like his wife, Rose Graubart, a painter, and his son and daughter, appear recurrently in his poems. He worked for many years as a businessman in his father's bindery, eventually becoming president, but, disliking business life, he disbanded the firm shortly after his father's death, and worked at a number of menial jobs. Since the dissolution of his business, he has largely been engaged as an editor and university teacher, most recently as visiting professor at Columbia and NYU.

Ignatow's poetry is highly autobiographical. His personal problems, dislike of business, strained family relations – particularly his efforts to resolve his ambivalent feelings about his father and his pain at the mental illness of his son – account for a great deal of his subject-matter. Despite his bleak view, a number of the poems in his third collection *Say Pardon* (1961), are religious, God, "...a sufferer like yourself," actually appearing to comfort the poet in "The Rightful One". The concluding poem in *New and Collected Poems, 1970–1985* (1986) is representative of Ignatow's recent work and portrays a man looking at his image in the mirror "... which reveals him to himself./If there is a god, this is he." indicating a quality of comfort in this existentially agnostic position.

Though not a practicing Jew, Ignatow is continually aware of his "guilt and pull towards" traditional life. In 1956, he wrote in his *Notebooks* that he had "...an insight into the Jewish religion. It is essentially a poetic one and it is only its poetry that sustains and nourishes it...." He worries he is "not worthy...to be called a poet in the same breath as the psalmists". In fact, he identifies with the American poets Walt Whitman and William Carlos Williams, both of whom he addresses in various poems.

The winner of two Guggenheim fellowships and numerous other honors, including the Bollingen Prize and the Wallace Stevens Fellowship from Yale University, he is the author of fourteen volumes of poetry, a prose collection, *Open Between Us* (1980), and his *Notebooks* (1973). Ignatow, rather late in his career, has achieved recognition as an important American poet.

FURTHER READING
Melange, G.: The art of poetry XIII: David Ignatow. *Paris Review* (1979) 55–79

ELIZABETH KLEIN

Ikor, Roger (1912–1986) French novelist.

Born in Paris of Lithuanian immigrant parents, he was educated there, eventually qualifying as a school teacher. Ikor, his family, and associates were among those Jewish immigrants who sought to assimilate as rapidly as possible into French society. This essential reality would later radically influence his literary creations.

His initial attempts as a novelist proved dismal failures. It was only in 1955 that Ikor had his first success with *Les fils d'Avrom* (1958; The sons of Avrom). Highly autobiographical, the novel is a naturalist tapestry depicting Jewish immigrant life in early twentieth-century Paris and the opportunities Jews had to evade their religious and cultural heritage. The various themes which are developed in the story have been compared to those found in the Yiddish works of Sholem ASH, I. B. SINGER and Der Nister (see KAHANOWITZ). Ikor strikes the particular position which glorifies French cultural values, viewing them as superior to the coarser Yiddish-peasant heritage. He seems to urge the "crude" Jewish immigrant to assimilate as rapidly as possible into the new host society. These views offered Jean-Paul Sartre adequate literary proof for the character of the inauthentic, assimilated Jew.

In 1968 Ikor published a powerful and profoundly disturbing essay, "Peut-on être juif aujourd'hui?", in which the author examines the viability of continued Jewish existence in secular cultures. He also considers the effect of assimilation in the wake of the reality of a reawakening of the Jewish consciousness after the Six Day War in 1967.

BIBLIOGRAPHY
The Sons of Avrom, trans. L. Friedman and M. Singer (New York: G. P. Putnam's Sons, 1958)

SIMON SIBELMAN

Imber, Shmuel-Yankev (1889–1942) Yiddish poet and critic. Born in Jezierna, East Galicia, the nephew of Naftali-Herts Imber (author of the *Hatikva*), Imber attended the *Gymnasium* in Zloczow and Tarnapol and studied philosophy in Lemberg. In 1912 he went to Palestine, but served in the Austrian army during the war. In 1918 he went to Vienna, visited the USA but returned to live in Lemberg and Krakow, receiving a doctorate. He was murdered in 1942, although the exact circumstances of his death are not known.

Imber was a significant innovator in Yiddish poetry, a neo-romantic lyricist who wrote poems of longing for Palestine, but he was also an important polemicist (in Polish, under the pseudonym Jan Niemiara) against anti-Semitism, and was the mentor and driving force behind a whole generation of Yiddish poets in Galicia. His publications include *Vos ikh zing un zog* (1909; What I sing and say) and *Esterke* (1911), which tells the story of the love of the daughter of a Jewish blacksmith for King Casimir. Imber was the editor of the important anthology of Yiddish poetry in Galicia *Inter Arma* (1918) and founded the neo-romantic journal *Nayland* (1918–19).

CHRISTOPHER HUTTON

Isaac, Jules (1877–1963) French historian, founding member of the Jewish–Christian Friendship Society. Coming from an assimilated Alsace-Lorraine family with strong army links, both his father and grandfather having been officers, Isaac had his first serious encounter with anti-Semitism during the Dreyfus Affair. Notwithstanding this and subsequent events which temporarily dimmed his faith in progress and emancipation, he pursued a successful teaching career in history during the interwar years, ultimately rising to the rank of chief inspector. He was the co-author (with Malet) of history textbooks used in French secondary schools until the Second World War. The Nazi occupation and Vichy shattered his professional and personal life (his wife and daughter perished). He devoted the last 18 years of his life to fighting anti-Semitism in what he saw as its deeply embedded roots: the Christian "teaching of contempt" for Jews and Judaism. He campaigned vigorously for an end to anti-Jewish interpretations of the scriptures, calling upon the Church to rethink its attitude towards Jewry and revise the offensive parts of the liturgy. His efforts, sympathetically received by Pope John XXIII with whom he personally discussed the matter, may have contributed to the Second Vatican Council declaration 1965. More obviously successful was the creation of the Jewish–Christian Friendship Society.

BIBLIOGRAPHY
Jesus et Israël (Paris: Albin Michel, 1948)
The Teaching of Contempt (Toronto: McGraw–Hill, 1965)

NELLY WILSON

Islam and modern Judaism Modern Judaism's relations with Islam must, on all sides, be understood against the background of pre-modern Judaism and its existence in the Muslim world. For the contrast between the earlier era and the modern world in this respect is precisely the point on which the modern situation gains its unique meaning and significance. This may in fact be true in one's analysis of almost any aspect of modern history; but as regards our particular subject, for reasons which will become clear, the strength of this claim is most compelling.

The religious and historical background
Muslim–Jewish contacts became prominent during the later, politically crucial, years of Muhammad's mission in the town of Medina. Here according to the well-known and oft-recited story prominent in Islamic sources, the Muslims and their prophet-leader found only disappointment and frustration in their dealing with Medina's Jewish tribes. For the teachings

emerging from the prophet's revelations had begun to tell the story of this new (Islamic) religion which, though an heir of the earlier revelations (chief among them the Jewish and Christian), had come to correct, to complete and to fulfil these previous, now distorted, truths. In Islam's view the Jewish tribes in Medina seemed oblivious of the truth of Islam's claim here; indeed, more than that, they opposed this truth and actively conspired with its other, pagan, opponents toward its destruction. For this reason did the Qur'an describe the Jews as the "strongest in their enmity toward the Believers" along with the pagans. And for this reason did the post-Qur'anic Islamic literary sources consolidate this portrayal of the Jews and Judaism for the generations. Here the Jews were in the main characterized as detractors and enemies of Islam during its early formative period, as allies of Islam's pagan Arab opponents, and as deniers of Allah's truth, and purveyors of their own distorted version of that truth. This characterization remained as the foundation of Islam's view of the Jews.

On the practical side, Islam with its prominent politicization of religion and its propensity to prove "on the ground" its self-proclaimed spiritual superiority and finality, assigned the Jews (and Christians) a special place and role of inferior status under Muslim rule. Politically, socially, and legally, Islam discriminated against its Jews through this institutionalized arrangement of the *dhimmah* or "protection" of Jewish communities. Seen through Islam's eyes, this status was a just one, as it maintained the Islamic sovereignty over the Jews which was enjoined by the Qur'an itself, while allowing them a modicum of communal autonomy. And while the general Islamic conception of this arrangement was as a means of humbling and humiliating the Jews for their unseemly arrogance in having rejected Islam's call and having worked against its prophet, the discriminatory treatment of the Jews was sometimes surprisingly easy, allowing them to flourish in a most remarkable manner. The so-called "Golden Age" of Jewry in Islamic Spain or the relative comfort of tenth-century Iraq are two examples of such positive times for the Jews under Islam. However, it is clear that as the Muslim world itself began to experience its long historical decline, which culminated in Islam's parlous situation in our century, the position of its Jews often became more uniformly bleak and corresponded with more unswerving fidelity to Islam's theoretical picture of Muslim–Jewish relations. The challenge of modernity, including the creation of a new Jewish state – one of modernity's great irritants to Islam – provided the setting for the worst relations yet between Judaism and Islam. These were to be comparable to and in in many ways worse than the notoriously bad relations between Islam and Judaism back in Medina.

Islam, modernity and Judaism

The gradual decline in Islam's political power and efficacy which began in the tenth century led to a general weakening of this great civilization. One aspect of this loss of vitality was a worsening of the position of the non-Muslim minorities, pre-eminent among them the Jews. As is often the case in such situations, minorities suffer from the losses and difficulties besetting their masters. General tensions, unrelated to minority problems, exacerbate these problems and promote an exaggeration of existing elements of conflict in majority–minority relations. The Jews of Islam in recent centuries have served as an interesting example of such a process. From the eighteenth century onward, with Islam's internal decline now being hastened and intensified by the inexorable pressure of the West as it gradually imposed its will on the Islamic Middle East, the situation of the Jews in these areas noticeably worsened. Edward Lane, the prominent nineteenth-century British orientalist, described Egyptian Jewry as he saw them in the early part of the century. It is worthwhile quoting him extensively:

> They (the Jews) are held in the utmost contempt and abhorrence by the Muslims in general, and are said to bear a more inveterate hatred than any other people to the Muslims and the Muslim religion. It is said, in the Kur-an, "Thou shalt surely find the most violent of (all) men in enmity to those who have believed (to be) the Jews...". On my mentioning to a Muslim friend this trait in the character of the Jews he related to me, in proof of

367

what I remarked, an event which had occured a few days before. – "A Jew," said he, "early one morning last week, was passing by a coffee-shop kept by a Muslim with whom he was acquainted, named Mohammed. Seeing a person standing there, and supposing that it was the master of the shop (for it was yet dusk), he said, 'Good morning, sheykh Mohammad;' but the only answer he received to his salutation was a furious rebuke for thus addressing a *Jew*, by a name the most odious, to a person of his religion, of any that could be uttered. He (the offender) was dragged before his highpriest, who caused him to receive a severe bastinading for the alleged offence, in spite of his protesting that it was unintentional." – It is a common saying among the Muslims in this country, "Such a one hates me with the hate of the Jews." We cannot wonder, then, that the Jews are detested by the Muslims far more than are the Christians. Not long ago, they used often to be jostled in the streets of Cairo, and sometimes beaten merely for passing on the right hand of a Muslim. At present, they are less oppressed; but still they scarcely ever dare to utter a word of abuse when reviled or beaten unjustly by the meanest Arab or Turk; for many a Jew has been put to death upon a false and malicious accusation of uttering disrespectful words against the Kur-an or the Prophet. It is common to hear an Arab abuse his jaded ass, and, after applying to him various opprobrious epithets, end by calling the beast a Jew. (E. Lane, *The Manners and Customs of the Modern Egyptians*, London, 1871, pp. 304–5.)

Lane's portrayal of early nineteenth-century Jewish life in Egypt reflects a modern worsening of the lot of Islam's Jews. Here with the diminution of Islam's own role and possibilities in this world, its Jews suffered the general Islamic decline as well as an exacerbation of the inherent anti-Jewish elements in Islam. No longer a leader of world history as its own teachings proclaimed its right and duty to be, Islam experienced a contraction of its power in which its Jews also got squeezed. With the almost total imposition of Western colonial power on Islam during the early years of the twentieth century, Muslims keenly felt not only their great loss but the total reversal of historical roles between Islam and the West. This was a reversal which to Islam was not only painful and unjust but which represented a betrayal and inversion of God's plan of human history.

This straitened situation inevitably resulted in a heightening of tensions between Muslims and Jews in the Islamic countries, as in all instances of social and political disruption which adversely affects majority–minority relations. One powerful factor contributing to this process in the Muslim–Jewish case here was the attempt by the European powers to institute an equalization of rights and opportunities (in keeping with Western notions of human rights) between Muslims and non-Muslims, in some areas which had come under European control. Jews were thereby enabled to achieve higher status and greater opportunities. And because this went so fiercely against the grain of Islamic doctrine and experience in Jewish matters, Muslim attitudes toward Jews further deteriorated. But it was Zionism and its end product of a Jewish state in the midst of the Islamic patrimony (Dar al-Islam) which finally fixed the form and quality of Muslim–Jewish relations in the latter half of the twentieth century.

Islam, the Jews and Israel

In Islam's view, no aspect of its painful encounter with modernity has been worse than Israel's presence in the Middle East. If the Western (Christian) domination of the area represented for Muslims an inversion of all that was right, good, and proper, then the creation of a Jewish state there was the most anomalous aspect of that generally anomalous situation. And this is really what is meant when we talk about modern Judaism and Islam. For Muslim thinkers and ideologues of our time, already preoccupied with the modern crisis and seeking ways to re-establish Islam's ancient glory, Israel and Zionism represent a recapitulation of Muhammad's early Jewish problems in Medina. And just as that earlier struggle with the Jews constituted Islam's foremost political and theological challenge, so then has modern Islam come to see its conflict with Israel as a microcosmic representation of Islam's modern predicament. And insofar as modern Islam seeks to rehabilitate itself now by reviving and re-establishing those aspects of its ancient tradition which led to wordly glory and success, it must include defeat of the Jews (in Israel) as a central element in that rehabilitation. For in any traditional reading of Islamic sources, Islam's defeat of Medina's Jews was crucial to its subsequent emergence as a regional and, later, a world power. And theologically, the defeat of this renegade earlier monotheism constituted in Islamic terms the proper corrective measure required to counteract Jewish falsification of religion and hatred of Islam. In a thought-world such as that of Islam, still integrated and not centrally affected by critical currents of modern thought in the West, one's understanding of Zionism's challenge to the Muslim world ineluctably took the form of reliance on early exemplars. And of these there were many, as we have seen.

The result of all this has been a new body of Islamic thought concerning the Jews and Judaism (and Israel), based mainly on the ancient sources but far exceeding these sources in ideological animosity and emotional hatred. Here, with some aid from the borrowed Western text of the *Protocols of the Elders of Zion*, the ancient Islamic thought on the Jews is pushed to a logical extreme and infused with a hatred which matches in intensity the seriousness of Islam's modern predicament and the repetition in a far worse form of the ancient Jewish threat. For most Muslim thinkers, the elimination of Israel, however accomplished, has thus become a necessary element in Islam's ultimate re-entry into a leading role in world-history.

Sayyid Qutb, the great and influential Muslim fundamentalist writer of the mid-twentieth century (d.1966), published a highly influential essay in the early 1950s entitled "Our Struggle With the Jews" which became a model for much of the subsequent highly elaborated Islamic thought on the Jews. A few quotations from this essay will provide a concise representation of the main motifs in this thought:

> The Jews have confronted Islam with enmity from the moment that the Islamic state was established in Medina...
>
> The Muslim community continues to suffer from the same Jewish machinations and double-dealing which discomfited the early Muslims...
>
> This is a war which has not been extinguished...for close on fourteen centuries, and which

continues until this moment, its blaze raging in all corners of the earth.

> ...the Jews will be satisfied only with the destruction of this religion (Islam)...(in R. L. Nettler, *Past Trials and Present Tribulations: A Muslim Fundamentalists View of the Jews*, Pergamon, Oxford, 1987, p. 34)

Since Sayyid Qutb this school of thought has continued. In response to the continuing and growing conflict between Israel and the surrounding Muslim countries, a proliferating Islamic literature has elaborated upon and explicated the basic framework story already in circulation in the early 1950s. In particular, this response has been prompted by certain landmark events in the history of the conflict, in conjunction with certain general trends of instability and internal social, economic and political dislocation suffered by these countries. The latter may generally be described as problems or (sometimes) failures in modernization. An example here may be seen in the Six Day War and its aftermath.

President Nasser's Arab Socialism, with its loud promises of dual success in internal reform and the struggle with Israel, was judged by the results of the Six Day War to have been a failure in both realms. And though Nasser had in fact successfully instituted certain economic reforms, the catastrophic outcome of the war had convinced the intellectuals and ideologues engaged in serious post-war self-examination that these reforms had been of little value, and too few, in light of the enormous challenges of modernization which as yet stood unmet. By a traditional logic derived from early historical exemplars, an integral link between the struggle for success in the world and the war against the Jews was now firmly established. In addition, subsequent to the Six Day War, and in part directly due to the war's outcome, the already established general trends of Islamic fundamentalism received an enormous boost. This in turn brought with it a further increase in the output of Islamic literature on the Jews, Judaism and Israel, as well as the further development of that literature's basic themes. As regards the latter, two examples will illustrate new motifs which were easily integrated into the earlier basic framework story: *The Protocols of the Elders of Zion* and the claim of collusion between Zionism and Communism against Islam.

Though present in the Arab Middle East since the early part of the twentieth century, and widely used in the more secular Arab nationalist writings against Zionism and Israel, the *Protocols* came into Islamic literary usage in prominent fashion mainly subsequent to the Six Day War. Almost invariably, when using the *Protocols* a Muslim writer will juxtapose his selected passage from the *Protocols* with one from the Qur'an or another traditional Islamic source, in such a way as to show how the *Protocols* here reflect the sacred teaching concerning the Jews.

The allegations of collusion between Zionism and Communism against Islam has become a common motif in the post-1967, and especially the post-1973, Islamic writings. Here Zionism is portrayed as the actual creator of Communism through the founder, himself a Jew, Karl MARX. And both movements then are said to rest securely on the foundation of Judaism, as this religion is known to Muslims first through their own ancient sources and then through the

Protocols. For the Muslim writers, all of this represents the old (Jewish) anti-Islam force in modern garb now purveying its wares in the form of socialism, Zionism and atheism.

With the continuation, and exacerbation, of the Arab–Israeli conflict, the strong and vital Islamic trends of the late twentieth century seem determined to maintain the Jews and Israel as a focus of their concerns. Literature and thought of the type described above continue to appear in prominent fashion, reflecting and further enhancing the deep motivation which produced them. Modern Judaism's relations with Islam have already been profoundly influenced in this process; and not for the better.

FURTHER READING

Lewis, B.: *Semites and Anti-Semites* (London: Weidenfeld and Nicolson, 1986)

Nettler, R. L.: *Past Trials and Present Tribulations: A Muslim Fundamentalist's View of the Jews* (Oxford: Pergamon, 1987)

Stillman, N. A.: *The Jews of Arab Lands* (Philadelphia: Jewish Publication Society, 1979)

RONALD NETTLER

J

Jabès, Edmond (b.1912) French writer. Born in Cairo, Jabès settled in Paris in 1957, becoming one of his adopted country's most influential writers. In Egypt he had participated in French literary circles, influenced by Max JACOB, while also initiating anti-Fascist political activities. Publishing poems in small editions in Cairo and Paris, he identified the struggle of writing with the Jewish condition only during his forced exile as a "French" writer. Henceforth, abandoning poetic forms, he developed an unclassifiable genre, a continuous meditation on writing as nomadic exile, God's absence, nothingness and silence, the impossibility of completing the "Book", and the historical realities of anti-Semitism and the Holocaust. The seven-volume series entitled *The Book of Questions* (1963–74), blends fragmented narrative, dialogues, self-contradictory aphorisms, commentaries, commentaries upon commentaries, and large, blank margins, comprising, on one level, post-religious responses to an unreachable and absent, "God". In 1970 Jabès was awarded the prestigious *Prix des Critiques* for his entire work.

The Jabès "Book", as it is usually called, consists of separately titled volumes, all published in Paris by Gallimard, which dynamically put into question basic humanistic notions of literature and truth. Edmond Jabès became internationally known after Jacques DERRIDA (1967) and Maurice Blanchot (1971) published essays on his work. His poetry of 1943–57 was collected in *Je bâtis ma demeure* (1959; I build my dwelling), with a preface by Gabriel Bounoure. While the original trilogy is made up of conversations, commentaries, and so on, by fictional rabbis and their disciples, all centered around a constantly interrupted story about the tragic love affair between Sarah Schwall and Yukel Sérafi, the following four develop more mythical, equally elusive meditations on the mysteries of writing, with less emphasis on specifically Jewish themes: *Yaël* (1967), *Elya* (1969), *Aely* (1972), and *El, or the last book* (1974). Nevertheless, questions of God, the Jewish people, and human meaning, far surpass the subversion of language and narrative structure which had attracted formalist and deconstructive critics.

A second seven-volume series, entitled *The Book of Resemblances* (1976–87), parallel to, and sometimes quoting from, the first, explicitly rejects exclusively theoretical interpretations of Jabès' work, while continuing the meditation on Judaism as writing. The last four volumes in particular gradually open the "Book" to community and meaning beyond literature. The author expresses himself directly in essays, *Le livre des marges* (1984; The book of margins), and conversations of Jabès with Marcel Cohen, *Du désert au livre* (1980; From the desert to the book).

FURTHER READING
Gould, E., ed.: *The Sin of the Book* (Lincoln: University of Nebraska Press, 1985)

EDWARD KAPLAN

Jabotinsky, Vladimir (1880–1940) Zionist leader. Born in Odessa to a middle-class family,

Vladimir Jabotinsky

ities for confronting Arab crowds with his troops in 1920. After much protest, he was released from Acre prison in 1921.

Jabotinsky's thinking was greatly influenced by Italian nationalism. His anti-socialist, militaristic philosophy put him at odds with mainstream Zionist theory and policies, leading to the formation of the Revisionist Zionist Organization and Betar Youth Movement in 1925, and the New Zionist Organization in 1935. These groups sought alliances with European governments to effect mass migrations of Jews to Palestine. Faced with increasing British resistance to Jewish settlement and statehood after 1920, Jabotinsky sponsored illegal immigration and supported anti-British terrorism by the Irgun.

Jabotinsky was also well known as a prolific essayist, poet, and translator in several languages. He died in 1940 while visiting a Betar summer camp in New York.

FURTHER READING

Avineri, S.: *The Making of Modern Zionism: The Intellectual Origins of the Jewish State* (New York: Basic Books, 1981)

JANE SHAPIRO

Jabotinsky attended Russian schools and studied law in Berne and Rome. He excelled as a journalist and linguist, and traveled widely as a columnist for several Russian newspapers.

Jabotinsky became an active Zionist in 1903. Faced with the threat of a pogrom in Odessa after similar events in Kishiniev, Jabotinsky helped organize a self-defense group. His fiery oratory was popular at Zionist congresses. Convinced during the First World War that the Ottoman Empire would be dismantled, Jabotinsky sought to form a Jewish legion to fight alongside the Allies in Palestine. His first attempt, the First Zion Mule Corps, fought at Gallipoli. They were succeeded in 1918 by the Thirty-Eighth through Fortieth Battalions which fought in Palestine. After 1920 these units became the Haganah which defended Jewish settlers against increasing Arab hostility. Jabotinsky was imprisoned by British author-

A man of letters and a polyglot, writing in seven languages, Jabotinsky remains in the history of Jewish culture above all as a Russian–Jewish publicist, prose writer, and poet. Not without reason, as he continued to create in Russian almost to the end of his life. He published first in his homeland, in Odessa in 1897. He contributed to the newspaper *Odesskie novosti* (Odessa News) abundantly and continuously, right up to the First World War. The pre-revolutionary Russian–Jewish periodicals that regularly published Jabotinsky included *Evreiskaia zhizn* (Jewish life), *Khronika evreiskoi zhizni* (Chronicle of Jewish life), and *Rassvet III* (Dawn III). During the war he was the foreign correspondent of Petrograd's *Russkie vedomosti* (Russian Gazette): after the war he wrote principally for *Rassvet* (Dawn), which began to be published anew in Berlin and then Paris, and which he ran for a period of 10 years, from 1924 to 1934. In the entire history of Russian–Jewish journalism there has not been a publicist equal to Jabotinsky. The strength and clarity of thought and the beauty, the harmony, and the maximally concentrated energy of style retain all their charm even up to the present time. The publicist and the ideologue subordinate the artist in his artistic prose as well, not to the benefit of the latter. As a poet, Jabotinsky became famous for his translations into Russian of H. N. BIALIK, *Pesni i poemy* (1911; Songs and poems). He himself collected the best of his articles in two books: *Feletony* (1913; Newspaper satires; 3rd rev. edn, 1922) and *Causerie* (1930; Chat). The publicistic character is also apparent in *Slovo o polku: Istoriia Evreiskogo legiona po vospominaniiam ego initsiatora* (1928; A word about the regiment: the story of the Jewish Legion according to the recollections of its pioneer). His artistic prose consists of the historical novel *Samson Nazorei* (Samson the Nazarite), which appeared first in *Rassvet* (1926–7); the collection *Rasskazy*, from various years (1930); and the novel *Piatero* (1936; Five), the story of an assimilated Jewish family in pre-revolutionary Odessa.

FURTHER READING

Schechtman, J. B.: *The Life and Time of Vladimir Jabotinsky*, vols 1–2 (Silver Spring: Eshel Books, 1987)
Nakhimovsky, A.: Vladimir Jabotinsky, Russian writer. *Modern Judaism* (May 1987)

SHIMON MARKISH

Jacob, Max (1876–1944) French poet, novelist, and avant-garde artist. Jacob was born at Quimper, Brittany, the son of a tailor. His family was descended from German Jews who had emigrated to France in 1816 at the beginning of the Emancipation. His Jewish roots were weak and held little significant meaning for him.

Jacob's childhood was most unhappy and led to three attempted suicides before the age of 17. A gifted linguist with a flair for writing, Jacob eventually allied himself with avant-garde literary and artistic circles dominated by such luminaries as Guillaume Apollinaire, Picasso, and André Salmon.

In 1909 Jacob experienced a vision of Jesus which forever altered his life. He wrote a mystery play, *St Matorel* (1911), in which he attempted to vent a degree of the ecstasy and anguish

he sensed in the wake of his mystical experience. His conversion to Catholicism in 1915 only appeared to provide him a limited degree of spiritual comfort. Undoubtedly this event sparked an outburst in his creative life as some of his most lyrical works were published. His religious emotions were given voice in *Extase, remords, visions, prières, poèmes et meditation d'un juif converti* (1919; The ecstasy, remorse, visions, prayers, poems, and meditation of a converted Jew). In 1921 Jacob retired to a monastery at St-Benoît-sur-Loire where he continued to write poetry and novels. In 1924 he published two intensely religious, mystical works, *Visions Infernales* and *L'Homme de Chair et l'Homme Reflet*.

In 1928 Jacob left the monastery and returned to Paris where he became a painter. After eight years in the worldly capital, Jacob again retired to the monastery in search of God and the Divine Will in his own life. After the Nazi Occupation of France, he was arrested and held at Drancy where he eventually died in March 1944.

SIMON SIBELMAN

Jacobs, Joseph (1854–1916) English historian, scholar, and folklorist. Born in Sydney, Australia, Jacobs was educated there until his emigration to England, where he studied at various universities, including Cambridge (1876). In 1877, after graduating, he went to Berlin to study with Moritz STEINSCHNEIDER and Moritz LAZARUS. On his return, he settled in England, becoming active as an author, journalist, and scholar. In 1890 he was called to the USA as a revising editor of the *Jewish Encyclopedia*.

Jacobs is recognized as a scholar – perhaps the first – who utilized statistical evidence in his articles on European Jewry. The articles were first published in the *Jewish Chronicle* and the *Journal of the Anthropological Institute* and reprinted in his book *Studies in Jewish Statistics* (1890). After his visit to Spain to pursue his research he published *Sources of Spanish–Jewish History* (1893). His study of early Anglo-Jewish history was followed by *Jews of Angevin England*, which also appeared in 1893. He wrote many books and articles on these topics as well as on folklore, becoming the editor of the periodical, *Folklore*, the honorary secretary of the International Folklore Council, the chairman of the literary committee of the Folklore Congress in London (1881) and the major English authority in this field.

His other writings include *As Others Saw Him* (1895), a novel on the life of Jesus, from a Jewish viewpoint. Among his other activities he edited and wrote introductions to some of the masterpieces of English literature, such as *Emma* by Jane Austen and *The History of Henry Esmond* by Thackeray.

DEBORAH SCHECHTERMAN

Jacobs, Louis (b.1920) English rabbi and theologian. Born in Manchester, he studied at the *yeshivot* of Manchester and Gateshead and at the University of London. He served as rabbi of the Central Synagogue, Manchester, and at the New West End Synagogue, London from 1954 to 1959. From 1959 to 1962 he was tutor at Jews' College, London. When Chief Rabbi I. Brodie vetoed his appointment as principal of Jews' College because of his heterodox views, Jacobs resigned as tutor. This led to a major controversy among British Jews. Jacobs's supporters created for him the position of director of a new Society for the Study of Jewish Theology. In 1963 the post of minister of the New West End Synagogue became vacant, but Brodie stopped Jacobs's appointment. Subsequently, many of the synagogue's members seceded from the United Synagogue and founded the New London Synagogue with Jacobs as their rabbi. From 1985 to 1986, he was a visiting Professor at the Harvard Divinity School, and since 1988 has been visiting Professor at Lancaster University, England.

BIBLIOGRAPHY

We Have Reason to Believe (London: Vallentine, Mitchell, 1957); *Principles of the Jewish Faith* (London: Vallentine, Mitchell & Co., 1964); *Hasidic Prayer* (London: Routledge & Kegan Paul, 1972); *A Jewish Theology* (London: Darton, Longman & Todd, 1973); *Theology in the Responsa* (London and Boston: Routledge & Kegan Paul, 1975); *Jewish Mystical Testimonies* (New York: Schocken Books, 1977); *The Talmudic Argument* (Cambridge: Cambridge University Press, 1984); *A Tree of Life* (Oxford: Littman Library, 1984)

DAN COHN-SHERBOK

Jacobson, Dan (b.1929) British novelist. Born in Johannesburg, South Africa, Jacobson was educated at the University of the Witwatersrand and moved to London in the mid 1950s. Since 1976 he has been teaching English literature at University College, London, where he is now a professor in English. In 1955 he published his first novel *The Trap* which was a naturalistic account of South Africa, based on his life there. His first set of short stories *A long way from London* (1958) won the Llewellyn Rhys Memorial Prize in 1959.

Continuing the themes of his first novel, *A Dance in the Sun* (1956) concerns the tension between black and white inherent in a small farm community in South Africa under the system of apartheid. Jacobson's stories are of human relationships which cross the boundaries of race, religion, and color. *The Price of Diamonds* (1957) is a comic treatment of dubious financial dealings by two elderly Jewish businessmen in a small South African mining town. This was followed by *The Evidence of Love* (1960) which concerns the question of intermarriage between a black man and a white woman in South Africa. Although many of Jacobson's short stories and some of his novels draw on his Jewishness, it was not until *The Beginners* (1966) that he was to deal in full with this aspect of his personal history. Set in South Africa, Israel, and England, Jacobson applies his economic use of language and gentle humor to a novel which spans three generations of a Jewish family. This family saga received considerable critical acclaim and demonstrated in full Jacobson's unhurried narrative technique and his cool, sensitive observation.

The Beginners, in fact, signaled a shift away from the naturalistic South African novels and short stories which Jacobson had produced in the 1950s and 1960s. The publication of *The*

Rape of Tamar (1970), in particular, crystallized this move from his South African fiction, by using the biblical story of the rape of King David's daughter by her half-brother, Amnon. The incisive analysis of relationships in *The Rape of Tamar* refers back to Jacobson's earlier fiction. *The Wonder-Worker* (1973), about a schizophrenic, experiments with narrative viewpoints which anticipates Jacobson's last novel, *The Confessions of Josef Baisz* (1977). This novel is set in an imaginary dictatorship and is narrated by the brutal yet sympathetic Baisz. It won the *Jewish Chronicle's* H. H. Wingate Award in 1978.

Jacobson has written travel literature and an autobiographical set of essays, *Time of Arrival and Other Essays* (1963). He has also produced a controversial analysis of the Bible from the viewpoint of literary criticism, *The Story of Stories: The Chosen People and its God* (1982) and a radio play based on the biblical story of David and Saul, *The Caves of Adullam* (1972). His most recent work is a collection of autobiographical stories, *Time and Time Again: Autobiographies* (1985), and a collection of literary essays, *Adult Pleasures: Essays on Writers and Readers* (1988).

FURTHER READING

The novels of Dan Jacobson. *The Jewish Quarterly* 14 (1966)
Roberts, S.: *Dan Jacobson* (Boston: Twayne, 1984)

BRYAN CHEYETTE

Jacobson, Howard (b.1942) British novelist. Born in Manchester, Jacobson was educated at Cambridge University where he was influenced by the English literary critic, F. R. Leavis. He subsequently lectured in English literature at Sydney University, Australia for three years and tutored at Cambridge University. Jacobson has also worked as a publisher, teacher, and retailer and in 1975 was appointed a lecturer in English at Wolverhampton Polytechnic. This experience provided the material for his first novel, *Coming from Behind* (1983).

The publication of *Coming from Behind*, set in Wrottesley Polytechnic, established Jacobson's reputation as a comic writer who had, according to many reviewers, transformed the English comic novel. In an interview published in the *Guardian*, Jacobson argued that he intended this novel to be "the last word in academic novels, about a rotten polytechnic in a rotten town". Instead, however, he goes on to say that he found himself "writing about gentleness, about what a foreign place England is to a Jew". In *Coming from Behind*, Jacobson seems to define Jewishness in misanthropic terms as a hatred of all that surrounds his central character, Sefton Goldberg.

With his more substantial second novel *Peeping Tom* (1984), Jacobson directly confronts this negative definition of Jewishness. In this novel Jacobson's persona, Barney Fugelman, is contrasted with "Peeping" Thomas Hardy and the English literary rural tradition – the supposed polar opposite of urban Jewish culture. Instead of simply opposing these two cultures Jacobson, with a considerable ironic punch, constructs his novel so that his fictional Jewish persona becomes Hardy's reincarnation. The culturally dispossessed Jew without Jewishness – who defines himself purely in relation to others – is therefore Jacobson's subject matter in *Peeping Tom*. This novel achieves a lasting seriousness with the comic realization that it is the "goyische" Hardy who enables Fugelman to call himself a "Jew".

Jacobson has also published a third novel, *Redback* (1986), based on his period of teaching at Sydney University. Before writing this novel Jacobson expressed his intention in a radio interview of writing a Jewish novel in which Jewish characters and situations are not explicitly defined. *Redback* can perhaps be read as an ambitious attempt at expressing a Jewish voice without an explicitly Jewish subject-matter. Jacobson is one of a new generation of British Jewish writers in the 1980s who, with a welcome self-assurance, directly address the question of their Jewish cultural disinheritance.

BIBLIOGRAPHY

In the Land of Oz (London: Penguin, 1988)

FURTHER READING

The funny side of Wessex country. *Guardian* (11 Oct. 1984)
Kiss me Hardy. *The Jewish Quarterly* 32 no.1 (1985)

BRYAN CHEYETTE

Jacoby, Hanoch [Heinrich] (b.1909) Israeli composer and musician. Born in Germany, he studied at the Berliner Hochschule with Paul Hindemith. In 1934 he immigrated to Palestine and settled in Jerusalem, where he was active as a leading violin and theory teacher at the Academy of Music, of which he became the director for several years. In 1958 he moved to Tel Aviv and joined the Israel Philharmonic Orchestra as a viola player. Jacoby combined in his compositions the powerful influence of Hindemith's polyphonic technique with traditional oriental Jewish music, having worked for a long period with Bracha ZEPHIRA. His works include a viola concertino (1941), three symphonies, and many chamber and instructional works.

JEHOASH HIRSHBERG

Jacoby, Johann (1805–1877) Prussian politician and doctor. Born in Königsberg, he studied medicine at Königsberg University between 1823 and 1827. He soon established a thriving medical practice and wrote his first articles, on the administration of medical schools and on the cholera epidemic which broke out in 1831. His researches formed the basis of the new government regulations on the prevention and treatment of cholera. In 1833 he published his first political pamphlet, *Über das Verhältnis des Königlich-Preussischen Oberregierungsrats Herrn Streckfuss zur Emanzipation der Juden*, in which he refuted Streckfuss's argument that the Jews should be content with the relative freedom bestowed on them by the 1812 reforms, declaring that equality was a right, not a favor. This was followed by articles such as *Über die bürgerliche Stellung der Juden in Preussen* (1833). He supported Jewish religious reform and was involved in the commission set up to deal with the reform of religious services, a subject dealt with in his *An den Vorstand der Königsberger Jüdischen Gemeinde* (1838).

Jacoby became increasingly involved in politics and his opinions on "the Jewish question" simply formed part of his wider view of the need for political reform in the struggle for a democratic Germany. Whilst continuing to write occasionally on medical issues he wrote many political essays, such as the anonymous address in 1841 to the provincial parliament, *Vier Fragen, beantwortet von einem Ostpreussen*, which claimed a constitution as a right. As a result of this he was arrested and sentenced to two and a half years in prison, but the sentence was quashed on appeal.

His liberal politics led him to become greatly involved in the events of 1848 and he formed part of the preliminary parliament convened to draw up a popular constitution. He was a member of the Prussian National Assembly until its dissolution, but in the reaction which followed the revolutionary uprisings he was again arrested, for treason. He was acquitted in 1849 and returned to medicine for some years, until the renewed liberal atmosphere of the late 1850s brought him back to the political arena. In 1859 he was elected to the Prussian Chamber of Deputies, where he was one of the more extreme members of the opposition. He spent six months in prison after denouncing militarism and the Junkers in 1863.

Jacoby's popularity, however, declined and his position became more isolated. He opposed Bismarck's militarist policies and in 1868 called for greater working-class involvement in government, as well as a more equal distribution of wealth. His ideas formed the basis of the program adopted by the Stüttgart Congress in 1868, but in 1870 he was arrested again for his opposition to the annexation of Alsace–Lorraine. He was elected to the Reichstag in 1874 but refused to take his seat.

BIBLIOGRAPHY
Gesammelte Schriften und Reden, 2 vols (Hamburg: 1872; suppl. 1889)

FURTHER READING
Silberner, E.: *Johann Jacoby* (Bonn–Bad Godesberg: Verlag Neue Gesellschaft, 1977)
Engelmann, B.: *Die Freiheit! Das Recht! Johann Jacoby und die Anfänge unserer Demokratie* (Bonn: Dietz, 1984)

CATHERINE PHILLIPS

Jakobovits, Immanuel [Baron Jakobovits of Regent's Park] (b.1921) Chief Rabbi of Great Britain and the Commonwealth. Jakobovits was born in Königsberg in Germany. He came to London as a refugee in 1936, received a BA (Hons) and Minister's Diploma from Jews' College, London, and a Ph.D. (for a thesis on a comparative and historical study of Jewish medical ethics) from the University of London.

Jakobovits entered the ministry at the age of 20, serving at Brondesbury Synagogue, London (1941–4), the South East London Synagogue (1944–7) and the Great Synagogue, London (1947–9). He was called to Dublin as Chief Rabbi of Ireland (1949–58) in succession to Dr Isaac Herzog, who became Chief Rabbi of Israel. Jakobovits remained in Ireland for 10 years, until his call to be the first Rabbi of New York's Fifth Avenue Synagogue (1958–67), one of America's best-known Orthodox synagogues.

He was installed in 1967 as Chief Rabbi of the United Hebrew Congregations of the British Commonwealth of Nations, with jurisdiction over some two hundred congregations in the United Kingdom and Commonwealth. A frequent visitor to America and Israel, his communal tours have taken him to most major communities in every continent, including Russia, Romania, and Hungary.

His offices include President of Jews' College, London; President of the Institute of Judaism and Medicine, Jerusalem; Governor of four universities in Israel and of Shaare Zedek Hospital, Jerusalem. He is Honorary Director of the Center for Jewish Medical Ethics at Ben Gurion University of the Negev, Beer Sheva, established and named in his honor. Jakobovits was awarded an Honorary Doctorate by Yeshiva University, New York, in 1977; made Fellow of University College, London, in 1984; DD (Lambeth) in 1987; D.Litt. (Hon.), City University, London, in 1986. He also has an honorary degree from Queen Mary College, London.

A noted authority on Jewish medical ethics, he is author of *Jewish Medical Ethics* (1959, 4th edition 1975), now widely recognized as the standard work on the subject; *Jewish Law Faces Modern Problems* (1965); *Journal of a Rabbi* (1966); *The Timely and the Timeless* (1977), and *"If Only My People..." Zionism in My Life* (1984). He is co-author of the *Jewish Hospital Compendium* (1963, 1965) issued by the Federation of Jewish Philanthropies of New York, the first manual ever published for the guidance of Jewish physicians and hospital staff. He has also published the Order of the *Jewish Marriage Service* (1950, 1959) and numerous contributions to learned and popular magazines on both sides of the Atlantic.

He was knighted by Queen Elizabeth II in 1981, and in 1988 was elevated to the Peerage. Lord Jakobovits is an outspoken proponent of traditional values in the face of society in moral flux. His traditional Orthodoxy is untempered either by fashionable liberal compromises on the one hand or by the new fundamentalism on the other.

SHIMON COHEN

Janco, Marcel (1895–1984) Israeli artist. Janco was born in Bucharest, Romania. Between 1914 and 1919 he studied painting with the prominent Romanian painter and draughtsman, Iosif Iser, a former colleague of the artist André Derain. From 1912 Janco was a member of a group of artists and poets who published an avant-garde journal, *Simbolul*, which expressed revulsion and contempt for the bourgeoisie. Janco was the publisher and graphic editor; at his side were the poets Tristan Tzara and Ion Vinea. In 1915, Janco left for Switzerland to study architecture at the Zurich Polytechnikum. In neutral Zurich he joined a multinational group of students: Hugo Ball, Hans Arp, Hans Richter, Tristan Tzara, Viking Egelling, Richard Huelsenbeck, who met at the newly opened literary cafe – Cabaret Voltaire, at Spiegelgasse no. 1. Here on 5 February 1916, the group of writers, poets, painters, dancers, and musicians founded Dada.

The group was involved in exhibitions, performances, and publication of an avant-garde magazine. Janco designed the masks, costumes, and stage settings for the "happenings", as well as serving as editor of the Dadaist magazines. 1918 Janco joined the Basel artists' group *"Das Neue Leben"* (The new life). An exhibition of its members' work opened at the Zurich Kunsthaus in January 1919. In the summer of 1921 Janco received his architecture diploma and joined the Dadaist Surrealist group in Paris. He then rejected the new tendencies of the group and returned to Romania. In 1922–41 he was engaged in many varieties of artistic activity: contemporary architecture in the spirit of functional architecture; publicistics, as editor and publisher of *Contimporanul*, a platform for the Romanian avant-garde; painting, as a member of the "Arta Nova" (New Art) group. With the advent of Fascism and pro-Nazi politics Janco was forced to leave Romania. In 1941 he emigrated to Palestine and settled in Tel Aviv. In 1948 Janco participated in the foundation of the "New Horizon" group, which sought to measure Israeli art by the standards of contemporary Western art, and in 1953 he founded the cooperative artists' village of Ein-Hod on the southern slopes of Mt Carmel. Cooperation between different art disciplines was to pave the way for the newly emerging Israeli Art. At the same time Janco founded the art department at "Oranim" – the kibbutz movement's Teachers College where he taught 1953–60. At the 1965–6 "Fifty Years of Dada" jubilee, Janco participated in exhibitions held in Paris, Zurich, Geneva, and Milan. In 1967 he was awarded the Israel Prize for Art, for his lifetime achievement. In 1978 Janco cooperated in the production of the film, *Janco, his Life, his Work*, which was awarded many prestigious prizes. In 1981 the Museum of Art, Bucharest, organized a special celebration in his honor. In 1982 the Municipality of Tel Aviv awarded Janco honorary Citizenship. In 1983, the President of Israel, Chaim Herzog, inaugurated The Janco–Dada Museum in Ein-Hod, dedicated to the life and work of Marcel Janco. Marcel Janco died at the age of 89 and was buried in Tel Aviv.

FURTHER READING

Mendelson, M. L.: *Marcel Janco* (Tel Aviv: Massadah Publishing Co., 1962)

JUDITH SHEN-DAR

Jaques, Heinrich (1831–1894) Austrian lawyer and politician. Born in Vienna, Jaques was the nephew of the banker Sigmund Wert-

heimstein. He studied law at Vienna and Heidelberg. In 1856 he became a director of his uncle's bank, and in 1869 became a lawyer. In 1879 he entered the Reichsrat as a German Liberal. One of the founders of Vienna's *Handelsakademie* (School of Commerce), Jaques was one of the most prominent lawyers in Vienna, and also an important liberal politician. One of his closest friends was Theodor GOMPERZ.

Jaques shared the assimilationist goals of his generation, understood as the result of emancipation. This can be seen in his emancipationist tract, *Denkschrift über die Stellung der Juden in Österreich* (1859; Treatise on the position of the Jews in Austria). In this essay, addressed to the authorities, Jaques argues not so much that Jews deserve their emancipation, as that, unless they are emancipated, Western society stands to be flooded by Jewish money and revolutionaries. The bar against Jews in the civil service would only lead to conversions made without conviction, thus promoting duplicity and dishonesty, at the expense of integrity. While he accepts that Galician Jews are uncivilized, he sees no connection between this and the case for civilized Western Jews. Furthermore, Jaques points to the barbarism of any group in Galicia, including the Polish nobility. What is needed is for Austria to fulfill its mission of bringing German culture to the East. Austria, in order to prosper, must find its men of talent anywhere it can, whether it be palace or *shtetl*. Jaques's argument for full emancipation is, in effect, a plea for the career open to talent.

STEVEN BELLER

Jastrow, Marcus Mordechai (1829–1903) Scholar, lexicographer, preacher, and rabbi. Born in Rogasen, Prussian Poland, Jastrow received a private Jewish education. In 1852 he graduated from the *Friedrich Wilhelm Gymnasium* at Posen, and continued his Jewish studies at Berlin University. There he was strongly influenced by Michael Sachs, who opposed the Protestant influence on the synagogue. In 1855 Jastrow received his doctorate from the University of Halle for his thesis *De Abraham ben Meir Aben Ezra Principiis Philosophiae* (The philosophy of Abraham ibn Ezra). In 1853 he received his rabbinical diploma and shortly after his ordination was appointed, on the recommendation of Heinrich GRAETZ, as a preacher to the progressive German congregation in Warsaw.

In Warsaw Jastrow immediately became involved in political activities. His first political work, *Beleuchtung eines ministeriellen Gutachtens über die Lage der Juden im Königreich Polen veranlasst durch Kaiserlichen Willen und bürokratische Willkür*, (1859) was published anonymously, and supported the cause of the Jews in Poland. He then continued to preach and write in favor of Polish nationalism. After participating in the political demonstrations of the Polish revolutionary movement (1860–1), he was arrested in November 1861, thus becoming the hero of a Polish legend and a poem. As he was a Prussian citizen, and with the help of the Prussian Ambassador, he was released in February 1862, but was forced to leave Poland.

Jastrow published several articles and books on the corruption of the Russian bureaucracy and the underlying causes of the Polish revolution. One of these, *Die Vorlaufer des Polnischen Aufstandes* (1864) was published anonymously and initially appeared as a series of newspaper articles. Hoping to return to Warsaw but needing to earn his living, Jastrow was appointed as a rabbi first at Mannheim and then for two years at Worms, at the same time publishing works on rabbinic history. When his Prussian passport was canceled, he realized that he would not be able to return to Warsaw and he emigrated to the USA in 1866.

Jastrow settled in Philadelphia as rabbi of Rodfei Shalom Congregation, becoming deeply involved in public life and one of the leaders of the Conservative movement in the USA. He founded a new synagogue, opposed the Reform and its leaders, primarily Isaac M. WISE and Samuel HIRSCH. He also taught philosophy of religion, Jewish history, and biblical exegesis at Maimonides College. A few years before he died he was forced to limit his public activities due to poor health, but he continued his scholarly activities. His major work *Dictionary of the Targumim, the Talmud Babli and Jerusalmi, and the Midrashic Literature* (1886–1903), which is un-

doubtedly his main contribution to scholarship, was completed during those years. At the same time, he was co-editor of the *Jewish Encyclopedia* and editor-in-chief of a new translation of the Bible into English.

DEBORAH SCHECHTERMAN

Jerusalem, Wilhelm (1854–1923)

Jerusalem, Wilhelm (1854–1923) Austrian philosopher. Born in Drenic, Bohemia, Jerusalem studied at Prague, and subsequently became a schoolteacher, while he continued his interest in the psychology of speech and the education of blind deaf-mutes. In 1891 he began lecturing in philosophy at Vienna, and from 1903 in pedagogics. In 1920 he was appointed professor in both. From 1894–1902 Jerusalem also taught at the *Jüdisch-theologische Lehranstalt* (Jewish Theological College).

Jerusalem held a positivist viewpoint, opposing the neo-Kantians, Husserl, and much of the thought of Brentano. His friends included Ernst Mach and Josef POPPER-LYNKEUS. One of his major works is available in English: *Einleitung in die Philosophie* (1899; *Introduction to Philosophy*, 1910).

His collection of essays, *Gedanken und Denker* (1925; Thoughts and thinker) shows Jerusalem's close identification with what he saw as the Jewish tradition. He was the son of very traditionalist Jews and, although he later went through a materialist phase, he came to accept a non-anthropomorphic idea of God, and the life-oriented teachings which he saw as the basis of Judaism. For Jerusalem Judaism was a form of "ethical monotheism" which was entirely compatible with a scientific view of the world. Thus, although he disagreed with Hermann COHEN's aprioristic approach, he shared his views on Judaism.

FURTHER READING

Eckstein, W.: *Wilhelm Jerusalem* (Vienna and Leipzig: 1935)

STEVEN BELLER

Jewish Publication Society

Jewish Publication Society Founded in Philadelphia on 3 June 1888, this was American

Jewry's third attempt to establish a publication society. Earlier efforts (1845, 1871) had ended in failure. From the start, the Society committed itself "to publish works on the religion, literature, and history of the Jews; and . . . to foster original work by American scholars on these subjects" (1888 constitution). Membership dues and contributions funded its operations, and members received books in return. Well over seven hundred different titles have been published to date. The Society's history may be divided into four periods.

1888–1916

Led by Judge Mayer Sulzberger, and by Henrietta Szold, who from 1893 to 1916 acted as editor, the Society established itself, and by extension the entire American Jewish community, as a major force in Jewish cultural life. It published important works by Heinrich GRAETZ, Israel ZANGWILL, Solomon SCHECHTER, Moritz LAZARUS, Louis GINZBERG, and Simon DUBNOW, as well as Helena Franks's pathbreaking translations from Yiddish literature. In 1899 it issued the first volume of the *American Jewish Year Book*, an annual it now co-publishes with the American Jewish Committee. In early 1917 it released a major Anglo-Jewish translation of the Bible, under the chief editorship of Max MARGOLIS.

1917–1935

Despite reverses, the Society, led by Cyrus ADLER, and editors Benzion Halper (1916–24) and Isaac Husik (1924–39), continued to publish significant books. The 17-volume Schiff Library of Jewish Classics (1923–36) stands as the chief contribution during this period. The Society also placed into operation a new and highly innovative Hebrew press, making it the foremost printer of quality Hebrew books in the USA. The press was transferred to private hands in 1950.

1936–1949

Under the leadership of Maurice Jacobs, with Solomon Grayzel as editor (1939–65), the Society rapidly expanded. Its list now focused on history, biography, literature, and children's books, and featured works by leading Jewish writers and thinkers. The Society and its press were particularly active in meeting the literary needs of Jews during the Second World War.

After 1950

Recent editors of the Society have faced new challenges accompanying the changing needs and interests of the American Jewish community, and the increasingly competitive character of the American Jewish book trade. In 1973 in a departure from past policies, the Society published the highly successful *Jewish Catalog*. In 1983 after three decades of effort, it completed its new translation of the Bible, issued in one-volume in 1985 under the title *Tanakh*.

FURTHER READING

Bloch, J.: *Of Making Many Books: An Annotated List of the Books Issued by the Jewish Publication Society of America, 1890–1952* (Philadelphia: The Jewish Publication Society of America, 1953)

Sarna, J. D.: *JPS: The Americanization of Jewish Culture: A History of the Jewish Publication Society, 1888–1988* (Philadelphia: The Jewish Publication Society of America, 1988)

JONATHAN D. SARNA

Jewish women, education of

Jewish education in its original form was purely religious education, the constant and unchanging study of *Mikra* and *Mishnah*, the written and oral law. As study for its own sake it was restricted entirely to makes. Women, because they were not obligated to observe most of the laws, were not obliged to study them either. The training offered to all girls was deliberately role-specific and took place for the most part in the home, where the mother acted as the role-model. Through her example and instruction the girl was taught the duties of the Jewish woman as wife and mother. She might learn to read and write some Hebrew, but, in Europe, rather more Yiddish than Hebrew, she would learn the laws of menstruation (*niddah*) of keeping a kosher home (*halah*) and observing sabbaths and festivals (*Had Rakat haner*). This was linked with explicit teaching of modesty, chastity, and charity. There were instances of very learned women, of girls attending the lowest level of *heder*, but, on the whole, there were no formal, institutional provisions for the education of Jewish girls until the beginning of the Emancipation period at the end of the eighteenth century.

It is one of the ironies of history that, with the advent of the modern era, Jewish women were better able to cope with secular life and secular education, because they did not accept the constraints imposed upon them by the dominant values of most Jewish communities. Certainly in central and western Europe women created an informal system of education for themselves which left them better equipped to deal with the social changes around them. Five factors of Jewish life enabled them to do so.

1   Many women were economically active. While they were at work in the market place or domestic service, their male children would attend formal educational classes while the females were left with a *Rebitsin*, an early version of a childminder who often provided the first experience of learning.

2   Many families in Europe would offer boys learning in *Yeshivot* "*Freitish*", free board in return for some tuition for their children, which often included the girls as well as the boys and was occasionally also the means of introducing secular subjects to the young.

3   The lack of religious education left a whole world of secular knowledge which girls could pursue more easily than boys and many families arranged for private tuition in music, drama, foreign languages, and geography for their daughters.

4   Since most families depended on trade in some form for subsistence, it was necessary in many instances to teach girls arithmetic and elements of bookkeeping.

5   The fact that most Jewish women were literate led to a vigorous production of religious and secular literature in Yiddish mainly, but also, for example, in Ladino. Women worked as typesetters, commissioned translations and new editions of popular works like the famous *Tzenna Urenna* and created a whole literature – all of it for and some of it by women. The rapidity with which women adapted to secular life and secular learning was, at least in part, a consequence of the neglect they had exprienced by the religious establishment.

Since the early years of this century there has been a considerable change in attitude and all Jewish learning is now open and available to all Jewish women.

FURTHER READING

Fishman, I.: *History of Jewish Education in Central Europe* (London: Edward Goldston, 1944)
Gamoran, E.: *Changing Conceptions in Jewish Education* (New York: Macmillan & Co., 1925)

JULIUS CARLEBACH

Jewish Studies Jewish Studies as an academic subject is entirely a modern development. It emerged gradually in the course of the nineteenth century, mainly at first in German-speaking Central Europe (see WISSENSCHAFT DES JUDENTUMS). Largely influenced in its approach by trends in the study of classical philology, history, and scripture, its essential impetus was derived from the movement for Jewish political emancipation and social re-integration. If Jewish existence were to be "normalized", if the Jews were to stand on their own feet as an element within European society, they must discover and interpret their own past. Important factors guiding the lines along which research was to develop were the various movements for religious reform within Judaism, the polemical Christian stance towards Judaism (particularly in relation to the origins of Christianity), and later political anti-Semitism, with its hostile stereotype of the Jew as an alien presence whose contribution to European civilization was entirely negative. Despite a fundamental commitment to scholarly objectivity and rigor, a certain apologetic tendency, whether tacit or openly avowed, was therefore built into the program from the start. It might be added that the emergence of Jewish Studies embodied some of the ambiguities of purpose which marked the whole movement towards

Jewish emancipation: was the ultimate purpose some kind of autonomy, or rather the contrary, a total normalization? Was the aim to establish Jewish Studies as an academic discipline in its own right, or simply to secure a proper attention to Jewish aspects within other disciplines?

This conflict of aims may not always have been perceived as such at the time. The general (often seemingly wilful) neglect of Jewish history among non-Jewish scholars (at a time when very few Jews were present in university faculties, and those for the most part chose to ignore or play down their Jewishness) meant that even a certain normalization required a very great effort. So in the revolutionary year of 1848 Zunz petitioned for the creation of a department of Jewish Studies in Berlin, a premature demand which had to wait a century to bear fruit in Germany. Meanwhile, however, the establishment of a network of rabbinical seminaries in Europe and (later) in America made it possible for a good number of talented Jewish scholars to devote themselves to research and to serious teaching, and so the subject was created at first outside the environment of the European universities, and within an essentially separate and religious environment. A notable exception was England, where a more pragmatic attitude led in the 1840s to the foundation of the Goldsmid Chair of Hebrew at University College London, and in the 1870s to the creation of a Readership in Rabbinic and Talmudic Literature at Cambridge for Solomon Schiller-Szinessy, a Hungarian refugee who had been teaching Rabbinic Hebrew there for some years. This undramatic move was to have far-reaching consequences: Schiller's successor was Solomon SCHECHTER, who not only secured the astonishing hoard of medieval manuscripts from the Cairo Genizah for Cambridge but later played a cardinal role in the building of Jewish studies in America as the first President of the Jewish Theological Seminary in New York.

By the time of the First World War, solid achievements had been marked, notably a considerable wealth of publications, including a good number of learned journals and a popular, but soundly-based, English-language Encyclopedia, the *Jewish Encyclopedia*. An important step forward in the inter-war years was the opening of the Hebrew University in Jerusalem in 1925, which for the first time offered Jewish Studies a sound independent academic base. Together with Zionist colonization of Palestine and the movement towards Jewish autonomy, it also encouraged a quickening of interest in the Land of Israel and its Jewish past. Abroad, a number of archives and research institutes were set up in various countries, enabling rapid progress to be made in the study of the Jewish past. The Second World War shattered Jewish life in Europe, and put an end to much of this activity. Some of the libraries and institutes were rescued, or reconstituted elsewhere, but much of the work was simply stopped dead, as witnessed by the incomplete (German) *Encyclopaedia Judaica*, and by the cessation of the venerable German periodical, the *Monatsschrift für Geschichte und Wissenschaft des Judentums*. The post-war decades have seen a significant revival of Jewish Studies, notably in the United States and Israel. In America departments of Judaica or Jewish Studies have been established in the majority of universities and scholars have a regular forum in the meetings of the Association for Jewish Studies. In Israel, where there is widespread public interest in developments in the subject, and some of the achievements have been recognized by the presentation of national awards, a four-yearly Congress brings together scholars from all over the world. Jewish studies has thus definitely "arrived" as a subject; the old questions, as to the autonomy or the ancillary nature of the subject, are still, however, far from being answered.

Constraints of space preclude a full survey of the subject here: in any case its personalities and preoccupations are scattered throughout the pages of this book. A few of the main areas of interest are singled out for brief mention below, together with some of the major names and also some of those for which space could not be found elsewhere.

Manuscript research

The "raw material" of a great deal of the historical and literary research, medieval Jewish manuscripts abounded in the libraries of Europe, generally uncataloged or poorly described. The enormous work of discovering and cataloging them is associated in particular with the name of Moritz STEINSCHNEIDER; credit is also due to A. Neubauer, S. M. Schiller-Szinessy, Moïse SCHWABE, Alexander Marx, and many others. Their catalogs are still in use; but more than this, their work laid the foundations for other research. Important private collections of books and manuscripts were formed, many of which eventually found their way into institutional or public libraries (see David OPPENHEIM, David KAUFMANN, Moses GASTER; other important collectors were David Guenzburg of St Petersburg, Meyer Sulzberger in the United States, Leser Rosenthal of Hanover, whose library is now in Amsterdam, and S. D. Sassoon.). In Jerusalem a microfilm library aims at making the world's Hebrew manuscripts available to researchers, and important new work on Hebrew paleography and codicology is associated with the names of Malachi Beit-Arié and Colette Sirat.

The discovery of the Cairo Genizah manuscripts marks a watershed in the modern history of Jewish manuscripts. The sheer size of this deposit (there are thought to be well over 200,000 fragments – very few manuscripts survived whole) only accounts for part of its importance: it is a source of manuscripts of types which were not previously available: documents, both private and public, texts of many previously unknown works, and many older manuscripts than those preserved in the European libraries. The Genizah gave an enormous stimulus to research, and it continues to be one of the main focuses of Jewish manuscript research. (Genizah research and publication is associated, among many others, with the names of Solomon SCHECHTER, Jacob Mann, S. D. Goitein, Alexander SCHEIBER.)

Another manuscript discovery which has revolutionized research has been the discovery of Jewish texts from the Greco-Roman period in the Judean Desert, beginning in 1947. Together with the papyri found in Egypt (see below), these are the earliest Jewish manuscripts we have, and they have made an immeasurable contribution to our understanding of Judaism in the late Second Temple period. Among the relatively few Jewish scholars associated with

this research are Geza VERMES, Yigal YADIN and Solomon ZEITLIN.

Hellenistic Judaism
This subject, of great interest to Christian scholars, also overlaps with other areas of study such as classical studies and ancient history. It is therefore far from being a Jewish monopoly. There have, however, been some notable Jewish contributions to the study of the major Jewish writings in Greek, such as the Septuagint (Max MARGOLIS, Harry ORLINSKY), Philo (Harry Austryn WOLFSON, S. Sandmel, V. Nikiprowetzky), Josephus (L. H. Feldman), and even the New Testament (C. G. MONTEFIORE, David DAUBE, David FLUSSER), as well as to the historical background (Jean Juster, A. D. MOMIGLIANO, E. BICKERMAN, B. Z. WACHOLDER). Collections of texts of Greek and Latin authors referring to the Jews were published by Theodore REINACH and more recently by M. Stern. In the area of Jewish papyrology the name of Victor TCHERIKOVER stands out, and among numismatists L. Kadman and Y. Meshorer. Research has focused for various reasons on the period up to the early second century CE, but Samuel Krauss did pioneering work on Greek loanwords in rabbinic texts, as well as Jewish aspects of the Greek Christian literature, while important evidence on later centuries has emerged from the work of epigraphists such as Moshe Schwab and Baruch Lifshitz. Synagogue ARCHAEOLOGY is also beginning to yield valuable clues.

Rabbinic literature
The early scholars confronted an urgent task of basic rescarch into the text-history and philological study of the foundation-documents of traditional Judaism (Mishnah and Talmuds, Targum, Midrash, and a host of ancillary texts), the study of which lagged a long way behind that of other ancient texts such as the Bible, the Greek and Latin classics, or even the Christian Patristic literature. But the study was itself highly controversial, and the technical problems were enormous. There is still no critical text of the whole Mishnah, the Babylonian Talmud or the Palestinian Talmud (the Yerushalmi): even specialist scholars tend to rely heavily on reprints of early, insufficiently critical editions. The Tosefta was edited by M. S. Zuckermandel

(to some extent rendered obsolete by the remarkable work of Saul LIEBERMAN). In the fertile field of Midrash the harvest is richer, and the editions of early scholars such as Solomon BUBER, S. Schechter, Meir Friedmann, Adolf Jellinek, are still serviceable today. The edition of *Genesis Rabba* by J. Theodor, completed by Ch. Albeck, is generally reckoned good of its kind. Among aids to study, the enduring monuments are Marcus JASTROW's dictionary of the rabbinic literature, the earlier lexicon by Jacob Levy, and Alexander Kohut's edition of the *Arukh*, a talmudic dictionary originally compiled in the twelfth century. It should be added, however, that many of the standard items in any modern library of rabbinics are due to Christian scholars, such as H. L. Strack, R. Travers Herford and (in France) J. Bonsirven, not forgetting the English translation of the Mishnah by H. Danby.

The even more controversial subject of the history of rabbinic tradition was pursued within the context of the reform of Jewish religion and the REFORM–ORTHODOX confrontation. Mention must be made of the pioneering work of Zecharias FRANKEL, Isaac Hirsch WEISS, Wilhelm BACHER, among many others. Since their time the investigation of the way in which the Mishnah and Talmud came into being and were "redacted" in their present forms has given rise to an enormous literature, among which the most substantial contributions in recent years are due to the American Jacob Neusner. In the special area of the emergence of the Hebrew liturgy the pioneer was Leopold ZUNZ, followed by Ismar ELBOGEN, and more recently E. D. Goldschmidt, J. Heinemann and J. J. Petuchowski.

Medieval literature

A great deal has been done, since the early days of research, on editing the texts (there is a useful compendious history in English by M. Waxman), but many important writings remain unpublished. Attention has focused in the main on a few important authors, in such areas as biblical commentary and philosophy. Poetry, both sacred and secular, has attracted special attention, particularly since the discovery of the Genizah, which revealed the enormous richness of Byzantine hymnography (*piyyut*), and gave us new texts of the classic medieval Hebrew poets. The names that stand out are Israel DAVIDSON, H. Brody, J. Schirmann, A. M. Habermann, and more recently D. Yarden, Dan PAGIS, E. Fleischer and J. Yahalom. Among many distinguished contributions to the study of the (mainly Arabic) philosophical writings, tribute must be paid to the work of Alexander ALTMANN, Georges VAJDA, and L. V. Berman.

History

By far the largest area of research, its productions range from the huge compendious works of Heinrich GRATEZ, Simon DUBNOW, and Salo BARON to detailed studies and publication of source documents. Since the beginning there has been a tendency for Jewish historians to study the history of their own country (e.g. Cecil ROTH in England, B. BLUMENKRANZ in France, Umberto CASSUTO in Italy, A. Scheiber in Hungary, or S. Dubnow in Russia), or else to focus on another country which has a glorious past or perhaps merely romantic associations (e.g. C. Roth for Italy, F. (Y.) Baer and E. Ashtor for Spain). Inevitably, other areas were neglected, notably the Byzantine empire (a useful start was made by Joshua Starr), Iran and the Arab world (although the Genizah has given rise to important medieval studies, and there is valuable work by W. J. Fischel, Bernard Lewis, and, for North Africa, H. Z. Hirschberg and André CHOURAQUI).

NICHOLAS DE LANGE

Jong, Erica (b.1942) American poet and novelist. Born in New York, Jong was educated at Barnard College, receiving her BA in 1963, and Columbia University, where she graduated MA in 1965. Her three marriages to Michael Werthman, Allan Jong, and Jonathan Fast (one child) ended in divorce. She achieved fame with the publication in 1973 of *Fear of Flying*, a landmark feminist novel not yet fully valued for its mythopoeic worth.

Jong's fiction is noted for its sensationally explicit sexuality and candor. *How to Save Your Own Life* (1977) and *Parachutes and Kisses* (1984), sequels to *Fear of Flying*, and her other raucous, wildly extravagant novels *Fanny: Being the True History of the Adventures of Fanny Hackabout Jones* (1980) and *Serenissima: A Novel of Venice* (1987) have largely obscured Jong's achievement as a poet, a social commentator, a serious woman writer and a Jew. In terms of suffering, she often equates these latter two aspects of being. Like her feminism, now less strident in maturity, her Jewishness is always near the surface, and on occasion it breaks through strongly as in her protagonist's tender expressions of familial affection for and identity with her aged grandfather whom she journeys to see in the old country in *Parachutes and Kisses*.

In her first book of poems, *Fruits and Vegetables* (1971), Jong established herself as a genuine poet, displaying a fertile imagination, concretion, gusto, sensitivity, a mastery of metaphor and myth, and a surpassing joy in the physical world. She has a marvelous comic sense. Her subsequent volumes of poetry have sustained and extended these gifts. Hers is a major talent, too often frittered away.

BIBLIOGRAPHY

The Poetry of Erica Jong (1976); *Megan's Book of Divorce* (New York: New American Library, 1984)

FURTHER READING

Reardon, J.: Fear of Flying: Developing the Feminist Novel. *International Journal of Women's Studies* 1 (1978)

Showalter, E., and Smith, C.: Interview with Erica Jong. *Columbia Forum* 4 (1975)

JOSEPH COHEN

Josephs, Wilfred (b.1927)   English composer. Josephs was born in Newcastle-upon-Tyne, England. He began his musical studies with Dr Arthur Milner in 1947, but soon stopped and qualified as a dental surgeon in 1951. After two years of national military service, he took up the serious study of music with Alfred Nieman as scholarship-holder at the Guildhall School of Music and Drama, London. After being awarded the Leverhulme Scholarship he was able to study in Paris with Max Deutsch, a pupil of Arnold SCHOENBERG.

Through his ensuing musical career, Josephs

produced a collection of works of remarkable variety, including opera, ballet, vocal and choral works, and over 40 chamber and instrumental works. He has written over 30 pieces for orchestra and 12 concertos. His style of composition has gradually progressed from serialism to the total harmony of his latest works.

Josephs's subject matter is as varied as his treatment of themes. Hugo Cole in *The New Grove Dictionary of Music and Musicians* comments that "Josephs has the confidence and the technical ability, as well as the persistence and will to treat great and universal themes". His ability has been shown in his adaptability and he has produced music for 25 feature films, 32 documentaries and over 100 television productions.

Possibly his most notable work is his *Requiem* Op. 39 for which he was awarded first prize in the First International Composition Competition of La Scala and the City of Milan in 1963. The Hebrew text of the *Requiem* is the Mourners' Kaddish, and the work bears the dedication "pro defunctis iudaeis". The work has met with international acclaim and is regarded as an important contemporary choral work.

Two later works incorporate Biblical themes: *Adam and Eve – An Entertainment* is a short piece for narrator and orchestral instruments. The text is by the well-known writer and storyteller, David Kossoff. *Spring Songs* (1981) draws its text from various writings and includes the biblical text of The Song of Solomon. The work was commissioned by the Cork Festival and first performed there in 1981.

JOHN MATTHEW

Josipovici, Gabriel (b.1940)   British novelist, dramatist, and literary critic. Born in France, Josipovici was educated at Victoria College, Cairo, and Oxford University. His first novel *The Inventory* was published in 1968 and his outstanding work of literary criticism *The World and the Book: A Study of Modern Fiction* was published in 1971. He has taught comparative literature at the University of Sussex since 1963 where he is now a Professor of English.

In both his fiction and criticism Josipovici

is writing in a European modernist tradition. His fiction, in particular, is influenced by the French writer Alain Robbe-Grillet. His delicate, vulnerable novellas aim to make art out of the everyday and discover "a thousand subjects for every moment of time" in the words of Pierre Bonnard, the subject of Josipovici's most recent work. Josipovici's early short fictions began by concentrating on developing a clean and sharp dialogue and it was not until the publication of *Migrations* (1977) that he was able to contrast the lightness and musicality of his dialogue with a series of haunting images of displacement.

Josipovici has also written 15 stage and radio plays which have emphasized the playful, experimental aspect of his modernism and have enabled him to question vividly what constitutes a work of art. In contrast, his most recent fiction balances the lightness of his earlier work with a more plangent note of distress. The novella, *Contre-Jour: A Triptych after Pierre Bonnard* (1986) has received considerable critical acclaim and was short-listed for the 1986 Whitbread Award. He has also recently published his collected short stories, *In the Fertile Land* (1987).

A distaste for fiction based on large historical questions means that Josipovici's novellas do not explicitly articulate Jewish themes. Nevertheless, his interest in questions of identity and displacement have led him to an understanding of Jewish writing in his literary criticism. After travelling to Israel to meet Aharon APPELFELD, Josipovici has recently written the introduction to the English edition of Appelfeld's *The Retreat* (1985). He is also a regular contributor to *European Judaism* and is on the editorial advisory board of *The Jewish Quarterly*. His criticism includes *Writing and the Body: The Northcliffe Lectures 1981* (1982) and *The Mirror of Criticism: Selected Reviews 1977–1982* (1983). His most recent work, *The Book of God* (1988), an important literary critique of the Bible, demonstrates the depth of Josipovici's interest in Jewish literature.

FURTHER READING

In conversation with Timothy Hyman. *The Jewish Quarterly* 32 (1985)

From game to silence. *Times Literary Supplement* no. 4441 (13–19 May 1988)

BRYAN CHEYETTE

Jost, Isaac Marcus (1793–1860) German historian and pedagogue. Born in Bernberg, central Germany, Jost received a traditional Jewish education and later studied at the universities of Göttingen and Berlin. He spent much of his life as a teacher at Jewish schools in Frankfurt-on-Main. In connection with these activities he published a young people's Pentateuch (1823) and a vocalized bilingual text of the Mishnah (1832–4). Jost was also active in such German–Jewish journalistic activities as *Zion* (with M. Creizenach, 1841–2) and *Israelitische Annalen* (1839–41). He belonged to the reform school in religious matters and helped to bring into being the second rabbinical conference at Frankfurt in 1845, where he also acted as secretary. Although much criticized by Heinrich GRAETZ and Abraham GEIGER for his alleged superficiality and dryness, and by S. D. LUZZATTO for his biblical criticism, Jost's status as a pioneer in Jewish historiography is secure. In his *Geschichte der Juden seit der Zeit der Maccabäer bis auf unsere Tage* (12 vols, 1820–47) and his *Geschichte des Judentums und seiner Sekten* (3 vols, 1857–9) he showed the ability to handle lucidly and without apology a wide range of source material. He distinguished strongly between a theological and an historical viewpoint, identifying the latter with the rationalism of the eighteenth century. This led him to dismiss the importance of the *kabbalah*. Jost's work also suffered from a certain vagueness in his conception of the Jewish people. In general, he gave more attention to institutional and social history than to intellectual history. The last three parts of his *Geschichte der Israeliten* covering the period 1815–46 are a valuable contemporary source.

FURTHER READING

Baron, S. W.: I. M. Jost the historian. In *History and Jewish Historians* (Philadelphia: The Jewish Publication Society of America, 1964)

Schorsch, I.: From Wolfenbüttel to Wissenschaft – the divergent paths of Isaac Marcus Jost and Leopold Zunz. *Yearbook of Leo Baeck Institute* 22 (1977) 109–28

LIONEL KOCHAN

Judeo-Arabic, modern Far from referring to a single, homogeneous linguistic entity, equally shared by all speakers within the hundreds of Jewish communities scattered throughout the Arab world, the term MJA (Modern Judeo-Arabic) is rather a useful label pointing to a plurality of Arabic dialects, differing in various degrees from one another, comprising various sociolects, language levels and registers. The only structural feature common to these dialects is their relative proximity to the lexical and grammatical structures of the various neighboring non-Jewish Arabic dialects spoken in the Near East and in North Africa during the last four centuries. No less important for the definition of the MJA dialects is the shared sociolinguistic characteristic, in that their entire linguistic repertory is used exclusively by Jewish speakers in their social interaction as well as in their socio-cultural life, including literary and journalistic production. All MJA dialects are written in Hebrew characters.

MJA is to be distinguished from medieval Judeo-Arabic which was more homogeneous, consisting of a kind of *koine*, the lexical and syntactic structures of which were close to those of Classical Arabic but included certain morpho-phonemic features of medieval Arabic dialects.

Until the recent virtually total dispersion of the various Jewish communities of the Arab world, MJA was used as the main language of the Jews of Yemen, Iraq, Syria, Lebanon, Palestine, Egypt, Libya, Tunisia, Algeria, and Morocco. Only in Morocco, Tunisia, and Yemen do a few thousand speakers remain in their natural discursive space. Today almost all speakers of the various dialects live in Israel, France, and Canada, with small numbers in the USA and Mexico. In the nineteenth and the beginning of the twentieth centuries, MJA blos-somed in Bombay and Calcutta, India, where Iraqi Jews had founded communities.

Some of these MJA dialects are the more or less direct heirs of medieval arabic dialects spoken by Jews in large, relatively stable communities like Sanaa, Baghdad, Damascus and Aleppo, Cairo and Alexandria, Tunis and Djerba, Algiers, Fes and Marrakech. These dialects still share certain features in common with ancient arabic dialects prior to Bedouin influence. Other dialects took shape after the sixteenth century in communities that were formed or revived with the arrival of Judeo-Arabic (JA) speakers from other communities.

MJA dialects are thus characterized by certain distinctive morpho-phonemic traits and by particular lexical items, very often stemming from their conservatism and their development in a Jewish context largely closed to the non-Jewish environment. They also exhibit

a) a rich *Hebrew-Aramaic* component,
b) a special variety of language – *aš-šarh* – reserved for traditional translation of biblical, talmudic, and para-liturgical texts, and
c) a *romanization* of the lexicon of some dialects.

As with other Jewish languages, the Hebrew-Aramaic component is a by-product of the permanent Jewish diglossia of traditional communities, within which operate, side by side, the local Jewish language and the Hebrew and Aramaic of the liturgical texts as well as the founding texts of traditional Jewish culture. It is not uniformly used in the different types of text, nor in the MJA discourse, nor by the various classes of speakers. This component is found particularly in rabbinical texts, be they exegetical, halakhic, didactic, or narrative. In everyday speech the Hebrew–Aramaic component undergoes morpho-phonemic transformations and alterations as a result of inter-linguistic and integrative interferences. These integrated lexical elements usually refer to particular Jewish cultural entities like the vocabulary of holy days, of the sabbath, of liturgical practice, of culinary acts, or of blessing and cursing formulas. In their interaction with non-Jews, male speakers sometimes use Hebrew–Aramaic elements for a special purpose: to create secret Jewish languages in order to hide certain meanings from third parties.

The "*šarḥ*" also concerns traditional Hebrew texts, for it purports to present directly in JA the original text irrespective of the syntax of the target language. Except for the Yemen where the classical translation of Rabbi Saadia Gaon (882–942) was maintained, all other communities of the Arab world have developed a literal and artificial system of translation, thus preserving the syntax of the original biblical text and using a more archaic and richer lexicon than that of daily speech.

In North Africa, after the arrival of thousands of Jews expelled from Spain and Portugal, hundreds of wordloans from JUDEO-SPANISH contributed to the romanization of the lexicon of certain urban dialects from the sixteenth century on. This roman influence increased considerably for most MJA dialects – except for the Yemen – in the nineteenth and the twentieth centuries in the aftermath of the French colonial presence in North Africa and the installation of the French–Jewish school system by the ALLIANCE ISRAÉLITE UNIVERSELLE throughout the Mediterranean basin.

By the fourth quarter of the nineteenth century, the need to publish Judeo-Arabic newspapers to cover the ever changing news scene and to adapt new or modern works taken from the modern Hebrew literary canon, from European literature or from Arabo-Islamic fiction has induced authors to use increasingly Islamic linguistic structures as they are lexically richer, and allow for the differentiation between the literary and the everyday languages. This Islamization of the literary language is particularly evident in the very rich Judeo-Tunisian literary production of the late nineteenth and the beginning of the twentieth centuries.

FURTHER READING

Blank, H.: *Communal dialects in Baghdad* (Cambridge: Harvard Middle East Monographs, 1964)

Chetrit, J.: Niveaux, registres de langue et sociolectes dans les langues judéo-arabes du Maroc. In *Les Relations entre Juifs et Musulmans en Afrique du Nord au XIX–XXe siècles*, ed. J. L. Miège (Paris: Éditions du CNRS., 1980) 129–142

——: Stratégies discursives dans la langue des femmes judéo-arabophones du Maroc. In *Massorot* (Jerusalem: Center for Jewish Languages, 1986) vol. 2, 41–66

Cohen, D.: *Le parler arabe des Juifs de Tunis*, vols 1, 2 (The Hague and Paris: Mouton, 1964, 1975)

JOSEPH CHETRIT

Judeo-Italian The term Judeo-Italian best applies to the linguistic expression which Italian Jews have been using – in a variety of contexts and for different purposes – from the origins of the Italian language up to the present time.

The earliest record of Judeo-Italian may be found in a limited number of tenth-century glosses to Hebrew texts. In the thirteenth century we have definite proof of the use of an Italian rather than an Aramaic *la'az* in the synagogal rite, and likely the first appearance of written translations of the Bible and of the Prayers Ritual, as well as of philosophical, scientific, and grammatical texts. The only original composition which we know for this period is the famous *Tishah Be'av Elegy*, published by Umberto CASSUTO.

Use of Hebrew characters, archaisms, and South Italian elements (the South being the most ancient centre of Jewish culture in Italy), may be considered the main features of early Judeo-Italian as well as of Judeo-Italian in general, for several centuries. Translations are very close to the original texts, but their esthetic value is often quite remarkable. This linguistic tradition continues in the Renaissance and late Renaissance periods, with more texts of the same kind, as well as *derashot* (sermons) and *Sifrei mitzvot* (moral books). The use of verse is often linked to a display of technical virtuosity – with both languages, Italian and Hebrew, appearing either alternatively or simultaneously in the same text: a composition by Leon Modena can be read both in Italian and in Hebrew. Spoken and written languages appear to be quite similar, as we can gather from transcripts of courtroom proceedings and from other outside sources.

Beginning from the seventeenth century, Judeo-Italian dialects were fixed in their modern forms with the institution of ghettoes and travel and mobility restrictions giving rise to contrasting phenomena. On one hand, the language of Italian Jews became increasingly related to the Italian dialect spoken in the same area; on the other, the strict physical isolation of the Jewish community encouraged the conservation of old words and structures, some of local origin, others relevant to previous centers of residence, the final result being a noticeable differentiation from the local speech, stressed often by a very particular lilt. During this period, the study and comprehension of Hebrew is generally on the decline, despite its continued presence in ritual readings of sacred texts and prayers, and in the religious aspects of everyday life. As a consequence, Hebrew words become subject to many changes and remarkable semantic shifts.

In this last respect the ritual field functions as the primary focal point. Hebrew words for prayers, festivities, ritual objects, and so on are used as figures of speech in everyday life, with a notable display of imagination and irony. Thus, *Tishah be'av* (the 9th of Av) is a mournful person, *megillah* (scroll) is a too-long text. When, in a couple, one partner is tall and thin and the other short and fat, they are said to be *lulav* and *etrog*. Sometimes the Hebrew expression, totally unrelated to its literal meaning, evokes a situation or a visual image: *faccia di anì aggever* is "a pale, sad face" – *anì aggever* [*ani haggever*] being the first words of a chapter of *Lamentations* read on *Tishah be'av*. As in other Jewish languages, Hebrew religious elements are often the central image of many picturesque proverbs: *Pesah non è, mazzà non c'è* Wait for Pesah before worrying about *mazoth* ("don't cross the bridge before you come to it").

Interference with Italian and with local dialects is discernible in:

a) phonetics: alien Hebrew sounds being replaced with more Italian-like ones: *hamor/ camor*; or words becoming similar to Italian equivalent

b) morphology: many Hebrew words acquire Italian morphemes: *hahamessa* (a clever wo-man), *scigazzella* (young girl), *acchaneffiarsi* (to flatter), *misvoddiero* (charitable), *bachione* (complaints), and vice versa: *schifitoddi* (effusions of love)

c) semantics: *shohet* "usurer".

There are also numerous cases of Hebrew–Italian compounds *malasa'a* (bad hour), *malmasal* (a person with negative qualities), *perdizeman* (idler), *masakinim* (lousy). Whereas the selection and adaptation of Hebrew words in Judeo-Italian is comparable to that of other Jewish languages, the subtle variations of humor in different parts of Italy, may be said to be a distinctly original trait.

Interest in Judeo-Italian dialects dates from the end of the nineteenth century and follows their decline due to the then-prevailing enthusiasm for assimilation to non-Jewish society. From this time on, available materials regarding Piedmont (Turin, Casale, and Moncalvo), Eastern Padania (Mantua, Modena, Ferrara, Lugo, Venice, and Trieste), Tuscany (Florence, Livorno [Leghorn], and Pitigliano), and Rome have been recorded and studied in various ways and on different levels. Additional data are available from non-Jewish authors such as Carlo Goldoni (Venice, eighteenth century), Giuseppe Berneri (Rome, seventeenth century), and Gioacchino Belli (Rome, nineteenth century) as well as from several anti-Semitic parodies.

Apart from a limited number of original compositions (from Turin and Modena), modern Judeo-Italian literature, whether in the from of drama or poetry, is invariably based on the spoken language and is intended to keep it alive. The most important examples are Benè Kedem, *La gnora Luna* (1932), B. Polacco, *Quarant'anni fa* (1972), *Pur io riderio*, the creation of a company called "Chaimme 'a Sore 'o Sediaro e 'a moje" (1985), as well as collections of verse by Del Monte (Rome) and Bedarida Several (Livorno).

Several Hebrew expressions of Judeo-Italian are also used by non-Jews, for instance *ganav* "thief", *taref* "unsuitable", *hamor* "ignorant", and *shamir* "homosexual". This phenomenon is important in Rome but may be found in Piedmont, Mantua, Livorno, and Venice.

Nowadays, Judeo-Italian dialects are almost completely extinct, the last terrible blow being dealt by (as is the case of other Jewish languages) the disappearance of Judeo-Italian speakers due to the Holocaust. A noteworthy exception is Judeo-Roman, a living language which still retains vigor and creativity.

MARIA MODENA MAYER

Judeo-Persian The term "Judeo-Persian" (JP) refers to any text in the Modern Persian language written in the Hebrew alphabet. Such texts are known from the very beginning of Modern Persian in eighth century CE, that is, postdating the Arab-Islamic conquest of Persian-speaking territory in the late seventh century. The very earliest dated texts that can be identified as "Modern Persian" that have been found are written in the Hebrew alphabet. The first major JP texts of any length, however, begin to appear only in the fourteenth century. One is the earliest known JP translation of the Pentateuch from a unique manuscript in the British Library bearing the date 1319. Though it does not contain the entire Pentateuch – the end of Genesis, all of Exodus, and the first chapters of Leviticus are missing – the manuscript contains 128 pages with extremely interesting Persian linguistic forms plus many references to medieval Hebrew grammatical doctrines, citations from Rashi, and quotations from the works of Maimonides. This translation is the oldest of a long tradition of independent JP Bible translations that extend well into the twentieth century.

The fourteenth century also gives us the works of the greatest of Jewish poets of Iran – Shāhin of Shiraz. Other poets of later centuries like Emrāni and many others show a continuing effort by Jewish writers to compose their works in the same forms used by contemporaneous Islamic writers in the Persian language, but on Jewish themes.

Numerous works of both poetry and prose are part of a very large extant JP literature by Jewish authors on Jewish subjects. However, JP literature also includes a great many transcriptions of classical Islamic Persian works into Hebrew script. Apparently, as in other Jewish language communities, Jews were not able to read the local script of the non-Jewish form of the language, but were thoroughly familiar with and appreciated the literary works that they heard in their speech community.

JP texts are known from all over Iran, Afghanistan, and Central Asia, that is from the entire area of Persian speech. In addition, some of the texts of the Chinese Jews of Kai-feng-fu also contain JP material.

Since the middle of the nineteenth century, the migration of Jews from cities like Bokhara, Samarkand, and Tashkent to Palestine provided the impetus to produce a large printed JP literature in Jerusalem. One of the leading authors, editors, and translators was Shim'on Hakham, who lived in Jerusalem during the last twenty years of his life (d.1910) and left a library of important JP texts.

FURTHER READING

Asmussen, J. P.: *Studies in Judeo-Persian Literature: Studia Post-Biblica 25* (Leiden: Brill, 1973)
Fischel, J.: Israel in Iran: a survey of Judeo-Persian literature. In *The Jews: Their History, Culture, and Religion*, ed. L. Finkelstein (New York: Harper & Bros., 1949) vol. 2, 1149–90

HERBERT PAPER

Judeo-Spanish Judeo-Spanish (JS) is a language of Hispanic stock spoken and written by Jews of Spanish origin. Its phonology, morphology, and lexicon derive, for the most part, from pre-sixteenth-century Spanish, and, as with other Jewish languages, the influence of Hebrew is felt, particularly in lexical areas associated with religious observance and practice, and, more restrictedly, in affective and taboo uses of Hebrew words and concepts. Through contact with the languages of those Mediterranean countries in which the Jews settled after their expulsion from Spain in 1492, a number of lexical items, as well as a smaller number of morphological and syntactical elements, have entered the language from Turkish, Arabic, French, and, to a lesser extent, Italian.

Upon leaving Spain whole communities of Jews headed east through Italy to the lands of the Ottoman Empire at the invitation of Sultan Bayazid II, and important centers, which survived until the Second World War, grew in present-day Turkey, Greece, Israel, and Egypt, with smaller ones in Yugoslavia, Bulgaria, Romania, and the island of Rhodes. Their speech is described by linguists as eastern JS. For a century or so prior to the Expulsion, persecuted Spanish Jews also found shelter in North Africa, and speech communities grew along the northern coast of Morocco. The speech of this region, which bears a marked resemblance to its eastern counterpart both phonetically and in the retention of Old Spanish lexemes, is denominated western JS. The twentieth century witnessed the annihilation of many of the eastern Mediterranean communities as a result of Nazi persecution, and in the late 1950s the fear of persecution also threatened many of the Moroccan communities. And so, with the displacement and dispersal of the old JS-speaking communities from their traditional centers, largely towards Israel but also to Europe, North and South America, speakers came into contact with, and eventually adopted, the language of their new surroundings.

A current debate on JS nomenclature raises some interesting points about linguistic evolution and linguistic consciousness. In the eastern Mediterranean the language is referred to by a variety of names. In general, two persons who speak the same language do not feel the need to identify to one another the language they are speaking; however, the need for identification does arise when they come into contact with non-native speakers. This could well explain why, following the break-up of traditional communities in the eastern Mediterranean in the early nineteenth century, the language is confusingly referred to by a variety of names. *Spanyol* is perhaps the most commonly used among speakers of the language, with its unmistakable reference to their linguistic and cultural origins. Its widespread use is confirmed by the Modern Hebrew coinage *Spanyolit* (*Spanyol* + Heb. suffix for forming language names), the name by which the language was referred to until quite recently in Israel. *Ladino*, probably the earliest attested name, has the widest cur-

rency today, and certainly so in Israel where the largest speech-communities in the modern world are to be found. The term has another application which is discussed below. The names *Judezmo* and *Judió/Jidió*, which are registered in some nineteenth- and early twentieth-century communal publications, clearly have the function of underlining a Jewish identification among speakers. *Judezmo* is the JS word for "Judaism", and, for this reason, is used by certain scholars today who wish, on ideological grounds, to draw a semantic equation between *Judezmo* and *Yiddish*; however, it seems rather late in the day to rename the language. Faced by this terminological plurality, scholarship has generally opted for the more descriptive and neutral "Judeo-Spanish".

In the western Mediterranean, the language is frequently referred to as *hakitía* (formed on Moroccan Arabic *haka* "to converse" + diminutive suffix), although it is interesting to note that with the renewed impact of Modern Spanish in this area in the nineteenth century, the term is reserved by speakers to describe an artificial language of humor which abounds in archaic forms of Spanish and Hispanicized arabisms, or else to the language as spoken in some distant past. However, though it is more similar to Modern Spanish than its eastern counterpart, the language continues to preserve many characteristic features.

Up to the beginning of the twentieth century the language was almost always written in Hebrew characters using the standard Hebrew alphabet with some modifications, mostly in the form of diacritical marks, to accommodate Hispanic phonemes. The earliest texts appeared in "square" characters either with or without vowels, but the bulk of printed material is in a cursive (rabbinic) script. Some early manuscripts preserve a cursive script known as *solitreo*, which is still in use among native speakers in personal correspondence, for example.

Two views about the origins of JS prevail. One holds that Jews in medieval Spain spoke the same language as their non-Jewish contemporaries, while drawing on Hebrew terms to express religio-cultural concepts not current in Spanish (for example *shabbat*), and preserving, at the same time, a number of archaisms. The language thus acquires a separate linguistic identity only after 1492. The second view, which is gaining greater currency, maintains that JS, while being essentially a form of spoken medieval Spanish, had linguistic features of its own long before 1492, owing not merely to the presence of Hebrew words, but also to the peculiar sociolinguistic conditions which affected Jewish communities during their long history in the Iberian Peninsula, and to the greater linguistic receptivity by Jews to the waning Arabic culture. Thus the Arabic borrowing *alhad* ("the first [day]") is retained for "Sunday" in preference to the Spanish *domingo* (from Latin *dies Dominicus* "the Lord's day"), with its Christian connotation; *alhad* appears in medieval texts and continues to be in use in both eastern and western JS.

The first editions of the JS Bible translations appeared in the sixteenth century, although these are believed to reflect an earlier tradition elaborated by the Spanish Jews long before their expulsion. The language of these texts is usually referred to in scholarship as *Ladino*: it is characterized by an artificiality which permeates, especially, the lexicon and syntax, and which is the result of a method of translation where the strictest adherence to the Hebrew original is the rule. It is generally accepted that these texts do not reflect the spoken language, although clearly they share common features with it. Two centuries later, the first complete Ladino translation of the Old Testament in Hebrew characters (1739–45) was edited in Constantinople by Abraham Assa, and editions of it continued to be produced throughout the eighteenth and nineteenth centuries. This highly literal method of translation was so widely accepted that it was even adopted by Christian missionaries in 1873 in their JS Bible translation. The same method is also reflected by translations of liturgical works which first appeared in the sixteenth century and have continued to do so up to the present. Among them are the Ladino translations of the daily and festival prayerbooks, manuscript fragments of which date from before the Expulsion, the *Haggadah*, and the *Pirkei 'avot*. Halakhic literature dating from the sixteenth century also displays this translation language and incorporates much Hebrew phraseology; however, the language does not show the same degree of rigid adherence to Hebrew as that found in the Ladino Bible and liturgical translations. Among these is a selection from Yosef Caro's *Shulhan arukh* entitled *Shulhan hapanim* (Salonica, 1568).

The reader of JS, as opposed to Ladino, literature may be struck by the fact that the language he is reading reflects a spoken rather than a literary variety. The sensation is of a strong tradition of oral literature, which is eventually committed to paper. A notable case is that of the traditional ballads known as *romances*, which comprise many medieval Spanish examples of the genre, as well as more recent ones based on the traditional model. But JS texts in Hebrew characters also number among the earliest witnesses of Spanish literary activity. The *kharjas* incorporated into the poetry of such major figures of the Golden Age of Hebrew verse in Spain as Yehudah Halevi in the eleventh and twelfth centuries, are an example of this as is a fifteenth-century fragment of an early JS poem on the biblical story of Joseph, *Coplas de Yoçef*.

The best-known and most widely translated JS work of the post exilic period is the *Me'am lo'ez* (1730), which was begun by Yaacov Khuli and continued over a long period, in series form, by a number of different authors writing under the same title. A midrashic work, the *Me'am lo'ez* is structured mainly on the Pentateuch and spans the sources of Jewish thought. The beginning of the nineteenth century saw the growth of a secular literature, which was popular, for the most part, and included a sizable corpus of original compositions such as novels, short stories, plays, and popular histories as well as adaptations of major European novels of the period, where the impact of French on JS is significantly felt. This is also observed in the JS press which began to flourish in the eastern Mediterranean at the same time; only a small number of newspapers continue to appear today.

There can be no doubt, therefore, as to the slow disappearance of JS as a spoken language. Traditional linguistic registers are gradually being overtaken by those of the co-territorial languages, and the language is no longer transmitted to succeeding generations in the normal manner. Today, only small clusters of native speakers, usually of an advanced age, are to be found scattered around the globe. However, although the spoken language may have been the principal vehicle for the transmission of JS culture up to now, as the language "dies", more and more people seem to be taking to the pen in order to write in and about it. At first sight this may appear paradoxical. However, a spoken language looks partly to the written word for conservation, and this becomes, in turn, a different vehicle for the transmission of a culture and guards against its annihilation.

FURTHER READING

Armistead, S. G. and Silverman, J. H.: *Folk Literature of the Sephardic Jews*, 1 (Berkeley: University of California Press, 1971)

Benabu, I. and Sermoneta, J., eds: *Judeo-Romance Languages* (Jerusalem: The Hebrew University & Misgav Yerushalayim, 1985)

Harris, T. K., ed.: Sociology of Judezmo: the language of the eastern Sephardim. *International Journal of the Sociology of Language* 37 (1983)

Stern, S. M.: *Hispano-Arabic Strophic Poetry*; ed. L. P. Harvey (Oxford: Clarendon Press, 1974)

ISAAC BENABU

K

Kabak, Aharon Avraham (1880–1944)
Hebrew novelist. Born in Smorgon, Lithuania,
Kabak traveled a great deal and lived in
Odessa, Constantinople, and France before
settling in Jerusalem in 1911. His novels,
influenced by French realism, predominantly
reflect the world of east European Jewry at the
turn of the nineteenth century, although he did
not use symbols and motifs from Judaic sources.
His early works describe the dilemmas of young
Jews caused by their having to choose between
Haskalah (Enlightenment), traditional Judaism,
assimilation, social revolution, and the Jewish
national movement.

Kabak is the only Hebrew writer to have
written a novel on Jesus, *Bamish'ol hatzar* (1937;
On the Narrow Path, 1968), probably his finest
work. He portrays Jesus in human terms as a
martyr and a Jewish personification of redemption. Having written it at the time of his return
to Jewish Orthodoxy, Kabak attempts to present, through the character of Jesus, the visionary who desires to bring redemption to the
world by means of his suffering. Kabak's actual
purpose was to stress the need for redemption
even in the period of national revival.

His three-volume work, *Shlomo Molkho* (1927–
9), similarly depicts the problem of the Messiah
and messianism, in addition to providing an
authentic evocation of Catholicism, the Reformation, the Marranos, and the Kabbalists of
Safed.

Kabak wrote many volumes of stories and
criticism and published translations from European languages. His later novels include the
unfinished cycle, *Toldot mishpahah 'ahat* (1942–

5; The history of one family) which reflected
Jewish life in eastern Europe and in Palestine
through the realistic portrayal of a Russian–
Jewish family.

GLENDA ABRAMSON

Kafka, Franz (1883–1924) Austrian novelist. Born into a Jewish family largely assimilated to the German-speaking community in
Prague, Kafka studied law at Prague University, and became one of the few Jews employed in
the public service when in 1909 he joined the
partially state-run accident insurance company
for industrial workers. After the diagnosis of
tuberculosis in 1917, he spent long periods of
leave in sanatoria, and took early retirement in
1922. His writing was done under unfavorable
circumstances, after work or on sick leave, and
the bulk of it was published only posthumously.

Kafka's earliest (1912) published works, the
sketches in *Betrachtung (Meditation*, 1949), are
sometimes fantasies, sometimes realistic evocations of aspects of everyday life. Much of the
major fiction Kafka wrote between 1912 and
1914 is set against a similarly ordinary background which helps persuade the reader to
accept the fantastic events described. In *Das
Urteil* (1913; *The Judgement*, 1949), a father sentences his son to death, whereupon the son
obediently drowns himself, while in *Die Ver-
wandlung* (1917; *The Transformation*, 1949), the
son of the household is transformed into an
unspecified insect. The tragi-comic *Der Verschol-
lene* (1927) shows an innocent European loose in

a fanciful version of the USA. Much grimmer is *Der Prozess* (1925; *The Trial*, 1937), in which a successful banker is charged with an offence that is never spelt out and falls under the power of a mysterious court which finally has him executed. And in *In der Strafkolonie* (1919; *In the Penal Settlement*, 1949) Kafka describes in minute technical detail how prisoners, condemned under an arbitrary judicial system, are tortured to death on a machine which inscribes on their bodies the law they have transgressed.

The shorter fiction written during the First World War hints at the decay of civilization. In *Der neue Advokat* (1917; *The New Advocate*, 1949), the war-horse of Alexander the Great settles for a quiet career as a lawyer; in *Ein altes Blatt* (1917; *An Old Manuscript*, 1949), nomads invade a Chinese-sounding capital which the Emperor can no longer protect; and in *Ein Landarzt* (1918; *A Country Doctor*, 1949) the doctor, unable to heal an apparently supernatural wound, is left stranded in "the frost of this most unhappy of ages". Convalescence in the country in the winter of 1917–18 gave Kafka leisure to ponder social and religious questions and express his conclusions in pithy and profound aphorisms (some available in English as "Reflections on Sin, Pain, Hope and the True Way", 1933).

After this turning-point, Kafka's fiction focuses more sharply on themes such as the situation of the artist ("First Sorrow", 1949, "A Hunger Artist", 1949, and "Josephine the Singer, or the Mouse-folk", 1949) or the seeker after knowledge ("Investigations of a Dog", 1933). *Das Schloss* (1926; *The Castle*, 1953) shows its hero trying to make contact with officials of the inaccessible Castle and to found a household with the village girl, Frieda, and failing in both.

Much is known about Kafka's tormented personal life from his copious diaries and letters and from the long, accusing "Letter to his Father" written (but not delivered) in 1919. His relationship with his authoritarian father obviously helped to inspire his fiction, as did the emotional difficulties that wrecked his relationships with Felice Bauer (to whom he was twice engaged, in 1914 and 1917), Julie Wohryzek, and his Czech translator, Milena Jesenská. In the last year of his life he seems to

Franz Kafka

have found comparative happiness with Dora Dymant, with whom he lived in Berlin in the winter of 1923–4. But his fiction contains more than personal themes. His legal training underlies the recurring metaphors of law, trial, guilt, and judgment, and his demonstrations of how authorities misuse legal machinery to incriminate the accused. His bureaucratic career inspired his grotesquely comic depictions of harassed and obstructive officials. And some of his later fiction reveals an interest in Jewish matters which was first aroused by Yiddish actors who visited Prague in 1911–12, and later by wartime refugees from Galicia. By 1917 he was in sympathy with Zionism and beginning to learn Hebrew, and he talked of emigrating to Palestine.

Kafka's literary originality consists in inventing multivalent, dream-like images, like the insect in *The Transformation*. This image releases many implications, sometimes mutually contradictory: it implies disgust with physical life, yet lets the hero revel in his new-found animality; it brings painful isolation, but also release from work and family pressures. These and other connotations are highlighted in turn. Elsewhere Kafka describes fantastic objects and institutions (the punishment-machine in *In the Penal Settlement*, the bureaucracy in *The Castle*) in meticulous and sober detail. Kafka also varies narrative with passages of argument and discussion in which people distort logic to serve their semi-conscious wishes and interests. Although his images recall Expressionism, his limpid, concise and understated style is modeled on classical nineteenth-century German prose.

BIBLIOGRAPHY

America, trans. W. Muir and E. Muir (London: Secker & Warburg, 1949; New York: Schocken, 1962); *The Trial*, trans. D. Scott and C. Waller (London: Picador, 1977); *The Castle*, trans. W. Muir and E. Muir with additional material translated by E. Wilkins and E. Kaiser (London: Secker & Warburg, 1953; New York Knopf, 1954); *Stories 1904–24*, trans. J. A. Underwood (London: Macdonald, 1981); *Diaries*, trans. J. Kresh et al. (London: Secker & Warburg, 1949; New York: Schocken, 1948–9); *Letters to Friends, Family and Editors*, trans. R. Winston and C. Winston (London: Calder, 1978)

FURTHER READING

Politzer, H.: *Franz Kafka: Parable and Paradox* (Ithaca: Cornell University Press, 1962)
Robertson, R.: *Kafka: Judaism, Politics, and Literature* (Oxford: Clarendon Press, 1985)

RITCHIE ROBERTSON

Kahan, Ya'akov (1881–1960) Hebrew poet and playwright. Born in Slutsk, Russia, he moved with his family to the vicinity of Lodz, Poland, where he was educated in a progressive Jewish school. Largely self-taught in Hebrew and world literature, he wrote Hebrew poetry and criticism at a young age and translated German lyrical poetry. Kahan acquired the reputation (being so acclaimed by Hayyim Nahman BIALIK in the famous essay *Shiratenu*

hatze'irah) as the most purely lyrical of Hebrew poets at the outset of the twentieth century.

Kahan's first collections of poetry appeared after he had moved to Berne, Switzerland, where he received a doctorate in 1909 for his thesis, "A critique of the concept of genius". According to A. Sha'anan, Kahan's poetry reflects the "vitalism" of his close friend, Ya'akov Klatzkin, and of Henri BERGSON, as well as the symbolism of Stefan Georg and Maurice Maeterlinck. This attraction to the non-rational is seen to account for Kahan's movement from his "silk-like" lyricism to poems of cultural revolt, and to such affirmations of militarism and Zionist Revisionism as these famous lines of his poem *Biryonim*: "Through blood and fire did Judea fall/ Through blood and fire will Judea arise".

During his years in Switzerland Kahan founded *Ivriyyah*, an international organization for Hebrew language and culture. He also edited the journal, *Ha'ivri hehadash*, which heralded a new Hebraic humanism of universal scope. His major editorial contributions were to the journals, *Hatekufah*, in Warsaw (where he arrived around 1919) and *Keneset*, in Palestine after his emigration there in 1934.

Kahan was extremely prolific as a playwright and translator. He composed nearly thirty plays, most of them in verse form, dealing with major personalities such as David, Solomon, and Elijah and their mythical or world-historical significance for Jewish destiny. According to Gershon SHAKED, most of Kahan's plays are "melodramas of ideas, which have an added dimension of the folk tale". His translations from Goethe are regarded as a tour-deforce.

FURTHER READING

Nash, S.: The Hebraists of Berne and Berlin circa 1905. In *The Great Transition*, eds G. Abramson and T. Parfitt (Totowa: Rowman & Allanheld, 1985)
Silberschlag, E.: *From Renaissance to Renaissance*, vol. 1 (New York: Ktav, 1983)

STANLEY NASH

Kahana (Hermann), Aharon (1904–1967) Israeli painter, ceramic artist, and muralist. Born in Stuttgart, West Germany, Kahana studied at the Academy of Art, and later in

Berlin and Paris. His early style was post-Cubist and in Paris Fauvism captured his imagination. He emigrated to Palestine in 1934 and continued (as in Berlin) as a window dresser. Together with his wife he studied ceramics in Paris in 1947. Kahana was founder member of the art group "New Horizons" (1947–8) which created a forum for the new generation of artists interested in Modernist–Abstract painting, distinct from the sentimentality of Jerusalem-based figurative artists. Subsequently he participated in all its group exhibitions until his resignation in 1957. From 1950 he divided his time between Paris and Israel and, together with his wife, made several decorative, ceramic abstract murals.

Kahana's early style was influenced by German Expressionism and the Paris School, and his themes were predominantly biblical. During the 1940s and 1950s his palette darkened and his compositions are of dense, complex forms, veering between Cubism and Primitivism. In the 1950s his style changed, and his forms became increasingly abstract. Eventually he evolved an abstract symbolism: his abstract forms were derived from archaeological finds and ancient pots, forms reminiscent of several ancient Mediterranean cultures, the so called "Semitic Symbolism". The same ideas also inspired his and his wife's ceramic work, such as the mural at the Hebrew University's Givat Ram campus in Jerusalem.

His stylistic transition can be exemplified by his series on the *Akedah* (the binding of Isaac), a subject he painted repeatedly between 1950 and 1955. Symbolism plays a crucial role in *The Large Akedah* (1951; The Stedelijk Museum, Amsterdam) through the omission of the ram. In an *Akedah* of 1954 the ram is depicted climbing on the altar. The fate of Israel and the Jews was close to his heart and he painted a series of "torso paintings" as a memorial to the Holocaust. His wife claimed that his premature death on the eve of the Six Day War was probably caused by his worry about the sacrifice the nation might have to make.

NEDIRA YAKIR BUNYARD

Kahana-Carmon, Amalia
Israeli author. Kahana-Carmon was born in Tel Aviv. In her stories of the 1960s, collected in the volume, *Under One Roof* (1966), Kahana-Carmon has shunned treatment of political themes, as well as any narrative expansion that would assist the reader's orientation. The reader is thus plunged directly into a world of private intensity, conveyed by an unadorned but rich language. The subjects relate to the author's own subjectivity, the feeling of the individual, and the difficulty and unpredictability of relationships. Although the sentences are usually short, they have to bear considerable weight.

The reflective consciousness of the stories and novels is female, both in relation to her own life, and to any other. Sometimes, a character is traced from youth in one work, through to later life in another, as in an early story in her first volume, and then in the novel, *And Moon in the Valley of Ajalon* (1971). Kahana-Carmon incorporated the story into the later novel, as an echo of what was still ringing in the characters' memories.

Concern with romantic attachment and its workings is played on too in the tryptich *Magnetic Fields* (1977) and in the historical/mythical story "Up in Montifer" (1984). The language is carefully shaped, and has a special place within the canon of Israeli fiction.

BIBLIOGRAPHY
Na'ima Sasson writes poems. In *Meetings with the Angel*, eds B. Tammuz and L. Yudkin (London: André Deutsch, 1973)

FURTHER READING
Yudkin, L. I.: *1948 and After: Aspects of Israeli Fiction* (Manchester: University of Manchester Press, JSS Monograph Series 4, 1984)

LEON I. YUDKIN

Kahanowitz [Kaganovitsh], Pinye [Pinkhes] [Der Nister]
(1884–1950) Yiddish novelist and short-story writer. Born in Berdichev, Ukraine, the young Kahanowitz was influenced by his elder brother, a follower of Bratslaver Hasidism, and by the hasidic stories of Reb Nahman of Bratslav, and was steeped in the study of Hebrew and kabbalistic literature. Unlike his literary contemporaries who held Hasid-

Pinye Kahanowitz [Der Nister]

earned money as a teacher of Hebrew. He traveled to Berlin where he published two volumes entitled *Gedakht*, (1922; Contemplations) in the style of Reb Nahman. He returned to the Ukraine where he published *Fun mayne giter* (1929; From my treasures) which displays a new-found pessimism and spiritual anguish. In *Di mishpokhe Mashber* (The family Mashber), his major work, (first volume Moscow, 1939) he abandoned his mystical style for the realism of the other Russian novelists. However, by placing the novel in the Berdichev of the 1870s he avoided the contemporary world from which he felt alienated. During the Second World War he wrote stories about Nazi-occupied Poland which were published in New York in 1957. His last novel, *Fun finftn yor* (From the fifth year), on which he had worked for nearly ten years, was published posthumously in *Sovetish heymland* in Moscow in January 1964. Der Nister was arrested in early 1949 and died following an operation in a prison hospital in 1950.

DEVRA KAY

ism in disdain, he admired the simplicity and piety of the committed devout as seen in his first volume *Gedanken un motivn*, (1907; Thoughts and motives). In 1908 he moved to Kiev where he became a leading member of the Kiev group of Jewish intellectuals. He was enthusiastically received by Peretz in Warsaw in 1910 but would not stay in a large city. His two books *Hekher fun der erd* (1910; Higher than the Earth), and *Gezang un gebet* (1912; Song and prayer) are concerned with kabbalistic themes and mysticism. His pseudonym which means "the concealed" alludes to his involvement in mysticism.

He remained apolitical during the First World War and the Russian Revolution, isolating himself from his contemporaries. To avoid the draft he lived under an assumed name and

Kahn, Gustave (1859–1936) French poet, novelist and critic. Born in Metz, his parents moved to Paris in 1870. Imbued with a love of literature and the arts, he followed the courses at the École des Chartes absentmindedly. Military service in North Africa (1880–4) came almost as a relief and was to prove an esthetically rewarding experience, providing him with the imagery and colors of the Orient, a prominent feature of his poetry and short stories, especially those with a biblical setting. As editor of *Vogue* (1886) and *La Revue Indépendante* (1887) and contributor to numerous literary and libertarian reviews (*La Revue Blanche, La Société Nouvelle, La Jeune Belgique, Idée Moderne, La Plume, La Nouvelle Revue, Le Mercure de France*, etc.) he quickly made his reputation. Later, he also wrote weekly columns on varied subjects for daily newspapers, notably *Le Quotidien* (1923–36). From 1932 until his death he edited the French–Jewish review *Menorah*.

Together with his friend Jules Laforgue, Kahn was one of the first to practice and defend the then revolutionary free verse (*vers libre*), which substituted natural rhythm for traditional rhyme, and lines of irregular numbers of syllables for regular, fixed metre. The emphasis in free verse, and in symbolist esthetics in general, on freedom from artificial constraints came close to anarchist aspirations although without the latter's social commitment. Kahn moved closer to socialism after the Dreyfus Affair, a move reinforced when he worked with Léon Blum during the First World War. The Affair was also instrumental in making him conscious of his Jewish roots, felt even more strongly in face of the anti-Semitism of the 1930s. Though different from André Spire and Edmond Fleg who went further along the same path, he belongs, with them, to a small group of writers who celebrated in French their Jewish heritage, thereby adding a distinct voice to modern French poetry.

BIBLIOGRAPHY

Contes Juifs (Paris: Fasquelle, 1926); *Terre d'Israël, Contes Juifs* (Paris: Fasquelle, 1933)

FURTHER READING

Ireson, J. C.: *L'Oeuvre Poétique de Gustave Kahn* (Paris: Nizet, 1962)

NELLY WILSON

Kalischer, Zevi Hirsch (1795–1874) Rabbi, messianic theorist and activist. Kalischer lived in the Posen district of Prussia and, financially supported by his wife, devoted himself to community service and scholarship. An expert in Talmud and knowledgable in Jewish philosophy, he wrote commentaries on the Talmud, Bible, Passover Haggadah, issues of contemporary Jewish law, and a treatise reconciling religion and philosophy. His most influential work was *Derishat tziyyon*, an essay and anthology of traditional halakhic and aggadic prooftexts showing that God desired human initiative in ending the Jewish exile and bringing the Messianic Age. This conviction contradicted the centuries-old dominant rabbinic tradition mandating messianic passivity.

In his works Kalischer argued that since God influences history in subtle ways without violating natural laws, both divine and human acts

Zevi Hirsch Kalischer

are necessary to bring the Messianic Age. Jews must initiate the process by agriculturally resettling the Land of Israel and restoring sacrificial worship there. God would then usher in the supernatural phase of the Messianic Age including the miracles foretold in biblical prophecies.

Kalischer's messianic activities began in 1836, when he drafted a plan to acquire the Temple Mount and restore sacrificial worship. While he continued to believe that the sacrifice renewal was central to the messianic process, he turned, in the 1860s, to the more popular task: the agricultural resettlement of Palestine. He worked independently and through the Kolonisations-Verein für Palästina (which he helped found) to gain support and raise funds for the establishment of religious agricultural communes. These activities have led some historians to describe Kalischer as a proto-Zionist.

Kalischer's writings and activities eventually helped legitimize messianic activism, and his formulation of it is used today by religious Jews who regard the State of Israel as a step toward the Messianic Age.

FURTHER READING

Katz, J.: Tsevi Hirsch Kalischer. In *Guardians of Our Heritage*, ed. L. Jung (New York: Bloch, 1958)

Myers, J. E.: Zevi Hirsch Kalischer and the origins of Religious Zionism. In *From East and West: Jews in a Changing Europe*, ed. F. Malino and D. Sorkin (Oxford: Basil Blackwell, 1989)

JODY ELIZABETH MYERS

Kalisky, René (1936–1981) Belgian essayist and playwright. He was born in Brussels, where a sympathetic family saved him from the camps. He studied and practiced journalism until 1971. With the encouragement of Jacques Lemarchand of Gallimard, who published his first plays, he settled in Paris in 1972 to devote himself to essays and drama. His work in both genres is marked by brilliantly original theories and keen interest in the gamut of Jewish history. Early essays include "L'Origine et l'essor du monde arabe" (1968; The Origins and development of the Arab world), "Le monde arabe à l'heure actuelle" (1968; The Arab world today), and "Sionisme ou dispersion?" (1974; Zionism or diaspora?).

The essay "Le Théâtre climatisé" (1971; The air-conditioned theater), censures the modern stage for abandoning its origins in sacred rite and metaphysics in order to make often facile political statements. As example, the representation of Hitlerism as a "military-sado-masochistic hiatus", ignores facets of Nazism which have no referent in our age. Art might better probe what Kalisky advances as the underlying cause of the National Socialist rise to power: its irresistible appeal to people whose "agonizing availability" ("angoissante disponibilité") forms the very foundation of our crisis-ridden civilization.

Jim le téméraire (1972; Jim the lionhearted), illustrates the point. Years after the war, Jim (Chaim), an enervated 40-year-old, lies abed, studying the mythological roots of Nazism.

Lacking all Jewish identity, ambition, and self-esteem, he is obsessed with ideologies which feed on the abnegation of the individual and views Hitler as a genuine messiah. The play also shatters conventional notions of time. It brings to Jim's bedside Hitler's wrangling acolytes and the Führer himself, whose unlikely ally Jim becomes. With the hindsight conferred by the quarter century that has passed, Jim is able to warn Hitler of his chieftains' schemes to betray his cause. The work bids us regard Jim as representative of those whose "agonizing availability" renders them vulnerable to fascination with totalitarianism.

It is perhaps in *Dave au bord de mer* (1978; Dave on the beach), that Kalisky most effectively defies time and space, at the same time illustrating Robert Aron's observation that there is a special confluence of past, present, and future for the Jew. Set in modern Israel, *Dave* reworks the biblical account of the troubled relationship between Saul and David. This Saul and his wife have prospered in the modern state they helped hew from the wilderness. Dave is a young musician from New York, where he had emigrated after a European childhood spent in hiding. Like characters in Pirandello's theater, these protagonists strive to change the course of their play; they struggle with one another, and against both their scriptural roles and the dangers that threaten contemporary Israel.

Other plays in which Kalisky demonstrates his conviction that there is no chronology man cannot overturn include *Sur les ruines de Carthage* (1980; On the ruins of Carthage), where specialists in ancient history join battle over professional and scholarly differences, and *Falsch* (1983), whose publication and premiere he did not live to see. Here the story of Joseph and his brothers is woven into the memories of Joe Falsch as he recalls his family's efforts to escape the Nazis.

In *Aïda vaincue* (1979; Aida defeated) the playwright draws on his own life to depict the reunion of a family whose patriarch had vanished in Auschwitz, as had Kalisky's father.

In his single long prose piece, *L'Impossible royaume* (1979; The impossible kingdom) the filming of the Maccabean Revolt serves as a frame for Kalisky's contention that the existence of Israel should not mean the end of Jewish universalism, nor should Israel be delegated authority for world Jewish affairs.

Kalisky was awarded the Belgian Society of Authors' annual prize for dramatic literature in 1974, and the Grand Prix Triennal for dramatic literature in 1975. The Belgian Society of Authors and Dramatic Composers paid posthumous homage to his work with its Prix Special in 1982. *Falsch* was awarded the Best Foreign Play prize by the German Theater Heute in 1987.

FURTHER READING

Schiff, E.: *From Stereotype to Metaphor: The Jew in Contemporary Drama* (Albany: State University of New York, 1982)

Willinger, D., ed.: *An Anthology of Contemporary Belgian Plays, 1970–1982* (Troy, NY: Whitston, 1984)

ELLEN SCHIFF

Kallen, Horace (1882–1974) American philosopher, writer, and teacher. Kallen was born in Berenstadt, Silesia (Germany), the son of a rabbi. He was brought to the USA in 1887, at the age of five. He was educated at Harvard (1899–1903), where his most important teachers were William James, George Santayana, and Josiah Royce. His first aspiration was to become a novelist and poet, and he taught English for two years (1903–5) at Princeton. He returned to Harvard to take his doctorate in philosophy in 1908 and to teach philosophy at Harvard and Clark from 1908 to 1911. He then taught psychology and philosophy for seven years at The University of Wisconsin, and he wrote a study of what he called contrasting theories of life: *William James and Henri Bergson*, published by The University of Chicago in 1914. He also published a striking and controversial study of *The Book of Job as a Greek Tragedy* in 1918. At the end of the First World War he published two volumes, *The Structure of Peace* and *The League of Nations, Today and Tomorrow*, and he became for a time an associate of Colonel House, who was an adviser to President Wilson at the Peace Conference in Versailles. In 1919 he helped to found The New School For Social Research in New York, along with

Charles Beard, John Dewey, James Harvey Robinson, and Thorstein Veblen.

He has been credited with two major contributions to social philosophy: his theory of cultural pluralism and his advocacy of consumer cooperation. Kallen was among the first to advise other immigrants to take pride in their national origins, to keep their native language as second to English, and to learn more of the history, literature, and customs of their own people as well as of the USA. The USA he argued, was less like Israel ZANGWILL's "melting pot" than it was like a symphony orchestra, to which various nationalities contributed their tonalities like different instruments. His theory may be compared to Walt Whitman's conception of America as "a nation of nations". America, Kallen thought, should not only tolerate but welcome differences (including racial differences); it should be strong and unified politically but culturally diverse. He was against forcing or hurrying the inevitable process of Americanization and assimilation. As an example, he was at the same time a loyal American, a loyal Jew, and an early Zionist. These loyalties, he thought (as Louis BRANDEIS did) reinforced rather than conflicted with each other.

FURTHER READING

Ratner, S., ed.: *Vision and Action: Essays in Honor of Horace Kallen on his 70th Birthday* (New Brunswick: Rutgers University Press, 1953)

Hook, S., and Konvitz, M., eds: *Freedom and Experience* (Ithaca: Cornell University Press, 1947)

MILTON HINDUS

Kaminska [Helpern]**, Ester Rachel** (1868–1925) Jewish theater and film actress. She made her debut in 1888 in Warsaw at the Eldorado, the theater of her future husband, Abraham Kaminski. In 1905, after great success in Petersburg, she was described as the "Jewish Soul". She also performed outside Poland and Russia, in various European countries and in North America. In 1913 she established the Abraham Kaminski Jewish Memorial Theatre. Her more distinguished creations include parts in plays by Jacob GORDIN (*Mirele Efros*), Avrom GOLDFADEN, Ibsen (*Nora*) and Dumas (*Camille*.

She also took part in Jewish films produced in Poland, for instance *Mirele Efros* (1912) and *Tkies-Kaf* (An Oath, 1924). Ester Kaminska became the most eminent actress in the history of the Jewish theater.

Her daughter, Ida Kaminska (1899–1978), also became a distinguished Jewish actress. She began performing in the theater of her father, Abraham, and continued her work in the Jewish theaters of Warsaw and other cities. During the years 1921–8, together with Zygmunt Turkow she ran the WIKT (Warshawer Jidisher Kunst-Teater), but after 1933 she established her own theater. At the beginning of the Second World War she took charge of the Jewish Theater in Lvov, but after the German invasion of the USSR she left for the Kirghis town of Frunze. There she organized a Jewish theater company which performed in many towns in Asia. She returned to Poland in 1947 and continued her work in the Jewish theaters of Lodz, Wrocław, and Warsaw. In 1955 the Warsaw Jewish National Theater, with which she also performed successfully abroad, was named in memory of her mother. Kaminska adapted for the Jewish stage Dostoyevsky's *The Brothers Karamazov* and E. Orzeszkowa's *Meir Ezefowicz*. She was noted for her parts in such plays as Jacob Gordin's *Mirele Efros*, Ibsen's *Nora*, and Brecht's *Mother Courage*. She emigrated to the USA in 1968.

MARIAN FUKS

Kaniuk, Yoram (b.1930) Israeli author. Kaniuk was born in Tel Aviv. His earliest published work, *The Acrophile* (1961), is a portrait of alienation. In this short novel, the objectively correlated situation is of the Israeli living in New York, dwarfed and distanced by the giant city. Written in the first person, the narrator becomes attached to the alienating situation, and falls in love with the vast heights, such a contrast to his own personal shortness.

Kaniuk is not a realistic novelist. Situations are exaggerated to grotesque proportions. The fictional marker is the telescope or the microscope. As the subjects are large, so the specific plot enlarges the figures still further. As the Jews were threatened with extermination, so he

relates in a massive novel, *Hayehudi ha'aharon* (1982; The last Jew), the story of that last Jew. But the other large subject that he treats is even more specifically Israeli, that of local alienation on the part of Israel's own inhabitants.

Confessions of a Good Arab (1984) is told from the point of view (although in the third person) of someone of who is half-Jew and half-Arab, distrusted and ultimately rejected by both communities. Both the anger and the expressed estrangement of Kaniuk's work find an appropriate theme in this novel, which, although still in the spirit of the grotesque, approaches realism. In the expression here, the linguistic aphorism becomes the paradox of plot.

BIBLIOGRAPHY
Himmo, King of Jerusalem (London: Chatto & Windus; New York; Atheneum, 1962); *Rocking Horse* (New York: Harper & Row, 1977); *His Daughter* (London: Peter Holban, 1988)

LEON I. YUDKIN

Kaplan, Mordecai Menahem (1881–1983) Rabbi, naturalistic theologian, and founder of the Reconstructionist movement. Kaplan was born in Svencianys, Lithuania, arriving with his family in the USA at the age of nine. He studied at the Jewish Theological Seminary and, after his ordination there, served as Rabbi to the Orthodox Kehillat Jeshurun Synagogue, a position he felt obliged eventually to relinquish because he could no longer accept the dogmas regarding the transmission of the Torah upon which Orthodoxy is based. In 1909 Kaplan was appointed dean of the Teachers' Institute at the Jewish Theological Seminary and he later served as Professor of Homiletics at the Seminary, influencing more than one generation of Conservative Rabbis. Kaplan founded the Reconstructionist movement to cut across the usual divisions into Orthodox, Reform, and Conservative. In the opinion of this movement Judaism is, to be sure, a religion but it is more than that. In the language of Kaplan's influential book, *Judaism as a Civilization* (1934) the Jewish religion embraces the whole of life, art, music, drama, folk customs, as well as religion in the narrow sense.

Kaplan's understanding of the Jewish religion is severely naturalistic. God, in this scheme, is the name one gives to the power in the universe that makes for righteousness. Faith in God does not mean belief in a supernatural Being or Person but involves the conviction that the universe is so constituted that ultimately righteousness will win out. The precepts of Judaism – the *mitzvot* – are divine commands only in the sense that they enable the Jew to draw on this power in the universe for the enrichment and ennoblement of life. Prayer is not an appeal to an undecided God out there but is an act by means of which the attention of the worshipper is directed to the highest within himself.

BIBLIOGRAPHY

Mordecai Kaplan on his hundredth year. *Judaism*, vol. 30 (1981) 5–103

FURTHER READING

Davis, M., ed: *Mordecai M. Kaplan Jubilee Volume*, 2 vols. (New York: Jewish Theological Seminary, 1953) 9–33

LOUIS JACOBS

Karavan, Dani (b.1930)   Israeli sculptor and environmental artist. Born in Tel Aviv, Karavan studied with Aharon AVNI, Streichman, Steimatzky, and Marcel JANCO, as well as at the BEZALEL SCHOOL OF ARTS AND CRAFTS. While a kibbutz member he worked in the style of Socialist Realism. After his studies of fresco technique in Italy (1955–7), his style changed. The Italian public squares, housing sculpture and surrounded by articulated walls, building fronts, their shapes at times irregular (as in Siena for example), stirred Karavan's work towards estheticism. Karavan is primarily a sculptor of abstract geometrical forms, initially in decorative walls, as, for example, the wall in the Assembly Hall of the Knesset, Jerusalem (1966–70). Among other public walls are one in Basel, and a wall relief at the El Al terminal, Kennedy Airport, New York.

The other aspect of Karavan's work is of larger scale, in three dimensions, creating complete artistic environments for the viewers to face or to enter, and to experience new sculptural forms and spaces, both as external squares or internal hollows. *The Monument to the Negev Brigade* (1963–8) near Beersheba, is such a structure. Built in concrete, it consists of watchtowers, canals, and aqueducts, constructed mainly in a composition of tubular forms, some upright, others horizontal, with varying openings, so that the visitors experience different spatial hollows or open cavities, with dramatic changes of the desert light and shade. In 1976 Karavan exhibited at the Venice Biennale. More recently his outdoor public works include laserbeam, as in his *Laserbeam Environment: La Défense – Tour Eiffel; Ars + Machina 3* in Rennes, France, all created during 1984–5. Other public works in Europe are a central court for the Ludwig Museum, Cologne; a central three-kilometer axis near Paris, environmental work for the sculpture garden of the Brera Museum, Milan; environment in Amsterdam; a square in Heidelberg.

Karavan exhibits extensively in Europe and Israel, both in Group Exhibitions and one-man shows, including a one-man show at the *Musée d'art Moderne*, Paris (1983), of an aluminum mirrors environment, and environments in Breda, Rotterdam, The Hague, and Kröller-Müller, Otterlo. In 1983 he contributed a "Bridge" for the Seventeenth Biennale for Sculpture, Antwerp. Karavan believes that it is essential that a sculpture should not become overpowering and thus self-imposing, but always considers the measurements in relation to the viewer, creating a human scale. An ironic reality of modern public sculpture is that the abstract forms are more acceptable among the traditional and religious sectors of Jewish society.

NEDIRA YAKIR BUNYARD

Kardos, György G. (b.1925)   Hungarian writer. Born to a Jewish middle-class family with bohemian leanings (his father was a journalist), as a young man he was called up for wartime "labor service" and sent to the German-run labor camp of Bor in Yugoslavia. He was liberated by the partisans and he left for

Palestine via Bulgaria. After the formation of the State of Israel he served in the Israeli army. In 1951 he returned to Hungary and worked in theaters in Győr and Budapest. Later he was on the staff of the weekly *Élet és Irodalom*, before becoming a freelance writer.

Kardos wrote three novels about his post-war experiences in the Middle East: *Avraham Bogatir hét napja*, (1968; *Avraham's Good Week*, 1975), *Hová tűntek a katonák?* (1971; Where have all the soldiers gone?) and *A történet vége* (1977; The end of the story). This "Palestinian trilogy", which deals with the situation in Palestine before and soon after the establishment of the State of Israel, was praised for its realism and warm humor; in these novels Kardos shows how ethnically and culturally diverse was the human material that made up the new state of Israel. Shunning idealization, he describes conflicts between *sabras* and newcomers, hard-fisted orthodox peasants from Eastern Europe and quick-witted young opportunists from the Orient. His own standpoint could be defined as that of a libertarian socialist. Kardos's shorter prose is also enjoyable, e.g. "Do You Like Théophile Gautier?" *New Hungarian Quarterly*, 3 g, 1970, pp. 63–71 and "The First Lines" in the anthology *Present Continuous*, ed. I. Bart, 1985, pp. 44–57.

GEORGE GÖMÖRI

Karni, Yehuda (1884–1949) Hebrew poet. Born in Pinsk, Karni wrote Hebrew, Yiddish, and Russian poetry from an early age. His early poetry is abstract and Romantic and is chiefly influenced by H. N. BIALIK and Saul TSCHER-NICHOWSKI. He was active in *Po'alei Zion* and served as a representative in various Zionist congresses. Prior to and immediately after the First World War Karni lived in Vilna and Odessa, where he worked for Hebrew and Yiddish journals. In 1921 he came to Palestine. From 1923 until his death he was an editor of *Ha'aretz*, where he published thousands of topical articles and poems. Karni's work is characterized by his deep moral and esthetic sensitivity. His poetry became increasingly concrete under the pressure of current events in Palestine. He

was among the first Hebrew poets who successfully adopted the Sephardic accent, thus bringing Hebrew poetry closer to spoken Hebrew. Jerusalem is a recurrent motif in some of his best work and is the subject of his collection *Shirei yerushalayim* (1948; Songs of Jerusalem). Among his other volumes of poetry are *She'arim* (1923; Gates), *Bishe'arayikh moledet* (1935; Homeland in your gates) and *Shir vedema'* (1948; Song and tears). In his late work, Karni laments the victims of the Holocaust.

DAVID ABERBACH

Katz, Menke (b.1906) Yiddish and English poet. Born in Tsvintsyan, Lithuania, Menke Katz was spiritually closer to the neighboring village of Mikhalishek, where he spent two years as a youth during the First World War, and was inspired to write poetry. He emigrated to the USA in 1920. His first poems were published in English in 1922 and he made his Yiddish debuts in the journals *Baginen* (1923) and *Tsuzamen* (1924), and, most importantly, with "Bowery" in the trilingual (Yiddish/English/Russian) *Spartak* (1925), co-edited by V. Mayakovsky. His early career was characterized by the ambivalence of being among the Jewish literary Left in New York, while steadfastly refusing to adhere to its dictates. His first book, *Dray shvester* (1932; Three sisters) created a sensation in New York Yiddish literary circles because of its personal, mystical, and erotic tones which clashed with "socialist realism". His reputation as a poet was dramatically enhanced by the two-volume epic work *Brenendik shtetl* (1938; Burning village) which traced his life, and ultimately that of multitudes of Jews, from the *shtetl*, through the First World War, to the Lower East Side of New York City. He replied to the sharp criticism that followed with the more daring *S'hot dos vort mayn bobe Moyne* (1939; My Grandmother Moyne speaks). In 1944 he co-founded the journal *Mir*, which campaigned for an end to political meddling in literature.

Katz severed ties with the leftist Yiddish writers of New York in 1953, when news of Stalin's 1952 murders of Yiddish writers was confirmed.

The break led to two major innovations in Katz's poetry. The first, was an embracing of universalist and pan-Jewish thematics, e.g. in *Inmitn tog* (1954; In the middle of the day). He spent several years in Israel (1954–6, 1959–60), completing *Tsfas* (Safad) in 1956, which was published much later, in 1979. The second was the launch of a career in English poetry.

In English, Menke Katz became known as an innovator in poetic form. He experimented with twin sonnets, twin narrative chant royals, new chant royals, and unrhymed unrefrained chant royals. His essay "A word or two against rhyme" (*Poet Lore*, 1966) led to the publication of *Aspects of Modern Poetry: A Symposium* (1967). His "World of Old Abe" won the 1974 Stephen Vincent Benet Award. A new English version of *Brenendik shtetl*, entitled *Burning Village* (1972) was nominated for the Pulitzer Prize. Since 1962 he has edited the poetry magazine *Bitterroot*. In 1978 he settled in a forest in upstate New York. The sharply contrasting civilizations of Mikhalishek, the mystic island *shtetl* on the Lithuanian Viliya River, and the New York metropolis, are recurring themes in his poetry.

FURTHER READING
Evory, A., and Metzger, L., eds: *Contemporary Authors* (Detroit: Gale Research Co., 1984) vol. 11, 285–8
Kay, E., ed., *International Who's Who in Poetry* (Cambridge: Melrose, 1974–5) 234

DOVID KATZ

Kaufman, Bel American author and educator. Kaufman was born in Berlin and raised in Russia. Her grandfather was the Yiddish writer, SHOLEM ALEICHEM. Her mother, Lola Rabinowitz, published more than two thousand short stories. Kaufman graduated *magna cum laude* from Hunter College, and earned an MA from Columbia. She taught in New York high schools for 20 years. From 1964 she was English instructor at several New York colleges, including the New School, and the Borough of Manhattan Community College. She made TV and radio appearances and she was the recipient of plaques from the Anti-Defamation League and the United Jewish Appeal. In 1965 Nasson College in Maine gave her an honorary doctorate.

Her novel, *Up the Down Staircase* (1965) was named a Book-of-the-Month Club selection. In its first month in paperback it sold 1,500,000 copies. In 1967 it was made into a movie by Warner Brothers. It was awarded both the Paperback of the Year by the National Booksellers Institute in 1966, and the Bell Movie award.

In 1977, *Love, etc.* was published. Short stories have also been printed in *Esquire*, *Collier*'s, and *Saturday Review*. She has written plays for television, and has translated Russian lyrics for musicals.

She is a member of the executive board of PEN, of the Dramatists' Guild, the Authors' Guild, and Phi Beta Kappa.

FURTHER READING
New York Times Book Review (February 14 1965)
Saturday Review (March 20 1965)

RUTH ROSENBERG

Kaufman, Shirley (b.1923) American poet and translator. Born Shirley Pincus in Seattle, Washington, she married her first husband, Bernard Kaufman Jr, in 1946, two years after receiving her undergraduate degree from the University of California, Los Angeles. After raising three daughters Kaufman received her MA from San Francisco State University in 1967. Her first book *The Floor Keeps Turning* (1970) won the 1969 International Poetry Forum United States Award in a competition for publication by the University of Pittsburgh Press. Although the poems in this volume do not exactly fall into the confessional mode, a substantial number are highly personal, including poems about marriage, and, most poignantly, about difficult relationships between mothers and daughters. Her strong Jewish interests emerge in poems representing biblical figures ("His [Lot's] wife" and "Rebecca") and numerous poems about Israel, including "The western wall" in which the poet not only visits but identifies with the Wall, as little papers with prayers that "...fall/from every hollow, every crack, / fall in the small pores of my skin, / and I am huge with prayers I cannot hold". She continued to explore these themes and, in a more direct style, a broad range of human relationships in her second book, *Gold Country* (1973), dedicated to the memory of her mother.

Her translation of Abba KOVNER's poetry *A Canopy in the Desert* (1973), done in consultation with the poet, preceded a translation of the work of another Israeli poet, Amir GILBOA.

In 1974, Kaufman divorced, remarried, and moved to Jerusalem. Her volume *From One Life to Another* (1979) continues to explore family relationships as well as Israeli and Jewish, contemporary, and biblical themes. She often combines these threads in one poem as in "Divorce", in which the concluding imagery of receiving the *get*, the traditional Jewish divorce paper, vividly captures the personal pain. The Israeli poet Yehuda AMICHAI writes that in this book, despite Kaufman's change of country with its attendant risks for her creative power, "...her voice [is] richer and fuller than ever before...".

FURTHER READING
Kinsman, C. D., ed.: *Contemporary Authors* (Detroit: Gale Research Co., 1975)

ELIZABETH KLEIN

Kaufmann, David (1852–1899) Scholar. Born in the ghetto of Kojetein in Moravia, Kaufmann was admitted to the Breslau rabbinical seminary, a great center of Jewish scholarship under Zacharias FRANKEL, at the age of 15. After gaining his doctorate at Leipzig, he was appointed to teach at the new Budapest rabbinical seminary in 1877. (At that time outside the UK there were no university posts in Jewish studies: Kaufmann became an outspoken proponent of the establishment of such posts.) A fortunate marriage gave him the means to indulge fully his penchant for research, for manuscript collection (his manuscripts, now in the possession of the Hungarian Academy of Sciences, include one of the most important texts of the Mishnah and several hundred fragments from the Cairo Genizah), and for encouraging the work of others. He mastered Hungarian, and firmly made Budapest his home for the rest of his life.

Considering that he was just 47 when he died, Kaufmann's output is quite astonishing. He published nearly thirty books and well over three hundred scholarly articles (over five hundred if one includes popular essays and book reviews). The range of his writings is also amazing, extending from medieval Hebrew and Arabic literature through Jewish genealogy and archaeology to modern European literature; he wrote in various languages, including Hebrew, for which he had a particular fondness. His most important work perhaps was his pioneering research in the area of Jewish art, a subject which simply did not exist before Kaufmann. He was involved in various projects concerning Jewish archaeology, art, and folklore. But his greatest achievement undoubtedly was to have made the Budapest seminary one of the main centers of Jewish research and teaching in Europe.

FURTHER READING
Brann, M., and Rosenthal, F., eds: *Gedenkbuch zur Erinnerung an David Kaufmann* (Breslau: 1900) [with biography and bibliography]

NICHOLAS DE LANGE

Kaufmann, Isidor (1853–1921) Hungarian painter. Kaufmann was one of a number of Jewish artists who found success in late nineteenth-century Vienna producing scenes of *shtetl* life. Born in Arad, Hungary, he studied in Budapest before moving to Vienna and attempting to practice as a history painter. However success eluded him until he began painting Jewish genre works of the kind already being produced by Leopold HOROWITZ. Thereafter his work found a ready home on the drawing-room walls of Vienna's large Jewish middle class, and he was awarded many Establishment honors.

Although he worked in an art-form noted principally for its mawkishness and lack of originality, Kaufmann was an artist of considerable talent. Even his early works are characterized by a strength of design and a seriousness of intention which distinguishes them from the more run-of-the-mill output of other artists in the field. He traveled to the *shtetls* of Poland, Galicia, and the Ukraine recording Jewish folk-art and customs (in accordance with the contemporary interest in ethnography), and the apparent accuracy of his depictions has meant that they are frequently used today to illustrate social histories of east European Jewry. However, Kaufmann's intention was not so literal, and his paintings are never a mere accumulation of picturesque detail. Underlying his work is a vision of an idyllic way of life founded on spiritual values, a romantic ideology which led without incongruity to Kaufmann's participation in BUBER's 1901 Exhibition of Jewish Art at the Fifth Zionist Congress in Basel.

Much of Kaufmann's finest work was produced after the turn of the century, when his subject matter and his approach to pictorial representation were already anachronistic. From this period date his boldly designed portraits of Jews in traditional costume, gazing at the viewer with sad, archetypal intensity. The tranquillity of his later scenes recalls Vermeer as women light the Sabbath candles or sit in luminous contemplation, the simplicity of their surroundings reflecting their piety. Kaufmann's work is imbued with nostalgic longing, but devoid of sentimentality.

FURTHER READING
Kleeblatt, N., et al., eds: *Treasures of the Jewish Museum* (New York: Universe Books, 1986)

LAURA JACOBUS

Kaufmann, Yehezkel (1889–1963) Israeli scholar. Kaufmann was born in Dunajevcy, Ukraine. After studying at the *Yeshivah Hagedolah* of Tchernowitz in Odessa, at the Academy of Baron David Guenzburg in St Petersburg (Leningrad), and gaining his doctorate at the University of Berne, he emigrated to Israel in 1928. He was a teacher at the Realli School in Haifa for more than 20 years. After retiring in 1949 he was appointed Professor of Bible studies at the Hebrew University in Jerusalem and became the teacher and master of an entire generation of biblical scholars, including Yigal YADIN. He dedicated his life to studying, and led a solitary existence, remaining unmarried, and establishing neither family ties nor close friendships. One of his famous sayings, demons-

trated his devotion to scholarship: "I have no biography, only bibliography".

Kaufmann is considered to be one of the greatest scholars f modern critical biblical scholarship, a field which had been almost entirely the province of Gentile scholars. In his first book, *Golah venekhar* (4 vols, 1929–30; Exile and alien lands) which is an historical and sociological study of Jewish history, he claimed that it was Judaism which maintained the identity of the people of Israel throughout the Diaspora. However, the peak of his creativity is undoubtably *Toldot ha'emunah hayisra'elit*, (1937–57; History of the religion of Israel, from ancient times to the destruction of the Second Temple). The book includes a fundamental critique of classical criticism, suggesting that the origins of Israelite monotheism are based on elements that were totally different from any that existed within the pagan world. The writing of this eight-volume book occupied nearly twenty years, but it remained unfinished according to Kaufmann's original plans.

His other writings include commentaries on the book of Joshua (1959) and the book of Judges (1962). For his great contribution to biblical scholarship he was awarded the Bialik Prize in 1933 and in 1956, and the Israel Prize in 1958.

FURTHER READING
Menahem, H., ed.: *Yehezkel Kaufmann Jubilee Volume* (Jerusalem: 1960)

DEBORAH SCHECHTERMAN

Kazin, Alfred (b.1915) American critic and memoir writer. Kazin was born and raised in the Brownsville section of Brooklyn. His parents were immigrants from Eastern Europe. He graduated from the City College of New York in 1935 and received an MA from Columbia in 1938. A "gypsy scholar" for nearly two decades, in 1963 he started teaching at the State University of New York at Stony Brook. He is a member of the American Academy of Arts and Sciences and the National Institute of Arts and Letters.

In the first volume of his autobiography, *A Walker in the City* (1951), Kazin describes his adolescent desire to move beyond the confines of "Brunsvil" and into the real America–represented by the excitement of Manhattan and by the grandeur of American literature and history. The second and third volumes of the autobiography, *Starting Out in the Thirties* (1965) and *New York Jew* (1978), chronicle his lifelong involvement in the New York literary establishment. He has written countless reviews, essays, and introductions, but his reputation as a critic rests on his first book, *On Native Grounds* (1942), an important reassessment of American literary history. In Grant Webster's words, Kazin believes that "American prose literature is a response to the crises of capitalism and industrialism in the 1880s and after", torn between a realistic absorption in everyday life and a transcendentalist idealism. A more recent book, *An American Procession* (1984), explores the tensions between writers' commitments to their inner lives and the demands of a vigorous but immature culture.

The lyrical countermelody throughout his autobiographical writing is the effort to recover and nurture the part of himself that remains the child of a Yiddish-speaking immigrant family.

FURTHER READING

Hazlett, J.: Repossessing the past: discontinuity and history in Alfred Kazin's *A walker in the city*. *Biography* 7 (1984) 325–40

Rubin, Louis: Alfred Kazin's American procession. *Sewanee Review* 93 (1985) 250–65

Webster, G.: *The Republic of Letters* (Baltimore: Johns Hopkins University Press, 1979)

MICHAEL SHAPIRO

Keesing [Hertzberg], **Nancy Florence** (b.1923) Australian writer, poet, critic, anthologist, social historian, and editor. Nancy Keesing was born a member of a prominent Sydney Jewish family that had an active role in synagogue life and her own interests reflect this family background.

Nancy Keesing is one of Australia's better known contemporary writers (she is the author or editor of some 26 volumes). While not much of her own work has direct reference to Jewish themes and affairs, she has been especially

active as a publicist in Jewish causes. She has been notable for encouraging talented young Jewish writers to work in the field of Australian Jewish literature. For her many services to literature and the arts in general she was awarded the Order of Australia in 1979.

Her literary directions are multifarious, but in all of them she tends to adopt Australian themes. She first became widely known as the editor, with Douglas Stewart, of the anthologies *Australian Bush Ballads* (1955) and *Old Bush Songs* (1957). She has written verse, children's novels, literary criticism, a book of memoirs, biography, has edited several anthologies of Australian bush ballads, and a historical volume relating to the search for gold in Australia. One of her successful works that is being reprinted is her anthology of Australian Jewish short stories, *Shalom* (1978). She also edited the section "The Jewish Contribution to Australian Literature", in *The Australia and New Zealand Jewish Year Book* (1985). Apart from her own four volumes of verse her poetry is represented in at least nine anthologies of Australian verse including *The New Oxford Book of Australian Verse* (1986).

In her biographical study, *John Lang and "The Forger's Wife"* (1979), she researched the career of the first native-born Australian writer of fiction, a scion of a Jewish (convict) family. Her *Lily on the Dustbin*, a study of Australian Women's slang (1982), has been reprinted three times and her feminist *The White Chrysanthemum* (1977), was reprinted under the title *Dear Mum* (1985). Her latest book, *According to my Memory* (Allen and Unwin), is autobiographical.

ALAN D. CROWN

Kemelman, Harry (b.1908) American mystery novelist. Kemelman has written a series of mystery novels whose hero and amateur detective, Rabbi David Small, uses talmudic logic and knowledge of Jewish tradition to help him solve murders. Within these novels, the complications of plot serve to dramatize the tension between the rabbi, his congregation, and his board, and to illuminate the sociological functioning of a contemporary American Jewish suburban community.

As he struggles with each mystery Rabbi

Small is often required to explain Jewish tradition to his gentile Yankee townspeople, and to stand in apposition to his assimilationist congregants. Although he gets along well with non-Jews, Rabbi Small firmly delineates the distinctiveness of the Jewish tradition rather than promulgating the melting-pot notion of the Judeo-Christian heritage. His integrity and firm convictions often put him in danger of losing his job. Rabbi Small's comfort with his thoroughly American nature and his equal comfort with his thoroughly Jewish nature make him almost unique among heroes in American Jewish fiction.

BIBLIOGRAPHY

Friday the Rabbi Slept Late (London: Hutchinson, 1964); *Saturday the Rabbi Went Hungry* (London: Hutchinson, 1966); *The Nine Mile Walk: The Nicky Welt Stories of Harry Kemelman* (London: Hutchinson, 1968); *Someday the Rabbi Will Leave* (London: Hutchinson, 1985)

SYLVIA FISHMAN

Kempf, Franz (b.1926)   Australian painter, printmaker, and teacher. Kempf studied at the National Art School, Sydney, at the Academy of Fine Art in Perugia, and printmaking in Israel in association with Jacob Pins. For some years he has taught at the South Australian School of Art. Kempf has been described by one critic of his work as "among the most consistent and powerful printmakers of Australia during the last quarter of a century". This description has been earned particularly for his lithographs with a Jewish content, often Holocaust related. His *Memorial I, II*, and *III* (1979), all in the National Gallery of Victoria, are moving examples of his involvement in things Jewish. All of them have somber colors yet in his contemporary lithographs Kempf shows himself to be a master of strong and vibrant colors.

He has held 11 solo exhibitions, has been involved in 26 other shows internationally, and has received 12 awards for his work (principally for his strongly designed prints). His paintings and prints are exhibited in almost every State and provincial gallery in Australia, the Victoria and Albert Museum in London, the Bezalel Museum, Israel, and a number of private collections including that of the Reserve Bank of Australia.

His Jewish themes are represented in his lithographs *Reflections on Bashevis Singer, Song of Esther, Golem of Prague, Kabbalists, The Chassidic Legend*, and *Dark Changes and the Baal Shem*.

Kempf is the author of *Contemporary Australian Printmakers* (1977).

ALAN D. CROWN

Kesten, Hermann (b.1900)   German author. Born in Nuremberg, Kesten had an extensive university education in the early 1920s. He made his literary debut with the novel *Joseph sucht die Freiheit*, (1927; Josef seeks freedom) depicting the disillusionment of an idealistic schoolboy through the discovery of his mother's and sisters' promiscuity. His next novel *Glückliche Menschen* (1931; Happy people) served to illustrate Kesten's notion that the ruthless build their happiness on the despair of others. In fact this entire literary output upheld threatened liberal values: *Scharlatan* (1932), typified everything the engaged humanist Kesten opposed.

The advent of Hitler in the following year caused him to flee Germany. He emigrated to Paris, making intermittent journeys to Amsterdam where he helped guide the affairs of two publishing houses that constituted the main outlet for emigre writers.

In exile, Kesten diversified his work; while continuing to treat contemporary reality he also turned to historical fiction as an allegory of the present. He produced a sequence on late medieval Spain which, besides focusing on the expulsion of the Jews, demonstrated the evils engendered by absolute rule. As a modern sequel he wrote about the fate of the Basques during the Spanish Civil War in *Die Kinder von Gernika* (1939; The children of Guernica). In 1940 Kesten fled to the USA where he worked for the Emergency Rescue Committee (which brought threatened writers out of Nazi Europe) and contributed, as formerly in France, to diverse emigre periodicals. In addition he wrote a biography of Copernicus and *Die Zwillinge von Nürnberg* (1937; The twins from Nuremberg) a novel with a contemporary post-war theme.

Returning to Europe in 1949 he eventually chose Rome as his permanent residence. His subsequent literary output intermingled biography with autobiography – a genre for which his own record as general factotum of the exiled German Republic of Letters provided ample material.

BIBLIOGRAPHY
Copernicus and His World, trans. E. B. Ashton and N. Guterman (New York: Roy Publishers, 1945)

RICHARD GRUNBERGER

Kingsley [Kirshner], **Sidney** (b.1906) Playwright. Born in New York, he attended public school on the Lower West Side, and graduated from Townsend Harris Hall High School in 1924, where he had written and directed plays. He won a scholarship to Cornell, where he won an award in 1928 for the best one-act play. After his graduation he acted in a stock company in the Bronx, then, in 1929 served as a play reader for Columbia Pictures. In 1933, *Men in White* opened at the Broadhurst Theater, directed by Lee Strasberg. It won a Pulitzer Prize in 1934 and was filmed by MGM with Clark Gable.

Kingsley's *Dead End* opened at the Belasco in 1935 and ran for 684 performances. It won the Theater Club Award in 1936 and was filmed by United Artists with Humphrey Bogart the next year.

His play, *The Patriots* opened in 1943 at the National Theater and won the New York Drama Critics Circle Award, among other prestigious awards. Kingsley used the conflict between Jefferson and Hamilton to allegorize the political positions of the 1940s.

His later plays, *Darkness at Noon* (1951), *Lunatics and Lovers* (1954), and *Night Life* (1962) were not critical successes. The playwright maintains an active role in New York's theatrical life, having served as president of the Dramatists Guild and as a member of the board of directors of the Experimental Theater Club of La Mama. In 1965 he was given the Yeshiva University Award for Achievement in Theater. The very qualities which made Kingsley's plays popular: exhaustively researched social realism, melo-

dramatic plots, and stereotypical characters make them seem outdated today.

FURTHER READING
Bailey, P. M.: Sidney Kingsley. *Dictionary of Literary Biography*, vol. 7 (Detroit: Gale Research Co., 1984)

RUTH ROSENBERG

Kipnis, Menachem (1878–1942) Singer and collector of Jewish folk music. Kipnis was born in the Polish town of Wolin and died of natural causes in the Warsaw ghetto. Orphaned at the age of eight he was raised by his brother who gave him singing lessons and a place in the choir of the local synagogue. Later he became a high tenor which allowed him to sing with such famous cantors as Berl Miler, Jakub Samuel Morogowski (Zaidel Rowner), and others. Accompanied by cantors he visited towns in Ukraine, Belorussia, Lithuania and central Poland. In the course of these travels he collected Jewish folk music and initiated a series of concerts devoted to folk songs.

At the age of 19 Kipnis arrived in Warsaw and joined the choir of the Warsaw Opera where he sang as first tenor for 16 years. His short, thin stature prevented a career as operatic principal and he eventually left the Opera choir, partly because of his commitment to collecting folk music, and partly in order to accompany his wife, a singer, on her tours. He continued collecting old synagogue, rabbinic, and ritual songs, many of which were sent to him in response to his appeals in the Jewish press. He often adapted these songs and performed them with his wife.

In his work he took full advantage of the phonograph, and later of the gramophone. As enthusiastic photographer, he supplemented his work by recording the life of Jewish people, in addition to collecting antiques, fine arts, and unique objects connected with Jewish culture. For many years, until the outbreak of war in 1939, he published his essays, articles, reviews, sketches, and memoirs in many Jewish journals, particularly in the celebrated Warsaw daily *Hajnt*. He published several books on Jewish musicians, KLEZMER, and Jewish folk songs, and two collections of Jewish folk songs. With the death of Kipnis and his wife their priceless collection of manuscripts together with the archives of Jewish songs perished.

MARIAN FUKS

Kirsch, Olga (b.1924)

The only South African Jewish Akrikaans poet. She was reared in the small Afrikaans-speaking Orange Free State farming village of Koppies, attending school there, and later in Bloemfontein. She attained her BA (Hons) degree at the University of the Witwatersrand, Johannesburg, in Afrikaans and Nederlands.

Her mother was English-speaking, while her father, a Lithuanian immigrant, was most comfortable in Yiddish. Although she was equally conversant in English and Afrikaans, her poetry could only be expressed in Afrikaans, the language of her early childhood.

Her first volume of poetry, *Die Soeklig* (The searchlight), was published in 1944, followed by *Mure van die Hart* (1948; Walls of the heart). While the first attracted attention because a Jew had written poetry in Afrikaans, the latter was acclaimed for the sheer excellence of the poetry.

The 1940s witnessed delicate relations between Jew and Afrikaner and, driven by her love of the Afrikaans language, she felt that she could convey in her poetry what could not, perhaps, be said by an Afrikaner. She could express conflict as an onlooker.

She settled in Israel in 1948, convinced that only her generation could be given the privilege of helping to build the Jewish State. She has not found it possible to write poetry successfully in Hebrew or English. In 1972 she broke her almost 25-year silence and *Negentien Gedigte* (Nineteen poems), appeared.

She visited South Africa in 1974 as a guest of the Afrikaans *taalfees* (Language festival) in Paarl, which inspired her to publish *Geil Gebied* (Lush territory) and *Oorwinteraars in die Vreemde* (Hibernators in strange lands). All her poetry from Israel reflects her three preoccupations: the call of Zion, black–white relations, and her own personal introspections.

JOCELYN HELLIG

Kirschen, Ya'akov (b.1938)

Cartoonist. Kirschen was born in Washington, DC, and was raised in Brooklyn, New York City. He was educated at Brooklyn Technical High School and Queens College, graduating with a BA in Art and Economics.

His first efforts as a freelance cartoonist were published in popular American magazines such as *Playboy* and *Esquire*. At the same time he wrote and illustrated children's books as well as becoming involved in corporate consultancy and local party politics.

In 1968 Kirschen emigrated to Israel and soon thereafter created "Dry Bones", a daily political comic strip which was taken on by the *Jerusalem Post* where it still appears today. The comic strip became hugely popular and has been reprinted in newspapers and magazines throughout Israel and the USA. The strip has been described as "lampooning everything and everybody from Yassir Arafat to Henry Kissinger, from the United Nations to Israel's own bloated bureaucracy". Kirschen himself sees Jewish humor as being traditionally based upon grotesquely desperate situations; he therefore, perversely, finds much in Israeli daily life and events to provide his inspiration.

Kirschen's involvement in, and experience with "Dry Bones" has led him to publish, in 1976 and again in 1979, collections of the best cartoons in book form. In 1978 he produced a video comic which appeared nightly on Israeli television news broadcasts. In the early 1980s Kirschen saw the possibility of marrying cartoon and computer. He started by creating video games that propagandized Jewish values and identification. From this he founded a company in Israel which undertakes creative work for many major manufacturers of personal computers worldwide.

JOHN MATTHEW

Kisch, Erwin Egon (1885–1948)

Journalist and essayist. Born into a middle-class Jewish family in Prague, he found out early in his life where his inclinations and talents lay. He served his apprenticeship as a journalist on the *Prager Tagblatt* in 1904–5 and from 1906 until 1913 he belonged to the staff of the *Deutsche Zeitung Bohemia*. During the First World War he

411

served first in a unit stationed in the Balkans, then in press units. In 1918 he actively participated in the "Red Putsch" in Vienna. From 1921 until 1933 he lived as a freelance journalist in Berlin. He was arrested after the Reichstag fire and freed only through the intervention of the Czech Government. He traveled extensively and lived in Paris until 1937; during the Spanish Civil War he served in the International Brigade; in 1939 he went to the USA and in 1940 moved to Mexico. In 1946 he returned to Prague.

Roughly one can distinguish three periods in Kisch's writings: the first between 1918 and 1925, when his articles showed no marked political tendency; the second, from 1926 until 1933, when he voiced his polemics against the "bourgeois parliamentary faction", and the third, between 1933 and 1947 when his disappointment in the scant left-wing influence – as he saw it – in world affairs led to a growing resignation.

The driving force of all Kisch's writings was his desire to discover the truth but he instictively knew what to delete and what to stress in order to convey his impression. He not only inaugurated a new type of reportage, he raised it to a higher literary level and some of his articles are novelistic masterpieces. Kisch was a chronicler of his time and perhaps at his best during that early period in which the conscientiousness and the painstaking care he took with details are not yet overshadowed by his later belief that the truth in reportage should serve a political–ideological aim.

In 1914 Kisch wrote a novel *Der Mädchenhirt* (The pimp) in which he pointed out the correlation of social strife and cultural hatred between the Germans and Czechs in the Prague of that time.

BIBLIOGRAPHY

Australian Landfall, trans. J. Fisher, I. Fitzgerald, and K. Fitzgerald (London: M. Secker & Warburg, 1937); *The Three Cows*, trans. S. Farrar (London: Fore Publications, 1939)

MARGARITA PAZI

Kishon, Ephraim (b.1924) Humorist and satirist. Kishon was born in Budapest. On completing High School he studied History of Art at the Budapest University. After the Second World War, escaping from German and Russian camps, he emigrated to Israel, where he learned Hebrew.

Kishon is considered to be Israel's national humorist. His books, plays, and films have spread his fame all over the world and made him a leading exponent of his country's artistic revival. He is probably the world's most published living satirical writer, reaching the top of the best-seller lists in many countries throughout the world. Kishon's plays, like the acclaimed *The Marriage License* (Haketubah), *His Friend At Court* and *It Was The Lark* and film comedies, like the Academy Award Nominees *Sallah*, and *The Policeman*, under his own production and direction, have scored all-time records in Israel and have been performed on stage and television in many important theatrical centers abroad.

Since 1952 Kishon has run a daily satirical column in Israel's leading daily *Ma'ariv*; He has written about 50 books, satires, novels, and plays in Hebrew. His books, such as *Look Back, Mrs Lot, So Sorry We Won, New York Ain't America*, and *My Family Right Or Wrong* have appeared in practically every Western language and have been sold in 27,000,000 copies, earning critical acclaim in the various translations, which include Korean, Finnish, Turkish, Esperanto, and others.

Kishon has been awarded the Israeli Herzl Prize, Jabotinsky Prize, and Nordau Prize for Literature, and the Sokolov Prize for outstanding journalistic achievements, the *Wider den tierischen Ernst* Award, the *Till Eulenspiegel Prize 1980, Ordre de St Fortunat*, and the *"Noble" Prize for Humor*, Paris 1981.

His films, written and directed by him, earned him many international awards, including two Golden Gate Awards of the San Francisco International Film Festival, three Golden Globe Awards of the Hollywood Foreign Press Association, the Cine del Duca Prize of Monte Carlo International Festival for Television, and the Gold Medal of the Atlanta International Film Festival.

JOHN MATTHEW

Kiss, József (1843–1921) Hungarian poet. Born at Mezöcsát he was the first Jewish poet whose work became an integral part of Hungarian poetry. His father, a village shopkeeper, sent him to a *yeshiva* but he escaped and attended first the Protestant school of Rimaszombat (now Rimska Sobota in Czechoslovakia) and then Debrecen. After the death of his father he earned his living as an itinerant teacher. In 1867 he moved to Pest where he lived (with the exception of 1876–82) for the rest of his life, working first as proofreader, then clerk, journalist, and finally, from 1890 onwards, as newspaper editor. He first made his name as a poet with ballads much influenced by the populist (*népi-nemzeti*) school of János Arany, but the subject-matter of some of these was more Jewish than Hungarian (*Zsidó Dalok* (1868; Jewish songs)). From 1882 his attention turned to the harsh life of the urban lower classes and his lyrical verse tackled problems of generational and social change, as well as personal identity. Some of his later verse also has Jewish protagonists, for example "Jehova", the graphic description of an irreconcilable conflict between the morality of strict Orthodoxy and the temptations of worldliness, and the nostalgic epic tale "Legendák nagyapámról" (1910; Legends about Grandfather), the hero of which, Reb Mayer Litvak, emigrated from Vilno to Hungary.

Kiss's mature poetry on the whole, however, eschews ethnic introspection for the affirmation of his personal choice: he regards himself as being as Hungarian as any other citizen of the country and in this spirit raises his voice against the wave of anti-Semitism following the ill-famed process of Tiszaeszlár. His love for his homeland does not dispel his doubts about the success of assimilation (this is expressed in the self-deprecating line "a beggar of a stranger who happened to settle here"), yet in "Reincarnation" he confesses "if it were up to me, I would be reborn here". In his two most famous poems Kiss prophesies great social upheavals and expresses sympathy with the rebellious Russian seamen of the 1905 revolution, "Tüzek" (Fires) and "A Knyáz Potemkin" (Kniaz Potemkin) respectively. Kiss's poetic language is largely traditional but there are innovative musical tendencies in his verse, and his irregular iambic lines are said to have prepared the ground for the modernization of Hungarian verse completed by the *Nyugat* generation.

Today Kiss is less remembered for his poetry than for his editorial work. In 1890 he launched the literary review *A Hét* (The Week) which became the leading "cosmopolitan" cultural review of the 1890–1908 period. Politically *A Hét* could be called liberal, although it would sometimes print contrasting views; artistically it tried to reflect the new trends in the literatures of Western Europe. Kiss's generosity as editor was matched by his sensitivity for artistic achievement and *A Hét* is generally regarded as a worthy predecessor of *Nyugat* (The West, begun in 1908).

BIBLIOGRAPHY
Smith, M., ed.: *Kiss József költeményei*, (New York: 1954) [with an English introduction and several poems in English translation]

GEORGE GÖMÖRI

Kitaj, R. B. (b. 1932) American painter. Born in Cleveland, Ohio, Kitaj studied at the Cooper Union Institute, New York, and at the Akademie der Bildenden Künste, Vienna, in the early 1950s and, under the terms of the G. I. Bill, at the Ruskin School of Art, Oxford (1958–9), and at the Royal College of Art, London (1959–62). He has lived in England during most of his working life and established his reputation as early as 1963 with his first one-man exhibition at the Marlborough Gallery, London. An important figure in the history of British Pop Art as an influence on fellow students such as David Hockney, he was never comfortable with that label, instead drawing inspiration from Surrealism, literary sources including the poetry of T. S. Eliot and Ezra Pound, iconographic studies by Aby Warburg and Fritz Saxl, and the history of socialism.

Kitaj was not raised as a Jew by his mother and stepfather, but from the mid 1970s he became profoundly involved with Jewish identity as a conscious and subconscious impulse. A

413

R. B. Kitaj The Jew Etc. *1977. Private collection*

major early painting such as *The Murder of Rosa Luxemburg*, 1960–2 (London, Tate Gallery) now seems to him more concerned with the anxiety and persecution of Jews even before Nazism than with the heroic failures of leftwing politics.

In paintings such as *The Jew Etc.*, 1976–9 (coll. the artist), a portrait of a man traveling in a train into presumed exile, Kitaj began to represent an invented character called Joe Singer as an "emblematic Jew". *If Not, Not*, 1975–6 (Edinburgh, Scottish National Gallery of Modern Art) introduced the gates of Auschwitz into a scarred landscape based on T. S. Eliot's *The Waste Land*. The Holocaust and the effect it had on the lives of Jews subsequently became Kitaj's most urgent subjects. In *Cecil Court, London WC2 (The Refugees)*, 1983–4 (London, Tate Gallery) the artist pictures himself in a London alleyway full of bookshops that at one time were run mainly by exiled Jews; behind him are real and imagined figures, including his recently deceased stepfather, Joe Singer, and nameless victims who appear to be swimming in desperation towards the safety of friendlier shores.

The condition of the modern Jew has been an obsessional subject in Kitaj's work of the 1980s, particularly in a group of *Passion* pictures initiated in 1985 with the explicit intention of using the chimneys of concentration camps as symbols of a Jewish passion equivalent to the Christian cross. Kitaj has continued to dwell on this almost untouchable subject both in his paintings and in his writings. In a long tract completed in 1987, *First Diasporist Manifesto*, he stressed his urge to "relate our past experience of Diaspora to a present understanding of it in painted, hopefully universal pictures which may speak to many people".

BIBLIOGRAPHY
First Diasporist Manifesto (London: Thames and Hudson, 1989)

FURTHER READING
Ashbery, J., Hayman, T., Livingston, J., and Shannon, J.: *R. B. Kitaj* (Washington DC: Hirshhorn Museum and Sculpture Garden, 1981; London: Thames and Hudson, 1983)
Livingstone, M.: *R. B. Kitaj* (Oxford: Phaidon; New York: Rizzoli, 1985)

MARCO LIVINGSTONE

Klausner, Joseph Gedaliah (1874–1958) Literary critic and historian. Klausner was born in Olkienik, near Vilna, but at the age of 11 moved with his family to Odessa. After having shown an interest in Hebrew at a very young age he became the youngest member of the *Sefatenu 'itanu*, a society for the revival of Hebrew, established in Odessa in 1891. In 1897 he went to Heidelberg to study Semitic and modern languages, history, and philosophy.

In 1898 he moved to Warsaw to succeed AHAD HA'AM as editor of *Hashiloah*, a post he held for 23 years, joined at times by H. N. BIALIK and Jacob Fichman. He befriended many of the young Hebrew and Yiddish writers such as Bialik, Saul TSCHERNICHOWSKI, Joseph Hayyim BRENNER, and MENDELE MOKHER SEFARIM, encouraging them by publishing their work. In 1907 Klausner returned to Odessa, where he taught Jewish history at the modern *yeshivah*, and he was appointed professor of Oriental History at the Odessa University in 1917, but left for Palestine in that year. When the Hebrew University was established he was appointed to the Chair of Hebrew literature and, in 1944, to the Chair of the History of the Second Temple. He died in Jerusalem.

Klausner's enormous literary output consisted of literary criticism, philology, and historiography. His essays on criticism, collected in the three-volume *Yotzerim 'uvonim* (1925–8; Creators and builders), inter alia discussed the functional tasks of Hebrew literature in the age of national renaissance and also the relationship between the renascent Hebrew literature and European literature. One of his most influential works was his six-volume *Historyah shel hasifrut ha'ivrit hahadashah* (1930–50; *History of Modern Hebrew Literature*, 1932). This masterly survey encompasses Klausner's views about the writer's contribution to the development of the Hebrew language, and the relationship between Hebrew literature and Jewish nationalism, and between Hebrew literature and world literature. Klausner's influence in the field of literary criticism and literary history is marked, and his monographs on Bialik and Tschernichowski remain a valuable source to this day, despite his positivist critical approach.

Klausner's other writing includes a study of Jesus, *Yeshu hanotzeri, zemano, hayyav vetorato* (1922; *Jesus of Nazareth*, 1925) which stresses the unaltered Jewishness of Jesus, and *Miyeshu 'ad Paulus* (1939; *From Jesus to Paul*, 1943) which traces the evolution of Christianity, using Jewish sources. His five-volume history of the Second Temple period, *Hahistoryah shel habayit hasheni* (1949; The history of the Second Temple) which, in his proposition that the past should be evaluated in the light of the values of the present, revealed his essentially Jewish approach and ardent nationalism. Philological writings include *Ha'ivrit hahadashah uve'ayoteha* (1952; The Hebrew language and its problems), in which Klausner stressed his belief in the development of Hebrew, by mishnaic and talmudic usage over biblical usage, and in which he encouraged the use of neologisms.

An active Zionist and nationalist, Klausner identified with the Revisionists, later the Herut party and stood as their candidate for the Presidency of the State of Israel in 1949.

FURTHER READING

Waxman, M.: *A History of Jewish Literature*, vol. 4 (New York: Bloch, 1960)

GLENDA ABRAMSON

Klein, Abraham Moses (1909–1971) Canadian poet and writer. Born in Ratno in the Ukraine, Klein moved with his family to Canada in 1910 and settled in Montreal. Educated in Protestant and Jewish schools, Klein pursued his academic studies at McGill University and the Université de Montréal. He was admitted to the Bar in 1933 and earned his livelihood as a practising lawyer while pursuing a literary career as poet and writer.

Klein's literary work is informed by sensitivity to the multicultural aspects of his environment. An ardent humanist, Klein strove to express the affinity between his Jewish heritage and the dominant English and French traditions in Montreal.

The first volume of poetry, *Hath Not a Jew* (1940), reveals Klein's deep attachment to Jewish tradition, in an array of folkstories, biblical motifs, and religious symbols. *Poems* (1944) deals almost exclusively with Jewish subject matter. Especially moving and impressive are the psalms in the first section of the collection, "The psalter of Avram Haktani". Stylistically, however, both collections demonstrate the dominant influence of the English romantics, imagists, and the Elizabethan poets. The deep impact of the eighteenth-century English satirists emerges in *The Hitleriad* (1944), Klein's vituperative attack on Nazism. Though quite severely criticized for its polemical and didactic approach, this long satiric poem represents the only poetic attempt in Canada to deal with the evolving Nazi horror.

The Rocking Chair (1948), Klein's best poetic achievement, focuses on social reality in Quebec. It presents a sympathetic view of French Canadian tradition and astute observations of the political reality in Quebec. In some of the poems, Klein transcends the local scene. The concluding "Portrait of the poet as a landscape" offers a striking vision of the poet as an alienated outcast in society.

Klein's only novel, *The Second Scroll* (1951), represents his final artistic and ideological statement. Soon after its publication Klein became reclusive and, due to mental illness, ceased to write altogether. The novel is based on Klein's visit to Israel in 1949. The birth of the State is presented as the ultimate vindication of Jewish suffering in the Holocaust. The sense of the materializing messianic promise of moral regeneration is enhanced through the structural parallel between the five chapters of the novel and the five books of the Torah.

Klein's need to reconcile humanistic universalism and Zionist particularism is also evident in many of the editorials, essays, and articles he published in Canadian and American journals. A prominent and respected public figure, Klein influenced other Canadian Jewish writers, such as Irving LAYTON and Mordecai RICHLER. Klein's work is well known in Israel. His poetry can be found in many Canadian and international anthologies.

FURTHER READING

Caplan, U.: *Like One That Dreamed: a Portrait of A. M. Klein* (Toronto: McGraw–Hill Ryerson, 1982)
Waddington, M.: *A. M. Klein* (Vancouver: Copp Clark Publishing, 1970)

RACHEL FELDHAY BRENNER

klezmer (pl. *klezmorim*) Yiddish term derived from the Hebrew words *klei zemer*, musical instruments, which at some stage took on both the identities of the musician and instrument, as well as being used to describe the genre of predominantly eastern European Jewish instrumental folk music.

The earliest references to the *klezmer* tradition in Europe date back to around the sixteenth century. *Klezmorim* were those itinerant musicians who, until well into the nineteenth century, served the needs of Jewish communities throughout Europe by accompanying the singing and playing dance music at weddings, much of which was improvised, as well as providing music for other special occasions such as minor festivals (for example, *Hanukah*, *Purim*) and

other celebrations. There were many occasions throughout this period when bands of Jewish musicians were preferred to their Gentile counterparts. This often led to the Jews being penalized by heavy taxes or requiring permits to perform music in specific towns. There were even instances of *klezmorim* being prevented from playing at Jewish weddings.

A typical *klezmer* band in an eighteenth-century Germanic territory consisted of three to five members, usually two violins and a violoncello to which a clarinet and/or *tsimbl* (portable hammered dulcimer) might be added. Although *klezmorim* in Germany were playing the clarinet by about 1800, it was only in the mid nineteenth century that the clarinet became popular with their eastern European counterparts.

Klezmorim were considered to have very low social status but were always in demand as entertainers, although they were often condemned to a life on the road, such was the uncertainty of their existence. Because Jewish musicians would also be familiar figures at non-Jewish weddings, *klezmorim* had to develop not only a traditional Jewish repertoire but also one of sufficient variety to satisfy the needs of those who hired them; this often depended on whether they were playing for nobility, land-owners, or peasantry and had to include salon music, peasant dances, local folksongs, ballads, and popular street songs.

As the *klezmer*'s repertoire changed, so did the instruments on which it was played. In the early nineteenth century the violin's predominance was challenged by the clarinet. By the end of the nineteenth century brass instruments had gradually been introduced into *klezmer* bands. This may well have been due to the increasing numbers of Jewish army conscripts choosing to play for, or being assigned to military bands. It was also a period which witnessed the demise of the *tsimbl* from the *klezmer* bands as these gradually developed into 12- and 15-piece ensembles featuring mainly wind, string, and brass instruments.

The music of the synagogue always had a profound influence on the music of the *klezmer* on both emotional and musical levels, which was reflected in his playing; both clarinet and

Klezmorim *(most of them members of the Faust family)*, *Rihatyn, Galicia, c.1912*

violin at times expressing remarkable closeness to the human voice. Eastern European *klezmer* music was much influenced by the existing folk music idioms of Romania, Russia, the Ukraine, Byelorussia, Poland, Hungary, and Bulgaria, as well as by Gypsy elements. It was dance-oriented music, featuring such rhythms as the bright *Bulgar* or *freylekh*, the slower *khosidl*, or the *doina* which would lend itself to a more rhapsodic treatment, not always with a fixed rhythmic pattern, together with additional improvisation and ornamentation.

To escape from economic, social, and religious oppression, many *klezmorim* left eastern Europe between 1880 and 1924, most of them settling in the USA. Whilst some found work in the Yiddish theater, others played for both Jewish and non-Jewish bands. Hundreds of recordings were issued prior to the 1940s, the majority between 1913 and 1930. These were purely commercial and not intended for preservation or posterity. With the rise of American popular music, *klezmer* music might have faded into obscurity but it has undergone a renaissance since the mid 1970s, particularly in the USA. This has mainly manifested itself in the reissue of early recordings and the formation of new professional *klezmer* groups who have, through their own performances and recordings, helped revive the musical tradition.

FURTHER READING

Idelsohn, A. Z.: *Jewish Music in its Historical Development* (New York: Schocken, 1967)

Sapoznik, H.: *Klezmer Music 1910–1942* (New York: Folkways Records FSS 34021, 1981)

——: *The Compleat Klezmer* (Cedarhurst: Tara Publications, 1987)

Sendrey, A.: *The Music of the Jews in the Diaspora* (New York: Thomas Yoseloff, 1970)

Slobin, M.: *Tenement Songs: The Popular Music of the Jewish Immigrants* (Urbana: University of Illinois Press, 1982)

——: *Old Jewish Folk Music: The Collections and Writings of Moshe Beregovski* (Philadelphia: University of Pennsylvania Press, 1982)

BARRY WEINBERG

417

Koch, Kenneth (b.1925)   American poet. It is largely due to Koch's influential textbooks, now in use worldwide, that poetry became teachable to children and senior citizens. Through his alliance with John Ashbery, with whom he forged a friendship when they were undergraduates at Harvard, the New York School of poetry was founded. Its ties with avant-garde art and theater led to experiments with finding verbal equivalents for abstract expressionism, as well as to off-off Broadway lyric productions. Koch's work for the stage was collected in *A Change of Hearts: Plays, Films, and Other Dramatic Works, 1951–1971* (1973).

Koch was born in Cincinnati, where he graduated from high school in 1943. He served as rifleman in the army for the next three years in the Pacific. *Ko, or a Season on Earth* (1959) was a comic epic inspired by his contact with Japanese culture. After graduating from Harvard in 1948 Koch taught at Rutgers and at Brooklyn College, as well as directing a poetry workshop at the New School from 1958–66. In 1971 he became a full professor at Columbia University.

From 1950 he collaborated with painter Larry RIVERS, who has illustrated several of his books. Koch's first publication *Poems* (1953) was followed by *Thank You and Other Poems* (1962) which contained "Fresh air" which expressed the need for poetry to revivify itself through fusions with the other arts. *The Pleasures of Peace and Other Poems* (1969) presented "Some South American poets" who were comic inventions, mock translations of nonexistent poems, and 18 other exuberant parodies. In 1975, Koch published another collection of poems, *The Art of Love*, as well as a novel, *The Red Robins*.

FURTHER READING

Howard, R.: *Alone with America: Essays on the Art of Poetry in the US since 1950* (New York: Atheneum, 1969)

Myers, J. B.: *The poets of the New York School* (Philadelphia: University of Pennsylvania Press, 1969)

RUTH ROSENBERG

Koestler, Arthur (1905–1983)   Author and systems theorist. Born in Budapest, of an assimilated Jewish family, Koestler studied at the Technische Hochschule in Vienna. A lifelong supporter of Israel, he was co-founder of the Austrian branch of Vladimir JABOTINSKY's Revisionist movement and in 1926 he went to work on a kibbutz in Palestine. He was a foreign and later science correspondent in Palestine, Cairo, Paris, and Berlin, and lived in France and the USA before settling in England. A member of the voluntary euthanasia society, he committed suicide aged 77. His career falls into two discrete periods: between 1931 and 1956 he was a political activist and writer, and after 1956 he devoted his energies to work on the history and philosophy of science.

From 1931 until 1938 he was a member of the Communist Party and his "conversion" and subsequent repudiation is recorded in his contribution to *The God that Failed* (1950). His disillusionment with Communism was the inspiration behind his first three novels, which explore the ethics of revolution. The most famous of these, *Darkness at Noon* (1941), is a savage indictment of Stalin's Russia, based on the Moscow trials. It became one of the most influential, widely read, and translated political novels of the time. The morally concerned protagonist, Rubashov, an old bolshevik, finally confesses, in prison, to crimes that he did not commit as a last logical act of loyalty to the party. Koestler's own imprisonment in Spain in 1937, and in France in 1939–40, are related in *Spanish Testament* (1937, abridged as *Dialogue with Death*, 1941) and *The Scum of the Earth* (1941), respectively.

He returned to Palestine as a newspaperman in 1945 and again in 1948 and wrote a novel about Jewish settlement, *Thieves in the Night* (1946) and an historical study, *Promise and Fulfilment: Palestine 1917–1949* (1949), the controversial epilogue of which gives all Jews, after the establishment of the state, an "historic" choice between immigration or assimilation. The starkness of this choice is indicative of Koestler's dialectical mode of arguing, a tendency reflected in all his writings. *The Thirteenth Tribe* (1976) seeks to establish that eastern European Jewry are, in fact, descended from the Khazars, a thesis rejected by almost all the scholars in the field.

Arthur Koestler

The Sleepwalkers (1959) traces the part played by creative intuition, chance, and irrational beliefs in the history of cosmology. Koestler, whilst accepting that determinism is "depressingly true but only up to a point" sees human freedom in creativity, and in *The Act of Creation* (1964) attempts to provide a synthetic model for all human creativity, by an analysis of humor, art, and scientific discovery. At the heart of the model is his concept of "bisociation", that is, the connections made between "previously unrelated dimensions of experience to attain a higher level of mental evolution". His attack on determinism is continued in *The Ghost in the Machine* (1967) which examines the rational and emotional elements of the human brain from the viewpoint of evolutionary physiology and offers an explanation of human destructiveness, in terms of the "pathological" separation of these two neurological elements. It also presents a systems model of the operation of the interwoven hierarchical structures which underlie all biological and social life, from the genetic code to symbolic thought. Extra-sensory perception and the paranormal are the subject of *The Roots of Coincidence* (1972) in which Koestler seeks a model to account for these phenomena.

Other works include *The Gladiators* (1939), *Arrival and Departure* (1943), *Insight and Outlook* (1949), *The Heel of Achilles* (1974), *Janus* (1978), *Bricks to Babel* (1980, annotated selections), *Kaleidoscope* (1981), *Arrow in the Blue* (1952, autobiography), *The Invisible Writing* (1954, autobiography).

FURTHER READING

Harris, H.: *Astride Two Cultures: Koestler at Seventy* (London: Hutchinson, 1975)

Levine, M.: *Arthur Koestler* (New York: Ungar, 1984)

Mikes, G.: *Arthur Koestler: The Story of a Friendship* (London: André Deutsch, 1984)

Sperber, M.: *Arthur Koestler: A Collection of Critical Essays* (New York: Garland, 1971)

PAUL M. MORRIS

Kohler, Kaufmann (1843–1926) Rabbi, scholar, and leader of American Reform Judaism. A deep piety running hand in hand with critical investigation of religious institutions reflects the divergent influences of Kohler's early years. Born in Bavaria, he grew up "in the atmosphere and under the influence of the ancient, ardent, and unsophisticated orthodoxy". As a *gymnasium* student he was a disciple of Samson Raphael HIRSCH. At university he underwent a radical change of outlook, which made him an ardent champion of advanced Reform Judaism for the rest of his life. Kohler's doctoral thesis, *The Blessing of Jacob* was considered so radical as to preclude any rabbinical appointment in Germany, and in 1869 he went to the USA and became rabbi in Detroit. In 1871 he moved to Chicago and in 1879 he succeeded his father-in-law, David EINHORN, as rabbi of Temple Beth El, New York.

In 1885 Kohler engaged in a widely noticed pulpit controversy with an eminent Conservative preacher, defending the universalist outlook of Reform against the view that the Mosaic–rabbinical system of observances was of the essence of Judaism. This controversy led Kohler to convene a conference of rabbis in Pittsburgh where a statement of principles was adopted virtually in the form in which he presented it. Though unofficial, the Pittsburgh Platform became the dominant note in American Reform Judaism; and ideas which in Germany had their practical impact blunted by the disposition of a conservative society could be carried to radical conclusions in the New World.

Kohler's various statements suggest that at this period his enthusiasm for American developments transcended the political sphere and became a belief that it was bringing messianic fulfillment. Contemporary intellectual currents provided the yardstick; only the moral laws of the Pentateuch were binding, and all such ceremonies as were not adapted to the views and habits of modern civilization were rejected; Judaism had to drop its orientalism and become truly American in spirit and form. This made prayers in Hebrew obsolete, and to pray for a return to Jerusalem was a lie upon the lips of every American Jew.

Kohler's influence was enhanced through his appointment as president of Hebrew Union College (1903). He reorganized the faculty and curriculum, shaping the College to train rabbis of a "Classical Reform" outlook.

Throughout his career – even after his retirement in 1921 – Kohler was assiduous in pursuing scholarly research. He contributed many articles to *The Jewish Encyclopedia* and was editor of its department of philosophy and theology. Kohler's major work, originally written at the request of a German organization for advancing Jewish scholarship, is *Jewish Theology* (English trans. 1918).

BIBLIOGRAPHY

Hebrew Union College and Other Addresses (Cincinnati: Ark Publishing Co., 1916); Cohon, S., ed.: *A Living Faith – Selected Sermons and Addresses* (Cincinnati: Hebrew Union College, 1948)

FURTHER READING

Blau, L.: *Judaism in America* (Chicago and London: University of Chicago Press, 1976)
Plaut, W.: *Growth of Reform Judaism* (New York: World Union for Progressive Judaism, 1965)

SEFTON D. TEMKIN

Kompert, Leopold (1822–1886) Austrian writer, editor, and journalist. Born in Mnichova Hradiste (Münchengrätz), Bohemia, Kompert studied at the university in Prague, associating with the literary circle "Young Bohemia", which advocated a liberal political stance. Owing to financial difficulties, he interrupted his studies and worked for a time as a private tutor in Hungary. He later became a member of the Vienna City Council, as well as member of the Board of the Jewish Community in Vienna. From 1848 to 1852, he edited the newspaper *Österreichischer Lloyd*. He was an enthusiastic supporter of the Revolution of 1848, believing that the Jewish community only stood to benefit from a revolutionary victory. In the same year he helped found the Austrian–Jewish journal, *Oesterreichisches Central-Organ für Glaubensfreiheit, Cultur, Geschichte und Literatur der Juden* (Austrian Central Organ for Jewish Freedom of Religion, Culture, History and Literature), which advocated Jewish civil rights. His despair in the wake of anti-Jewish riots and setbacks in the struggle for full emancipation and equality led him call for mass Jewish immigration to the USA as a more realistic solution to the Jewish problem in Central Europe. Kompert is best known for his literary depictions of provincial Bohemian Jewish life and as one of the originators of Jewish ghetto literature.

In his *Aus dem ghetto* (1848, From the ghetto), *Böhmische Juden* (1851; Bohemian Jewry), *Neue Geschichten aus dem Ghetto* (1860; New stories from the ghetto), and *Geschichten einer Gasse* (1865; Stories of a street), he presented a consistently sympathetic and partially romanticized version of provincial Jewish life. The unique patterns and particulars of Jewish life are shown to be quaint, if foreign and somewhat unenlightened, but certainly worthy of respect and understanding. He treated issues concerning Jewish and gentile relations, such as intermarriage and anti-Semitism, never failing to depict the majority of his Jewish characters with sympathy and as potential modern citizens of a multi-national Austro-Hungarian state. In his novel *Am Pfluge* (1855; At the plow), he appears to advocate that Jews take up agriculture.

BIBLIOGRAPHY

The silent woman. In *Yisroel. The First Jewish Omnibus*, ed. J. Leftwich (London and New York: Thomas Yoseloff, 1952) 254–63; Off to America! In *The Jew in the Modern World*, eds P. R. Mendes Flohr and J. Reinharz (New York and Oxford: Oxford University Press, 1980) 366–8

MARK H. GELBER

Konrád, György (b.1933) Hungarian writer and essayist. Born at Berettyóujfalu in eastern Hungary, Konrád studied literature at the University of Budapest. After 1956 he was a social worker, later researching urban sociology. Since the publication of *A látogató* (1969; *The Case Worker*, 1973) he has been a full-time writer. He has traveled extensively in Europe and the USA. In 1984 he was awarded the Austrian Herder Prize, and in 1986 the Swiss Ch. Veillon Prix for the best European essay. At present he is regarded as the most impressive spokesman for the Hungarian opposition within Hungary.

Konrád's best novel is probably *A látogató* which, describing the routine working day of a Hungarian social worker, gives unusual insight into the life of the underprivileged in Socialist society. Reality and fantasy are, to some extent, intertwined in *A látogató* but the latter gains upper hand in *A városalapító* (1977; *The City Founder*, 1977) the personal notebook of a townplanner which is, in fact, a long poetic monologue, linking clusters of suggestive images. In *A cinkos* (1982; *The Loser*, 1986) the pendulum swings back to the social and historical theme. This novel relates the life of an ex-Communist intellectual whose vicissitudes reflect the violent changes in the life of an eastern European society since the collapse of the Austro-Hungarian monarchy. Konrád was also the co-author (with sociologist Iván Szelényi) of the long essay *Az értelmiség útja az osztályhatalomhoz* (1979; *The Intellectuals on the Road to Class Power*, 1979) a controversial attempt to reinterpret the classstructure of Eastern European societies, which led to the authors' brief arrest in Hungary and Szelényi's subsequent emigration to the West. *Az autonómia kisértése*, (1980; The temptation of autonomy) is a less coherent, but thoughtful collection of political notes, axioms, and suggestions; the somewhat similar *Antipolitika* (1982; *Antipolitics*, 1984) has not yet found a Hunga-

rian publisher. Since 1978 Konrád's books have not been published in Hungary, with the exception of the *samizdat* publications, yet he is still a member of the Hungarian Writers' Association.

Konrád is an agnostic rationalist but believes that "the culture of the Jewish–Christian Bible has been the shared value of Europe for nearly 2000 years" and attributes more power to religion than to secular ideologies, including Marxism. The hero of *The Loser* is a Jew, and in the different attitudes and aspirations of three generations Konrád sketches a typical enough tendency: Grandfather is a respectable Jewish merchant in a small town, Father, a somewhat enervated bourgeois with little interest in religion, and the son (also the narrator) is a skeptical rebel turning into a professional revolutionary who finally breaks with his comrades for the sake of intellectual autonomy. The son's career is to a certain extent typical of Communist intellectuals of Jewish origin. As for Konrád himself, he regards the uprising of 1956 as an important turning-point in his life; while freedom of expression is his overriding concern, his Hungarian local patriotism is strong enough to temper the temptation of cosmopolitan life in the West and keep him in his native country. He is the unlicensed critic of a regime which is attempting to project a civilized and attractive image to the West, as long as this ambition prevails, Konrád can live his "double life".

FURTHER READING

Birnbaum, M. D.: An armchair picaresque: the texture and structure of George Konrád's *The Case Worker*. In *Fiction and Drama in Eastern and Southeastern Europe*, eds N. Birnbaum and T. Eekman (Columbus: Slavica, 1980) 61–85

Sanders, I.: Freedom's captives: notes on George Konrád's novels. *World Literature Today* 57 (1983) 210–14

GEORGE GÖMÖRI

Kook, Abraham Isaac Hacohen (1865–1935) Zionist rabbi and mystic. Kook was born in Lativa and emigrated to Palestine in 1904 where he became chief rabbi of Jaffa. After spending part of the First World War in London, he returned to Palestine and was appointed the first Ashkenazic chief rabbi of Palestine in 1921. He established a *yeshivah*, Merkaz Harav, where particular attention was paid to study of texts regarding settlement of the land of Israel and the sacrificial laws which would be practiced once the Temple was rebuilt.

Kook developed close relationships with the secular labor Zionists and evolved a religious theory that accepted non-religious Jews as partners in the national enterprise of building the land. He held that the Zionist movement represented the "beginnings of messianic times", since a material substrate was necessary for the coming of the Messiah. This substrate was the land of Israel. Borrowing the talmudic saying that "in the footsteps of the Messiah insolence (*hutzpah*) will increase", Kook argued that the secular pioneers were playing a necessary role by settling the land. Their irreligious "insolence" was not an unwanted byproduct of the messianic drama, but a required factor in creating the correct material conditions. The secular Zionists unwittingly fulfilled God's intention even though they denied the authority of the religious tradition. In arguing for the legitimacy of human action in bringing the Messiah, Kook identified with a long tradition articulated by Moses Maimonides in the twelfth century and by Zvi Hirsch KALISCHER in the nineteenth; yet by giving such a positive role to the secular, Kook took this activist messianism a step further.

Kook regarded the land of Israel as intrinsically holy and he believed that its holiness would penetrate even the most irreligious Jews. Once the secular had fulfilled their material function, they too would return to the Orthodox fold. Thus, despite his openness to the secular Zionists, Kook never advanced a pluralistic theory of Judaism.

Kook's Zionism was rooted in his mysticism. He held that holiness requires a dialectical synthesis of the sacred and the profane; there is no such thing as pure spirituality devoid of a profane substrate. The goal of mysticism is to unify the fragmented world, to harmonize the secular and the sacred. The mystical perspective (*hasodiyut*) understands the secret unity between all things. Kook was more interested in his mystical writings in human psychology than

in theosophy, an emphasis that he shared with Hasidism.

Kook also believed that the modern theory of evolution does not contradict Jewish teachings since it teaches, like Jewish mysticism, that human beings progress from lower to higher forms. Kook thought that the hand of God lay behind evolution, just as divine "cunning" explained the role of the secular Zionists in fulfilling God's plan. Thus, although evolutionary theory emphasized blind chance, a mystical interpretation of evolution could find evidence of God's providence.

Finally, Kook sought a reconciliation of nationalism with universalism. Jewish nationalism was the key to bringing peace and harmony to the nations; the Jews were the chosen people since God had elected them to fulfill a universal role.

Kook's thought was the major influence on the messianic Zionist movement, *Gush Emunim*, which advocated settlement of the lands occupied in the 1967 war; his son, Zvi Yehuda Kook, was the main ideologue of this group until his death in 1981. But Kook was also quoted by those on the more moderate side of the Israeli political spectrum who referred to his universalism as a religious source for reconciliation with the Arabs.

BIBLIOGRAPHY

The Lights of Penitence, Lights of Holiness, The Moral Principles, Essays, Letters and Poems, trans. B. Z. Bokser (New York: Paulist Press, 1978)

FURTHER READING

Agus, J. *High Priest of Rebirth* (New York: Bloch, 1972)

Bergmann, S. H.: *Faith and Reason* (Washington DC: Bnai Brith Hillel Foundation, 1961)

DAVID BIALE

Kops, Bernard (b.1926) British novelist, dramatist, and poet. Born in London, Kops left school at 13 and worked in a variety of jobs in London's East End. He first began to write poetry after the Second World War, later published as *Poems* (1955) and *Poems and Songs* (1958). His literary breakthrough was achieved with the production of his first play *The Hamlet of Stepney Green*, (first produced in 1957). This play was one of a number of "kitchen sink" dramas in the 1950s which challenged the traditional middle-class theater of reassurance. By utilizing his working-class background, Kops was inevitably related to the stark naturalism of the new wave of playwrights in the 1950s. Nevertheless, he was also to develop a specific voice and set of concerns during this period. *Goodbye World* (produced 1959), *The Dream of Peter Mann* (produced 1960) and *Change for the Angel* (produced 1960) are all distinguished by a mixture of fantasy and naturalism and by a tone of poetic exuberance and apocalyptic rejection. Another important element of Kops's early drama is an idealistic hero who is forced to confront and compromise with the realities that have shaped him. Above all, Kops's main concern is the bitter-sweet familial relationships which are the core of his plays and which he developed in his novels of the late 1960s and 1970s.

Kops draws heavily on his own working-class Jewish background and early life in London's East End, most clearly in his autobiography *The World is a Wedding* (1963). Phrases and scenes from this book are often reused in Kops's imaginative work. Because of his central exploration of fantasy and inner states of being, and his use of dream logic, some critics have argued that radio drama is, in fact, Kops's true métier. Certainly, some of his most important work such as *Home Sweet Honeycomb* (1962), *The Lemmings* (1963) and *Ezra* (1980) take the form of radio plays. Other successful plays such as *Enter Solly Gold* (1962) were written for both the stage and radio. In all, Kops has written 17 radio and 10 stage plays.

Kops's novels were written as an extension of his work as a poet and dramatist. Central elements of his fiction, such as the destruction of the Jewish East End, the spiritual loss which accompanies embourgeoisment, the dying father-figure, and the oedipal mother-figure are all taken from his drama. *Yes From No-man's Land* (1965) and *The Dissent of Dominick Shapiro* (1966) are, like Kops's earlier plays, concerned with the painful ambivalences caused by the loss of one's family and community. And

Settle Down Simon Katz (1973), like *Enter Solly Gold*, contrasts the exuberant world of the East End with the dull conformity of North West London. The oedipal fixation of Kops's early Hamlet-figures is also given its fullest account in *By the Waters of Whitechapel* (1969). This novel is Kops's most successful treatment of the breakdown of personality, a theme running through most of his work and based on his own mental breakdown as a young man. Kops has written nine novels and most recently, two television serials *After the Big Time* (1985) and *Children of Mean Streets* (1987). He has also published *Neither Your Money Nor Your Sting: An Offbeat History of the Jews* (1985).

FURTHER READING

East Ender: Bernard Kops. *The Jewish Quarterly* 33 (1986)

BRYAN CHEYETTE

Kopytman, Mark (b.1929) Israeli composer. Born in the Soviet Union, he studied music and medicine, but after gaining his MD degree he turned to music, graduating from the Moscow Conservatory in 1958. In Russia he composed large-scale works, among them string quartets and a full scale opera, *Casa Mare*, which was produced there. In 1972 he immigrated to Israel, where he soon assimilated, acquainting himself for the first time with Jewish culture and heritage. He became a professor of composition at the Rubin Academy of Music in Jerusalem. His style underwent significant changes as a result of his encounter with contemporary western music and Jewish traditional chant and songs. He developed heterophonic textures in his chamber and orchestral works, with quotations from traditional Jewish cantillation, and powerful qualities of recitative, as in the series of *Canti* for chamber ensembles. His *Memory* for orchestra utilized the voice of a Yemenite folk singer, Gila Bashari, who performs a Yemenite song whose melody and intonation serve as the basis for elaborate heterophonic development. *Memory* won Kopytman the Koussevitzky Award for the outstanding recording of 1986, and was performed in the USA and Europe.

His chamber works have reached the Eastern bloc countries.

JEHOASH HIRSHBERG

Korda, Alexander (Sándor László Kellner) (1893–1956) British film producer and director. Korda was editing film journals while still at school in Budapest. By 1919, he had directed 25 films. He went to Vienna, Berlin, and, in 1927, to Hollywood, directing and sometimes producing a further 20. When he returned to Europe he finally settled in England. Korda created London Film Productions in 1932 and launched the British cinema on to the international stage. The success of *The Private Life of Henry VIII* (1933) enabled him to expand and to build, at Denham, the most prestigious studio in Europe, although, by 1938, he was in financial difficulties and had lost it. Although he continued as an executive producer, he directed only three films after 1939, the last, a version of Oscar Wilde's *An Ideal Husband,* in 1947.

His personal reputation for extravagance was mirrored in his production methods. *Things to Come* (1936) was a costly *"succes d'estime"* and *The Thief of Bagdad* (1940) had to be finished in Hollywood, where Korda remained from 1941 to 1943, and where he made the patriotic *That Hamilton Woman* (1941) which Churchill admired. He suggested the double characterization of Hitler and the Jewish Barber which Chaplin adopted for *The Great Dictator* (USA 1940) and was executive producer on the most brilliant anti-Nazi satire of the Second World War, Lubitsch's *To Be Or Not To Be* (USA 1942). At this time he was also working for British Intelligence – as he had before the war – and for which, probably in combination with Churchill's debt to him for supporting and employing him during the 1930s, he was knighted.

He returned to Britain in 1943 and, after the war, attempted to rebuild London Films by acquiring British Lion but state loans could not sustain it and, in 1954, Korda found himself, once more without a studio base.

Other films include: *Seine Majestät das Bettelkind* (Austria, 1920), *The Private Life of Helen of Troy* (USA 1927), *Rembrandt* (1936).

FURTHER READING

Dell, J.: *Nobody Ordered Wolves* (London: Heinemann, 1939) [novel]

Kulik, K.: *Alexander Korda: The Man Who Could Work Miracles* (London: W. H. Allen, 1975)

Tabori, P.: *Alexander Korda* (London: Oldbourne, 1959)

KEVIN GOUGH-YATES

Kornfeld, Paul (1889–1942) Playwright and essayist. Born into a well-to-do Jewish family in Prague, he was probably the most controversial of the writers of the "Prague circle". In his expressionistic dramas, *Die Verführung* (1917; The temptation) and *Himmel und Hölle* (1919; Heaven and hell), he illustrated the theory he had proclaimed in 1918 in his manifesto *The Soulful and the Psychological Man,* which served as a guideline to a great many of his literary contemporaries. In the manifesto Kornfeld denies the need for "convincing characters, because reality is but a mistaken conception and only within emotions the truth might be found". By sheer force of his language and agility of thought he became a great influence during the period of literary expressionism.

Like many expressionistic playwrights he turned to comedy and in the first of his comedies, *Der ewige Traum* (1922; The eternal dream), he ridiculed the notions he had so fervently defended until then. *Palme oder der Gekränkte* (1924; Palme or the offended one) was followed by *Kilian oder die gelbe Rose,* (1926; Kilian or the yellow rose), his most successful comedy. In the comedy *Smither kauft Europa* (Smither buys Europe), written in 1929 and never published or performed, Kornfeld pours out his disappointment with Europe, the shallowness of its society and the unethical manner of literary critics. Smither, like Palme and the protagonist of *The Temptation* are outsiders, condemned to loneliness, and the motif of the outsider, in an historical frame, is also at the core of Kornfeld's last drama *Jud Süss* (1930; Jew Süss). Here Kornfeld took great liberties with the historical figure of the Duke to stress the similarity between Jud Süss's reactions and those of Kornfeld's contemporaries. It is not the desire for riches but love and admiration for the Duke and the land that keep Süss from leaving while he still could do so.

During the years 1929–32 Kornfeld lived in Berlin, publishing many essays which proved his grasp of political matters and his mistrust of politics. For family reasons he went to Prague in 1932 and of his own volition remained there after 1939 when his sisters' families went to England. In a small room in a suburb of Prague he continued writing his only novel until he was deported. *Blanche oder das Atelier im Garten* (Blanche or the study in the garden) was published in 1957; it is a compilation of loosely connected reflections about art, love, God, life, with death as the main motif. Kornfeld left the manuscript with a Czech friend who sent it to his family after the war.

MARGARITA PAZI

Korngold, Erich Wolfgang (1897–1957)

American composer. He was born in Brünn, Moravia (now Brno, Czechoslovakia) and his father was the music critic Julian Korngold (1860–1945). Erich's musical ability manifested itself when he was still a child and, at the suggestion of Gustav Mahler (who heard one of Korngold's compositions, the cantata *Gold*, in 1907), he began to take composition lessons. When he was still only 11 he composed the pantomime *Der Schneemann*, which scored a great success at its first performance in Vienna in 1910. A number of eminent composers and musicians took an interest in Korngold's music: Artur Schnabel adopted the Piano Sonata in E (1910) into his repertoire; Richard Strauss praised the Sinfonietta (1912); and Puccini expressed his admiration for the opera *Violanta* (1916). The finest of Korngold's operas, *Die tote Stadt*, was premiered simultaneously in Cologne and Hamburg in 1920 and was widely performed in Europe and the USA.

In the 1920s Korngold taught opera and composition at the Vienna State Academy. His reputation as a composer continued to grow and in 1934 he went to Hollywood, where he wrote a number of superlative film scores, including those for *Robin Hood* and *Anthony Adverse*. He settled in the USA and after the war returned to composing symphonic music; these works include the Violin Concerto (1945), the Cello Concerto (1946), the Symphonic Serenade for strings (1947) and the Symphony in F Sharp (1952).

FURTHER READING
Hoffmann, R. S.: *Erich Wolfgang Korngold*, (Vienna: 1922)

SYDNEY FIXMAN

Kossoff, Leon (b.1926)

British painter. Kossoff was born in London to Russian–Jewish immigrant parents who ran a bakery in the East End. He studied at St Martin's School of Art during the day between 1949 and 1953, and in the evenings between 1950 and 1952 attended David BOMBERG's classes at the Borough Polytechnic, where he was profoundly influenced by the older Jewish painter's self-professed search for the "spirit in the mass". He became a postgraduate student at the Royal College of Art in 1953, and himself taught in various art schools until the late 1960s.

Kossoff's work has much in common with that of Franz AUERBACH, a close friend of his. The surfaces of his paintings are heavily impastoed and colors, until recently, have tended to be somber. His repertory of motifs is limited: either family and friends or anonymous passers-by in the anonymous public spaces of London's less glamorous districts. Although his paintings have affinities with a British urban realist tradition best represented by Sickert, his approach to the human figure can also be seen as deriving in part from his Jewish heritage. Helen Lessore has described Kossoff's work as follows: "The idealizing is in the direction of moral qualities, above all, of endurance ... one often feels a heroic spirit almost bursting out of its inadequate or hampering body ... Kossoff has painted his own people, giving them something approaching mythological status".

FURTHER READING
Leon Kossoff: Paintings from a Decade 1970–1980 (Oxford: Museum of Modern Art, 1981) [exhibition catalog]
Leon Kossoff: Recent Work (London: Fischer Fine Art, 1984) [exhibition catalog]

MONICA BOHM-DUCHEN

Kovner, Abba (1918–1988) Hebrew poet. Born in Sevastopol in the Crimea, Kovner was raised from the age of 8 in Vilna where he studied in a modern Hebrew *gymnasium* and was active in the *Hashomer Hatza'ir* movement. He began writing Hebrew poetry before the war and was also a student of sculpture. At the outbreak of the war, Kovner remained in Vilna. For a brief period, he was sheltered by nuns in a Dominican convent, the memories of which are reflected in his poems, notably *Ahoti ketanah* (1967; My sister is little). Later, he moved to the Vilna ghetto where he became one of the leaders of the Jewish resistance. With the liquidation of the ghetto, Kovner escaped and continued as a leader of the Jewish partisan groups in the Rudniki forests near Vilna. His poem *Ad lo 'or*, (1947; Until no light) is set against this background. Having survived the war, Kovner became one of the organizers of the illegal Jewish immigration into Palestine. Captured by the British secret police, he was imprisoned in Cairo. Upon his release, Kovner returned to Palestine and joined the kibbutz *Ein hahoresh*. During the War of Independence, he served in the Givati Brigade, an experience recounted in his prose trilogy *Panim 'el panim*, (1953, 1955; Face to face).

Kovner's most important poems deal mainly with the two most powerful experiences of his life: the Holocaust and the birth of the State of Israel. Apart from the works mentioned, his volumes of poetry include: *Preidah mehadarom*, (1949; A parting from the south), *Admat hahol*, (1961; Sandy soil), *Mikol ha'ahavot*, (1965; From all the loves), *Hupah bamidbar*, (1970; A canopy in the desert) and *Hasefer hakatan*, (1973; The little book). His poetry is characterized by its painful fusion of personal experience and Jewish history and its complex, yet precise, lyric–dramatic modernist style. A selection of his poems in English, *A Canopy In the Desert*, has been translated by Shirley Kaufman (1973). A collection of Kovner's Hebrew essays, *Al hagesher hatzar* (On the narrow bridge) appeared in 1981, edited and with a biographical and critical afterword by Shalom Luria.

FURTHER READING
Carmi, T., Spicehandler, E., and Burnshaw, S., eds:

Abba Kovner. In *The Modern Hebrew Poem Itself* (New York: Holt Rinehart Winston, 1965)

DAVID ABERBACH

Kozakov, Mikhail (1897–1954) Russian prose writer, also partially (in the 1920s) involved with Russian–Jewish literature. The most significant of his works are the narrative tales "Abram Nashatyr, soderzhatel gostinitsy" (1926; Abram Nashatyr, hotel landlord) and "Chelovek, padaiushchii nits" (1928; The person kissing the ground). These are Jewish in terms not only of their theme and point of view, but also in the vigilance and intrepidity of the views on the most acute problems of Jewry in post-revolutionary Russia: the déclassé process, poverty, criminal enrichment, and anti-Semitism). Mercilessness of vision ranks him together with Isaak BABEL. It is interesting and instructive to observe Kozakov's declining attention to Jewry while writing his major book, the historical novel (from the pre-revolutionary era) *Deviat tochek* (Nine points; the first four parts, 1929–37; the final version, under the title *Krushenie imperii*, The downfall of the Empire, 1956).

SHIMON MARKISH

Krakauer, Leopold (1890–1954) Israeli architect and draughtsman. Krakauer was born in Vienna where he studied architecture and engineering. In 1920–1 he helped design the Parliament building in Belgrade, Yugoslavia. Architecture was his professional vocation, while drawing his leisure activity. However, in Vienna, where he was associated with such Modernist painters as Oskar Kokoschka, he painted flowers in black and white, and attempted abstractions under the influence of Kandinsky's theories. Portrait drawings of *c*.1919 indicate a knowledge of Cubism. In 1924 Krakauer emigrated to Palestine, settled in Jerusalem, and won an architectural prize. Initially Krakauer and his wife belonged to the circle of Jerusalem that focused around the Ticho family, and which included S. Y. AGNON, Martin BUBER, Zalman Schocken, Hugo Bergman and others. Only following the wave of German immigration during the 1930s did Krakauer increase his links with the Bezalel artists. He participated in the *Migdal David* exhibition of 1926, and in the 1949 opening of the Artists' club, *Beit ha'omanim* in Jerusalem.

Krakauer designed several private houses and public buildings. Dr Bonem House, today a branch of Bank Leumi in Jerusalem, is one of his more famous buildings and a clear indication of his affiliation with the modern International style of the time. It is a classical example of modernist architecture, clearly defined square masses, intercepted by asymmetrical openings and doors. During the early 1930s he designed dining halls, cultural centers, and children's houses for collective settlements, commissioned by the *Keren kayemet leyisra'el* (the Jewish National Fund) and *Keren hayesod*. In his architecture he was always conscious of the local materials and attempted to harmonize with the landscape through simplicity of line and volume. He designed a cultural center for Hanita, incorporating an Arab ruin and using the local traditional stone rustication for the façade, a texture to which he returned frequently. From 1948 he concentrated mainly on town planning, for small or larger settlements.

Krakauer's main pictorial themes, drawn from memory, are landscapes, or details relating to the Jerusalem landscape; they are often executed in black or sepia on yellowish or blue paper. Other subjects are olive trees, especially their dramatic trunks, and thistles, which he kept in his study, or close at hand. All these were drawn with energetic, winding, and changeable line, often without any articulation of the background. While his line can be seen as belonging to the Viennese Expressionists like Kokoschka and Egon Schiele, his themes are a unique symbolic attempt at combining Christian cultural symbols with the Jewish prophetic mood of loneliness. Krakauer's sober, unsentimental style is exceptional in Israeli figurative art. In 1931 he exhibited in Amsterdam; in 1954 he participated in the Venice Biennale.

NEDIRA YAKIR BUNYARD

Kramer, Jacob (1892–1962) British painter. Born in Klintsy in the Ukraine, he lived in Leeds from 1900. Kramer was unusual in coming from an artistic family: both his father and his uncle were successful court painters, while his mother was a distinguished opera singer. His formal artistic training began in 1907, when he attended evening classes at the Leeds School of Art; a year later, he won a scholarship to study there full-time. In 1912, supported by the Jewish Educational Aid Society, he became a student at the Slade School of Art in London.

Exposed during these years to avant-garde influences, he gradually abandoned the naturalism of his earliest works (most of which were portraits) in favour of a radically simplified, hieratic style indebted to the example of his friend Mark GERTLER. The works for which he became best known were depictions of Jews at prayer or deep in studious contemplation (see illustration on p. 428); rhythmically powerful and somber in colour, these paintings are intensely devotional, even though Kramer ceased early on to be an observant Jew. He himself wrote of his "endeavor to create a purely spiritual form".

Financial necessity, however, impelled Kramer to continue producing sensitive naturalistic portraits. Israel ZANGWILL and Jacob EPSTEIN, both close friends of the artist, were among those who sat for him. His later work is less innovative, although a commission in the late 1940s to design book jackets for the Soncino Books of the Bible enabled him to recapture something of the graphic boldness of the work produced between 1916 and the early 1920s. Leeds, which remained his home, honored him posthumously by renaming its art college the Jacob Kramer College.

FURTHER READING

Kramer, M.: *Jacob Kramer: A Memorial Volume* (Leeds: E. J. Arnold & Sons, 1969)
Jacob Kramer Reassessed (London: Ben Uri Art Gallery, 1984) [exhibition catalog]

MONICA BOHM-DUCHEN

Kraus, Karl (1874–1936) Austrian essayist, dramatist, and poet. A native of Jičin (Bohe-

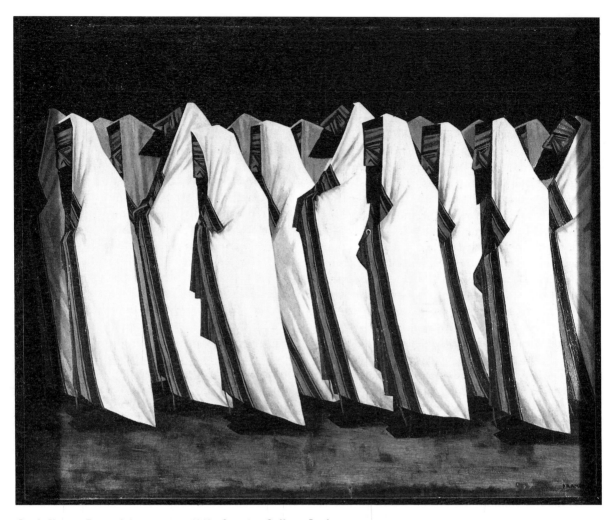

Jacob Kramer Day of Atonement *1919. City Art Gallery, Leeds*

mia), Kraus spent almost his entire life in Vienna, a city with which he, like Sigmund FREUD, had a love–hate relationship. After studying at the University of Vienna without taking a degree, and making an unsuccessful debut as an actor (for which he later compensated with 700 spellbinding readings of his own works as well as one-man performances of entire plays and operettas), Kraus contributed to a number of journals before founding his own satiric periodical, *Die Fackel* (The Torch), in 1899. From 1911 on Kraus wrote the entire contents of this irregularly published journal with an inimitable satiric *genius loci* himself.

Quotation was the hallmark of Kraus's satire,

and in its use he was guided by the conviction that what was most unspeakable about his age could be spoken only by the age itself. Most of his books – from *Sittlichkeit und Kriminalität* (1908) to *Literatur und Lüge* (1929) and including nine volumes of poetry *Worte in Versen* (1916–30) as well as several books of aphorisms – first appeared in the pages of *Die Fackel*. A foe of the pernicious press and the feuilletonism of a Heinrich HEINE, Kraus fought for purity of language, thought, and action, in a "language-forsaken" age. His aphorism "My language is the common prostitute that I turn into a virgin" (H. Zohn, ed., *Half-Truths and One-and-a-Half Truths*, 1976; 1985) illuminates both the mission and the method of a man who discerned an absolute congruity between word and world, language and life.

Kraus's most characteristic work was produced in wartime, and the most important of his plays, the monumental but virtually unperformable "phonomontage" *Die letzten Tage der Menschheit* (1922; *The Last Days of Mankind*, Engl. abridgments 1974, 1976) may be the most powerful pacifistic statement ever made. *Die Dritte Walpurgisnacht*, Kraus's chilling adumbration of the full fury of the Nazis, did not appear in its entirety in the author's lifetime. In his last years the essentially apolitical satirist chose what he regarded as the lesser of two evils and supported the clerico-fascist regime of Engelbert Dollfuss. In resignation, Kraus increasingly concentrated on his translations of Shakespeare and his *Sprachlehre*, including his unique "comma problems".

Kraus's convoluted Jewishness is a controversial matter. He has been called everything from "a shining exemplar of Jewish self-hatred" (Theodor LESSING) to an "arch-Jew" (Berthold Viertel). As early as 1899 Kraus left the Jewish fold, then secretly converted to Catholicism in 1911 and publicly left the Church again in 1922 as a protest against its perceived collusion with the commercialism of the Salzburg Festival. In Kraus's writings embarrassingly anti-Jewish statements alternate with the exhortations of a latter-day Old Testament prophet.

FURTHER READING

Iggers, W. A.: *Karl Kraus: A Viennese Critic of the Twentieth Century* (The Hague: Martinus Nijhoff, 1967)

Timms, E.: *Karl Kraus: Apocalyptic Satirist* (New Haven and London: Yale University Press, 1986)

Zohn, H.: *Karl Kraus* (New York: Twayne, 1971)

HARRY ZOHN

Kreitman, Esther [Hinde] (1891–1954) Yiddish writer. Kreitman was born in Bilgoray, Poland, the eldest child of Bathsheba and Pinchos Mendel Singer. Her father was a rabbi, as were both her grandfathers, her mother's father being the magisterial Rabbi of Bilgoray. Esther grew up in Leoncin (moving subsequently to Radzymin and Warsaw), frustrated by the convention of Orthodox Jewry which proscribed education for females. When she asked her parents what she would be her mother replied, "What *can* a girl be", while her father answered, "What are *you* going to be one day? Nothing, of course". Such enquiries of her three brothers occasioned more considered responses. Two of them became world-famous novelists; Israel Joshua and Isaac Bashevis SINGER. They wrote memoirs too – the former's being *Of A World That Is No More* (1987), the latter's *In My Father's Court* (1966) – which show Esther as a somewhat manic adolescent. Yet she was the first of the siblings to start writing. All her early stories, however, were destroyed when she took the train to Berlin to meet Avraham Kreitman, her future husband. The arranged match was a disaster, made worse by the disruptions of the First World War, during the course of which the Kreitmans fled to England. Here Esther began to write again, inspired by a post-war visit to her brothers in Warsaw. In her lifetime she published two novels, *Der sheydem-tants* (1936) and *Brilyantn* (1944) and a collection of stories – *Yikhes* (1949). Of these only *Deborah* (as *Der sheydem-tants* became known) has been translated into English. Published in 1946, it was forgotten until Virago, a feminist imprint, reissued it in 1982. It is an autobiographical novel, the story of how a young woman determines to make something out of nothing. This Esther Kreitman did, but at the cost of her health.

FURTHER READING

Sinclair, C.: *The Brothers Singer* (London: Allison & Busby, 1983)

CLIVE SINCLAIR

Krochmal, Nachman [Renak] (1785–1840) Philosopher and historian. One of the founders of the Jewish Enlightenment (*Haskalah*), Krochmal was among the first modern Jewish thinkers to develop an historical study of Judaism and try to fit it into a systematic philosophical framework greatly influenced by Herder and Hegel.

Trained in his native Brody (Galicia) in rabbinical studies, Krochmal was one of the first Eastern European Jewish scholars who came under the influence of the writings of Moses MENDELSSOHN. His major work, *Moreh nevokhei hazeman* (Guide of the perplexed of our time), was published posthumously by Leopold ZUNZ in 1851. Consciously modeled on Maimonides' attempt to integrate Aristotelian philosophy into normative Judaism, it tries to offer an understanding of the development and eternity of the Jewish people within Hegelian philosophy of history. In *Haruhani hamuhlat* (Absolute spirit) Krochmal sees, following German idealist philosophy, a rational explication of the Divine. History is its objective manifestation, and it occurs as a successive unfolding of "national spirits". Each such successive national spirit (*ruah 'uma*) expresses a higher degree of consciousness and, following Herder, Krochmal recognizes three stages of development in every "national spirit": growth, flowering, and decline. All historical nations follow this pattern, and the epitome of each nation is when it adds its contribution to world history – and disappears, just at the height of its civilization which then becomes integrated into world culture. Jewish history, however, is different according to Krochmal – it is cyclical rather than linear. Like all nations, the Jewish nation also goes through three stages – but at the end of the third stage, rather than disappear into the universal horizon of mankind, the Jewish people starts afresh. The reason for this difference in the Jewish case is, according to Krochmal, because all other national spirits express the Absolute only in varying particular modes and hence in limited forms, whereas the Jewish "spirit of the nation", which is the Torah, is itself coeval with the Absolute Spirit. Hence every Jewish period of decline – the destruction of the First, or Second Temple, for example, is followed by a new explosion of historical energy. The Jewish people is thus *'am 'olam* – both an eternal and a universal people.

Krochmal's thinking historicized the understanding of Judaism while claiming for Judaism an identity with the Absolute Spirit of Hegelian philosophy which enabled the Jewish people to transcend history while being constantly active

in it. In this, Krochmal contributed to the intellectual underpinning of the WISSENSCHAFT DES JUDENTUMS, as well as providing an answer to the conventional Young Hegelian contention, rather popular among first-generation Jewish *maskilim*, that Judaism had fulfilled its role with the emergence of Christianity.

In his studies of *halakhah* and *aggadah*, Krochmal also contributed to the understanding of both as two different modes of conveying the eternal rational kernel of the Torah within given historical contexts.

FURTHER READING

Schechter, S.: *Rabbi Nachman Krochmal and "The Perplexities of the Time"* (London: Jews' College Literary Society, 1887)

Rotenstreich, N.: *Jewish Philosophy in Modern Times* (New York: Holt, Rinehart & Winston, 1968) chapter 5

SHLOMO AVINERI

Kronenberger, Louis (1904–1980)   American drama critic, editor, and novelist. Kronenberger was born in Cincinnati, Ohio, to German–Jewish parents. Educated in the public schools, he graduated from the University of Cincinnati in 1924. He worked for the New York *Times* until, in 1926, he obtained an editorial job with Boni and Liveright, the publishers of O'Neill, Anderson, Faulkner, Hemingway, and Dreiser. From 1933–8 he worked as an editor for Alfred A. Knopf, and served as a member of the board of editors of *Fortune* Magazine. From 1938–61, he served as the drama critic for *Time*.

His numerous academic appointments include City College (1953), Stanford (1954), New York University (1958), Harvard (1959), Oxford (1959), Princeton (1961), Berkeley (1968), and Brandeis, where he was professor of theater arts from 1952–70. These lectures were published as a study of stage comedy in *The Thread of Laughter: Chapters on English Stage Comedy from Jonson to Maugham* (1952). He also edited the annual volume of *Best Plays* from 1952 to 1961.

Kronenberger's collections of critical essays were admired for their urbanity and sophistication and his novels were lauded for their civility and charm. He began his literary career with *The Grand Manner* (1929), followed by *Grand Right and Left* (1952), and *A Month of Sundays* (1961). His play, *The Heavenly Twins* was produced at the Booth Theater on Broadway in 1955.

He also achieved acclaim as a biographer of Sarah Churchill in *Marlborough's Duchess: A Study in Worldliness* (1958) and of *Oscar Wilde* (1976). He was awarded a Guggenheim fellowship in 1969.

BIBLIOGRAPHY

No Whippings, No Gold Watches: The Saga of a Writer and his Jobs (Atlantic, 1970)

FURTHER READING

Kinsman, C. D., ed.: *Contemporary Authors*, vol. 2 (Detroit: Gale Research Co., 1967)

RUTH ROSENBERG

Kuhn, Walt (1877–1949)

Kuhn, Walt (1877–1949) American painter. The son of immigrants from Bavaria, Walt Kuhn was born in Brooklyn, New York. He began his artistic career as a newspaper cartoonist and magazine illustrator. In Europe in 1901 he studied in Amsterdam, in Paris at the Academie Colarossi, and in Munich at the Academy. Back in New York in 1903, he became allied with the Ashcan group of painters, who organized against the conservative academic art establishment, and developed a realist style to paint the urban social scene.

Kuhn's role as the principal organizer of the famous Armory Show (New York 1913), which introduced such European modernists as Picasso, Matisse, and Duchamp to the American public, prompted him to experiment with Fauve color and Cubist abstraction in his own work. The development of his own distinctive mature style was slow, however. With the development of a near fatal stomach ulcer in 1925, Kuhn resolved to pursue his painting to the exclusion of all other activities. Within several years he painted his first portraits of show people, a subject which had always attracted him and which was to preoccupy him artistically until his death in 1949. Bold outlining and the massing of volumetric solids endows his showgirls, acrobats, and clowns with a robust energy and physicality. These portraits earned Kuhn undivided critical favor during the 1930s and 1940s.

Although his art fell out of favor after his death, a number of significant posthumous exhibitions of his work have been organized. In 1987 the Whitney Museum of American Art in New York presented an exhibition of his paintings of show people.

FURTHER READING

Adams, P. R.: *Walt Kuhn, Painter* (Columbus: Ohio State University Press, 1978)

Phillips, L.: *Walt Kuhn: The Entertainers* (New York: Whitney Museum of American Art, 1987) [exhibition catalog]

KRISTIE A. JAYNE

Kumin, Maxine (b.1925) American poet, novelist, and children's author. Born Maxine Winokur in Philadelphia, Kumin received BA and MA degrees from Radcliffe College. The mother of three children, whom she addresses in many poems, she has taught at Tufts, Columbia, and Princeton among other schools. The winner of many prestigious honors, she received the Pulitzer Prize in 1973 for her fourth collection of poetry *Up Country* (1972) and has served as Poetry Consultant to the Library of Congress.

Often associated with her close friend, the poet Anne Sexton with whom she wrote a children's book, *The Wizard's Tears* (1975), Kumin, unlike Sexton, cannot be called a confessional poet although she addresses personal and familial issues in her poems. She and Sexton do share an exploration of common themes: the role of women as daughters, mothers, and wives; religious identity (Sexton was Catholic); and the fragility of human life, with a concomitant fascination with death. But Kumin's perspective is instructed by her affinity with the natural world's recurrent cycles of loss and renewal, a subject she writes about frequently and unsentimentally in poems about her New Hampshire farm.

Kumin is sometimes uneasy with but never indifferent to her Jewish identity. In her first collection, *Halfway* (1962), she recalls, "On being asked to write a poem for the centenary of the Civil War" that her "... only link with" the event is her immigrant great-grandfather, "a Jew, and poor", who made his fortune tailoring Confederate Army uniforms. His persistent, if "erratic", commitment to Jewish and family values, celebrated in a later poem from the collection, *The Nightmare Factory* (1970), is her legacy. The Jewish identity embodied in her family history, eulogized in poems like "The Pawnbroker", "Sperm", and "The Chain", is comfortable; however, in her personal connection to Jewish life Kumin almost always sees herself in contrast to a dogged, discomforting other. A self-declared agnostic for whom "[w]ords are the only holy ...", she finds no comfort in religion, a skepticism reaffirmed in her 1985 collection, *The Long Approach*.

In addition to her poetry, four novels, short stories, and several collections of essays, Kumin has published more than 20 children's books.

BIBLIOGRAPHY
Through Dooms of Love (New York: Harper, 1965), repr. as *A Daughter and Her Loves* (London: Gollancz, 1965)

FURTHER READING
Ludvigkson, S.: Maxine Kumin, in *Dictionary of Literary Biography*, vol. 5 part 1 (Detroit: Gale Research Co., 1980)

ELIZABETH KLEIN

Kunitz, Stanley (b.1905) American poet. Born in Worcester, Massachusetts, of immigrant Russian–Jewish parents, Kunitz was the third child and first son of a dress manufacturer who committed suicide shortly before the poet's birth. The trauma of that loss and the quest to find its meaning have marked Kunitz's life and poetry. At Harvard, from which Kunitz took a BA degree in 1926 and a master's degree a year later, he won his first poetry prize, an award which was to usher in a lifetime of honors. In 1958 he married his third wife, the artist, Elise Asher.

For nearly two decades Kunitz edited literary reference works. After military service in the Second World War, he held a series of academic posts. He became a venerable dean of American poets for the superb quality of four collections of poetry: *Intellectual Things* (1930), *Passport to the War* (1944), *Selected Poems 1928–1958* (1958), and *The Testing Tree* (1971). Additional poems appear in *The Wellfleet Whale and Companion Poems* (1983) and *Next-to-Last Things: New Poems and Essays* (1985).

Never a coterie poet, Kunitz followed his own bent, probing his life experiences for insights into himself and the meaning of the universe. His poems are marked by their intensity, wonder, passion, craftsmanship, clarity, and strength. Poetry is his religion but Jewishness is implicit in his work; the best example is to be found in his most famous poem, "Father and Son".

BIBLIOGRAPHY
The Poems of Stanley Kunitz, 1928–1978 (London: Secker & Warburg, 1979); *A Kind of Order, A Kind of Folly: Essays and Conversations* (1975)

FURTHER READING
Busa, C.: The art of poetry XXIX. Stanley Kunitz. *Paris Review* 24 (1982)
Orr, G.: *Stanley Kunitz: An Introduction to the Poetry* (New York: Columbia University Press, 1985)

JOSEPH COHEN

Kurzweil, Baruch (1907–1972) Hebrew literary critic. Born in Pirnice, Moravia (Czechoslovakia), Kurzweil studied in Frankfurt at the Breuer *Yeshivah* and at the University of Frankfurt, where he received a doctorate in 1933 for a thesis on Goethe. This merger of German–Jewish Orthodoxy and Germanic humanism was to reflect itself in Kurzweil's literary and cultural criticism.

After teaching in a Hebrew *gymnasium* in Brno, Kurzweil went to Palestine in 1938. He was assisted in this by Martin BUBER, whose influence on Kurzweil remained formative. After serving as Buber's research assistant in Jerusalem, Kurzweil taught at prestigious secondary schools in Haifa and finally, from 1956, at Bar–Ilan University.

As a pre-eminent literary critic, Kurzweil's name is linked primarily with his diagnosis of the crisis of faith in the works of such major writers as H. N. BIALIK, S. Y. AGNON, and Uri Zvi GREENBERG, but also, generally, in the totality of "modern" Hebrew literature as well. His provocative and influential *Sifrutenu hahadashah – hemshekh 'o mahapekhah* (1959 and 1971) assessed the rupture dividing centuries of religion-dominated thinking from Hebrew letters of the modern era. In evaluating contemporary Israeli writing Kurzweil was frequently harsh in dismissing it as unripe and shallow.

A brilliant polemicist, Kurzweil extended his critical sweep from the purely literary to issues of historiography, attacking, for example, the stature of AHAD HA'AM in Jewish thought, and the widely acclaimed scholarly views of Gershom SCHOLEM. With his broad erudition Kurzweil frequently embraced authors such as Franz KAFKA, Goethe, Heidegger, Otto WEININGER, and Karl KRAUS. He also dealt with problems of the European novel, as in his widely acclaimed *Masekhet haroman* (1953). Most of all, however, Kurzweil made his mark in his very fine close readings of Agnon's stories (particularly, the surrealistic *Sefer hama'asim*); of the poetry of Bialik and Saul TSCHERNICHOWSKI (in his *Mekharim beshiratam*, 1960); and of Uri Zvi Greenberg and related modernist poets (in *Bein hazon leven ha'absurdi*, 1966 and 1973). A collection of his articles on younger writers appeared posthumously in the volume *Hippus hasifrut hayisra'elit* (1982).

As a dynamic teacher, literary personality, and columnist (in *Ha'aretz* and elsewhere), Kurzweil's influence extended beyond his writing. His disciples at Bar–Ilan continue his work on Agnon, *Haskalah* satire, and, generally, on the nexus between literature and Jewish identity.

FURTHER READING

Diamond, J.: *Barukh Kurzweil and Modern Hebrew Literature* (Chico: Scholars Press, 1983)

Nash, S.: Criticism as a calling. *Prooftexts* 5 no. 3 (1985) 281–7 [review of Diamond's book]

STANLEY NASH

Kutscher, Eduard Yechezkel (1909–1971)

Hebrew and Semitic linguist. Kutscher was born at Topoltshani, Slovakia (Czechoslovakia), and went to Israel in 1941. He studied Hebrew language and Talmud, joined the teaching staff of the Department of Hebrew Language at the Hebrew University, and later taught in the corresponding department of the Bar-Ilan University in Ramat-Gan, where he was active in establishing a body for the production of a lexicon for the language of the Mishnah and Talmud, and other works of that period.

His first article was published in 1935, on a biblical subject, as were his publications until 1940. His MA thesis in 1941 was on Aramaic texts from Elephantine, and from then onwards he dedicated himself mainly to Aramaic and to Mishnaic Hebrew. In 1942 he became a secretary of the Hebrew Language Council, and remained an active member of that body, which later became the Academy of the Hebrew Language. About 1967 he became an active corresponding member of the editorial board of the third edition of the Köhler-Baumgartner Lexicon to the Bible.

With the discovery of the Qumran documents in the late 1940s, Kutscher began to devote much of his time to the language of those texts. His main study is the detailed analysis of the spelling of the Hebrew text of Isaiah found at Qumran and its light upon the development of post-biblical Hebrew. *The Language and Linguistic Background of the Isaiah Scroll* appeared in Hebrew in 1959 and in English in 1974, followed by several articles and discussions.

From 1964 until close to his death, Kutscher worked on his *History of the Hebrew Language*, which was edited in 1982 by his son Raphael and some of Kutscher's disciples, and published by The Magnes Press and E. J. Brill. This is the first detailed description of the changes that have occurred in the Hebrew language during the 3,000 years of its existence.

CHAIM RABIN

Kvitko, Leyb (1890–1952)

Yiddish poet. Kvitko was born in Aleskov, Ukraine. He was a disciple of Der Nister (P. KAHANOWITZ) and one of the triumvirate of the Kiev Group, the other being Dovid Hofshteyn and Peretz Markish. All three perished at the hand of Stalin. Leaving the pogrommed towns of Russia for Berlin Kvitko decided to return to Kiev in 1925 when Yiddish education and culture began to receive official encouragement and support. He wrote both stories of communist heroes with a social conscience and enchanting tales of animals for schoolchildren in Yiddish schools, following the existing Soviet narrative formula. His poems, written for, and sung in kindergartens show his capability for originality. In spite of his patriotism and devotion to Yiddish in Russia he was imprisoned in 1948 by Stalin and was shot four years later. His anthologies of poetry include: *Trit* (1919; Steps) and *Gezang fun mayn gemit* (1947; Songs of my moods). His *Geklibene verk* (1937; Selected works) was dedicated to his executioner-to-be, Stalin.

DEVRA KAY

L

Lamdan, Yitzhak (1899–1954) Hebrew poet, editor, and translator. Born in Volhynia, Ukraine, Lamdan emigrated to Palestine in 1920. He had gone through his formative experiences during the First World War and in the civil war following, which, for the Jews of Southern Russia, was a period of pogroms and general destruction. Such images made their profound impact on his original poem, *Massadah* (1927), an expressionist work, imaging the options and threats facing Jewry, as well as the glimpse of a hope of survival in a resurrected Israel, here called *Massadah* (paradoxically, the scene of the Jews' final defeat by the Roman Empire). This epic came to epitomize the Zionist struggle against the forces of nature, history, and the outside world.

Lamdan founded the monthly journal *Gilyonot* in 1934, and edited it until his death. It opened up a channel for the publication of new Hebrew work, and took pride in being politically nonpartisan. Lamdan's own poetry also appeared there, now rather more conventional than *Massadah*, but still obsessed with his primary theme, the Jewish fate in history. The striking effect of his first great work was not repeated, but the powerful concern still comes over in his later volumes.

FURTHER READING

Yudkin, L. I.: *Isaac Lamdan: A Study in Twentieth-Century Hebrew Poetry* (London: East & West Library, 1971)

LEON I. YUDKIN

Landa, Myer Jack (1874–1947) English journalist, novelist, and playwright. Born in Leeds, Myer Landa moved in 1904 from provincial journalism to the London *Daily Mail* and subsequently the *Daily News*. In 1919 he became editor of the Zionist Organization's daily bulletin, and remained a committed Zionist all his life. A visit to Palestine in 1931 led to a series of articles, later collected in *Palestine As It Was* (1932). Of his 50 years in journalism, 25 were spent as a Parliamentary correspondent, and from 1943–4 he was a distinguished Chairman of the Gallery Committee. At one time editor of the *Jewish World*, he contributed articles of Jewish interest to the general press, as well as book reviews and essays to the *Jewish Chronicle*. A keen interest in Jewish immigration and indignation over the Aliens Act led him to publish *The Aliens Problem and its Remedy* (1911).

One of his consuming passions was the theater, and in particular the Jewish play. He was the author of *The Jew in Drama* (1926), still a standard work on the subject, and *The Shylock Myth* (1942) in both of which he campaigns against the stereotyped stage Jew as "simply an enslaved buffoon, condemned to outlandish gesticulation, to a specific make-up which must at least border on the foreign". In 1904 he married Gertrude, sister of Samuel Gordon, the novelist; she, as Aunt Naomi, became known for her articles for children in the *Jewish World* and the *Jewish Chronicle*, and for the popular *Jewish Fairy Tales and Fables* (1908). She shared Myer's enthusiasm for the theater, and together they encouraged early efforts to present Jewish drama, and wrote several plays of Jewish interest. They also collaborated on four novels, the first of which, *Jacob Across Jabbok* (1933), while deficient in characterization, treats many contemporary problems, such as relations between Jew and Gentile, and between East End and West End Jews. *Kitty Villareal* (1934), is a historical romance based on the life of the daughter of a wealthy eighteenth-century Sephardi family who married an English country gentleman and was mother to the first Jewess to marry into the English aristocracy.

VERA COLEMAN

Landau, Judah Leo (1866–1942) South African rabbi, writer, and scholar. Born in Galicia, he was influenced by its conflicting currents in Jewish life: rabbinism, Hasidism, enlightenment, and Jewish nationalism. Educated initially in Galicia, he moved to Germany where he matriculated in the German *gymnasium* in Brody in 1893, and then to Vienna where he received his rabbinic diploma from the Rabbinical Seminary in 1898.

His first literary work, the *New Haskalah*, was published in Lemberg in 1883 when he was only 17, and was a polemic against assimilation. He later wrote powerful Hebrew plays with heroic themes such as *Bar Kochba* (1884) and *Herod, King of the Jews* (1887), and is regarded as one of the pioneers in the field of modern Hebrew drama.

Having imbibed Galician Jewishness and cultured Austrian refinement, the third influence on his life emanated from the Anglo-Jewish world. In 1900 he went to London to represent the journal *Hamaggid* at the fourth Zionist Congress. After two years as rabbi to an orthodox congregation in Manchester, he became rabbi in Johannesburg in 1903. He served the Johannesburg Jewish community, first as spiritual head of the Johannesburg Hebrew Congregation, and, after 1915, as chief rabbi of the United Hebrew Congregation until his death. In 1915 he was also appointed to the chair of the newly established Hebrew department at the University of the Witwatersrand.

He interpreted his rabbinic post in Johannes-burg as a mission and in the face of the eroding forces of assimilation he acquainted South African Jewry with the legacy of its history and tradition. Attempting to teach Jewish history through dramatic representations of its spiritual leaders, he wrote a series of Hebrew dramas, the best being *Don Isaac Abrabanel* (1919) and *Yisra'el Ba'al Shem* (1925). The first represented the ideal in Jewish leadership and the second assessed the rise of modern Jewish pietism.

His scholarship embraced many branches of Jewish learning. He played a prominent role in the editorship of the first Hebrew Encyclopedia, *Otzar Yisra'el* (1906–13), also contributing some 40 articles covering a range of topics. His collection of Hebrew poems *Neginot 'ufo'emot* was published in Warsaw in 1933. Two of its main themes are his *Weltschmerz* and passionate love of Zion. Johannesburg's distance from the main centers of Europe probably resulted in his failure to achieve due recognition in the world of Hebrew letters, for it was in this sphere that his main influence lay. His literary interest was protean and he was at home in Hebrew, German, and English literature. His multifarious interests and range of knowledge are reflected in his library, housed at the University of the Witwatersrand, Johannesburg, which today forms the nucleus of the "Landau Collection".

FURTHER READING
Saron, G., and Hotz, L., eds: *The Jews of South Africa: A History* (Cape Town: Oxford University Press, 1955)

JOCELYN HELLIG

Landauer, Gustav (1870–1919) German anarchist philosopher. Born in Karlsruhe Landauer studied literature and philosophy in Heidelberg and Berlin. Novelist, social philosopher, literary critic, and anarchist thinker, he discovered Judaism – and his own Jewish identity – through reading Martin BUBER's hassidic tales. In the essay "Are these heretical thoughts?" (1913), he explained his conception of the revolutionary and messianic mission of the Jews: because they wait for the Messiah in exile and dispersion, they are destined to be the

Messiah of the peoples. The redemption of the Jew and the redemption of humanity itself will be one and the same.

A romantic revolutionary, Landauer abhorred the modern State – "this supreme form of the non-spirit" – and the industrial capitalist civilization, and harked back with nostalgia to the old peasant community and medieval Gothic culture. His vision of socialism as a decentralized network of collectivist rural communities – inspired by Proudhon and Kropotkin – had a considerable influence on Buber himself, as well as on certain currents of the Zionist–socialist youth in Central Europe.

In his best known work, *Aufruf zum Sozialismus* (1911; *For Socialism*, 1978), he celebrated the *Mosaïc Jubiläeum* as a great and holy institution, because it makes permanent upheaval and revolution the foundation stone of the social constitution.

For a few days in 1919 Landauer became People's Commissar for Culture in the ephemeral Bavarian Council's Republic. Following the defeat of the revolution in Munich he was killed by the army on 2 May 1919.

FURTHER READING

Lunn, E.: *Prophet of Community. The Romantic Socialism of Gustav Landauer.* (Berkeley: University of California Press 1973)

Breines, P.: The Jew as Revolutionary. The case of Gustav Landauer. In *Yearbook of the Leo Baeck Institute* 13 (1967)

MICHAEL LÖWY

Landstone, Charles (1891–1978) English dramatist, critic, and novelist. Brought to London from Vienna at the age of four, Charles Landstone's lifelong passion for the theater started with his first pantomime. A foundermember of the Jewish Drama League in 1925 and for several years its secretary, he always retained a warm interest in Jewish dramatic and literary endeavor. He worked in the People's Theatre Movement at the Fortune Theatre, and three of his plays – *Behind Your Back* (1937) *Ruby Morn* (1938) and *On a Summer's Day* (1939) – were produced on the London stage. Associated with the Arts Council from its inception, he was in 1947 awarded the OBE for his work as its associate drama director, and was, until 1952, general manager and London representative of the Bristol Old Vic, which he had helped to found. Landstone had many other theatrical appointments and his encyclopedic knowledge of his subject was legendary, as his books *You and the Theatre* (1948) and *Off Stage* (1953) testify. From the 1920s he had reviewed fiction for the *Jewish Chronicle*, and after the war he became its main theater critic, an appointment which was to last for 37 years.

The title of his first novel, *Blue Tiger Yard*, (1927), was a thin disguise for Black Lion Yard, the Hatton Garden of the East End, where the hard-working, thrifty Lakarin family has prospered mightily in the jewellery trade. The action takes place just after the First World War, which wrought profound economic and social changes in the East End, and the book was praised for its authenticity, characterization, and humor. Landstone's own experiences, when his family moved to the then totally non-Jewish suburb of Muswell Hill, are reflected in *The Kerrels of Hill End* (1929). It describes theatrical activity among the young, and a wonderfully evocative visit to the Yiddish theater in Whitechapel, but the main interest of the book lies in its depiction of expanding Jewish suburbia in the 1920s. Because of theatrical commitments, *The Man from Butlers* (1930), based on Landstone's work as a courier for Thomas Cook, was his last novel. An immensely readable autobiography *I Gatecrashed* (1976), was published to coincide with his 85th birthday.

VERA COLEMAN

Langer, Georg [Jiři Mordechai] (1894–1943) Czech-born writer and Hebrew scholar. Langer was the son of a Prague Jewish assimilated family and brother of the famous Czech author and playwright František Langer. Mordechai Langer became interested in Hasidism and hasidic teachings and lived for many years in hasidic surroundings in Hungary and also at the "court" of a hasidic Rabbi in Galicia. After his return to Prague he continued to follow the hasidic tradition and way of life. He was well aquainted with Franz KAFKA and Max BROD and became their Hebrew teacher, and he advised and guided Brod in kabbalistic and Jewish lore. He wrote in German, Czech, and Hebrew; his most important books are *Die Erotik der Kabbala* (1923; Eroticism of the *kabbalah*), which has been translated into many languages, and *Devet bran* (1937; *Nine Gates*, 1961).

Langer left Prague in 1939 but shortly after his arrival in Tel Aviv he became gravely ill. In one of his last Hebrew poems he remembers Kafka and pays tribute to the purity of his soul.

MARGARITA PAZI

languages, Jewish Languages, or special forms of existing languages which are spoken by Jews. These are generally developments of languages spoken in countries where a Jewish community exists, or existed formerly. Some, however, flourish or flourished mainly after that community had left the country and settled among a population speaking another language. The outstanding examples of this are YIDDISH and JUDEO-SPANISH. But most others either continue in their original countries, or are spoken to some extent in countries to which the Jews had migrated, with a restricted use as spoken language, and in some cases for comic entertainment within the community.

The causes of the rise of a Jewish language are twofold. Firstly, the community, because of its difference in behavior, or simply because they are aliens, do not mingle with the native majority and concentrate in separate quarters in order to defend themselves, if necessary. Secondly, the Jews live according to religious prescriptions and food-laws which necessitate living apart from the local population. To this add the duty, at least of the male Jews, to learn Hebrew and Aramaic in order to read the prayers, the Bible, and the later works on religious matters, especially the Mishnah and the Talmud. Through this, large numbers of Hebrew and Aramaic words are constantly used, and the more learned a person, the higher the percentage of Hebrew–Aramaic words and phrases in his speech. Moreover, men were expected to write to other men in Hebrew, while letters to women were usually in the Jewish language.

The Jews who emigrated to Palestine before the rise of Zionism continued using their Jewish language among compatriots, but in the nineteenth century developed a Hebrew idiom in which Jews from different countries could talk to each other in the market and on communal affairs, without any intention of replacing their Jewish dialect with Hebrew. At the same time they used Hebrew for writing, including public announcements on walls and later in newspapers.

After the development of Modern Hebrew as the language of the Zionist immigrant community, the Orthodox population kept largely to its Jewish Languages and to writing traditional Hebrew, although they are able to speak Israeli Hebrew to outsiders and, especially among the women, ability to read contemporary literary Hebrew is widespread.

There is extensive publication of translations from Yiddish and Judeo-Spanish. Jewish languages are taught in Israeli universities, and especially Yiddish literature – in the original – is widely studied, as is the medieval literature of other Jewish languages. On the other hand, in the relevant communities the interest of the younger generation for the traditional language of their ancestors tends to diminish, and their use is coming to be restricted to the older generation.

CHAIM RABIN

languages, Jewish secret These are in a way the counterpart of JEWISH LANGUAGES, and their characteristic is the use of Hebrew words in sentences of the local non-Jewish language, the Hebrew words being grammatically treated according to the local language, for example Hebrew *akhal* ("he ate") appears as a pseudo-German perfect form *"er hat geakhelt"*. This hebraization applies mainly to nouns and verbs of importance to the message intended. Thus place-names are often literally translated into Hebrew.

The purpose of this is to discuss matters in non-Jewish surroundings, especially at markets, in such a way that the bystanders should not understand what was being said. Because of its high percentage of Hebrew words, such a language was, at least in theory, less intelligible to outsiders than the Jewish language spoken in the community. This assumption proved, however, to be wrong: the market men picked up words, and so did the thieves in the market. When, in the eighteenth century, a Prussian official produced a dictionary of thieves' language, it turned out that many of the words were traceable to Hebrew. This was interpreted by contemporary anti-Semites as proof that the Jews were involved in crime. However, in Germany Jews in villages often employed non-Jewish workers, and used the secret language (called in Germany "*loshen khodosh*", that is, "new language", to distinguish it from "*loshen kaudesh*", "holy language", the name for Hebrew). The workmen picked up the language and used it as a secret language among themselves, and remnants of it can still be heard in some districts.

The best-known instance of such a language among a non-Jewish group was discovered at Schopfloch in northern Bavaria some years ago by a librarian who heard it from butchers' assistants at the local public house, discovered the Hebrew element in it, and published a list of words and some samples of conversation.

Words from the Jewish secret language can be found in lists of words from the secret languages of itinerant elements in Germany, which likewise contain many gypsy words. Some have also penetrated into the general everyday language, for example Austrian and Swiss "*Beisel*" for a pub, from ashkenasi Hebrew "*bayis*" = a house, with the diminutive suffix -el, together "a little house". Similar borrowings from Jewish secret languages exist also in Dutch, where inhabitants of Amsterdam use for their town the slang word "*de mokem*", literally, in Hebrew, "the place", along with other slang words from Hebrew sources.

CHAIM RABIN

Lanzmann, Claude (b.1925)   French writer, political activist, and film maker. Born into a petit-bourgeois family in Paris, Lanzmann re-ceived his early education in that city, then attended university at the Sorbonne. His family background and native inclinations gradually drew him first into Zionist activities and then into contact with the existentialist teachings of Jean-Paul Sartre and Simone de Beauvoir. From 1952, Lanzmann became one of the regular figures around Sartre and de Beauvoir in the setting of Saint-Germain-des-Près. He was also one of the youngest contributors and editors for Sartre's journal, *Les Temps Modernes*.

Through his connections with Sartre and *LTM*, Lanzmann became involved in numerous activities for justice and equality in France and around the world. During the 1960s Lanzmann's attentions were gradually drawn to Jewish causes and also to the enormity of the tragedy of the Holocaust. In the mid 1970s, just as Sartre was retiring from the helm of *Les Temps Modernes* thus projecting Lanzmann into the position of chief editor and subsequently director, Lanzmann set upon his scheme of producing a film which would attempt to offer some explanation for the events which had befallen the Jewish people during the Holocaust. The result was Lanzmann's internationally acclaimed film *Shoah*, which has proven to be not simply a film about the Holocaust, but about the ruthless, inhuman bureaucratic machinery which permitted the Final Solution to occur.

Lanzmann and his family live in Paris where he is director of *Les Temps Modernes*.

SIMON SIBELMAN

Lasker-Schüler, Else (1869–1945)   German–Jewish poet. She was born into a well-to-do, assimilated Jewish family in Elberfeld in the Rhineland. Both her marriages – to the doctor Berthold Lasker, from 1894 to 1903, and to the editor and art critic Georg Levin (better known as Herwarth Walden) from 1903 to 1910 – ended in divorce. Thereafter she had no settled home, but lived a Bohemian life in Berlin and Munich, mingling with leading Expressionist writers and artists. Her oriental costumes and impulsive behavior gained her a reputation for eccentricity, while her generosity and

Else Lasker-Schüler

improvidence ensured that she was always short of money. Her son Paul, a gifted artist, died of tuberculosis in 1927, aged 28. After physical ill-treatment by the Nazis, she moved to Switzerland in 1933. She twice visited Palestine briefly before settling there for good in 1939.

Throughout her life Else Lasker-Schüler remained child-like in her love of play and disguises, her unworldliness, her frankness, and her emotional vulnerability. She constructed an exotic fantasy-world in which she figured first as Tino of Baghdad, later as Yussuf, Prince of Thebes. Her Oriental fantasies are prominent in her prose works, for example *Die Nächte Tinos von Bagdad* (1907; The nights of Tino of Baghdad) and *Der Malik* (1919), in which she and her friends appear under pseudonyms. Her semi-naturalistic play *Die Wupper* (1909), named after the river at Elberfeld where it is set, was first performed in 1919 in Max REINHARDT's Deutsches Theater in Berlin. Her other play, *Arthur Aronymus* (1932), a mythical account of her father's early life, was performed in Zurich in 1936.

The wealth of colorful, inventive imagery in her poems does not render them inaccessible. They often express adult emotions with a child's disconcerting directness. Her many fine and touching love poems combine simple, concise statement with psychological sensitivity. Many poems express sorrow and loneliness. Some evoke the lost paradise of her childhood, while others are addressed to her mother, whose sudden death in 1890 gave Else Lasker-Schüler a shock from which she never fully recovered. Her pride in her Jewishness is conveyed in *Hebräische Balladen* (1913), which present Old Testament figures like Abraham and Isaac, Jacob and Joseph, and in the story *Der Wunderrabbiner von Barcelona* (1921; The miracle-working Rabbi of Barcelona). Later poems, especially her last collection *Mein blaues Klavier* (1943; My blue piano), record her gradual discovery of emotional solace in an idiosyncratic relation to God. Despite its affinities with neo-Romanticism and Expressionism, her poetry is too original to be easily categorized; this has probably delayed her recognition as an outstanding poet.

BIBLIOGRAPHY

Your Diamond Dreams Cut Open My Arteries: Poems by Else Lasker-Schüler, trans. R. P. Newton (Chapel Hill: University of North Carolina Press, 1982)

FURTHER READING

Cohn, H. W.: *Else Lasker-Schüler: The Broken World* (Cambridge: Cambridge University Press, 1974)

RITCHIE ROBERTSON

Lassalle, Ferdinand (1825–1864) German sociologist, political theorist, and activist. Lassalle was born in the ghetto of Breslau, the only son of Heyman Lassal who became an adherent of the Jewish Reform movement. After studying at Berlin University, where his brilliance earned him the title of *Das Wunderkind*, Lassalle joined the group of Young Hegelians and settled down to a scholarly career. Between 1843 and 1845 he developed his ideas of democratic and industrial socialism. His meeting with the Countess Sophie van Hatzfeldt in 1846 led to his law studies and extraordinary prosecution of her suit against her husband throughout the next nine (some claim variously eight or eleven) years. Apart from a short period of imprisonment in 1848 for his revolutionary activities Lassalle spent the next few years in study and the completion of his three most famous works. It was at this time, too, that he began his correspondence with Karl MARX. He helped Marx publish his writings, but differences in their political attitudes later caused their relations to cool. In 1857 he published *Die Philosophie Herakleitos Des Dunklen von Ephesos*, a study of Heraclitus from the Hegelian point of view; this was followed, in 1859, by a pamphlet on the Italian war and Prussia's mission, in which Bismarck's policy is foreshadowed, and *Das System der erworbenen Rechte* (1861) a treatise on property.

In the following year Lassalle began the activity which was to gain him historical significance. He called on the German workers to form their own party and concentrate on their political and economic emancipation. The two main points in his program were universal suffrage and a form of State socialism. He believed that the workers' salvation lay in social reforms that would enable them by education and civil liberties to participate in political life. His proposals were intially rejected by most of the organized working clubs but in 1863 Lassalle founded the *Allgemeiner Deutscher Arbeitverein* (General German Workers Association), the embryo of the German Social Democratic Party.

He died in 1864 from a wound received in a duel at Carrouge, Geneva, and was buried at the Jewish cemetery in Breslau. It is as a propagandist who successfully placed a socialist program before the German workers, and who succeeded in forming the first effective socialist party, that he is chiefly remembered.

In his youth Lassalle took an interest in Judaism but later turned against it. Some have considered his political philosophy to have been derived from his awareness of Jewish disabilities and of Jewish apathy. As a young man he had aspirations for freeing the Jews, pushing towards Jewish self-help and an end to passivity, along the lines of Israel ZANGWILL. Later in his life, however, Lassalle disavowed contact with Jews, who did not enter his social concerns. This did not protect him from anti-Semitic attacks and, in fact, the duel that led to his death was provoked by the anti-Semitic attitude of his fiancée's family.

BIBLIOGRAPHY

The Working Man's Programme, trans. E. Peters (London: The Modern Press, 1884)

GLENDA ABRAMSON

Lattes, Dante (1876–1965) Italian writer, journalist, and rabbi. He was born in Pitigliano in the province of Grosseto and studied at the Collegio Rabbinico of Livorno with Elia Benamozegh. He contributed to the Trieste-based *Il Corriere Israelitico*, and was its director from 1904 to 1916. In Florence he founded, with a group of scholars, the weekly *Israel*. In 1925 he published the first volume of *La Rassegna Mensile d'Israel*, one of the most widely circulated Italian Jewish literary periodicals, and he continued as its director until his death.

Lattes was a fervent Zionist from an early age; he served as president of La Federazione Sionista Italiana (The Italian Federation of Zionists) and was a founding member of the World Jewish Congress (1933). Through the publication of numerous translations he helped to divulge the thoughts of some of the most prestigious Jewish leaders, including AHAD HA'AM, Leon PINSKER, Moses HESS, and Chaim WEIZMANN. His popularizing gifts are ably demonstrated in his essay Il Sionismo (1928).

He was forced to leave Italy because of the racial laws and settled in Palestine, returning to Italy in 1946 in order to resume his work as a writer and educator. He was active in the Unione delle Comunità Israelitiche Italiane (Union of Italian Jewish Communities), serving as its vice-president from 1952 to 1956.

Lattes retired to Dolo (near Venice), where he dedicated the last years of his life to the diffusion of the Jewish ideal. As a man and a Jew, Lattes was a singular figure: despite the fact that he hardly ever acted in his capacity as rabbi and rarely worked as a teacher, he exalted both professions in numerous writings through which he communicated his thoughts to a wide public.

GABRIELLA MOSCATI-STEINDLER

Lauterbach, Jacob (1873–1942) American academic scholar and Talmudist. Born in Galicia, Lauterbach studied at German universities and received ordination from Berlin's *Rabbinerseminar*. Arriving in the United States in 1904, he became an editor of the *Jewish Encyclopedia*, to which he contributed 260 articles on talmudic and rabbinic literature. After several years as a congregational rabbi, in 1911 he was appointed Professor of Talmud and Rabbinics at the Hebrew Union College in Cincinnati, a post he occupied until his retirement in 1934. Trained in traditional methods of study and in modern scientific techniques, Lauterbach produced a critical edition, introduction, and translation of the tanaitic midrash *Mekhilta derabbi Ishma'el* (1933), perhaps his most lasting contribution to the field of talmudic research. His interest in the early rabbinic period led to important historical studies, many of which are included in *Rabbinic Essays* (1951), an anthology edited by his colleagues and students. A number of these, such as "The Sadducees and the Pharisees" (1913), "The Pharisees and their teachings" (1929), and "Midrash and Mishnah" (1915), explored the development of a crucial sectarian controversy and its effects upon varying approaches to the study of Torah and the *halakhah*. A later collection, *Studies in Jewish Law, Custom, and Folklore* (1970), brings together his investigations of such practices as the naming of children, *Tashlikh*, and the covering of one's head during worship. Talmud teacher to several generations of American Reform rabbis, Lauterbach served as chairman of the Committee on Responsa of the Central Conference of American Rabbis from 1923 to 1933. Unlike his predecessors in that role, Lauterbach assumed a broadly affirmative attitude toward the rabbinic halakhic literature as a source of guidance for determining Reform Jewish practice.

FURTHER READING
Freehof, S., ed.: *Rabbinic Essays* (Cincinnati: Hebrew Union College, 1951)

MARK WASHOFSKY

Lavry, Marc (1903–1967) Israeli composer and conductor, one of the founders of the national school of modern Israeli music. Born in Riga, Latvia, Lavry was active as composer and conductor in Berlin (1929–34). With the rise of the Nazi regime he returned to Riga, where the growing anti-Semitism aroused in him an awareness of his Jewishness that had been dormant. He composed a symphonic poem named *The Wandering Jew*, and emigrated to Palestine in 1935. He became active as conductor, as composer, and arranger of incidental and light music in folk style, a field in which he was a master. With the beginning of radio broadcasts in 1936 he became a program director, and after the foundation of the State of Israel he controlled the musical broadcasts to the Diaspora. During his final years he became an honorary citizen of the city of Haifa where he was invited to reside. Lavry was the active spokesman for the ideological trend which emphasized the importance of a popular, easily accessible musical style as a prerequisite for the formation of a new national style. He claimed that he endeavored to write for the audience and wanted to be understood by his listeners, and he stressed the centrality of melody as the predominating factor in his music. His first important work written in Palestine was the song, *Emek*, incorporated into a symphonic poem, widely performed as representative of Israeli music. Lavry developed the folk song known as the Israeli *horah* and made it into a national emblem which appeared in most of his own compositions and became associated with Israeli music in general. His most ambitious works were the oratorio, *Song of Songs* (1940) and the opera *Dan the Guard* (1945) based on a play by the poet Sh. Shalom and adapted as a libretto by Max BROD. This was the first opera performed in the country in which the contemporary problems of a frontier kibbutz were presented and contrasted with a personal drama of a young kibbutz member. Much influenced by the European genre of national operas, Lavry made use of distinct styles as symbols, contrasting Eastern European Jewish tunes with Yemenite and Arabic songs, *horah*, and Puccini-like operatic patterns. Lavry was an extremely prolific composer in all genres of popular and art music.

JEHOASH HIRSHBERG

law, Jewish, in Israel Upon its establishment in 1948, the new State of Israel officially adopted the legal system in force at the time. Under this system, matters affecting the personal status of members of recognized religions were decided by their own religious courts; all other legal issues were governed by an amalgam of English, Ottoman, and Muslim law, and mandatory ordinances. Much of this amalgam has since been replaced by new Israeli legislation, but the divided structure has been retained. What emerges is that in modern Israel, the only area in which Jewish law is officially binding is that of the personal status of resident Jews. Rabbinical courts, staffed by religious judges steeped in traditional Jewish law (*halakhah*), possess exclusive jurisdiction over Jews in matters of marriage, divorce, and, under certain circumstances, maintenance. In other aspects of status law, e.g. adoption and succession, rabbinical courts enjoy a limited concurrent jurisdiction with the general courts system. Secular provisions govern all other areas of Israeli law, even where issues of a Jewish religious nature are involved.

The High Court's interpretation of the Law of Return (1950) in the celebrated case of *Rufeisen* v. *Minister of the Interior* H.C. 72/62 *P.D.* 16 (1962) provides a striking example of secular treatment of a law possessing Jewish significance. The Law of Return grants every Jew an automatic right to Israeli citizenship. Rufeisen, also known as Brother Daniel, was born a Jew. During World War Two, he converted to Christianity, and eventually became a Carmelite monk. On being refused citizenship under the Law of Return, Rufeisen petitioned the High Court to overturn the decision of the Minister of the Interior, inter alia on the grounds that under the *halakhah*, he was still a Jew. The petition was dismissed: the Court made it quite clear that a secular interpretation would be given to the word "Jew" in the Law of Return – a secular law. Such an interpretation would not allow for a Carmelite monk to be considered Jewish, no matter who his mother was.

Various pieces of Israeli legislation deal with matters of Jewish import, such as pig-breeding, missionary activities, Sabbath as an official rest day, etc. Secular courts have exclusive jurisdiction over such matters, and administer them without reference to the *halakhah*.

At a more informal level, the Israeli legal system is influenced by Jewish law in diverse ways. Some laws are based upon concepts derived from traditional Jewish sources. The biblical injunction to pay the wages of a hired labourer immediately upon the completion of his working day (Leviticus xix.13; Deuteronomy ii.14) is reflected in the Wage Protection Law (1958) which prohibits delay in the payment of wages. The source of the Severence Pay Law (1963) may also be traced to a biblical precept to the effect that a Hebrew slave must receive a substantial gift upon the completion of his term of service (Deuteronomy xv.14).

Changes in existing Israeli Legislation have also been influenced by the Jewish legal tradition. Formerly all witnesses were required to swear to tell the truth, unless good reasons existed for waiving the oath. In the case of *Becker* v. *Eilat* H.C. 172/78 *P.D.* 32 (1978), an agnostic witness appealed against a magistrate's refusal to exempt him from taking the oath. Elon J. observed that in Jewish law, an oath imposed upon a witness for the purpose of making him tell the truth did not exist, since everybody was bound to observe the Sinaitic commandment "not to bear false witness against one's neighbor" (Exodus xx.13; Deuteronomy v.17). Witnesses' oaths were therefore superfluous. In the wake of the court's decision upholding the petition, the law was changed, and under the Evidence Law Amendment (Warning of Witnesses and Removal of Oath) Law (1980), the administration of the oath is now a matter for the judge's discretion, to be imposed only if it is felt that it will help in uncovering the truth.

Undoubtedly the most significant recent development in relation to the application of Jewish law is the enactment of the Foundations of Law Act (1980). Under this law, a judge finding that "a question requiring a decision cannot be answered by reference to an enactment or a judicial precedent or by way of analogy" must turn to "the principles of freedom, justice, equity, and peace of the heritage of Israel". A judge learned in Jewish law is thus provided with an official channel for introducing that system into legal decisions. Indeed, in a recent case, Elon J. propounded a solution based upon the *halakhah* relating to lost property; in a further hearing, however, the introduction of *halakhah* by means of the Foundations of Law Act was rejected in this particular case, since existing law already contained an answer to the issue before the Court (*Kupat Am Bank Ltd* v. *Hendeles* F.H. 13/80, 35 P.D. 785).

Hebrew is the official legal language of Israel, and much Israeli legal terminology is therefore derived from halakhic sources. The halakhic background will often be invoked by judges for the purpose of interpreting these terms, e.g. the requirement of "good faith" (*tom lev*) is s.39 of the Contracts (General Part) Law (1973) (*Roth* v. *Yeshufeh Building Co. Ltd* C.A. 148/77, 33(1) *P.D.* 617). In some cases concepts drawn from Jewish law are used to illuminate statutory provisions. According to s.31 of the Contracts (General Part) Law (1973) a contract which is void on grounds of immorality may, in certain circumstances, be enforced. Elon J. explained this apparent inconsistency in the light of the talmudic concept of *ma'aseh haba ba'averah*, i.e. an act may be legally binding even if it was carried out in forbidden circumstances, such as a contract drawn up on the Sabbath.

Recourse to halakhic sources in order to derive fresh principles from a statutory provision is well illustrated by the case of *Cohen* v. *State of Israel* C.A. 91/80, in which the court held that a husband could be charged with raping his wife. English Common Law, upon which the relevant Israeli statute was based, did not recognize this possibility, but the court, in upholding a novel interpretation of s.345 of the Penal Law (1977) invoked halakhic sources prohibiting coercive sexual relations between a husband and wife. Bekhor J. observed that in this particular respect, the attitude of Jewish law towards the welfare of married women was superior to that of the Common Law of England.

Finally there are various practical channels through which Jewish law influences the legal system of modern Israel. All draft bills are submitted to the Jewish Law Department of the Ministry of Justice for amendment in the light of halakhic sources. Jewish law courses constitute an integral part of the Israeli law degree curriculum, and all Israeli law schools have Jewish law departments in which academic research plays an important role. Traditionally at least one justice of the Supreme Court is an expert in Jewish law, and many lower court judges, as well as a large number of lawyers, also possess expertise in this area.

Even in the absence of its official incorporation into Israeli law in areas other than personal status, therefore, it is clear that Jewish law exercises a powerful and pervasive influence upon the legal system in modern Israel.

FURTHER READING

England, I.: *Religious Law in the Israel Legal System* (Jerusalem: Hebrew University Press, 1975)

Jackson, B. S., ed.: *Modern Research in Jewish Law* (Leiden: E. J. Brill, 1980)

Shava, M.: The nature and scope of Jewish law in Israel. *Jewish Law Annual* 5 (1985)

DANIEL B. SINCLAIR

law, modern Jewish Prior to the Emancipation, every aspect of Jewish life was governed by Jewish law. Not only were the private lives of all Jews shaped by the *halakhah* (traditional Jewish law), but their communal institutions were also molded by rabbinic opinion. The vast majority of *responsa* (solutions to practical problems of Jewish law) written by the great authorities of the Middle Ages deal with communal and administrative matters such as fair taxation and the regulation of commerce. Purely ritual concerns such as sabbath observance and *kashrut* (the dietary laws) only make up a small proportion of medieval *responsa*. Jewish judicial autonomy was not only a matter of conviction on the part of the Jews: it also suited their non-Jewish rulers, whose primary concern was the most efficient method of taxing their Jewish subjects. The autonomous status of the Jewish community was ideal for this purpose, hence the support lent by non-Jewish authorities to Jewish courts when the internal sanctions of fining and the imposition of the *herem* (ban on social contact with the offender) failed to bring a recalcitrant member of the community to order.

All this changed quite drastically with the Emancipation of European Jewry which began in the eighteenth century. Emancipation involved the abolition of both the judicial autonomy of Jewish communities and the use of the *herem* by their rabbinic authorities. No longer were eminent halakhists required to deal with question of communal administration involving the welfare of the community at large. Civil litigation, too, passed out of rabbinic hands into those of non-Jewish courts. As a result, the status of Jewish courts in civil matters was reduced to that of arbitral bodies rather than official courts of law. The prominent rabbis of the day fought this trend, but to no avail. In general, the influence of non-Jewish culture, and the rise of the Reform movement early in the nineteenth century, combined to put traditional Judaism on the defensive. The major concern of halakhists in the eighteenth and nineteenth centuries was, therefore, to adapt Jewish law to modern conditions while still preserving the integrity of the *halakhah* in this era of rapid social and technological change. In the early twentieth century, Jewish law as a binding way of life was rapidly disappearing, particularly in new centers such as the United States and Great Britain. The development of Jewish law in the period under discussion thus proceeded along much narrower lines than it had done during the Middle Ages. In struggling to synthesize traditionality and modernity, however, the great halakhists of this era provided the intellectual basis for the application of Jewish law as a living system in the second half of the twentieth century, especially in the State of Israel.

The special nature of the development of Jewish law from the eighteenth to the early twentieth centuries is best illustrated by the *responsa* literature of this period. Although the struggle against the Reform movement tended to inject a polemical element into any discussion of the alteration of traditional practices or the adaptation of *halakhah* to modern conditions, some of the *responsa* demonstrate a highly sensitive approach to the problems of life in the modern era. One such *responsum* is that of Rabbi Solomon Kluger of Brody, Galicia (1785–1869) permitting divorce by post. The background to this novel ruling was undoubtedly the Czarist policy of forcible conscription of young, often newly married Jews, for lengthy periods of military service far from their homes. Many potential recruits fled to Galicia. Their Russian wives were thus left without any possibility of remarriage, since the husbands could never return in order to present them with a *get* (bill of divorce) as required by Jewish law, nor could the *get* be sent through an agent, as no Galician Jew was prepared to enter Russia, nor, apparently, could it be posted, as the postal services were all run by non-Jews, who cannot act as agents for the transfer of a *get*. Rabbi Kluger overcame this obstacle to the mailing of a *get* by distinguishing between the designation of a non-Jew as an agent for the specific purpose of its delivery, which is prohibited, and the impersonal nature of the postal services, in which case the prohibition does not apply (*Sheirei Taharah* 3 nos 1–2).

The desire to prevent women being chained to their marital status even after the death or disappearance of their husbands underlies the permissive stand adopted by two other Galician luminaries to the admissibility of photographic evidence in establishing the death of a married man. Rabbi Isaac Schmelkes of Lemberg (1828–1906) was prepared to accept such evidence in the absence of any other proof (*Responsa Bet Yitzhak, Even Haezer* no. 87), and Rabbi Shalom Shvadron of Brezen (1835–1911) admitted it where the other evidence was of a conflicting nature (*Responsa Maharasham* 3 no. 256).

Rabbi Isaac Schmelkes also dealt with the purely ritual question of using electricity for sabbath and *Hanukkah* lights. Although he is prepared to permit electricity for sabbath lights, he prohibits it for those of *Hanukkah*, inter alia because there would not be a sufficient distinction between the festive lights and those in everyday use. Characteristically Rabbi Schmelkes's view regarding sabbath lights was rejected in the following century by authorities who doubted whether a blessing could be recited over electrical sabbath lights.

One modern invention which caused a storm in rabbinic circles in the nineteenth century was the mechanized process for baking *matzah* (unleavened bread) for use on Passover. The *matzah* baking machine was introduced to the Galician city of Krakow from Germany, but the *matzot* baked in it were declared unfit for Passover use by Rabbi Solomon Kluger. A permissive ruling was, however, issued by Rabbi Joseph Nathanson of Lemberg (1810–75), and the two authorities published pamphlets rejecting each other's views. The debate was joined by many of the leading halakhists of the time, and the main arguments advanced by the prohibitionists were that the performance of a *mitzvah* (ritual act) such as the baking of *matzot* required intelligence which machines did not possess, and that every time the machine stopped, the great heat in the ovens would cause the dough to rise and become leaven. Those in favor of permitting machine-baked *matzot* maintained that it was sufficient that the machine was operated by an intelligent person, and that the risk of the dough rising was much greater in the hand baking process because of the army of untrained helpers who made it difficult for the baker to comply with the halakhic requirements of *matzah* baking. The dispute raged on for many years, but machine-baked *matzot* eventually became the norm, especially in the United States and Western Europe.

Another issue which sparked off a major dispute amongst rabbinic authorities was that of innovations in the synagogue services, for example, use of the organ and praying in the vernacular. In the first half of the nineteenth century, these issues were still discussed in the context of rabbinic *responsa*, since the decisive split between Orthodoxy and Reform had not yet come about. The permissive views on these two issues were published in a collection known as *Nogah hatzedek* (1818) and, interestingly, contain the opinion of a senior member of the Orthodox rabbinical court in Budapest. The prohibitionists, however, included in their ranks the outstanding halakhic luminaries of the day, with Rabbi Moses Sofer of Pressburg, Hungary (1762–1839), and Rabbi Akiva Eger of Posen (1761–1837) heading the list. In their pamphlet entitled *Eleh divrei habrit* (1819) Rabbi Sofer argued that the projected innovations constituted a serious breach with tradition, and would open up the way for major reforms of the *halakhah*, culminating in its eventual rejection as the normative expression of Judaism. The polemical background to these *responsa* is evident on every page, and portends the shape of things to come.

The problems discussed in the *responsa* literature of this period cover all aspects of life and modernity, and attest to the efforts of Galician rabbis in particular to achieve a synthesis of the two. The preponderance of *responsa* literature originating from this part of the Austro-Hungarian Empire, as opposed to Russia or Germany, may be accounted for by the fact that Galicia constituted a bridge between the closed and highly traditional Jewry of the Czarist realm, and the open and relatively tolerant German Jewry. The Galician authorities shared both the serious commitment of their Russian co-religionists to the *halakhah*, and the interests of their German colleagues in modernity. Although the pursuit of *halakhah* in Russia was more intense than any other European country, its rabbinical scholars devoted themselves to talmudic novellae and the codification of the law, rather than to its application in a modern context. The outstanding respondents of the nineteenth century were, therefore, predominantly Galician.

Finally mention must be made of the development of Jewish law in Eastern centers during this period. Unlike the West, emancipation in the East was a much more gradual process, and Jewish communities such as those of Algeria and Tunis preserved their judicial autonomy well into the twentieth century. As a result, *halakhah* continued to flourish in all areas of Jewish life in these countries, and the *responsa* of their rabbis include much civil and administrative law. The persecution of Jewry in Arab lands immediately prior to, and consequent upon, the establishment of the State of Israel, brought this long and glorious tradition to an abrupt end.

FURTHER READING
Baron, S.: *The Jewish Community* (Philadelphia: The Jewish Publication Society of America, 1942)
Freehof, S.: *The Responsa Literature* (Philadelphia: The Jewish Publication Society of America, 1955)

DANIEL B. SINCLAIR

Layton, Irving (b.1912)   Canadian poet. Born in Romania, Layton went to Montreal with his family in 1913. He was educated in Canadian universities and earned a BSc. in agriculture and an MA in economics and political science. During the war Layton served in the Canadian Army. He taught at a Jewish school in Montreal, and later was appointed English professor at York University, Toronto.

Though his career as a poet began rather late, Layton is probably the most prolific Canadian poet. Since 1934 he has published over 40 volumes of poetry. Layton also appears to be one of the most controversial literary figures in Canada. Though he has complained of being misunderstood, his stance as a rebel preaching unrestricted sexuality has shocked the Canadian community. Layton has attacked social conventions and often presented women as subservient to men. Poetic imagination, according to Layton, combined Apollonian spirit and Dionysian freedom: this dialectic affirms life, but is considered dangerous to social order; therefore, the poet is a social outcast.

Layton has often antagonized his Jewish readers. The volume *For My Brother Jesus* (1971), shocked the Jewish community and in his essays, *Taking Sides* (1977), he presents a harsh criticism of Israel, and claims that Germany's crimes against the Jewish people should have been long forgiven.

At the same time Layton's work manifests strong identification with Jewish heritage and suffering. He remembers his parents and their faith with love and respect. In his memoir,

Waiting for the Messiah (1985), childhood experiences of anti-Semitism are recalled with pain. Layton reacts with anguish to the Holocaust and blatantly accuses Christianity for "having prepared the ground on which Europe's gas chambers and crematoria flourished". The proper response to hatred is demonstrated by Israel. In his poem "For my two sons, Max and David", Layton forbids his children to perpetuate Jewish helplessness and tells them to "be gunners in the Israeli Air Force".

Some of Layton's best poems appear in *The Collected Poems of Irving Layton* (1971), *The Darkening Fire 1945–68* (1975), and *The Unwavering Eye* (1975).

FURTHER READING
Cameron, E.: *Irving Layton: a Portrait* (Don Mills: Stoddart, 1985)
Mandel, E: *Irving Layton* (Toronto: Forum House 1969, rev. 1981)

RACHEL FELDHAY BRENNER

Lazarus, Emma (1849–1887)   American poet. Born in New York City, the daughter of well-to-do Sephardic parents, Lazarus was educated at home by private tutors. *Poems and Translations* (1866), published when she was just 17, attracted the attention of Ralph Waldo Emerson, with whom she began an extended correspondence. Her second collection, *Admetus and Other Poems* (1871), included the poem "In the Jewish synagogue at Newport". It was soon reprinted in *The Jewish Messenger*, a periodical that subsequently published her translations of Ibn Gabirol and Judah Halevi.

She was part of a long-established, native-born American Jewish community, free from fear of persecution, and her concern was aroused when Russian pogroms of the early 1880s brought floods of East European Jews to America. Following publication of *Songs of a Semite* (1882), encounters with displaced Jewish immigrants inspired her to remember Emerson's advice that she "...show the celestial element in the despised Present...".

Her sonnet "The New Colossus", written in 1883 to help raise funds for construction of the pedestal for the statue of Liberty, captured last-

Emma Lazarus

ing public acclaim. The poem, inscribed on a bronze plaque, was placed at the statue entrance in 1903. The concluding lines of this work, familiar to most Americans, are a beloved expression of the national ideal the statue symbolizes:

> . . . Give me your tired, your poor,
> Your huddled masses yearning to breathe free,
> The wretched refuse of your teeming shore.
> Send these, the homeless, tempest-tost to me,
> I lift my lamp beside the Golden door!

BIBLIOGRAPHY

Emma Lazarus: Selections from her Poetry and Prose, ed. M. Schappes, 3rd edn (New York: Emma Lararus Federation of Jewish Women's Clubs, 1967)

ELIZABETH KLEIN

Lazarus, Moritz (1824–1903)   German philosopher and psychologist. Lazarus made a deep impact upon the Jewish and general community of his time. When the Jewish community decided to form a (Reform) Synod in Leipzig (1869), Lazarus was elected to be its president. A noted professor of philosophy (first in Berne and later in Berlin until 1896) who also taught psychology, political science, and education, he was also known to be a profound Jewish scholar concerned with all aspects of Jewish life. His final work, *The Ethics of Judaism* (i, 1898; 2nd edn 1899) became a standard work in Jewish libraries. In the general community, he was best known for his work on the psychology of nations (*Völkerpsychologie*), a discipline he developed with his brother-in-law H. H. Steinthal through a journal (*Zeitschrift für Völkerpsychologie*). His best known work of psychology was the three-volume *The Life of the Soul* (1893–7) – and a popular text proclaiming the superiority of the Prussian people.

The Ethics of Judaism demands an "objective–immanent" rather than the "constructive–speculative" of Saloman FORMSTECHER and Samson Raphael HIRSCH: one must study Jewish sources rather than introduce philosophy from the outside. Yet Lazarus does use Kant's moral philosophy to interpret Jewish ethics. He preferred moderate rabbinical thinking to prophetic fervor, and creates a gentle nineteenth-century bourgeois philosophy. Lazarus used the language of Kant's autonomy of moral demands, but at the same time demanded that this act should arise out of the love of God. Judaism makes God the source of the moral law. Lazarus tried to combine Kantian autonomy with his theology by making God subject to the moral law; and was rightly charged with inconsistency. Nevertheless, the text and the author remain a mirror of much that was noble and kind within German Jewry at the end of that century.

ALBERT H. FRIEDLANDER

Lebensohn, Abraham Dov [Adam Ha-Kohen] (1794–1878)   Hebrew poet, playwright, scholar, and publicist. Born in Vilna, he became a leading *maskil* and a teacher of Bible in the city's rabbinical school for 20 years. His first collection of poems *Shirei sefat kodesh* (i, 1842, ii, 1856; Poems of the holy language) was followed by an enlarged edition (1869–70), while in 1895 a posthumous collection of his poems and those of his gifted but tragic son, Micah Joseph LEBENSOHN, appeared in six volumes entitled *Kol shirei Adam 'umikhal* (Collected poems of Adam and Mikhal). Emotional, lofty, and euphuistic, his poetry was highly regarded by contemporary readers, but has since been virtually forgotten. His allegorical drama *Emet ve'emunah* (1867; Truth and faith) – one of the many imitations of Moshe Hayyim LUZZATTO's *Leyesharim tehillah* (1743; Praise to the righteous) – was published 25 years after its completion and aroused a painful literary controversy. Between 1849 and 1853 Lebensohn collaborated in a second edition of Moses MENDELSSOHN's commentary on the Bible, *Bi'ur*, and he published additional materials in *Be'urim hadashim* (1858; New commentaries). He also composed a Hebrew Grammar (1874). He was a regular contributor to many of the leading Hebrew periodicals in which he advocated the ideals of Moses Mendelssohn and the "Berlin" *Haskalah*. Although ephemeral, his work deserves a place in the history of modern Hebrew literature.

DAVID PATTERSON

Lebensohn, Micah Joseph (Mikhal) (1828–1852)

Hebrew poet. The son of Abraham Dov LEBENSOHN, Mikhal received an intensive Hebrew education but was also taught European languages and began his literary activity by translating German poetry into Hebrew. Ill with tuberculosis, Mikhal was sent to Berlin for medical treatment, where he attended Schelling's lectures in natural philosophy, made the acquaintance of Leopold ZUNZ, and came into contact with the current literary movements.

His poetry shows evidence of the influence of Romanticism. His *Shirei bat tziyon* (Songs of the daughter of Zion), published by his father in 1851, contained six poems on subjects drawn from ancient and medieval Jewish history. The first of these, "Shelomo vekohelet" (Solomon and Ecclesiastes), is composed of two poems which contrast the life of the youthful shepherd, Solomon, and the disillusioned old man he has become, who proclaims that all is vanity. Other poems in this collection deal with Samson, Jael and Sisera, and Judah Halevi. Mikhal's third volume, *Kinnor bat tziyon* (1870; The lyre of the daughter of Zion) contains a number of short poems which deal with the sadness of the young man at the imminence of death, others about love and nature, and many translations, of Virgil, Schiller, Goethe, and Mickiewicz, among others.

Mikhal's poems in this volume constitute a departure in Hebrew poetry by their adherence to romanticism, by their self-referentiality and by their unusual and sincere evocations of human love. Mikhal died in Vilna at the age of 24.

GLENDA ABRAMSON

Leeser, Isaac (1806–1868)

American religious leader. Born in Neuenkirchen, Westphalia, Leeser was orphaned at an early age. He received a traditional but limited Jewish education and later studied at the Münster *gymnasium*. In 1824, at the request of a maternal uncle, he resettled in Richmond, Virginia, and planned to go into business. His plans changed after he published two articles in a local newspaper in which he defended Jews and Judaism against the aspersions of a British missionary. In 1829 he agreed to serve as hazzan of Philadelphia's Mikveh Israel Congregation. After a series of contract disputes, he resigned in 1850 and for the next seven years, traveled and wrote extensively before returning to the pulpit. He then served at Beth El Emeth, a congregation organized for him by friends, until his death on 1 February 1868. A complex and uneven individual, Leeser never married and poured his energy and personal resources into his work.

Leeser's extensive literary and communal activities were animated by his vision of a unified, dynamic American Jewish community. He

Solomon Nunes Carvalho Isaac Leeser *1857. Private collection*

Jewish Sunday School movement, founded the first American rabbinical seminary (Maimonides College, 1867), and encouraged the development of many Jewish communal institutions. A proto-Zionist, he favored the development of a modern Jewish society in Palestine.

Acclaimed by both Conservativism and Modern Orthodoxy, Leeser represented a mode of traditional American Judaism which did not survive the nineteenth century. He believed that the Americanization of Judaism was desirable so long as neither the *halakhah* nor the Maimonidean Creed were violated. His ideas were later perpetuated by a number of distinguished disciples including Mayer Sulzberger and Moses Aaron Dropsie.

FURTHER READING

Sussman, L. J.: Another look at Isaac Leeser and the first Jewish translation of the Bible in the United States. *Modern Judaism* 5 (1985) 159–90
Whiteman, M.: Isaac Leeser and the Jews of Philadelphia. *Publications of the American Jewish Historical Society* 48 (1959) 207–44

LANCE J. SUSSMAN

coined the phrase "Catholic Israel" but was best known for his monumental publications including *The Occident* (1843–69), the first successful Jewish newspaper in the United States; an English translation of the entire Hebrew Bible (1853); and 10 volumes of sermons, *Discourses on the Jewish religion* (1867). Included among his other publications were *The Jews and the Mosaic Law* (1834), translations of Sephardi (1837) and Ashkenazi (1848) prayerbooks, a catechism, and a rendition (1852) of Moses MENDELSSOHN's *Jerusalem*.

Leeser was deeply involved in Jewish communal affairs and worked indefatigably to defend Jewish rights at home and abroad. In 1841 he sponsored the first attempt to organize American Jewish life on a national basis. In 1848 and 1855 he even joined Isaac Mayer WISE, his arch rival, to promote American Jewish unity. Later he was elected the first Vice President of the Board of Delegates of American Israelites (1859). Leeser also helped launch the

Leibowitz, Yeshayahu (b.1903) Israeli scientist, scholar, and philosopher. Leibowitz is a unique figure, who has placed his seal upon Israeli life. Born in Riga, Latvia, he was educated at the University of Cologne, received his doctorate from the University of Berlin, and completed his medical studies at the University of Basle. He emigrated to Israel in 1935 and immediately began teaching at the Hebrew University, being appointed Professor of organic chemistry, biochemistry, and neurophysiology in 1961. Leibowitz is a rare phenomenon for having served on several faculties, including the Medical School, the Faculty of Natural Sciences, and the Faculty of Humanities, at the same time, while concurrently holding numerous other academic posts. With his characteristic humor he commented that because he has seven doctorates and is extended over so many subjects he has not excelled in any field. Yet he has also claimed that had he concentrated on one field he would have won a Nobel Prize.

Leibowitz has written on a wide range of scientific subjects, including organic chemistry and physiology, in addition to Maimonidean commentaries, Jewish Orthodoxy, and Israeli politics. His books, for example, *Torah 'umitzvot bazeman hazeh* (1954; Torah and *mitzvot* in our time) and *Yahadut, 'am yehudi 'umedinat yisra'el* (1975; Judaism, the Jewish people, and the State of Israel), collections of his articles and lectures, set out what is termed Leibowitz's "unorthodox orthodoxy". While he regards Judaism as strictly *halakhah*, he presents a radical criticism of the traditional authorities responsible for the religious law. In general, in his articles, as well as in other public activities, Leibowitz has criticized the Israeli government, national institutions, religious leaders, and a number of Israeli political parties. After the Six Day War, for instance, he attacked the Israeli foreign policy and at the start of the Lebanon war he called upon the Israeli Army to refuse to serve in Lebanon.

Leibowitz is therefore one of the most controversial personalities in Israel, considered by some to be an intellectual giant, comparable to Bertrand Russell or Jean-Paul Sartre. Others regard his ideas as erroneous and confusing to the public who do not understand his philosophic and scientific terminology. However, it is not only his ideas, but his provocative style which arouses opposition, for instance his characterization of Golda Meir, the fourth Israeli Prime Minister, as "a wicked old lady" or the *kotel* (The Wailing Wall) as the Golden Calf.

Leibowitz's contribution to Jewish philosophy is in his studies of Maimonides. His *Sihot 'al shemonah perakim larambam* (1986; Conversations on eight chapters of Maimonides) is a record of his lectures on the subject. Other lectures are collected in *Emunato shel harambam* (The faith of Maimonides).

DEBORAH SCHECHTERMAN

Lessing, Theodor (1872–1933)

German cultural historian, philosopher, and writer. Lessing was born in Andorten near Hanover and studied philosophy, history, and medicine in Bonn, Munich, and Freiburg, where he converted to Protestantism (Lutheran). He received his Ph.D. (Erlangen) in 1899 and married an aristocrat in 1900. He returned to Judaism with the rise of Zionism and joined the socialist movement. He sought academic posts and eventually received an appointment as professor at the Technical University in Hanover. Intellectually embattled throughout his career, he caused controversy when he publicly opposed Hindenberg and was subsequently forced to suspend his lectures in 1926. After receiving verbal threats on his life with the Nazi takeover, he sought refuge in Czechoslovakia, only to be murdered in Marienbad by Nazi assassins in 1933.

He wrote poetry and fiction, as well as literary and theater criticism, associating early on with Maximilian Harden, the editor of the influential and respected German journal, *Die Zukunft*. As an earnest disciple of Nietzsche, Lessing devoted himself to cultural–historical studies. His book, *Untergang der Erde am Geist: Europa und Asien* (1915; The decline of the earth by spirit: Europe and Asia), contained an historical–anthropological argument which viewed the Jews as performing a mediating function between dionysian–mystical Asia, on one hand, and intellectual–technological Europe, on the other. He also wrote a book about, and lectured on, the triumvirate Schopenhauer, Wagner, and Nietzsche throughout his academic career. Later he developed a version of the science of "characterology" (*Prinzipien der Charakterologie*) which utilized ethnological and proto-racialist studies of the nineteenth century, which divided humanity into categories according to national characteristics. Although much interested in aspects of human psychology, he attacked Freud and psychoanalysis as typical Jewish deviations. He also excoriated East European *shtetl* life in a series of articles published in the *Allgemeine Zeitung des Judentums* (1909). After returning to Judaism, he publicly confessed his "Jewish self-hatred"; he published the first major study of this phenomenon, *Der jüdische Selbsthass* (1930; Jewish self-hatred). In this work, in addition to a psychological, philosophical, and cultural–historical introduction to the topic, he presented six case studies focusing on, among others: Otto WEININGER, Arthur Trebitsch, and Maximilian Harden. In his post-humously published memoirs, *Einmal und nie wieder* (1935; Once and never again) and in his last work, *Deutschland und seine Juden* (Germany and its Jews), he professed unabashedly his tripartite identity as German, Zionist, and Communist.

BIBLIOGRAPHY

Jewish self-hatred. In *The Jew in the Modern World*, ed. P. Mendes–Flohr and J. Reinharz (New York and Oxford: Oxford University Press, 1980) 237–9

FURTHER READING

Liptzin, S.: *Germany's Stepchildren* (Philadelphia: The Jewish Publication Society of America, 1944) 165–9

MARK H. GELBER

Levanda, Lev [Jehuda-Leib] (1835–1888) Russian–Jewish publicist and prose writer. He was born in Minsk, graduated from the rabbinical school in Vilna, and from 1860 was the Jewish expert to Vilna's governor-general. His literary legacy is extraordinarily vast and has yet to be collected. He wrote for all the Russian–Jewish periodical publications and for several Russian ones. In his articles he consistently adhered to the ideas of the *Haskalah*, primarily assimilation and Russianization. However, the pogroms of the years 1881–2 compelled him to repudiate his former convictions: he joined the *Hibbat Zion* movement, whose slogans, "self-preservation" and "self-help", became his own.

The publicist prevailed over the artist in Levanda's fictional works, the best known of which was the novel *Goriachee vremia* (1871–3; Turbulent times), depicting the Polish uprising of 1863–4 and urging Jews to take the side of Russia in its discord with Poland. Artistically superior is his prose portraying morals and manners (partly autobiographical): for example, such essays, short stories, and narrative tales as "Ocherki proshlogo" (1870; Essays of the past), "Putevye vpechatleniia i zametki" (1873; Travel impressions and notes), "Tipy i siluety" (1881; Types and silhouettes), "Iashka i Ioshka" (1881), and "Dve semeinykh idillii" (1886; Two family idylls). In 1880 his novel *Ispoved deltsa* (Confession of a smart dealer) appeared, a satire on the fever of business profiteering, which began during the period of Alexander II's reforms and became a noticeable theme in Russian satirical literature (for example the satires by Saltykov-Shedrin and Nekrasov). Levanda also composed two historical novels: *Gnev i milost magnata* (1885; The wrath and mercy of a magnate) and *Avraam Iesofovich* (1887).

FURTHER READING

Lvov-Rogachevsky, V.: *A History of Russian Jewish Literature* (Ann Arbor: Ardis, 1979)

SHIMON MARKISH

Levertin, Oscar Ivar (1862–1906) Swedish poet and literary critic. Born in Gryt, near Norrköping, Levertin grew up in a closely knit family. His mother took the main responsibility for keeping a Jewish household. His father was a dealer in art and antiques.

From 1893 Levertin lectured at Stockholm's Högskola (now the University), from 1899 as professor of literary history. His main interest as one of Sweden's greatest historians of literature was the eighteenth century, to which a considerable part of his brilliant essays are devoted. In 1903 his best known collection of essays, *Svenska gestalter* (Swedish figures) appeared, which contained a number of psychological portraits of Swedish eighteenth- and nineteenth-century poets.

During the main part of his professional life he was a leading critic of the *Svenska Dagbladet*, the most prestigious Stockholm newspaper. On account of his perceptive readings, his ability to interpret poets on their own terms, and in spite of his formal traditionalism, he broke new ground. Levertin's reviews became trendsetters in middle and right-wing Sweden.

In the 1880s he joined Unga Sverige (Young Sweden), a group of young poets of what was then the radical persuasion. In his two collections of stories, *Småmynt* (1883; Small change), and *Konflikter* (1885; Controversies), he demonstrated his social concerns, using a contemporary narrative mode. His friendship with Carl Gustaf Verner von Heidenstam, with whom he collaborated on *Pepitas bröllop* (1890; Pepita's wedding), a literary manifesto about the creative genius, the joy of life, and fin-de-siècle esthetic, had a profound influence on him. The result of this influence was *Legender och visor* (1891; Legends and songs), a collection of poems marking his artistic breakthrough. A number of years later he published *Nya dikter* (1894; New poems); and later still, *Dikter* (1901; Poems).

Levertin's poetry shows influences ranging from Nietzsche to French symbolism. A certain estheticism is conspicuously present in his highly personal lines. A fascination with medieval Christianity, coupled with religious moods makes his poetry typical of its period; but together with poems with Christian themes it contains a number of Jewish poems.

Levertin had in mind recent political events such as the new upsurge of anti-Semitism, when he wrote about Jewish messianic longings in one poem, and in another, transformed Shylock into an image of persecuted Jewry. "Ahasverus", the longest of the Jewish poems, ends in reconciliation when the Wandering Jew meets Christ and is urged to join in a meal. That Jewish and Christian themes were equally valid to Levertin is a function of the syncretism, the trend towards leveling of oppositions, that he shared with his contemporaries.

Levertin was firmly rooted in Swedish middle-class culture, a fact which had a profound effect on his tastes and sympathies. Despite knowing little about Jewish history and culture he was consciously Jewish and throughout his entire life endeavored to unite his Swedish and his Jewish legacies.

Whereas in his first poems he seldom reached a level comparable to other writers of the 1890s, he achieved, in his last collection, the cycle of *Kung Salomo och Morolf* (1905; King Solomon and Morolf), a lyrically balanced wholeness unique in his generation. Themes from the "Song of Songs" and "Kohelet" are here interwoven with fairy-tale themes and themes out of medieval poetry. Levertin's Solomon becomes the ultimate Meditative Wisdom – a Faust in oriental garb.

JUDITH WINTHER

Levi, Carlo (1902–1975)

Italian writer and painter. Born in Turin, Levi trained as a doctor but did not practice for long, turning instead to painting, in which he quickly won a national reputation, exhibiting at the Venice *biennale* in 1924 and 1926. He also took an active interest in politics, Turin being the main center of intellectual opposition to Fascism. He was a member of Piero Gobetti's *Rivoluzione liberale* group and then of Carlo Rosselli's *Giustizia e libertà*.

It was as a leading member of Rosselli's group that he was arrested in 1934 and sent into internal exile in Basilicata, first in Grassano and then in the even more remote village of Aliano, from which he was released in 1935 under an amnesty celebrating the fall of Addis Ababa. *Cristo si è fermato a Eboli* (1945; *Christ stopped at Eboli*, 1948) is his remarkable account of that year *in confino*. It was an immediate success in Italy, where it was seen as revealing the human misery and deprivation still existing in the south, the problems of which Fascism had officially declared to be solved. It was also translated into several foreign languages. Its lasting success is due not only to Levi's perceptive account of peasant society, but also to his claim to have discovered in that society certain qualities – freedom from the artificial constraints of the calendar, fellowship, and a sense of the numinous – which he saw as lacking in urban mass society, alienated and alienating, which he believed to be responsible for the rise of Fascism and Nazism. These themes are developed in the essays collected in the volume *Coraggio dei miti: scritti contemporanei, 1922–1974* (1975). Levi's Jewish consciousness was indirectly expressed, but he derived his sense of the numinous from his constant reading of the Bible. *Cristo* was the subject of a lyrical film directed by Francesco Rosi.

Levi's other works include a novel centered on his resistance experiences (*L'orologio*, 1950; *The Watch*, 1952) and several volumes describing his travels in Sicily, Germany, and Russia: but he always considered himself first and foremost a painter, excelling at landscape and portraiture, especially of leading Italian writers such as Gadda, Saba, and Vittorini.

FURTHER READING

Hughes, H. S.: *Prisoners of Hope: The Silver Age of Italian Jews* (Cambridge: Harvard University Press 1983)

BRIAN MOLONEY

Levi, Israël (1856–1939)   French scholar and chief rabbi. He was ordained as a rabbi by the Rabbinical Seminary of Paris in 1879. In 1919 he was appointed chief rabbi of France, having been previously assistant to the chief rabbi in Paris (1882), professor at the Paris Seminary (1892), and lecturer at the École Pratique des Hautes Études (1896). Levi was also one of the founders and the spiritual leader of the Société des Études Juives. On its establishment in 1880, he became its secretary, as well as the general manager of the *Revue des Études Juives*, for which he wrote numerous articles. In 1892 he took charge of its bibliographical section.

Levi's main contribution to modern scholarship is to be found in several areas of Jewish studies. He wrote and published on the Bible, the Apocrypha, and rabbinic literature, as well as on the history of the Jews in France and on the religious controversies between Jews and Christians. He also wrote reviews on almost every publication in those fields. His main works include *Le Roman d'Alexandre* (1887) and *Le Péché originel dans les anciennes sources juives* (1907). To the *Semitic Studies Series*, edited by Chottheil and Marcus JASTROW, Levi contributed his *Ecclesiasticus* (1903) which includes the Hebrew text with English notes and an English–Hebrew vocabulary. For *L'Ecclésiastique ou la sagesse de Jésus, fils de Sira* (1901), the original Hebrew text with notes and translation, he was awarded a prize of the Académie des Inscriptions et Belles Lettres, in 1902.

DEBORAH SCHECHTERMAN

Levi, John (b.1934)   Australian rabbi, historian, biographer, and teacher. Levi was born in Melbourne, the grandson of Nathaniel Levi, the first Jew in the Victorian parliament. He is the first Australian Jew to be ordained as a rabbi and to return to Australia and serve a congregation there. He was educated at Melbourne University, the Hebrew Union College at Cincinnati, and at the Hebrew University, Jerusalem. He earned a second MA with a thesis on Australian Jewish history at Monash University in 1974. Ordained in 1960, he was inducted in the same year as the rabbi of Temple Beth Israel in Melbourne where he has served since. Because of his personality and involvement in the broader community in a variety of leadership positions, he has been instrumental in giving Liberalism a more respectable image among the Jews of Melbourne than was thought to be possible in the nominally Orthodox but divisive Australian religious scene.

He has been one of the pioneers of Jewish broadcasting in Victoria and, since 1974, he has edited and produced a weekly radio programme on the Victorian ethnic station. Active in interfaith work he serves on the staff of the Yarra Theological Union (A Catholic seminary) and is an examiner for the Melbourne College of Divinity. Working in conjunction with the Orthodox rabbinate he was able to reactivate the Council of Christians and Jews, moribund since the establishment of the State of Israel.

Amongst his numerous historical writings were his co-writing of *Australian Genesis*, the classic study of the convict origins of the Australian Jewish community, and *The Forefathers*, a dictionary of the biography of Australian Jewry (1788–1930). In 1981 Levi was appointed a Member of the Order of Australia.

ALAN D. CROWN

Levi, Primo (1919–1987)   Italian writer and chemist. After graduating in chemistry *summa cum laude* from the University of Turin in 1941, Levi worked in Milan until the fall of Mussolini and the Nazi assumption of power forced him into hiding in the Aosta mountains with the aim of joining the Resistance. Captured on 13 December 1943, he was imprisoned at Fossoli and subsequently transferred to Auschwitz. He owed his survival to the scientific qualifications which enabled him as an "economically useful Jew" to be employed in the laboratory of a rubber factory for which prisoners were the labor force. Freed by the Russians and transferred to the Ukraine, he eventually set out for Turin, which he reached after a long and difficult journey.

He turned to writing both as a means of therapy and as a civic duty, to bear

Primo Levi

witness to the atrocities he had witnessed and also to the survival of human decency and brotherhood even in the most adverse circumstances. *Se questo è un uomo* (1947; *If This is a Man*, 1960), describes his concentration camp experiences in a style full of echoes of Dante's *Inferno*. *La tregua*, (1963; *The Truce*, 1965), relates his journey home. Levi's account of Auschwitz is not chronological: he groups his material under headings such as "Work" and "Beyond good and evil", moving from the particular to the general, seeking to understand the process of dehumanization imposed in Auschwitz and the rationality and self-awareness that enable people to preserve their humanity. His conclusions were akin to those of Bruno BETTELHEIM's *The Informed Heart*, (1961). Levi's autobiography, *Il sistema periodico* (1975; *The Periodic Table*, 1986), consists of episodes named after the elements in the periodic chart and is of interest for its account of Levi's education, in which the verifiable certainties of science liberated him

from the abstractions of Italian education and served as "an antidote to Fascism", and also his post-war professional contacts with the German scientist in whose laboratory he worked in Auschwitz. *Se non ora, quando?* (1982; *If Not Now, When?* 1985), is fictional, narrating the vicissitudes of the Russian–Jewish mechanic Mendel, who fights his way across Europe to reach Italy in 1945 in order to sail to Israel. Levi has also written several volumes of short stories, of which *La chiave a stella* (1978; *The Wrench*, 1987), is the most notable, picaresque in tone and celebrating the world of work: bridges and gorges are to Levi's hero, Tino Faussone, what ships and the sea were to Conrad. Levi crosses, in a way unprecedented in Italian literature, the divide between science and art.

FURTHER READING

Gunzberg, L. M.: Down among the dead men: Levi and Dante in Hell. *Modern Language Notes* 6 no. 1 (1986) 10–28
Hughes, H. S.: *Prisoners of Hope: The Silver Age of Italian Jews* (Cambridge: Harvard University Press, 1983)

BRIAN MOLONEY

Lévi, Sylvain (1863–1935) French Indologist. Parisian born and bred, Lévi came from a humble, pious family of Alsatian origin. Intellectually brilliant and encouraged by such eminent scholars as Renan, Lévi quickly made his reputation as one of the foremost authorities on Indian and Far Eastern cultures. His scholarly works on Buddhism, *Dictionnaire du Bouddhisme* (1928) and *Système de Philosophie Bouddhique* (1932), together with his extensive study tours of India, China, Vietnam, and Japan, contributed greatly to the West's understanding of the East. He held distinguished teaching posts (Sorbonne, Ecole des Hautes Etudes, Collège de France), founded the French School of the Far East in Hanoi and the French–Japanese Institute in Tokyo. From 1920 until his death he also played a leading part in Jewish affairs as president of both the ALLIANCE ISRAÉLITE UNIVERSELLE and the *Société des Études Juives*. Given Lévi's hostility to Zionism it is strange, and indeed still mysterious, why he should have

Sylvain Lévi and his wife in Japan

appeared as a member of the Zionist delegation at the Versailles peace conference in 1919. WEIZMANN and SPIRE understandably felt betrayed by their fellow delegate. (For an account of Lévi's evidence at the conference and of his attitudes in general, see CHOURAQUI, André: *L'Alliance Israélite Universelle et la renaissance juive contemporaine, 1860–1960* Paris: Presses Universitaires de France (1965) pp.203–64, 472–81).

NELLY WILSON

Lévi-Strauss, Claude (b.1905) French ethnologist. A great-grandson of Isaac Strauss, an orchestral conductor at the courts of Louis-Philippe and Napoleon III, Lévi-Strauss belonged to the intellectual Jewish bourgeoisie of Paris, and can be described as an assimilated Jew. When he mentions his relationship with Judaism, the only link with it of which he is aware is the image of the ritualized and severe Judaism of his childhood, lacking in any message or teaching, as symbolized by his grandfather, then chief rabbi of Versailles. However, Lévi-Strauss did inherit from that intellectual middle class the taste for study, which constitutes a translation of the traditional virtues into secular terms. He studied in the Faculty of Law at the Sorbonne, passing the *agrégation* examination in philosophy in 1931. He was averse to dogmatic positivist philosophy on account of its subject matter, and his methodological approach was influenced by geology, psychoanalysis, and Marxism. He left France in 1935 to become Professor of Sociology at the University of São Paulo in Brazil.

If he was influenced by Marcel MAUSS, from whom he inherited in particular a sense of the importance of exchange as "a total social factor", his scientific career is in sharp distinction to that of those Jewish intellectuals who, like Mauss and Sylvain LÉVI, secularized their Judaism and turned to the study of foreign societies for institutional and cultural reasons. His appointment as Deputy Director of the Musée de l'Homme in 1946; his lectures in 1950 at the École Pratique des Hautes Études on "The comparative religion of societies without a written language"; his appointment to the Collège de France, where he became Professor of Social Anthropology in 1959; the triumphant progress during the 1960s of structuralism of which he is considered the progenitor, and to which the success of *Tristes Tropiques* (1955; *A World on the Wane*, 1962), and in particular of *Anthropologie Structurale* (1958; *Structural Anthropology*, 1963), bear witness; and finally his election to the Académie Française in 1977, all represent the career to be expected of a great intellectual.

Can Lévi-Strauss be situated in the line of descent of rationalist Jewish thinkers? He was opposed both to Anglo-Saxon empirical sociology, which sees structure as inherent in reality, and to idealistic structuralism which sees structure as corresponding to nothing real. Instead Lévi-Strauss re-establishes the structure of thought as something essentially rationalist by relating the idea of social structure not to empirical reality but to models constructed according to it. Basing it on the linguistic model – an epistemological discovery set out in a famous article in *Word* (1945) – Lévi-Strauss applies this structural model to economic and matrimonial systems of exchange, and to primitive thought (*Le totemisme aujourd'hui*, *La pensée sauvage*), which, contrary to the ideas of Lucien LÉVY-BRUHL, he establishes as having its own discernible logic, instead of being an uncivilized mode of thinking, as well as to the analysis of myths to which he devotes the four volumes of *Mythologiques* (1964–71).

From the importance of method in Lévi-Strauss's theories derives the position he adopts towards Judaism. It is in effect a methodological condemnation which is indebted to Edward Leach's attempt to apply structural analysis to Judaism. This, according to Lévi-Strauss, is not a legitimate process except in an ethnographic context, independent of the sources analyzed. Contrary to Mauss, in whose works religious proximity and philological methodology preceded the scientific process, Claude Lévi-Strauss, who had neither an intellectual affinity with religion nor any personal religious misgivings, never considers Judaism in his scientific proceedings; his methodological presuppositions exclude it. He thus sets up against Judaism a scientific attitude of extreme rationalization.

BIBLIOGRAPHY

The social use of kinship terms among Brazilian Indians. *American Anthropologist* 45, no. 3, (1943); L'analyse structurale en linguistique et en anthropologie. *Word* 1, no. 2 (1945); *Les Structures Élémentaires de la Parenté* (Paris, 1949). Trans. as *Elementary Structures of Kinship* (London: Eyre & Spottiswoode, 1968); *A World on the Wane* (London: Cape, 1963); Structural Anthropology (New York: Basic Books, 1963); *Paroles données* (Paris: Plon, 1984); *La Potière jalouse* (Paris: Plon, 1985)

FURTHER READING

Marc-Lipiansky, M.: *Le Structuralisme de Lévi–Strauss* (Paris: Payot, 1973)

PERRINE SIMON-NAHUM

Levin, Hanoch (b.1943)

Israeli playwright and story-writer. Born in the shabby southern quarters of Tel Aviv to lower middle-class immigrants from Poland, Levin's background has provided inspiration for many of his plays and stories. While still a student he began publishing satirical poems.

Levin's first work for the stage was a political cabaret: *At ve'ani vehamilhamah haba'ah* (1968; You and I and the next war). It was followed by two further satirical reviews in the same vein: *Ketchup* (1969), and *Malkat ha'ambatya* (1970; Queen of the bathtub). The main target of his satire was post-Six-Day-War Israeli society, addicted to euphoria, false patriotism, and materialism. *Queen of the Bathtub* caused a national uproar and performances were suspended.

Levin's first play was *Solomon Grip* (1969). *Hefetz*, produced in 1972, was a major theatrical event which provoked extreme reactions: some condemned its alleged nihilism while others hailed it as an original contribution to Israeli drama. *Hefetz*, as most of Levin's later plays, is a stylized black comedy inhabited by caricatures: a petit-bourgeois family of grotesque characters who engage in a game of humiliation. Victimizers and victims alike take part in it willingly as it is their raison d'être. Levin's next and most successful play was *Ya'akobi veleidental* (Yaacobi and Leidental). It was first staged in 1972 and has since enjoyed several revivals, in Israel and abroad: in Britain in 1974 under the name *Dominoes* (directed by Hayyim Topol), at the Fringe Festival in Edinburgh (1980), with the original Israeli cast, and at the Young Vic Studio, 1981. Levin's characters move mechanically and recite in monotonous voices, and stage props are minimal, as in the Theater of the Absurd. While Levin continues to view humiliation and torture as the main factors of human relationships, he also introduces blunt, explicit references to basic bodily functions with which the characters are preoccupied. These two aspects become the major characteristics of Levin's plays. Death is another recurring theme, as a final inescapable stage in human life which is a process of degradation, disintegration, and defeat.

In 1988 Levin became Israel's Cameri Theater's house playwright.

BIBLIOGRAPHY

Ya'acobi and Leidental (Tel Aviv: Institute for the Translation of Hebrew Literature, 1979); *Hefetz* (Tel Aviv: Institute for the Translation of Hebrew

Literature, 1981); *Rubber Merchants* (Tel Aviv: Institute for the Translation of Hebrew Literature, 1983)

FURTHER READING

Levi, S.: The Gospel according to Hanoch. *Theatre Research International* 13 no. 2 (1988) 146–54

Ofrat, G.: The archetypal structure of Hanoch Levin's plays. *Modern Hebrew Literature* 1/2 (1985) 34–8

RIVKA MAOZ

Levin, Harry (b.1912)   American critic and Professor of Comparative Literature. Levin was born in Minneapolis, Minnesota, and educated at Harvard where he received his AB in comparative literature in 1933. He was awarded honorary degrees by Syracuse, St Andrews University (Scotland), and the University of Paris. In 1988 Levin was the Babbitt Professor of Comparative Literature at Harvard, a position he had held since 1960. In addition to his numerous books, which range from Shakespeare to Hawthorne, Joyce and beyond, Levin taught at a number of universities throughout the world, including Oxford, Cambridge, Tokyo University, University of Puerto Rico, and the Chinese University in Hong Kong. Levin published widely but he is best known for his work on Elizabethan drama, the modern novel, and literary criticism. Some of his better known books include his edition and critical introduction to *The Portable James Joyce* (1947), *Contexts of Criticism* (1957), *The Power of Blackness: Hawthorne, Poe, Melville* (1958), *Refractions: Essays in Comparative Literature* (1966), *Grounds for Comparison* (1972), and *Shakespeare and The Revolution of the Times* (1976). In *Playboys and Killjoys* (1987), Levin explored comic theory and practice. Levin's work has been praised by both scholars and ordinary readers alike in that he adds an "instant and immanent wit" to his consistent scholarly accuracy. Many compare his work to Edmund Wilson, the famous American literary and social critic, for Levin brings "breadth, richness, and sensitivity" to a wide scope of topics.

RANDALL BEEBE

Levin, Meyer (1905–1981)   American writer. Born in Chicago to immigrant parents, Meyer Levin became well known for his ambitious naturalistic fiction and passionate sense of Jewish experience. His earliest novels – *Reporter* (1929) and *Frankie and Johnny* (1930) – ignored Jewishness, but in the mid 1920s Levin began his attachment to Zionism and in 1931 produced *Yehuda*, the first novel in English to reflect kibbutz life. His work thereafter unfailingly adumbrated Jewish concerns and sympathies.

In 1932 Levin completed a collection of Hassidic Lore, *The Golden Mountain* (republished in 1975 as *Classic Hassidic Tales*). A proletarian novel, *The New Bridge*, appeared in 1933, and in 1937 Levin published his *magnum opus*, *The Old Bunch*, a lengthy, journalistic account of young Jews in Chicago at the time of the Jazz Age and the Great Depression. The *New York Times* reviewer applauded it as "a landmark in the development of the realistic novel", although a romantic like Ludwig LEWISOHN saw in the novel evidence of "violent Jewish self-hatred". Another proletarian novel, *Citizens* (1940), has for its protagonist a character from *The Old Bunch*, but, says S. J. Rubin, it shows "an unusual understanding of the ambiguous situation of the black man in America".

Levin, active as a journalist in British Mandatory Palestine and in Civil War Spain, served as a war correspondent during the Second World War and also produced documentary films. After the war he helped smuggle Jewish émigrés into Palestine. In 1947 *My Father's House*, a meditation on the Jewish fate in Nazi Europe and in Palestine, appeared as both film and novel. Two other Zionist films belong to these years: *The Illegals* and *Voyage of the Unafraid*.

Levin's splendid autobiography, *In Search* (1950), was followed in 1952 by his dramatization of the Anne Frank diary. This led a year later to litigation and a court finding that a version by Albert and Frances Hackett had plagiarized Levin's script. *Compulsion* (1956), Levin's evocation of the Leopold–Loeb case, proved to be his greatest popular success. A series of Holocaust novels, *Eva* (1959), *The Fanatic* (1963), reflecting his Frank diary troubles, and *The Stronghold* (1965), followed. In 1968 came his one venture into the realm of humor, *Gore and Igor*. Levin's last notable works were a second autobiographical volume, *The Obsession* (1973), and a two-volume evocation of the Zionist experience, *The Settlers* (1972), and *The Harvest* (1978).

Levin had believed that "a book about Jews" would never "be regarded as in the direct mainstream of American writing", but his career belied his prophecy. The best account of that career is Steven J. Rubin's *Meyer Levin* (1982).

STANLEY F. CHYET

Lévinas, Emmanuel (b.1905) French philosopher. From a background of Lithuanian Judaism, the severity and sobriety of which he likes to emphasize, born into a middle-class intellectual Orthodox family steeped in traditional Russian and Jewish culture, Emmanuel Lévinas came to France in 1923 to study with Blondel, Guéroult, and Halbwachs at the University of Strasbourg. In 1928–9 he was the pupil of Edmund Husserl and Martin Heidegger at Freibourg, and introduced their ideas to France by publishing a *Théorie de l'Intuition dans la Phénoménologie de Husserl* in 1930, and translating the *Méditations Cartésiennes*. In 1932 he published *Martin Heidegger et l'Ontologie*, the first French study of Heidegger.

Lévinas' philosophy has thus from the first been situated in the line of Husserlian methodological reflection. Of Heidegger's notion of being, Lévinas retains the separation between being and the state of beings, which in his work becomes that between existence and the existent, analyzing being through the notion of "il y a" (there is), and trying to discover how an "existent" arises in the neutral and impersonal "existence" expressed in that phrase. He seeks the break with "there is" in the interhuman relationship, in what he calls the "epiphany" of the face of another person. The face in effect constitutes the moment when the other transcends the idea of the other in oneself. But the other person ·is not, as in Martin BUBER, absorbed into the consciousness of the exchange as "you". It is a one-way relationship. Lévinas takes the description of subjectivity to its uttermost limits, defining it on the basis of responsibility to another person.

In emphasizing the contribution of this system of thought in relation to the Kantian criticism and epistemological doctrines of the nineteenth century, Lévinas is brought to define its limits. To do so, as his post-1960 writings bear witness, he appeals both to Cartesian metaphysics and the biblical inspiration which inspires ethical Jewish thought. The process set out in *Au-delà de la Phénoménologie*, passing from existence to the existent and from the existent to another person, consists of reaching a metaphysic which derives its meaning from the ethical element of existence.

It is in passing from ontology (concern for the being) to ethics (concern for another) and to the word of God, that the connection between philosophy and religion appears, understood in the face of another, although the religious element is not revealed to oneself. Lévinas situates the law in which Judaism is rooted, as a kind of sacrifice to the other person, in a relationship of fidelity without fideism, allowing Judaism no meaning except as an ontological category, that is to say, raised from the singular to the universal, denying any recourse to dogma and faith. The ethical relationship determines access to the idea of God and defines its specific transcendence, its "thatness". Lévinas thus transforms the relationship between sacred and secular texts. Insofar as it shows a commitment to another person, a secular text is in effect potentially sacred.

This phenomenology is developed in a critical approach to history. In the wake of Franz ROSENZWEIG, Lévinas denounces the illusions of historicity. He sets out his very radical criticism in *Totalité et Infini* (1961), which is devoted to the phenomenology of the face.

No doubt there is ambiguity and paradox in the echoes set up by this system of thought, more philosophical than Jewish (Lévinas is regarded as a philosophical master in contemporary French Judaism), a system of thought which, arising from German phenomenology at a time when the question of "otherness" was posed in tragic terms, rejects any sociohistorical analysis of the contemporary era.

BIBLIOGRAPHY
Difficile Liberté (Paris: Albin Michel, 1963); *Quatre lectures talmudiques* (Paris: 1968); *Totalité et infini.*

459

Essai sur l'extériorité (The Hague: Martin Nijhoff, 1971); *Du sacré au saint. Cinq nouvelles lectures talmudiques* (Paris: Les Editions de Minuit, 1977); *Du Dieu qui vient a l'idée* (Paris: J. Vrin, 1982); *L'au-delà du verset. Lectures et discours talmudiques* (Paris: 1982)

FURTHER READING

Forthomme, B.: *Une Philosophie de la Transcendance: La Metaphysique d'Emmanuel Lévinas* (Paris: Vrin, 1979)

PERRINE SIMON-NAHUM

Levine, Jack (b.1915) American painter. Born in Boston of immigrant Jewish parents, Levine was raised in the city's South End. His family background, poor financial circumstances, and art education paralleled that of Hyman BLOOM. Levine's formal art studies began in high school under Boston's public school program at the Boston Museum of Fine Arts. He also studied at the Roxbury, Massachusetts Settlement House under Harold Zimmerman who exposed him to the expressionist works of Georges Rouault and Chaim SOUTINE. From 1929 until 1931 Levine, like Bloom, studied with Denman Ross at Harvard; Ross customarily looked for new talent among the poorer youth of Boston.

Levine is considered part of the Boston School of Figurative Expressionism. The arts in Boston had a tradition for conservatism, and although Levine remained a representational painter, his bold use of color and exaggerations of form were considered controversial.

From 1935 until 1940, Levine was employed by the Works Progress Administration (WPA) as part of Massachusetts' easel painting project. Throughout his career, he focused on issues of social consciousness, an attitude shared by a number of American–Jewish artists until about 1950. Levine has consistently been a critic of the American lifestyle – its politicians, its wealthy, its inequitable system of reward.

It was not until the Second World War and the tragedies of the Holocaust that Levine painted works with specifically Jewish content. Some works such as *The Passing Scene* (1941; Museum of Modern Art, New York) and *Apteka* (*c.*1940) commented on the uncertainties of life in the USA for Jewish immigrants. In reaction

to the Holocaust, Levine painted *Tombstone Cutter* (1947), with the image of an emaciated artisan engraving the tombstone in memory of the Jews of Europe. In 1969 he created *To An Unknown German* (Kennedy Galleries, New York), a lithograph based on archival Holocaust photographs. During the 1940s Levine also began a series of miniature paintings of kings from the Bible and scholars from Jewish history. Included in the series of strongly characterized personalities from the ancient past are images of King Solomon and his architect of the Temple, Hiram of Tyre, King Saul, King David, King Asa, Hillel, and Maimonides. In each of these paintings, the name of the principal characters is inscribed in Hebrew. Levine continued to paint biblical themes. His more recent works, including *Jacob Wrestling with the Angel* (1975), *David and Goliath* (1977), and *In the Valley of Kidron* (1983) are created on a grander scale placing more attention on narrative.

FURTHER READING

Getlein, F.: *Jack Levine* (New York: Harry N. Abrams Inc., 1966)

Kampf, A.: *Jewish Experience in the Art of the Twentieth Century* (South Hadley: Bergin & Garvey Publishers Inc., 1984)

BARBARA GILBERT

Levine, Philip (b.1928) American poet and teacher. Philip Levine's birth in Detroit to Russian–Jewish immigrant parents has informed nearly all his poetry with a unifying theme – the isolated individual striving to survive and embrace a world that seems to treat his presence with disdain. In treating this theme Levine has sounded a truly authentic urban voice, both toughened and sensitized by experience. He worked at a number of menial jobs before attending Wayne State University in Detroit, where he studied under John Berryman and eventually earned a BA in 1950 and an MA in 1955. Before finishing his graduate work there, he married Frances Artley, by whom he had three sons. From the highly regarded program of the University of Iowa Levine received an MFA in creative writing in 1957. He began teaching at California State University, Fresno, in 1958 and stayed there until the late 1960s when, after active opposition to the war in Vietnam, he and his family moved to Barcelona. Later he returned to teach at Fresno once again.

Levine's poetry has moved from the tight syllabics and rhyme of his first volume, *On The Edge* (1963), to the looser, narrative form of his latest poems in *Sweet Will* (1985). But while he has pushed against the restrictive forms of his early work and opted for a more flamboyant language, he has never been an innovator. His intention has been focused squarely on uttering "vivas for those who have failed", on the people who inhabit the work, whether as speakers or subjects. Ever distrustful of dogma, Levine creates poetry that is political in its very inception, in its overriding concern with these working-class lives, one excellent example being "The Midget" from *Not This Pig* (1968). While some promise of a grander human society is suggested, that promise can only be embodied in the individual who persists doggedly against great odds. Human nature, then, is the foundation of Levine's faith. His Jewishness is a matter of cultural heritage rather than religion and expresses itself as "a celebration of courage and integrity and the difficulty of life wherever it takes place".

BIBLIOGRAPHY
Don't Ask (1981); *Selected Poems* (London: Secker & Warburg, 1984)

FURTHER READING
Mills, R. J., Jr.: "The True and Earthy Prayer": Philip Levine's poetry. In *Cry of the Human* (Urbana: University of Illinois Press, 1975) 251–65
Yenser, S.: Bringing it home. *Parnassus* 6, 1977 101–17

NELSON HATHCOCK

Levy, Amy (1861–1889) British novelist and poet. Born in Clapham, South London, Levy was educated at Cambridge University and was the first Jewish woman to reside at Newnham College. While at Cambridge she published a story about a half-Jewish woman "Euphemia, a sketch" in *Victoria Magazine* and also her first collection of poems *Xanthippe and Other Verse* (1881). The title poem of this volume is a defense of the wife of Socrates, which demonstrates an early sympathy for the nascent feminist movement in England. Levy published extensively in journals throughout her life and her second collection of poems, *A Minor Poet and Other Verse*, (1884) had for the most part been previously published in literary magazines. Levy's characteristic *weltschmerz* is especially apparent in this volume. Such melancholia, however, contrasts starkly with the lightness of tone of her first novel *The Romance of a Shop* (1888).

Levy began writing a series of articles on Jewish themes for the *Jewish Chronicle* in 1886. This led to the publication of her second novel *Reuben Sachs: a Sketch* (1888), which is about the impact of materialistic values on two upper-middle-class London Jewish families. This work, which quickly went into a second edition, is Levy's most accomplished and telling novel largely because it is written from the viewpoint of the novel's heroine, Judith Quixano. Israel ZANGWILL was profoundly influenced by *Reuben Sachs* and obliquely referred to it in his *Children of the Ghetto* (1892). His Jewish family in *The Melting Pot* (1908), was also, pointedly, called Quixano. Close friends of Levy's such as Eleanor Marx and Olive Schreiner were also influenced by this novel, although it did cause an outcry within Anglo-Jewry.

As well as writing regularly for Oscar Wilde's *Woman's World* and other journals, Levy published her third novel *Miss Meredith* (1889), whose lightness of tone, as with *The Romance of a Shop*, is a deliberate counterpoint to her darker poetry and to *Reuben Sachs*. In the same year she also published her most successful collection of poems *A London Plane Tree and Other Verse* (1889). She corrected the proofs of this volume only a week before her suicide. Her best short story "Cohen of Trinity", published in *The Gentlemen's Magazine* (1889) is about a successful Jewish novelist who committed suicide in the midst of his publishing success. Only when faced with material success was Levy's hero able to realize that he had not achieved what he wanted. For this reason, this story has been rightly regarded as Amy Levy's epitaph. Her suicide at the age of 28 ranks with Isaac ROSENBERG's untimely death as a profound loss to the corpus of Jewish and English literature in general, before the Second World War.

FURTHER READING

Amy Levy. *Transactions of the Jewish Historical Society of England* 11 (1924–7)

Wagenknecht, E.: *Daughters of the Covenant: Portraits of Six Jewish Women* (Massachusetts: 1983)

BRYAN CHEYETTE

Lévy, Bernard-Henri (b.1947)   French philosopher and writer. Born in Béni-Sof, Algeria, Lévy's family emigrated to Paris when he was a child. Educated at two of Paris's most prestigious *lycées*, the Lycée Pasteur and the Lycée Louis-le-Grand, he was awarded his degree at the exclusive *École normale supérieure*. There Lévy began his studies of the philosophies of Jean-Paul Sartre and Raymond ARON, the leading thinkers of the day. Lévy found both men and their respective schools of thought to be responsible for a certain impoverishment of life, as well as for the general politicization of various aspects of Western life. Moreover, *l'homme Sartron*, or adherents of either Sartre's or Aron's views, tended to be in opposition to authentic Jewish views of man, of the world, and of God.

Though formerly a disciple of the Jewish–French educator and philosopher, Emmanuel LÉVINAS, Lévy's evolving antirationalist attitudes heralded a new era of thought in the Francophone world. The leftist and rationalist philosophies of the university student were utterly abandoned in two of Lévy's early works, *La Barbarie à visage humain* (1977) and *Le Testament de Dieu* (1979). In both volumes, the *enfant terrible* of the "new philosophers" denounced Marxism and Fascism as well as those schools of Western thought which were seen as inheritors of classical Platonic philosophy. Lévy postulated that such movements sought to demystify life and likewise denigrated other modes of thought, notably the particular Jewish vision of life. Moreover, in his sweeping condemnation of French cultural and political ideas, *L'idéologie Française* (1981), Lévy argued that anti-Semitism in all its guises is consub-stantial with French and occidental culture, despite so-called liberal attitudes and the limited historical evidence of emancipation.

These general philosophical attitudes were refined somewhat in Lévy's first novel, *Le Diable en Tête* (1984). The book stands as a more passionate investigation on a personal plane of Jewishness, its being the "devil" in the psyche of the protagonist. A quasi-autobiographical book, it follows a contemporary Jewish intellectual through a series of attachments to contemporary non-Jewish movements, and views his Jewishness from a number of perspectives.

Lévy currently (1988) works for the publishers Bernard Grasset, serving as chief editor and director of the *Collection Figures*, a series of works written by some of those writers associated with Lévy's "new philosophy", as well as others who are active in the present renaissance of Jewish belles-lettres in France.

SIMON SIBELMAN

Levy, Emmanuel (1900–1985)   English painter. Born in Manchester of Russian immigrant parents who had settled there at the end of the nineteenth century, Levy first studied at the Manchester School of Art, under Adolphe Valette. Later he went to London where he continued his studies at the St Martins School of Art, and subsequently in Paris. A fellow student in Manchester, although 13 years his senior, was L. S. Lowry. Levy's portrait of this artist now hangs in Salford Art Gallery. Levy was an excellent teacher, especially of drawing, and taught from the time he completed his studies and throughout his adult life: in Manchester at the School of Architecture in the late 1920s, and at Stockport School of Art. After settling in London in 1963, where he lived until his death, he had many private pupils and held a teaching position at the Battersea School of Art. His work was first exhibited in Manchester; Salford City Art Centre held a retrospective exhibition in 1948 and Manchester's Tib Lane Gallery gave him an exhibition in 1979. In London several one-man exhibitions were held at the Ben Uri Art Society and the Fieldborne Galleries. His works are in private and the following public collections: National Portrait Gallery, London; the Ben Uri Art Society, London; and the Tel Aviv Museum of Art and Ein Harod Museum, Israel.

MURIEL EMANUEL

Lévy-Bruhl, Lucien (1857–1939) French philosopher and anthropologist. In addition to being a respected teacher of philosophy (for example at the Lycée Louis le Grand and the Sorbonne) and editor of the *Revue philosophique de la France et de l'étranger*, Lévy-Bruhl wrote extensively on anthropological subjects to which he brought a positivist view of the development of socio-cultural phenomena, based on Auguste Comte's law of the three stages, combined with modern sociological methods. His views on primitive societies and on the a-rational nature of preliterate mentality came increasingly to be challenged.

NELLY WILSON

Lewisohn, Ludwig (1882–1955) German–American novelist and author. His was a career of impassioned proselytizing, public scandal, and prolific literary endeavor. Of his novels, *The Case of Mr Crump* (1926), still retains misogynistic energy as an autobiographical portrait of a disastrous marriage. (Thomas Mann likened the novel to works by Strindberg.) Lewisohn told his own story in *Up Stream* (1922) and *Mid-Channel* (1929), one of the most fascinating autobiographies by an American Jew. Going decidedly against the optimistic grain of narratives by Mary ANTIN, Jacob Riis, and others, Lewisohn described his bitter disillusionment with the cause of assimilation. Raised in South Carolina, and strongly influenced by its Methodist culture "at the age of 15, I was an American, a Southerner and a Christian", Lewisohn emancipated himself intellectually through Darwin and the promise of cultural pluralism in America. Denied academic employment by Columbia University, and the victim of anti-German sentiment during the First World War, by the 1920s Lewisohn rejected the "promises" of American life which were denied to Jews like himself. He became an astringent critic of American culture in the pages of *The Nation*, before fleeing to Europe in the mid 1920s to seek a divorce. In Europe he became converted to the cause of Zionism. Lewisohn's *Israel* (1925), written at the behest of Chaim WEIZMANN, sought to heighten the awareness of his fellow American Jews to the achievements and needs of Jewish colonists in Palestine. His many books, which include a widely read study of *Expression in America* (1932), were marked by an impassioned advocacy of the need for frankness and freedom in sexual matters, a dedication to Zionism, and a natural combativeness. After his return to America in 1934, he became honorary secretary of the Zionist Organization of America. Lewisohn was appointed Professor of Comparative Literature when Brandeis University was founded in 1948.

ERIC HOMBERGER

Leyvik, Halper [Leyvik Halpern] (1888–1962) Yiddish poet and dramatist. Born in Igumen, Belorussia, Leyvik had a strong traditional education, but came under the influence of modern ideas, and read contemporary Hebrew literature. Leyvik became active in revolutionary politics, joining the Jewish–socialist *Bund* and organizing demonstrations and meetings. He was arrested in 1906 for his activities in Minsk, spent two years in prison awaiting trial, and was then sentenced to a period of hard labor followed by life exile in Siberia in 1912. Leyvik escaped from Siberia and reached the United States, where he worked as a paperhanger, even after he had become a well-known literary figure. In 1925 he toured Europe and the Soviet Union, but broke with the New York communist newspaper *Di frayhayt* over the Palestine pogrom. In 1937 he visited Palestine, and Zionist thinking became a strong influence, particularly after the Second World War.

Much of Leyvik's early poetry is autobiographical, dealing with an unhappy childhood, his prison experiences and road to exile, for instance *Hintern shlos* (1918; Behind the lock). He had links with the *Yunge* group of poets, but

463

turned increasingly to a visionary poetic voice, in a response to the pogroms in Eastern Europe and to his own personal suffering. He gives poetic expression to themes of moral struggle, redemption through suffering, and a longing for justice, human dignity, and salvation. His most celebrated work, the verse drama *Der goylem*, appeared in 1921 and embodies Leyvik's aspiration to use Jewish themes and messianic longings as symbols for universal human problems. Other plays include the "realist" prose drama *Shmates* ("Rags", vol. 5 of *Geklibene shriftn*, 1928) which deals with generational and class tensions in a Jewish family in New York.

FURTHER READING

Landis, J. C., ed. and trans.: *The Dybbuk and Other Great Yiddish plays* (New York: Bantam, 1966)

Roskies, D.: *Against the Apocalypse: Responses to Catastrophe in Modern Jewish Culture* (Cambridge: Harvard University Press, 1984)

CHRISTOPHER HUTTON

Liberman, Serge (b.1942)   Australian novelist, editor and essayist. Born in Fergana, Russia, Liberman emigrated to Australia in 1951 after spending some time in a DP camp, an experience that is reflected in some of his writing. His literary career began with his editorship of student Jewish magazines, later of the *Melbourne Chronicle*, a bilingual, Yiddish–English, cultural magazine (1977–84). He is the associate editor of the literary periodical, *Outrider*.

He began writing short stories, essays, reviews and articles for Australian and overseas Jewish and literary periodicals in the 1970s and has been published in the more important Australian journals. Since 1980 his stories, which have received substantial critical acclaim, have begun to appear in anthologies of current Jewish or multicultural writing, for example *Ethnic Australia* (1981), *Jewish Writing from Down Under* (1984), and *Joseph's Coat: An Anthology of Multicultural Writing* (1985). He has published three anthologies of short stories, *On Firmer Shores* (1981), *A Universe of Clowns* (1983), *The Life that I have Led* (1986), and his *Bibliography of Australian Judaica* (1987). These works have brought Liberman recogni-

tion in the form of two major Australian literary awards: the Alan Marshall Award for separate collections of fiction which he has won three times, (1981, 1984, and 1985), and the New South Wales Premier's Literary Award (Ethnic Section, 1984).

Most of Liberman's stories move us through an event, or series of events, which are typically urban, middle class, often identifiably Australian in setting. They tend to have visionary or autobiographical motifs and critics have described him as the "citizen moralist". About half of them have identifiably Jewish motifs. A common theme in his work is the exploration of what it is like to be treated as the stereotype Jew. Other stories focus on the Jewish immigrant and memories of the Holocaust.

FURTHER READING

Burns, G.: Review of *A Universe of Clowns*. *Australian Book Review* (Dec./Jan. 1984) 33

Keesing, N.: The Jewish contribution to Australian literature. *Australia and New Zealand Jewish Year Book* (1985)

ALAN D. CROWN

Lieberman, Saul (1898–1983)   American talmudic scholar and historian. Born in Belorussia, he received his talmudic training at the Slobodka *yeshivah* and at the Hebrew University of Jerusalem, where he served as instructor in Talmud from 1931 to 1940. In 1940 he was appointed Professor of Talmud at the Jewish Theological Seminary of America in New York, teaching there until his death.

Lieberman's books and articles display his vast knowledge of classical and rabbinic literature. In *Greek in Jewish Palestine* (1942) and *Hellenism in Jewish Palestine* (1950), he argued that Palestinian Jewry of the first four Christian centuries, including its rabbinic leadership, participated in and was profoundly influenced by the surrounding intellectual culture. He produced important researches on the rabbinic literature of the period, including an attempt at a critical edition of and modern commentary on the Palestinian Talmud. His *Hayerushalmi kifeshuto* (1934), covers only three tractates, interrupted by his conclusion that such a project must await a systematic clarification of the earlier tanaitic texts which form the basis for talmudic discourse. To this end he began his work on the Tosefta, culminating in his magnum opus, a critical edition of the Tosefta accompanied by a brief commentary and, in separate volumes, a comprehensive commentary (*Tosefta kifeshutah*, 1955–73, covering orders *Zera'im*, *Mo'ed*, and *Nashim*). In this work, Lieberman expressed his preference for the traditional rabbinic approach, which explains its subject from within the text itself, as against an overreliance upon textual variants, emendations, and source criticism. In it he included, besides historical and philological materials, an analysis of citations of Tosefta passages found in the later rabbinic authorities. The work thus constitutes a thoroughgoing commentary, not only on Tosefta, but on rabbinic literature as a whole and is accepted among scholars as an indispensable tool in talmudic research.

MARK WASHOFSKY

Liebermann, Max (1847–1935) German painter and graphic artist. Born in Berlin in 1847 into a family of millionaire Jewish manufacturers, Max Liebermann entered the Weimar Art Academy in 1868. He lived in Paris from 1873 to 1877, during which time he visited Barbizon and became acquainted with Millet, Corot, and Daubigny, contacts which strengthened his predilection for proletarian subject matter.

Liebermann's role in nineteenth-century German art is comparable to that of Manet for France: his roots lie with Realism and he developed into the leading German Impressionist. Initially inspired by mid-nineteenth-century German realists, seventeenth-century Dutch genre, and plein air painting, and the work of his contemporary, the Dutch genre painter Josef Israëls, Liebermann depicted the rural and urban working classes in a straightforward, candid manner, eschewing both sentiment and propaganda. In the 1880s, under the influence of French Impressionism, he loosened his brushstroke and lightened his palette, yet his commit-

Max Liebermann Memorial Service for Kaiser Friedrich at Kosen *1888. Tate Gallery, London*

ment to proletarian themes never wavered. Living in a period of rapid assimilation and emancipation for Jews, Liebermann did not generally exploit Jewish themes. In 1884, however, with vivid memories of the visits he had made a decade earlier to Amsterdam's Jewish quarter, he initiated a series called the *Judengasse* (street scenes of the Jewish quarter), which he worked on for the next 20 years.

Although Liebermann made Berlin his home again in 1884, throughout his life, he traveled constantly between the major French, German, and Dutch cities, exhibiting regularly in art academies and annual salons and in several major one-man shows. In 1899 he was instrumental in the founding of the Berlin Secession, a group which rejected academic painting and advocated greater artistic freedom. In 1920 he was appointed president of the Prussian

Academy of Art. After the rise of Nazism in 1933 he resigned his presidency.

A major posthumous retrospective of Liebermann's work was organized in 1980 by the Nationalgalerie in Berlin.

FURTHER READING
Koeppen, W.: Max Liebermann – Juden in der deutschen Kunst. In *Porträts zur deutsch-jüdischen geistesgeschichte*, ed. T. Koch (Cologne: 1961)
Max Liebermann in seiner zeit (Berlin: Nationalgalerie, 1979) [exhibition catalog]

KRISTIE A. JAYNE

Lilien, Ephraim Moses (1874–1925) German artist. He was born of humble origins in Drohobycz in eastern Galicia. At first apprenticed as a sign-painter, later, with the help of rich relatives, he went to study at the Art Academy in Krakow with the well-known Polish painter of patriotic and historical subjects, Jan Matejko. From there he went to Munich, but found the atmosphere too confining. In 1899 he settled in Berlin, where he became associated with the Zionist movement and such noted Zionist personalities as Berthold FEIWEL and Martin BUBER. In 1902 Lilien, together with Martin Buber, Davis Trietsch and Berthold Feiwel, founded the Berlin publishing house *Jüdischer Verlag*. Its purpose was to create "a center for the promotion of Jewish culture and the encouragement of art and culture". In the same year Lilien illustrated *Songs of the Ghetto* by Morris ROSENFELD. The poems by Rosenfeld dealt with poverty, exploitation, and hard labor – themes that must have appealed to Lilien because they probably reminded him of his own childhood experiences.

In 1905 at the Seventh Zionist Congress he, along with such distinguished Zionists as Boris Schatz and Otto Warburg, helped to establish the BEZALEL SCHOOL OF ARTS AND CRAFTS in Jerusalem. When the Bezalel school opened in 1906 Lilien traveled to Jerusalem and served for a short time on its faculty.

Lilien's oeuvre consists primarily of ink drawings. These were in the fluid, lyrical, and decorative style called Jugendstil. From 1905 on he turned to etching. Some of his etchings show views of his native Galicia, but most depict the sites and the diverse and colorful inhabitants of the Holy Land. Lilien produced many Ex Libris designs for famous Jews, such as Stefan ZWEIG and Martin Buber. His last major work was to have been a ten-volume illustrated Bible for the Braunschweig publisher Georg Westermann, but only three volumes actually appeared.

Neither a noted master nor an innovator, his contribution lies primarily in his having made Jews conscious of their artistic heritage.

FURTHER READING
Gutmann, J.: *Jerusalem by Ephraim Moses Lilien* (New York: Ktav, 1976)

JOSEPH GUTMANN

Lilienblum, Moses Leib (1843–1910) Hebrew writer and political journalist, leader of the *Hibbat Zion* movement. Born in Kedainiai, Lithuania, Lilienblum received an Orthodox education but later studied secular subjects. He became attracted to the *Haskalah* and in 1863 published the article "Orhot hatalmud" (The ways of the Talmud) in which, while adhering to the spirit of Talmud, he urged major reforms in talmudic law. This so aroused the local Orthodox community that Lilienblum was compelled to move to Odessa in 1869, where he eked out a living as a bookkeeper. A year later he published his political satire, *Kehal refa'im* (The community of the dead), in which he advocated his belief that Jewish participation in agricultural labor, and in commerce and industry would solve the Jewish problem. His autobiography, *Hate'ot ne'urim* (1876; The sins of youth), is a major testament to Russian Jewry's cultural dilemma and to Lilienblum's own struggles with conflicting ideologies. The book, a frank description of his early life, education, marriage and maturation, also documented the growth of his socialism and his views on the failings of the *Haskalah*.

The pogroms of 1881 led Lilienblum to the conviction that there was no remedy for anti-Semitism in the Diaspora, and that settlement in the historic homeland was the only solution to the problem of east European Jewry: "We are aliens everywhere; we have to return home!'' In 1883, together with Leon (Judah Loeb) PINSKER, he founded the Zerubbabel Zionist Society; in 1884 he was elected secretary of the Odessa Committee, the governing body of *Hibbat Zion*. From 1889 he developed the ideology of *Hibbat Zion* in the pages of *Hamelitz* and *Hashahar*, firmly establishing himself as its ideological mentor.

Lilienblum's literary criticism was largely subordinated to his political writing. Like many *Haskalah* critics, he believed in the functionality of all art, emphasizing its usefulness to society. For example, his review of Avraham MAPU's *Ayit Tzavu'a* stressed Mapu's lack of utilitarianism.

FURTHER READING

Raisin, J. S.: *The Haskalah Movement in Russia* (Philadelphia: The Jewish Publication Society of America, 1913)

Slouschz, N.: *The Renascence of Hebrew Literature 1743–1885* (Philadelphia: The Jewish Publication Society of America, 1909)

GLENDA ABRAMSON

Lind, Jakov (b.1927) Austrian writer. Born in Vienna, he went to the Netherlands in 1938. Under the Nazi occupation he first worked as a gardener, and escaped deportation by the acquisition of false papers and finding employment inside Germany. Having spent the early post-war years in Palestine he studied theater arts in Vienna, after which he did a succession of jobs before finally settling in London.

He first attracted attention with the collection, *Seele aus Holz* (1962; Soul of wood), surreal tales whose fantastic elements transmuted the horror of the Holocaust. Pushing paradox to its extreme, Lind depicts a totally amoral world in which the monstrous has become everyday. By writing in a manner which suggested that the twentieth century was not insane but "reasonable", he began – in the words of one critic – to utter the first syllable of the unspeakable. The eponymous soul of wood was Lind's metaphor for the conscience of a peglegged male nurse to whose tender mercies a couple of Auschwitz-bound Jews entrusted their handicapped child.

Another story in the same collection had two Jews hidden in an Amsterdam attic debating religion, with a Christian convert defending his new faith by recourse to talmudic *pilpul*.

The concreted-over landscape from which Lind's 1963 novel, *Landschaft aus Beton*, derived its title, was the tidy antidote a Wehrmacht NCO had dreamt up to the mud in which so many of his regimental comrades had met their end. The same monomaniac notion to tame nature obsessed the protagonists of *Eine bessere Welt* (1966). 1970 saw the appearance of Lind's autobiography, *Counting my Steps;* this, the first book he had written in English, was shot through with rueful humor and quirky humanity.

BIBLIOGRAPHY

The Death of the Silver Foxes (1974); *The Trip to Jerusalem* (London: Johathan Cape, 1974)

RICHARD GRUNBERGER

Lipchitz, Jacques [Chaim Jacob] (1891–1973) French–American sculptor. Lipchitz was born in Druskieniki, Lithuania, into a wealthy banking family. His father, a building contractor, intended his son for a career in engineering; his mother and uncle, encouraged by the artistic talent he had displayed while still at school, supported his ambition of studying in Paris. Arriving there in 1909, he enrolled first at the École des Beaux-Arts and then at the Académie Julian and the Académie Colarossi. As important as his formal studies, however, was his "discovery" of ancient, medieval, and non-western art. In 1912–13 he met and became friends with Max JACOB, Amedeo MODIGLIANI, and Chaim SOUTINE, as well as Diego Rivera, who introduced him to members of the Cubist group.

Lipchitz's earliest mature works, rhythmic and energetic, date from 1913 to 1914. In 1915 to 1916 he subordinated his natural exuberance to the more severe, geometric esthetic of Cubism, and until the mid 1920s was one of the main exponents of Cubist sculpture. During this period he restricted himself to the limited repertory of subjects characteristic of Cubism:

Jacques Lipchitz The Prayer *1943. Philadelphia Museum of Art*

primarily harlequins and musicians, musical instruments, and still lifes. Around 1925, however, he reverted to more fluid, curvilinear forms and extended his subject matter to include biblical, mythological, and symbolic motifs. Political events of the late 1930s provoked an obsession with the theme of violent struggle against mythical monsters: Prometheus, Theseus, and the Rape of Europa became favorite subjects.

In 1941 Lipchitz emigrated to New York. Continuing in a richly baroque idiom, his elaborate late bronzes are more allusive in their imagery, many of them – particularly in the immediate post-war period – full of pathos and suggestive of religious ritual practices. In 1948 he accepted a commission to sculpt a Virgin for the church of Assy only on the condition that the following inscription be placed on the statue: "Jacob Lipchitz, Jew, faithful to the religion of his ancestors, has made this Virgin to foster understanding between men on earth, that the life of the spirit may prevail". A frequent visitor to Israel, Lipchitz was buried in Jerusalem.

BIBLIOGRAPHY

Lipchitz, J.: *My Life in Sculpture* (London: Thames & Hudson, 1972)

FURTHER READING

Hammacher, A. M.: *Jacques Lipchitz* (New York: Harry N. Abrams Inc., 1975)

MONICA BOHM-DUCHEN

Lipiner, Siegfried [Salomon] (1856–1911) Austrian writer. Born in Jaroslaw, near Lemberg in Galicia, Lipiner attended the *gymnasium* in Tarnow, and subsequently the *Sperlgymnasium* in Vienna. He studied philosophy at Vienna. His first work was the epic poem, *Der Entfesselte Prometheus* (1876; The unbound Prometheus). This was followed by other works, including the libretto to Karl GOLDMARK's opera, *Merlin* (1886). Lipiner also translated the works of Mickiewicz from the Polish. From the mid 1880s until his death, Lipiner worked on his Christ poem, of which only the prologue, *Adam* (1911) was ever completed. He was the librarian of the Austrian *Reichsrat* (parliament) from 1881.

Lipiner is the *éminence grise* of much of *fin de siècle* Viennese culture. While a student he became a prominent figure in the Wagnerian group around Victor ADLER and Engelbert Pernerstorfer. Among the colleagues he impressed was Sigmund FREUD. Nietzsche and Wagner were initially great admirers of Lipiner's work, and he exerted a great deal of influence on another Wagnerian, Gustav MAHLER.

Lipiner converted to Protestantism in 1891, and it is clear that he was preoccupied with the question of Christ long before that. Lipiner tried to avoid the question of his Jewish descent, but descriptions of him reveal a man whose deep religiosity seems to have stemmed from his Jewish childhood. Paul Natorp certainly saw it that way, and although Lipiner's actual background is unclear it is perhaps helpful to compare his attitudes to those of Joseph EHRLICH, another *Ostjude* who assimilated in Vienna. It is also ironic that the circle around Mahler and Lipiner was largely composed of people of Jewish descent, such as Fritz Löhr and Bruno Walter.

FURTHER READING

McGrath, W. J.: *Dionysian Art and Populist Politics* (New Haven: Yale University Press, 1974)

STEVEN BELLER

Lipton, Seymour (b.1905) American sculptor. Born in New York City, Lipton received his dental degree from Columbia University in 1927. Throughout his higher education, he had been interested both in art history and in sculpture. His first forays into sculpture were clay portrait heads. He gradually spent more time working in direct plaster and carving in wood, and by the mid 1930s gave up dentistry for sculpture. His early work, semi-abstract sculptures concerned with social and political issues, was exhibited throughout New York in the 1930s at the John Reed Club Gallery, the ACA Gallery, the World's Fair, and the American Artists Congress Show. Between 1940 and 1965 Lipton taught sculpture at the New School for Social Research in New York. In the mid 1940s Lipton began to experiment with direct metal, welded sculpture, and by 1949 he arrived at his signature technique of brazing (melting) metal rods onto sheet metal with an oxyacetylene torch. The resulting works are highly textured, angular, and expressive in form.

Shortly after arriving at his mature style, Lipton was commissioned by architect Percival Goodman in 1953 to design three objects of ceremonial art for Temple Israel in Tulsa, Oklahoma: a *ner tamid*, a monumental seven-branch *menorah*, and an abstracted, vine motif

that is placed along the top of the Torah Ark. Goodman again commissioned Lipton to design five ceremonial objects in 1955 for Temple Beth-El in Gary, Indiana.

A few works of the 1940s represent Lipton's response to the Holocaust: *Refugee* (1940), a mournful figure carved in limestone; *Moloch #1, #2,* and *#3* (1945–6), and *Exodus* (1947). In the late 1950s and 1960s, Lipton created several hieratic, non-objective sculptures that, from their titles and commanding presence, allude to ancient Jewish concepts. Included among these works are: *Sanctuary* (1950, Museum of Modern Art, New York); *Prophet* (1959); *High Priest* (1960); and *Scroll* (1960).

FURTHER READING

Elsen, A.: *Seymour Lipton* (New York: Harry N. Abrams Inc., 1974)

Kampf, A.: *Contemporary Synagogue Art* (Philadelphia: The Jewish Publication Society of America, 1966)

BARBARA GILBERT

Litvinoff, Emanuel (b.1915) British novelist and poet. Born in London, Litvinoff left school and worked in tailoring, cabinet-making, and the fur trade before the outbreak of the Second World War. During his army service he began writing poetry and published three volumes of war poems. Many of Litvinoff's poems were avowedly Jewish, which was unusual for a British war poet. His best known poem "To T. S. Eliot" is a dignified rejoinder to the anti-Semitism of T. S. Eliot's poetry of the 1920s, and was published in *Notes for a Survivor* (1973), Litvinoff's only volume of verse since 1948. Eliot was accidentally present at a public reading of this poem in 1951, which caused a literary scandal at the time.

Litvinoff's fiction, like his poetry, is informed by what he has called "the guilt and obsession of a survivor". His first novel *The Lost Europeans* (1960) is a major statement of this theme. Set in post-war Berlin, Litvinoff examines both German guilt and the spiritually "lost" generation of Jewish survivors. *The Man Next Door* (1968), his second novel, enacts the xenophobia of an English suburban man whose personality disintegrates. This was followed by Litvinoff's trilogy, *A Death out of Season* (1973), *Blood on the Snow* (1975), and *The Face of Terror* (1978), which achieved much critical acclaim. Moving from London's East End to the impact of the Russian Revolution and the horrors of Stalinism, Litvinoff examines a group of young revolutionaries whose ideals are gradually eroded. As in *The Lost Europeans* and his most recent novel, *Falls the Shadow* (1983), Litvinoff uses many of the conventions of the popular thriller and detective story to give his historical narrative an added piquancy.

Litvinoff has also published a collection of quasi-autobiographical short stories, *Journey Through a Small Planet* (1972), which evokes the pain and pleasure of growing up in London's Jewish East End. He is also the editor of the collection, *The Penguin Book of Jewish Short Stories* (1979), and has published extensively on the plight of Soviet Jewry through his journal, *Jews in Eastern Europe*, which he founded after a visit to Moscow.

BIBLIOGRAPHY
A Crown for Cain (London: Falcon Press, 1948)

BRYAN CHEYETTE

Loeb, Isidore (1839–1892) French rabbi and scholar. Born and educated in Alsace–Lorraine, Loeb became a well-known figure in Parisian Jewish circles. He was one of the founders of the *Société des Études Juives* (1880) and a frequent contributor to its review. As secretary of the ALLIANCE ISRAÉLITE UNIVERSELLE for 23 years (1869–92), he did much to enrich its library, augment the number of its schools abroad, and encourage its intervention on behalf of persecuted Jews in Eastern Europe.

NELLY WILSON

Lothar, Ernst (1890–1974) Austrian writer and stage director. Born in Brünn, Moravia (now Brno, Czechoslovakia), Lothar studied law at Vienna and took up a career as a civil servant. In his early years he was overshadowed by his brother, Hans Müller, but in the inter-

war years Lothar became a prominent theater critic and, in 1935, the director of the *Theater in der Josefstadt* and played a large role in Max REINHARDT's other Austrian concern, the Salzburg Festival. Although Lothar converted to Catholicism and attempted complete assimilation, his Jewish descent meant that he had to leave Austria in 1938. He found refuge in the USA before returning to Vienna as a cultural officer in the US army in 1945. He played a large role in the reconstruction of Austrian cultural life, taking up where he left off as a stage director.

In one respect, however, his views had changed. His book *Der Engel mit der Posaune* (1946; *The Angel with the Trumpet*, 1946) describes the history of an intermarriage between an established Catholic family and a Jewish one. The hero of the book, Hans Alt, as well as his Jewish mother, are used by Lothar to illustrate the problems, and successes of assimilation. The book ends with the Anschluss of 1938, the denial of what Lothar saw as the "Austrian idea" of tolerant pluralism. The final passage is written as an underground broadcast by Hans Alt but is in effect a eulogy of the Viennese Jewish assimilation, which stresses the huge contribution which the "Jewish bourgeoisie and intelligentsia" made to Viennese culture. Hofmannsthal is a notable inclusion in the list.

BIBLIOGRAPHY
Das Wunder des Überlebens (Vienna: 1966)

STEVEN BELLER

Louvish, Simon (b.1947) British writer. Born in Glasgow, Louvish was moved to Israel in 1949 where he was educated until the age of 18. His Israeli army service from 1965 to 1967 included the Six Day War, during which he was a military cameraman. In 1968 he attended the London School of Film Technique where he began a series of political documentaries. His films included *End of the Dialogue* about apartheid in South Africa, *Greece of the Christian Greeks* on the Colonels' regime in Greece, and *To Live in Freedom*, a documentary about the Israeli occupied West Bank and Gaza Strip.

Louvish has also published *A Moment of Silence* (1979), an autobiographical account of his life in Israel.

It was not, however, until the publication of his first novel, *The Therapy of Avram Blok* (1985), that Louvish found a wide readership in England, and achieved critical acclaim. This novel reflects Louvish's political radicalism but also an interest in literary fantasy – especially science fiction and South American literature. It is a deliberately iconoclastic and grotesque account of the myths and taboos which the post-1967 Jewish State has generated. In this novel a lunatic asylum in Jerusalem has become a metaphor for a world where the line between fantasy and political reality has become increasingly blurred. Louvish's strength is that he is able to utilize Israeli street humor in an imaginative context, which results in a cross-cultural literary voice unique in the English language.

Louvish's second novel *The Death of Moishe Ganef* (1986), avoids the nihilistic construction of his first novel and instead uses the form of a comic thriller. Set in Israel after the 1982 invasion of the Lebanon, this less ambitious novel enacts the bizarre fantasies of the Israeli secret service which Louvish depicts with savage humor. His fiction has generated a good deal of interest in Israel and *The Therapy of Avram Blok* is currently being translated into Hebrew.

FURTHER READING

Simon Louvish: an interview. *The Jewish Quarterly* 34 no. 4 (1987)

Madness now and to come. *Times Literary Supplement* no. 4463 (14–20 Oct. 1988)

BRYAN CHEYETTE

Lozowick, Louis (1892–1973) American painter, graphic artist, and art critic. He was born in Ludovinka, a small village in the Kiev district of Russia. From 1903 to 1905 he studied art in Kiev. One of his most influential teachers was Ilya Repin (1844–1930) a leader of the Russian nationalist art group "The Wanderers" that was committed to portraying the Russian people in real-life situations. This influence surfaced later with Lozowick's concern for the laborer and the common man.

In 1906 he arrived alone in the United States and resumed art studies from 1912 to 1915 at the National Academy of Design. Between 1915 and 1918 he studied at Ohio State University in Columbus, Ohio, earning a Bachelor of Arts degree. In 1919 he took a trip through the United States which served as a basis for his paintings glorifying cities and modern industrialization. Between 1920 and 1924 he took an extended trip to Europe, traveling to Paris where he met the Cubist painters Juan Gris and Fernand Léger who also glorified the machine. In 1920 he became acquainted with El Lissitsky and the other expatriate Russian Constructivists in Berlin who dealt with the Machine-style esthetic. It was in Berlin that he learned the technique of lithography and also began to write about art and literature for the international magazine *Broom*.

Upon returning to New York in 1924, he began to participate in exhibitions of the Jewish Art Center, a secularist–Jewish institution that founded a gallery in 1920 on the Lower East Side to support Jewish artists. Although a supporter of Jewish artists, Lozowick did not feel that they should be tied to particular themes or styles, but that they should attempt daring formalist breakthroughs. According to Lozowick "there can be Jewish artists but no Jewish art, unless there be a social need for it" (Louis Lozowick, "Jewish Artists of the Season," *Menorah Journal*, July 1924). His major contribution to Jewish art was a series of articles for the *Menorah Journal* on the works of Jewish artists working in both the United States and in Europe. His book, *One Hundred American–Jewish Painters and Sculptors* (1947), represents the only comprehensive study of modern American-Jewish art. He also wrote for several periodicals with left-wing sympathies, including the *New Masses*, *The Nation*, *The Union Builder*, and art journals including *The American Magazine of Art*.

During the Depression Lozowick focused on the image of the laborer. He worked for the WPA Graphics Division and for the Treasury Relief Art Project for which he painted two large oils, *Lower Manhattan* and *Triborough Bridge*, for a post office on 33rd Street in New York.

His themes were more traditional during the 1950s and 1960s and included landscapes, figure studies and vignettes from trips. His visits to Israel (1954, 1964, 1968) were the source for several lithographs including, *Gate to Knesseth, Jerusalem* and the *Wailing Wall*. Some of these works were commissions for Jewish organizations in New Jersey: *Safed #2* (1957 and 1964), *Safed #1* (1962), and *Lone Worshipper* (1966).

FURTHER READING

Flint, J.: *The Prints of Louis Lozowick: A Catalogue Raisonné* (New York: Hudson Hills Press, 1982)

Kampf, A.: *Jewish Experience in the Art of the Twentieth Century* (South Hadley: Bergin & Garvey Publishers Inc., 1984)

BARBARA GILBERT

Lublinski, Samuel (1868–1910)

German author, literary historian, dramatist, and critic. Born in Johannisburg in East Prussia, Lublinski worked in the book trade until he gravitated in the 1890s to Berlin and associated with a circle of writers, intellectuals, and artists led by Ludwig Jacobowski and Rudolf Steiner and including Peter Hille, Elsa LASKER-SCHÜLER, and Stefan ZWEIG. By the end of the decade, he had embarked upon an ambitious career as a writer, penning numerous works in several genres.

His first book-length publication was a literary study of Jewish characters in the work of three major nineteenth-century writers: *Jüdische Charaktere bei Grillparzer, Hebbel, und Otto Ludwig* (Jewish characters in [the work of] Grillparzer, Hebbel, and Otto Ludwig). He characterized this work as "a small contribution to German literary history from the point of view of a Jewish temperament". According to Lublinski, Hebbel's *Judith*, a biblical drama, evidences deep insight into the Jewish "Volksseele" (soul of the nation). His approach in this study, as well as in his *Literatur und Gesellschaft im 19. Jahrhundert* (1900; Literature and society in the nineteenth century), was literary–sociological. At the same time, he wrote a number of tragedies, novellas, and major studies, both literary–critical, and cultural–historical in nature. For example, in two far-ranging works, *Die Bilanz der Moderne* (1904; The balance sheet of the modern), and *Der Ausgang der Moderne* (1908; The exit of the modern), he investigated the decline of Naturalism and neo-Romanticism, while attempting to locate the modern element, and pointing out future trends in cultural production. He also wrote a massive two-volume study of the mythology of early Christianity, claiming that there was no historical Jesus.

Lublinksi was an early adherent of the modern Zionist movement, and he contributed essays and criticism to Zionist publications. He appreciated Zionism as a movement which stimulated artistic and cultural energies among a broad spectrum of acculturated and assimilating Jews. Still, he had little hope for the success of political Zionism and he took leave of the movement publicly in a letter published in *Die Welt* in 1899. He subsequently tended to favor assimilation as a more reasonable solution to the Jewish problem in Europe.

MARK H. GELBER

Lukács, György [Georg] (1885–1971)

Hungarian philosopher and literary critic. Born into a rich Jewish family, he was educated in the Lutheran Grammar School of Budapest, and at the universities of Budapest and Berlin where he studied law and philosophy. His first books of literary essays such as *A lélek és a formák* (1910; *Soul and Form*, 1974), as well as *A modern dráma fejlödésének története*, (1911; The history of the evolution of the modern drama), were still influenced by Wilhelm Dilthey's anti-positivism. Between 1912 and 1918 he lived in Heidelberg where he became associated with Max WEBER and was influenced by the philosophy of Emil Lask. During the First World War Lukács's political thinking became radicalized to the point of joining the newly founded Hungarian Communist Party in 1918 and serving as Commissar for Education during the Hungarian Soviet Republic. In 1919 Lukács fled to Vienna where he lived for 10 years. During this period he published important works both in literary and political theory: *Die Theorie des Romans* (1920; *The Theory of the Novel*, 1971), and *Geschichte und Klassenbewusstsein*

(1923; *History and Class Consciousness*, 1971). The latter work, subsequently repudiated by Lukács, gave a dialectical but also strongly "elitist" interpretation of the role of the Communist Party in the labor movement.

After 1919 Lukács wrote mainly in German. He lived in exile until 1945, in Moscow and in Berlin. In the USSR Lukács worked for Russian, German, and Hungarian cultural reviews but published comparatively little. After the war he returned to Hungary, where he lectured at the University. He was awarded the Kossuth Prize in 1955. His essays on realism were collected in *A realizmus problémái* (1948; *Studies in European Realism*, 1950), but he also published works on the Enlightenment *Goethe und sein Zeit* (1947; *Goethe and His Time*, 1967) and on the development of the novel in the nineteenth century *A történelmi regény* (1947; *The Historical Novel*, 1962). In these works Lukács held up the "critical realist" model and rejected modernism which in his view reflected the "decadence" of Western society.

As for philosophy, Lukács attributed great importance to his book *Der junge Hegel* (1948; *The Young Hegel*, 1975), in which he established links between Hegel's dialectics and the economic conditions of early nineteenth-century German society. *Az ész trónfosztása* (1954; *The Destruction of Reason*, 1980), was a polemical attempt to prove how the "irrational" trend in German philosophy paved the way for National Socialism. After his involvement in anti-Stalinist activities in 1956 (when, during the Hungarian uprising, he was a member of Imre Nagy's government), and short internment in Romania, Lukács withdrew from politics, turning his attention to a esthetics and philosophical theory. The result of this was the two-volume work *Az esztétikum sajátossága* (1965; *Esthetics*) and his unfinished attempt to create a Marxist ontology, *A társadalmi lét ontológiájáról* (1970; *Ontology of Social Being*, I, 1978). In the 1960s Lukács rejoined the Hungarian Communist Party, but this did not prevent him from writing a long essay on Solzhenitsyn (1970; *Solzhenitsyn*, 1970) whom he regarded as a genuine Socialist realist.

Although he was a professed atheist, Lukács's philosophy and career show signs of a quasi-religious commitment. Prior to 1914 he sensed a crisis in European culture, man being in the state of "transcendental alienation", but could not offer a solution. In Heidelberg Lukács's interest grew in early Christianity, as well as in Jewish mysticism. His "conversion" to Marxism–Leninism in 1918 further accentuated the messianic element in his thinking: in *Geschichte und Klassenbewusstsein* the proletariat appears as the "chosen people" whose struggle will redeem mankind. While later Lukács repeatedly paid tribute to Stalinist dogma, on balance he can be regarded as the upholder of Hegelian dialectics, always ready to make tactical adjustments in support of "the march of the World Spirit".

BIBLIOGRAPHY

Studies in European Realism (London: Hillway Publishing Co., 1950); *Goethe and His Age* (London: Merlin Press, 1968); *The Theory of the Novel* (London: Merlin Press, 1971); *Soul and Form* (London: Merlin Press, 1974); *Ontology of Social Being* (Atlantic Highlands: Humanities Press, 1983)

FURTHER READING

Lichtheim, G.: *Lukács* (London: Fontana/Collins, 1970)

Heller, A., ed.: *Lukács Revalued* (Oxford: Basil Blackwell, 1983)

Kiralyfalvi, B.: *The Aesthetics of György Lukács* (Princeton: Princeton University Press, 1975)

Parkinson, G. H. R. et al.: *Georg Lukács, the Man, his Work, and his Ideas* (Reading, Reading University Press, London: Weidenfeld & Nicholson and New York: Random House, 1970)

GEORGE GÖMÖRI

Lunel, Armand (1892–1977) French novelist and librettist. Lunel was born at Aix-en-Provence into a family of Provençal Jews whose roots in the south of France dated back over at least five centuries. Lunel was well acquainted with the many Jewish legends which had evolved in Provence as well as the way in which those stories were framed by the folktales of the non-Jewish Provençal community. Many of his works are centered on the town of Carpentras and its unique Jewish quarter, the *carrière*.

Educated in the region, Lunel eventually took

a degree in law and spent some time as a teacher of philosophy in Monaco. Writing, however, was his passion. His stories are sensitive and colorful portrayals of Provence and its Jewish and non-Jewish inhabitants. His literary talent permitted him to transcribe many of the dialects he heard, especially the unique patois of the Jewish population. In 1924, his novel *L'Imagerie du Cordier* met with great critical acclaim. Some of the critics compared him to Marcel Pagnol, the French writer whose stories of "old Provence" preserved a way of life soon to disappear.

Lunel's second success was his novel *Nicolo-Peccavi, ou I'Affaire Dreyfus à Carpentras* (1926), which combined historical fact, authorial imagination and regional legends. In 1937 he published a series of short stories entitled, *Jérusalem à Carpentras*. In this slim volume of tales, Lunel evokes a mystical Carpentras which seems to contain within it an image of Jerusalem. Sadly, none of Lunel's later works of fiction ever measured up to his earliest novels and stories. Later in his life, Lunel began writing libretti for musical compositions penned by his childhood friend Darius MILHAUD. His first attempt was with *Esther de Carpentras* (1926) which was later to become an *opéra-bouffe*, *Barba Garibo* (1950). This particular piece was based on an ancient Provençal Purim play which had evolved from the Jewish humor and folktakes of medieval Carpentras.

SIMON SIBELMAN

Lustig, Arnošt (b.1926) Czech author. Born in Prague, he spent a large part of the Second World War in concentration camps such as Auschwitz, where his father died in the gas chambers, and Buchenwald, and then returned to Prague and studied journalism at the College of Political and Social Sciences. He worked as a journalist until 1968, covering the Arab–Israeli War in 1948–9 and editing several teenage periodicals, as well as writing screenplays for film and television. After the end of the Prague Spring in 1968 he emigrated briefly to Israel, moving on to the USA in 1970. He has held several university lectureships, and has been Professor of literature and creative writing at the American University in Washington since 1973. He has also lectured on film studies and participated in film festivals; many of his stories have been filmed and he has written several documentaries.

His writings draw largely on his childhood experiences in the camps, as in the collections of short stories *Noc e naděje*, (1959; *Night and Hope*, 1962) and *Démanty noci* (1958; *Diamonds of the Night*, 1962), and his best known work, the novel *Modlitba pro Kateřinu Horovitzovou* (1964; *A Prayer for Katerina Horovitzova*, 1973), which was made into a film. His television documentaries include *Theresienstadt* (1965) and, more recently, *The Most Precious Legacy* (1984).

Other works include the novels *Darkness Casts No Shadow* (1976) and *Z deníku sedmnáctileté Perly Sch.* (1978; From the diary of seventeen-year-old Perly Sch.), the essay "The Holocaust and film arts" (1980), and the text for *The Beadle of Prague*, a cantata with music by Herman BERLINSKI (1983). His collected works have appeared as a series entitled *Children of the Holocaust* (from 1977). He has received many awards including the National Jewish Book Award in 1980.

BIBLIOGRAPHY
Diamonds of the Night (New York: Artia, 1962;) *Night and Hope* (New York: Dutton, 1962); *A Prayer for Katerina Horovitzova* (New York: Harper, 1973); *Darkness Casts No Shadow* (Washington: Inscape, 1976)

FURTHER READING
Contemporary Authors (Detroit: Gale Research Co., 1981)
Washington Times (2 June 1986)
Washington City (4 July 1988)
Washington Post (9 August 1988)

CATHERINE PHILLIPS

Luzzatti, Luigi (1841–1927) Italian politician and economist. He was born in Venice and graduated in law at the University of Padua in 1863. He was anxious to improve the lot of the underprivileged classes and decided to dedicate himself to the study of the economic sciences. He lived in Milan briefly, working as a schoolteacher, but returned to the Veneto in 1867 in order to take up the Chair of Constitutional Law at the University of Padua. He was elected to the Italian Parliament in 1871, thus beginning a brilliant political career in which he held the posts of economic adviser to Prime Minister Minghetti, Minister of Finance in 1891, Chancellor of the Exchequer, and Minister of Agriculture. He became Prime Minister in 1910, holding office for one year.

As an economist he maintained that the State should be actively involved in solving society's ills, and to this end he promoted the setting up of credit institutions and formulated legislation to protect women and children at work. During and after the First World War Luzzatti advocated a monetary peace and the creation of an organization which would aid economic standardization on an international scale. Although Luzzatti was not a practicing Jew, he attempted, through diplomatic channels, to aid the oppressed Jews of Eastern Europe.

He was a gifted orator and, as well as economical treatises, he also wrote important works on philosophy and the history of religion. His memoirs, published in Bologna in 1931 under the title *Memorie autobiografiche e carteggi*, give an indication of the personality of this statesman.

GABRIELLA MOSCATI-STEINDLER

Luzzatto, Moshe Hayyim [Ramhal] (1707–1746)

Italian kabbalist, writer, and playwright. He was born in Padua into a well-to-do and illustrious family of scholars and rabbis. He received a secular education, acquiring a profound knowledge of Latin and Italian. He was taught Hebrew by the famous teachers Isaac Hayyim Canterini and Rabbi Isaiah Bassan, who introduced him to the *kabbalah*. While still a young man, Luzzatto decided to dedicate himself to a study of both the theoretical and practical aspects of this discipline and with this object in mind, he and a group of devotees met daily at his home. His works of this period, however, show a more purely literary interest: he was not yet 20 when he wrote his rhetorical treatise, *Leshon limmudim* (The language of scholars), in which the breadth of his classical cul-

ture is amply demonstrated, while his biblical drama, *Ma'aseh Shimshon* (The story of Samson), exemplifies the concepts expounded in this treatise.

In 1725 Luzzatto composed his first dramatic masterpiece: *Migdal 'oz* (Tower of strength) was written as a wedding present for his friend, the son of Isaiah Bassan. This work was not published until a century later, by F. Delizsch in Leipzig, with a preface and notes by S. D. Luzzatto and Meir Halevi Letteris. The drama has a Jewish theme with allegorical and mystical overtones: the story of a love of a spiritual kind is related in four acts, and contrasts sharply with Italian dramatic works of the same period, despite the influence of the pastoral drama of Giovanni Battista Guarini (1537–1612). The Hebrew style of Luzzatto's work is a clear indication of the author's linguistic competence.

Luzzatto's fascination with the *kabbalah* led him to undertake, together with an increasingly numerous group of disciples, an enthusiastic study of its hidden meanings. He experienced visions in which a *maggid* appeared and dictated mystic writings to him, including the *Zohar tinyana* (The second Zohar). News of these activities reached the ears of the Venetian rabbis who, encouraged by their German colleagues, aware of Luzzatto's youth and conscious of the spiritual crisis precipitated by the Shabbetai Zevi movement, strongly opposed him. The rabbinate appealed to Isaiah Bassan to divert his young student from studies of this nature, with their overtones of messianic expectations. Luzzatto was forced to hand over his writings to his teacher who acted as his guarantor. He was forbidden to involve himself in matters of a mystical nature until his 40th year. In 1731 Luzzatto married Tzipporah, the daughter of the rabbi of Mantua, but his continued dispute with the Venetian rabbis and his family's precarious financial situation persuaded him to move to Amsterdam in 1735. On the way there he stopped in Frankfurt-am-Main where the chief rabbi took out an injunction against him, forcing him to deposit all the mystical manuscripts in his possession, many of which were then burnt.

In Amsterdam Luzzatto was given a warm welcome by the Sephardi community. There followed a period of tranquil family life, during which Luzzatto continued his studies and earned his living grinding optical lenses. From this atmosphere were born two important works which brought fame and prestige to their author: his allegorical drama in three acts, *Leyesharim tehillah* (1743; In praise of the righteous) which reflects his personal experience and his own fight for the acceptance of his ideas. Fifty editions of the work were published in his lifetime. The composition, written in verse, attests to Luzzatto's mastery of the Hebrew language and was an important influence on future generations of writers. Luzzatto is considered by some critics to be the father of modern Hebrew literature.

The second work, his moral treatise, *Mesillat yesharim* (1743; *The Path of the Righteous*, 1936), was published during the author's lifetime and was praised both for its style and for the ethical content of its admonitions. Eager to continue his mystical studies, Luzzatto traveled with his family to the Holy Land. A few years later, in 1746, he caught the plague and died in Acre. He was buried in Tiberias.

GABRIELLA MOSCATI-STEINDLER

Luzzatto, Samuel David [Shadal] (1800–1865) Italian religious thinker, historian of Hebrew literature, and poet. Shadal was born in Trieste and received an intensive traditional Jewish education from the time he was three. He continued to teach himself after illness forced an end of formal study at the age of 13. He already deduced that Hebrew vowels and biblical cantillation were post-Talmudic, meaning that Simeon bar Yohai could not have written the Zohar. In 1818 he began *Torah nidreshet*, on the truth of divine law from the perspective of philosophical inquiry. His poem *Helek kehelek yokheilu* appeared at this time, describing how every individual's life contains equal portions of joy and sorrow. In 1819 Shadal prepared a study of synonyms (in *Bikkurei ha'ittim*) and in 1821 he translated the prayerbook into Italian. In 1825 he wrote *Vikuah 'al hokhmat hakabbalah* (ultimately published in 1852), attacking the social dangers of

esoteric mysticism. His *Tzelem Elohim* (1828), explains that like God, man has comprehensive powers. Man also possesses freedom to act according to his will and a rational ability. But more important is man's ability to feel the pain and pleasure of others as well as his own. It is to these emotions that Torah's supernaturally-rooted divine imperatives are directed.

In 1829 Shadal was appointed to the new Rabbinical College in Padua, and remained there until his death. In 1840 he published the poems which Judah Halevi wrote during his journey to Palestine (*Betulat bat Yehudah*) and *Yesodei hatorah* (*The Foundations of the Torah*, 1965) on the distinction between "Abrahamitic" and "Mosaic" revelations. In 1848 he published *Judaism Expounded* (Italian) about the universalistic dimension to Judaism. In 1856 his Italian translation of *Isaiah* and introduction to the Italian *makhzor* appeared, and in 1860 his Italian translation of the *Pentateuch* and *Haftarot*. In 1832 he began writing *Lectures on Israelite Moral Theology* (Italian) for students entering the College, which he completed in 1872. His last work was the publication of Judah Halevi's *Diwan*. Shadal was known as a beloved pedagogue, a writer of voluminous letters and someone anxious to share all he knew with fellow scientific students of Judaism.

Shadal speaks of Abrahamitic revelation which is in harmony with autonomous moral consciousness, and Mosaic revelation which provides forms for it in order to satisfy the new state constitution. The revealed laws, with their reward and punishment, relate to the human emotions of compassion for others, and of self-love. Shadal attacks Maimonides for allegedly stressing idea at the expense of deed, whereby he makes immortality of the soul without the body a matter of intellectual achievement (in *Kerem hemed*, 1838). He attacks Spinoza for identifying man exclusively in intellectual terms and discounting feeling in general and compassion in particular (in *Mehkerei hayahadut*, 1847–65). Generally Shadal considers philosophy a useless exercise which fosters moral depravity and suicidal depression. He delineates two forces of civilization. "Atticism" promotes philosophy, reason, and love of beauty. Judaism promotes religion and morality of the heart and soul, and love for the good. Ultimately Judaism will attract mankind because of the unquenchable thirst for goodness, and philosophy will disappear.

FURTHER READING

Harris, M.: The theological-historical thinking of Samuel David Luzzatto. *Jewish Quarterly Review* (1962)

Margolies, M.: *Samuel David Luzzatto*. In *Traditionalist Scholar*, (New York: Ktav, 1979)

Motzkin, A. L.: Spinoza and Luzzatto: philosophy and religion. *Journal of the History of Philosophy* (1979)

GERSHON GREENBERG

M

Mahler, Gustav (1860–1911) Austrian composer and conductor. Mahler was born in Kalischt, Bohemia. His compositions belong to the final phase of the Romantic era and are often described as post-Romantic because of their harmonic and orchestral influence on twentieth-century composers such as Arnold SCHOENBERG, Alban Berg, and Anton Webern. His music combines mastery of large forms, sensitive orchestration, and forward-looking harmony, with a broad variety of melodic types, ranging from folk elements and even street music to highly sophisticated styles deriving from opera and the art song. At times, folk elements (especially those in symphonic movements in the minor mode) have been mistakenly singled out as specifically Jewish. To the extent that we may identify a Jewish vein in Mahler's music, it would seem to lie in the direction of his symbolic use of popular melody as a means of ironic and even bitter commentary on western culture.

From 1875 to 1878 Mahler studied composition at the Conservatory of the Gesellschaft der Musikfreunde in Vienna, where he also gained his first conducting experience. Mahler subsequently enrolled in the University of Vienna, coming into contact with the composer Anton Bruckner. Although Mahler began composing in childhood, his first significant work, the cantata *Das Klagende Lied*, dates from 1880, the same year in which he took his first position as a conductor. Composition and conducting remained central to Mahler's career as a creative artist throughout his lifetime. Between 1880 and

1887 he primarily composed orchestral songs. He completed his First Symphony in the fall of 1888 and immediately started work on the opening movement of his Second Symphony. From the beginning his songs and symphonies were intimately connected; thus, songs from the autobiographical cycle, *Lieder Eines Fahrenden Gesellen* (1885), provided musical content for movements I and III of his First Symphony. Mahler's life assumed a characteristic pattern during these years: he composed during the summer and worked as a conductor during the winter. Between 1880 and 1887 Mahler held a series of minor conducting positions in Austria, Germany, and eastern Europe. From 1888, however, with his appointment as Director of the Royal Hungarian Opera in Budapest, Mahler's fresh interpretations of operas from Mozart to Wagner attracted increasing attention. He was offered first conductorship of the Stadttheater in Hamburg in 1891 and in 1897 conductorship of the Imperial and Royal Court Opera in Vienna. It was in order to be accepted to this latter post that Mahler converted to Catholicism in the early months of 1897.

Despite his conversion, Mahler's Jewishness continued to figure prominently in his career. His relations with the Vienna Philharmonic Orchestra, which he conducted from 1898 to 1901, were complicated by anti-Semitic feelings among some of the players. Similar prejudices often colored reviews of Mahler's performances and, more importantly, evaluations of his music. His famous remark that he felt three times homeless – as a Bohemian among Aus-

Gustav Mahler

purely instrumental works. Mahler's monumental Eighth Symphony, 1906, however, once again includes vocal movements within the framework of the symphony.

In 1902 Mahler married Alma Schindler (1879–1964), who bore him a daughter in 1902 and another in 1904. The sudden death of their elder daughter in 1907, diagnosis of Mahler's heart disease, and his resignation as conductor of the Vienna Opera induced a state of severe personal crisis. In the winter of 1907, he sailed for America to conduct the Metropolitan Opera in New York and later the New York Philharmonic Orchestra. Mahler spent the next three conducting seasons in New York, returning to Europe in the summers to compose. His late works are the important song-symphony, *Das Lied von der Erde* (1909); his Ninth Symphony (also 1909); and his uncompleted Tenth Symphony (begun in 1910). Mahler's personal life remained extremely troubled throughout much of this period, and in 1910 he visited Sigmund FREUD for marital counseling. Mahler became ill in the early spring of 1911 and died in Vienna on 18 May.

BIBLIOGRAPHY

Selected Letters of Gustav Mahler, trans. E. Kaiser, B. Hopkins, and E. Wilkins; ed. K. Martner (London: Faber, 1979)

FURTHER READING

Bauer-Lechner, N.: *Recollections of Gustav Mahler*, trans. D. Newlin; ed. P. Franklin (London: Faber Music, 1980)

Blaukopf, K.: *Mahler. A Documentary Study*, trans. P. Baker, S. Flatauer, P. R. J. Ford, D. Loman, and G. Watkins (London: Thames & Hudson, 1976)

Mitchell, D.: *Gustav Mahler. The Early Years* (London: Rockliff, 1958)

——: *Gustav Mahler. The Wunderhorn Years* (London: Faber, 1975)

Newlin, D.: *Bruckner – Mahler – Schoenberg* (rev. edn New York: Norton, 1978)

BETH SHAMGAR

trians, an Austrian among Germans, and a Jew among the rest of the world – gives some indication of the composer's alienation.

Prior to his appointment to the Vienna Opera, Mahler had already completed both his Second (1894), and Third (1896) Symphonies. Two years later he concluded work on the last song in the cycle, *Des Knaben Wunderhorn* (1898), and he finished his Fourth Symphony in 1900. These four compositions form a stylistic unit: each of the symphonies has melodic links to the Wunderhorn songs, and each contains at least one vocal movement. Mahler's next three symphonies, (the Fifth, 1902; the Sixth, 1904; and the Seventh, 1905) inaugurated a new style period. Although they incorporate melodic references to Mahler's orchestral songs to texts by Friedrich Rückert (the cycle, *Kindertotenlieder*, was completed in 1904), these symphonies are

Mailer, Norman (b. 1923) American novelist, essayist, and journalist. Although raised in the ethnic enclave of Brooklyn's Crown Heights, the Harvard-educated Mailer has termed himself a "non-Jewish Jew". Unlike his contemporaries Bellow, Malamud, and Roth, he is seldom thought of as a Jewish–American writer, for specifically Jewish characters appear only in his best-selling first novel, *The Naked and the Dead* (1948). More than thirty subsequent works have earned similar commercial success, but only the non-fiction *Armies of the Night* (1968), and *The Executioner's Song* (1979) have enjoyed comparable critical acclaim.

Like Hemingway, Mailer is a self-dramatist, who embodies the romantic conception of the larger-than-life writer. With his six marriages, acrimonious squabbles, televised pronouncements, leftist activism, violent episodes, and other escapades, he spent the 1950s and 1960s as an *enfant terrible*, at once admired and deplored. Often assailed by feminists, he has now assumed the mantle of tough-guy patriarch, a role that found its most damaging expression in his ill-fated championing of Jack Henry Abbott, a convict–writer released from jail after securing Mailer's mentorship, but soon re-imprisoned for murder. Such events, coupled with Mailer's excursions into New Journalism, have tarnished his reputation, fueling his detractors' claims that he has won notoriety at the expense of artistic credibility. Mailer's position was further weakened when *Ancient Evenings* (1986), his long-awaited "big book", received mixed reviews. Nevertheless, many critics still revere him, citing his versatility, his stylistic virtuosity, and the significance of his recurring themes (for example, the alienated individual in existential conflict with external forces), explored in such noteworthy books as *Advertisements for Myself* (1959), *An American Dream* (1965), and *Why Are We in Vietnam?* (1967). Perhaps the most controversial figure in current American letters, Mailer is unquestionably a major literary personality.

FURTHER READING

Lennon, J. M., ed.: *Critical Essays on Norman Mailer* (Boston: G. K. Hall, 1986)

Manso, P.: *Mailer: His Life and Times* (New York: Simon & Schuster, 1985)

GEORGE J. SEARLES

Maimon, Salomon (1754–1808) Jewish philosopher. Born in Sukoviboeg near Mir in Poland, Maimon felt oppressed by his intensive *heder* education, and left at 14 for Berlin in a quest for free pursuit of knowledge. Initially turned away by the Jewish community because he carried Maimonides' treatise on logic (*Bi'ur millot hahigayon*), he eventually was accepted through Moses MENDELSSOHN's circle. In 1778 he wrote *Heshek Yehoshua* to reconcile scientific study with the principles of Torah. In 1789 he started to develop a rabbinic philosophy with a Kantian elaboration of Maimonides' commentary on *Mishnah avot* III/21 (*Sayings of the Jewish Fathers*, 1877). He translated Mendelssohn's *Morgenstunden* into Hebrew, of which chapters 13 and 14 are preserved in *Givat ha-moreh*, 1791. The latter work introduces and comments upon Maimonides' *Moreh nevukhim* (*Guide to the Perplexed*, 1881–5), and thereby brings Maimonides' philosophy into the modern epoch. Maimon wrote his autobiography, *Salomon Maimon's Lebensgeschichte* (1792–3; *Salomon Maimon: an Autobiography*, 1888). He also wrote several philosophical works of Kantian character (Salomon Maimon, *Gesammelte Werke*, six volumes, 1965–76).

Maimon defines religion in general as the expression of gratitude and reverence to the source of human benefit. The religious personality recognizes the impossibility of identifying this ultimate cause. Since God is infinite essence, the ideal of infinite perfection, it cannot be said whether God is or is not, real or not real. How may the religious thinker then approach this God? Maimon speaks of an upper level beyond temporal sequence and a lower level of multiplicity and temporality, which are synthesized by the idea of the power of infinite understanding or of the infinite ability to know. The final link in knowing God is the act of reflection upon the infinite ability of consciousness (*Lebensgeschichte; Philosophisches Woerterbuch*, 1791; *Kritische Untersuchungen ueber den menschlichen Geist*, 1797).

According to Maimon, Judaism begins with the Sinai covenant between man and the metaphysical idea of unidentified ultimate cause. At first silent, the covenant is soon expressed by the symbol of the supreme being's name, by the covenant, by the system of Mosaic law, and then by the Temple. Originally intended to capture the silent moment and make it available in history, the symbols eventually turn opaque and block the original experience from expression. The obstacles become solidified as a result of the quest for power over access to them by rabbis and mystics. Their control must be removed, so that the original encounter with the metaphysical idea may be liberated and reconnected to history through transparent, rational symbols. Maimonides' *Guide* is the perfect vehicle.

FURTHER READING

Atlas, S.: *From Critical to Speculative Idealism: The Philosophy of Salomon Maimon* (The Hague: 1961)

Jacobs, N. I.: Salomon Maimon's relation to Judaism. *Yearbook of the Leo Baeck Institute*, 8

GERSHON GREENBERG

Malamud, Bernard (1914–1986) American novelist. Born in Brooklyn, New York, Malamud was educated at Erasmus High School in Brooklyn and the City College of New York. He taught in New York City's evening high schools while completing the requirements for an MA degree at Columbia University in 1942. He subsequently taught English at Oregon State University (Corvalis, Oregon) from 1949 to 1961. While at Oregon State, Malamud published four books: *The Natural* (1952), *The Assistant* (1957), *The Magic Barrel* (1958), and *A New Life* (1961), the last set in Cascadia College, a Pacific Northwest school not unlike Oregon State. Malamud joined the faculty at Bennington College, Vermont, in 1961 and he continued to be associated with that school throughout his life. He received numerous awards for his writing, including the Pulitzer Prize for *The Fixer* (1966), a National Book Award and a Pulitzer Prize for *The Magic Barrel*, and the 1981 Brandeis Creative Arts Award.

Malamud once described himself as a chronicler of "simple people struggling to make their lives better in a world of bad luck". His father, a Russian–Jewish immigrant, ran a small grocery not unlike the one depicted in *The Assistant*. Other characters exist in a timeless, placeless world that resembles a Depression of the spirit. Through it all, however, Malamud's fables, with their alternating currents of realism and fantasy, keep pointing towards the moral wisdom gained through suffering.

Malamud's early works occupy an important place in what has come to be called the "American–Jewish renaissance", and he often found himself linked with Philip ROTH and Saul BELLOW. But the label of "Jewish writer" never fitted him comfortably. He may, or may not, have actually claimed that "all men are Jews", but he did insist that he had "interests beyond all that" and that he felt that he was "writing for all men". For Malamud, what mattered was the story: "The story will be with us as long as man is".

Other collections include *Rembrandt's Hat* (1973), and *The Stories of Bernard Malamud* (1983). Other novels include *Dubin's Lives* (1979), and *God's Grace* (1982).

FURTHER READING

Astro, R., and Benson, J., eds: *The Fiction of Bernard Malamud* (Corvalis: Oregon State University Press, 1977)

Hershinow, S. J.: *Bernard Malamud* (New York: Ungar, 1980)

Richman, S.: *Bernard Malamud* (Boston: Twayne, 1966)

SANFORD PINSKER

Mamet, David (b.1947) American playwright. Mamet was born and raised in a middle-class Jewish home in Chicago, and carries the sensibility of an urban ethnic, at once comfortable with the disadvantaged and minorities, attracted to but circumspect of the wealthy and "cultured". His college education in the rural east (distinctly not Ivy League), provided freedom and opportunity to explore the world of his artistic imagination which had been frequently and continually stimulated by working in theaters (including study at New York's Neighborhood Playhouse). His first success came in the mid 1970s with the New York production of two one-act comedies *Duck Variations* and *Sexual Perversity in Chicago*, and with deepening skill in the longer *American Buffalo* (1975), and the Pulitzer Prize-winning *Glengarry Glen Ross* (1983).

In one of his short essays collected in *Writing in Restaurants* (1986), Mamet noted how Jews have "constant *acute* awareness" of "being completely dependent on the vagaries and good will of their environment". Mamet's skill lies in his ability to create an environment of threat and then filling it with people who resist their vulnerability within it. Importantly, this environment need not be explicitly created, and, in fact, Mamet is most skillful in creating it verbally, without resorting to stage appurtenances. Much of Mamet's career has been spent working in the much-neglected field of radio drama and his greatest strength lies in the evocative quality of his language. The power of his writing conveys the effort of inarticulate characters to express their thoughts, a condition which lends a tremendous propulsive quality to the often vulgar dialog. Levene's opening monolog in *Glengarry* is, typically, an interrupted aria, written with him seated in a restaurant booth, forcing the actor to liberate his character's comic and violent energy vocally, in a confined space. Mamet's love of the sounds of things asks us to receive his best plays as we might the riff of an improvising jazz musician.

Mamet's theater includes the same man's world of poker games and pool halls which he remembers so fondly from his own life. The pawn shop of *American Buffalo* and the sleazy real estate office of *Glengarry Glen Ross* are venues of significance (as is Al Capone's Chicago in Mamet's screenplay for *The Untouchables*, 1987), places of tribal competition and community breakdown inhabited by people desperate in their search for respectability or success. Mamet repeats this nasty condition in the world of Hollywood producers in his most recent stage success, *Speed the Plow* (1988).

At his best, Mamet cuts often although rarely deeply. He has one of the most distinctive voices in the American theater, and needs only to gain some intellectual weight to make an even heavier contribution to it.

ROBERT SKLOOT

Mandelstam, Osip Emilyevich (1891–1937 or 1938)

Russian poet. Born in Warsaw to a father who intended to become a rabbi, Mandelstam grew up and was educated in St Petersburg. After completing his studies he traveled to Germany, France, and Italy, and later joined the poetic movement, Acmeism, which proposed to set Russian poetry on a new course, preferring clarity and directness to the vagueness and mysticism predominant in Symbolist poetry. Mandelstam composed some of the programmatic articles of the new movement, such as "The Dawn of Acmeism" (1913), the year in which he published his first collection of poems, *Stone*. It was, however, his second collection, *Tristia* (1922) which established his position as one of the most important voices in twentieth-century Russian poetry.

Mandelstam's initial attitude towards the Bolshevik Revolution was positive, but the first signs of a rift between him and the Soviet authorities appeared in the mid 1920s. In 1934 he was arrested for the first time, having written an antagonistic poem about Stalin. Three years of persecution followed, ending with Mandelstam's exile in Siberia and, ultimately, his death, the exact date and cirumstances of which are still unclear. Mandelstam's martyrdom was described in detail by his widow, Nadezhda, in her two volumes of memoirs.

Mandelstam regarded the classical tradition and its evolution in Christianity as the framework of his poetry, the themes of which are often cultural and literary. His outlook implied the rejection of the Orthodox Judaism of his ancestors. Yet while he described his attitude as "a flight from Jewish chaos" his poetry often refers to things Jewish, sometimes in deep, elegiac mood (as in the 1916 poem "This night cannot be remade"), and sometimes quasi-humorously (as in the poem about a musician, "Alexander Hertsovitch", 1931).

BIBLIOGRAPHY

The Eyesight of Wasps, trans. J. Greene (Angel, 1989); *The Noise of Time*, trans. C. Brown (Quartet, 1989)

FURTHER READING

Brown, C.: *Mandelstam* (Cambridge: Cambridge University Press, 1973)

Mandelstam, N.: *Hope Against Hope*, trans. M. Hayward (London: Collins & Harvill, 1971); *Hope Abandoned*, trans. Hayward, (London: Collins & Harvill, 1974)

YORAM BRONOWSKI

Mané-Katz The Musicians. *The Mané-Katz Museum, Haifa*

Mané-Katz [Emmanuel (?) Katz] (1894–1962) French painter. Born in Kremenchug in the Ukraine, the son of a synagogue beadle, Mané-Katz received a religious education and was destined for the rabbinate. Having learnt to draw from a friend who attended the Russian school in Kremenchug, his early efforts were spotted by a visiting art student. At the age of 17 he left his home town to study first at the Vilna and then at the Kiev School of Fine Arts.

He arrived in Paris in 1913, where, enrolled as a student at the École des Beaux-Arts, he met Chaim SOUTINE and Marc CHAGALL. In 1914 he returned to Russia, and in 1917 was appointed a professor at the Academy of Fine Arts in Kharkov. In 1921 he was back in Paris, which remained his home, in spite of extensive travels, especially to Israel (where he died), and his wartime residence in the United States.

With the notable exception of Chagall, Mané-Katz is one of the few members of the *École juive* (see PARIS, JEWISH SCHOOL OF) to have specialized in images of overtly Jewish significance. Although he did produce nudes, still-lifes, landscapes, and Old Testament scenes, he is best known for his colorful depictions of the Jewish world of his childhood – of talmudic scholars, rabbis, musicians, weddings, and other ceremonial occasions. His early work was heavily painted, clearly indebted to the example of Fauvism and Expressionism, with a strong tendency to melancholy. The surfaces of his paintings gradually became smoother, the forms reduced to their bare essentials, the mood more serene. Although his style and subject matter have been much imitated and his own output varied considerably in quality, his best work has a life-affirming, almost baroque intensity.

FURTHER READING

Mazars, P.: *Mané-Katz* (Geneva: René Kister, 1962)

Werner, A.: *Mané-Katz* (Tel Aviv: Masada Publishing Ltd, n.d.)

MONICA BOHM-DUCHEN

Manger, Itsik (1901–1969)

Manger, Itsik (1901–1969) Yiddish poet. Born in Czernowitz, Bukovina, Manger was educated in a German-language school and came under the influence of German literature, although his family background also brought him into close contact with Yiddish folk culture. He went to Yasi in 1912 and became acquainted with intellectual life and socialist ideas in Romania. He began to write in Yiddish, and in the early 1920s published widely in Warsaw and New York literary journals. In 1928 he went to Warsaw and lectured on Yiddish and European literature. His first collection of poetry, *Shtern afn dakh* (1929; Stars on the roof), was a great sucess. Manger was in Paris when the Nazis occupied France and he fled to London where his collection, *Volkns ibern dakh* (1942; Clouds above the roof), was published. After a period in the United States, he went to Israel in 1958.

Manger achieved great popularity and critical acclaim during his lifetime. He appealed both to the reading public and the academic Yiddishist by virtue of a brilliant if unthreatening synthesis of a European poetic vocabulary, with Eastern European Jewish *shtetl* culture. In his poetry with biblical content he likewise assimilated Biblical figures to a *shtetl* background. Manger drew on secondary academic sources about older Yiddish literature on religious themes, thus somewhat artificially welding himself on to a long tradition of Yiddish interpretations and elaborations of sacred texts. This poetry is published as *Medresh Itsik* (1984). Manger also wrote a considerable amount of prose, with legendary or folk-tale themes, but often with a polemical Yiddishist tone. Many of Manger's poems have been set to music, some reaching the status and popularity of traditional folk-songs. The accessible lyricism and wistfulness of Manger's poetry made him perhaps the most widely read Yiddish poet.

FURTHER READING

Howe, I., and Greenberg, E.: The adventures of Herschel Summerwind. In *Treasury of Jewish Stories* (New York: Schocken, 1965), 438–46
Leftwich, J.: *The Golden Peacock – A Worldwide Treasury of Yiddish Poetry* (New York: Thomas Yoseloff, 1961) 541–70

CHRISTOPHER HUTTON

Mani Leib

Mani Leib [Mani Leib Brahinski] (1883–1953) Yiddish poet. Born in Nyezhin, Chernigov, Ukraine, Mani Leib was trained as a cobbler, but became active in various socialist and revolutionary organizations, and was arrested in 1904. He fled to England, and reached the United States in 1905. He became the most famous Yiddish lyric poet, and the dominant voice in the Yunge group of poets, although he also wrote some of the most celebrated Yiddish literature for children, including *Vunder iber vunder* (1930; Wonder upon wonder), Mani Leib was co-editor of the collection *Indzl* (1918), and of the monthly of the same name. Influenced by Russian and German literature, his poetry is concerned with private emotions and impressions, solitude, and melancholy moods, although he also wrote in folk-ballad style. The Yunge poets reacted against the didacticism of the sweatshop poets of New York, and were influenced by European movements, such as romanticism and art for art's sake. Mani Leib's poetry was collected in two volumes as *Lider un baladn* (1955).

CHRISTOPHER HUTTON

Mankowitz, Wolf

Mankowitz, Wolf (b.1924) British novelist, dramatist, and screenwriter. Born in East London, Mankowitz was educated at Cambridge University after his army service in the Second World War. After teaching literature and the publication of some award-winning poetry, he worked in London selling fine china and pottery and became an authority on Wedgwood. He was to incorporate his knowledge of fine china into his first novel *Make Me an Offer* (1952) which became a best seller. This work contrasts the seamy side of dealing in antiques with the beauty and passion which a genuine Portland Vase can evoke. *A Kid for Two Farthings* (1953), Mankowitz's second novel, was also a best-seller and established a wide readership

Wolf Mankowitz with his son Gered

for his characteristic blend of Yiddish story-telling, pathos, and worldly cynicism. In this novel Mankowitz was to rewrite the Passover song *Had gadya* in his unique voice, as a paean to the lives of London's East End poor. The seamy side of London is also the subject matter of the novel *My Old Man's a Dustman* (1956). Mankowitz's short stories of this period such as "Laugh till you cry" (1955), and *The Mendelman Fire and Other Stories* (1957) universalize the Eastern European Yiddish tradition which informed much of his early writing. This tradition was applied to the West Indies in *The Biggest Pig in Barbados: A Fable* (1965).

Many critics have argued, however, that Mankowitz's true *métier* has proved to be as a dramatist and screenwriter. He has successfully adapted much of his early fiction for both the stage and screen, and throughout his career has produced many accomplished screenplays. Perhaps his most important screenplay was *The Bespoke Overcoat*, a reworking of Nikolai Gogol's novel *The Overcoat* (1842), which was first pro-

duced as a stage play in London in 1953. This play dramatized Mankowitz's bitter-sweet worldview, and the theme of exploitation which informs much of his early fiction. As a screenplay, *The Bespoke Overcoat* won an Oscar and other major awards for the best short film of 1956. In *Expresso Bongo: a Wolf Mankowitz Reader* (1961), Mankowitz describes this play as "an over-long Jewish joke". Mankowitz's other plays such as *It Should Happen to a Dog* (1955) also utilized Jewish folk-tradition, in this case the biblical story of Jonah. After writing many successful screenplays in the 1960s, Mankowitz published a bitter novel *Cockatrice* (1963), about the film industry. In the 1970s he moved to Eire as a tax exile and this move resulted in the screen- and stage-play *The Irish Hebrew Lesson* (produced London, 1978) which brought together a rabbi and a member of the Irish Liberation Army.

In recent years Mankowitz has increasingly returned to fiction with the publication of *Raspberry Reich* (1979), *Abracadabra!* (1980), *The Devil*

485

in Texas (1984), and *Gioconda* (1987), which all demonstrate his characteristic mixture of fantasy, pugnacious exuberance, and satiric erudition. Mankowitz has had an extraordinary, varied, and prolific career and has produced 9 novels, 3 volumes of short stories, and 18 plays, as well as nearly 30 screenplays for film and television, and a children's book. Surprisingly, he has published only one volume of verse, *XII poems* (London: Workshop Press, 1971) although he began his career as a prize-winning poet.

FURTHER READING

Sonntag, J., ed.: *Jewish Perspectives: 25 Years of Jewish Writing* (London: Secker and Warburg, 1980)

BRYAN CHEYETTE

Mapu, Abraham (1808–1867)   Hebrew novelist. Born in Slobodka, a suburb of Kovno, Mapu was an impoverished elementary teacher all his life, but combined profound talmudic learning with knowledge of several languages and considerable secular learning. He is best known for his first and most successful novel *Ahavat Zion* (1853: The love of Zion), an historical romance set in ancient Israel at the time of Isaiah, which represents a turning point in modern Hebrew literature. Published in at least 16 editions and translated into at least 9 languages, this short novel, the labor of 20 years, exerted a profound influence on many contemporary and later Hebrew writers. A second novel, long and somewhat rambling and in five parts *Ayit tzavu'a* (1858–69; The hypocrite), was set in contemporary Lithuania, went into some 10 editions, and became a model for most Hebrew novels over the next 20 years. Of a third long novel, *Hozei hezyonot* sent to the Russian censor in 1858, only a fragment of seven chapters remains. Mapu reverted to the biblical romance for his final novel *Ashmat shomron* (pt. 1, 1865, pt. 2, 1866; The guilt of Samaria) which also achieved some 10 editions. A lifelong pedagogue, Mapu published three Hebrew textbooks of which *Amon pedagog* became a standard work. Mapu's novels combine both strongly imitative and highly original features. The influence of Hebrew writers such as M. H. LUZZATTO, N. H. WESSELY, J. Perl, and I. Erter,

as well as of French romantic novelists such as Alexandre Dumas the elder and Eugène Sue, is clear. Mapu's originality lies in the conception of a biblical novel – the first in any literature – depicted in a striking neo-biblical style with sincerity and skill. For the Hebrew reader Mapu's first novel opened the prospect of a free and independent life to a people hopelessly fettered by political, social, and economic restrictions, and promoted an imaginative awareness of art and life.

FURTHER READING

Patterson, D.: *Avraham Mapu. The Creator of the Modern Hebrew Novel* (London: East and West Library, 1964)

DAVID PATTERSON

Margolis, Max Leopold (1856–1932) American biblical and Semitic scholar. Margolis was born in Meretz, Government of Vilna, where he achieved early proficiency in Jewish and general studies under the tutelage of his father Isaac, rabbi of the community. In 1885 he entered the Leibnitz *Gymnasium* in Berlin where he excelled in classical studies. At the age of 23 he joined his family who had emigrated to the United States. At Columbia University he studied Semitics and wrote his doctoral dissertation on the text of the talmudic tractate of 'Erubin on the basis of variant readings in Rashi's commentary, 1891.

Margolis had a distinguished academic career, beginning with his appointment as Assistant Professor of Hebrew and biblical exegesis at Hebrew Union College (1892–7). In 1893 he published a work on Hebrew grammar and phonetics entitled *An Elementary Text-Book of Hebrew Accidence*. Following a year at the University of California at Berkeley (1897), he returned to Hebrew Union College to serve as Professor of Bible until 1910. In that year he was was led to resign because of a controversy over his Zionist views.

Margolis then went to Europe were he completed his *Manual of the Aramaic Language of the Talmud*, which appeared in both English and German (1910). He settled in Philadelphia, where he was invited by Dropsie College to serve as Professor of Bible, a post he occupied with distinction until his death. In Philadelphia he became editor-in-chief of the new translation of *The Holy Scriptures*, published in 1917 by the JEWISH PUBLICATION SOCIETY. In 1924 he spent a year in Jerusalem as annual professor at the American School of Oriental Research, and as visiting professor at the newly organized Hebrew University.

Margolis soon achieved recognition as an unsurpassed textual critic of the Bible and as an authority on biblical grammar. He devoted himself to establishing the text of the Septuagint and published a critical edition of *The Book of Joshua in Greek* (1931). His biblical commentaries include: *Micah* (1908) and *Zephaniah and Malachi* (in Hebrew 1930). Among his popular works are: *The Story of Bible Translations* (1917), and *The Hebrew Scriptures in the Making* (1922). In 1927 he published, in collaboration with Alexander Marx, an authoritative *History of the Jewish People*.

FURTHER READING

Adler, C.: Max Leopold Margolis. *American Jewish Year Book* 35 (1933) 139–44

Gordis, R., ed.: *Max Leopold Margolis* (Philadelphia: Alumni Association, Dropsie College, 1952) [memorial volume containing appreciations and bibliography]

Marx, A.: Max Leopold Margolis. In *Essays in Jewish Biography* (Philadelphia: The Jewish Publication Society of America, 1947) 265–9

JACOB KABAKOFF

Markfield, Wallace (b.1926) American novelist. Born in Brooklyn, Markfield was educated at Brooklyn College and New York University. Jules Farber, the stand-up comic and protagonist of *You Could Live If They Let You* (1974), speaks as much for Markfield as for himself when he declares: "I got a terminal case of aggravation". Indeed, several years earlier, Philip ROTH had mentioned Markfield in precisely this connection when Alexander Portnoy thinks: "The novelist, what's his name, Markfield, has written in a story somewhere that until he was 14 he believed 'aggravation' to be a Jewish

word". The story is entitled "The Country of the Crazy Horse", but its theme – aggravation comically rendered – spreads equally across Markfield's canon.

To an Early Grave (1964), is a relentless, pointed satire of the New York Jewish intellectual crowd. Ostensibly a comic tale of how a group of disparate mourners attend the funeral of fellow literary journalist, Leslie Braverman, the novel cut narrow, but deep. Those who saw themselves reflected, and ridiculed, in Markfield's portraits were not amused; and at least part of the general neglect that Markfield has suffered had its origins in his decision to satirize Jewish–American book reviewers rather than Jewish–American mothers.

Markfield's second novel, *Teitelbaum's Window* (1970), was both larger in scope and more conventional in posture. It tells the story of Simon Sloan, a boy growing to manhood in Brooklyn's Brighton Beach during the 1930s. The result was a study in the popular culture of that time, that place, and a novel top-heavy in predictable nostalgia.

Markfield dedicated his novel, *You Could Live If They Let You*, to "the wisest men of our time – the stand-up comics", and the novel itself is an extended exercise both in imitation and appreciation. But it is also an instance of finding himself at a dead end: he told an interviewer "I've grown tired, after three novels, of chronicling the Jewish experience in America" and he vowed to "tell no more Jewish jokes which they neither get nor care to get, drink no more egg creams, enter no more candy stores, stay away from talk of *shtetls*, stop salting and peppering my speech with all that Yiddish." Up to 1988 Markfield has been as good as his word; unfortunately, it is also true that he has not finished a single new novel.

Other works include essays and short stories in magazines such as *Partisan Review*, *Commentary*, *Midstream*, and *Esquire*.

FURTHER READING

Bruccoli, M. J.: Wallace Markfield. In *Conversations with Writers I* (Detroit: Gale Research Co., 1977) 216–36

Friedman, M. J.: Jewish mothers and sons: the expense of chutzpah. In *Contemporary American–Jewish*

Literature, ed. I. Malin (Bloomington: Indiana University Press, 1973) 156–74

SANFORD PINSKER

FURTHER READING
Markish, E.: *The Long Return* (New York: 1978)

ALICE NAKHIMOVSKY

Markish, David (b.1938) Russian novelist. Markish is the younger son of the Yiddish poet Peretz MARKISH, executed in 1952 (his elder brother is the critic and scholar, Shimon Markish). After the arrest of Peretz Markish, the family was exiled to Kazakhstan. They returned to Moscow after Stalin's death, where Markish attended the Literary Institute and began writing fiction and poetry. He left for Israel in 1972, where he became a prolific novelist and journalist.

The experience of coming to age in exile formed the basis for Markish's first book, the novel *Priskazka* (1976; *The World of Simon Ashkenazy*, 1976). Though it lacks the artistry of his later books, *Priskazka* is interesting for its straightforward identification with Jews, linked with the romantic belief in a Jewish future outside of the Soviet Union. In Markish's later books, the romanticism diminishes but the identification remains, tempered by a sharp eye for historical irony.

Markish's recent fiction reveals him as a writer with a gift for plot and design. Though his novels vary widely in theme, he shows a constant fascination with the interplay of national psychologies on a background of Russian history. *Shuty* (1982; The jewters), is set in the court of Peter the Great at the imaginative source of Russian–Jewish relations. *Pes* (1984; The dog) is set by contrast in the latest emigration, when there are no longer many differences between Russians and Jews.

Relations between national groups is a theme of many of Markish's books. *Granatovyi kolodets* (1986; The crimson well), is a spy story that deals, in part, with a Soviet national let loose in Israel. Here the interchange is depicted satirically. But in a different, unusually lyrical book, the same phenomenon is permeated with sadness. Also published in 1986, *V teni bol' shogo kamnya* (In the shade of the great rock), is an impressionistic account of the consequences of Soviet power in a remote corner of Azerbaijan.

Markish, Peretz (1885–1952) Yiddish poet and novelist. The youngest member of the Kiev triumvirate was Peretz Markish, the others being Dovid HOFSHTEYN and Leyb KVITKO. With the other two Markish produced the joint anthology *Eygns* in which the authors expressed their joy at the fall of the Tsar and the liberation of the Russian Jews. His early works include; *Shveln* (1919; Threshholds), and the acclaimed *Di kupe* (1922: The mound). In Warsaw in 1922 he edited with Israel Joshua SINGER the first of two anthologies entitled *Khalyastre* (Gang), the uncomplimentary title given by the editor of the Warsaw daily newspaper *Moment* to Markish and his group of Expressionist young poets. The group took on this title with pride and produced a second anthology under the same name in Paris in 1924 under the editorship of Markish and Varshavsky. Marc CHAGALL supplied its illustrations. Markish was received at his public poetry readings in Berlin, London, and Paris as something of a superstar. He was extremely handsome with an expressive and excitingly dramatic voice and delivery. Like the rock stars of today, he was looked upon by older critics with disdain. They insisted that the unseemly hysteria of his admirers would disappear when the poet grew in maturity and self-discipline in his work. He was a dedicated and enthusiastically optimistic Marxist. He returned to the Soviet Union in 1926 where his song *Mayn dor* (1927; My generation), glorified the Communist regime and its imminent liberation of the rest of the world. In 1928 he composed a celebratory song for May Day. His novels include: *Dor oys, Dor ayn* (1929; One generation after another); *Brider* (1929; Brothers); and *Eyns af eyns* (1934; One plus one). Later poetic works include: *Poeme vegn Stalinen* (1940; Poem about Stalin) and an epic poem *Milkhome* (1948; War). Like the other members of the Kiev Group, his loyalty to Stalin did not prevent his arrest in 1948, his imprisonment, torture, and subsequent shooting in 1952. His unfinished epic poem *Yerushe* (Herit-

Peretz Markish (4th from left) with other members of Di Khalyastre *(The gang): Mendl Elkin, Peretz Hirschbeyn, Uri Zvi Greenberg, Markish, Melekh Ravitsh, and Israel Joshua Singer, Warsaw, 1922*

age) was published posthumously in Buenos Aires in 1959.

DEVRA KAY

Martin, David [Ludwig Detsinyi] (b.1915) Australian novelist, critic, and poet. Martin, who was born in Hungary, had a chequered and fruitful career before emigrating to Australia where he rapidly became established as a prolific and diverse novelist and poet. In his youth he was an active member of the Communist Party and that affiliation has colored his attitude to Judaism all his life. Though he is deeply conscious of his Judaism (as reflected in his writings), Martin considers himself to be an atheist. From Hungary he went to Germany and in 1935 went on *hakhsharah* to a youth camp in Holland and then emigrated to Palestine. After a short stay in Palestine he went to Spain where he saw active service with the fifteenth International Brigade. During the war he worked as a radio monitor for the BBC at Glas-

gow. It was here that he had his first book of poetry published. In 1949 he moved to Sydney, where he became editor of the *Jewish News* until 1955.

His first Australian novel was *The Young Wife* (1962) in which he explored the theme of creativity versus destructiveness, expressed through the psychological turmoil of adjustment to a new culture. Unlike other Jewish immigrant novelists there was no simple equation in Martin's work of the old world representing decay and death and Australia representing life; Australia, rather, became the battlefield for these forces. Martin returned to the theme of the search for identity in a foreign land in his *Where a Man Belongs* (1969). In this work, a German Jew and an Australian confront each other in representation of the old world and the new.

His poetry has met with a mixed reception. His early poetry shows traces of his non-native English origin, but his poems on the Spanish Civil War are said to be among the best he has written. Reviewers of his Australian poetry have compared him with Blake "meaning and emotion explodes from and beyond the written word" and his poem *Dirge for a Press Lord*, has been described as the best poem written in Australia. Martin is a prolific writer, having published more than 29 books of poetry and fiction.

FURTHER READING

Brissenden, R. F.: The Poems of David Martin. *Meanjin* 17 342–3

Haddock, Y.: The prose fiction of Jewish writers of Australia, 1949–1969, II. *Australian Jewish Historical Society* 8 no. 1 (1975)

ALAN D. CROWN

Marx, Karl (1818–1883) German social thinker and revolutionary. Born in Trier, a non-industrial, vineyard city of some 15,000 inhabitants in the Mosel valley of the Rhineland, Marx had a thoroughly Jewish genealogy, with a long line of rabbis on both sides of his family, going as far back as the fifteenth century. Marx's paternal grandfather was rabbi of Trier as was his uncle. But Marx's father, growing up under the impact of the Irideas of the French Enlightenment, was less influenced by his religious ancestry and turned to the legal profession. In order to retain a state position he converted to Protestantism, a year or so before Marx's birth. In Trier Marx received a humanist education, and in 1835 was sent to study law at the University of Bonn. Within a year, however, he transferred to the University of Berlin and studied towards a doctorate in philosophy. Here he came under the influence of the Young Hegelians, became a radical in his outlook and wrote his first, tentative critiques of German society and politics. His radicalism made a university career impossible and he turned instead to journalism as editor of the *Rheinische Zeitung* in Cologne. When the paper was closed down in 1843 by the Prussian authorities, Marx emigrated to Paris (having in the meantime married Jenny von Westphalen, the daughter of a prominent and ennobled, but liberal, Trier Protestant family). In Paris Marx met and befriended Friedrich Engels – a personal and intellectual friendship that would last until Marx's death – became a communist, and wrote socio-philosophical essays which, though still much fashioned by the Hegelian legacy, contained the seeds of his later thought. Expelled from Paris, Marx moved to Brussels in early 1845 and, on the eve of the 1848 revolutionary eruptions in Europe, he and Engels drafted the *Communist Manifesto*. By now Marx had formulated the fundamental tenets of a world view – historical materialism – that would govern all his subsequent intellectual work. But in 1849, as the revolutionary movement began to decline, Marx, having returned to Germany and radical journalism, fled to London where he spent the rest of his life. Aside from his activities as one of the founders of the First International in 1864, Marx's 34 years in England were uneventful, except that they produced that huge corpus of thought and writings that would become one of the dominant social and political theories of the twentieth century.

There is no precedent for the direct impact that this intellectual edifice has had on world history. Early in his life Marx had declared that the aim of philosophy should be to change the world; and, indeed, his philosophy had precisely this consequence, even if in a manner that would have surely provoked his sense of irony. Looked at individually, Marx's writings are for the most part detailed, scholarly, and sometimes quite tedious analyses of particular problems of history, economics, and society. But the whole is animated by a strikingly original thematic synthesis, utilizing the main currents of thought prevalent in Marx's time – German philosophy, French sociology, and British economic theory. He created a system of thought that made possible a consistent way of reflecting upon the social world – and of acting upon it. This element of theory and practice was central to everything he wrote and in an industrial, scientific, and secular age – one, moreover, in which a substantial intellectual class was coming into being – it had immense appeal for those who believed that modern man was now in a position both to understand history and control it, and thereby make the natural world subservient to the social through a ubiquitous science of society.

Historical materialism, the theoretical foundation of Marx's social science, advanced the view that the manner in which human beings engaged in economic production determined the character of their social, political, and cultural lives. Simply put, this meant that economic needs and possibilities were the paramount force in history, the direct progenitor of all human relations and forms of social organization. As such needs and possibilities (or "forces of production") changed over time – primarily through scientific and technological progress, itself motivated by material interests – so human relations and forms of social organization had to be adapted accordingly, in functional conformity. In a sense, Marx proposed the notion that human history was no more than this continuous process, the adaptation of relations to forces of production. However, his grasp of this was not mechanistic; on the contrary, adaptation took place slowly, unevenly, and in conditions of conflict and violence. Those who had most to lose from change were those who controlled, and thus benefited from, the existing economic and social structure. They were a ruling economic class and they would invariably resist every social transformation that threatened to undermine their privileged position. Hence Marx's concomitant view that history was primarily a tale of fierce struggle, of outright war in the end between old and emerging economic classes, a protracted social revolution culminating in political upheaval. Change in this sense, therefore, was ultimately inevitable, Marx believed, no matter how powerful the resistance to it. Its pace, he conceded, depended on human beings themselves, on their capacity for understanding this or that conjunctural predicament, and on the institutional and organizational resources they could mobilize. Even so, the "superstructure" of society – state, law, nation, religion, political ideologies, culture in its various forms – was not the driving force of history but rather the consequence of economic exigencies.

However unhappy a picture of the past, Marx's deterministic materialism was nevertheless saturated with the promise of better things to come. In the first place, he perceived each stage of change as one of progress, since it opened up new human possibilities and expanded economic and social resources. But, above all, he also believed that men were not doomed to follow for ever the course of conflict

he had described. The modern age, he thought, was on the verge of a scientific–technological transformation so immense and qualitatively different from the past that, for the first time in human history, there appeared the prospect of the complete eradication of economic scarcity, and hence of classes, of exploitation, of oppression, of the state and of all social antagonism. Industrial–capitalist society, at present limited to certain European societies but bound to engulf the whole of the world because of its advanced methods of production and thus military power, was the last stage of class history. The necessary triumph of the proletariat over the bourgeoisie – the socialist revolution – could usher in a new human history, of rational economic production and affluence, and thus of freely determined social relations.

This chiliastic vision of the future has long been seen as both the strength and the weakness of Marx's thought – strength, because it exercised a powerful hold upon actual and potential followers; weakness, because it had more in common with Old Testament-like prophecy than modern social science. But the scientific and messianic, the descriptive and prescriptive, cannot easily be separated in Marx's intellectual temperament and the interplay between the two, as that between reflection and action, tells us something about the European and the Jewish historical contexts from which he sprang, and in which his personality was fashioned. The European Enlightenment made possible, as in the case of Marx, the liberation of Jews from their religious and communal traditions and their entry into the larger Gentile society. But their roots remained suspect and their socio-economic position marginal and vulnerable, and they felt the iniquities of the larger society both more subtly and more heinously than others. Marx never wrote about his own Jewishness or Jewish ancestry, but among his earliest writings is an essay, "On the Jewish Question" (1843), which analyzes the peculiar status and economic role of Jews in capitalist society. It does not make for pleasant reading: Marx attacks Jews for embodying the worst attributes of a mercenary civilization and he does so in language which is, on the face of it, clearly anti-Semitic ("What is the worldly cult of the Jew? Huckstering. What is his worldly god? Money") Yet if this essay betrays "self-hatred", it also makes manifest Marx's hatred for the Christian society which had in effect inflicted upon the Jews their situation.

During these early years Marx was also preoccupied with the writing of exploratory philosophical essays, in particular the so-called "Economic and Philosophical Manuscripts" (1844), where the concept of alienation plays a central role in his analysis of the condition of modern man in general. There is no mention of Jews here, but the Jew as the paradigm case of this alienated modern man, as Marx describes the latter, unmistakably springs to mind: emancipated in principle yet constricted in practice; useful in the service of capitalism yet estranged from his labor; prepared to embrace a secular, rationalistic ethic yet subjected to a mendacious Christian morality; enjoying free legal status yet rejected and repelled by the social, political, and cultural powers that be. This dissonance between promise and fulfillment – so characteristic of the European Jew's situation then and later but grasped by Marx as a universal human phenomenon – was to animate the whole of Marx's intellectual output, as well as its manner. His methods were scientific and analytical but his tone was one of rage and fury. Not surprisingly, Marxism was to attract many Jews, even if – or perhaps because, as in the case of its founder – they had in one way or another abandoned Judaism as such.

The intellectual enterprise is by its very nature a universal one, and it allowed those Jews who pursued it to escape their constricting particularism. But the chiliastic side of Marx's thought, linked inextricably to a seemingly rigorous social science and method of analysis, appealed to a wider audience as well, disenchanted with the unfulfilled realities of modern society. In a sense, Marx's thought was so strikingly original for being the most thoroughgoing, systematic attempt at doing away with dissonance and at making fulfillment conform to promise.

BIBLIOGRAPHY

The Marx–Engels Reader, ed. R. C. Tucker (New York: Norton, 1978); *The Portable Karl Marx*, ed. E. Kamenka (Harmondsworth: Penguin Books, 1983)

FURTHER READING

Avineri, S.: *The Social and Political Thought of Karl Marx* (Cambridge: Cambridge University Press, 1968)

Berlin, I.: *Karl Marx: His Life and Environment*, (Oxford: Oxford University Press, 1963)

Cohen, G. A.: *Karl Marx's Theory of History: A Defence* (Oxford: Oxford University Press, 1978)

McLellan, D.: *Karl Marx: His Life and Thought* (London: Macmillan, 1973)

BARUCH KNEI-PAZ

Marxism, Jews and A study of Jewish revolutionism (and especially Marxism) in nineteenth-century Europe reveals a structural division into two basic categories: the one tried to relieve the Jews of their plight, while the other tried to be relieved of their Jewishness. Both saw the Jewish way of life – in the Pale of Settlement, the ghetto and the anti-Semitism it suffered – as a perpetual state of the scapegoat and underdog. Whereas the former revolutionary group took as its responsibility the welfare of the people and its fate, the latter, "extra"-Jewish group sought deliberately to lose its Jewishness not only with the hope that this would serve as an entrance ticket to the Gentile world, but, in addition, adopting its issues and problems to boot.

The "extra"-Jewish revolutionaries withdrew from the Jewish fate, and aimed at saving the whole world; by redeeming all mankind they would automatically save also those who were of Jewish extraction. These Jewish revolutionaries adopted universal socialist ideologies, and especially Marxism, centering themselves mainly in the German and Russian Social Democratic movements, and were even largely instrumental in the formulation of these movements.

The sociological factor

Jewish radicalism grew under the influence of two seemingly contradictory climates: the emancipation of Western liberalism and the ceaseless pressure in the Jewish townships of the White Russian Pale of Settlement. Nevertheless, the sociological impact within these two frameworks was similar: the Russian Jew felt himself depressed within the Pale of Settlement, and alienated should he attempt to escape it. In Germany, the promise of emancipation bore within it the frustration of non-realization, liberalism was offered to the Jews on condition that they relinquish completely their unique identity, while at the same time the Emancipation carried along waves of fierce anti-Semitism on the part of the various conservative ideologies.

The assimilation of the Jews into the liberal–bourgeois milieu of that period was an attractive dream more than an operative goal. The Jewish activist, intellectual, assimilationist was accordingly cut off from both sides: he relinquished his Jewish tradition in favor of an enlightened German identity, but this same enlightened German world remained closed before him despite all his efforts. Thus a guaranteed path to absorption within Europe did not exist, and the inevitable results were compromise, disappointment, or alienation.

The feeling of alienation was the basic factor which pushed the Jew into the arms of revolutionary–radical ideologies. Just as the general Russian intelligentsia was motivated by a sense of vacuum, of an absence of framework, and any sense of belonging, (and indeed these served as a cornerstone of Marx's revolutionary program regarding the growing proletariat), so too did these factors cause those Jews, who yearned to become a part of Europe, to want to change Europe. Since assimilation was not possible, they began to nourish a dream for a new world, redeemed and united, in which they would automatically belong. Thus the Jews' universalist idealism grew out of the vacuum caused by an absence of roots and identity.

The liberal movements were not sufficiently radical; the "bourgeois" middle path could not satisfy – even if it were philo-Semitic – the need for a total redemption, which was the inevitable result of a total alienation. At the same time, the European nationalist movements, were, by their very nature, exclusivist.

The Russian populist movement *Narodnichestvo*, for example, was anarchistic and radical, yet anti-Semitic to the core. It was only the universalist anational socialism found in the Marxist movement of late nineteenth-century Russia and Germany which permitted complete assimilation irrespective of racial origin, and which did not propose a closing of the ranks as part of their ideological aim.

The psychological factor

The degree of assimilation–alienation and revolutionism developed by the intellectual Jews, thirsty for freedom and seized with a longing for assimilation into the humanist world, was dependent upon the degree of openness of this world towards them. This in turn was related to the deep-rooted and problematic psychological phenomenon of the anti-Semitic tradition. This hatred towards Jews, which was an integral part of the development of European culture, became more than an external shield of the Gentile towards the Jew; it also grew to become an immanent psychological factor in the form of self-hatred. This explained the rejection by the revolutionary Jew of the Jewish world and the Jewish fate; it also explained the desire to escape a ghostly world and integrate into a world of cultured people.

Yet this self-hatred was only one form of Jewish reaction to the phenomenon of anti-Semitism, for at the same time a tremendous amount of bitterness at this alienating world was built up. This brought in its wake a rejection of the world as it existed and the search for a radical–revolutionary solution by destroying the existing world and building a better one in its place. This desire for destruction in turn contributed not a little to fanning the fires of antagonism between the frustrated Jew and the rest of the world.

Yet this rejection of the world, and the deep-felt need to change it, came not only as a reaction to anti-Semitism, but also from the immanent Jewish tradition which the Jews carried with them; the sense of introversion of the Jew from the follies of the world. The sociological situation thus acted as a catalyzing agent in strengthening traditional emotional motives: conditions of history placed the enlightened, intellectual, assimilationist, radical Jews in a state of perpetual alienation – from their original culture and society and also from their adopted ones. This resulted in a double set of attitudes: by absorbing the standards of Western culture, the Jews were able to look on their Jewishness

493

with foreign, anti-Semitic, eyes; at the same time, they carried with them the deep-seated Jewish revulsion of Gentiles and compulsive introversion for the sake of guarding the treasures of the Torah.

The other face of this Jewish rejection of the world was embodied in the Jewish sense of mission to correct the world's failings. There was a self-awareness of ethical elitism that must be guarded from the perversions of the world in order to enlighten and show a path in that same world. This Jewish elitism led to universalism and the sense of mission as bearers of the truth.

Even though the revolutionary radicals abandoned their Jewishness, the dialectical phenomenon of rejection versus a mission of salvation nonetheless remained in force. The traditional Jewish introversion was translated into an ideological activism of destruction, while the sense of mission was projected to an awareness of self as a revolutionary avant-garde.

The ideological factor

Anti-Semitic thinkers correctly explained the Jewish elitism as stemming from an ideological principle of the "Chosen People" which had set itself above the global history of mankind. Yet they were not aware of the duality within the idea of the chosen. This idea is based on a two-dimensional outlook in the Jewish tradition, which calls for other-wordliness on the one hand and full involvement in world history on the other. The Jewish principle of "a nation that dwells unto itself" existed side by side with the even more ancient principle of "a light unto the nations" and "by you will be blessed all the families of the earth". The "elitism" in Jewish ideology was thus never anti-historical or anti-human. An interpretation of complete isolation from the world would be missing the point of Jewish ethical leadership, prophecy, "Torah from Zion", and the establishment of faith on earth. Indeed such an interpretation is negated by Judaism as much as is total absorption and assimilation.

This point occasioned a paradoxical development: despite the fact that the radical revolutionary threw off his Jewish milieu, despite his identification with the anti-Semitic denigration

of the "Chosen People" syndrome, he continued to feel the sense of mission of the "sons of Priests" and of the "holy people", in its secular translation as the avant-garde destined to bring about liberty, equality, and fraternity.

In addition to the dialectical attitude of Jewish ideology towards the world, one must not ignore the dialectic within Jewish messianism. This was based on the belief in an apocalyptic destruction ordained by God, followed by a universal redemption. It was this belief in a Messiah which in fact enabled the Jews to exist in the stifling ghettoes under the threat of oppression. Jewish origin was a fertile breeding ground in which to nurture an identification with the responsibility for the good of the world as a whole, and the certainty in the coming of the Messiah. Jewish theology had disappeared, replaced, however, by a broad-scoped and binding *Weltanschauung*. The world was still viewed as a deterministic framework whose redemption would surely be realized in the end; so too remained the elitism and sense of mission of the revolutionary avant-garde. Revolutionary radicalism, then, served as an entrance ticket to a world in which the Jew had no place. It also neutralized the hidden complexes of guilt and betrayal of their people, and the desire to take revenge on that closed-in world sinking in its own superstitions. Yet in the same way it must be seen as a new and revolutionary expression of the deep-rooted historical consciousness of messianic belief. Without a God, and rejecting any conscious identification with the Jewish people, the Marxist revolutionaries of Jewish origin continued to carry on their shoulders the Jewish consciousness and tradition.

The degree to which this brand of revolutionism is similar to that of consciously Jewish revolutionism is quite astonishing. Two basic factors were at work in Jewish thought and history during the Exile: the oppression of the Jews and their ultimate mission – the fate and the vision. Zionist revolutionaries sought to free themselves of the Jewish fate and at the same time realize the Jewish dreams of redemption. The aims of the Jewish radical-univeralists ran parallel: the drives to change and be changed were similar, as was the drive towards redemption. The main difference lay in the contents – the release of Jews from their trouble gave way to the releasing of mankind from the limitations of Judaism, and national redemption gave way to the universal redemption of all mankind – the scope of the redemption was in keeping with the extent of the renunciation.

Thus, in a sublimated form, the rejected Judaism continued to serve as an emotional and ideological source with permanent implications even in the new frames of reference. Just as revolutionary radicalism among Jews sprang from an attempt to reject Jewish uniqueness in favor of the new unity of mankind, so too was it bound up with the very roots of the Jewish uniqueness.

It was natural that Jews should turn to revolutionary radicalism and especially to Marxism. The traditional Jewish form of life, the stifling life of the Jewish township versus the signs of European emancipation with all its ambivalence towards the Jews – all these stimulated its growth. The permanent ideological dimension nourished the sociohistorical phenomena, and was transformed by them into a new context. The relevance of static interpretations indicating a permanent messianic or a perpetual revolutionary mentality must be balanced against the dynamic sociohistoric forces.

FURTHER READING

Carr, E. H.: *The Bolshevik Revolution* (London: Macmillan & Co., 1954)

Cuddihy, J. M.: *The Ordeal of Civility: Freud, Marx, Levi-Strauss and the Jewish Struggle with Modernity* (New York: Basic Books, 1974)

Deutscher, I., *Trotsky: The Prophet Armed*, (Oxford, 1954)

Feuer, L.: The conversion of K. Marx's father. *The Jewish Journal of Sociology* 14 (1972)

Keep, J. H.: *The Rise of Social Democracy in Russia* (Oxford: Clarendon Press, 1963)

Lichtheim, G.: Socialism and the Jews. *Dissent* (Jan.–Feb. 1968)

Nedava, J.: *Trotsky and the Jews* (Philadelphia, 1972)

Silberner, E.: *The Anti-Semitic Tradition in Modern Socialism* (Jerusalem: 1953)

Tucker, R.: *Philosophy and Myth in Karl Marx* (Cambridge: Cambridge University Press, 1971)

ELLA BELFER

Marxism, Judaism and In determining the possible comparison between Marxist and Jewish thought several basic questions must be asked: What conception of the world do these two hold? How do they see humanity, its role in the world, and its influence upon the future? Do they see revolution or redemption as the bridge between their conception of the world and their conception of humanity?

Some scholars find that Judaism and Marxism offer largely alternate answers to these two questions. Thus it is no coincidence that such a large proportion of Jews figure among the founders of the Marxist tradition, and that so many Jews have found their places, following MARX himself, within that revolutionary movement, in communist parties and Trotskyite groups. For example, most members of the first Russian revolutionary group, the "Emancipation of Labor group", were Jews. Ultimately, because of the similarity between these two doctrines, these Jews would not have had the impression of truly changing their intellectual code in joining the Marxist stream.

Others hold that Judaism and Marxism offer radically opposite perspectives, both upon the world and upon humanity. They see the Jewish tradition as essentially theocentric and ethnocentric, whereas the Marxist tradition is anti-religious, collectivist, and universalist. Thus, for those who defend this second point of view, the persecutions suffered by the Jews on the part of Marxist regimes and the fundamental hostility of the Soviet Union towards Zionism are quite natural and logical like the self-denial of the "non-Jewish" Jews, to use Isaac DEUTSCHER's expression.

But it can be said that both of these opposing views sin in their extremism: Judaism and Marxism are both parallel and antagonistic. In general, while these views seek to answer similar questions about the relation of humanity to the world and the relation of people to each other the paths of these two cross in an interesting alternative, meeting at certain points which are problematic, difficult, and uncertain.

On the first question, regarding the view of the world, Marxism seeks to combine two perspectives. On the one hand, it is clear that

Marx and his followers sought to define the world in absolute terms, the world in its Truth. Hence their desire to establish unchanging, total, and eternal rules. Here we definitely find the contribution of Hegel. Marx takes from Hegel, on the one hand, his global *Weltanschauung*, his deep belief in history; on the other hand, his profound interest in people and freedom of conscience and thought. But, where Hegel very well distinguishes these two perspectives, Marx tries to link one with the other, because he does not intend to renounce one or the other. The originality of Marx's thought is precisely in this linkage between voluntarism and determinism. He is a determinist, when he tries to define absolute concepts, to tell what is the truth, to define the laws of the world, to be objective. He is a voluntarist, when he says that revolutionary forces are what can move the world. But he sees a permanent link between both: revolution is part of the laws of the world, voluntarism is part of determinism. In this particular perspective, Marx is different from other socialist thinkers (like the anarchists) who renounced determinism. However, on the other hand, and this is the dialectical character of Marxism, this ideology accepts change, incorporates the existence of a dynamic force, and, in the final account, accepts relativity.

In the perspective of Marx and the Marxists, this coexistence of the absolute and the relative does not constitute an insoluble contradiction. On the contrary, it is precisely the essence of the world and of human existence to be simultaneously truth and change.

Indeed, Marxism considers that it possesses an absolute, eternal truth, and it believes it is capable of predicting that which, sooner or later, must necessarily take place: the war of the classes, the victory of the proletariat and its party, the dictatorship of the proletariat, and a classless society. However its reflection is inserted into history. Marxist thought is not a-historical: for history is changing, dynamic, uncertain. The field remains free for human will, for individual initiative and commitment. That is one of the aspects which appears most paradoxically for those who view Marxism from the outside: the revolution must take place. However, one cannot know when or where, and the

accomplishment of the revolution depends on the initiative and organization of the proletariat. In short, we have here a mixture of the most exacerbated Hegelianism and the ideas and principles of the individualist French philosophers of the eighteenth century, which led to the French Revolution.

On this level, one must recognize a relative similarity to the dialectic structure of Jewish harmony between God's omnipotence and human will, between *yedi'ah* and *behirah*. Judaism claims to possess and reveal an absolute truth. A moral code whose acceptance by the Jewish people is defined as the *sine qua non* of the existence of the world. The Torah is *'emet*, that is, truth. Thus, it contains a fair amount of determinism, because the Jewish people had to be exiled in Egypt, had to leave Egypt, and to receive the Torah at Sinai, had to enter the Land of Israel, and so on, until the advent of the Messiah, who must necessarily appear, which is an article of faith. But, like Marxism, Judaism also does not renounce history. It is situated within history, in the material world, in the concrete.

It is not a matter of indifference whether or not Jews obey the commandments. It is not a matter of indifference if Jews sanctify the name of God in the face of pogroms and persecutions, or that they return one day to the Land of Israel and recreate their sovereignty. Thus in Judaism one finds a mixture between the desire not to renounce absolute truth and the Kingdom of Heaven, and also unwillingness to renounce history, the concrete human domain.

There is a similarity, but one which appears debatable, when one notes the deterministic or voluntaristic content of these two ways of thinking. The truth which Marxism and Judaism claim to possess refers to two different absolutes. For Marxism, truth is of the human order, it is materialism. Nothing exists besides people. It is they who are transcendent. For the Torah, truth is beyond humanity, on the level of the single God. Thus, it is a truth that does not depend on humans, but rather a transcendental, exterior factor. The Torah is God's message to the world. The Jewish tradition exists only on the basis of that transcendence outside of human beings, while Marxism exists only on the basis of a total immanence; omnipotence situated within human history. It must be stressed that the problems of faith Marxism and Judaism encounter are opposite. Marxism is bound to answer the following question: How is it possible to believe in history as "absolute" while not believing in God? Judaism tries to answer the following question: How is it possible to preserve the freedom of man, while believing that everything is in God's hand? The answer of Maimonides is that Judaism is harmony: it teaches us both the knowledge of the Almighty God, and man's freedom of choice.

A more important difference appears in the fashion in which the two "doctrines" combine their deterministic and voluntaristic perspectives. In Marxism, the absolute and history clearly form a whole, and the separation made by the commentator between truth revealed by the doctrine and the dynamic of human action exists only in his mind. In the writings of Marx these two aspects are constantly united in a remarkable symbiosis. In contrast, Judaism does not fuse the quest for the absolute and the value of human action. The two poles exist, and remain quite separate: on the one hand God and the Torah meta-historical and meta-physical; on the other hand, there are man's inscription in history: the wanderings and adventures of the patriarchs, power, war, persecutions, exile. The Jew lives on both these levels: Torah as a condition of existence of the world.

The other area in which the Jewish and Marxist worlds should be compared is that of their conception of humanity's role with respect to the future. The idea of revolution and the idea of redemption (ge'ula) have much in common. They aim to constitute a bridge between the conception of the world and the conception of man. One finds a fundamental similarity in the necessity, affirmed by both doctrines, to have the world changed by man. The Hebrew word *tikkun*, expresses this idea perfectly: it means "repair". Humanity is called upon to repair the world, to act on the world, to change the course of history. The similarity lies in the perception of humans as beings who are not passive, inactive, or immobile, but rather as ones who can alter their environment, in time

and in space. Here again, from this angle of this similarity one can understand how the Jew who has lost his faith in God might be tempted to pass over to the Marxist camp. There, in his new camp, he knows he will also be called upon to act, though not to observe the commandments, but to fulfill a role in history. This is not conversion to a new religion, a contemplative one, like the oriental religions.

Where is the difference in this area? In what sense is the *tikkun* demanded by Marxism different from that demanded by the Jewish tradition? Since Marxism acknowledges no authority or responsibility beyond man, or, if you will, humanity is its divinity, from the start the people's possibilities of changing the world are unlimited. Henceforth there are no limits to human liberty, and the responsibility for the final goal of human action: the revolution. There remains but one scandal – since humanity is invincible – the fact that it is bound by circumstance. It is, perhaps, the impossibility of a total conquest of nature which gives Marxism its human face and a certain modesty: man cannot be a superman.

In the Jewish tradition this struggle for absolute liberty, absolute change, and for total revolution does not exist, because the Jew knows he has natural limits. The throne of God reigns above history. Thus, in some sense, heaven limits human action. From the start the Jewish tradition accepts that limitation of the power of *tikkun* which a person can exercise in the world. The ultimate solution to history is in the hands of divine providence. Hence a fundamental difference of method. The commentators have noted that both Judaism and Marxism use the dialectical method. History, according to both, advances by accentuating contradictions and harmony. These are not Manichean doctrines, in which good and evil are rigorously antagonistic, in which history must end with the victory of one or the other force. These two ways of thinking speak of dialog. However, that dialog is not exactly between the same poles.

In Judaism there is a dialog between the universal, humanity, on the one hand, and the Jewish people, the chosen people, on the other: the relationship of the people who have receiv-

497

ed the Torah and has the mission of transmitting it, and the world, which must incorporate it, and benefit from it, is at the center of the Jewish dialectic. In Marxism, the dialog places the universal, humanity in confrontation not with a chosen people but with the working class, the proletariat, the vanguard of the people. It is true that in both cases, for both doctrines, there is a vanguard that makes the world progress, marching at the head of the others. But the nature of this vanguard is different. In Judaism, the vanguard, the Jewish people is not only functional, it has a reality by itself. In Marxism, the vanguard is a "chosen class", which means that it has a functional justification only as long as history is the history of classes.

The difference resides also in the way and the means which the vanguard can use. Marxism admits the possibility that the dialectic might be destructive, or, in other words, that the vanguard might be led to destroy, demolish, ruin, lay waste. In the final analysis the Marxist movement gives the proletariat the right to be radically destructive: the end justifies the means. The revolution may be radical, bloody, and cause the death of a large number of people; the dictatorship of the proletariat may be a dreadful period, while one creates the "tomorrow" or, one might say that in Marxism creation does not, in an a priori sense, condemn destruction.

The Jewish dialectic does not admit that the *tikkun* of the world, the dialectic between the chosen people and humanity, may pass through destruction, because it is not mankind who created the world, but rather God. God has the right to destroy, and He does destroy in fact (in the Torah he destroys Sodom and Gomorra and drowns Pharaoh's army). Humankind however, does not have the right to destroy. It may only repair. Here the concept of *ge'ula* (redemption) enters Judaism, the final liberation, the end of time. Certainly *ge'ula* is presented as a time which can bring destruction, but only God is capable of bringing on destruction and redemption. Humanity in the Jewish tradition, must pave the way. They are asked to live their lives, in the sphere of the relative, acknowledging

their lack of ultimate sovereignty over the outer limits of existence.

In summary, the similarity and the contrast focus on man and his role in the world. Both share an anthropocentric view of the world, and that human activism which derives from it in realizing the messianic future. Yet therein lie the fundamental differences: Jewish thought is in essence transcendental, centered as it is on the Covenant between man and God, leading to the perpetual need for humility and divine aspiration at one and the same time. Marxist ideology, on the other hand, categorically exorcises the "Kingdom of Heaven" both from its ultimate humility and its process of revolutionary dynamics, whence the revolutionary radicalism which is incorporated into a system of totally human responsibility and freedom.

These philosophical points do not, of course, fully encompass all of the fundamentals and their ramifications, be it of the Jewish world or the Marxist ideology. Marxism, in its broader sense, includes economic criticism, political theory, an egalitarian vision of social justice and human liberty, a revolutionary dogma, revolutionary movements, and even Communist societies and states. The Jewish entity and experience are based upon dual definition of religion and nationality, and cover, therefore, the *halakhah*, philosophy, a comprehensive system of social law and communal behavior, national memories, and aspirations of kingdom and prophecy – all these fused together over an extraordinarily long and unique history.

Breadth of scope and totality of experience notwithstanding, both have as their cornerstones a profoundly professed faith and a firm commitment to ideological principles. This being the case, the issues of *Weltanschauung* (even in their most general form) are central to all aspects of both these phenomena.

FURTHER READING

Bergman, S. H.: *Faith and Reason* (New York, 1963)

Guttmann, J.: *Philosophies of Judaism* (London: Routledge & Kegan Paul, 1964)

Maurer, C. B.: *Call to Revolution* (Detroit: Wayne State University Press, 1971)

Scholem, G.: *Messianic Ideas in Judaism & Other Essays*

on Jewish Spirituality (New York: Schocken Books, 1971)

Schaeder, G.: *The Hebrew Humanism of Martin Buber* (Detroit: 1973)

Urbach, E. E.: *The Sages, their Concepts and Beliefs* (Jerusalem: Magnes Press, 1982)

ELLA BELFER AND ILAN GREILSAMMER

Matsa, Joseph (1919–1986) Greek literary scholar, Hebrew teacher, local historian, and folklorist. Matsa was born in Ioannina, Greece, educated at the ALLIANCE ISRAÉLITE UNIVERSELLE and the Greek Zosimaia High School in Ioannina. He continued his studies at the University of Thessaloniki where he majored in literature and philosophy. After receiving his BA degree, he accepted an appointment to teach Greek literature in a High School in Ioannina. He also continued to teach Hebrew and religion to the children of pre-school age in the Jewish community.

When the Germans occupied Greece in 1941, Joseph Matsa joined EPON (Panhellenic Organization of Youth), a national resistance union, and fought with the rebel forces of ELAS (National People's Liberation Army) stationed in Vermio, where he served in the cultural unit until the liberation. In 1945 Matsa returned to Ioannina and devoted his time to solving the problems of his decimated community. As General Secretary of the Jewish Council of Ioannina, he helped to rehabilitate the Jewish survivors of that city, and continued teaching the Talmud to the community.

Joseph Matsa returned briefly to his schoolteaching until 1946/7, when he took over the family business, a glass store.

Matsa wrote two small books: *Yianniotika Evraika Tragoudia* (1953; The Hebrew songs of the Jannina Jews), and *Ta Onomata ton Evraion Sta Jannina* (1955; The names of the Jews of Ioannina). *Yianniotika Evraika Tragoudia* contains 16 hymns, 13 of them previously unpublished, which Matsa discovered in two unpublished manuscripts dated 1853 and 1870. They are written in Hebrew characters in the Judeo-Greek dialect of that epoch spoken by the Jews of Ioannina. Because the vocalization was missing in the 1853 manuscript, Matsa took care to supply the accents according to the meter and the pronunciation of the Ioannina idiom. He transliterated these original hymns, then translated them into Greek for Greek readers. The melodies of all these hymns have been influenced by the rhythm of the vernacular songs of the province of Epirus.

Matsa compiled *Ta Onomata ton Evraion Sta Ioannina* from registrations relating to births, marriage contracts, the book of the dead, and from tradition. The male given names and their diminutives are purely Hebrew. Feminine given names are taken from a variety of sources, for example Hebrew (Esther), Greek (Eftychia), Italian (Gratsia), and Spanish (Delicia). As for surnames, the Jews of Ioannina had no surnames other than Cohen and Levy identified with their Hebrew tradition. Matsa lists surnames originating in other lands, surnames of Greek and Hebrew origin; surnames derived from nicknames, occupations, physical characteristics and character traits.

Joseph Matsa participated widely in folklorist and other philological conferences. He became a founder of the *Society for Epeirotic Studies*, and he wrote articles in *Chronika, Epeirotiki Estia, Epeirotikes Selides*, and the Hebrew *Sefunot* published in Israel. He wrote studies of Greco-Jewish culture, and Judeo-Greek poetry, and he investigated the literary achievements of the Jews in his native Iaonnina.

FURTHER READING

Dalven, R.: The names of the Jannina Jews. *Sephardic Scholar*, Series 3 (1977–8)

——: *The Jews of Ioannina* (New York: Cadmus Press, 1988)

RACHEL DALVEN

Matsas, Nestoras (b.1932) Greek author, painter and film director. He was born in Athens. After the deportation to Auschwitz in 1943 of his father, a rabbi, Matsas was hidden in the home of a Greek Orthodox family and shortly afterwards was baptized into the Greek Orthodox Church. His Jewish background and the sufferings of the Occupation have, however, found expression in several of his books, sometimes as a revelation. In 1950 he published three plays; among them *Fleghomeni batos* (Burning bush), and *Yiom Kipur*. His first novel, *Klisti ourani* (1955; Closed heavens), is set in the Athens slums which Matsas portrays as the source of social evil. He also published several volumes of short stories: *I meghali irini* (1957; The great peace), is dedicated to the memory of his father "who sleeps in the barren earth of Auschwitz". It consists of three short novels about three Jewish families in Athens and their problems before the deportation and after the liberation. *O Messias* (1959; The Messiah) describes the tragic fate of a Greek Jew who survives imprisonment in Dachau, but who, on his return to Greece, entertains the delusion that he is the Messiah. Later works include a novel on the life of a Greek artist, verse, stories, and an anti-war novel, *O mikros stratiotis* (1967; The little soldier).

Matsas has been active in bringing about closer relations between Israel and Greece. He has written scripts for documentary films and directed feature films. He is one of the best-known Greek writers of post-war years.

RACHEL DALVEN

Mauss, Marcel (1872–1950) French ethnologist. Brought up in Orthodox Judaism in Alsace, and a nephew of Émile DURKHEIM, who influenced his career, Marcel Mauss is one of the most notable examples of those figures in the intellectual Jewish society of Paris who contributed to the development of the social sciences in France. Following Durkheim's example, he elected to study philosophy. He was doubly representative of the intellectual Jewish middle classes, in that he devoted himself to the study of religious subjects within relatively marginal institutions (the École Pratique des Hautes Études and then the Collège de France), more by his own choice of disciplines than for any reason of exclusion. He studied the history of religion in the department of historical and philological sciences and in the department of religious sciences. From 1895 to 1898 he trained himself in philology, undertaking in turn the

study of Sanskrit, Pal, Hebrew, Zend, and the Christian liturgy. An active Dreyfus supporter, like the majority of the *Année Sociologique* team, he was also an active socialist all his life.

Like many Jewish intellectuals, he made rapid headway in a discipline he had helped to create. As professor of the history of the religions of non-civilized peoples, a post he held until the end of his career, he taught the history of religions and the philosophy of pre-Buddhist India until 1902. In 1925 he founded the Ethnological Institute of the University of Paris, where he lectured until 1939, and he also taught at the Collège de France from 1930 to 1939.

His familiarity with the Hebraic tradition, from which he had parted company on the religious plane at the age of 18, predisposed him to take an objective interest in religious subjects, although his thesis on Leone Ebreo, Spinoza, and prayer was never completed. This inclination to religious studies showed both in a Durkheimian perspective and a specifically Jewish approach. Indeed, the work of Mauss is inseparable from that of Durkheim, with whom he published "De quelques formes primitives de classification" in 1903, and from that of the contributors to the *Année Sociologique*.

Demonstrating the fragility of philosophical concepts of religion, Mauss saw it as arising from the very nature of society. The substitution of the term "rite" for that of "religion" also calls for an enlargement of the semantic range of the concept, defined henceforth less as a collection of factors with a specific function than as the social sphere par excellence. This transition from the science of religions to ethnology underlies all Mauss's pre-war work.

At the same time as the theory of religions was losing its central position in the post-war ethnological debate, Mauss, who had become head of the École since Durkheim's death in 1917, turned to the study of the conditions of sociability and general sociology. His masterpiece, the *Essai sur le Don* (1925), the first systematic and comparative study of exchange and the first to develop the relationship between forms of exchange and the social structure, sets out the idea of the "total social factor", of "potlach" and of "mana" which were to influence subsequent ethnographical works. His own later works extended these concepts, with the publication of *L'Effet physique chez l'individu de l'idée de mort suggérée par la collectivité* (1926) and other works. Mauss also published general sociological articles of a methodological character.

The incontestable influence of Mauss on modern ethnology is hard to define precisely. He himself never attempted to develop any systematic theory (and no book by him was published in his lifetime), but he was always multiplying original approaches and indicating directions for research. In this respect, Mauss figures more as a precursor than as the leader of a school of thought.

PERRINE SIMON-NAHUM

Maybaum, Ignaz (1897–1976) Theologian. Born in "Freud's Vienna" (as he termed it in a memorable description of the city in his book *Creation and Guilt*), Maybaum served as rabbi successively in Bingen on the Rhine, Frankfurt on the Oder, and Berlin, and in the last years before the outbreak of the Second World War and the annihilation of German Jewry, he was active in giving spiritual guidance and moral support to the doomed Berlin community. In 1939 he settled in London, where eventually he became minister of the Edgware Reform Synagogue. He was among the group of survivors of the Berlin *Hochschule* who in 1956 founded Leo Baeck College, the Reform rabbinic seminary in London, where he taught theology.

Maybaum came to see himself as the disciple and mouthpiece of Franz ROSENZWEIG, interpreting his thought for a post-war, English-speaking generation. However the Nazi Holocaust stands at the center of Maybaum's experience and thinking, masking the relationship with Rosenzweig, and giving a particular direction to his work. Maybaum's theological reflections on the Holocaust are presented most directly in his book *The Face of God After Auschwitz* (1965), but the topic is ever-present in his other works, such as *Creation and Guilt* (1969, subtitled "a theological assessment of Freud's father–son conflict", but really a study of the Christian roots of anti-Semitism), or *The Sacrifice of Isaac* (1959), a powerful pamphlet. Particularly vivid is the phrase "Hitler my servant": the destruction is interpreted as a deliberate act of God, sweeping away the past and clearing the way for necessary progress. Maybaum's confidence in the traditional understanding of God as the author of history led him to moderate his anti-Zionist position somewhat after the establishment of Israel. However, he always emphasized the Jewish mission to be a light to the nations, and he was a staunch proponent of dialog and cooperation between Jews and Christians, extended in his later work to "trialog" involving the Muslims as well.

FURTHER READING

de Lange, N.: Ignaz Maybaum and his attitude to Zionism. In *Tradition, Transition and Transmission*, ed. B. D. Fox (Cincinnati: 1983)

NICHOLAS DE LANGE

Mayer, Carl(chen) (1894–1944) German screenwriter. Mayer was the greatest screenwriter of the German cinema. Among his associates were Erich Pommer, Friedrich Murnau, Lupu Pick, Erich Freund, Walter Ruttman, Berthold Viertel, and Karl Grune. He wrote exclusively for the cinema and was responsible for *Das Kabinett des Dr Caligari* (1919), *Genuine* (1920), *Scherben* (1921), *Erdgeist* (1923), *Der letze Mann* (1924), and *Sunrise* (1927). He visualized his screenplays as expressions of the camera. In *Caligari* he created a madman's outlook of the world, and designed *Der letze Mann* to incorporate the moving camera and convey, first, the strength of the central figure (Emil Jannings), and then to reveal his humiliation when he loses his job as a senior hotel porter. His scripts are models of structure and continuity.

His success did not, as it did for many others, take him to Hollywood. When he wrote his only Hollywood film, *Sunrise*, he composed it from Europe. His career declined when sound was introduced in 1928 and he took only one screen credit after he came to England in 1932, on a virtually unseen documentary for Paul Rotha, *The Times* (1939). However, he advised on *Pygmalion* (1938) and *Major Barbara* (1941), and

Filippo del Guidice used him as a scenario supervizer at one of the major production companies of the late 1930s and 1940s, Two Cities, where he guided many young writers. The films of Erich von Stroheim, Charles Chaplin, and G. W. Pabst, owe something to his influence.

FURTHER READING

Daugherty, F.: The screen's greatest poet. *Films in Review* (Mar. 1953)

Kracauer, S.: *From Caligari to Hitler* (Princeton: Princeton University Press, 1947)

Rotha, P.: It's in the script. *World Film News* (Sept. 1938)

KEVIN GOUGH-YATES

Mayer, Sigmund (1831–1920) Austrian merchant, politician, and writer. Born in Pressburg, Hungary, Mayer was educated at the *Schottengymnasium* in Vienna, and studied law at Vienna and Prague, before becoming a merchant. In 1880 he became a city councillor, and from 1894 was active in efforts to defend Jewish interests in Austria.

A prominent figure in Viennese liberal politics, Mayer provided two of the most important sources for understanding the history of the Viennese Jews in the late nineteenth century: his autobiography *Ein jüdischer Kaufmann, 1831–1911* (1911; A Jewish merchant) and the history *Die Wiener Juden: Kommerz, Kultur, Politik 1700–1900* (1918; The Viennese Jews: commerce, culture, and politics). These books give a liberal Jew's (sympathetic) view of traditional Jewish life, describe the success of assimilation, but also the gathering gloom from the 1880s. Mayer was deeply disillusioned by the spread of racial anti-Semitism, was scathing about the Christian Socialists, and stressed in his book the general social isolation of Jews which anti-Semitism caused. Mayer attacked Sombart's view that Judaism was a capitalist religion, and saw the moral life of Jews as superior to that of the surrounding Christian populace. On the other hand Mayer disliked the idea of Jewish nationalism and saw *Ostjuden*, especially the Hasidim, as a reactionary element. His hope for the future was that Jews would, as the opponents of nationalism, become the "earliest

citizens of the coming world". As such Mayer was a typical representative of the Jewish liberal bourgeoisie.

STEVEN BELLER

Mazar, Benjamin (b.1906) Israeli scholar, archaeologist, and historian of the biblical period. Mazar was born in Ciechanowiec, Russia, and after graduating from the *Gymnasium* in the Crimea and Berlin, studying at the universities of Berlin and Giessen, and receiving his doctorate in 1928, he emigrated to Palestine in 1929. In 1931 he participated in his first archaeological excavations at Ramat Rahel, and soon after continued to participate in, and later directed, various archaeological excavations, including Bet She'arim (Galilee), Tell Qasile, En-Gedi (the Dead Sea), and the south and west of the Temple Mount in Jerusalem. In 1943 he began teaching at the Hebrew University of Jerusalem. In 1951 he was appointed Professor of Archaeology and Biblical History, in 1952 a rector, and in 1953 the president, a post he held for eight years, retiring in 1961 for health reasons.

Mazar's main contribution to modern scholarship is in the field of the archaeology and historical geography of the people of Israel in the biblical period. In 1930 his dissertation, *Untersuchungen zur alten Geschichte und Ethnographie Syriens und Palästinas* was published, and since then he has published more than 400 works in Hebrew, English, German, and French. His book *Canaan and Israel* (1980), first published in Hebrew, which is a collection of articles on the history of the biblical period and the archaeology of Israel, became a fundamental text for every scholar and reader in this field of inquiry. He also published excavation reports such as *Bet She'arim* (1973) and the graphic historical atlas *Israel in Biblical Times* (1941).

A scholar of great modesty and concern for others, Mazar has been involved in many other academic activities, such as editing a large number of works, and has inspired and encouraged an entire generation of younger scholars. For his various academic activities and his contribution to a better understanding of Israel and its culture in the early biblical period he has been honored by several universities and institutions in Israel and the USA. He is Hon. President of the Israeli Exploration Society and a member of the Israel Academy of Science and Humanities. He has been awarded a great number of prizes, including the Israel prize in 1968.

DEBORAH SCHECHTERMAN

medicine, Jews in   Jews have always been prominent in medicine wherever they have lived. In the past it was not considered ethical for Jews to teach the word of God for gain, and medicine was a popular alternative to trade as a means for the rabbi to earn his bread. Yet, although individual physicians were often protected by princes and popes, Jews were generally subject to restrictions on the academic study of medicine and sometimes even on its practice, and these hindrances were only gradually removed, as part of the general process of emancipation.

Up to relatively recent times, however, scholarly medicine, as practiced by Jews, Christians, and Muslims alike, was essentially a clinical discipline, based on ancient Greek concepts, which remained untouched by religious dogma over the centuries. It could be pursued and even mastered, if necessary, without any institutional backing. Yet, as judged by their writings, Jews seem to have played little part in the progress of medicine before the end of the nineteenth century. They were renowned mainly for the care of their patients. As late as the eighteenth century the enlightened Jewish physician of the period is epitomized by Marcus Herz (1747–1803), well-known as a clinician in his time but now remembered chiefly for his influence on the philosophy of Kant.

Yet the eighteenth century marked the end of the "Hippocratic" era and the beginning of the modern period, when medicine gradually abandoned the study of symptoms and their palliative treatment, and began to focus on the diagnosis and specific cure of "diseases". Hence medical progress came to depend less on the individual physician and his patient and more on the institutional aspect of disease, as encoun-tered in the hospital ward and in the laboratory above all.

The professional emancipation of the Jews coincided, in point of time, with an institutional revolution throughout the West: an enormous expansion of medical and scientific facilities of all kinds, public and private. Jews, like Christian "dissenters", avidly took up the newly available posts, which were at first largely ignored by members of the established religions, who preferred the traditional careers. This released a flood of medical and scientific talent, and from that time Jews came to play such a vital part in medical research that some 20 percent of those who have received the Nobel Prize in medicine and physiology up to the 1980s were Jews or of Jewish descent. In fact the space allotted here to this question is insufficient even to list – let alone describe – the main Jewish contributions in this field, so that this review must be confined to a tiny selection of some entirely new aspects of medicine which Jews have helped to pioneer.

In clinical medicine Jews at first tended to engage in the less popular – and often less remunerative – fields, such as dermatology and psychiatry. Sigmund FREUD and his pupils devised methods of psychoanalysis by which they tried to explain the workings of the mind, healthy as well as sick. While their findings are not accepted by all, it is apparent that the greatest triumphs of clinical medicine in our era have so far depended on the study of the normal processes of the body. Advances in the basic medical sciences, in which biochemists and biologists of all kinds, rather than physicians, are now being ever more involved, have led to new methods of conquering disease.

Thus in 1930 K. Landsteiner (1868–1943) was awarded the Nobel Prize for his discovery of the human blood groups. This resulted in safe blood transfusion and thus saved innumerable lives, as did a number of fundamental contributions by Jews in the field of nutrition, such as the discovery of vitamins by C. Funk (1884–1967), or the studies of the normal metabolism of the body for which H. A. Krebs (1900–81) received the Nobel Prize in 1953.

Judaism has always manifested a strong messianic element, which in recent times seems often to have become sublimated into secular visions of imminent Utopia, here on this earth. While Marx and Trotsky preached socio-economic redemption, Jewish physicians and scientists sought to better the human condition by medical means. The end of the nineteenth century was marked by one of the greatest revolutions in medicine: the discovery that specific microorganisms were responsible for so many of the great scourges of mankind. Paul Ehrlich (1854–1915) openly aspired to conquer communicable disease by means of "magic bullets": specific chemical missiles targeted on the microorganisms concerned. His dream was largely to be realized after his death by the discovery of drugs such as the antibiotics. E. B. Chain (1906–79) received the Nobel Prize in 1945 for his part in the development of penicillin, and in 1952 it was awarded to S. A. Waksman (1888–1973) for the discovery of streptomycin, which helped to conquer tuberculosis.

Ehrlich also helped to develop specific antisera, to assist the natural defenses of the body to overcome specific organisms. W. M. W. Haffkine (1866–1930) similarly devised vaccines against cholera and plague, and more recently J. E. Salk (b.1914) and A. B. Sabin (b.1906) have done the same for poliomyelitis. In 1958 J. Lederberg (b.1925) received the Nobel Prize for his work on bacterial genetics, which paved the way for further advances in genetic engineering, including the synthesis of vaccines, as well as of life-saving hormones and drugs. It has also contributed to the extraordinary progress now being made in other fields of molecular biology, including cancer and other genetically determined conditions: not least by the Medical Research Council's Laboratory of Molecular Biology in Cambridge, UK, headed by Sir Sidney Brenner (b.1927).

It seemed somewhat ironical at the time that Ehrlich shared the Nobel Prize in 1908 with Elie Metchnikoff (1845–1916) who, having detected the presence in the body of certain *non*-specific cellular defenses aimed at bacterial pathogens in general, opposed Ehrlich's idea of specificity. The implications of Metchnikoff's findings were largely ignored for many years, in favor of Ehrlich's approach, and only of late has

it been shown that both views must be taken into account. In 1957 A. Isaacs (1921–67) first demonstrated the existence of natural intracellular defenses against viruses, known today as the interferon system. This has now been found to act in a non-specific manner against viral invasions of all kinds, both the acute infections and those great plagues of our own time: the long-term and possibly opportunistic infections such as AIDS, and many neoplastic conditions.

Jews were also largely responsible for the fact that in the 1930s the center of gravity of medical progress shifted from Europe to the USA. In 1910 A. Flexner (1866–1959) issued a report criticizing the quality of medical education in North America. He himself helped to initiate the subsequent reforms. Standards then rose still higher with the arrival in America of large numbers of Jewish physicians and scientists from Europe, fleeing from Nazi oppression.

Yet no essentially Jewish element can be discerned in any of these outstanding achievements by Jews, and the advances in medicine are becoming ever more international in scope. On a much smaller scale, however, Jewish physicians, mainly from Russia, established their Jewish identity around the turn of the century on emigrating to Palestine. There, stimulated by the Czarist *zemstvo* system of rural medical care which they had left behind, they played a vital – and practically undocumented – role in the creation of the future State of Israel. Without their care Jewish settlement on the land, by means of which the State was largely established, would have been defeated by the onslaught of malaria, trachoma, and other endemic diseases.

This service, moreover, formed the basis of a contributory system of medical care by salaried staff, the Workers' Sick Fund of the General Federation of Labor, which, founded in 1912, was the most comprehensive in the world until the establishment of the British National Health Service in 1948. It played an essential part in the absorption of large numbers of sick and disabled immigrants in the early years of the State.

However, even such a triumph of the spirit under harsh pioneering conditions pales before the conduct of a number of Jewish physicians under Nazi rule. One outstanding example was that of Dr Elchanan Elkes, a leading internist in Kovno, who, in the true tradition of the caring physician of the Jewish past, went to his death in Dachau in 1944, rather than abandon his community.

FURTHER READING

Ackerknecht, E. H.: German Jews, English dissenters, French Protestants: nineteenth-century pioneers of modern medicine and science. In *Healing and History*, ed. C. E. Rosenberg (Folkestone: Dawson, 1979) 86–96

Sourkes, T. L. *Nobel Prize Winners in Medicine and Physiology, 1901–65* (London: Life of Science Library, 1967) [Sourkes's revision of L. G. Stevenson's *Nobel Prize Winners in Medicine and Physiology, 1901–1950*]

ELINOR LIEBER

Megged, Aharon (b.1920) Israeli novelist, playwright, and journalist. Born in Poland, Megged came to Palestine in 1926. The nine years he lived with his family in the farming settlement of Raanana loom large in his later work, overshadowing his ostensibly formative years as a kibbutz member of Sedot Yam from 1939 to 1950. His early stories, in the collections *Ruah yamim* (1950; Sea spirit) and *Yisrael haverim* (1955; Israel friends) indeed depict the kibbutz environment, but Megged's renegade and misfit heroes prefigure his disenchantment. The satirical novel, *Hedvah va'ani* (1954; and as a play, 1964; Hedvah and I), chronicles the transition of a kibbutz yokel to city life. This and the immensely popular play *I Like Mike* (1956) treat ideological trends of great moment with the characteristically light touch which occasionally disguises Megged's distinctive seriousness as a writer.

Equally inaccurate is the stock assessment of Megged as a "Palmach" or "generation of 1948" author. Megged's first major work, the surrealistic novel, *Mikreh hakesil* (1960; *Fortunes of a Fool*, 1962), was followed by the three novellas in *Haberihah* (1962; The flight) and the novel *Hahai 'al hamet* (1965; *Living on the Dead*, 1970). These books adumbrate the ethical–

psychological drama in much of Megged's fiction. Problems of identity, emotional strength, and individual responsibility in a collectivist society and "ideocracy", such as Israel, pervade his work. So, too, does another recurrent theme, the gap between reality and literary or ideological stereotypes. Megged has produced intriguing variations on these ideas in novels including *Hahayyim haketzarim* (1972; *The Short Life*, 1980), *Asahel* (1978; *Asahel*, 1982) and in his most recent book, *Ma'aseh meguneh* (1986; An indecent incident).

Four other recent books by Megged differ from the above. *Masa' be'av* (1984; A father's journey in the month of Av) is a stream-of-consciousness account of a father's bereavement; *Hagamal hame'ofef vedabeshet hazahav* (1982; *The Flying Camel and the Golden Hump*, 1986) is a spoof on writers and their critics; *Masa' hayeladim el ha'aretz hamuvtahat* (1984; The voyage of the children to the promised land) is inspired reportage about the lot of young Holocaust survivors; and *Ezor hara'ash* (The turbulent zone) is a sampling of Megged's work as a columnist. In the latter category of journalistic and critical writing (largely in *Lamerhav and Davar*), Megged has written well over 1,000 articles. He was also cultural attaché in London from 1969 to 1971.

Megged's short story, *Yad vashem* (1956; *The Name*, 1962), has been widely anthologized in English, and represents part of Megged's abiding concern for the residual influences of the Holocaust, also evident in his play, *Hannah Senesh* (1952, 1958), and in his recent story, "Bikur hageveret Hilda Hoffer" in *Ma'aseh meguneh*.

FURTHER READING

Abramson, G.: *Modern Hebrew Drama* (London: Weidenfeld and Nicolson, 1979)

Fuchs, E.: *Encounters with Israeli Authors* (Marblehead: Micah Publications, 1982)

Nash, S.: Reflections on Israeli literature based on recurrences of the *"Akedah"* Theme. *Edebiyat*, 2 (1977) 29–40

STANLEY NASH

Mehutan, Hava (b.1925) Israeli sculptress. Born in Philadelphia, she studied at the

Pennsylvania Academy of Fine Arts, and since 1946 she has lived in Israel. Her early sculptures were created out of wood, retaining the natural shape and feel of the tree-trunk, and worked in a linear fashion, modeling simplified human figures, often on the theme of "mother and child". In 1959 an exhibition of her work was held at the Tel Aviv Museum. During the 1960s her work was permeated with the themes of sacrifice as a tribal activity, motherhood, and death.

Mehutan's more recent work indicates a shift towards the abstract, and great internalization of the desert landscape surrounding her home town, Beersheba. Her *Har Sdom Event* (1984) was an open-air environmental work in which 47 shallow rectangles were dug out, in a grid of 7 rows, the earth of each of the rectangles (900 × 600 mm and about 200 mm deep) placed into a sandbag, which in turn was placed parallel, alongside its square thus creating another grid of sandbags. At the end of the symposium the earth was returned to its original square. The location was near the Dead Sea, and the work had overt burial and ritualistic significance. In similar works she uses tree-trunks, only slightly shaped, and, placing them in an open landscape, she creates a visual association of dead or mutilated bodies, as well as funerary rituals.

FURTHER READING
Tal, M.: Three women artists. *Ariel* 21 (1967–8)

NEDIRA YAKIR BUNYARD

Meijer, Jacob [Jaap] (b.1912) Dutch–Jewish historian, author, and poet. Meijer was born in Winschoten, in the north-eastern province of Groningen, to a traditional provincial Jewish family. His father, a poor merchant, died when Jacob was 10 years old. As an unusually bright and promising Jewish boy Meijer was enabled, by a grant from a Jewish foundation, to study at the Ashkenazi Rabbinical Seminary in Amsterdam. Thereafter he studied history at the University of Amsterdam, at the same time continuing his studies at the Seminary. His membership of the Mizrahi Youth organization and later, of the Zionist Students Organization in Amsterdam, influenced him greatly. In 1938 he broke off his rabbinical studies. In 1940 he married Liesje Voet, the daughter of a prominent, socialist, non-religious Jewish family and he took his Ph.D. degree a year later, one of the last Jewish students able to do so under the German occupation. From 1941 to 1943 he was a history teacher at the Jewish Lyceum in Amsterdam which had been established for Jewish pupils and teachers who were no longer allowed to attend general schools. In 1943 he, his wife, and baby son, were taken to Westerbork, and from there, in February, 1944, to Bergen-Belsen, which they survived, unlike most of his friends.

After the war, Meijer taught history in Amsterdam and in Paramaribo, Surinam, returning to teach in Haarlem until his retirement.

Having written many articles, mainly in the Dutch Zionist Youth monthly *Tikwath Jisraeel* before 1940, his main publishing activity began after 1945, concentrating chiefly on the pre-war history of the Jews of the Netherlands. The list of his publications, both articles and books, published in *Neveh Yaakov*, which appeared on the occasion of his seventieth birthday in 1982, and dealing only with publications on Jewish subjects in prose, contains more than 260 items. His vast literary activity spans many topics: Netherlands–Jewish social and political history; a contribution to the earliest history in English of the Jewish colonization of America (*Pioneers of Pauroma*, 1954); Jewish life in Amsterdam; literary biography; a series of Cahiers (1971–81) on primarily nineteenth-century Dutch–Jewish literary figures, and on the historiography of the Jews of the Netherlands (1981).

Since 1967, under the pen-name of Saul van Messel, Meijer has published many small volumes of poetry, several in limited and often bibliophile editions, in Dutch and in the Groningen dialect of his childhood. These deal with the memories of what was irrevocably destroyed during the Second World War.

HENRIETTE BOAS

Melnikoff, Avraham (1892–1960) Israeli sculptor. Born in Russia, from 1917 to 1918 Melnikoff studied sculpture in Chicago and in 1918 he emigrated to Palestine. In 1926 he moved to Metula, at that time one of the northernmost points of Israel, and in 1928 he was commissioned to erect a monument to Joseph Trumpeldor and his comrades who were killed there.

Melnikoff was the pioneer of modern Israeli sculpture, and his monument in Tel Hai, the first modern public monument in the country, is his most famous work. Formally and thematically it drew from ancient archeological prototypes of the region. The choice of rough stone, not pliable for intricate details, left the form of the roaring lion on a high plinth, a simple monolith, in the simple shape of a tapering cone, the details of the mane and head only outlined on the surface. The contained and static composition is related to Mesopotamian sculpture, even though the emotional content is more recent and European in its symbolism. The monument has become the earliest visual symbol of suffering and defiance in Israeli society.

Melnikoff's later work, like the portrait of Zeev Ben Zvi of the 1930s, indicates a stylistic shift towards Cubism.

NEDIRA YAKIR BUNYARD

Memmi, Albert (b.1920) Tunisian-born French author, essayist, and sociologist whose family claimed Berber ancestry. Memmi fought with the Free French Forces during the Second World War, and after Liberation returned to North Africa to pursue his university education. Awarded his degree in philosophy from the University of Algiers, Memmi continued his doctoral research at the University of Paris where, in 1950, he was awarded a Ph.D. Memmi opted to remain in France and since 1966 has been professor of sociology at the École Pratique des Hautes Études in Paris.

Memmi's primary field of interest is the social and psychological effects of colonization. Through his research into this question, he uncovered similar attitudes and reflections upon identity between Jews and other colonized peoples. As such, Memmi was an ardent supporter of the liberation of the countries of the Maghreb though he also knew one of the bitter consequences would be an exodus of North African Jewry. Such an eventuality

strengthened Memmi's belief in the necessity of a Jewish state: "Israel is our only solution, our one trump card, our last historical opportunity".

Memmi's writings, be they his fiction or his essays, are primarily concerned with the author's search for authentic identity. Many of his early novels are cast in the brilliant sun of North Africa, and obviously owe a certain debt to Camus. His first novel, *La Statue de Sel* (1953; *Pillar of Salt*, 1955), is highly autobiographical and traces the story of a young North African Jew who emerges from the narrowness of Jewish society into the culture of the French colonialists, only to have his fundamental human and religious beliefs shattered by the conflict between these two civilizations. A similar battle for identity underlies Memmi's 1955 novel *Agar* (*Strangers*, 1958), although the conflict is more painful as the isolated Tunisian Jew is rejected by the French and the Arab. The Jew (who apparently has no role to exercise in world events) is cast as a shadowy figure on the fringes of universal human history. The bitterness and anguish which characterize these early novels is missing in later works such as *Le Scorpion* (1969) and *Le Désert* (1977). Although the titles themselves project the negative aspects of seeking one's true identity, the novels are filled with the warmth of folk-tale and simple wisdom, and appear to present a convincing image of the Jew and the society in which he found himself at the end of the French protectorate.

Memmi's search for identity has also been highlighted in his lengthy works of non-fiction. In *Portrait d'un Juif* (1962; *Portrait of a Jew*, 1963), and *La Libération du juif* (1966; *The Liberation of the Jew*, 1966), Memmi has meticulously delineated the path which the Jew in Diaspora communities has chosen to pursue. Highly autobiographical, the essays nevertheless have a remarkable sense of clarity and universal application.

SIMON SIBELMAN

Mendele Mokher Sefarim [Mendele Moykher-Sforim; Sholem-Yankev Abramovitsh] (1836–1917) Hebrew and Yiddish novelist, short-story writer, playwright, critic, and popu-

Mendele Mokher Sefarim (center) on a visit to the Jarosinski trade school in Lodz, 1909

larizer. Mendele's career can be seen as a Hegelian triptych. The first phase follows the fairly typical pattern of the Hebrew *Haskalah*: born and raised in the Lithuanian *shtetl* of Kapulie (described in *Shloyme reb Khayims/Bayamim hahem* (1899; *Of Bygone Days*, 1973), Mendele was orphaned at a young age, spent a few trying years in the Slutsk *yeshivah*, then headed south with a professional beggar. He ended up in Kamenets-Podolski where A. B. Gottlober (1810–99) introduced him to *Haskalah* literature, oversaw his secular studies, and published his first Hebrew article.

Remarried and settled in Berdichev, the commercial hub of the Ukraine, Mendele launched his literary career in earnest by trying to breathe new life into Hebrew literary criticism with *Mishpat shalom* (1860; The judgment of peace) and *Ein mishpat* (1866; The fount of judgment); by translating and adapting a comprehensive textbook of zoology, *Toledot hateva'* (1862–72; Natural history, 3 vols); and by writing a "realistic" Hebrew novel, *Limdu hetev* (1862; Learn to do good; rev. as *Ha'avot vehabanim*, 1868).

Then, moved by the prospect of effecting real change in Jewish society by exposing its manifold follies, Mendele turned to writing in Yiddish. He launched a new career under the guise of Mendele, the peripatetic bookpeddler who hawked his traditional wares through a fictional geography of satirically named towns. Mendele began with openly didactic works that had at their core a confessional autobiography, be it that of Avrom-Yitskhok the Power Broker in *Dos kleyne mentshele*, (1864, 1879; *The Parasite*, 1956), of Hershele from Beggarsburgh in *Dos vintshfinger* (1865; The wishing ring [*Be'emek habakhah*] 1907–9) or of Fishke in *Fishke der krumer* (1869; *Fishke the Lame* 1960).

In 1869 Mendele moved to Zhitomir where he continued to publish occasional essays in Hebrew. It was in Yiddish, however, that he produced two of his artistically most accomplished and ideologically most radical works: his complex allegory on the universal exploitation of Russian Jews, *Di klyatshe* (1873; *The Mare*, 1976), and his mock-epic *Masoes Benyomin hashlishi* (1878; [*Mas'ot Binyamin hashelishi*, 1896] *The Travels of Benjamin III*, 1979), which parodied Jewish immobility against the backdrop of European expansionism.

The third, synthetic phase of Mendele's career was preceded by a personal crisis (the death of his daughter and the exile and subsequent conversion to Christianity of his son) and by the first cycle of pogroms in Russia (1881–2). When Mendele finally broke his silence, he did so from his new and secure vantage point as the head of the Talmud Torah in Odessa. He also achieved two syntheses in one: he created a modern Hebrew prose style drawn from all historical strata of the language, including Aramaic and Yiddish, which he perfected in a series of allegorical short stories dominated by the Mendele persona. In Yiddish he greatly expanded his earlier novels to produce what many consider his finest work: the revised version of *Fishke der krumer* (1888) and the preface to *The Wishing Ring* (1888). Furthermore, from 1905 until his death, Mendele was engaged in revising and translating his entire bilingual corpus, producing two completely distinct canons that shaped the future course of modern Hebrew and Yiddish prose.

Volumes of Mendele's writing in English include: "Of bygone days", in *A Shtetl and other Yiddish Novellas* (1973, 1986), ed. Ruth R. Wisse; "Shem and Japheth on the train", trans. Walter Lever in *Modern Hebrew Literature* (1975), ed. Robert Alter; "The Mare", in *Yenne Velt: the Great Works of Jewish Fantasy and Occult* (1976, 1978) and "The Travels of Benjamin the Third", in *The Shtetl: a Creative Anthology of Jewish Life in Eastern Europe* (1979), the last two trans. Joachim Neugroschel.

FURTHER READING

Miron, D.: *A Traveler Disguised: a Study in the Rise of Modern Yiddish Fiction in the Nineteenth Century* (New York: Schocken, 1973).

Neiman, M.: *A Century of Modern Hebrew Literary Criticism 1784–1884* (New York: Ktav, 1983)

DAVID G. ROSKIES

Mendelssohn(-Bartholdy, Jacob Ludwig) Felix (1809–47)

German composer, conductor, pianist, and scholar. He was the son of Lea (née Salomon) and Abraham Mendelssohn. Abraham, a successful banker, had at first espoused full emancipation for Jews and opposed conversion to Christianity. Later, however, he and Lea decided to have Felix and their other children baptized and brought up as Protestants, in order to improve their social opportunities. The parents delayed their own formal adoption of Christianity because of likely problems regarding family inheritance. However, they decided to take the step in the wake of anti-Semitic experiences – both personal and political – and because 'it is the religious form acceptable to the majority of civilized human beings' according to Abraham, in a letter to his daughter Fanny). The name Bartholdy was taken from a long-deceased Mayor of Neuköln whose former estate had been inherited through Felix's maternal great-grandfather; and it was added to the family name because, according to Abraham, "a Christian Mendelssohn is an impossibility". Indeed, he put enormous pressure on his son to use the professional name "Felix M. Bartholdy", and even had visiting cards printed for him in that style. Felix, who was usually obedient towards his father, refused absolutely and let himself be known throughout his life as Felix Mendelssohn. Although he, his wife Cécile (née Jeanrenaud, daughter of a Pastor), and their five children followed a sincerely Christian way of life, he remained conscious of the heritage handed down through the literary and philosophical legacy of his grandfather Moses MENDELSSOHN , and through certain members of the *Gesellschaft der Freunde* – an enlightened circle of celebrities who met in the cultivated atmosphere of Abraham's home.

Musical examples of his Jewish consciousness include a quotation from the popular "Leoni" *Yigdal* tune in one of his early String Symphonies; a variation of a High Festival motif in his oratorio *Elijah*; and a setting of Psalm 100 in German for the Reform Temple in his native Hamburg. There were plans for an oratorio on Moses but these came to nothing.

Mendelssohn felt a special affinity not only for Jewish-born classically trained musicians of his period such as Ignaz MOSCHELES and Ferdinand David, but also for individuals like Michael Gusikow, an Orthodox instrument-maker and KLEZMER musician, whom he described as "a terrific fellow", "a true artist", and "a genius". In a wider context he wrote with great enthusiasm about the laws passed by Parliament in 1833 which brought emancipation to British Jews. Significantly, the Jewishness of his music was as strongly emphasized by the important Jewish writer and composer Max BROD in his book *Die Musik Israels* as by Richard Wagner in his anti-Semitic pamphlet *Das Judenthum in der Musik*. But many musicians and musicologists flatly oppose this view. Persuasive criteria are selected to support either position. The debate continues.

FURTHER READING

Werner, E.: *Mendelssohn: A New Image of the Composer and his Age*, trans. D. Newlin (New York: Free Press of Glencoe/Macmillan/Crowell-Collier, 1963)

Werner, J.: *Mendelssohn's "Elijah": An Historical and Analytical Guide to the Oratorio* (London: Chappell, 1965)

ALEXANDER KNAPP

Mendelssohn, Moses (1729–1786) German philosopher, intellectual spokesman for German Jewry, and symbol of the age of Emancipation. Mendelssohn's life epitomized the eighteenth-century renaissance of Jewish culture that culminated in the *Haskalah* and not, as commonly thought, the migration from an atrophied ghetto Judaism to a cosmopolitan European culture and society. Born in Dessau, Mendelssohn received the predominantly talmudic education typical of his time, yet before his *bar mitzvah* had also begun to lay the foundation of his later interests – esthetics, *belles-lettres*, and metaphysics – through a study of the Bible, Hebrew grammar, and Maimonides. When he followed his teacher to Berlin in 1743, he studied at a *Bet midrash* but also joined a circle of young Jews who, educating themselves in Jewish and general culture, helped him to learn classical and modern languages and to

continue his philosophical studies (of, for example, Leibniz, Locke, Wolff, and Spinoza). Of equal importance, they introduced him to leading figures of the Berlin Enlightenment (such as Lessing and Nicolai) who became lifelong friends and eased his entrance into the world of German letters.

Mendelssohn was singular not because he acculturated, then, but because he became one of the most important philosophers and noted personalities of the German Enlightenment while remaining an observant Jew. In *Briefe über die Empfindungen* (1755; Letters on the sentiments), and *Philosophische Schriften*; (1761; Philosophical writings), he helped redefine esthetics by arguing that judgements about beauty are independent of logical criteria or ethical purposes, and he applied these views in numerous reviews in leading periodicals. In his *Treatise on Evidence in the Metaphysical Sciences*, which won first prize in the Prussian Royal Academy of Science's competition (1763), he defended metaphysics against the inroads of science, that is, the claim that its evidence for the existence of God and the principles of morality do not attain the certainty of mathematics. His Platonic dialogue *Phaedon* (1767), gained him a European reputation as a philosopher and stylist with its "Socrates redivivus" who elegantly articulated the Enlightenment's fundamental belief in the immortality of the soul. His last work, *Morgenstunden* (1786; Morning hours), was devoted to the demonstrability of God's existence and defending his friend Lessing against charges of atheism. Mendelssohn became a Berlin landmark, the German Socrates whose wit, charm, and penetrating intelligence attracted dignitaries and intellectuals from all Europe.

Mendelssohn also wrote in Hebrew, and the fundamental agreement between his works in the two languages attests to the unity of his thought. Hoping to revive Hebrew and propagate an enlightened understanding of Judaism, Mendelssohn produced two issues of the first Hebrew-language journal, the *Kohelet musar* (1758; The preacher of morals), for which he translated contemporary poetry into Hebrew and wrote essays that integrated rabbinic dicta with Enlightenment philosophical categories. In

510

Moses Mendelssohn at home, with Lavater and Lessing

1760–1 he wrote a commentary on Maimonides' treatise, *Millot hahiggayon* (Logical terms); in 1769 a Hebrew essay that reproduced the central argument of the *Phaedon*; and in 1770 a commentary on the book of Ecclesiastes. A nervous debility that prevented strenuous philosophical studies, as well as cultural and social changes in Prussia, led him to translate the Pentateuch into German (printed in Hebrew letters) with a Hebrew commentary (*bi'ur*) that drew on the medieval rationalist tradition. In calling this translation, which a number of leading rabbis opposed, the "first step toward culture", he did not mean that it would lead the Jews to German or European culture, but rather to a cultural renaissance based on Hebrew and the Bible.

As a prominent philosopher and a believing Jew, Mendelssohn naturally became a spokesman for the Jews and Judaism. In 1769–70 he deflected the conversionary challenge of a Swiss theologian, Lavater. He interceded on behalf of Jewish communities (Schwerin, 1772; Switzer-land, 1775; Dresden, 1777) with authorities with whom he often had influence. He also served the Prussian government as a consultant on Jewish law, first in regard to matrimonial laws touching on property *Die Ritualgesetze der Juden* (1778; Ritual laws of the Jews), and then on the question of oaths (1782). A call for aid from Alsatian Jewry led Mendelssohn to persuade Dohm, a Prussian civil servant and journalist, to write his famous tract *Über die bürgeliche Verbesserung der Juden* (1781; On the civic amelioration of the Jews). Not wholly in agreement with Dohm's views, Mendelssohn published his ideas in an introduction to a translation of Menasseh ben Israel's *Vindiciae judaeorum* (1781), which, in turn, elicited an anonymous response (1782), accusing Mendelssohn of inconsistency in not converting to Christianity. Mendelssohn's reply, *Jerusalem; oder, Über religiosse Macht und Judenthum* (1783; *Jerusalem: or On Religious Power and Judaism*, 1983), delineated both a political theory of emancipation (church–state relations in a secular society) and, in keeping with it, a philosophy of Judaism (a "revealed legislation" and not a "revealed religion"). Mendelssohn thought Judaism could best survive as a voluntary association divested of all aspects of corporate autonomy.

Mendelssohn was one of those rare figures who become the symbol of an era. For German Jewry he was an avatar of the culture that served as a surrogate citizenship; through his friendship with Lessing a model for social integration; and by virtue of his *Jerusalem* a touchstone for the reform and rethinking of Judaism in the nineteenth century. Whether Mendelssohn is made to represent the boon of emancipation or the bane of assimilation (a number of his children converted to Christianity), he remains the emblematic Jew of the age of Emancipation.

BIBLIOGRAPHY

Jerusalem: or, On Religious Power and Judaism, trans. A. Arkush (Hanover and London: University Press of New England, 1983)

FURTHER READING

Altmann, A.: *Moses Mendelssohn, a Biographical Study*, (Alabama: University of Alabama Press, 1973)

Meyer, M. A.: *The Origins of the Modern Jew*, (Detroit: Wayne State University Press, 1967)

Sorkin, D.: *The Transformation of German Jewry, 1780–1840*, (New York: Oxford University Press, 1987)

DAVID SORKIN

Mendès-France, Pierre (1907–1982)

French politician. Pierre Mendès-France, like Raymond ARON, illustrates the emergence of a new type of Jewish intellectual in contemporary France. Originating from a middle-class Marrano family, which can be traced back to the beginning of the sixteenth century, he had a secular childhood, broken only by a short-lived mystical crisis when he was 13, at the time of his *bar mitzvah*. His childhood was also Republican, in a family on which the Dreyfus Affair had left a considerable mark.

He studied at the École Libre des Sciences Politiques (1923–5), became a doctor of law in 1928, and was called to the Bar of Paris in 1926. Elected the youngest deputy in France in 1932, representing the Département de l'Eure, he was Mayor of Louviers in 1935, and was active in the left wing of the Radical party. At the start of his political career he displayed a powerful rationalism, inherited from the tradition of French Judaism, which had no time for Utopian notions and was to determine all his theoretical, institutional, and political thinking. Mendès-France applied this rationalism, combined with a profound desire for justice, to the new science brought over from the United States. In his two books published in 1928 and 1930, *L'Oeuvre Financière du Gouvernement Poincaré* and *La Banque Internationale: Contribution à l'Étude des Problèmes des États-Unis d'Europe*, he criticized economic privileges and came out in favor of more egalitarian state internationalism. His post as Under-Secretary of State at the Treasury in the BLUM government of 1937 enabled him to begin putting Keynesianism into practice.

A fervent patriot, he left France for North Africa on board the Massilia on 21 June 1940. He was arrested for treason at Rabat in August 1940, and transferred to Clermont-Ferrand, whence he escaped on 21 June 1941, reaching England in March 1942. He was the provisional Government's spokesman on economic affairs, subsequently becoming Economics Minister, a post he resigned on 5 April 1945, after a disagreement on the economic policy to be adopted.

The disaster of Dien Bien Phu alone explains why Mendès-France was elected Prime Minister on a platform of withdrawal from Indo-China, ratified by the Geneva agreements of July 1954. The rise to power of Mendès-France signaled the revival of an anti-Semitism which had been taboo since 1945, and which found its official organs in the Press and the right-wing parties, as well as the ranks of the Communists. Recalled to government after the victory of the Republican Front in January 1956, Mendès-France resigned in May. He was beaten in the 1958 parliamentary elections and barred from the Radical Party in 1959. The publication in 1962 of *La République Moderne*, a statement of his political convictions illustrates the gap between his ideas and the practice of the Fifth Republic. His governmental experiment, despite some ambiguous practice, was to retain validity, and Mendèsism lives on as the myth of a period when politics and ideals coincided.

The trials of the war and the virulence of the anti-Semitic attacks on Mendès-France in his rise to power reshaped his Judaism. The existence of the State of Israel offered a focal point for the crystallization and rationalization of that sense of Jewishness which eluded scientific definition. While the attitudes of Pierre Mendès-France towards the Suez operation in 1956 were those of the politician rather than the Jewish intellectual, a journey to Israel in 1959 was to reawaken unreserved enthusiasm in him. He subsequently took the Israeli equation into account in his definition of the French Jew. He tried to promote the same dialog he had encouraged with the people of the Maghreb in the 1950s between Arabs and Israelis in the years 1968–73 (*Dialogues avec l'Asie d'aujourd'hui*).

FURTHER READING

De Tarr, F.: *The French Radical Party: from Herriot to Mendès-France* (Toronto: Oxford University Press, 1961)

PERRINE SIMON-NAHUM

Meyer, Ernst H. (1905–1988) German composer. Meyer came to Britain as a refugee from Nazism in 1933, working as musical journalist and as a lecturer in music. Umberto Cavalcanti took him into the GPO Film Unit in 1937, as an expert on sound effects. He was the only important émigré of the period to find more than passing work in the British documentary movement. Later, during the war, he composed music for the cartoons of Halas-Batchelor. He had supported his musical education in Berlin by playing piano and violin in dance bands. Amongst his tutors were Hanns Eisler and Paul Hindemith, both of whom were interested in the cinema. In England, as a Communist driven out of Germany, he was politically committed to the defeat of Nazism and was an active member of the Free German League of Culture. He became a seminal influence on British musicology with his work on English Chamber music, which was published after the war.

His concept of film music derives from his political principles and attempts to relate the composer closely to reality rather than to impose purely musical concerns on to images. It led him to carry out location research before composing the score for *North Sea* (1938). His music for the Jewish Agency of Palestine's *Collective Adventure* (1940), for *A Few Ounces a Day* (1941), and for *When The Pie Was Opened* (1941) was described as "orchestrated sound". The authentic effects which were used on *Roadways* (1937) is a model of the way in which music and sound can combine with the visual image and transform it in unexpected ways.

In 1948, Meyer became professor and director of the Institute for Musicology at Humbolt University, Berlin (GDR) and played an important role in East German music. Some of his film music has been incorporated into the *Orchestral Suites* (1959).

Other films include: *The Londoners* (1938), *Swinging the Lambeth Walk* (1940), *Subject for Discussion* (1943), *Die Auftrag Höglers*, (1949), *Chronik des Aufstiegs* (1950).

FURTHER READING

Huntley, J.: *British Film Music* (London: Skelton Robinson, 1947)

Sadie, S., ed.: *The New Grove Dictionary of Music and Musicians* (London: Macmillan, 1980)

KEVIN GOUGH-YATES

Meyerbeer, Giacomo (Jakob Liebmann Beer) (1791–1864) German composer. He was the son of a wealthy banker in Berlin. He was an infant prodigy at the piano, taught by Clementi; he then studied in Darmstadt where his friend and fellow pupil was Carl Maria von Weber. His first successes were operas in Italy in the style of Rossini. He then moved to Paris and conquered the fashionable world with the first of his lavish productions, *Robert le Diable* (Robert the Devil), complete with a spectacular ballet for the ghosts of nuns who died in carnal sin. He developed his taste for religious themes in *Les Huguenots* (1836), based on the St Bartholemew's Day Massacre, and *Le Prophète* (1849) on the rising of the Münster Anabaptists under John of Leyden.

In 1842 the King of Prussia appointed him General Music Director in Berlin where he used his influence to help Wagner, and staged the premieres of *Rienzi* and *Der Fliegende Holländer*. It is said that Wagner's anti-Semitism was nurtured by his jealousy of Meyerbeer's wealth and success. Meyerbeer's last and perhaps his best opera, *L'Africaine* (The African maid), with a libretto by Eugene Scribe, was not performed until after his death.

CAROLE ROSEN

Meyerson, Émile (1859–1933) French philosopher, director of the Jewish Colonization Association. Born in Lublin, he was the son of Malvina Meyerson, a Jewish Polish novelist of some distinction and a descendant of a long line of talmudic scholars. After studying chemistry at Heidelberg, he settled in Paris in 1882, worked as translator and editor for the Havas news agency and devoted his energies to Jewish relief work as administrator, and subsequently director general, of the Jewish Colonization Association. With the help of numerous correspondents, Meyerson conducted the first systematic enquiry into the situation of the Jews in Russia (1898–1903). Its first publication in St Petersburg, in 1904, was followed by a French edition, in 1906–8, entitled *Recueil de Matériaux sur la Situation Économique des Israélites de Russie*.

Meyerson was a great friend of BERNARD-LAZARE. He retired from the JCA in 1923, owing to ill health, and devoted the remaining years to developing his philosophy. Starting with a severe critique of rational positivism, he endeavored to find a synthesis between idealism and scientific reasoning. In *Identité et Réalité* (1908) Meyerson had already argued that total rational explanation is illusory because reality and nature resist the human mind's urge to identify, reduce, and rationalize. In the later works he tried to prove the impossibility of total rational explanation by systematically examining the nature of scientific reasoning as evidenced in the natural sciences, particularly in modern physics. His work won world-wide acclaim in philosophical and scientific circles. EINSTEIN publicly congratulated Meyerson on his understanding of relativity theory and its philosophical implications.

BIBLIOGRAPHY

La Déduction Relativiste (Paris: Payot, 1925); *De l'Explication dans les Sciences* (Paris: Payot, 1927)

FURTHER READING

La Lumia, J.: *The Ways of Reason: A Critical Study of the Ideas of Emile Meyerson* (London: Allen and Unwin, 1967)

NELLY WILSON

Mieses, Matisyohu [Matthias] (1885–1945)

Yiddish semiologist. He was born in Pshemeshl, Galicia, to a well-to-do family of illustrious rabbinic ancestry, and was educated in both traditional Jewish and modern subjects. He developed multifarious scholarly interests, usually on 'exotic' subjects, and throughout his career excelled in assembling large bodies of data as a point of departure for highly original views. He preferred pioneering new subjects, with all the inherent risks, to being a 'scholarly worker' in established disciplines. He began publishing journalistic and essayistic pieces, mostly in Hebrew, in 1904. One of the very few Hebrew writers to defend Yiddish, he debated the language question with N. Sokolow in *Ha'olam* (1907) and AHAD HA'AM in *Heatid* (1910). Most of his later work was written in German.

Mieses studied the roots of anti-Semitism and published a number of controversial studies on racial questions, including *Germanen und Juden* (1917) and *Zur Rassenfrage* (1919).

He took the world of Yiddish by storm when, at the age of 23, he delivered the first-ever scientific analysis of Yiddish to be written in the language itself, at the Chernowitz Language Conference of 1908. It included an impassioned plea for the rights of the language: "The nineteenth century created the rights of man, the twentieth has the responsibility of creating the rights of languages. Affording Yiddish the right to develop is a sacred national cause and a contribution to the progress of humanity". Mieses's paper caused a major sensation and not a little controversy, and was finally published in 1931. His *Entstehungsursache der jüdischen Dialekte* (1915) established, in a stroke, the academic field of comparative Jewish linguistics. His was the first work to conceptualize the rise and development of all the Jewish languages in the framework of linguistic and cultural creativity within a religious civilization. This was a sharp contrast to the prevailing views of the day, which looked down upon most Jewish languages as "corruptions" of non-Jewish languages, and reflections of a "ghetto mentality". His *Die jiddische Sprache* (1924) is an exciting and daring, but not wholly reliable work on the history of Yiddish. *Die Gesetze der Schriftgeschichte* (1919) is a classic work on the interrelationships between writing systems and human beliefs which deserves far more scholarly attention than it has attracted to date. Mieses had completed several volumes of his lifework – a comparative study of religion, apparently with emphasis on the phenomenon of racism – when he fell victim to the Holocaust.

FURTHER READING

Goldsmith, E. S.: *Architects of Yiddishism at the Beginning of the Twentieth Century* (London: Rutherford and Associated University Presses, 1976) 139–58, 200–9, 236–45

King, R. D.: Matisyohu Mieses. In *History of Yiddish Studies*, ed. D.-B. Kerler (Chur: Harwood Academic Publishers, in press, 1990)

DOVID KATZ

Milhaud, Darius (1892–1974) French composer. Born of an affluent Jewish family long settled in Provence, Milhaud began to study the violin at the age of seven and, soon after, to compose. He entered the Paris Conservatoire in 1905, primarily as a violinist but soon began to concentrate on composing. His teachers included Paul DUKAS and Widor. He first achieved recognition in the theater with his incidental music to Claudel's *Protée* (1913–19) and the opera, *La Brebis Égarée* (1910–15). Of particular importance is incidental music for *Les Choëphores* (1915 – Claudel's translation of the Choephori of Aeschylus – where polytonality became the norm of Milhaud's harmonic language.

Paul Claudel, when appointed French Ambassador to Brazil, invited Milhaud to accompany him as his secretary. Milhaud stayed for nearly two years (1917–18) where he was much influenced by South American folk and popular music, this influence manifesting itself in such works as the ballet *L'Homme et son Désir* (1918) and two dance suites *Saudades do Brasil* (1920–1). On returning to Paris in 1918 Milhaud became involved in the group of writers, artists, and composers associated with Jean Cocteau. His ballet, *Le Boeuf sur le Toit*, was composed in 1919. In 1920 he became a member of Les Six, a loosely based association of six composers with similar esthetic ideals.

In 1920 on a visit to London he first heard and was much attracted to American jazz, and later (1922) on a visit to the USA he experienced black jazz in Harlem, which influenced such works as the piano work *Trois Rags Caprices* (1922) and the ballet *La Création du Monde* (1923), regarded as one of his most important works. While traveling extensively during the 1920s and 1930s, Milhaud composed a large number of works of all kinds. In 1940, at the fall

Darius Milhaud

of France, he went to teach at Mills College, Oakland, California returning to France in 1947, when he became Professor of Composition at the Paris Conservatoire. In 1949 he was one of the founders of the Aspen Music Festival (USA).

Milhaud's awareness of his Jewish heritage inspired him to create many works of particular Jewish significance. The *Poèmes Juifs* (1916) and *Service Sacré* (1947) must be counted amongst his finest scores.

Milhaud's other Jewish works include two operas, *Esther de Carpentras* (1925) and *David* (1952). Choral works include *Psaume cxxxvi* (1919), *Psaume cxxvi* (1921), *Liturgie Comtadine: cinque chants de Rosh Hashanah* (1933), *Barechu-Shema* (1944), *L'Choh-Dodi* (1948), *Trois Psaumes de David* (1954), *Service pour la Veille du Sabbat* (1955), *Cantate de l'Initiation* (bar mitzvah) (1960), *Cantate des Psaumes* (1967), *Ani Maamin un Chant Perdu et Retrouvé* (1972); Solo vocal:

Psaume cxxix (1919), *Six Chants Populaires Hébraïques* (1925); *Prières Journalières a l'Usage des Juifs du Comtat Venaissin* (1927); Piano: *Le Candelabre à Sept Branches* (1951); Radio: *Le Dibbouk* (1953); *Samuel* (1953).

FURTHER READING

Beck G.: *Darius Milhaud* (Paris, 1949)
Collaer P.: *Darius Milhaud* (Geneva and Paris: Editions Slatkine, 1982)

SYDNEY FIXMAN

Miller, Arthur (b.1915) American playwright. Miller was born in New York City. Shortly before the Great Depression, his father's business failed and the family moved to Brooklyn. Two years after high school he enroled in the University of Michigan, graduating in 1938. Miller worked briefly with the Federal Theater Project, wrote radio scripts, had a lackluster New York debut with *The Man Who Had All the Luck* (1944), and published a journal, *Situation Normal* (1945), of visits to army camps. *Focus* (1945), a novel, is about an anti-Semite thought to be a Jew.

Miller's career blossomed with *All My Sons* (1947), winner of the New York Drama Critics Circle Award, about a man who sells defective airplane parts to the US Army, causing 21 deaths. His favored son, a flyer believed dead, discovers his father's duplicity and writes an accusing letter, which the surviving son reveals, driving the father to suicide.

Death of a Salesman (1949), Miller's best-known play, won a second Circle Award, as well as the Pulitzer Prize. One of Miller's few departures from naturalism, its characters drift from reality into memory or fantasy. The salesman, Willie Loman, whose evasions and self-deceptions have worn threadbare, is driven to suicide when finally forced by his elder son to confront himself. Critics disagree as to whether Willie is a tragic hero or a pathetic victim, as well as over the Lomans' Jewishness, despite Miller's effort to universalize the characters. He had stopped writing about Jews, fearful that the most minor human failings of Jewish characters would be used to fan the flames of anti-Semitism.

In subsequent work, Miller addressed various forms of moral responsibility. He adapted Ibsen's *An Enemy of the People* (1950) and wrote *The Crucible* (1953), about witch trials in Puritan New England with unmistakable reference to current anti-communist hysteria. (Miller was later convicted of contempt for refusing to implicate others before the House Un–American Activities Committee, but was acquitted on appeal.) *A View From the Bridge* (1955; revised 1956), a tale of repressed incest and fear of homosexuality, set among Sicilian immigrants in Brooklyn, won a third Circle Award. His screenplay for *The Misfits* (1961) was intended as a vehicle for Marilyn Monroe, then his wife. His political and marital troubles supplied raw material for *After the Fall* (1964), in which the protagonist feels his self-image assaulted by figures from his past. In *Incident at Vichy* (1964), a Nazi officer and suspects awaiting interrogation probe meanings of idealism and moral responsibility. These issues are transposed to a fraternal conflict in *The Price* (1968), and examined from a playful cosmic and theological perspective in *The Creation of the World And Other Business* (1972). *The American Clock* (1980), adapted from Studs Terkel's *Hard Times*, looks back at the 1930s. *The Archbishop's Ceiling* (1980) considers the artist's role in a totalitarian society, as does the television drama *Playing for Time* (1980) based on Fania Fenelon's Auschwitz memoir.

BIBLIOGRAPHY

Timebends: A Life (New York: Grove, 1987)

FURTHER READING

Brater, E.: Ethics and ethnicity in the plays of Arthur Miller. In *From Hester Street to Hollywood*, ed. S. B. Cohen (Bloomington: Indiana University Press, 1983)
Welland, D.: *Miller: The Playwright* (London; Methuen; 1985) [3rd edn]

MICHAEL SHAPIRO

Millin, Sarah Gertrude (1889–1968) South African writer. She was born in Zagar, Lithuania, and died in Johannesburg. Before her marriage to the lawyer Philip Millin in

1912, she had spent most of her life on the Vaal diggings near Kimberley. It was here that her fascination with race and the Bible began, and it is her presentation of the topic of race through biblical imagery, as seen in her best-selling novel, *God's Stepchildren* (1924), which makes her contribution to South African literature unique.

In 1926 Millin wrote her first non-fiction work, *The South Africans*, and in 1933 she published a biography of Cecil Rhodes. The latter was a great success and allowed her access to the highest literary and political circles in South Africa and Great Britain. It also led to her friendship with General Jan C. Smuts, whose biography she completed in 1936.

Millin's international reputation is derived in the main from her biographies, and her autobiography, *The Night is Long* (1941), rather than from her fiction. Nevertheless, her novels, for example *The Coming of The Lord* (1928), provide a valuable commentary on both South African affairs and the Jewish Question. Her awareness that as a Jewess she was "not exactly" South African is revealed in her fictional work by her identification with the plight of minorities: the Blacks, the Coloreds (mixed race), and the Jews. This insight is the key to her character and her actions as she became increasingly concerned with the fate of the Jews and the development of a Jewish state.

Millin's post-war writing is devoted to defending Israel and South Africa against their many critics. It is precisely this element of dual loyalty which links her work to that conflict of loyalties and *Zerrissenheit* which is one of the distinctive characteristics of modern Jewish literature.

FURTHER READING

Rubin, M.: *Sarah Gertrude Millin: A South African Life* (Johannesburg: A. D. Donker, 1977)
Snyman, J. P. L.: *The Works of Sarah Gertrude Millin* (Johannesburg: The Central News Agency, 1955)

LAVINIA BRAUN

Mises, Ludwig von (1881–1973) Austrian economist. Born in Lemberg, Galicia, Mises was educated in Vienna at the *Akademisches Gymnasium*, where he was a schoolmate of Hans Kelsen. He studied economics at Vienna, and went on to teach there from 1913. In 1918 he became assistant professor, a post which he held until 1938. Mises also taught at Geneva, 1934–40. In 1940 he arrived in the USA, where he established his brand of liberal economics.

Mises is best known as one of the founding fathers of monetarism, providing the link between the Austrian school of Menger and liberal economists such as Friedrich von Hayek, who was the most prominent member of Mises's famous private seminar. Mises's theory is elaborated in his works, which include: *The Theory of Money and Credit* (1934); *Socialism* (1936); and *Human Action* (1949). There is also his memoirs, *Notes and Recollections* (1978), in which he discussed his main ideas. Mises paralleled Kelsen in rejecting the prevalent historicist approach. Instead he adopted the Austrian, subjective approach to classical economics. His most important insight was that money was not a neutral factor in economic relations. He opposed the trend to economic planning because he saw tampering with the market as ill-advised, and socialist control as immoral. In this view he was confirmed by his pupil Hayek.

Hayek has remarked that in inter-war Vienna Mises, a Jewish intellectual who actually defended capitalism, was regarded as a monstrous paradox. Mises himself said very little about his being Jewish, although comments he makes in his memoirs about the demise of Koerber, the Austrian Prime Minister, suggest that he was conscious of his descent as a barrier to promotion. It is worthy of note that Mises's family was prominent in the Jewish community – his father being a member of the *Gemeinde*'s elected board.

STEVEN BELLER

Mishkovsky, Zelda Schneerson (1914–1984) Hebrew poet known as "Zelda". Born in Chernigov in the Ukraine to a famous hasidic family (Lubavich) of intellectual bent, she came to live in Jerusalem at the age of 11, and later taught there in a religious school for girls. Her education prepared her to be conversant not only with religious texts but with modern Hebrew and Russian literature as well. An unusual blend of ultra-Orthodox and modern sensibilities distinguishes her poetry and contributes to her popularity with a diverse readership. Although she began writing poetry in her teens, Zelda first published two poems in *Ha'aretz* in November 1965. These were later included in her immensely successful first volume *Pnai* (1967; Time to spare).

Her verse combines a convincing mysticism of everyday experience with a potential for psychological catharsis amidst twentieth-century anxieties. Her rich but relatively simple language makes palatable her sermonic posing of challenges to one's humanity through encounters with misery, deformity, unfounded suspicion, abuse, loneliness, and political injustice. Zelda's poetic response moves from the placidly contemplative to the ecstatically transcendent. Nature – plant life, in particular – offers solace, and intimations of the divine stir in unexpected places.

BIBLIOGRAPHY

Poems in: *The Penguin Book of Hebrew Verse*, ed. T. Carmi (New York: Penguin, 1981); *Contemporary Israeli Literature*, ed. E. Anderson (Philadelphia: Jewish Publication Society, 1977)

FURTHER READING

Barzel, H.: Elegiac Romanticism and Ironic Romanticism. *Modern Hebrew Literature* 2 no. 1 (1976) 10–16

Morris, B.: Ultra-orthodox Jewish Poet. *Present Tense* 10 no. 1 (1982) 16–19

STANLEY NASH

modernity, Judaism and An ethnographic approach. To speak of Judaism in an ethnological sense today means both taking as a subject Jews in the widest sense of the term – those who profess or claim to be Jews, in whatever relation they stand to the orthodoxy of the religion – and considering the structures of a specific culture as well as its long history. It means examining the continued existence of a historical consciousness, transmitted by memory, even if that memory is of a secular nature. This relatively recent view of Judaism arises not only from the general evolution of the science of ethnology, which takes a growing interest in complex historical societies, but also from the creation of Israel as a state with a society made up of groups of various ethnic origins and with access to political power.

If some would see the present occupation of positions in the liberal professions, in the intellectual world, and in leading areas of medical research as the sign of acceptance into the modern world, the Jews of the Diaspora still face the problem of preserving and handing on their specific identity.

Where Israel is concerned, it is a case of gaining recognition as a state like any other. In fact, the will behind the creation of a modern society uniting the most ancient of biblical and Jewish sources with technically highly advanced structures has to take account of ethnic variations. The social, economic, and cultural diversity of Israeli immigrants, coming mainly from Christian and Muslim countries, or owning as marginal an obedience as do the Ethiopians, the Karaites, or the B'nai yisrael, means that cultural as well as economic choices must be made.

On the other hand, new technology and the sciences – including biology – have created new problems which the Jewish ethic finds itself confronting, and to which it must find answers both in Israel and in the Diaspora. One may thus ask what system of values will serve as a common point of reference for Judaism in the whole context of modern society.

A situation of compromise

Among the Jews of Communist countries, as well as Jews who have had to leave their countries because of anti-Semitism, war, or decolonization, and indeed for Jews still living in countries with quite a large Jewish population, the same kind of compromise is found between adopting the language, culture, educational system, and values of the dominant society on the one hand and on the other, maintaining a Jewish tradition of a more or a less distinctive nature, a tradition which may be enfeebled, indeed almost non-existent, and often differs from its original form. In France the Lubavitch movement, founded by the Ashkenazi, now numbers among its adherents 90 per cent of Sephardi Jews of Maghrebi origin. The Central Board of Jewish Communities of Hungary has a program of Jewish research which is unique in the Communist bloc, trains rabbis for the Soviet bloc in the Neological Rabbinical Seminary, runs an abattoir providing kosher meat for other Eastern countries, and so on. In the USSR, certain Mishnaic treaties have been translated and analyzed by Marxist Talmudic scholars. Naturally, this compromise affects both community and family structures.

Community structures

Two types of systems act as models for the community as a whole: the Anglo-Saxon model, where communities are autonomous, rule themselves, and train their own rabbis according to their particular observance (Orthodox, Conservative, Reform, Liberal, Reconstructionist); and the consistorial French model, which has been in existence since the time of Napoleon I, and imposes a synthetic form of Judaism, neither Orthodox nor Liberal, on all communities. Rabbis come from the Seminary set up on the old model of the seminaries of Berlin and Breslau. These two models confront similar situations: first, a traditional community system with its official staff which once consisted of rabbis, *hazzanim* (officiating ministers), *mohalim* (to perform circumcisions), *shohatim* (to perform ritual sacrifice), *mashgihim* (supervisors of the slaughtering and preparation of animals for kosher meat), and *shammashim* (vergers) as well as functionaries to officiate at burials, but is now reduced to the bare minimum (a rabbi or officiating minister); and second, a re-organized and extended system in countries where the dominant religion itself is highly structured or forms part of the public domain.

Community responsibilities

This restructuring of the community, subject to its political and social background, has entirely changed the relations between the community leaders, the rabbis, and ordinary community members. The general tendency is to confront the problems discussed in the dominant society more directly. There is a trend towards more equality insofar as a certain freedom of relationships exists within the community. The community system arranges for the practice of Jewish law within the framework of the public domain, for worship in synagogue, for the abattoir, the cemetery, the situation of Jews in the army or at school, Jewish festivals, and the civil application of rabbinical legislation in family law (marriage, divorce, the custom of the levirate). In the Diaspora, the Beth Din (rabbinical tribunal) generally has an advisory role, and intervenes only in strictly religious matters.

The synagogue service is almost wholly conducted by professionals and not ordinary believers. The tendency to give trainee rabbis general education as well, often even at university level, is becoming common in most rabbinical schools, whatever their affiliation. The professionalization of the rabbi's function gives rise to phenomena similar to those found in other professions and the rabbi's social role often becomes more important than his strictly religious function.

Separation of the sexes is still observed in Orthodox synagogues, but feminist demands are now being made in conservative American circles, the aim being to create a place for women in the form of worship and the liturgy in general, with the inclusion of women in collective prayer, recitation by women of the same prayers as men, wearing of the *tallit* and the *tefillin* by women, and the composition and use of specific prayers to celebrate peculiarly female occasions: childbirth, the *bat mitzvah*. The Liberal Jewish movements in the USA and Great Britain also train women rabbis.

The introduction of music (the organ), driving to the synagogue on the Sabbath, and sometimes even the postponement of the Sabbath service until Sunday, are all adaptations to the modern age, though they are still set in the framework of the community.

Social welfare

Of recent years, the roles and responsibilities of community structure have undergone relative diminution in the social sphere, now that there is more state welfare. In those countries where state social cover is still deficient (as in India and Burma) or is controlled by authorities which are often of a religious nature, as in the

USA, the community structure retains some of its traditional prerogatives in connection with the *mitzvah* (commandment) of charity: social security, giving dowries for poor girls, visiting the sick, the *hevrah kaddisha* charitable associations providing for burials. The community takes up social welfare only where state welfare ends: the JWB in the UK and the Limited Jewish Philanthropic Fund in France run aid and welfare programmes for the old and the handicapped. The ORT (Organization for Rehabilitation and Training) makes its own contribution to countering unemployment in the UK by agreement with a government agency. A large number of philanthropic associations, such as the B'nai B'rith and Wizo, take part in immediate or long-term humanitarian actions. The charity (*tzedakah*) peculiar to the institution of the Jewish community is mainly practiced today through educational and cultural patronage.

Education and culture

The number of Jewish schools (at all educational levels) and their staff has increased considerably since the beginning of the 1970s (e.g. the Tarbut School in Mexico, the Yabné in Paris, the JFS Secondary School in London, Mt Scopus College in Melbourne.) These schools integrate the educational programmes in force in their respective countries with Jewish material (history, Hebrew, religious subjects, costumes, holidays). Their objectives are sometimes very different from those of pre-war schools, when the main endeavor (and this was particularly so in France) was to inculcate the culture of the host country into the children of immigrants, so as to integrate them rapidly into the dominant society. Today, the main concern is to give children from all backgrounds a specifically Jewish education and culture. School thus becomes the place where Jewish culture is learned, a culture that parents are often unable to pass on themselves. However, the Talmud–Torahs (supplementary schools), like the youth movements, have not disappeared. In Israel, emphasis is placed on those elements common to Ashkenazi, Sephardi, and Oriental cultures, so that no single one of them is privileged above the others.

The development of Jewish press and radio has run a parallel course almost everywhere. Large numbers of newspapers, magazines, and periodicals are published – mainly in English and French – and reach a very wide public which is not interested in Yiddish or Hebrew papers. When private radio stations were authorized in France in 1981, Jewish radio stations were set up in over twenty cities. There are also television programs at certain times of day in the USA and Canada. Almost throughout the Western world, Judaism can be seen to be opening up, becoming culturally known and recognized in the non-Jewish world, a relatively new phenomenon of religious and cultural externalization.

The family

The texture of life as a whole influences the community structure, and also has profound repercussions on the structure of the family, though one must remember that the typical "Jewish family" does not exist, any more than the typical "Jewish institution".

The Jewish family, in which *parental roles* were very distinct (with the purity of the family ensured by the mother, and the education of the children – or at least of the sons – by the father) has changed a great deal. Originally very extended, it has now shrunk almost everywhere to the unit consisting of parents and children. This development has been slower than in the society surrounding the Jewish family, but from the 1970s onward there has been a rise in the number of one-parent families, fewer marriages (particularly religious marriages) and a lower rate of fertility, with an increase in the number of divorces.

The authority of the head of the family, the husband and father, is still upheld in certain circles, but it is under attack not only from legislation but also from such integrating forces as schools and the army, as well as by new educational methods developed in the kibbutzim of Israel.

The constant rise in the number of mixed marriages (between 40 and 60 per cent in the West) creates problems insofar as the children of non-Jewish mothers are not recognized as Jews by either the *halakhah* or the State of Israel.

Criteria of religious standards

It is difficult to define the criteria of individual people's religious standards. Those which are most categorical in traditional Jewish society will be the chief ones mentioned here.

Outside certain communities (such the Hasidim of Antwerp, or the adherents of the Lubavich movement in New York and Israel), attendance twice a day at synagogue for communal prayer is obviously no longer a fact of life in a mainly urban Judaism. Even if the liturgy has not changed, and the family *minhag* is observed, with the saying of prayers and the wearing of tephillin still practiced in the home, the meaning of prayer itself has been considerably modified. Respecting the *shabbat* and devoting that day to study and prayer is still one of the strongest principles of Orthodox Judaism almost everywhere. In Israel the religious movements are campaigning to have the sabbath observed by everyone, and to have traffic banned on that day. The most common way of observing the sabbath is often limited to the lighting of candles, the *kiddush* (blessing the wine) and the careful preparation of the Friday evening meal.

Two different sets of vessels (one for meat and the other for milk dishes) are still kept by certain traditionalists outside Orthodox circles. We often see the observance of kosher cooking and the eating of kosher food in the home, the last stronghold of tradition, coexisting with the eating of "local" food, the food of "others", in the world outside. The rise in the number of shop counters selling kosher products in vast areas of Canada and the USA is spreading to Western Europe, and setting off new reactions in circles where observance had slackened. A thousand kosher meals a day are cooked in one Budapest canteen.

The *mikveh*, the purification ritual practiced chiefly by married women after the state of *niddah* (menstrual impurity), and scarcely observed in Europe and the USA, is being revived in Canada with the influx of a considerable number of Jewish immigrants from Morocco. Several establishments have recently been constructed in Montreal according to the rules laid down in the *halakhah*. In Israel, observance of the ritual is principally linked to the family's weak integration or its geographical origin (it chiefly affects families from Asia and Africa).

Festivals

There is widespread participation by the Jewish population in a certain number of festivals, although the great majority of the people are not involved with the Jewish community or with religion (in Israel, 53 per cent of Jews originating from Europe describe themselves as not being religious). Of the principal holidays, Hanukkah, Pesah, and Purim are observed for various reasons, as family festivities, symbolic and historical moments; Sukkot and Shavuot are observed as festivals of nature, particularly in the kibbutzim and among secularized Jews, both in Israel and the Diaspora. The activities of going to the synagogue and taking part in festivals culminate in Rosh Hashanah and Yom Kippur; the latter, which with Tisha B'Av is one of the most austere of Jewish holy days, enables many people who hardly practice Judaism any more to celebrate the ritual fast and come to hear the blowing of the *shofar*. For others, the calendar of festivals has become reduced to festive meals. Maintaining family conviviality is one way of ritualizing the Jew's difference from the dominant society.

Some festivals peculiar to certain ethnic groups are becoming popular: Mimouna, the Moroccan Jewish observance of the end of Pesah, is being celebrated more and more frequently both in Israel and the Diaspora; the Seged may become a great festival of the affirmation of Judaism, of initiation and of Jewish education, as it already is among Ethiopian Jews (it was celebrated in Israel for the first time in November 1982).

Rites of passage

Similarly, the rites of passage linked to birth, the attaining of religious majority, marriage, and death are quite widely observed by people not closely connected with any community. If the number of religious marriages and funerals is falling almost everywhere there is no recourse to a religious authority, the practices of circumcision and the naming of daughters, followed by the *bar mitzvah* or *bat mitzvah*, are still flourishing, even in circles where there is little Jewish observance.

Changing values

These practices pose the problem of what is chosen or retained when the traditional structure has disappeared and secularization is omnipresent. We are now seeing a change in traditional values, which are not systematically transferred to other objects, but applied to the facts of modern life. For instance, Zionism can be linked to the messianic movement which is an essential component of Judaism. The use of Hebrew as an everyday language means that part of the symbolism connected with the prestige of a sacred, liturgical language is preserved. Israel has become a modern myth, as the Holy Land was in its time. Literature, research in every field, investment in scholarship, go to realize the aspirations once aroused by study of the Torah and the Talmud.

In a way, it is a system of equivalences between certain values of the past and others that are wholly modern. It is a mutation brought about, to a certain extent, by secularization.

The anthropology of Judaism

Various research workers of the twentieth century have been fascinated by Jewish customs and practices: Moses GASTER in Great Britain, S. AN-SKI in Russia, Balaban in Poland and Alexander SCHEIBER in Hungary have provided Jewish folklore with some remarkable archives which have still scarcely been explored, but until the 1960s anthropological work was mainly limited to local or partial studies, particularly in the Ashkenazi world.

Several Israeli institutes and universities (the Ben-Zvi Institute for Research on Oriental Jewish Communities, the Center for the Study of Sephardi Culture, the Yeshurun Institute, Haifa University, etc.) have undertaken research. The many varied fields of ethnological study opened up in Israel and in the Diaspora are arousing the interest of numerous research workers. The Sephardi and Oriental worlds are no longer forgotten.

Investigation is going on not only into folklore (with the help of musicology, linguistics, ethnography, the cinema, etc.) but also into the classics of Judaism, with the analysis of certain

ideas, beliefs, and myths according to the interpretational models of Tylor, Émile DURKHEIM, Lucien Lévy-Bruhl, Radcliffe-Brown, Evans-Pritchard, Claude LÉVI-STRAUSS, etc. These works in progress should give Judaism indispensable conceptual tools for all anthropological analysis.

To make an ethnological work of collecting and analyzing what seems to be disappearing may perhaps be a sign that modernity is carrying the day, but it also unveils those intrinsic values thanks to which Judaism has survived.

FURTHER READING
Aviad, J.: *Return to Judaism: Religious Renewal in Israel* (Chicago: University of Chicago Press, 1983)
Chazan, B.: Jewish education towards the end of the 20th century. *Encyclopedia Judaica Yearbook* (1983–5) 77–83
Cohen, S: *American Modernity and Jewish Identity* (London and New York: Tavistock Publications, 1983)
Goldberg, H., ed.: *Judaism Viewed From Within and From Without Anthropological Studies* (New York: State University of New York Press, 1987)
Lipmann, Sonia and Vivian, eds: *Jewish Life in Britain 1962–1977* (New York: K. G. Saur, 1981)
Neusner, J.: I am a parrot (red). *History of Religions* 11 (1972) 391–413
——: The bare facts of ritual. *History of Religions* 20 (1980) 112–27
Yosha, N.: The heritage of oriental Jewry in Israeli education and culture. *Encyclopedia Judaica Yearbook* (1983–5) 106–18

PATRICIA HIDIROGLOU

Modiano, Patric (b.1947) French novelist. Born in Paris, Modiano has become the leading voice of a group of young French Sephardi writers who are based largely in and around Paris. Modiano recognizes his Jewish roots, although a sense of confusion and frustration arises in his fiction when it considers Jewish identity. His protagonists alternate between passive acceptance of the Jewish experience and the reality of its *Leidensgeschichte*, and a degree of self-hatred and abnegation for being Jewish. His novels create a surreal atmosphere through which his characters somnambulate toward some realization of "the self".

Modiano's novels have met with great critical

acclaim in the Francophone world, though he remains virtually an unknown personality in the English-speaking world save his work with Louis Malle in writing the scenario for the film *Lacombe Lucien*. French critics have frequently considered him as an inheritor of the traditions of the existential authors of the immediate post-war Saint-Germain-des-Près era. His fiction teems with desperate characters in search of themselves and of that inner truth which will relieve their suffering. This quest for identity is universally bound up with an obsessive desire to give sense and significance to the Jewish condition. His first novel, *La Place de l'Étoile* (1968), is a nightmarish, almost Kafkaesque fantasy in which conventional plot is sublimated to the search for identity. The story is likewise haunted by the German occupation of France and the Holocaust, themes which predominate in Modiano's fiction. These themes and techniques are used frighteningly and exceptionally well in his second novel, *Les Boulevards de ceinture* (1972), for which he won the Grand Prix du roman de l'Académie française. In this work Modiano commences a search for his missing father. This quest is taken up in his third novel, *Rue des boutiques obscures* (1978), for which Modiano was awarded the Prix Goncourt. In both novels, the father is a phantasmagorical figure whose existence would provide vital information to the protagonist-son. This spectral father-figure is a cross between a negative stereotyped Jew and a more "Aryan" Frenchman. Somehow Modiano's son-figures hope to uncover the source of their authentic identities in this father. One must stress that despite all negative images which arise in the novel, Modiano seems to possess a genuine affection for the father-character.

Modiano's fiction sounds a desperate note frequently echoed in the fiction of other French–Sephardi writers of the post-war era. Like them, he is neither French nor Jewish and agonizes under a mantle of attempting to determine his essential identity.

BIBLIOGRAPHY

Trace of Malice, trans. A. Bell (Henley-on-Thames: Aidan Ellis, 1988)

SIMON SIBELMAN

Amedeo Modigliani Chaim Soutine. *Staatsgalerie, Stuttgart*

Modigliani, Amedeo (1884–1920) Italian painter & sculptor. Modigliani was born in Livorno to a once wealthy and prominent Sephardi family. His health was weak from childhood. He entered a local art school at the age of 14, and studied art in Florence and Venice before settling in Paris in 1906, where, beginning to indulge in drink and drug-taking, he soon became a well-known figure in Montmartre avant-garde circles. He moved to Montparnasse in 1909, mixing mainly with fellow émigrés. Chaim SOUTINE, whom Jacques LIPCHITZ introduced to Modigliani in 1915, became a particularly close friend. Modigliani's financial situation remained precarious in the extreme; his love life was no less troubled. In early 1920 he was stricken with tubercular meningitis, and died in a charity hospital. Jeanne Hébuterne, the girl with whom he had been living, committed suicide the following day.

In contrast to his turbulent life, Modigliani's art is serenely sensual, although many of his portraits betray an inner melancholy. Relatively unaffected by the radical art movements of the day, Modigliani's paintings are strongly indebted to the Italian Renaissance for their classical simplicity of form. His use of color is deeply sensuous, and his nudes of 1917 and 1918, while never prurient, are almost shockingly frank in their sexuality. The sculptures he produced between 1901 and 1914 are clearly inspired by the example of primitive carvings. Although Modigliani's Jewishness never featured directly in his work, he seems to have remained fiercely proud of his origins and deeply sensitive to anti-Semitism. In the romantic myth that has grown up around his life, his Jewishness is frequently used to "explain" his exotic otherness, his tragic alienation from respectable society.

FURTHER READING

Fifield, W.: *Modigliani: The Biography* (London: W. H. Allen, 1976)

Modigliani, J.: *Modigliani, Man and Myth* (London: André Deutsch, 1958)

MONICA BOHM-DUCHEN

Moissis, Asher (1899–1975)   Greek communal leader, translator, Zionist, and writer. Born in Trikkala, Greece, Moissis studied law, a profession he practiced in Athens throughout his life. In 1817 he founded the monthly *Israel* which he edited for the two years of its existence. He served as President of the Jewish National Fund (1930–8), of the Salonika Jewish community (1934–6), and of the Greek Zionist Federation (1936–8). Among Moissis's works on Jewish subjects published in the 1930s were those particularly concerned with Greco-Jewish relations throughout history; also a work detailing the author's impressions of Palestine following his first visit there, an introduction to the sources and history of Jewish civil law, and a translation into Greek of Leon PINSKER's *Auto-emancipation* (1934).

During the occupation of Greece, Moissis, as President of the Central Council of Jewish Communities of Greece, pleaded forcefully but unsuccessfully with the Nazi-approved Prime Minister Logothetopoulos to save the Jews from deportation. After the war Moissis was one of the community's legal representatives in the trial of Logothetopoulos who was found guilty and imprisoned until 1951.

Following the liberation of Greece in 1945 Moissis resumed his literary activities which included a number of distinguished translations, among them selections from Theodor HERZL's *Diaries*, Jewish liturgy, Joseph KLAUSNER's *A short history of modern Hebrew literature*, and a parallel-text version of the Psalms of David. Moissis also translated the *Haggedah* into rhymed Greek verse and wrote an extensive historical and explanatory introduction (1971). His *Ellenoyoudhaikye Melete* (1958; Hellenic–Jewish studies), traces the ancient and modern history of Greeks and Jews with special emphasis on common points of reference; *Istoria Kye Thrili yiro apo to Tikhos ton Dhakrion* (History and legends concerning the Wailing Wall), written after the Six Day War in 1967, was translated into Italian and English, and *I Onomatologia ton Evraion tis Ellados* (1973; The names of the Jews of Greece), contains the origin, history, and meaning of the names of the leading families in the Greek–Jewish community.

Asher Moissis was honorary Consul General for Israel in Athens from 1948 to the time of his death.

RACHEL DALVEN

Moldova, (Reiff) György (b.1934)   Hungarian writer. Born in a working-class district of Budapest, Moldova was educated at the Academy of Theatrical and Cinematographic Arts. After 1956 his political convictions prompted him to take up manual work for some years, but at the end of the 1950s he wrote film scripts. Although his first stories were published in the mid 1950s, his first novel *Az idegen bajnok* (The strange champion) was not published until 1963. Since then he has published a number of novels on contemporary themes, of which perhaps *Malom a pokolban* (1968; Mill in hell) and the pseudo-historical novel *Negyven prédikátor* (1973; Forty preachers) were the most accomplished. His growing popularity, however, was less due to his novels than to his satires, satirical sketches, and reportages; of the last, probably *A szent tehén* (1980; The sacred cow), a critical but good-humored inquiry into the problems of the State-owned Hungarian textile industry, elicited the greatest popular response.

Moldova's interest in matters Jewish stems from his own background, although this element is only marginally dealt with in the majority of his books. In the *Szent Imre-induló* (1980; Saint Emeric March), and *Elhúzódó szűzesség*, (1981; Innocence prolonged), however, where the plot is largely autobiographical, the situation of Hungarian Jews during the Second World War and the first post-war years is discussed extensively. *Szent Imre-induló* reflects the helplessness of Budapest Jews in the wake of Hungary's German occupation in March 1944, but it also describes the heroism and martyrdom of such people as Jan Koterba, a Polish doctor working in the Budapest ghetto in the last months of the war. As in his other novels, Moldova here eschews psychological introspection for the sake of a fast-moving, anecdotal plot and brief, realistic characterization. In *Szent Imre-induló* he is critical of the wartime mentality of most Hungarian Jews, their facile optimism and political conformism; he is also skeptical of the "educational" effect of suffering. Moldova's feelings about his own Jewishness are ambivalent – while not denying the past, he does not appear to believe in the uniqueness of Jewish suffering nor in the superiority of Jewish values. Moldova twice won the Attila József Prize and once (1983) the Kossuth Prize for his writings.

FURTHER READING

Sanders, I.: Sequels and revisions: the Hungarian Jewish experience in recent Hungarian literature. *Soviet Jewish Affairs* 14 no. 1 (1984) 30–45

GEORGE GÖMÖRI

Molnár, Ferenc (1878–1952) Hungarian writer and playwright. Born to a middle-class Jewish family in Budapest, Molnár was educated in the Calvinist Grammar School and at the University of Budapest where he studied law. His lack of zeal in pursuing his studies forced his father to send him to Geneva and it was here that he wrote his first story. After his return to Budapest he became a full-time journalist in 1896, changing his family name (Neumann) to the more Hungarian-sounding Molnár. He worked on the staff of *Budapesti Napló* and made his name as a talented journalist before publishing his first novel *Az éhes város* (1901; The hungry city). This was followed by several prose collections. In his early stories and novels Molnár appears as a sharp-eyed critical observer of city life and social convention. He also wrote a delightful children's story which became a classic of its genre: *A Pál utcai fiúk* (1907; *The Paul Street Boys*, 1927). As a playwright he made his debut with *A doktor úr* (The lawyer) in 1902 but he scored his first great success with *Az ördög* (1907; *The Devil*, 1908), a witty, impish social comedy which opened on Broadway a year after its European premiere. This was the first of Molnár's plays to reach New York, and the beginning of a success story which lasted until his death. In 1909 Molnár wrote *Liliom* (*Liliom*, 1921), the bitter-sweet story of a barker-bouncer in a Budapest amusement park and a shy servant girl, a mixture of naturalism and sentimental romanticism (later turned into the musical *Carousel*), which became Molnár's most popular play. Alfred Kerr deemed it "genius . . . with an element of *kitsch* in it". One of his later plays, *Játék a kastélyban* (1926; The play's the thing), adapted by P. G. Wodehouse in 1926, was re-adapted in the 1980s by Tom Stoppard and staged at the National Theatre in London.

Molnár made New York his home in 1940, living in the Hotel Plaza until his death. During this period he did not write anything noteworthy, with the possible exception of *Utitárs a számüzetésben* (1958; *Companion in Exile*, 1950), a somewhat disjointed, anecdotal, nostalgic tribute to his secretary and companion for many years, Wanda Bartha. Since most of his plays take place in the milieu of the old European aristocracy or the rich middle-classes, it seems that his world collapsed in the cataclysm of the Second World War.

Molnár is sometimes described as "a typical product of a patriotic generation of Jewish intellectuals" (C. Györgyey) in a Hungary of the old Austro-Hungarian monarchy. Until 1918 this generation sincerely believed in the possibility of assimilation, and embraced Hungarian habits and tradition with few reservations. But Molnár was also the product and chronicler of metropolitan life with its strongly Jewish bourgeois coloring, and a Bohemian by temperament. He appears to have had no interest in Judaism and in the mid 1930s came close to embracing Christianity, although his efforts to write "Christian" plays (such as *Csoda a hegyek között* (1933; *Miracle in the Mountain*, 1947), or *A király szolgálólánya* (1941; *The King's Maid*, 1941), brought only feeble and unconvincing results. The play *Liliom* was criticized on account of some anti-Jewish barbs by the characters, but in fact the Jews appearing in the play are either "good" (Hugo) or "indifferent" (Litzmann). Molnár's social criticism before 1914 was often directed at the Jewish bourgeoisie which aped the Hungarian ruling classes and alienated the masses, thus providing new arguments for "popular" anti-Semitism. On the credit side stand Molnár's acerbic wit and excellent sense of humor which characterized the Bohemian Jewish milieu of Budapest coffee-houses. Apart from his consummate theatrical skill it was probably this attitude which made him such a long-standing success on Broadway.

BIBLIOGRAPHY

All the Plays of Molnár, ed. L. Rittenberg (New York: Vanguard Press, 1929; 1937); *Stories for Two* (New York, 1950)

FURTHER READING

Gergely, E. J.: *Hungarian Drama in New York: American Adaptations 1908–1940* (Philadelphia: University of Pennsylvania Press, 1947)

Györgyei, C.: *Ferenc Molnár* (New York: Twayne, 1980)

Reményi, J.: Ferenc Molnár, Hungarian playwright. In *Hungarian Writers and Literature* (New Brunswick: 1964) 348–62

GEORGE GÖMÖRI

Molodovsky, Kadye (1894–1975) Yiddish

poet. Born in Kartuz-Bereze, Lithuania, Kadye Molodovsky was a teacher by profession and taught in Warsaw and Odessa and later in the USA. Her talents also found expression as a critic, novelist, and dramatist. Her first volume of poems *Kheshvndike teg* (1927; Autumn days), is filled with the tenderly expressed concerns of women. She was a member of the Kiev group of Jewish intellectuals which included Dovid BERGELSON, Nakhmen Mayzl, Peretz MARKISH, and Der Nister. They published an anthology *Eygns* in 1918 which gave expression to the general eupohoria at the fall of Czarism and the liberation of the Jewish people in Russia. Her lyrics for children in *Kinder-mayselekh* (Children's stories) were sung in schools of pre-war eastern Europe. She settled in New York in 1935 where she died. In *Dzike gas* (1933), a Warsaw street inhabited by poor parents of the children she taught, and in *Freydke* (1935), she portrays the plight of the unemployed or striking Jews in Warsaw whose emigration from Poland was enforced. Her novels include *From Lublin to New York* (1942), *Grandparents and Grandchildren* (1944) and *On One's Own Soil* (1957). In 1943 Molodovsky founded and edited the journal *Svive* (Environment), a literary quarterly which closed due to her ill-health but resumed in 1960. In 1949 she traveled to the newly founded state of Israel where she wrote her play *Nokhn got fun midber* (1949; After God of the desert). In Israel she also edited the periodical *Heym* (Home) from 1950 to 1952 and her songs celebrating the new state *In yerusholayim kumen malokhim* (Angels enter Jerusalem) were published. Following her return to New York her published works include: *Af di vegn fun tsien* (On the roads to Zion) and a collection of short stories *A shtub mit zibn fentster* (A house with seven windows). *Der meylekh Dovid aleyn iz geblibn* (1946; Only King David remained), and *Lider fun khurbn* (1962; Songs of the Holocaust), convey her grief at the Holocaust and its victims which included her family and friends, but also stress her eternal faith. Her 1965 volume of poems, *Light from the Thornbush*, received the Kovner Award.

FURTHER READING

Kagan B.: *Lexicon of Yiddish Writers*, (New York: 1986) 355–60

DEVRA KAY

Momigliano, Arnaldo Dante (1908–1987)

Italian historian. Born in Caraglio, he held professorships in Rome, Turin, Pisa, London, and Chicago, and his wide learning and immense productivity gave him a unique position in his generation. By the age of 25 he had a reputation in at least three distinct fields of ancient history; work on the Maccabees and on Judaea as a Roman province broke new ground in the history of the Second Temple period. Later in life, factual investigations came to interest him less. He turned to historiography, and his interests ranged from questions of method to the background and interests of individual historians and theorists; at times it seemed that the whole of European intellectual history was his province. A mass of individual papers, in English and Italian, are collected in his *Contributi alla Storia degli Studi Classici e del Mondo Antico* (1955–87); smaller English selections may be found in *Studies in Historiography* (1966) and *Essays in Ancient and Modern Historiography* (1977). Some of these are of specifically Jewish interest; a paper on Jacob Bernays, one of the first Jews to accommodate conventional scholarship to his own interests, is particularly worth attention. Broadly, he saw the most characteristic feature of Jewish scholars as the urge to preserve and transmit tradition. The Italian Jewish situation naturally concerned him; his parents and other figures of his youth died in concentration camps, and some of his latest work went beyond the study of scholarship and has a strongly autobiographical tinge.

In his later scholarly work, Jews and Judaism became ever more prominent. They play a substantial role in *Alien Wisdom: The Limits of Hellenisation* (1975), a masterly and very readable study of Greek understanding of foreign cultures. As Grinfield Lecturer at Oxford University from 1978 to 1982, he returned to the Maccabean and intertestamental periods, not now to establish a factual framework, but rather to examine how Jewish authors of the period used and developed traditional categories of writing and thought to accommodate the widening world of their time. But he was too diverse a figure to be described as only a Jewish or only an Italian historian, and he was certainly not only a historian; he has shown us

how Europeans have thought about their world and its past for more than two millennia.

FURTHER READING

Finley, M. I.: The historical tradition: the *Contributi* of Arnaldo Momigliano. In M. I. Finley, *The Use and Abuse of History* (London: Chatto & Windus, 1975)

Murray, O.: Arnaldo Momigliano. *Journal of Roman Studies* 87 (1987) 11–12

DAVID LEWIS

Montefiore, Claude Joseph Goldsmid

(1858–1938) Theologian and founder of Liberal Judaism in England. Montefiore, scion of a prominent Anglo-Jewish family, studied at Balliol College, Oxford, where he came under the influence of Benjamin Jowett's religious modernism, and at the Hochschule in Berlin, where he met a fellow-student, Solomon SCHECHTER, whom he brought to England to act as his private tutor in Rabbinics. Montefiore founded the radical Reform movement Jewish Religious Union in 1902, which led to the establishment of the Liberal Jewish Synagogue in 1911. Montefiore, determinedly anti-Zionist in the belief that this movement is detrimental to Jewish universalism, tried, in his capacity as president of the Anglo-Jewish Association (1895–1921), to prevent the signing of the Balfour Declaration.

Among Montefiore's works are *Bible for Home Reading* (1897–9), *The Synoptic Gospels* (1909–27), *Rabbinic Literature and Gospel Teaching* (1930), and, in collaboration with the Orthodox scholar Herbert Loewe, *A Rabbinic Anthology* (1938).

Montefiore's work on the New Testament led him to the belief that, in certain respects, the Christian ethic is superior to the Jewish, and in looking forward to the day when the best in both religions (and in other religions) will be combined. But he never contemplated accepting the doctrinal claims of Christianity and steadfastly refused to place the New Testament in any way on a par with the Old. Montefiore also sought to demonstrate that the acceptance of biblical criticism need not lead to any rejection of the Hebrew Bible as devotional literature of the highest order. In Montefiore's view, the greatest contribution to civilization made by the Jews was in keeping theism alive in the life of ordinary Jews throughout the ages.

FURTHER READING

Cohen, L.: *Some Recollections of C. G. Montefiore* (London: Faber and Faber, 1940)

Jacob, W.: *Judaism* 19 no. 3 (1970) 328–41

LOUIS JACOBS

Morpurgo, Rahel (1790–1871)   Italian poet. She was born in Trieste into the famous Luzzatto family and was a cousin and friend of Samuel David LUZZATTO. She received an exclusively Hebrew education from private tutors and teachers: after learning the Pentateuch she began the study of the Babylonian Talmud at the age of 14.

Morpurgo entered the Judeo-Italian tradition and wrote poetry in Hebrew, some inspired by everyday scenes and some in praise of famous men. Her work is pervaded by a profound religious spirit while the images she created recall values and themes belonging to the biblical tradition. Morpurgo's preference was for the sonnet form and Iambic meter, and her often precious rhymes confer elegance upon her poetry.

A poem composed in response to another by her cousin Samuel David Luzzatto was sent by him to the periodical *Kokhevei Yitzhak* (The stars of Isaac) and published in 1816. Morpurgo was thus revealed to be a gifted poet and her work became known in Italy and abroad. Despite the protracted opposition of her parents, she married Giacomo Morpurgo, and bore three sons and a daughter, Penina. On her mother's death, Penina entrusted the manuscripts and letters to Vittorio Castiglioni who, on the occasion of Morpurgo's centenary, published them with a preface and biographical notes under the title *Ugav Rahel* (1890; Rachel's harp).

In her lifetime Morpurgo enjoyed the esteem of many scholars and men of letters who sought her advice on literary matters.

FURTHER READING

Kobler, D.: *Four Rahels* (London: Federation of Women Zionists, 1947)

GABRIELLA MOSCATI-STEINDLER

Moscheles, Ignaz (1794–1870)   German–Czech pianist, conductor, and composer. Born in Prague, he was taught piano from the age of 10 by the director of the conservatory there. After moving to Vienna in 1808 he studied with Albrechtsberger and Salieri and began to establish himself as a pianist. Before long he was one of the favorite performers in Vienna; his virtuoso compositions for piano, which well represent his own playing, made a mark and were taken into the repertoire of a number of eminent pianists. His stature as a composer is evidenced by his being commissioned by the publisher Artaria to make a piano arrangement of Beethoven's *Fidelio* under the composer's supervision. Between 1815 and 1825 Moscheles performed in the major musical centers throughout Europe before settling in London, where he taught at the Royal Academy of Music and was appointed conductor of the Philharmonic Society – he gave a number of successful performances of works by Beethoven. In 1846 he took up the post of Professor of Pianoforte at the Leipzig Conservatory at the invitation of his friend MENDELSSOHN. His most important compositions were written for the piano, his sonatas being particularly notable. His orchestral works include *Symphony No. 1 in C*, and eight piano concertos. He also composed chamber music and songs.

FURTHER READING

Roche, J.: Ignaz Moscheles 1794–1870. *Musical Times* 111 (1970)

SYDNEY FIXMAN

Mosenthal, Salomon Hermann (1821–1877)   German writer and dramatist. Born in Kassel, Mosenthal studied in Karlsruhe and associated with members of the Swabian school of German poetry. After he received his doctorate at the university in Marburg in 1842, he assumed a position as a private tutor in Vienna. There he wrote his most successful work, *Deborah* (1849), which made him famous for a short time throughout Central Europe. Subsequently, he was accepted into the State Civil Service, despite restrictions on Jewish entrance into the ranks. He worked for the Austrian Ministry of Culture and Education and became Chairman of Library Services of the Ministry. He received various promotions and was eventually admitted to the aristocracy in 1871.

Mosenthal produced some poetry, many dramas, and short fiction in the tradition of Jewish ghetto literature, in his case, depicting the particular form of life characteristic of Hessian Jewry he observed in his childhood and formative years. His *Erzählungen aus dem jüdischen Familienleben* (1878; Stories from Jewish family life), contain precious sociological information concerning provincial Jewish life in Central Germany, as well as documenting changes in that life over the course of several years. Mosenthal's Jewish characterizations are consistently positive, if variegated, and tend to depict traditional Jewish life as valuable to a degree, if foreign to modern ways.

Mosenthal's tragedy, *Deborah*, is a powerful drama set in Styria, where powerful and blind prejudices characteristic of the Christian and Jewish communities contribute to thwart a passionate love between a Jewish refugee and an "enlightened" Christian, nearly destroying both. The presentation of a wide spectrum of relatively positive and negative characters from both the Jewish and Christian sides tends to illuminate the complexity of Jewish–Christian relations, as reflected in drama, in the mid nineteenth century in Central Europe. One of the more progressive Jewish voices in the play expresses a readiness to abandon some potentially offensive Jewish traditional formulations, such as the messianic hope to return to Zion. Yet, given a substantial residue of recalcitrant Christian anti-Semitism, Mosenthal, in the play, seems to view emigration to America as the most reasonable option for a bright Jewish future.

Mosenthal also wrote many opera libretti, a genre in which he became quite well known. For example, he wrote the libretti for Nicolai's *Die lustigen Weiber von Windsor* (The merry wives of Windsor), Flotow's *Der Müller von Meran* (The miller from Meran), and Rubinstein's *Die Makkabäer* (The Maccabees), among others. Several of Mosenthal's own poems were set to music, by such composers as Dessauer, Felix MENDELSSOHN, Nicolai, and Kalliwoda.

MARK H. GELBER

Moss [Levetus]**, Celia** (1819–1873); **Moss** [Hartog]**, Marian** (1821–1907)   English writers. Celia and Marian Moss together wrote two three-volume sets of stories, *The Romance of Jewish History* (1840) and *Tales of Jewish History* (1843), the earliest Anglo-Jewish works of fiction. Like their contemporary, Grace AGUILAR, they sought, in the era preceding Jewish emancipation in England, to arouse in their readers sympathy and understanding for Jews. Their didactic and highly sentimental tales, set in a vague biblical or medieval past, portray noble and self-sacrificing Jews, although a very few base characters, always pariahs, are included to demonstrate that Jews are susceptible to human weakness. Although they occasionally include England in their complaints of anti-Semitism, their stories of past persecution implicitly flatter the more tolerant and liberal English society in which they seek to gain total freedom.

In the preface to *The Romance of Jewish History* they state as their motivation "the fact that the English people generally, although mixing with the Jews in their daily duties, are as unacquainted with their history, religion, and customs, as if they still dwelt in their own land, and were known to them but by name". Readers of these tales, alas, will remain unacquainted with Jewish religion and customs, although they may glean a modicum of the history. Religious practices are described in the vaguest terms, if at all, and the whole emphasis is on demonstrating, in highly melodramatic plots, the steadfastness and integrity of exemplary historical Jews.

The Moss sisters also wrote a book of poems, *Early Efforts* (1838), and were editors of a short-lived periodical, the *Jewish Sabbath Journal* (1855).

VERA COLEMAN

Muñiz, Angelina (1936)   Mexican novelist. She was born in France of Spanish parents

529

fleeing the Civil War. She became lecturer in literature at the Colegio de México and the Universidad Autónoma de México. Muñiz gained the Magda Donato prize in 1972 for her first novel, *Morada interior*. This is based on the life of St Teresa of Ávila and focuses on an inner conflict which might have been engendered by her Jewish ancestry. The secret integration of Jewish prayers and beliefs into the mystic's Catholic faith is explored imaginatively.

Rafael, the protagonist of her second novel, *Tierra adentro*, also searches for a way of affirming both his Jewish and his Spanish identity in sixteenth-century Spain. When his parents are burnt by the Inquisition, the boy sets off on foot for Israel, so he may preserve the values they died for, and transmit them to future generations. His wanderings recall the picaresque novel, but this model is subverted by the spiritual nature of the quest. Moreover, Jews are shown to be more marginal than picaros or criminals, rejected even by these social outcasts, who see Rafael as a moral offender, solely by being a Jew. The book is written to bear witness to the survival of Jewish cultural and religious values, despite persecution over the ages. The emphasis throughout is on the need to integrate spiritual beliefs in the active life of the community.

Similar themes inspired her next novel, *La guerra del Unicornio*, which is a form of miniature epic or prose poem dramatizing the conflict between the forces of good and evil. Set in the time of the troubadours, the novel is closely modeled on the romances of chivalry, but through deliberate anachronisms it becomes timeless. Cruelty and lust for power which continually thwart the human search for knowledge and peace are incarnated in archetypal figures who also constitute allusions to the Spanish Inquisition, the Nazis, and the Spanish Civil War. Moreover, the predominantly Christian ethos of medieval literature is here refocused, since Jewish beliefs and customs play a crucial role in the story. The social and intellectual importance of Jews in the Middle Ages is thus reinstated in literature.

Muñiz won the Villaurrutia prize for the novel in 1985 with *Huerto cerrado, huerto sellado*.

(The title comes from Song of Songs iv.12.) Several of these stories or prose poems concern Jewish life or beliefs.

BIBLIOGRAPHY
A Garden Enclosed, a Garden Sealed Off, trans. L. Parkinson Zamora, serialized in: *Mississippi Review* 10 no. 1 (1981), 13 nos 1, 2 (1984); *Pacific Quarterly Moana (NZ)* 8 no. 2 (1983)

FURTHER READING
Contemporary Women Authors of Latin America, (New York: 1983)

ANN DUNCAN

Munk, Solomon (1803–1867) French specialist in Semitic studies. Munk was one of several German-born scholars who settled in France in the first half of the nineteenth century. His speciality lay in Semitic languages and literature which he taught at the Collège de France (1864), and to which, especially in the field of Hebrew and Arabic literature in Spain, he made important contributions (in spite of total blindness). He was responsible for a three-volume critical edition of the original text of Maimonides' *Guide of the Perplexed*, accompanied by a French translation (1856–66). He identified Solomon ibn Gabirol as the author of *Fons Vitae*, hitherto attributed to Arabic writers.

NELLY WILSON

music, Jewish What is Jewish music? Is it the same thing as music created by Jewish-born composers? The difficulty in finding a large enough umbrella under which all kinds of Jewish music can be brought together arises because the three main branches of the Jewish people (Ashkenazi, Sephardi, Oriental) have lived and developed their arts in culturally distinct regions; and representatives of each group have migrated to other parts of the world, taking the music of their heritage and environment with them. Acculturation is the result, and it plays havoc with any attempt at making a rigorous definition of Jewish music.

In his opening lecture to the First International Congress of Jewish Music in Paris in 1957, the eminent ethnomusicologist Curt Sachs defined Jewish music quite simply as "that music which is made by Jews, for Jews, as Jews". This statement has many implications. Does each of the three conditions have to be satisfied in each case? Does the definition apply to art music as well as to liturgical and folk music? Would it be true to say that anything composed not by Jews, not for Jews, not as Jews, is *ipso facto* not Jewish music? Can we tell, just by listening, for example, to Prokofiev's *Overture on Hebrew Themes* or Shostakovich's songs *From Jewish Folk Poetry*, that these works are by celebrated twentieth-century Russian non-Jews? Can we tell, just by listening to Ernest BLOCH's *Sacred Service*, that although the composer was Jewish, this work was not parochially conceived, but rather intended as a gift for the whole of humanity? Can we tell, just by listening, that Felix MENDELSSOHN's Violin Concerto was written by a Jewish-born musician who had embraced Christianity? In other words, are genetics and ideology the only criteria for determining Jewishness in music? What about the content and sound of Jewish music, and its appearance when notated? Hugo WEISGALL, the important American–Jewish composer and scholar contends in his definition that "there are no specific, objective musical qualities which make a piece Jewish or not". (Jewish music in America. *Judaism: A Quarterly Journal*, vol. 3, New York: JTSA/AJC, 1954).

But the enormously wide diversity of styles can, to some extent, be garnered if a more geographical historical approach is adopted: "that music which traces its origins directly or indirectly to the Temple Chant of some 2,000 years ago, but which has over the centuries been subjected to the innumerable non-Jewish influences of the Diaspora". But even if this is acceptable in the context of liturgical and folk music, we must ask again how relevant it is to Jewish Art music which, with certain notable anticipations, came into being in the wake of the French Revolution, that is, only some 200 years ago. This is an extremely short time-span in relation to the development not only of Jewish music, but also of Western Art music; and it helps to explain why the proportion of

internationally recognized Jewish composers has been comparatively small, until fairly recently.

Access to the necessary training in the early to mid nineteenth century gave rise to an interesting paradox: many European ethnic groups that had previously been kept politically and culturally in thrall now chose to rediscover and consolidate their national identity and character. The Jews, however, who had suffered enforced nationhood behind ghetto walls for centuries, chose to internationalize themselves by identifying with all the host nations among whom they lived.

Whereas Jewish-born composers of this period tended to contribute to the culture of their environment despite their Jewishness, rather than because of it, the twentieth century was different. In 1908, for example, a group of professional Jewish composers sought consciously to express themselves in specifically Jewish terms. And so the "Society for Jewish Folk Music" was founded in St Petersburg, with the full support of Rimsky-Korsakov. Important developments were taking place at this time in North America; also in Palestine where, by the time the State of Israel was established, there were several highly organized "schools" of composition.

Today, Jewish composers are working in Jewish centers and elsewhere throughout the world. To what extent do they share common values and characteristics? To what extent is the configuration of qualities and traits exhibited by each individual unique? Is the fact of their Jewish birth significant to them and to their musical creativity? How far does their wider environment influence them? To what extent, if any, do they proclaim their Jewishness in the choice of titles for their compositions, in books, articles, and correspondence about music in general and their works in particular? What traditional materials, if any, do they use? How do they, consciously or subconsciously, incorporate them? Is it easy or difficult to trace a dividing line between works based on folk tunes and "original" compositions? Do the latter contain scales and modes derived from the Near East, oriental ornamentation of melody, accumulations of short, irregular phrases, influences of West Asian instrumental color, improvisation techniques, extreme dynamic levels and moods? These are some of the typical traits of traditional Jewish music. How are they reconciled with, and integrated into, Western formal and harmonic structures?

Perhaps some answers to these many questions will emerge from the music entries in this book.

FURTHER READING

Heskes, I.: *The Resource Book of Jewish Music* (London: Greenwood Press, 1985)

Idelsohn, A. Z.: *Thesaurus of Hebrew and Oriental Melodies*, 10 vols (New York: Ktav Publishing House, 1973)

Nulman, M., ed.: *Concise Encyclopedia of Jewish Music* (New York and London: McGraw-Hill, 1975)

Werner, E.: *The Sacred Bridge*, vol. 1 (London: Dennis Dobson and New York: Columbia University Press, 1959; rev. 1970), vol. 2 (New York: 1984)

ALEXANDER KNAPP

music, Polish–Jewish At the root of Jewish music in Poland there were two elements: religious culture and folklore. Various influences penetrated religious music, among them songs of east and west European Jews as well as the music, of the nations amongst which the Jews were living. Itinerant cantors, frequently surrounded by a small choir which provided vocal accompaniment, carried over old and new melodies of prayers and religious songs which were never free from regional folkloristic influences – not only Jewish. In the Polish territories, some of the cantors acquired legendary fame, winning popularity and recognition not only among the faithful, but also among the non-Jewish musical elite. They included the 13-year-old cantor Joel Dawid Jaszuński, called Baal-Beysyl (d.1850), who was admired by Stanisław Moniuszko and other Polish musicians of the mid nineteenth century.

What contributed to the flourishing of Jewish vocal music in Poland was, above all, the construction of new synagogues in the nineteenth and early twentieth centuries. The more magnificent the temple, the more arduous were the efforts to ensure a high vocal quality of religious services. Thanks to an improvement of the financial situation of the Jewish community and the affluence of the synagogue committees, a whole galaxy of cantors appeared in Poland, their skills matching those of the best opera singers. Many of the cantors gained worldwide renown, and numerous synagogues in west Europe and both Americas were anxious to engage them.

An important position in the field of sacral vocal culture was held by Warsaw's High Synagogue in Tłomackie Street, which functioned from 1878 until the tragic days of the Nazi occupation. During services on especially festive holidays, apart from members of the congregation, chiefly the progressive Jewish elite, only holders of special invitations were admitted to the Synagogue. Such invitations were solicited by outstanding Polish musicians and singers, clergymen, and government representatives. It is worth adding that the High Synagogue in Tłomackie Street was one of the few in Poland that possessed a Reformed (i.e. German) character, admitting, next to the choir, organ music accompaniment. There were other synagogues whose cantors and choirs won world renown in the interwar period. One could mention the Nożyk synagogue in Warsaw (functioning to this day in Twarda Street), as well as synagogues in other towns, such as Cracow, Lodz Białystok, Lublin, Lvov, or Vilna.

The most famous of Polish cantors was Gershon Sirota (1877–1943), called "the king of cantors" and "a Jewish Caruso". He frequently performed in concert halls and had in his repertoire secular as well as religious music, including arias from well-known operas. Opera companies from many countries sought to engage him, but in vain; he remained faithful to the synagogue. During the uprising in the Warsaw ghetto, he and his family were burnt in their flat at 6 Wołyńska Street.

Naturally, synagogue music was not confined merely to the activity of the cantors. The Polish synagogues were famous for their excellent choirs. Depending on the size of the synagogue, the choirs numbered several or several score members. The choir of Warsaw's High Synagogue, for example, included over a hundred persons and several soloists. There were hundreds of such choirs, which were also present in secular music life. For instance, the excellent choir of the synagogue in Tłomackie Street, directed until the outbreak of the war in September 1939 by David Ajzensztadt (who was killed in the Warsaw ghetto together with his daughter, Marysia, a talented singer) frequently performed in concert halls, its repertoire comprising religious and secular works: stylized Jewish folk songs, fragments of operas, and oratorios. The Ajzensztadt choir also performed before the microphones of the Polish Radio.

Bordering on folk music was hasidic music. It was played at the courts of hasidic *tzaddikim*, or saintly rabbis. The hasidic religious festivals were marked by the adoration of God, combined with singing, music, and dancing. This specific hasidic ideology was thus characterized by one of its advocates Nahman Braslawer, 1772–1811 (NAHMAN OF BRATSLAV): "Come, I'll show you a new way to God. Not through speech, but through song. We shall sing, and the heaven will understand us..." The hasidic songs and dances were filled with ecstasy and exaltation. Their authors were mostly devout Hasidim. Some of these interesting works have been preserved until this day, either in collections or on gramophone records.

The rich Jewish folk music was for the most part the work of anonymous authors. Numerous songs have survived until today, orally transmitted to posterity. A number of collections of these songs have been published, coming chiefly from the countries of eastern Europe, in particular from the Polish territories. These are historical, love, and family songs, lullabies, as well as soldiers' songs and songs created during the Second World War, sung by partisans and the people in the ghettos. Their specific beauty and emotional contents took on a particular significance after the war. Many interesting folk melodies have been forgotten. At the close of the nineteenth century, it was realized that the relics of Jewish folk music should be recorded and cultivated. Folk songs began to be collected and published. Before the war, such collections were brought out by Marek Ginzburg, Noe Prylucki, Yoel ENGEL, and Menachem KIPNIS (1878–1942), a popular Warsaw collector and

propagator of Jewish lore, who throughout his life collected Jewish ritual and folk songs and maintained lively contacts with Jewish folk singers.

The origins of Jewish folk songs were diverse. One can discern the influence of the nations amongst which the Jews were living, and thus also influences of Polish folklore. Significantly, the latter were mutual influences, as Polish folklore, too, assimilated Jewish motifs, if only those popularized by KLEZMER bands playing in Polish inns, at weddings, and even in manors. Quite a number of songs were created by folk poet-singers. There were many such folk artists. The last of them was Mordecai GEBIRTIG, a Cracow resident, carpenter by profession, poet, and songster, whose songs were taken down by fellow musicians, as he himself did not know the notes. His songs would frequently become hits sung by popular Jewish actors and were presented on the stages of small Jewish theaters. In 1920 the first volume of his songs, entitled *Folksstimlech* (In a folk tune), appeared, and in 1936 a collection of 50 works, *Mayne lider* (My songs), marking the thirtieth anniversary of his activity. Gebirtig carried on his work in the Cracow Ghetto, but the songs he created there contained less sentiment and joy, and more suffering. He was shot and killed on 4 June 1942, while being conducted, together with other ghetto inhabitants, to the railway station to be deported to Bełżec. During the Nazi occupation, his song *S'Brent, Undzer Shtetl Brent* (Fire, our town is on fire), written in 1938, became the hymn of the fighting ghettos and a call to fight.

Folk music was co-created by the *klezmerim*, who first appeared in the Polish territories in the sixteenth century. As members of manorial or folk bands, they played in inns and at weddings, both Jewish and Polish. They were self-taught musicians who did not know the notes, but nevertheless their masterly playing aroused admiration. There were also *klezmerim* who would become a sensation in palaces and large concert halls. One of them was Józef Michal Gusikof (1806–37), a virtuoso of *strobfiedel*, a variation on today's xylophone. His playing fascinated the most outstanding musicians of the epoch, among them Karol Lipiński, Frédéric Chopin, Felix MENDELSSOHN, Ferdinand

David, Franz Liszt, and also George Sand and Lamartine. He thought himself to be a Polish Jew although he came from Szklow in Byelorussia. He played his own fantasias on Polish themes: mazurkas, polonaises, Polish, Byelorussian, and Jewish folk melodies. His performances at fairs and in Warsaw courtyards launched him on a career that was to lead him to the great concert halls of Europe, including the Paris Opera. The Polish, German, and French press of the time wrote about him extensively. Fascination with the sound of his strange instrument resulted in its introduction in the symphony orchestra under the name of xylophone.

The playing of some of the *klezmerim* often served as a model for outstanding professional musicians. The talent and mastery of those folk artists were, in some way, phenomenal, and thus the magnates were eager to employ them in their palatial orchestras, where they gave concerts or played dance music. Józef Elsner, a Polish composer of the early nineteenth century, director of the Warsaw Opera, wrote in 1805, in a letter to the *Allgemeine Musikalische Zeitung* in Leipzig: "Jewish musicians play the polonaise in such a perfect Polish spirit that no one is likely to match them". The Czech composer František Benda, together with many other violinists, among them the famous Leopold Auer, recall that in their youth they learnt the proper way of holding the fiddlestick from Jewish *klezmerim*.

The Jewish community took an active part in musical life in its various forms. The opera houses and concert halls were frequented by large numbers of Jews. The Jewish community, however, also attended events organized by local Jewish Music Societies, some of which (for example the Warsaw Society) had their own orchestras. The orchestra of the Warsaw Society gave concerts, among other places, at the Nowości theater, with the participation of well-known conductors and soloists. In the 1930s there was a Jewish Music Institute; Jewish music schools and courses existed, as well as chamber ensembles and orchestras, both amateur and professional. Every Jewish theater was, at the same time, a music theater, availing itself of original works by Jewish composers, among them Icchaak Szlosberg, Dawid BAJGIEL-

MAN, Józef Kamiński, Izrael Szejewicz, and Henoch Kon. A significant contribution to Polish music was made by Jewish composers and composers of Jewish descent. Although their works, like the works of many an erstwhile composer, have now fallen into oblivion, they played an important role in their time. Among them were: Henryk Wieniawski (1835–80), a great violin virtuoso, and composer: Adam Mincheimer (Münchheimer, 1830–1904), a composer and conductor, and – after Moniuszko's death – director of the Warsaw Opera; Ludwik Grossman (1835–1915), the author of such operas as *The Fisherman from Palermo*, staged in Warsaw and Paris, and *The Voivode's Ghost*, which became a success in Warsaw, Lvov, St Petersburg, Vienna, and Berlin; Gustaw Adolf Sonnenfeld (1837–1914); called "a Polish Offenbach"; Leopold Lewandowski (1831–96), a violinist, composer, and conductor, was the most outstanding author of dance music in nineteenth-century Poland. Called "a Polish Strauss", he wrote over 300 works, the most popular of which were his temperamental mazurkas, fiery obereks, dolorous kujawiaks, and elegant polonaises. Maurycy Moszkowski (1854–1925), a pianist and composer of the turn of the nineteenth century, was the father of the so-called salon music and the author of the *Spanish Dances*, popular to this day.

The twentieth century can likewise boast several outstanding composers. They include Poland's first dodecaphonist, Józef Koffler (1896–1944); Karol Rathaus (1891–1954), the author of the ballets *The Last Pierrot* and *A Lion in Love* and the opera *Foreign Land*; Szymon Laks (1901–1985); and Aleksander Tansman of Lodz (1898–1986), one of the most prominent contemporary composers, the author of symphonic music, oratorios, and operas.

Jews were active not only in the field of "great music"; they also made a significant contribution to what we call show business today. It is worth noting, for example, that the phonographic industry in Poland was fathered by Juliusz Feigenbaum, the founder of the Syrena Record factory. This diversified show business, including numerous vaudeville theaters and night clubs, needed light music. In this domain, the composers and the authors of texts were almost exclusively Jews – at least, those whose names are still known today were Jews. Among them were the precursors of jazz in Poland, the authors of fashionable dances and song hits. All these composers were unusually inventive and prolific. Albeit the fame of those musicians was transitory, they nevertheless constitute an important chapter in the history of Polish music. Their influence, though frequently short-lived, was not insignificant in their epoch. On the other hand, the great masters of serious music of world-wide renown have secured for themselves a permanent place in the history of Polish music.

MARIAN FUKS

music, popular American–Jewish Were it not for composers and lyricists of Jewish origin, the American musical theater would be much the poorer. The "turning-point works", those which advanced the Broadway musical into the realm of higher art, have not been matched by the output of non-Jewish writers. Moreover, the sheer quantity of Jews who have shaped the course of music on Broadway suggests it would be simpler to cite those non-Jews who were significant contributors. The latter group with a proven track record would include George M. Cohan (his Jewish-sounding family name is actually of Celtic origin), Victor Herbert, Johnny Mercer, Cole Porter, Harvey Schmidt and Tom Jones, Meredith Willson, and Vincent Youmanns, among five or six others. But no score written by a member of this group (with the possible exception of Porter's *Kiss Me Kate*) had the "leap forward" impact on Broadway history as those produced by Jews.

An issue of vital concern to Jews as a people, whether induced by biblical values or by concerns of personal survival, has always been that of social justice. In the musical theater this has been translated by book writers into themes which take a stand or risks, involving large stakes. The following works (all by Jews, unless otherwise indicated by NJ – non-Jewish) not only reflect this communality, but they also are among those that have become landmarks: mis-

cegenation in *Show Boat* (Kern and Hammerstein), ghetto life in *Porgy and Bess* (the GERSHWIN brothers and Heyward, NJ), racial injustice in *South Pacific* (Rodgers, Hammerstein, and Logan, NJ), pro-unionism in *The Cradle Will Rock* (Blitzstein), the anti-war stance of *Bloomer Girl* (Arlen, Harburg, Saidy, and Herzig), apartheid in *Lost in the Stars* (Weill and Anderson, NJ), the urban angst of *Street Scene* (Weill and Hughes, NJ), the vicissitudes of tradition borne by *Fiddler On the Roof* (Bock, Harnick, and Stein), anti-capitalism in *Finian's Rainbow* (Lane, Harburg, and Saidy), society dancing-on-the-edge in *Cabaret* (Kander, Ebb, and Masteroff), juvenile delinquency in *West Side Story* (Bernstein, Sondheim, and Laurents) and the decline and fall of the American dream in *Follies* (Sondheim and Goldman).

There are at least 17 shows about or including the Black experience written by Jews. It is tempting to speculate that in some instances these were masks to cover up a natural urge to use Jewish content. Perhaps Black subject matter was perceived as having greater commercial value than parochial Jewish topics. In any case, there is no doubt that Blacks and Jews have shared histories of oppression, and some of this mutuality is also to be found in their respective musics, spiritual and otherwise.

The specific striving for *Jewish* justice is associated, of course, with the search for homeland (not necessarily the yearning for Zion). This may, in some way, account for the superior quality of many shows by Jews with a non-American setting. The offspring of the "Wandering People" have been adept at simulating nationalist styles, sometimes going beyond pastiche, from the Occident to the Orient. The most comprehensive is to be found in the global range of Bernstein's *Candide*. Cole Porter is a special exception. However, more than one observer has noted the Jewish quotient of this Episcopalian's musical style, and, what's more, he did write à la "Russian", "French", and "Latin" in various shows.

The centrality of book-learning in Jewish conditioning must have also affected the quality of show books. Some of the results are as important to Broadway history as the social justice works listed above. They not only contributed toward elevating the "girlie show" reputation of the musical on to a higher level of artistic accomplishment, but did so without diminishing its entertainment value.

Musicals with Jewish subject matter constitute a sub-category of the American musical. Almost all of them came to the fore after the Yiddish Theater of New York had atrophied. Thus the assimilated theatergoer had the best of the old and new worlds: *Yiddishkeit* wrapped in nostalgia. It should be noted that most of these works were written after the creation of the State of Israel, as if that act legitimized Jewish topics for musical comedy. Among this mixed bag of approximately 40 shows are those on themes taken from American-Jewish life, such as *I Can Get It for You Wholesale* and *Wish You Were Here*; biblical themes, such as *The Apple Tree* and *Two By Two*; biographies such as *Minnie's Boys* (the Marx Brothers) and *Funny Girl* (Fanny Brice), Israeli themes such as *Ari* and *Milk and Honey*, and many more. In addition there are many non-Jewish bread-and-butter works, not necessarily distinguished, but, nevertheless, vital contributions to the American musical by Jewish journeymen writers.

If Jewish musical creators associated with Hollywood, (background scores and incidental songs), as well as with the commercial venue known as TIN PAN ALLEY (authors, publishers, promoters) were added to the list, the percentage of Jews who have molded the development of American popular music would be completely disproportionate to their numbers in the general American population. What are the reasons for the extraordinary statistical phenomenon? Has the musical content of American popular music been affected by Jewish source materials? The answers lie in, respectively, Jewish history itself, and the role theologians have played in stifling the evolution of (sacred) music. The 50-year period in the USA between 1914 (the start of the First World War and the year of Irving Berlin's first full score, *Watch Your Step*) and 1964 (the premiere of *Fiddler On the Roof*) is informed by a musical legacy from Yiddish folk and theater songs and from Ashkenazic synagogue modes and tunes.

FURTHER READING

Gottlieb, J.: *Funny, it Doesn't Sound Jewish: A Look into American Popular Music* (forthcoming)

JACK S. GOTTLIEB

music, Russian–Jewish The history of Russian–Jewish art music begins at the turn of this century and has its roots in the nationalist tendencies that pervade the works of late nineteenth-century Eastern European composers. The initial impetus for such a movement is usually the collection and arrangement of folk songs. The Jewish musical renaissance began the same way, when the gentile music critic Vladimir Stasov encouraged the otherwise assimilated composer Yoel ENGEL (1862–1927) to search the treasures of Jewish folk music for inspiration.

Engel, whose teachers included Taneiev and Ippolitov-Ivanov, became an avid collector and arranger of Jewish folk tunes, promulgating his enthusiasm through his compositions and scholarly writings as well as by organizing concerts of Jewish music. In 1900 the Imperial Ethnographic Society invited Engel to lecture on the first fruits of his research. Before long, Engel's work attracted a large circle of eager followers, including Michael Gnessin (1883–1957), Shlomo Rosowsky (1878–1962), Lazare SAMINSKY (1882–1959), Joseph Achron (1886–1943), Gregory Krein (1880–1955), and his brother Alexander (1883–1951). This group went on to create the Jewish Folk Music Society in 1908 with the aim of furthering interest in their research.

The outbreak of the First World War, however, virtually paralyzed the group's activities, although it did enjoy a short-lived revival after the Russian Revolution. In spite of its brief existence, the Jewish Folk Music Society saw the collection, arrangement, and publication of thousands of folk songs from all over Russia and Eastern Europe. Ultimately the upheavals of a world war and a national revolution resulted in the disintegration of the group, with many members leaving the country.

Several participants, including Engel, went to Berlin, where they organized the Juval publishing house in 1923, continuing abroad the work they had begun in St Petersburg. Engel eventually moved to Palestine; Saminsky and Achron went to the USA. Michael Gnessin and the Kreins remained in the USSR after the Revolution, becoming part of the new musical establishment.

As a composer, Gnessin, a student of Rimsky-Korsakov, hoped to create an individual style uniting his Russian training with his Jewish heritage. Political expediency, however, necessitated a different approach. Nevertheless, Gnessin became one of the most influential educators of his generation, teaching, among others, Tikhon Khrennikov and Aram Khachaturian. Along with his four sisters, the best known being Elena (1874–1967) and Yevgenia (1870–1940), the Gnessin family established a private music school in 1895. This is now Moscow's second conservatory. In 1975, a new multi-story building was added to the Gnessin Institute, a tangible tribute to the rare esteem in which the Gnessins are held.

While an emphasis on their Jewish roots characterizes the compositions of the older generation of Russian–Jewish composers, a less ethnic, more international style marks the work of the younger generation, including Gregory Krein's son Yulian (b.1913), Lev Knipper (1898–1974), and Moissei Vainberg (b.1919).

Born in Warsaw, Vainberg received his musical training in Poland. When the Germans invaded his homeland in 1941, he fled to Moscow. Vainberg's Jewish heritage has a neutral influence on his compositions. Some works, such as the *Sinfonietta* (1948), reflect elements of Jewish folk music; most adopt a musical language akin to Bartók and Shostakovich. According to Boris Schwartz, Vainberg receives many performances and commissions. He is well-liked and one of the few Soviet composers of Jewish origin to have achieved equality among his colleagues.

FURTHER READING

Rabinovitch, I.: *Of Jewish Music; Ancient and Modern*, trans. A. M. Klein (Montreal: The Book Center, 1952)

Rothmüller, A. M.: *The Music of the Jews* (South Brunswick: Thomas Yoseloff, 1967)

Schwartz, B.: *Music and Musical Life in Soviet Russia, 1917–1981* (Bloomington: Indiana University Press, 1983)

ORLY LEAH KRASNER

The establishment of the Hebrew Habimah Theater and the Yiddish State Theater of Moscow (GOSET) in the 1920s stimulated the creation of Jewish musical pieces for the theater such as Engel's music to Sh. AN-SKI's drama, *Hadybbuk* (1922; The Dybbuk), performed by Habimah, and Lev Pulver's music for *Two Hundred Thousand, Bewitched Portrait, The Journey of Benjamin the Third*, and *Uriel Acosta* performed by Goset (1883–1970)

In the 1930s, Jewish music as such was declared incompatible with the ideological doctrine of the state, "speeding up of the building of a socialist society". Jewish composers had to branch out in two directions. Some began to cultivate folk songs and national styles of art of the Russian outskirts which had no background of art-music in the European sense. Yevgeny Bruselovsky (b.1905) wrote the first Kazakh operas; Mikhail Raukhverger (b.1900) a Kirghiz ballet and an opera; Pavel Berlinsky (b.1900) the first Buryat musical drama; Boris Shekhter (1900–61) the first Turkman opera in 1941 and so on. The second direction was the so-called mass song which includes patriotic and love songs. Born mostly in Ukraine and Moldavia, the composers transformed Jewish folklore and elements of the "Blatnaya pesnya" (thieves' chant), and introduced the mixture into the new Soviet songs. The most famous composers of "mass songs" in the 1930s and 1940s were Isaac Dunaevsky (1900–55), the brothers Pokrass, Matvey Blanter (1903–74), Veniamin Basner (b.1925), Mark Fradkin (b.1914), and Y. Frenkel (b.1920).

Constantly growing, the anti-Semitic state policy reached its peak after the Second World War in 1948–53, when all Jewish cultural organizations were violently dissolved and numerous Jewish intellectuals arrested. After Stalin's death, in the so called "thaw", the persecutions ended, but Jewish music as such remained half-legal, a state of things which continues to the present time. This is one of the reasons for the intensive emigration of Jewish composers to Israel and to the West in the 1960s and 1970s.

A new generation of Jewish composers in the USSR have found a means of incorporating Jewish tunes into their works through different musical genres. This can be seen in the works of Sergey Slonimsky's opera (The *Master and Margarita* on the text by M. Bulgakov); in the mono-opera *Anna Frank's Diary* (1970) by Grigory Frid (b.1915). Some elements of Jewish themes can be found in the music of Alfred Shnittke (b.1934) and Boris Tishchenko (b.1939).

Another form of Jewish participation in musical life emerged at the beginning of the 1960s, when the officially accepted "mass songs" were ousted by new songs where composers wrote not only the music but the lyrics as well. These poet-songwriters were not recognized by official and semi-official organs, but gained wide recognition among the public by means of cassette recordings. One of the fathers of song poems of this type was Alexander Ginsburg (GALICH) who emigrated in 1974. Now many such bards occupy a conspicuous place in Russian informal culture, the percentage of Jews among them being very high.

FURTHER READING

Braun, J.: *Jews and Jewish Elements in Soviet Music: A Study of a Socio-National Problem in Music* (Tel Aviv: Israeli Music Publications, 1978)

Smith, G. S.: *Songs to Seven Strings. Russian Guitar Poetry and Soviet Mass Song* (Bloomington: Indiana University Press, 1984)

RUTH ZERNOVA

music in Israel Throughout the history of Israel and especially during the *vishuv* period (1880–1948), folk and art music acquired symbolic functions beyond mere artistic involvement or entertainment. Folk music served as a means for the unification of social groups, for the faster spread of the knowledge of modern Hebrew, and for the dissemination of national feelings, whereas art music was a source of national pride and a sense of revival and independence. Musical life on all levels, performance and composition, was dominated by strong ideology, which, however, was also a source of polemics and disagreement as to the desired character of Israeli music. The ideology was directional, regarding each event as another step toward the slow formation of musical style and musical activity in the future, so that musicians were the target of constant pressure and criticism. At the same time, there was no clear line to follow and frequently they formed their own criteria regarding the definition of an Israeli style.

During the period of Turkish rule in Palestine there began to be a certain distinction between amateur communal activity and professional work. A fine community orchestra was formed in 1895 in the settlement at Rishon Lezion and pianos were imported from Europe, symbolizing the penetration of Western music. At the same time, the contact of farmers in the settlements with neighboring Arab villagers brought them in touch with Arab tunes, which were sometimes combined with new texts in Yiddish. Yet most of the folk songs of the first *Aliyah* were Russian, with either Russian or Hebrew words, or else Russian-influenced melodies.

In 1910 the first music school opened in Jaffa. Its founder, the German-born singer Shulamit Rupin, used the Central European conservatory as a model, with piano, violin, and theory classes as its central activities. The musical director, the violinist M. Hopenko, named the School "Shulamit" following the death of its founder in 1912. A branch in Jerusalem and another school in Tel Aviv followed the same educational approach, thus setting the pattern for music education in Palestine which has followed the European model ever since.

The musical heritage of Sephardic and Yemenite Jews, who formed a substantial part of the small Jewish population, became the focus of a thorough research project by Abraham Zvi IDELSOHN who settled in Jerusalem in 1906. Yet no actual living contact between the musical heritage and way of life of the family-oriented Sephardic and Yemenite Jews and the institutional, concert-oriented musical life of immigrants from Europe could be formed without a long process of mediation, and intermediate stages.

The First World War was disastrous to musical life in the impoverished *Yishuv*. It was only after the war, and with the implementation of the British Mandate over Palestine, that musical life resumed. The two most ambitious projects immediately following the war were the foundation of the opera and the transference of the activities of the Society for Jewish Folk Music from Russia to Palestine. In 1923 the distinguished opera conductor, Mark Golynkin, then conductor of the St Petersburg opera, emigrated to Palestine, following a long period of planning and preparation. While in Russia, Golynkin outlined an ambitious plan for a "temple for the arts", combining opera, theater, ballet, a school for performance, and a research center which would make Palestine an international artistic center. The contrast between vision and reality forced him to begin with a modest opera house, with fine singers from Russia but a small student orchestra, a movie house as theater, and hardly any funds for productions. Nevertheless the opera house opened and presented a series of operas, all in Hebrew translation, among them, standard masterpieces like *La Traviata* as well as works by Jewish composers such as Giacomo MEYERBEER and Anton RUBINSTEIN. After four years of precarious activity, and despite the enthusiastic support of audiences, the opera collapsed for lack of funds. Revivals and occasional productions continued in the 1930s and a new company was founded in 1948, but opera continued to suffer for many years from lack of funds and never became an integral part of the musical life of the country. The realization of biblical music was, however, more consistently attempted through oratorio, with masterpieces such as Haydn's *The Creation* and Felix MENDELSSOHN's *Elijah* performed in Hebrew under the direction of Fordhaus Ben-Zissi.

Between 1922 and 1924 several of the founders of the Society for Jewish Folk Music (founded 1908 in St Petersburg, with a branch in Moscow started in 1914) settled in Israel, including the pianist Arieh Abileah (Nisvitzky), the scholar Solomon Rosowsky, the composer Jacob Weinberg, and the distinguished founder of the society, Yoel ENGEL. Engel made Tel Aviv the center of his Jewish publishing house, Yuval. He was very active in elementary music

education and the composition of songs, but the lack of financial support forced him to make his living as a teacher until his untimely death in 1927. His work was continued by his friends, chiefly the pianist and teacher David Schorr, who coordinated a large-scale project of lectures and concerts, publications, and the organization of amateur choirs. Schorr was highly motivated by an ideology combining socialism, the dissemination of music to the masses of workers and agricultural settlements, and the vision of making Palestine a center that spread the idea of music as a humanitarian, unifying art throughout the Western world. The composer Weinberg wrote an ambitious nationalistic opera, *The Pioneers* advocating kibbutz life, agricultural work, and the abandonment of a diasporan way of life, and quoting Arabic and Yemenite melodies. Lack of funds prevented a production in the country and Weinberg emigrated to the USA in 1927.

Several attempts were made at organizing a symphony orchestra during the 1920s. Ad hoc orchestras composed of all the professional musicians in the country and strengthened with amateurs performed occasionally in front of huge audiences numbering 3,000 on a sand hill in Tel Aviv, but no regular establishment was formed while the *Yishuv* was small, during a period of economic depression and armed clashes with Arabs.

The situation changed with the beginning of the large scale immigration from central Europe in the early 1930s. Well-educated listeners, many of them with fine German pianos, professional performers who had lost their positions in leading orchestras, teachers, and experienced composers came to the country and effected a radical change on the musical scene within a short time. The main event was the founding of the Palestine Philharmonic Orchestra (now the Israel Philharmonic) in December 1936. The orchestra was organized almost singlehandedly by the violinist Bronislaw HUBERMAN. A pan-European in his world view, Huberman regarded the deterioration in Europe as an indication that the international center for music should move to the east, and his initial idea was to form a comprehensive performing art center. The orchestra project soon became an emergency tool for saving Jewish refugees whose admission to the ensemble allowed them to receive the immigration certificate from the British authorities. The first concert series under Arturo Toscanini was a national celebration, and the orchestra maintained high artistic standards, performing with the best conductors and soloists in the world. The pianist and educator Leo Kestenberg was its musical director during the war years.

During the 1920s and 1930s Hebrew folk song underwent considerable stylistic changes. The Russian-influenced tunes and texts were replaced by labor and landscape songs, with optimistic march and dance rhythms, sometimes betraying imitations of Arab singing, such as the song *Gamal gamali* (My cameleer) by Yedidiah Admon, or agricultural songs, such as *Gozu gez* (Cut the wool of the sheep) by Emanuel Amiran. A mediation process of much significance was begun in the 1930s by the Yemenite singer Bracha ZEPHIRAH, a brilliant natural talent educated for a brief period in Germany, who performed in concerts before western-educated audiences, singing traditional songs of various ethnic groups from Palestine, including Arabs, accompanied by the pianist, Nahum Nardi and later with players from the Philharmonic orchestra, thus establishing direct contact between the traditional music of Sephardic Jews and the western concert tradition.

Musical life centered in Tel Aviv and Jerusalem, but local activity of a special kind developed in many of the *kibbutzim* where local composers, such as Yehudah Sharet, created a tradition of community celebrations of festivals. Passover, for example, was celebrated by a unique combination of the traditional text of the *Haggadah* with new texts and music adapted to the agricultural reality of the settlements, thus reviving the ties to the ancient Biblical land with texts from Song of Songs and Psalms as an important source.

Some twenty professionally trained composers emigrated to the country during the period 1931–8, completely changing the musical scene with intensive compositional activity and professional instruction in theory and composition. They did not form a unified school but represented different approaches to the ideological question of the nature of the emerging national style and the role of the composer in the new society. U. A. BOSCOVITCH formulated a comprehensive theory according to which the composer should consider himself a spokesman and representative of the collective. His way of writing must be determined by the dialectics of the place and the time in which he operates; that is, the musical language of the Jewish composers in eastern Europe cannot suit the reality of life in Palestine. Music should reflect the oriental and Mediterranean atmosphere and sounds. Boscovitch's theory, strongly supported by the critic, author, and musician Max BROD, was termed "eastern Mediterranean". Representative works of this kind searched for sonorities derived from Arabic music, dance tunes, Arabic modes, harmonies which resulted from heterophonically doubled melodic lines, and avoidance of subjective, romantic, and personal expression. A totally contrasting approach was that of the German-educated E. W. STERNBERG who supported the right of the composer to express his personal world, and the need to maintain contact and accept inspiration from progressive trends in European music, such as those of Arnold SCHOENBERG and his circle. Some of the composers received musical ideas through joint work with Bracha Zephira, who commissioned arrangements for her traditional songs from most of the composers active in the country in the 1940s. She worked mostly with the most prolific of them, Paul BEN-HAIM who, while avoiding theorizing on national music, found the way to work concurrently on several levels, maintaining his ties to the western tradition in which he had been educated, while absorbing inspiration from folk and traditional music, sonorities of Arabic music, heterophonic techniques, the sound of the Hebrew language, and the Eastern Mediterranean ideology. Mark LAVRY endeavored to make art music easily accessible and popular among the audience at large, stressing tuneful melodies and euphonic sound. His opera *Dan Hashomer* (Dan the guard), based on a play by the poet Sh. Shalom with libretto by Max Brod, is the most salient example of a national opera addressing itself to contemporary social and political problems, presented through a popular love story set on a kibbutz. Other important composers active then were Menahem AVIDOM, Mordechai SETER,

Joseph TAL, Oedeon PARTOS, joined in the late 1940s by Haim ALEXANDER, Zevi AVNI and Ben-Zion ORGAD.

During the 1930s and 1940s the academies of music, first in Jerusalem and later also in Tel Aviv, began to provide professional musical education in the country. The ethnomusicologist, Robert Lachmann, was very active during the four years of his activity in Jerusalem (1934–8) which ended with his sudden death, and his work has been continued by Esther Gerson-Kiwi, arranging the extensive collection of ethnic recordings now comprising the enormous sound archives in the National Library at the Hebrew University.

The foundation of the State of Israel was reflected through a new surge of folk songs directly related to the war and to the Israeli military forces, some written for the military entertainment groups. After several years of wars and economic hardship Israeli society opened to outside influences. The Philharmonic orchestra and fine soloists toured Europe and the USA and composers were exposed to new music. Joseph Tal, the representative of the Israeli avant-garde, founded the first studio for electro-acoustic music, joined later by Avni and others. Some composers, like Partos and Boscovitch, combined contemporary serial and dodecaphonic techniques with modal patterns related to the Arabic *maqam* (Partos's *Maqamat*) or serialization of the rhythms of the Hebrew language (Boscovitch's *Ornaments*). With the normalization of Israeli statehood the ideological pressures diminished and Israeli music in the 1960s and 1970s showed signs of integration into world music, with a similar wide array of styles and technique typical of contemporary music in general. Yet composers still continue to utilize traditional melodies and Hebrew texts, with the influence of non-European musical techniques such as elaborate heterophony, as in Mark KOPYTMAN's *Memory*, in works by Ami Ma'ayani and by Haim Alexander, who integrates folkish, even Mediterranean inspiration with sophisticated serial techniques. During the 1980s attempts at integration of East and West also presented themselves in the field of light and popular music, combining oriental instruments and the style of the *ud* and *kanun* with electric guitars.

From the 1950s new orchestras were founded in Israel, mainly municipal (Haifa, Be'er Sheva) or dedicated to special repertory (Israel Chamber Orchestra). After a long break a new opera company was started in 1986. Since 1965 three musicology departments have been established (Hebrew University, Tel Aviv, and Bar-Ilan Universities) in which extensive research has been done, both in traditional musicology and in ethnomusicology, for which Israel, with its unique concentration of Jewish, Arab, and Christian ethnic groups, serves as a living laboratory for scholars, including visiting researchers from abroad. Israel enjoys a large, interested audience, and concerts, whether in the traditional symphonic realm or in specialized fields such as ancient music, are met with much interest and enthusiasm. Since 1985 professional performance training has expanded to include courses in the performance of non-European music, such as Arabic, Indonesian, and Japanese, symbolizing once again Israel's unique position as a bridge between East and West.

JEHOASH HIRSHBERG

musical performance, Jews in The pervasive role of music in Jewish life from biblical times to the present can hardly be denied. Similarly, the quantity and quality of the Jewish contribution to music in general, while harder to define in many respects, is equally undeniable, especially in the period from the eighteenth century to the present. Why this is so, however, has long been a subject of discussion.

In an attempt to isolate those Jewish genes that lead to creative excellence, Gdal Saleski cites the Jews' extraordinary powers of concentration and analysis, zeal and endurance, appreciation of the poetic and dramatic, and deep emotional responsiveness. Unfortunately, this analysis does not account for the common misconception that the Jewish contribution to music is unequally distributed between performers and composers. One is tempted to phrase the question, "Are there any Jewish composers of a stature equalling Bach or Beethoven?". A quick survey indicates that many composers in the pantheon of immortals were indeed of Jewish or partly Jewish ancestry. More noteworthy is the fact that most of them are from the nineteenth and twentieth centuries, constituting a distinct historical bias. The answer lies in a consideration of Jewish history and customs as well as the shifting relationship of the Jewish community to its Gentile neighbours.

The first place to look for an explanation to the discrepancy between performers and composers lies in the synagogue itself. Music for the service depends upon the *hazzan*, whose role is primarily interpretive. Bound by musical traditions and rabbinic strictures, the synagogue provided little encouragement for new compositions; those by Salamone Rossi at the end of the sixteenth century proved to have no long-term effect. Composers like Bach, however, habitually found a creative outlet – and employment – in the church. The niche in Jewish secular music was also filled by performing artists relying largely on their powers of improvisation, once again minimizing the need for formal compositions.

Another essential consideration is the nature of the training needed to become a musician. With interaction between Jews and Gentiles severely limited throughout much of history, musical tutelage would have had to be obtained within the community from other Jews, thus creating an insularity of knowledge and technique. Cantors learned their art within the confines of the synagogue. Secular performers were similarly taught by local masters. Since formal compositions had no place in the social fabric, the community had no framework for learning or transmitting the necessary background. The desire to pursue such knowledge at all would have been highly irregular and the possibility of acquiring it in the Gentile world was virtually non-existent.

Furthermore, opportunities for either performers or composers outside the Jewish community were rare. Musicians in general were considered socially inferior for many centuries and the combination "Jewish musician" would have been acceptable only under the most tolerant of circumstances. Music's chief patrons were the church and the nobility, neither of which had much inclination towards hiring Jewish musicians. Noteworthy exceptions in this context are the medieval minnesinger Süsskind of Trimberg, and Salamone Rossi, who found favor at the renaissance court of Mantua. In general, however, a milieu accepting Jewish participation would not exist until concerts were accessible to the larger public and a liberal education not grounded in the church became available to all. These two hallmarks of the rising middle class reflect the changing politics and attitudes of the eighteenth century, an era which saw a radical shift in Jewish–Gentile interactions.

The granting of civil liberties after the French Revolution encouraged Jews to assimilate into a larger social environment, one which allowed them access to broader musical currents. For example, it was not unheard of for a *hazzan* to also be an opera singer. Such was the case of Meyer Leoni (1740–96) (see BRAHAM), cantor at the Great Synagogue in London. His dual role frequently perturbed his congregation, and he was ultimately fired when he insisted on singing a performance of Handel's *Messiah*. The most important Jewish contributions to eighteenth-century culture, however, occurred in other realms such as finance and philosophy. Music, like a tree with deep roots, took until the nineteenth and twentieth centuries to reach its most impressive fruition.

A composer whose own family roots epitomize this cultural soil is Felix MENDELSSOHN. While his musical contribution is firmly embedded in the nineteenth-century romantic tradition, his grandfather, Moses MENDELSSOHN ranked as one of the best-known thinkers of the late eighteenth century. Felix Mendelssohn also typifies a knotty problem: the distinction between musicians of Jewish parentage and Jewish music.

Although the question remains under debate, it certainly did not prevent people of Jewish extraction from becoming composers. Unfortunately, nineteenth-century prejudices often did. Although there was seldom anything in the music of these romantic Jewish composers to so identify it, their creator's ethnicity was often enough to hamper its acceptance and hinder job possibilities. The answer for many, including Gustav MAHLER and Arnold SCHOENBERG, was conversion.

Paradoxically, while many musicians were turning away from Judaism to further their creative endeavors, others were seeking a means of revitalizing the synagogue tradition. Just as Salamone Rossi used the secular renaissance musical idiom in his synagogue music, nineteenth-century musicians tried to incorporate the styles of the day. The Viennese singer and composer Solomon SULZER (1804–90), whose singing impressed Franz Liszt, went so far as to commission Franz Schubert to compose a choral psalm-setting in Hebrew. In Paris, Samuel Naumbourg (1815–80) created a synagogal style reflecting contemporary operatic taste.

While the problems of acquiring a musical education and social acceptance slowed any large-scale contributions by nineteenth-century Jewish composers, performers fared much better. Unlike composers who had no historical background within the community from which to draw, a high level of technically proficient performers already existed, especially on traditional instruments like the violin. Once piano lessons became a standard part of middle-class cultural attainment, Jewish pianists soon made their mark as well. Perhaps, too, the performer's interpretive role was less likely to invoke the prejudices of an audience.

Many of the problems facing Jewish musicians in the nineteenth century were alleviated in the twentieth. Increased opportunities, especially in the USA, to pursue musical studies and then earn financial remuneration for one's efforts, coupled with a more socially tolerant environment, led to a substantial increase in the number of Jewish composers. Their works span the entire compass of contemporary styles, from the serialism of Schoenberg to the film scores of Max Steiner, and in many cases indicate a conscious reliance on a Jewish muse for inspiration.

Performers, too, have infiltrated every possible avenue. No longer limited to membership in the "kosher nostra", the violin coterie around Isaac Stern, Jews can be found in classical circles on almost any instrument, either in the orchestra or leading it. The improvisations of KLEZMER music from the *shtetl* have been transplanted to jazz. The cantorial tradition discovered a home in opera. Jews become popular artists, folk-singers, musicologists. The ever-increasing contribution of Jews in music from the eighteenth century to the present may very well be the expression of a natural impulse compensating for all the silent years when our harps hung from the willows of Babylon.

FURTHER READING

Di Cave, L.: *Mille Voci Una Stella; Il Contributo degli Esecutori Vocali Ebrei o di Origine Ebraica alla Musica Operistica e Classica* (Rome: Carucci Editore, 1985)
Gradenwitz, P.: *The Music of Israel; Its Rise and Growth Through 5000 Years* (New York: W. W. Norton & Company, 1949)
Idelsohn, A. Z.: *Jewish Music in its Historical Development* (New York: Schocken Books, 1967)
Saleski, G.: *Famous Musicians of Jewish Origin* (New York: Bloch Publishing Company, 1949)
Sendrey, A.: *Bibliography of Jewish Music* (New York: Columbia University Press, 1951; repr. New York: Kraus Reprint Co., 1969)

ORLY LEAH KRASNER

mysticism, modern Jewish The Jewish mystical tradition began in the second century within the framework of talmudic literature, and was known in the Middle Ages as the *kabbalah*, the largest and most influential school of Jewish mysticism. It produced one central phenomenon in the modern period – modern Hasidism, founded by Rabbi Israel BA'AL SHEM TOV (1700–60) in eastern Europe, and which is to this day the strongest and best-organized segment in Orthodox Judaism. However, Hasidism is not the only modern Jewish mystical movement: to it we should add the Sabbatean movement, which still flourished in the eighteenth century, and the traditional followers of the *kabbalah*, especially among the opponents of Hasidism in eastern Europe and among the Jews in the Middle East and North Africa.

The spiritual crisis which followed the conversion of Shabetai Zevi to Islam in 1666, when belief in his messianic mission was almost universal among all Jewish communities, divided Jewish mystics into various sects. Some tried to return to pre-Sabbatean *kabbalah*, primarily that of Rabbi Isaac Luria of Safed (d.1572), and to follow conservative, orthodox mysticism; some followed their messiah Shabetai Zevi in conver-

"Gate of the Broken Vessels" from chapter 8 of Etz Hahayyim, *a kabbalistic treatise by Rabbi Hayyim Vital (early 18th century)*

sion to Islam, mainly those who formed the Donmeh sect of Sabbateans which flourished in Turkey up to the twentieth century; others formed secret Sabbatean sects within Judaism, expressing their messianic devotion by repeated attempts to settle in Jerusalem (like the large group which followed Rabbi Judah the Pious in 1700), while still others remained "underground" in various parts of Europe. One such sect received attention because of the controversy concerning the Sabbateanism of Rabbi Jonathan Eibeschutz, the great Rabbi of Prague in the first half of the eighteenth century. Other mystics who derived some of their ideas from Sabbatianism were those gathered around Rabbi Moshe Hayyim Luzzatto of Padua (1707–47). He regarded himself as a Messiah

and he and his circle produced meaningful messianic–mystical literature. The most notorious group of mystics was the one gathered around Jacob Frank in Poland. Frank, who saw his mission as a continuation of the messianic role of Shabetai Zevi, created a sect of nihilistic heretics who, after being excommunicated by the rabbinic establishment, converted to Christianity in 1760. The Frankists continued their nihilistic activities after their conversion, and some of them took part in upheavals following the French Revolution and the Napoleonic wars.

Hasidism derived some of its ideas from Sabbatean mysticism although it transposed them into an Orthodox framework. The main new mystical institution introduced by Hasidism, the adherence to the *tzaddik*, the mystical leader of the community, is based on the idea of a superhuman redeemer, although usually in Hasidism the *tzaddik*'s redeeming role is limited to his followers in his own area during his lifetime. Some hasidic rabbis, however, saw their messianic role as engulfing the people of Israel as a whole, such as Rabbi NAHMAN OF BRATSLAV (d.1810), thus returning to the original Sabbatean framework. Most hasidic leaders, however, were content to follow traditional kabbalistic study, some of them producing important commentaries to the Zohar and other ancient kabbalistic works. The Hasidim were also active in the printing of medieval kabbalistic works, and so helped spread the knowledge of the sources of Jewish mysticism.

The opponents of Hasidism (the *Mitnagdim*), led by Rabbi Elijah the Gaon of Vilna in the last quarter of the eighteenth century, concentrated on the study of the Zohar and the Lurianic *kabbalah*, while restricting it to adults under suitable tutorship. The main avenue of kabbalistic expression was, in these circles, as in those of the Hasidim, the *Derashah* (homily or sermon); hundreds of collections of such *Derashot* were printed in the eighteenth and nineteenth centuries, mainly in eastern Europe, dedicated to teaching ethical behavior reflecting a theological basis that is purely kabbalistic. The same phenomenon is also to be found in Morocco, Egypt, Syria, and other Jewish communities in the Ottoman Empire. Some rabbis wrote kabbalistic works, while most of them preached traditional Jewish ethics relying heavily on kabbalistic symbolism. Some *yeshivot* (rabbinic academies) became centers for the study of *kabbalah*, like the Beth El *yeshivah* in Jerusalem. It should be noted, however, that during the last four centuries no Jewish theological system has appeared within Orthodox Judaism to replace the *kabbalah*.

The opposition of the Jewish Enlightenment to Hasidism and the *kabbalah* did not weaken the adherence of Orthodox Judaism to this ancient mystical system. When new Orthodox Jewish centers were established in the USA, Europe, and Israel after the Holocaust, the traditions of the Hasidim and the Mitnagdim were revived and continue to develop along the old lines. The major new phenomenon of the last generation is the emergence of one hasidic sect, *Habad* (Lubavitch), led by Menachem Mendel Shneursohn in New York, an order which attempts to convert all Jews, everywhere, to its ranks, and which expresses a renewed messianic zeal.

There are a few circles of kabbalists active today outside of the hasidic and mitnagdic schools, most notable among them being the followers of Rabbi Yehudah Ashlag, who wrote a detailed commentary on the Zohar in the first half of this century. Portions of this commentary are published today in separate books and studied by a small group of disciples.

The modern, scholarly study of Jewish mysticism which was begun by Gershom SCHOLEM in 1921 also created a renewed interest in Kabbalah. Scholem's many scholarly works have been published in Hebrew, English, German, and French, and several circles of students, in the USA, UK, and France, have read them as if they were original works of *kabbalah* rather than scholarly studies; several such groups of "kabbalists" exist today. These, however, do not reflect the enormous spiritual force within the *kabbalah* which shaped Jewish culture in previous centuries. The only active and creative element of Jewish mysticism in modern times is to be found within Hasidism, especially in the Lubavitch sect.

FURTHER READING

Dan, J.: *Gershom Scholem and the Mystical Dimension in Jewish History* (New York: Press, 1987)

Scholem, G.: *Major Trends in Jewish Mysticism* (New York: Schocken, 1954)

JOSEPH DAN

N

Nahman of Bratslav (1772–1810) Hasidic rabbi. He was born in Medzhibozh, Ukraine. His mother, Feige, was the granddaughter of the BeShT (Israel Ba'al shem tov, the founder of the hasidic movement). His childhood in Medzhibozh is described in his biography, *Hayyei Moharan* (The life of Rabbi Nahman). In these stories we find a lonely child keenly aware of the conflict between the ideal world, based on his reading and studying, and reality. At the age of 13 he was married, and moved to Usyatin. His life in this village and his encounters with nature were later expressed in his sermons, *Likutei Moharan*, and in his stories.

When he was about 20 he moved to Medvedevka where he became a self-appointed public leader and teacher. In 1798, Nahman decided to go to the Holy Land, an amazing episode that has generated considerable commentary. Arthur Green, in his biography of Nahman, notes that the sequence of events takes the shape of a paradigmatic rite of passage with its order of danger, a journey to the center of the world, and a passage through water as a prelude to rebirth.

In the summer of 1799 after a long, adventurous journey, Nahman returned home. His life now became very difficult. Declaring himself to be the *tzaddik* of the generation (*tzaddik hador*), the true *tzaddik*, he aroused the anger of Rabbi Aryeh Leib of Shpole (referred to as the *Zeide* – the Old Man). The *Zeide* of Shpole represented the mainstream belief that Hasidism was an ideology of deeds and self-example. In 1802 Nahman moved to Bratslav to become a leader of a small group of Hasidim. By the summer of 1803 both Nahman's reputation and his isolation, were firmly established but he and his Hasidim were excommunicated by the major hasidic leaders.

In Bratslav he composed his main literary work which was set down in writing by Rabbi Nathan Sternhartz, Nahman's pupil, scribe, and secretary. He was affected during this time by the death of his son in 1806 for whom he had had messianic expectations, the death of his wife, Sosia in 1807, his own illness (tuberculosis), and the frustration of his messianic expectations based on his belief that he himself was a messiah, the son of Joseph, who would usher in the period of redemption. Seeking a remedy for his illness he moved from place to place. He died and was buried in Uman.

Rabbi Nahman's doctrine was based on the kabbalistic tradition of Isaac Luria, the most seminal figure in Safedic Mysticism. According to this messianic mystical tradition, man, in order to be redeemed, must seek the truth. This was the primary activity of a human being and it occurred within his soul. Nahman, trying to explain his own messianic failure, maintained that his generation was not prepared for the messianic age. To prepare the hearts of his contemporaries and arouse in them a desire to worship God, he turned to telling stories which symbolically describe the world of the divine, on the one hand, and reality, on the other. Within his stories, we find mythical, folkloric, and autobiographical motifs. Their principal motif is that of search and struggle: a general struggle to redeem the world from evil; a national struggle to redeem the nation of Israel from exile; and the human struggle for liberty.

BIBLIOGRAPHY

The Tales, trans., with introduction and commentaries by A. J. Band (New York: Paulist Press; Toronto: Ramsey, 1978)

FURTHER READING

Green, A.: *Tormented Master: A Life of Rabbi Nachman of Bratslav* (Alabama: University of Alabama, 1979)

Rapoport-Albert, A.: Confession in the circle of Rabbi Nahman of Bratslav. *Bulletin for the Institute of Jewish Studies* 1 (1973) 65

MICHAL ORON

Naquet, Alfred Joseph (1834–1916)

French Republican politican. Naquet was born in Carpentras. After his initial scientific work as a chemist (*Principes de chimie fondés sur les théories modernes*, 1865), Naquet played an important part in Republican politics, first as secretary to Léon Gambetta and editor of *La démocratie du Midi* and later as radical deputy for the Vaucluse and member of the Senate. He promoted the bill legalizing divorce (1884) known as the "Naquet law". Unlike other prominent French Jews and in spite of being totally assimilated, a militant atheist with no links with the Jewish community, he spoke out against pre-Dreyfus Affair anti-Semitism, condemning it as a retrograde force likely to halt the process of assimilation. His subsequent opposition to any form of Zionism sprang from a similarly assimilationist stance.

NELLY WILSON

Nathan, Isaac (1790–1864)

English composer. Nathan was born in Canterbury, where his father, Menahem Mona, was cantor to the small Jewish community. He later claimed that his father was the illegitimate son of Stanislaus Poniatowski, the last king of Poland, and an unknown Jewish mistress. He was originally designated for the rabbinate and attended the Reverend Solomon Lyon's boarding school in Cambridge, but at the age of 18 he moved to London as apprentice singer and composer to Domenico Corri, the most fashionable Italian music teacher of the day. He quickly won favor with his good looks and pleasing tenor voice, and was appointed singing teacher to Charlotte, Princess of Wales, and Musical Librarian to her father (later George IV).

In 1814 he persuaded Lord Byron to write a series of poems which he would set to "very beautiful melodies sung by the Hebrews before the destruction of the Temple of Jerusalem". Byron's "Hebrew Melodies" were published with "appropriate Symphonies and Accompaniments by John BRAHAM and Isaac Nathan". Braham's name provided invaluable publicity although he took no part in the actual composition. Despite Nathan's claim for authenticity, the music has little recognizable Jewish liturgical content, but nevertheless proved very popular with contemporary audiences. Nathan also wrote incidental music and light operas which were performed at Covent Garden. He published a *History of Music*, subtitled *Musurgia Vocalis* (1835) and the first biography of the Spanish soprano, Maria Malibran (1836).

CAROLE ROSEN

In 1841 Nathan emigrated to Australia to escape his debts and brought with him new standards of musical knowledge and professionalism, as the newspapers of the day were quick to point out. Little serious music had been written in Australia before Nathan's arrival and he soon assumed the role of musical laureate to the colony. The consistent public interest in Nathan's work probably stems not so much from its quality as from the fact that music and dancing were the principal forms of recreation in the Australia of the period.

Despite his deep involvement with church music circles, his work contained many Jewish themes. What may be his best known work, *The Southern Euphrosyne and Australian Miscellany Containing Oriental Moral Tales, Original Anecdotes,*

Poetry and Music, etc., includes tales from the Talmud, episodes from Jewish history, quotations from the Rabbinic commentators, and a collection of Aboriginal songs. His fascination with Aboriginal music earned no sympathy and it was publicly stated that good music was spoiled by its thematic connections.

Nathan arranged the music for the consecration of the York Street Synagogue, Sydney, in 1844, but the opening *Barukh Haba* and the concluding *Halleluyah* are both now lost, allegedly destroyed by his second wife, with all his unpublished compositions which had Jewish associations, as part of her attempt to erase memories of Nathan's Jewish background. His numerous works include the opera *Don John of Austria*, the first opera to be written in Australia, and several patriotic Australian songs, most of which were written from financial necessity.

FURTHER READING

Burwick, F., and Douglas, P.: *A Selection of Hebrew Melodies, Ancient and Modern by Isaac Nathan and Lord Byron* (University of Alabama Press, 1988)

Levi, J. S. and Bergman, G. F.: *Australian Genesis* (Sydney and Melbourne, 1974) 176–82

Wentzel, A.: Early composers of music in Australia. *Quadrant* 22, 29–36

Mackerras, C.: *The Hebrew Melodist: A Life of Isaac Nathan* (Sydney: Currawong Publishing Co., 1963)

ALAN D. CROWN

Nathan, Robert (1894–1985) American author. Robert Nathan was born to a Jewish family in New York city but was not typically concerned with those issues characteristic of Jewish writers. His writings for the most part represent the thoughts of an assimilated Jew. He was educated at home and in Switzerland, eventually graduating from Phillips Exeter Academy. He then attended Harvard, where he edited the *Harvard Monthly* but dropped out of college when he decided to marry. After leaving Harvard, he started employment at a New York advertising agency, publishing his own work in various magazines and papers at the same time.

Robert Nathan characteristically writes ironic fantasies which explore the boundaries of time. His first novel, *Peter Kindred* (1919) is semi-

autobiographical. It traces the intellectual growth of a young boy at preparatory school and at Harvard. The novel also shows how the conversation of "nice" people reveals bitter prejudice. *Autumn* (1921) depicts the life of a Vermont schoolmaster whose very compassion towards his fellow man lends him the qualities of a secular rabbi. *Jonah* (1925), a retelling of the biblical tale, suggests that like other Jewish writers, Nathan consistently questions rather than blindly accepts his own heritage and in *Road of Ages* (1935), Nathan recounts the struggles of Jewish exiles. His most important novel, *A Portrait of Jennie* (1940), weaves a romantic love story which moves outside the constraints of time. *A Star in the Wind* (1962) examines the affects of Zionism, and symbolically retells the story of man's search for a home.

BIBLIOGRAPHY

The Bishop's Wife (Indianapolis: The Bobbs-Merrill Company, 1938) [short novel]; *The Devil with Love* (New York: Alfred A. Knopf, 1963) [short novel]

FURTHER READING

Benet, S. V.: The world of Robert Nathan. Introduction to *The Barley Fields: A Collection of Five Novels by Robert Nathan* (New York: Alfred A. Knopf, 1938)

Laurence, D. H.: *Robert Nathan: A Bibliography* (New Haven: Yale University Press, 1960)

DEBRA MORRIS

Nathansen, Henri (1868–1944) Danish playwright and novelist. Nathansen was born in Hjørring, Jutland. He practiced law (1892–1902), first as Assistant Judge, then as a High Court defense counsel but always felt a strong attraction towards literature and the stage. In 1899 he made his debut as a prose writer with "Sommernat" (A night in summer).

Nathansen was at his best depicting the struggle of Jews to transplant their heritage into modern times. His basic mood was expressed by characters such as Daniel Hertz, in the play of that title (1909), "I was smiling at the New, while in my heart the Old was in tears".

Nathansen's one major novel, the four-volume *Bildungsroman, Af Hugo Davids liv* (The life of Hugo David), appeared in 1917. It is a portrait of several stages in the life of a contemporary Jewish Dane, of his awareness of having a specific ethnic and cultural background, and his concomitant attempts to be accepted in Danish Gentile society. The attempted reconciliation fails. The novel contains the most perceptive analysis of Jewish minds in Danish literature. His second large work of fiction, *Mendel Philipsen og Søn* (1932) is centered round a single family and its milieu.

His most popular work is the play *Inden for Murene*, (1912; Within the walls), whose dominant themes are the tensions between Danish and Jewish lifestyles, between Jewish and Danish members of the bourgeoisie, and between the old and the new. It is a skillfully wrought, post-Ibsenian play, the best of its kind in Denmark, and a Royal Theater staple. His sensitive, insider's portrayal of a Jewish family has secured this play a steady success.

Dr Wahl (1915) is Nathansen's most passionately ideological play. For its anti-clerical, anti-royalist, and anti-militarist protagonist he borrowed some of the features of Georg BRANDES and his brother Edvard. Later, in 1929, Nathansen published a "portrait" of Georg Brandes, in which his model's Jewish contours are drawn particularly sharply. Nathansen was involved in Jewish politics in Denmark, but did not declare himself a Zionist until the 1930s.

During the Nazi occupation of Denmark, 1940–5, Nathansen with his wife, like the majority of the Danish Jewish population, had to take refuge in Sweden. There he ended his own life.

FURTHER READING

Borum, P.: *Danish Literature* (Copenhagen: Det Danske Selskab, 1979) 59–60.

JUDITH WINTHER

Neher, André (1913–1988) French rabbi, scholar, and philosopher. Neher was born in Obernai, Alsace, into a family of modern, practicing Jews. Prior to and after the Second World War, he taught German in secondary schools in Alsace. During the war Neher and his family immersed themselves intensely in Jewish studies. He emerged from the experience as an original and highly captivating Jewish thinker. By the early 1960s, he had established himself as the spiritual and philosophical leader for an entire generation of young Jewish intellectuals in the Francophone world. His influence was so profound that David BEN GURION named him as one of the Sages of Israel in 1957. In that same year, Neher was elected a member of the influential Executive Committee of the International Union for Jewish Studies (Jerusalem).

His first published work, *Transcendence et immanence* (1946), projected his fundamental belief as a philosopher and Jew. Neher stressed the necessity for reasoned belief in all matters of Jewish and human life, combined with an abiding respect for tradition. His own thought was strongly influenced by the teachings of Rabbi Judah Loëw ben Bezalel, the *Maharal* of Prague, who preached about the vital "alliance of God with Man, in particular with the People of Israel". Such views were given broad definition in Neher's study of the Maharal, *Les Puits de l'Exil, la théologie dialectique du Maharal de Prague* (1966).

In 1948 Neher was elected to the Chair of Jewish Studies at the University of Strasbourg. Within that community, he assisted in the development of a strong local and regional commitment to Jewish life and responsibilities. He actively convinced the Catholic and Protestant communities of the legitimacy of Jewish aspirations, most especially Zionism. In fact, it was his own Zionist beliefs which led Neher to emigrate to Israel in 1967. He settled in Jerusalem with his wife, Renée Neher–Bernheim, and assumed a teaching post at the Hebrew University. He continued to interpret the totality of the Jewish spiritual inheritance to a predominantly French public until his death.

Works in English include: *Moses and the Vocation of the Jewish People* (1959), *The Prophetic Existence* (1969), and *The Exile of the Word* (1981).

BIBLIOGRAPHY

Moses and the Vocation of the Jewish People, trans. I. Marinoff (New York: Harper; London: Longmans, 1959); *The Prophetic Existence*, trans. W. Wolf (London: Thomas Yoseloff, [1969]); *The Exile of the*

World, trans. D. Maisel (Philadelphia: The Jewish Publication Society, 1981)

SIMON SIBELMAN

Nemerov, Howard (b.1920)   American poet, novelist, short story writer, essayist, and literary critic; US poet laureate. Before he graduated from Harvard College in 1941, he had distinguished himself as a talented writer: he won the Bowdoin Essay Prize, and his senior essay on Thomas Mann received praise from Mann himself. Following graduation he enlisted in the Royal Canadian Air Force as a fighter pilot, and later (1944–5) served with the Eighth US Army Air Force. He served as associate editor of *Furioso* magazine from 1946 to 1951 and was consultant in poetry to the Library of Congress from 1963 to 1964. He has taught on the faculties of Bennington College (1948–66), Hollins College (1962–3); Brandeis University (1966–9), and has been teaching at Washington University in St. Louis since 1969, where he is the Edward Mallinckrodt Distinguished University Professor of English.

Nemerov is primarily known as a poet, and he has won many literary prizes including induction into the American Academy and Institute of Arts and Letters (1977), the Pulitzer Prize for Poetry (1978), and the National Book Award (1978). His verse is lucid, neat, finished, and witty, and often constructed in blank verse. He writes much nature poetry; in his verse, precisely visualized, evocative descriptions of natural phenomena lead both inward, to insights on human nature, and outward, to reflections on human existence. Nemerov's reflective nature poetry at its most profound occurs in the poetic sequence "Runes", in *New and Selected Poems* (1960). He is keenly aware of the artistic illusion which creates its own enchanted world, where the "real" world of "the sickbed and suffering" are excluded. Yet in Nemerov's poetry, death and darkness always have at least a symbolic presence; the tension between art's elegant surface and gross mortality, between the stories and the facts behind the stories, provides Nemerov's poetry with much of its depth and bite.

Biblical themes and images reverberate frequently in Nemerov's *oeuvre*, and he treats Jewish subjects directly in several works, including a novel, *The Homecoming Game* (1957), two verse dramas, "Cain" and "Endor", and poems such as "Lot Later". In the biblical pieces, Nemerov's heroes are the characters conventionally conceived as villains or losers. When writing of the modern scene, he tends to satirize modern mores. Yet despite his skepticism and irreverent attitude toward the dogmas of religion, science, and art, Nemerov maintains a deep respect for the mysteries of man and nature, and he has a basically conservative approach to society.

SYLVIA FISHMAN

Németh, Andor (1891–1953)   Hungarian writer and critic. He studied philology at the University of Budapest. His poetic play *Veronika tükre* (Veronica's mirror) was staged in 1913. In 1914 he visited Paris and was interned by the French authorities during the war. In 1919, on his way back to Hungary, he stopped in Vienna and became (almost by chance) the Press Attaché of the Hungarian Soviet Republic in Austria. Between 1919 and 1926 he lived in Vienna, contributing poems, book reviews, and articles to most Hungarian émigré publications. After his return to Budapest in 1926 he worked both for the popular press and for small left-wing cultural reviews, and became the close friend of the great socialist poet Attila József. Between 1936 and 1939 Németh was a contributor to *Szép Szó*, József's review, but in 1939 he moved to France. During the German occupation he lived in the South of France. After the liberation he lived in Paris for two years and it was there that he published the essay *Kafka ou le mystère juif* (1947). In 1947 he returned to Hungary where he was offered the editorship of the cultural review *Csillag* but after a few years he retired and spent the final period of his life in almost complete isolation. His last book, a historical novel about the famous Transylvanian printer Miklós Kis, *A betű mestere* (1954; The master of letters), was published posthumously.

Németh was a versatile and extremely well-read writer; his "Emlékiratok" ("Memoirs") first printed in the collection *A szélén behajtva*

(1973; *Turned down at the corner*) teem with literary anecdotes and colorful real-life adventures. A friend of the Hungarian humorous writer Karinthy, as well as Arthur KOESTLER, Németh is above all a literary *connoisseur* and an outstanding popularizer of literature. Not only his interpretations of Attila József's poems are of lasting value, but also his perceptive reading of Franz KAFKA's work. He stresses the role of Jewish mysticism in Kafka's work and discusses the structure of Kafka's myths. With the exception of this book and some short stories Németh's Jewishness is expressed not so much in the choice of his themes as in his wistful and melancholy humor, and his total involvement with imaginative literature.

FURTHER READING
Koestler, A.: *The Invisible Writing* (London: Hutchinson, 1969) 205–11.

GEORGE GÖMÖRI

Nemoy, Leon (b.1901)   Librarian and scholar in the field of Judeo-Arabic and Karaite studies. Born in Balta in Russia, he studied classical and Slavic languages at Odessa University. Before emigrating to the United States in 1923 via Poland, he served successively as librarian of the Society for the Propagation of Knowledge (Odessa, 1914–21), the Academic Library of Odessa (1919–21), and the University Library (Lvov, 1922–3). He pursued his studies in Semitic languages under Charles Torrey at Yale University (1924–9), where he became curator of Hebrew and Arabic Literature and principal rare-book cataloger at the Sterling Memorial Library until his retirement in 1966. He centered his scholarly interests on Karaite history and literature, and besides his diverse catalogs of the Yale Arabic and Hebrew collections, he contributed numerous articles, studies, and reviews written in English, Hebrew, and Yiddish to various scholarly journals on Karaitica, Arabic philology, and the History of Jewish and Arabic medicine. His major work was the monumental edition of al-Qirqisânî's Code of Karaite Law, the *Kitâb al-anwâr wal-marâqib* (5 vols, 1939–43), based on manuscripts in Leningrad and London. He also produced for the Yale Judaica Series, of which he became, after 1956, one of the principal editors, a *Karaite Anthology* (1952), a valuable collection of sectarian texts, translated from Arabic, Aramaic, and Hebrew into English with introductions and notes. Upon retirement from Yale, he moved to Philadelphia where he became Research Professor in Karaite Literature at Dropsie College. In 1976 he was awarded a DHL *in honoris causa* by the Hebrew Union College.

FURTHER READING
Brunswick, S., ed.: *Studies in Judaica: Karaitica and Islamica presented to Leon Nemoy on his Eightieth Birthday* (Ramat–Gan, 1982)

PAUL B. FENTON

Netherlands, Jewish art in the   The role of the visual arts in Judaism has long been a minor one. This is because of the biblical second commandment which states that "no graven images shall be made, nor any likeness of what is in the heaven above or the earth beneath". However, the absolute prohibition was against the making of idols. This explains why both Tabernacle and Temple, the oldest European synagogues and medieval manuscripts are decorated and illustrated. Meaning and content are based on biblical and rabbinical explanations but the actual form is adapted from the surrounding culture. In 1796 all Jews in Holland were declared Dutch citizens. Since this Declaration of Civil Equality, all Jews have been free to interpret their Jewishness in their own way.

The Dutch environment, Jewish religion, persecution and survival, the establishment of the state of Israel, all play different parts in the lives of different artists. Several seventeenth- and eighteenth-century portraits and illustrations of Jewish texts form the earliest examples of Jewish art. Thus there is a portrait by Salom Italia (1619–after 1655) painted in 1642 of the learned rabbi Menasseh ben Israel (1604–57). Jewish ceremonial objects, such as Torah scroll finials, were made in those days by non-Jews, since Jews could not be guild members.

In the nineteenth century the first generation

551

of Jewish artists emerged who followed the style and subject matter of their Dutch contemporaries. The landscapes and townscapes by S. L. Verveer (1813–76) a then famous painter, and the genre painting by D. Bles (1821–99) and M. Calisch (1819–70) are inspired by the works of the Dutch Golden Century, which was a great inspiration to many nineteenth-century artists. These painters scarcely dealt with Jewish topics. The major figure from the second half of the nineteenth century is Jozef Israëls (1824–1911). He was inspired by Judaism and gave expression to the new ideals of his age, gaining international recognition for his work. He chose to work in the rustic village of Laren, near Amsterdam, where pupils followed him, giving rise to the Laren School of painters (*c*.1900). There were several Jewish artists in this Laren School, including E. S. van Beever (1876–1912), D. Schulman (1881–1966), B. Laguna (1864–1943), and S. Garf (1879–1943).

Impressionism was an important influence on the following generation, of whom Jozef's son Isaac Israëls (1865–1934) was the most successful. The principle of art for art's sake made its appearance and the number of works produced in this period with specifically Jewish subject matter is also limited. Towards the close of the nineteenth century several artists began to protest against the very dated forms used in industrial art and design and believed that the old crafts should be restored to their former respected place. A good example of a graphic designer who experimented with printing techniques and developed his own unique style is S. Jessurun de Mesquita (1868–1944). That struggle to achieve a harmony between form and function can also be seen in a sculpture of J. Mendes da Costa (1863–1939). At roughly the same time, popular realism is represented in the work of M. Cohen (1901–43) and S. Meyer (1877–1965).

E. Frankfurt (1864–1920), M. Monnickendam (1874–1932), and his pupil Marianne Franken (1884–1943), gained popularity during the interbellum. P. Citroen (1896–1983) became popular with his realistic portraits. In the years between the two world wars Jewish artists recognized their own emancipation in the struggle for socialism and Zionism. Jewish artists such as E. Smalhout (1889–1939), M. Bleekrode (1896–1943) and Fré Cohen (1903–43), together with non-Jewish colleagues, worked to produce propaganda for a better world. Other artists, such as Else Berg (1877–1942), M. Schwarz (1876–1942), M. van Dam (1910–43), and B. Hanf (1894–1944) sought and found connections with the avant-garde in other countries. Many of these artists were killed by the Nazis during the Second World War. There are a few drawings, such as those by L. Kok (1923–45) and J. H. Gosschalk (1875–1952), that have been preserved from Westerbork, a Dutch transit camp. They give an impression of the life in this imprisoned society, set in a dreary, comfortless landscape.

After the liberation Jews returned to a country that had to rebuild itself: their place in Dutch society was difficult, their memories filled with grief. This can clearly be seen in the work of such artists as W. Couzijn (b.1912) and Frieda Tas (1896–1977). The children of the survivors experience the effects of the war indirectly. In their highly personal style of painting they show themselves deeply influenced by their Jewishness. Characteristic of the post-war period is the variety of styles: the dramatic expression of Chaja Polak (b.1942) stands in sharp contrast with the abstract art of E. Content (b.1943). Commenting on his work, Content once said: "I am a Jew and I make abstract paintings because I feel impelled by my religion to free people from the addiction of the image". The wheel has come full circle; producing a paradoxical link between art and the biblical second commandment.

EDWARD VAN VOOLEN

Neugeboren, Jay (b.1938) American fiction writer. Born in Brooklyn, New York, Neugeboren was educated at Columbia University and gained an MA at Indiana University. He taught at a wide variety of institutions – including New York City public schools, Stanford University, and SUNY – Old Westbury – before becoming writer-in-residence at the University of Massachusetts, Amherst. Neugeboren is a prolific writer of novels, short stories, autobiography, and drama. But it was *The Stolen Jew* (selected as the best novel of 1981 by the American Jewish Committee) that made the difference. It is a thick, complicated novel about the inextricable connections between personal memory and Jewish history, between the patterning that art makes possible and the insistencies of life, between an aging ex-writer named Nathan Malkin and his obligations to those, living and dead, who comprise his "family". The result is a novel-within-a novel, as Nathan rewrites "The Stolen Jew", hoping to sell the manuscript at a high price on the Russian black market thus raising money to aid the refuseniks. Whole chapters of Nathan's novel are interspersed with Neugeboren's; each refracts upon the other.

With *The Stolen Jew*, Neugeboren found "a *subject*, a subject that comes from deep personal wells within me". The defining subject is, of course, his Jewishness, and the result has been one of the more important searches currently being conducted for an authentically Jewish–American esthetic. In this quest he joins other Jewish–American writers such as Arthur A. Cohen, Hugh NISSENSON, and Cynthia OZICK.

In Neugeboren's case, however, experimentation means raising questions about "the relation of art to life", but "without losing the nineteenth-century novel – without losing character, history, story, the love of these things". *Before My Life Began* (1985) is an ambitious effort to make good his manifesto. The novel is the story of a man forced by circumstances to live "two" lives – one as the David Voloshin who grows up in Brooklyn during the years immediately after the Second World War; the other, as Aaron Levin, a civil rights activist during the mid 1960s.

Identity has been Neugeboren's abiding subject. But to the old, old question of "who am I?" he has added "Jew" and "product of history" to the traditional list of "son", "father", and "man". Other novels include *Big Man* (1966), *Sam's Legacy* (1974), and *An Orphan's Tale* (1976).

FURTHER READING

Candelaria, M.: A decade of ethnic fiction by Jay Neugeboren. *MELUS* 5 (1978) 71–82

Moran, C.: Parentheses. *Massachusetts Review* 11 (1970) 613–16

SANFORD PINSKER

Neumann, Alfred (1895–1952) German writer. Born in Lautenburg, West Prussia, he attended the universities of Berlin and Geneva, interspersing his studies with wartime army service. In the mid 1920s he became a freelance writer and settled in Italy, and then France. Escaping to the USA in 1940 he found employment in Hollywood for a while. After the war he undertook extensive European tours and died at Lugano, Switzerland.

Neumann's forte was the historical novel to which he gave contemporary relevance by focusing on the drive for power and the workings of dictatorship. He gained a wide readership by garnishing his work with touches of lurid horror and Expressionistic psychodrama. Success came to him early with the award of the 1926 Kleist Prize for the ancien régime novel *Der Teufel* (The devil), while *Der patriot* (1925; The patriot), about the assassination of Czar Paul, was turned into a film. In the 1930s Neumann published a trilogy on Napoleon III's climb to power as well as a novel about Queen Christina of Sweden, stressing her sexual proclivities. During the Second World War he switched his focus from past Liberation movements to the contemporary German student resistance with *Es waren Ihrer Sechs*, (1944; There were six of them). In addition to his prolific novelistic output Neumann published poetry of his own, as well as translations of French Romantic poets.

RICHARD GRUNBERGER

Neumann, Robert (1897–1975) Austrian novelist and satirist. Born in Vienna, Neumann switched as an undergraduate from medicine to German philology. After 1918 he worked at numerous jobs but the Inflation left him penniless. In the mid 1970s he traveled the world as a merchant seaman before gaining literary acclaim with *Mit fremden Federn* (1927; Under false plumage), a collection of parodies in the style of other writers. His first novel described the hectic turmoil of the Great Inflation which he had experienced at first hand. His subsequent work also dealt with contemporary themes of chicanery and injustice as seen through the prism of a liberal conscience – but treated in the soberly distancing manner of Neue Sachlichkeit (new objectivity). *Die Macht* (1932; Mammon) was an example of this genre.

In 1934 Neumann, like Stefan ZWEIG (with whom he maintained a literary feud) left authoritarian Austria for England. Here he wrote a biography of Basil Zaharoff which constituted a powerful pacifist indictment of the international arms trade. In *Struensee*, (1935; The queen's doctor) he depicted the struggle between the Rousseau-influenced eighteenth-century reformer and the decadent and brutal Danish aristocracy. *The Waters of Babylon* (1939), written after the Austrian Anschluss, treated of the contemporary Jewish refugee problem within a structure reminiscent of Thornton Wilder's *The Bridge of San Louis Rey*.

During the war when, released from internment, he worked briefly alongside Dylan Thomas for the Ministry of Information, Neumann began to write in English, earning plaudits for the mastery with which he handled his second language. His themes, however, remained, as before, the fate of refugees and events in Europe. (At the same time his publishers set up Hutchinsons International Authors specifically to handle Neumann's work.)

In the late 1950s he produced an autobiography centered on his house in Kent as a prelude to moving to Switzerland. Proximity to Germany prompted him to write a Pictorial History of the Third Reich as well as two documentaries analyzing the relationship between the Germans and the Nazi regime. Prolific in output and stylistically inventive to the last, Neumann died at Munich.

RICHARD GRUNBERGER

Neurath, Otto (1882–1945) Austrian philosopher and sociologist. Born in Vienna, the son of Wilhelm NEURATH, Neurath studied at Vienna and Berlin. He taught at the *Handelsakademie* 1906–14. After the war Neurath was in charge of planning in the short-lived Bavarian Republic; after the latter's collapse, Neurath returned to Vienna, where he became prominent in the housing policy of the socialist city administration. In 1924 he founded the Social and Economic Museum, where he developed the new method of statistical representation now known as isotypes. Neurath was also heavily involved in the Vienna Circle of philosophers, being the main author of the circle's manifesto, *Wissenschaftliche Weltauffassung* (1929; The scientific concept of the world). He left Austria in 1934 for Holland, and in 1941 fled to England, spending his last years in Oxford.

Neurath resembles a figure from the Enlightenment. His goals included restoring to science a unified language, using rational planning to increase human happiness and freedom, and the destruction of intolerance and dogmatism through the tool of logical positivism. As such he had no obvious Jewish identity. Baptized a Catholic with a North German Protestant mother, Neurath had no formal religious upbringing, in line with his father's progressive ideas. Nevertheless it can be argued that this enlightened, progressive approach is itself the product of the Jewish assimilation started by his father, and that Otto Neurath is part of a phenomenon of the assimilated, left-leaning Jewish intellectual, of which friends of his such as Heinrich GOMPERZ, Otto BAUER and Max Adler were a part as well.

BIBLIOGRAPHY
Empiricism and Sociology (Dordrecht and Boston: D. Reidel Publishing Co., 1973)

STEVEN BELLER

Neurath, Wilhelm (1840–1901) Born in St Miklos, near Pressburg in Hungary, Neurath spent his youth as a wandering scholar, earning his keep by private tutoring. He went to Vienna in 1866. In 1871 he gained his doctorate, and in 1881 he started teaching economics at Vienna's Technical High School; in 1889 he transferred to the Agricultural College, where he became a professor in 1894.

Neurath, a prominent economist in his day, was especially concerned, as was his friend Josef POPPER-LYNKEUS, with the moral dimension of economic life. He regarded economic planning and social control as necessary in the interests of social justice, seeing society in terms of a giant limited company. Ironically, Neurath's ideas formed the basis of Karl Lueger's municipalization program.

Neurath's autobiographical notes, reproduced by Otto NEURATH in *Empiricism and sociology* (1973), describe how Neurath, starting from a curiosity sparked by the views of his deeply religious Jewish father on God and Nature, went on to understand "God's ways" by studying a whole range of academic disciplines, from physics to philosophy. Although this secular education was acquired in spite of his religious parents, and although his studies at one point persuaded Neurath to be an atheist and materialist, the religious springs of his studies are quite evident from these notes. This religious side became ever more evident in his later work and contemporaries came to see him as a religious leader. Neurath formally converted to Catholicism on marriage in 1881, but this did not change his attitude to religion, or to his former acquaintances, as his fulsome letters to Ludwig August Frankl show.

FURTHER READING

Johnston, W. M.: *The Austrian Mind: an Intellectual and Social History, 1848–1938* (Berkeley: University of California Press, 1972)

Mayer, S.: *Ein jüdischer Kaufmann, 1831–1911: Lebenserinnerungen* (Leipzig: 1911)

STEVEN BELLER

Nevelson, Louise (1899–1988) American sculptor. Born in Kiev, Russia, she came, with her family, to the USA in 1905, settling in Rockland, Maine, where her father was in the building and lumber business. She studied at the Art Students League in New York and for a brief period in Germany with Hans Hoffman, whose non-objective, Cubist-inspired paintings may have influenced Nevelson's ultimate style of sculpture. Returning to the USA in 1932, she worked as an assistant to muralist Diego Rivera. During the Depression she was employed by the Works Progress Administration (WPA) and also taught at the Educational Alliance School of Art.

Nevelson first worked in sculpture in the 1930s; the resulting pieces were primitive human figures. She gradually evolved her mature style, creating environmental, monochromatic sculptural assemblaged walls comprising a series of rectangular, box-like units that are in turn filled with abstract fragments of objects. Though not intentionally Jewish in content, her skill in woodworking is a continuation of a traditional Jewish craft of Eastern Europe. The inclusion of disjointed fragments from real life – chair legs, turned balusters, wood spools – may possibly be interpreted as nostalgia for Jewish life at the turn of the century.

Commissioned sculptures offer Nevelson's only overt use of Jewish themes. In 1964 she was commissioned to design a work in memory of the Holocaust. *Six Million* (Brown University, Providence, Rhode Island) is a monochromatic, black wall sculpture. In this instance the fragments that fill the regular pattern of boxes recall those Jews killed in the Holocaust.

FURTHER READING

Glimcher, A. B.: *Louise Nevelson* (New York: E. P. Dutton & Co. Inc., 1972)

Louise Nevelson: Atmospheres and Environments (New York: Clarkson N. Potter Inc., 1980) [intro. by E. Albee]

BARBARA GILBERT

Newman, Barnett [Baruch] (1905–1970) American painter and sculptor, precursor of the Color Field School of painting of the 1950s and 1960s. He was born in New York City to immigrant parents; his father, Abraham, who first sold sewing machines and then later manufactured men's clothing in the Bronx, was a staunch Zionist and secularist. Although they were not observant Jews, there was in the family the traditional Jewish respect for learning and education. Barnett and his siblings studied Hebrew as a living language at the National Hebrew School in the Bronx. While a senior in high school, Barnett studied art concurrently at the Art Students League. He then attended the

City College of New York to satisfy his father who was opposed to his pursuing the career of an artist. After graduation from college, Newman agreed to work for a brief time in his father's business. However, the Depression of the 1930s forced him to change his plans, and he continued to work for the now failing business until 1937. He taught art on a substitute basis at a high school during the same period. This set of circumstances isolated Newman from the majority of American artists who were working for public art projects during the Depression

Newman's goal as an artist was to place art intellectually and emotionally on a level with philosophy and world thought. He wanted to free art from the restrictions of subject and form of the past, believing that art had a purpose higher than esthetic satisfaction or decoration. He attempted in his large-scale paintings, covered with an even, consistent layer of paint and punctuated by vertical stripes at carefully calculated intervals, to evoke parallels with ultimate creation. Basic Jewish concepts were continuously at issue in his work. He was concerned with the idea of monotheism, with the various states of creation, with the kabbalist concept of a sacred place, and with biblical personalities. His titles such as *Onement* (1948), *Covenant* (1949), *Abraham* (1949), and *Adam* (1950–1) often confirmed his spiritual and Jewish intentions. In 1963, Newman was invited to participate in an exhibition on Recent Synagogue Architecture at the Jewish Museum in New-York. In the synagogue model that he submitted, Newman was concerned with the creation of a sacred space rather than the design of an actual building. He experimented with the kabbalist concept of *tzimtzum* (the contraction of God to allow room for creation) with zig-zag forms evoking a sense of spiritual contraction.

FURTHER READING

Hess, T. B.: *Barnett Newman* (New York: Museum of Modern Art, 1971)

Rosenberg, H.: *Barnett Newman* (New York: Harry N. Abrams, 1978)

BARBARA GILBERT

Niger, Sh(muel Tsharni) (1883–1955) Yiddish literary critic and historian. Born in Dukor, near Minsk, Niger as a youth startled contemporaries with his talmudic prowess, but soon came under the influence of Zionism and the revolutionary movements. Niger began his uninterrupted literary career in 1906–7 in Vilna, and in 1908 he teamed up with members of other Jewish parties to launch the first modern Yiddish literary periodical, *Literarishe monatsshriftn*. He settled in Bern in 1910 to write a thesis in philosophy, while maintaining, via essays and correspondence, his position of authority in the Yiddish literary world of Eastern Europe. He returned to Vilna in 1912 to edit *Di yidishe velt*, further cementing his own reputation as literary critic. In 1913, he edited *Der pinkes*, which signalled the rise of modern Yiddish scholarship (see BOROKHOV). His own contribution to that volume was a landmark study in the history of older Yiddish literature, demonstrating the centrality of women in the rise and growth of that literature. He settled in St Petersburg in 1916, returning to Vilna in 1918. He and two colleagues, Leyb Yafe and A. Vayter, were arrested; Vayter was shot. Shortly thereafter, Niger left for New York.

In New York, Niger worked for the *Jewish Daily Forward* for several weeks, but soon switched to the more intellectually oriented *Tog*, where he remained literary critic for the rest of his life, assuming BAL-MAKHSHOVES's erstwhile role of unofficial "overseer" of the directions and perspectives of Yiddish literature. He edited numerous books and periodicals, led a number of Yiddish culture organizations, and played an active role in the Yiddishist movement. His constant journalistic responsibilities diluted what had started as a career of a higher-planed literary theoretician. The vast scope of his coverage, however, made him, above anybody else, the "official chronicler" of modern Yiddish literature for roughly half a century.

Among his major works (some assembled posthumously from his widely scattered writings) are: *Vegn yidishe shrayber* (1912; About Yiddish writers, 2 vols); *Lezer, dikhter, kritiker* (1928; Readers, writers, critics) *Dertseylers un romanistn* (1946; Storytellers and novelists, 2 vols); *Bleter geshikhte fun der yidisher literatur* (1959; Pages from the history of Yiddish literature).

FURTHER READING
Reyzen, Z.: *Leksikon fun der yidisher literatur, prese un filologye*, vol. 2, B. A. Kletskin (Vilna: 1927) 539–51
Leksikon fun der nayer yidisher literatur, vol. 6 (New York: Congress for Jewish Culture, 1965) 190–210

DOVID KATZ

Nikel, Lea (b.1916)   Israeli painter. Born in the Ukraine, Nikel arrived in Palestine at the age of two years and later studied with Hayyim Gliksberg, and in the late 1940s with Streichman and Steimatzky. She is probably the most dynamic, and the only true abstract, painter in "The Goup of Ten" which dominated the modernist Israeli art scene until the mid 1950s. She traveled to Paris regularly and worked in Paris, Rome, and New York, exhibiting during the 1950s in Paris and Amsterdam, and gaining the acclaim of international art critics. In the 1960s she won the *Migdal David* prize, and represented Israel at the 1964 Venice Biennale. In 1972 she won the Sandberg prize, and exhibited extensively in Canada, New York, Rome, and Milan. Her art is highly individualistic in its use of thick impasto, brush strokes, totally uninhibited and free in movement and shapes, and vivid color. With time her forms moved from the linear to more elaborate and controlled compositions but still with highly saturated colors brilliantly juxtaposed. Unlike most Israeli abstract painters, Yosef ZARITSKY for instance, her abstractions do not derive from the figurative or landscapes, but are pure geometrical abstractions. Because of the energetic qualities of her brush strokes and colors, her art cannot be grouped with the rest of Israeli lyrical abstraction. She has exhibited in the Netherlands, Rome, Milan, Paris, London, and New York.

FURTHER READING
Tal, M.: Three women artists. *Ariel* 21 (1967–8)

NEDIRA YAKIR BUNYARD

Nissenson, Hugh (b.1933)   American novelist and short story writer. Nissenson, a descendant of Polish Jews, was born and grew up in New York City but was educated at Swarthmore and Stanford. *A Pile of Stones* (1965), his first collection of stories, won the Edward Lewis Wallant Award. It was followed by a second collection, *In the Reign of Peace* (1972). Both volumes explore the difficulties of maintaining religious belief in the modern age. Other stories, especially those set in Israel, analyze conflicts between a modern, secularist, pragmatic sense of survival at any cost, and a traditional but often complex, personal piety and faith in providentially ordained values.

In his longer fiction, Nissenson considers the problem of survival from a different perspective – the moral and emotional costs to witnesses and victims. His first novel, *My Own Ground* (1976), set in 1912 on the Lower East Side, is a violent tug-of-war between a pimp and a socialist intellectual for the body and soul of a rabbi's daughter, seen through the eyes of a 15-year-old boy. *Tree of Life* (1985) is a novel in the form of a diary for 1811–12 kept by a man who forsook his Protestant ministry after the death of his wife and moved to the Ohio frontier. He and his neighbors struggle to preserve their lives, their sanity, and their values amidst personal doubt and despair, physical hardship, child mortality, and sadistic brutality committed by both Indians and American settlers and soldiers.

The same issues inform some of Nissenson's journalism. In 1961 he covered the Eichmann trial in Jerusalem for *Commentary*, while *Notes from the Frontier* (1968) is a memoir of visits to a kibbutz on the Syrian border before and during the Six Day War.

FURTHER READING
Goldman, L. H.: Hugh Nissenson. In *Dictionary of Literary Biography*, vol. 28 (Detroit: Gale Research Co., 1984)

MICHAEL SHAPIRO

Noah, Mordecai Manuel (1785–1851) American journalist, playwright, politician, and diplomat. Born in Philadelphia, and orphaned at the age of seven, he also lived in Charleston, and for most of his life, New York City. He was the best known American Jew of his day, lived both as an American and as a Jew, and sought to mediate between both of his worlds.

In his youth Noah published journalistic pieces, a political pamphlet, two plays (*The Fortress of Sorrento*, 1809, and *Paul and Alexis, or the Orphans of the Rhine*, 1812), and a sophomoric critique of Shakespeare (*Shakspeare [sic] Illustrated*, 1809) – all before being appointed consul to Tunis in 1813.

Recalled in 1815 in the wake of a scandal, he published *Correspondence and Documents* (1816) in his own defense, followed by *Travels in England, France, Spain and the Barbary States in the Years 1813–14 and 15* (1819), his most important book, and the first of its kind by an American diplomat. It describes his experiences abroad, and contains valuable information on early nineteenth-century Tunisian Jewry.

Thereafter, he concentrated on journalism, editing such important New York newspapers as *The National Advocate*, *The New York Enquirer*, *The Evening Star*, and *The Sunday Times and Noah's Weekly Messenger*. He also wrote several plays, most significantly, *She Would Be A Soldier* (1819). He is, however, best remembered for notable published addresses, including one dedicating his proposed Jewish colony ("Ararat") on Grand Island, New York (1825); another arguing that the Indians were the "lost ten tribes" (1837), and a third, frequently reprinted, entitled *Discourse on the Restoration of the Jews* (1845).

FURTHER READING

Goldberg, I.: *Major Noah* (Philadelphia: The Jewish Publication Society of America, 1936; repr. New York: Alfred A. Knopf, 1937)

Sarna, J. D.: *Jacksonian Jew: The Two Worlds of Mordecai Noah* (New York and London: Holmes & Meier Publishers, 1981)

JONATHAN D. SARNA

Nordau, Max [Simon Maximilian Suedfeld] (1849–1923) Zionist leader, social philosopher, and journalist. Nordau was born in Hungary. The son of a rabbi, he ceased to be an observant Jew in his late teens. He pursued a career in journalism, at the same time as studying medicine, and settled in Paris as a practicing doctor in 1880. Nordau wrote books of social, artistic, and literary criticism, many of which

Max Nordau with his daughter Maxa in Spain

became international best-sellers which aroused great controversy (he has been called "the most brilliant philistine of his day"). His output also included plays and short stories.

In the 1890s Nordau met Theodor HERZL, another Hungarian-born Jew. The two men, both Paris correspondents for German-language newspapers at a time when anti-Semitism was a major issue in French affairs, discussed the Jewish question and found an immediate rapport: "Each took the words right out of the other's mouth. I never had such a strong feeling that we belonged together", wrote Herzl in his diary. In 1895 Nordau was one of Herzl's first converts to the idea that the solution was a Jewish state. In spite of his seniority to Herzl in years, and his greater fame, Nordau played a supporting, though major, role in the Zionist movement. He helped draft the "Basle program" at the first Zionist Congress (1897) and served as president of the seventh to the tenth congresses. His masterly surveys at the congresses, of the situation of world Jewry, became famous among Zionists.

Nordau supported Herzl wholeheartedly in the latter's dispute with AHAD HA'AM about the nature and aims of Zionism. He believed that political Zionism was essential to avert a major disaster for the Jews, and he was, therefore, also opposed to the "practical" Zionism of Chaim WEIZMANN and others. His public support for Herzl over the East Africa (so-called "Uganda") project was given reluctantly; nevertheless, it led to an attempt on his life.

After the Balfour Declaration, Nordau believed that a Jewish majority must be built up quickly in Palestine. When his proposal for the immediate transfer of 600,000 Jews from the pogrom-stricken Ukraine was rejected as unrealistic, Nordau retired from active Zionist work.

FURTHER READING
Ben-Horin, M.: *Max Nordau, Philosopher of Human Solidarity* (New York: 1956)

Elon, A.: *Herzl* (New York: Holt, Rinehart and Winston, 1975)

Vital, D.: *The Origins of Zionism* (Oxford: Clarendon Press, 1975)

——: *Zionism: The Formative Years* (Oxford: Clarendon Press, 1982)

GEORGE MANDEL

O

Odets, Clifford (1906–1963) American dramatist and screenwriter. Odets was born in Philadelphia, but lived mostly in New York. His parents had come from Eastern Europe as children and achieved modest affluence. After leaving high school, Odets acted in radio and with several minor companies before joining Theater Guild productions.

In 1931 he became a charter member of the GROUP THEATER, a company of young dramatic artists (most of them Jews) influenced by Stanislavsky. His first play for the Group, *Waiting for Lefty* (1935), was a strident one-act protest against capitalism, which captured the mood of the Great Depression. That year the Group also produced *Awake and Sing*, *Till the Day I Die*, and *Paradise Lost*, plays resonant with speech rhythms of working-class New York Jews. Alfred KAZIN describes the impact of *Awake and Sing*: ". . . it would at last be possible for me to write about the life I had always known. In Odets's play there was a lyric uplifting of blunt Jewish speech, boiling over and explosive . . . Everything so long choked up . . . was now out in the open, at last, and we laughed . . . watching my mother and father and uncles and aunts occupying the stage . . . by as much right as if they were Hamlet and Lear. . ." (pp.80–2). *Paradise Lost* also depicts Jewish families clinging to their integrity as the economic noose tightens, and sometimes failing. Odets wrote three more plays for the Group, *Golden Boy* (1937), *Rocket to the Moon* (1938), and the ill-fated *Night Music* (1940). All but the last work appeared in *Six Plays* (1939; reprinted 1979). His relations with the company soured and he refused to give them his next play, *Clash by Night* (1941).

In the late 1930s he began to spend more time in Hollywood writing screenplays and he settled there in 1942. Cited for contempt by the House Un-American Activities Committee and fearful of being blacklisted in Hollywood, he returned to New York in 1948 and wrote three more plays: *The Big Knife* (1949) and *The Country Girl* (1950) assess the casualties of the entertainment industry, while *The Flowering Peach* (1954) is a playful updating of the Noah story. In 1955 he returned again to Hollywood, where he worked on film and television scripts until his death.

FURTHER READING
Brenman-Gibson, M.: *Clifford Odets, American Playwright* (New York: Atheneum, 1981)
Kazin, A.: *Starting Out in The Thirties* (Boston: Little, Brown, 1965)
Weales, G.: *Clifford Odets, Playwright* (New York: Pegasus, 1971)

MICHAEL SHAPIRO

Ofek, Avraham (b.1935) Israeli painter. Born in Burgus, Bulgaria, Ofek was orphaned at the age of seven months, separated from his two brothers and adopted. He and his parents emigrated to Israel in 1949. His adolescence was spent in Kibbutz Ein Hamifratz where he began to paint under the tutelage of Aryeh Rothman. In 1953 Ofek served in the Israeli armed forces in the division of *Nahal*.

Ofek's art constantly draws upon these early

personal experiences: the search for his family and true identity, the hardships of life in Israel in the 1950s, survival that is dependent upon a strong army, the idealistic pioneering dream that moved the spirit of the country at that time, of the kibbutz in particular and the constant struggle to define Jewish life and modern Israel. The major breakthrough that allowed Ofek to express these dramatic themes on a monumental scale came at the time he went to Florence, Italy, in 1959 and studied the art of fresco painting. Examples of this form of expression, which is one of Ofek's main contributions to Israeli art, can be seen in the paintings that cover the walls of Kfar Uriah (1970), the Jerusalem Central Post Office (1972), the Agron and Stone Schools in Jerusalem (1973 and 1974), the Tel Aviv University Library (1976), and, most recently and perhaps the most definite statement of his fresco work, the entrance to the main building of the University of Haifa.

Although many elements of Ofek's murals can be compared to such Mexican muralists as Orozco and Rivera, in terms of scale, symbolic meanings, and social criticism, Ofek's iconography and style is personal. Nowhere can this be seen more clearly than in his 1987 work for Haifa University. In this 1,800 square feet of rough concrete (the largest ever done in Israel) there seems to be a summing up of the two themes that permeated Ofek's earlier drawings and paintings: Israel's rise (*'aliyah*) and development, and the disappointments and failures that invariably accompany such a process. Jewish mysticism and Israeli realism, the two themes that have preoccupied Ofek all of his life are clearly presented on these walls.

Ofek is well known both in Israel and abroad. He taught at the BEZALEL SCHOOL OF ART until 1976, then became a Professor of Art at the University of Haifa. He has exhibited both in Israel and abroad since the 1960s.

ELAINE SHEFER

Offenbach, Jacques [Jakob Levy Eberst] (1819–1880) German/French composer. He was born in Cologne, where his father, known as *Der Offenbacher* from the town of his birth,

Jacques Offenbach

was a poor music teacher and synagogue cantor. He soon showed a prodigious talent for the cello and when he was 14 his father took him to Paris where Cherubini accepted him for the Conservatoire. To pay for his studies, Offenbach played in the orchestra of the Opéra-Comique where he was befriended by Jacques HALÉVY.

After some years as musical director of the Comédie-Française in 1855 he opened his own small theatre, Les Bouffes-Parisiens, for the performance of his witty musical entertainments. Leaders of Parisian high society could laugh at themselves being lightheartedly caricatured. Empress Eugénie referred to the whole brilliant epoch of the Second Empire as "just one great Offenbach operetta". Renowned for the brilliance and vivacity of his music, his phenomenal output of nearly 100 works for the stage, either full-length operettas or curtain-raisers, included *Orphée aux Enfers* (1858; Orpheus in the Underworld) and *La Vie Parisienne* (1866). *La belle Hélène* (1864), *La Grande Duchesse de Gerolstein* (1867), and *La Périchole* (1868). Many starred the charismatic and scandalous Hortense Schneider, whose Jewish father had come from Strasbourg to Bordeaux.

Despite his enormous success, Offenbach hankered for recognition as a composer of grand opera. Sadly, he did not live to see this aim achieved; his last work *Les Contes d'Hoffmann* (The Tales of Hoffmann), a romantic opera based on the adventures of the German author and composer, was produced a year after his death.

CAROLE ROSEN

Olman, Israel J. (1883–1968) Dutch–Jewish composer and choirmaster. A son of Jacques Olman and Rachel Hamel, he came (on his mother's side) from an artistic family, active in the fields of the stage and music. His cousin, Jacob Hamel, likewise became a choirmaster and a composer, mainly of music for children, and became known nationwide as the conductor of a radio children's choir for the AVRO Broadcasting Company.

Israel Olman studied the violin at the Musical Academy in Amsterdam, then choir conducting, and composition under Bernard Zweers, and later under Evert Cornelis. He wrote his first composition at the age of 15. Aged 22 he became choirmaster of a local synagogue in Amsterdam and later also of the Santo Servicio choir of the Sephardi Synagogue and adviser to the choir of the Amsterdam Great Synagogue. During the last years of the life of Chief Cantor Isaac Heymann, the latter considered him as his successor as composer of synagogue music, and Olman frequently assisted him.

He was also choirmaster to a number of general choirs, both male and mixed, and wrote compositions for them as well. Among his over 100 compositions are works for male and mixed choirs, operas, two symphonies, chamber music, and songs. Among his compositions are the Jewish liturgical *Jigdal*, the choirs *Populus Sion* and *Jerusalem*, and compositions for Jewish choirs on the occasion of visits of members of the Royal family to Amsterdam in which he combined Jewish liturgical and Dutch national motifs.

He was the teacher of Samuel M. Englander (1896–1943), who, from 1916 until his death, was the conductor of the famous choir of the Amsterdam Great Synagogue.

Olman, who survived the Nazi occupation because after the death of his first wife he had married a non-Jewish woman, no longer wrote music for Jewish choirs or conducted them after 1945. He remained active as a choirmaster of general choirs and as a composer until an advanced age. In later years, however, his music was largely forgotten.

HENRIETTE BOAS

Olsen, Tillie (b.1913) American fiction writer and essayist. Born Tillie Lerner in Omaha, Nebraska, to poor Russian immigrant parents, Olsen was influenced early by her family's socialist views. Forced to leave high school to work during the Depression, she became a political activist and union organizer, and moved to California. Although she had begun her uncompleted novel *Yonnondio: From the Thirties* (1974), and published a small section and several essays before her marriage to Jack Olsen in 1936, her writing career languished for years, while she raised four children.

Encouraged in the 1950s by a Stanford University creative-writing fellowship, she won a Ford Foundation grant for work on the poignant title story of *Tell Me a Riddle* (1961), which won the O. Henry Award for the best story of 1961. The collection established her as a passionate portrayer of working people. Her acclaimed collection of essays, *Silences* (1978), discussed the "cost of discontinuity" to writers, particularly women, who must constantly confront "responsibility to daily matters". Winner of an Endowment for the Arts grant and a Guggenheim fellowship among other awards, Olsen has taught at many universities including Amherst and Stanford.

Although not a writer greatly concerned with Jewish issues, her characters include the old Jewish couple in "Tell Me a Riddle", and Anna Holbrook, burdened mother in *Yonnondio*, who recalls her grandmother making the Sabbath blessings. But it is to American women writers, whose feeling for Olsen Margaret Atwood calls "reverence", that her small body of published work speaks most eloquently.

ELIZABETH KLEIN

Opatoshu, Joseph (1886–1954) Yiddish novelist and short-story writer Opatoshu was born in Stupsker Vald, Poland to an established hasidic family. His first novel, *A roman fun a ferd-ganev* (1917; Story of a horse-thief) was based on his acquaintance with a horse thief who was killed defending Jews who were ill-treated by Poles in their own market-place. When he was 19 he went to study engineering in France but returned home penniless two years later. He received encouragement from PERETZ whom he visited in Warsaw. Arriving in New York in 1907 to escape Russian pogroms he completed his degree in engineering while teaching Hebrew to earn a living. From 1910 he was a member of the *Yunge*, a group of young Jewish Eastern-European immigrant writers in New York who sought to discard the established conventions of the older generations of Yiddish poets, but nevertheless preferred to continue writing in Yiddish rather than adopt English.

Opatoshu is famous for his long historical novels, and their skillful narrative, the most famous of which is *In poylishe velder* (1921; In Polish forests) set in Poland in the mid nineteenth century. A sequel, *1863*, was published in 1929. He achieved international fame through translations of his books into many languages including English, German, Hebrew, Russian, Polish, and Romanian. His novel *A tog in Regensburg* (1933; A day in Regensburg) is set in the age of Yiddish minstrels or *shpilmener* who entertained with ballads of medieval, knightly romances including the *Morte d'Arthur*. Opatoshu uses a specially contrived archaic Yiddish dialect to depict a medieval wedding day of rejoicing in Regensburg. He was critical of what he regarded as too much emphasis on the persecution of Jews in standard historical works. He preferred to portray the joyful side of Jewish life. The characters he depicted were mainly crafty, criminal adventurers who used their guile to overcome difficulties and crises. They had their own code of moral behavior which was never judged by the author. He completed his final historical novel, *Der letster ufshtand* (The last uprising), set in Roman Palestine, just before his death in 1954.

DEVRA KAY

Oppen, George (1908–1984) Poet, publisher. Born in New Rochelle, New York, to a German–Jewish family who shortened their name from Oppenheimer, and who moved, when he was five, to San Francisco, Oppen was educated in the California public schools, and briefly, at Oregon State University (1926–7). From 1929–33, he and his wife, Mary Corby, published poetry in France, including *An Objectivists Anthology* (1932) containing poems by Oppen, Pound, Williams, and Eliot. Objectivism sought a philosophical grounding from Imagism by objectifying or making an object of the poem.

In the 1930s, the Oppens worked as organizers for the Workers' Alliance in Brooklyn. In the 1940s, he was a tool and die maker in a Detroit factory. Drafted in 1942, he served for three years in the infantry, and was wounded in battle. After his discharge he worked as a cabinet-maker and builder. Not until the 1960s did he turn his sense of design and craftsmanship back upon poetry. In 1960 he won the American Arts and Letters Award for excellence in literature. In 1969 he was given the Pulitzer Prize for *Of Being Numerous* (1968). The title poem probes the problem of sustaining one's humanity in crowded cities. The second long poem in this volume, "Route", states his esthetic. The sparsely defined, economically crafted simplicity at which he aimed was that of "A limited, limiting clarity". Oppen is valued by other poets for his workmanship. Ezra Pound had written in his preface to Oppen's first book: "I salute a serious craftsman."

Oppen's later work was assembled in London by the Fulcrum Press, *Collected Poems* (1973), and in New York by New Directions, *The Collected Poems of George Oppen* (1975).

FURTHER READING
Oppen, M.: *Meaning a Life* (Santa Barbara: Black Sparrow Press, 1978)

Power, K.: Conversation with George and Mary Oppen, May 25, 1975. *Texas Quarterly* 21 (1978) 35–52

RUTH ROSENBERG

Oppenheim(er), David (1664–1736) Rabbi, scholar and bibliophile. Born in Worms, he studied with Gershon Ashkenazi of Metz and Isaac Benjamin Lipman of Landsberg, who ordained him rabbi at the age of 20. Nephew of the Austrian court financier, Samuel Oppenheimer, who left him part of his fortune, he married into the aristocratic Behrends family. At the age of 25 he was called to the post of Chief Rabbi of Moravia at Nikolsburg, where he founded a rabbinical academy, which attracted numerous students. He was later appointed Chief Rabbi of Prague and Landrabbiner of Bohemia, a position which he occupied until his death. Under the title "Prince of the Holy Land", he assumed responsibility for the collection and transference of funds for the Jews of Jerusalem. Author of numerous responsa, Oppenheim was hailed not only as an eminent authority on the intricacies of rabbinical and halakhic literature, but also as a mathematician. He was involved in serious disputes with both the Hakham Zevi on a Sabbatean issue and with Jonathan Eybeschütz, over permission to print the Talmud in Prague, where Eybeschütz was a resident at the time. The latter quarrel was eventually quelled by the intervention of the Emperor Charles VI. Oppenheim patronized Jewish scholarship and granted subsidies towards the printing of several talmudic and halakhic works. An ambitious collector from his earliest youth, he possessed one of the greatest private libraries of his time, with an estimated 7,000 volumes, including 1,000 manuscripts. Although they were acquired at great expense, he readily made his manuscripts available to scholars, and encouraged their publication. Fearful of the censors in Prague, Oppenheim placed his library in Hanover. A frequent visitor there was the Christian bibliographer, J. C. Wolf, who gathered most of the information for his monumental *Bibliotheca Hebraea* from Oppenheim's books, of which several catalogs were published. After his death the library, which contained innumerable unique copies, was put up for sale by his heirs. Though valued at 60,000 thalers it was finally purchased in 1829 for the absurdly underestimated sum of 9,000 thalers by the Bodleian Library in Oxford, where it was to constitute the substantial part of the Hebrew collection.

FURTHER READING

Marx, A.: *Studies in Jewish History and Booklore* (New York: Jewish Theological Seminary of America, 1944) 213–19; 238–55

PAUL B. FENTON

Oppenheim, Moritz Daniel (1800–1882) German painter. Called the "Rothschild among painters and the painter of Rothschild", Moritz Oppenheim was born to an Orthodox family in the Jewish quarter of Hanau near Frankfurt-am-Main, Germany. He is probably the first professional Jewish painter to emerge on the nineteenth-century scene. He attended the local Talmud Torah and later the *gymnasium*, but yearned to be an artist. Hanau, however, proved too provincial and Oppenheim decided to study at the well-known Art Academy in Munich, where he became proficient in the relatively new craft of lithography. In addition, he chose to apprentice himself to Jean-Baptiste Regnault, a famous Paris artist who painted in the popular academic style. From Paris Oppenheim went to Rome where he spent four years. Though remaining an Orthodox Jew, he associated himself with the "Nazarenes" – a group of Catholic Germans who attempted to revive the naive and simple, yet pious, depictions of medieval Christianity. He was even awarded a prize in 1823 for his drawing *Christ and the Samaritan Woman at the Well* until it was discovered that he was a Jew. Tired of living abroad, he returned to settle in Frankfurt.

He painted imaginary portraits of deceased German emperors and popular literary, historical, and religious figures. He also did portraits of such Jewish personalities as the poet Heinrich HEINE and the politician Gabriel Riesser. Oppenheim is best known for his genre paintings of "Pictures of Traditional Jewish Family Life" which once hung in most German–Jewish homes. Made between 1865 and 1880, these meticulous depictions of the Jewish life cycle and holiday celebrations nostalgically recalled a religious life that was rapidly disappearing. The life of this artist is beautifully captured in his autobiography entitled *Erinnerungen* (1924) – the first autobiography by a Jewish artist.

FURTHER READING

Werner, A.: *Pictures of Traditional Jewish Family Life by Moritz Daniel Oppenheim* (New York: Ktav Publishing House, 1976).

Cohen, E., ed.: *Moritz Oppenheim: The First Jewish Painter* (Jerusalem: The Israel Museum, 1983) [exhibition catalog]

JOSEPH GUTMANN

Orgad, Ben-Zion [Buschel] (b.1926)   Israeli composer and educator. Born in Germany, he emigrated with his parents to Palestine in 1933. He studied composition with Paul BEN-HAIM, Mordechai SETER, and later with Aaron COPLAND in the USA. He has been a superintendent of music education in Israel, making a lasting contribution to the formulation of educational programs, and training music teachers for schools throughout the country. His composition is strongly motivated by national ideology, stressing the deep relationship between music and Hebrew poetic texts, both biblical as in *Mizmorim* (1967), and modern such as in *Shirim baboker baboker* to Amir GILBOA's poems. Orgad has also been active as a poet.

JEHOASH HIRSHBERG

Orlinsky, Harry (b.1908)   American Bible scholar. Born in Toronto, Canada, Orlinsky graduated from University of Toronto and earned a Ph.D. at Dropsie College in Philadelphia. In 1943 Orlinsky was invited by Stephen WISE to the faculty of Jewish Institute of Religion in New York, (merged in 1950 with Hebrew Union College).

Orlinsky was at the forefront of Bible studies for four decades. He served as president of the interconfessional Society of Biblical Literature in 1970. As the only Jewish member of the ongoing committee that prepared and continues to update the Protestant *Revised Standard Version* of the Bible, Orlinsky has championed both the plain sense of the text and Jewish interpretative tradition. He also was editor-in-chief of the JEWISH PUBLICATION SOCIETY's translation of the Torah, (1962) and co-editor with H. L. GINSBERG of Prophets (1978). Other scholarly contributions range from detailed technical studies in the text of the Greek Septuagint to Job, through the history of American Jewish Bible scholarship to syntheses such as *Understanding the Bible through History and Archaeology* (1972).

Orlinsky has always been an independent thinker. Repeatedly, his articles have compelled scholars to rethink notions that had become axiomatic, such as "universalism" in the prophets and the "suffering servant" in second Isaiah. He demonstrated the textual unreliability of the St Mark's Isaiah scroll at a time when it was being hailed as a reliable source of precious Hebrew variants to the received texts of Isaiah. In a like manner, he repeatedly pointed out the severe shortcomings of the standard *Biblia Hebraica*. He was one of the few scholars to mount an early challenge to the characterization by Albrecht Alt and Martin Noth, of pre-monarchic Israel as a sacral league along the lines of the Greek amphictyony.

BIBLIOGRAPHY

Essays in Biblical Culture and Bible Translation (New York: Ktav, 1974)

FURTHER READING

Miller, P.: A selective bibliography of the writings of Harry M. Orlinsky. In *Eretz Israel* 16 (Jerusalem: Israel Exploration Society, 1982)

S. DAVID SPERLING

Orloff, Chana (1888–1968)   French sculptor. Orloff's family emigrated from the Ukraine, where she was born, to Palestine in 1905 and although she settled in Paris in 1910, she was to retain strong emotional and physical links with that country. Attending drawing classes at the École Nationale des Arts Decoratifs and studying sculpture at the Académie Russe, she soon became an important member of the group of artists, many of them Jewish, known as the *École de Paris* (see PARIS, JEWISH SCHOOL OF).

From the start, wood was her preferred medium (although she also worked in stone, marble, and bronze); and portraits, mothers and children, nudes and animals her preferred subjects. Although influenced to some extent by Cubism, her close friend Amedeo MODIGLIANI, and the vogue for the "primitive", she soon established a distinctive idiom: essentially naturalistic, but tending to a decorative simplification of form and a love of smooth, rounded surfaces. In the early 1920s she gained a considerable reputation as portraitist of the Parisian cultural elite; she was appointed Chevalier de la Légion d'Honneur in 1925.

She lived in occupied Paris until 1942, when she was forced to flee to Switzerland. She returned to Paris in 1945 where her work became more impressionistic and emphatically textured. In later years she worked increasingly in bronze, both for public commissions and for more intimate studio pieces, her forms becoming more and more elegantly attenuated. A warm respect for human and animal dignity pervades her work of all periods. Orloff was to spend an increasing amount of time in Israel, creating numerous public monuments, such as the *Mother and Child* at Kibbutz Ein Gev, which are now an integral part of the landscape.

FURTHER READING
Gamzu, Haim et al.: *Chana Orloff* (Brescia: Shakespeare & Company, 1980)
Chana Orloff (Tel Aviv: Musée de Tel Aviv: Pavillon Helena Rubinstein, 1968) [in French & Hebrew; exhibition catalog]

MONICA BOHM-DUCHEN

Ornitz, Samuel (1890–1957) American novelist and screenwriter. Ornitz was born and grew up on the Lower East Side of New York City. His parents had emigrated from Poland. He studied in local schools and at City College of New York. His first novel, *Haunch, Paunch, and Jowl* (1923; reprinted 1985), is narrated by Meyer Hirsch, a street urchin who eventually becomes a judge. Hirsch sees life as a jungle and claws his way to wealth and power, without the redeeming features of many picaresque heroes – such as vitality, raffish charm, or late pangs of conscience.

Ornitz published another novel, *A Yankee Passionel* (1927), highly critical of the Catholic Church, and then went to Hollywood to work as a screenwriter. Before and during the Second World War, he was active in social protest movements and anti-Fascist organizations. One of the "Hollywood Ten", he was sentenced to a year in prison for contempt before the House Un-American Activities Committee. His last novel, *Bride of the Sabbath* (1951), is also a *bildungsroman* set on the Lower East Side; its hero, a dreamy Jewish idealist, eventually converts to Catholicism. The narrative is slowed by intrusive disquisitions on Jewish history and belief.

FURTHER READING
Miller, G.: Samuel Ornitz. In *Dictionary of Literary Biography*, vol. 28 (Detroit: Gale Research Co., 1984)

MICHAEL SHAPIRO

Ornstein, Leo (b.1895) American composer and pianist. He was born in Kremetchug, Russia, where his father was a cantor. When Leo was three years old his father started his piano lessons and at the age of 10 he was accepted at the St Petersburg Conservatory. As a result of the pogroms sweeping Russia, the family decided to emigrate to the USA in 1907. The young Ornstein studied piano with Bertha Feiring and composition with Percy Goetschius at the New England Conservatory and later on attended the Institute of Musical Art in New York. From 1911 until 1933, Ornstein gave many concerts throughout the USA and also in Norway, Denmark, France, and the UK. Some of his recitals featured "futuristic music", which meant Debussy, Ravel, Scriabin, and Ornstein. By 1935 he ceased his appearances and became head of the piano department of the Zeckwen Hahn School in Philadelphia. Subsequently he established his own school, the Ornstein School of Music, where he taught until his retirement in 1955, occasionally also teaching some composition at Temple University.

Despite his successes as a piano virtuoso, Ornstein's compositions did not fare too well after about 1930, and, except for a performance of *Nocturne and Dance of the Fates* by the St Louis Symphony, are seldom performed. Ornstein settled in Brownsville, Texas, and some newer recordings of his works have spurred a renewed interest since the late 1970s.

His principal works include: a symphony (1934); several shorter orchestral pieces; four piano sonatas; *Hebraic Fantasy* (1929) for violin and piano; *Five Songs* (1935) for voice and orchestra; *Six Water Colors* (1935) for piano; *Ballade* (1953) for saxophone and piano.

SAMUEL H. ADLER

Orpaz, Yitzhak (b.1927)   Born in the USSR, Orpaz emigrated to Palestine in 1938. In his novels, he uses symbols to try to create a myth of resurrection. In *Daniel's Trials* (1969), a young soldier returns home, and attempts to rediscover himself through unification with the sea, through the discovery of a new community, and through the renaming of all his friends. The sea is a reminder of eternity and as such, and of its own nature, is constantly flowing. The climax of this novel, as of many other of his works, is expressed in the state of wonder springing from the most commonplace of experiences.

A Charming Traitor (1984) counterpoints the mundane with the aspiration to eternal truth. The Orpaz hero is usually locked into a position of adolescent conflict with and rebellion against the outside world of parental authority and conventional attitudes. His objective is to "transcend time".

As in much Israeli fiction, the author's characters are concerned primarily with their own subjectivity and often appear adolescent, mystical, escapist, and indulge in mystic fancies. Orpaz expresses this tendency through symbolistic devices, and, sometimes, through allegory.

BIBLIOGRAPHY
The Death of Lysanda (London: Jonathan Cape, 1970)

FURTHER READING
Yudkin, L. I.: *Escape into Siege* (London: Routledge & Kegan Paul, 1974) 182–4

LEON I. YUDKIN

Orthodox Judaism   Contemporary Jewish religious life is largely defined by the denominational beliefs and practices of the three major religious groupings – Orthodox, Conservative, and Reform – and, to a far lesser extent, by the Reconstructionist Movement, the smallest of the groupings. The movements themselves are not monolithic. Each is characterized by a substantial variety of intradenominational differences in doctrine and practice. What they stand for and how they differ from one another – and from other groupings within their own denomination – is determined by their position on the nature of divine revelation, religious authority, and their attitudes to the contemporary situation. These positions determine their relationships to one another and to the outside world.

At the center of Orthodox Jewish teaching is the conviction that God revealed the entire Torah to Moses at Sinai, and that the Torah is unchanging. Although various Orthodox groups articulate the manner of revelation differently – some maintaining that the contents were dictated verbally to Moses, and others maintaining that the method of inspiration cannot be comprehended or articulated within the context of normal human experience – all are united in the conviction that what is recorded in the Torah is of exclusively divine origin.

The Orthodox utterly reject the Reform view that the Torah is a fundamentally humanistic document, representing an amalgam of outdated local custom and practice and ongoing, increasingly sophisticated religious inspiration, a view which permits the selective observance and rejection of different parts of the Torah. The Orthodox even reject the non-Orthodox view that the Sinai experience was simply an encounter between God and Moses, and that the Torah is the inspired human record of that encounter.

In the Orthodox view, God revealed not only the written Torah (*Torah shebikhetav*) but also

567

Lubavitch Hasidim completing a Torah scroll

the oral interpretation of its contents (*Torah shebe'al peh*). The former is incomprehensible without the latter. Thus, for example, there is no explication within the Written Torah of the imperative, "Thou shalt slaughter of thy herd and of thy flock which the Lord hath given thee as I have commanded you" (Deuteronomy xii.21). Yet the ritual slaughter of sacrificial animals occurred at least twice daily according to intricate instructions delineated in the Oral Torah.

As the divine *logos*, all knowledge and truth is immanent in the Written Torah. That knowledge and truth is recoverable by the application of the hermeneutical rules which were revealed simultaneously with the revelation of the Written Torah, by rigorous logical analysis of the text, and by building upon previously recovered precedents. The comparison of the Torah to a mine which contains all knowledge and truth compels the view that the entire corpus of divine law (the *halakhah*), both that which has already been "mined" and which will be recovered in the future derives from the Torah. On this view, it follows that the *halakhah* is a unitary and binding religious, legal system.

In addition to the original oral interpretation of the Written Torah, and what was subsequently derived from the Written Torah, the Oral Torah contains rabbinic injunctions, ordinances, and prohibitions, whose binding authority, in turn, also derives from the Written

Torah (Deuteronomy xvii.11). Originally an exclusively unwritten tradition, the Oral Torah was, for various reasons recorded in literary form: as the Midrash, the Mishnah and its *gemara* (the Talmud), the Codes, and the Responsa (see TALMUD).

Piety, in the Orthodox view, is the infusion of every aspect of human life with religious significance. Eating, sexual behavior, bio-medical decisions, business practice, and so on, are of no lesser religious significance than worship and meditation. Every facet of life is governed and defined by the *halakhah*, and all reflect the ubiquitous influence of a continually expanding Oral Torah on every aspect of the life of the observant Jew. The leading question of the Orthodox Jew is: "What does the Torah say about...?" The answers to such questions as the permissibility of organ transplantation, *in vitro* fertilization, and insider trading are provided by rabbis who are expert in the halakhic process.

The expertise and the acceptance of these rabbis is a function of the Orthodox perspective on rabbinic authority. Originally, the acceptance of a halakhic decision was determined by a majority of the Sanhedrin, a cathedocracy selected by peers. Since the disappearance of the Sanhedrin, halakhic authority is based upon the acclaim of qualified peers. No great decisor is elected as such, rather he emerges by dint of the universal acceptance of his halakhic decisions. The authorities of each generation are simply recognized by those who are trained to judge rabbinic acumen.

The Orthodox have no collective organizational halakhic authority akin to the Conservation Committee on Law and Standards, whose majority decisions determine Conservative practice, but whose minority decisions are also acceptable. The Orthodox certainly reject the Reform notion of individual autonomy, which allows individuals to accept some imperatives and to reject others.

Although Orthodox Jews are bound by the halakhic system disclosed by the halakhic process, and accept the authority of the Talmud and Codes (notably the *Shulhan arukh*) and subsequent rabbinic authorities, religious practice is, nevertheless, varied because, provided that a Jew bases his halakhic practice upon a recognized authority, his behavior is acceptable. Variations in halakhic practice among the Orthodox Jews reflect the custom of their communities of origin and domicile as well as their reliance upon their chosen halakhic authorities, some of whom are more strictly constructionist than others, and some more unyielding than others.

The selection of their halakhic authorities also determines their attitudes to those major questions which divide the Orthodox subgroups from one another. There are three such major questions.

Orthodoxy is divided in its attitude to secularity. Most hasidic groups have existentially insulated themselves from the potentially corrupting outside world. They eschew secular studies and enter the secular society only to the degree that it is a locus of their livelihood. The Modern Orthodox, on the other hand, currently led by Rabbi Dr Joseph SOLOVEITCHIK, influenced by the philosophies of Rabbi Samson Rafael HIRSCH and Rabbi Abraham Isaac KOOK, and, for the most part, trained or touched by Yeshiva University in New York, believe that Jewish values can transform the world, and that it is a religious imperative to live in two civilizations. The Modern Orthodox claim to be the heirs of such unchallenged rabbinic masters as Saadia Gaon and Maimonides. Other Orthodox groups mediate between these positions.

The attitude to the State of Israel is another dividing issue, and the divisions are on the same lines. The right wing of Orthodoxy believes that only the Messiah can validate the State and that its establishment on currently secular lines is in defiance of Judaism. They therefore refuse to recognize its existence and some actively campaign for its delegitimization and ultimate disappearance. The left wing of Orthodoxy believes that the establishment of the State is a precondition of the messianic process and that it is of ultimate religious significance. The in-between positions regard the State of Israel as having no special theological significance, but as of great importance as the home of millions of Jews who command their concern and assistance.

If the Orthodox right wing rejects the outside world as potentially corrupting, it regards errant Jews as actually corrupting, especially groups which have rejected the *halakhah* and redefined Jewish personal status as patrilinear. Consequently, they allow no recognition of non-Orthodox leaders and permit no significant contact with members of the non-Orthodox groups. The Modern Orthodox, on the other hand, cooperate both with heterodox and secular Jewish groups in matters of common interest, such as philanthropy, communal defense, and support for the State of Israel. They conduct outreach programs to the non-Orthodox and unaffiliated.

Currently, religious orthodoxy appears to be on the increase. It has succeeded in attracting significant numbers of alienated Jews (*ba'alei teshuvah*). These penitents, in search of authenticity and in rejection of their past, tend to gravitate to the Orthodox right. Indeed, the rightward trend is a tendency which characterizes contemporary orthodoxy as a whole, and which, in turn, influences the intra- and inter-denominational postures of both the Orthodox and non-Orthodox.

ABNER WEISS

Oz, Amos (b.1939) Israeli novelist and social critic. Born in Jerusalem to his scholarly father, Yehuda Aryeh Klausner, and to his mother, Fanya, who committed suicide in 1952, Oz left Jerusalem to be educated in Kibbutz Huldah. He was a member of the kibbutz for many years.

Oz's first book of short stories, *Arsot hatan* (1965; *Where the Jackals Howl*, 1981) and his first novel, *Makom'aher* (1966; *Elsewhere Perhaps*, 1973) are set in the kibbutz environment; his enormously successful *Mikha'el shelli* (1968; *My Michael*, 1972) takes place in Jerusalem. These two locales – the kibbutz and Jerusalem – represent the major focuses of Oz's literary universe, microcosms which he has exploited so fully as to achieve world-wide acclaim.

The "jackals" represent a world of subconscious drives and fears given mythic force. Very much like the eruption of passions and violence on the fringe of insanity in the stories of BERDY-

Amos Oz

CZEWSKI, Oz's stories challenge the facade of order and "decency" in such bastions of Israeli society as the kibbutz and the Jerusalem academic establishment. Like Berdyczewski, too, Oz depicts incestuous relationships and primitive, pre-Noahide, killing of animals with lust as a radical literary device. The resurgence of primitive, irrational, behavior is posed as an inexorable part of man's fate, as if gods or demons were laughing at man's illusion of a sane and staid existence. In *My Michael* the forces of insanity assume a political thrust in the form of Hannah Gonen's hallucinatory fears about the Arab twins she grew up with. Oz's depiction of Hannah is widely accepted by critics as a metaphor for pre-1967 Jerusalem under siege.

Oz's preoccupation with anti-Semitism as another demonic world force led him to write his powerful novella, *Ad mavet* (1971; *Unto Death*, 1975), a moral allegory about a band of crusaders obsessed by the need to exorcise the Jew in their midst. The novel *Laga'at bamayim, laga'at baru'ah* (1973; *Touch the Water, Touch the Wind*, 1974) describes the ultimate migration, romance, and mythical (underground) merging into the kibbutz of two extraordinary post-Holocaust Jews – one, a mathematical genius from Poland, the other, a woman who had achieved a high post in the KGB. Generally, it appears to some that after 1967 Oz moves from "self-negating" exploration of the mythic unconscious in Israel to more global themes.

A later novel, *Menuhah nekhonah* (1982; *A Per-*

fect Peace, 1985) merges Oz's kibbutz microcosm of human pettiness – the need to dominate and insult, the restless inroads of mental imbalance, Oedipal revolt against a father's ideological tyranny – with his broader perception of the need to absorb constructive Diaspora influences into the kibbutz (that is, into Israeli society at large).

As a publicist Oz has had considerable appeal. His collection, *Be'or hatekhelet ha'azah* (1979; In the powerful blue light), contains charming personal reminiscences with pointed critiques of the abuse of rhetoric and "myth" in the political arena. A well-known "dove", Oz has appealed, above all, for sobriety in the evaluation of historical and political realities. With his frequently quoted assessment that Israel is an intellectual theater of debate among lunatic fringes and even "psychopaths", Oz has pursued his curious odyssey of peace-making through the airing of competing extremist views. He has done this most effectively in *Po vasham be'eretz yisra'el bistav* (1982; *In The Land of Israel*, 1983).

In the novel *Kufsah shehorah* (1987; *The Black Box*, 1988) Oz utilizes a satirical epistolary style to depict a tormented heroine, reminiscent of the female protagonist of *My Michael*, and some intriguing new problems in the semi-retarded and violent sabra son and his Sephardic Orthodox and maximalist step-father.

BIBLIOGRAPHY

In The Land of Israel, trans. M. Goldberg-Bartura (London: Fontana, 1983)

FURTHER READING

Alter, R.: *Modern Hebrew Literature* (New York: Behrman House, 1975)

Fuchs, E.: *Israeli Mythologies: Women in Contemporary Hebrew Fiction* (Albany, NY: SUNY Press, 1987)

STANLEY NASH

Ozick, Cynthia (b.1928) American novelist, short-story writer, and essayist. She was born and brought up in New York City, and educated at New York University, from which she graduated in 1949, and Ohio State University, where she received an MA in 1950. Her Mas-

ter's thesis was on Henry James, whose influence on her was to be seen for several years. During the 1950s, her apprentice years, Ozick began an intensive study of the literature, history, and philosophy of Judaism. Although she had spoken Yiddish at home and learned Hebrew in college, she developed her direction at the age of 25 when she first read Leo BAECK, Martin BUBER, Franz ROSENZWEIG, and Hermann COHEN. In writing her first published novel, *Trust* (1966), she began as an American novelist and ended as a Jewish novelist.

Trust was the result of seven years of unrelenting toil. Concerned with an American innocent who had just graduated from college and traveled through the Nazi camps, the novel focuses on her mother Allegra Wand's "Trust" and Allegra's second husband, Enoch, a Jew aspiring to be both a prophet and an atheist. This long novel is infused with philosophy, psychology, religion, history, and literature, to demonstrate that the characters are torn between what Ozick calls the pagan and the sacred, between nature worship or idolatry of art, and Judaism.

The Pagan Rabbi and Other Stories (1971) received extraordinarily high praise when it was published. Having found her true narrative voice, Ozick begins "The Pagan Rabbi" with the evocative sentence: "When I heard that Isaac Kornfeld, a man of piety and brains, had hanged himself in the public park, I put a token in the subway stile and journeyed out to see the tree". Kornfeld, whose soul was warring with his desire for nature, strayed from the holy path into one suffused with nature. Ravished by the dryad that inhabited the tree, from which he then hanged himself, the man of religion succumbed to the blandishments of Pan. Other excellent stories in the collection are "The Dock Witch", "Envy: or Yiddish in America", and "Virility".

Her next work, *Bloodshed and Three Novellas* (1976), includes "A Mercenary", "Bloodshed", "An Education", and "Usurpation", each of which carries further Ozick's concern with the differences between the religious and the pagan. Similarly, in *Levitation: Five Fictions* (1982), Feingold, who is Jewish, and his wife, Lucy, a convert, throw a party to find themselves, only to find that Lucy's converter and his friend, a survivor who has the face of Jesus, are the means by which the Jewish guests levitate. Lucy, however, chooses nature, the god she formerly knew. The point is that only the Jews ascend, the pagans will always remain rooted below. In this title story, it seems that mere conversion cannot assure ascension, cannot make a pagan holy, cannot bridge the gulf between the history of the Jews, the Holocaust, and the "other". In the two Puttermesser stories, Ruth Puttermesser, a civil servant in New York, dreams of Eden, of a connection with a rich Jewish past. Unfortunately, Ruth, in her misery, calls on a golem, an automaton in Jewish myth – a female golem, named Xanthippe – to help her, only to see the Messiah-like golem become a false Messiah.

The Cannibal Galaxy (1983), Ozick's second novel, and one of her most brilliant works, is a short, taut tale about a school principal who aspires to be God by deciding which students will succeed and which will not. In *Art and Ardor* (1983), a book of essays, Ozick explores the dimensions of the holy, especially why and how she believes as she does. Covering literature, feminism, politics, religion, she asks: What is holy, pagan, Judaism? A truly religious woman, she disagrees with many of the practices that penalize or stigmatize women, even as she constantly searches out her own pagan proclivities.

Finally, in *The Messiah of Stockholm* (1987) Ozick asks not only if there is a Messiah but how would one know it if the Messiah did appear. As indicated earlier, Ozick is very Jewish, but she is also very much sited in the twentieth-century USA. As we know, Terach was a maker of idols, but Abraham broke his father's idols. It is very likely that Ozick is an Abraham among the idol-worshippers and god-usurpers.

FURTHER READING

Pinsker, S.· *The Uncompromising Fictions of Cynthia Ozick* (Columbia: University of Missouri, 1987)

Rainwater, C., and Scheik, W., eds: Cynthia Ozick. *Texas Studies in Language and Literature* 6 (1983)

Cole, D.: Cynthia Ozick. In *Twentieth Century American Jewish Fiction Writers,* ed. D. Walden (Detroit: Gale Research Co., 1984) 213–25

Walden, D., ed.: The world of Cynthia Ozick. *Studies in American Jewish Literature* 6, (1987)

DANIEL WALDEN

P

Pagis, Dan (1930–1986) Israeli poet and scholar. Dan Pagis was born in Bukovina, Romania. Educated in Vienna, he was imprisoned in Nazi concentration camps during the Second World War, before emigrating to Israel in 1947. He spent some time on Kibbutz Merhavia, then in the Kibbutzim Seminary and on Kibbutz Gath. Pagis devoted a considerable part of his time to academic research and was professor of medieval Hebrew literature at the Hebrew University of Jerusalem until his death.

Pagis's first poems were published in 1949. However it was not until 1959 that his first book, *She'on hatzel* (The sundial), appeared. The theme of the Holocaust is prominent in Pagis's poetry, sometimes quite explicitly, at other times implicit. Nonetheless the poems are perhaps better described generally as introverted and intimate rather than public. Life and death are recurrent subjects although the dead are never quite fully dead nor the living quite fully alive. Grim contents contrast sharply with a uniquely witty and playful presentation, a tone which is not unlike that of Auden's poetry. In subsequent volumes (*Shehut me'uheret* (1964), *Millim nirdafot* (1972), *Moah* (1976)) Pagis gradually adopts simpler diction and imagery, draws further away from literary allusion and generally closer to prose syntax and rhythm.

Pagis published several scholarly works on the subject of Hebrew literature, among them a collection of the poems of Ibn-Ezra (1970), *Kehut hashani*, an annotated anthology of Hebrew love poetry from Spain, Italy, Turkey, and the Yemen, from the tenth to the eighteenth centuries (1979) and others. *Points of Departure*, a collection of his poems in English translation was published in 1983 by the Jewish Publication Society of America.

AHUVIA KAHANE

Paley, Grace (b.1922) American short-story writer and poet. Born Grace Goodside in New York City, the daughter of Russian immigrants, she was greatly affected by their strong leftist political sensibilities, the household conversation, and the storytelling of her physician father, whose role in her literary imagination she acknowledges at the beginning of her second collection, *Enormous Changes at the Last Minute* (1974). She was educated in New York City schools and colleges but received no degree. At 19 she married Jess Paley, and was mother of two children, housewife, and typist when she studied poetry with W. H. Auden before turning to short-shory writing. Divorced in the 1960s, she married Robert Nichols. After the publication of her first collection of short stories, *The Little Disturbances of Man: Stories of Women and Men at Love* (1959), she taught writing at Columbia University and Syracuse University, and later at Sarah Lawrence College.

On the strength of her slim first volume, she was hailed as having the "daring and heart of a genuine writer". With a sure voice, idiomatic and individual, she explores deep feelings in short, often plotless stories, or serio-comic monologues. Characters and themes introduced in the first book recur in the second collection

573

and in a third volume, *Later the Same Day* (1985). Concerned with love and the plight of those without love, her stories are generally set in the urban world of immigrant Jews, or their second- and third-generation American children. Her character, Faith – Jewish, close to other women, and a social activist, divorced, later remarried, mother of two sons, and child of aging parents – is an alter ego. She is present in all Paley's collections, and women like her appear in stories such as "A Conversation with my Father" and "Enormous Changes at the Last Minute".

Among her best known stories is "The Loudest Voice", about a Jewish child's participation in a school Christmas pageant, and "Goodbye and good luck", in which an older woman recounts her youthful love affair with a star of the Yiddish stage. Throughout her work Paley portrays Jews as feisty underdogs. But injustices happen not only to Jews, but to women, to blacks, and to others. Whoever suffers claims her attention. "I cannot keep my mind on Jerusalem" – a traditional metaphor for Jewish concern – Paley muses ironically in a poem from her first poetry collection, *Leaning Forward* (1985). "It wanders off. . . / to whatever city lies outside my window. . ."

Among many honors, Grace Paley has won a Guggenheim fellowship, a National Endowment for the Arts grant, and election to the American Institute of Arts and Letters.

FURTHER READING

Sorkin, A. J.: Grace Paley. In *Dictionary of Literary Biography*, vol. 28 (Detroit: Gale Research Co., 1984)

ELIZABETH KLEIN

Pap, Károly (1897–1945)   Hungarian writer. His family name was Pollák and his father the Chief Rabbi of Sopron, near the Austrian border. He completed his secondary education in Sopron and volunteered for army service in the First World War. After the collapse of Austro-Hungary he joined the revolution, serving in the Hungarian Red Army and becoming commander of the town of Murakeresztúr. After being imprisoned by the counter-revolution, he emigrated to Vienna in 1923 but did not stay there

long; for a while he was a traveling actor in Hungary but around 1925 settled in Budapest. In 1930 he was to have been awarded the prestigious Baumgarten Prize but the authorities barred him from receiving it because of his "Communist" past. In the 1930s he published three novels: *Megszabaditottál a haláltól* (1923; You have delivered me from death), *A nyolcadik stáció* (1933; The eighth station of the cross), and *Azarel* (1937), and several collections of short stories.

In his best fiction Pap grapples with his deeply felt but "constricting" Jewish identity, reflects on the conflict between vision and reality, individual destiny and a longing for a community. His first novel takes place in the Near East, in ancient "Libbania"; its central hero is Mikhael, the carpenter–prophet who, in his search for salvation, defies not only the authorities but also clashes with his own people. *Azarel* is innovative with its psychological insights into the mind of a young boy first raised by his Orthodox Jewish grandfather and later by his "reformed" rabbi-father. Gyuri Azarel rebels against the "hypocrisy" and respectable standards of his father with the passion of an emotionally deprived child. Though his rebellion is in a Jewish context, critics have pointed out that it has "universal validity". Pap wrote a pamphlet *Zsidó sebek és bűnök* (1935; Jewish wounds and sins) which dealt with the problems of assimilation, in a tone often very critical of Jews. Of his two biblical plays, *Betséba* (1949; Bathsheba) and *Mózes* (1942), only the former was staged. In 1944 Pap was deported to Buchenwald and is believed to have died in the concentration camp of Bergen-Belsen.

Several of Pap's stories were translated into English: "The Organ" in *Twenty-Two Hungarian Short Stories* (1967), and "Blood" in *New Hungarian Quarterly* 36 (1969).

FURTHER READING

Boldizsár, I.: A Lost Generation. *New Hungarian Quarterly* 36 (1969) 25–9

GEORGE GÖMÖRI

Paris, Jewish School of   Although Paris's position as undisputed center of the avant-garde in late nineteenth and early twentieth-century

Marc Chagall Zelfportret met zeven vingers *1912/13.*
Stedelijk Museum, Amsterdam

western culture naturally attracted a large number of non-Jewish foreigners, a disproportionate
number of those who came from around 1905
onwards were Jews. So conspicuous were they
that, by the 1920s the notion of an *École juive* as
a subdivision of, or even an alternative to, the
less specific *École de Paris* had gained common
currency. The better-known names among the
Jewish émigrés include Marc CHAGALL,
Georges Kars, Michel Kikoïne, Moïse Kisling,
Pinchus Krémègne, Jacques LIPCHITZ, MANÉ-
KATZ, Amedeo MODIGLIANI, Chana ORLOFF,
Jules Pascin, Chaim SOUTINE and Ossip Zad-
kine. A second generation, which arrived in the
1920s and 1930s, included artists such as Sigmund Menkés, Abraham Mintchine and future
Israelis Arie Aroch, Moshe Castel, Avigdor
Stematsky, Yeheskel Streichman, and Yosef
Zaritsky. The First World War marked a
hiatus, as many of the artists returned to their
home countries; while the advent of the Second
led to the emigration of some and the extermination of approximately eighty others.

The term *École juive* is useful primarily as a
sociological one. Although by no means all

these artists came from a milieu hostile to the
visual arts, as is often claimed, by far the majority hailed from Russia and Eastern Europe: for
them, Paris spelt not only artistic, but also social and religious freedom. Tending to gather in
the same cheap studio complexes, notably La
Ruche and La Cite Falguière, they tended also
to share a similar lifestyle, often on the poverty
line, frequenting the same Montparnasse cafés,
supported by the same benefactors, promoted
by the same critics, and partaking – in many,
though not all cases – of a strong community
spirit. Russian and Yiddish were far more likely
to be heard than French.

The fact that many of these artists – notably
Soutine, Pascin (né Pincas) and Modigliani –
led colorful and often tragic lives gave rise to
the myth of the Jewish *peintre maudit*, regardless
of the fact that their oeuvre, unlike that of Chagall or Mané-Katz, makes no explicit reference
to their Jewishness. The only collective attempt
to create a specifically Jewish art was instigated
in about 1912 by a group called the *Machmadim*
(Precious Ones), comprising such relatively
minor figures as Krémègne, Henri Epstein, Leo
Koenig, and the sculptor Léon Indenbaum.
Joseph Tchaikov, the graphic artist who lived in
La Ruche between 1910 and 1914, and then
returned to Russia, formed an important link
between this group's activities and those of Jewish artists in Russia. Although Chagall later
expressed scorn for the *Machmadim*, claiming
that he held aloof from all group activities, recent evidence suggests a closer involvement
than was hitherto supposed.

The presence of so many Jewish artists in
Paris, in addition to a large number of prominent Jewish dealers and critics, aroused frequent
comment. In many cases the response was
overtly anti-Semitic, especially in the 1920s'
"call to order" period of nationalist retrenchment
and conservatism. A 1925 article in the respectable *Mercure de France*, for example, claimed:
"The day that painting became for the many a
speculative business, the Jew came in, and the
ancient calligrapher of the Talmud went out to
buy canvas and colors". Less objectionably,
attempts were made by Jews and non-Jews
alike to characterize the work of Jewish artists
in Paris as essentially expressionist, angst- or
nostalgia-ridden, irrespective of subject matter,

575

which more often than not consisted of emotionally "neutral" landscapes, portraits, and still-lifes.

FURTHER READING

The Circle of Montparnasse: Jewish Artists in Paris 1915–1945 (New York: Jewish Museum, 1985) [exhibition catalog]

Marevna: [pseud. of M. V. Rosanovitch] *Life with the Painters of La Ruche* (London: Constable, 1972)

Warnod, J.: *La Ruche et Montparnasse* (Geneva and Paris: Weber, 1978)

MONICA BOHM-DUCHEN

Partos, Oeden (1907–1977) Israeli composer, violinist, viola player, and teacher. One of the founders of the modern Israeli school of composition, Partos was born in Budapest to an assimilated Jewish family. He began violin lessons at an early age and at the age of 12 was accepted to the Liszt Music Academy as a pupil of Jenö Hubay (violin) and Zoltan Kodály (composition). Upon graduation at the age of 17 Partos became the concert master of a Swiss orchestra and in 1928 began work in Berlin as a composer of popular and film music, and as a chamber violinist specializing in new music. In 1933 he was forced to leave Germany. He returned to Budapest, and in 1934 obtained a teaching position in Baku, Russia. In 1938 he was invited by Bronislaw HUBERMAN to join the newly founded Palestine Philharmonic Orchestra as the leader of the viola section. He met the singer Bracha ZEPHIRAH for whom he wrote a series of arrangements which formed his first encounter with Eastern ethnic Jewish musical traditions. His exposure to folk-song research in Hungary and his work in the Crimea made him more amenable to non-European music than the other immigrant composers in Israel, and he was especially interested in the elaborate Yemenite songs. In 1951 he became the director of the music academy in Tel Aviv, where he had already established himself as a prominent violin teacher. In 1954 he received the Israel prize for his symphonic poem, *Ein Gev*. He performed extensively as a virtuoso viola soloist and wrote several solo works for viola.

Partos's works written in the 1940s and 1950s, among them his *Song of Praise*, represented his attempts at synthesizing Eastern patterns of melody and rhythm and sophisticated contrapuntal forms. In the 1960s he turned to dodecaphonic and serial techniques which he considered closer to the Arabic *maqam* technique, as in his *Maqamat* for flute and strings. His style is dramatic, with strong recitative-like rhetoric and dense contrapuntal, dissonant harmony. As an active performer and a teacher he left an important mark on the musical life of modern Israel.

JEHOASH HIRSHBERG

Pastan, Linda (b.1932) American poet. Born Linda Olenik in New York, Pastan received her undergraduate degree from Radcliffe College in 1954, an MLS from Simmons College, and an MA from Brandeis University. She was winner of the *Mademoiselle* Dylan Thomas Poetry Award in her senior year in college – a competition in which Sylvia Plath was runner-up – although her first book, *A Perfect Circle of Sun*, did not appear until 1971. Her fourth collection, *The Five Stages of Grief* (1978), won the Poetry Society of America's di Castagnola Award for work in progress, and *PM/AM: New and Selected Poems* (1983) was a nominee for the American Book Award.

Pastan is married and the mother of three children, and explores domestic life as a central landscape in her poetry, using direct, straightforward diction. She is concerned with how a woman retains herself while waging "a war between desire / and dailiness". Though dailiness may win, it includes the painful as well as the placid: watching death come to aging parents; marriage in which the partners no longer offer solace to one another; and the inevitable growing away of parents and children. Family life, she tells us, is "the dangerous life".

With an unflinching eye, she addresses the most difficult of these feelings in highly accessible poems. To her dying father, she "long[s] to say, Father let go / and death will hold you up". Confronted by loss, she passes through "the five stages of grief ": denial, anger, bargaining, depression, and acceptance, only to discover that "grief is a circular staircase". Loss is never resolved but only lived through, ordered, like the "knotted chaos of yarn" traditionally given to "each Jewish bride" which she must untangle to learn patience.

Although she uses classical as well as biblical allusions, Pastan's Jewish inheritance is clearly a primary source of her poetic sensibility. In "Ark" she finds a metaphor for the limitations and renewals of life in Noah's voyage. In "Passover" she perceives her adolescent son, slouching at the *seder*, "his hair...long: / hippie hair, *hasid* hair, how strangely alike..." holds within himself the wise, wicked, simple, and unasking sons of the Passover parable. She treats spiritually complex issues with similar gentle irony as in "A short history of Jewish thought in the twentieth century". While Jewish metaphor is found throughout her work, even in *A Fraction of Darkness* (1985), it is most heavily concentrated in her early collections.

Although Pastan is sometimes criticized for a lack of breadth in her subject matter, she succeeds in enlarging the imagery of "dailiness" in a manner reminiscent of Emily Dickinson. Her reputation grows in recognition of her steady, unsentimental, and penetrating poems.

FURTHER READING

Franklin, B. V.: Linda Pastan. In *Dictionary of Literary Biography*, vol. 5 part 1 (Detroit: Gale Research Co., 1980)
Washington Post Book World (5 July 1981; 7 November 1982; 2 February 1986) [reviews]

ELIZABETH KLEIN

Pasternak, Boris Leonidovich (1890–1960) Russian poet.

Born in Moscow, Boris Pasternak was the son of the Russian Jewish painter Leonid Pasternak. He was baptized at an early age by his nursemaid and expressed his Orthodox Christian faith in his poetry, regarded as among the best in twentieth-century Russian literature. Pasternak was educated at the universities of Moscow and of Marburg, where he studied philosophy under the Neo-Kantian, Hermann COHEN. For Pasternak, poetry was the intellectual's private world and the "draught of history" blew in only on the margins of his existence. He did not write on Jewish subjects and, indeed, in later years evaded discussion of his Jewish origins. Having translated the two prototypal Georgian Odes to Stalin, and reacted with shock to the slighting references to the ethnic origins of the Soviet leader in Osip MANDELSTAM's *Ode to Stalin*, telling Mandelstam that a Jew should not have written this.

The Jewish Question is dealt with directly in *Doktor Zhivago* (published abroad, 1959; *Doctor Zhivago*, 1958) an epic novel of Russia in war and revolution. Through the eyes of Yurii Zhivago and in the characterization of Misha Gordon, Pasternak expressed among his views of history and revolution, nature and the poet, his belief that nations were rendered anachronistic by Christianity and that the Jews would only bring upon themselves further calamities if they clung to their exclusivity and did not assimilate. It has been variously suggested that Pasternak's theology in the novel betrays Judaic concepts or that he transferred the ideas on Judaism in his father's monograph on Rembrandt to the Russian people.

Pasternak was awarded the Nobel Prize in 1958 and refused it amid a press campaign against him in the Soviet Union and a storm in the West. *Doctor Zhivago* and other works have since been republished in the USSR.

BIBLIOGRAPHY

I Remember: Sketch for an Autogiography, trans. D. Magarshack (Cambridge and London: Harvard University Press, 1959); *The Voice of Prose: Boris Pasternak*, ed. C. Barnes (Edinburgh: Polygon, 1986)

FURTHER READING

Ivinskaya, O.: *A Captive of Time: My Years With Pasternak* (New York: Doubleday, 1978)
de Mallac, G.: *Boris Pasternak: His Life and Art* (Norman: Oklahoma University Press, 1981)

EFRAIM SICHER

Patterson, David (b.1922) Hebrew British and Judaic Scholar.

Born in Liverpool, Patterson has been the Cowley Lecturer in Post-Biblical Hebrew at Oxford University since 1956 and President of the Oxford Centre for

Postgraduate Hebrew Studies since 1972. Over the last three decades he has been the outstanding figure in modern Jewish studies in the UK: his range of scholarly expertise is remarkable – spanning 2,000 years and a variety of geographical *loci*. His service to this field of study has not been restricted to his teaching at Oxford but has also included the Anglo-Jewish and international community at large, through countless contributions to conferences, seminars, synagogue symposia, and many visiting professorships in the USA and Australia. He has made a great contribution to a scholarly understanding of nineteenth-century Hebrew literature and virtually introduced this subject to English readers with no knowledge of Hebrew. In addition to many articles on Hebrew literature and allied subjects, some of which have been collected in a new volume – *A Phoenix in Fetters* (1989), he has written two major studies: *Abraham Mapu* (1964) and *The Hebrew Novel in Czarist Russia* (1964), as well as translating the novel *The King of Flesh and Blood* by Moshe SHAMIR. As the general editor of two important series *Studies in Modern Hebrew Literature* (East and West Library and Cornell University Press) and *Jewish Heritage Classics* (Viking) he has played a further role in the remarkable growth of an academic literature on modern Jewish studies in the English language over the last few decades.

Patterson's crowning achievement to date has been the development of his field of study at Oxford from rather humble beginnings, and particularly his establishment of the Oxford Centre for Postgraduate Hebrew Studies in 1972. The Centre has become one of the most important institutions of Jewish learning in the world (certainly the most important one in Europe) and has fulfilled one, at least, of his hopes for it: that it should help to replace those centers of Jewish scholarship which were destroyed during the Second World War.

Patterson has been the recipient of a number of honors and awards, including a Rockefeller Foundation Award (1959) and the National Brotherhood Award of the Conference of Christians and Jews in the USA (1978); he was elected a Fellow of the American Jewish Academy of Arts and Sciences and of the Society for the Humanities, Cornell University (1983). He received the Stiller Prize in Jewish Literature (1988), and was recently awarded honorary doctorates by Baltimore Hebrew University (1988) and Hebrew Union College (1989).

TUDOR PARFITT

Pearl, Cyril (1904–1986)

Pearl, Cyril (1904–1986) Australian Journalist and social historian. Pearl was born in Melbourne and brought up in a traditional Jewish family and educated at private schools in Melbourne and Perth. However until late in his life, he wrote little that was of Jewish interest, opting instead to work as a journalist. His literary career began at the University of Melbourne where he edited *Virago* and then started a new literary journal called *Stream*. After freelancing for the Melbourne *Herald* he joined the staff of *The Star* (1933) and then the Sydney *Daily Telegraph*. In 1939 he founded the *Sunday Telegraph* which he edited for 10 years. He subsequently became editor of the *Sunday Mirror* until 1961.

A prolific writer, Pearl produced 25 books of which only one, *The Dunera Scandal* (1983), later to become a television film, had substantial Jewish interest. That book showed that a substantial number of the Jewish professionals and writers in Australia were European refugees in Britain who had been rounded up for internment in Australia and were transhipped on the infamous *SS Dunera*.

ALAN D. CROWN

Pearlstein, Philip (b.1924)

Pearlstein, Philip (b.1924) American painter. Born in Pittsburgh, Pennsylvania, Pearlstein attended college there at the Carnegie Institute of Technology. After receiving his Bachelor of Fine Arts in 1949, he moved to New York City where for the next eight years he worked as a typographer and mechanical draftsman for industrial catalogs and earned his MA degree in art history at New York University's Institute of Fine Arts.

During his first years in New York, Pearlstein's primary artistic preoccupation was landscape. He focused on aspects of nature – clusters of rocks and tangles of roots – that lent themselves to the all-over compositional emphasis of Action Painting. While on a Fullbright scholarship in Italy in the late 1950s, his paintings displayed a decided preference for realism. He began working directly from models in 1962, and within a few years had developed his mature painting style, with its abrupt cropping of figures, pronounced foreshortening, and crisp, precise rendering of forms. In his work the human form is treated almost as a still-life object: nudes, posed either alone or in pairs are bathed in a sharp, artificial light that avoids any suggestion of beauty or eroticism.

Pearlstein has exhibited extensively since the 1950s in group and one-man exhibitions. He has lectured extensively and taught at a number of schools. In 1970, the Georgia Museum of Art at the University of Georgia in Athens gave Pearlstein his first museum retrospective. In 1983 a traveling retrospective was sponsored by the Milwaukee Art Museum.

FURTHER READING

Bowman, R., Pearlstein, P., and Sandler, I.: *Philip Pearlstein: Retrospective* (New York and London: Milwaukee Art Museum; Alpine Fine Arts Collection, 1983) [exhibition catalog]

KRISTIE A. JAYNE

Perec, Georges (1936–1982) French novelist, playwright, radio and film producer, translator, poet, and theoretician of literature. Perec, renowned for the striking variety of his work, was considered one of the foremost contemporary French intellectuals until his literary career was abruptly brought to an end by his death at the age of 46.

Perec, whose family had come from Poland, was born in Paris, where he spent his early childhood until his mother had to send him away to escape deportation by the Nazis. She subsequently died in Auschwitz. Although Perec is not commonly perceived in France as a specifically Jewish writer, his mother's disappearance and the persecution of French Jews, which he witnessed as a child during the German occupation, had a significant influence on his creative work.

Around 1960 Perec joined the experimental literary workshop *Oulipo* (Ouvroir de Litterature Potentielle) founded by Queneau. There he practiced experimental writing, dismantling language structures, and escaping from traditional psychology in fiction. His first novel, *Les Choses*, where he describes the everyday life of a young French couple and criticizes the consumer society and its resulting alienation, was extremely well received: it won the prestigious *Prix Renaudot* in 1965 and gained Perec public recognition.

His subsequent novel *La vie mode d'emploi* (1978, *Prix Medicis*) is his major work and masterpiece. The meticulous descriptions or inventories of objects, a desire to capture everyday reality in all its aspects, a form of extreme realism, bring it close to the attempts of the *Nouveau Roman*, but at the same time the originality of Perec remains the feeling of virtuosity created by unexpected situations and effects of language.

It is in *Woule souvenir d'enfance* (1975), that Perec directly reveals his Jewish identity in a narrative which is partly autobiographical and partly fictional. He describes the life of his family and his Parisian childhood in extremely simple and moving terms, yet at the same time the themes of disapppearence, war, extermination, and absence are omnipresent.

FURTHER READING

Motte, W. F.: *The Poetics of Experiment: A Study of the Work of Georges Perec* (Lexington: French Forum Publishers, 1984)

PATRICIA TOUTON-VICTOR

Peretz, I(saac) L(eyb) (1852–1915) Yiddish and Hebrew short-story writer, playwright, poet, essayist, and ideologue. Peretz can be considered the chief architect of Jewish modernism in eastern Europe. He mastered every genre but the novel and adapted such diverse movements as Naturalism, Neo-Romanticism, and Symbolism to Jewish literature. Born in Zamosc in the south of Poland, he was virtually self-taught in secular studies and European languages. For 10 years he practiced as a lawyer in Zamosc until he was disbarred on false charges.

During this period be published occasional poems and short stories in Hebrew. His Yiddish debut came in 1888 with the mock-heroic poem *Monish*, published in SHOLEM ALEICHEM's prestigious *Di yidishe folksbibliotek*. Peretz then moved to Warsaw where he put out his own literary almanac, *Di yidishe bibliotek* (1891–5) in which he launched a vigorous campaign for modernity in literature as in life. The first volume also featured his masterly *Bilder fun a provints-rayze* (1906; Travel pictures), a panorama of the *shtetl*'s spiritual and economic decline within a framework of psychological breakdown. Entering a radical phase in 1893, Peretz wrote concurrently for the New York *Arbayter tsaytung* and published subversive, anticlerical poems and stories in his own *Yontef-bletlekh* (1894–6; Holiday folios). Sobered, however, by a brief stint in prison for attending an illegal workers' rally, and heartened by the appearance of *Der yid*, the first highbrow newspaper in Yiddish, Peretz abandoned his mimetic approach and turned instead to the hasidic monologue, the medieval romance and the folktale. He used these stylized narratives to extoll such humanist values as individual freedom, doubt, and selfless love as well as to address, in allegorical fashion, many of the great social issues of his day.

Indeed, Peretz came to dominate the Jewish cultural scene in Poland as an orator, polemicist, defender of Jewish national interests, mentor of young writers, and advocate of a modern Jewish theater. It was in drama that he experimented most radically, beginning with naturalistic plays about Jewish urban life, for example *Shvester/bashefel* (1904–06; *The Sisters*, 1929), then moving on to his celebrated visionary drama *Di goldene keyt* (1907–13; The golden chain), and culminating with his symbolist verse drama *Bay nakht afn altn mark* (1906–15; At night in the old market-place). This most encyclopedic of Peretz's writings was also his most despairing, for in it he confronted the total collapse of traditional values and modern ideologies alike. Nevertheless, Peretz held out some hope for individual self-transcendence, notably, at the conclusion of his *Memoirs* (1913–14; trans. 1965).

A guide to English translations of Peretz's writings can be found in *The Field of Yiddish: Studies in Yiddish Language, Folklore, and Literature*, ed. Uriel Weinreich (New York: Linguistic Circle of New York, 1954). Later volumes of Peretz's writings in English translation are: *A Treasury of Yiddish Stories* (1954, 1973), ed. Irving Howe and Eliezer Greenberg; *In this World and the Next: Selected Writings* (1958), trans. Moshe Spiegel; *The Book of Fire: Stories* (1960), trans. Joseph Leftwich; and *Selected Stories* (1974), ed. Irving Howe and Eliezer Greenberg.

DAVID G. ROSKIES

performing arts, Jews in It is not coincidental that the growth and development of the motion picture precisely corresponds to the era of mass emigration of Jews from Europe (especially eastern Europe) to the USA. While it is perhaps entirely accidental that Thomas Edison in the USA, William Friese-Greene in Great Britain and the brothers Lumière in France were developing and perfecting their respective apparatuses for recording and projecting motion on photographic stock at the same time that one third of eastern European Jewry left their homes, it is not at all accidental that many of these same Jews would utilize these inventions in a manner completely beyond the wildest dreams of these pioneering inventors. Films were first an urban phenomenon, centered in New York. When the Motion Picture Patents Company (MPPC) was formed in New York in 1908, there were approximately one million Jews living in that city. The early appeal of the films themselves were to working and immigrant classes; one's inability to read, or to read and speak English, was no hindrance to enjoying the wordless, soundless flickering images appearing daily at neighborhood nickelodeons. It was easy for Jews to enter the burgeoning film business, as there was no one there before them to keep them out: and if film was initially seen as a risky business, that too was of little concern to many newly Americanized Jews — they had little to risk, little to lose, and a tradition of starting over to back them if they failed.

At the same time Jews were making their presence felt in the early years of the twentieth century in the newly emergent film industry, they were also gravitating toward that other great urban and ethnic popular art form: Vaudeville. Jewish songwriters, singers, and comics, especially, found a welcome home amongst their own in the downtown theaters springing up to compete with and provide an alternative to Broadway, uptown. Although the Yiddish theater was flourishing (and would continue to do so until the late 1920s), many immigrant and first-generation Jews set their sights on the slightly wider world, even making fun of their background, their families, and themselves in order to enter it. Jewish songs and jokes reflect the feelings of cultural dislocation, alienation, conversion, and assimilation. As Jews found that by the middle 1910s, film exhibition, distribution, and production was open to them, so too, Jewish entertainers were finding open arms on the Vaudeville circuit. Indeed, the theater-owning Schubert Bros, and the owners of the Orpheum theater circuit were more than happy to book acts handled by agents Klaw and Erlanger, all of whom were Jewish.

As Jewish movie moguls like Louis B. Mayer (born in Minsk on 4 July 1885), Marcus Loew (born in 1870, the son of Jewish–Austrian immigrants), William Fox (born of Jewish–German parents in Hungary in 1879), Adolph Zukor (born in Hungary in 1873), and Carl Laemmle (born in Germany in 1867) who later founded and headed MGM, Fox (later 20th Century Fox), Paramount, and Universal studios – were solidifying their hold on the movie industry in the mid 1920s, Jewish songwriters and composers branched out from their downtown New York haunts and made their mark on Broadway. So that by the time that Jewish performers like Al Jolson, George Jessel, Eddie Cantor, Fanny Brice, George Burns, Sophie Tucker, Jack Benny, and the Marx Brothers found Vaudeville to be a dying form, they, too, could make their way uptown and sing the songs of Irving Berlin, Jerome Kern, Oscar Hammerstein II, Richard Rodgers, Lorenz Hart, Harold Arlen, and George and Ira GERSHWIN, in shows produced by Florenz Ziegfeld, among others. For by the Jazz Age and through the era of the Great Depression, Broadway, too, had become the province of the Jews.

Movies, Vaudeville, Broadway – although by no means the exclusive province of immigrant and first-generation American Jews in the first half of the twentieth century, are inconceivable without Jewish participation, even domination, and are part and parcel of the Jewish experience in the USA. The world of the performing arts, of show business in general, continued to exert an appeal to Jews as the century progressed; radio (in many ways an extension of Vaudeville in the 1930s and 1940s), nightclubs and hotel lounges (especially the "Borscht Belt" circuit in New York's Catskill Mountain resort area), and television all welcomed Jews, by now the children and grandchildren of the eastern European émigrés. While comics like Milton Berle, Jack Benny, George Burns, Sid Caesar, and Phil Silvers entertained television audiences nightly, their Jewish brethren like Henny Youngman, Shecky Green, Alan King, Jackie Mason, Don Rickles, and Jack E. Leonard kept nightclub and hotel patrons equally amused. And on Broadway, *Show Boat* (1927), *Porgy and Bess* (1935), *Oklahoma!* (1943) *Carousel* (1945), *Guys and Dolls* (1950), and *West Side Story* (1957) filled Broadway theaters over the years with native New Yorkers and tourists alike. Yet an examination of most of these forms (save for the short-lived Vaudeville), these mass media, these popular arts, reveals on the one hand, a seeming avoidance of overt mention, overt confrontation with Judaism on the part of these Jewish creators, and an equally paradoxical inability to recognize such roots on the part of critics and historians.

For instance, Chaim BERMANT, like many social critics, or theater and film historians, has noted that most of the creators of stage and film musicals were Jewish. But he believes that, until *Fiddler on the Roof* (1964), there was usually little that was "noticeably Jewish" about their productions. Bermant goes on to point out that, before *Fiddler*, Jewish composers and lyricists had created "a Negro folk opera, *Porgy and Bess*..." and "[that] in the post-war years Irish themes were treated in *Finian's Rainbow* (1947), Scottish in *Brigadoon* (1947), Italian in *Fiorella* (1959), and Puerto Rican in *West Side Story*". He also notes how *Fiddler* shares something of the "splendid evocation of an earlier trouble-free America [found in] *Oklahoma!*, *Carousel*, and *Annie Get Your Gun* (1946)".

Broadway Musical historian Martin Gottfried acknowledges the fact that many Broadway composers were, or are, Jewish, but claims, too, that nothing noticeably Jewish appears in their work:

> Like *Oklahoma!* it [*Carousel*] deals with a rural, white, Protestant America. This was an image with which the country had long identified itself, an image that sustained America through the Second World War – the image of a clean-living, morally authoritarian, agricultural country. Just what Rodgers and Hammerstein had to do with that America is hard to understand since they were big-city, Jewish boys. Contrary to the old writing rule, nothing they wrote had anything to do with their background.

Gottfried's discussions of Frank Loesser, Jule Styne, Leonard BERNSTEIN, and Stephen Sondheim, among others, never mention the word Jew. He even feels compelled to speak in a kind of code. Discussing Sondheim, he mentions that he was "[b]orn to a well-to-do family and raised in the brittle milieu of the garment industry and show business...". Only the American garment industry was more completely Jewish than show business!

While both Berman and Gottfried are right that little overtly Jewish appears in the majority of the works of these Jewish playwrights, composers, and lyricists, it is possible to see a metaphoric quality to these works, or what Freud, in his *Interpretation of Dreams*, call "displacement". In both metaphor and displacement, something else stands in for the actual image, issue, or thing at hand. Metaphor is, of course, a strictly creative idea, whereas displacement is the manifest content created by a mechanism in the mind which tries to repress the unpleasant, unresolved issues which, Freud postulates, are the latent content of the dream. That Jewish creators of films, musical plays, and television shows should have consciously or unconsciously relied on displacement as a creative strategy provides a clue to a struggle within American–Jewish life, a fear of being too manifest, too overt, conflicting with a need to express the tensions created by such fears. Thus we might note that *Show Boat*, *Porgy and Bess*, and *West Side Story* deal fundamentally with racism, as does *South Pacific* (1949); that *Finian's Rainbow*, *Brigadoon*, and *Fiorella*, deal, at least in part, with ethnicity and cultural origins, as does *Flower Drum Song* (1958). Fears of, and the struggle against, anti-Semitism are thus dis-placed on to the related issue of racism, against Blacks, Puerto Ricans, and other non-whites, and on to questions of maintaining cultural distinctiveness within a larger, dominant culture – the struggles of other races and other cultures.

Displacement is only one of the characteristics of the Freudian "dreamwork". Another important component is the concept of "overdetermination". When something appears in a variety of disguised forms. While displacement might be used, for instance, to explain a preponderance of *shtetl*-like locales for many musicals (*Brigadoon* providing only the most obvious example), how to account for the noteworthy frequency of what Gottfried called "rural, white, Protestant America... [the] clean-living, morally authoritarian agricultural country"? Perhaps only the desire to be perceived as essentially American, as an insider, can account for such settings in rural New England (*Carousel*), the South (*Show Boat*), Southwest (*Oklahoma!*), and in the mythical American farm town (*The Most Happy Fella*, 1956). Indeed, Gottfried himself notes this overdetermination, this overcompensation in less Freudian terms, when he discusses Cole Porter:

> Unlike Kern, Rodgers, Berlin and Gershwin, Porter was not a Jewish New Yorker. Perhaps this is why he didn't try as hard as the others to be American and write American-sounding music. At a time when so many Jews were recent immigrants, "Americanism" was often an important matter to them... This might be the reason other composers tended to do shows set in America, while Porter's were as often as not set on the Continent.

We might understand this desire to "sound American" as owing as much to a desire to reject Europe, from whom they or their parents had emigrated due to intolerable living conditions, as to appear desperately to fit in with the American mainstream.

Displacement and overdetermination may be taken as unhealthy symptoms, reflecting, on the one hand, fears of being singled out as Jewish, and attacked, and, on ther other hand, an intense desire to avoid being Jewish. This is perhaps most clearly seen in the growth and development of the film industry. Whereas America's silent films of the 1910s and 1920s boast an enormous number of movies devoted

A scene from the film The Jazz Singer *(1927) with Al Jolson (left)*

to Jewish issues and characters, not the least being *The Jazz Singer* (1927), which instituted the move to talking pictures, with its story of a cantor's son who wants to be a popular singer, the 1930s show a decline in such portrayals. The movie moguls' fears of public backlash against Jewish control of the film industry (revealed in periodic efforts to institute self-censorship to keep governmental and public interference to a minimum) combined with an overt identification with American values and interests. American largesse and openness had enabled these men to become rich. They were, in the words of screenwriter Michael BLANKFORT, "accidental Jews, terribly frightened Jews, who rejected their immigrant background to become super-Americans". On the other

hand, Rabbi Edgar Magnin maintains that they were not ashamed of their Jewishness, "and they gave very generously to local Jewish causes". Such ambivalence is precisely the cause of displaced and overdetermined portrayals of American life and problems.

Certainly, there is no reason to claim that works by Jews should be in all, or even in many cases, somehow Jewish. Also to say that immigrant or native-born Jews are not Americans (or British, or French, etc.) is unfair, unnecessary, and probably anti-Semitic. Yet it is precisely the overt avoidance of Jewishnees, the positive ban on Jewish themes, issues, and characters that mark mainstream, mass entertainment that is notable. Such an avoidance, a fear of being marked as Jewish, has also had tragic conse-

583

quences for world Jewry. Concurrent with the rise of the Nazi party in Germany, and the institution of anti-Semitic laws in the middle 1930s, movie moguls banned Jewish issues and characters from American screens. Novels and plays which focused on Jewish characters were changed in their film version, and even anti-Nazi films of the late 1930s and early 1940s skirted mention of anti-Semitic laws and concentration camps. Movie executives overtly stated that American films must not be perceived as anti-Nazi and hence pro-Jewish, lest it be felt they were propagandizing for the USA's entry into the war; they simply felt that the USA would not fight to save European Jewry and that movies must not agitate for such entry. When war was declared, Hollywood was involved in the war effort both overseas and on the home front. Jews reappear in mainstream movies, but always expressing American values, always expressing their America-first attitude. Even after the war and into the 1950s, Hollywood was reluctant to confront the issue of the Holocaust. Few films made before 1960 deal in any way with the death camps or Nazi war crimes. Stanley Kramer's *Judgment at Nuremberg* (1961) marks the first major effort on Hollywood's part to tell the world about the destruction of European Jewry. Similarly, the number of films produced about, or even alluding to, the formation of the State of Israel is miniscule, at least until Otto Preminger released *Exodus* in 1960.

The clearest example of Jewish fears of anti-Semitism, beside the banishment of Jews from American screens at precisely the same moment that world Jewry was imperiled, may be found precisely in the short-lived wave of anti-anti-Semitism films of the immediate postwar era. It is not surprising that two important films decrying anti-Semitism released in 1947 were made by non-Jews: *Crossfire*, directed by Edward Dmytryk, a politically aware filmmaker born to Ukrainian immigrant parents in Canada (and one of the Hollywood Ten jailed in the Red Scare, blacklist era) and *Gentleman's Agreement*, directed by Elia Kazan, of Greek birth and ancestry. It is further worth noting that the big-budget *Gentleman's Agreement*, from the novel by Jewish–American writer Laura Z. Hobson,

was produced at 20th Century Fox, then the only studio controlled by a non-Jewish executive. And it may be taken as equally revealing that this cycle came to an end after only two films, when *Home of the Brave*, from the Arthur Laurents play, changed the central character of a Jew to a Black in this story of discrimination in the army of the Second World War.

Of course we may take the idea of displacement in a positive light – that discrimination against Jews gave Jewish popular artists a sensitivity toward the plight of other minority groups. This notion is manifested in a general way in Jewish participation in the Civil Rights struggles by Blacks in the 1960s. Producer –director Stanley Kramer is noteworthy for the creation of sympathetic portrayals of black–white relations in *The Defiant Ones* (1958) and *Guess Who's Coming to Dinner* (1967). Jewish producers like Herbert Brodkin in the 1950s and Norman Lear in the 1970s were the first to introduce controversial issues of racial discrimination to television. This notion is also manifested by a greater sensitivity on the part of Jewish filmmakers toward homosexuals. We see, for instance, the sympathetic portrayal of a gay, black character (named Bernstein!) in Paul Mazursky's autobiographical comedy-drama, *Next Stop Greenwich Village* (1976), and the recognition that both Jews and homosexuals were singled out for extermination by the Nazis in Mel Brooks's remake of *To Be Or Not to Be* (1983).

A survey of Jews in the performing arts in the USA reveals that in the more specialized, limited audiences of Vaudeville, radio (because of its great variety), legitimate theater, and the nighclub and "Borscht Belt" circuit, expressions of Jewishness and Judaism were quite frequent. Examination of the content of these media reveals the entire network of Jewish–American tensions, from the prizing of one's background and roots (the use of *Yiddishkeit* and Yiddishisms, for instance to create a communal sense, an "in group") to a self-denigration of one's status as alienated and outside of the mainstream, to the disturbing area of self-hatred and intense desires for assimilation. Although Jewish involvement in the more mass media of Broadway musicals (whose expense and hoped-for national tours seem to require a more "lowest common denominator" attitude), film, and television is just as significant, the range of Jewish issues is more limited. Only recourse to the ideas of displacement and overdetermination allows us to see specifically Jewish elements in these seemingly "all-American" productions. The 1960s found a more open expression of Jewishness among American filmmakers. The death of most of the original movie moguls and the breakdown of the studio system, combined with the USA's embrace of racial and ethnic differences, allowed individual Jewish filmmakers to express Jewish life with the kind of variety previously seen in the smaller world of Jewish-oriented entertainment. The 1960s, for instance, saw the beginning of the film careers of Mel Brooks (*The Producers*, 1968), and Woody ALLEN (*Take the Money and Run*, 1969), a successful film biography of Broadway and radio comedienne Fanny Brice (*Funny Girl*, William Wyler, 1968), and the adaptation into film of Wallant's *The Pawnbroker* (Sidney Lumet, 1965), Bernard MALAMUD's *The Fixer* (John Frankenheimer, 1968) and Philip ROTH's *Goodbye, Columbus*, (Larry Peerce, 1969) among others. While the notion of displacement is still an important one in understanding the reluctance of the still Jewish-dominated mass media to address more serious issues, for the most part the status of Jews in the USA is such that this analysis is primarily historical. Jews seem no longer to feel as much need to displace their problems onto related issues, or to overcompensate their Americanness. That is, there seem to be few problems with being Jewish in the USA; that American Jews have become an integral part of the American scene, as comfortable in America as America is comfortable with them. With this recognition of Jewish assimilation into the American mainstream comes the related recognition that perhaps there will in future no longer be a distinctively unique Jewish contribution to American culture.

FURTHER READING

Bermant, C.: *The Jews* (New York: Times Books, 1977)
Friedman, L.: *Hollywood's Image of the Jew* (New York: Frederick Ungar, 1982)
M. Gottfried: *Broadway Musicals* (New York: 1979)

Howe, I.: *World of Our Fathers: The Journey of the East European Jews to America and the Life They Found and Made* (New York: Simon and Schuster, 1976)
Insdorf, A.: *Indelible Shadows: Film and the Holocaust* (New York: Vintage Books, 1983)

DAVID DESSER

philosophy, nineteenth-century Jewish

"Modern Jewish thought" designates both a chronological category and a mode of discourse. Chronologically, the onset is generally identified with Spinoza (seventeenth century) and the termination with the Second World War. The mode of modern Jewish thought is characterized by its reflexive nature; that is, it explores modernity from a Jewish perspective, and Judaism from the viewpoint of modern intellectual currents. More than in previous periods in history, Jewish thought in the modern period was composed not only for Jews, but for Christians as well. That dual audience shaped both the kinds of issues addressed and the approach taken to them.

The two major figures who stand at the onset of the modern period are Barukh Spinoza (1632–77) and Moses MENDELSSOHN. Spinoza, whose *Tractatus Theologico-Politicus* (1670) ultimately led to his excommunication from the Jewish community on the grounds of heresy, nonetheless was admired by subsequent generations of *maskilim* (Jews promoting secular enlightenment) because of the position of respect he attained among modern non-Jewish thinkers, and because he did not convert to Christianity after his excommunication, but was able to live as a secular Jew, that is, unattached to the formal Jewish community. Spinoza's *Tractatus* itself was significant for its critique of the Bible and of traditional Jewish beliefs, especially the commandments, and provided ammunition both for modern Christian attacks on Judaism and for Jews demanding radical change within Judaism.

It was, however, Moses Mendelssohn who more formally introduced the modern period of Jewish thought, both by virtue of his personality and his writings. Living in Berlin, Mendelssohn became the first modern Jew accepted into non-Jewish intellectual circles and who won the

585

respect of the most important thinkers of the day. His life was taken as a model for what emancipation of the Jews could accomplish, and he became the figure upon whom the Enlightenment philosopher Gotthold Ephraim Lessing (1729–81) based his famous play of religious tolerance, *Nathan the Wise* (1779).

In regard to emancipation, however, Mendelssohn's writings were ambiguous. Some of his Hebrew writings to the Jewish community encouraged modification of Jewish observance in accord with the demands of modern life, while his German writings, in particular his book of esssys on Judaism, *Jerusalem* (1783), insisted that no changes in Judaism should be made in exchange for emancipation. His understanding of Judaism itself was also ambiguous. In defining Judaism as a religion of revealed legislation, Mendelssohn intended to demonstrate its superior ability to adjust to the modern state. In contrast to Judaism, Christianity, he argued, teaches dogmas which conflict with religious liberty, the foundation of modernity. Judaism, however, is a religion of reason which teaches ceremonial laws designed to inculcate symbolically universal truths of reason. Mendelssohn's intention of fortifying traditional Judaism in the face of modernity was misunderstood almost from the outset by both radical reformers and Orthodox opponents. His own disciple, David Friedlaender (1750–1834), argued, shortly after Mendelssohn's death, that if Judaism commanded only religious practices, not beliefs, a level of agreement could be achieved between non-practicing Jews and liberal Protestants who, under the influence of the Enlightenment, had abandoned traditional Christian dogma. He even proposed that the Protestant Church accept a mass conversion of Jews without requiring their acceptance of Christian dogma.

Subsequent leaders of Orthodoxy, including Hatam Sofer (1762–1839) and Samson Raphael HIRSCH, contended that Mendelssohn was responsible for the modern decline in religious observance, and accused him of throwing away Judaism in favor of secularism. By distinguishing between beliefs and laws, they claimed, Mendelssohn had rendered Jewish law meaningless and superfluous. Hirsch, who developed modern Orthodoxy, sought to demonstrate that an Orthodox lifestyle would not hinder participation in business and other secular affairs; his slogan was *Torah 'im derekh 'eretz* (Torah and the ways of the world). Much of nineteenth-century Jewish thought was concerned with finding an accommodation of Judaism and modern life, especially justification of the major synagogal and liturgical reforms carried out by the laity. By the 1840s, the Reform movement was an established reality in Central Europe, and Jewish thinkers hurried to recast traditional doctrines in modern form. Solomon FORMSTECHER and Samuel HIRSCH were two of the prominent rabbinical leaders of the Reform movement and each used the philosophies of Schelling and Hegel to develop an apologetics for liberal Judaism. The idea of an inner dynamic propelling the historical unfolding of truth, taken from idealist philosophy, legitimated change within Judaism, although not its separateness within society.

The need to show that Jews were just like every other historical people, yet at the same time justify their particularism, was a central conflict in the historical study of Judaism (WISSENSCHAFT DES JUDENTUMS) which arose in Europe during the nineteenth century. The results of historical investigations were often put to use in the struggle for emancipation, as well as to support innovative religious practices. For example, that preaching was always an intrinsic aspect of synagogue worship was demonstrated by Leopold ZUNZ, one of the most important historians of the nineteenth century. His conclusions were used to reassure German authorities that the Reform movement was not a politically radical and dangerous movement, and to justify to the Jewish community that the proposed liturgical changes fell into the mainstream of Judaism's historic development. The earliest generation of Reformers, in the first decades of the 1800s, wrote traditional responsa, based on rabbinic texts, to justify their proposed changes, such as inclusion of an organ in the synagogue. Subsequent generations and leaders who were more radical, however, rejected such efforts at rabbinic justification and looked, instead, for more over-arching theological principles for reform. Abraham GEIGER, the most important ideologue of the Reform movement in Germany and a historian of note, argued that Pharisaic Judaism, embodied in the Talmud, represented a principle of progressive development and liberalization during the period of the Second Temple and following its destruction. Modern Reform Judaism, he contended, was simply the continuation of that Pharisaic principle. Geiger justified his argument in his major study of Judaism in the Second Temple and rabbinic periods, *Urschrift und Ueberstzungen der Bibel* (1857), in which he argued that variations in biblical texts and translations represented deliberate alterations of the text which, when properly analyzed, gave evidence for the internal political and spiritual struggles between conservative and progressive forces within the Jewish community in antiquity.

A central concern of nearly every modern Jewish thinker was Christianity and its relation to Judaism. Heinrich GRAETZ whose monumental 11-volume *History of the Jews* (1853–76) was widely read by European Jews, saw Jewish history in terms of suffering and persecution through the centuries at the hands of anti-Jewish Christians. Other thinkers, particularly within the nascent Reform movement, developed what came to be known as the "mission theory", in which Christianity was understood to have undertaken a historic mission on behalf of Judaism, bringing Jewish monotheism and ethics to the pagan nations of the world. The Jews, according to this theory, had to remain isolated and surround their faith with a fence of Jewish law in order to maintain its purity and keep it from the kind of syncretism to which, in their view, Christianity ultimately fell victim. This argument, which takes the Pauline view of Jewish particularism opposed to Christian universalism and gives it a pro-Jewish slant, is only one of the many examples of Jewish adaptation of Christian theological motifs in the modern period. In Jewish hands, however, Christian motifs are inverted so that Judaism becomes the superior religion out of which Christianity developed. While Christian theologians in the nineteenth century promoted the idea that Christianity was superior by virtue of its later, and thus more refined, stage of historical development, Jewish thinkers such as Samuel

Hirsch and Geiger argued for Judaism's superiority on the basis of its position as the original, and hence more authentic, religious teaching.

Mendelssohn's distinction between Judaism as a religion of law and Christianity as a religion of dogma had led to Immanuel Kant's criticism that Judaism consisted of an externally imposed ethical system, not an autonomous ethic which would foster moral consciousness in the individual. Kant's criticism came under attack by late nineteenth-century efforts of Jewish thinkers, such as Moritz LAZARUS and Hermann COHEN, who sought to prove that Judaism was, in fact, a religion of superior ethical commitment. Lazarus presented what he called *The Ethics of Judaism* (1898–1911) embodied by the commandments of rabbinic literature which foster, he argued, precisely that autonomous moral consciousness held up by Kant as the highest form of a religion. Cohen, the most important Kantian philosopher of his generation, began writing about Judaism only at the end of his life, and also sought to reconcile Judaism with Kant's ethical idealism. According to Cohen, in his posthumously-published *Religion of Reason out of the Sources of Judaism* (1919), Judaism is the supreme religion of reason in which God functions as the correlator of human beings. In becoming aware of God's love and concern, human beings are motivated to emulate divine qualities, becoming co-workers in the process of creating the ever-changing world.

The modern Jewish concern with Christianity and secular philosophy arose in large measure as a response to the pressures surrounding the emancipation process. If Germany, along with other European nations, was understood to be a Christian nation, how could Jews be both Germans and Jewish? While some Jews responded by devising a schema in which Christianity was an extension of Judaism, other Jews responded by asserting Jewish national identity even more forcefully. For some Jews, anti-Semitism would never be overcome so long as Jews remained within Christian countries; only a Jewish state would permit full expression of Jewish culture and nationality. ZIONISM, born in nineteenth-century Europe, expressed both the political and cultural longings of Jews unwilling to make compromises for the sake of emancipation and anxious to develop non-religious forms of Jewish expression.

Stimulated in large measure by the rise of the Zionist movement, Jewish thinkers during the first third of the twentieth century in Central Europe began a revisionist movement against the formulations of Jewish history and theology of the preceding century. They opposed the rejection by *Wissenschaft des Judentums* of Jewish mysticism as an aberration, and began an effort to recapture the mystical and hasidic traditions within Judaism. In the *belles-lettres* of writers such as Micha BERDYCZEWSKI the essays of Martin BUBER, and the philosophical writings of Franz ROSENZWEIG, Judaism was increasingly defined less in terms of ethics and philosophy than of faith, popular piety, and mysticism. Existentialism was increasingly incorporated as the language of Jewish thought, with Rosenzweig, in his magnum opus, *The Star of Redemption* (1921), emphasizing the unique situation of each individual who is addressed by God. Buber at first presented hasidic stories as universally applicable existential parables, and later, in *I and Thou* (1922), developed an understanding of revelation as dialogue. Rosenzweig and Buber differ, however, in their understanding of the response to God's approach to the individual. According to Rosenzweig, that response takes the form of fulfilling God's commandments; indeed, the *mitzvot* themselves are signs of God's love, since only a lover, Rosenzweig writes, can command love of the beloved. For Buber, by contrast, the commandments serve as a hindrance to the I–Thou encounter with God, because they prevent the spontaneity necessary to be open to God's initiation of dialogue.

FURTHER READING

Cohen, H.: *Reason and Hope. Selections from the Jewish Writings of Hermann Cohen*, trans. E. Jospe (New York: Viking, 1971)

Graetz, H.: *The Structure of Jewish History and Other Essays*, trans. and ed., I. Schorsch (New York: Jewish Theological Seminary, 1975)

Hirsch, S. R.: *Horeb: A Philosophy of Jewish Laws and Observances*, trans. I. Grunfeld, 2 vols (London, 1972)

Lazarus, Moritz: *The Ethics of Judaism*, trans. H. Szold (Philadelphia: The Jewish Publication Society of America, 1900–1)

Mendelssohn, M.: *Jerusalem: or, On Religious Power and Judaism*, trans. A. Arkush (Hanover and London: University Press of New England, 1983)

Wiener, M., ed.: *Abraham Geiger and Liberal Judaism: The Challenge of the Nineteenth Century*, trans. E. J. Schlochauer (Philadelphia: The Jewish Publication Society of America, 1962)

SUSANNAH HESCHEL

Pinsker, Leon [Yehuda Leib] (1821–1891) Leader of *Hibbat Zion*. Pinsker's education was unusually secular for a Jew in Czarist Russia at the time. He was brought up in Odessa speaking German and Russian, but knowing little Hebrew, and was one of the first Jews to enroll in a Russian university. After a false start in law – which, as a Jew, he could not practice – Pinsker became a doctor. His upbringing, and the relatively liberal climate in the early part of Alexander II's reign, made him a natural adherent of the party that wanted to see the cultural and social barriers between Jews and Russians dissolved, and hoped for equal rights for Jews. Pinsker helped to establish the first Jewish journal to appear in Russian, and was active in the Society for the Promotion of Culture among the Jews of Russia.

The pogroms of 1881 led to a profound change in Pinsker's outlook. The following year he produced a pamphlet called *Autoemancipation* which has become a classic of Zionist literature. Pinsker argued that anti-Semitism would not be cured by any advance towards liberalism and humanism by society at large. Its causes lay very deep, and were closely linked to the peculiar status of the Jews as a group with some residual characteristics of a nation, yet without a territory of its own. Emancipation, even when granted, was at best a gift flung by a rich man to a beggar, which did not raise the latter to the status of the former. The only solution was for the Jews to have a territory in which they would be the majority, where they could support themselves, and whose status would be politically assured.

Pinsker hoped that the leaders of the wealthy and emancipated Jewish communities of western Europe would try to put his plan into action. However, they failed to respond, and

Leon Pinsker, 1880

Pinsker was persuaded by M. L. LILIENBLUM and other Russian *Hovevei Zion* (Lovers of Zion) to join them and, indeed, become their leader. Pinsker agreed because the *Hovevim* believed as he did in self-help and were moved by a desire to raise the national, not just the individual, status of the Jews. He did so in spite of important differences between his ideas and theirs, including the fact that they saw Palestine as the only possible location for the enterprise, whereas Pinsker seems to have remained a territorialist at heart. Although he came to see settlement in Palestine as important in itself, he doubted that it could ever lead to more than a spiritual center – to use AHAD HA'AM's term – for the Jewish people.

BIBLIOGRAPHY

Road to Freedom. Writings and Addresses by Leo Pinsker, ed. and intro. B. Netanyahu (New York: Scopus Publishing Company, 1944)

FURTHER READING

Vital, D.: *The Origins of Zionism* (Oxford: Clarendon Press, 1975)

GEORGE MANDEL

Pinter, Harold (b.1930) British dramatist and screenwriter. Born in Hackney, London, Pinter left school at 17. He studied briefly at the Royal Academy of Dramatic Art and was a conscientious objector after the Second World War. From 1949 to 1960 he became a professional actor and in 1950 began to publish poetry under a pseudonym. His first one-act play *The Room* was produced in Bristol in 1957 and his first full-length play *The Birthday Party* was produced in London in 1958 but taken off after a week. It was not until the production of *The Caretaker* (1960) that Pinter's reputation was established both in England and abroad. He is now widely regarded as Britain's foremost postwar dramatist.

The initial critical hostility towards *The Birthday Party* reflects the inability of English critical opinion in the 1950s to assimilate a voice which remains peculiarly continental. Much of Pinter's early drama, like Anton Chekov's best known work, communicates through the absence of direct explanation. Existential insecurity and a vague sense of threat in these early "comedies of menace" relates Pinter directly to the fiction of Franz KAFKA. More distinctly, Pinter was aiming to develop a dislocated theatrical language which both concealed reality and, at the same time, complemented the alienation of his characters. His debt to the Music Hall – reminiscent of Samuel Beckett – is also reflected in *The Caretaker* which juxtaposes both high and low theater. And his use of rootless working-class and Jewish characters in *The Room* and *The Birthday Party* is in part autobiographical, especially his experience of anti–Semitic violence in Hackney. Nevertheless, much of Pinter's Jewishness and Jewish background is universalized in his early plays and this is especially true of his third full-length play *The Homecoming* (1965). After this play, explicit references to his Jewishness are eschewed in his drama.

From the beginning of his career Pinter wrote simultaneously in a number of literary forms, all of which he has mastered. Dramas such as *A Night Out* (1961) were written as radio plays and successfully moved to television. With the radio performance of *A Slight Ache* (1959) Pinter, for the first time, adopted a middle-class idiom which culminated in *The Collection* (1962), a television play which successfully transferred to the stage. Throughout the enormously productive period of the 1960s, Pinter continued to experiment with lyrical monologues as in the radio play *Landscape* (1968) and *Silence* (1969) and other situational dramas such as *Old Times* (1971), his fourth full-length play. Pinter has continued to produce many short dramas for both the stage and radio, and has also adapted many of his works as screenplays, most recently, *Betrayal* (1978). This play's naturalism and upper-middle-class social setting indicates the extent that Pinter has eschewed his earlier low-life comedies of menace. On the other hand, *Family Voices* (1981) does pointedly refer back to Pinter's earlier drama.

Since the 1960s Pinter has been the recipient of over 14 major literary awards, and his plays have constantly remained in print.

FURTHER READING
Baker, W., and Tabachnick, S.: *Harold Pinter* (Edinburgh: Oliver & Boyd, 1973)
Esslin, M.: *Pinter: The Playwright* (London: Methuen, 1982)

BRYAN CHEYETTE

Pissarro, Camille (1830–1903) French painter. Born Jacob Abraham Camille Pizarro on St Thomas in the Virgin Islands to parents of Sephardi extraction and remoter Marrano origin, Pissarro was to become one of the pivotal figures in the French Impressionist group and an important father-figure to younger artists like Cézanne and Gauguin. Ironically, though, for a painter usually celebrated as the greatest of all nineteenth-century Jewish artists, Pissarro painted not a single Jewish subject; his Jewishness seems scarcely to have impinged on his consciousness, artistic or otherwise. (The only reference to matters of Jewish concern in the letters he wrote to Lucien is to the Dreyfus Affair.)

Like so many assimilated Jews in the modern period, however, Pissarro's Jewishness can be seen to manifest itself in a broader, less sectarian way: above all, in his left-wing ideals and deeply humanitarian stance, both of which find artistic expression in his many renderings of rural workers, and the moral seriousness with which he regarded the Impressionist enterprise of making ordinary people's lives into fit subject matter for art. It was this, perhaps, combined with his biblical appearance that caused his contemporaries at the Café des Nouvelles Athènes to say: "Here comes Moses bearing the Tablets of the Law". The violent attacks directed at Pissarro's art were often motivated less by artistic than by political outrage tinged with anti-Semitism.

BIBLIOGRAPHY
Letters to his Son Lucien (Mamaronek, NY: Paul P. Appel, 1972)

FURTHER READING
Camille Pissarro (London: Hayward Gallery, 1980–1) [exhibition catalog]

MONICA BOHM-DUCHEN

Pissarro, Lucien (1863–1944) British painter. The eldest of Camille's six children (all of whom were artists), he was not legally a Jew, since his mother came from a French farming family. (This proved problematic when, in 1892, he married Esther Bensusan, whose father was an Orthodox Jew.) To a large extent Lucien followed in his father's Impressionist footsteps, and, in moving to England in 1890, became an important link between the French and English avant-garde. In the 1890s, presumably under the influence of his wife, he also produced a number of lyrically decorative wood engravings on biblical themes which were published by his own Eragny Press. Lucien's daughter, Orovida (1893–1968), was also an artist of distinction.

FURTHER READING
Meadmore, W. S.: *Lucien Pissarro* (London: Constable & Co. Ltd., 1962)

MONICA BOHM-DUCHEN

Podhoretz, Norman (b.1930) American writer, editor, and political analyst. Norman Podhoretz has stood in the midst of controversy for most of his career. "I was raised intellectually to believe there was something admirable in taking risks", he observed, "but the people who raised me, in effect, punished me whenever I did what I was raised to do".

He was born to eastern European immigrant parents living in Brooklyn, and graduated from high school at 16. He simultaneously enrolled at Columbia and at the Jewish Theological Seminary, the latter to please his parents. Studying under Lionel TRILLING, Podhoretz took his BA in English from Columbia in 1950, as well as a BHL from the Seminary. Earning a Kennett Fellowship and Fullbright, he spent two years at Cambridge, under the English critic, F. R. Leavis.

Returning to the USA, Podhoretz joined the staff of *Commentary*, the intellectual monthly published by the American Jewish Committee and edited by Elliot Cohen. Among those working at the magazine were a number of individuals associated with the New York intellectual community, including the art critic Clement Greenberg, the sociologist Nathan Glazer, the political commentator Irving Kristol, and the cultural critic Robert Warshow. Becoming a younger member of this group, Podhoretz's first public acknowledgment came from a critical review of Saul BELLOW's *The Adventures of Augie March* in *Partisan Review*. Podhoretz married Midge Decter, an editor and political analyst, in 1956.

After suffering severe depression for several years, Cohen committed suicide in 1959. His job was ultimately offered to Podhoretz, despite his youth. Accepting the position, he began a short-lived flirtation with the emerging New Left, publishing critical assessments of the cold war, Vietnam, and American domestic life, including excerpts from Paul GOODMAN's *Growing Up Absurd.*

Podhoretz has chronicled his own career, evoking controversy in his wake. His 1968 memoir, *Making It,* resulted in an enormous furore, deriving in part from his assertion that the "dirty little secret" of New York intellectual life was "the lust for success which ... replaced sexual lust". Many of his contemporaries disputed this and attacked the book.

As the majority of American intellectuals began to move left in the middle 1960s, Podhoretz began to move back toward the center, and then the right. By the early 1970s literary interests had taken second position to his political analysis as he became a leading spokesman for neoconservatism, along with Irving Kristol, Midge Decter, Daniel Patrick Moynihan, and Daniel Bell. (The last two are no longer identified closely with neoconservatism.)

During the 1980s, Podhoretz has continued his analysis of American politics, and especially American foreign policy. Despite support for Ronald Reagan, two years into Reagan's presidency Podhoretz wrote of "the neoconservative anguish over Reagan's foreign policy". In 1982 he accused critics of Israeli policy not just of anti-Semitism "but of the broader sin of faithlessness to the interests of the United States and...Western civilization as a whole". He has continued to be controversial, although his topics and audiences have changed dramatically over the course of his career.

FURTHER READING

Bloom, A.: *Prodigal Sons: The New York Intellectuals and Their World.* (New York and Oxford: Oxford University Press, 1987)
Steinfels, P.: *The Neoconservatives* (New York: Simon & Schuster 1979)

ALEXANDER BLOOM

Poliakov, Léon (b.1910)   Historian of anti-Semitism. Poliakov was born in St Petersburg but lived in France from 1920. He read law at Paris, worked as a journalist, and after service in the French army during the Second World War studied history at the Sorbonne. His thesis, submitted in 1964, was published by the École Pratique des Hautes Études the following year as *Les Banchieri juifs et le Saint-Siège du XIIIe au XVIIe siècle (The Jewish Bankers and the Holy See,* 1977).

His preoccupation with anti-Semitism, which resulted in his major *Histoire de l'antisémitisme* (1955–77; *History of Anti-Semitism,* 1974–85), was presaged by his participation in the foundation of the Centre de Documentation Juive Contemporaine in 1944 (he headed its research department after the war) and his investigation of Nazi war crimes during the Nuremberg Trials.

It emerged in his first book, *Bréviaire de la haine* (1954; Harvest of hate), on French Jewry under German occupation.

That year he joined the École Pratique des Hautes Études, then directed by the eminent historian, Fernand Braudel and widely identified with the *annales* school of history. Poliakov's work reflects the ethos of the school in its multidisciplinary approach and wide range of sources. It is most apparent in the history, which covers a period of nearly 2,000 years in four volumes: *Du Christ aux Juifs de Cour* (*From Roman Times to the Court Jews*), *De Mahomet aux Marranes* (*From Mohammed to the Marranos*), *De Voltaire à Wagner* (*From Voltaire to Wagner*); and *L'Europe suicidaire, 1870–1933* (*Suicidal Europe, 1870–1933*). Also multidisciplinary is his *Le mythe aryen* (1971; *The Aryan Myth: A History of Racist and Nationalist Ideas in Europe*, 1974), written when he was research fellow at Sussex University from 1964 to 1968. In 1975 the book received the annual Anisfield–Wolf award for research on race relations given by the Cleveland Foundation.

Poliakov is currently honorary director of research at the Centre National de la Recherche Scientifique, which first appointed him research fellow in 1952.

BIBLIOGRAPHY
History of Anti-Semitism (London: Littman Library, 1974–85); *The Jewish Bankers and the Holy See* (London: Littman Library, 1977)

MIRIAM KOCHAN

Polotsky, Hans Jacob (b.1905)

Israeli professor of Egyptian and Semitic linguistics. Born to Russian parents in Zurich, Polotsky attended the universities of Göttingen and Berlin, where he studied Egyptology and Semitic languages. Furthermore, he participated in the *"Göttingen Septuaginta Unternehmen"* and also edited Manichean texts in Coptic. Since 1934 he has been teaching at the Hebrew University of Jerusalem, where he was appointed full professor in 1948. During his long and illustrious career, he has been the recipient of numerous awards, among them the Israel Prize in Humanities (1965).

Polotsky's work is internationally acknowledged for its penetrating analysis of linguistic structures and his outstanding contributions to the study of several language families. His foremost achievements are in the field of Coptic, where he solved the problem of the so-called second tenses through a comparison with the Greek Vorlagen and English and French parallels. Moreover, he substantially contributed to Neo-Aramaic linguistics, applying comparative dialectology and meticulous syntactic methodology. He was also able to decipher Greek papyri from Massada which had hitherto resisted proper understanding.

BIBLIOGRAPHY
Collected Papers (Jerusalem: Magnes Press, 1971)

FURTHER READING
Ullendorff, E.: *The Two Zions* (Oxford: Oxford University Press, 1988)

MAREN NIEHOFF

Pommer, Erich (1889–1966)

American film producer. Pommer is the major formative figure of the German film industry. With his skill as a producer, his shrewd commercial grasp, and his eye for talent, he can be said to have rescued the German film industry three times, immediately after the First World War, in the late 1920s and after the Second World War. Numerous actors, directors, writers, designers, and other technicians owe their careers to him.

Pommer came from Hildesheim and worked in Germany, France, England, and the USA. Immediately after the First World War he produced *Das Kabinett des Dr Galigari* (1919) with its stylized sets and expressionist performances. It was made inexpensively and brilliantly promoted. Films, including: *Die Spinnen* (1919–20), *Der Müde Tod* (1921), *Dr Mabuse, der Spieler* (1921), *Der letze Mann* (1924), and *Faust* (1926) followed. A short period in Hollywood was followed by *Der blaue Engel* (1930), *Der Kongress tanzt* (1931), and *Stürme der Leidenschaft* (1931). As head of production for UFA, Germany's largest film company, with a brilliant eye for talent, he was an important figure in the careers of many figures of "Germany's golden age".

He resigned from UFA the day Hitler became Chancellor, and went via Paris to Hollywood. By 1936, he was in England, working with Alexander KORDA and producing the patriotic *Fire Over England*. In 1937, he and the actor Charles Laughton created Mayflower Pictures which made Hitchcock's *Jamaica Inn* (1939) and for which he produced and himself directed, for the only time, the sometimes admired *Vessel of Wrath* (1937).

During the Second World War, in Hollywood, he produced without distinction. When he returned to Germany afterwards, he was in US army uniform, with the responsibility of removing Nazi and Communist elements from the film industry. Once more he started young talent on its way. His final film, set at the end of the war, *Kinder, Mutter und ein General* (1955) portrays the consequences of militarism for the young.

FURTHER READING
Eisner, L.: *The Haunted Screen* (London: Thames & Hudson, 1969)
Luft, H.: Erich Pommer. *Films in Review*, Oct./Nov. 1959)
The Times 13 May 1959 [obituary]

KEVIN GOUGH-YATES

Popper-Lynkeus, Josef (1838–1921)

Austrian polymath. Born in Kolin, Bohemia, Popper studied at the polytechnics of Prague and Vienna. He worked for the railways, before an invention of 1867 for defurring sugar-beet boilers ensured his material success. While continuing a career as an inventor, Popper turned to social reform, and wrote a number of books, including *Die allgemeine Nährpflicht als Lösung der sozialen Frage* (1912; see H. I. Wachtel, *Security for all and free enterprise*, New York, 1955). He was also the author, under the pseudonym of Lynkeus, of the volume *Phantasien eines Realisten* (1899; Fantasies of a realist), which made Popper a widely known figure.

He was a close friend of Ernst Mach and shared his positivist viewpoint. His approach to society, which inspired the social reform movement in Vienna around 1900, was to see it in terms of a "social technology". Popper insisted that life must be the primary good, and so embraced pacifism and a form of the Welfare State. Popper saw this as the logical outcome of his individualism.

It is notable that Popper saw the connection between individualism and social duty as stemming in his case from a talmudic saying (Belke, 1978). When young, Popper was not formally religious, but in the 1880s, when anti-Semitism became prevalent, he identified with his fellow Jews. Although Popper could not accept Zionism, and remained true to his enlightened principles, he came to see the social ethical tradition of Judaism as of central importance; in his will he donated his library to the Jewish National Library.

BIBLIOGRAPHY
Selbstbiographie (Leipzig, 1917)

FURTHER READING
Belke, I.: *Die sozialreformerischen Ideen von Josef Popper-Lynkeus, 1838–1921* (Tübingen: Mohr, 1978)
Wittels, F.: *An End to Poverty*. (London: G. Allen & Unwin, 1925)

STEVEN BELLER

Porush, Israel (b.1907)

Australian rabbi, author, spiritual leader. Born in Jerusalem, Porush was educated at the Yeshiva Etz Chayim and went to Germany for his schooling where he graduated from the universities of Berlin (mathematics and philosophy) and Marburg (Ph.D.) and rabbinics at the Hildesheimer Rabbinical Seminary in Berlin (1932). Porush moved to England in 1934 where he was appointed Rabbi of the Finchley synagogue.

He emigrated to Sydney in 1940 where, as a traditional, Orthodox Rabbi with a solid western as well as a rabbinic education, he laid the foundation for the future mainstream Rabbinate in Australia. The Rabbinate of the larger Australian congregations had tended to be of the Anglo-Jewish type somewhat remote from Zionism. Porush was able to exercise wide ecclesiastical and communal leadership working towards his goal of establishing the Great Synagogue as the centre of a real *Kehillah*. By espousing the cause of refugees from the Holocaust and through his active role in the Zionist movement, he was instrumental in breaking down the barriers between the Anglo-Jews and the newcomers. He understood that religious pluralism and a wide range of identification with Judaism made positive contributions to a vital Jewish life.

Porush was able to undertake a number of initiatives which greatly strengthened the Jewish community and helped develop relationships with the broader Australian community. In 1943 he approached the Australian churches to recruit their aid in the fight to rescue European Jewry, and reopened the friendly cooperation between Australian Jewry and the various churches that had been the mark of nineteenth-century Australian Jewish life. He instituted a program of regular broadcasts over the national radio network, (the ABC), at festival times, now an annual event.

ALAN D. CROWN

Potok, Chaim (b.1929) American novelist. Born in New York of Polish–Jewish parents, Potok was educated at Yeshiva University, BA 1950, the Jewish Theological Seminary, MHL 1954, and the University of Pennsylvania, Ph.D., in philosophy, 1965. He was an instructor at the University of Judaism, Los Angeles, in 1957–9, and the Jewish Theological Seminary in 1963–4. An ordained rabbi, he served as a chaplain in Korea in 1956–7. In 1965 he became an editor for the Jewish Publication Society. He married Adena Sarah Mosevitzky in 1958. They have three children.

Among American–Jewish writers, Potok has become the central exponent of the joys and sorrows of traditional Judaism's encounter with Western secularism. The basic conflicts and tensions permeating Potok's novels involve Hasidism and Jewish Mysticism versus legalistic, rabbinic orthodoxy, the efforts of fathers literally to direct their sons' lives, and the rebellion of the children tantalized by various secular lures, clinical psychology, modern exegetical criticism, and art. Frequently a set of young friends is pitted against their parents and, in turn, against each other until their differences are painfully resolved, as in Potok's first and best known novel *The Chosen* (1967) and its sequel *The Promise* (1969). His third novel, *My Name is Asher Lev* (1972) deals with the agonized maturation of a Ladover Hasid, who, although he remains an observant Jew, determines to be an artist in the face of monumental parental and communal opposition. *In the Beginning* (1975) concerns a Jewish son who must confront and deal with strident anti-Semitism.

Yet the extent of Jewish suffering, massive and prolonged, which marks these works and Potok's subsequent novels is counterbalanced and softened by the rich portrayals of Jewish family life, the lucid dramatization of Jewish study and scholarship, an emphasis on piety and ethics, a love of Israel, and faith in humankind.

In his most recent fictions Potok has employed the same formulas but broadened his scope. *The Book of Lights* (1981) explores the implications of nuclear holocaust while *Davita's Harp* (1985), an intricately woven, sophisticated work with Kafkaesque overtones, ponders the role of the Jew in socialist and radical circles of the USA in the years leading up to and following the Spanish Civil War.

BIBLIOGRAPHY

Wanderings: Chaim Potok's History of the Jews (London: Hutchinson, 1978); *Tobiasse: Artist in Exile* (1986)

FURTHER READING

Leviant, C.: The Hasid as American hero. *Midstream* 13 (1967)
Walden, D., ed.: *Studies in American Jewish Literature* 4 (1984) [Chaim Potok Issue]

JOSEPH COHEN

Poznanski, Samuel Abraham (1864–1922) Judaic scholar and bibliographer. Born in Lubraniec, Poland, Poznanski became interested in the modern scholarly study of Judaism through Moritz STEINSCHNEIDER, whom he met in Berlin, where he studied at the University and the Hochschule für die Wissenschaft des Judentums. Later, as rabbi of the Tlomacka synagogue in Warsaw, he became involved in Hebrew education and established and directed a government-aided, Jewish teachers' seminary.

An enthusiastic Zionist and delegate to the First Zionist Congress, together with Ignaz GOLD-ZIHER, he was to have headed a peace mission in 1921 to the Arabs at the instigation of Nahum Sokolov.

Despite his communal occupations, Poznanski made an outstanding contribution to Jewish scholarship in the form of books, articles, and reviews in Hebrew, German, French, English, Yiddish, and Polish. Together with others, he was responsible for the relaunching of the Mekizei Nirdamim Society, and he carried on an extensive correspondence with the foremost Judaic scholars of his time, who sought his advice on learned matters. His rabbinic learning, his extensive knowledge of Arabic, his scientific acumen, and his use of unpublished manuscript sources led to pioneering studies in his areas of interest. The latter included biblical exegesis and the history of Hebrew grammar in the medieval period, Jews in Arab lands, and Judeo-Arabic literature. Poznanski was among the first scholars to publish material from the Cairo Genizah. His doctoral thesis had been devoted to the philological and exegetical works of Moses Ibn Chiquitilla (Leipzig, 1895) and he wrote *Zur jüdisch-arabischen Literatur*, (Berlin, 1904) as a supplement to Steinschneider's *Arabische Literatur der Juden*. However his most significant contribution was in the field of geonic history and the cognate area of Karaite studies. In addition to numerous contributions on the foregoing subjects to encyclopedias and scholarly journals, special mention must be made of his *Karaite Literary Opponents of Saadiah Gaon* (1908), his *Babylonische Geonim im nach-gaonäischen Zeitalter* (1914) and an edition of M. Sultanski's *Zekher Zaddikim* ("Karaite Chronicle", 1920). Poznanski also compiled a comprehensive bio-bibliographical dictionary of Karaite writers, containing over 8,000 entries. The unpublished manuscript together with his personal archives are preserved in the Jewish National and University Library in Jerusalem.

FURTHER READING

A. Marx and E. Poznanski. In *Hommage à S. Poznanski* (Warsaw: 1927)

PAUL B. FENTON

Praag, Siegfried van (b.1899) Dutch writer. Born in Amsterdam, the youngest son of Herman van Praag, a diamond manufacturer and broker, and his wife, Grietje de Jongh, together with his older and brilliant brothers, grew up in the middle-class, predominantly Jewish "Sarphati" neighborhood of Amsterdam, where many of his novels are set. From childhood he developed an interest in the world of the circus and also a close affinity with French culture. Several of his historical novels, many of which have a woman as their central character, are situated in eighteenth-century France. Although not very Orthodox, Praag's father was a traditional Jew and an early Zionist who strongly influenced his sons in their attachment to Judaism and Zionism, and he maintained contact with colleagues whose origins were in eastern Europe. Praag combined many of these elements in a single novel, for example *Maria Nunes* (1927) about one of the first Sephardi women to have settled in Amsterdam; *La Judith* (1930), about a Jewish circus artist, and *Het Huisaltaar* (1978; The domestic altar), about east European Jewish immigrants who made their way in cabaret and theater in Amsterdam. Most of his novels, however, are about Amsterdam-born Jews between 1900 and 1935, his own time.

In 1924 Praag married Hilda Sanders, an economic journalist and together they were instrumental in bringing exiled German–Jewish authors into contact with the Allert de Lange Publishing House in the 1930s. After a short while as a teacher of French at a secondary school Praag decided to devote himself to writing. In 1936 he, his wife and children settled in Brussels. During the German invasion of Belgium they reached London where he worked in the Dutch and Belgian sections of the BBC as a translator. At the end of the war they returned to Brussels, where Praag continued to live.

The main theme of Praag's forty or so novels is Jewish life in Amsterdam before and after the Second World War. Among the post-war novels pride of place must be given to *Jeruzalem van het Westen* (1961; Jerusalem of the West [i.e. Amsterdam]) which, to some extent, is a *roman à clef*. Some of his later novels and essays are autobiographical, such as *De Arend en de Mol* (1973; The eagle and the mole) and the essay "De oude darsjan" (1971; The old *darshan*). Volumes of essays include *De West-Joden en hun Letterkunde* (1926; The west European Jews and their literature), *In eigen en vreemde spiegel* (1928; Jews through their own and non-Jewish eyes) and *Mokum-aan-de Amstel. Een goed huwelijk* (1976; Mokum-on-the Amstel: a good marriage).

Partly due to his having lived outside Holland for over 50 years Praag was increasingly outside the mainstream of Dutch literature and its modern developments. However, several of his novels have been reprinted in recent years. Praag was made an "officer" of the Académie Française in 1939.

HENRIETTE BOAS

Prawer, Siegbert Salomon (b.1925)

German scholar and writer. Prawer is a towering figure among contemporary scholars, and one of the few Germanists to be known outside of his subject. He was born in Cologne, Germany, and went to England in 1939. While at school he won a Major Open scholarship to Jesus College, Cambridge, where he studied English and Modern languages. As a student he won a number of prizes and was awarded a Research Studentship at Christ's College which he relinquished for a teaching post at the University of Birmingham in 1948.

Prawer was appointed Professor of German at London University in 1964, and Head of the department of German language and literature. In 1969 he became Taylor Professor of German at the University of Oxford, and Professor Emeritus on his retirement in 1986.

Prawer has held Visiting Professorships at numerous universities, including the University of Chicago (1957–8), University of Cincinnati (1963–4), Harvard (1967–8), and Brandeis (1981–2). In 1980 he was Visiting Fellow at the Humanities Research Centre, Australian National University.

A brilliant critic and lecturer, Prawer is renowned as a scholar whose many publications are not only informative but elegantly composed. In recognition of his studies of German poetry, language, and culture he has been awarded a Litt.D. from Cambridge, a D.Litt. from Oxford and a D.Phil. *honoris causa* by the University of Cologne in 1984. Among his many other honors he was elected Fellow of the British Academy in 1982 and President of the British Comparative Literature Association in 1984.

Although Prawer's research has covered German literature of the nineteenth and twentieth centuries, including studies of writers as diverse as Möricke, E. T. A. Hoffman, Paul CELAN, and Günter Grass, a substantial element of his thought concerns the Jewish contribution to German literature. The starting point of his analysis is Heinrich HEINE, whose work he has examined in the context of German–Jewish culture and in the light of the relationship of the creative writer to history. In his recent study, *Heine's Jewish Comedy: a Study of his Portraits of Jews and Judaism* (1983) he demonstrates Heine's importance as a poet–historian, through his satirical portraits which allow a clear insight into the attitudes of his time.

Prawer's studies involve English-language writers as well, including Shakespeare, Yeats, Faulkner, and Golding. He is currently engaged in writing a book-length study of the works of W. M. Thackeray. He has an interest in Yiddish language and literature and is the author of a chapter on Yiddish poetry in *Kontroversen, alte und neue* (1986; Old and new controversies), and a short analysis of the poetry of Avrom Nokhem STENCL.

Prawer has an international reputation as a learned and meticulous scholar who pays disciplined and subtle attention to the finest details of literary texts. His books, written with a grace and fluency unusual in critical scholarship, reveal the extraordinary range of his intellectual interests. As gifted a graphic artist as he is a scholar, Prawer is currently active as a portraitist and illustrator.

BIBLIOGRAPHY

Seventeen Modern German Poets (Oxford: Oxford University Press, 1971); *Comparative Literature Studies* (Oxford: Duckworth, 1973)

JOHN MATTHEW

Preil, Gabriel Yehoshua (b.1911)

Preil, Gabriel Yehoshua (b.1911) Hebrew and Yiddish poet. Born in Estonia, Preil is the grandson of Yehoshua Josef Preil (1858–96), an Orthodox rabbi who nonetheless published articles in *Haskalah* journals such as *Hamelitz*. Gabriel Preil spent his early childhood in Lithuania. He lost his father at an early age. In 1922 he emigrated, with his mother, Clara, to New York City, where he remained.

Preil's first poem was published in *Hadoar* in 1936. Since 1944 he has published nine volumes of poetry and a number of articles on Hebrew and Yiddish. He has translated verse (from Hebrew to English and vice versa) and written essays on literary matters in Hebrew, Yiddish and English. He is said to have been influenced by American poets as varied as Walt Whitman, Robert Frost and Carl Sandberg. His Hebrew is remarkably Israeli in diction and phrasing, although he first went to Israel only in 1967.

Preil perceives himself as the product of three very different environments: Lithuania, the land of his childhood; New York, the place of his adult residence, and *Eretz Yisra'el*, his essential locus of identification.

BIBLIOGRAPHY
Selected Poems of Gabriel Preil (St Louis: Cauldron Press, 1979); *Sunset Possibilities and Other Poems* (Philadelphia: The Jewish Publication Society, 1985)

FURTHER READING
Feldman, Y.: *Modernism and Cultural Transfer: Gabriel Preil and the Tradition of Jewish Literary Bilingualism* (Cincinnati: The Hebrew Union College Press, 1986)

ZILLA JANE GOODMAN

press, Hebrew

press, Hebrew The Jewish press in general and the Hebrew press in particular developed in Holland at the start of the eighteenth century out of the relationship between the Jews of Amsterdam and the Dutch press, and for reasons peculiar to the city's heterogenous Jewish community. It comprised Ashkenazic and Sephardic Jews, both including Marranos (forced Christians) who had returned to their ancestral faith. The many questions they asked about the modern world in which they found themselves led to the appearance, in 1691, of the first Hebrew paper in Holland, *Pri etz hahayyim*.

To the mid-nineteenth century: a drafted press

The Jewish Enlightenment sought to effect a radical change in Jewish perceptions, and to inculcate Jewish life with the spirit of humanism and modernity. The early nineteenth-century press, epitomized by the periodical *Hama'assef* (1784–1811), devoted itself single-mindedly to this goal. Influenced by contemporary philosophies and a growing historicism, it proposed to place man and nature squarely in the center of a thinking and creative world. Therefore, although the articles in these periodicals differed widely, their intentions were the same: to change Jewish perceptions even in those fields that were clearly traditional, such as scriptural interpretation.

Everything that appeared to defy common sense in traditional interpretation, including the importance of legend, was pushed aside in a new mindset that celebrated victory over tradition.

Meir Halevy Letteris's *Hatzefirah* (1823), which appeared in Galicia, is another typical example of the Enlightenment press. This "monthly" (only one issue ever appeared), had an ambitious agenda rooted in Enlightenment rationalism and humanism. Its columns were to include poetry, scriptural "clarifications", and literature, as well as the "history of the Jews and the great men of Israel". *Hatzefirah* is one of the more extreme examples of a press drafted to the goals of the Hebrew Enlightenment.

The appearance of *Zion* (1840–1) in Frankfurt-am-Main caused a minor revolution. Its approach was genuinely historicist, and therefore secular. This was in direct contrast to the transcendent and religious outlook prevalent in Jewish life to that time. While it resembled its predecessors in terms of content, *Zion* was a well-organized and edited periodical that appeared every month for two years. Additionally, *Zion* reacted journalistically in its reporting of current events in the Jewish world close to the time that they occurred.

The Hebrew weeklies in Europe 1856–1886

Hebrew readers were bombarded with weeklies

during the second half of the nineteenth century. The first of these was the influential *Hamagid*, which appeared in the Prussian city of Lyc. It was followed by periodicals such as *Hamelitz, Hakarmel, Hazefirah, Halebanon, Hahavazelet,* and *Hadekel*. These weeklies were the beginning of the Hebrew press proper, and were true journals in the modern sense. They began to concentrate increasingly on news delivery, relinquishing their literary activities to the monthlies and quarterlies. *Hamagid*'s circulation and influence in the Jewish world outstripped any other weekly and many other periodicals copied its format and its style, such as the handwritten *Hadover*, edited by Baruch Moshe Mizrachi, that appeared in Baghdad in 1870. *Hamagid* pioneered both the printing of actual news and the modern feature article. These were written in a concise, lucid Hebrew by such as *Hamagid*'s editor, D. Gordon. The weekly was also the first paper to have a recognizable graphic style. *Hamelitz*'s editor, Alexander Tsederboym, invented the modern editorial and developed the paper into an outspoken and aggressive journal.

In the second half of the nineteenth century, the Hebrew press became more diverse, and less single-mindedly devoted to Enlightenment goals. Doubts about the movement's methods began to creep into the press, even among the papers that had been the Enlightenment's most faithful supporters. The intellectual and militant *Hamelitz*, for example, ranged itself against the more traditionalist *Hamagid*, especially in scriptural matters. *Hamagid*, however, turned to nationalism, and even to Zionism, before *Hamelitz*, and certainly before the birth of the Zionist movement.

The Hebrew press outside Europe at the end of the nineteenth and beginning of the twentieth centuries

In Jerusalem, *Halebanon*, (1863), published and edited by Joel Brill, was the first Hebrew journal in Palestine. It was followed that same year by *Hahavazelet*, edited by Israel Bak, and Israel Dov Frumkin. The paper was published for about fifty years and reflected Jewish life in the city and later in the newly established settlements. When the Ottoman authorities closed both papers, *Halebanon* transferred to Paris.

Eliezer BEN-YEHUDA, the founder of modern spoken Hebrew, also wrote for *Havazelet*, but resigned and between 1885 and 1910 put out his own papers, *Hazvi, Ha'or,* and *Hashkafa*. Ben-Yehuda's papers tried to be innovative and were therefore severely criticized. But the modern Hebrew press, which moved from Jerusalem to Tel Aviv in the early 1920s, derived both from their influence and from the criticism levelled against them. *Ha'aretz* was the first of these modern papers, followed by *Davar* and *Do'ar hayom*.

In America, Hebrew periodicals and papers began with the arrival of the first Jewish immigrants from Russia in the 1880s, in New York, Chicago, Baltimore, and Boston. They dealt with the immigrants' daily life in their new country, the fight against missionaries, and America's history and constitution, as well as with events in Europe. Apart from the material on America, the American Hebrew press closely resembled its European counterpart, and many European journalists wrote for it. This press flourished until after the beginning of the twentieth century, but today only two periodicals exist. These are the literary magazine *Bitzaron*, and the political weekly *Hado'ar*.

From a weekly to a daily press

Yehuda Lev Kantor put out *Hayom*, the first Hebrew daily, in St Petersburg in 1886. The weeklies, afraid of losing their readers, quickly followed suit. Essentially they did not change, but as communications in Europe improved, they began to receive the news more quickly, and events in both the Jewish and non-Jewish world were reflected in the Hebrew press with greater intensity. The Friday papers allotted a small section to culture, but the literary and cultural aspect expressed itself mainly in bonus supplements from the daily press to its readers. This format remains a constant in today's Israeli press, which is a direct descendant of the press revolution at the end of the nineteenth century.

MENUCHA GILBOA

press, Israeli According to the Central Bureau of Statistics, 75 percent of Israelis read

מכתב עתי משמיע חדשות

יוצא לאור אחת בשבוע, מאת
חיים וֶעֶלִין סלאניסמסקי

№ 13. | וַארשויא, רח ניסן תרמ"ו | Варшава, 25 Марта (6 Апрѣля) 1886. | שנת השלש עשרה

הודעת המו"ל

הגליון הזה הוא האחרון לרבע השנה הנכחי , והנו מודיעים לקוראינו הנכבדים כי קבלנו רשיון מהממשלה
להוציא את הצפירה מדי יום ביומו , ומראשית הרבע הבא הלאה , היינו מיום 1 (13) אפריל , הוא יום ג'
ח' ניסן הבעל , תשוב הצפירה את פנֶיה להיות מכתב עתי יומי . . .

a daily newspaper (many of them reading two
or more). This is hardly surprising in view of
the avid interest the Israeli public shows in the
news. TV news coverage lasts longer (in ratio to
all programs) than in any other western country; there are radio broadcasts on the hour,
every hour, throughout the day on two networks. It is not surprising, therefore, that the
print medium has such a following and has
created such a rich assortment of newspapers
and periodicals in Hebrew and in a multitude of
other languages. Although television had a certain deleterious effect on newspaper sales in its
first years, the two media now live in happy
coexistence and probably serve to boost each
other.

Historically, the nation's political movements
have been anxious to ensure that their particular ideological viewpoints reach as wide a
public as possible, and many of the country's
newspapers were, in the past, linked or indeed
owned outright by one or another political
movement or party. As time has progressed, the
reading public has grown more sophisticated
and less prepared to be fed politically-strained
news and analysis and most of these papers are
now defunct. Such was the fate of *Haboker*
(General Zionist), *Lamerhav* (Ahdut HáAvodá),
Hayom (Herut), *Hayom Hazeh* (edited by Moshe
Dayan), and the Likud weekly *Yoman Hashavua*.

The quality of the Israeli press is, by and
large, fairly high. There is no daily paper
equivalent to the "yellow" journalism of the
New York Daily News or the *Sun* or *Daily Mirror*
in UK. Even the advent of the *Hadashot* afternoon paper (a misnomer, as all three "afternoon" papers are actually on sale at about 9.00
a.m.) in 1984, did not have the feared effect of
"pulling down" the quality of the others. It did,
however, inject a strong additional element of
competition into an already turbulent situation
and make for shorter stories and "snappier"
and colorful news presentation.

Not surprisingly, in view of the Israelis' concern for the news, several of the newspaper
editors as well as some of the leading journalists
have become powerful and influential – some
observers would say more than is healthy in a
democratic society. To be fair, however, there
are very few examples of this power having
been abused. Several journalists have successfully made the transition from print to the electronic media and become television or radio
personalities in their own right – such as M. K.
Amnon Rubinstein and Dan Margalit of
Ha'aretz, Yeshayahu Ben Porat, Gideon
Reicher, and Didi Menusy of *Yedi'ot Aharonot*,
Hanna Zemer of *Davar*, and Nahum Barnea of
Koteret Rashit, a high-quality weekly magazine
that unfortunately ceased publication at the
beginning of 1989.

The whole of the Israeli press – whether
printed, the wire services or the electronic
media, is subject to state censorship. This censorship is calculated to prevent leaking of secrets which could be injurious to the country's
security, although in the late 1980s there has
been an increasing number of charges of use of
the censorship weapon where issues other than
security were involved.

In a nation facing Israel's particularly sensitive military situation there is widespread
agreement with the need to maintain some form
of press censorship. The correct relationship of
the censorship authorities vis-à-vis the media,
and of the media vis-à-vis the censor, is over-
seen by the Editors' Committee. This committee, composed of the editors of the daily
newspapers and the heads of the Broadcasting
Authority, acts as a sort of supreme watchdog

and its rulings tend to be followed by the rest of the press.

The Arab press in Jerusalem, Samaria, and the Gaza District are not represented on the Editor's Committee and are subject to different censorship regulations. By and large, however, the Arab press is free to publish hostile material about Israel and to criticize Israel and its government and authorities, as long as it does not call for civil insurrection or incitement. Again, however, in the late 1980s there have been an increasing number of actions designed to muzzle or at least to limit the freedom of the Arab press, and some journals have even been closed down temporarily. This phenomenon must worry anyone concerned for the freedom of the press.

Israel has no official body corresponding to the Bureau of Audit in the USA which monitors and publishes audited circulation figures. However, the Israel Association of Advertisers does try to ascertain circulation figures for the major papers. On the basis of these figures – the accuracy of which cannot be considered either scientific or reliable – it draws up suggested advertising rates schedules.

A phenomenon which has become increasingly prevalent over the last few years is the burgeoning of local newspapers. The first of these, the Jerusalem-based *Kol Ha'ir* and its Tel Aviv sister, *Ha'ir*, both published by *Ha'aretz*, are a tremendous success story and they have created in their wake a string of others – in Tel Aviv, Haifa, the Dan area, Beersheba, and virtually every major town.

The most important daily newspapers are as follows:

Ha'aretz (morning). Unequivocally recognized as Israel's most distinguished paper, *Ha'aretz* is required reading for all senior civil servants and government employees, industrialists, businessmen, lawyers, academics, and people in public affairs. It is fiercely independent, jealously guarding its journalistic freedom and that of its staff of journalists. It aspires to a high level of writing and has often been compared to such papers as the New York *Times*, *The Times* of London, *Le Monde*, or *Die Welt*, in the seriousness and responsibility of its editorial coverage, reporting and analysis.

Davar (morning). *Davar* is owned by the Histadrut (The General Federation of Trade Unions). As such it is clearly associated with the Labor Party and is also widely read by members of the kibbutz and moshav movements. However, despite its affiliation, the newspaper adopts an independent editorial line, not fearing to criticize the Labor Party and its institutions if it sees fit.

Jerusalem Post (morning). Founded in 1932, the *Jerusalem Post* was, for 56 years, Israel's only English-language newspaper. Although by no means the widest-read or the highest circulation paper in the country, it is certainly the most important in the terms of diplomats, foreign correspondents, non Hebrew-speaking residents, visitors from overseas, and tourists, and presumably key figures in neighboring Arab states. While the Israel Government Press Office prepares daily translations in English of articles in the Hebrew press which are circulated to foreign journalists, wire services and diplomatic missions, it is clearly the *Jerusalem Post* to which the non-Hebrew reader first turns.

Yedi'ot Aharonot (afternoon). This paper, founded in 1939, is today Israel's undisputed leader in circulation figures with some 200,000 copies per day and about 350,000 copies of the Friday weekend edition. It suffered a near-fatal blow on 14 May 1948 (the day independence was declared) when most of its journalists, under the leadership of Dr Azriel Carlebach, walked out without warning to found *Ma'ariv*. *Yedi'ot Aharonot* today is a ramified business empire with manifold interests in book and magazine publishing, printing, real estate, football pools and so on.

Ma'ariv (afternoon). After the split from *Yedi'ot Aharonot* (see above), *Ma'ariv* enjoyed many years as the undisputed leading circulation newspaper in the country. However, over the past few years, *Ma'ariv*'s fortunes have waned drastically and it is now making strenuous efforts to recapture its share of the market. *Ma'ariv* owns a major book publishing house and *At*, a women's monthly magazine.

Hadashot (afternoon). Owned by the *Ha'aretz* morning paper, its sister paper is its complete antithesis. Bright and breezy, its trademark is short, punchy articles with catchy headlines and lavish use of color. There is a strong emphasis on human interest stories, light entertainment, gossip, and sport. Despite Cassandra-like predictions for its future, it has certainly carved out a place for itself on the Israeli newspaper scene, especially with a newer generation of newspaper readers.

The Nation. The second daily English-language newspaper started as a weekly in 1988 and became a daily in 1989. As of writing, there is considerable doubt over the future of this attempt to set up a competing newspaper to the firmly entrenched *Jerusalem Post.*

The leading weekly magazines are:

Ha'olam Hazeh. Widely considered to be purely a scandal sheet, this magazine has created a reputation over the years for its revelations of affairs in governing circles in Israel and its glimpse into the private (especially sex) lives of leading Israeli personalities. The paper has survived countless lawsuits but at the same time has often revealed events which turned out to be only too true. The paper's maverick founder and editor, Uri Avineri, founded a political party also called *Ha'olam Hazeh* "This World" and was elected to the Knesset in 1965. Avineri is no longer in the Knesset, but the magazine continues its crusading, markedly anti-religious and strongly left-wing approach.

La'isha. Israel's largest-selling weekly magazine, this is a traditional-formula women's magazine owned by the *Yedi'ot Aharonot* daily newspaper. It covers all subjects usually associated with a women's magazine but has enough general articles to appeal to mixed audiences.

In addition to the daily and weekly newspapers and magazines there is a huge range of monthly, quarterly, and irregular publications in both Hebrew and other languages, covering every aspect of life and interest, from magazines for young children to specialist scientific, medical, literary, sporting, and trade journals, and so on, of which there are several hundred.

ASHER WEILL

press, Jewish, in Australia
Proportionate to its size among Jewish communities in the English speaking world, the Australian Jewish community has been in the forefront of Jewish

periodical publication. A recent survey of its output runs to 161 pages, and a bibliography of Australian books of Jewish interest runs to 569 pages and shows a substantial range of topics.

The natural concern of the community has been to develop a literary medium that would inform the community of the activities of its members, mediate information of concern to Australian Jews, bring news from the Jewish Diaspora, and provide a vehicle for individual expression of opinion. Perhaps the isolation of Australia intensifies these needs, accounting for the 19 attempts at publishing community newspapers either on the state or national level.

The first attempt to publish a Jewish newspaper was early in the nineteenth century even before the Jewish community was large enough to sustain it. Jewish communal life in the colony had begun in the 1820s and in 1842, despite the small number of Jews, an Australian edition [subtitled *The Hebrews' Monthly Miscellany, Sydney Edition*] of *The Voice of Jacob* (a London newspaper) began to appear. When it ceased publication, after three issues, the editor noted that the community was too small to sustain a newspaper. The second newspaper, the eight-page weekly, *The Australian Israelite*, survived for four years, 1871–5.

Throughout the nineteenth century, newspapers and broadsheets came and went, some short-lived and others with longer lives. Most were published in New South Wales or Victoria which always had the largest concentration of Jewish settlers. Some had particular leanings at their birth, such as *The Australasian Hebrew* which proclaimed itself to be "Orthodox with a tendency to liberality" and others adopted stances on various issues, especially in relation to the development of Zionism, which made them the focus of community attention.

The Hebrew Standard of Australia, first published in 1895 was embroiled in communal controversy throughout the 1940s. Later, this weekly became the *Jewish Times*, then *The Australian Jewish Times*, and is still extant today, incorporating the international edition of the *Jerusalem Post Weekly*. This Sydney-based newspaper has national distribution and is equivalent to the Melbourne-based *Australian Jewish News*.

The states with smaller Jewish populations produced a variety of periodicals, some of them of

601

literary merit, as exemplified by *The Westralian Judean*. Today, the smaller states have lost any independent press that they may have had; they are represented either by synagogue journals which serve the whole community rather than their own parochial interests or else by community roof organization journals. Among such we note the weekly *Maccabean*, (West Australia) and monthly *Shalom* (Queensland), *Hamerkaz* (Australian Capital Territory), *South Australian Jewry*, and the *Tasmanian Jewish Times*.

It is frequently suggested, within the Australian Jewish community, that it is immature and parochial, a Diaspora outpost. Yet the periodical listings tell rather a different story. There is a vigorous synagogue press, with some 32 newsletters, magazines or journals (nearly all of them established in the post-war period) as well as the recent periodical publications, (some six in number), of the *Yeshivot* and *Kollelim*. Since the publication of *The Dialectic* (Jewish monthly, Melbourne 1875) no less than 48 periodicals have been launched with an overt cultural purpose. Some, such as the Journal of the *Australian Jewish Historical Society*, have had a specialized but culturally important role. The majority journals such as *Unity* or *The New Citizen*, appeared in the post-war period and represent the literary aspirations of migrant European Jews who transferred cultural leanings and social predilections from the old world. In the 1960s and 1970s one saw the reappearance of the same cultural influences, refreshed and reinvigorated by post-war Anglo-Jewish migration, in such journals as *Contact* and *The Bridge*.

The distribution of the Yiddish publications in Australia must give rise to caution in evaluating the role of post-war emigration from Europe in the development of the Australian Jewish press. Of the 20 Yiddish periodicals which have been published in Australia, 10 began their publication before the Second World War. Virtually the only surviving Yiddish publications today are supplements to the newspapers or other periodicals. No Hebrew newspaper has ever been published although *Brit Ivrit Olamit* issues newsletters.

There is some periodicity in the listings. Six journals published by the Jewish Council to Combat Fascism and anti-Semitism appeared in the immediate post-war period and ceased publication in 1964 by which time the Australian Jewish community had subdued its interest in the issue of the migration of Nazi war criminals to Australia and it was no longer the sole target for racist attacks on post-war migrants as Australia began its slow progress towards its current multi-culturalist ideology. Zionist publications tend to be concentrated in the period between 1929 (when the Zionist Federation of Australia and New Zealand was established) and the years immediately after the establishment of the State of Israel. The 1970s and 1980s marked the rise of eight journals devoted to Australia–Israel cultural affairs news briefing.

The younger generation was active in the development of Australian attitudes towards the Zionist movement, especially in the war years. The Zionist youth movements have published 38 periodicals, many of them between 1942 and 1950. In the last two decades, as the tertiary education system expanded and the Jewish student population grew, the Jewish student press expanded with 30 titles appearing in print.

Apart from the newspapers there has been no specialized commercial Judaica publisher in Australia. Cultural organizations and synagogues have been their own publishers, some being remarkably productive. Scholarly Jewish publications have been published by the international commercial presses or their Australian subsidiaries. The Australian Jewish Quarterly Foundation and the Mandelbaum Trust have been active publishers on a small scale and, in the last year, there appeared the first scholarly journal of Judaica in Australia, *Menorah*.

FURTHER READING

Goldhar, P.: The Yiddish Press in Australia. *Australian Jewish Almanac* (1937) 258–74

Marks, P. J.: The Jewish Press of Australia Past and Present. *Periodical Publications from the Australian Jewish community*, ed. A. D. Crown and M. Dacy (Sydney: University of Sydney, 1986)

Rutland, S.: *Seventy Five Years: The History of a Jewish Newspaper* (Sydney: The Australian Jewish Historical Society, 1970)

ALAN D. CROWN

press, Jewish, in South Africa   The Jews of German, and more especially of English, extraction, who established the Jewish community of South Africa, generally used English as their common language. During the nineteenth and twentieth centuries the English press reported in some detail on matters of Jewish communal interest. The need for a distinctively Jewish press, more particularly in Yiddish, therefore only became acute after 1880, with the mass immigration of Yiddish-speaking, eastern-European Jews. As a sizeable proportion of all the Jewish immigrants settled in Cape Town and Johannesburg, it followed that the Jewish press came to be concentrated in those two cities.

The founding of the Jewish press in South Africa is attributed to Nehemia Dov Hoffman, an east European immigrant. He published the first Jewish newspaper in the country, an eight-page Yiddish weekly, *Der Afrikaner Israelite*, which appeared for six months, from the beginning of 1891, in Johannesburg. Hoffman subsequently moved to Cape Town where he was associated with *Haor* (1895–7), *Der Yiddisher Herald* (1896–8), *Der Afrikaner Telegraph* (1898–1902) and *Die Judishe Folkzeitung* (September–October 1905). In 1905 he edited a Hebrew bi-weekly *Kineret*, which later appeared as a Hebrew supplement in his monthly Yiddish publication *Der Afrikaner* (1909–14).

David Goldblatt, an associate of Hoffman's on *Der Afrikaner Telegraph*, edited and published the country's first Yiddish daily newspaper *Der Kriegstaphet*. It appeared from 16 October 1899 to 213 December 1899 in Cape Town and carried news of the Anglo-Boer War. Later Goldblatt edited *Der Yiddisher Advocate* (1909–14). Amongst its contributors was his daughter Sarah, who was the private secretary of Senator C. J. Langenhoven, author of the South African national anthem. One of the founders of the Cape Jewish Board of Deputies, Goldblatt fought tirelessly and successfully for the specific recognition of Yiddish as a European language in terms of the Cape's Alien Immigration Act of 1902.

Whilst Hoffman and Goldblatt were active in Cape Town, a vigorous Yiddish press also developed in Johannesburg. Among many weekly newspapers published were *Die Afrikaner Yiddishe Gazetten* (1896–7), *Der Express* (1898), *Hakochav* (1903–7), *Die Judishe Fohn* (1909–13),

Die Yiddishe Shtime, (1910), *Wechentliche Naies* (1912), *Der Strom* (1917–19), *Dorem Afrika* (1921–3), and *Yiddishe Shtime* (1924). The Yiddish dailies included *Die Johannesburg Tageblat* (1912–13), *Die Naie Heim* (1913), and *Dorem Afrikaner Yiddishe Shtime* (1938). In marked contrast to the brief lifespan of the aforementioned Yiddish newspapers, which, in some instances, were the journalistic efforts of individuals, the *Afrikaner Yiddishe Zeitung* was published from 1931 to 1982. Funded through a shareholding company, it was a modern newspaper in a broadsheet format which was distributed in all the country's major towns and cities. In 1934 it incorporated *Der Afrikaner* (1911–33), and in 1937, it amalgamated with *Der Yiddisher Express* (1934–7). From 1936 to 1942 it appeared twice a week, thereafter being published weekly, its demise due largely to the natural loss of a Yiddish reading public.

The first Anglo-Jewish newspaper, the *S A Jewish Chronicle*, founded and edited by Lionel Goldsmid, was published as a fortnightly in Cape Town from 1902 to 1904. It reappeared in Johannesburg in May 1905 and continued as a weekly until December 1927. In January 1928 it was removed to Cape Town where it was taken over by members of the *Dorshei Zion* Association, and became the official organ of the Zionist Federation in Cape Town.

In August 1959 the *S A Jewish Chronicle* was merged with the *Zionist Record*, the official newspaper of the South African Zionist Federation in Johannesburg. The *Zionist Record* which was first published as a monthly in November 1908, initially contained extracts of the minutes of the Federation's Executive Council and reports from affiliated Zionist Societies. In 1923, in order to enable the newspaper to develop into a fortnightly journal of Jewish interest, an editorial board, chaired by Benzion Hersch, was established, and a separate office opened. In 1924 it became a bi-weekly, and in 1926 a weekly, which it has remained. On special occasions it appears in an enlarged form, with annuals to mark certain festivals and *Yom Ha'atzmaut*. Whilst still the official mouthpiece of the Zionist Federation, its contents also include international Jewish news and reports on communal activities.

The first issue of the *S A Jewish Times*, founded

by Leon Feldberg, appeared in July 1936. At its inception it merged with *The Ivri* (1923–36), the official organ of the Jewish Guild and the Hebrew Order of David. An independent weekly newspaper, it carried articles of specific Jewish and general interest and became the widest circulating Jewish newspaper in Africa. In 1986, in the interests of rationalization and economy, it merged with *The Jewish Herald*.

The Jewish Herald was launched in May 1937 by the New Zionist Association (Zionist Revisionist Organization) at the instruction of Ze'ev Jabotinsky. Until November 1937 it was called *The Eleventh Hour*, which alluded to the prevailing situation of Jews in Europe and the *Yishuv* at that time. Unlike other party publications in Yiddish, such as *Unzer Weg* (monthly organ of *Po'alei Zion*)(1919–21) and *The Yiddishe Post* (organ of the Zionist Socialist Party) (1937–8), *The Jewish Herald* attracted subscribers from supporters of the Revisionist Party and the wider Jewish public. This could possibly be ascribed to the fact that whilst championing Zionist Revisionism, it also carried news of general Jewish interest.

Following the merger of the *S A Jewish Times* and *The Jewish Herald*, the *Herald Times* came to be the most largely distributed Jewish newspaper in the Republic. Published weekly, with supplements and annuals to mark special events, it tends to be strongly Zionist and communal in content, without generally being contentious on matters of a local political nature. Its first editor formerly edited *The Jewish Herald* and the national chairman of the Zionist Revisionist Organization chaired its editorial board.

Less widely distributed but still important national publications include the *S A Jewish Observer* (formerly *Our Future*), published since 1942 by the *Mizrahi* Organization of South Africa, and *Jewish Tradition* (formerly the *Federation Chronicle*) published by the Union of Orthodox Synagogues of South Africa. A number of monthly newspapers serving regional interests and featuring local communal and social news are also published. They include *Hashalom*, issued under the auspices of the Durban Jewish Club, the South African Zionist Federation (Natal), and the Council of Natal Jewry, the *Pretoria Jewish Chronicle*, published by the Pre-

toria Council of the South African Jewish Board of Deputies, and the *Cape Jewish Chronicle*, issued by the Western Province Zionist Council and the Cape Council of the South African Jewish Board of Deputies.

FURTHER READING

Dorfan, M.: The community and the media. In *South African Jewry, A Contemporary Survey*, ed. M. Arkin (Cape Town: Oxford University Press, 1984)

Gitlin, M.: *The Vision Amazing: The Story of South African Zionism* (Johannesburg: Menorah Book Club, 1950)

Judelowitz, J. S.: The Jewish Press in South Africa. In *The South African Jewish Year Book Directory of Jewish Organisations and Who's Who in South African Jewry 1929*, ed. M. de Saxe (Johannesburg: Radford, Adlington Ltd, 1929)

Poliva, J. A.: *A Short History of the Jewish Press and Literature of South Africa from its Earliest Days until the Present Time* (Johannesburg: Prompt Printing Co., 1961)

STEPHEN COHEN

press, Yiddish Before the birth of the periodical press among Yiddish-speaking Jews, news was spread by travelers and by letters (many of which are extant, especially from the seventeenth century and after). A major function of the Yiddish historical ballad in the seventeenth and eighteenth centuries was to disseminate news. The first printed items in Yiddish which relayed news at fixed periods were the Amsterdam *Dinstogishe kuranten* and *Fraytogishe kuranten* (Tuesday/Friday Current News, 1686–7). These, as well as a few other ephemeral efforts, constitute the prehistory of the Yiddish press, whose history proper begins with Aleksander Tsederboym's *Kol-mevaser* (Odessa, 1862–73) and was spurred by this remarkable publisher's *Yudishes folks-blat* (St Petersburg, 1881–90).

These seminal weeklies accustomed Yiddish-speakers to read newspapers, which became the favorite (and often sole) reading matter of many; they also attracted important writers who had been wary of publishing in Yiddish, since it then lacked prestige. Modern Yiddish literature and the modern Yiddish press are intimately related. When *Kol-mevaser* published Mendele mokher sefarim's *Dos kleyne mentshele*

(1864; The Mannikin), a landmark of modern Yiddish literature, it began a tradition which continues to this day. The literature–press symbiosis also included "the world of ideological–political efforts", (Fishman, 1981). Few Yiddish periodicals were simply business ventures, and few lacked an ideological or partisan dimension.

In the 125 years since *Kol-mevaser*, thousands of Yiddish periodicals of every description have appeared throughout the world (several thousand in Poland, two hundred in Britain, one hundred in Belgium, etc.). Arising first in eastern Europe, the modern Yiddish press appeared wherever Yiddish-speakers settled, founding a major center in North America and active also in western Europe (especially Paris and London), Latin America (especially Buenos Aires), Israel, South Africa, Australia, and elsewhere (Turkey, Egypt, Manchuria, etc.).

The geography of the Yiddish Press

Russia   The infant Yiddish press in Czarist Russia was opposed by Jewish reformers and assimilationists as well as by the central authorities. Tsederboym published his papers by stealthy maneuvering within a corrupt system. The weekly *Der yud* [Der yid] (1899–1903), the most significant periodical to follow Tsederboyms's *Yudishes folks-blat*, while edited in Warsaw, had to be published in Krakow (Austria–Hungary) and smuggled across the nearby Russian border. In the last two decades of the nineteenth century, numerous socialist periodicals were illegally circulated throughout Russia. The first Yiddish daily in Russia, *Der fraynd* (St Petersburg and Warsaw, 1903–14, also at certain times called *Dos leben* [Dos lebn]), was frequently suspended. With the October Revolution, the Yiddish press in Russia flared into activity and flourished through the 1920s. Purges dampened its development in the 1930s and it was in deep trouble in the 1940s. During the Second World War the Yiddish press was reactivated, since the Soviet state saw it as a useful tool to mobilize world Jewish support for the Soviet war effort. In 1948, purportedly to stem an upsurge of Jewish nationalism and driven by paranoid fears of Jewish power, Stalin ordered the suppression of all Yiddish cultural institutions, including the press. On 12 August 1952 the leading Yiddish writers and journalists were executed. Today all that remains of the Soviet Yiddish press is the substantial monthly *Sovetish heymland* (from 1961) and the insignificant daily *Birobidzhaner shtern* (from 1930).

Poland   The leading center of Ashkenazic culture in modern times, Poland supported a highly developed Yiddish press (including two great mass-circulation dailies, the Warsaw *Haynt*, 1908–39, and *Der moment*, 1910–39). Through the years of the occupation a Yiddish illegal press operated underground. At the end of the war, Polish Jews repatriated from the Soviet Union tried valiantly to revive Yiddish culture, including the press. The resilience of Polish anti-Semitism, however, as shown in the 1946 Kielce pogrom, drove the majority of Jews out of Poland. The rather thin Warsaw bi-weekly *Folks-shtime* (from 1945) contrasts sadly with the rich Yiddish journalistic tradition which once thrived in Poland.

USA   Two decades before *Der fraynd* appeared in Russia (after eight years' lobbying for a publishing permit), Kasriel-Tsvi Sorezon (after two false starts in 1881 and 1883 with his *Yudishe gazetten* [Yidishe gazetn]) started the daily *Yudishes tageblat* (1885–1928) in New York City, the major western center of Yiddish publishing. Sorezon's daily later merged with the Orthodox daily, *Der morgn-zhurnal* (founded 1902), which in 1952 merged with the liberal independent *Der tog* (founded 1914), which closed in the early 1870s, leaving the *Forverts* (from 1897) the only Yiddish daily in the USA (in 1924 Abe Kahan's great newspaper had a daily readership of a quarter of a million). In the USA in 1986 there were three Yiddish weeklies (including the now weekly *Forverts*) with a combined circulation of about 125,000, and a dozen monthlies with a combined circulation of around 75,000, but no dailies. A significant number of the current readership is ultra-Orthodox.

Jewish interests and the Yiddish Press

Kol-mevaser, like its Hebrew-language contemporaries, reported news from a Jewish point of view. The Yiddish press has been mainly an instrument for discussion within the Jewish community. Virtually every Jewish interest group has had its own organ. Not only did the Yiddish press orient its readers ideologically, leading them through the many crises that have beset Jews as Jews, but it also initiated mutual aid and political organization. In the immigrant centers, it helped them adjust to their new homes, teaching them laws, history, customs, and traditions. The dailies, especially, have been political schools upon which modern Jewish movements like Zionism have depended heavily.

The natural rhythms of growth and decline, rather than trauma, have characterized the Yiddish press in countries of immigration: during the peak immigration years and until the second generation established a Jewish press in the vernacular and the acclimated immigrants learned to read the local non-Jewish language, Yiddish periodicals dominated the Jewish press and virtually all Jewish dailies were in Yiddish. Thus, until the First World War, Yiddish dominated the South African Jewish press. Increased costs and competition from other media have figured in the decline of Yiddish periodicals, but the major reason has been loss of readers by language shift or, more typically, by death. Yet the Yiddish press struggles on. A Yiddish daily (*Letste nayes*) and a fine literary quarterly (*Di goldene keyt*) still appear in Tel Aviv.

FURTHER READING

Bar, A., ed.: *The Jewish Press That Was* (Tel Aviv: World Federation of Jewish Journalists, 1980)

Fishman, J. A., ed.: *Never Say Die! A Thousand Years of Yiddish in Jewish Life and Letters* (The Hague/Paris/New York: Mouton Publishers, 1981)

Howe, I.: *World of Our Fathers* (New York and London: Harcourt Brace Jovanovich, 1976)

Prager, L.: *Yiddish Literary and Linguistic Periodicals and Miscellanies: A Selective Annotated Bibliography*, with the help of A. A. Greenbaum (Darby: Norwood Editions, 1982)

Shmeruk, C.: The Yiddish press in Eastern Europe. *The Jewish Quarterly* 33 vol. 1 (1986) 24–8

LEONARD PRAGER

Pressburger, Emeric (1902–1988) British film producer, screenwriter novelist. Pressburger, who was born in Hungary, began as a journalist and was soon working in the film industry at UfA, Germany's largest film company, in Berlin. Unable to work in Germany after 1933, he left for France and arrived in England in 1935. Korda brought Pressburger and the director, Michael Powell, together for *The Spy in Black* (1939) and launched a partnership. They created the production company The Archers and took equal credits on a number of "commercial" but experimental films. Pressburger created the scripts, which were rewritten by Powell; Pressburger did most of the producing; Powell did all of the directing.

Pressburger is the most autobiographical of all British screenwriters and many of the films disclose his concerns about his dislocated life as well as his problems with the English language. His most personal script, for *The Life and Death of Colonel Blimp* (1943), incorporates a key sequence, in which a German refugee of conscience (Anton Walbrook) is interrogated at immigration control. The awkwardness which Pressburger felt, as a stranger, was never to leave him. In *I Know where I'm Going*, made at the end of the war, he transforms this personal preoccupation into an entirely British story when a girl travels to Scotland for a soulless marriage on a remote Scottish island. She never arrives, for the elements conspire against her, she is disturbed and irritated by the Gaelic language, which she does not understand, by the temperament of the people, and by their customs, until she discovers that she has fallen in love with them.

After the war, Powell and Pressburger explored color with a series of brilliant films, including: *A Matter of Life and Death* (1946), *Black Narcissus* (1947), *The Red Shoes* (1948), and *The Tales of Hoffmann* (1951) but their partnership, except for a film for children made in 1972, faded out in 1956. Pressburger turned to writing novels; *The Glass Pearls* (1966) is the story of a Nazi concentration camp doctor permanently haunted by the fear of being hunted down.

FURTHER READING

Gough-Yates, K.: *Michael Powell in Association with Emeric Pressburger* (London: British Film Institute, 1971)

Powell, M.: *A Life in Movies: An Autobiography* (London: Heinemann, 1986)
The Times, 5 February 1988 [obituary]

KEVIN GOUGH-YATES

Presser, Jacob [Jacques] (1899–1970) Dutch–Jewish historian and author. He was the son of middle-class parents with little Jewish identity. After Presser had completed secondary school, a non-Jewish patron enabled him to begin studying history at the University of Amsterdam in 1920, which brought him into contact with the world of music and the arts. In 1926 he obtained his Ph.D. cum laude. In the same year he became a history teacher at the newly established Municipal Vossius *Gymnasium*. Around 1930 Presser came into contact with the Dutch Marxist historian, Jan Romein, who greatly influenced him. In 1936 he married Deborah Appel, also of Jewish origin, one of his former pupils, and 15 years younger than he.

In November 1941 Presser, like all teachers of Jewish origin working in government or Municipal schools, was forced to leave the Vossius *Gymnasium* but was immediately appointed a teacher at the Amsterdam Jewish Lyceum which had been established for Jewish pupils and teachers no longer admitted to general schools, under the German occupation of the Netherlands. In 1943, his wife was arrested and sent to Westerbork and from there to Sobibor. Through non-Jewish friends Presser hid in the village of Wageningen where, under the pseudonym of J. van Wageningen, he wrote poetry about the loss of his wife which, originally clandestinely circulated, was published as *Orpheus and Ahasverus* in 1946.

In September 1945 he returned to the Vossius *Gymnasium* and in 1947 became a lecturer at the newly established Faculty of Political Sciences at the University of Amsterdam. Although the University offered him and two others professorships, these appointments were delayed until 1949, due to the Marxist views of the candidates.

In 1950 Presser was commissioned by the Netherlands State Institute for Documentation on the Second World War (RIOD), in Amsterdam, to write a history of the Jews in the Netherlands during the German occupation. Owing to many other preoccupations and the magnitude of the task this history appeared only in April 1965, as *Ondergang. De vervolging en verdelging van het Nederlandse Jodendom, 1940–45* (*Ashes in the Wind* [abridged], 1968). Its publication caused a sensation since the subject had largely been forgotten by the general public. Professional historians, both non-Jewish and Jewish, criticized its subjectivity and also Presser's consideration of himself as "the voice of those who perished and whose indictment can no longer be heard", an indictment not only of the Germans but also of the *Joodse Raad* ("*Judenrat*") who, according to him, sacrificed the Jewish proletariat in order to save themselves. The work was anecdotal rather than systematic, and ignored certain important aspects such as the nature of the Netherlands Jewish community prior to 1940.

In 1957 Presser published a short novel on life in the Westerbork concentration camp, *Nacht der Girondijnen (Breaking Point*, 1958) which achieved great success. Since he had never been in Westerbork, he based the story largely on the diaries of Etty HILLESUM, part of which were kept at the Netherlands State Institute for War Documentation to which he had access, and which were then still unpublished.

His works on historical subjects, such as *Napoleon* (1946) and *Amerika* (1949) reveal his vast reading and also his inclination to debunk his subject.

BIBLIOGRAPHY
Ashes in the Wind (London, 1968)

HENRIETTE BOAS

Prilutski [Pryłucki], **Noyakh** (1882–1941) Yiddish scholar and Jewish rights activist. Prilutski was born in Berdichev, and grew up in Kremenitz. He won a gold medal at a Warsaw secondary school and went on to study law at the University of Warsaw. An early activist in the campaign for Jewish access to higher education, he was arrested by Czarist police in 1904 and expelled from the university in 1905. He set up a private law practice in Warsaw in 1909, founded the Warsaw Yiddish daily *Moment* in

1910, was elected to the Warsaw City Council in 1916 and to the Polish Parliament, as a member of the Folkist Party, in 1918. When, in 1919, he exposed Polish officers responsible for the murder of 34 Jews, his enemies had his election nullified on grounds of his "foreignness". When his citizenship was restored, he won his seat back in 1922. Prilutski became the leading spokesman in defense of Jewish rights in Poland and abroad, and saved many from unjust expulsion or death by his personal interventions. In 1921 he visited the USA on behalf of the homeless in the Ukraine, and was received by President Warren G. Harding in Washington.

In addition to the foregoing, Prilutski found time to become one of the leading Yiddish scholars of the century, specializing in dialectology and folklore. He was, moreover, one of the acknowledged leaders of Yiddish culture in interwar eastern Europe. Inspired by the Chernowitz Conference of 1908 to devote himself to Yiddish culture, he was pivotal in the establishment of the infrastructure of Yiddish culture in Poland. He founded the *Yidisher shul un folks bildungs fareyn*, which established a network of Yiddish-speaking schools in Poland; organized the first Yiddish cultural conference in Poland (1917); and founded the *Yidishe folks bildungs lige* which established schools and libraries in rural areas (1922). In 1925 he delivered an address in Yiddish at the Congress for National Minorities in Geneva.

Prilutski published a long array of massive volumes in Yiddish scholarship, all part of the series *Noyakh Prilutskis ksovim* (Noyakh Prilutski's writings), including *Tsum yidishn vokalizm* (1920; On Yiddish vocalism) in which he proposed the first classification of Yiddish dialects for the whole of the European Yiddish speech territory. His work still awaits cartographic interpretation, which will result in an invaluable atlas of Yiddish language and culture in eastern Europe before the Second World War.

In addition to his pure scholarship, Prilutski was active in building the emerging field of Yiddish Studies through editing or co-editing major collective volumes. With Max WEINREICH and Zalmen REYZEN he edited *Yidishe filologye* (1924; Yiddish philology); with Sh. Lehman *Arkhiv far yidisher shprakh-visnshaft* (1926–33; Arch-

ive for Yiddish linguistics), and on his own, edited Yivo's last scientific journal, *Yidish far ale* (1938–9; Yiddish for all), to appear before the war. His series of folkloristic collections known as *Noyakh Prilutskis zamlbikher* (Noyakh Prilutski's collective volumes), were launched with his *Yidishe folkslider* (1911; Yiddish folk-songs).

Prilutski's abilities to pinpoint the exact origin of any Yiddish speaker were legendary. Isaac Bashevis SINGER, in his *Mayn tatns bezdn shtub* (1956; My father's court), recounts his father visiting Prilutski's law office in Warsaw to seek his help in countering a swindler. After hearing the elder Singer utter two words, Prilutski asked if he was a native of the district of Lublin. He was. He asked further if he was a native of the village of Tomashov. He was.

When the Nazis invaded Poland in the Second World War, Prilutski fled to Vilna. During its Soviet occupation, he published a book on Yiddish phonetics and became professor of Yiddish at the University of Vilna. Unable to flee the German invasion of Vilna because of pneumonia, Prilutski was captured, tortured, and forced to classify the archives of the Yivo for the Nazis. In the summer of 1941, he was stripped of his university position and on 18 August 1941 he was murdered by the Gestapo.

FURTHER READING

Hutton, C.: Prilutski as philosopher of language. In *History of Yiddish Studies*, ed. D.-B. Kerler (Chur: Harwood, in press, 1990)

Katz, D.: On the second winter symposium. In *Dialects of the Yiddish Language*, ed. D. Katz (Oxford: Pergamon, 1988) 1–5

DOVID KATZ

Proust, Marcel (1871–1922) French writer. Born in Paris of traditionally Catholic stock on his father's side and a Jewish family on his mother's side, Proust has often been compared, from several points of view, with Montaigne whose mother too was Jewish. Biographers and critics have attempted to relate Proust's inner conflicts to his dual heritage, ascribing to his beloved mother's Jewishness an important role in the development of his personality. Proust, however, grew up in a liberal Catholic environment, attending the exclusive Lycée Condorcet where he began his literary activities by contributing to school magazines. This early phase, marked also by a fervent social life, reached its apogee with the publication in 1896 of his first book *Les Plaisirs et les Jours*, (1896; *Pleasures and Regrets*, 1950). The charm of these early stories and essays was rediscovered many years later, when Proust had achieved an assured, mainly posthumous, fame. From the manifold, and mostly rather frivolous, activities of his so-called "social phase" one should single out Proust's passionate involvement in the Dreyfus Case. Proust even claimed to be "the first Dreyfusard", having approached Anatole France to secure his signature on the famous petition of the intellectuals. The case figures prominently in the abandoned novel Proust was writing during the last years of the nineteenth century, *Jean Santeuil*, discovered years later among his papers and published in 1952. Even more important was the impact of the case on his great novel, particulary its final part, "Time Regained" (in fact, written first).

This novel, considered by many to be the greatest modern work of fiction, is called, in its English version, *Remembrance of Things Past*, a title rejected by Proust himself, its Shakespearean reference notwithstanding, because it lacked the idea of a quest conveyed by the original title *À la Recherche du Temps Perdu* (In search of lost time). A sort of fictional autobiography, this novel consists of 15 parts, in 7 volumes, the bulk of which depicts the narrator's years lost in the pursuit of life in upper-class French society with its illusory pleasures; the smaller part is devoted to the miracle of regaining this lost time by means of memory and art. This general framework holds within it an entire world of events and ideas on a variety of subjects, blending realism with poetry and achieving a brilliant summary of the main traditions of French literature, while retaining throughout an absolutely individual style and tone. One critic, Georges Cattui, even attempted to detect, somewhat fancifully, a streak of talmudic Judaism in the very eccentric, but always profoundly French, style of the great novel.

Marcel Proust

In the vast and variegated universe of the novel a few obsessive themes or *leitmotifs* (Wagner's operas had a considerable influence on Proust) stand out and appear in different guises in every section. These are topics such as the constant lure of the old French aristocracy, embodied in the family Guermantes; the topic of sexual perversion in general and of homosexuality in particular, dealt with mainly in the volume entitled "The Cities of the Plain", and the associated topic of love which Proust considers to be a sort of illness; and the most important topic, that of Time, the great transformer, the ultimate master of the human – and therefore Proustian – universe. It is on account of these *leitmotifs* or obsessions that Proust's novel is not a series of novels, loosely interconnected, like Balzac's *Human Comedy*, but a piece of extraordinary architecture, justly compared by Proust himself to a gothic cathedral.

Jews and Jewishness play an important role, or roles, in the vast drama of the narrator's search for lost time. Unlike Proust, however, the narrator, Marcel, is not a Jew, and his grandfather often indulges in anti-Semitic remarks. The narrator's attitude to the various Jewish characters in the novel varies: some, like Charles Swann, are sympathetically portrayed while others, such as Bloch, are the embodiments of the worst social qualities. The role played by Jews and Judaism in the novel should not be exaggerated, yet it is even less appropriate to speak of Proust's "anti-Semitism", as some have done. Proust did not consider himself Jewish in any religious or spiritual sense, but there is profound sympathy, in his description of the Jews as a persecuted and paranoid minority, "the cursed race" to be compared with homosexuals (in "The Cities of the Plain"). The first volume of the novel appeared in 1913, the last in 1927, five years after Proust's death.

BIBLIOGRAPHY

Remembrance of Things Past, trans. C. K. Scott-Moncrieff, with emendations by T. Kilmartin (Harmondsworth: Penguin, 1981)

FURTHER READING

Painter, G. D.: *Marcel Proust: A Biography*, 2 vols (London: Chatto & Windus, 1959, 1965)

YORAM BRONOWSKI

psychoanalysis, Jews in During the first five years of its existence (1902–6), all 17 members in the psychoanalytic circle around Sigmund FREUD (initially known as the "Psychological Wednesday Society") were Jewish. They were, moreover, fully aware of their Jewishness and maintained a sense of Jewish purpose and solidarity. Without grasping the intensity of their Jewish attachments, it is scarcely possible to see how the circle acquired the impetus which took it far beyond the usual bounds of a detached scientific endeavor.

So powerful were these attachments that the history of psychoanalysis has been, in part, a running debate between those who have suppressed their existence and those who have magnified them. Freud's biographer and dis-

ciple, Ernest Jones, regarded any attention paid to the sectarian tendencies in the movement as a distraction from the psychoanalytic advancement of truth. He once omitted Freud's expression of gratitude to "those of our faith" in a then-unpublished letter Freud had addressed to his fiancée in 1884. Like Jones, Peter Gay, a more recent critic, apparently sees nothing significant in the Jewish attachments of Freud and those who followed him.

Arguments for their significance are sometimes no less specious. A. A. Roback, an American–Jewish admirer of Freud from the 1920s, argued that the analytic and introspective method, as well as the emphasis on realism and the concrete, were manifestations of a "Jewish bent of mind". Other writers, such as Thorstein Veblen, Lewis Feuer (Feuer, 1963), and Frederic Grunfeld see a relationship between the social marginality or political homelessness of Jews and the revolutionary creativity of the psychoanalytic pioneers. A few critics have exaggerated the Jewish aspect of the early movement to disparage or discredit psychoanalysis. Most notorious were the Nazi ideologues. Friedrich Walter, for example, vilified Freud and other Jews for exposing to public view "the filth of the gutter". That perception resulted in the final dissolution of Freud's psychoanalytic movement in Vienna. When the Nazis identified Freud in 1938 as a member of the B'nai B'rith, they ordered his removal from the city and the abolition of the *Internationaler Psychoanalytischer Verlag*.

All critics, whether they under- or overestimate the significance of the movement's Jewish origin, agree on one premise: a sectarian loyalty cannot be fully reconciled with the scientific or artistic temperament, which is universal in substance and purpose. Either the early analysts were sectarian or they were not. The writings and activities of the analysts themselves, however, show that they were both.

To be sure, no one in Freud's circle observed Jewish practices, beliefs, or customs. On the contrary, they ridiculed or rejected traditional Jews and Judaism. Freud explicitly repudiated Jewish orthodoxy and, like Fritz WITTELS, thought about converting to Christianity. Others in the circle did convert: Alfred Adler

Otto Rank, Karl Abraham, Max Eitingon, Ernest Jones (standing). Sigmund Freud, Sandor Ferenczi, Hanns Sachs (seated), 1922

became Protestant and Otto RANK became Roman Catholic. (Rank later returned to Judaism.) In general, the early analysts regarded Judaism as irrelevant and anachronistic. They delighted in reducing religious beliefs to a "universal obsessional neurosis" (for example, Freud's *Obsessive Actions and Religious Practices*, written in 1907).

Their rejection of "unassimilated" Jews from east Europe, just as adamant as their opposition to the religion, might seem to have left little in Judaism to which they could cling. But they did not sever their ties altogether. As Freud once remarked, "Enough else remained to make the attraction to Judaism and Jews so irresistible".

The debate over the significance of the Jews in Freud's circle must rest on what exactly to make of this remaining part of their Jewishness. To Freud, his attraction to Jews and Judaism alone offered reassurance, if not inspiration. In a letter to Karl Abraham, expressing his pleasure at having Jews in the movement, Freud attributed their intellectual affinity to their "racial kinship". (Abraham reflected the sentiment by commenting that psychoanalysis appeared to show some talmudic qualities.) Freud often acknowledged the Vienna lodge of the B'nai B'rith, where he gave a number of lectures on psychoanalytic themes between 1897 and 1902, as a sympathetic and supportive environment for developing his earliest views. As a member of the lodge, he enlisted at least two others who eventually joined his psychoanalytic circle–Oscar Rie, a longtime friend, and Eduard Hitschmann.

Many others, and quite possibly Freud himself, believed that Jews formed a heroic minority destined to reinvigorate humanity. Members of Freud's lodge, for example, felt that their cultural and philanthropic activities would preserve "the ideal of humanity through the [current] period of moral degeneration". They were referring to the strife among nations and the hostility toward Jews that polarized the Austro-Hungarian empire (by the turn of the century anti-Semitism in Vienna had become virulent).

For Freud's early followers, psychoanalysis represented the ideal of humanity. Rank believed that only Jews could find the "radical cure" of neurosis. Wittels felt that Jews, instilled with the "lofty passion of the oppressed", should lead the way toward achieving justice for all mankind. Isidor Sadger, who was critical of east European Jews, fostered the German–Jewish struggle for a humanitarian way of life. Victor Tausk asserted that the "progress of psychoanalysis" rested with the Jews. He shared the premise with other like-minded Jews before the First World War that, as outsiders, Jews were not contaminated by bankrupt moral conventions and, as a result, embodied mankind's last hope.

For the early analysts, it was possible to reconcile a sectarian Jewish loyalty with their expeditions into psychoanalysis because there was nothing specifically Jewish in the way they thought about their analytical endeavors. Their Jewishness was nominal. It was really nothing more than a basis for affirming their faith in humanity and the quest for relieving its neurotic misery. But for them, that was crucial: by believing that, as Jews, they were special and privileged, they could affirm their faith and quest with a renewed confidence and a resolve which they might otherwise not have had.

FURTHER READING

Feuer, L.: *The Scientific Intellectual* (New York: Basic Books, 1963)

Gay, P.: *A Godless Jew: Freud, Atheism, and the Making of Psychoanalysis* (New Haven: Yale University Press, 1987)

Grunfeld, F. V.: *Prophets Without Honour: A Background to Freud, Kafka, Einstein, and their World* (London: Hutchinson and Co., 1979)

Jones, E.: *The Life and Work of Sigmund Freud*, 3 vols (New York: Basic Books, 1953, 1955, 1957)

Klein, D. B.: *Jewish Origins of the Psychoanalytic Movement* (Chicago: University of Chicago Press, 1985)

Roback, A. A.: *Jewish Influence in Modern Thought* (Cambridge: Sci-Art Publishers, 1929).

Veblen, T.: The intellectual pre-eminence of Jews in modern Europe. In *Essays in Our Changing Order*, ed. L. Ardzrooni (New York: A. M. Kelly, 1964)

Walter, F.: *Wien: Die Geschichte einer deutschen Grossstadt an der Grenze* (Vienna: Verlag Adolf Holzhausens Nachfolger, 1940–4)

DENNIS B. KLEIN

psychoanalysis, Judaism and Psychoanalysis, a discipline that concerns itself with understanding human behavior and its disorders, and with the treatment of these disorders, was established by a Jew, Sigmund FREUD, who made the initial and major discoveries; and it was developed by his disciples, most of whom were Jews. From the outset and to this day, the discipline was associated in the minds of both its supporters and detractors, with the Jews and with Judaism. In fact psychoanalysis suffered a fate similar to the fate of the Jews in the Holocaust. The Jewish members of the psychoanalytic profession were driven out of Germany. The discipline itself was denounced, but it was exploited after it had been diluted and its name changed.

Why is psychoanalysis associated with Judaism? Its originator, Sigmund Freud, was a Jew, who, in an age when professionals and academics were assimilating and converting for the sake of expediency, openly wrote in his autobiography, "My parents were Jews, and I have remained a Jew myself".

In the exposition of his theories, he did not hesitate to present material from his personal experiences. For example, he expounded the theory of dream interpretation using his own dreams as illustrations. In the discussion of these, he mentioned issues of anti-Semitism which troubled him, Zionism, and the nature of Jewish society. Autobiographical material pervades many of his papers, in which his attitude toward his Jewishness and toward anti-Semitism is boldly stated. In a well-known document, his 1926 address to B'nai B'rith, he said that what made "the attraction of Jewry and Jews irresistible", were "many obscure emotional forces, which were the more powerful the less they could be expressed in words, as well as a clear consciousness of inner identity, the safe privacy of a common mental construction. And beyond this there was a perception that it was to my Jewish nature alone that I owe two characteristics that have become indispensable to me in the difficult course of my life. Because I was a Jew I found myself free from many prejudices which restricted others in the use of their intellect; and as a Jew I was prepared to join the opposition and to do without agreement with the 'compact majority'".

Vienna, the home of Freud and many of his early disciples, at the turn of the century was the locus of cultural turmoil, as an avant-garde introduced new concepts and new approaches to the arts, and new values and standards in literature and thought. As is true in most such instances, the innovations met with resistance on the part of those conservatively disposed. Psychoananlysis was doubtless seen as one of the disturbing innovations that threatened customary ways of thinking about oneself, about society and about religion. It seemed to threaten the delicate balance between individual drives for achieving sexual gratification, and socially imposed and generally accepted constraints upon such gratification. Although psychoanalysts at no point advocated rejection of conventional restraints – except perhaps with respect to masturbation – nevertheless open discussion (psychoanalysis) of intimate sexual behavior and fantasies, and its ascription of some neurotic symptoms and behavior to conscious sexual suppression and unconscious repression, earned it the erroneous reputation of a force for the repudiation of conventional restriction of sexual behavior. Therefore it attracted the hostility, not only of those opposed to change in general, but especially of those who could not with comfort even consider the idea of change in sexual mores.

The admission of Jews from their literal, social, and cultural ghettos into Christian society seemed, to many Christians, to undermine that society and the values associated with it. Therefore resistance to cultural change and to the emancipation of the Jews were usually found together, and mutually reinforced each other. Accordingly, the fact that the founder of psychoanalysis and most of his disciples were Jewish, brought those who were concerned about the loosening of sexual morality the support of anti-Semites; and vice versa. "Rest assured", Freud wrote to Karl Abraham, one of his earliest disciples, "that if my name were Oberhuber, in spite of everything, my innovations would have met with far less resistance".

The argument can be given a somewhat different emphasis noting that both psychoanalysis and Jews were considered marginal. Jews were considered marginal socially. The Jews of central Europe were struggling to extend their political emancipation and to defend themselves against anti-Semites who impeded their entry into Christian society and the Christian business, commercial, and industrial elites. Psychoanalysis was considered marginal scientifically. It could not demonstrate its findings with the rigor achievable in the basic sciences. Its entry into science in general, and even into medicine, was resisted, on the surface because of its lack of demonstrability, but beneath the surface because of its implicit challenge to accepted attitudes, toward human thought and behavior in general, and to sexual behavior in particular. Their common marginality facilitated an antagonism between those who saw Jews and psychoanalysts as presumptuous boundary-crossers, and those who indeed did yearn to cross the boundary. While conservative Christians, including members of the medical establishment, denounced Jews and psychoanalysts virtually in the same breath, Jews, in response, tried to undermine the boundary that kept them apart. They did this by defending themselves against anti-Semitism, and striving upward politically, socially, artistically, and financially. But psychoanalysis also attacked the boundary by positing an identical psychology that prevailed among all peoples, all races, and all religions, that transcended boundaries. The veneer of inherited nobility, power, and wealth concealed the same conflicts, hypocrisies, sordid and shameful sexual fantasies, and secrets as those that prevailed among both the lower social and economic classes, and the unwelcome, newly liberated Jews, and other outsiders. Psychoanalysis was a democratizing influence.

However, the anti-Semitism that the Jewish analysts encountered did not leave them untouched. Probably even before they became psychoanalysts, most of them had turned away from their traditional religion, and saw themselves as emancipated from it, as well as from the social inferiority that was associated with it. Their attitude toward religious observance of any kind was patronizing and contemptuous. At meetings of the Vienna Psychoanalytic Society in the earliest days of psychoanalysis, in discussions of religion, only Freud made remarks that were less than derogatory. Yet none of them permanently converted. Freud said that he had considered conversion at one point, but had rejected the idea.

Although Freud did attend a Jewish religious school and venerated one of the teachers whom he encountered there, nevertheless he professed to know nothing of the Hebrew language, and early in his career and writings, made no reference to Jewish history. In fact, however, review of his life discloses an increasing interest in the Jewish religion and increasing public identification with the Jewish people and their destiny. Not many others among the Jewish psychoanalysts followed in this path. Yet a few associated themselves with the Jewish youth movement (Blau–Weiss) that assumed the role of a Jewish counterpart to the German youth movement (Wandervogel) in the 1920s and 1930s. Seigfried Bernfeld, a distinguished psychoanalyst of the second generation, actively organized Zionist youth and established a journal to promote his program. He was joined in this effort by another distinguished analyst, Willi Hoffer.

Starting in the late 1920s and early 1930s, a few of the Jewish analysts went to Israel. Max Eitingon was perhaps the best known of these. M. Wulff, Erich Gúmbel, and Heinz Winnik were among the earliest. In 1933 the Israel Psychoanalytic Society was established and it continues to this day.

With the coming of the Holocaust Jewish analysts were forced to confront their association with the destiny of the Jewish people.

Those in the free world managed to help their unfortunate colleagues to find refuge, with the generous assistance of many non-Jewish colleagues in the USA, UK, and elsewhere. Upon their arrival at their new homes, a number took up the issue of anti-Semitism in papers and books on a psychoanalytic view of the phenomenon. For the most part these were only superficial discussions based upon no serious studies, and they were soon forgotten. More serious studies are being undertaken only now.

It would be an error to assume that with the suppression of their interest in religious Judaism, the early analysts shook off its influence upon them. Though they disdained the specific religious forms and observances, they nevertheless identified themselves with the prophetic, humanistic ideals of Judaism, and became "non-sectarian" humanitarians. In this way they preserved an unacknowledged identification with the universalistic component of Judaism, while maintaining a declared rejection of its particularistic aspects.

The association of Judaism with psychoanalysis is reinforced by the fact that the principal method of study in each discipline is textual exegesis. A religion that is based upon a fixed ancient scripture, as Judaism is, can accommodate itself to changing circumstances only by continual reinterpretation of its basic texts. The discontinuities and hiatuses that mark Jewish history have each required alterations in the details of religious observance and each has left its mark in the accumulated liturgy of Judaism and in its religious practice. Probably the most striking reinterpretation of Judaism was that achieved during the talmudic period, beginning perhaps as early as 200 BCE, and coming to an end during the sixth century CE. That reinterpretation was committed to writing first in the corpus of the Mishnah, and later in an enormous commentary on the latter, namely, the Gemarah. The Talmud, comprising these two components, establishes the format of rabbinic Judaism which differs strikingly from the forms that had preceded it. As time went on, the Gemarah itself was interpreted and reinterpreted. These interpretations yielded both religious cultic and religious civil law, but also discussions of ideals and values embodied in legend, parable, debate, and admonition. The appearance of the typical page of the by now standard Vilna Edition which developed out of the precedent-setting Venice Edition of the Talmud, printed by Daniel Bomberg in the sixteenth century, with its clearly printed central text, the voluminous commentaries surrounding it, and the marginal notes, is familiar to most educated people in the West. It would be no exaggeration to say that the Jewish religion as practiced today is set in the interpretation and reinterpretation of its ancient scripture.

Professor Ismar Schorsch has observed that whereas Greek thought is analytic in type and idea-centered, Jewish thought is exegetic in type and text-centered. Exegesis is also the principal method of psychoanalysis. It is concerned not only with making the past relevant to the present, but with ascertaining concerns and intentions embedded and concealed within an explicit statement. The interpretation of dreams, "the royal road to the unconscious", relies primarily upon exegetic technique. Individual words in the dream text are explored with the dreamer for their conscious resonances in his life, recent and childhood. Figures within the text are examined for their universal symbolic significance. Relevance of the dream text to recent experience and behavior is explored. Out of all of these considerations, one attempts to construct the principal strivings that gave rise to the dream. A similar approach applies to the analysis of the significance of spontaneous mental activity: slips of speech, inaccurate remembering, inadvertent behavior, and creative products.

Not only does the technique of the one discipline resemble that of the other, but the assumptions in each case resemble each other too. Namely that the text is so constructed as to convey an exoteric meaning, but also an esoteric meaning that can be apprehended only by a specially skilled, learned interpreter.

Several categories of exegesis, and a large number of methods are conventionally recognized among students of the Jewish religion. First, one must ascertain the plain meaning of the text, exoteric message. Second, one attempts to draw reasonable inferences that one assumes are implied. Third, the text may be

explored for its homiletic value. Finally, the text may lead to insights into the mystical world. In psychoanalysis it is assumed that a text results from the thrust of unconscious strivings, distorted for the purpose of concealment and censorship, by a superimposed conscious intention. In both cases it is assumed that an esoteric intention is concealed within an exoteric statement. In the one case that assumption is based upon religious belief, in the other upon attempts at scientific study.

Recent years have seen two opposite tendencies operative in the relation of psychoanalysis to Judaism. On the one hand, the discipline has attracted large numbers of non-Jewish practitioners. In many places, Jews represent a minority among the psychoanalysts. I have been told that the psychoanalytic movement is growing especially rapidly in West Germany, for example, where there are very few Jews. On the other hand, the 1985 Congress of the International Psychoanalytic Association in Hamburg, the first meeting of the International Psychoanalytic Association on German soil since the Second World War, has been the occasion for examining the behavior of the non-Jewish analysts in Nazi Germany toward their Jewish colleagues, and toward their profession. Many difficult and complex issues have been raised. Did the German psychoanalysts who remained in Nazi Germany after the Jews were driven out, repudiate Freud? Did they become anti-Semites? How have they indoctrinated their students, knowingly and unknowingly? How much of the defensiveness and protectiveness towards the wartime generation represents anti-Semitism, and how much simply loyalty to parents and teachers? As one might expect, these issues deter a full and unreserved reconciliation between Jewish psychoanalysts and their German colleagues, but they have also generated a good deal of suspicion, recrimination, and defensiveness among the German analysts themselves.

While in his earlier years as a psychoanalyst, Sigmund Freud turned to the classical world rather than to Judaism for his images and metaphors, nevertheless the first hospitable audience for his early discoveries was the local B'nai B'rith, which he served as program chairman. In addressing them years later, he expressed his attraction to them in terms of "common identity" as noted above. (It is of some interest that the use of the term "identity" in psychoanalysis appears here for the first time, that is, with reference to Jewish identity.) When Freud was forced to flee Vienna he finally identified himself with a Jewish hero, Rabbi Johanan ben Zakkai, saying, "After the destruction of the Temple in Jerusalem by Titus, Johanan ben Zakkai asked for permission to open a school at Jabneh for the study of the Torah. We are going to do the same. We are, after all, used to persecution by our history, tradition and some of us by personal experience". It is the common fate as well as the common origin of psychoanalysis and the Jews, that in the end establishes their community.

FURTHER READING

Ostow, M.: *Judaism and Psychoanalysis* (New York: Ktav, 1982)

MORTIMER OSTOW

publishing, Jewish, in the UK Jewish publishing in the United Kingdom may be conveniently divided between books and pamphlets on one hand, and newspapers and periodicals on the other. The principal center for these activities has been in London which, since the Resettlement in 1656, has contained the largest Jewish population. Jewish publishing outside of the capital, with the exception of Oxford, has been relatively insignificant and, for the most part, restricted to the local communites such as Manchester, Leeds, Liverpool, Birmingham, and Glasgow.

Though the definition of the term "Jewish publishing" lays itself open to various interpretations it would be fair to assert that among the earliest examples of Jewish publishing in Great Britain since the Middle Ages were the Cartwright Petition requesting the readmission of the Jews to England of 1648–9, and the Humble Address of Menasseh Ben Israel of 1655. The former was printed in London and the latter in Amsterdam. This claim, however, ignores the works of such great Christian Hebraic and Talmudic scholars as Pococke and Lightfoot whose publications also appeared in the mid seventeenth century, while texts in Hebrew had been printed in London and Oxford since the end of the previous century.

With the arrival of Jews from the Continent in the second half of the seventeenth century Jewish publications, in the strict sense, soon began to appear, although not from Jewish publishers. In 1688 the first volume of sermons preached by Rabbi Joshua da Silva in Spanish at the Creechurch Lane synagogue was published in London. By the beginning of the next century there was an increasing flow of books intended for Jewish readers, and mainly of a religious character. The year 1705 saw the publication of the first book printed entirely in Hebrew in England, containing Haham Jacob Zvi Ashkenazi's vindication of Haham David Nieto, who had been accused of following the heretical views of Spinoza. Six years later, Haham Nieto himself published *The Rod of Dan and Cuzari*.

From these early beginnings an increasing output developed during the eighteenth century, coinciding with the increase in the size and prosperity of the Anglo-Jewish community. The first Jewish printer to establish a business in London appears to have been Alexander Alexander, who also acted as translator and publisher, and produced a considerable number of books and pamphlets, chiefly of a devotional nature, including the first English translation of the Jewish Prayer Book, published in 1770. When he died in 1807 Alexander was succeeded by his son, Levy, who died in 1853. The Alexanders catered for both the Sephardi and Ashkenazi communities and in 1822 Levy published a Hebrew-English Bible in five volumes, translated by himself. He also produced in 1808 a volume of Anglo-Jewish social scandals.

During the nineteenth century, as was to be expected, Anglo-Jewish publishing expanded rapidly although not to the same degree as on the Continent. A considerable stimulus to the publishing of books of Jewish interest was provided by the sympathy shown by a section of the British people for the yearning of the Jews for the Holy Land. This was reflected in much English literature of the period and nowhere more forcefully than in Lord Byron's *Hebrew Melodies* of 1814 which were translated into

Hebrew and Yiddish and set to music by John BRAHAM and Isaac NATHAN. Similar thoughts were expressed by novelists such as Benjamin Disraeli and George Eliot who were widely read in the Anglo-Jewish community. A further stimulus to Jewish publishing was provided by the activities of missionary societies like the London Society for the Promotion of Christianity among the Jews, who were busily distributing their own literature aimed at the Jewish reader and achieving no little success in proselytising.

The challenge posed by the missionaries also played a part in the creation of the Anglo-Jewish press though the precedent set by communities on the Continent – in Holland, Germany and France – was, perhaps, a more significant factor. Conversionist publications had been appearing since the second decade of the nineteenth century and were causing some concern to the small Anglo-Jewish community which felt the need for an organ which could speak on its behalf and, at the same time, spread news of the community's activities. The result was the appearance, on 1 January 1823, of *The Hebrew Intelligencer*, a private enterprise launched as a monthly publication, edited anonymously and printed and published in London by J. Wertheimer whose name was connected with Jewish publishing for many years. The paper, however, soon ran into difficulties and survived for only three issues. But it was a beginning and it was succeeded 11 years later by a literary monthly called *The Hebrew Review and Magazine of Rabbinical Literature*, edited by Dr Morris Jacob Raphall, which survived for three years. Six years later the need was again recognized to establish a periodical "for the promotion of the spiritual and general welfare of the Jews by the disseminiation of intelligence on subjects affecting those interests and by the advocacy and defence of their religious institutions". The result was the arrival, in September 1841, of *The Voice of Jacob*, a fortnightly publication. It was edited by its founder, Jacob Franklin, and secured a little financial support from the Montefiores and Rothschilds among others. The new periodical was a more sophisticated publication than its predecessor but it soon had problems. Two months after its appearance, a rival entered the scene. In November 1841, the

Jewish Chronicle issued its first number, printed and published by Isaac Vallentine, and edited by David Meldola and Morris Angel. Clearly, there was no room for two newspapers in the limited field and, after an uneasy initial relationship, they merged after three years under the single title of the *Jewish Chronicle* to which was appended (for 20 numbers only) *and Working Man's Friend*. The new proprietor was Joseph Mitchell and the printing was transferred to Wertheimer. The paper was now set on a steady course which it still pursues, having earned, among other tributes, the commendation of the organizers of the tercentenary Anglo-Jewish Art and History Exhibition of 1956 as "the doyen of the Anglo-Jewish Press and probably one of the greatest unifying forces in Anglo-Jewry". Although a number of Jewish newspapers and periodicals have appeared from time to time, the *Jewish Chronicle* has survived all its competitors and has rarely been seriously challenged by them. Today, rejoicing in its independence, it is probably more firmly based than ever before.

In 1956 the catalog of the Tercentenary Exhibition noted that there were over 50 Anglo-Jewish papers in London and the Provinces, representing various viewpoints. Only one wholly Yiddish paper, *Dos Yiddisher Folk*, managed to survive in London until 1988 to represent a once flourishing press. The list of papers would have included weekly newspapers catering for local communities, such as the *Jewish Gazette* in Manchester or the *Jewish Echo* in Glasgow as well as synagogue bulletins and publications belonging to Zionist institutions such as the *Jewish Observer and Middle East Review* or to societies such as the Anglo-Jewish Association which published *The Jewish Monthly*. The founding of the *Jewish Quarterly Review*, in the year following the Anglo-Jewish Exhibition of 1887, deserves to be recorded, for it maintained a high standard of scholarship and continued this tradition after being transferred to Philadelphia in 1910. Important contributions to learning have also been made since the Second World War by such journals as the *Journal of Jewish Studies*, the *Jewish Journal of Sociology*, the publications of the Institute of Jewish Affairs, and the *Jewish Quarterly*. Annuals like the *Jewish*

Year Book, the *Zionist Year Book* and the Year Books of the Leo Baeck Institute have also served a useful purpose.

If Anglo-Jewry can boast the oldest and most prestigious Jewish newspaper in the world, its record in the field of book publishing is less impressive than that of its counterparts in Germany until the Second World War, and in the USA. Although Jewish writers and authors were increasingly productive during the course of the nineteenth century, Anglo-Jewish publishing remained at a modest level. Under Benisch's editorship, the *Jewish Chronicle* published a number of books of general Jewish interest and, coinciding with the Exhibition of 1887, when Asher Myers was editing the paper he published three volumes connected with the Exhibition including the *Bibliotheca Anglo-Judaica*. Jewish authors, for the most part, were content to be published by general publishers such as Macmillan or Heinemann.

About the turn of the century a number of Jewish publishers appeared in London, specializing in works of Jewish interest in English and in Yiddish. Among these may be mentioned Shapiro, Vallentine, a direct descendant of the family printing and publishing business begun by Isaac Vallentine, as well as M. Cailingold, R. Mazin, and E. Goldston, all of whom were established in the East End of London. Outstanding among the new arrivals was the Soncino Press, founded in the 1920s by Jacob Davidson who set an altogether higher standard as a publisher specializing in Jewish books. Among other works, between 1935 and 1948, he produced a 34-volume edition of the Talmud in English, the *Midrash Rabbah* in 10 volumes and a one-volume edition of J. H. HERTZ's *Pentateuch and Haftarot*, all excellently printed and bound. Among the arrivals from the Continent in the 1930s was the publisher Bela HOROVITZ from Vienna who brought with him the Phaidon Press together with its Jewish branch, the East and West Library which also maintained a high standard, both editorially and of production.

Soon after the Second World War the *Jewish Chronicle* founded a publishing house under the name of Vallentine, Mitchell, thus honoring its first two proprietors. Its contribution to Jewish publishing included *The Diary of Anne Frank*, Stein's *Balfour Declaration*, and English translations of Israeli authors. In 1973 it merged with the publisher, Frank Cass, and continues to produce works of Jewish interest.

In addition to those mentioned, many general publishers have made something of a speciality of publishing Jewish books. Foremost among them for many years was Routledge, later known as Routledge and Kegan Paul, which was controlled by the Franklin family who published the well-known *Festival Prayer Book*. Other houses which have been prominent in this sphere, some of whose owners have been Jews, have been Victor GOLLANCZ, Weidenfeld and Nicolson, Thames and Hudson, the Oxford University Press (the Littman Library of Jewish Civilization), Eyre and Spottiswood (Singer's Prayer Book), while many others have included books of Jewish interest in their lists from time to time. Finally, mention should be made of the Jewish Historical Society of England which has been responsible for publishing many fine books of historical interest.

FURTHER READING

Catalogue of an Exhibition of Anglo-Jewish Art and History (London: East & West Library, 1956)

The Jewish Chronicle 1841–1941: A Century of Newspaper History (London: The Jewish Chronicle, 1949)

Magna Bibliotheca Anglo-Judaica (London: The Jewish Historical Society of England, 1937)

Nova Bibliotheca Anglo-Judaica (London: The Jewish Historical Society of England, 1961)

Fraenkel, J.: *The Jewish Press of the World* (London: World Jewish Congress, 7th. edn, 1972)

DAVID F. KESSLER

publishing, Jewish, in the USA Prior to 1794 there is no record of a Jewish book published by a Jew on American soil. The first was a reprint of the London edition of David Levi's *Letters to Dr Priestley*, issued in New York for Benjamin Gomez. It launched a controversial series of books defending Judaism, a theme that dominated early American–Jewish literature for many years. Two additional parts appeared in 1797–8 and were printed for Naphtali Judah, Gomez's brother-in-law. Numerous works reflecting christological interpretations of Jews and Judaism had appeared with the beginning of New England printing. Two Hebrew prayer-books and four sermons by Jews had been published by non-Jews, in sharp contrast to the preponderance of publications about Jews by Christians.

Solomon Jackson was the major Jewish printer–publisher in the early decades of the nineteenth century. His work was largely confined to constitutions of synagogues and reports for Jewish societies. Two items, intrinsically Jewish, stand out in an otherwise pedestrian career. *The Form of Daily Prayers* (1826) was the first prayer book in Hebrew and English. The Passover service of 1837, also an American milestone, carried the unusual Hebrew imprint, "New York, Next Year in Jerusalem". This edition relied on the English–Hebrew version of David Levi.

Imprints so distinctively Jewish were not to be repeated until the late nineteenth century when Hebrew publishing reflected the interests of east European immigrants. Jackson actively defended Jews against missionaries and their arguments in his short-lived periodical, *The Jew*, in 1824.

Not until 1830, shortly after Isaac LEESER arrived in Philadelphia to minister to Congregation Mikveh Israel, was a serious Jewish publication program introduced. Leeser as editor, journalist, advocate of traditional Judaism, and publisher, awaits a full study. More than 115 items, exclusive of reprints, can be credited to him. As publisher he introduced the young Englishwoman, Grace AGUILAR, to an American public in 1842; as a minister he influenced a broad community when he preceded all others with a series of sermons published in the USA. Leeser launched the first successful Jewish journal in the western world, *The Occident and American Jewish Advocate* in the spring of 1843. Twenty-five volumes appeared under his editorship.

Two years later Leeser founded the American Jewish Publication Society with the aid of Hyman Gratz and Abraham Hart. The new society emulated the London Cheap Jewish Library and, to a lesser degree, the Christian publications of the American Sunday School Union. The society failed. It came to a dismal end because of a lack of interest in its 14 volumes by European authors and two disastrous fires that destroyed many of Leeser's publications.

Hart, who was associated in this unhappy endeavor, was a publisher in his own right. He brought Bulwer-Lytton, Thackeray, and other English writers to an American audience. It was he who first published Charles Dickens's *A Christmas Carol* in 1844 in Philadelphia. These major introductions of English writers cannot be compared to his Jewish publications, of lesser interest, translated by Leeser. One example, perhaps the most significant Jewish book published in nineteenth-century America, is Joseph Schwarz's *Descriptive Geography and Brief Historical Sketch of Palestine* (1850).

Leeser, in addition to counseling Hart, engaged himself in the publication of prayer books for both Sephardim and Ashkenazim, and the publication of his own translation of the Pentateuch in 1845. His complete translation of 24 books of the Bible, which appeared in 1854, served the English-speaking world until 1917 when a new version under Jewish auspices appeared.

The rapid increase of the Jewish population in the USA in the middle decades of the nineteenth century demanded more than an individual could provide. In New York Robert Lyon founded his own press in 1849; in Cincinnati Isaac Mayer WISE, mentor of Reform Judaism, began publication of his journal *The Israelite* in 1854 and soon thereafter one in German, *Die Deborah*. In the late 1850s the Jewish press reached California and by 1900 the Jewish population could draw upon 20 Jewish newspapers in German, approximately 50 in English, and a wide choice in Yiddish with a few in Hebrew. From the presses of the Jewish newspaper publishers came a variety of books. Wise engaged his brother-in-law, Edward Bloch to print fiction, interpretations of Christianity, and essays on such subjects as Judaism, temperance, and politics. They attained little popularity and the extent of their distribution is unrecorded. But the firm of Bloch & Company established itself successfully. Since the 1890s it has operated from New York and in the course of its history has issued more than 2,000 titles,

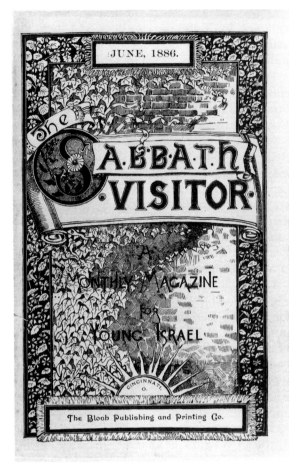

The Sabbath Visitor, *one of the magazines produced by Bloch & Company*

many by authors prominent in Jewish scholarship. The forerunner of such presses as the Hebrew Publishing Company at the beginning of the twentieth century, Ktav toward the end of the century, and others which sprang up yearly, Bloch & Company is a champion in American–Jewish publishing.

Jewish ventures into publishing at the beginning of the twentieth century were largely commercial, organizational, and institutional. Seminaries founded their own presses and from the faculties of the Hebrew Union College, the Jewish Theological Seminary, the former Dropsie College, and Yeshiva University came a constant flow of scholarly books. Books that may not have been published elsewhere brightened the intellectual mind of America. Sabato Morais, Solomon SCHECHTER, Louis GINZBERG,

Bernard Revel, Kaufmann KOHLER, and Max Margolis are a few who altered the course of Jewish scholarship in the USA.

Major universities, although not yet concerned with such studies, gradually emulated this program and subsequently broadened it to include aspects of Jewish History unanticipated in the nineteenth century. Columbia, Yale, Michigan, Princeton, and Harvard Universities introduced Jewish publishing programs, random at first and gathering force by the mid twentieth century.

Organizations like B'nai B'rith and the American Jewish Committee represented their aims and purposes by an independent series of publications which would not tempt other publishers. Julius H. Greenstone of Philadelphia was one of many individuals who established their own presses. Greenstone introduced a major bibliographical study in David Werner Amram's *The Makers of Hebrew Books in Italy* (1909).

Men like Greenstone were innovators; they were booksellers and printers and it is difficult to liken them to commercial publishers with an editorial staff and a system of distribution. But they were a venturesome lot without whom many interesting manuscripts may have been lost forever. Their books were published helter-skelter. Many that found their way into print were ephemeral. Authors like Emma LAZARUS, published by commercial houses as well as such Jewish innovators as Philip Cowen of the American Hebrew Publishing Company, were few. A feeble attempt to reintroduce a publication society for Jews in the 1870s met with failure after the publication of four volumes. But in 1888 after a simmering discontent among a new generation of sophisticated, Jewish-spirited men, the first steps were taken to establish firmly a non-commercial society for the publication of Jewish literature for English-reading Jews in the USA.

From the very beginning frustration confronted the new JEWISH PUBLICATION SOCIETY (JPS). To obtain worthwhile manuscripts, to edit and publish them was difficult at first. The people of the book had no books to offer. As Leeser and his predecessor Jackson had done earlier, the new Society turned to England and then to Germany. Drawing upon the work of Lady Magnus, the Society offered its first selection, *Outlines of Jewish History* (1890). It was revised for an American audience and went into several editions.

The Society's first major intellectual effort was the publication of a new edition and translation of Heinrich GRAETZ's *History of the Jews* which appeared in five volumes between 1891 and 1895. Dependency on authors like Israel ZANGWILL, father of immigrant ghetto fiction, was necessary. Judge Mayer Sulzberger encouraged Zangwill to pursue this aspect of writing. It was the initial interest of the JPS to publish fiction but bow to the new field of American scholarship. Its list grew impressively and the level of its scholarship rose in proportion. Although it was able to entice Zangwill after Macmillan accepted his *Children of the Ghetto* (1892), the JPS rejected contemporary works of a similar nature. It would have been inconceivable for the JPS to publish Henry ROTH's *Call It Sleep* in 1934 because of the author's political views, but understandable to reprint it in 1987 once it had been rediscovered by others. If there have been weaknesses in the Society's editorial program, long a matter of debate, it has evinced unequaled strengths in other areas.

Beyond any question its major contribution has been and is its intense devotion to Bible translation. The 1917 translation which succeeded the individual work of Leeser was the first turning point in modern Jewish translation. A more recent translation, divorced totally from the King James and other versions, and drawing upon the roots of newer knowledge, appeared in three parts in 1962, 1978, and 1982. Currently a translation of the commentary is in progress.

In addition to numerous histories which have entered scholarship as standard works, the *Social and Religious History of the Jews* by Salo W. BARON, co-published with Columbia University Press from 1937 to 1983 in 18 volumes thus far, can be described as a remarkable and eloquent achievement. The *American Jewish Year Book*, published jointly with the American Jewish Committee, provides an ongoing record of worldwide events affecting Jewry.

While the Jewish Publication Society con-

tinued to seek a definition for itself during the 1960s – to stand apart from the commercial and university presses who competed for similar manuscripts – it gradually evolved different series of programs. Juvenile literature, which had been neglected, belles lettres, and translations of modern Israeli literature are among these. It maintained its program of biblical and rabbinic translation for which there was only a meager market but a critical need.

Although the JPS no longer monopolizes the field, it can boast some of the best histories on the vanished communities of Europe and the vanishing communities of the Arab world. On the other hand, it is still weak in the area of American Jewish history which has attracted the attention of the university presses. In spite of the limitations of a non-profit-making publishing house it continues to redefine its program for the changing intellectual taste of its American readers.

Recognition of the great potential for Jewish books is not limited to the century-old Jewish Publication Society. The activity of other Jewish publishers and the eagerness with which the university presses search out what they consider worthy contributions has vastly altered the world of Jewish books.

Entry into the field of literary and political journalism came early. But with the debut of journals like *Commentary* and a host of quasi-Jewish imitators, Jewish periodicals underwent considerable transformation. They operate under Jewish auspices but are never exclusively Jewish. In 1953 an unheralded author–translator combination, Isaac Bashevis SINGER and Saul BELLOW, both recipients of the Nobel Prize for literature, appeared with "Gimpel the Fool" in the *Partisan Review*, a non-Jewish journal.

In 1962 the Association of Jewish Publishers was founded. Its effect can be seen, more than 25 years later, in the publication of its combined Jewish catalog, offering recent titles and improved distribution methods. There are more than 20 independent Jewish publishers, most universities have some Jewish titles on their lists while commercial publishers are in lively competition with one another. If Isaac Leeser's initial proposal failed, Jewish publishing in the late twentieth century has become a grand success.

FURTHER READING

Bloch, J.: *Of Making Many Books: An Annotated List of the Books Issued by the Jewish Publication Society, 1890–1952* (Philadelphia: The Jewish Publication Society of America, 1953)

Freud, B.: The Jew as a publisher. *Jewish Exponent* (1955) [21 parts]

Madison, C. A.: *Jewish publishing in America: The Impact of Jewish Writing on American Culture* (New York: Sanhedrin Press, 1976)

Rosenbach, A. S. W.: *An American Jewish bibliography* (New York: American Jewish Historical Society, 1926)

Whiteman, M.: A century of Jewish journalism: the *Jewish Exponent,* 1887–1987. In *A People in Print: Jewish Journalism in America* (Philadelphia: National Museum of American Jewish History, 1987) 7–25

——: Isaac Leeser and the Jews of Philadelphia. In *Publication of the American Jewish Historical Society* (1959) 207–44

MAXWELL WHITEMAN

Q

Querido, Israel (1872–1932) Dutch–Jewish author. He was born of parents who were proud of their Sephardic origin. His formal education ceased at the age of 14, when he became an apprentice, first to a watchmaker and then to a diamond worker.

He began his literary career with two volumes of poems (1893 and 1894), under the pen-name of Theo Reeder, and was strongly influenced by the hypersensitive poetry of Herman Gorter. He then became a literary critic, under the pseudonym Joost Verbrughe or J. V.; his reviews were collected in book form in 1897. As J. V., he also contributed to the journal *Le Rêve et l'Idée* edited by Maurice Blondel, the son-in-law of Émile Zola, who strongly influenced him. In 1897 Querido joined the Dutch Socialist Party, SDAP, and from 1898 wrote literary reviews in the socialist periodical *De Jonge Gids,* edited by Herman Heijermans. For many years he was also a literary reviewer of the daily *Algemeen Handelsblad.*

Many of his novels were influenced by the naturalism of Émile Zola. *Levensgang* (1901) describes the world of the predominantly Jewish Amsterdam diamond workers; *Menschenwee* (1903) describes the miserable working conditions of laborers in the bulb flower fields. His novels *Zegepraal* (1904) and *Kunstenaarsleven* (1906) and his play *Aron Laguna,* all situated in an Amsterdam Sephardi milieu, are largely autobiographical. *De Jordaan,* in four volumes (1912–24), is situated in the Amsterdam lower-class non-Jewish district of that name.

Querido turned later to the Old Testament and to ancient history for his inspiration – for the play *Saul and David* (1914), and novel *Simson* in two volumes (1927–9), and in his three-volume epic *De Oude Wereld* (The ancient world).

In 1927 he established, together with the non-Jewish socialist A. M. de Jong, the socialist literary periodical *Nu* (Now), in which they sharply criticized the over-individualistic approach of the younger generation of Dutch authors; the periodical existed for only two years. At that time Querido began a large cycle *Het Volk Gods* (God's people) on the history of the Jews of Amsterdam, of which two volumes appeared in 1931 and 1932. His flamboyant style and language made much of his work inaccessible to his contemporaries, and make it outdated today.

His brother, Emanuel Querido (1871–1943), a bookseller, established the Querido Publishing House which still exists, and which in the 1930s published many novels by exiled German authors.

HENRIETTE BOAS

R

Rabikovitch, Dalia (b.1936) Israeli poet and writer. Born in Ramat Gan, Dalia Rabikovitch is best known for her poetry, although she has published short stories, children's prose, and essays as well. Rabikovitch is perhaps the first woman modernist poet in Hebrew. She was educated on Kibbutz Geva, in Haifa, and also studied at the Hebrew University in Jerusalem. Rabikovitch began publishing in the late 1950s. Her first book, *Ahavat tapuah zahav* (1959; The love of an orange) gained considerable success. Among the prizes she has won are the Shlonski Prize, the Ussishkin Prize, and the Bialik Prize. Following the publication of her third book, Ravikovitch maintained a public silence for some 10 years, finally publishing her most recent book in 1986.

The main body of her poetry is intensely personal and introspective. It is characterized, as some Israeli critics have put it, by the ability to center on the smallest details of reality. Her first book was dominated by a mixture of exuberant joy and solemn mourning, a central theme being the longing for her dead father. Rabikovitch may in some ways be considered a feminist poet, often describing distinctly feminine experiences.

A synthesis of opposites is characteristic not only of Rabikovitch's themes but also of her language and forms, where a combination of biblical words and constructions can be found alongside the current Hebrew idiom. At times she uses traditional forms such as the sonnet, at other times she abandons formal order altogether. Among those who have influenced her writing she counts Yehuda AMICHAI, Nathan ZACH, T. S. Eliot, and W. B. Yeats.

In subsequent collections of poetry, *Horef Kashe* (1964; A rough winter) and *Hasefer hashelishi* (1969; The third book), the tone grows more mature. "The poet must have a highly developed capacity for wonder", Rabikovitch said at one point. The fairy-tale tones heard in her earlier work are now invaded by a stronger air of disillusion and greater simplicity. Dalia Rabikovitch's most recent collection of poems, *Ahava 'amitit* (1986; True Love), makes a considerable shift towards public life, with a stronger, manifest political and social element.

AHUVIA KAHANE

Rabin, Chaim (b.1915) Israeli scholar of language and linguistics. Born in Giessen, Germany, Rabin was educated in the Jewish tradition, first at the Jewish elementary school, and then at several institutes such as Hirschche Realschule, Philanthropin, and Staatliches Kaiser–Friedrichs–Gymnasium in Frankfurt and at the Höhere Jüdische Schule in Breslau. In 1933, after taking his matriculation in Frankfurt, he went to Israel, and continued his studies at the Hebrew University where he was a student of Harry TORCZYNER (later Tur-Sinai). After receiving his doctorate on ancient Arabic dialects from the University of London in 1939, he taught Hebrew and Arabic at the University of Oxford, and in 1942 received a second doctorate there. In 1965 Rabin was appointed professor of Hebrew language at the Hebrew University. His academic posts and activities have been numerous, including chairmanship of the Committee for Research Students (1961–6), Chairman of the academic committee of J. L.

Magnes Press (1965–9), Chairman of the Institute of Jewish Studies (1970–6), as well as President of the Israel Association for Applied Linguistics (from 1974) and member of the Hebrew Language Academy (from 1968).

Rabin's major contribution to modern scholarship is in the field of linguistics. He published his early research, a comparative study of Hebrew grammar and that of other Semitic languages, including the groups of Akkadian and Syrian–Canaanite languages, Arabic, and Ethiopian. His *Otzar hamillim, millim, tzerufim va'amarot mesudarim lefi tehumei mashema'ut* (1970) is a thesaurus of Hebrew words, similar to Roget's *Thesaurus of English Words and Phrases* (first published in 1852). Rabin's thesaurus includes words from the Bible and rabbinic literature, as well as from modern Hebrew literature. Among his other books are also *Ancient West-Arabian* (1951) and *Qumran Studies* (1957; 1975).

Rabin has written a large number of articles on a range of subjects, such as Qumran Hebrew, Aramaic, biblical Hebrew, and normative modern Hebrew. Generally, his approach to linguistic studies is sociological and functional, that is, he studies the function and development of language in everyday life.

DEBORAH SCHECHTERMAN

Rabinovich, Osip (1817–1869) Russian–Jewish prose writer and publicist, the founding father of Russian–Jewish literature. He was born in the small town of Kobelyaki in the Poltava province and spent his entire creative life in Odessa. His first publication was in 1847. His legacy of fiction includes five narrative tales and a novel (published during the period 1849–65), among which a special place is occupied by the tale "Shtrafnoi" (1859; The penal recruit), the history of the ruin of a Jewish family during the final years of Nicholas I's government. The tale astounded both the Russian and the Jewish reader: for the first time the persecution of the Jews in the Russian Empire was talked about publicly. In literary terms, "Shtrafnoi" was the first example of the creation of a Jewish character in a specifically Jewish situation; the experience was augmented and enriched in the next tale, "Nasledstvennyi podsvechnik" (1860; Hereditary candlestick), published in the first

Russian–Jewish periodical, the weekly *Rasvet* (The dawn; Odessa, 1860–1). Rabinovich was the editor and an unfailing author of editorials, which in aggregate make up the most important part of the publicistic legacy of the writer-maskil, that is, in the Russian conditions of that time: a fighter for enlightenment and civic equality; and a convinced assimilator. These convictions were shaken by the failure of the journal which was closed because of the Odessan management's gross interference. Rabinovich's last narrative tale, "Istoriia o tom, kak reb Khaim-Shulim Feigis puteshestvoval iz Kishineva v Odessu, i chto s nim sluchilos" (1865; The story of how Reb Khaim Shulim Feigis traveled from Kishinev to Odessa, and what happened to him) was of its kind "a return to the ghetto": it is Rabinovich's most national work and at that time the most perfect artistically.

FURTHER READING
Lvov-Rogachevsky, V.: *A History of Russian Jewish Literature* (Ann Arbor, Mich.: Ardis, 1979)
Orbach, A.: *New Voices of Russian Jewry, A Study of the Russian–Jewish Press in Odessa in the Era of the Great Reforms, 1860–1871* (Leiden: 1980)

SHIMON MARKISH

Rabinowitz, Sholem See SHOLEM ALEICHEM.

Rabinowitz, Louis Isaac (1906–1984) South African rabbi, scholar, and communal leader. Born in Edinburgh, he was educated at the University of London where he attained his Ph.D. He received his Jewish education at Jews' College and the Yeshiva Etz Chaim, London. He was awarded his rabbinic diploma in 1930 and later received *semikha* from Chief Rabbi Abraham KooK of Palestine.

After ministering successively to three major synagogues in London, he served as senior Jewish chaplain to the British army in the Middle East and Normandy during the Second World War. In 1945 he emigrated to Johannesburg, South Africa, subsequently being appointed as Chief Rabbi of the United Hebrew Congregation of Johannesburg and of the Federation of Synagogues of the Transvaal and Orange Free State, and chairman of the Beth Din. He was also appointed Professor of Hebrew at the University of the Witwatersrand.

He was a forceful orator and conducted his ministry with courage and vigor. In 1947 he protested against British policy in Palestine, discarding his war decorations publicly. He denounced the South African government's apartheid system in a forthright manner. He was an ardent Zionist and aligned himself with the Revisionist movement. A staunch champion of Jewish orthodoxy, he unified the South African orthodox community under the aegis of the Federation of Synagogues. His leadership determined the nature of Jewish religious expression in South Africa. He laid the basis for public kosher catering in the large centers of South Africa and, in 1948, he instituted the use of the Sephardic pronunciation in the liturgy.

In 1961 he settled in Israel where he became deputy editor-in-chief of the *Encyclopedia Judaica*, and, on its completion, editor of its Year Books. From 1975 to 1977 he served as Jerusalem's Deputy Mayor and in 1980 received the distinction of Worthy Citizen. He was also a governor of the Hebrew University. He was a frequent contributor to the columns of the *Jewish Chronicle,* the *Jerusalem Post*, and the *South African Jewish Herald*. His publications include *Soldiers from Judea* (1942), *Jewish Merchant Adventurers* (1948), *Far East Mission* (1952), and volumes of his sermons.

JOCELYN HELLIG

Radnóti, Miklós (1909–1944) Hungarian poet and translator. Radnóti was born in Budapest into a middle-class Jewish family. Orphaned young, he was brought up by relatives. After finishing trade school he studied for some time in Liberec (Reichenberg), Czechoslovakia, and, from 1930, he studied Hungarian and French literature at the University of Szeged in Hungary. His first book of poetry *Pogány köszöntő* (1930; Pagan greeting) consists mostly of idylls and elegies; the poet's rebellious feelings towards society are indicated by his expressionism. During the Szeged years Radnóti had socialist sympathies and maintained ties with a group of young populists, but he was also influenced by the Catholic priest–poet Sán-

dor Sík who taught Hungarian literature at the university. In 1935 Radnóti married and settled in Budapest, working as a freelance poet and translator. By the time his collection of poetry, *Járkálj csak, halálraitélt* (1936; Keep walking, you, the death-condemned!), was published, Radnóti's poetry, though in some ways more openly political, had lost its shrill, provocative edge while gaining a new, broader dimension.

His theme from this volume onwards is the inevitability of violent death in a new war which will engulf Europe. The fate of Federico Garcia Lorca, murdered by Fascists, stands as a memento for him; in his interpretation Lorca had to die because he was a poet, a spokesman for the forces of life. As to formal aspects the mature Radnóti's poetry is characterized by a return to classicism: the axis of his last, posthumous collection, *Tajtékos ég* (1946; Foaming sky), is his cycle of eclogues the subject-matter of which is often very personal, the seventh being a lyrical report from the forced labor camp of Bor in Yugoslavia where Radnóti worked in 1944. In September 1944 the camp was evacuated and the Jewish laborers sent on foot westward in a forced march about which Radnóti wrote one of his most moving final poems. Around 9 November 1944 those men in the march who were too weak to continue walking towards Germany were shot and buried in a mass grave near the village of Abda. Radnóti's last poems were found in the pocket of his raincoat when the body was exhumed.

Radnóti is now recognized as one of the finest poets of his generation and an authentic voice of anti-Fascism. He manages to transmute the horrors of his time into poems of beauty and serenity. While he personally broke away from Judaism (he was converted to Catholicism in 1943), the structure of his poetic vision is Judeo-Christian in the sense that he frequently draws upon prophets of the Old Testament to articulate his views. His protest against war and totalitarian regimes is often couched in "humanistic" terms but ultimately he returns to the Bible, as in "Fragment" (1944).

Radnóti was an excellent translator of Latin, French, English, and German poetry, his collection of translations *Orpheus nyomában* (1942; In Orpheus' footsteps) attesting to his impeccable taste and poetic skill. His only prose piece of interest is *Ikrek hava* (1940; *Under Gemini*, 1985), an impressionistic collage of the poet's childhood memories and his visit to Paris in 1939. Radnóti is now the most translated Hungarian poet into English: since 1972 several collections of his poetry have been published in the UK and the USA, including a volume of *The Complete Poetry* edited and translated by Emery George (1980).

BIBLIOGRAPHY

Under Gemini, trans. K. McRobbie, Z. McRobbie, and J. Kessler (Budapest: Corvina Kiadó, 1985)

FURTHER READING

George, E.: introduction to *Miklós Radnóti: The Complete Poetry* (Ann Arbor: Ardis, 1980)

Wilmer, C., and Gömöri, G.: introduction to *Miklós Radnóti: Forced March* (Manchester: Carcanet New Press, 1979)

GEORGE GÖMÖRI

Rahv, Philip [Ivan Greenberg] (1908–1973) Literary critic and political intellectutal. Philip Rahv, co-founder of one of the most influential cultural journals in the USA, was born in Galicia. Emigrating to the USA at the age of 14, he attended high school in Providence, Rhode Island, before heading west, where he worked in advertising and as a Hebrew teacher. Returning to New York in 1930, he read in public libraries, slept in parks or friends' homes, grew increasingly politicized, and in 1932 joined the Communist Party, taking the name Philip Rahv.

Interested in questions of literature and radicalism, Rahv and William Phillips, founded *Partisan Review* in 1934. They announced that the magazine would "concentrate on creative and critical literature, but ... shall maintain a definite viewpoint – that of the revolutionary working class ... the defense of the Soviet Union is one of our principal tasks".

Growing doubts about the quality of much radical literature and about the role of intellectuals within the radical art movement ultimately led Rahv and Phillips to take *PR* out of the Communist cultural circle in 1936. They revived the magazine in 1937 as an independent radical journal. Around the magazine grew an intellectual community and Rahv became, in the words of the critic Alfred Kazin, the "the Doctor Johnson of his small group of radical intellectuals". In 1940, Rahv married Nathalie Swan, an architect.

The American entry into the Second World War redefined the political view of the *Partisan Review* editorial board. Initially opposed to the war as an example of competing bourgeois states, Rahv led the move of the magazine toward qualified support of the war effort. While many of his contemporaries moved to liberalism and anti-Communism in the post-war years, Rahv grew angry at the capitulation of many American intellectuals to the status quo.

In 1957, despite not having ever taken any college degree, Rahv was offered a position at Brandeis University. Married for a second time, Rahv settled in Boston but maintained ties to New York and the *Partisan Review*. The distance and changing cultural context of the 1960s strained the relationship between Rahv and Phillips. He wrote critical attacks on old friends and intellectual allies. His fortunes declined in the late 1960s. In 1968 his house was gutted by fire and his wife suffocated. In 1969 he resigned from *Partisan Review*, planning to launch a new journal. Marrying for a third time, life appeared to be turning up, but his marriage failed as did his new journal. Only six issues of *Modern Occasions* appeared, marked mostly by their caustic tone toward contemporary culture and cultural figures.

Rahv's published work is small. His academic career came late and he never fully adjusted to the role. His greatest skills were talking and editing. He lived at the center of an intellectual world which began to recede, even as it gained notoriety in the 1950s. Rahv died at the age of 65 – without *Partisan Review*, without many of his old friends, and disconnected from the intellectual community he had helped create.

FURTHER READING

Bloom, A.: *Prodigal Sons: The New York Intellectuals and Their World* (New York and Oxford: Oxford University Press, 1987)

Gilbert, J.: *Writers and Partisans* (New York: John Wiley & Sons, 1968)

ALEXANDER BLOOM

Rank, Otto (1884–1939)   Austrian psychoanalyst. Born in Vienna, Rank was a devoted
and creative member of Sigmund FREUD's
psychoanalytic circle from 1905 to 1926. Raised
in Vienna's lower-middle-class and Jewish–
immigrant second district (the Leopoldstadt),
and saddled with the burden of achieving material security, Rank delayed his formal higher
education until 1908. He received his doctorate
from the University of Vienna in 1912. His
doctoral thesis, *Die Lohengrinsage,* a precocious
study of Richard Wagner's operatic hero
Lohengrin, was the first dissertation anywhere
utilizing the psychoanalytic method of interpretation.

The large corpus of Rank's work that remains
untranslated or poorly translated reflects
neither the importance of his contribution to the
nascent psychoanalytic movement nor the sheer
quantity of his intellectual output. Between
1910 and 1913 alone, Rank published 46 pieces,
including three major contributions to the
psychaoanalytic literature: *Die Lohengrinsage*
(1911), in which he argued that Wagner's protagonist's relationship with Elsa achieved a
reunion with the pure and holy mother of Wagner's childhood; *Das Inzestmotiv* (1912), and
"Die Nacktheit in Sage und Dichtung" (1913),
both works elaborating on his first book, *Der
Künstler* (1907). From the beginning, Rank distinguished himself as a psychologist of the
artist.

Rank is best known for his sensational book,
Das Trauma der Geburt (1924), his first open challenge to psychoanalytic orthodoxy that led to
his break in 1926 from the circle around Freud.
In contrast to Freud's restraint and preference
for self-understanding, Rank believed in the
value of unfettered self-expression. In *Das
Trauma,* he argued for its therapeutic possibility
as well, by urging a return to prenatal existence
(the mother now forming the center of his
theory), and an analytic "acting out" of the
patient's fantasies. Rank's significance for
psychoanalysis is the introduction of these ideas
(and others, such as the separation crisis, or
primal anxiety) into the mainstream of the field.

Despite their tensions, Freud and Rank
formed a close father–son relationship from the
moment Rank joined Freud's small circle in
1905–6. Acquiring an abiding filial loyalty to

Otto Rank

Freud (consistent with his sometimes desperate
search for a more satisfying father), Rank
appeared to his associates as Freud's closest
protégé and as Freud's likely successor to the
leadership of the movement. In 1912–13, Freud
appointed Rank as founding coeditor (with
Hanns Sachs) of *Imago,* the psychoanalytic journal of the arts, and the *Internationale Zeitschrift
für Psychoanalyse,* the most important periodical
of psychoanalytic literature published in German. Freud also invited Rank to revise and
contribute to later editions of *The Interpretation of
Dreams* (1914–22). Until their final and bitter
rift, Freud was impressed with Rank's mastery
of the esthetic, as opposed to the medical or
scientific side of psychoanalysis.

There is little in Rank's life, and nothing
in his publications, that betray his powerful,

if eccentric self-understanding as a Jew. He appeared to have repudiated everything that was Jewish. In 1903, Rank formally severed his ties with the Jewish confession. Aware of the Jewish sound of his family surname, Rosenfeld, and uncomfortable with it (for legal as well as for personal reasons), he changed his name, in 1909, to Rank. The year before, he had converted to Roman Catholicism. He returned to Judaism in 1918, when he married Betty Münzer, the first of two wives.

Although Rank was dissatisfied with his Jewish heritage, he was not indifferent. The most illuminating expression of his inner Jewish conflict is an impetuous and unpublished five-page essay he wrote in 1905 called "Das Wesen des Judentums". Written on the verge of joining Freud, it offers unusual insight into the predilection of an assimilated Jew on the way toward shaping one of the twentieth century's most influential and enterprising intellectual movements.

According to Rank, Jews possessed special creative powers: As outsiders, they had been immune from dispiriting, civilized morality and therefore able to maintain a direct and energizing relation to "nature, primitive sexuality". Recently, however, Jews had encountered a repression of their sexuality, both from the surrounding world (anti-Semitism) and from within (assimilation). As a result, Jews had become as neurotic as the rest of civilized humanity. But, due to their close affinity with nature and the suddenness of their search for renewal, Jews embodied mankind's last hope. They could go beyond momentary relief (by "discharging affect" in artistic creativity) to the "radical cure" of neurosis. They could become the "physicians" for mankind.

It is impossible to see what is Jewish in Rank's defense of Jewish culture and his own part in it. What is crucial, however, was his belief that, as a Jew, he was destined to help regenerate humanity. Adopting (and reinterpreting) psychoanalytic ideas for the essay, and poised for deeper engagement, Rank would draw on this belief in a heroic Jewish minority for self-confidence and the resolve for ambitious work. How deeply Rank's Jewish self-conception imbued the rest of his life and work may never be known, but there is no doubt

that it supplied a major impetus to his early psychoanalytic endeavors.

FURTHER READING

Klein, D. B.: The psychology of the follower: Otto Rank. In *Jewish Origins of the Psychoanalytic Movement* (Chicago: University of Chicago Press, 1985)
Lieberman, E. J.: *Acts of Will: The Life and Work of Otto Rank* (New York: Free Press, 1985)
Taft, J.: *Otto Rank: A Biographical Study* (New York: The Julian Press, 1958)

DENNIS B. KLEIN

Raphael, Frederic (b.1931) British novelist and screenwriter. Born in Chicago, Illinois, Raphael moved to England at the age of seven and was educated at Charterhouse School and Cambridge University where he was influenced by John Wisdom, a follower of the philosopher Ludwig Wittgenstein.

It was not until the publication of his third novel *The Limits of Love* (1960) that Raphael gained wide recognition as a novelist. The protagonist of this novel is Paul Reisman, an assimilated Jew, who is forced to confront the existential implications of the Holocaust. The tension between bourgeois accommodation and conformity and the dark subterranean underworld of modern society – as represented by the Holocaust – is a theme in many of Raphael's novels. His characteristic word-play and flamboyant philosophizing is both the civilized obverse of these dark forces and a means by which Raphael's heroes are able to cope with the horrors of modern living. His seventh novel *Lindmann* (1963), in particular, explicitly deals with these tensions with reference to the Holocaust. In this novel James Shepherd, a British civil servant, assumes the identity of Jacob Lindmann who was one of two survivors from a ship of doomed Jewish refugees prevented by Shepherd from landing safely in 1942. By identifying Shepherd with Lindmann, Raphael is able to demonstrate the dark realities beneath the veneer of the civilized Englishman. The Lindmann/Shepherd duality is a sustaining moral viewpoint – albeit not always in a specifically Jewish context – throughout many of his novels.

Raphael has frequently argued that his kind

of Jewishness is the feeling that he is "alien from everyone". The discovery of Jewishness for Raphael's rather alienated protagonists can often, therefore, be a bitter-sweet refuge from displacement. This is the case in *A Wild Surmise* (1960), Raphael's fourth novel, and, especially, *Orchestra and Beginners* (1967). In this, his ninth novel, Leonard Strauss, an assimilated Anglo-Jew, discovers his Jewishness against the backdrop of the Second World War. The contradictory pulls of assimilation and anti-Semitism, which help characterize Raphael's Jewish protagonists, often result in telling portraits. Adam Morris in *The Glittering Prizes* (1976), Raphael's fifteenth novel, is both a representative civilized man and is, at the same time, alienated from himself and society at large by the spectre of the Holocaust and continuing anti-Semitism. Raphael's most recent novel, *Heaven and Earth* (1985), brings together the complacent Stephen Hellman and the civilized Gideon Shand in an apocalyptic novel which is Raphael's most ambitious examination of this duality to date.

Raphael has published 16 novels and four volumes of short stories. He is also an Oscar-winning screenwriter and has written 10 television plays. *An Early Life* (produced Leicester 1979), the first section of *The Glittering Prizes*, has been turned into a successful stage play and examines Adam Morris's encounter with English anti-Semitism as a public schoolboy. Six other plays by Raphael have been staged and, more recently, two radio documentaries have been broadcast. His reviews and articles have also been republished in *Cracks in the Ice: Views and Reviews* (1979) which includes an account of his long and fruitful involvement with the London *Jewish Quarterly*.

BIBLIOGRAPHY

The curiousness of Anglo-Jews. *The Jewish Quarterly* 31 no. 2 (1984)

FURTHER READING

Sonntag, J., ed.: *Jewish Perspectives: 25 Years of Jewish Writing* (London: Secker & Warburg, 1980)

BRYAN CHEYETTE

Rapoport, Solomon Judah (1790–1867)

Chief Rabbi of Prague and pioneer of modern Jewish scholarship. Born to a moderately circumstanced family in Lemberg, where he spent the first half of his life, Rapoport was 47 before he obtained rabbinic office. He had early shown distinction as a talmudist, but was supported either by his father-in-law or by secular occupations. The *Haskalah* (Enlightenment) movement, which had originated in Germany and which in its various manifestations had included the revival of Hebrew letters, belief in secular studies, and the scientific examination of the Jewish past, had spread to Galicia. Rapoport was an early participant, being particularly influenced by his neighbor Nachman KROCHMAL. A biography of Rashi (1829), based on original research and objective in its approach, followed by others of similar character, secured his place as one of the founders of the WISSENSCHAFT DES JUDENTUMS.

Rapoport's acceptance of free enquiry in the realm of research involved him in contacts with non-Orthodox workers in the field, but he was adamant in his condemnation of REFORM JUDAISM. Nevertheless, he incurred the violent hostility of the ultra-Orthodox of Galicia. In 1837 Rapoport became Rabbi of Tarnopol, and in 1840 Chief Rabbi of Prague. He maintained contact with Jewish scholars throughout Europe, but his literary output was limited. *Erekh Millin* (1852) was intended as a talmudic encyclopedia, but only a small part appeared.

Considering the importance of the Prague Jewish community, Rapoport appears to have exercised little influence as Chief Rabbi. *Yeshiva* learning decayed in Bohemia, but no modern institute of Jewish scholarship was set up to replace it. Probably his blend of modern research with Orthodox practice helped to prevent the Reform movement from taking hold, but the communities appear to have contented themselves with corrections to the externals of the synagogue service.

FURTHER READING

Mendes-Flohr, P. R., and Reinharz, J.: *The Jew in the Modern World – A Documentary History* (New York: Oxford University Press, 1980)

Zinberg, I.: *A History of Jewish Literature* Eng. trans. (Cincinnati and New York: 1977)

SEFTON D. TEMKIN

Rapoport, (O.) Yehoshua (1895–1971)

Australian Yiddish essayist, translator, and editor. Born in Bialystok, Rapoport emigrated to Australia in 1947 after spending the war years in Shanghai. He arrived with an established reputation having published his first works in Poland. His subject matter was belles lettres, public affairs, and the whole field of Jewish studies, especially Bible and Talmud. He translated works from Russian, German, French, and Hebrew into Yiddish.

In Australia he became editor of the *Yiddishe Neies*, setting new standards for local community journalism, turning the paper into a well-informed news sheet for such immigrants as were yet unable to read English. A man of considerable political foresight, he saw many of his predictions fulfilled. Because of his anti-Soviet stance, strong opinions, and merciless printed criticisms of some of his fellow writers, his writing was often resented. He gave a good deal of encouragement to gifted young writers and especially to those who had taken refuge in Australia from Nazi Europe, demanding that they record their experiences for posterity. He argued that Europe was morally bankrupt, that its literature had not responded to the tragedy of the Holocaust, and that it was up to the new generation of Australian Jewish immigrant writers to create a new, moral protest literature. Though some of his work has appeared in translation in *Quadrant* the majority is available only in Yiddish in his collected essays, some of which were published outside Australia, in Israel or Argentina.

FURTHER READING

Kahan, I.: Three Australian Yiddish writers. *Australian Jewish Historical Society* 7 no. 4 (1973)

ALAN D. CROWN

Rappaport, Solomon I. (1905–1986)

South African rabbi and scholar. Born in Lemberg, Galicia, he and his family fled to Baden, near Vienna with the advent of the First World War. He qualified as a rabbi at the Vienna Jewish Theological Seminary in 1926, studying simultaneously at the Vienna University where he attained the degrees of D. Juris. (1929) and Ph.D. (1930). He subsequently became a lecturer at the Maimonides College for Judaic Studies in Vienna. In 1938, with the Austrian Anschluss with Nazi Germany, he and his wife sought refuge in London. He began his rabbinic career at the Reform Sheepcotes Synagogue in Birmingham.

In 1943 he emigrated to South Africa where he served as rabbi to the Orthodox North Eastern Hebrew Congregation, Johannesburg, for over 30 years. He joined the Department of Hebrew at the University of the Witwatersrand in 1949, becoming professor and head of the department in 1969. On his retirement in 1973 he became professor emeritus. Under his leadership the department grew to be one of the largest foreign-language departments in the University. In 1978 he was honored by his congregation and appointed rabbi emeritus. In 1985 a Festschrift was published in honor of his eightieth birthday.

He was a man of wide-ranging scholarship, having imbibed the fructifying scholarly atmosphere of Vienna between the wars. Steeped in Jewish learning and scholarship and in Hebrew language and literature, he also displayed a remarkable knowledge of and interest in art, music and literature. He was recognized as one of the finest and most versatile Jewish scholars in South Africa, and gave public lectures and published prolifically on a variety of topics. It was the combination of the best in Western civilization – music, art, and philosophy, and the best of Judaism – ethics, morality, religious contemplation, and devotion, that characterized Rabbi Rappaport.

He wrote in English, Hebrew and German on many topics. His publications include: *Antikes Zur Bibel Und Agadah* (1937), *Rabbinic Thoughts on Race* (1951) and *Jews and Gentiles – The Philo-Semitic Aspect* (1980).

JOCELYN HELLIG

Raskin, Saul (1886–1966)

American artist and art writer. Born in Nogaisk, Russia, Raskin traveled and studied in Germany, France, and Italy and emigrated to the USA in 1904.

Raskin was a Yiddishist and Zionist whose paintings, book illustrations, and art criticism reflected the attitudes of secular Yiddish culture that for a large group of immigrants had supplanted traditional Jewish observance and ritual in the USA. Stylistically conservative, Raskin's paintings show the influence of late nineteenth-century Post Impressionism, particularly the experiments with spatial relationships and color of Paul Cézanne. Thematically, Raskin attempted to evoke a nostalgic view of Yiddish domestic and neighborhood life in New York on the Lower East Side in the early twentieth century. In 1921 he traveled to Israel, painting scenes of Jewish life there including lithographs on Jerusalem. Raskin was active as an illustrator of Hebrew texts and Yiddish tales including *Pirkei Avot* (1940), the *Haggadah* (1941), Psalms (1942), the *Siddur* (1945), the *kabbalah* called *Kabbalah in Word and Image*, and *Hebrew Rhapsody* (1959).

Raskin was an active participant in the thriving Yiddish culture that blossomed on the Lower East Side of New York. In 1911 he was responsible for conceiving the first exhibition exclusively for Jewish artists. During the 1920s he was active in the Jewish Art Center.

FURTHER READING

Kampf, A.: *The Jewish Experience in Art of the Twentieth Century* (South Hadley: Bergin & Garvey Publishers Inc., 1984)

BARBARA GILBERT

Rathaus, Karol [Leonhard Bruno] (1895–1954) American composer. Austrian by birth, Rathaus once exercised "an influence on the whole trend of modern music". He taught and composed in the late-Romantic idiom under the influences of his tutor Franz Schrecker and of Karol Szymanowski. His works were performed by Erich Kleiber and Wilhelm Furtwängler and at the Berlin State Opera. After 1933, he went via Paris to England, where he remained until he emigrated to the USA 1938. His compositions for the cinema, concert hall and the theater include symphonies, ballets, orchestral suites, and chamber works, many of which have been performed at music festivals, including the American League of Composers and Jewish Music World (Israel).

His film score for Fedor Ozep's *Der Mörder Dimitri Karamasof* (1931) has been described as "a model of film symphonic art" for he success-

fully associated film rhythm and music rhythm for the first time in the cinema. His intellectual approach to creating an organized form which which would support the structure of the film was influential throughout the industry, but in Europe he had the opportunity to compose from the script, before shooting began, and not simply for a completed film. This "luxury" was not offered to him in Hollywood. In Britain he composed the scores for *The Dictator* (1935) and for *Broken Blossoms* (1936). He was opposed to using film music as a shapeless mosaic of background fragments and was concerned with preserving its form inside a medium which had the unique quality of the sudden appearance and disappearance of music.

Other films include: *Hallo, Hallo, hier spricht Berlin* (1932), *Dame de Pique* (1937), *Let Us Live* (1939).

BIBLIOGRAPHY

Music in films, a composers' symposium (with others). *Films* 1 no. 4 (1940)

FURTHER READING

London, K.: *Film Music* (London: Faber & Faber, 1936)

KEVIN GOUGH-YATES

Ratosh, Yonatan [Uriel Halperin] (b.1909) Hebrew poet. Ratosh was born in Russia, educated exclusively in Hebrew and arrived in Palestine in 1921. He had spent some of his early childhood in Odessa, and absorbed the atmosphere which had so intensively fed Hayyim Nahman BIALIK on whom Ratosh wrote a number of scholarly essays.

Although Ratosh is a poet of some innovative influence, he is best known for his championing of the short-lived "Canaanite" ideology and for his "Manifesto to Hebrew Youth". A so-called "primitivist" even in his poetry, Ratosh saw contemporary Hebrew youth as strong, healthy, and heroic, opposed to the Diaspora-afflicted Jews whom he characterized in conventional and stereotypical anti-Semitic terms. He idealized the ancient Hebrews and proposed a Hebrew divested of Diasporan accretions, as a living language.

The non-religious, anti-Zionist but ultranationalist movement, "Canaanism", was launched in 1948 with the establishment of the periodical, *Alef*. The most extreme manifestation of the division of "Hebrew" and "Jewish" culture, it saw Jewish history after the Bar Kokhba revolt as "an irrelevant intrusion into the present" and it therefore rejected the Diaspora together with its intellectual achievements. Ratosh's "Canaanite" political program was somewhat grandiose: the liberation of all peoples living in the Fertile Crescent, the occupation of Damascus and Cairo, and the imposition of a benign Hebrew dictatorship. The new nation would be the cultural descendant of the ancient Hebrew/Canaanite nation, powered by Hebrew, not Jewish, culture and language. The movement did not preclude violence.

Ratosh wrote several volumes of poetry, the early works in particular distinguished by his recreation of the ancient Canaanite world and its mythology. *Huppah shehorah* (1941; Black canopy) introduced his Canaanite motifs. These were crystallized in *Shirei herev* (1969; Songs of the sword), which presented, in accordance with his beliefs, imagery and vocabulary dating back to biblical times.

GLENDA ABRAMSON

Ravitsh, Melekh [Zekharye-Khone Bergner] (1893–1976) Yiddish poet and essayist. Born in Radymno, East Galicia, Ravitsh left home as a young man and traveled widely throughout his life. He was active in Yiddish literary circles in Warsaw in the 1970s, and in the 1930s visited Australia, Argentina, the USA, and Mexico. From 1941 onwards he lived in Montreal, although he spent the years 1953–6 in Israel.

In Warsaw he was, with Uri GREENBERG and Peretz MARKISH, a member of the so-called *Khalyastre* poetic group, which took a strongly anti-realist position in poetics and was expressionist in orientation. Thus, in the collections *Nakete lider* (1921; Naked songs) and *Di fir zaytn fun mayn velt* (1929; The four sides of my world), Ravitsh turned away from the regular rhyme and metrics of his early poetry. However the collection, *Kontinentn un okeanen* (1937; Continents

and oceans), marked a return to song and ballad forms. Ravitsh was a poet of philosophical ("idealist") aspirations as well as lyricism, and the author of criticism, memoirs and a three-volume biographical work on Yiddish literature, *Mayn leksikon* (1945–58).

CHRISTOPHER HUTTON

Ray(-Rapaport), Rudolf (b.1891) Austrian painter. Born in Latvia, Ray went to Vienna in 1896, where he studied law. His interest in painting stemmed from his earliest childhood, and he was always deeply preoccupied with science, philosophy, and religion. He took up painting seriously in 1920. In 1927 he visited India where he met Tagore, among others. In 1929 Ray was in Paris, where he met Soutine and Duchamp. 1933 saw the publication of *Super-Realismus in der Portraitmalerei von Rudolf Ray* (Super-realism in the portraiture of Rudolf Ray) by Stephan Pollatschek, and Ray became known for penetrating psychological studies. Kokoschka, an admirer, called him a "pure expressionist". In France again in 1938, Ray emigrated to the USA in 1942, where he developed the technique of over-painting to provide, in his view, spiritual as well as physical depth to his art. In 1956 he was again in India, in 1960 in Mexico, and he later lived in London.

Ray's art is highly spiritual in its aims, an art of the inner self according to Herbert Read. Ray ascribed much of this spirituality to his Orthodox Jewish background; in the 1930s he painted the portrait of H. N. BIALIK, and was deeply impressed by his conversation with the Hebrew poet.

FURTHER READING

International biographical dictionary of Central European émigrés, 1933–45 (Munich: 1983)

Kolb, L.: The Vienna Jewish Museum. In *The Jews of Austria*, ed. J. Fraenkel (London: Vallentine Mitchell, 1967)

STEVEN BELLER

Reconstructionism The only indigenous denomination in American Judaism, it looks upon Judaism as an evolving religious civilization rather than a supernaturally revealed teaching and law.

Reconstructionism is a carefully articulated ideological system created by Rabbi Mordecai KAPLAN in response to the challenges raised by modernity to traditional faith. The son of a Lithuanian talmudist, Kaplan earned a BA degree from City College and an MA from Columbia while studying for the rabbinate at the Jewish Theological Seminary. He taught at JTS from 1909 to 1963, heading its Teacher's Institute and teaching homiletics and philosophy to rabbinical students. He exerted a profound influence upon the liberal wing of the Conservative rabbinate and served a term as the president of its rabbinial organization.

During his youth, Kaplan read deeply in the writings of Émile DURKHEIM, John Dewey, and William James. His encounter with scientific naturalism and critical historiography shattered his faith in traditional Jewish theism and in its personal God who intervened in history and revealed Himself to humanity through the prophets. In a cosmos bound by natural law and devoid of a supernatural element, religion was revealed to be an organic expression of a culture's innermost values and desires. Determined to nurture the tradition he loved and to foster its creativity, Kaplan found a key to its reconciliation with modernity in AHAD HA'AM's spiritual Zionism. In his magnum opus, *Judaism as a Civilization* (1934), he argued that the starting point for a modern Jewish identity must be peoplehood. The Jewish people were the heirs of a great civilization, rooted in a land with a distinctive history and culture. Kaplan defined Judaism as an evolving religious civilization, animated by a profound vision of God and a hunger for social justice and holiness. Spiritual sensitivity should remain at the center of Jewish identity.

Kaplan's interpretation of Jewish theology is highly naturalistic. Religion derives from humanity's quest for salvation. This is not the attainment of eternal life but, rather, the development of human creative and moral powers to their highest potential. The inherent psychic forces that support our moral drives – the power that makes for salvation – is symbolized through the concept of God. The Bible is a human document, recording Israel's deepening spiritual maturity, while Jewish rituals are sancta, time-honored folkways expressing significant values, rather than divinely ordained commandments.

Kaplan called for the reconstruction of Jewish life and belief along these lines. Synagogues should be complete centers for all aspects of a flourishing Jewish culture: arts, music, and athletics as well as prayer and study. He was an advocate of women's rights and the creator of the *bat mitzvah* ceremony. Kaplan's congregation, the Society for the Advancement of Judaism (est. 1922) served as a vehicle for his ideas.

Despite growing frustration with the official Conservative movement's legal and theological traditionalism, Kaplan, throughout much of his career, preferred to view Reconstructionism as an intellectual movement in American Judaism, rather than a fourth institutionalized denomination. However, he became intensively involved in liturgical reform, publishing a Reconstructionist *Haggadah* (1941) and prayerbook (1945). A congregational organization was established in 1954 and a new rabbinical school, the Reconstructionist Rabbinical College, with a curriculum organized around the major eras of Jewish history, opened in Philadelphia in 1968.

Reconstructionism is entering a period of great creativity. Kaplan's influence remains significant. Much energy is being devoted to feminism, social justice, and peace issues, while the past decade has witnessed a significant resurgence of interest in spirituality.

FURTHER READING

Goldsmith, E., and Scult, M.: *Dynamic Judaism: The Essential Writings of Mordecai M. Kaplan* (New York: Schocken Books, 1985)

Kaplan, M.: *The Meaning of God in Modern Jewish Religion* (New York: Reconstructionist Press, 1962)

Libowitz, R.: *Mordecai M. Kaplan and the Development of Reconstructionism* (New York: The Edwin Mellen Press, 1983)

SETH L. BRODY

Reform Judaism The organized branch of the Jewish religion that has been most concerned to harmonize Jewish tradition with modern life and culture. Today it numbers well over a million adherents, mainly in North America, but also in other centers of Jewish life in the West, including the State of Israel.

Reform Judaism began as a movement for religious change in central Europe during the late eighteenth and early nineteenth centuries. In an age of increased tolerance, advancing social and cultural integration, and secular knowledge among Jews, the early European reformers attempted to remove the perceived conflict between the prevalent ghetto Judaism and their newly discovered intellectual and esthetic environment. They attempted to create a Jewish theology that could withstand Christian thinkers' claims that only their faith was suited to modern times and they sought to reshape the institutions of Judaism in such a way as to appeal to the transformed religious sensibilities of an acculturating Jewry. Crucial to the beginnings of the movement was the subjectivization of religious consciousness, which made the personal experience of prayer and ritual for the individual, rather than the fulfillment of the commandments given at Sinai, the principal criterion determining liturgy and observance.

The early Reform services stressed order and decorum in line both with Christian practice and the newly internalized belief that the synagogue, as a sanctuary, required an atmosphere of reverence. Sermons now stressed moral and religious themes that would edify congregants (female as well as male), rather than points of Jewish law. To heighten the esthetic value of worship, the Reformers introduced organ music and the harmonic singing of mixed choirs. Some of the prayers were recited in the vernacular so that all would be able to understand their meaning. While references to Zion were not wholly expunged from the liturgy, those passages in the traditional prayerbook that expressed the hope of return to Palestine and re-establishment of animal sacrifices were altered or eliminated, along with prayers that spoke vengefully about the suffering of Jews at the hands of Gentiles.

Beginning in the 1830s a new generation of talented German rabbis, the most notable of whom was Rabbi Abraham GEIGER, began to formulate an ideology for religious reform. They understood revelation as a continuing process that brought Judaism to ever higher levels of consciousness of the divine will. They stressed the doctrine of ethical monotheism and that Jews, as custodians of that doctrine, were charged with a "mission" to bring it to the full awareness of non-Jews.

In the USA, where Reform Judaism found an intellectual climate far more hospitable to religious individuality than in Europe, it was able to spread rapidly, spurred by the immigration of German Jews during the nineteenth century and their integration into American life. Under the mediating leadership of Rabbi Isaac Mayer WISE, the American Reform movement was able to create a congregational union (1873), a rabbinical seminary, the Hebrew Union College (1875), and a rabbinical association (1889). The period of the late nineteenth and early twentieth centuries, today called "Classical Reform", was characterized by an absolute minimum of tradition and decided opposition to Jewish nationalism. Since the end of the First World War, however, Reform Judaism has moved increasingly away from its earlier position. Due in part to the growing influx of east European Jews into its ranks, it has reintroduced many traditional practices, given much greater attention to Hebrew, and become ardently Zionist.

While Reform Judaism today continues to move in the direction of tradition, giving serious consideration to Jewish law and the significance of ritual commandments, it maintains its liberal orientation in such matters as allowing wide autonomy to individual rabbis and congregations, insisting upon full equality of the sexes, and departing from the consensus where Jewish law seems in conflict with religious conscience and sensibility.

FURTHER READING

Meyer, M. A.: *Response to Modernity: A History of the Reform Movement in Judaism* (New York: Oxford University Press, 1988)

Philipson, D.: *The Reform Movement in Judaism* (New York: Macmillan Co., 1907; 3rd repr. New York: Ktav, 1967)

MICHAEL A. MEYER

Steve Reich at the Metropolitan Museum of Art, New York

Reggio, Isaac [Yashar] (1784–1855) Italian rabbi and thinker. He was born in Gorizia, and studied at first with his father, receiving a secular and Hebrew education. He inspired and promoted the Collegio Rabbinico Italiano which was opened in Padua in 1829 with the aim of ensuring that all future rabbis received Jewish philosophical and legalistic instruction. He was an exponent of the illuminist movement and his works bear the stamp of that epoch. Following the example of Moses MENDELSSOHN, Reggio published an Italian translation of the Pentateuch with a commentary in Hebrew (1821). This was preceded by *Ma'amar torah min hashamayim* (1818; The Law revealed), in which he discusses the divine law according to the speculations of the period. After his father's death, Reggio suceeded him as the rabbi of Gorizia in 1846.

Reggio's rationalism is evident in his most important work, *Hatorah vehafilosofiah* (1827; Law and philosophy). Here he addresses those readers who are still bound to the faith and attempts to demonstrate to them that the study of philosophy and of the sciences does not conflict with divine law. At the same time he defends the sacred text from its detractors. His analysis of the scroll of Esther, which he carried out in a critical spirit, publishing a Hebrew edition in 1841, is a work of great originality in which Reggio also utilizes archaeological sources. It prompted bitter criticism from Mendelssohn. Reggio had a profound knowledge of Italian Hebrew literature: he published editions of Elia del Medigo's *Behinat hadat* (Examination of religion) in 1833, and two essays by Leone da Modena under the title *Behinat hakabbalah* (Examination of tradition) in 1852, both with prefaces and notes. He was a friend of S. D. LUZZATTO, whom he saw as being one of the few scholars in Italy at that time; the two men carried on a close correspondence. Other writings by Reggio include *Mazkeret Yashar* (1849; an autobiography), and *A Guide for the Religious Instruction of Jewish Youth* (1855).

GABRIELLA MOSCATI-STEINDLER

Reich, Steve (b.1936) American composer, conductor, and percussionist. He was born in New York City and educated at Cornell University, where he majored in philosophy and took some music courses. During his college days he did a great deal of performing with jazz bands, playing a trap set. He received a BA in 1957 and moved back to New York City, where he studied privately with Hall Overton, then entered the Juilliard School to work with Vincent Persichetti and William Bergsma. While studying composition he also kept up his percussion playing and was greatly influenced by John Coltrane, whom he befriended during those years. In 1961 Reich enrolled as a graduate student at Mills College in California, where he continued his compositional studies with Darius MILHAUD and Luciano Berio. He became fascinated with African music systems through A. M. Jones' *Studies in African Music*. After receiving his master's degree in 1963 he settled in San Francisco, writing music for the San Francisco Mime Troupe, and presenting concerts at the San Francisco Tape Music Center. He formed a five-man ensemble specializing in free and controlled improvisation. For this ensemble, he wrote *Pitch Charts* (1963), which gave all the players the same notes to play but with a free rhythm. After less than a year's experience with this ensemble, Reich came to dislike this kind of improvisation and he returned to fully notated scores through "phase-shifting" exemplified by *It's Gonna Rain* (1965) he slowly developed his own kind of "minimalism" which is different from that of other "minimalist" composers. The new direction which Reich charted for himself is perhaps best seen in the works *Music for Eighteen Musicians* (1974–6), *Music for a Large Ensemble* (1978), and *Tehilim* (1980), in which new approaches to rhythm, harmony, and instrumentation combine with new structures, and even pseudo-biblical cantillation in *Tehilim*.

Steve Reich has become one of the most influential voices in the USA today, having written many works for various combinations, instruments, and voice, and including *Clapping Music* (1972) for two musicians clapping.

SAMUEL H. ADLER

Reinach, Joseph (1856–1921) French politician. In contrast to his two brothers, Joseph showed little interest in Jewish affairs. On the other hand, he took a brave public stand over the Dreyfus Affair, exceptional for a conservative Republican, an assimilated "Israelite of France", and a Reinach to boot, nephew and son-in-law of the notorious baron Jacques de Reinach implicated in the Panama Company scandal (1892). Undeterred by vicious attacks, official humiliation, and the loss of his parliamentary seat (at Digne for the period 1898–1906), he continued to play a crucial role on and off the Dreyfusard stage, determined to win a battle that had to be won. His seven-volume history of the Affair (*L'Histoire de l'Affaire Dreyfus*, 1901–8) remains indispensable even if its central thesis (Colonel Henry's treason) is now generally rejected. The Dreyfus Affair inspired a number of his other writings.

NELLY WILSON

Reinach, Salomon (1858–1932) French archeologist and historian. Prominent scholar, teacher (École du Louvre), curator of the Musée des Antiquités Nationales de Saint-Germain-en-Laye, author of authoritative works on ancient Greece and on the history of religions, Salomon made his most noteworthy archaeological contribution in his early twenties, as a member of the School of Athens (1879–82), with important archaeological discoveries at Myrina in Turkey. He was accused in certain Jewish circles of destroying Judaism with his erudition. There is some truth in the charge and it could be leveled against other scholars, Jewish and non-Jewish, who in the name of "sciences religieuses", a flourishing subject at that time at the École des Hautes Études, examined and compared sacred texts as if they were esoteric historical records to be deciphered and evaluated. This did not prevent Salomon from serving for many years on the council of the Jewish Colonization Association (1894–1932) and for even longer on the central committee of the ALLIANCE ISRAÉLITE UNIVERSELLE. His silence during the Dreyfus Affair is more curious but not uncharacteristic of the Jewish establishment. He at least seems to have been active behind the scenes. If, as is likely, he is the author behind the anonymous "archivist" who compiled *Drumont et Dreyfus, études sur la Libre Parole de 1894 à 1895* (1898), then he has left us one of the best-documented analyses of

Salomon Reinach

the climate which preceded and produced the Dreyfus Affair.

BIBLIOGRAPHY
Orpheus, a history of religions (1909), (London: Routledge, 1931)
Cultes, Mythes et Religions vols 1–5 (Paris: Leroux, 1905–23)

NELLY WILSON

Reinach, Théodore (1860–1928) French historian and numismatist. He was a man of many talents: lawyer, archaeologist, historian, notably of religion and ancient civilizations which he professed (École des Hautes Études). He directed *La Revue des études grecques* (1888–1907), *La Gazette des Beaux Arts* (1906–28), and the publication of the complete works of Josephus in French translation (1900–4); he translated Aristotle, Plutarch, and Shakespeare. He even tried his hand at politics (deputy for the Savoie 1906–14). His most original contribution was to numismatics which he taught

(Collège de France) and popularized (*Les Monnaies Juives*, 1887; *L'Histoire par les Monnaies*, 1902). In French–Jewish circles he is best remembered perhaps for his outspoken, total assimilationist stance. In *L'histoire des Israélites depuis leur dispersion jusqu'à nos jours* (1885) he claims that French–Jewish history came to an end in 1791; henceforth it is inappropriate to speak of French Jews; they are French citizens professing the Israelitic religion. And since the latter consists essentially of an ethic of justice, it is perfectly assimilable into French traditions. Few have taken Franco-Jewish symbiosis further back into history: he discerned its first manifestation in the Middle Ages. The Dreyfus Affair temporarily shook his faith but never his love. "Continue to love France", he told an audience of Jewish school children at the height of the Affair, "as one loves a mother even when she is unjust" (Quoted in: Phillippe, Béatrice: *Les Juifs dans le monde contemporain*. Paris: MA Editions, 1986, p.86).

NELLY WILSON

Reinhardt, Max (1873–1943) Austrian theater producer and director. Born in Baden bei Wien, Reinhardt became an actor in his teens and gained his first post at 17 as assistant director at the Salzburger Stadttheater. In 1894 he was engaged by Otto Brahm for the Deutsches Theater in Berlin, where Reinhardt soon gained a large reputation. In 1905 Reinhardt succeeded Brahm and proceeded to dominate the theater world of Berlin until the 1930s. After 1918 Reinhardt was also a major force in Viennese theater, and was a co-founder of the Salzburg Festival. From 1934 Reinhardt was often in the USA, and from 1937 he was in permanent residence there.

Reinhardt is one of the dominant figures in modern theater. He has been seen as having attempted to integrate the Baroque tradition of Vienna with the literary and intellectual tradition of Berlin. Although the importance of the Viennese influence on him has been contested, it is clear that Reinhardt took German theater away from Naturalism towards a more imaginative use of the stage, where the subjective will of the director became of paramount importance.

Max Reinhardt, c.1910

He pioneered innovations in the theater such as the revolving stage, and ensemble acting. His greatest innovation was the phenomenon of the star director of which he was the first, as a result of his epoch-making production of *A Midsummer Night's Dream* in 1905. Other famous productions include *The Miracle* (1911), *Oedipus Rex* (1910), and *Jedermann* (1920).

Reinhardt remained a professing Jew until his death. Although this rarely intruded directly on his work in the theater, Reinhardt was plainly conscious of his Jewishness and of that of others, as entries in his diary show. He rejected

Zionism, but the extent of his identification with the Jewish people is shown in his agreeing to produce *The Eternal Road* in New York in 1937. A response to a plea to help the Jewish cause, this play is not without its ambiguities. Reinhardt chose Franz WERFEL, a quasi-Catholic, to write the script, Kurt WEILL, a Marxist atheist, to write the music, and the anti-Semitic Norman Bel Geddes as stage designer. Despite this the production was a great critical success, although certain negative aspects of Werfel's text did not go unnoticed.

FURTHER READING

Reinhardt, G.: *The Genius: A Memoir of Max Reinhardt* (New York: Knopf, 1979)

STEVEN BELLER

religious thought, twentieth-century Jewish

The twentieth century marks a bold new chapter in Jewish religious thought. It is a period in which Jewish thinkers endeavored to free themselves of the apologetic motive that burdened their immediate predecessors who labored under the shadow of the struggle for emancipation and acceptance. Eager to hasten the exit of their brethren from the ghetto and its indignities, Jewish intellectuals since Moses MENDELSSOHN were understandably sensitive to the image of Judaism prevailing in the host society; accordingly, they sought to present Judaism in its most appealing attire before the forum of Gentile opinion and judgement. To be sure, responding to the challenge to explain oneself to others can often be an instructive and illuminating exercise, as indeed it was. The apologetic motive stimulated much that was productive and enriching. With an eye on the ethical idealism and universal values of the Enlightenment and liberal opinion of the nineteenth century, Jewish thinkers identified aspects of Israel's religious and spiritual heritage that might otherwise have remained inchoate. Thus, nineteenth-century Jewish thinkers highlighted the ethical components of Judaism as well as its universal mission and significance; moreover, by often formulating their understanding of Judaism with the inflections and categories of the then regnant philosophical discourse, they served to renew the venerated tradition of Jewish philosophy largely dormant since the late middle Ages. The danger of such apologetics, however, is that they may lead one to adopt the criteria – the perspective and vocabulary – of the opposing cultures and faith systems to evaluate one's own tradition. Adjudging one's own culture and religion through the prism of the other may be distorting and perhaps lead one to a disaffection with one's ancestral heritage and faith.

Twentieth-century Jewish religious thinkers are increasingly cognizant of this danger. Clearly, they are inspired by the renascence of Jewish life whose initial energy came largely from Zionism – the movement of Jewish national self-assertion and pride that formally came into being when Theodor HERZL convened the First Zionist Congress in Basel, Switzerland, in August 1897. To uplift the downtrodden people of Israel, Herzl placed emphasis on the reappropriation of political power and sovereignty: other Zionists – such as AHAD HA'AM and Martin BUBER – felt Jewish pride would be rekindled by the renewal of Jewish culture. These "cultural Zionists" noted the paradox that ever since the Jews had left the ghetto and pursued the goal of social and political acceptance by fervently adopting the high culture of the host society they became proportionately illiterate in Judaism. With astounding celerity, the children and grandchildren of rabbis joined the forefront of European arts and sciences and, in the process, lost their knowledge of Judaism, its teachings, and literature.

The cultural Zionists advocated the reacquistion of Hebrew as essential to the reeducation of the Jews. Yet they were also profoundly aware that Hebrew and a knowledge of the literary sources of Judaism of themselves would no longer be sufficient to engage the soul and imagination of the Jew. For having once experienced the modern world – which in its deepest sense, of course, cannot be construed as the mere province of the Gentiles but as an unprecedented opening of the human spirit sponsored, perchance, by the Gentiles – the Jew cannot, indeed for the most part, will not renounce it. As the late Robert Weltsch (1891–1982), a leading proponent of cultural Zionism in Germany, observed:

Sometimes it is argued that for Jews emancipation and assimilation, i.e. the entry into the modern world, was a disaster which should have been rejected; all contact with the modern world necessarily produces the inducements to desertion and/ or heresy . . . In our post-emancipation age not many will share this view . . . It would be quixotic to try to arrest the march of time or to shut the door to the modern world. Most Jews of our age are convinced that they have been immeasurably enriched by the modern culture and would not want to miss it. As to Judaism, the decisive question was whether it could be fitted into the new pattern of life. (Editor's introduction, *Leo Baeck Institute Year Book* VI, 1961).

Indeed, as denizens of the twentieth century, the overarching question confronting Jews is how to remain active participants in the modern, "secular" world and still be passionate, self-respecting, and responsible Jews. With respect to religion, whose revealed authority one is to accept, the question has a particular twist. To be a believing Jew, indeed a religious person in general, in the twentieth century, as R. J. Zwi Werblowsky of the Hebrew University of Jerusalem has put it, means that one "is fully aware of living after Darwin, Karl MARX, Sigmund FREUD, Weber, and Émile DURKHEIM. He is also aware of living after Kant, Hegel, Nietzsche, Dostoyevski and Kierkegaard". In affirming Judaism one can discard neither modern biblical criticism nor the critical perspectives that inform the modern sensibility. Hence, the modern Jew of faith "no longer wastes time on arguing with Wellhausen, or Freud, or Marx, or Darwin. Whatever his reservations regarding major or minor details, he takes them all for granted. And taking them for granted he asks: where do we go from here?" (*Beyond Tradition and Modernity*, London: 1976.)

New strategies were thus required for affirming the tradition as an intellectually compelling and personally meaningful mode of divine service. In particular, for those trying to find their way back to Judaism, a new approach to the study of the religious texts of the tradition was required, a manner of reading these texts that would allow one to behold their sacrality – their divine dimension – without surrendering the integrity of one's "secular" experience and understanding. Such an interpretative or hermeneutical strategy was elaborated by Martin

Buber and his younger colleague Franz ROSENZWEIG, two German–Jewish religious philosophers who set the tone of much of twentieth-century Jewish thought.

Buber and Rosenzweig spoke of reading the texts as a dialogue: listening to the texts – and to listen properly, of course, one has to understand them properly, optimally in the original Hebrew – and allow their voice to be heard unencumbered by the preconceptions and bias of the age, while at the same time not denying one's own consciousness and sensiblity. One conducts, so to speak, a dialogue with the texts. Reading is thus pre-eminently an act of, to use Buber's expression, "I and Thou".

Rosenzweig sought to extend the concept of dialogue to the *mitzvot*, the ritual precepts enjoined by the tradition as the Word of God. Rosenzweig – whose journey to Judaism from the threshhold of conversion to Christianity singularly inspired his and subsequent generations – insisted that Jewish faith must be grounded in *Offenbarungsglaube*, a belief in revelation as an existential reality. As a divine address, he affirmed, revelation is a not an abstract, eternal occurrence, but an address to a particular human being who "has a first and last name", it is an address of the divine I to a human Thou. Buber concurred. The question was whether the *mitzvot* were in fact the revealed Word of God. Rosenzweig insisted that they indeed constituted God's address to the Jew. In contrast to Orthodox Jews, however, he could not accept the *mitzvot* on the basis of rabbinic authority, for as he once remarked, "faith based on authority is equal to unbelief". His approach to "the Law", as he explained in a now famous open letter to Buber, was rather to encourage each individual Jew to explore the sacramental and existential possibilities of the *mitzvot*, so determining which of the precepts one personally feels called upon by God to fulfil. As he further elaborated his position to Buber with reference to a rabbinic commentary to Isaiah liv.13, we are not only God's obedient "children" (*banayikh*), but also his "builders" (*bonayikh*): every generation has the opportunity, indeed the task, of re-creating the Law for itself. (Cf. "The Builders. Concerning the Law" (1925), in Rosenzweig, *On Jewish Learning*, 1965).

Buber demurred. God, "the Eternal Thou", he held, addresses one through varied and protean life-experiences – from the ephemeral and seemingly trivial to the grand and momentous – that demand a dialogical response, or a confirmation of the Thou, the unique presence, of the other who stands before one. God's address is refracted, that is revealed, through the addressing presence of the Thou who stands before one. As a response to the continuously renewing presence and address of the other-cum-God, dialogue must be born ever anew. The I–Thou response, Buber emphasized, thus requires spontaneity, and cannot be determined by fixed expressions, gestures, and formulations. Authentic service to God – and this is the core of Buber's teaching – is then found in such spontaneous responses to the Eternal Thou who turns to one through the flux of life. Not surprisingly, he could not accept Rosenzweig's proposition that the *mitzvot* bear God's address. "I do not believe that revelation is ever a formulation of law", he explained to his friend. "I cannot [accept] the law . . . if I am to hold myself ready as well for the unmediated word of God directed to a specific hour of life" (ibid.).

Buber and Rosenzweig respectively represent two alternative conceptions of Jewish spiritual renewal. Defying denominational labels, Rosenzweig's undogmatic traditionalism, guided by a phenomenological reconstruction of the existential meaning of Jewish observance, was focused on the synagogue as a community of study, prayer, and ritual. Buber celebrated Jewish spirituality as it appertains to the troubled secular realm of everyday life of interpersonal and intercommunal relations. Within the "common landscape" of Judaism both Buber and Rosenzweig encouraged diversity of expression.

Their sanction of diversity conforms with the sociological reality of twentieth-century Jewry. This diversity is no longer comprehended simply by the denominationalism introduced in the previous century: it crosses such boundaries and reflects the relentlessly dynamic character of an age that constantly generates new ideas, insights, values, communal demarcations, and affiliations, and even new identities. The pluralism, which is said to be one of the salient emblems of the age, does not simply characterize the diversity of cultures and religions within a given society; as the sociologist Peter Berger has observed, in its most profound sense this pluralism is within the individual. The modern individual, Berger points out, consciously lives within plural and ever shifting "worlds" of ideas, interests, and perceptions. In that there is often a discontinuity between these "worlds", it may be said that the abiding challenge to modern Jewish thought, religious and secular alike, is to illuminate for the individual Jew how a continuity of Jewish identity and community may be maintained while accommodating the irrefrangible reality of this discontinuity and ever-unfolding pluralism. (Cf. P. Mendes-Flohr, "Jewish Continuity in an Age of Discontinuity", in P. Mendes-Flohr, *Divided Passions: The Jewish Intellectuals and The Experience of Modernity*, 1989.)

It is Rosenzweig's and Buber's greatness that they recognized this challenge and established Jewish religious thought as a serious discourse – unfettered by sermonic appeal and apologetic contrivance – addressed to the modern Jew who finds himself or herself firmly rooted in the contemporary experience. They inspired, both in terms of agenda and tone of discourse, the unprecedented galaxy of Jewish religious thinkers, representing virtually every stream of organized Jewish life, that has emerged, especially in the post-Second World War period. Voices like Arthur A. Cohen (1928–86), Emil L. FACKENHEIM, Abraham Jehoshua HESCHEL, Louis JACOBS, Mordecai KAPLAN, Joseph Dov SOLOVEITCHIK were clearly emboldened by their earnest and urbane endeavor to formulate Judaism as an existentially and intellectually engaging mode of existence and divine service.

Buber and Rosenzweig may also be credited with introducing into twentieth-century Jewish thought an unabashedly theocentric orientation. In his very first essay on religious matters, Rosenzweig observed that, bereft of a belief in divine revelation, theology arrives at the strange anthropocentric brew concocted by the nineteenth century which, in placing religion within the realm of human sensibility alone – be it called "spiritual experience", "moral consciousness", or "national soul" – "is in effect godless". (Cf. "Atheistische Theologie", Rosenzweig: *Kleinere Schriften*, 1935.) This theocentric orientation permits the religious imagination to stand over against culture – the secular sphere – in a dialectic relation. Bound to a transcendent reality, revealed through and in the Torah, one may relate to the world without being submerged in it.

The emerging critical tension between the religious and the temporal is most poignantly raised by Zionism. Sponsoring the Jews' return to history – to the ranks of the politically sovereign protagonists of history – Zionism has been regarded by some Orthodox Jews as an act of divine providence. As the first Chief Rabbi of Palestine, Abraham Isaac KOOK declared, God has chosen Zionism, despite its emphatically secular character, as his instrument of redemption. Viewing history from the perspective of the kabbalistic teaching that external events are but symbolic reflections of a deeper, hidden reality, Rabbi Kook firmly believed that the restoration of the people of Israel to their ancient patrimony was a messianic event, and that the many wordly problems attendant to Zionism – power politics and its moral ambiguities, war and conflict with the Arabs – would thus be miraculously resolved by the imminent arrival of the messiah. Other Orthodox thinkers, such as Yeshayahu LEIBOWITZ, strenuously reject any eschatological "mystification" of Zionism. Leibowitz resolutely refuses to ascribe any messianic significance to Zionism and the State of Israel. He is particularly fond of citing Maimonides' admonition that one should desist from messianic speculations, for "they lead neither to the fear [of God] nor to love of [him]" (Melakhim xii.2). Assuming a rigorously theocentric view of Judaism, he further contends that those who attribute religious or any other intrinsic value to the state are committing the cardinal sin of idolatry (*'avodah zarah*), the worship of false gods. The state and the Zionist movement have but an "instrumental" value, that is to fulfill certain pragmatic functions on behalf of the Jewish people. Accordingly, Leibowitz sternly rebukes the "modern Sabbateans" (that is the followers of the seventeenth-century pseudo-messiah Shabatai Zevi) for whom "the nation has become God, and the homeland Torah" (*Judaism, the Jewish People and the State of Israel*, 1975 [Hebrew]).

Leibowitz does not wish to gainsay the achievements of Zionism. Although an instrument devised by human beings and thus of no intrinsic religious significance, Zionism is acclaimed by him as the movement for the political liberation of the Jewish people. Concomitant to this achievement is the restoration of the unity of the Jewish people and the sense of mutual responsibility – a principle evoked by Herzl when he ceremoniously exclaimed at the Basel congress of 1897, "We are one people".

This principle – unity of the Jewish people – may be said to have become axiomatic for Jewish thought, Zionist and non-Zionist, in the twentieth century. The American theologian Mordecai Kaplan even integrated the principle as central motif of his view of a Judaism as a "civilization". As a civilization, Judaism is, for Kaplan, pre-eminently the life of the Jewish people for whom religion serves the pragmatic function of enhancing its well-being and dignity, as well as giving expression to its collective consciousness, shared values, and sense of history.

The affirmation of unity and mutual responsibility of the Jewish people has been decisively reinforced by the Holocaust and the tragic sense that all Jews everywhere are "survivors" bound by a common fate. This feeling has been most forcefully articulated by Emil Fackenheim who discerns in Auschwitz a commandment to Jews to endure and to ensure the survival of Judaism, lest Hitler be granted a "posthumous victory" (*Quest for Past and Present*, 1968).

Reflecting on the nature of Jewish unity and community, post-Holocaust Jewish thinkers have given new focus on the covenant as the matrix of a two-fold responsibility to God and one's fellow Jew. The covenant, as the French philosopher Emmanuel LÉVINAS argues, is the basis of a biblical humanism that Jews are enjoined to preserve tenaciously not only in the wake of Auschwitz but also in the face of the self-serving egotism that presently masquerades as liberty in Western culture. The wisdom of the covenant is that the Jew attains transcendence and thus liberty by paradoxically living under the law of God's covenant which requires of one ethical and social responsibility for the other. As custodians of biblical humanism, Lévinas avers, Judaism defiantly proclaims to the contemporary world that liberty entails responsibility and obligation.

FURTHER READING

Bergman, S. H.: *Faith and Reason: An Introduction to Modern Jewish Thought*, trans. A. Jospe, (New York: Schocken, 1963)

Cohen, A. A., and Mendes-Flohr, P., eds: *Contemporary Jewish Religious Thought: Original Essays On Critical concepts, Movements and Beliefs*, (New York: Scribners, 1986)

Jacobs, L.: *Jewish Thought Today*, (New York: Behrman, 1970)

Katz, S. T., ed.: *Jewish Philosophers*, (Jerusalem: Keter, 1975)

Mendes-Flohr, P.: Jewish thought and philosophy: modern thought. *The Encyclopedia of Religion* (New York: Macmillan & Free Press, 1987) vol. 8, 70–82

PAUL MENDES-FLOHR

Reyzen [Reisin, Raisin], **Avrom** (1876–1953) Yiddish poet and story writer. Born in Koydenev, White Russia, Reyzen was the son of a poor wheat merchant who wrote poems in both Hebrew and Yiddish. He was the older brother of Zalmen REYZEN, compiler of the four-volume *Leksikon* of Yiddish writers, and of Sarah, the poetess. In his childhood he received a traditional Hebrew education. He also learned Russian and German. He began tutoring aged 14 to earn extra money for the family. In 1890, aged only 15, he sent samples of his writing to I. L. PERETZ in Warsaw. To his delight, Peretz published one of his poems "Ven dos lebn iz farbitert" (When this life is embittered) in *Yidishe biblyotek* (The Yiddish library) in 1891. Drafted into the Russian army for four years aged 21, he was released from unpleasant duties when he joined the regimental band. A 48-page volume of his poems was published in 1902 entitled *Tsayt-lider* (Current songs). This was well received and was also published in New York where a review in the daily Yiddish newspaper *Forverts* sang its praises. He attended the Yiddish Language Conference in Chernovitz in 1908 where he strongly defended Yiddish as national Jewish language. Visiting the USA in 1911 he edited a new literary weekly *Dos naye land* (The New Country) for several months. Many of his works were published in periodicals in Europe and the USA. He settled in New York at the outbreak of the First World War, where he contributed regularly to Yiddish papers and magazines. His poems are written in simple quatrains. He crafted his literary Yiddish into lyrical poetry while retaining natural, flowing idiomatic language. The central figures of his poems and stories are the poor and rejected members of society about whom nobody cares. He evokes their plight, not in a depressing manner but by instilling them with gentle dignity. In New York, new hopeful Yiddish writers came to Reyzen in the Europa Café on East Broadway where he sat most days with other Yiddish literary figures. There they would read their poetry or prose to him hoping to win his approval. He received them all with patience and kindness. He died in New York in 1953 where he was popular among his peers both as an author and as an amiable man.

DEVRA KAY

Reyzen [Reisen, Raizin], **Zalmen** (1887–c.1941) Yiddish scholar. Born in Koydenev, White Russia, Reyzen spent time as a youth in Mohilne and Vinitse (in the Ukraine), and in Minsk. He moved to Vilna in 1915 where he quickly became a leader of the new Yiddish culture movement. He edited the Yiddish daily *Vilner tog* from 1919 to 1939, and was lecturer in Yiddish and Yiddish grammar at the Folk University and the Vilna Yiddish Teachers' Seminary.

Reyzen published an experimental Yiddish grammar in 1908, and a vastly more sophisticated work, *Gramatik fun der yidisher shprakh* (Grammar of the Yiddish language) in 1920 in which he standardized modern Yiddish orthography. His *Fun Mendelson biz Mendele* (1923) is a cardinal work on the origins of modern Yiddish literature. He was one of the editors of the pioneer journal *Yidishe filologye* (1924; Yiddish philology) and a co-founder of the Yivo Institute for Jewish Research in 1925. Author of a large number of linguistic and literary studies, Reyzen is best known for his *Leksikon*, a biographical and bibliographical encyclopedia of Yiddish literature. The first one-volume edition (1914) included old as well as modern Yiddish literature, and a list of Yiddish periodicals and pseudonyms. The now classic four-volume edition, *Leksikon fun der yidisher literatur, prese un filologye* (1926–9), restricted to modern Yiddish literature, documented the phenomenal growth of Yiddish belles lettres to the end of the first quarter of the twentieth century. To this day, it remains the best source of comprehensive, accurate, and unbiased information on modern Yiddish literature. Reyzen's love of Yiddish was legendary. His role in winning universal acceptance of the notion "modern Yiddish literature" as an acknowledged fact rather than a dream was crucial in the twentieth-century rise of modern Yiddish culture.

Reyzen was arrested by the Red Army in September 1939, and murdered by Soviet forces in the early 1940s.

DOVID KATZ

Reznikoff, Charles (1894–1976) American poet and author. Born in Brooklyn of immigrant parents, whose story he movingly told in *Family Chronicle* (1969), Reznikoff from early manhood wanted to be a writer. He studied journalism at the University of Missouri, and law at New York University, in neither case finding a profession compatible with his wish to write. Legal training enabled him to work in various editorial and journalistic posts. Although he wrote steadily from 1918, when his first small book, *Rhythms*, appeared, until his death, it was only in the 1960s that he had public recognition. His poetry, strongly influenced by Ezra Pound and the spare doctrines of Imagism, remained largely of a piece through nearly six decades, exemplifying the prose virtues of direct statement. The subject matter of Reznikoff's verse altered dramatically: he began as an observer of the urban tenement-dweller, but from the late 1920s, began a study of Hebrew, Jewish liturgy, and history, making himself into a consciously Jewish poet. He also wrote *Testimony* (prose version 1934; verse, 2 vols, 1965–8), poems based upon United States legal reports. His "cold impartiality" upset critics who were unaccustomed to such themes in contemporary verse. The same objectivity formed the basis of Reznikoff's association with the Objectivist movement (Louis ZUKOFSKY, GEORGE OPPEN, and Rakosi) in the 1930s, and enabled him to write unadorned, deeply moving poems about the Holocaust (1975). A gentle man, revered for his humanity, he had an ability to confront directly the worst of humankind. Although for most of his adult life he had no publisher or audience and was forced to print his verse in small private editions, at the time of his death, Reznikoff was acknowledged as the leading poet in the English language to have so directly engaged with the meaning of his religion and the history of his people. He married the author and Zionist Marie SYRKIN in 1930.

FURTHER READING

Hindus, M., ed.: *Charles Reznikoff: Man and Poet* (Orono: National Poetry Foundation/University of Maine, 1984)

ERIC HOMBERGER

Ribalow, Menachem (1895–1953) Hebrew essayist and editor. Born in the Volhynian town of Chudnov, Ribalow studied at a *yeshivah* and at the University of Moscow before emigrating to the USA in 1921. In 1923 he was appointed editor of the New York Hebrew weekly *Hado'ar*, a position he held until his death. Ribalow was influential in progagating the cause of Hebrew in the USA and was co-president (with Yitzhak BEN-ZVI) of the World Hebrew Union. Under the pseudonym M. Shoshani he published hundreds of articles, mostly on Hebrew poetry. These essays were collected in five volumes: *Sefer hamassot* (1928; Book of essays), *Soferim veishim* (1936; Writers and personalities), *Ketavim 'umegillot* (1942; Writings and scrolls), *Im hakad el hamabu'a* (1950; With the pitcher to the spring), and *Me'olam le'olam* (1955; From world to world). Ribalow also edited a number of Hebrew annuals and anthologies. A selection of his essays appeared in English, *The Flowering of Hebrew Literature* (1959).

DAVID ABERBACH

Rice, Elmer [Elmer Leopold Reisenstein] (1892–1967) American dramatist. Rice was born in New York City, the grandchild of immigrants from Germany. He attended night school after the age of 14 and was admitted to the bar but gave up law in 1913 to write plays.

In the next year he achieved commercial and critical success with a courtroom drama, *On Trial*. He wrote over 50 plays, most of them produced on Broadway, where he was also active as an adaptor and collaborator, and later as a director and producer. He also wrote screenplays, some adapted from his own dramatic work. Dissatisfied with Broadway, he was briefly associated with the Federal Theater Project and helped form the Playwrights' Company.

Although Rice once rivaled O'Neill as America's greatest dramatist, most of his plays now seem competent rather than brilliant, and somewhat dated in their political and economic views. A few, more experimental in their time, have historical value: *The Adding Machine* (1923) and *Street Scene* (1929), for example, introduced such formal innovations to the American stage as, respectively, Expressionism and Naturalism. a Pulitzer Prize winner, *Street Scene* is essentially a mosaic of vignettes drawn from the lives of families representing the city's ethnic diversity; it includes a stereotypical Jewish family, the Kaplans – Marxist father, poetic son, and schoolteacher daughter, who are among the few Jewish characters Rice ever created. In *Counsellor-at-Law* (1931), however, he presented a Jew as an outsider in conflict with the dominant American ethos.

BIBLIOGRAPHY

Minority Report: An Autobiography (New York: Simon & Schuster, 1963)

FURTHER READING

Behringer, F.: Elmer Rice. In *Dictionary of Literary Biography* vol. 7 (Detroit: Gale Research Co., 1981)

Chametzky, J.: Elmer Rice, liberation, and the great ethnic question. In *From Hester Street to Hollywood*, ed. S. B. Cohen (Bloomington: Indiana University Press, 1983)

MICHAEL SHAPIRO

Rich, Adrienne (b.1929) American poet. Rich's poetry, initially tightly controlled and restrained, brought her early recognition by critics and other poets. Her first book of verse, *A Change of World*, was chosen by W. H. Auden for the Yale Younger Poets Award and published in 1951; a Guggenheim Fellowship followed in 1952–3, when she traveled in Europe and England. In 1960 Rich won the National Institute of Arts and Letters Award for poetry, and was awarded another Guggenheim Fellowship in 1961–2, which took her to the Netherlands for a year. In 1962 she won a Bollingen Foundation grant for translation of Dutch poetry.

During this period, Rich married Alfred H. Conrad, an economist who taught at Harvard, and had three sons. When not traveling overseas they lived in Cambridge, Massachusetts, and Rich served as Phi Beta Kappa poet at William and Mary College, at Swarthmore College, and then at Harvard College. In 1966 Rich and her family moved to New York City and she grew active in protests against the war in Vietnam. Rich's poetry became radicalized as well, moving away from the neatly honed blank verse which had been her trademark, to freer forms of expression. In 1969 she published a book of verse entitled *Leaflets*; the name expressed her new conviction that the goal of her art is to illuminate present life at the moment it is lived, rather than to be held back, worked, and reworked, with the goal that it will last forever.

In 1970, Rich's husband died. She became increasingly involved in the radical feminist movement. When she was awarded a National Book Award for her 1973 book of verse, *Diving into the Wreck*, she refused to accept the award as an individual, and instead accepted it in the name of all women.

Rich continues to produce volumes of verse. *Poems: Selected and New* was published in 1975. Her most recent book, *A Wild Patience Has Taken Me This Far*, was published in 1981. A self-proclaimed lesbian poet, she writes frequently of historical women, such as Willa Cather and Ethel Rosenberg, and she often uses imagery drawn from female experience to illuminate the task of writing poetry as well as the tasks of living life.

SYLVIA FISHMAN

Richler, Mordecai (b.1931) Canadian

novelist. Richler is a third-generation Canadian born in Montreal. As a young man, Richler went to Europe to become a writer. His first novel, *The Acrobats* (1954), takes place in Spain and reflects the influence of Hemingway and the French existentialists. Richler subsequently settled in London for two decades working as novelist, journalist, and screenwriter. In 1970 he returned to Montreal.

Richler has become a controversial figure in both Gentile and Jewish circles. The Canadian community has found it difficult to accept his often dismissive view of Canadian culture manifested in many of his articles, essays, and the satiric novel *The Incomparable Atuk* (1963). The bestseller *The Apprenticeship of Duddy Kravitz* (1959), was denounced in the Jewish community. Richler's portrayal of a Jewish boy who establishes his financial empire through ruthless manipulation and conniving was perceived as evidence of the novelist's Jewish self-hatred. Nonetheless, many critics have considered the novel a successful satiric criticism of today's society at large. It was adapted as a movie which won several international prizes. Richler's satiric outlook reaches its extreme in *Cocksure* (1968) which presents an absurd vision of the world taken over by a self-reproducing tycoon, while the subplot of this black comedy depicts Jewish characters who exploit and victimize their Gentile counterparts.

Richler's consciousness of Jewish history of suffering emerges in his 1971 critically acclaimed novel, *St Urbain's Horseman*. The protagonist's obsessive preoccupation with the fantasy of a heroic avenger of the Holocaust initiates an examination of the self-image of the North American Jew today. The scrutiny is pursued in *Joshua Then and Now* (1980), which tells a story of a Canadian Jew obsessed with the desire to avenge his own defeat in an encounter with an ex-Nazi officer.

Deeply rooted in the Montreal "ghetto", Richler struggles to resolve the ambivalence of post-war Jewish identity. He often identifies himself as "the loser's advocate", a moralist, and a staunch believer in liberal humanism; at the same time, his writing reveals preoccupation with Jewish vulnerability in today's world.

BIBLIOGRAPHY

The Son of a Smaller Hero (London: André Deutsch, 1955); *A Choice of Enemies* (London: André Deutsch, 1957); *Shovelling Trouble* (London: Quartet Books, 1973); *Notes on the Endangered Species* (1974); *Home Sweet Home* (1985)

FURTHER READING

Darling, M., ed.: *Perspectives on Mordecai Richler* (Toronto: ECW Press, 1986)

Woodcock, G.: *Mordecai Richler* (Toronto: McClelland & Stewart, 1971)

RACHEL FELDHAY BRENNER

Rivers, Larry [Yitzroch Loiza Grossberg] (b.1923) American painter and sculptor. He works in a wide range of often experimental techniques and unorthodox media; he also produces stage designs, video, and poetry. He combines an impressive technical virtuosity with an irreverent attitude to the sanctity of art.

Born in the Bronx, New York, he began his career as a professional jazz saxophonist. He began to paint in 1945 and in 1947 studied at art school; in 1951 he graduated from New York University with a BA in art education. Whilst the modern movement was dominated by abstraction, Rivers remained a dedicated figurative artist. Early influences included Pierre Bonnard, Chaim SOUTINE and Willem de Kooning – whose *Woman* series sparked off a series of paintings by Rivers (1952). In 1951 he began producing sculpture. As the Pop artists were to do, he took well-known images and used them in unexpected ways, but the images he used were often those dear to the American people, and he gave new meaning to the phrase "history painting": his 1954/5 painting, *Washington Crossing the Delaware* (damaged 1958; new version 1960; New York, Museum of Modern Art), was based on the work by Emanuel Leutz in the Metropolitan Museum, New York. In 1965 he produced the monumental *A history of the Russian Revolution: from Marx to Mayakovsky* (Hirshhorn Museum and Sculpture Garden, Smithsonian Institute, Washington, DC). In the 1970s he became more involved in working with video.

While Rivers's works are in many ways autobiographical, the Jewish element has appeared only sporadically; he is not a traditional believer but he has always been conscious of the Jews' spiritual and ethnic heritage. In 1954 he produced designs for a series of the Ten Commandments for a synagogue in Connecticut, but they

were rejected. In the 1950s and 1960s Rivers produced a number of works based on family photographs, such as *Europe II* (1956) and *Bar Mitzvah photograph painting* (1961). His major work in this area, however, is *The History of Matzah (The story of the Jewish People)* (1982–5). This vast triptych covers nearly 4,000 years of Jewish experience, with over sixty scenes drawn from various sources and incorporating pieces of text, all set against the tan and brown background of the matzah, which serves a multiple purpose: not only is it a symbol of deliverance from oppression but it is dry and burnt and featureless like the desert through which the Jews wandered, and its flat two-dimensional quality perfectly fulfils the requirements of modern painting, unifying the picture plane.

BIBLIOGRAPHY

with C. Brightman: *Drawings and Digressions* (New York: Clarkson N. Potter, 1979)

FURTHER READING

Kleebatt, N. L., and Friedman, A.: *History of Matzah: The Story of the Jews*, (New York: Jewish Museum, 1984) [good bibliography]

CATHERINE PHILLIPS

Rogers, Bernard (1893–1968) American composer, educator, and critic. He was born in New York City and died in Rochester, New York. He was educated at the Institute of Musical Art in New York City and the Cleveland Institute. In 1927 he went to London to study with Frank Bridge and in 1928–9 to Paris to work with Nadia Boulanger. Rogers became an editor and the chief critic of *Musical America* 1913–24, and during 1926–7 he taught at the Hartt School of Music. He was appointed as an instructor at the Eastman School of Music in Rochester, New York, in 1929 and taught there until 1967, when he retired as head of the composition department.

Bernard Rogers was one of the most revered teachers on the American scene and honored by the National Institute of Arts and Letters (1947), and was awarded the Lillian Fairchild Award (1962); he received honorary doctorates from Valparaiso University and Wayne State University, and commissions from the Koussevitsky Foundation, the Ford Foundation, and the Juilliard School, among many others.

Biblical and esoteric subjects, and paintings of both the Eastern and Western worlds were the inspiration for most of Rogers's output. Though he often used unconventional rhythms and complex sonorities, his music is mostly of a conservative nature, beautifully crafted, extremely colorful in orchestration, and deeply rooted in traditional practices and structures. He was a most prolific composer and wrote many dramatic works.

SAMUEL H. ADLER

Rosenberg, Harold (b.1906)

American Art critic. Born in Williamsburg, Brooklyn, Rosenberg was educated at City College, and at St Lawrence University, from which he graduated with a law degree in 1927. He became one of the socially conscious Greenwich Village intellectuals whose art attempted to serve Depression-era causes. In 1947 he founded an art magazine, *Possibilities*, with Robert Motherwell. He also served as national art editor for the WPA American Guides series from 1938 to 1942.

The Tradition of the New (1959) depicted the pressures put upon artists to innovate. The demands of the market forced artists to exceed their own resources, and resulted in a response called Action Painting. The canvas ceased being a space upon which an object was represented, and became an arena in which to act.

In 1967 Rosenberg became art critic for the *New Yorker*. His weekly columns were later published in a number of collections.

Rosenberg taught at the University of Chicago, the University of California, Berkeley (1962), Princeton (1963), and Southern Illinois University (1965). He has been the recipient of two honorary doctorates, and the Frank Jewett Mather Award of the College Art Association of America (1964).

RUTH ROSENBERG

Rosenberg, Isaac (1890–1918)

English poet and painter. Rosenberg was born in Bristol. In

Isaac Rosenberg Self Portrait *1911. Tate Gallery, London*

1897 the family moved to the peripheries of the Jewish ghetto in the East End of London. His sister, Annie Wynick, said that the move was prompted by their expectation of becoming better-off, but they became poorer, and Rosenberg's health (his lungs), never robust, became worse. The family's first lodging was above a carpenter's workshop, and was visited by rats (Cohen says, "at the back of a rag-and-bone shop"). Thus the rat in one of Rosenberg's most celebrated so-called "Trench" poems, "Break of Day in the Trenches", is a creature endowed with a powerful fanged intelligence, yet is seen without horror, as a familiar. Of more positive value to Rosenberg was the Jewish intellectual activity in the East End and, rooted in this, was Rosenberg's friendship with Joseph Leftwich, John Rodker, and Samuel Winsten c.1911. Rosenberg was later to form friendships with the painters David BOMBERG and Mark GERTLER, all three of them at the Slade School of Fine Art. It was, in fact, through the generosity of three Jewish ladies that Rosenberg attended the Slade School in 1911–14, but even by 1912, Rosenberg, in reply to criticism from one of these patrons, declared, with respect to his art, "I believe I have begun too late". However, another different, if related, growth was taking place in Rosenberg. By the end of 1915 he wrote to another of his patrons, Edward Marsh, "I think I get more depth into my writing". Rosenberg's first known poem was written in 1905. By 1914–15 he had produced mature representative poems such as "None have seen the Lord of the House" and "Midsummer Frost".

Rosenberg enlisted in October 1915. By August 1916 he was in the trenches of the Western Front, and had apparently written, in the trenches, "Break of Day in the Trenches". Rosenberg refused promotion and remained a private. In return, the war destroyed him in some obscure operation on 1 April 1918.

Rosenberg paid for three pamphlets of his work to be privately printed: *Night and Day* (1912), *Youth* (1915), and *Moses* (1916) which contains both poems and the verse play *Moses*, this latter unfolding some of his finest poetry. The best of Rosenberg's poems however, notwithstanding the clear indication of dramatic power, are the "Trench" poems which include "Break of Day in the Trenches", "Returning, we hear the Larks", "Daughters of War", and, arguably the best "war" poem written during the war in English, "Dead Man's Dump". A part of Rosenberg's strength as a poet could be gathered under the heading of synecdoche. Thus the "suntreaders", so vividly predicated in "Chagrin", may be seen as representing the predicament of Anglo-Jewry, and that of the wounded, rescued, and then destroyed soldier in "Dead Man's Dump" as embodying the predicament of all soldiers. Rosenberg's remarkable achievement, however, is to have maintained a particularized vitality of the creature he re-created and, at the same time, to have made that creature instantial and representative, without compromising either aspect of this fusion. To put it differently, the singular dilemma of Jews, which becomes of universal significance, is extrapolated into an "all-eyed" perception of the predicament of the many.

His powerful, compact, often wiry poetry has permanent value. Some readers have found it "difficult". One critic, Randall Jarrell, thought it had no value.

A selection of his poetry edited by Gordon Bottomley was first published in volume form by Heinemann in 1922. It contains a fine photograph of Rosenberg, in uniform. *The Complete Works*, edited by Gordon Bottomley and Denys Harding, was published by Chatto and Windus in 1937. Chatto and Windus also published *The Collected Works*, edited by Ian Parsons (1979), but after that Rosenberg went out of print.

JON SILKIN

From an early age Rosenberg had wanted to be an artist, and at the local board school his artistic talents impressed his masters who encouraged him to attend weekly London County Council art classes. He continued to attend evening classes during his apprenticeship to an engraver (1904–10), and frequented the Whitechapel Art Gallery and Library where he met Bomberg and Gertler who were to become fellow students at the Slade. It was Gertler who introduced him to the Café Royal gatherings and Bomberg who organized an important exhibition of modern art at the Whitechapel Gallery in 1914 in which Rosenberg participated. Suffering from ill-health after he had left the Slade in 1914, Rosenberg spent a year in Cape Town. On his return to London he was without work and in despair. Tired of begging help from friends, and despite pacifist leanings, he enlisted in the Army, serving in the Bantam Battalion and the Royal Engineers after having tried, unsuccessfully, to transfer to the Jewish Battalion. He left for France in 1916. Towards the end of 1917 Rosenberg's poor health necessitated a period in military hospital, but he was sent back to the front line where he was killed on 1 April 1918.

Major one-man exhibitions were held posthumously: in 1937 the Memorial Exhibition at the Whitechapel Art Gallery, London; in 1959, at Leeds University; in 1975, at the National Book League, London. Works by Rosenberg

649

are to be found in many private collections; at the Tate Gallery, London; National Portrait Gallery, London; Carlisle Museum and Art Gallery, and other museums and art galleries throughout the United Kingdom.

FURTHER READING

Cohen, J.: *Journey to the Trenches: The Life of Isaac Rosenberg* (London: Robson Books, 1975)

Liddiard, J.: *Isaac Rosenberg: The Half Used Life* (London: Victor Gollancz, 1975)

Moorcroft Wilson, J.: *Isaac Rosenberg: Poet and Painter* (London: Cecil Woolf, 1975)

Parsons, I.: *The Collected Work of Isaac Rosenberg: Poetry, Prose, Paintings and Drawings* (London: Chatto and Windus, 1976)

MURIEL EMANUEL

Rosenfeld, Isaac (1918–1956)   American essayist and fiction writer. Rosenfeld's literary legacy is small: one novel published during his lifetime, *Passage from Home* (1946); posthumously, one collection of short stories, *Alpha and Omega* (1966; 1967); one volume of reviews and essays, *An Age of Enormity: Life and Writing in the Forties and Fifties* (1962); and the collection *Preserving the Hunger: An Isaac Rosenfeld Reader* (1987). Despite this limited output, Rosenfeld enjoys a considerable reputation as an essayist and fiction writer. His stories are uneven in quality; however, the best like "The Hand That Fed Me", are of lasting quality. Similarly, despite the limited scope and length of many of his reviews and essays, his non-fiction is noteworthy for his brilliant, provocative ideas and direct, pungent style.

Rosenfeld was the only child of a lower-middle-class Jewish family in Chicago. The death of his mother when he was less than two years old and the subsequent alienation from his father and stepmother resonate throughout his life and fiction, especially in *Passage from Home,* a loosely autobiographical *Bildungsroman* about a sensitive adolescent's search for meaning and love.

Yiddish, Rosenfeld's first language, and *Yiddishkeit* were major interests throughout his career. Despite his often widely fluctuating enthusiasms (including Gandhi, Franz KAFKA,

Tolstoy and Wilhelm Reich), Rosenfeld maintained a lifelong interest in Jews, Judaism, and Jewish life in America and Europe, which are the subjects of some of his most memorable essays.

The 1940s were Rosenfeld's most productive decade, and few careers looked more promising in these early years. However, by the end of the decade he was extremely blocked and turned to the theories of Wilhelm Reich as a solution and world view. In 1951 he left New York City, a symbolic gesture, as the city represented the intellectual hub and the scene of his youthful success. He died of a heart attack five years later, at 38. Friends like Saul BELLOW believe Rosenfeld experienced a breakthrough at the very end of his life, and "King Solomon", one of his best stories was written during his last months. But the overall pattern is one of depression and withdrawal.

FURTHER READING

Shechner, M.: Isaac Rosenfeld's world. *Partisan Review* 43 no. 3 (1976) 524–43

Solotaroff, T.: introduction to *An Age of Enormity* (Cleveland: World, 1962)

BONNIE LYONS

Rosenfeld, Morris [Moyshe Yankev Alter] (1862–1923)   Yiddish poet and socialist propagandist. Born in Bolkshein, Suwalki, Poland. Rosenfeld learned German and Polish, and read contemporary as well as classical Hebrew literature. In 1882 he went to the USA, but quickly returned, and lived for a time in London, where he lived in poverty working as a tailor. He returned to USA in 1886, working in sweatshops and publishing poetry of agitation and social criticism. Throughout his life in America Rosenfeld struggled to escape the sweatshops and illness brought on by overwork. His published collections include *Di gloke* (1888; The bell) and *Dos lider bukh* (1897; The song book). This collection marked a turning point in Rosenfeld's career: it showed him to be more than the creator of rhymed socialist ballads, capable of poetry of greater subtlety and sophistication. Rosenfeld's importance was recognized by Leo Wiener, who translated *Dos lider bukh* (*Songs from the Ghetto*, 1898) and thus brought him to the attention of a much wider public. A growing reputation as a journalist and public figure led to a tour of eastern Europe in 1908, but ill-health and bitterness against the Yiddish literary establishment (Rosenfeld was dismissed from the *Forverts* in 1913) brought a sense of isolation and melancholy to his later work. In addition to being the "poet-laureate of labor", Rosenfeld wrote criticism and dramas, and works on Heinrich HEINE and Yehuda Halevi. His collected works were published in 1908–10 as *Shriftn*.

FURTHER READING

Leftwich, J.: *The Golden Peacock – A Worldwide Treasury of Yiddish Poetry* (New York: Thomas Yoseloff, 1961) 101–4

Madison, C.: *Yiddish Literature – Its Scope and Major Writers* (New York: Schocken, 1971)

CHRISTOPHER HUTTON

Rosenthal, Erwin Isak Jakob (b.1904)

Biblical scholar, Arabist, and Islamicist. Born in Heilbronn, Rosenthal studied Semitics at the Universities of Heidelberg and Berlin, where he was the pupil of the German–Jewish orientalist, E. Mittwoch. He wrote his D.Phil. dissertation on Ibn Khaldun's political thought. He also studied at the Berlin Hochschule, where his teachers included Leo BAECK and J. Guttmann. Upon the rise of Nazism, he emigrated with his wife to England in 1933, where he obtained a post as Lecturer in Hebrew at University college, London. In 1936 he was appointed Special Lecturer in Semitic Languages and Literatures at Manchester University, where he edited *Saadya Studies* (1943) in commemoration of the thousandth anniversary of the great Ga'on's death. After the war, during which he had worked for the Foreign Office, he was appointed in 1948 to the newly created Hebrew lectureship at the University of Cambridge. After having been awarded a Litt.D. for his distinguished contribution to scholarship, he became Reader in Oriental Studies at Cambridge in 1959, a post which he held until his retirement

in 1971. Though Rosenthal wrote on various themes, including Judaism, biblical exegesis, and Medieval philosophy, he was particularly interested in Islam as a political philosophy. Besides his numerous contributions in this field to scholarly periodicals, he also wrote a number of books of which the most noteworthy are: *Averroes' Commentary on Plato's Republic* (1956), *Political Thought in Mediaeval Islam* (1958), *Griechisches Erbe in der jüdischen Religionsphilosophie der Mittelalters* (1960), *Judaism and Islam* (1961), and *Islam in the Modern National State* (1965).

FURTHER READING

Emerton, J. A., and Reif, S. C., eds: *Interpreting the Hebrew Bible: Essays in Honour of E. I. J. Rosenthal* (Cambridge: Cambridge University Press, 1982)

PAUL B. FENTON

Rosenzweig, Franz (1886–1929)

German religious philosopher and educator. Born in Cassel, Germany, Rosenzweig learned Hebrew privately. After graduating from the local *Gymnasium*, he studied medicine for two years at the universities of Göttingen, Munich, and Freiburg, and then philosophy, theology, art, literature, and classical languages at the universities of Berlin and again at Freiburg. He completed his dissertation on Hegel's political theory under Friedrich Meinecke's inspiration in 1912. He was drafted into the army for a brief time and then studied jurisprudence at the University of Leipzig under Eugen Rosenstock-Hüssy. Dismayed by a seeming absence of absolutes in Judaism which clarified itself during discussions with Rosenstock, Rosenzweig sought to convert to Christianity. He chose to do so not from neutral rational ground, rather on the basis of the consummation of Judaism, as reflected in *mitzvot*. This led him to High Holiday services in an Orthodox *shul* in Berlin, and there his lonely encounter with God made conversion no longer important.

In 1914 Rosenzweig dedicated himself to reading Hebrew texts and to writing *Atheistische Theologie* (in *Zweistromland. Kleinere Schriften zur Religion und Philosophie*, 1926) a critique of contemporary Jewish and Christian theology for

651

ignoring the concept of revelation. He then volunteered for the German army and served in Berlin, France, the Balkans, and near Warsaw. From the Balkans in 1917 he wrote *Zeit ists* (1917; *It Is Time*, 1955), addressed to Hermann COHEN, on the need to upgrade Jewish education through direct contact with Hebrew texts. He also published *Das aelteste System Program des deutschen Idealismus* (1917) on Schelling's pioneering plan for a united system of German idealism. In 1918, while confined to military hospitals in Leipzig and Belgrade, he completed his systematic religious philosophy, *Der Stern der Erloesung* (1921; *Star of Redemption*, 1971).

When Rosenzweig returned home he committed himself to bringing *Der Stern* "into life" by establishing the *Freies Jüdisches Lehrhaus* in Frankfurt. He wanted to institute a "new learning", to bring Jews back from the apologetic periphery to the Torah-center, and to have them live an authentic Jewish life in communion with their predecessors and successors. Besides Rosenzweig, the faculty included Martin BUBER, Erich FROMM, Leo STRAUSS, Nathan BIRNBAUM, Gershom SCHOLEM, Ernst SIMON, and Leo BAECK. In 1921 Rosenzweig became partially paralyzed but he continued his writing, his worship, and his communion with fellow thinkers from the attic to which he was confined. He translated Yehuda Halevi's poetry (1927) and introduced Hermann Cohen's *Jüdische Schriften*. In 1925 he wrote *Das neue Denken* (*The New Thinking*, 1953). With Buber, he began to translate Hebrew scripture into German (1925–9).

In his last year, Rosenzweig journeyed through all he had done and purified it, as if bringing his own life into the eternal center of the star of redemption. He prepared a second edition of *Der Stern* and had a portion translated into Hebrew. He placed his son into the hands of a Torah teacher. He read through the themes of election, covenant, and knowledge of God in *Isaiah*. He replaced Moses MENDELSSOHN's translation of YHWH as *der Ewige* (the eternal) with "I shall become what I shall become", to convey divine hiddenness and revealed-ness together (*"Der Ewige". Mendelssohn und der Gottesname, Gedenkbuch fuer Moses Mendelssohn*, 1929). He opposed the Mendelssohnian direction

of Jews entering German culture in favor of Jews returning to their own sources. He rejected the term "Bible", with its implied historical judgment of favoring "New" Testament over "Old", in order to preserve the authentic present which is not subject to history which *Tenach* offers.

In Rosenzweig's "new thinking" the three entities of God, man, and world retain their respective integrities. They also relate dialogically: God and world in creation, man and God in revelation, and man and world in redemption. In creation, God's infinite substance breaks into the cosmos and the cosmos responds with definition into particular entities. In revelation, God breaks through time to man in love, and man responds by declaring his presence and thereby reaching into eternity. In redemption, revelational love will flow through all humanity. In the messianic universe, the three dialogues will be orchestrated into a single trialogue.

Rosenzweig's Judaism is of eternity and history together. It resides in the center of the star, outside history. Each born Jew has an apperception of God from within eternity; the people reside beyond time within God's sacred countenance. But Judaism also perceives God from within history, God revealing Himself within temporal experiences and irradiating them. Christianity, which is rooted in redemption but capable of moving into history's own terms, conveys Judaism as eternity/history together into time, and builds the eternal way between creation and redemption.

FURTHER READING

Freund, E.: *Franz Rosenzweig's Philosophy of Existence*, trans. S. L. Weinstein and R. Israel (The Hague: M. Nijhoff, 1979)

Glatzer, N. N.: *Franz Rosenzweig: His Life and Thought* (New York: Schocken, 1953)

GERSHON GREENBERG

Rosowsky, Shlomo (1878–1962)   Composer and musicologist. One of the proponents of Jewish national music, Rosowsky was an active member of the Society for Jewish Folk Music founded by Yoel ENGEL in 1908. He emigrated to Palestine in 1925. There he composed incidental music for the Hebrew theater, with an especially elaborate score for *Jacob and Rachel* produced by *Haohel* theater in the 1920s. In the 1930s he settled in Jerusalem and turned to research and teaching of Jewish music, publishing a monograph on the cantillation of the Bible, in which he endeavored to continue A. Z. IDELSOHN's pioneering work. In his latter years Rosowsky lived in the United States and taught at the Jewish Theological Seminary in New York.

JEHOASH HIRSHBERG

Rosten, Leo (Calvin) [Leonard Q. Ross]

(b.1908)   American Jewish humorist and social scientist. Born in Lodz, Poland, Rosten emigrated to the US with his parents at the age of three, settling in Chicago. With the intellectual curiosity typical of his acculturating American Jewish generation, Rosten pursued a secular education, graduating from the University of Chicago with a Ph.D. in Political Science and International Relations. As a student during the Great Depression of the 1930s, he took several part-time jobs, most notably as a teacher in a Chicago night school. His students, immigrant adults learning English for the first time, caught his linguist's ear. Though much of Rosten's professional career includes sociological research and writing, he is best known for his humorous writings in which Yiddish language and diction is contrasted with proper English usage.

Rosten's first humorous work, *The Education of H*Y*M*A*N K*A*P*L*A*N* (1937), appeared for three years in *The New Yorker* before being published in book form. His hilarious presentation of an immigrant world which turns the English language on its ear became an instant classic. His Hyman Kaplan was an earnest new American whose every foray into our language became incursion rather than excursion. Built upon dialect jokes, absurd puns, and malapropisms, Hyman Kaplan captured the comic personality of Jewish self-perception.

*The Education of H*Y*M*A*N K*A*P*L*A*N* is a classic work of the immigrant generation because it captures the anxieties of acculturation with good humor and charm. It has also lasted in popularity because the characters Ros-

ten created, the irrepressible Hyman Kaplan and his cohorts, are larger than life, bantering malapropists whose chatter is zany, self-effacing, and ironic. They represent the Americanization of classic Yiddish stock characters or, as Rosten labels his intra-cultural blendings, "Yinglish" and "Ameridish".

Rosten has made other attempts at humor; he has written screenplays, potboiler novels, and even *The Return of H*Y*M*A*N K*A*P*L*A*N*. As a "serious author", he has written on religion and sociology for national publications. He has also taught at Columbia, Yale, and Berkeley. Still, Rosten is best known as the creator of Hyman Kaplan and as the compiler, editor, and writer of *The Joys of Yiddish* (1968), a lexicon of Yiddish in English. In this popular lexicon, Rosten exploits the nostalgia of second-generation Americans for their lost *Mamaloshen*. Through example, monologue, and serious explication, he reintroduces Yiddish to an American audience, while ruminating linguistically about bygone days. This serendipitous and chatty volume has established his reputation as the world's lay authority on the modern care and feeding of Yiddish.

Rosten has had many successful publications in a prolific career. Of these, only *The Education of H*Y*M*A*N K*A*P*L*A*N*, The Return of H*Y*M*A*N K*A*P*L*A*N* (1959), and *The Joys of Yiddish* seem of lasting import.

BIBLIOGRAPHY

The Leo Rosten Bedside Book (London: Victor Gollancz, 1965); *The Joys of Yiddish* (London: W. H. Allen & Co., 1970)

ELLEN GOLUB

Rotenstreich, Nathan (b.1914)

Israeli scholar and philosopher. Rotenstreich was born in Sambor, Poland, and, after graduating from the *Gymnasium* in Lvov, emigrated to Palestine in 1932. He completed his studies at the Hebrew University, receiving his MA in 1936 and his doctorate two years later. After being a postdoctoral fellow at the University of Chicago, and a Principal of the Youth Aliyah Teachers Training (1944–51), he was appointed a research associate in philosophy at the Hebrew

University in 1949. He became a senior lecturer in 1951, a professor of philosophy in 1955, a founding member of the Israel Academy of Sciences and Humanities in 1959, and a member of the International Institute of Philosophy in Paris in 1959. He served as dean of the Faculty of Humanities of the Hebrew University (1958–62) and its rector (1965–9).

Rotenstreich, considered one of the pioneers among Israeli creative philosophers, is also deeply involved in public and academic life. He was an activist in the Mapai party and one of the founders of the *min hayesod* movement opposing David BEN GURION. An extraordinarily prolific writer, he has published over 500 works on a variety of topics, such as Zionism, Judaism, the State of Israel, sociology, and education. *Bein 'adam lemoladeto* (Between a man and his homeland) is, for instance, a collection of several articles on modern Jewish identity. His *Spirit and Man: an Essay on Being and Value* (1963) deals with the terms by which the individual is able to establish his own philosophy of morality and human behavior. Rotenstreich's unorthodox approach allows him to deal with man and his place in the universe. Other books include *On the Human Subject: Studies in the Phenomenology of Ethics and Politics* (1966) and *Man on his Dignity* (1983). He is also the author of *Tradition and Reality: the Impact of History on Modern Jewish Thought*, as well as *Philosophy, History, and Politics: Studies in Contemporary English Philosophy of History* (1976) and *Order and Might* (1988). With S. H. Bergman, Rotenstreich co-translated Kant's three *Critiques* and *On Eternal Peace* into Hebrew, and published the critical edition of *Giv'at hamoreh* by Solomon MAIMON.

His scholarly work has gained the unequivocal appreciation of the academic world, for its originality and attention to detail. He has been honored by several universities, such as The Jewish Theological Seminary of America and Hebrew Union College. For his great contribution to modern scholarship he was awarded the Israel Prize for the Humanities in 1963.

DEBORAH SCHECHTERMAN

Roth, Cecil (1899–1970) English historian, Reader in Jewish Studies at Oxford University from 1939 to 1964. Cecil Roth was the most outstanding of a succession of scholars who both represented Judaism in the English universities and presented Jewish history and civilization to a wider English readership. A formidable historical researcher, he also had a gift for vivid self-expression which made his most serious articles a pleasure to read.

Roth's output was prodigious: his bibliography contains some 600 items, including translations of his works into several languages, and the range of his interests was enormous. "The trouble with being a Jewish scholar", he is quoted as saying, "is not that you have to know something about everything, but that you have got to know everything about everything". He devoted himself especially to the history of the Jews in England. Among his many writings on the subject, his *History of the Jews of England* (3rd edn 1964) became a classic, and he published an important bibliography, *Magna Bibliotheca Anglo-Judaica* (1937). He was President of the Jewish Historical Society of England no fewer than nine times.

Italian history was another of his interests: his first major work was *The Last Florentine Republic* (1925), and he later published a *History of the Jews in Italy* (1946). Having resigned his membership of Italian learned academies in 1938 in protest at the Fascist racial laws, he was delighted to be honored towards the end of his life with the title of *Commendatore* of the Italian Order of Merit.

It was in Italy that he first became interested in Jewish art, and its importance for the study of Jewish history. He wrote a number of pioneering studies in this subject, published numerous facsimile editions and illustrated works, and built up a splendid collection of objects, which he eventually sold to the Beth Tzedec Synagogue in Toronto. (His collection of books and manuscripts went mainly to the University of Leeds.)

After retiring from Oxford Roth was briefly visiting Professor at Bar Ilan University in Israel. It was an ill-judged move: his religious outlook (enlightened English Orthodoxy) was not that of his colleagues, and attacks on his work broke his health. For the last four years of his life he divided his time between Jerusalem and New York, as editor-in-chief of the *Encyclopedia Judaica*

NICHOLAS DE LANGE

Roth, Henry (b.1906)   American writer. He was taken to New York from Austrian Poland at the age of 18 months. The family, initially settled in Brownsville, moved to the Lower East Side in 1910 and in 1914 to Harlem. Roth graduated from the City College of New York in 1928 and for 10 years lived with Eda Lou Walton, an anthropologist of Pennsylvania Quaker ancestry, who supported and encouraged him as he wrote the novel, *Call It Sleep*, on which his fame rests. The lengthy novel was published in 1934 and, though generally well received at the time, was soon forgotten and had to wait a generation, until the 1960s, to become recognized as a work of genius.

Call It Sleep, autobiographical in conception, is set in Roth's childhood Brownsville and Lower East Side, and unfolds with exceptional lyricism the experience of its main character, a youngster named David Schearl, who, says Roth's biographer, Bonnie Lyons, "is at once a sensitive child and a mystic longing for divine illumination", and whose immigrant parents seem caught in a wretchedly unhappy marriage. David sides with his mother against his father in a classic oedipal struggle. What lends the novel so extraordinary a power is the "bilingual" sensibility Roth brilliantly fashioned, in alternating a crude, impoverished immigrant English with a lyrical, high-flown English diction meant to evoke the speaker's native Yiddish. Roth thus achieved in language, as well as plot, a remarkable layered, analytical effect. According to Leslie FIEDLER, "no one has ever distilled such poetry and wit from the counterpoint between maimed English and the subtle Yiddish of the immigrant. No one has reproduced so sensitively the terror of family life in the imagination of a child caught between two cultures".

Though in 1933 Roth joined the Communist Party, he was never deeply committed to political activity. He claimed to have been "in a sort of general mystical state" during the three and a half years he worked on his novel – "the most

distinguished single proletarian novel", Walter B. Rideout called it. Bonnie Lyons says of *Call It Sleep* that it "transcends all limiting categories and is, first and foremost, a great work of art", though she concedes its "Joycean" character and sees it as "a profoundly Jewish novel in its language and allusions". Ultimately, the book, which sold some 4,000 copies in 1934, would, as a paperback 30 years later, sell over a million copies.

Roth has published little since 1934 and nothing comparable to *Call It Sleep*, though a highly accomplished short story, "The Final Dwarf" (1969), also focuses on conflict between father and (adult) son. The JEWISH PUBLICATION SOCIETY of America issued in 1987 *Shifting Landscape*, a retrospective collection of Roth's short pieces: stories, essays, and memoirs he allowed to be published since 1934.

The revival of *Call It Sleep* in the 1960s enabled Roth to visit Mexico, Europe, and Israel. The Israeli victory in the 1967 war aroused his enthusiasm and reportedly led him to contemplate immigration. In 1968, however, the Roths left Maine for New Mexico where Roth was named D. H. Lawrence Fellow at the University.

FURTHER READING

Lyons, B.: *Henry Roth: The Man and His Work* (New York: Cooper Square Publishers, 1976)

STANLEY F. CHYET

Roth, Joseph (1894–1939)   Austrian writer. Roth was born in the frontier town of Brodi in Eastern Galicia, in an area remarkable for its mixture of races and cultures, mainly Polish, Ukrainian, and Jewish. Roth himself was unsure whether his mother was a Ukrainian or a Jewess and knew less about his father, other than what he learnt from his grandfather, in whose house he grew up. Brodi had a large Jewish population and Roth came to learn a great deal about Jews and their customs. He knew Yiddish and some Hebrew, as well as Polish and German, the language of his education in the high school of Brodi, and the universities of Lemberg (Lvov) and Vienna, and subsequently the language of his writing. In 1913 he moved to Vienna and began publishing poetry and articles in the Viennese press. At the outbreak of war Roth joined the army. His war experience was fundamental to his development, and its outcome in the disintegration of the Habsburg empire was to become an obsessive theme of his novels and stories. His first published novel, *Hotel Savoy*, appeared in 1924, when Roth was living in Berlin and working as a journalist. In 1930 his novel *Job*, a story of a Jewish family in a small town in Galicia, was published to wide acclaim. The family saga, *The Radetzky March*, followed in 1934, undoubtedly Roth's masterpiece. At the time of its publication Roth was already an exile in Paris, writing against the Nazi regime, describing its atrocities in many articles. He died of alcoholism shortly before the outbreak of the Second World War.

While not a major novelist, Roth was a gifted writer, with an individual style. His was an elegiac voice, lamenting the disappearance of human values embodied for him in the lost empire of his beloved Franz Joseph.

BIBLIOGRAPHY

The Radetzky March (Harmondsworth: Penguin, 1982); *Hotel Savoy*, trans. J. Hoare (London: Chatto & Windus, 1986) [containing "The Emperor's Bust" and "Fallmereyer the Stationmaster"]

YORAM BRONOWSKI

Roth, Leon (1896–1963) British historian of philosophy. He held a lectureship in philosophy in the University of Manchester from 1923 to 1927, and moved to the Ahad Ha'am Chair in Philosophy at the Hebrew University of Jerusalem in 1928. He served as Rector of the University, 1940–3, and resigned the Chair in 1953, having previously left Israel for England as a result of his disapproval of the exclusively Jewish character of the State.

His work can be divided into two categories. First, he was very interested in the seventeenth-century rationalists, and his *Spinoza, Descartes, and Maimonides* (1924) and *Spinoza* (1929) represent part of his contribution to this area. He presents the views of the philosophers clearly and concisely, with particular detail on the con-

text within which they were working. He also wrote a number of books on Jewish philosophy, the most successful being his *The Guide for the Perplexed* (1948) in which he represents the views of Maimonides and relates them to current concerns and developments. Throughout his writings on Jewish philosophy he argued that it is possible to reconcile the principles of Judaism with the conclusions of philosophy. One of his most important contributions to the development of philosophy in Israel was his sponsorship and organization of the translation of a large number of the classical texts into Hebrew. Although by no means a highly original thinker, his work exhibits wit and clarity when dealing with very complex issues.

FURTHER READING

Jessop, T.: *Proceedings of the British Academy* 50 (1965) 317–29
Loewe, R. ed.: *Studies in Rationalism, Judaism and Universalism. In memory of Leon Roth* (London: Routledge & Kegan Paul, 1966) ix–xiii, 1–11

OLIVER LEAMAN

Roth, Philip (b.1933) American novelist, short-story writer, and essayist. Roth is in many ways the quintessential American–Jewish writer. As a boy in New Jersey, both his Jewishness and his Americanness seemed a sine qua non, as he notes in memoirs. Both of them shaped his perceptions of the world. Roth's novels and short stories recount the often tormented struggles of American Jewish men with the conflicts between the demands of their Jewish heritage – as embodied by other Jews – and the allure of the dominantly Christian American culture.

Partially because he often casts these struggles in a sexual context, and partially because of his devastatingly funny portrayals of American Jewish "types", Roth's work has frequently been controversial, inspiring both vehement condemnation and ardent praise among critics and lay readers alike. Before he had left his twenties, Roth had won a Houghton Mifflin Literary Fellowship, the 1958 Aga Khan Prize for Fiction, and a National Book Award designating *Goodbye Columbus* the best American fiction published during 1959. He has since won Guggenheim Fellowships and a Ford Foundation Grant in playwriting. Roth was elected to the National Institute of Arts and Letters in 1970, and he has taught at several universities, including the University of Chicago, Princeton, and the University of Pennsylvania.

While his defenders have praised his strong voice and exceptional ear for dialogue and the nuances of human motivation and behavior, his detractors have angrily denounced him as a self-hating Jew. Roth writes knowingly of urban Jews and their angst in works such as "The Defender of the Faith", "The Conversion of the Jews", and *Letting Go* (1962), all of which explore the ambiguities of modern American Jewish definitions of Jewishness and Jewish behavior. In *The Anatomy Lesson* (1983) Roth utilizes ribald hilarity to struggle with the concept of Jewish chosenness, and the Jewish preoccupation with persecution and suffering.

Roth often writes of complex and painful family relationships in a humorous vein. The relationships of sons to mothers, sons to fathers, and men to their wives and mistresses are described in evocative and bitterly funny details. The guilt which a rebellious but loving son feels toward a hardworking or ailing father, the struggle of men who want to control their own existence against females who have other agendas are frequent themes in Roth's fiction. *Goodbye Columbus* (1959) gave the American reading public one of the prototypes of the "Jewish American Princess", an epithet now in such wide usage that it has become an anti-Semitic cliché. Most of Roth's later protagonists are intelligent, accomplished men who focus almost exclusively on the charms of non-Jewish women. The most famous such sexually obsessed intellectual is probably Alex Portnoy of *Portnoy's Complaint* (1969). Like *Goodbye Columbus*, *Portnoy's Complaint* also launched an attack on Jewish womanhood, with a lethally funny dissection of the "Jewish mother", Sophie Portnoy.

Roth's themes include not only the complex interactions of what he was later to call "the oedipal swamp" but also the internal world of the artist and the act of creation in novels such as *The Breast* (1972), *My Life As A Man* (1974), *The Ghost Writer* (1979), and *Zuckerman Unbound* (1981).

Philip Roth

All of Roth's themes coalesce brilliantly in *The Counterlife* (1986). Within the four parts of the novel, Roth plays with the alternative routes which life – and art – can follow. Areas which Roth has left fallow since the stories in *Goodbye Columbus* are picked up in *The Counterlife*, as Roth explores the meaning of contemporary Jewish experience in Israel and the Diaspora.

Other books by Roth include: *When She Was Good* (1967); *Our Gang* (1971); *The Great American Novel* (1973); *Reading Myself and Others* (1975); *The Professor of Desire* (1977); and *A Philip Roth Reader* (1981).

BIBLIOGRAPHY
The Facts: A Novelist's Biography (London: Jonathan Cape, 1989)

SYLVIA FISHMAN

Rothenstein, William (1872–1945) English painter. The Rothenstein family had originally come from the German village of Grohnde, near Hanover, but by the time William was born, in Horton, Yorkshire, his father, who had become a British citizen, was already a prosperous wool merchant. William grew up in the countryside around Bradford, leaving for London in 1888 to study drawing under Professor Alphonse Legros at the Slade. After a year he left for Paris where he formed a close friendship with Whistler and continued his studies at the Académie Julian. At this time his work consisted mainly of male portraits which were much admired by Degas and Camille PISSARRO; Degas particularly expressed a wish to meet the young Englishman. Having received a commission to paint several portraits, Rothenstein spent a year in Oxford before settling in London in 1894. His subject matter and style changed considerably during the first decade of the twentieth century, and it was during this period that he worked on his only religious and Old Testament subjects. He traveled in Italy, India, and the USA during the years 1906 to 1912 and, on his return to England, found a home in Far Oakridge, Gloucestershire, where he lived until his death.

Rothenstein was an official war artist in both World Wars; he inaugurated the Chair in Civic Art at Sheffield University in 1917, and was Principal of the Royal College of Art from 1920 to 1935. He was knighted in 1931.

During his lifetime his works were exhibited regularly at many London galleries. They are in the collections of the Tate Gallery and Imperial War Museum, London; Walker Art Gallery, Liverpool; National Gallery of Victoria, Melbourne; Musée d'Art Moderne, Paris; Metropolitan Museum, New York; and other museums, art galleries, and many private collections.

BIBLIOGRAPHY

Men and Memories, 3 vols (London: Faber & Faber, 1931–9)

FURTHER READING

Lago, M., ed.: *Men and Memories 1872–1938* (London: Chatto & Windus, 1978) [abridged edn]
Speaight, R.: *William Rothenstein: The Portrait of an*

Artist in his Time (London: Eyre & Spottiswoode, 1962)

MURIEL EMANUEL

Rothko, Mark [Marcus Rothkowitz] (1903–1970) American painter. Born in Russia, he emigrated with his family to the USA in 1913, settling in Portland, Oregon. He attended Yale University from 1921 to 1923 on a scholarship. He left to study art at the Art Students League with Max Weber as one of his teachers. In the early years of his career, Rothko retained his ties with the Jewish community through his skills as an artist and a draftsman. In the late 1920s he drew maps for a book on popularized biblical history for a rabbi from Portland. Between 1929 and 1952, he taught art at the Brooklyn Jewish Center.

During the 1930s, he was employed by the easel division of the WPA Federal Art Project. During the 1920s and 1930s Rothko absorbed the many stylistic possibilities open to him, experimenting with a Cézannesque form of social realism as well as biomorphic Surrealism. By the late 1940s he gradually evolved his signature style, replacing semi-abstract, biomorphic imagery with non-objective pulsating planes of color. He devised a format which comprised vertical rectangular shapes divided by horizontal passages of contrasting colors. Although not specifically religious in content, the paintings project an aura of spirituality and invite contemplation on the part of the viewer. To Rothko, the spiritual dimension of painting was paramount to the extent that it was rumored that he wore a *kipah* (skullcap) while painting. In 1964 Dominique and John de Menil commissioned Rothko to paint a series of 14 paintings for the non-denominational chapel in Houston that bears his name. There is no overt subject matter of any kind referred to in the immense purple-hued canvases. Rather, it is the large scale, the subtle variations of tone and shape in the paintings, and the serial effect that evoke a contemplative response.

FURTHER READING

Waldman, D.: *Mark Rothko, 1903–1970: A Retrospective* (New York: Harry N. Abrams Inc., in collaboration with the Solomon R. Guggenheim Foundation, 1978)

BARBARA GILBERT

Roziner, Felix (b.1936)   Russian writer and journalist. Roziner was born in Moscow and lived there until his emigration in 1978. Like many of his contemporaries, he spurned an early inclination for art and music to take up engineering (the contrast between Soviet philosophical materialism and the world of art would become a frequent theme). In 1969 he quit his job to write. Making use of a strong musical background, he published biographies of Grieg and Prokofiev, in addition to articles on music. At the same time he wrote poetry and prose not intended for publication. A major novel, *Nekto Finkelmaier* (A certain Finkelmayer) became well known in typescript. While still unpublished, it won the prestigious Dahl Prize (Paris) for 1980. The Russian text appeared in London in 1981.

A Certain Finkelmayer is set in Moscow in the late 1950s and early 1960s, and makes fictional use of some of the era's history, most notably the trial of Joseph BRODSKI. The novel's central concern is that of the Jew as Russian intellectual and the Russian intellectual as Jew. Roziner's hero, the bearer of an extravagantly Jewish name, is by nature and fate a Russian poet, heir to Pushkin. The incongruity between the poet's calling and his name is briefly played for comedy, but soon becomes natural and later tragic.

Out of the USSR, Roziner published a volume of short stories *Vesennie muzhskie igry* (1984; The spring games of men) and has published frequently in journals. His interest in history and human relations is apparent in *Lilovyi dym* (1985; Lilac smoke), a novella about postwar Lithuania. Other works, notably an antiutopian satire, *Medved' Velikii* (1977; The great bear) and a play, *Siamskie bliznitsy* (1981; The siamese twins), take a more experimental stance.

Of Roziner's nonfictional works, the most striking are two memoirs. *Serebryannaya tsepochka* (1983; The silver cord) was written for an Israeli competition entitled "My Fathers' Home in Russia", in which it won an award. The book covers seven generations and follows the family's migrations to and from the *shtetl*, the Russian capitals, Palestine, and eventually Israel; it incorporates the autobiography of his grandfather, translated from archaic Hebrew. *Triptikh* (1986; Triptych) is similar in its concern with the author's roots, but on this occasion, the past evoked with love and sadness is wholly Russian.

ALICE NAKHIMOVSKY

Rubens, Bernice (b.1927)   British novelist. Born in Cardiff, Rubens was educated at the University College of South Wales and Monmouthshire. She subsequently became a schoolteacher in Birmingham, and a documentary film writer and director for the United Nations and other institutions. Her prize-winning films were generally about marginal or disadvantaged groups and individuals, and the dual themes of marginality and disablement were carried over into Rubens's fiction. Her first novel *Set on Edge* was published in 1960. This was followed by *Madame Sousatzka* (1962), *Mate in Three* (1965), and *The Elected Member* (1969). The last of these novels, republished in America as *Chosen People*, won the Booker Prize and established Rubens as a noteworthy post-war British novelist.

Rubens's first four novels were all set in a Jewish environment and were concerned with the extremes of middle-class Jewish life, especially the depiction of exploitative and destructive marital and familial relations. In Rubens's early fiction, children are condemned to partial lives by their parents – especially their mothers – and are unable to function outside of the family circle. Her characteristic tone is one of black humor as demonstrated in her fifth novel, *Sunday Best* (1971), which is the story of a transvestite pursued for his own alleged murder. The disabled personality dominates Rubens's fiction and this can lead to an irredeemably gloomy view of the world, as in *Go Tell the Lemmings* (1973). In her seventh novel, *I Sent a Letter to My Love* (1975), Rubens situates the theme of destructive familial and erotic relationships in a specifically Welsh context.

The publication of *A Five Year Sentence* (1978) and *Spring Sonata* (1979) signalled a return to the emotional claustrophobia of Rubens's earlier novels as well as a greater emphasis on the bizarre in her fiction. In *Spring Sonata* Buster, a child still in the womb, decides to remain unborn rather than face the crippling family expectations that await him. Conversely, in *A Five Year Sentence*, a lonely spinster is condemned to live longer than she wishes. *Brothers* (1983) proved to be sui generis as it situated the Jewish family, perhaps not altogether successfully, against the background of European Jewish history. Continuing this expansiveness, *Our Father* (1987) examines the metaphysical dimension of the disabling family by humorously introducing the figure of "God" into the scarred pysche of the novel's central character.

Rubens's novels vary from being comedies of manners to bleak accounts of family expectations. Her dark early Jewish novels, as a recent commentator has noted, contrast significantly in tone and perspective from her non-Jewish novels which increasingly contain a spirit of comic redemption.

FURTHER READING

A novelist of family life. *The Jewish Quarterly* 34 no. 3 (1987)

BRYAN CHEYETTE

Rubenstein, Richard Lowell (b.1924)

American Holocaust and "death of God" theologian. While studying to become a Reform rabbi at the Hebrew Union College, Cincinnati, the disclosures of the horrors of the Nazi death camps led to his disillusionment with Reform Judaism's anti-Zionist stance and its optimism concerning humanity. Constrained by various factors from studying for the Orthodox rabbinate, he was ordained as a Conservative Rabbi at the Jewish Theological Seminary, New York, in 1952. He attained his Ph.D. at Harvard University in 1960. His thesis, a psychoanalytic study of the *Aggadah*, revealed the fears and strivings of the rabbis who laid the foundations for the reconstruction of the Jewish community in the face of powerlessness after the defeat of 70 CE. It was later edited and published as *The Religious Imagination*.

In *After Auschwitz* (1966) he formulated his "death of God" theology. If the omnipotent God of history existed, how could one explain the murder of six million of his chosen people? The idea that Hitler could be God's instrument was too obscene for Rubenstein to accept. He declared the death of the God-who-acts-in-history and in his stead posited God, the Holy Nothingness, the Cannibal Mother, who gives birth to all only to consume all, a concept which owes much to kabbalistic thought and bears a strong resemblance to Freud's Thanatos. It is accompanied by cyclic repetitiveness. There is no afterlife and no Messiah. Life is "bracketed between two oblivions" and death is the Messiah. Because the Holocaust is the culmination of Jewish powerlessness, he stresses the need for Jewish political power and supports Zionism. *After Auschwitz* spoke of religion in the time of the death of God. With strong Freudian underpinning, Judaism is interpreted as the particular way in which Jews confront the ultimate questions and crises of life. Religion functions psychologically. *Rites de passage* should be celebrated in the most authentic and archaic way and the Jewish tradition needs to be passed on to succeeding generations intact and without changes. The sacrificial aspects of religion are asserted over the prophetic, because sacrifice, even if only verbal, channels aggression and helps people to assuage guilt.

Rubenstein was "bureaucratically excommunicated" from the Jewish community. In 1970 he accepted an academic post at the Florida State University. *The Cunning of History* (1975) marked a change in his orientation. Turning from the Holocaust's theological implications for Judaism, he now explores its more global implications. He has come to see the Holocaust as one of a series of bureaucratically administered programs of mass population riddance in the face of the modern world's most intractable problem, population explosion and consequent population redundancy.

Perceiving Diaspora Judaism as doomed, he exhibits extreme pessimism. Intent on exploring the kind of world in which a Holocaust could take place, his work retains theological import inasmuch as he continues to probe the "godless" world in which we live.

JOCELYN HELLIG

Rubin, Reuven (1893–1974) Israeli artist. Rubin was born in a remote village in Romania to an Orthodox family. His natural gift for drawing was recognized at an early age, but he had to go to work in order to help finance his impoverished family. In 1912 he was accepted by the newly founded BEZALEL SCHOOL OF ARTS AND CRAFTS in Jerusalem where he remained for a year before leaving for Paris and the École des Beaux-Arts. After the First World War Rubin lived in Italy, Romania, and the USA where his first New York exhibition was sponsored by the American photographer Alfred Steiglitz, in 1921. Rubin returned to Palestine in 1922, settling first in Jerusalem then in Tel Aviv where he became a leading figure on the local Israeli art scene, eventually becoming one of Israel's best-known painters.

The themes of Rubin's paintings are numerous but all of them are concerned with the life and landscape of his newly acquired homeland. The impact of the Orient on the western-born artists who settled and worked in Palestine/Israel was a major factor in the art history of the country. Rubin's figurative art is important because of its response to the new and exciting vistas, both human and topographic that the land offered: Arabs riding their donkeys or leading camels, boys playing the flute, Yemenite Jews in their traditional dress, Hasidim, and pioneers. Yet reality was merely the starting point for Rubin's art; he created an idealized world, sometimes containing an element of fantasy. His compositions are static, harmonies of pinks, blues, and whites, particularly in his landscape paintings which comprise the most important part of his oeuvre. As his human figures lost their specific identity the landscape became increasingly dreamlike and mysterious.

One of Rubin's best known paintings is his *Seder in Jerusalem* (1950), a mystical portrait of a man in biblical dress, a Yemenite family, an east European rabbi, and a Palmach soldier gathered round a Passover table, with a vision of Jerusalem seen through an open window.

Now a museum, the Rubin House in Tel Aviv contains his major works and serves as a venue for temporary exhibitions of Israeli art. Much admired by H. N. BIALIK and the pianist Artur Rubinstein, among others, Rubin's paintings are to be found in many important international collections.

SARAH HACKER

Rubinstein, Anton (1829–1894) Russian pianist, composer, and teacher. Rubinstein was one of the greatest pianists of the nineteenth century. He received early piano lessons from his mother, giving his first concert in 1839. Between 1840 and 1843, he toured Europe as a child virtuoso, and in Paris played before Chopin and Liszt. In 1844–6 he moved to Berlin where he studied composition, meeting MENDELSSOHN and MEYERBEER. In 1846–8 he lived in Vienna, and in 1848–9 returned to Russia where he enjoyed the patronage of the Czar's sister-in-law. In 1849–54 he composed much music, including three Russian Operas, *Dmitry Donskoy* (1852), *Tom the Fool* (1853), and *The Siberian Huntsman* (1854). In 1859 he became director of the Russian Musical Society and in 1862–7 founded and was Director of the St Petersburg Conservatory. Between 1867 and 1887 he returned to concert life; while continuing as Director of the Conservatory. He died in Peterhof.

Rubinstein's influence on both performance and education was of the greatest importance to Russian musical culture. He composed throughout his life – his works include operas, choral works, orchestral works (his Second Symphony, *The Ocean*, was at one time much played), chamber, and piano music.

FURTHER READING

Bowen C. D.: *Free Artist – the Story of Anton and Nicholas Rubinstein* (New York: Random House, 1939)

SYDNEY FIXMAN

Rukeyser, Muriel (1914–1980) American poet, prose writer, and translator. Born in New York City of German–Jewish descent, Rukeyser delineated the city's social forces and technological strains in her *Theory of Flight* (1935) the first of 16 volumes of poetry. Her childhood in the city incarnates social consciousness for the poet which, together with her father's role in the construction industry and her emotional distance from his life-style, become the themes of *The Life of Poetry* (1949) the second out of six prose works, and *Elegies* (1949) a volume of poetry. From Fieldston School and Vassar (1929–31), Rukeyser moved to the left-wing Theater Union which produced political plays in the 14th Street Theater and later wrote a play, *The Colors of the Day*. During the Civil War, she traveled to Spain to cover the Counter-Olympics in Madrid and narrowly escaped death at the hands of the secret police. At the University of California in Berkeley during 1938, she was concerned with the question of American actions against the Nazis in Europe. However, her volumes of poetry *A Turning Wind* (1939), *Beast in View* (1944), and *The Green Wave* (1945) center around less purely political concerns and more deeply personal experiences. Her *Body of Waking* (1958) announced her awakening to artistic, physical, and intellectual powers. From 1957 to 1967 Rukeyser worked as a poetry adviser at Sarah Lawrence. Meanwhile, she published *Waterlily Fire: Poems 1935–1962* (1962) and *The Speed of Darkness* (1968), both works imbued by political themes. In 1967 she wrote poems based on the legends of her ancestor Rabbi Akiba which, together with essays and short stories, appeared in the *American Judaism Reader*. Then she joined the War Resister's League, and in 1975 as president of the writers-in-prison committee of International PEN she went to South Korea to plead for poet Kim Chi Ha's life, an adventure presented in *The Gates* (1976). Furthermore, Muriel read "On Being a Jew in the Twentieth Century" and other poems on Paul Kresh's radio programs "Treasury of 100 American Jewish Poets Reading Their Own Poems" and "Adventures in Judaism" and was offered full-scale recognition. Muriel Rukeyser received an honorary doctoral degree from Rutgers University in 1961 and the Copernicus and the Shelley Memorial Awards in 1977 for "her contribution to poetry as a cultural force".

FURTHER READING

Gould, J.: *American Women Poets: Pioneers of Modern Poetry* (New York: Dodd, Mead & Co., 1984)

Craft interview with Muriel Rukeyser. *New York Quarterly* 11 (1972) 15–39

LIANA SAKELLIOU-SCHULTZ

Russian–Jewish culture before 1917

As in other countries where Jews were dispersed, the beginning of Russian–Jewish cultural activity was connected with the emergence and development of the Jewish Enlightenment (see HASKALAH). In the region of the Russian empire, peculiarities of this development led to the first Russian–Jewish printed work appearing almost half a century before the birth of Russian–Jewish literature, that is the apologetic work *Vopl dshcheri Iudeiskoi* (1803; The lament of the daughter of Judea) in St Petersburg by Leiba Nevakhovich (Yehuda Leib ben Noakh, 1776–1831). Addressing the educated Russian reader, he complains about the distressing situation of the Jewish people.

Osip RABINOVICH should be viewed as the founding father of Russian–Jewish literature. His creative work and that of his younger contemporary and collaborator Lev LEVANDA brought about the definition of the necessary indicators of the Russian–Jewish writer's affiliation: a Jewish consciousness, a full and integral sensation of oneself as a Jew; a thorough familiarity with and integral connection to Jewish civilization, resulting in the treatment of Jewish themes; and a social representativeness, that is the writer's capacity and responsibility to represent the community either as a whole or at least in its essential components. To this definition the twentieth century added another indicator.

In 1910 the publicist Iosif Bikerman (1867–1945) coined the phrase "not split but doubled" ("Natsionalizm i natsiia", *Evreiskii mir*, no. 2–3, 1910, p. 151), which anticipated by more than twenty years Mordecai Menahem KAPLAN's famous thesis about contemporary Jewry's twofold civilization in the Diaspora. This fourth constitutive indicator – a twofold civilized affiliation, with both halves equally necessary – has become both universal and obligatory from 1917.

As a sociocultural phenomenon, Russian–Jewish literature is divided into periods according to the movement of Jewish history in Russia and the shifts in Russia literary trends.

The first period (1850s–1882)

This period, starting with the two above-mentioned writers, lasted from the middle of the 1850s to the years 1881–2; it thus coincides with Alexander II's liberal reign, which superseded Nicholas I's oppressive regime. This time was characterized by recollections of past calamities; of hopes for full emancipation in the near future, which presupposed the complete equalization of rights and obligations with those of the indigenous population and on the other hand the repudiation of Jewish isolation and of traditional modes of life as well as adoption of the Russian language and Russian culture: in short, the full assimilation in every field except religion. Just as in the case of Russian literature, this time was one of "exposure" and of "civil spirit" applied to the Jews, of the unreserved denial of all that enlighteners (*maskilim*) called medieval prejudice and fanaticism (in practice, of the whole life of the old ghetto); it was also one of an unconditional call to serve the "homeland", the Russian nation and Russian interests, to amalgamate with them in spirit and thought.

For Russian–Jewish fiction writers and publicists, both the negative and the positive halves of this program proved to be all the more acceptable in that they concurred with the *Haskalah's* ideas both in its primary "Berlin" form and in the first stage of its existence on Russian soil (1820s–40s). After Rabinovich and Levanda, the most outstanding figure of this period was Grigori Bogrov.

Both during this period and later, the periodical press played a role in collecting and organizing literary talent. *Rassvet* (The dawn) was the first Russian–Jewish journal, a weekly, which was issued in Odessa (1860–1) and which was replaced by *Sion* (Zion, 1860–2). Osip Rabinovich directed *Rassvet*, and among the managers of *Sion* was Leon Pinsker (1821–91), subsequently one of the leaders of the *Hibbat Zion* movement in Russia and in western Europe. Also in Odessa the weekly *Den* (The day) appeared and proclaimed itself the direct successor to *Rassvet* and *Sion*. *Den* was published by the Odessa branch of the Society for Promotion of Culture among Jews in Russian. The society, founded in 1863 in St Petersburg (to October 1917), achieved a great deal in giving Jews access to Russian culture and, consequently, in molding the Russian–Jewish intelligentsia.

The second period (1881–1897)

The second period in the history of Russian–Jewish culture began under the aegis of the great pogroms of the years 1881–2. For Russia this was the period of transition from the liberal reforms under Alexander II to the reaction under Alexander III. For the Jewish people (not only the Russian Jews) the great pogroms were exceptionally important: they led to massive emigration, to the beginning of new centers of the Diaspora, including the United States and, in a more distant perspective, to the birth of political Zionism and the rebirth of Israel. Assimilationist ideas, which inspired the Russian–Jewish intelligentsia of the first generation, proved untenable and the longed-for "confluence with the indigenous population" proved chimerical.

Hence, the two basic motifs of the second period are the bitterness of forfeited illusions and the return to the rejected values of the patriarchal ghetto. It should be borne in mind that the transition to the new period began within the framework of the first literary generation: for example Osip Rabinovich's narrative tale "Istoriia o tom, kak Reb Haim-Shulim Feigis puteshestvoval iz Kishineva v Odessy, i chto s nim sluchilos" (The story of how Reb Haim Shulim Feigis traveled from Kishinev to Odessa, and what happened to him); and Lev Levanda's late publicism. The Russian–Jewish intelligentsia was not cognizant of the conflict between the "fathers and sons" nor of the total repudiation of Enlightenment's ideas of assimilation: in the notion of the "Russian Jew", the first half ("Russian") remained no less important than the other half.

At the center of Russian–Jewish culture stood the capital, St Petersburg. There, in 1879, two weeklies opened, both of which stayed in print until 1884: *Rassvet* (in order to distinguish it from the Odessa publication of 1860–1 of the same name, it adopted the designation *Rassvet. II*; and *Russkii evrei* (The Russian Jew). Many well-known (not only in Jewish circles) men of letters were on the editorial board of *Rassvet*, including Mikhail Kulisher (1847–1919), Nikolai Minski (Vilenkin, 1855–1937), Semyon Vengerov (1855–1920), Pavel Levenson (1837–94), and Grigori BOGROV (who for some time was also the publisher and editor of the journal).

Many of those who subsequently became celebrated writers made their debut in these two weeklies, such as Semyon FRUG; BEN-AMI; the historian and publicist Simon DUBNOW (1860–1941); the literary critic and art historian Akim Volynski (Haim Flekser, 1863–1926); and some, who began well but then disappeared without a trace, like Gershon-ben-Gershon (Grigorii Lifshits), a gifted essayist and prose writer who completely left literature in the 1890s.

In January 1881, on the eve of the great pogroms, the monthly *Voskhod* (The sunrise) was launched. Its publication was concomitant with *Nedelnaia Khronika Voskhoda* (The weekly chronicle of the sunrise) from 1882 to 1897 which was subsequently renamed *Khronika Voskhoda* (The chronicle of the sunrise). In 1899 the weekly came to be called *Voskhod* and the monthly *Knizhki Voskhoda* (The books of the sunrise). The weekly and the monthly existed until 1906, setting a long-standing record among Russian–Jewish periodicals and remaining in its history as the most authoritative and prestigious organ of the press.

For a little less than 20 years the publisher and editor was Adolf Landau (1842–1902), and among the collaborators were all outstanding Jewish men of letters, writing in Russian. Besides those already mentioned, one must include S. An-ski (Shloyme Zanvil Rapaport), the prose writers Nikolai Pruzhanski (b.1844) and Sergei Yaroshevski (d.1907), the publicists and fiction writers Jakov Rombro (1858–1922) and Gershon Badanes (Grigori Gurevich, 1854–?). As before, the poetry of the period was of little interest, with two exceptions: Frug and Minski.

Russian–Jewish publications reached the Russian reader only to an insignificant degree; one has to admit that the Russian–Jewish intelligentsia did not care much for those publications either. Therefore especially noteworthy is the long short story by N. Naumov (Naum Kogan, 1863–93) "V glukhom mestechke" (In a godforsaken *shtetl*), which was published in the popular St Petersburg monthly *Vestnik Evropy* (The European herald) in November 1892. Both the Russian and, following it, Russian–Jewish critics responded enthusiastically, perceiving not only the opening in the approach to material (the spiritual wealth of patriarchal Jews, the unbearable conditions of existence, and the relationship of the Russian authorities to the Jewish masses), but also in the manner of writing, simultaneously rigid and lyrical. It is possible *mutatis mutandis* to compare the appearance of Kogan's short story with the publication of Osip Rabinovich's *Shtrafnoi* (The penalized). It is characteristic, however, that the editor of *Vestnik Evropy* called for the replacement of an author's typical Jewish family name by a pseudonym sounding fully Russian.

The third period (1897–1917)

The third and final period covered the last 20 years before the Russian Revolution. Its beginning may be arbitrarily combined with the literary debut of the most significant writer of this period, Semyon YUSHKEVICH, who became known to readers in 1897 in *Russkoe Bogatstvo* (Russian richness), a magazine of the Populists, in which Ivan Bunin, Leonid Andreev, Maksim Gorky, and Aleksandr Kuprin were publishing. In its way this was an omen: in the pre-revolutionary decades Russian–Jewish literature for the first time attracted the Russian reading public's earnest attention, yet an attention that was far from always being sympathetic. During the second half of the 1890s, voices began to be heard about the Jews' dominance in Russian literature; in so doing, they meant both Russian–Jewish writers and Russian writers of Jewish origin.

The birth and the growth of Zionism on the one hand, and of the Russian revolutionary movement, on the other, reinforced not only social and political motifs in literature, but also a sharp demarcation among writers according to these motifs. From the artistic, esthetic point of view Russian literature experienced, conventionally speaking, a symbolist revolution, which led to the flourishing of Russian culture at the beginning of the twentieth century, a period which has been called the "silver age". Similar developments also occurred in Russian–Jewish literature, which, as in previous periods, found itself artistically dependent on Russian literature. Both aspects in the evolution of Russian–Jewish literature are distinctly visible, in the shape of such important figures as David AIZMAN and Vladimir JABOTINSKY.

But the less visible figures, who are half-forgotten today, are highly interesting. Miron (Meir) Ryvkin (1869–1915), a prose writer and publicist, wrote chiefly for Russian–Jewish publications. His short stories and essays were collected in *V dukhote* (Out in the stuffy air), which was rather successful, with the first edition appearing in 1900 and several thereafter. This was psychological, Chekhov-like prose, the material of which was the hermetically sealed world of the *shtetl* in the Jewish Pale. During his last 10 years, Ryvkin also wrote in Yiddish. He created a novel in two versions about the blood libel affair of 1823–35, in Russian *Navet* (1912) and in Yiddish *Der velizher blut-bilbul* (which appeared in 1912–13 in the Warsaw newspaper *Fraind*, and in a separate edition in 1914). It was the first experiment in creating a modernist historical novel, one that was sympathetically received by the most prominent Russian–Jewish critic of the first three decades of the twentieth century, Sergei (Israel) Zinberg (1873–1938).

Aleksei Svirski (1865–1942), on the other hand, began as a Russian writer (1892) and for many years did not turn to Jewish themes (conceivably, the fact that Svirski was baptized in his youth played a part). In the first two decades of the twentieth century, three collections of his stories about the Jewish poor appeared; at the end of the 1920s, in a review of a multi-volume collection of Svirski's work, one Russian critic observed that in his entire creative work the greatest artistic value was represented by his Jewish stories. As an artist, Svirski is closer to early Gorky (for example his writing about morals and manners). He also wrote for the

theater; his plays (one co-authored with Kuprin) were successful and were staged in Moscow and St Petersburg. Svirski's last work, the autobiographical novel *Istoriia moei zhizni* (1929–40; The story of my life), exceeded the limitations of this period. However, its manifest twofold affiliation must be noted: on the one hand, with the tradition of Russian–Jewish autobiographical prose (Levanda, Bogrov, Ben-Ami); on the other, with the characteristic Russian biography of the twentieth century, such as Gorky's autobiographical trilogy.

Another prose writer close to the Gorky trend was Aleksandr Kipen (1870–1938), one of the best stylists in Russian–Jewish literature and a master of the classical landscape (in the spirit of Turgenev) and of characterization by means of style of speech. His narrative tale "V oktiabre" (1906; In October) was especially renowned; it is about the 1905 Revolution, the pogroms, and Jewish self-defense. However, more convincing and more palpable is the new Jewish type represented in the story "Liverant" (1910). Aron Gets, the story's hero, is the direct predecessor of BABEL's characters. In equal measure, Kipen feels at home both in Russian and in Jewish surroundings, and his material draws more or less uniformly from both environments.

Osip Dymov (Perelman, 1878–1959) was a journalist, prose writer, humorist, and dramatist almost exclusively Russian, but the pogroms of 1905 turned him toward the Jews: the short story "Pogrom" (1906), the drama *Slushai, Izrail!* (1907; Listen, Israel!), and the drama *Vechnyi strannik* (1913; The eternal wanderer). The public received the latter with such enthusiasm that the author was invited to the United States, where the play was produced on the Jewish stage in the same year, 1913. Osip Dymov never returned to Russia, and very quickly went from Russian to Yiddish, becoming one of the leading figures in the Jewish theater in New York during the inter-war period. As a matter of fact he belonged to Russian literature and to Jewish (Yiddish) literature, with Russian–Jewish literature serving only as a short bridge for the passage from the first to the second.

The period under review was the time of the blossoming of Russian–Jewish culture. More than 60 different periodicals appeared during these years. An entire school for the study of Jewish culture and historiography took shape (Meir Balaban, Iuli Gessen, Shaul Ginzburg, Petr Marek, Sergei Zinberg). The Society for the Promotion of Culture among the Jews in Russia established a special historico-ethnographic commission in 1892, which was transformed into the Jewish Historico-Ethnographic Society in 1908, a center of research, publishing, and lecturing activities. In 1907 there appeared a Jewish institution for higher education, which functioned in the Russian language, giving courses in Oriental Studies in St Petersburg. During the period 1908–13 *Evreiskaia entsklopediia* (The Jewish encyclopedia) was published in 16 volumes; it has remained the most important source of information about Russian Jewry up to the present time.

It is important to bear in mind that during this period many young writers began their careers, a number of whom were committed to Russian–Jewish literature but who were torn from it by the Bolshevik revolution (through emigration and a forced change in political and literary orientation). This particularly applied to poetry, which had just begun to gather strength. Two of the most gifted Russian–Jewish poets of this time were Lev (Leib) Jaffe (1876–1948) and Samuel Marshak (1887–1964), both active Zionists. Both wrote a great deal for Zionist-oriented periodicals (Jaffe from 1902 and Marshak from 1904) up to the end of the period under review. But in 1918 Jaffe emigrated and subsequently almost entirely devoted himself to politics; Marshak irrevocably broke with politics and with Jewry.

FURTHER READING

Lvov-Rogachevsky, V.: *A History of Russian Jewish Literature* (Ann Arbor, Mich.: Ardis, 1979)
Zipperstein, S. J.: *Odessa, A Cultural History* (Stanford, Calif.: Stanford University Press, 1985)

SHIMON MARKISH

Ryback, Issachar (1897–1935) Russian artist. Issachar Ryback was born in the small Ukranian town of Elisavetgrad (now Kirovo) in 1897. When he was a child his father was murdered by a Cossack band in a pogrom. In 1916, following five years of study at the Kiev Art School, Ryback and El Lissitzky received financing from the Jewish Historical and Ethnographic Society to make an ethnographic tour of the Dnieper River. Inspired by the contemporary belief that a modern Jewish art based on Jewish folk art was possible, they explored the art and architecture of the wooden synagogues of the area, making plans and colored drawings, and gathering inscriptions.

In Ryback's mature paintings and drawings, Cubism and Expressionism provided the language with which to manipulate Jewish folk themes. Cubist devices were employed not to analyze or fracture forms, but to distort and abstract the subject matter – a synagogue or rabbi, for example – for expressive and dramatic effects. His art, albeit more somber and tragic, bears comparison with that of Chagall. In addition to drawings, paintings, and prints, Ryback created a series of small ceramic figures based on folk types of the *shtetl*.

After the Revolution of 1917, Ryback together with Lissitzky and Joseph Tchaikov, founded an art section in the Jewish Cultural League in Kiev. In Berlin between 1921 and 1925, Ryback illustrated children's books in Yiddish and published the albums *The Shtetl* (1923) and *The Jewish Types of the Ukraine* (1924). His visit to the Jewish settlements in the Ukraine on his return to the USSR provided him with visual material for his portfolio, *On the Jewish Fields of the Ukraine* (1926).

Ryback moved to Paris in 1926. The art dealer, Georges Wildenstein, planned a large retrospective of his work for 1935; Ryback died the day before the exhibition opened. In 1962, the artist's widow, Sonia, helped to establish a small museum in Ramat Yosef in Israel for the permanent display of Ryback's work.

FURTHER READING

Kampf, A.: In quest of the Jewish style in the era of the Russian Revolution. *Journal of Jewish Art* 5 (1978) 48–75
Tradition and Revolution: The Jewish Renaissance in Russian Avant-Garde Art, (Jerusalem: The Israel Museum, 1987) [exhibition catalog]

KRISTIE A. JAYNE

Rybakov, Anatolii Naumovich [Anatolii
Aronov] (b.1911) Soviet writer. Rybakov was
born in Chernigov, Chernigov Province, Russia,
the son of an engineer of Jewish origin. In 1919
his family moved to Moscow where, on completing his secondary education, Rybakov
worked for two years in factory labor as a steve-
dore and driver. He entered the Moscow Transport Institute in 1929. In his final year he was
arrested on a trumped-up charge and sentenced
to three years internal exile in Siberia. Released
on 5 November 1935, he was prohibited from
living in any large city and spent from 1936 to
1941 making his way slowly back towards European Russia, working as a ballroom-dancing
teacher, auto mechanic, and driver in places
such as Ufa, Kalinin, and Ryazan. Mobilized as
a private in June 1941, he was commissioned in
the field and, as a major in charge of transport
in the IV Guards Rifle Corps, entered Berlin
with the first Red Army units.

He began writing, under his Jewish mother's
name of Rybakov, while still serving in the
occupying forces at Reichenbach, Germany. His
first novel *Kortik* (The dirk) was published in
1948 and established him at once as a writer of
children's adventure stories. In 1950 he published *Voditeli* (The drivers), for which he won
the Stalin Prize. His further writing includes:
Ekaterina Voronina (1955); *Bronzovaya ptitsa* (1956;
The bronze bird), the sequel to *Kortik*; *Prik-
lyuchenie Krosha* (1960; The adventures of
Krosh); *Leto v Sosnyakakh* (1964; Summer in Sos-
nyaki), an anti–Stalinist novel; *Kanikuly Krosha*
(1966; Krosh on holiday); *Neizvestnyi soldat*
(1970; The unknown soldier), the final part of
the *Krosh* trilogy); *Vystrel* (1975; The shot, ending the *Kortik* trilogy). In 1978 he was the first
Russian writer of Jewish origin to approach the
subject of the Russian Jewish past and of the
Holocaust in the USSR in his *Tyazhelyi pesok*
(*Heavy Sand*, 1981). His *Deti Arbata* (*Children of
the Arbat*, 1988), written in 1966 but not published until 1987, was the first critical treatment
in a permitted publication, whether in fiction or
non-fiction, of the early years of the Stalinist
terror. Most of his books have been adapted for
either TV or cinema, and translated into 22
Soviet and 23 foreign languages.

BIBLIOGRAPHY
Heavy Sand, trans. H. Shukman (London and New
York: Penguin/Viking, 1981); *Children of the Arbat*,
trans. H. Shukman (New York and London: Little, Brown/Century Hutchinson, 1988)

HAROLD SHUKMAN

S

Sachs, Nelly (1891–1970) German–Jewish poet. Born to an assimilated middle-class Berlin family, she was scarcely conscious of her Jewishness until the Nazi period. In 1940 she narrowly succeeded in escaping with her mother to Sweden, where she spent the rest of her life. Her poems were published in periodicals from 1929, but she refused to let these early poems be reprinted. Her major poetry was first written in the war years in order to come to terms with the sufferings of the Jewish people. Her other works are a number of short plays, in which music and visual effects are prominent. They include the mystery-play *Eli*, inspired by hasidic legends; *Der magische Tänzer* (The magic dancer); and the kabbalistic *Beryll sieht in die Nacht* (1969; Beryll sees in the night). She also translated much modern Swedish poetry. From the late 1950s she received numerous literary prizes in Sweden and West Germany. In 1966 she was awarded the Nobel Prize for Literature, jointly with S. J. AGNON.

Nelly Sachs knew little of poetry since Hölderlin and the Romantics, but she had read widely in mysticism. Beginning with the German Romantics and Böhme, she moved on to the oriental and medieval mystics, and finally to Buber's hasidic legends and passages from the Zohar. Her poetry is itself mystical, and was often composed in ecstatic states. "Death was my teacher", she wrote; "my metaphors are my wounds". She tried to pare language down so as to restore its original purity. Her syntax is fragmented and hesitant; her vocabulary concentrates on a small number of image-clusters.

Her poems of the 1940s allude directly to the Holocaust, placing it in the context of Jewish history whose main figures, for her, were Abraham and Job. Thereafter her poetry enlarged its scope. She evoked fear, loneliness, pursuit, and martyrdom, placing them in a cosmic setting by her imagery of stars, planets, wind, and night. The recurrent image of wandering through desert sand evokes the Israelites' journey through Sinai as well as the Diaspora; it also suggests the kabbalistic image of "exile" for man's estrangement from God. Old Testament and hasidic references accompany Christian allusions; the BA'AL SHEM TOV appears alongside St Francis. Though her poems are populated by persecutors and victims, many of them circle round a tentative hope for the transcendence of suffering, often expressed by the image of the butterfly.

Nelly Sachs's intense personal engagement in her poetry, and her arresting and often appalling themes, have made it difficult to attain a balanced view of her achievement. While her elegies on Holocaust victims are deeply moving, assessments of her later poetry vary widely: some critics have hailed her as a prophetess, others doubt whether her poetry consistently attains enough verbal freshness and precision to let the reader share her religious perceptions.

BIBLIOGRAPHY

Gedichte, 2 vols (Frankfurt: 1961, 1971) [poems]; *Zeichen im Sand* (Frankfurt: 1962) [plays]; *O the Chimneys. Selected Poems. Including the Verse Play "Eli"*, trans. M. Hamburger et al. (New York:

Farrar, Straus and Giroux, 1967; London: Cape, 1968)

RITCHIE ROBERTSON

Sadeh, Pinhas (b.1929) Israeli author. Sadeh was born in Tel Aviv. His work is reflective, autobiographical, and mystical, both in prose and in poetry. The genres are not distinguished from each other; each item contains the author's reflections, either through an account of his own life and thoughts, or, more rarely, through the fictional other.

His first work, *Hahayim kemashal* (1958; *Life as a Parable*, 1966), sets out the program. Life is a voyage of discovery, and it stands for something other. That other is God, the object of the parable. This, as Sadeh understands it, is what it means to be religious. For him, literature should recover its initial Hebrew purpose, to clear the way for the Lord.

The author's function is also, in consequence, to grasp man's condition. His poetry expresses ineffable longing for the ungraspable, and his poetic language abounds with terms for yearning, longing, aspiration to what he calls "the baptism of the soul". Man's condition is to experience this aspiration and thus acquire a taste of the Godhead. Literature exists in the service of this attempt at mystical union, beyond the tawdry, everyday concerns of life and of most current literature.

BIBLIOGRAPHY
Life as a Parable (London: Anthony Blond, 1966)

FURTHER READING
Yudkin, L. I.: *Escape into Siege*, (London: Routledge & Kegan Paul, 1979)

LEON I. YUDKIN

salon women, Jewish Two centuries ago, in Berlin and Vienna, a tiny circle of wealthy Jewish women entertained the cream of high society in their drawing rooms. Although the number of Jewish women who mixed in salon society in both cities was quite small – probably under fifty – the episode was distinctive in several ways. To begin with, the extraordinary wealth of the women's fathers freed the daughters from Jewish women's traditional work roles in the family's commercial enterprises. Inspired by Moses MENDELSSOHN and his followers, the daughters used their leisure to conquer the secular intellectual world. Even with their fathers' wealth and their own acculturation, it was not to be presumed that nobles in either city would be willing to socialize with Jews. But for three reasons, nobles did indeed deign to visit Jewish homes in these two settings. First, there was a temporary economic crisis among the nobility, which Jewish loans alleviated. Second, there was no efficient banking system for anonymous loaning, so to get a loan one had to socialize with the Jews. Third, there was an ideology of emancipation which was favorable to individual acculturated Jews, if not to Judaism itself.

The Berlin salons

In Berlin, the first salon opened in 1780, led by Henriette Herz, wife of the physician Markus Herz. The most popular salon met at Rahel Levin's home; Levin later married the diplomat and writer Karl August Varnhagen von Ense, and her posthumously published correspondence remains important in German literary history. Moses Mendelssohn's daughter Dorothea, later Dorothea Schlegel, was a prominent member of salon circles but never actually hosted her own salon. The less famous salon women included Philippine Cohen (née Hitzel Zuelz), Rebecca Friedlaender and her sister Marianne Saaling (both née Solomon), Sara von Grotthuss and her sister Marianne von Eybenberg (both née Meyer), Amalie Beer (née Wolff), and Sara Levy (née Itzig). The intellectual level of the salon women varied considerably. Dorothea Schlegel published a novel (under Schlegel's name); Henriette Herz mastered several languages; Rahel Levin's letters were widely admired for their sharp opinions and innovative style. Other women had only mastered oral culture, which was nonetheless crucial for hosting a salon. Salon experiences led in many cases to the women's conversions and

Rahel Levin Varnhagen

intermarriages, which were the final confirmation of their entree into the Gentile world.

The Vienna salons

In Vienna Jewish salon culture was literally a Berlin export. In Vienna, as in Berlin, there were nobles and commoner writers willing to attend a Jewish salon. But the difference between the two cities was that the Viennese Jewish community obviously was not in the cultural and intellectual situation to "produce" the Jewish hostesses. And so Vienna's salons began when two daughters of the powerful Itzig family in Berlin, Fanny and Cacelie, moved to Vienna when each married an ennobled Austrian Jewish financier. The salon hosted by Fanny von Arnstein was for many years Vienna's only real salon. By the time of the Vienna Congress in 1814 and 1815, several more exclusive noble salons had opened. But observers still praised the atmosphere in her salon as the most "free" in Vienna. Indeed, during the many months while the Vienna Congress was in session, Fanny von Arnstein's salon also had its political function, since it was a central meeting place for Prussian diplomats working at the Congress.

Decline after 1815

The salon tradition did not completely disappear either in Berlin or Vienna after 1815, but beginning in that decade both writers and nobles increasingly found other public arenas for socializing, albeit not with each other. As the intelligentsia grew . and its institutions became more formalized, the coffeehouse, the newspaper, the lecture hall, the professional association, and the club took over the functions of the salon. And there was also a shift in the sort of homes where high society gathered. Gradually the Jewish women began to find their drawing rooms quite empty, as high society in both cities became more exclusively noble. In Berlin, especially, the Jewish salons were victims of the new patriotic anti-Semitism, whose ideologues explicitly attacked the Jewish salon women for the very assimilation of which they were so proud.

The Jewish salons disappeared also because of developments inside the Jewish world. As more and more career opportunities opened to Jewish men, it was they and not the Jewish women who were tempted to leave the faith to enter the wider world. But not all of those who were tempted succumbed, for the formation of Reform Judaism meant that conversion and intermarriage were no longer the only paths away from traditional Judaism. All in all, the price the Jewish salon women were asked to pay for their social success was a high one, for in gaining this emancipation they also lost the warmth and the faith of their families and communities. Yet for all its costs, theirs was not an opportunity offered to every generation, because the constellation of social structures and ideological trends which made their salons possible was fragile and evanescent.

FURTHER READING

Arendt, H.: *Rahel Varnhagen: The Life of a Jewess* (London: East & West Library, 1958; repr., New York, 1974)

Hargrave, M.: *Some German Women and Their Salons* (London: T. Werner Laurie, [1912])

Hertz, D.: *Jewish High Society in Old Regime Berlin* (New Haven and London: Yale University Press, 1988)

Kayserling, M.: *Die juedischen Frauen in der Geschichte, Literatur und Kunst* (Leipzig: P. A. Brockhaus, 1879)

Meyer, B.: *Salon Sketches* (New York: Bloch, 1938)

DEBORAH HERTZ

Salten, Felix [Siegmund Salzmann] (1869–1945)   Austrian writer. Born in Budapest, Salten was educated in Vienna, and studied philosophy there. He became a well-known feuilletonist, and one of the central figures of Young Vienna, along with Arthur SCHNITZLER and others. A friend of HERZL, he succeeded him to the post of feuilleton editor of the *Neue Freie Presse*. His main reputation was as a drama critic, his own plays generally being unsuccessful. He is claimed as the author of *Josephine Mutzenbacher*, the most famous pornographic novel of fin-de-siècle Vienna. He is most famous, however, as the author of *Bambi* (1926; *Bambi*, 1928). Salten left Vienna in 1938 for the USA, and in 1945 returned to Switzerland. He died in Zurich.

Salten has received little attention as a figure in Vienna 1900. He appears to have been a typical esthete, and his feuilletonistic style made him a favorite target for Karl KRAUS's satire. (Salten assaulted Kraus in 1899 for the latter's jibes at him.) Salten followed his colleagues Herzl and Richard BEER-HOFFMAN in combining his estheticism with a strong Jewish identity. He was a very early supporter of Herzl's Zionism, and saw the need to remain true to one's Jewish self as paramount, at one point attacking Mahler for having surrendered his. Salten dealt with Jewish themes in at least two of his works: *Neue Menschen auf alter Erde* (1925; New people on ancient soil) and *Simson* (1928).

STEVEN BELLER

Salvador, Joseph (1796–1873)   French Philosopher. Born in Montpellier, son of a Catholic mother and Jewish father of Iberian origins, ardent admirer of the French Revolution, and attracted by Utopian socialism, Salvador is one of the most original messianic thinkers, an early, highly imaginative Zionist whose New Jerusalem of truth, justice, science, and law was placed in Palestine, in ancient Jerusalem whose gates (renamed Moses, Jesus, Mohammed, Brahma, Voltaire, and Rousseau) are open to all. In this ecumenical *aliyah*, the Jewish people and revolutionary France play a special role. The first, because they are the custodians of the rational and just laws of Moses, uncorrupted by Rome and the Roman Church. The second, because the French Revolution ushered in an irresistible and universal return to mosaism and a liberation from Rome. At the heart of Salvador's Utopia lies a defence of Judaism as a rational religion unjustly held in contempt by a semi-pagan, metaphysically orientated, spiritually oppressive Church, remote from the teachings of Jesus. These ideas, developed in numerous works, found their most eloquent expression in *Paris, Rome et Jérusalem, ou la Question Religieuse au XIXe siècle* (1860).

NELLY WILSON

Saminsky, Lazare (1882–1959)   American composer, conductor, and musicologist. He was born near Odessa, Russia, and died in Port Chester, New York. He studied mathematics and philosophy at the University of St Petersburg, composition with Rimsky-Korsakov and Liadov, and conducting with Nicolas Tcherepnin at the St Petersburg Conservatory, graduating in 1910. While he and a group of other Jewish students were studying with Rimsky-Korsakov, they founded "The Society for Jewish Folk-Music". During his military service he was stationed in Tiflis, where later (1915–18) he conducted symphonic concerts and taught briefly at the People's Conservatory (1917–18). Saminsky left Russia in 1919, traveling first to Palestine, then to Paris and London, finally settling in New York City in 1920. In 1923 he was a co-founder of the League of Composers and, in 1924, assumed the position of music director of Temple Emanu-El in New York City, a position which he held until his death in 1959. During his tenure at Emanu-El he established the Three Choir Festival, which was especially famous for its presentation of new liturgical music in his frequent appearances as guest conductor all over the world.

Musically, Saminsky's style follows the

romantic tradition both in sound and structure, but Hebrew subjects and tunes often play a most important role in his works. Very little of his music still remains in the secular repertory, but his liturgical works for the synagogue are still frequently heard. This is especially true of his *To Zion* (1948), a choral fantasy; *Ten Hebrew Folk Songs and Dances; Three Hebrew Song Cycles*; a *Sabbath Morning Service; High Holyday Service*; and *By the Waters of Babylon*. His secular works include four operas, five symphonies, many shorter orchestral works, chamber music, and songs.

Saminsky was also a prolific musicologist, critic, and writer on scientific subjects. Some of his books contain harsh criticisms of some of the major musical figures on the American scene. This did not endear him to the musical establishment of the middle of the twentieth century.

SAMUEL H. ADLER

Samuel, Maurice (1895–1972)   American writer and lecturer.

Samuel was born in Macin, Romania, from which his family emigrated before the end of his fifth year. After a two-year stay in Paris, the family settled in Manchester, England, where his father earned his livelihood as a shoemaker. Maurice proved to be an exceptionally able student and won a number of competitive scholarships at the University of Manchester, where his teachers included the Nobel Prize-winning physicist Ernest Rutherford, and the chemist Chaim WEIZMANN, with whom Samuel was later to be associated in the Zionist movement. Weizmann credited him with being very helpful in the preparation of his autobiography, *Trial and Error*.

In the summer of 1914 Samuel was visiting Paris and witnessed the outbreak of the First World War and the assassination of the Socialist leader, Jean Jaurès. At the end of 1914 Samuel sailed for the USA where he was to spend most of the rest of his life. In 1917 he was drafted into the American Army and went with the American Expeditionary Force to France. He did intelligence work in Bordeaux and, after the armistice, in Paris. In 1919 he served as secretary and interpreter (from the Yiddish) for the Morgenthau Pogrom Investigation Commission in Poland. This experience, he later wrote, "had a permanent effect on my already developed Jewish interests".

Between the two World Wars, he became the most popular oral expositor of Zionist ideas, not only in the USA and Canada, but as a lecturer in South Africa and in Palestine, where he settled for a number of years during the period of the British Mandate.

The most popular of his 25 books has proved to be *The World of Sholem Aleichem*, which was published in 1943 at the very moment when the Yiddish-speaking communities of eastern Europe were being destroyed. This was the first of three books he published on the general subject of Yiddish literature, the second being *Prince of the Ghetto* (on I. L. PERETZ), published in 1948, and *In Praise of Yiddish*, published in 1971.

Samuel was an accomplished linguist who was fluent in French, German, Hebrew, Yiddish, and English. In order to write his book on the Mendel Beilis Case, *Blood Accusation*, he learned Russian as well. He was a distinguished translator into English of many authors, including Sholem ASH, Isaac Bashevis SINGER, and Hayyim Nachman BIALIK.

In addition to his popularity as a lecturer, he became known to many thousands of American radio listeners as the host of the program *The Eternal Light* (in which he conversed with the poet Mark Van Doren), sponsored by the Jewish Theological Seminary of America. This program produced two books, edited after his death by Edith Samuel, as well as his own volume, *Certain People of the Book* (1955).

In addition to those books already mentioned Samuel published an autobiography, *Little Did I Know* (1963) and several novels, a polemic, *The Professor and the Fossil* (published 1956), aimed at Arnold Toynbee's *The Idea of History*, and several books on Zionism.

FURTHER READING
Hindus, M., ed.: *The Worlds of Maurice Samuel*, intro. M. Hindus (Philadelphia: The Jewish Publication Society of America, 1977)

MILTON HINDUS

Schach, Leonard (b.1918) South African actor and theater director. His early career was focused in Cape Town where he was educated at the South African College School and the University of Cape Town. He attained his MA and studied law. His career began during the Second World War when he directed *The Middle Watch* while serving in the navy.

In 1947 and 1948 he traveled to the USA and Europe on a two-year study of theater arts. In 1948 he represented the Smuts government at the inaugural Conference of the International Theatre Institute, prior to the setting up of South Africa's National Theatre, predecessor to its four provincial performing-arts councils. He established himself as a producer and director with his production of Tennessee Willams's *The Glass Menagerie* (1948) and subsequently directed plays for, and established several South African theater societies.

He settled in Israel where in the late 1980s he was directing important productions in Hebrew and English. Among these are Arthur Miller's *After the Fall*, Harold Pinter's *The Birthday Party*, and Peter Shaffer's *Equus*. Having worked on theater and film direction in several countries, he has been called South Africa's only "international" director.

JOCELYN HELLIG

Schaeffer, Susan Fromberg (b.1941) American novelist and poet. Born in Brooklyn, New York, Schaeffer was educated at Simmons College and received her BA, MA, and Ph.D. degrees from the University of Chicago. A member of the English faculty at Brooklyn College since 1967, Schaeffer has also taught at other American universities. Married to Neil Schaeffer, in 1970, and the mother of two children, Schaeffer has been a prolific writer. Since her first book of poetry, *The Witch and the Weather Report* (1972), and her first novel, *Falling* (1973), named one of the 10 best novels of that year by *Time*, she has published five more collections of poetry, and seven volumes of fiction, including a children's novel. In 1974 she won the Edward Lewis Wallant Award and the Friends of Literature Award for her novel *Anya*, and received a National Book Award nomination for her poetry collection, *Granite Lady*. She has since received additional honors, including a Guggenheim fellowship.

As a fiction writer, Schaeffer creates her narrative landscapes through a rich accretion of detail which allows the reader to become immersed in the world of the characters. In *Falling* Elizabeth Kamen, a young Jewish woman attempts suicide, then struggles back to mental health with the help of psychoanalysis, reaching through reflections of her childhood memories, family stories, and her own romantic involvements to, in Wayne C. Booth's words, "an acceptance of all that has been done against her and all that she has done to destroy herself". Similarly, in *Anya*, Schaeffer makes the reader live the loss imposed by the Holocaust on her protagonist, by painting a vivid picture of Anya's comfortable, protected, assimilated life as an upper-middle-class Jew in pre-war Vilno, Poland, from which the reader tumbles with Anya into the devastating degradation of the ghetto, the camps, and the separation from her daughter, before beginning a new life in the USA. In *Anya*, as in *Falling*, the intimacy of Jewish family life, its obsessive quality, is a determining force in the lives of her characters, but a quality to be judged cautiously.

Although she claims not to be "a Jewish writer . . . trying deliberately to write on Jewish themes", Schaeffer acknowledges her Jewish sensibility, present throughout. After *Anya*, however, her next novel *Time in Its Flight* (1978), again a chronicle which explored a nineteenth-century New England family's sensibilities, received relatively poor reviews for its tedious detailing of happy family life. A collection of short stories *The Queen of Egypt* (1980) includes several with Jewish themes: "His daughter's house", "Advice", and "Antiques". Subsequent novels: *Love* (1980), *The Madness of a Seduced Woman* (1983), and *Mainland* (1985) have been received with critical interest.

FURTHER READING

Mazurkiewicz, M.: *Contemporary Authors* vol. 18 (Detroit: Gale Research Co., 1986) 402–5

Ribalow, H. U., ed.: *The Tie that Binds: Conversations with Jewish Writers* (San Diego: A. S. Barnes, 1980)

ELIZABETH KLEIN

Schalit, Heinrich (1886–1976) American composer, pianist, and organist. He was born in Vienna and died in Evergreen, Colorado. He began his musical studies with Jacob Labor at the age of 11. In 1903 he entered the Staatliche Musikakademie in Vienna, where he studied with Robert Fuchs and piano under Leschetitzky. After winning many of the most coveted student prizes, Schalit went to Munich where many of his early non-liturgical works were first performed. In Munich also, he continued his studies on the organ, which were begun in Vienna. The First World War caused a hiatus in his career, and thereafter, as a musician, he grew increasingly conscious of his Jewish heritage. It began with the setting, opus 16, of texts by Yehuda Halevy called *Seelenlieder* for baritone and piano. These Halevy texts continued to inspire Schalit for the rest of his creative life. From 1927 to 1933 he was organist at the large Munich Liberal synagogue and became acquainted with the Sulzer, Lewandowski, Kirschner tradition of German liturgical music. He rebelled against it, feeling that his study of the works of Idelsohn, biblical cantillation, psalmody, and the ancient modes made these "romantic" models spurious. In 1932 Schalit composed his *Freitagabend Liturgie*, a complete Sabbath Eve Service which he later revised and to which he added several numbers before publishing it in the USA in 1951.

From 1933 Schalit was in transition, first becoming organist and music director at the central synagogue in Rome, then living in London for a short while until 1940, when he emigrated to the USA to take a position at Temple B'rith Kodesh in Rochester, New York, and then at temples in Providence, Rhode Island, and in Hollywood. In 1948 he moved to Evergreen, Colorado to devote himself exclusively to composition.

Schalit began his career as a very prolific composer, writing chamber and piano works in quick succession between 1906 and 1917. However, once he began the works with Jewish content, his output slowed considerably and he often revised a work several times until it lived up to his standard of excellence.

Among his most important mature works are: *In Eternity* for chorus and strings (1929); *Chassidic Dances* for violin and piano (later written for string orchestra) (1936); *Builders of Zion* for unison chorus and piano (1944); *Sabbath Morning Liturgy* (1954); *Songs of Glory*, a suite of anthems (1963); and a few individual anthems, prayers and organ preludes.

A book in tribute of the composer was published by his son Michael, called *Heinrich Schalit, the Man and his Music*.

SAMUEL H. ADLER

Schechter, Solomon (1847–1915) Scholar, theologian, and president of the Jewish Theological Seminary of America. Schechter was born in Fascani, Romania, where his father, a *Habad* Hasid, was a *shohet* (hence the family name). After the usual traditional course of study in the Talmud and Codes, Schechter took courses at the University of Berlin and the Berlin Hochschule. Soon after his arrival in England to be the private tutor to C. G. Montefiore, Schechter won a reputation as a scholarly exponent of traditional Judaism, in a felicitous English style he had acquired through wide reading in English literature. In 1892 Schechter was appointed reader in Rabbinics at Cambridge University and, in 1899, he also became Professor of Hebrew at University College, London.

Schechter established his scholarly reputation by the publication of *Avot According to Rabbi Nathan* (1887), and, especially, by his discovery of the Cairo Genizah, of which he brought to Cambridge over 100,000 fragments. The investigation of these shed new light on the history of medieval Jewry. Schechter's three-volume *Studies in Judaism* (1896–1924), and his *Some Aspects of Rabbinic Theology* (1909) fast became classics of the genre.

Schechter was appointed President of the Jewish Theological Seminary in New York, a position he occupied until his death. Here he was responsible, more than any other, for the training of Conservative Rabbis with an

Solomon Schechter studying fragments from the Cairo Genizah in the Cambridge University Library, c.1898

approach to traditional Judaism based on the ideas of Zecharias FRANKEL. Judaism, in this view, is a developing religion, with its authority vested ultimately not on this or that sacred book, but on the historical experience of what Schechter called "Catholic Israel."

BIBLIOGRAPHY
Aspects of Rabbinic Theology, intro. L. Finkelstein (New York: Schocken Publishers, 1961) vi–xx

LOUIS JACOBS

Scheiber, Alexander (1913–1985) Hungarian rabbi and scholar. Born in Budapest, Scheiber was ordained at the Budapest Jewish Theological Seminary where he later became professor (1945) and director (1950). Many of the world's greatest scholars in Judaica, including Wilhelm BACHER, Ignaz GOLDZIHER and Bernard HELLER, had at some time taught or studied there, and under Scheiber's directorship it was transformed into an international center of Jewish Studies. Scheiber considered himself to be a link in the great tradition of Jewish studies in Hungary, and he concentrated on the spiritual and cultural revival of the remnant of Hungarian Jewry after the Second World War. He fought to preserve Jewish life in post-war Hungary and superintended the resuscitation of a number of synagogues and the revival of Jewish communities.

Scheiber's scholarship was vast; he published major works on Jewish history, primarily the history of Hungarian Jewry, Jewish literature, comparative folklore, Jewish liturgy (*piyyut*), bibliography and the history of Jewish art. Another of his fields of specialization was the study of a collection of over 700 *genizah* fragments in the library of the Austrian scholar, David Kaufmann, which Scheiber began publishing in 1949. During several stays in England, mainly at Cambridge, he discovered many other important *genizah* fragments. In 1975 *Folklór és Tárgytörténet* (Folklore and history of motifs) was published, his collected papers issued by the Board of Representatives of the Jews in Hungary. Its focus was folklore, biblical legends, and the history of literary motifs, but it included formidable material on the work of Hungarian–Jewish folklorists, and on biblical and Jewish motifs in Hungarian literature from the sixteenth century. Scheiber's purpose in the book was to demonstrate the past glory of a great Jewish community and its contribution to the culture of its host nation.

Scheiber served as visiting professor at universities in the United States and the United Kingdom, including Cambridge, Oxford, and the Oxford Center for Hebrew Studies. He was offered the directorship of Jews' College in London but chose to remain at the Theological Seminary in Budapest, considering its wellbeing his major priority. He was awarded the Order of the Hungarian Flag in 1983.

GLENDA ABRAMSON

Schlesinger, John (b.1926) British film director. Schlesinger caught the mood of the 1960s with his feature films, *A Kind of Loving* (1962), *Billy Liar* (1963), and *Darling* (1965). The story of the first of these is told through the eyes of the central character and suggests one of Schlesinger's recurring themes, a hero who is constitutionally unable to conform to society. He directs also for the theater and, most interestingly, for television.

Having begun his career as an actor, he went to the BBC, where he worked on *Tonight* and *Monitor* and after which he directed the greatly admired documentary, *Terminus* (1960). He soon emerged as an "international", bankable, director with British roots, although *Far From the Madding Crowd* (1967) and *The Day of the Locust* (USA, 1974) failed badly. His work is sometimes considered merely fashionable and *Marathon Man* (1976), while pursuing the theme of Nazi-hunting, is unbalanced with cliché and surprisingly grotesque acting. On the other hand, *Sunday Bloody Sunday* (in which Peter Finch plays a homosexual Jewish medical practitioner) draws on his skills and patience with actors and elevates the theme of isolation to one of personal concern. The doctor is desperate to find acceptance but is forever doomed to remain outside Jewish and Gentile heterosexual life. Schlesinger draws parallels with the obligatory black guest who is invited to a Sunday lunch, skilfully distancing him in the frame and emphasizing that he is not genuinely accepted.

Schlesinger had another huge success with *Midnight Cowboy* (USA, 1969), another story of outsiders. The young, naive John Voight arrives in New York expecting to make his fortune, primarily as a gigolo. He finds himself ruthlessly exploited by women, men, religious cranks, and others. Other film include *Honky Tonk Freeway* (1981) and *Madame Sousatzka* (1989).

FURTHER READING

Walker, A. *Hollywood England: The British Film Industry in the Sixties* (London: Michael Joseph, 1974)

KEVIN GOUGH-YATES

Schnitzler, Arthur (1862–1931)   Austrian playwright and novelist. Born in Vienna, Schnitzler was the son of the laryngologist Johann Schnitzler, and was related to the Schey family. He was educated at the *Akademisches Gymnasium*, and subsequently studied medicine at the university. After gaining his doctorate he pursued the career of a physician; it was only in 1893, with the success of *Anatol* (first published in English, 1911) that he became a full-time writer. His subsequent career made him one of

Arthur Schnitzler

the most prominent figures in Young Vienna, and hence of fin-de-siècle Vienna.

Although he is seen nowadays as the chronicler of the decadent charm of the declining years of the Habsburg Monarchy, his contemporary reputation rested on his innovative approach and to a significant degree on his critical view of society. His play *Liebelei* (1895; *Dalliance* 1986) had the distinction of being the first play in Viennese dialect to be performed in the Burgtheater. His short story, *Leutnant Gustl* (1900) was the first in German to use the stream-of-consciousness approach, an idea which Schnitzler adopted from Dujardin's *Les lauriers sont coupés*. *Gustl* caused a scandal, and led to Schnitzler losing his reserve officer commission. Other works which caused a furore were *Der grüne Kakadu* (1899; *The Green Cockatoo*, 1913), *Reigen* (1900; *La Ronde*, 1959) and *Professor Bernhardi* (1912; *Professor Bernhardi*, 1927).

The last of these is one of the works in which Schnitzler's attitude to the Jewish predicament in Vienna is most evident. The other work in which the Jewish question plays a large, indeed dominant, role, is his only major novel, *Der Weg ins Freie* (1908; *The Road to the Open*, 1913) His autobiography *Jugend in Wien* (1868, *My Youth in Vienna*, 1970) also deals with this issue. Schnitzler had little connection with the formal aspects of Judaism, and did not consider himself a "Jewish writer", but rather a German one. However, he was very conscious of being a Jew in an age of anti-Semitism, and he identified the Jewish tradition with the Enlightenment. In his view Jews represented the "other" in European society, and as such symbolized the possibility of a new humanity, albeit born of suffering. Schnitzler was thus contemptuous of those who converted to Catholicism to complete the assimilation, regarding them as renegades; for him such a course of action was shirking one's responsibility as a (Jewish) individual.

This image of the Jewish role in Vienna is evident in both *Professor Bernhardi* and *The Road to the Open*. In the former a Jewish doctor, in trying to be humane, earns the wrath of the Catholic church, and succumbs to the political machinations of Viennese anti-Semitism. In the latter, Jewish individuals in the assimilated liberal bourgeoisie are shown attempting to escape the predicaments which the failure of assimilation has caused. Zionism, socialism, simple estheticism, and conversion are all shown to be inadequate solutions; only the look within, recognition of the self, can free the individual from the oppressive environment. Understanding the soul is the way to freedom. It is in this sense that Schnitzler saw the Jews as "the ferment of humanity".

FURTHER READING

Liptzin, S.: Arthur Schnitzler. In *Germany's Stepchildren* (Philadelphia: The Jewish Publication Society of America, 1944)

STEVEN BELLER

Schoenberg, Arnold (1874–1951)

Austrian and (after 1941) American composer. Born in Vienna, Schoenberg began his musical studies with violin lessons at the age of eight. Except for a brief period of study with Alexander von Zemlinsky, he was entirely self-taught as a composer.

His early compositions gradually attracted the favorable attention of musicians. His String Quartet in D Major (1897) was recommended by Zemlinsky to the Wiener Tonkünstlerverein which then gave it a public performance. The success of this work brought further recognition and marks the beginning of Schoenberg's public life as a composer. During the next few years compositions appeared in rapid succession: five sets of songs, opp. 1, 2, 3, 6, and 8, *Verklärte Nacht*, op. 4, *Gurrelieder, Pelleas and Melisande*, op. 5, String Quartets Nos 1 and 2, opp. 7 and 10, and the Chamber Symphony, op. 9. These compositions established Schoenberg's reputation as one of the most innovative composers of his day.

Each successive composition from this period is characterized by more and more intensive use of chromaticism, ever more tightly controlled motivic development, freer and more adventurous treatment of dissonance, longer and more extended excursions into remote keys: Schoenberg was pushing to the limits of tonality. Although then – as always – a small, enthusiastic group of supporters formed around him, the vast majority of the Viennese musical public reacted with growing hostility to his music.

This hostility turned to horror and outrage, when Schoenberg, feeling compelled by what he saw as the inner logic of his material, abandoned tonality and wrote the first atonal compositions: the *Klavierstücke*, op. 11 and the *George Lieder*, op. 15 (1908–9). To Schoenberg, the free treatment of dissonance and the intensive use of chromaticism – characteristic of the late Romantic style – had loosened the structural functions of tonality and made inevitable the coming of atonality. In a remarkable series of compositions, including the Five Pieces for Orchestra, op. 16, *Erwartung*, op. 17, and *Pierrot Lunaire*, op. 21, he wrestled with the special problems of coherence posed by his new material.

However, Schoenberg was never completely satisfied with the ad hoc compositional logic of his atonal period. In particular he was concerned that he felt incapable of writing large abstract forms: he noticed that all of his compositions were either very short or that the form was dictated by a text. Between 1914 and 1923 he gradually evolved a new method of composition, one designed to replace the structural functions of tonality. In a burst of enthusiasm he remarked to a friend: "I have just discovered something which will assure the supremacy of German music for the next 100 years". This was his method of 12-tone composition in which a 12-tone "set" (or "row" or "series") – that is, a particular ordering of the 12 chromatic pitch classes – acts as the source for all of the material in the composition. In the following years, Schoenberg refined his use of this new method and was inspired to write some of his most enduring masterpieces: the Variations for Orchestra, op. 31, the Concerto for Violin, op. 36, the Fourth String Quartet, op. 37, the String Trio, op. 45, and *Moses and Aron*.

In 1933, with the coming to power of the Nazis, Schoenberg emigrated to the USA, eventually settling in Los Angeles. Although in his early manhood (1898) Schoenberg had converted to Lutheranism, his conversion was not an attempt at assimilation: in Catholic Austria Lutheranism was scarcely more tolerated than Judaism. Rather, this conversion should be understood as evidence of Schoenberg's lifelong spiritual search. Moreover, he was never totally happy with his choice, and when he returned formally to Judaism – in 1933 – it was the culmination of a long process. Schoenberg's return to Judaism is reflected in his compositions: he retold (and reinterpreted) episodes from Exodus in *Moses and Aron*, set the *Kol Nidre*, op. 39, gave tribute to the heroes of the Resistance in his *Survivor from Warsaw*, op. 46, and celebrated the rebirth of Israel with *Israel Exists Again*.

One of the most important musical figures of all time, Schoenberg is universally acknowledged to have transformed musical thought in the twentieth century. His compositions have influenced – directly and indirectly – virtually every composer working today. The innovations he promulgated, the ideas he disseminated, the concepts he created have penetrated to every corner of our musical consciousness, altering totally and irrevocably our notions of musical

Arnold Schoenberg teaching at the University of California

coherence. Indeed, it is fair to say that in historical importance, and in the scope of the effect of his ideas, he has no peer in this century and can reasonably be compared only to such figures as Dufay, Monteverdi, or Beethoven.

That a composer of such paramount importance was Jewish is a mark of the extraordinary transformation of social life in Europe in the nineteenth century. In earlier eras composers were trained and employed by church or court, environments hardly suitable for a Jewish composer. But with the decline of royal and ecclesiastical patronage and the rise of the middle class, Jewish musicians began to have opportunities to participate actively in the musical life of Europe. Schoenberg's career is both a reflection of that social change and an indication of the contribution Jews could make to musical culture once they were permitted to participate actively in it.

BIBLIOGRAPHY

Style and Idea: Selected Writings of Arnold Schoenberg, ed. L. Stein; trans. L. Black (New York: St Martins Press, 1975) *Letters*, ed. E. Stein, trans. E. Wilkins and E. Kaiser (Berkeley and Los Angeles: University of California Press, 1987)

FURTHER READING

Stuckenschmidt, H. H.: *Schoenberg: His Life, World and Work*, trans. H. Searle (New York: Schirmer Books, 1978)

Perle, G., Neighbour, O., and Griffiths, P.: *The New Grove Second Viennese School* (London: Macmillan, 1984)

ETHAN HAIMO

Scholem, Gershom (1897–1982) Israeli historian of Jewish mysticism. Gershom Scholem almost singlehandedly created the field of academic study of Jewish mysticism (*kabbalah*) which had previously had the status of an unwanted stepchild of Jewish historiography. By transforming this largely neglected and denigrated subject into the main actor on the stage of Jewish history, Scholem radically changed the perception of the "essence" of Judaism. Where nineteenth-century historians and philosophers had considered Judaism to be a rational and legal religion, Scholem showed that it also contained irrational and ecstatic elements; at times, he even argued that mysticism was the vital force in Jewish history and that without it, law and philosophy would have turned rigid and sterile.

Scholem was born to an assimilated family of printers in Berlin. In his youth, Scholem rebelled against the assimilationist culture of his parents. One of his three brothers, Werner, who later became a Communist delegate to the Reichstag during the Weimar Republic, had a major influence on his rebelliousness. He was attracted to the Zionist youth movement Jung-Juda and fell under the influence of Martin BUBER in the years before the First World War. During the war, he broke with Buber over support for the war and identified with the small pacifist camp led by the anarchist Gustav LANDAUER. Scholem's pacifism was based on radical Zionist principles: the Jews had no part in Europe's war and should emigrate to Palestine.

Scholem initially undertook to study mathematics and philosophy, but abandoned these fields for Jewish mysticism. He had educated himself in the reading of Hebrew texts and completed a doctoral dissertation on the *Sefer bahir* at the University of Munich in 1922. In 1923 he emigrated to Palestine where Hugo Bergmann, who was the chief librarian of the nascent Hebrew University, hired him as Judaica librarian. When the university opened in 1925, Scholem was appointed lecturer in Jewish mysticism and was promoted to Professor several years later. He served in this capacity until his retirement in 1965. Scholem's academic career therefore overlapped with the history of the Hebrew University to whose development he made a singular contribution. As a result of his work and his training of students, *kabbalah* became a central focus of the curriculum in Jewish studies at the university. Beyond his specific discipline, Scholem was one of the most influential figures in the life of the university and in the Jewish intellectual world in general.

The main outlines of Scholem's history of Jewish mysticism can be discerned best in *Major Trends in Jewish Mysticism*, which was delivered as series of lectures in 1938 and published in 1941. Here, Scholem developed the idea that the history of religions, and the Jewish religion in particular, has three stages: the mythical period of immediacy with God, the legal and philosophical period when the revelation of the first period is institutionalized, and the third period of mysticism when an attempt is made to recover the immediacy of the religion's origins. The dialectical structure of this theory is characteristic of Scholem's thought and reflects his German intellectual heritage. Mysticism, he argued, comes to revitalize a religion in danger of losing its mythic forces.

In this work Scholem also proposed a solution to one of the outstanding problems of Jewish historiography: the dating of the *Zohar*, the classical work of *kabbalah*. Although he had argued in the 1920s that the *Zohar* was an ancient work (as it itself claims to be), in *Major Trends* he proved definitively that it dated from the late thirteenth century and was the work of Moses de Leon.

At the heart of Scholem's historiography is the belief that myth is crucial to the vitality of a religious tradition. He identified the central myth of the *kabbalah* with Gnosticism. He argued that as early as late antiquity, Jewish mystics developed a monotheistic version of Gnostic dualism. This Jewish Gnosticism persisted in underground traditions and made its way from Babylonia via Italy and Germany to southern France where it surfaced in the *Sefer Bahir* and thence to the *kabbalah* of Provence and Spain. Gnostic themes could be found later in sixteenth-century Lurianic *kabbalah* and in the heretical messianic Sabbatian movement of the seventeenth century. Indeed, it was the very heretical potential of the Gnostic myth in Judaism that made the *kabbalah* at once a force of vitality and also a source of danger. In Sabbatianism, the Gnostic myth exploded and caused an outburst of antinomian heresy.

Scholem's studies of Sabbatianism were among his most pioneering. He regarded this movement, which had previously been considered marginal, as central to any understanding of Jewish history. He argued that Sabbatianism captured the imagination of much of the Jewish world and profoundly shook the hegemony of the rabbis. It was therefore the great watershed between the Middle Ages and modernity, foreshadowing the rise of antinomian secularism. Scholem held that subsequent Jewish movements, including Hasidism and the Enlightenment, were all reactions to Sabbatianism. Thus the rise of modern Judaism was a consequence of a catastrophe within the Jewish religious tradition and not simply the result of outside influence.

Although Scholem rejected the nineteenth-century rationalist bias, he wrote a similar kind of *Geistesgeschichte* (history of ideas). He held that Jewish history is driven by the dialectic of ideas developed by intellectual elites and he generally ignored the role of social forces. Similarly, he was more interested in the theoretical *kabbalah*, rather than in its folkloristic or popular side.

Scholem was not a mystic, but he believed that the mythic and mystical impulses of the *kabbalah* remain hidden forces in Jewish history into the twentieth century. He suggested frequently that Zionism itself may have taken its vital energies from the same sources. Yet he also made clear his personal ambivalence about these forces. Zionism might end up in the same catastrophe as Sabbatianism if it failed to "neutralize" potentially nihilistic forces. Scholem's own political activities were informed by this analysis. In the 1920s he was active in the *Brit Shalom* which sought a policy of compromise with the Arabs. At the end of his life, he denounced the "Sabbatianism" of the messianic *Gush Emunim* (the religious nationalist movement). Thus, although attracted to such revolutionary forces in the Jewish past, he felt uneasy about them in the present.

BIBLIOGRAPHY
Major Trends in Jewish Mysticism (3rd edn, New York: Schocken, 1961); *The Messianic Idea in Judaism and Other Essays in Jewish Spirituality* (New York: Schocken, 1971); *From Berlin to Jerusalem* (New York: Schocken, 1980) [autobiography]

FURTHER READING
Biale, D.: *Gershom Scholem: Kabbalah and Counter History* (Cambridge: Harvard University Press, 1979; 2nd edn, 1982)

DAVID BIALE

Schreiber, Moses [Hatam Sofer] (1762–1839) German–Hungarian rabbi, halakhic scholar, and Orthodox community leader. Born in Frankfurt and a student of the mystic Nathan Adler, Schreiber followed his teacher when the latter was forced by community pressure to abandon the city. He occupied rabbinic posts in Dresnitz and Mattersdorf, Moravia, establishing his reputation as an outstanding talmudist. In 1806 he was appointed rabbi of Pressburg, Hungary, a community divided between traditionalists and those open to the intellectual influences of the Enlightenment. Through his spiritual and organizational leadership Pressburg and Hungary became bastions of an Orthodoxy which rejected almost all inroads of modernism. He established a *yeshivah* in Pressburg which attracted numerous students and exerted profound pedagogical influence over all the other Hungarian academies. From this school, and by means of his frequent public sermons, Schreiber expounded a systematic ideology of religious conservatism. To him, the entire tradition, including customs of relatively recent origin, was sacred; the preservation of the tradition, in its entirety, was the prerequisite for the survival of Judaism. He fought all attempts toward leniency in observance, liberal educational reform, and rationalistic interpretation of Judaism under his motto: "all innovations are forbidden by the Torah". He took a leading role in opposition to the emerging movement for religious reform, particularly in connection with the Hamburg liberal temple controversy of 1819. An Orthodox leader of international stature, he was the prototype for a new style of Orthodox rabbinate, relatively free of traditional community controls, which exerted enormous influence in Hungary in the struggle against liberalizing tendencies. Schreiber's lasting influence is his outstanding reputation as a Jewish legal scholar. His *responsa*, collected in seven volumes, remain a leading source of authority in halakhic matters.

FURTHER READING

Burak, M. J.: *The Hatam Sofer* (Toronto: Beth Jacob Congregation, 1967)

MARK WASHOFSKY

Schulz, Bruno (1892–1942) Polish writer. Born in the town of Drohobycz, then under Austrian rule, Schulz, intending to become a painter, went to Vienna to study at the Academy of Art. The artistic mood of the Viennese fin-de-siècle was later to be found not only in his drawings, with their tendency towards perverse and sado-masochistic subjects, but also in his stories which grew, in part, out of his drawings. He began writing in the early 1920s, having completed his studies and returned to his native town, remaining there until his death in the Ghetto of Drohobycz during a Gestapo raid. He was always a deliberate provincial, in love with the sleepy atmosphere of his town which pervades many of his stories. He would not leave Drohobycz even when the literary success of his first book, published in Warsaw in 1934, made him a celebrity. This was the book of interconnected short stories, *Sklepy Cynamonowe* (Cinnamon shops; trans. as *Streets of Crocodiles*, 1980). The beauty and originality of these stories impressed the Warsaw literary milieu

and the modest provincial artist found himself, to his surprise, fêted as one of the leaders of the avant-garde, and an exponent, together with Witold Gombrowicz, of the "new Polish prose", to be recognized in the West, many years afterwards, as one of the most brilliant contributions to modern literature. In Poland Schulz's writings were republished after many years of semi-official ban on "decadent literature", and are now recognized as among the most significant events in Polish art and literature.

Schulz's output was small: apart from the above-mentioned book, he published a second collection of stories in 1938, *Sanatorium pod klepsydra* (Sanatorium under the sign of the hourglass), and a number of literary essays and reviews. His correspondence, painstakingly collected several years ago and published in Krakow, indicates that during the last years of his life he proceeded to write a full-scale novel entitled *Mesjasz* (The Messiah).

Often compared to Franz KAFKA, the Polish translation of whose novel, *The Trial*, Schulz signed but did not in fact translate (having lent his already famous name to a translation by a friend), Schulz is different from his contemporary Austro-Hungarian. Where Kafka's prose is "lean", Schulz's is opulent and baroque, poetic and "scientific" at the same time. The qualities the two writers have in common may partly be due to their common heritage of Jewishness, for example their use of the Bible as a source of inspiration, particulary important in Schulz's case. His technique of "mythologizing reality", as he termed it, meant, in one case, recreating the Book of Genesis, translating it, as it were, into the everyday life of a small town in Galicia with the figure of the Father its main protagonist, taking God's place ("The Book of Books", 1934).

English translations of his work by Celina Wieniewska were published by Hamish Hamilton in 1979 and subsequently in Picador (by Pan Books) in 1980.

YORAM BRONOWSKI

Schwabe [Schwab], **Moise** (1839–1918) French scholar and librarian. Schwabe was born in Paris, and educated at the Jewish

School and the Talmud Torah in Strasbourg. In 1868 or 1869 he became a member of the staff of the Bibliothèque Nationale, having been previously secretary to Salomon Munk (1857–66) and an official interpreter at the Paris Court of Appeals (1867).

Schwabe was a prolific writer who contributed numerous articles to the Jewish press. He wrote on a wide range of subjects within the field of Jewish studies, including bibliographical studies. In 1880 he was sent to Bavaria and Württemberg to study early Hebrew printing, and in 1883 he published *Les Incunables Hebraïques et les Premières Impressions Orientales au Commencement du XVIe Siècle*. He also described the Hebrew manuscripts and incanabula in several libraries in France and Switzerland. However, his main contribution to rabbinic scholarship is considered to be *Talmud de Jerusalem* (1871–90) which comprises 11 volumes, and is the first translation of the *Talmud yerushalmi* into French.

His other writings include *Repertoire*, a bibliography of articles published on Judaism between 1665 and 1900, and the biography of Salomon Munk, *Salomon Munk, sa Vie et ses Oeuvres* (1900).

DEBORAH SCHECHTERMAN

Schwartz, Delmore (1913–1966)

Schwartz, Delmore (1913–1966) American poet, critic, and short-story writer. Schwartz was born and raised in New York City, the child of Jewish immigrants from Romania. He attended Wisconsin, New York, and Harvard Universities. He taught English Composition at Harvard from 1940 to 1947, held a series of brief visiting appointments at Princeton, Chicago, and other universities, and taught at Syracuse University from 1962 until his death. From 1943 to 1955 he was an editor of *Partisan Review*, and from 1955 to 1957 was poetry editor and film critic for *New Republic*. His family life was painful. His parents separated frequently and finally divorced, and his father amassed considerable wealth but left him a modest inheritance. Schwartz's two marriages ended in divorce. His latter years were afflicted by severe self-doubt, dependency on drugs and alcohol, and deepening paranoia.

The title story of Schwartz's first book, *In Dreams Begin Responsibilities* (1938), had appeared in *Partisan Review* in the previous year. The protagonist dreams he is watching a film depicting his parents' courtship. It is a more successful attempt to explore his Jewish family life than his ponderous verse drama *Shenandoah* (1941) and his unfinished poem *Genesis, Book One* (1943). Several stories in *The World is a Wedding* (1948) analyze immigrant Jews and their alienated intellectual children. His poetry combines lyric deftness and philosophical density in both traditional and experimental forms. It appeared in his first published book, as well as in *Vaudeville for a Princess, and Other Poems* (1950), *Summer Knowledge: New and Selected Poems* (1959), and *Last and Lost Poems* (1979). In 1960 his poetry won the Bollingen and Shelley Prizes. In his *Selected Letters* (1984), as in the many accounts of his prodigious conversational skills, he was at his best a generous and stimulating influence on other writers. Saul BELLOW has drawn his portrait in *Humboldt's Gift* (1975).

FURTHER READING
Atlas, J.: *Delmore Schwartz: The Life of an American Poet* (New York: Farrar Straus Giroux, 1977)

Goldman, M.: Delmore Schwartz. In *Dictionary of Literary Biography* vol. 28 (Detroit: Gale Research Co., 1984)

McDougall, R.: *Delmore Schwartz* (New York: Twayne Publishers Inc., 1974)

MICHAEL SHAPIRO

Schwarz-Bart, André (b.1928)

Schwarz-Bart, André (b.1928) French novelist and activist. Schwarz-Bart was born in Metz of Polish immigrant parents who had emigrated to France seeking a better, freer life. His life, education, and childhood were interrupted by the Second World War. At the age of 15 he joined the Maquis, only to be arrested by the Nazis, but he was able to escape and joined the Free French forces, fighting with them until the Liberation of France. Upon his return home, he learned that his family had perished in the Holocaust.

The post-war years proved a period of privation and suffering for Schwarz-Bart. He moved to Paris where he became a student at the Sorbonne. These years of silence, solitude, and contemplation were broken by the publication in 1959 of his critically acclaimed novel, *Le Dernier des justes* (*The Last of the Just*, 1961). The book is not merely a reflection on the Holocaust and Schwarz-Bart's personal tragedy but it is also a passionate and poetic meditation on Jewish fate through the ages. The use of the *lamed-vovniki*, the 36 just men on whom the continuance of the world depends, is the mystical and mythical point of departure for this remarkable work. But, despite its brilliance as a literary piece, *Le Dernier des justes* does present certain problems with regard to Jewish theology and identity. It is not so much the poetic licence Schwarz-Bart takes in making the *lamed-vovnik* an hereditary possession, but rather the overt Christian element of a sacrificial lamb suffering for the rest of the world and for God's greater glory. What appears to transpire in the story is the utter end of a world of mystery, myth, and legend, a world of faith in the Creator and faith in the Jew's mission, and the emergence of another world which has no place for a "just man".

In the non-French-speaking world, Schwarz-Bart's reputation relies solely on his first novel. In France and the Francophone world, however, he has been a constant social and political activist, and has been a champion of society's outcasts, especially non-white minorities who suffer prejudice and injustice, and has sought to assist them in a restoration of dignity and full emancipation. Such interests have led him to begin a seven-part epic novel, *La Mulatresse Solitude*, which he is writing with his wife, Simone.

Schwarz-Bart was awarded the Prix Goncourt for *Le Dernier des justes* in 1959, and he was given the Jerusalem Prize for the same work in 1966.

SIMON SIBELMAN

Schweid, Eliezer (b.1929) Hebrew scholar and critic. Schweid was born in Jerusalem. Having studied in Israel, he embarked upon an academic career, accepting a professorship at the Hebrew University, Jerusalem in 1961. He still held this post in the late 1980s.

Schweid has dedicated his studies over the past 25 years to the field of Jewish Philosophy.

His studies have embraced a modern Jewish philosophy dealing with the problems of Jewish nationalism, Jewish identity in the present generation, the status of the Land of Israel in Jewish thought, and the Holocaust.

A second limb to Schweid's work is the history of Jewish philosophy. He has lectured and published extensively on aspects of medieval Jewish philosophy and the history of Jewish philosophy in the nineteenth century. He has also undertaken detailed studies of individual philosophers such as Maimonides, Joseph Albo, Saadia Gaon and Moses MENDELSSOHN.

A third facet of Schweid's work as a Jewish scholar is in his analysis of Hebrew literature, including the poetry of H. N. BIALIK and Saul TSCHERNICHOWSKI. His interest in traditional Judaism has led him to explore the question of Jewish faith, the philosophy of the holy days and the *halakhah*.

JOHN MATTHEW

Schwob, Marcel (1867–1905) French writer. Marcel's remarkable father, descendant of a long line of rabbis, was active in literary and Fourierist circles before going to Egypt as secretary to the Egyptian Foreign Minister. Shortly before Marcel's birth the family returned to France, eventually settling in Nantes (1876) where the father bought two newspapers, *Phare de la Loire* and *Petit Phare*. From 1891 to 1905, when he was living in Paris, Marcel wrote nearly 2,000 editorials (*Lettres Parisiennes*) and articles for the family papers. He was an unusually gifted man, writing beautiful French, and reading English and German literature by the age of 11. Later he translated R. L. Stevenson, Wilde, Defoe, Richter, Nietzsche, and others. While still a student struggling in vain to pass examinations, he published linguistic studies (*Éude sur l'argot français*, 1889; *Le jargon des Coquillards en 1455*, 1890), lectured at the *Société de linguistique* and the *Sociétés Savantes* to an appreciative audience of distinguished scholars (BRÉAL, his teacher; Saussure, Gaston Paris, among them), and wrote a widely acclaimed study of François Villon (*Revue des Deux Mondes*, 15 July 1892). His wide knowledge and erudition were also appreciated by fellow writers: Jarry and Valéry, who dedicated *Ubu Roi* and *L'Introduction à la méthode de Léonard de Vinci*, respectively, to him; Apollinaire whom Schwob and his scholar uncle, Léon Cahun, befriended; even the anti-Semitic Léon Daudet admired his friend's ability to animate and associate diverse branches of knowledge in "his immense and precise imagination". The latter lies at the heart of his creative writing, short stories which lyrically evoke rather than studiously recreate past and present cultures and figures in a highly polished but never obscure style of "complex simplicity". Quietly independent, Schwob was drawn to heretics and outsiders both in life and literature. An ardent Dreyfusard, he was not spared vicious attacks in the anti-Semitic *Libre Parole* (19–20 October 1899). Even more painful was the break with Valéry, Daudet, and other literary friends. One of his last great triumphs was his translation of *Hamlet* (1899; in collaboration with Eugène Morand) made famous by Sarah Bernhardt. Illness virtually paralyzed creative efforts during the last 10 years of his brief but intense life.

BIBLIOGRAPHY

Chroniques, ed. J.A. Green and J. Alden (Geneva: Droz, 1981); *The King in the Golden Mask and Other Stories*, trans. I. White (Manchester: Carcanet New Press, 1982); *Correspondance Inédité*, ed. J. A. Green (Geneva: Droz, 1985).

NELLY WILSON

Sciaky, Leon (1893–1958)   Greek progressive teacher and historical novelist. Sciaky was born in Salonica to an upper-class family during Turkish rule. When he was eight he attended the Shalom school where he was taught Turkish and later attended the Mission Laïque Française School which led to the Baccalauréat. After a visit to the USA in 1908 he continued his studies at home where he was tutored in English. In 1915 he and his family emigrated to New York. He studied mechanical engineering but worked as an engineer for only a short time. After his marriage to Frances Hellman, and the birth of his son, he settled in the vicinity of Cold Spring, USA, and taught in public schools, until he and his wife, both of whom were freethinkers, established a camp for young children. From 1952 they accompanied groups of children on study visits to Mexico, and continued doing so every year until Sciaky's death in Mexico in 1958.

Farewell to Salonica (1946), his only novel, is a nostalgic and affectionate recollection of the city where he and his two sisters were born and raised, as well as an authentic historical account of the struggle for independence of national groups, Bulgarians, Albanians, Vlachs and Greeks, and the subsequent dismemberment of Turkey.

The first part of the novel is devoted to Sciaky's antecedents, his great grandmother Bisnona Miriam (of the Arditti family), her sister, and his illiterate grandfather Nono, who lived in the Bulgarian village of Kilkis. He expresses sympathy for the many groups living in Salonica, each group remaining faithful to its own language, customs, traditions, and national consciousness. He briefly traces the history of the Salonica Jews, favored in the community since Sultan Bayezit II (1481–1512) had welcomed some 25,000 Spanish émigrés from the Iberian Peninsula. These enjoyed an autonomous lifestyle in communities arranged according to their province of origin in Spain, and which evolved their own fiscal system, judicial courts, and commercial consulates. In his novel Sciaky also discusses the influence of the self-proclaimed Messiah, Shabetai Zevi (1626–76), on the Jewish community of Salonica.

RACHEL DALVEN

sectarian trends in modern Israel Sociologists and political scientists in Israel are in agreement that for an understanding of Israel's politics, culture, and international relations it is increasingly important to understand religious developments in the country. In this respect, at least three trends may be discerned – the changing influence of the *Gush Emunim* movement, the rise of the religious extremism of ultra-Orthodox groups, and the growth of the Repentance Movement (*Hazarah betshuvah*). Though these trends are at times depicted as if arising from a common source, their origins, characteristics, and social impact are different, and should be understood as such.

The Gush Emunim *movement*

The spate of political activism shown by the *Gush Emunim* movement in the decade following 1974 has brought unprecedented forms of political activity to the Israeli scene. Though *Gush Emunim* was formally founded only in 1974, it has a pervasive – at times traumatic – impact on Israeli society.

Gush Emunim's origins have been traced to a young cadre of national-religious *yeshivah* students – the *Gahelet* group. During the 1950s they met regularly and developed an active religious and political stance towards both the secular center of the Zionist movement and Jewish orthodoxy. During the 1960s the group moved to Jerusalem and "adopted" as their spiritual guide, Rav Zvi Yehuda Kook (1891–1982), son of Abraham Itzhak Hacohen Kook (1865–1935). Zvi Yehuda, until then a neglected and marginal figure in religious circles, offered them a unique interpretation of his father's writings, and in the *Merkaz Harav yeshivah* he and his followers developed their theology, political outlook, and forms of social organization.

Gush Emunim's ideology is based on the relationship between three fundamental elements: the Jewish people, the land of Israel, and Torat Israel. The peculiar ideology, developed and fervently espoused by members of *Gush Emunim*, rests on the unique synthesis reached in Rav Abraham Kook's doctrine as interpreted by his son. This dialectic synthesis seems to bridge orthodox messianic theology and secular Zionist symbols. Rav Kook interpreted Zionism – in the spirit of the *kabbalah* – as a religious manifestation of God's will, a first step towards redemption. Accordingly, earthly happenings are interpreted as religious signs ("lights") endowed with a fundamental and transcendental meaning: they all convey messages about the oncoming redemption of the world – *ikvita d'mashiha*. Hence, the secular Zionists are conceived as genuinely religious people (if unconscious of the fact), endowed with a "divine spark"; their actions too are deemed to have religious significance.

In accordance with this dialectic view, members of *Gush Emunim* felt obliged to help, in almost magical terms, in bringing the messianic age. Believing the greater land of Israel has religious significance, they protested against the territorial withdrawal associated with the peace treaty negotiated with Egypt (1977). Before 1977, they had forcibly settled in Judea and Samaria as a reaction to Henry Kissinger's visits to Israel and the attempts to reach an agreement with the Arab states. Although in the 1970s their impact on Judea and Samaria was mainly symbolic, their demographic growth and new settlement projects have set up economic, demographic, and symbolic barriers to withdrawal from the region.

Since in their eyes the ultimate values of secular Zionism and Orthodox Judaism are theologically almost synonymous, members of *Gush Emunim* have felt confident in proclaiming themselves more Zionist than the secular Zionists, and at the same time more devout than the ultra-Orthodox. Indeed, the unique "Kookist" ideological synthesis has served as a basis for securing legitimation from wide strata in Israel, and many latent activists, secular and religious alike, have participated in *Gush Emunim* activity.

Rav Zvi Yehuda Kook and his followers translated their theology into a concrete social organization and a politically active movement. They were religiously motivated but also politically oriented. Their goal was the conquest of, and hegemony over, Israel's core value system. Since 1974, *Gush Emunim* has participated – both directly and by the fact of their presence – in political decision making, especially in international policy. The main thrust of its activity has been directed at the extensive settlement of Judea and Samaria, though its struggle came to a climax in the period preceding the withdrawal from Sinai in 1982. It was in this traumatic experience that its much acclaimed ideological synthesis – and those who bore it – began to falter.

Gush Emunim is undoubtedly a political, as well as a religious, phenomenon. Indeed, immanent in its ideology is the view that politics and religion are inseparable – two sides of the same coin. Thus, *Gush Emunim*'s political activity is aimed at bringing redemption through political activism. Consequently, its activities have been at times alien to the "rules of the game" of Israeli politics – since it was, in fact, playing a different game. Evidently, the extreme activities today associated with *Gush Emunim*, such as the assassination of Arab mayors and the attempt to bomb mosques in Jerusalem, are expressions of its theo-political ideology.

The unique "Kookist" linkage of opposing ideological concepts may perhaps have contained the seeds of its own destruction. Its move into political activism – culminating in the struggle between the *Gush*'s members and soldiers of the Israel Defence Army during the withdrawal from Sinai and Yamit in 1982 – has led to internal contradictions. Faced by these extreme actions, secular Zionists felt that they – and their precious secular symbols – were being used for religious reasons. In contrast, Orthodox Jews feared that *Gush Emunim* were using religious symbols for political and secular interests.

Gush Emunim was initially considered as marginal but heroic, and as an expression of pure Zionism suffused with religiosity. Yet recently, it has begun, especially in leftist secular circles, to be seen as a pervert, deviant group.

Ultra-Orthodoxy in Jerusalem

Jerusalem's social history is rife with conflicts between secular and ultra-Orthodox Jews. These conflicts are usually associated with local infringements of one group's territorial and cultural claims on the other. In the first half of the twentieth century the conflict was largely a reaction of ultra-Orthodox groups against intentional provocation by secular Zionists. Yet, since the 1960s, it has been largely dominated by the expansion of the ultra-Orthodox and their conquest of urban areas as well as by their battle to stop secular trends in Jerusalem.

The most characteristic feature of Israel's ultra-Orthodoxy – at times the only common ground between its different subgroups – is the denial of the state of Israel as the legitimate Jewish state. Historically unchanging, this ideological rejection of the state is manifested in a repudiation of its symbols (e.g. the flag), civic duties (e.g. army service), and rituals (e.g. the commemorative siren for Israel's fallen soldiers,

ignored by the *Haredim* or ultra-Orthodox). This long-held rejection is based on traditional interpretations of the *halakhah*. From this perspective, Zionism, Israel's secular religion, is regarded as idol worship – *'avodah zarah*; it is therefore imbued with demonic significance. Actually, the ostracism of the state is of paramount importance for the construction of the social identity of ultra-Orthodoxy. In the most extreme circles, refusal to eat state-secured "kosher" foods, and a complete reliance on self-sustained religious services, are used both to consolidate identity and as a status symbol. Significant differences in the repudiation of Israel are associated with specific subgroups, such as the *Neturei Karta*, the *Eduh Hacharedit* etc.

In spite of ultra-Orthodoxy's reluctance to provide information for social research, several investigators have succeeded in shedding some light on life in their highly individual world.

Jewish history and national continuity have been shaped by the unique educational settings arranged for the young – the *heder* and the *yeshivah*. Although the social history of these institutions has benefited from recent research, contemporary study patterns in ultra-Orthodox educational frameworks are largely unexplored. Nevertheless, the schooling patterns of the *'edah haharedit* (ultra-Orthodox community) in Jerusalem have recently been described. Boys' study patterns seem to be in line with eighteenth-century customs, characterized by a sectarian attitude towards the broader social environment, with Yiddish being the main language. Yet, in contrast, there seems to have been a broadening of – and even a modern orientation for – educational provision for girls, which was deemed essential for the preservation of the ultra-Orthodox world. Thus, the *yeshivot* for boys and the *beit Yahacob* for girls currently form the main educational framework of modern ultra-Orthodoxy.

Studies in the High Yeshivah are at present carried until after the age of marriage, for many even after the age of 30. Whereas formerly the High Yeshivah was mainly for a small elite, today it is mandatory for all, even for the lessable. Thus, all the young must devote themselves to the study of sacred texts, and instead of being an achieved role, the *yeshivah bocher* is currently an ascribed role. S. C. Heilman found that the study of sacred texts is dissociated from mundane realities, having a relevance of its own. By extension, the prolongation and intensification of religious studies may be the cause of the rise in idealism (or religious extremism) expressed in young *haredi* (ultra-Orthadox) circles.

It has been claimed that the conflicts between ultra-Orthodox and secular in Jerusalem should be understood on the basis of the urban expansion of ultra-Orthodox neighborhoods. According to one estimate, 70,000 ultra-Orthodox residents are spread throughout Jerusalem. Due to a relative high fertility rate, a larger *haredi* population needs housing more than ever before. Consequently, secular residents are persuaded – violently at times – to move out of a particular neighborhood, in order to free new housing for the ultra-Orthodox community. This demographic trend is correlated with a reduction in the mean age of the population. By implication, educational frameworks – High Yeshivah in particular – are gaining in prominence and their role as keepers of the faith will become all the more intense as larger segments of the community fall under their control.

This transformation of the age structure of ultra-Orthodox Judaism in Jerusalem – implying a less productive population – may explain, at least to a certain extent, the growing political involvement of *haredi* political parties in Israel's government. The rising need to secure fundings, yet retain social segregation and educational autonomy, has paradoxically forced them into integration into the very political machinery which the ultra-Orthodox ideology so flatly rejects.

Another important factor is the change in the ethnic composition of the *haredi* community. Whereas it was previously dominated by Polish and Hungarian Jewry – with the special Jewish sectarian attitudes of *prushim* and Hasidim – it is increasingly dominated by Asian and African groups. This change may help to explain the rise of ethnic political–religious parties, which aim to promote local and ethnic interests. This ethnic development may also explain the growing openness of ultra-Orthodox groups to influences exerted by non-Orthodox groups (e.g. the adoption of magical conceptions from Moroccan Jewry).

To conclude, demographic developments in Jerusalem have strengthened sect-like tendencies in various *haredi* sub-groups, while at the same time forcing a church-like openness (especially in the political arena) on the ultra-Orthodox community at large. There can be little doubt that ultra-Orthodoxy, its religious behavior, and its residential patterns will be influenced by further demographic developments.

The Repentance Movement

Since the Yom Kippur War of 1973, the Repentance Movement (*Hazarah betshuvah*) has drawn into its orbit many people of diverse social, ethnic, and educational backgrounds and has aroused intense concern in Israel. Since it is viewed in symbolic terms as a duel between secular Zionism and religious orthodoxy – and since secular Zionism is numerically the loser – it is no surprise that members of the kibbutz movement in particular have been traumatized by the "betrayal" of their sons and daughters. Accordingly, the repentance movement is usually portrayed as resulting from a weakness in secular Zionism and as arising in response to the erosion of socialist ideals. In response, education boards as well as a government committee have studied the phenomenon and tried to suggest ways to slow this "wave of conversion". Indeed, it was found that conversion-like processes are more likely to occur in Israeli families than in non-native families.

Yet, whereas the Repentance Movement tends to be grouped by those who hold this view with sectarian and cult-like groups in Israel and abroad, it should be seen rather as "church-like" behavior on the part of ultra-Orthodoxy. Only in the past decade have the ultra-Orthodox displayed this willingness both to be in contact (during the conversion process), and live (at the inclusion phase) with ex-secularists. This openness testifies to the intensification of the religious feeling of the young cohort which grew up in the educational frameworks described above.

One scholar who has studied the recruitment tactics of the Orthodoxy focused on "the problem of meaning" troubling young secular American youth arriving in Jerusalem. He found that the tactics adopted by those preaching repentance: desperation inducement, hope infusion, and the supply of theological solutions, are all processes backed by social pressures to conform to the all-embracing – yet supportive – religious environment. Thus, the openness of the repentance movement is only apparent – its actual orientation is towards a closed sectarian view.

Ultra-Orthodoxy in the Diaspora

It is somewhat misleading to view Israel in isolation from the Jewish world in the Diaspora. It is all the more erroneous to regard the ultra-Orthodox groups, especially hasidic dynasties, as separated from the interlocking social and international networks they compose. After the Holocaust and the destruction of the east European Orthodox centers, small, yet vital, centers of Jewish Orthodoxy were constructed throughout the world. London and Melbourne, Antwerp and New York, Vienna and Zurich – all became new strongholds of ultra-Orthodox and hasidic groups.

Most hasidic courts (or dynasties) – like Satmar, Belz, Ger, and others – are remarkable in the strong sectarian attitudes they maintain in their social surroundings. Although essential contacts are maintained with less religious Jews and non-Jews in the cities, these concern only economic affairs. The growing ultra-Orthodox population enables the Hasidim to maintain and strengthen their internal cohesion. Thus, as in Jerusalem, the major cities are currently experiencing a religious revival. And, again as in Jerusalem, this revival is not a response to new religious interpretations, nor an indication of greater religious scholarship but is primarily a response to the unprecedented social and economic possibilities available to religious communities. As in other religions, Jewish religious behavior is partly a by-product of mundane and non-religious causes. In this respect, urbanism and religion are essentially connected.

Although most hasidic groups are essentially sectarian, the Lubavitcher Hasidim are noteworthy in their missionary zeal and the fervent activities they arrange for non-observant Jews throughout the world. Lubavitcher Hasidim

cater both for the religious needs of many far and forgotten Jewish communities, and with the other hasidic groups they constitute the "collective conscience" of many non-observant Jews in the major cities.

It may be in fact that the relaxed Jewish observance of many communities is currently a precondition for the identity formation of most ultra-Orthodox groups in Judaism. On the whole, the diversification of the "religious market" in Judaism has had a pervasive impact on the formation, maintenance and possible transformation of Jewish identity in the twentieth century.

FURTHER READING

Aran, G.: From religious Zionism to Zionist religion: the roots of Gush Emunim. In *Studies in Contemporary Jewry II*, ed. P. Y. Medding (Bloomington: Indiana University Press, 1986) 116–43

Freidman, M.: Religious zealotry in Israeli society. In *On Ethnic and Religious Diversity in Israel*, ed. S. Poll and E. Krausz (Ramat Gan: Bar–Illan University, 1975) 91–111

——: Haredim confront the modern city. In *Studies in Contemporary Jewry II*, ed. P. Y. Medding (Bloomington: Indiana University Press, 1986) 74–96

Heilman, S. C.: *The people of the book* (Chicago: University of Chicago Press, 1983)

Leibman, S. C., and Don-Yehiya, E.: *Religion and politics in Israel* (Bloomington: Indiana University Press, 1984)

Marmorstein, E.: Religious opposition to nationalism in the Middle-East. *International Affairs* 28 no. 3 (1952) 344–59

GAD YAIR

Segal, George (b.1924) American sculptor and environmental artist. Segal was born in the Bronx area of New York, the son of a kosher butcher. From the time of his birth until the Second World War, the Bronx was the favored neighborhood of the growing Jewish middle class. In 1940 Segal's family moved to another area where many Jews lived, South Brunswick, New Jersey, where his father started a chicken farm. In 1946, after marrying the daughter of a neighbor, Helen Steinberg, Segal bought a chicken farm directly across the road from his

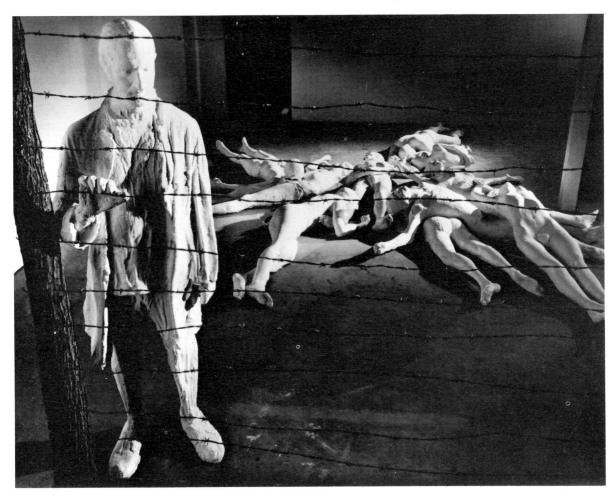

George Segal The Holocaust *1982 (plaster – eleven life-size figures – wood and wire). Sidney Janis Gallery, collection of the Jewish Museum, New York*

parents. The chicken coop area has since been rebuilt into a studio. Segal continues to prefer this way of life. He studied first at Cooper Union (1941–4), then at Rutgers University, next at the Pratt Institute of Design in Brooklyn (1947–8), and finally at New York University (1948–9). At NYU two of his fellow students were Larry RIVERS and Alfred Leslie, young artists who were experimenting with the integration of the large scale of Abstract Expressionism with objects and elements from everyday life. Segal's meeting with Allan Kaprow, the creator of art Happenings, and the integration of art with life had a profound influence on him.

Segal began as a painter but gradually integrated free-standing plaster sculptures with the paintings, creating a total environment. He eventually moved to working just in sculpture, creating environments from real life which are populated by human figures cast in plaster. Most of his subjects are drawn from real life situations: a gas station; a cafe; an old woman in her kitchen. Some refer specifically to his Jewish background. *The Butcher Shop* (1955), Art Gallery of Ontario, Toronto, is a memorial to his father Jacob Segal. A plaster cast figure of a woman within about to slaughter a chicken represents his mother.

Segal has occasionally diverged from the re-creation of scenes of contemporary life and has commented on subjects from the Bible. His first exhibited body of environmental works was a

689

series on *The Legend of Lot* (1958). Combined in the environment were four large-scale semi-abstract paintings and roughly-modeled plaster figures. In 1966 Segal again depicted *The Legend of Lot* (Kaiser Wilhelm Museum, Krefeld); this time fully three-dimensional and with greater specificity of detail, openly showing the unsettling events of the story of Lot, his wife, and his daughters. Segal also chose biblical subject matter as a point of reference to contemporary events for two public sculpture commissions – both on the themes of Abraham and Isaac. In 1973 he was commissioned by the Tel Aviv Foundation for Literature and Art to create a public sculpture. Later in 1978 he re-interpreted the theme in his commission for Kent State University's memorial to the students who were killed by the National Guard during an anti-war protest. One of Segal's most celebrated commissions is *The Holocaust* (1982) commissioned by the Committee for a Memorial to the Six Million Victims of the Holocaust in San Francisco. Segal attempted to give an accurate portrayal of the concentration camp, basing his images on archival Holocaust photographs and even using a friend who survived the Holocaust as the model for the dominant, standing figure in the work.

FURTHER READING

Hunter, S., and Hawthorne, D.: *George Segal* (New York: Rizzoli, 1984)

Tuchman, P.: *George Segal* (New York: Abbeville Press, 1983)

BARBARA GILBERT

Segal, Lore (b.1928) American novelist, children's writer and translator. Born Lore Groszmann in Vienna, Austria, Segal survived the Holocaust, arriving in England as part of the children's transport, soon to be followed by her parents. She received a BA with honors from Bedford College, London, in 1948. A candid, unsentimental account of her life in England, her parents' transformation as refugees, and her years in the Dominican Republic before arrival in America in 1951 is presented in her autobiographical novel *Other People's Houses* (1964), and concludes with her marriage to

David I. Segal in 1961. She has two children.

A regular contributor to journals such as *The New Yorker* and *Commentary*, Segal's other novels are *Lucinella* (1978), which John Gardner called "the best book I know about how poets and novelists really are", and *My First American* (1985) in which she explores the "parallel experience" of Jews and blacks embodied in a young Jewish survivor and her middle-aged black intellectual lover. She has written a variety of children's books, among them *Tell Me a Mitzi* (1970), winner of an American Library Notable Book Award; a translation, with poet Randall Jarrell, of Grimm's *The Juniper Tree and Other Tales* (1973); and *The Book of Adam to Moses* (1987), a collection of Bible stories. Winner of a Guggenheim fellowship, Segal teaches creative writing as a professor of English at the University of Illinois at Chicago Circle.

ELIZABETH KLEIN

Segal, Moshe Zvi (1876–1968) Hebraist and Bible scholar. Born in Myshad, Lithuania, Segal studied at local *yeshivot* before emigrating to Britain at the age of 17. For a while he was a journalist in London, where he met HERZL and other Zionist leaders. He was critical of Herzl's political Zionism and numbered himself among the followers of AHAD HA'AM. In 1901 he moved to Oxford and studied Semitics while acting as Minister of the Jewish congregation. He and his wife, who had spent her girlhood in Ottoman Palestine (where her father, the scholar, Rabbi Arye Leib Frumkin, was among the founders of Petah Tikvah), were united in their devotion to Hebrew, and used it as their everyday language; indeed, their two eldest children spoke Hebrew before they learnt English. In 1918, after eight years as Minister at Newcastle-upon-Tyne, Segal went to Palestine as member of the Zionist Commission with Chaim WEIZMANN. In 1926 he was appointed to a Lectureship at the Hebrew University at Jerusalem and elected to a Chair in Bible and Semitic Languages in 1939; he was an active member of the *Va'ad halashon* (later, Hebrew Language Academy), and was awarded the Israel Prize in 1959. He retired from the University in 1959.

The first of Segal's academic writings was a seminal article in the *Jewish Quarterly Review* in 1908, which later was expanded and developed into his *Grammar of Mishnaic Hebrew* (1927). This volume remains the standard work on the subject. (A revised Hebrew edition appeared in 1935.)

The distinctive features of Segal's attitude towards Bible criticism emerge most clearly in his *Mevo hamikra* (1946–50; *Introduction to the Hebrew Bible*, 1967). Traditionalist in his approach and moderate in his views, he nevertheless did not reject out of hand even the extreme theories of the Documentary Hypothesis, but submitted them to the same logical treatment as less radical opinions. On the authorship of the Pentateuch he held that numerous sections of the Torah are post-Mosaic; they were, however, erroneously attributed by tradition to Moses, just as many additions to the Oral Law were attributed to Moses. Segal's style of writing was economical, even terse; significantly he valued Rashi the most highly among Jewish commentators. This approach to Bible studies was to have profound influence on generations of students, and Segal's commentaries long remained popular classroom textbooks in Israel. In the field of Bible scholarship mention should be made of his *Parshanut hamikra* (1944, Interpretation of the Hebrew Bible), and two volumes of collected essays, *Masoret uvikoret* (1957, Tradition and Criticism), and in English *The Pentateuch: Its Composition and Authorship* (1967).

A pioneering work was Segal's *Yesodei hafonetikah ha'ivrit* (1928; The sources of Hebrew phonetics) the first scientific analysis of Hebrew phonetics, which laid the base for the wide development of the subject that was to follow. Segal was editor of two volumes (nos. 8 and 9, 1928–9) of the revised Hebrew dictionary of Eliezer BEN-YEHUDA, where his knowledge of Hebrew sources was invaluable. He turned afterwards to the composition of Hebrew–English and English–Hebrew dictionaries, notably in collaboration with Herbert Danby and Merton Dagut. Segal edited Ecclesasticus (*Sefer Ben Sira hashalem*, 1953) and made important contributions to the study of the Dead Sea Scrolls and cognate literature.

J. B. SEGAL

Segall, Lasar

Segall, Lasar (1891–1957) Russian–Brazilian painter. Segall was born in Vilna, where his father was a Torah scribe, and at the age of 15 he traveled alone to Berlin to study art at the Academy. He was soon drawn into the more vital circle of the *Freie Sezession* and thereafter became involved with the German Expressionist movement, founding the *Dresden Sezession Grupe* in 1919 with Otto Dix and others. His work at this time already dealt with the themes of poverty, suffering, and powerlessness which were to recur in his later work. The people he painted were not substantially different from the low-life characters depicted by other Expressionist painters but he endowed them with a dignity which, he implied, belongs only to the dispossessed.

In 1923 Segall settled in Brazil, but continued to exhibit internationally for the remainder of his life. He was to exercise considerable influence over the development of Modernism in Brazil, and was in turn motivated to lose the harsher elements seen in his German style.

Segall's portrayal of individuals continued to demonstrate his affinity with the powerless, and his ability to detect humanity in the despised, but from the mid 1930s these themes are treated on a larger scale. Whole communities are seen to be suffering from upheaval and persecution in works like *Pogrom* (1936–7) and *Ship of Emigrants* (1939–41), yet their humanity remains intact.

The human flotsam in *Ship of Emigrants* comfort one another wordlessly as the sea threatens to engulf them; the congregation of corpses in *Pogrom* nestles closely together, and a new plant grows sturdily amid the devastation. Rooted in Jewish experience, such works are universal in their concern with suffering and endurance. Only *Concentration Camp*, painted by Segall in 1945, is a painting of the unendurable.

FURTHER READING

Lasar Segall (Brazil: Museu de Arte Moderna, 1967) [exhibition catalog]

Lasar Segall: Watercolours, Drawings, Engravings (Sao Paolo: Museu Lasar Segall, 1978) [exhibition catalog]

LAURA JACOBUS

Seiber, Mátyás (1905–1960) Composer, teacher, and writer. Born in Budapest Seiber began to learn cello as a child. From 1919 to 1924 he was a student at the Budapest Academy of Music, studying cello, and composition with Kodály. From 1925 he taught at the Frankfurt Conservatory, but in 1927 he took a post as a ship's musician on a cruise liner. His experience in this capacity may well have influenced his later interest in jazz and popular music. After his return to Frankfurt in 1928 he introduced a pioneering course in jazz theory and performance. Due to the rise of Nazism he went to England in 1935, where he lectured and wrote music for films, including the outstanding score for the cartoon film of Orwell's *Animal Farm*. In 1942, at the instigation of Michael Tippett, he became a teacher at Morley College, teaching composition, harmony, and appreciation, and gaining a reputation as one of the most outstanding teachers of composition in Britain. In 1943 he was active in the founding of the Society for the Promotion of New Music (SPNM). In 1946–7 he composed his best-known and much admired work, the cantata, *Ulysses* (first performance 1949). His interest in jazz manifested itself in several of his compositions, notably in his work with John Dankworth, which resulted in the *Improvisations for Jazz Band and Orchestra* (1959). In 1960 he was tragically killed in a car crash in South Africa.

FURTHER READING

Keller, F.: Mátyás Seiber 1905–60. *Tempo* (1960)
Wood, J.: The music of Mátyás Seiber. *Musical Times* (1970)

SYDNEY FIXMAN

Seligson, Esther (b.1942) Mexican critic and novelist. Seligson studied at the Escuela Yavné in Mexico City, the University of Paris, the Institute for Hebraic, Sephardic, and Oriental studies in Madrid, the Martin Buber Center at the Free University in Brussels, the University Center for Jewish Studies in Paris, and at a *yeshivah* in Jerusalem. A student of philosophy as well as literature, the *kabbalah*, and the Talmud, she has translated Cioran into Spanish and lectured on diverse subjects including Jew-

ish traditional thought and medieval art and history. She is an editor of the bi-monthly review of Jewish culture *Aqui estamos* published in Oaxaca, Mexico.

Judaism is important in three of her seven works of poetic prose fiction, centering on themes of nostalgia, and a search for harmony and the ideal. The first one, *Otros son los sueños* (Dreams are different) gained the Premio Villaurutia for the novel in 1973. It is a drama of a woman's search for her identity within the couple, the family, her cultural heritage in Judaism. It is a poignant monologue, blending with dialogue and chorus, to express the collective and historical nature of the quest.

The eponymous story in *Luz de dos* (Double light) mirrors the relationship of a modern couple with the story of a Jewish Portuguese girl in the fourteenth century, whose tragedy is bound up with that of European Jewry at the time. *La morada en el tiempo* (Abode in time) evolves on several different time schemes simultaneously, although the setting is predominantly biblical. It symbolizes the Jewish search for a collective identity and ideal throughout the ages. Like Seligson's other works it is condensed and poetic.

BIBLIOGRAPHY

Luz de dos, trans. D. Pritchard. In an anthology of Latin American Jewish Writings, ed. R. Kalechofsky (Massachusetts: Micah, 1980)

FURTHER READING

Duncan, J. A.: *Voices, Visitors and a New Reality, Innovations in Mexican Narrative Since 1970* (Pittsburgh: 1986)

ANN DUNCAN

Senator, Ronald (b.1926) British composer and music educator. Senator was born in London, the son of Polish–Jewish immigrants. He studied composition at Oxford with Egon Wellesz, a distinguished pupil of Arnold SCHOENBERG, and he has been Professor of Music at London University (1964–79), the University of Europe (1979–81), and most recently the Guildhall School of Music in London. He has also been visiting professor at universities in the USA, Australia, and Canada.

While at London University Senator developed the system of "Musicgramma", whereby a basic set of musical operations is postulated for all kinds of musical structures, as an aid to musical education. The system enjoyed widespread acceptance and popularity, and has been used in many schools and colleges in the USA, Europe, and Australia. This has earned Senator a reputation as a leading innovator in the teaching of music.

Senator composes inventively, drawing upon widely varied sources as themes for his music. He has used as texts Chinese classical lyrics, as well as the writings of W. B. Yeats and W. H. Auden. His compositions include five operas, oratorios and cantatas, chamber and orchestral music, and two song cycles. His most notable composition on a Jewish theme is his *Kaddish for Terezín*, a large-scale oratorio which combines surviving poems and diaries from the camp with liturgical texts. The text was compiled jointly with Rabbi Dr Albert Friedlander, the director of the Leo Baeck School in London. Although the work was primarily written to commemorate the children who died in the Holocaust, it was inspired by the memory of the composer's late wife who was a survivor of Auschwitz. The work had its première at Canterbury Cathedral in 1986 as part of the B'nai B'rith Festival and it was also co-promoted by the United Nations, the West German government, and the Council of Christians and Jews. It has subsequently been broadcast and widely performed in the USA.

JOHN MATTHEW

Sereni, Enzo Hayyim (1905–1944) Italian Zionist, pioneer, and writer. He is justly considered "the first Jewish pioneer in Italy". Sereni was born in Rome into a family of intellectuals who had been resident in the city since classical times. His cultural formation was Italian and secular. His elder brother's chance participation at the Zionist congress of Karlsbad (1921) determined Sereni's adhesion to the movement, as is revealed by an autobiographical article entitled "Ritorno al Congresso" in *La Rassegna Mensile d'Israel* of 1931. A year later Sereni became the secretary and the driving force of the socialist-inspired Zionist group *Avodah*. His speech "La Palestina e noi" (reproduced in *Israel*, 1924), delivered at the *Congresso giovanile ebraico* (Jewish Youth Congress) held in Livorno in 1924, underlined his conception of a proletarization of the Jewish people who would settle in Palestine to work the land. After taking his degree in philosophy at the University of Rome Sereni emigrated to Palestine with his wife, Ada Ascarelli. He settled first at Rehovot and was one of the founders of the Givat Brenner kibbutz. He was active in the *Histadrut* and particularly in the *Hakibbutz hame'uhad* movement. At the same time he was aware of the dramatic events in Europe and in 1931 and 1932 he traveled to Germany in order to organize Jewish young people and to prepare them for working in Palestine. As a delegate at the Zionist Congress of Lucerne in 1937 Sereni persisted in his attempt to save his brothers in the Diaspora. At the outbreak of the Second World War he was in Egypt where he broadcast anti-Fascist propaganda on the radio and contributed to the *Corriere d'Italia*. On his return to Palestine, Sereni worked on a project to train parachutists who were to have brought help to the survivors of the Holocaust. In 1944 he went to Italy for a training course and after a parachute jump near Florence, he was captured by the Germans and sent to Dachau where he died in November 1944.

Many of Sereni's articles appeared in the weekly *Israel* and in *La Rassegna Mensile d'Israel* between 1922 and 1935. His writings attest to his profound idealism. Sereni was not opressed by anti-Semitism; he was perfectly integrated into Italian society and was motivated only by his egalitarian vision and the desire to see a rebirth of the Jewish people. Among his books written in Italian, Hebrew, and English, are *Jews and Arabs in Palestine* (1936); and *Mekorot hafascism ha'italki* (1951; translated by Dante Lattes).

GABRIELLA MOSCATI-STEINDLER

Seter [Starominsky], **Mordechai** (b.1916) Israeli composer. Born in Russia, Seter emigrated to Palestine with his family in 1926. After initial music studies in Tel Aviv he went to Paris for advanced composition training (1932–7). In 1940 he composed his first important work, the *Sabbath Cantata*, in which he quoted traditional Jewish tunes from A. Z. IDELSOHN's collection of songs of the Babylonian Jews, which were elaborated by strict contrapuntal technique and contemporary, dissonant diatonic harmony. This work already established his lasting tendency for concentrated, economic textures, linear counterpoint and intense expression. A series of chamber works for strings, such as the *Violin Sonata* (1953) are characterized by meditative expression, very slow rhythmic values, and a synthesis of the model of the Bach solo sonata with improvisatory, Arabic-type instrumental style. Seter also composed a series of works for choir a capella, mostly for the Rinat Choir, founded by the conductor Gary Bertini. Seter was a professor of theory and composition at the Music Academy in Tel Aviv, later part of Tel Aviv University. He has remained an introverted personality, dedicated to his compositional work and reluctant to make any ideological statement as to the nature of Israeli style.

JEHOASH HIRSHBERG

Shabtai, Jacob (1934–1981)

Shabtai, Jacob (1934–1981) Israeli author. Shabtai was born in Tel Aviv. He had been known as a minor composer of short stories, some of which were collected in *Hadod peretz mamri* (1972; The spotted tiger), sketches, and one or two plays. But then the novel *Zikron devarim* (1977; *Past Continuous*, 1983) appeared. The public was slow to grasp the significance of this innovative work, brilliant and precise in its language, mordant, witty, and penetrating. Making no concessions to the reader, it is related in one ongoing paragraph, a *roman fleuve*, passing through the consciousness of each of the characters to the others. It covers the passing time of nine months, marked out by two deaths, the initial death of Goldmann's father, to Goldmann's own suicide. So death is proposed as the central theme, the starting point and the conclusion. And yet the novel is hilarious and non-self-pitying, transmitting a tragic sense of the past, as well as the futility of the future.

This bleakness is concentrated and deepened in the posthumous novel, *Sof davar* (1984; Past perfect) where all focus is concentrated on one character, Meir. Rather than the abundance of incident we have here a variety of narrative techniques. The first part takes up the brilliant tone of the earlier novel, but then the narrative moves into a minor key, following the illness and death of the mother. Meir himself falls sick whilst on tour, and surrenders to fantasies, and, finally, the surrealistic experience of another world, a paradise. The different types of narrative convey different mental experiences.

BIBLIOGRAPHY
Past Continuous (Philadelphia: The Jewish Publication Society of America, 1983)

FURTHER READING
Yudkin, L. I.: *1948 and After*, JSS Monograph Series 4 (Manchester: Manchester University Press, 1984)

LEON I. YUDKIN

Shaffer, Peter (b.1926)

Shaffer, Peter (b.1926) British dramatist. Born in Liverpool, Shaffer was educated in St Paul's School, London, and at Cambridge University. He was a conscripted coal miner in 1944–7, and, after this, worked in the New York Public Library. He has also worked for a music publisher and as a literary and music critic in London. Shaffer first became known for his television plays *The Salt Land* (1955) and *Balance of Terror* (1957). *The Salt Land* is set in a contemporary Israeli kibbutz and concerns the philosophical conflict of two immigrant brothers. A strong emotional, social, or cultural conflict is central to most of Shaffer's subsequent drama which is distinguished by its classical construction, fluent, crisp dialogue, and realistic characterization. The successful production in London and New York of his first stage play *Five Finger Exercise* in 1958 established Shaffer as an important post-war British dramatist. In this play, the inner tensions of a supposedly comfortable middle-class family are exposed by a mysterious German interloper. Shaffer, in this way, universalizes the Jewish family and the specific cultural conflict of *A Salt Land*.

Shaffer has had an enormously varied output which includes a successful modern epic *The Royal Hunt of the Sun* (1964) which he has described as "the search for a definition of the idea of God", and an excellent modern farce, *Black Comedy* (1965). In recent years he has written two popular stage plays *Equus* (1973) and *Amadeus* (1979) which has been rewritten as a successful screenplay. His most recent play *Yonadab* (produced London 1985), is an adaption of Dan JACOBSON's novel *The Rape of Tamar* (1970), and is Shaffer's first stage play to utilize an explicitly Jewish story.

Shaffer has written twelve plays, one radio play *The Prodigal Father* (1957), and three novels with his twin brother, Anthony. He has been one of Britain's most consistently popular postwar dramatists who has also received considerable critical acclaim.

FURTHER READING
Russell Taylor, J.: *Peter Shaffer* (Harlow: Longman for the British Council, 1974)

BRYAN CHEYETTE

Shaham, Natan (b.1925) Israeli novelist and dramatist. Shaham was born in Tel Aviv, the son of the writer, Eliezer Steinman. After serving in the Palmach, he joined kibbutz Beit Alfa in 1945. A member of the so-called Palmach generation of writers, Shaham's early fiction and drama concentrated on highlighting the various ills perceived by many writers to be afflicting the new Israeli society. His play, *Hem yagi'u mahar* (1950; They will arrive tomorrow), based on one of his own stories, was a daringly realistic exposé of divisive forces in the Israeli army, and can be read as an analogy of similar divisiveness in Israeli society. Other plays, such as *Kra li Siomka* (1950; Call me Siomka), which deals with government corruption, were similarly representative of the "problem" literature of the time.

Despite its air of social realism, most of Shaham's writing has an idealistic orientation. It focuses on problematical areas of Israeli society without the pessimism and disillusionment en-

countered in the works of his contemporary, S. YIZHAR. *Halokh vehazor* (1972; To and fro) airs the re-evaluation of the heroine's Israeli identity and ideology. A number of novels followed, including *Demamah dakah* (1983; A still small voice), which, while contrasting the Israeli milieu with that of a foreign country, shifts its focus to a marital relationship. *Revi'iyat Rosendorff* (1987; The Rosendorff quartet), an interesting exercise in documentary fiction, is an authentic evocation of the *yishuv* of the 1930s, seen through the eyes of four musicians, European immigrants and members of the new orchestra founded by Bronislaw HUBERMAN.

Shaham has written nine novels and six collections of stories, in addition to plays and travel books.

BIBLIOGRAPHY
Coming home. In *Firstfruits*, ed. J. Michener (Philadelphia: The Jewish Publication Society of America 1973) 253–65; *The Other Side of the Wall*, trans. L. Gold (Philadelphia; The Jewish Publication Society of America, 1988)

GLENDA ABRAMSON

Shahar, David (b.1926) Israeli storywriter and novelist. A fifth-generation Jerusalemite, Shahar grew up among the ultra-Orthodox anti-Zionists, but attended secular high school. Shahar participated in the War of Independence. Exposure from early childhood to internal conflicts and tensions within Israeli society and between it and the Arab population has had a strong impact on his writings.

His first story appeared in 1946. In 1959 he published his first collection of stories *Al hahalomot* (On dreams) – followed by several other collections. His writing is remarkably different from that of the mainstream War of Independence writers. Shahar does not furnish his protagonists with socionational solutions. His stories are mainly the childhood recollections of a first-person narrator in Mandatory Jerusalem which strives to become "The Jerusalem of heaven". It is inhabited by a varied cast of marginal, idiosyncratic characters: mystics, sensualists, utopians, and madmen, artists, prostitutes, and shrews. It is a spectacle of the tragic and the sublime but also of the ridiculous and the grotesque – described in an affectionate, sardonic tone of remembrance of things past.

Shahar's first novel, *Yareah hadevash vehazahav* (1959; A moon of gold and honey), caused a controversy. It provided, in a rather new vein in Israeli fiction, a satirical portrayal of Israeli society on "the morning after" – once the Zionist dream had been realized and the State established.

Between 1969 and 1986 Shahar published a sequence of five novels: *Heikhal hakelim hashevurim* (The palace of shattered vessels). The title refers to the kabbalistic concept of the inadequacy of material to contain spiritual richness. According to it, God once bestowed his light on earthly vessels but they shattered. Man's goal is to try to retrieve that light.

Shahar is well-known abroad. The French have pointed out his affinities with Marcel PROUST – especially in his treatment of time and memory. He is a recipient of the Medicis Prize.

BIBLIOGRAPHY
Stories from Jerusalem (London: Elek, 1976)

FURTHER READING
Morahg, G.: Piercing the shimmering bubble: David Shahar's *The Palace of Shattered Vessels*. *AJS Review* (Fall 1985) 211–34
Telpaz, G.: *Israeli Childhood Stories of the Sixties*, (Chico, CA: Scholars Press, 1983) 87–120

RIVKA MAOZ

Shahn, Ben (1898–1969) American painter and graphic artist. Shahn was born in Kovno, Lithuania, to a family of woodcarvers and potters. The tradition of secular socialist and political activism prevalent among eastern European Jews was present also in his family. Shahn's father, afraid of being exiled for his strong anti-Czarist activities, fled first to South America and then to the USA, where his family joined him in 1906. At the age of 14 Shahn was apprenticed to a lithographer, receiving his first training in the artful integration of image and text – a skill in which he excelled throughout his career. He received formal art training in New York at Art Students League, New York University, City College of New York, the National Academy of Design, and the Educational Alliance, the settlement school attended by most immigrant Jewish artists. In the 1920s Shahn traveled to Europe and North Africa where he recorded his impressions of exotic Jewish life on the island of Djerba. While in Paris he read contemporary accounts of the case of Alfred Dreyfus, the French–Jewish military officer who between 1898 and 1906 was falsely accused and imprisoned for treason. After returning to the USA, Shahn in the late 1920s did a series of paintings based on original photos of the parties involved in the Dreyfus Affair. It was the first instance of Shahn creating a body of art work that made a plea against criminal injustice. In 1931, incensed by ethnic prejudice apparent in the case of Nicola Sacco and Bartolomeo Vanzetti, two poor Italian immigrants who where falsely accused and executed for killing a Massachusetts paymaster, Shahn painted 23 works that dealt with the participants and facts of the case. The case of West Coast labor leader Thomas J. Mooney who was found guilty for a bombing and then later pardoned was the basis for a series of 16 paintings between 1931 and 1932.

During the Depression, Shahn, like many American artists, was subsidized by the government. During the 1930s he was a photographer for the Farm Security Administration (FSA), taking more than 6,000 photographs of the unemployed, the poor, of government homestead projects, and of small-town life in the USA. Many of these served as models for easel and mural paintings documenting the plight of the American unemployed. Under a subsidy from the WPA, Shahn also painted several murals for public institutions on the East Coast.

Shahn shared the outrage against Nazi persecution felt by many American–Jewish artists. He painted *Concentration Camp* (1944), focusing on the sense of despair felt by victims. During the Second World War he designed posters for the Office of War Information including *This is Nazi Brutality* (1942) designed in memory of Lidice, Poland, the village that had been wiped off the map by the Nazis. He continued to exploit the propaganda value of the poster medium after the war when he served as

Ben Shahn The Bitter Herbs *1933. (Haggadah for Passover, p. 77) Jewish Museum, New York*

the Director of Graphic Arts for the Congress of Industrial Organizations, designing posters intended to recruit members into the labor union.

Until about 1950 Shahn was concerned with social realism, using an intentionally direct style to speak out for the common man. After 1950 he turned inward, creating allegorical and symbolic works that responded to his personal and religious convictions. The works tend to be more complex in their medium, combining gold foil collage, rich coloration, and graceful, arabesque calligraphy. His early training in Hebrew calligraphy and in lithography served as a valuable background for this late work. During the 1930s Shahn concentrated briefly on the illustration of Hebrew texts with the 12 ink and watercolor images from the *Haggadah* (1931, Jewish Museum, New York) and the text from the scroll of Ecclesiastes (1931). During

the 1950s and 1960s he gave this impulse full range with the playful integration of image and text in such works as *Pleides* (1959); *The Tenth Commandment* (*c.*1960); *The 133rd Psalm* and *The 150th Psalm*; *We Kindle These Lights* (1961); and *Decalogue* (1961). In his series of interpretive illustrations to the *Alphabet of Creation*, the legend from the *Zohar* on the origin of the relationship of the Hebrew alphabet to divinity, Shahn created his own expressive approach to the Hebrew letter.

Shahn's skills were also translated into large scale through a number of commissions for synagogue decoration. *Call of the Shofar*, a mosaic mural in the vestibule of Temple Oheb Shalom in Nashville, Tennessee (1949), is based on a biblical quote from Malachi ii.10 which pleads for racial equality. It is appropriate that Shahn, who has consistently worked against prejudice, designed this mural with images of people from a number of races at a time when the fight against racial segregation in the USA was in a stage of infancy. In 1960 Shahn was commissioned to design Ark doors for Temple Mishkan Israel in Hamden, Connecticut. The result was his joyful interpretation of the Ten Commandments, merging elegant Hebrew calligraphy with sprightly floral imagery. In 1965 he designed stained glass windows based on the story of Job (Job xxxviii.4–7) for Temple Beth Zion in Buffalo, New York.

FURTHER READING

Prescott, K. W.: *Ben Shahn: A Retrospective 1898–1969* (New York: The Jewish Museum and the Jewish Theological Seminary of America, 1976)

——: *The Complete Graphic Works of Ben Shahn* (New York: Quadrangle/New York Times Book Co., 1973)

BARBARA GILBERT

Shaked, Gershon (b.1929) Hebrew critic and literary scholar. Shaked was born in Vienna. His family emigrated to Palestine 10 years later, where he completed his schooling in Tel Aviv. He went on to study Hebrew literature and Bible at the Hebrew University in Jerusalem, graduating *summa cum laude* in 1960. His Ph.D. thesis was on the Hebrew historical

697

drama in the age of national renaissance (1880–1948), and he undertook postdoctoral studies in German, French, and English Literature at the University of Zurich in Switzerland.

In 1959 Shaked accepted a teaching post at the Hebrew University, where he was appointed Professor of Hebrew Literature in 1978. During his distinguished academic career, he has been visiting professor at universities in the USA, Canada, South Africa, and Brazil. He has also lectured extensively at international conferences and seminars. Since 1964 he has been awarded the Warburg Grant, the Talpir Literary Award (1974), Academy of Sciences Grant (1981–2), and the Bialik Literary Prize (1986), among many others.

An extraordinarily active and prolific writer, Shaked's central academic interest is Hebrew literature and drama, ranging from Bialik to the contemporary writers in Hebrew. He is currently preparing the fourth volume of *Hasifrut ha'ivrit; 1870–1980* (Hebrew narrative fiction, 1870–1980), the volume dealing with Israeli literature (1940–80). He is also working on a new approach to the works of S. Y. AGNON and has recently published an enlarged edition of his classic *Lelo motza*, a selection of essays on literature and society. Shaked's studies of Hebrew literature have revealed a concern with the relationship between the literary work and its readership, and he has done pioneering work in Israel on literary reception.

Shaked's work as comparatist has also led to his profound examinations of European literature, including a study of Joseph Roth. Always a champion of the translation of Hebrew literature into European languages, he is a member of the Board of the Directors of the Israeli Institute for the Translation of Hebrew Literature.

BIBLIOGRAPHY

The double confrontation of renascent literature. *Ariel* 22 (1968) 41–62; Hebrew prose fiction after the War of Liberation. *Modern Hebrew Literature* 5, nos 1–2 (1979); *The Shadows Within – Essays on Modern Jewish Writers* Philadelphia: The Jewish Publication Society, 1987)

JOHN MATTHEW

Shamir, Moshe (b.1921) Israeli author. Born in Safed, Shamir was raised in Tel Aviv. From 1941 to 1947 he was a member of kibbutz Mishmar ha'emek and in 1944–5 served in the Palmach. Since the 1940s he has edited a number of Hebrew literary magazines, including *Yalkut hare'im, Daf hadash, Massa, Bamahaneh, Basha'ar* and *Moznayim*. He has also been among the most politically active of Israeli writers, at first as a member of the national board of *Hashomer Hatza'ir*, and later as a member of Likud in the Knesset.

Shamir is a leading member of the first generation of native Israeli writers. Although he is also a poet, playwright, and short-story writer, Shamir is best known for his novels of the 1940s and 1950s. The novels give a rich, variegated portrayal of Israel's struggle for independence and self-definition, the difficulties inherent in adapting to new-found power, the evolution of the *sabra* character, and the tension between collective and individual destiny in time of crisis. In the novel *Hu halakh basadot* (1947; He walked in the fields), Shamir gave expression to the quintessential stereotype of the *sabra*: an idealist, rugged and unintellectual, a born leader, strong, honest, and compassionate, hating war but capable of cruelty if necessary. Another of Shamir's well-known portraits of native Israelis is Alik, hero of *Bemo yadav* (1951; *With His Own Hands*, 1970), based on Shamir's brother who died in the War of Independence.

Shamir's historical novels, *Melekh basar vadam* (1954; *King of Flesh and Blood*, 1958), and *Kivsat harash* (1956; *David's Stranger*, 1964), provide Shamir with much scope for an indirect critique of modern Israel, through the portrayal of the tyrant Alexander Yannai and of King David respectively. *Melekh basar vadam* is also notable for its successful imitation of mishnaic style and its skilful weaving of history and talmudic legend.

Shamir's later work, such as *Hagevul* (1966; The border) is more overtly critical of the collective values of the fledgling state: in this respect, he has followed the general trend in Israeli literature.

During the 1940s and 1950s Shamir was one of the most popular Hebrew writers but was displaced by younger writers who gave a more energetic and profound expression to Israel's rapidly changing society.

BIBLIOGRAPHY

King of Flesh and Blood, trans. D. Patterson (London: East and West Library, 1958); *With His Own Hands* (Tel Aviv: Institute for the Translation of Hebrew Literature, 1970)

FURTHER READING

Silberschlag, E.: The historical novel. In *From Renaissance to Renaissance II* (New York: Ktav Publishing House, 1977)
Yudkin, L.: Flight of the hero in Israeli fiction. In *Escape Into Siege* (London: Routledge & Kegan Paul, 1974)

DAVID ABERBACH

Shapero, Harold (b.1920) American composer. Born in Lynn, Massachusetts, he began his piano studies at a very early age, and, during his high school years, worked extensively as a jazz pianist and arranger. He studied harmony with Nicolas Slonimsky before attending Harvard University in 1937 where he worked with Walter Piston and Ernst Krenek, and with Paul Hindemith at the Berkshire Music Center in 1944. In 1941, after graduating from Harvard magna cum laude, he received the Prix de Rome for his *Nine Minute Overture*. Thereafter, he worked for two years with Nadia Boulanger. Shapero considers his Boulanger studies as well as his own analysis of the works of the classical masters as his most important musical education.

Shapero has received a great many awards and prizes besides his first Prix de Rome in 1941. In 1955 he was commissioned by the American Jewish Tercentenary Committee to write a work. The result of this commission was a piece for solo voices, chorus, trumpet, flute, violin, harp, and organ entitled *Until Night and Day Shall I Cease* to poems of Yehuda Halevy.

In 1952 Shapero was appointed Professor of Composition at Brandeis University, and since 1967 he has devoted himself primarily to writing electronic music. He has collaborated with the engineers Melville Clark and David Luce in developing a synthesizer called "the Orchestron", which can "duplicate electronically the sounds of all familiar orchestral instruments".

Among his most important works are *Serenade in D* for string orchestra (1945), *Symphony* for classical orchestra (1950), *Until Night and Day Shall I Cease*, a Hebrew cantata (1955), *Four Pieces in B flat* for synthesizer and piano (1970), and *Two Hebrew Songs* for tenor, strings, and piano (1978).

SAMUEL H. ADLER

Shapey, Ralph (b.1921) American composer and conductor. He was born in Philadelphia and he began the study of the violin with Emanuel Zetlin and composition with Stefan WOLPE. In 1938 he began his conducting career as assistant conductor of the Philadelphia National Youth Administration Orchestra and remained in that post until 1942. During the Second World War Shapey served in the US Army but continued to compose and even guest conduct. After the war his compositional activities increased greatly, and his first serious orchestra piece, *Fantasy* (1951) won an honorable mention in the George Gershwin Memorial competition. While living in Florence, Italy, he completed his *Concerto* for clarinet and chamber group, which brought him to the attention of a greater public. The work was chosen to represent the US at the festival of the International Society for Contemporary Music at Strasbourg, France, in 1958.

In 1969 Shapey announced that he would never again submit any of his works to anyone for performance or publication. This was his protest and his expression of frustration against what he considered "to be steadily deteriorating ethical standards in the musical world and the world in general". He reversed himself in 1976 when his oratorio, *Praise*, was performed and recorded to great acclaim.

Shapey is a most prolific composer and at the same time a great advocate of the music of his fellow contemporary creators. He has taught at the University of Chicago since 1964, and, as conductor of the Contemporary Chamber Players, has performed hundreds of new works. He has received many prestigious awards.

His style employs serial procedures, but mostly adheres to classical structures. Eric Salzman describes Shapey's work *Discourse* as a typical example of his cumulative form: "large, contrasting, blacklike ideas set forth in broad planes and constantly returning in great overlapping phrased cycles".

SAMUEL H. ADLER

Shapiro, Harvey (b.1924) American poet and newspaper editor. Born in Chicago, Illinois, Shapiro received his BA from Yale and MA from Columbia. He married in 1953 and is the father of two sons. Following stints on the editorial staffs of *Commentary* and *The New Yorker*, he moved to the *New York Times*. As editor of the *New York Times Book Review* from 1975 to 1983, Shapiro held one of the most influential positions in the shaping of American literary tastes. He is currently the editor of *The New York Times Sunday Magazine* and a *Times* literary critic.

The author of eight collections of poetry, Shapiro remarks that his early work was "marked by a preoccupation with Jewish (Hebraic) themes", and in his later work he follows "mainly chassidic teachings" to discover "the right way of living". The poems, generally free verse, anecdotal and urban, often reveal despair and disillusioned love, particularly in the late collection, *The Light Holds* (1984). Influenced by the straightforward, colloquial school of William Carlos Williams, Shapiro's language is direct and unadorned yet attempts to convey the mystical power of the word "to move a bit of air". Poems in his first major collection, *Battle Report* (1966), reflect grimly on his sense of failure and are haunted by images of the Holocaust. Even in despair at hopes for Jewish survival, he manages to find renewal on reading the Torah. As he writes in *This World* (1971), "The parchment before me / Was like a beginning".

ELIZABETH KLEIN

Shapiro, Karl Jay (b.1913) American poet, novelist, editor, and teacher. Born in Baltimore,

Maryland, Karl Jay Shapiro – the son of a small businessman, a southerner, and a Jew – was introduced early to conflicting influences which, along with sheer force of will, would shape his career profoundly. His secondary education was sporadic and undistinguished; he had to resign after single semesters at the University of Virginia and Johns Hopkins. However, during this apparently aimless youth, he was learning the hard lessons of racial and class prejudice.

In 1941 Shapiro was drafted, beginning a period of artistic activity that firmly established him as a poet. He served as a Medical Corps clerk in the South Pacific, seeing enough of the war to grant his subsequent writing an emotional verisimilitude. *The Place of Love* (1942) gave way to the powerful *Person, Place, and Thing* (1942), which marked the actual beginning of his poetic career. Adroit dramatic monologues alternating with the commentary of wryly detached observers characterize the poems of *V-Letter and Other Poems* (1944), which earned Shapiro the Pulitzer Prize and created a reputation for him to return to from the war.

In the following years, through his poetry and his public appearances, Shapiro presented himself as a renegade, an unabashed exponent of sensation in the line of Whitman and W. C. Williams, clearly at odds with the cult of impersonality he felt had been engendered by Eliot, Pound, and the New Criticism. He chose the poetry of "situation", leading him to confront and embrace his own Jewishness in *Poems of a Jew* (1958). By turns combative and conciliatory, this book examines both the heritage shared by Judaism and Christianity and what Shapiro sees as Christian repressiveness. While he was a master of varied poetic forms, in the mid 1960s he veered toward a prosaic poetry with *The Bourgeois Poet* (1964), interesting as an autobiography presented through free association. Later, in *Adult Bookstore* (1976), he produced some of his most polished verse.

Although at odds with academe throughout his career, Shapiro has taught at a number of major universities, including the University of California, Davis, where he still works, and he has edited two influential journals, *Poetry* and *Prairie Schooner*.

BIBLIOGRAPHY
In Defense of Ignorance (New York: Random House, 1960); *Collected Poems 1940–1978* (New York: Random House, 1978)

FURTHER READING
Malkoff, K.: The self in the modern world: Karl Shapiro's Jewish poems. In *Contemporary American–Jewish Literature*, ed. I. Malin (Bloomington: Indiana University Press, 1973) 213–28
Stepanchev, S.: Karl Shapiro. In *American Poetry Since 1945* (New York: Harper and Row, 1965) 53–68

NELSON HATHCOCK

Shapiro, Lamed [Leyvi-Yehoyshue] (1878–1948) Yiddish short-story writer and literary theoretician. Born in Rzshishtshev, in the district of Kiev, in the Ukraine, Shapiro had ambitions at a very young age to become a Yiddish writer, and, as was the custom of the day for aspiring Yiddish writers, he made the pilgrimage to Warsaw in the 1890s to Tsigliana 1, the address of I. L. PERETZ, seeking advice and support. Peretz encouraged the young writer, and his first pieces were a realistic short story and a pro-Yiddish article in the then-raging language controversy (both in 1904). In 1906 he emigrated to the USA and published a number of short stories which portrayed with unmitigated horror the events of the pogroms of 1905. The best known are "Der tseylem" (The cross) and "Der kush" (The kiss), both of which appeared in 1909. These stories made Shapiro famous. He had captured the dread of the pogroms as no-one else had. Shapiro's meticulously crafted Yiddish – condensed, precise, and starkly beautiful – was very different from anything else known in Yiddish stylistics. All his work was created in the spirit of impressionism.

After the pogrom stories, Shapiro's star faded for a time. He returned to Warsaw around 1909, worked for the Yiddish newspaper *Der fraynd*, specializing in translations from world literature into Yiddish, some of which later appeared in book form. He left for Zurich in 1910 where he and his wife managed a restaurant, then returned to the USA. One or two of the stories from that period were to attract acclaim, but Shapiro left the field of Yiddish

literature, moved to Los Angeles in 1921, and spent years trying to develop color movies.

Lamed Shapiro returned to New York in 1928, brokenhearted at the death of his wife, and increasingly alcoholic. During this latter New York period, he returned to writing Yiddish, and produced his most brilliant collection of short stories – *Nyu-yorkish* (1931; New Yorkish). The book starts with the story "Nyu-yorkish", the first work in which a Yiddish writer demonstrated that Yiddish could, for literary purposes, be universalized to the extent of having no ethnic content while preserving its native idiomaticity intact. The atmosphere of New York around 1930 is masterfully captured and the impressionistic devices perfectly constructed. In 1934 Shapiro published three issues of *Studio*, a journal for experimental Yiddish literature.

In 1939 Shapiro returned to Los Angeles where he published *Der shrayber geyt in kheyder* (1945; The writer goes to school), a collection of critical and theoretical essays. It is probably the most penetrating study of Yiddish literature, stylistics, sociolinguistics, and literary history ever written by a Yiddish author. His short stories and essays alike are characterized by his flowing modernistic Yiddish, an impressionistic tone, and a perfect architectural structure.

FURTHER READING
Frank, E.: *An Analysis of Four Short Stories by Lamed Shapiro* [*Working Papers in Yiddish and East European Jewish Studies*, 28] (New York: Yivo Institute for Jewish Research, 1978)
Leviant, C.: *Lamed Shapiro: Master Craftsman of the Yiddish Short Story* (MA thesis, Columbia University, 1957)

DOVID KATZ

Shaw, Irwin (1913–84) American novelist Irwin Shaw was born in New York City. He began his professional career after graduation from Brooklyn College in 1934 by selling radio serial scripts while writing an anti-war drama about six soldiers who refuse burial, *Bury the Dead* (1936), which became his first published book. But it was as a fiction writer, Hemingway's heir, that Shaw won recognition. His first collection of short stories, *Sailor off the Bremen* (1939; 1940), included many set in New York that critics have found his most successful and defined his literary strengths: vivid detail, sharp characterization, concise episode, graceful style, and lively talk.

After spending the Second World War in Africa and Europe in the Army Signal Corps, Shaw resumed his career with *The Young Lions* (1948, 1949), concerning three soldiers, two Americans and one German. His strongest novel, its outrage at cruelty and prejudice and its respect for human worth indicated Shaw's major themes. After a second novel about a television producer blacklisted during the McCarthy period, Shaw moved permanently to Switzerland, continuing to produce fiction, drama, and screenplays. Despite *Two Weeks in Another Town* (1960), which the author regarded his best book, critics repeatedly found his works disappointing and facile, and accused him of selling out for popular success. *Rich Man, Poor Man* (1970), a family chronicle, renewed his critical reputation as consummate craftsman. In his last 15 years, Shaw published 13 books. He died in Switzerland after nearly half a century of storytelling.

BIBLIOGRAPHY

The Troubled Air, (New York: Random House; London: Cape, 1951); *Beggarman, Thief* (New York: Delacorte; London: Weidenfeld & Nicolson, 1977)

FURTHER READING

Giles, J. R.: *Irwin Shaw* (Boston: Twayne, 1983)

ADAM J. SORKIN

Shemi, Yechiel (b.1922)   Israeli artist. Born in Haifa, Shemi was among the founders of Kibbutz Beit Ha'arava in the Negev (1939); after the War of Independence, he and friends from Beit Ha'arava founded Kibbutz Kabri in the western education; in the early 1960s he traveled to Europe and the USA, where he encountered works of modern art that had a marked influence on his own work. Especially influential were Julio Gonzales, David Smith, and Anthony CARO. Since his early works in the 1940s, Shemi has worked in a variety of materials: stone and wood, used iron scraps, and cast iron. Today he combines iron with cement and wood.

The diversity of materials is an indivisible part of this artist's formal language, which is, for him, the essence of art. Shemi shuns literary or symbolic significance; the meaning of a work of art resides, to use his terminology, in its being "art net". His stone and wood sculptures, although highly geometricized, are almost naturalistic; they also contain renderings of the human figure, as in *Father and Son* (1948) or *Head of a Young Warrior* (1956). These works, according to Shemi, were strongly influenced by ancient Middle Eastern art, especially Egyptian and Assyrian. His early iron sculptures were expressionistic, made of used materials, "torn" scraps of metal, or as the artist saw it, of material already "pregnant" with meanings. *Sea Iron-Scraps* (1964), for example, was sculpted from the remains of an ancient boat raised by underwater explosives from the seabed. The industrial cast-iron sculptures used regular geometric shapes, as in the monument to the 8th Regiment of the 'Palmach' near Ben-Gurion Airport (1972).

The surrounding space is a determining factor for Shemi. In his early works the accord between a work of art and nature was achieved through the use of local materials: stone and wood. Later works take into account the environment, the actual placement of the work. Thus, *Sea Iron-Scraps* is an integral part of the open sea north of Naharia and of the ancient rocks. The monument near the airport integrates and, at the same time contrasts, with industrial architecture. The artist encourages the visitor to go in and out of the sculpture, to follow, as it were, the process of its making.

For Shemi the forms evolve in the course of their execution. They are, for him, "a journey into the unknown". The spectator is made aware of the sculpting process by the visible joints and the big screws, which themselves thus become a part of the finished work of art.

ESTHER LEVINGER

Shlonski, Avraham (1900–1973)   Hebrew poet and literary editor. Born in Poltava

(Ukraine) to a hasidic family who were nonetheless followers of AHAD HA'AM's cultural Zionist philosophy, Shlonski received a secular Hebrew as well as religious education. At the age of 13 he went to study at the Herzlia *Gymnasium* in Tel Aviv but after the outbreak of the First World War he returned to Russia where he completed his high school education. He returned to Palestine in 1921 as a pioneer, working on road building and construction in the Jezreel Valley. In 1924 he spent some time in Paris, studying comparative literature and back in Palestine he became a literary journalist on a number of Hebrew language newspapers and periodicals. He was a founder and editor of *Sifriat Hapo'alim*, the Workers' Book Guild.

Closely associated with the Mapam party Shlonski headed Israel's literary left and was regarded as Israel's own revolutionary poet. His major rebellion, however, was against classicism and the challenged the authority of no less a master than Hayyim Nahman BIALIK. Shlonski's own work, influenced by the experimentalism of Blok and Yesenin, expresses the transition from the rhetorical, didactic poetry of the European Hebrew poets to the modernist tendencies of the Palestinian and Israeli poets. His greatest achievement was as a linguistic innovator (whom Bialik mocked as "Lashonski" – *lashon*: language). Shlonski introduced the newly revived and spoken idiom into his poetry, coined neologisms, related unrelated words to create amazing imagery and experimented with language by creating puns and plays on words. At the same time he employed the vocabulary and form of biblical and liturgical Hebrew, uniting the language of past and present in a unique and entirely original poetic idiom. Because of this Shlonski is regarded as the only Hebrew poet of the twentieth century to have created a poetic school.

His poetry is not exclusively concerned with Jewish themes although much of his best known and best loved verse relates to the Palestinian landscape which he glorifies both in itself and as a sign of hope for the future. One of his most famous poems, "Amal" ("Toil"), is a fine representation of his tendency to fuse ancient vocabulary with the newly encountered Palestinian landscape, and which well expresses the pioneering messianism. He expressed the horror of Nazism and the Holocaust in *Shirei hamapolet vehapiyus* (1938) and *Al Milet* (1947). However, much of his verse, such as *Avnei bohu* (1934), is deeply pessimistic, evoking the torment of modern man in his urban environment, or reflecting on life and death (*Mishirei haperozdor ha'arokh*, 1968).

In addition to producing nine major collections of poetry, Shlonski translated over 73 books and plays including *Eugene Onegin, Colas Breugnon, Hamlet, King Lear, Tartuffe*, and many other major works of European literature.

FURTHER READING

Burnshaw, S., Spicehandler, E., and Carmi, T., eds: *The Modern Hebrew Poem Itself* (New York: Holt, Rinehart & Winston, 1965)

Silberschlag, E.: Avraham Shlonski: the revolutionizer of the Hebrew language. In *From Renaissance to Renaissance II* (New York: Ktav Publishing House, 1977) 67–71

GLENDA ABRAMSON

Shlonski, Verdina

Shlonski, Verdina Israeli composer and pianist. Born in Russia, she studied piano with Arthur Schnabel in Berlin. She then went to Paris to study composition with Nadia Boulanger, Darius Milhaud, Max Deutsch, and Edgar Varèse. Already in her first composition, a series of songs to poems by her brother, Avraham SHLONSKI, entitled *Images Palestiniennes* (1929–31) she established an early model for the Eastern Mediterranean school later advocated by U. A. BOSCOVITCH, with elaborate oriental ornamentation, imitations of Arabic desert chant harmony of open fifths, and careful accentuation of the Hebrew texts. In 1931 she emigrated to Palestine, where she was active as piano teacher, composer, and performer. She maintained a strong personal style, combining the clarity of French-influenced forms with elaborate serial technique in her many piano and chamber works, while contributing at the same time to the field of folk song, and writing music for the political cabaret theater Hakumkum. Among her works are two sonatas for violin and piano and a song cycle *Al Milet* to poems by Avraham Shlonski.

JEHOASH HIRSHBERG

Shmeruk, Chone (b.1921)   Yiddish scholar. Shmeruk was born in Poland and as a young man emigrated to Israel where he was able to further his studies. In 1961 he accepted the position of Professor of Yiddish Literature at the Hebrew University, Jerusalem.

His first published works were examinations of aspects and examples of Yiddish literature in such scholarly journals as *The Field of Yiddish* and *The Jewish Quarterly*. He developed an interest in the Jewish literature of the USSR and is currently the editor of the books *Jewish Publications in the Soviet Union, 1917–1960*, and *A Shpigl oyf a Shteyn: An Anthology of Poetry and Prose by Twelve Soviet Yiddish Writers*.

Shmeruk has also concentrated on individual Yiddish writers, such as Joseph Perl and I. L. PERETZ. He has written extensively about the life and works of both SHOLEM ALEICHEM and Isaac Bashevis SINGER.

Shmeruk has been greatly acclaimed for his work: in 1973 he received the Y. Yefroykin Award, in 1983 the Itzik Manger Award and the Sholem Aleichem Award in 1984. From 1974 to 1977 he was head of the Center for the Research of Eastern European Jewry, and from 1982 has been Chairman of the Center for Research on the History and Culture of Polish Jewry. In 1986 he was elected to the Israel Academy of Science.

Shmeruk published, as co-editor, *The Penguin Book of Modern Yiddish Verse* (1987) and is Chief Editor with H. H. Paper of a new full and revised edition of the works of Sholem Aleichem.

JOHN MATTHEW

Shneour Zalman [Ben Barukh of Liady] (1747–1813)   Founder of the Habad movement in Hasidism. Born in Liozna, Belorussia, Shneour Zalman joined the hasidic movement at the age of 20 as a pupil of the *maggid*, Rabbi Dov Baer of Mezirech. He succeeded Rabbi Menahem Mendel of Vitebsk as the movement's leader in 1777. He played a leading role in the controversy with the opponents of Hasidism, the *mitnagdim*, led by ELIJAH BEN SOLOMON, Gaon of Vilna. As a result of accusations of treason by his opponents he was twice arrested and imprisoned by the Russian authorities, but was later declared innocent and released. In 1804 Shneour Zalman settled in Liady (Lozna), where he became known as the "Rav of Liady". With the approach of Napoleon's armies during the Franco-Russian war Shneour Zalman fled to Pyern in the Russian interior but died on the journey.

A great talmudic scholar and charismatic leader, Shneour Zalman considered himself a hasid but differed from other hasidic leaders in his emphasis on the importance of study and his refusal to assume the title of *tzaddik*, rejecting the *tzaddik's* reputed ability to work miracles. He wished to confine the *tzaddik's* role as intermediary between man and God to spiritual matters only. He sought to place Hasidism on a rational rather than emotional basis, emphasizing theoretical and intellectual teachings. He stressed the cultivation of wisdom (*Hokhmah*), understanding (*Binah*) and knowledge (*Da'at*); his followers therefore became known as *Haba-d*.

His works include a code of laws, and *Likkutei 'amarim* (Collected sayings), popularly known as the *Tanya*, his interpretation of the *kabbalah* and exposition of Hasidism, in which he expounded upon his own school of hasidic thought.

GLENDA ABRAMSON

Sholem Aleichem [Sholem Rabinowitz] (1859–1916)   Yiddish novelist, dramatist, and story writer. *Sholem-Aleichem*, the words of traditional Yiddish greeting meaning "peace be with you", is the pseudonym of Sholem Rabinowitz, one of the triumvirate of Yiddish classicists who created modern Yiddish literature, the others being MENDELE MOKHER SEFARIM and I. L. PERETZ. Sholem Aleichem's instinctive genius for story-telling and character depiction in Yiddish served to establish Yiddish as a language for the finest literature. He was born in Pereyaslav, Ukraine, and grew up in Voronkov which he later immortalized as Kasrilevke, a symbolic Jewish *shtetl*. His early life is depicted in the autobiographical *Fun yarid* (1916; From the fair). His first published articles appeared in the Hebrew periodical *Hamelits* in 1881. He also tried his hand at Russian sketches which were

Sholem Aleichem (right) with the popular Yiddish writer and editor Mordkhe Spektor

rejected by editors. After 1883 he wrote mainly in Yiddish following the acceptance of his first short story by Alexander TSEDERBOYM in the *Folksblat*. He was a government rabbi in Lubni until his marriage in 1881. He began writing plays, one-act comedies in 1887 with *A khosn, a doktor* (A bridegroom, a doctor), *Der get* (1888; The divorce), and *Di asife* (1889; The assembly). A financially advantageous marriage and his wife's inheritance on the death of his father-in-law enabled him to finance two volumes of the Yiddish literary annual *Folksbiblyotek* (1888–9) which included works of his own and those by Mendele and new young writers who were

for the first time given the opportunity of a literary forum. Before the third volume could be published Sholem Aleichem lost his money in stock speculation in 1890. His disastrous career attempts as insurance agent, stockbroker and commission merchant led him to discover that he could depend only upon his writing for a living.

Throughout the 1890s he created sketches of his two most famous characters. One is Tevye, the poor, hard-working, deeply honest and religious Jewish milkman, who is plagued by having no son, but seven daughters for whom to arrange marriages. He travels between "Kasrilevke" and "Yehupets" delivering milk, and his experiences exemplify eastern European Jewish life where the Jew could be persecuted without reason and at any time. Tevye uses his own homespun philosophy to explain the nature of man and the world. While seemingly naive, he has a natural, uncomplicated wisdom. The stories of Tevye and his daughters were dramatized on stage in New York in 1919 and in Moscow in 1943 among many other performances. The popular musical and film *Fiddler On the Roof* is based on the Tevye stories. Menakhem Mendl, Sholem Aleichem's other beloved protagonist, is the man about town, who dreams of fortunes almost within his reach but who is always luckless in his speculations.

Sholem Aleichem's experience of a pogrom in Kiev in 1905 drove him from Russia. He gave readings of his works all over Europe. He arrived in New York in October 1906 but was unhappy and returned to Europe where he settled in Geneva in 1907. In the following year, on a lecture tour of Russia, he collapsed and had to live during the next six years in various health resorts on the Italian Riviera, South Germany, and the Swiss Alps. These were years of intense literary creativity and ever increasing fame. At the same time he was constantly engaged in a struggle against illness and poverty. His use of satire and of the Yiddish language in dialogue intonation is masterly. He instills each deeply drawn character with established, recognizable gestures. Even when writing about poverty and hardship he always did so using ironic comedy. He could be relied upon to extract some humor from the most poignant situations. His readers laugh with the Jewish characters, not at them, because the characters display great fortitude and dignity in adversity. To Sholem Aleichem is attached the reputation of the greatest ever writer of Yiddish fiction and the greatest Yiddish humorist.

DEVRA KAY

show business, Jews in Jews have been involved in what for the past century has been known as "show business" ever since the first fiddlers on the roof. In many ways the Jewish entertainers mirror the life of the Jewish people from whom they stem – ghetto personalities, in their way almost as important as all the other ghetto characters, the butchers, the innkeepers, the horse dealers and those most vital of all public servants, the marriage brokers.

Probably the earliest form of Jewish entertainment was the Purimspiel, originally a dramatic representation of the struggle and triumph of the Jews of ancient Persia as told in the Book of Esther. From this developed the art of creating irony and proof that it could be represented on a stage. The Purimspiels demonstrated that the stage was something in which the Jews could excel.

The first recorded organized Jewish theater appears to have been the Corso Degli Ebrei which entertained at carnivals throughout medieval Italy. And so it continued – the Jews, never settled more than two or three generations in one place, were entertained by the strolling players, although there is much evidence to indicate that rather than stroll, the wandering Jewish minstrels ran or drove their horses and carts at speeds that demonstrated fear of Cossacks rather than enthusiasm to reach the next temporary theater, a village or two away.

It was Avrom GOLDFADEN who, in 1876, started the first permanent Yiddish theater in the Romanian city of Jassy (Bucharest, the Romanian capital, today boasts one of the few Yiddish playhouses still surviving). His first play, *The Green Tree Garden*, was a box-office sensation, with the result that he established a genre which was quickly imitated throughout eastern Europe, especially in Russia and Poland. The Yiddish theater provided the means by which Jews, with their celebrated sense of humor, could laugh at almost all their deprivations, the taxes, the quarrels with their rabbis, and the always constant fear of the next pogrom.

When the Jews moved westward the Yiddish theater moved with them. By the time they settled in the USA and western Europe the Jewish entertainer was representative of a well-honed craft. In London's Whitechapel and on Second Avenue in New York these *mameloshen*-speaking and singing actors and their writers and directors, such as Boris Thomashefsky,

Maurice Schwartz, and Jacob Adler, were the stars of their world and were treated accordingly. In both London and New York the audiences took precious moments away from their 14-hour days in the sweatshops to fill the stalls and balconies.

Before long the exponents of the Yiddish theater were moving into the wider world. Suddenly American vaudeville, British music hall, the world of the Broadway musical, and the boardrooms of Hollywood were proving that show business was also a Jewish business. It was from the environment of the vibrant Yiddish theater that the Jewish contribution to show business stemmed – and many a refugee from the Yiddish stage moved westwards to Broadway and, further away still, to Hollywood. They did so with varying degrees of success, but Muni Weisenfreund became Paul Muni and Emanuel Goldenberg, Edward G. Robinson. They arrived not long after Theda Bara (Theodosia Goodman) had "vamped" on the screen as the world's first sex symbol. More important, she was the first Jewish film star. Generations later, Lauren Bacall, Shelley Winters, John Garfield, Barbra Streisand, and George Segal would follow her example. But it was the other side of the film business that became – and has, to some extent, remained – a Jewish business. With the exception of Twentieth Century Fox, which was known as the "Goyishe Studio", Hollywood was run by the Jewish moguls; studio heads who had been fur salesmen (Adolph Zukor), glove makers (Sam Goldwyn), or butchers (the Warner Brothers).

A similar entrepeneurial spirit was probably responsible more than anything else for the biggest Jewish contributions to showbusiness – the world of musical comedy and vaudeville, to say nothing of its downmarket brother, burlesque, largely dominated by the Minskys. From the time Sophie Tucker, Fanny Brice, Nora Bayes, and Eddie Cantor were dominating the Ziegfeld Follies – contrary to general belief, Flo Ziegfeld was not Jewish – it seemed that Jews had appropriated this area of the theater for themselves.

With George Jessel speaking to his mother on stage on that new invention, the telephone, the picture looks complete. But it wasn't. The five –

then four and eventually three – Marx Brothers were causing organized mayhem on the Broadway stage long before they did it in Hollywood. Comedians like Smith and Dale (the original models for The Sunshine Boys by Neil Simon) and the Ritz Brothers followed similar routes. In London, Bud Flanagan – born Robert Winthrop (or Weinthrop) – led the Crazy Gang and was probably England's favorite comedian. In France – where Sarah Bernhardt had been the star of a very different stage – Marcel Marceau heard applause without opening his own mouth.

In Switzerland Grock became perhaps the most famous clown of the last two centuries – although possibly in Britain Coco, another outstanding Jewish circus performer, would offer competition for that title. In the USA they seemed to go for more bizarre performances – like those of Harry Houdini, son of a Hungarian rabbi.

It was in the USA that everything seemed to happen. Jerome Kern ushered in a new age of musical comedy with *Show Boat*, which was followed by a series of hits including Sheldon Harnick's and Jerry Brock's *Fiddler On the Roof* (later filmed, starring the Israeli actor Topol), and Jerry Herman's *Hello Dolly* (the film of which starred Barbra Streisand with Walter Matthau). Leonard Bernstein's Broadway contributions with *West Side Story* and *Candide* have been as significant as his more serious works.

George Burns and Jack Benny were among the greatest names on radio as well as on stage before they became important Hollywood names. Then came Danny Kaye, rarely seen specifically as a Jewish entertainer, although everything about him bespoke his early years in that nursery of so many Jewish stars, the "Borsht Belt" of the Catskill Mountains. Twenty years later, Woody Allen and Mel Brooks were to acknowledge their debt to this same area of New York State where they themselves cut their entertaining teeth. Above them all however, towered the presence of a man born in the Lithuanian *shtetl* of Srednicke in 1885 as Asa Yoelson whom the world came to know as the Jazz Singer, Al Jolson, star of the first talking picture in 1927, and for 40 years billed as "The World's Greatest Entertainer".

707

FURTHER READING

Freedland, Michael: *So Let's Hear The Applause, The Story of the Jewish Entertainer* (London: Vallentine Mitchell, 1984)

——: *The Secret Life of Danny Kaye* (London: W. H. Allen, 1985)

——: *The Goldwyn Touch* (London: Harrap, 1986)

——: *The Warner Brothers* (London: Harrap, 1984)

——: *Jolie, The Story of Al Jolson* (London: W. H. Allen, 1985).

MICHAEL FREEDLAND

Shteynbarg, Eliezer (1880–1932) Yiddish fable writer. Shteynbarg was born in Lipkan, Bessarabia, into a hasidic family. In 1919 he was invited to Chernowitz to become leader of Yiddish cultural activities. There he worked on the socialist publications *Dos naye lebn* and *Di frayhayt*. He is renowned for his Yiddish fables which are usually in the form of dialogues between characters which are either inanimate objects or more often animals and plants which are assigned human traits. These characters engage in disputes regarding etiquette in various human situations. The fables were collected from periodicals after his death in Chernowitz and published in a Yiddish volume which was later translated into Hebrew and several other languages.

DEVRA KAY

Shtif, Nokhem [Bal-Dimyen] (1879–1933) Yiddish scholar. Born in Rovne, Volhynia, Shtif's early education covered both traditional and modern subjects, and he went on to study chemistry and engineering in Kiev. He founded a radical Zionist group in 1902, was arrested as a result, and later led in the organization of Jewish self-defense groups in the wake of the Kishenev pogrom. He completed his doctorate in jurisprudence in 1913, around which time he published a number of amateurish Yiddish academic studies, using the pseudonym "Bal-Dimyen" ("Master of Imagination").

In March 1914 Shtif became manager of Kletskin's Vilna publishing house, the world's premier Yiddish publisher, and dedicated the rest of his life to Yiddish, first to the Yiddishist movement, and later to Yiddish scholarship. Works of the earlier period include *Yidn un yidish: Ver zaynen yidishistn un vos viln zey?* (1919; Jews and Yiddish: Who are the Yiddishists and what do they want?). The later period in his work was launched by his *Humanizm in der elterer yidisher literatur* (1922; Humanism in older Yiddish literature). Shtif grew remarkably as a scholar, becoming one of the international leaders in the field by the mid 1920s. In 1922 he left the USSR for Berlin, where he concentrated on Yiddish linguistics and literary history. His essay "Di organizatsye fun der yidisher visnshaft" ("Organization of the science of Yiddish") was crucial in effecting the rise of the Yivo (Yiddish Scientific Institute) in 1925 (see Max WEINREICH).

In 1926 Shtif returned to the USSR, accepting an invitation to head the Yiddish department at the Ukrainian Academy of Sciences in Kiev. He edited the scholarly journals *Di yidishe shprakh* (1926–30) and its successor, *Afn shprakhfront* (1930–3) and contributed major studies to the Minsk journal *Tsaytshrift* in 1926 and 1928.

Accused of "bourgeois Yiddishism" by Soviet authorities, Shtif was compelled to recant his "errors" in "Mayne felern" ("My errors"), in 1932. He was found dead at his desk a year later.

DOVID KATZ

Shtok, Fradl (1890–1930) American poet and short-story writer. Born in Skala, Galicia, little is known about her personally. She is reputed to have been exceptionally beautiful and very learned. In 1907 she arrived in the USA. She was one of the most talented Yiddish poets of the period and also wrote short stories. She was first in introducing the sonnet form into modern Yiddish poetry. However, due to a negative revue of her Yiddish book of short stories she decided to switch from Yiddish to English. Her attempt at a book of short stories in English was unsuccessful. Dogged with what she regarded as failure, she became mentally ill and depressive and died in a sanitarium. Her poems appear in *Dos naye land* (1911–12; The new country); *Di naye heym* (1914; The new home); *Fun mentsh tsu mentsh* (1916; From person to person); and she is included in M. Basin's *500 yor yidishe poezye* (500 years of Yiddish poetry), vol. 2, 1917. Her stories are collected in *Gezamlte dertseylungen* (1919; Collected stories).

DEVRA KAY

Sidgwick, Cecily Ullman [Mrs Alfred Sidgwick; Mrs Andrew Dean] (1855–1934) English novelist of German origin. Her one book of short stories, *Scenes of Jewish Life* (1904), and eight of her novels deal entirely with Jews or have some Jewish characters. In these the scene often moves between England and Germany, enabling her to draw a comparison between the ingrained and virulent anti–Semitism of the German upper and middle class, and the more tolerant attitude of the English. All the English Jews in her novels are of German origin, forming a closely-knit society in London and maintaining contacts with their German relatives, which enable them to exchange visits.

Mrs Sidgwick is a romantic novelist, and her plots invariably describe the machinations of middle-class parents to marry off their children to partners they deem suitable. She shrewdly, and often quite humorously, portrays the affluent, largely secularized German–Jewish society in which the men work to provide opulent homes and fashionable clothes and jewelry for their domineering wives.

Exposure of foreign anti-Semitism to English readers is an important element in these novels, and her last, *Refugee* (1934) begins dramatically with the escape from Nazi Germany and arrival in England of a young girl whose father has died of ill-treatment in prison, and whose brother has committed suicide rather than endure the same fate. At first there is some discussion of events in Germany, but disappointingly romance takes over and leads to a sentimental resolution.

VERA COLEMAN

Silberschlag, Eisig (1903–1988) Poet, translator, historian, and critic of Hebrew literature. Born in Stryj, within the Austro-Hungarian Empire, he emigrated to the USA in 1921, and received a Ph.D. at the University of Vienna in 1926. Until he began teaching in the USA in 1931, he spent time between Vienna and Paris, where he wrote the first of his seven books of Hebrew poetry (*In Lonely Paths*) which was subsequently translated into French and English. In 1931 Silberschlag began teaching Hebrew literature at Hebrew College in Boston. He was the college's dean from 1947 to 1968 and then president from 1968 to 1970. From 1970 to 1973 he was visiting professor at Emmanuel College, where he held the first Hebrew Chair. He was then invited to lecture at the University of Texas at Austin as visiting Gale Professor. He lectured at the World Congress of Semitic Learning in Jerusalem and in 1963 spent three months touring and lecturing at universities in South Africa. He received literary awards, both in the USA and in Israel.

In addition to his poetry, Silberschlag is well known for his work on Saul TSCHERNICHOWSKI and a two-volume work on Hebrew literature (*From Renaissance to Renaissance*, 1973, and *Thirty Years of Hebrew Literature under Independence*, 1981). In *From Renaissance to Renaissance* he places the date of modern Hebrew literature from the time of the later Renaissance, just as other modern European literatures are dated from this time. He emphasizes that the usual eighteenth-century date of the *haskalah* in Germany as the beginning of modern Hebrew literature dismisses the contributions of other Jewish populations to the European Renaissance, first in Spain, then Italy in the sixteenth century, and of the Low Countries during the seventeenth century.

Among Silberschlag's many notable accomplishments are his translations of the Greek comic writers into Hebrew, *Ahat'esreh komediyot* (The eleven comedies of Aristophanes) in two volumes, and, more recently, the dramas of Menander.

To the time of his death he was researching the work of Elias CANETTI, 1981 recipient of the Nobel Prize in Literature.

Other works include: *Igrotai el dorot aherim* (1971; Letters to other generations); *Yesh reshit lekhol aherit* (1976; Each end has a beginning); *Ben alimut uven adishut* (1981; Between violence and indifference); and *Hebrew Literature: An Evaluation* (1959).

BIBLIOGRAPHY

Saul Tchernichowsky: Poet of Revolt (London: East and West Library, 1968) *From Renaissance to Renaissance II* (New York: Ktav Publishing House, 1977)

VERONICA HAYDEN EASTABROOKS

Silkin, Jon (b.1930) English poet. Silkin was educated at Wycliffe and Dulwich colleges but rejected his comfortable Home Counties background and worked as a laborer. In 1952 he founded *Stand*, a magazine of committed writing, and in 1958 was appointed to a poetry fellowship at Leeds University. A distinct voice in post-war British poetry, Silkin has used the heritage of Jewish suffering as part of a larger universal concern with the inhumanity of mankind. He has done this in his explorations of the animal world (*Peaceable Kingdom*, 1954) and the world of flowers (*Nature with Man*, 1965), suggesting surprising correspondences with the human situation. *The Psalms With Their Spoils* (1980) juxtaposes the Hellenistic deification of nature with its desanctification in Judaism, and affirms the need for poetry in confronting the modern predicament. Silkin increasingly draws on Jewish historical experience, including the Holocaust and the martyrdom of York Jews in 1190. *Footsteps on a Downcast Path* (1984) is a tunnel-vision of Jewish history from Roman times to the present. One of his finest poems is "Death of a Son" (1954), based on the personal tragedy of the loss of an infant in a mental hospital.

Silkin's world is a barbaric kingdom awaiting a messiah, where meaning is often defined by loss and exile. His admiration for Isaac ROSENBERG is telling in his treatment of war and violence, as well as in his critical studies of First World War poetry. Silkin has translated much from modern Israeli poets and has assimilated both Hebrew literature and the Israeli scene in some of his own verse.

BIBLIOGRAPHY

Selected Poems (London: Routledge & Kegan Paul, 1980); *The Ship's Pasture* (London: Routledge & Kegan Paul, 1986)

FURTHER READING

Poetry Review 69 no. 4 (special issue)
Sicher, E. *Beyond Marginality: Anglo-Jewish Literature After the Holocaust* (Albany: State University of New York Press, 1985)

EFRAIM SICHER

Simon, (Akiba) Ernst (1899–1988) Israeli educator and religious thinker. Born in Berlin, he grew up in an assimilated family. He attended the universities of Heidelberg, Frankfurt, and Berlin, studying Hebrew and other subjects in the Humanities. From 1923, he co-edited (with Martin BUBER) the magazine *Der Jude*. In the wake of National Socialism, he was in many other ways involved in the process of familiarizing young adults with their Jewish tradition. Being an active Zionist from 1918, he emigrated to Palestine in 1928. There, he continued his work as a teacher and co-director of secondary schools and seminars. In 1935 he joined the Hebrew University of Jerusalem, where he became a professor of education in 1955. Between 1961 and 1966 he was also co-editor of the *Encyclopedia of Education*.

Simon's religious thought revolves around the term "religious humanism", a concept which attributes crucial importance and responsibility to man, but always remains focused on the ultimate value: God. Thus, Simon maintained that, although the religious path requires total devotion, it could not turn into a totalitarian system because it is centered on a true value. Simon's return to Judaism began with the experience of being excluded, on grounds of his Jewishness, from the German society of the First World War. Three teachers were especially influential in shaping his intellectual personality: Rabbi Nobel who first introduced him to Halakhah; ROSENZWEIG who promoted the issue of Jewish existentialism and made Simon aware of the spiritual–personal significance of the Halakhah; and Buber, who, despite Simon's criticism of him, influenced his notions of peoplehood and nationhood. Buber also drew his attention to the increasingly urgent issue of Arab–Jewish dialogue.

Simon's pedagogic activities in Israel were guided by several convictions: at a time of crisis and reconstruction, the young generation must be the focus and the hope of society. Extolling young Israelis' idealism and civic courage, he was convinced that this was the best youth the Jewish people had perhaps ever had. Second, he hoped to be able to convey the German Jewish experience of democracy and its failure and to teach effectively the lessons of history as he saw them. Finally, he had a cautious but positive attitude towards military service. He believed in its unifying and otherwise pedagogically useful function, but was not blind to the danger of Israel's turning into a "Sparta". Through his religious education and broad humanitarian outlook, he hoped to transmit sufficient values to create a vibrant Jewish state in cooperation with the Arab population.

FURTHER READING
Kraft, W.: *E. Simon und die deutsche Kultur* (Berlin: Neue Deutsche Hefte, 1979)

MAREN NIEHOFF

Simon, (Marvin) Neil (b.1927)   American playwright and screenwriter. Simon is a native New Yorker, who attended DeWitt Clinton High School in the Bronx. He left New York University before attaining a degree, when the Army Air Force Reserve stationed him in Colorado. He began his career in 1948 writing for many television comics including Sid Caesar on "Your Shows of Shows". Since 1961 when his first Broadway show, *Come Blow Your Horn*, was produced, Simon has had unprecedented success in the American theater. And while a dozen of his plays have been adapted for the movies, most frequently by Simon himself, he has been almost as prolific writing original screenplays.

Simon's popularity and appeal may be due to his ability to capture the humor in everyday life, and his focus on ordinary people in ordinary situations: young marrieds relating to each other, older married couples coping with declining interests or the vicissitudes of urban life, friends trying to remain friends, mature, world-weary people trying to open up to new experiences and romance, and so on. Simon also relies on autobiographical situations and settings. Many plays are set in New York City, and many are drawn from his personal experiences.

Neil Simon, 1969

Chapter Two (1977) dealt with his feelings for his deceased first wife and his remarriage to actress Marsha Mason, while his trilogy *Brighton Beach Memoirs* (1983), *Biloxi Blues* (1985), and *Broadway Bound* (1987) is directly and overtly autobiographical. A number of his plays, like *Plaza Suite* (1968), *The Sunshine Boys* (1972), and *California Suite* (1976), and the original film *The Goodbye Girl* (1977) are set in a show-business milieu.

Despite the autobiographical concerns, Simon has been reluctant to confront directly the Jewish experience in America. In this sense he is emblematic of American Jewish popular artists. While his characters are often Jewish by implication, by setting, and by their verbal facility and wit, Simon strives for universality of experience and feeling, repressing Jewish particularity. In *God's Favorite* (1974), a modern-day adaptation of the biblical Book of Job, Simon avoids any religious dimension at all! This was the case in his theater works until his 1980s trilogy, especially *Biloxi Blues* where Simon's autobiographical hero directly confronts anti-Semitism and his own weaknesses in dealing with it.

Simon did, however, script a film which directly and perceptively confronts two dominant issues of American Jewish life: Jewish self-hatred and the shiksa archetype. *The Heartbreak Kid* (1972, directed by Elaine May) adapted from Bruce Jay FRIEDMAN's story "A Change of Plan", tells of Lenny Cantrow who meets, courts, and weds Lila Kolodny, but is quickly disillusioned by her coarse, loud behavior and annoying insecurities. On their honeymoon he becomes infatuated with honey-blonde, blue-eyed Kelly Corcoran, and despite her father's overt anti-Semitism, courts and wins her. On their wedding day, Lenny realizes that the WASP ideal is a hollow illusion.

Other plays include *The Odd Couple* (1965); *Last of the Red-Hot Lovers* (1969); *The Prisoner of Second Avenue* (1971); and *I Ought to Be in Pictures* (1980).

FURTHER READING

Johnson, R. K.: *Neil Simon* (Boston: Twayne, 1983)
McGovern, E. M.: *Neil Simon: A Critical Study* (New York: Frederick Ungar, 1979)

DAVID DESSER

Simonsen, David (1853–1932) Danish rabbi, scholar, bibliophile, and philanthropist. Simonsen was born in Copenhagen. From 1874 he studied at the Jewish Theological Seminary of Breslau (Wrocław), and was ordained in 1879. In 1892 he was appointed Chief Rabbi of Copenhagen, the first to have been born in Denmark, a position he held until 1902, when he resigned in order to dedicate himself to scholarly activity and to inter-European humanitarian work, mainly during and after the First World War.

Simonsen was a versatile scholar whose knowledge was legendary. His literary achievement spans such diverse fields as philology, general history, history of religion, and bibliophily, emphasizing the centrality of their Jewish aspects. His production consists of a large number of articles and minor contributions to foreign as well as Danish journals.

The versatility of Simonsen's writings applies equally to his library. At the time of his death, this comprised about 40,000 volumes of Hebraica and Judaica for the most part. This was bequeathed to the Royal Library of Copenhagen and, as the Biblioteca Simonseniana, came to form the basic stock of the present Judaica Department. Simonsen's collec-

tion came to no harm during the Nazi occupation of 1940–5 and is now of international importance.

JUDITH WINTHER

Simpson, Louis [Aston Marantz] (b.1923) Jamaican-born American poet, critic, editor, novelist, dramatist, and non-fiction writer. The son of a prominent attorney and an actress, Louis Simpson could draw from both Gentile and Jewish heritage, his mother being a Russian Jew from Volhynia. Simpson himself grew up knowing nothing of Jewish life and culture and says that only when he emigrated to the USA at the age of 17 and met his mother's family did he begin to understand that side of his being. His distinguished preparatory school and university career was interrupted by service in the US Army from 1943 to 1945, during which time he saw extensive action with the 101st Airborne in Europe and was decorated for bravery. Upon his return he continued studies at Columbia where he earned a BS in 1948, an MA in 1950, and a Ph.D. in comparative literature in 1959.

Simpson has written extensively about his experience as a soldier and the ways in which war transforms man into child and then paradoxically robs that child of growth; about American culture, scrutinizing and criticizing its character; and about his Russian–Jewish ancestry. *The Arrivistes: Poems 1940–1949* (1949), *Good News of Death and Other Poems* (1955), and *A Dream of Governors* (1959) contain the bulk of his war poetry and present Simpson as one of the major interpreters of that conflict. In the Pulitzer-prize-winning *At the End of the Open Road* (1963), with allusions to Whitman throughout, he observes the USA from what he calls his "offshore" perspective and sees a dream gone wrong, an urge for growth stymied by the lack of physical frontiers and turned back upon itself. Not surprisingly the dominant tone of the volume is that of a lament. Many of the poems of *Adventures of the Letter I* (1971) and *Caviare at the Funeral* (1980) recreate the Volhynia province of his Jewish ancestry through the narrative method that he opts for most frequently in his latest work. The latter collection earned a 1981 Jewish Book Council award.

Since 1967 Simpson has lived on Long Island Sound and has been Professor of English at State University of New York at Stony Brook.

BIBLIOGRAPHY

Riverside Drive (New York: Atheneum, 1962) also published in the US as *North of Jamaica* (1972) and in Great Britain as *Air with Armed Men* (1972); *A Company of Poets* (Ann Arbor: Michigan University Press, 1981)

FURTHER READING

Cox, C. B.: The poetry of Louis Simpson. *Critical Quarterly* 8 (1966) 72–86

Moran, R.: *Louis Simpson* (New York: Twayne Publishers Inc., 1972)

NELSON HATHCOCK

Sinclair, Clive (b.1948) British novelist.

Born in London, Sinclair was educated at the University of East Anglia and Santa Cruz, the University of California. At Santa Cruz he began his first novel *Bibliosexuality* which was published in 1973. This novel postulates an imaginary neurotic disorder which is the desire for an unnatural relationship with a book. After the publication of *Bibliosexuality*, Sinclair worked as an advertising copywriter in London and began to publish short stories in various journals including *Encounter*, *London Magazine*, and *Quarto*. The publication of his story, "A Moment of Happiness", in *Encounter* proved to be Sinclair's literary breakthrough. His first collection of short stories, *Hearts of Gold* (1979) marked the emergence of an original Jewish literary voice in England, and in 1981 Sinclair was the recipient of the prestigious Somerset Maugham Award. With the publication of *Bedbugs* (1982), his second collection of short stories, Sinclair was one of twenty writers included in the Book Marketing Council's "Best of young British novelists" campaign.

Sinclair's stories draw mainly on the literature and history of Eastern Europe, the USA, and Israel. He has developed a disturbing literary voice which has enabled him to re-create these other-worlds in his own terms. With the publication of his second novel *Blood Libels* (1985), Sinclair situates his Jewish persona in both England and Israel. This work blends references to the Israeli invasion of Lebanon and its imagined repercussions in Israel with paranoid fantasies concerning the rise of anti-Semitism in England. Using many of the themes of his short stories – such as the relationship between personal illness and the ills of society – Sinclair has created an imaginary world which transcends the communal, biographical, and national limitations of his personal history.

Significantly Sinclair has described himself, in an interview in *The Jewish Quarterly*, as a Jewish writer in "a national sense". He is clearly indebted in his fiction to many Jewish writers such as Isaac ROSENBERG, Philip ROTH and Isaac Bashevis SINGER. A Jewish "national" identity, moreover, has enabled Sinclair to eschew the parochial forms of expression and concerns of the traditional British Jewish novel.

Other works include, *The Brothers Singer* (1983), a literary biography of Esther KREITMAN, Isaac Bashevis Singer, and Israel Joshua SINGER, and *Diaspora Blues: A View of Israel* (1987), a semi-autobiographical account of his relationship with Israel and his literary and intellectual counterparts in Israel.

FURTHER READING

Profile: Clive Sinclair. *Fiction Magazine* 2 no. 2 (1983)

On the edge of the imagination. *The Jewish Quarterly* 31 nos 3–4 (1984)

BRYAN CHEYETTE

Sinclair, Jo [Ruth Said] (b.1913) American

novelist, born in Brooklyn. Her parents had fled from Russia to Argentina, their expenses paid by a baron whose land they worked. When Ruth was three, they moved to Cleveland, Ohio. She took the commercial course, shorthand and bookkeeping at John Hay High School, where she edited the school newspaper. She graduated as the class valedictorian.

In 1930 she worked as a clerk–typist by day, and took a playwriting course at Cleveland College at night. During the Depression, she did historical research for the WPA for five years.

In 1938 she sold stories to *Esquire, New Masses,* and *Coronel.* In 1942 four of her plays were broadcast on the radio.

In 1946 *Wasteland* won the Harper Prize for the best novel, and became the Book Find Club selection. It told the story of John Brown's acceptance of his immigrant Jewish origins through a series of therapy sessions whic end with his resumption of his real name, Jake Braunowitz. Three other novels followed: *Sing at My Wake* (1951), *The Changelings* (1955), and *Anna Teller* (1960).

Her play *Folk Song America* was produced at Cleveland College in 1940. *The Long Moment,* was performed at the Cleveland Play House in 1951.

FURTHER READING

Gitenstein, R. B.: Jo Sinclair. *Dictionary of Literary Biography* vol. 28 (Detroit: Gale Research Co., 1984)

RUTH ROSENBERG

Singer, Isaac Bashevis (b.1908) Yiddish author. Singer would hardly approve of an entry such as this (indeed, he has successfully resisted inclusion in any Yiddish-language literary lexicon), since a substantial portion of his oeuvre has been devoted to obscuring distinctions between the historical and the imaginative.

We are, for example, given complementary/contradictory views in the memoiristic fiction (*In My Father's Court, A Little Boy in Search of God, A Young Man in Search of Love,* and some seven as yet untranslated serial works) of Singer's early years in Bilgoray, Poland (Singer was born in nearby Leoncin), where his father, a hasidic rabbi, held rabbinical court. The contrast between his father's mystical–textual "glosses" and his mother's rational–experiential "explanations" of the (often extraordinary) events recounted by litigants and petitioners has, Singer often suggests, served as formal and conceptual dialectic in his work as a whole.

In 1923 Singer moved to Warsaw, joining his elder brother (Israel Joshua SINGER) on the staff of the *Literarishe bleter,* interbellum Poland's most prestigious intellectual journal. Nearly

Isaac Bashevis Singer

from the start – and to the consternation of his seniors – Singer demanded a place in the literary canon: he rewrote works by reigning laureates; parodied works by others; translated novels by Thomas Mann and Stefan ZWEIG, suggesting thereby that his own belong in their company. And, indeed, these strategies met with notable success: Singer's first work of prose fiction, *Af der elter* (1925; In old age), submitted anonymously to the *Literarishe bleter,* won not only publication, but the journals's contest for prose fiction; Singer's first novel, *Satan in Goray,* was selected as inaugural volume to a series published by the Yiddish PEN Center.

Upon his arrival in New York City in 1935, Singer began an association with the *Jewish Daily Forward* (*Forverts*) which continues to the present day. Though Singer pretends to recall a lengthy period of literary "amnesia" during which "entire works fell apart in [his] hands", these were, in fact, years of immense productivity: by the mid 1940s, Singer was responsible for some 20 percent of the *Forverts*'s non-reportorial prose. To publish so prolifically under a single name would, however, have tested the limits of even so intensely personal an institution as the Yiddish periodical press; in response, Singer added to his previous pseudonymous persona, Yitskhok Bashevis, two additional ones, Yitskhok Varshavski, and D. Segal. (Only one of Singer's approximately three thousand publications has appeared under his orthonym.) These were fully elaborated fictional personalities with distinct personal proclivities, temperaments, and quirks of style; from time to time, one persona would address the other in the pages of the *Forverts*. (On 24 September 1946, Varshavski complained on Bashevis' behalf – and ostensibly without his knowledge – that the latter had not received royalties for the American reprint edition of *Satan in Goray*!)

If the ambitious debutante announced his presence by rewriting literary staples, the mature author set about rewriting his own oeuvre – or, more precisely, writing multiple versions of that oeuvre. Thus, for example, Shosha is at once a childhood playmate of the author, visited once years later but left behind on the eve of his emigration to America (in Varshavski's *A Day of Pleasure*), and the child–woman married by a strikingly Singer-like Aaron Greidinger (in Bashevis' *Shosha*) who, for her sake, chooses to remain in Poland.

Singer's reputation rests largely upon the dissemination of his works in English translation. English and Yiddish texts – and, especially, endings – often stand in ironic juxtaposition to one another, calling, it would seem, for a readership equally versed in both.

With the award of the 1978 Nobel Prize for Literature, Singer's early bid for inclusion in the international literary canon met with unambiguous success.

BIBLIOGRAPHY

Satan in Goray (New York: Noonday, 1955; Yiddish: *Der sotn in Goray*, 1935); *Gimpl the Fool and Other Stories* (New York: Noonday, 1957; Yiddish: *Gimpltam*, 1945); *Short Friday and Other Stories* (New York: Farrar, Straus and Giroux, 1964; Yiddish: *Der kurtser fraytik*, 1945); *In My Father's Court* (New York: Farrar, Straus and Giroux, 1966; Yiddish: *Mayn tatns bezdn-shtub*, 1956 rev.); *A Day of Pleasure: Stories of a Boy Growing up in Warsaw* (New York: Farrar, Straus and Giroux, 1969; Yiddish: *Eyntogglik*, 1966); *Alone In the Wild Forest*, (New York: Farrar, Straus and Giroux, 1971); *A Little Boy in Search of God: Mysticism in a Personal Light* (Garden City: Doubleday, 1976); *A Young Man in Search of Love* (Garden City: Doubleday, 1978); *Shosha* (New York: Farrar, Straus and Giroux, 1978; Yiddish: *Neshome-ekspeditsyes*, 1974)

FURTHER READING

Miller, D. N.: *Fear of Fiction: Narrative Strategies in the Works of Isaac Bashevis Singer* (Albany: State University of New York Press, 1985)
——, ed.: *Recovering the Canon: Essays on Isaac Bashevis Singer* (Leiden: E. J. Brill, 1986)

DAVID NEAL MILLER

Singer, Israel Joshua (1893–1944)

Yiddish novelist, journalist, and playwright. Born in Bilgoray, Poland, the son and grandson of rabbis, Singer received a traditional Jewish education with a strong hasidic orientation. At the same time he secretly read forbidden books in Hebrew and Yiddish. Refusing to become a rabbi, Singer left home at 18 and tried to establish himself as a painter in Warsaw, where he studied Polish, Russian, German, and other non-Jewish subjects until 1914. In order to avoid conscription, in keeping with his ideological opposition to the war, Singer went into hiding, as chance would have it, in a sculptor's studio. There Singer painted and wrote stories set in a hasidic milieu, one of which became his first publication when it appeared in the Orthodox weekly *Dos yidishe vort*.

Initially inspired by the Russian Revolution, Singer moved to Kiev in 1918, and remained there for three years, during which time he became progressively more disappointed with the Soviet regime. This disillusionment later found bitter expression in two novels, *Shtol un ayzn* (1933; Blood harvest) and *Khaver Nakhmen* (1939; East of Eden). The publication, in 1921, of his story *Perl* in Warsaw, marked the turning point in Singer's career, for it was noticed by Abraham Kahan, who printed it in *Forverts*, and offered Singer a permanent position as the newspaper's Polish correspondent.

From 1922 until 1928 Singer was at the center of Yiddish literary and cultural life in Poland. In 1928 he co-edited *Di yidishe velt* for the Vilna publisher, B. A. Kletzkin, but resigned after the appearance of the first issue, in reaction to a series of attacks against him in the Yiddish press. For the next five years Singer continued to contribute to *Forverts* in New York and *Haynt* in Warsaw, but published no fiction until *Yoshe Kalb* in 1932, (*The Sinner*, 1933) in which he portrays the courts of hasidic *rebbes* in nineteenth-century Galicia. *Yoshe Kalb* was also successful as a play dramatized in New York by Maurice Schwartz, as were Singer's other major novels. His best known work, *Di brider Ashkenazi* (1936; The brothers Ashkenazi) is a three-volume epic novel about the gradual domination of the textile industry in Lodz by Jewish entrepreneurs, here represented by the Ashkenazi family, and their destruction by war and Polish anti-Semitism. His last novel *Di Mishpokhe Karnovski* (1943; *The Family Carnovski*, 1943) depicts the disastrous effects of the doctrine of Enlightenment on European Jewry, in a setting reflecting the tensions of the Hitler period.

In 1933 Singer settled in New York City, where he died suddenly at his home in 1944. He was the elder brother of Isaac Bashevis SINGER, and the younger brother of the novelist, Esther KREITMAN.

FURTHER READING
Madison, C.: *Yiddish Literature. Its Scope and Major Writers* (New York: Schocken, 1971)

DAFNA CLIFFORD

Sinkó, Ervin (1898–1967) Hungarian writer and essayist. Born into a Jewish merchant family in Apatin (now Yugoslavia), he became acquainted with socialist ideas as an adolescent. His first writings were printed in Kassák's avant-garde reviews (*Ma, Tett*) as well as in the Communist periodical *Internationale*. After serving in the Austro-Hungarian army from 1916 to 1918, in the autumn of 1918 Sinkó left for Budapest and there befriended the young radical intelligentsia. During the Hungarian Soviet Republic he was commander of the House of Commissars (*Szovjetház*) and later, military commander of the town of Kecskemét. After the fall of the Soviet Republic he fled to Vienna and lived there until 1926, editing the review *Testvér* (Brother) in 1924–5. Between 1926 and 1932 he lived with his wife, a medical doctor, in Yugoslavia, Paris, Zurich, and Moscow. During the Second World War Sinkó returned to Yugoslavia, living first in Sarajevo, then in the territory occupied by the Italians, and finally in the area liberated by Tito's partisans. After the war he settled in Zagreb where he maintained friendly relations with the Croatian writer Krleža. In 1959 he was appointed to the Chair of Hungarian Studies at the University of Novi Sad where he taught Hungarian literature.

Although Sinkó began as a poet, only his prose is really important. His major novel *Optimisták* (1953–5; Optimists), the first draft of which was written in the 1920s, casts light on the ideas and dilemmas of Leftist Hungarian intellectuals active in the Soviet Republic of 1919. *Egy regény regénye* (1961; The novel of a novel) translated into German as *Roman eines Romans* (1962), is in fact a fascinating account of Sinkó's stay in Moscow where he witnessed the impact of Stalin's purges on Soviet cultural life. Sinkó met many Hungarian Communist émigrés in Moscow and he also befriended Isaac BABEL, later a victim of the purge. Sinkó's short stories, mostly dealing with ethical problems, were collected in *Aegidius útrakelése* (1963; Aegidius sets out on his way); also published were essays on Hungarian literature and a collection of diverse essays including pieces on Dostoevsky, Bakunin, Babel, and Krleža (published posthumously: *Szemben a biróval*, 1977; Facing the judge).

Sinkó's basic beliefs were founded on a secular version of Jewish messianism. His chiliastic, but morally motivated Leninism of 1919 changed into a "Christian" faith in the possibility of "real brotherhood" in the Viennese years, and that was transformed in turn into his "religious atheism" in the 1930s. Throughout his life, Sinkó's social radicalism was motivated by ethical, rather than economic considerations; the messianistic element in his faith caused him to react strongly against the discrepancy between revolutionary theory and practice. While the persecution of the war years forcefully reestablished Sinkó's Jewish identity, later he found a new model in the internationalism and anti-Stalinism of Tito's revolution. On the other hand, Sinkós whole life was a creative oscillation between the poles of faith and skepticism – a common enough syndrome of central European Jewish intellectuals of the period.

BIBLIOGRAPHY
Gömöri, G.: A Hungarian Don Quixote in Moscow. *Problems of Communism* 11 no. 3 (1962) 63–4

GEORGE GÖMÖRI

Smolenskin, Peretz (1842–1885) Hebrew novelist, editor, and publicist. A leading exponent of *Haskalah* in its later period and an early advocate of Jewish nationalism, Smolenskin founded and edited the Hebrew monthly *Hashahar* (The dawn) – 12 volumes in all – from 1868 until his death. Born in Monastyrstchina (White Russia) into privation, Smolenskin studied at a *yeshiva* in Shklov for five years before wandering through southern Russia to Odessa in 1862, where he spent five more years teaching Hebrew, and embarking on a literary career. After further wanderings in central Europe he finally settled in Vienna in 1868, devoting himself entirely to his monthly in which he published six novels, and a spate of articles on the main issues of contemporary Jewish life.

Through *Hashahar* Smolenskin endeavored to heighten his readers' awareness of their terrible plight, strengthen their internal resources, and foster genuine enlightenment, while attacking the falsities of the "Berlin" *Haskalah*, and any hypocritical pretensions of Orthodox Judaism or Hasidism. The journal reflected his passionate loyalty to Hebrew language and literature, and to Jewish national aspirations. The pogroms in Russia in 1881 convinced Smolenskin that any hope of emancipation was chimerical while spiritual nationalism was inadequate.

Henceforth he became an ardent advocate of a physical return to the land of Israel, while his dire warnings of increasing anti-Semitism proved chillingly prophetic.

An impassioned defender of the Jewish cause and a ferocious critic of Jewish failures, Smolenskin used his novels as vehicles to convey his ideas. His attempts to combine exciting tales with didactic ideas and social criticism resulted in a hybrid form whose disparate elements nestle together uncomfortably. But melodramatic exaggerations and tortuous plots are enlivened by zest and humor. Of his novels the long autobiographical *Hato'eh bedarkhei hahayyim* (The wanderer in the paths of life) is the most important. His stories and articles have an assured place in the history of modern Hebrew literature, and the development of modern Jewish nationalism.

DAVID PATTERSON

Sobol, Yehoshua (b.1939) Israeli playwright. Born in Tel Mond, Israel, and a member of Kibbutz Shamir from 1957 to 1965, Sobol studied philosophy at the Sorbonne in Paris, and served as a correspondent of the leftist Israeli newspaper *Al hamishmar*. Back in Israel in 1970 he wrote a satirical column in the same newspaper and began teaching and writing drama. From the end of 1984 to 1988 he served as an art director of the Haifa Municipal Theater together with Gedalia Besser. Sobol has been an active member of left "doveish" parties in Israel.

Sobol's first two plays were documentary. *Sylvester '72* (1974; New Year's Eve '72), is his first non-documentary drama. It explores the father–son conflict and exposes the corruption and degeneration of the pioneering fathers' ideals in Israeli materialist society after the Six Day War. In *Leyl ha'esrim* (1976; The night of the twentieth), Sobol turned to history – he reconstructed the night of 20 October 1920, during which a newly arrived group of young European pioneers, members of the Bitanya collective, engage in a confessional discussion, exposing their innermost feelings, caught between their individual needs and their involvement in the Zionist enterprise.

Two distinctive trends emerge in Sobol's prolific writing: on the one hand he explores the negative aspects of contemporary Israeli society; on the other, he tries to understand the roots of modern Judaism and Zionism while searching for clues to ancient and more recent Jewish history. To the first trend belong many plays – some of them short-lived satirical reviews on current issues; to the second belong, among others, plays which have been performed in many countries and which have won Sobol international acclaim: *Nefesh yehudi* (1982; Soul of a Jew) and *Ghetto* (1984). *Soul of a Jew*, chosen to open the Edinburgh Festival in 1983, is based on the life and ideas of the anti-Semitic, misogynist Jewish philosopher Otto WEININGER, who committed suicide at the age of 23. The play reveals the drama of the Jewish identity crisis. *Ghetto* depicts life in the Vilna Ghetto through the development of a theater group there. Like other Sobol plays, it is based on historical fact and is about Jewish combat, both physical and mental, with Nazism.

BIBLIOGRAPHY

The Night of the Twentieth (Tel Aviv: Institute for the Translation of Hebrew Literature 1978); *Soul of a Jew* (Tel Aviv: Institute for the Translation of Hebrew Literature 1983); *Ghetto* (Tel Aviv: Institute for the Translation of Hebrew Literature 1986).

FURTHER READING

Feldman, Y. S.: Zionism: neurosis or cure? The "historical" drama of Yehoshua Sobol. In *Prooftexts 7* (Baltimore: The Johns Hopkins University Press, 1987) 145–62

Ofrat, G.: Modern Hebrew drama: Sobol's Night of 1903. In *Modern Hebrew Literature* (Fall–Winter 1983) 34–41.

RIVKA MAOZ

sociology, modern Jewish Sociology is not a homogeneous, unified body of thought, Jews are not a homogeneous group, and Judaism, with its several ontolgies, theories of knowledge, and variety of ethics, cannot be regarded as a uniform world view. A Jewish sociology, modern or otherwise, must therefore be problematic. In absolute numbers and proportionately, Jews tend to be overrepresented in sociology. They have made important contributions to sociological theory (for example, Marxism, phenomenology, structuralism, and ethnomethodology) yet Jewish sociology is strikingly devoid of theory. It tends to be empirical, functional, or, perhaps more accurately, instrumental, and "applied". Although the origins of a Jewish sociology were determined by Jewish ethnicity and minority status in the Diaspora, sociology in modern Israel, a self-consciously Jewish state, shows the same concerns and preoccupations as is shown by the Jews in the Diaspora.

There is a biblical sociology in the detailed and precise regulation of social relations, in the constant and penetrating critiques of society and the apodictic insistence that social disadvantage (poverty, deprivation, and loss) should never be equated with, or explained by social inadequacy. This led to a tradition, perpetuated in talmudic and rabbinic Judaism, calling for a sustained interest in, and concern for, governance of social relations to ensure a common wellbeing. Reinforced all too often by external hostility and a deeply held conviction that the fate of the Jewish people is always in some way a consequence of their own actions (an early formulation of the social construction of reality?), this classical tradition persisted until it was overtaken by a modern secularized sociology which emerged around the turn of the twentieth century and which has, for the most part, discarded its links with the original source of its deliberations. Nevertheless, Jewish life and experience has been the impetus for the dominant interests of modern Jewish sociology, which we might consider under five headings: demography, socio-economic analysis, social philosophy, the influence of related disciplines, and problem-based studies.

Two factors in particular led to an intense interest in demography at the turn of the twentieth century: The destabilization of the world's largest concentration of Jews in eastern Europe, the subsequent migration from there, and the rapid and often total assimilation of Jews in the more settled communities in the West. Joseph Jacobs (UK) led the way in 1891 with *Studies in Jewish Statistics*. This was followed in 1904 by Arthur Ruppin's *Die Juden der Gegenwart*. In 1905 Ruppin edited the first Jewish social science journal, *Zeitschrift für Demographie und Statistik der Juden*, which dealt with Jews worldwide, and was published until 1919. Following the First World War, interest in demography appears to have declined, and, with some notable exceptions, remained quiescent until the 1950s, when it enjoyed a vigorous revival under the leadership of the Institute of Contemporary Jewry of the Hebrew University in Jerusalem. (An attempt was made to establish an office for Jewish Population Research in the USA in 1945. In Britain, the Board of Deputies of British Jews established a Demographic and Statistical Unit led by Barry Kosmin in 1965.) Jewish demography has made, and continues to make many important contributions and can boast such well known names as Roberto Bachi and Usiel Schmelz, Sergio DellaPergola and Calvin Goldscheider.

Ruppin subsequently extended his analyses and propounded a *Soziologie der Juden* (1931) which was the first major work on the subject, but owes much to contemporaries like Werner Sombart and attempts to find racial characteristics of Jews which would explain their problems and achievements.

The 1920s and 1930s saw a number of more genuinely sociological approaches to the study of Jews. Kurt Zilenzieger (*Juden in der deutschen Wirtschaft,* 1930), Alfred Marcus (*Die Wirtschaftliche Krise des deutschen Juden,* 1931) and Jakob Lestschinsky (*Das wirtschaftliche Schicksal des deutschen Judentums,* 1932) looked to a neo-Marxist type of analysis to account for the curious position of the Jews of Germany where integration and assimilation were at a peak, while the dark clouds of Nazism were gathering on the horizon, heralding an unprecedented storm of anti-Semitism. In the tradition of Bruno Bauer and Karl Marx, they tried to locate the Jews in the social structure, explaining both past progress and present discomfort by linking their exonomic role with the evolution of capitalism. The Jews, so they thought, had accomplished their entrepreneurial role as the agents of capitalist innovation. The Gentile trader, banker, and financier, having no further use for Jews, were seeking to eliminate them from society in which they had, in any event, no recognized position in the class structure. A similar view was taken by Max HORK-HEIMER, leader of the Frankfurt School in his essay on the *Jews of Europe* (1939), but neither he

nor anyone else at that time had an inkling of the excesses of the Nazi regime, and this line of enquiry petered out in the face of an incomprehensible reality. Yet this period of early maturity did represent a more genuinely theoretical formulation of modern Jewish sociology. This was also apparent in the more philosophical approach to sociology of men like Martin BUBER (the first head of Sociology at the Hebrew University) whose interest in utopias reflected some despair about the social evils of his time, and Morris Ginsberg, a leading sociologist in Britain who argued for a value-free social science, but saw social issues in moral terms of good and bad. In 1939 Salo BARON in the USA succeeded in establishing the prestigious journal *Jewish Social Studies*, while in Britain, Morris Ginsberg and Maurice Freedman produced the influential *Jewish Journal of Sociology* in 1959.

It took some time for the Jews to recover from the shock of the Holocaust and sociological studies of it were slow in appearing. Jewish survival remained the central theme as in Mark Wischnitzer's *To Dwell in Safety* (1948) Maurice Freedman's (ed.) *A minority in Britain* (1955), or the pessimistic Nathan Glazer in *American Judaism* (1957). American–Jewish sociology tends generally to be more sophisticated, more professional in its approach to research, but primary concerns are much the same as elsewhere. There are well-known studies like Bezalel Sherman's *The Jew Within American Society* (1965), Sidney Goldstein and Calvin Goldscheider's *Jewish Americans* and Marshall Sklare's *American Jews* (1971) which reflect some of the intensive, though mainly parochial, work which has been done. As yet little has been written about Jews outside the European–American orbit. The formidable five-volume study, *A Mediterranean Society* by S. D. Goitein (1967–85), based on documents in the Cairo Genizah, is raw data which underlines the need for systematic sociological analysis.

Modern Jewish sociology in Israel in not distinguishable from its Diaspora counterpart, except, for the large number of contributions on the sociology of the kibbutz, which is a uniquely Israeli institution. It has been led for many years by Shmuel Eisenstadt, a rare theoretician who had a profound influence which extends beyond the boundaries of his country. As we have already noted, Israeli scholars took the lead in reviving Jewish demography on a global scale. Apart from that, education, the family, ethnicity, and rural studies are primary concerns; and shared with the Americans a relatively new and promising field of political sociology which, at present is the most prominent field in Israel. There is a wholesome attempt by the Israel Sociological Society to draw together the more important contributions of Israeli–Jewish sociology in Ernest Krausz (ed.) *Studies of Israeli Society* (3 volumes to date).

It has been stated that sociology does not represent a uniform body of thought and it is not surprising therefore that many excellent contributions to modern Jewish sociology came from related disciplines, notably from social history, social anthropology, and political science. In history we have massive contributions not only from Simon DUBNOW's *History of the Jews* and Salo Baron's *Social and Religious History of the Jews*, there is also Baron's *The Jewish Community* (1948). More specific studies like those of Jacob Katz, Jacob TALMON, George and Werner Mosse, Michael Mayer, and Ismar Schorsch, have contributed immeasurably to a more sociological approach to Jewish history. In social anthropology, studies like Mark Zborowski and Elizabeth Herzog *Life is With People* (1952), Solomon Poll *The Hasidic Community of Williamsburg* (1962), and Samuel Heilman *Synagogue Life* (1976) have created new dimensions for a sociology of Jewish societies, while scholars like Daniel Elazar *Community & Polity* (1976) represent the growing interest in the political dimensions of Jewish life. Finally another encouraging development is one in which professional sociologists investigate very specific Jewish issues, like Percy Cohen's *Jewish Radicals and Radical Jews* (1980) and Julius Gould's *Jewish Commitment* (1984).

JULIUS CARLEBACH

Solomon Family of English painters. Until the emergence of three painters from a single family, the number of significant Anglo-Jewish artists could be counted on the fingers of one hand. Abraham (1823–1862), Rebecca (1832–1886),

and Simeon (1840–1905) were all born in Bishopsgate, London, into a prosperous and assimilated family of Ashkenazi origin. Their father was a hatter, and the second Jew to be made a Freeman of the City of London; their mother is reputed to have shown considerable artistic talent.

Abraham was the most conventionally successful of the three. After studying at Mr Sass's School of Art in Bloomsbury, he entered the Royal Academy Schools in 1839, exhibited there regularly thereafter, and was elected an Associate of the Academy in 1863, on the very day of his untimely death at the age of 38. He remained an observant Jew to the end, while outwardly appearing the perfect English gentleman. Although a few of his earliest paintings depicted Jewish subjects, these were soon abandoned in favor first of literary genre scenes set in the eighteenth century, and then of the contemporary genre scenes, meticulously realistic in style, anecdotal in implication, and usually moralizing in intention, for which he became best known.

Rebecca, as a woman, had to content herself with studying at the Spitalfields School of Design and, later, with becoming a pupil of her already successful older brother; her early work, comprising both historical and contemporary genre scenes, shows clear signs of his influence. She seems to have earned her living as a copyist and drapery painter for such well known figures as W. P. Frith and J. E. Millais. Her later work is less anecdotal, more atmospheric and evocative – closer to that of Simeon. Said to have exercised a stabilizing influence on her younger brother, and to have supervised his regular attendance at synagogue, she seems to have retained a strong Jewish faith even after her increasingly bohemian lifestyle and alleged alcoholism denied her a place in respectable Anglo-Jewish society. Rebecca exhibited nothing after 1869, and died in obscurity at the age of 54.

Simeon's career was undoubtedly the most colorful. He entered the Royal Academy Schools at the age of 15; by the age of 20 he was producing drawings of considerable finesse, many of them on Old Testament themes, and had scored his first major success at the

Simeon Solomon Carrying the Scrolls of the Law. *Whitworth Art Gallery, University of Manchester*

Academy with a painting entitled *The Mother of Moses*. The year 1860 also saw his introduction into Pre-Raphaelite circles, where Edward Burne-Jones is reputed to have exclaimed: "You know, Simeon, we are all schoolboys compared to you". In the early 1860s Simeon delighted Anglo-Jewish society by producing relatively realistic depictions of Jewish ceremonial practices for popular non-Jewish illustrated magazines. Under the influence of Swinburne, Pater, and others involved in the Anglo-Catholic Oxford Movement, however, he moved away from his Jewish roots and an adherence to specific religious beliefs, towards an obsession with ritual per se, and with the mystique of religion, whether Jewish or Catholic. In 1873 Simeon was arrested in a public urinal and charged with several homosexual offences. A social outcast thereafter, he died in a London workhouse, of heart failure aggravated by alcoholism. His late work treats pagan, Christian, and Jewish themes alike, all of them subsumed in a dreamy, spiritualized sensuality which was to find considerable favor with the Esthetic Movement.

FURTHER READING

Solomon: A Family of Painters (London: Geffrye Museum, 1985) [exhibition catalog]

Reynolds, S.: *The Vision of Simeon Solomon* (Stroud: Catalpa Press, 1984)

MONICA BOHM-DUCHEN

Solomon, Solomon J. (1860–1927) English painter. The Salamon family originated from Amsterdam, and had, at some time, changed the spelling of their name. Born in London, Solomon studied at Heatherley's Art School in 1876 and, in 1877, was enrolled at the Royal Academy Schools. He continued his studies at the École des Beaux-Arts, Paris, and later in Munich. He traveled in Italy, Spain, and North Africa before settling in London. In 1906 he was appointed Royal Academician, only the second Jew to be so honored, and in 1918 became President of the Royal Society of British Artists. He produced *The Practice of Oil Painting* which was published in 1910. During the First World War he served as a Lieutenant Colonel with the Royal Engineers. His contribution to the war effort was immense: he had created the system of camouflage in 1914 before any other country involved in the war had thought of it. He was sent to France to instruct army officers and his book on the subject, *Strategic Camouflage*, was published in 1920.

Solomon was a founder and first president of the Maccabeans and died in Birchington, Kent, where he had settled in 1906. During his lifetime his work was shown at the Royal Academy of Arts; in 1946 the Ben Uri Art Society, London, exhibited his work, together with that of his sister, the painter Lily Delissa Joseph.

FURTHER READING

Phillips, O. S.: *Solomon J. Solomon: A Memoir of Peace and War* (London: Herbert Joseph, 1933)

MURIEL EMANUEL

Soloveitchik, Joseph Dov (b.1903)
American talmudist, halakhic authority and
philosopher. The leading exponent of traditional Jewish thought in the United States, Soloveitchik continues his Lithuanian family tradition but links it to contemporary life. He was
born in Pruzhan, Poland, and trained in his
family tradition of analytic and incisive Talmud
study based upon Maimonides. Privately educated, he came to the University of Berlin and
wrote his doctoral dissertation on Hermann
COHEN, Kant's disciple. Soloveitchik emigrated
to the United States in 1932 and became rabbi
of the Orthodox community in Boston. In 1941
he succeeded his father as professor of Talmud
at the Rabbi Isaac Elchanan Theological Seminary of Yeshiva University in New York City,
and also served the Graduate School as professor of philosophy. He has published little, but
his teaching has guided the American Orthodox community, which responded to the
existentialist-flavored anthropology of a great
orator, who combined the most profound knowledge of Jewish law with the subtle insight of
contemporary disciplines within philosophy.

Man stands at the center of Soloveitchik's
teaching. Two major essays – "The Man of the
Halakhah" (1944) and "The Lonely Man of
Faith" (1965) present a typology of the human
being who is both active and passive, cause and
effect, subject and object, and who needs the
discipline of Jewish Law to control existence
and to break out of habit and routine. Halakhic man is contrasted with "religious man"
and "rational man", and the profoundly moving portrait of "the lonely man of faith" is defined by the Adam figure in Genesis seen on
two levels: Adam the First and Adam the
Second. From the fundamental statement "I am
lonely" Soloveitchik moves to "I believe therefore I am (credo ergo sum)", celebrating the
human being who can move beyond the majestic figure of the First Adam and his creative and
intellectual powers to the Second Adam who
exists within him. That Adam surrenders his
powers and pride, withdraws from society and
returns to his loneliness where he comes to encounter God and enters into the covenantal relationship of faith. In his later lectures,
Soloveitchik comes to present an additional
type: "repentant man" in whom the talent for
creation merges with the longing to draw near
to God.

Much of this parallels Kirkegaard's existential Christianity, but beyond the emphasis on
esthetics, on the need to surrender, to break
through the flux of time to the Divine guarantor
of human identity, Soloveitchik adds the Jewish
emphasis upon the dialogue between man and
God: prayer and prophecy, the first initiated by
man, the second by God. Radical loneliness is
not irredeemable here. In prayer, one stands
before God and discovers one's insignificance as
well as one's worth. Within the Halakha, partial redemption takes place for those who accept
it, and the loneliness is tempered by the life
within the community sharing in the Covenant.
Modern traditional Judaism has welcomed this
champion of Jewish law, and the searching non-
Orthodox Jew also feels addressed here. For
students outside the Jewish tradition, Soloveitchik becomes a witness to a way of faith
which makes the loneliness of humanity the
area where God is most often encountered.

FURTHER READING

Oppenheim, M.: Kierkegaard and Soloveitchik.
Judaism (Winter 1988)

Peli, P.: *On Repentance in the Thought and Oral Discourses
of Rabbi Joseph B. Soloveitchik* (Jerusalem: Oroth,
1980)

Soloveitchik, J. B.: The lonely man of faith. *Tradition*
(Summer 1965)

ALBERT H. FRIEDLANDER

Sonntag, Jacob (1905–1984)   Scholar and
editor. Born in Wiznitz (Northern Bukovina) in
1905, Sonntag grew up in Vienna from 1917
and arrived in England in 1938, a refugee from
Nazi Europe with no knowledge of English.
However, by spring 1953, he had launched *The
Jewish Quarterly* to which he single-mindedly dedicated the rest of his life. His first editorial
promised its readers that the magazine would
be "open to free expression of opinion" and
devoted to "reevaluating . . . our great cultural
heritage whilst [also] encouraging new creative effort in every field". He also set out to
"revive the tradition of serious debate and discussion on . . . vital issues confronting the [post-
Holocaust] Jew" in an era following the birth of
the State of Israel, in a world divided by the

"cold war" and where persecution of Jews still occurred. The first issue of the *Quarterly* included drawings by Josef HERMAN; an article by Joseph Leftwich on Anglo-Jewish literature; one on the future of Jewish education; "Hebrew Opera" by Martin Lawrence; poetry, prose, and drama by great Yiddish writers, translated by Sonntag; "Outlook for New Playwrights" by Frank Jackson and Alexander Baron; a short story by Emanuel LITVINOFF; poems by Dannie ABSE; photographs of Joseph EPSTEIN sculptures accompanying an article on the artist; a documentary piece on Halberstadt, based on evidence by that German town's only surviving Jew; and reviews of new books. This blend of past, present, and future in literature, the arts, and documentary was typical of the kind of balance to which Sonntag aspired and succeeded in achieving throughout the magazine's 31 years under his editorship.

Sonntag frequently expressed the necessity and desirability of forging cultural ties between Israel and Anglo-Jewry. On a few occasions he devoted entire numbers to Israeli writing and issues. In 1966 he organized, with the Israeli Writers' Association, a marathon dialogue in Jerusalem, the first of its kind, between Anglo-Jewish and Israeli writers. But when he felt that the ideals of a just and tolerant society were being betrayed by Israel's own statesmen, as in the case of the Lebanon war, he would say so and gave space to like-minded writers and historians from within and outside Israel. On the other hand, when the State's existence was severely threatened, as in 1967, he was quick to rally support for Israel amongst Anglo-Jewish writers.

Sonntag firmly believed that the State of Israel (or the Jewish religion, for that matter) was not the be-all-and-end-all of Jewish fulfillment and that, as his life's work reflected, helping Jewish culture to flourish outside Israel was not only important, but vital to the Jewish people. To promote further the exchange and stimulation of ideas, Sonntag frequently organized and chaired live symposia for his readers and writers, on a variety of subjects ranging from "The music of the Jews" to "The place of the kibbutz in present-day Israeli society" to "Jewish survival and resistance".

The task of producing regular issues of the magazine while maintaining its uncompromising independence and high standard of writing was a lonesome path, beset with problems. Jacob Sonntag gave his all to Anglo-Jewry through *The Jewish Quarterly*, but the number of loyal benfactors that Anglo-Jewry could muster to support financially this important journal was lamentably small. However, the establishing in 1976 of the Jewish Literary Trust Ltd. gave Sonntag at least partial reprieve from such financial concerns. Following Sonntag's death in 1984, the journal has continued under younger editorship and new, businesslike management.

BIBLIOGRAPHY

ed., *Caravan: A Jewish Quarterly Omnibus* (London & New York: Thomas Yoseloff, 1961); ed., *Jewish Writing Today* (London: Vallentine Mitchell, 1974); ed., *New Writing from Israel* (London: Corgi Books, 1976); ed., *Jewish Perspectives, 25 Years of Jewish Writing* (London: Secker & Warburg, 1980); intro. and trans., *Siberia, A Poem by A. Sutzkever* with eight illustrations by Marc Chagall (London, New York, Toronto: Abelard-Schuman, 1961)

RUTH SONNTAG

South African Jewry

Jewish links with South Africa stem from the contribution made by Jewish cartographers, astronomers, navigators, and crewmen to the Portuguese voyages of discovery around the Cape. Persons of Jewish descent found their way to the Cape from the beginnings of White settlement by the Dutch East India Company in 1652. Owing to the Company's policy of only employing Protestant Christians, Jews who wished openly to practice their faith could not settle at the Cape until religious tolerance was introduced by the British in 1795, and reaffirmed by the Batavian Republic. Following the second British occupation of the Cape in 1806 a trickle of individual Jews, mainly from England and Germany, began to arrive in the Colony. In the absence of an organized Jewish community those that remained generally assimilated into the wider population.

With the arrival of the British "1820 Settlers" the foundations of Jewish life were laid in the Eastern Cape. It was in the Cape Town home of one such settler, Benjamin Norden, that the first religious service took place in 1841, on the eve of the Day of Atonement. This led, in turn, to the creation of a Hebrew congregation, *Tikvath Israel*. As British influence in the region expanded Jews came to be amongst the pioneer settlers of Natal and the Orange Free State. The discovery of diamonds in 1867 and the main Witwatersrand gold reef in 1886 attracted prospectors and fortune hunters, including Jews, who established Jewish life in Kimberley and Johannesburg. Some of these Jewish immigrants were amongst the founders and developers of the diamond- and gold-mining industries. The gold rush coincided with the immigration of Jews from eastern Europe, principally Lithuania. That immigration, which continued until 1930, swelled the size of the Jewish community, altering its composition and influencing its character, structure, and direction. The final wave of immigration comprised approximately 6,000 refugees from Nazi Germany during the 1930s. The further growth of the Jewish population came principally through natural increase, with Jewish immigrants from Zimbabwe and Israel offsetting, to some extent, the loss incurred by the community through emigration.

Once widely distributed across the country, South African Jewry, which numbers approximately 110,000, is today concentrated in six districts: Pretoria, the East Rand, Cape Town, Durban, and Port Elizabeth, with more than half the Jewish population resident in Johannesburg and its environs. In its communal life South African Jewry is well organized and highly centralized, with bodies which cater for all its varied interests. In the main, South African Jews belong to Orthodox congregations with about a fifth being members of Progressive congregations. The Union of Orthodox Synagogues of South Africa is the umbrella body for Orthodox congregations. The coordinating body for Reform congregations is the South African Union for Progressive Judaism.

The central representative institution of the community is the South African Jewish Board of Deputies to which most Hebrew congregations and Jewish societies are affiliated. The Board seeks to safeguard the religious and civil rights, status, and welfare of the Jews of the Republic. It acts on behalf of the community in all matters affecting its relationship with the Government, provincial, and municipal authorities. In recent times it has come to speak out increasingly on moral, as opposed to political, issues, and has gone on record in rejecting apartheid.

The extensive range of Zionist activities in the Republic are coordinated through the South African Zionist Federation, the largest communal organization, to which Zionist parties, organizations, and societies are affiliated. It has various departments which maintain liaison with individual Zionist bodies, disseminate information, foster youth movement activities, provide audiovisual material, and promote *aliyah*.

Over the years, in addition to a network of Hebrew nursery schools, Jewish day schools have been established in the main centres, affiliated to the South African Board of Jewish Education. A considerable number of Jewish children in state schools receive a supplementary Jewish education through a *heder* or the Hebrew and Religion classes of the Reform temples. Hebrew and Jewish Studies at a tertiary level are taught at the Universities of South Africa, Cape Town, Natal, and the Witwatersrand.

The spectrum of Jewish communal work is broad. Jewish welfare agencies operate in all the major centers to care for the needy, and the community maintains a number of institutions for the aged, orphaned, and handicapped.

South African Jews are spread over a wide range of occupations. Studies have revealed that in comparison to the white population as a whole, a significantly larger proportion of Jews are employed in commerce, manufacturing, finance, and service industries. They are more concentrated in the professional, administrative, and sales occupational groups, with the majority of those professionals in the service sector being medical, educational, or community workers. Jews, furthermore, are employed almost exclusively in the private sector, where they comprise a relatively larger share of employers than the white population as a whole.

In their individual capacities Jewish writers

and poets have contributed to the English literature of South Africa. Jews have made an extraordinary contribution to every facet of the theater and have been generous patrons of music and the arts. Jewish artists have distinguished themselves as painters and sculptors, and through the efforts of Jewish-owned galleries international art has been promoted in the country.

Jews also play a significant part in South African public life, unhampered by any political disabilities. Traditionally mainly active in opposition politics, Jews are today found among the members and supporters of most political parties. There have, over the years, been Jewish Members of Parliament, although only one Jew has attained Cabinet rank. Jews have also served in the Senate, and as members of Provincial Councils and have been particularly active in local government, serving as mayors, city, and town councillors. There have been several Jews among the Bar's Senior Counsel, and on the Bench. Since the 1930s anti-Semitism has not been a central issue of political life. Anti-Semitism today emanates from elements on the extreme right and left of the political spectrum, and is closely monitored by the Board of Deputies.

The dominant issue in South African life remains the search for an equitable solution to the racial problems of the country. The Jewish community holds no collective view on that issue, and shares with other South Africans the various hopes, fears, and concerns regarding any future political dispensation. Whilst some have chosen to emigrate on account of the uncertainties regarding the sociopolitical and economic situations, a majority have chosen to remain in the country, for a variety of reasons, including the hope that the political situation will be resolved peacefully.

FURTHER READING

Arkin, A. Economic activities. In *South African Jewry, A Contemporary Survey*, ed. M. Arkin (Cape Town: Oxford University Press, 1984)

Bernstein, E.: A Bird's-Eye View of South African Jewry Today. In *South African Jewry 1967–68*, ed. L. Feldberg (Johannesburg; Fedhill, n.d.)

Herman, L.: *A History of the Jews in South Africa* (London: Victor Gollancz, 1930)

Saron, G., and Hotz, H., eds.: *The Jews in South Africa. A History* (London: Oxford University Press, 1955)

Shimoni, G.: *Jews and Zionism. The South African Experience 1910–67* (Cape Town: Oxford University Press, 1980)

STEPHEN COHEN

Soutine, Chaim (1893–1943) French painter. Soutine was born in Similovitchi, in the Lithuanian part of western Russia, into a large, extremely poor, and Orthodox family (his father was a mender of clothes). The story goes that Soutine stole from the household to buy a colored pencil, and was locked up in the cellar as punishment; that he made a drawing of the village idiot and then – rashly – asked the rabbi to pose fo him. Soutine was so severely beaten up by the rabbi's son that the rabbi was obliged to pay his mother damages: ironically, this money enabled him in 1909 to leave Smilovitchi in order to attend art school in Minsk.

In 1910 he moved to Vilna, where for three years he studied at the School of Fine Arts, and became friends with Pincus Krémègne. He childhood friend and fellow student Michel Kikoïne recalled that "he was one of the most brilliant students at the Academy. The subjects of his sketches always carried a suggestion of morbid sadness (Jewish burials, desolation, misery, suffering), and they were painted from life . . . Soutine was unconsciously attracted by the tragic".

In 1913 Soutine and Kikoïne left for Paris, and settled in La Ruche (see PARIS, JEWISH SCHOOL OF) where they lived in dire poverty. From 1915 he was a close friend of Amedeo MODIGLIANI; the latter's early death in 1920 prompted Soutine to paint a series of men at prayer, which, although non-specific, contain the only religious references to be found in his mature oeuvre. In 1916 he moved to the Cité Falguière, continuing, in spite of the support of Polish dealer Léopold Zborowski, to suffer financial hardship. In 1922–3, however, he was "discovered" by American collector Albert C. Barnes, and thereafter enjoyed financial security. Soutine spent the years 1940–3 in hiding from the Nazis in the French countryside, but

Chaim Soutine The Road up the Hill c.*1924. Tate Gallery, London*

died in Paris of natural causes.

Although Soutine's repertory consisted chiefly of portraits (both of friends and anonymous, humble members of Parisian society), still lifes, landscapes, and "copies" of Old Masters in the Louvre, his nervously expressionistic handling of paint, the emotional intensity with which he imbued these subjects, and his own complex, almost haunted personality have caused many commentators, past and present, Jewish and non-Jewish, to view him as the quintessential Jewish *peintre maudit*.

FURTHER READING
Chaim Soutine (London: Hayward Gallery, 1982) [exhibition catalog]
Forge, A.: *Soutine* (London: Spring Books, 1965)

MONICA BOHM-DUCHEN

Soviet–Jewish culture Since the *Haskalah* Jewish culture in Russia has been trilingual: Russian, Yiddish, and Hebrew. The disloca-

tions of the First World War and the Czarist decrees disrupted Hebrew and Yiddish printing, and the emancipation of Russian Jewry after the February Revolution in 1917 resulted in a plethora of books, journals, and newspapers. After the first few years of unprecedented liberty and experiment, however, the Bolshevik regime gradually repressed Jewish cultural activity.

Yiddish literature
Yiddish literature on the eve of October 1917 was dominated by the ideological tasks of the Bund and other socialist movements. The 1908 Czernowitz conference had declared Yiddish the national Jewish language and, unlike Hebrew, it appealed to the masses. Before it was itself liquidated, the Jewish section of the Communist Party, the *Evsektsiya*, purged nationalist and religious tendencies. A secular communist Yiddish culture with its publishing houses and educational as well as research institutes thrived well into the 1930s but declined during the Stalinist purges.

Soviet Yiddish writers were not all conformists. Some had matured before the Revolution (Pinye KAHANOWITZ, Dovid BERGELSON), some had spent several years abroad before returning to the Soviet Union (Kahanowitz in 1926, Dovid Bergelson in 1933). Novelist and playwright Moshe Kulbak, critic Maks Erik and others even emigrated to the USSR, believing it to be the only viable center of Yiddish writing. The fundamental ambivalence and excellence of some Soviet Yiddish writers may be gauged by the Kiev group in the *Eygns* collections (1918–20). The heated debates in Soviet culture in the 1920s affected Yiddish literature too, particularly the struggle for domination by hardline Marxists and attacks on fellow travelers, but exacerbated by the extraterritorial status of Soviet Jewry, notwithstanding the desultory attempt to establish a Jewish autonomous area in Birobidzhan, and by the failure to forge a new Jewish culture "socialist in content and national in form".

Writers who felt nostalgic for the *shtetl* or did not sing enthusiastically of the new life were severely criticized and often persecuted. The 1929 Zamyatin and Pilnyak affairs had their parallels, erupting over Peretz MARKISH's *Dor oys, dor eyn* (A generation goes, a generation comes) and his poem *Brider* (Brothers), and over Leyb KVITKO's satirical attacks on Moshe Litvakov, editor of the party newspaper *Der Emes* (Truth). None of their invective against Hebrew and nationalistic elements saved Litvakov and other *apparatchiki* who were arrested during the Purges along with their adversaries. From 1934 socialist realism required Yiddish writers to toe the line, something that was particularly difficult for such a gifted symbolist as Der Nister (Kahanowitz), whose satire *Unter a ployt* (Under a fence) was emblematic of the Yiddish writers' plight. Kulbak, in the second volume of his *Zelmenyaner* (1933–5), and Bergelson, in his *Bam Dnyeper* (1940; On the Dnieper), did try to adapt to the requirement that Jewish heroes be shown as part of the general revolutionary struggle and not primarily as Jewish revolutionaries.

The Molotov–Ribbentrop pact enforced silence on Nazi persecution of Jews, but the German invasion in 1941 allowed Yiddish writers to voice a Jewish national pride and solidarity in the face of the Holocaust. Mikhoels and Markish, along with Ilya EHRENBURG were included in the Soviet Jewish Antifascist Committee, organized to rally world Jewry to the Soviet war effort. Avrom SUTSKEVER was among the partisans and refugees who swelled the ranks of Yiddish writers in the Soviet Union at this time. The Zhdanov clampdown and the anticosmopolitan campaign after the war, unfortunately, signalled further arrests and the final destruction of Soviet Yiddish culture. Mikhoels was murdered in 1948 and the Yiddish press and theater closed down. A number of the most prominent Yiddish writers, among them Dovid Bergelson, Peretz Markish, Leyb Kvitko, Itzik FEFER and Shmuel Persov were executed 12 August 1952.

After the XX Party Congress, some Yiddish authors were released or posthumously rehabilitated and their works slowly and partially began to reappear. From 1961 an official periodical, *Sovietish heymland*, was issued in Moscow, edited by Aron Vergelis.

Hebrew in the Soviet Union

Hebrew was attacked by Bolsheviks and Jewish socialists as "clerical", "bourgeois", and a Zionist tool of British imperialism. The Hebrew press in Russia was banned at the end of 1919 and many Hebrew authors, as well as readers, emigrated, as did H. N. BIALIK and the Habimah Theater. Some idealists attempted to synthesize a Hebrew communism and a few books and anthologies were permitted, *Ga'ash*, (1923), *Tziltzelei shema* (1923), and *Bereshit* (1926). But at the end of the 1920s there remained only the clandestine activities of *Tarbut* and *Hehalutz* or the efforts of a few courageous individuals who risked death and labor camps.

Avraham Freeman's *1919*, published in Tel Aviv, where it earned a Bialik prize, is an epic of Jewish self-defense in the civil war; Freeman (1890–1953) was imprisoned for ten years from 1936. Elisha Rodin (1888–1947) was a poet who turned from Yiddish to Hebrew. Exceptionally, the Soviet authorities allowed his poems to his son, killed on the Kalinin front, to be published in Palestine (1943). Special mention should be made of Hayyim Lensky, the "nightingale without a nest", who made an outstanding contribution to modern Hebrew poetry. Arrested in 1934, Lensky continued to write in Siberia.

In the awakening of Jewish culture in the 1970s, Hebrew symbolized the hope of young activists and refuseniks. Hebrew teachers were harassed and arrested, among them Iosif Begun, but seminars and samizdat joined underground religious literature in a remarkable chapter of Jewish culture. Gorbachev's *glasnost* policy allowed the opening of a Jewish cultural center in Moscow (1989), cultural exchanges with Israel, and permission for family visits to Israel, as well as relaxation of emigration restrictions.

Jewish writing in Russian

Russo-Jewish literature had, since the 1860s, established a polemical style that sought both to speak for Jewish civil rights and criticize the Jewish community. Radical social and demographic change, emancipation, the emigration and death of Russo-Jewish writers – all helped to remove the raison d'être of Russo-Jewish literature. A new generation of assimilated and acculturated Jews entered the scene, some, like Isaac BABEL and Ilya Ehrenburg, before the Revolution. None looked back with any nostalgia to Czarist days but they differed in outlook and identity. Firstly, there were those who identified fully with Russian culture, but wrote to varying extents on Jewish themes, such as Andrei Sobol (1888–1926) or Ilya Ehrenburg. Isaak Babel is exceptional for the intensity of his Jewishness in his short stories. There is little outwardly Jewish in the poetry of Boris PASTERNAK and Osip MANDELSTAM, except inasmuch as rejection of Judaism determines their poetic identification with Russian Christianity and affects their artistic consciousness.

A large group of Jews totally cut themselves off from their origins and in some cases changed their names, such as Mikhail Golodny (Epstein, 1903–49) or Vladimir Lidin (Gomberg, born 1894). Mikhail Svetlov (1903–67), in his *Stikhi o rebbe* (1923; Verses on the rebbe) and Iosif Utkin (1903–44), in *Povest' o ryzhem Motele* (1926; Tale of red-haired Motele) referred to the Jewish past only to sing of the new life which replaced it. Eduard Bagritsky (Dzyuba, 1893–1934) also rejected the Jewish past in his poetry. Countless Jews were active in all spheres of Russian society and some were "unmasked" during the anticosmopolitan campaign which had distinctly anti-Semitic overtones.

The Holocaust awakened Jewish sentiments in Boris Slutsky (born 1919), Margarita Aliger (born 1915), and Pavel Antokolsky (1896–1981). Vasilii GROSSMAN collaborated with Ilya Ehrenburg on a *Black Book* of Nazi genocide, which included contributions from several Russian Jewish authors, and he later devoted his novels *Vse techet* (1972; Forever flowing) and *Zhizn' i sud'ba* (1985; Life and fate) to the atrocities under Stalin and Hitler. Anatoly Rybakov's *Tyazhelyi peski* (1978; *Heavy sands*, 1981) also describes the fate of Soviet Jews in the Holocaust, but in general the Soviet authorities scorned emphasis on the Jewish identity of Holocaust victims.

Yuli Daniel (b.1925) and Aleksandr GALICH (1919–77) are examples of Jews who have participated in the cultural expression of the larger human rights movement.

Jews from the USSR have also made up the Third Wave of Russian émigré culture, among them David MARKISH, a son of the executed Yiddish writer.

Other languages

Jews have written in Ukrainian (Natan Rybak) and Belorussian (Zmitrok Biadula, alias Shmuel Plaunik, 1886–1941; Vladimir Bill'-Belotserkovsky, 1885–1966). Besides a Georgian Jewish culture, there is also a Tat Jewish culture in the Caucasus which has a rich folk literature, as have the Judeo-Tadzhik speaking Bukharan Jews.

The arts

Marc CHAGALL, El Lissitsky (1890–1941), Issachar RYBACK, Robert Falk (1886–1958) – to name but a few – related their awareness of Jewish folk art to the experimentation of the first post-revolutionary years in painting, book-illustration, and stage design. Emigration and the impact of the different trends of modernism complicate the picture, and one cannot judge their contribution to Jewish culture without considering also their interaction with literature, cinema, and theater. Socialist realism forced modernists into silence, though Iosif Chaiko and Isaak Brodsky conformed. The wraps were lifted from modernism during the Thaw, but significantly the picture which angered Khrushchev at the 1962 Manezh exhibition was a nude by Falk. Since then Jewish cultural activists have exhibited unofficially in such groups as Alef, the Group of Eight, and others, and have had to contend with bulldozers and the KGB. Among hundreds of artists who left the Soviet Union are Ernst Neizvestny (b.1926), who defended his artistic principles in the confrontation with Khrushchev at the Manezh exhibition, and Oskar Rabin (b.1928).

Chagall, Altman, and Lissitsky undoubtedly left their mark on the Soviet Jewish theater. The Hebrew Habimah started as an amateur group under Nakhum Tsemakh and David Vardi, and later was attached to the Moscow Art Theater under Stanislavsky's pupil Vakhtangov, who knew no Hebrew but brilliantly produced S. AN-SKI's *The Dybbuk* and Leivick's *The Golem*. Habimah did not return from a foreign tour and settled in Tel-Aviv in 1931.

Aleksandr Granovsky, a disciple of Meyerhold in the Russian theater, directed the first Yiddish drama studio in Petrograd, then moved to Moscow, where the Yiddish theater with its GOLDFADEN comedies and Purimspiels was revolutionized by investing the Yiddish classics with class ideology, circus-style satire and avant-garde expressionism. In 1928 the Moscow Yiddish State Art Theater (GOSET) lost Granovsky to Hollywood and its star actor Solomon Mikhoels took over. There were some twenty government-sponsored Yiddish theaters and traveling companies, as well as amateur groups, but as the 1930s wore on ideological scrutiny of the repertoire tightened. The 1938 denunciation of Meyerhold and his arrest boded no good, but the end was interrupted by an influx of Yiddish actors and writers during the Nazi occupation of eastern Europe and the evacuation to central Asia. The end came with the murder of Mikhoels and the closure of the Moscow Jewish theater in 1949. Jewish drama in recent years has been confined to amateur groups.

FURTHER READING

Gilboa, Y.: *A Language Silenced: The Supression of Hebrew Literature and Culture in the Soviet Union* (Rutherford: Fairleigh Dickinson University Press, 1982)

Howe, I., and Greenberg, E., eds.: *Ashes out of Hope: Fiction by Soviet–Yiddish Writers* (New York: Schocken, 1977)

Kochan, L., ed.: *The Jews in Soviet Russia Since 1917* (3rd edn, Oxford: Oxford University Press, 1978)

Miller, J., ed.: *Jewish Contributions to Soviet Culture* (Brunswick: Transaction Books, 1984)

EFRAIM SICHER

Soyer, Raphael (1899–1988) American painter and graphic artist. Born in Borisoglebsk, Russia, the son of Abraham Soyer, a Hebrew writer and part of the Russian–Jewish intelligentsia. Raphael, his twin brother Moses (1899–1974), and their younger brother Isaac, all became professional artists. This was perhaps because of their early exposure to Renaissance and Baroque art through their father who brought them small reproductions of famous paintings and took them to museums in Moscow.

The Soyer family came to the USA in 1913, first to Philadelphia, and finally to the Bronx where their father worked as a Hebrew teacher. Their home continued to be a meeting place for secular Jewish intellectuals.

Both Raphael and Moses received their first art training at the Educational Alliance School. Beginning in 1915, Raphael wanted to establish an art identity separate from that of his brother and attended the National Academy of Design. Periodically from 1920 he studied at the Art Students League under George Luks and Guy Pene du Bois. He visited the Metropolitan Museum of Art on a regular basis and credits the collection of masters one of his greatest sources of inspiration. Soyer participated in exhibitions at the Jewish Art Center, although, like many secular Jewish artists, there was little overt Jewish subject matter in his work.

Raphael Soyer was a realist and an intense observer of contemporary life in New York. Throughout his career he painted genre scenes of immigrant and urban life and portraits of family, friends, and fellow artists. In *Dancing Lesson* (1926) Soyer painted in a direct, almost primitive manner, about his family's attempts at Americanization. In the painting *Artist's Parents* (1932) Soyer was less factual, focusing on the personalities of his parents. During the 1930s he turned his attention to the unemployed who spent their days in the city park or waiting for relief in government offices. At the same time he painted numerous examples of women who were employed in low-class jobs, such as secretaries, clerks, and shopgirls. He continues (1988) to paint about life in New York, commenting on contemporary life in Greenwich Village, with its artists, writers, and young bohemians.

Soyer was consistently a realist painter. He believes that if art is to survive, it is incumbent upon the artist to describe real people in actual situations. During the 1950s he was responsible for organizing a group of fellow representational painters who had resisted the current abstractionist trends. With Edward Hopper, Kuniyoshi, Ben Shahn, and Evergood he published a manifesto opposing abstraction in the short-lived periodical *Reality: A Journal of Artists' Opinions*, 1953–5.

BIBLIOGRAPHY

Self Revealment: A Memoir (New York: Maecenas Press, Random House, 1967)

FURTHER READING

Berman, A.: Raphael Soyer at 80: "Not painting would be like not breathing". *Art News* (1979) 38–43

BARBARA GILBERT

Sperber, Manès (1905–1984)   Austrian writer. Sperber was born in Zablotov, Galicia, and grew up there. His family moved to Vienna in 1916 as refugees from the war. Educated in Vienna, Sperber became involved in the Zionist movement, as well as becoming assistant to Alfred Adler. From 1927 to 1933 he taught Individual Psychology in Berlin, and was also active in the communist movement. From 1934, with a short interval in Switzerland during 1942–5, Sperber lived in Paris.

Sperber produced several collections of essays, including *Churban oder die unfassbare Gewissheit* (1979; Holocaust, or the unimaginable certainty); a biography of Adler, *Alfred Adler* (1970; *Masks of Loneliness*, 1974); the novel trilogy *Wie eine Träne im Ozean*, (1961; *Like Tears in the Ocean*, 1987), and his autobiographical trilogy *All das Vergangene* (1974–7; *All our Yesterdays*, 1986–7).

Brought up in the very Jewish environment of the *shtetl* of Zablotov in Eastern Galicia, Sperber retained a very positive attitude to his Jewish identity, as is quite clear from both *Like Tears in the Ocean* and *All Our Yesterdays*. The first volume of the latter, *Die Wasserträger Gottes* (*God's Water Carriers*, 1986), provides a vivid picture of *shtetl* life. Sperber stressed the religious life of the *shtetl*, and the difference of the Jews from the surrounding populace, in terms of the level of education especially. He also shows how, in his case, Jewish traditions of messianism and the search for ethical truth influenced his later attitudes to society, including his attraction to communism. The figure who dominates the recollection of his earliest years is his great-grandfather, Reb Boruch, a very strict Jew who spent all his time reading Holy Scripture in search of the real truth of God's Word. Sperber used Reb Boruch as the basis for one of the central characters of *Like Tears in the Ocean*, Rabbi Bynie, who represents the spiritual strength of Judaism, even in Jewry's darkest

hours. André Malraux called this novel trilogy "one of the Jewish people's greatest stories".

FURTHER READING

Roder, W., et al., eds: *International Biographical Dictionary of Central European Émigrés 1933–45*, 3 vols (Munich: Saur, 1980–3)

STEVEN BELLER

Spicehandler, Ezra (b.1921)   Hebrew scholar and literary analyst. He was born in Brooklyn, New York. He was ordained as a Rabbi and awarded the Masters of Hebrew Letters at the Cincinnati branch of Hebrew Union College – Jewish Institute of Religion in 1946. In 1952 he was awarded the degree of Doctor of Philosophy and accepted the post of Professor of Modern Hebrew Literature at Cincinnatti. He also received the National Defense Education Fellowship in Oriental Languages. The following year he received a Fulbright research grant for study in Iran.

In 1966 Spicehandler was appointed Director and then Dean of the Hebrew Union College at Jerusalem. He has been visiting professor at the Hebrew University in Jerusalem, at the University of Oxford, and the University of the Witwatersrand in South Africa, and has served as visiting Fellow at the Centre for Hebrew Studies in Oxford. He has been Vice President of the World Union for Progressive Judaism, and, in 1982, he was elected National President of the Labor Zionist Alliance. He is currently a member of the executive board of the World Congress of Jewish Studies, and is an active member of the Council of the World Zionist Organization, serving on its Praesidium.

Spicehandler has published articles on modern and medieval Hebrew literature, on Zionism, Judeo-Persian studies, and talmudic history in a variety of distinguished scholarly publications. He is co-author, with Dr Jacob Petuchowski, of *Perakim beyahadut* (1965; Chapters in Judaism). *The Modern Hebrew Poem itself* (1965), which he co-edited with Stanley BURNSHAW and T. CARMI, provides a stylistic and thematic guide through nineteenth- and twentieth-century Hebrew poetry. He has also edited a dual language anthology of modern

Hebrew stories (1971) and he has written on J. H. Schorr (1970) and on the Jews of Iran.

Spicehandler served as Divisional Editor of modern Hebrew literature of the *Encyclopedia Judaica*, and wrote several of its articles in that field, including the comprehensive article on modern Hebrew literature.

Apart from his organizational activities, Spicehandler is distinguished by his wide-ranging contribution to many fields of Jewish Studies, unusual in an age of specialized concentration. His broad knowledge of modern Hebrew fiction and poetry, for example, has allowed him to play an invaluable part in the creation of an awareness and understanding, outside Israel, of modern Hebrew literature. He has also done pioneering work on H. N. BIALIK and is undoubtedly among the finest of Bialik scholars.

BIBLIOGRAPHY

Ed.: *New Writing in Israel* (New York: Schocken, 1966); A descriptive list of Judeo–Persian manuscripts (Klau Library of the Huc). *Studies in Bibliography and Booklore* 8 nos 2–4 (1968); Odessa as a literary center of Hebrew literature. In *The Great Transition*, ed. G. Abramson and T. Parfitt (Totowa: Rownan and Alanheld, 1985) 75–90; Bernhard Felsenthal letters to Osias Schorr. In *Essays in American Jewish History* (Cincinnati: 1958) 379–406

JOHN MATTHEW

Spiegelman, Art (b.1948) American cartoonist. Spiegelman was born in Stockholm, Sweden, the son of Wladek (William) and Andzia Spiegelman. An artist who, as one critic put it, "redefines the comic book", Spiegelman enriched the field of cartooning as artist, editor, and designer, and has carried the medium itself to a public that had never before suspected its creative potential.

Spiegelman was set on a career as cartoonist from childhood, his earliest interest being in such satirical magazines as *Mad*. At 13 he was drawing for his school newspaper and, a year later, selling sports and political cartoons, illustrations, and covers to the *Long Island Post*. Spiegelman studied cartooning in high school but decided against a career in drawing conventional comic strips. He majored in art and philosophy at Harpur College (now SUNY at Binghamton) where he drew for the college newspaper and began contributing to the *East Village Other* and other alternative publications. By the time he left college in 1968 underground comics were evolving into a distinct sub-genre in which he had become solidly established, editing and contributing to a number of magazines. However, he preferred simple satire to the sex, violence, drugs, and scatology, the stock-in-trade of the underground press. In 1980 he and his wife, Françoise Mouly, created *Raw*, a yearly magazine of avant-garde comics. They saw a need for a periodical that provided "comics unselfconsciously redefining what comics should be, by smashing formal and stylistic, as well as cultural and political taboos". *Raw* established itself as the leading comic periodical of the avant-garde and sells 20,000 copies a year. It has elevated Spiegelman from a cult hero of the underground to a figure of mainstream American literature.

Spiegelman's international fame to date rests on his full-length cartoon strip, *Maus*, which originated as a three-page story in a 1972 underground comic book called *Funny Aminals* [sic]. Spiegelman turned to his own experience as the son of concentration-camp survivors and created a moving and terrifying tale of the Holocaust around the metaphor of Nazis as cats and Jews as mice. The true story of the artist's father, a survivor of Auschwitz, and of his own relationship to him, *Maus* evolved into a complex literary, multi-layered parable, rich in historical resonance, in addition to being a new departure in autobiography. The starkness of its black and white images had an immediate and powerful impact and the book became a popular and critical success, now translated into over a dozen languages.

Spiegelman has been the recipient of a number of awards, including the Annual *Playboy* Editorial Award for best comic strip, 1982; Joel M. Cavior Award for Jewish Writing (for *Maus*), 1986; Certificate of Excellence, *Design* magazine, 1986; nominated for the National Book Critics Award for Biography (for *Maus*), 1986; Best Foreign Comics Album, Netherlands, 1987. He has exhibited his work in many countries apart from the USA, including the UK, Japan, Canada, France, and Sweden.

GLENDA ABRAMSON

Spiel, Hilde (b.1911)

Austrian writer. Born in Vienna, Spiel studied there under Moritz Schlick and Karl Bühler. She was one of the up-and-coming young writers in Austria in the early 1930s, but left in 1936 for Britain. Since 1946 she has lived in Vienna and London, writing for various newspapers and journals. She is regarded by many as the grande dame of Austrian contemporary literature. Her works include a major biography, *Fanny von Arnstein* (1962), and the volume which she edited, *Wien: Spektrum einer Stadt* (1971). She has recently returned to the theme of Vienna in two works: *Früchte des Wohlstands* (1981; The fruits of prosperity), and *Vienna's Golden Autumn, 1866–1938* (1987).

Although Spiel is a Roman Catholic she has retained a strong interest in the Jewish world from which she came. *Fanny von Arnstein* is a sensitive description of the emancipation and the Jewish contribution to the Enlightenment. In a related essay she has stressed the central place of Jewish women in Viennese culture (Spiel/Fraenkel, 1967). *Früchte des Wohlstands* describes another stage in the integration of the Jewish bourgeoisie in Vienna around 1860. In *Vienna's Golden Autumn* the role of the Jews is again given a high profile.

BIBLIOGRAPHY
Jewish women in Austrian culture. In *The Jews of Austria*, ed. J. Fraenkel (London, 1967)

STEVEN BELLER

Spielvogel, Nathan Frederick (1874–1956)

Historian of Australian (especially Ballarat) Jewry, essayist and writer. Spielvogel is regarded as the first Australian writer of Jewish origin to concern himself extensively with Jewish life and subjects.

Born and educated in Ballarat, Victoria, he became a pupil teacher to support his siblings on his father's death in 1891. He was obliged to teach in small outposts of outback Victoria where his experiences (along with his strong commitment to, and outspoken identification with, Judaism) provided the principal themes on which he was to write until the end of his long and highly productive life. His numerous pieces center on the life of Jews in small Australian communities, the outback and its life, and his experiences as a teacher.

The majority of his writings appeared first in essay or short-story form and were collected and republished. Only two of these books are on specifically Jewish themes. The first of these in his privately circulated, *History of the Ballarat Hebrew Congregation* (1924); the second, *Selected Short Stories of Nathan Spielvogel* (1956), edited by L. E. Fredman, was an edition of Spielvogel's short stories about Ballarat Jewry. Of his numerous published poems, "The call of the wandering Jew", *The Bulletin* (1909), has been republished as an independent work.

Typical of his descriptive writing of Jewish life in Australia is his account of his father's career, "On the road, 1830–91", which appeared in September 1935 in the *Westralian Judean*, to which he was a regular contributor. At the end of his life he was heavily involved in community activities being the president of numerous civic organizations, as well as president of Ballarat Hebrew Congregation where he also conducted services and taught Hebrew.

FURTHER READING
Blake, L.: Nathan Spielvogel. *Australian Jewish Historical Society* 9 no. 6 (1984) 403–17
Fredman, L. E.: How my life was spent – autobiography of Nathan Spielvogel. *Australian Jewish Historical Society* 6 no. 1 (1964) 1–26

ALAN D. CROWN

Spire, André (1868–1966)

French poet. Born into a wealthy middle-class industrialist family in Lorraine, Spire belongs to that current of French Judaism which turned aside from the traditional Jewish professions to enter the great public bodies. In 1891 he enrolled at the École Libre des Sciences Politiques, and became an auditor in the Council of State in 1894. A specialist in problems of employment at the Ministry of Labor from 1898 to 1902, he then held the post of Inspector General in the Ministry of

André Spire

Agriculture until his retirement. Politically committed, Spire took part in the philanthropic movement, creating the "Society of Visitors" in 1896, and with, Daniel HALÉVY, founding the People's University of Mutual Education.

The discovery of the working-class Jewish world, together with the Dreyfus Affair, constituted a twofold shock for Spire, making him both the spokesman of French Zionism and trustee of the literary ambitions of the WISSEN-SCHAFT DES JUDENTUMS and its French heirs. A double revolution was required before the poet could find his own voice: first, one of form, when for several years he pursued studies at the laboratory of experimental phonetics at the Collège de France, underlying his collection published in 1949, *Plaisir poétique et plaisir musculaire*; the other revolution was one of political attitude, when he was sent to London to study the sweated labor system, and discovered the city's ghetto. In 1904 a reading of Israel Zangwill's novella *Had Gaddya* confirmed Spire's London experience.

The Dreyfus Affair crystallized his attitude to Judaism. He made himself the advocate of a national Jewish renaissance, giving his support first to the self-defense organizations of Russian Jews, then creating the "Young Jews' Association" to help new immigrants. His activities became politicized with his attendance at the Zionist congresses of Basel in 1911 and Vienna in 1912. From then on he led the French Zionist movement, founded the "League of Friends of Zionism" in 1918, after the Balfour Declaration, represented French Zionists at the Paris peace conference, and then on a journey to Palestine in 1920. This position within French Judaism typified all his activities from the 1920s. After resigning his official functions following a disagreement with Chaim WEIZMANN, and retiring from public service in 1926, Spire devoted himself wholly to literature.

The search for a system of poetics seeking to substitute the idea of laws for that of rules, and questioning conventions of rhyme and rhythm, and the importance Spire placed on the oral nature of his language, find a parallel in a concept of Judaism which makes the Bible central to its preoccupations, an attitude inherited from the *Wissenschaft des Judentums*. Spire's prophetism is of the senses. The "free verse" he used, supported by a concrete vocabulary, is inspired both by the Bible and by song. His subjects are taken from the world of the working classes (*Et vous riez...*, 1908), but his sentiments and expression refer more and more frequently to Judaism (*Versets*, 1909; *Vers les routes absurdes*, 1911; *Le secret*, 1919), some works constituting a direct testimony to French Judaism (*Quelques juifs et demi-juifs, Les juifs et la guerre*).

During the war Spire took refuge in the USA, where he taught French literature, but he did not give up his Zionist activities.

Writing for a large audience within the French Jewish community, André Spire nonetheless occupied a marginal position throughout his life: a Zionist in a community with deep roots in France, the successor of philologists at a time when the discipline of philology was disappearing.

FURTHER READING

André Spire. *Europe* 467 (1968)

Aubery, P.: *Milieux juifs de la France contemporaine* (Paris: Plon, 1957)

PERRINE SIMON-NAHUM

Spoliansky, Mischa (1898–1985) British film and theater composer. Spoliansky, who left Germany for Britain in 1933 and was naturalized in 1946 was best known for the songs which were written for Paul Robeson to sing in *Sanders of the River*, but his career spanned 70 years. He was born into a musical family and studied piano and composition in Russia and Berlin, where he became a prominent member of the musical scene and the pianist and composer for the cabaret *Schall und Rauch*. He worked with Max REINHARDT, Friedrich Hollander, Marcellus Schiffler, and Margo Lion and, in 1926, composed the music for Reinhardt's production of Somerset Maugham's *Victoria*.

Many cabarets and cabaret–operas followed and, in Britain, he was soon composing film music for the major companies. His capacity to incorporate stylistic variation made him an admired, yet unflamboyant composer, who never felt the need to force the music onto a film. During the Second World War, apart from composing for the cinema, Spoliansky was active in the BBC, broadcasting and sometimes singing (under the name of Tony Galento) his "forbidden music" into Nazi territory for the program *Aus der Freien Welt*. After the war he continued to compose for the cinema and the stage.

Other films include: *Over the Moon* (1938), *Mr Emmanuel* (1944), *Fiddlers Three* (1944), *Temptation Harbour* (1947).

FURTHER READING
Dell, J.: *Nobody Ordered Wolves* (London: Heinemann, 1939) [novel]
The Times, 3 July 1985 [obituary]

KEVIN GOUGH-YATES

Starer, Robert (b.1924) American composer, pianist, and educator. He was born in Vienna, Austria, and began piano lessons at the age of four. When he was 13 he entered the Vienna State Academy to study piano with Victor Ebenstein, while still continuing his academic studies in high school where he majored in Greek and Latin. When the Nazis annexed Austria in 1938, the Starers fled to Palestine where Robert entered the Jerusalem

Conservatory with Joseph TAL and Oedon PARTOS. Between 1941 and 1943 he became staff pianist for the BBC Palestine but soon enlisted in the Royal Air Force, serving until 1946. During his airforce service he wrote his first major work, a *Fantasy* for strings, 1945. Following his discharge from the service, Starer went to New York to continue his musical studies at the Juilliard School, working with Frederick Jacoby. After receiving his diploma in 1949 he stayed on as an instructor until 1975, and in 1963 he also became professor of composition at Brooklyn College.

Starer has experimented in some of his compositions, with fusing Eastern and Western music, with dodecaphonic techniques, and with superimposing non-tonal and tonal elements upon one another. He has also shown an interest in the music of the synagogue, composing a complete Friday Evening Service, and many settings of psalms and liturgical cantatas, such as *Kohelet* (1952), *Ariel* (1959), and *Joseph and his brothers* (1966). Robert Starer has also been a successful ballet composer, beginning with *Secular games* (1954), *The Dybbuk* (1960), *Samson Agonistes* (1961), and *Phaedra* (1962). Besides his prolific musical output, he has written many articles and published two books: *Rhythmic training* (1969) and an autobiography, *Continuo: a life in music* (1987).

His other major works include three symphonies, three piano concertos, concertos for various instrumental groups; three operas, ballets, orchestral works, many shorter choral pieces, piano pieces, songs, and chamber music.

SAMUEL H. ADLER

Steinberg, Ben (b.1930) Canadian composer, conductor, organist, and educator. He was born in Winnipeg, son of Cantor Alexander Steinberg. He was educated at Toronto's Royal Conservatory of Music, and the University of Toronto. For many years Steinberg taught music in the public schools of Toronto. Since his childhood he has been involved in synagogue music, first as a choir conductor and now as a noted composer, organist, and lecturer. Presently (1988) he is director of music of

Temple Sinai in Toronto, and he lectures frequently on the history of Jewish music throughout the USA and Canada. He has been awarded a great many prizes and honors, including the Gabriel Award in 1979 for outstanding creativity in broadcast programming, the Kavod Award from the Cantors Assembly in 1983, the Composer's Award in 1978 from the American Harp Society, and two invitations from the artist-in-residence program of the City of Jerusalem.

Steinberg is one of the most frequently performed liturgical composers in the North American Synagogue. His three complete Friday Evening Services and many settings of prayers for all liturgical occasions are favorites in both Reform and Conservative synagogues. Besides these, he has five cantatas for chorus and orchestra, including the prizewinning work entitled *Echoes of Children*, commemorating the children who perished in the Holocaust; instrumental chamber works; and solo songs. Steinberg has also published a book on synagogue youth choirs and has conducted a series of broadcasts for the CBC, which features newly discovered music for the synagogue during the Baroque period. Other programs included nineteenth-century Russian synagogue music, as well as works by contemporary Jewish composers.

SAMUEL H. ADLER

Steinberg, Milton (1903–1950) American rabbi and novelist. Born in Rochester, NY, Milton Steinberg was ordained by the Jewish Theological Seminary in 1928. In 1933 he became rabbi at Park Avenue Synagogue in New York. In his writing Steinberg was concerned with a philosophical approach to Judaism and was initially influenced by Mordecai KAPLAN. Later, however, he became a critic of RECONSTRUCTIONISM. In his novel *As A Driven Leaf* (1939), he dealt with the heretic Elisha ben Abuyah and the conflict between religion and philosophy in the Hellenistic period. In the novel Elisha comes to see that both religion and philosophy are equally based on undemonstrated basic principles; this realization pre-

vents him from denouncing religion as inferior. In *The Making of the Modern Jew* (1934), Steinberg discussed the meaning of history for a Jew in the modern world. This work was followed by *A Partisan Guide to the Jewish Problem* (1945), which depicts the type of Jew he believed would emerge from the conflict of past and present realities. Another book, *Basic Judaism* (1947), outlines the basic themes of the Jewish faith. Steinberg was also an active Zionist. His reflections on Zionism are contained in *A Believing Jew* (1951), and *Anatomy of Faith* (1960).

DAN COHN-SHERBOK

Steinberg, Saul (b.1914) American painter and graphic artist. Born in Ramnicul-Sarat, Romania, Steinberg moved with his family to Bucharest when he was child, where he attended elementary and high school, and then studied Philosophy and Letters at the University of Bucharest. Between 1933 and 1940 Steinberg lived in Milan, where he studied architecture at the Politecnico Facoltà di Architettura. From the mid 1930s, he concurrently published cartoons in *Bertaldo*, a bi-weekly humor magazine. These two strains – his architectural training and his gift for satirical cartooning – have consistently surfaced throughout his oeuvre. Following graduation as a "Dottore in Architettura" in 1940, Steinberg fled Nazi Europe by way of Portugal and the Dominican Republic, arriving in the USA in 1942.

Much of Steinberg's work is autobiographical, revealing his search for self-identity. His own experiences as a refugee are often integrated into his works. He incorporates unintelligible rubber stamps and false passports as reminders of forged rubber stamps he himself was forced to use on the passport that enabled him to flee to the USA.

FURTHER READING

McCabe, C. J.: *The Golden Door: Artist Immigrants of America, 1876–1976* (Washington: Smithsonian Institution Press for the Hirshhorn Museum and Sculpture Garden, 1986)

Rosenberg, H.: *Saul Steinberg* (New York: Alfred A.

Knopf, in association with the Whitney Museum of American Art, 1978)

BARBARA GILBERT

Steiner, George (b.1929)

Author and critic. Born in Paris and educated at the Sorbonne and at Chicago, Harvard, and Oxford universities, Steiner is presently (1988) an extraordinary fellow of Churchill College, Cambridge and Professor of Comparative Literature at Geneva University.

Steiner's widely acclaimed critical works include *Tolstoy or Dostoevsky* (1959), and *The Death of Tragedy* (1960) which traces the tragedy from its Greek origins to its present demise due to the anti-tragic metaphysics of Christianity and Marxism. Although he leaves open the possibility of a future revival or transformation of the tragedy, he raises the question of whether contemporary tragedies can be adequately encapsulated in this classical literary form. This concern with the effects of the tragedies of our century led Steiner to one of his major recurrent themes. He asks if, after world wars, totalitarianism, and in particular, the Holocaust, we can entertain the claim that education and the cultivation of the arts actually humanize and civilize humanity. In *Language and Silence* (1967) Steiner explores this theme in connection with language, in terms of our new understanding of the linguistic nature of human awareness and behavior, and the erosion of humanist ideals conveyed in language violated by political propaganda, pornography, and Marxism. He maintains that silence is the "only decent response" to the monstrosities of our age. In *In Bluebeard's Castle* (1971) he further argues that there is, in fact, an intimate connection between the "disinterested abstraction" of the sciences and the humanities, and our indifference to political and social realities.

The "language" theme is developed in *Extraterritorial* (1971) and in *After Babel* (1975), a major study of human speech, which attempts, via an investigation into meaning inside and between languages, to offer a model for the act of understanding itself, in that the process of translation is to be found in every act of comprehension, and that the exclusive diversity of languages is an integral feature of language.

The thesis that Jewish monotheism and its opposition to natural polytheism and animism is the source of anti-Semitism and the Holocaust, even if once removed as Christianity, or twice as Marxism, first found in *In Bluebeard's Castle*, reappears in Steiner's controversial novella, *The Portage to San Cristobal of A. H.* (1981, dramatized 1982). Here Hitler, captured after the war in South America by the Israelis, declares in his defense that he took the doctrines of the absolute command, the chosen race and the destiny of the nation from the Jews, and that as "the Reich begat Israel" might he, in fact, not be the long-awaited messiah.

Steiner understands his work to be the legacy of European Jewish humanism, in particular of Ernst BLOCH, Theodore ADORNO, and Walter BENJAMIN.

BIBLIOGRAPHY

Anno Domini (London: Faber & Faber, 1964); *On Difficulty and Other Essays* (Oxford: Oxford University Press, 1978); *Antigones* (Oxford: Clarendon, 1984); *George Steiner: A Reader* (Harmondsworth: Penguin, 1984)

PAUL M. MORRIS

Steinheim, Salomon Ludwig (1789–1866)

Philosopher. Steinheim was a physician, poet, and independent thinker whose fresh and original approach challenged most Jewish thinkers of his time. Born in Bruchhausen, Westphalia, he served as a doctor in Altona from 1813 to 1845, and then settled permanently in Rome. His major work was *Revelation According to the Doctrine of the Synagogue* (1835–65; 4 vols, with the final volume appearing much later). The work stressed personal experience against theory, and fought against the cool rationalism of Moses MENDELSSOHN's school. Its main thesis was that revelation manifests truth that human reason could never have constructed but which reason can then test and accept. Rational speculation on its own leads to dualism, but the Bible reveals *creatio ex nihilo* and the absolute unity of God, and stresses freedom against the rational system of mechanical necessity. Attacking rational thought, the elements of faith given by revelation – God, freedom, and immortality – are nevertheless identical with the postulates implied by moral reason according to Kant. Steinheim attacked Hegel's "World Spirit", Schelling's pantheism and Samuel Raphael Hirsch's sanctification of religious law, and made himself unpopular with both Reform and traditional Jewish thought. Yet his apparent irrationalism avoids romanticism and reaches forward towards modern scientific methods. Some view him as a forerunner of existentialism. Steinheim's second volume *The Doctrine of the Synagogue as Exact Science* views religion as a feature of reality, subject to the same divergence between the mathematical basis of experience and its empirical contents, and in its demonstration capable of the same degree of certainty – its secret can be unlocked in the same way as the geologist discovers the power inherent in a stone. In his time, Steinheim was regarded as a curiosity; now, he is seen as a challenge.

ALBERT H. FRIEDLANDER

Steinschneider, Moritz (1816–1907)

Czech–German bibliographer. Born in Moravia, he had an early *yeshivah* education and was further educated in Prague and Berlin. His existence was financially precarious until his appointment in 1859 as Director of the Jewish Girls School in Berlin. He is outstandingly important as a bibliographer of medieval Jewish and Islamic texts. Until he started producing his bibliographies there existed very little in the way of scholarly catalogs of such texts, and this served as an obstacle to research in the area of medieval orientalism.

He was an extremely prolific writer, especially of bibliographies. His *Die hebräischen Übersetzungen des Mittelalters und die Juden als Dolmetscher* (1893), remains an excellent guide to Hebrew translations of medieval texts and their interpretation by Jewish writers. He was particularly concerned with the ways in which one medieval culture received and transmitted Greek philosophy and science, and then passed it onto a different medieval culture. He produced important bibliographies of Arabic translations from

Greek. He wrote on Jewish and medieval culture, the role of Jews in the Middle Ages and the medieval approach to science, medicine, and mathematics. He founded the journal *Hebräische Bibliographie*. Two of his important books have been translated into English: *Jewish Literature from the Eighth to the Eighteenth Century* (1965), and *Introduction to the Arabic Literature of the Jews* (1901).

Steinschneider produced catalogs of Hebrew books in the Bodleian Library at Oxford, and Leiden, Munich, Hamburg, and Berlin libraries. He is in many ways the founder of modern orientalist bibliography. His work enabled a great deal of research on texts to take place, which previously would have been difficult, if not impossible, to accomplish.

FURTHER READING

Marx, A.: *Essays in Jewish Biography* (Philadelphia: The Jewish Publication Society of America, 1947) 112–84
Baron, S.: *Alexander Marx Jubilee Volume* (Philadelphia: The Jewish Publication Society of America, 1950) 83–148

OLIVER LEAMAN

Stencl, Avrom-Nokhem (1897–1983)

Yiddish poet. Stencl was born in Tsheladzh, near Sosnovits in Poland, into a rabbinic family. At an early age he organized a *HeChalutz* group in nearby Tshenstokhov, although he was not a Zionist. He spent two years in the Netherlands (1919–21) working as a laborer and farmer. Inspired by Yiddish author Wolf Vevyorke to start writing Yiddish poetry, Stencl moved to Berlin in 1921 in search of a literary environment. There he joined the circle of east European émigré Yiddish writers. He was encouraged to pursue a literary career by master Yiddish literary critic Bal Makhshoves, and soon the young Stencl became known for his Expressionist poetry, both in the Yiddish authors' "colony" in Germany and in some German literary circles where his work became known in translation. His writing benefited from his relationship with German–Jewish author Elsa Lasker-Schüler, who wrote a hymn in his praise in the Berlin *Tageblatt*. He never fully recovered from their break-up, and remained a bachelor all his days. He published over a dozen works in Berlin and Leipzig, the best known of which was *Mayn fisherdorf* (1935; My fisherman's town), which drew the critical acclaim of Thomas Mann.

Stencl was rescued from Nazi rule by a literary admirer and arrived in the Whitechapel district of London in 1936. For the rest of his life, much of his poetry centered upon Whitechapel, a bustling and poverty-stricken immigrant section of London, home to several generations of east European Jewish immigrants. Stencl romantically elevated Whitechapel to the status of the "last Yiddish *shtetl*". During the war years he edited and distributed journals under various names. They became known as *Shtentsls heftlakh* (Stencl's little journals), and crystallized after the war into the journal *Loshn un lebn* which he edited until his death. For over forty years he led weekly Saturday afternoon literary gatherings, the *shabes-nokhmitiks*, which became known internationally. Among his best known London-era works are *Londoner sonetn* (1937; London sonnets) and *Vaytshepl shtetl d'Britn* (1961; Whitechapel, *shtetl* of Britain).

Stencl was one of the few Yiddish writers to acquire near-guru status among his followers. Living in harsh poverty, and alone, in a slum tenement not far from the Thames in East London, Stencl radiated happiness and fulfillment deriving, he would tell visitors, more from the Yiddish language itself than from his writing, which some critics believe had declined sharply in the London years. Stencl's mystical personality and his anti-materialism inspired a number of young Yiddishists to embark on writing and research careers. An annual lecture in Oxford was established in his memory in 1983.

FURTHER READING

Prawer, S. S.: *A. N. Stencl: Poet of Whitechapel. The First Annual Avrom-Nokhem Stencl Lecture in Yiddish Studies*, (Oxford: Oxford Centre for Postgraduate Hebrew Studies, 1984)

DOVID KATZ

Stern, Gladys Bertha (1890–1973) English novelist. Born in London and educated at Not-

ting Hill High School, G. B. Stern studied at the Academy of Dramatic Art, but forsook her acting ambitions to continue the writing she had begun as a small girl. The year 1920 saw the publication of *Children of No-Man's-Land*, with a background of the First World War, in which Richard Marcus, son of a German Jew living in England, is born in Germany and by an oversight not included as a minor when his father is naturalized. When war breaks out he finds himself regarded with suspicion in the country he loves, and chooses internment rather than wear khaki without being allowed to carry arms. In another strand of the plot his sister, Deborah, becomes part of an "emancipated" group of women, but rejects their libertarian code just in time, to marry a Jew and lead a strictly conventional life. There is a genuine attempt to analyze their respective struggles and internal conflicts.

Of her vast output, probably the best known are the chronicles of the exotic and cosmopolitan Rakonitz–Czelovar clan, a far-flung tribe based, as Stern reveals in the semi-autobiographical *Monogram* (1936) on her own family. The first three volumes of this saga, *Tents of Israel* (1924), *A Deputy was King* (1926), and *Mosaic* (1930), were published together in 1932 as *The Rakonitz Chronicles*. A reader groping his way through the complex family tree provided with the novels will encounter wealthy, light-hearted, self-absorbed characters with few recognizable Jewish traits except perhaps for their intense interest in one another's affairs. With close family and business connections in the Austro-Hungarian Empire whence they originate, and their sense of security in secular society, they form a sharp contrast to the uneasy mass of European Jewry. Contemporary reviews suggest that these novels were welcomed as faithful representations of Jewish tribal life, and they were described on the dust-jacket of *Mosaic* as "the great Jewish saga of our time."

BIBLIOGRAPHY

Tents of Israel repr. as *The Matriarch* (London: Virago 1987); *A Deputy was King*, repr. (London: Virago 1988)

VERA COLEMAN

Sternberg, Erich Walter (1891–1974) Israeli composer. Born in Germany, he studied law at Kiel university, and in 1918 moved to Berlin in order to dedicate himself solely to professional music training with Hugo Leichtentritt as his teacher of composition. He was much impressed with the innovative trends in music prevalent in Berlin in the 1920s. From 1924 he made annual visits to Palestine, each time remaining for a few weeks. His early works, notably his first string quartet, reflect the strong influence of Alexander von Zemlinsky and the early works of Arnold SCHOENBERG in their dense texture, contrapuntal writing, powerful contrasts, and excited melodic rhetoric. Yet, he combined this strictly German technique with quotations from Jewish folk tunes and songs of eastern Europe, and the traditional cantillation of *Shema Israel*. This dichotomy of central and east Europe paradoxically represented for Sternberg the synthesis of his pedantic technical training with his Jewish, Eastern heritage, as represented in his piano composition, *Visions from the East*. In 1931 Sternberg settled permanently in Palestine, being the first professional composer among the immigrants from Germany. The powerful ideological pressures prevalent in Palestine during the 1930s and 1940s alienated Sternberg from the trend of collective-nationalism and the Mediterranean style. In the periodical *Musica Hebraica*, he published an ideological pamphlet claiming that "the composer should ignore any request for Israeli folklore, or synagogal chant, or Russian-orante tunes; he should rather walk his own path and speak his personal language, emanating from himself" (1938). His works composed in Israel represent his individuality. In his large-scale orchestral works, *Joseph and his Brethren* and *The Twelve Tribes of Israel*, he turned to the late romantic tradition of chromatic, expanded tonality, following Reger and Brahms in his employment of traditional procedures such as fugue and choral variations, and Hindemith in his harmony. His more intimate works for piano and chamber ensembles, such as the toccata and the sonata for violin and piano, preserved his earlier, avant-garde tendencies. His insistence on high technical proficiency has had a profound effect on the maintenance of high artistic standards in the newly developing and heterogenous Israeli style. Sternberg was the President of the Israeli Composers' League, but otherwise he avoided public duties and concentrated on composition.

JEHOASH HIRSHBERG

Strauss, Leo (1899–1973) German–American political philosopher. Born in Germany, he started working on Jewish philosophy at the Academy of Jewish Research in Berlin in 1925. He came to have great influence in the USA when he moved first to the New School for Social Research, New York, and then to the University of Chicago. He covered a very wide area in his books and articles, but the theme of the conflict between Athens and Jerusalem, between faith and religion, is frequently present. This theme is explored in his *Philosophie und Gesetz* (1935), and continued in his very last works on Xenophon and Plato's *Laws*. His interests were very broad and not limited to the reception and adaptation of Greek philosophy by medieval Jewish and Muslim writers. His *What is Political Philosophy* (1959), *Natural Right and History* (1965), and *Liberalism: Ancient and Modern* (1968), embody a conservatism which has made him a very influential thinker in the USA.

His influence on the development of the study of Islamic and Jewish medieval thought has also been very powerful, and his *Persecution and the Art of Writing* (1952), has persuaded a large number of scholars to study the way in which medieval texts have been constructed, rather than the arguments of the texts themselves. This is because of his thesis that there is a long tradition of writers not declaring their real views openly, but hiding those views under a veil of confusing and apparently orthodox language. His "How to begin to study Maimonides' *Guide of the Perplexed*" has been very important in directing students of Maimonides to investigate what might be hidden in the *Guide* and how its author may have used contradiction to instruct the wise and avoid challenging the faith of the vulgar. This hermeneutic approach is also supported by a large number of other books and articles which seek to support the general thesis that there is a long tradition of writing which conceals its real heterodox views under a camouflage of literary techniques that have to be prized open to reveal the authors' real views.

FURTHER READING

Altmann, A.: Leo Strauss 1899–1973. *Proceedings of the American Academy for Jewish Research* 41–2 (1973–4) xxxiii–xxxvi

Leaman, O.: *Introduction to Medieval Islamic Philosophy* (Cambridge: Cambridge University Press, 1985) 182–201

Lerner, R.: Leo Strauss. *American Jewish Year Book* 76 (1976) 91–7

OLIVER LEAMAN

Stutschewsky, Joachim (1891–1981) Israeli cellist, composer, teacher, and historian of Jewish music. Stutschewsky was a leading personality in the formation of musical life in Israel. Born in the Ukraine, he graduated from the Leipzig conservatorium. Between 1914 and 1924 he was active as a cellist in Switzerland, and in Vienna he founded the Austrian String Quartet, with Rudolf Kolisch as first violinist, which participated in premier performances of masterpieces such as Alban Berg's Lyric Suite. In Vienna he contributed essays on Jewish music to the Jewish periodical *Die Stimme*. He was in constant correspondence with close friends in Palestine, and after the Nazi Anschluss of Austria in 1938 he emigrated to Palestine. As a brilliant cello teacher he published an innovative book of method, *Das Violoncellspiel*. He engaged in historical research on the hasidic musicians (*klezmerim*) on whom he published a monograph. In Tel Aviv he organized a pioneering series of concerts of Jewish music for which he commissioned new works. In addition to many works for the cello he wrote numerous songs, pedagogical works, and arrangements of folk songs.

JEHOASH HIRSHBERG

Sukenik, Eleazar Lipa (1889–1953) Israeli archaeologist. Founder of the Department of Archaeology at the Hebrew University of Jerusalem (1927), Sukenik turned Jewish archaeology, which until then had been a small part of Palestinian archaeology, into a field of its own.

Born in Bialystok (then in Russia, now in Poland), Sukenik settled in Palestine in 1911 and studied at a teachers' seminary in Jerusalem. In 1922 he was accepted as a student at Kaiser Wilhelm University in Berlin where he studied for two years. Upon his return to Palestine in 1924, Sukenik began his career in archaeology in earnest, centering his research and excavations on the ancient Palestinian synagogues, an area of research that became one of his central interests. Over a number of years Sukenik was engaged in the excavation of synagogues at Beth-Alpha, Hamat-Gader, Salbit, and Japhia, as well as four synagogues in Greece. In 1926 Sukenik was awarded a Ph.D. by Dropsie College, Philadelphia, for his research on these ancient synagogues.

Sukenik's interest in archaeology was by no means restricted to one period – a factor evident in the title of the lectureship he received in 1934 at the Hebrew University (Lecturer in Archaeology of *Eretz Israel* from the Bronze to the Byzantine period). Sukenik participated in excavations at Hadera and Afula which contributed to a better understanding of the Chalcolithic period. In Samaria he was involved in the uncovering of the citadel of the kings of Israel and in 1925 he, together with L. A. Mayer, began excavating the "Third Wall" of Jerusalem, which led to a better understanding of the topography of Jerusalem in the Second Temple period. Sukenik was also very interested in the inscriptions found on ossuaries. In 1938 he was appointed Professor of Archaeology at the Hebrew University.

Of all his archaeological activities, Sukenik is probably best known as the first person to acquire some of the Dead Sea Scrolls and recognize their importance (1947). He devoted the rest of his life to the study of the scrolls he acquired and, as a result, was the first person to suggest that the scrolls belonged to the Essenes.

Sukenik published many books and articles. He was responsible for the publication of the periodical *Qedem* (first published in 1942) and was the Chief Editor of *Encyclopedia Biblica*.

One of Sukenik's three sons was Yigal YADIN,

also an archaeologist in addition to being a soldier and politician.

FURTHER READING

Eretz-Israel 8 (1967) [Sukenik Memorial Volume]

DEBRA JANE ROSEN

Sulzer, Salomon (1804–1890) Austrian synagogue composer and cantor. Born in Hohenems, in the Vorarlberg, Sulzer was the first musician since Salomone de' Rossi to raise the standards of composition and performance in the synagogue. Three outstanding qualities made him well-known among the Jews of western Europe: first, his baritone-tenor voice drew admiration not only from the Viennese community whom he served as Obercantor from 1826 to 1881, but also from scholars and musicians (including Giacomo MEYERBEER, Schubert, Schumann, and Liszt); second, his fiery temperament created a vogue among contemporary cantors, who tried to imitate his singing style and his deportment; and third, and most significant in the development of Jewish music, his compositions became the model upon which almost every newly emancipated congregation based its synagogue ritual. *Schir Zion* (Zion's song: songs for the Israelite religious service), published in two separate volumes (1838–40 and 1865–6), constitutes the earliest complete and thoroughly organized repertory in Hebrew to be set for cantor and four-part male choir.

Sulzer was a professor at the Vienna Imperial Conservatoire and received honors from the Royal Academy of St Cecilia in Rome. In 1868 he became Knight of the Order of Franz Josef.

FURTHER READING

Idelsohn, A. Z.: *Jewish Music in its Historical Development* (New York: Henry Holt & Co., 1929) 246–60.

Mandell, E.: Salomon Sulzer, 1804–90. *Journal of Synagogue Music* 1 no. 4 (1968) 3–13.

ALEXANDER KNAPP

Summerfield, Woolfe [Ben Mowshay] (1901–1976) English lawyer and novelist. A Manchester-born solicitor, Woolfe Summerfield wrote several legal textbooks, and also *An Outline of English Law for Laymen* (1931). In the *Jewish Chronicle* of the 1920s his articles appeared regularly on aspects of the law as they affected Jews, with such titles as "New names for old – and the Law" and "Some Anglo-Jewish Marital Cases". Under his pseudonym, Ben Mowshay, he published two novels set in Kidston (Manchester in disguise) which chart the progress of his hero, Abraham Bear Davis. As in most Anglo-Jewish fiction of this period, there is a strong autobiographical element, with first-hand accounts of Jewish life and institutions in a provincial city and London suburbia. *Fraudem Bear* (1928) was compared in the *Times Literary Supplement* with ZANGWILL's *Children of the Ghetto*, but while he may aim at depicting a section of society in all its aspects, Mowshay lacks not only Zangwill's skill, but his humanity and compassion. Indeed, the faults and weaknesses of his fellow-Jews are exposed and castigated as severely as those of the Gentile world.

Fraudem Bear follows Arthur from his birth to immigrant parents, through success at grammar school, despite the added burden of daily *heder*, and a scholarship to Oxford. *The Seeker Finds* (1929) takes him from a humble job as a solicitor's clerk to his own practice, then to a dazzling career in the City, London's Wall Street. In a highly improbable plot he loses the woman he loves, which provokes a total alteration of his outlook, causing him to devote himself to somewhat nebulous Zionist activities. Faulty and pretentious as these novels may be, they offer valuable insights into the sensibilities, struggles, and aspirations of a second-generation Jew in a secular society, striving towards the goal of Anglicization while still retaining his Jewishness.

VERA COLEMAN

Sussmann, Heinrich (1904–1986) Austrian painter. Born in Tarnopol, Galicia, Sussmann came to Vienna in 1914, fleeing with his family before the Russians. He went to study art in Paris in 1925, and in 1927–8 was back in Vienna studying stage design under Oskar Strand in Vienna. The years 1929–33 saw him in Berlin, primarily as a stage designer, but in 1933 he left for Paris. From 1940 Sussmann became involved in the French Resistance, until his arrest by the Gestapo in 1944. Sent to Auschwitz, Sussmann survived, but his experience there dominated much of his subsequent work.

Sussmann came from a traditionalist Jewish family, and he received the usual religious education at an early age. The extent of his Jewish identity only became really apparent, however, with his post-Auschwitz work, which, apart from attempting to deal with the horror of the death camps, also returned to other themes of the Jewish Diaspora, including reminiscences of his Galician childhood.

STEVEN BELLER

Sutskever, Avrom (b.1913)   Yiddish poet. Born in Smargon, Belorussia, Sutskever spent his childhood in Siberia, where his family fled to escape the war. In 1920, on the death of his father in Omsk, they returned to live near Vilna. Sutskever studied Polish and Hebrew literature and literary criticism, coming under the influence of the intellectuals around the Yiddish Scientific Institute. He became associated with the group of writers known as *Yung vilne* (Young Vilna), but also spent time in Warsaw, his earliest lyrics being published in the *Vokhnshrift far literatur* there. The American poet A. Glants-Leyeles recognized his talent and published his work in the USA. Sutskever's first collection, *Lider* (Songs) appeared in Warsaw in 1937 (Bibliotek fun yidishn pen-klub), and a collection of nature poems, *Valdiks* (Sylvan) appeared in Vilna in 1940 (Yiddisher literatur fareyn un pen-klub). Sutskever was in the Vilna ghetto under the Nazi occupation, and escaped and joined Jewish partisans. In 1944 he was airlifted to Moscow, where he had become known through Peretz MARKISH. In 1946 Sutskever returned to Poland, and then, after staying in France and Holland, he went to Palestine in 1947. In 1949 he became the editor of the Tel Aviv literary journal *Di goldene keyt* which he was still editing in the late 1980s.

Much of Sutskever's prolific output involves the depiction of his childhood, especially of his mother, and of his experiences during the war and immediately after. *Di festung* (The fortress) was published in 1945 and contains poems written during the war; the ghetto experiences also underlie the collections *Lider fun geto* (1946; Songs from the ghetto) and *Geheymshtot* (1948; Secret town). The collection *Sibir* (1953; *Siberia*, 1961) deals with Sutskever's childhood in Siberia. The collected poems were published in 1963 in two volumes (Tel Aviv, Sutskever yubiley-komitet) as *Poetishe verk*.

Although Sutskever might with justice be characterized as a lyric poet, his work is complex and innovative. Sutskever uses neologisms and striking juxtapositions in his search for a poetic language to match the complexity and dislocated nature of his experiences. He is faced with the problem of creating out of the past and of memories, of poeticizing experience whilst remaining true to its story. The combination of lyricism and verbal brilliance, the evocation of psychological compression through a multi-layered structuring of the narrative, and the creation of a poetic memory to set alongside the historical and factual memory, make Sutskever one of the most significant Yiddish writers of the century.

FURTHER READING
Leftwich, J.: *Abraham Sutzkever – Partisan Poet* (New York: Thomas Yoseloff, 1971)

CHRISTOPHER HUTTON

Suzman, Helen (b.1917)   South African politician and spokesperson for civil rights. She was educated in Johannesburg at the Parktown Convent and at the University of the Witwatersrand. She served as a statistician for the War Supplies Board during the Second World War until 1944, when she became a lecturer in economic history at the University of the Witwatersrand. Her involvement in economic history led her to a political career, for it made her increasingly aware of the socioeconomic problems and labor laws of South Africa. In 1947 she represented the Institute for Race Relations at an inter-nation Conference on human rights in London. On behalf of the Institute she prepared evidence for the Fagan Commission on

Native laws. This led her to want to ameliorate conditions actively.

In 1953 she was elected United Party Member of Parliament for Houghton, Johannesburg, subsequently representing this constituency for the Progressive Federal Party. In 1959 she was a founder member of the (then) Progressive Party, in 1961 being its only member in Parliament, a situation which continued for 13 years, until, in 1974, six more members of her party were elected. Until she resigned in 1989, she was the longest-serving Member of Parliament. An indefatigable and courageous fighter for human rights, she has received world-wide recognition for her struggle against apartheid and has been awarded several honorary doctorates by prominent universities among which are: Oxford (1973), Harvard (1976), Witwatersrand (1976), and the Jewish Theological Seminary of America (1986). She is an honorary fellow of St Hugh's College, Oxford, and of the London School of Economics. She has been nominated twice for the Nobel Peace Prize. In her Oxford citation she was regarded as the "pride of authentic Africa ... the voice of the people, however isolated, the defender of civil and academic freedom ... like a cricket in a thorn-bush with always the same tune in implacable defiance of apartheid".

FURTHER READING
Strangwayes-Booth, J.: *A Cricket in the Thorn Tree*, (Johannesburg: Hutchinson, 1976)

JOCELYN HELLIG

Svevo, Italo [Aron [Ettore] Schmitz] (1861–1928)   Italian writer. Born an Austrian citizen and brought up in Trieste speaking the local dialect, Svevo was educated partly in his native city and partly in Germany, near Würzburg. He thus had his cultural roots in continental Europe rather than in Italy, which in the late nineteenth century was somewhat provincial. Because of the strong cultural links between Vienna and Trieste, Sigmund FREUD's theories found an interested audience in the latter city, and Svevo became the first novelist to use Freudian theories and techniques for narrative purposes. His first novel, *Una vita* (1892; *A Life*, 1963) is cast in the naturalist mold but takes naturalism into the realm of the subconscious. It deals with the suicide of an unsuccessful bank clerk and includes a study of the phenomenon for which Freud was later to use the term "family romance". His second novel, *Senilità* (1898; *As a Man Grows Older*, 1932), is a study of self-deception and egoism. Svevo's parents were observant Jews, although he was not. His letters to his wife show that he was always conscious of his Jewishness (James Joyce used him as one of the models for Leopold Bloom in *Ulysses*). Although this consciousness finds no direct expression in his work, it is possible to see Zeno Cosini, the central character of his third novel, *La coscienza di Zeno* (1923; *The Confessions of Zeno*, 1930) as based on the traditional figure of the schlemiel. Zeno's engaging humor and optimism make *La coscienza* a comic masterpiece, but since its action is set in the period ending in 1915, when Italy entered the First World War, it is also a radical critique of European civilization akin to Thomas Mann's *The Magic Mountain* and Robert Musil's *Man Without Qualities*.

FURTHER READING
Gatt-Rutter, J: *Italo Svevo: A Double Life* (Oxford: Clarendon Press, 1988)
Moloney, B.: *Italo Svevo. A Critical Introduction* (Edinburgh: Edinburgh University Press, 1974)

BRIAN MOLONEY

synagogue composers in the USA   Impetus for the prolific musical creativity in American synagogues was twofold: the unique position occupied by religion in the general American society, and the development of the Reform and Conservative movements in the American Jewish community.

Tradition and Sephardic Jews
Although a small group of Sephardic Jews settled in New Amsterdam (now New York) in the middle of the seventeenth century, the bulk of Jewish immigration did not reach large proportions until 200 years later. The Sephardic Jewish community, even though many of its

members became the "Grandees" of American Jewish society, remained very small in number. There are still a handful of Sephardic congregations throughout the USA. These communities have had little musical growth, but fashion their service songs after the synagogues in Amsterdam and London, and they have pretty much codified their music and its performance. As with most traditions, it is faithfully rendered as if it were changeless, although the harmonies pointedly show the influences of the Ashkenazic synagogue song.

Reform in the nineteenth century

The immigration of the German Jews during the middle of the nineteenth century brought with it the spirit of liberalism which had been spreading throughout central Europe since the French Revolution. The German immigrants established the first Reform temples and brought with them the music which had been composed for the Hamburg Reform Temple. The first such congregation in the New World was the Reform Society of Israelites in Charleston, South Carolina, in 1824. Its aim was "not to overthrow but rebuild, not to destroy but to reform". This congregation published the first American prayer book with English hymns (1830). Music for these hymns was taken from the Hamburg Hymnal and also from non-Jewish sources. The success of the congregation was quickly followed by the establishment of other Reform congregations in Baltimore, New York, and many other cities.

Service music was usually that found in SULZER's *Shir Zion* or Naumbourg's *Zemirot Israel*. Very few cantors or even Jewish singers were available in those early years in the USA, therefore non-Jews were employed as soloists and choristers in the temples. Organists also were non-Jewish. However, by the end of the nineteenth century, even though still heavily influenced by the German Reform tradition, some indigenous American Jewish music was emerging. Two Reform cantors, Alois Kaiser and William Sparger, published a collection called *The Principal Melodies of the Synagogue*. Sigmund Schlesinger (1835–1906) published a four-volume *Musical Service for Sabbath and Holy Days*, followed by others: Max Graumann (1871–1933) *Song of Prayer* ("Sabbath" and "Musical Service for New Year and Day of Atonement"); Fred Kitzinger *Songs of Judah*; Max Spicker (1858–1912) *Services for Sabbath Evening and Morning*; Edward Stark (1863–1918) *Sefer Anim Zemirot*. Added to this "service music" was the appearance of a succession of hymnals published by the Central Conference of American Rabbis (Reform). The third revised edition of this hymnal was edited by A. W. Binder in 1932 and, though it contained a few of the "traditional German Reform hymns", it was dominated by tunes written by authentically Jewish composers such as Weinberg, Schalit, Beimel, Achron, Alman, Gerovitch, and others. It also contained many original hymns by A. W. Binder, as well as tunes of the "classical" composers Sulzer, Lewandowski, and Naumbourg.

The development of a native school

In the twentieth century there has been a tremendous growth and productivity of music for the American synagogue by American-born composers, as well as the many who fled to the USA during the 1930s and 1940s and earlier. In addition to A. W. Binder, Frederick Jacobi, Joseph Achron, Gershon Ephros, Jacob Weinberg, and Reuven Korsakoff, were Lazare Saminsky, and Lazare Weiner, both of whom settled in New York City and became music directors at Temple Emanuel and Central Synagogue, respectively. Isadore Freed, Heinrich Schalit, Jacob Weinberg, Eric Werner, Max Janowsky, Herbert Fromm, Hugo Adler, Julius Chajes, Erwin Jospe, Max Helfman, and Herman Berlinsky formed the next generation that contributed a significant number of works to the American synagogue.

After the war, while many of the above-mentioned composers reached the height of their creativity, younger men and women followed in their footsteps, Robert Starer, Samuel Adler, and Yehudi Wyner, among others, following the "classically-oriented" composers wrote prodigiously for the synagogue. Others, though writing some music in the traditional synagogal style, were greatly influenced by youth movement and folk elements that have come into the American synagogue.

The patronage of Conservative synagogues

The American Conservative synagogue has also been greatly instrumental in encouraging composers to write music for use in its services. Although most American Conservative congregations do not use instrumental music, many cantors serving these communities have developed mixed choirs, especially for High Holy Day services. During the earlier portion of this century, most of the music used was by such eastern European composers as Leo Low, A. Dunayevesky, Z. Zilberts, Alter, Novokovsky, Weisser, and Roitman, and a sprinkling of a generous number of "traditional" pieces by Sulzer, Lewandowsky, Birnbaum, and others. The Ephros anthology is widely employed, and it introduced many of the composers who had written for the Reform synagogue to the Conservative ritual. Composers who wrote "secular" Jewish music and music for the Yiddish theater have also contributed to the music of the Conservative synagogue.

Individual Conservative cantors must be credited for encouraging and commissioning major composers to write synagogue music, among them Jewish and non-Jewish composers who had never written for the synagogue, such as Bernard Rogers, Leo Smit, Paul Dessau, Kurt Weill, Roy Harris, and many others.

The music of the Orthodox synagogue in America has shown little creativity. It is, of course, very strongly "*Hazzan* oriented", with some male choirs or combinations of boys' and men's choruses supporting the *Hazzan*. Most Orthodox *Hazzinim* slavishly imitate the style, the melodies and, with their choirs, the practices and harmonies of their great eastern European models: Rosenblatt, Koussevitsky, Kwartin, Glantz, Vigoda, and others. At best they are influenced by cantor-composers who codified and purified some of the most important recitatives and composed some outstanding works frequently used in the American Orthodox synagogue.

Among important synagogue collections which have appeared in America are the five-volume collection by Gershon Ephros for Sabbath, High Holy Days, and Three Festivals; the two collections by Chemjo Vinaver; The High Holyday collection titled *Yamim Nora'im* by Samuel Adler.

In this connection one must mention the 1987 Hymnal published by the CCAR and Transcontinental Music Publishers, entitled *Sha'arei shirah* edited by Charles Davidson. It contains many new hymns, songs, and responses especially written for the new Reform prayer books *Gates of Prayer* and *Gates of Repentance*.

SAMUEL H. ADLER

Syrkin, Marie (1899–1988) American journalist, editor, poet, and teacher. Marie Syrkin was one of the great spirits in twentieth-century Zionist and Jewish intellectual life in the USA. Brought up in the thick of classic labor Zionist ideology (her father, Nachman Syrkin, helped found the Labor Zionist movement), Marie Syrkin provided a passionate, sustained, eloquent voice on behalf of Jewry in Israel and around the world for over half a century.

Syrkin brought her broad awareness of Jewish history to her essays and books. Many Americans know her best by her broad-ranging essays in *Commentary*, the *Nation*, *Midstream*, *Dissent*, *Saturday Review*, the *New York Times Magazine*, and the *New Republic*, as well as for her work as an editor of the *Jewish Frontier*. A generous selection of these essays have been collected in *The State of the Jews* (1980). Syrkin's essays have an extraordinary combination of carefully researched factual detail, coherent historical argument, and deep feeling for the heights and depths of contemporary Jewish experience.

Syrkin also wrote biographies of major historical figures, and translated poetry for and edited anthologies.

BIBLIOGRAPHY
Nachman Syrkin, Socialist Zionist: A Biographical Memoir (New York: Herzl Press, 1961); *Golda Meir: Woman With A Cause* (New York: G. P. Putnam's Sons, 1963)

SYLVIA FISHMAN

Szichman, Mario (b.1945)   Argentine novelist. Having left law school after three years, Szichman began a lifelong career as a journalist. In 1967 he left Argentina for Colombia, and shortly thereafter he settled in Venezuela until 1971. Szichman wrote his first two novels, *Crónica falsa* (1969) and *Los judíos del Mar Dulce* (1971) in Caracas. Upon returning to Buenos Aires, and until 1975, he served as foreign reporter for Jacobo TIMERMAN's *La opinión*, and as correspondent for the Italian news agency, Interpress. During that time he produced a collection of short stories (*Náufrago de tierra firme,* never published), a critical book on Venezuelan writer Arturo Uslar Pietri (*Uslar: Cultura y dependencia*, 1975), and a new version of his first novel (*La verdadera crónica falsa*, 1972). Szichman returned to Caracas in 1975, he contributed to several local news magazines and directed the literary supplement of *Ultimas noticias*. In 1975 he published a second, and equally polemical, critical book on a major Venezuelan figure (*Miguel Otero Silva: Mitología de una generación frustrada*), and in 1981 the novel, *A las 20:25 la señora entró a la inmortalidad* (At 8:25 Evita became immortal). Since September 1980 he has lived in the USA, first in New York, and later in Washington, DC (1983–6) as a correspondent for United Press International. He is currently an editor for Associated Press (New York), and a contributor to several Latin American and US-based Spanish publications. His latest novel is *La tercera fundación de Buenos Aires*. He is currently completing a volume of short stories, *Cuentos para la hora del davenen*.

Szichman's novels re-enact the saga of the "schlemiel-schlimazl" Pechof family, from humble eastern European origins through the initial and flawed attempts to adapt to Argentina as the promised land. These works, centered on collapsed immigrant dreams, can be seen as a direct response to the "New Zion" heralded by Albert GERCHUNOFF's classic *Los gauchos judíos* (1910). With sarcastic, merciless, humor and biting satirical prose, Szichman demythologizes both Argentina's official history and its recent myths, notably some dear to textbook Socialists and partyline Peronists, as well as attempts to create a venerable Jewish past where the marginal was all-pervasive. In a violent and anti-Semitic society, Szichman suggests, unfathomable survival seems to be the final lot for those Pechofs who plunder their own identity and build upon the burnt remnants of national projects.

SAÚL SOSNOWKSI

Szigetti, Imre (1879–1975)   Australian graphic artist, cartoonist, and illustrator. Szigetti was born in Budapest, the son of an assimilated and wealthy Jewish family. He arrived in Australia in 1939 after spending a period in jail for his anti-Nazi satires. He studied art at the State Art Academy, Berlin, in 1917 and combined his art studies with a career in journalism, using his drawings to illustrate his satirical comments. From the time of his arrival in Australia his delicate, open line drawings added a vivacious and decorative flavor to the contemporary art of Sydney. He held nine solo shows in Australia between 1946 and his death, and was involved in numerous group exhibitions. He received three major graphic prizes. However, he is better known in the USA than in Australia, where he was frequently "rediscovered".

Szigetti was heavily influenced by his observation of Jewish life in Hungary. Many of his drawings depict Hungarian Jews, especially Orthodox Jews, talking, praying, and reflecting Jewish history. Among his best works are *Five Jews in Conversation* and *Erev Shabbat*. Many of these drawings were done with his eyes closed so that he was not influenced by visual impressions from his immediate surroundings.

His work is represented at various Australian state galleries, galleries in New Zealand, the Budapest City Art Gallery, and numerous private collections. He illustrated over one hundred books, including editions of the works of Edgar Allen Poe and Baudelaire.

ALAN D. CROWN

Szlosberg, Icchak (1877–1930)   Polish composer. Szlosberg was born into a family of synagogue cantors (*chazen*): both his grandfather and father were cantors. He began his musical career in Vilnius at the age of 13. At that time he had already conducted a choir and a small instrumental ensemble. A few years later he left for Warsaw to study music at the Warsaw Conservatoire. He supported himself by giving private classes in music. After the departure for the USA, in 1919, of Leo Liow, the conductor of the choir of the Warsaw Central Synagogue in Tlomackie, Szlosberg assumed his post and contributed greatly to the development of the choir.

He was also employed in Warsaw as a music director in Fiszzon's Jewish Theater, a touring company, with which he visited many towns of Poland, the Ukraine, and Russia.

He composed for numerous Jewish theatres, often using old Jewish tunes whether in their original form or modified and rearranged. It has been calculated that he composed music for 80 Jewish plays and operettas. These were performed throughout the country by such troupes as, for instance, Wilner Trupe, Kaminski's Theater and WIKT (Warszawer Jidiszer Kunst-Teater). Szlosberg's excellent orchestral adaptations were also used by Polish music theaters.

MARIAN FUKS

Szomory, Dezső [Mór Weisz] (1869–1944) Hungarian writer and playwright. Born into a lower middle-class Jewish family, he attended a Catholic grammar school. Later he studied music at the Academy of Music in Budapest but abandoned his studies for the sake of journalism. In 1889, to escape military service, he left for Paris and remained there until 1906 sending back correspondence to a number of Budapest journals. In 1907–8 he visited London and Oxford. Although his play *Péntek este* (Friday night), the romantic love-affair of a rabbi's wife with a mysterious non-Jewish figure, was staged in the Hungarian National Theater in 1896, he scored his first real success with the historical play *A nagyasszony* (1910; The grand dame) which centers around the Empress Maria Theresa. This and Szomory's later his-

torical plays (for example *II József*, 1918; Emperor Joseph II) show his rhetorical, rather than dramatic, talent. His social comedies, such as *Györgyike, drága gyermek* (1912; Georgina, dear child), reflect the longings and frustrations of women ruled by the power of money. Szomory's early stories were influenced by French naturalism; later, symbolism and Art Nouveau affected his writing, although his richly embroidered style is often tempered by wit and irony. His best collection of stories is probably *A mennyei küldönc* (1926; Heavenly envoy), although the loosely constructed *Levelek egy barátnőmhöz* (1927; Letters to a lady friend) and the equally autobiographical, nostalgic *A párizsi regény* (1929; The novel of Paris) have also been acclaimed by critics.

In spite of the Jewish theme in *Péntek este*, the young Szomory had little interest in specifically Jewish problems. This began to change in 1917 when he published the article-pamphlet "Egy levél alkalmából" (Apropos of a Letter) in the literary review *Nyugat*. In this he bemoaned the considerable obstacles which, in his view, Hungarian society had put in the way of Jewish assimilation. While he professed non-involvement in social affairs, some of his post-1920 stories are critical of the accommodation of the rich Jewish bourgeoisie to the authoritarian, and initially openly anti-Semitic Horthy regime. In the ironic miniatures of *Horeb tanár úr* (1934; Professor Horeb) Szomory condemns the attitude of the social climber who rejects his Jewishness for the sake of more rapid advancement. His last play, *Sába királynője* (The Queen of Sheba), written some time in the 1930s was never performed; it was first printed in the posthumous collection *Szinház* (1973; Theater). This is an imaginative, although over-poeticized attempt to portray the love of King Solomon for Belkis, Queen of Sheba. Some of Szomory's stories were translated into English, for example "The Divine Garden" in *22 Hungarian Short Stories* (1967).

BIBLIOGRAPHY

The divine garden. In *22 Hungarian Short Stories*, trans. I. Farkas (Budapest: Corvina, 1967)

GEORGE GÖMÖRI

T

Tabatznik, Mendel (1894–1975) Yiddish essayist and poet. Born in Kletsk, in the Minsk area of White Russia, Mendel Tabatznik was director of a Yiddish elementary school in Mir. He emigrated to Johannesburg, South Africa, in 1927, where he taught Yiddish. He began to publish articles on pedagogical matters around 1920. In later years Tabatznik turned to poetry, publishing *Mentsh un zayn arum* (1963; Man and his environs); *In shpete shoen* (1965; In late hours); and an autobiographical novel, *Kalmen Bulon* (1968–70). His memoirs appeared in 1973.

DEVRA KAY

Tal [Grünthal], **Josef** (b.1910) Israeli composer, pianist, and teacher. Tal was born in Posen and studied at the Hochschule für Musik in Berlin. His composition teacher, Heinz Tiessen (1887–1971), was deeply committed to the avant-garde technique of Arnold SCHOENBERG, and the encounter with the innovative milieu of Berlin in the 1920s left a lasting mark on Tal's personality, He emigrated to Palestine in 1934, settling first on kibbutz Gesher and then in Haifa, but soon moved to Jerusalem which remained his home. During the 1940s he was active as a solo pianist, performing with the Philharmonic orchestra, and as a theory teacher. His early works written in the 1940s were chamber and piano pieces, in which he established himself as the representative of a personal, individual approach to composition in Palestine, and of high technical standards of contemporary European composition. Yet he also tried to achieve a synthesis of Western harmony and form with Eastern melodies and ancient tradition. In the 1950s and 1960s he turned to elaborate serial techniques stressing the parameter of sound as a central structural element. He was one of the founders of the Academy of Music in Jerusalem, and in 1960 he started the first studio for electronic music in Israel.

In 1960 Tal began to lecture on music at the Hebrew University in Jerusalem, and he was the first chairman of the Musicology Department (founded 1965). In his electronic music he combined traditional instruments with synthesized sounds, as in his series of concertos for piano and tape. In 1971 his opera *Ashmedai* (libretto by Israel Eliraz) was produced at the Hamburg Opera and later at the New York City Opera. More operas followed, and in 1987 he was commissioned as a member of the Berlin Akademie to compose an opera for the festival commemmorating 750 years of Berlin. In 1970 he received the Israel Prize and, in 1983 the prestigious Wolf Prize.

Throughout his work as a musician he maintained his uncompromising commitment to sincere and innovative style, regarding the emerging Israeli music as the natural result of historical continuity and everyday involvement in musical life, resisting any external ideological pressures.

JEHOASH HIRSHBERG

Talmon, Jacob Leib (1916–1980) Israeli scholar and historian. Talmon was born in Rypin, Poland, and emigrated to Palestine in

748

1934. He completed his MA degree at the Hebrew University in 1939 and continued his studies at the London School of Economics where he received his doctorate in 1943. Six years later, in 1949, he was appointed a lecturer at the Hebrew University and in 1961 he was appointed Professor of Modern History and became a member of the Israel National Academy of Sciences.

Talmon's book *The Origins of Totalitarian Democracy* (1952) which deals with the history of Europe in the modern period, and intended for a universal reading audience, gained him the Israel Prize for the Humanities in 1956. Talmon's main contribution in this book, as in all his works, was to the history of ideas which he approached with the fundamental assumption that there is a mutual influence between ideas and processes of history. In his *Romanticism and Revolt* (1967) which is primarily an historical study, he devoted a complete chapter to a discussion of the ideas of philosophers and writers who, in Talmon's view, contributed to specific behavioral structures and influenced the processes of history. He believed that the tendency to turn history into statistical research and sociological analysis was excessive. It is therefore no wonder that his research, based on his different outlook, caused controversy among international historians. These controversies also led to differences of opinion about Talmon's interpretation of various historical events.

Other works dealing with these problems are *Political Messianism: the Romantic Phase* (1960) the topic of which is the conflict between various types of democracy, and *The Myth of the Nation and the Vision of Revolution* (1981) the last of Talmon's works to have appeared after his death. In it he discussed the sources of the ideological polarization of the twentieth century.

He also published books and many articles on the problems of Jewish identity, the Arab–Jewish conflict, as well as problems of religion and State. Among these is *The Nature of Jewish History: Its Universal Significance* (1957) and *The Unique and the Universal* (1965) a volume of articles.

DEBORAH SCHECHTERMAN

Talmud in modern Judaism The Hebrew Bible and Talmud together constitute the classical sacred literature of Judaism. From the perspective of traditional Judaism, the Bible and Talmud are interwoven, the latter interpreting the former, and reflecting and determining its normative, philosophical, and ethical content. All subsequent Jewish religious literature is an extension, elaboration, or application of the Bible and Talmud.

In the classical Jewish view, the Torah is the divine *logos*. As such, all knowledge is immanent in the Torah. It can be compared to a mine containing an infinite variety of precious jewels. The function of the study of Torah is the recovery of these hidden treasures.

Part of the hidden content of the Torah was immediately accessible. According to tradition, the Written Torah was revealed to Moses, together with its unwritten interpretation, without which much of the normative content of the Written Torah would be incomprehensible. In addition to this original divine interpretation of specific laws, Moses was entrusted with hermeneutical rules for deriving further legal information from the Written Torah. These rules, and the rigorous logical analysis of the written text, were the tools of the rabbis in "mining" the hidden treasures of the Torah. This method of disclosing the divine *logos* was called *midrash*. The normative content of the Midrash is known as *midrash halakhah*, and the non-normative as *midrash 'aggadah*.

By applying the *midrash* method, the answer to questions of religious law could be derived from the Written Torah. Obviously, the widespread acceptance of the derived law was a reflection of the high communal standing of the rabbis who used the *midrash* method, and also reflected the assent of their peers to their rulings. Together with purely rabbinic decrees and prohibitions, the original oral interpretation and the Midrash constitute the foundations of the Oral Torah (*Torah shebe'al peh*). To preserve its dynamic, developing character, the writing down of the contents of the Oral Torah was proscribed.

The product of centuries of midrashic interpretation was a vast accumulation of rabbinic expositions of the written text of the Torah, lengthy and unorganized. For practical purposes, the organization and preservation of the conclusions of the midrashic process – its purely normative content – was an increasing necessity, particularly for use in Jewish courts of law (see LAW, JEWISH, IN ISRAEL). The normative conclusions of the midrashic process, preserved and separated from the *midrash halakhah*, constitute the Mishnah.

The rabbis who produced the Mishnah were called *tanna'im*. The Mishnah was organized into six orders (divisions) by Rabbi Akiva (*c.* 50–135 CE) and his school. *Zera'im* (seeds) deals with prayer and agricultural subjects; *Mo'ed* (appointed seasons) with Sabbaths and festivals; *Nashim* (women) with family law; *Nezikim* (damages) with civil and criminal law; *Kodashim* (holy things) with the Temple in Jerusalem and its sacrifices; and *Toharot* (purities) with ritual purity and impurity. These orders were divided into 63 tractates, themselves subdivided into chapters and individual paragraphs (*mishnayot*).

As part of the Oral Torah, the Mishnah was originally transmitted orally. Only the possibility of its disappearance, a consequence of the martyrdom of its transmitters, persuaded Rabbi Judah the Prince (*c.*200 CE) to edit the written edition of the Mishnah. The Mishnah is written in relatively simple, extraordinarily economical Hebrew. Its language is far closer to contemporary Hebrew than to the Hebrew of scripture.

Much of the tana'itic material was not included in the Mishnah. Some was later preserved in a parallel work, the *Tosefta*. Other tana'itic material was preserved orally. Tana'itic materials not included in the Mishnah are known as *baraita*.

The Mishnah became *the* text selected for study by subsequent generations of teachers in Palestine and Babylon. These teachers were called *amora'im*, and their analysis of the Mishnah is known as *gemarah*. The *gemarah* on a particular *mishnah* usually consists one or more of the following elements: reverse *midrash* – the tracing of the *mishnah* to its scriptural origin; resolutions of contradictions between various tana'itic materials, or between *tana'im* themselves; the conceptual analysis of halakhic (normative) materials; and, sometimes, at a later phase of talmudic development, the determination of the *halakhah* (law).

To be sure, the *gemarah* is not monolithic. Halakhic analysis is interspersed with aggadic philosophical, ethical, and diadactic comments. The *gemarah* represents the shorthand notes of several centuries of students of the Mishnah, reflecting the tangential discussions which characterize all classrooms, and demonstrating the organization of ideas by association.

The Mishnah and the *gemarah* together constitute the Talmud. In fact, there are two versions of the Talmud. The schools of Jerusalem and Babylon produced different *gemarah* on identical *mishnayot*. In addition, each sometimes commented on *mishnayot* not analyzed by the other and, in some instances, completely neglected to comment on some tractates of the Mishnah. The recension of the *gemarah* was motivated by the same considerations which produced the written edition of the Mishnah.

The Jerusalem version was edited *c.*400 CE, and the Babylonian version *c.*500 CE. The former is called the *Talmud Yerushalmi*, and the latter the *Talmud Bavli*. The language of the *gemarah* is an admixture of Hebrew and of the Aramaic of Jerusalem and Babylon respectively.

The *Bavli* is the fuller, better-edited, and more authoritative of the Talmudim. It therefore became the basis for most subsequent talmudic developments. These were essentially of three kinds. The first was expository and analytical. The commentary of the talmudic exegete par excellence, Rabbi Shlomo Yizhaki (Rashi), the analyses of medieval talmudists known as the Tosafists, and the works of other medieval scholars (*Rishonim*) exemplify this genre. The second consisted of halakhic digests, codes, and responsa, for example, the work of Maimonides and Rabbi Joseph Caro (*Shulhan arukh*), among others. The third was the development of an aggadic digest (*Ein ya'akov*) and expositions on the '*aggadah*.

The standard, printed edition of the Talmud reflects some of these developments. The first page of any tractate or chapter of the *Bavli* contains a *mishnah* and its *gemarah*. The *gemarah* may, in fact, occupy many of the following pages, until the analysis of the *mishnah* is completed, and the next *mishnah* is presented with its *gemarah*. The *gemarah* on a given *mishnah* may sometimes occupy only a few lines, so that a single page of the Talmud may be made up of several pieces of *mishnah*, each followed by its own *gemarah*. A typical page also contains Rashi's commentary and the analytical comments of the Tosafists. In addition, each page contains scriptural and talmudic cross references, references to the Codes, notations with suggested emendations, and, in some cases, other medieval commentaries.

The traditional study of the Talmud has been dialectic/homiletical. Contradictions between passages have been resolved, the interpretations of medieval commentators analyzed and compared, and their conceptual bases minutely examined. The latter approach has been dominated in recent times by the analytic method of the great Soloveitchik family, beginning with Rabbi Chaim of Brisk (1853–1918) and continuing to the giant of this generation, Rabbi Dr Joseph B. SOLOVEITCHIK of Boston.

In contemporary times, new directions in Talmudic study have been explored. Philosophers such as Emanuel LÉVINAS have used the Talmud as the basis of their thought, and scholars such as Abraham Weiss and David Weiss Halivni have developed talmudic text criticism.

The almost universal daily study of a double folio page of Talmud by groups of laymen is a comparatively recent development, attesting to the present widespread popularity of talmudic study. The newly vocalized, translated, annotated, and elucidated text of the Talmud by Adin Steinsaltz has enhanced the process of popularization and has made the Talmud accessible to almost anybody with a basic grasp of Hebrew. Happily, an English version of the Steinsaltz edition of the Babylonian Talmud is now in preparation. Steinsaltz's publication of the first volume of the *Talmud Yerushalmi* undoubtedly presages the opening of that previously all but closed work to the masses in much the same way as his work on the *Bavli* had done.

In all, contemporary fascination with the Talmud is as great as ever, and its study probably more widespread.

FURTHER READING

Neusner, J.: *Invitation to the Talmud* (New York: Harper & Row, 1973)

Steinsaltz, A.: *The Essential Talmud* (London: Weidenfeld & Nicholson, 1976)

Strack, H. L.: *Introduction to the Talmud and Midrash* (New York: Harper & Row, 1959)

ABNER WEISS

Tammuz, Benjamin (b.1919) Israeli novelist, editor, art critic, and sculptor. Born in Kharkov in the Ukraine, Tammuz emigrated to Palestine with his family in 1924. He studied at the Herzlia secondary school in Tel Aviv, and then at the Sorbonne, where he specialized in the history of art. In Israel Tammuz was long associated with the newspaper *Ha'aretz*, in which he wrote the satirical column "Uzi ve shut" in 1949–50, and later served as literary editor for many years.

Under the influence of Yonatan RATOSH, Tammuz became an active devotee of the "Young Hebrew" or "Canaanite" movement from 1939 to 1950. Both Tammuz's satirical tendencies and his lyrically nostalgic or utopian early stories may be traced to Canaanism's critique of Israeli society. Tammuz republished most of these stories in *Angioxyl, terufah nedirah* (1973; *A Rare Cure*, 1981).

The allegorical novella *Hapardes* (1971; *The Orchard*, 1984), is a powerful tale with a blend of mystical and ideological overtones. In it two half-brothers, one Jewish, one half-Arab, vie for the affections of the girl Luna, also of mixed blood, and for possession of an orchard, which is symbolic of the land. The novella develops more fully a theme of Tammuz's well-known story, *Taharut sehiyah* (1952; *The Swimming Race*, 1953), the elusive dream of peace between Arab and Jew in all its tragic complexity. The essential problem of Tammuz's work (in the words of Nurit Gertz) is "the ideological polarization between a pragmatic–materialistic Israeli society and an ethical–spiritual Jewish essence". Tammuz expresses this polarity through the experiences of a naive picaresque hero, Elyakum in a lengthy trilogy, completed in 1969, vol. 2, *Besof ma'arav* (1967; *Castle in Spain*, 1973).

In his other novels Tammuz continues this theme, either through internal conflict in a central personality or through conflict between generations. We see the former technique especially in *Ya'akov* (1971; a segment translated in B. Tammuz and L. Yudkin, *Meetings with the Angel*, 1973). Here Tammuz details his conception of the need for renewing Jewish identity through a new encounter between the archetypal Jew, Jacob–Israel, and the angel who marked Israel's destiny and character at the inaugural juncture of its history. The latter technique is especially well executed in *Requiem lena'aman* (1978; *Requiem for Na'aman*, 1982), Tammuz's strongest novel of disenchantment with Israel's promise. *Mishlei bakbukim* (1975; Bottle proverbs) suggested a corrective through resumption of Judaism's spiritual, if ethereal, posture as a universal, Diaspora, people. *Minotaur* (1980; *Minotaur*, 1981), is a novel of intrigue, which Y. Oren has shown to be an equally intricate continuation of Tammuz's ideological critique. Tammuz's latest novel, *Pundako shel yirmiyahu* (1984; Jeremiah's inn) is a vehement and farcical satire about the intrusion of fanatical religious elements into Israeli politics.

FURTHER READING

Diamond, J.: *Homeland or Holy Land? The Canaanite Critique of Israel* (Bloomington: Indiana University Press, 1986)

Yudkin, L.: *Escape into Siege* (London: Routledge & Kegan Paul, 1974)

STANLEY NASH

Tcherikover, Victor [Avigdor] (1894–1958) Israeli historian. He was born in St Petersburg and graduated in Moscow, but his grounding in the techniques of ancient history came from the still great school of post-First-World-War Berlin. Eduard Meyer gave him understanding of the broader canvas, and Ulrich Wilcken introduced him to Hellenistic history and to the new fields opened by the Greek papyri from Egypt. His first book, *Die hellenistische Städtegründungen* (1927) surveyed the new cities founded during the centuries of the spread of Greek civilization. His writing career took a more specialized turn when, in 1925, he came to the Hebrew University. Eventually becoming the first Professor of Ancient History there, he founded a strong department.

The attractions of ancient history to the student in Jerusalem were obvious. Many were found to share Tcherikover's enthusiasm for the thorough examination of questions concerning Jewish life and thought in the Hellenistic and Roman worlds. The main interest, which all could identify with, was on the position of the Jews among alien cultures. Modern experience could provide clues, but the danger that it would dominate interpretation was combated by Tcherikover's rigorous scholarship; he seldom read into a text more than was there. His own concentration was on the Jews of Egypt, where he was fascinated by the help papyri could give in illuminating the questions of Jewish status and the nature of everyday life; although he made valuable contributions to the study of apologetic literature, even Philo sank into the background. His fullest treatment is in *Hayehudim bemitzrayim batekufah hahelenistit haromit l'or hapapirologyah* (1963; The Jews in Egypt in the Hellenistic and Roman period in the light of papyrology); the English reader is served in a different way by the *Corpus Papyrorum Judaicarum* (with Alexander Fuks and Menahem Stern, 1957–64), which occupied the closing years of his life. Five hundred and twenty Greek papyri of the most varied nature were edited, translated, and equipped with a masterly introduction and careful commentary; it is a worthy memorial. Jews outside Egypt were not neglected, and his original training was indispensable here. His *Hellenistic Civilization and the Jews* (1959), expanded from a Hebrew version (1930), is still outstanding for the solidity of the historical background against which the Jewish story is deployed. Tcherikover was a giant figure among those who transplanted European scholarship to Jerusalem, but he had other sides. Visitors who admired the labor which had obviously gone into his trim garden in Bethakerem were firmly told that it was this which constituted the real building of the Land.

DAVID LEWIS

Terezín, music in The Bohemian town of Terezín (Theresienstadt), evacuated of its local population by the Germans in late November 1941, served as a transit–concentration camp until early May 1945. Some 140,000 Jews, including 15,000 children, were brought to Terezín and while about 34,000 died there, most of the remainder perished in the gas chambers of Auschwitz and Treblinka. The largest number came from Czechoslovakia, but Jews also arrived from Austria, Germany, and other occupied countries, collectively representing much of western and central Europe's cultural and intellectual elite. Forced in their detention and isolation to draw entirely on their own resources, the cultural activities in which they engaged became a spiritual resistance, the breadth and intensity of which even the Germans could not stop.

The first clandestine and carefully guarded musical performances began in late 1941 in attics and basements of living quarters, a continuation, in fact, of private concerts and lectures held in Prague after September of that year, when the SS banned music by Jewish composers and public performances by Jewish musicians. By mid 1942 a *Freizeitgestaltung* (free-time organization) was formed in Terezín, in the framework of the Council of Jewish Elders, to administer theater, music, lectures, library, and sports. The music section was responsible for coordinating opera, recitals, concerts, cabaret, and musical instruments.

The nature and extent of this activity was dictated by the unpredictable but inevitable turnover of personnel, caused by the continuous transports east. Despite this, however, an unbelievable schedule of events was maintained: piano, violin, and vocal recitals, chamber, choral, and orchestral concerts, oratorios and operas, as well as semi-classical and light music. Amidst terrible conditions of overcrowding, insufficient food, disease, deaths, and the uncertainty of their ultimate fate, Terezín inmates could hear a Beethoven quartet, a Verdi opera, Dvořák songs, contemporary works presented by the Studio for New Music, jazz by the Ghetto Swingers and cabarets in the style of Jaroslav Ježek's well-known music from the Liberated Theater in Prague before the war – momentary respite from the pressures of the ghetto.

The Germans' biggest deceit occurred in the summer of 1944 when Terezín was readied for a visiting delegation of the International Red Cross. Freshly painted houses, newly planted gardens, orderly streets, false store fronts, and temporarily better-fed and clothed residents awaited the guests, who also witnessed several musical programs. In showing off their "model Jewish community", the Germans sought to deflect attention from increasing rumors of the genocide taking place elsewhere. They also took advantage of the occasion to produce a propaganda film, *Der Führer schenkt den Juden eine Stadt*. Of course, after the departure of the Red Cross members and the completion of the filming, most of the "cast", including the performing musicians, made their own terminal exit as well.

Excerpts from several works by Terezín composers were included in the film, preserving at least a few precious moments of their music in actual performance. In addition, a substantial number of original manuscripts were saved. These compositions reveal influences of post-romanticism, Viennese expressionism, Czech folk music, and post-First World War musical theater. There are also a number of instances of musical protest in the form of subtly encoded thematic materials.

Ich wandere durch Theresienstadt by the poet and amateur musician Ilse Weber, is a folk-like song of touching simplicity; Gideon Klein, a supremely gifted young pianist and composer, based one movement of his *String Trio* on a nostalgic Moravian song, *The Kňeždubsk Spire*; Pavel Haas, who studied with Janáček in Brno, composed *Four Songs on Chinese Texts*, inflecting the poetry of homesickness with motifs drawn from patriotic Czech chorales; Egon Ledeč's *Gavotte* for string quartet has an elegance of old Vienna; and Viktor Ullmann's *Fifth Piano Sonata*, "From my youth", radiates an expansive

Composer Pavel Haas acknowledging applause after a performance of his Study 1944 *(From the film* Der Führer schenkt den Juden eine Stadt)

nineteenth-century pianism. Ullmann, a former pupil of Arnold SCHOENBERG in Vienna and a conducting assistant to Alexander Zemlinsky at the New German Theater in Prague, also composed in Terezín a string quartet, songs, choral pieces, and an opera, *Der Kaiser von Atlantis.* This ambitious work, owing much to Kurt WEILL, Hindemith and the Second Viennese School, is a powerful and highly individual music-drama. Rehearsed in the autumn of 1944, the quickening transports removed most of the singers, musicians, and the composer, precluding any actual performance. A Terezín audience would have well understood Ullmann's quotation of the angel of death motif from Suk's *Asrael Symphony,* and his distorted versions of *Deutschland über alles* and the Lutheran chorale, *Ein' feste Burg ist unser Gott,* whose substitute text admonishes that death should

dignify life's end and not result from mindless killing. Hans Krása's *Brundibar,* a children's opera written in Prague in 1938 and orchestrated in Terezín, portrays the victory of two youngsters over a bullying organ grinder. Its more than fifty performances had tremendous impact on participants and audiences alike. Karel Švenck's popular *Terezín Hymn,* from his first cabaret, *The Lost Food Ticket,* inspired some hope and is still remembered by many Terezín survivors.

Zionist orientation and Jewish awareness is evident from some of the music which was performed, arranged, and composed. Perhaps it was for the Subak Chorus, which regularly sang liturgical, Yiddish, and Palestinian songs, that Ullmann arranged melodies from the *Jüdisches (Makkabi) Liederbuch* (Berlin, 1930), though what prompted his use of Yehuda Sharett's song *Rachel* for variations and a fugue in the finale of his *Seventh Piano Sonata* is not known. Other original Jewish pieces included Haas's *Al s'fod*, Zikmund Schul's *Two Chassidic Dances* and a *Cantata Judaica*, and Carlo Taube's *Ein Jüdisches kind*.

The music of Terezín is a monument not only to the spiritual strength and heroic courage of its senselessly martyred creators, performers, and listeners, but it is also of considerable, even exceptional, value in its own right, and Viktor Ullmann most fittingly and eloquently evaluated his, and others', experience, when he wrote that

> . . . it must be emphasized that Theresienstadt has served to *enhance*, not impede, my musical activities, that by no means did we sit weeping on the banks of the waters of Babylon, and that our endeavor with respect to Art was commensurate with our will to live. And I am convinced that all those who, in life and in art, were fighting to force form upon resisting matter, will agree with me.
>
> Bloch, 1979.

FURTHER READING

Bloch, M.: Viktor Ullmann: a brief biography and appreciation. *Journal of the Arnold Schoenberg Institute* 3 no. 2 (1979) 151–77

Ehrmann, F., Heitlinger, O., and Iltis, R., eds: *Terezín* (Prague: Council of Jewish Religious Communities, 1965) [Memorial volume]

Karas, J.: *Music in Terezín 1941–1945* (New York: Beaufort Books, 1985)

DAVID BLOCH

theater, Yiddish The Yiddish theater came into existence largely through the efforts of one man, Avrom GOLDFADEN. Until the last decades of the nineteenth century, it was impossible to talk of a Yiddish theater. With the exception of performers such as the *badkhn* ("wedding bard") and of the *purimshpil* (Purim play, enacting Esther's triumph over Haman), drama was not a part of Jewish life. It was only under the influence of Moses MENDELSSOHN's *Haskole* (*Haskalah*, Jewish Enlightenment) that things began to change. Certain disciples of Mendelssohn such as Etinger, Aksenfeld, and Gotlober wrote highly didactic Yiddish plays which were widely read by the 1860s. Nevertheless, Goldfaden's creation, although influenced by the *purimshpil* and *Haskole* dramas, was largely a creation out of nothing.

1876 is regarded as the year the Yiddish theater was born. In Jassy, Romania, Goldfaden found his first actors, Israel Grodner and his assistant, Sakher Goldstein. Grodner was a *Broderzinger*, a type of cafe entertainer who performed songs and monologues about everyday Jewish life. Goldfaden's first plays were semi-improvised musicals which imposed a certain continuity on the traditional *Broderzinger* format. He began touring all over Europe, writing more substantial plays for his ever-expanding company. With certain exceptions they were of little literary worth, as Goldfaden himself admitted. But their folk quality and their mixture of melodrama, music and moralizing made them extremely popular.

Goldfaden had achieved his goal. He had created a Yiddish theater and, almost single-handedly, provided it with a repertoire. New companies evolved rapidly, often headed by graduates of Goldfaden's troupe. By the turn of the century, growing anti-Semitism and the Czar's prohibitive edicts had driven over a million Jews to the New World. New York became the major center for Yiddish theater. Competition was fierce and standards not always very high. Playwrights such as Hurwitz and Lateiner "baked" (that is, mass-produced) domestic melodramas and bombastic operettas. The partisan public was much more interested in the personalities of David Kessler, Jacob P. Adler, Boris Thomashevsky, and the other stars than in the roles they were playing. It was the era of *shund* (literally: "rubbish, trash"), of poor quality, "popular" theater.

War was declared against *shund* by Jacob GORDIN (1853–1909). His plays, many of them adaptations of European works, were often mediocre. But they possessed a realism of character and situation which was new to the Yiddish theater. Gradually, audiences and actors came to appreciate Gordin's demands for a more naturalistic acting style and greater respect for the text. The Gordin era, the so-called "Golden Age" of the Yiddish theater, had begun.

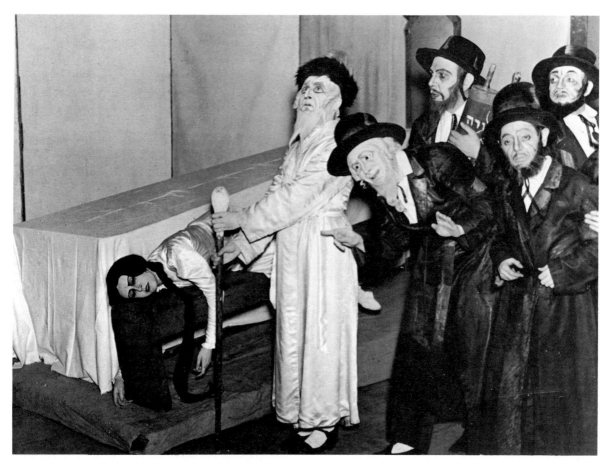

Performance of S. An-ski's The Dybbuk *by the Habimah Theater Company*

By the first decade of the twentieth century, Yiddish literature was flourishing under the leadership of the three classicists MENDELE MOKHER SEFARIM (1834?–1917), SHOLEM ALEICHEM (1859–1916) and I. L. PERETZ (1852–1915). Writers such as Sholem ASH, Kobrin, Pinski, Peretz HIRSHBEYN, and later, H. LEYVIK, were writing plays which ranged in style from the naturalist to the symbolist. The heirs of *Haskole* idealism and didacticism, they explored contemporary Jewish concerns, especially the question of Jewish identity and the relationship with tradition. Their works, often written from a left-wing perspective, examined the plight of the Jew and the individual's duty to society.

However, it was not until 1908 that there was a Yiddish theater capable of performing this repertoire. It was then that one of the new generation of dramatists, Peretz Hirshbeyn, formed the first Yiddish art theater, touring mainly in and around Odessa. It disbanded less than two years later, but the troupe's commitment to serious drama bore fruit. By the 1920s, the Yiddish art theater was thriving in every Yiddish-speaking community, drawing on and contributing to the developments in the European theater.

The new movement had its flag-bearers. The Vilna troupe under David Herman, best known for their 1920 premiere of S. AN-SKI's *Tsvishn tsvey veltn: der dibek* (Between two worlds: the Dybbuk), toured all over the Yiddish-speaking world between 1916 and 1924. The Moscow Yiddish State Art Theater (known by the acronym GOSET), founded in 1919, was the most influential of some twenty state-subsidized companies in the Soviet Union. Both the Vilna troupe and GOSET became identified with an expressionist style which, for many, became almost synonymous with "serious" Yiddish drama. Poland, despite ever stricter censorship, could boast Weichert's highly experimental *Yung teater* ("Young Theater") as well as the Kaminska family's Warsaw Yiddish Art Theater (or VYKT). The American Yiddish stage was dominated by Maurice Schwartz's Yiddish Art Theater, which opened in 1918 and survived until 1950. Though not always faithful to the principles of the European art theater, Schwartz fought to maintain a high standard and provided dramatists with a theater for their new plays. Also worthy of note were the amateurs of the socialist ARTEF under Benno Schneider.

The Holocaust, Stalin's purges and the abandonment of Yiddish brought about a rapid decline in the Yiddish theater. State Yiddish theaters in Poland, Romania, and, more recently, Israel, still perform to dwindling numbers, whilst, elsewhere, small groups of actors continue to tour, presenting mostly musical comedies. Nevertheless, the revival of interest in Yiddish culture means that the future of Yiddish theater, though uncertain, is by no means bleak.

FURTHER READING

Beck, E.: *Kafka and the Yiddish Theater* (Madison: University of Wisconsin, 1971)

Hapgood, H.: *The Spirit of the Ghetto* (London and New York: Funk & Wagnalls Co., 1902)

Landis, J. C.: *The Dybbuk and Other Great Yiddish Plays* (London, New York and Toronto: Bantam, 1966)

Lifson, D. S.: *The Yiddish Theater in America* (Cranbury: A. S. Barnes, 1965)

Sandrow, N.: *Vagabond Stars: A World History of Yiddish Theater* (New York: Limelight, 1986)

The Drama Review: Jewish theater edition (New York: New York University and MIT Press, 1980)

DAVID SCHNEIDER

Ticho, Anna (1894–1980) Israeli artist. Born in Brünn (Brno), Moravia, she had her first drawing lessons at the age of 12 and went to art school in Vienna at 15. She emigrated to Jerusalem in 1912 and married the Austrian ophthalmologist Dr Ticho. After a short absence during the First World War, they both returned to Jerusalem in 1919 where they lived permanently except for short trips to Paris, Amsterdam, London, and New York.

Anna Ticho brought to Palestine memories of such painters as Gustav Klimt, Egon Schiele, and Oskar Kokoshka. Their psychological probings and expressionistic distortion of line can also be seen in her art. At first the new landscape was difficult for Ticho to master, but slowly, through her natural gift of draughtsmanship, her surroundings took on a special appearance. For Ticho, who lived through the growth of Jerusalem from a small village to a major capital, Jerusalem became the ultimate symbol of Israel itself. This is expressed in the countless drawings she made of its majestic Judean landscape. Relying primarily upon pencil, charcoal, or sometimes brown and red chalk, the forms emerge out of rough chaotic lines whose internal parts are filled with details of gnarled natural shapes. Hundreds of drawings later, Ticho did not need the actual landscape in front of her in order to depict it. In 1955, when her husband's illness forced her to work indoors, she drew the landscape endlessly from memory. (In the 1960s, when she went to Paris for a few months, she found herself sitting by the Seine drawing the mountains of the Judean landscape.) After the death of her husband these later drawings, done on large sheets, were no less authentic and majestic than the original ones done in earlier years. In her later years, with failing eyesight, Ticho forsook the large paper and began to draw on small pads. This same landscape now became even more abstracted since the small pads enabled her to show the essence of the landscape she loved with very few lines.

Ticho's work was not limited to landscape. Between the 1930s and the 1950s she became involved with figurative drawings inspired by the old, infirm patients who attended her husband's clinic. Ticho brought to these expressive faces not a mere distorted contour line but their suffering. Her expressionistic approach, where the personality of the sitter penetrates the outer shell, is directly related to such influences as Klimt and Schiele and the psychoanalytical theories of Sigmund FREUD which permeated the Austrian capital of Ticho's youth.

Anna Ticho was awarded the prestigious Israel prize in 1980, shortly before she died.

ELAINE SHEFER

Timerman, Jacobo (b.1923) Argentinan journalist. Born in Russia in a village where all the Jews were exterminated by the Nazis in 1942, Timerman emigrated to Argentina with his parents in 1928. He became a political journalist in 1947 and founded the newspaper *La Opinion* in Buenos Aires in 1971. He campaigned tirelessly for human rights in spite of threats from death squads. He was arrested in 1977 by military extremists, tortured, and held secretly for six months in prison, which was followed by two years of house arrest. No charges were ever brought against him.

He describes this experience and the political background to it in *Prisoner Without a Name, Cell Without a Number* (1981), which was made into a television film in 1986. This book analyzes the causes behind the political violence and terrorism in Argentina during successive military governments. It also analyzes the covert anti-Semitism in Argentina which became open with the pro-Nazi military government which took over in 1976. Much of the torture and ill-treatment Timerman suffered in prison was motivated by the blind anti-Semitism of his captors, who openly expressed their admiration of the Nazis. Timerman explores the reasons for hatred of the Jews, analyzing the different motives behind political extermination and genocide. He commented. "The enemy can be converted; he wasn't born an enemy. The Jew was born a Jew" (p.67) and "Some things cannot be proven. And one of them . . . is the right of Jews to exist". He declares that "The Jew is a man under total suspicion" (p.145). He adumbrates his reasons for espousing Zionism in the 1940s and the political and moral conflicts facing people at the time. He concludes that "The most important lesson of the Holocaust does not lie in the horrors committed by the Nazis . . . it will be understood not so much for the number of victims as for the magnitude of the silence" (p.141), which he clarifies as both the Jewish silence and the silence of the majority whenever their survival is endangered by their protest.

This is an important book for understanding the phenomena of torture and political terrorism, particularly in the context of Latin America. It also provides a cogent analysis of the meaning of being Jewish in the eyes of non-Jews.

Timerman was deprived of his Argentine citizenship, had his goods confiscated, and was expelled from the country.

BIBLIOGRAPHY
Prisoner Without a Name, Cell Without a Number, trans. T. Talbot. (London: Weidenfeld and Nicholson, 1981)

ANN DUNCAN

Tin Pan Alley Cole Porter, the most WASP-ish of White Anglo-Saxon Protestants, once approached the Jewish songwriter Sammy Cahn – who wrote *It's Magic, I'll Walk Alone,* and *All The Way*, as well as *Bei Mir Bist Du Schon* – and told him: "I wish I'd been born on the Lower East Side like you. Just think what I might have produced!" There is no doubt that the Lower East Side of New York and its Jewish inhabitants had a tremendous influence on the popular musical tastes of America for more than half a century. Nor was this only in the songs that, on the surface, "sound" Jewish, such as *Bei Mir Bist Du Schon*, or perhaps Ziggy Elman's *And The Angels Sing*.

Irving Berlin might have written *Cohen Owes Me 97 Dollars*, but he is better known for the best-selling Christmas song of all time, *White Christmas*, which by 1986 had sold something like 300 million record copies, more than any other popular song in history. Add to that notable achievement, *Easter Parade, God Bless America*, and *There's No Business Like Showbusiness*, and one has some idea of the significance of a songwriter who has produced no fewer than 3,000 tunes – more hits than anyone else, although, as he put it to this writer, "more flops too". Yet

Sheet-music cover of one of Irving Berlin's early compositions

Berlin began his musical career singing in the choir of the synagogue where his father was cantor – in Cherry Street on the Lower East Side, to which the Baline family had moved from Siberia.

It was a familiar route. Al Jolson, George Burns – both of whom would claim to have written many songs – and Harold Arlen, who wrote *Over The Rainbow*, *Stormy Weather*, and *That Old Black Magic*, were all cantorial sons. So the link between the synagogue and the world of popular music was well established. Jerome Kern, who came from very different, almost patrician, Jewish stock, recognized the supremacy of Irving Berlin in his own field. "Berlin", he said, "has no place in American music. He IS American music".

There was a time when four out of the top five songwriters in what became known as Tin Pan Alley were all Jews – Berlin, Kern, Richard Rodgers, and, of course, George GERSHWIN.

When Gershwin, the writer of *Swanee*, *Rhapsody In Blue*, and *I Got Rhythm*, produced his black folk opera, *Porgy and Bess*, one critic said that it really wasn't Negro music he had written at all: "It's Jewish music". Gershwin wrote *Swanee* for Al Jolson with his Jewish lyricist Irving Caesar, who went on to produce *Is It True What They Say About Dixie?* (The Jewish connection with the Deep South, Black and White, was plainly quite prodigious).

Jews have inhabited the Alley all the way from Gus Kahn – *Toot Toot Tootsie* – through such established names as Johnny Green – *Body and Soul* – and David Raksin – *Laura* – right up to Simon and Garfunkel and Bob Dylan. They were all heirs of those Jewish fiddlers, the *klezmorim* (see KLEZMER), who went from town to town, wedding to *bar mitzvah*, some of whom earned the traditional penalty for not pleasing their audiences – the sound of a crashing tin pan in the alleys where they played.

MICHAEL FREEDLAND

Tobias, Lily (1887–1984) Welsh novelist. Born in Swansea, one of a large family of Orthodox immigrants, she was the only Welsh voice among the Anglo-Jewish novelists of inter-War years. After leaving school she started writing in her teens, influenced by her unfashionably Zionist father and by the swirl of Socialist activity in the Swansea Valley. She found outlets for her early pieces in the local Socialist newspaper, and, later, in the *Zionist Review*. Her pacifist views, confirmed by the imprisonment of her two brothers in the war, are expressed in her novel *Eunice Fleet* (1933).

Wales provided the background for her short stories *The Nationalists and Other Goluth Studies* (1922), which show how awakening Jewish consciousness can lead to an interest in Zionism encouraged, in several instances, by the Welsh conception of Jews as "the people of the Book". In her first full-length novel, *My Mother's House* (1931), the setting moves between Wales, London, and Palestine, and presents, as well as the spiritual pilgrimage of the protagonist, a panorama of contemporary Anglo-Jewry, portraying with penetrating psychological insight its var-

759

ious political, religious, and cultural milieux. The heroine's work in Palestine provokes much discussion of Jewish race and nationality, as well as interesting accounts of the struggle to tame the land. Its sequel, *The Samaritan*, was started in 1937 but published only in 1939 due to the tragic death of Tobias's husband in the Arab riots of 1938. The first-hand portrayal of life under the Mandate, the tensions between Arabs, Jewish settlers, and British administrators, and among the Jews themselves, are all illuminating.

Lily Tobias was a life-long communal worker both in Britain and in Israel, where she settled, writing newspaper and magazine articles until her final years.

VERA COLEMAN

Toch, Ernst (1887–1964) American composer, pianist, and educator. He was born in Vienna and died in Los Angeles. Toch was a student of medicine and philosophy, and taught himself music by studying the scores of the great masters. In 1909 he won the Mozart Prize, in 1910 the Mendelssohn Prize, and in four successive years won the Austrian State Prize for composition. On going to Germany in 1909 he studied piano with Willy Rehberg in Frankfurt, and, in 1913, became a teacher at the Hochschule in Mannheim. In 1921 Toch received a Ph.D. with a dissertation on the study of melody. This was published in Berlin in 1923 as *Melodielehre*. From 1929 to 1933 he lived in Berlin, teaching both composition and piano. Upon the rise of the Nazis he left Berlin, first going to Paris, and then settling in the USA in 1935. In 1937 he moved to Los Angeles to teach at UCLA and later, at the University of Southern California. From that time he wrote several film scores.

One of this century's most prolific composers, and one of the few to win two Pulitzer Prizes, Toch was honored in Europe as well as in the USA, receiving the Cross of Honor for Science and Art from the Austrian government, and elected member of the National Institute of Arts and Letters. In 1975 UCLA founded an Ernst Toch Archive of his manuscripts, books, and memorabilia. Besides the hundreds of composi-

tions, Toch wrote a textbook, *The Shaping Forces in Music* (1948).

Toch was never averse to experimentation, but his inspiration was definitely romantic. His music is profoundly emotional, yet always carefully structured. The idiom is mostly tonal with great emphasis on melodic flow and rhythmic vitality. He was master of the orchestra and produced great textures in his orchestral compositions.

SAMUEL H. ADLER

Torczyner, Harry [Naphtali Herz Tur-Sinai] (1886–1975) Israeli philologist and Bible scholar. Torczyner, born in Lemberg and educated in Vienna, emigrated to Palestine in 1933, and taught at the Hebrew University in Jerusalem.

Torczyner translated several books of the Bible into German. A highly original Bible scholar, he rejected Wellhausen's documentary hypothesis in favor of a more radical theory of his own. Torczyner posited an ancient epic-historical framework, no longer extant, in which our surviving biblical materials were once set. Thus, the poems in the book of Psalms belonged originally to a grand narrative about King David, while Proverbs had been part of a Solomonic biography.

Torczyner's approach to biblical and Semitic textual interpretation was equally original. He wrote three major commentaries to Job, respectively in German, Hebrew, and English. Although his theory that Job is a translation of an Aramaic original has not won general acceptance, his studies have shed more light on Job than any previous work. His book on Proverbs, *Mishlei Shelomo* (1947), is also extremely valuable. Torczyner's collected essays on biblical texts and institutions, rabbinic Hebrew, problems in the history of the Hebrew language, and related subjects, are available to the Hebrew reader in *The language and the book*, 3 vols (1951–6). Torczyner's *Peshuto shel mikra* (1962–8; Plain sense of scripture), was modeled on the like-named *Mikra kifeschuto* of Arnold EHRLICH.

Torczyner was both a historian of Hebrew

and a contributor to its development as a modern language. His book *The Lachish letters* (1938) deciphered a collection of Hebrew letters from the biblical period. He completed the seventeen-volume historical dictionary of Hebrew begun by the founder of Modern Hebrew, Eliezer BEN-YEHUDA. Torczyner, who coined the modern Hebrew word for flatware, edited the periodical *Leshonenu*, and served as president of the Academy of the Hebrew Language, the ultimate authority in Israel on proper Hebrew usage.

BIBLIOGRAPHY

Tur-Sinai, N. [Torczyner, H.]: *The Book of Job, a New Commentary* (Jerusalem: Kiryath Sepher, 1967)

S. DAVID SPERLING

Treinin, Avner (b.1928) Israeli poet and scientist. Avner Treinin was born in Tel Aviv and trained in the natural sciences at the Hebrew University and in Cambridge, England. Treinin is now professor of physical chemistry at the Hebrew University of Jerusalem. Apart from scientific publications and his volumes of poetry he has written several school textbooks on chemistry.

Treinin's first collection of poems, *Azovei kir* appeared in 1957. The poems very often view the collective and are particularly concerned with the Holocaust and the recent events in the history of the Jewish people. Treinin has won several important prizes, among them the Jerusalem prize (1979) and the Brenner prize (1986).

Treinin occasionally incorporates scientific knowledge into his poetry to form original images, almost always, however, accessible to the layman. In Treinin's poems man confronts his fate, and Treinin himself confronts his past. Images are an important element in the poems, particularly landscape images. Among his other books are *Hasha'ar hasatum* (1975), *Hama'arakha hamakhzorit* (1978), *Leket shiheha* (1982), and *Hahzarot* (1988). Individual poems have appeared in English translation in various publications and anthologies.

AHUVIA KAHANE

Trilling, Lionel (1905–1975) American literary critic and novelist. Trilling once praised Edmund Wilson for making the literary life handsomely real. The same should be said about Trilling: although a professor of English literature at Columbia University in New York, he transcended the role of "New York intellectual" and university teacher by devising a style, a way of thinking about culture, which gave a glimpse of the drama and integrity of a mind fully engaged with the age. After his death his diaries began to appear in journals, and a steady stream of studies of Trilling's achievement were published. What was revealed was a moving story of a struggle against anti-Semitism in the university, and of the discovery by the son of lower-middle-class immigrant Jewish parents of a way towards acculturation and entry into the cosmpolitan world of high culture.

The "we" of a Trilling essay reached beyond Jewry, beyond his university and New York, to a community of literary intellectuals which he in no small part invented. Jewishness was central to an understanding of Trilling's cosmopolitanism, although after an early association with Elliot Cohen's *Menorah Journal*, Jewishness was noticeable by its almost complete absence from his work. In 1944 he argued that Jewishness was basically irrelevant for anyone seeking to become an American artist or intellectual. Trilling sought the capacious, grave tones of an Oxford don, and published books (*Matthew Arnold*, 1939; *E. M. Forster*, 1943) which are calculatedly remote from the fierce internecine literary and political struggles around him. His novel *The Middle of the Journey* (1947), which portrayed the moral and intellectual dilemmas of the appeal of Communism, was a powerful vehicle for his political concerns. In *The Liberal Imagination* (1950), Trilling emerged as an essayist of power, learning, and subtlety. The horizons of his thought always seemed grandly redolent of concern for culture and the role of the intellectual. These concerns were central to his last book, *Sincerity and Authenticity* (1974), which ended with a passionate denunciation of the adversary culture of the 1960s. Not a systematic thinker – he had an allergy to closure of discussion – he left a legacy rich in humanistic complexity.

761

FURTHER READING

Krupnick, M.: *Lionel Trilling and the Fate of Cultural Criticism* (Evanston: Northwestern University Press, 1986)

ERIC HOMBERGER

Tschernichowski, Saul (1875–1943) Hebrew poet and translator. Though traditionally coupled with H. N. BIALIK as one of the great poets of the modern Hebrew renaissance, Tschernichowski has not maintained the attention he once enjoyed. His poetry does not fit easily with the normative generational markers: Bialik, Natan ALTERMAN, Yehuda AMICHAI. His output was too massive, too varied in both subject and form, and thus defies easy categorization.

Tshernichowski's background differs from that of most modern Hebrew poets. Born and reared not in the heartland of eastern European Jewish settlement, but at its fringe, in Mikhailovka in the southern Ukraine, not in a *shtetl* but in a village, he was more open to foreign, natural, and cultural influences than any of his contemporaries. When he was sent to Odessa for his *gymnasium* education, he already knew both Hebrew and Russian well and could thus enter the dynamic cultural life of that community, one of the centers of Hebrew creativity and modern, secular nationalism. Adept at learning languages, he added German, French, English, Latin, and Greek to his repertoire during his Odessa years (1890–9). The impact of his wide reading of poetry – Romantic poetry, in particular – in Russian, German, and English can be seen in his first two volumes, *Hezyonot umanginot* (Visions and melodies); Part One: 1898; Part Two: 1900). These early poems already evidence two characteristic features: a relative freedom from echoes of rabbinic sources and a fascination with a variety of European prosodic forms.

Tschernichowski's residence in Heidelberg and Lausanne (1899–1906), where he studied medicine, exposed him to the world of German literature, particularly to Geothe and the Nietzschean vitalism in vogue in those years. His cultivation of the ballad, the sonnet, the idyll, and the long narrative poem evolves from that period, as does his espousal of the enjoyment of the sensual world. Though he yearns nostalgically in his idylls for the warmth of his childhood (*Levivot, Brit milah, Kehom hayom*), he writes savagely about the terrors of Jewish history in *Barukh mimagentza*. His poems sympathetic to Hellenic ideals or the "false prophets" of the Hebrew Scriptures infuriated many of his readers.

Returning to Russia, Tschernichowski had difficulties in finding employment as a doctor and, after several years of wandering, finally established himself in St Petersburg in 1910. In 1914 upon the outbreak of the First World War, he was called to serve with the army at the front. His experience in the war and in the general turmoil in Russia in the years following the Bolshevik Revolution jolted him towards the pole of alienation. The poetry of the period often embodies the tension between his perception that civilizations are crumbling about him, and his will to believe in the redemptive power of art. His two great sonnet cycles of the period, *Lashemesh* (1919; To the sun) and *Al hadam* (1923; On the blood) are the result of these conflicting impulses.

Having been released – together with a group of Hebrew writers from the Soviet Union in 1922, Tschernichowski settled in Berlin where he worked at writing and editing. He devoted most of his energies to short stories, often keenly erotic, and numerous masterful translations from world classics; several essays; a play; and the preparation of his collected works for the Berlin edition. The latter, a ten-volume opus published between 1928 and 1934, established him firmly as one of the classic writers of modern Hebrew literature.

Tschernichowski finally settled in Palestine in 1931 and remained there until his death. Residing first in Tel Aviv where he worked as a physician in the municipal schools, he moved in 1936 to Jerusalem where he wrote the last two volumes of his poems. His adaptation to the new environment was remarkable. In his verse he was able to shift from the Ashkenazic, penultimate stress to the Sephardic, ultimate stress, a feat few other Hebrew poets achieved successfully. He found a renewed belief in nature and vitalism embodied, this time, in the

Saul Tschernichowski

burgeoning new Jewish community, particularly in the phenomenon of life on the land. And yet, the troubles of the time – the rise of Nazism and the Arab riots of 1936–9 – inform and energize the poems of those years. His political commitment was intensely nationalistic, often drawing upon a mythic past. His last two volumes, *Re'i adamah* (1940; See earth) and *Kokhevei shamayim rehokim* (1944; Stars of distant skies) contain some of his finest poetry. His narrative, confessional poem, *Amma dedehava* (1943; The golden people), is a summation of his life-long beliefs embodied in a description of people resettling the land.

ARNOLD J. BAND

Tsederboym [Zederbaum, Tsederbaum], **Aleksander** (1816–1893) Polish publisher, ed-

itor, and author. Born in Zamosc, Poland, Tsederboym studied Jewish and general subjects with private tutors and was influenced by the *maskilim* (enlighteners) who met often in his parents' home. Following his marriage at 19, he lived in Lublin for five years, directing his own education, and in 1840 settled in Odessa to engage in business. In this bustling port city he discovered his talents as an intercessor with government officials on behalf of Jewish causes. Endowed with immense energy and zealous to reform Jewish life, he used his lobbying skills to win permission to issue periodicals in Hebrew, Yiddish, and Russian.

At a time when most of his fellow enlighteners urged the use of German, Tsederboym advocated the shift to Russian (which he himself knew imperfectly). Yet in 1860 this Russifier founded the Hebrew weekly *Hamelitz* (The mediator). Later appearing biweekly and finally daily, this served for more than four decades as a central organ of the Enlightenment in eastern Europe, printing the works of virtually every important contemporary Hebrew writer and, after 1885, championing the *Hovevei Zion* (Lovers of Zion) movement, whose legalization in Russia was largely Tsederboym's work.

In 1862 he began to issue *Kol mevaser* (Herald), a supplement to *Hamelitz* "in plain Yiddish so that ordinary people, and even women, may learn what is happening in the world" (*Hamelitz*, xxiv, 1862). S. J. Abramowitz (MENDELE MOKHER SEFARIM) and Y.-Y., Linetski with great consequence for Yiddish literature, published their first Yiddish works here.

Moving to St Petersburg, then a budding center of Jewish life in Russia, Tsederboym established the first Russian–Jewish periodical in the capital, the *Vyestnik russkikh yevreyev* (Messenger to the Jews of Russia), which lasted from January 1871 to summer 1873, and, in 1881, the first modern Yiddish periodical, the *Yidishes folks-blat* (Jewish People's Journal), whose importance for Yiddish literature cannot be exaggerated.

"Erez" (Cedar), as Tsederboym signed himself, was an astute publicist, one of the earliest Yiddish literary critics, and an innovator in trying to standardize Yiddish spelling and forge a style close to spoken (essentially southeastern)

Yiddish. The grandfather of Julius Martov (the Menshevik leader), he opposed radical assimilationists as much as he did fanatic pietists. Author of forgotten anti-hasidic tracts, a crotchety editor who appended long comments to contributor's articles, a figure who was often lampooned for his bad Russian and was not always taken seriously by his contemporaries, Tsederboym nevertheless achieved much and should be better known.

FURTHER READING

Getzler, I.: *Martov; a Political Biography of a Russian Social Democrat* (Cambridge: Cambridge University Press; Melbourne: Melbourne University Press, 1967)

LEONARD PRAGER

Tsinberg [Zinberg], **Yisroel** (1873–1939) Literary historian. Born in a village near Lanovits, Volhynia, to a well-to-do merchant family, Tsinberg acquired his early education from private tutors. He studied chemical engineering in Karlsruhe, and the University of Basel, where he completed his doctorate in 1898. That year he moved to St Petersburg where he became head of the chemistry laboratory of one of the leading railway-car factories in Russia, a position he held until his arrest in 1938. His enormous scholarly output in the field of Jewish literature results from his work in his free time.

Tsinberg launched his literary career with a popular science book in Yiddish in 1899, which he followed with numerous critical and literary-historical studies, written in Russian, Yiddish, and, occasionally, Hebrew. He was responsible for the first-class representation of modern Hebrew and Yiddish literature in the 16-volume Russian *Yevreiskaya entsiklopediya* (1908–13).

After the Russian Revolution Tsinberg withdrew from active academic and literary affairs, publishing next to nothing in Soviet Yiddish periodicals, but continuing to publish his work in non-Soviet Yiddish publications. It was during the early Soviet years, and, it is said out of literary loneliness, that Tsinberg embarked on his multivolume masterpiece, *Di geshikhte fun der literatur ba yidn* (History of Jewish literature). After writing four volumes in Russian, Tsinberg

decided, apparently in 1919, to publish the whole of his magnum opus in Yiddish. He reworked the completed volumes and set out on the rest. The eight volumes of the *Geshikhte* were published in ten books in Vilna, appearing between 1919 and 1937. The work takes the history of Jewish literature from the Middle Ages through to the Enlightenment movement in Russia, and remains one of the fundamental sources for students and scholars of Jewish literature.

Tsinberg had completed the first part of volume nine but had not yet sent it to his Vilna publishers when he was arrested. A committee of Yiddish writers was established in New York to rescue him, but to no avail. He was sent to exile in Vladivostok, where he died, sick and weary, after a cruel journey. Years later Brandeis University succeeded in acquiring a microfilm of Tsinberg's surviving unpublished manuscripts from Leningrad, and finally, volume nine was published in New York in 1966.

FURTHER READING

Reyzen, Z.: *Leksikon fun der yidisher literatur, prese un filologye*, vol. 3, B. A. Kletskin (Vilna: 1929) 310–17

Leksikon fun der nayer yidisher literatur, vol. 7 (New York: Congress for Jewish Culture, 1968) 585–95

DOVID KATZ

Tucholsky, Kurt (1890–1935) German essayist, critic, and poet. A native of Berlin, Tucholsky took a doctorate in law at the University of Jena in 1915. His three-and-a-half years of military service turned him into an ardent pacifist. In 1913 he began to contribute to *Die Schaubühne* (renamed *Die Weltbühne* in 1918), becoming a close associate of this important journal's founder, Siegfried Jacobsohn, and its sometime editor, Carl von Ossietzky. For his essays, poems, reviews, and aphorisms that appeared in *Die Weltbühne* as well as numerous other journals and books, Tucholsky used his own name, as well as the pseudonyms Peter Panter, Theobald Tiger, Ignaz a Wrobel, and Kaspar Hauser – a situation that he called "gay schizophrenia". After 1924 Tucholsky lived in

Germany only sporadically, residing mostly in France, Switzerland, and Sweden, and considering Sweden his home from 1929. Ailing and profoundly depressed by the course of events in Germany, Tucholsky fell silent and took his own life at Hindås shortly before his 46th birthday.

Tucholsky's satiric oeuvre is flanked by two charming romantic idylls with autobiographical elements, *Rheinsberg: ein Bilderbuch für Verliebte* (1912), and *Schloss Gripsholm* (1931; *Castle Gripsholm*, 1985). His satirical sallies were directed against nationalism, militarism, the injustices of the state, and the dehumanizing tendencies of the age, as well as against human stupidity, cupidity, and indifference in their myriad guises. Tucholsky's contributions to the fabled Berlin cabarets enlisted the services of the foremost composers and performers of the time. One of his most controversial books, *Deutschland, Deutschland über alles* (1929; trans. 1972), a mordant critique of the Weimar Republic, featured the photomontages of John Heartfield. Having left the Jewish fold in 1911, Tucholsky painted, in 16 monologues, an unflattering portrait of "Herr Wendriner", an assimilationist, opportunistic, spiritually empty German Jew.

Since the end of the Second World War Tucholsky's work has been deemed to be of undiminished timeliness and validity, and in both East and West Germany he is published in a manner befitting a modern classic.

FURTHER READING

Poor, H.: *Kurt Tucholsky and the Ordeal of Germany, 1914–1935* (New York: Scribner's, 1968)

Grenville, B. P.: *Kurt Tucholsky: The Ironic Sentimentalist* (London: Oswald Wolff, 1981)

Soldenhoff, R. von, ed.: *Kurt Tucholsky* (Berlin: Quadriga, 1985) [picture/biography]

HARRY ZOHN

Tumarkin, Yigal (b.1933) Israeli artist. Born in Dresden, Tumarkin was brought to Palestine in 1935. He started to study art seriously in 1954 with the sculptor Rudi Lehman, in the artists' village, Ein Hod, south of Haifa. In 1955 he left for East Berlin (his father, a non-Jew, was a film director there), and later lived in Amsterdam and Paris until 1961, when he returned to Israel. In Berlin Tumarkin worked for the Berliner Ensemble (the Bertolt Brecht company) as set decorator. Tumarkin's artistic activities include sculpture (usually monumental), painting, drawing, stage decoration, graphics, and jewelry design.

Tumarkin is highly aware of all the manifestations of twentieth-century art, and his work has undergone many and frequent changes. It exhibits, however, two salient characteristics: anti-estheticism and Expressionism. Both are artistic and political choices. For ten years, from the late 1950s to the late 1960s, Tumarkin's canvases consisted of collages of a single or of several heterogeneous everyday objects. *Panic over a Pair of Trousers* (1961), for example, features a pair of real trousers. By the end of the 1960s the artist incorporated casts of human and animal body parts. *Portrait of the Artist as a Tortured Saint* (1965) consists of a cogwheel, the cast of a hand and a head projecting out of a hollow body.

The expressivity and anti-estheticism of the dissected body parts used by Tumarkin are politically oriented. Thus *He Walked in the Fields* (1966) is named after a well-known novel (see SHAMIR, MOSHE) that glorified the Israeli hero in the War of Independence. In contrast, the artist wished in this representation to arouse repugnance and horror, and therefore to denounce the devastation of war. Similarly, the incorporation of weapons or their parts in Tumarkin's monuments to the fallen, was another means of political opposition. *The Big Chief* (1968) a monument to the Israeli occupation of the Golan Heights that was erected in the northern Galilee town of Kiryat Shemona, consists of three enemy cannons painted in vivid primaries – red, yellow, and blue – standing in front of a tall black sculpture made of casts of different war instruments, such as rifles, bullets, and helmets.

For Tumarkin excessive order and clarity serve to express pain and disaster. One example is *Monument to the Holocaust and Revival* (1975) in Tel Aviv's Malkhai Israel Square. The monument consists of an inverted pyramid constructed of metal bars and glass. According to the artist, the narrow inverted tip creates a feeling of enclosure and hence depression, contrasted by the soaring height of the base of the pyramid connoting the burst of happiness and liberty. The dark glass reflects the surrounding environment: movement, dynamism, and constant change.

The stylistic clarity and transparency of this artist's work was shortlived. From the mid 1970s Tumarkin's sculptures have been made of earth. "Earth Art" has been in vogue in much contemporary western art since the mid 1960s, but in Tumarkin's hands these works also acquire a pronounced local political significance: a reference to the "Earth of Israel" and the importance of The Land in much of early Zionist ideology. This meeting between two trends is indeed the core of Tumarkin's art – the universal, which finds expression in the profusion of modernist styles, and the local, the constant involvement in Israeli reality and politics.

ESTHER LEVINGER

Tuwim, Julian (1894–1953) Polish poet. Born in Lodz to a family well assimilated into Polish society, Tuwim moved to Warsaw in 1916, and soon afterwards embarked on his literary career. With four of his friends he founded, in 1920, the literary monthly *Skamander* which gave its name to the poetic movement whose recognized leader he became. The Skamander group stood in the forefront of Polish literature until the outbreak of the Second World War.

Along with his lyric poetry, vitalistic yet with metaphysical and even macabre undertones, Tuwim wrote many satires in verse as well as in prose, often directed towards the extreme nationalistic party, with its anti-Semitic tendencies. He was himself a target of its anti-Semitic propaganda, which often described him as a foreigner who defiled the Polish language. Tuwim responded with brilliant spite, but he directed his satire also at the Jewish nationalists and particulary at the Zionists. Jewish themes often appear in Tuwim's pre-war poetry, often characterized by a kind of self-hatred. Only during the Second World War, when he was an exile in New York, did he compose what amounts to a proud assertion of belonging to his

Julian Tuwim

race: *We, Polish Jews* was written in April 1944, a unique document, dedicated "to my mother in Poland or to her beloved shadow". In New York Tuwim completed his long poem "Flowers of Poland" which was published in 1947, after his return to Poland, and which appeared to be his total acceptance of the new Communist regime. He did not in his later work achieve anything comparable to his pre-war poetry fed, as it was in large measure, by his Jewish complex.

BIBLIOGRAPHY
Voices Within the Ark: The Modern Jewish Poets, ed. H. Schwartz and A. Rudolph (New York: 1980); *We, Polish Jews* (Jerusalem: Magnes Press, 1984)

YORAM BRONOWSKI

766

U

Ullendorff, Edward (b.1920) British scholar of Semitic languages. Ullendorff was born in Zurich and received his schooling in Berlin. He attended the Universities of Jerusalem (MA) and Oxford (D.Phil.). After graduation from the Hebrew University in 1942 Ullendorff worked for the British Military Administration in Eritrea, serving at the same time as Ethiopian correspondent of the Hebrew newspaper *Ha'aretz*. After a brief period with the British Mandatory Government in Palestine (1947–8) Ullendorff moved to the United Kingdom, where he has been resident ever since: Lecturer/Reader in Semitic Languages, University of St Andrews, 1950–9; Professor of Semitic Languages and Literatures, University of Manchester, 1959–64; Professor of Ethiopian Studies, University of London, 1964–79, Professor of Semitic Languages, 1979–82. He is now Emeritus Professor, and a fellow (Vice-President 1980–2) of the British Academy.

For fully 40 years Ullendorff has been an active and influential scholar in Semitic studies, particularly in the Ethiopian field. His books on Ethiopian subjects include: *Exploration and Study of Abyssinia* (1945); *The Semitic Languages of Ethiopia* (1955); *The Ethiopians* (1960, 1973); *An Amharic Chrestomathy* (1965, 1978); *The Autobiography of Emperor Haile Sellassie I* (1976); *A Tigrinya Chrestomathy* (1985). He has also published catalogs of various collections of Ethiopian manuscripts.

Much of Ullendorff's writing is devoted to Semitica in general and to Hebraica and Judaica in particular. He is, for example, co-author of *An Introduction to the Comparative Grammar of the Semitic Languages* (1964). His work on Hebrew is concerned mainly with the biblical language, especially the manner of its elucidation with the help of other Semitic languages (e.g. Ugaritic). However, he has also published mediaeval Hebrew texts in *The Hebrew Letters of Prester John* (co-author, 1982) and several items dealing with Israeli Hebrew. The contents, as well as the language, of the Hebrew Bible have been the subject of a number of articles from Ullendorff's pen. He has also dealt with the question of Ethiopian Jewry ("Falashas"), for example in *Ethiopia and the Bible* (1968), a book which contains much important information on both Biblical and Ethiopian topics. He has shown a marked penchant for the Queen of Sheba, on whom he has written, as in J. B. Pritchard (ed.), *Solomon and Sheba* (1974).

Two volumes of Ullendorff's collected articles have appeared: *Is Biblical Hebrew a Language?* (1977) and *Studia Aethiopica et Semitica* (1987). He has published a volume of reminiscences of Jerusalem and Ethiopia in *The Two Zions* (1988). A Festschrift in Ullendorff's honor appeared in 1989.

FURTHER READING
Barr, J.: *Journal of Semitic Studies* 26 (1981) 115ff

SIMON HOPKINS

Ulpan The Ulpan (the word is derived from the root *alef* – to teach, instruct) is an institution for teaching Hebrew to adults. The Ulpan was established in September 1949 by the

Israeli government shortly after the foundation of the State, out of the need to teach Hebrew effectively and within a short period of time to large numbers of immigrants. The Ulpan has played a central role in the dissemination of modern Hebrew and also helped immigrants to adjust to Israeli society. Between 1949 and 1987 about eight hundred thousand to a million adults learnt Hebrew by the Ulpan method.

The standard Ulpan runs for over six months, is based on a six-day, 30-hour academic week. Ulpanim in absorption centers offer accommodation for entire families for the period of their studies. A second type is the external Ulpan, where students come to study during the day. The *kibbutzim* offer working Ulpans, where students work for four hours a day and study Hebrew for four hours. University Ulpans have special programs that prepare students for academic studies. A less intensive institution is the Ulpanit which meets for four to ten hours of instruction weekly. The Ulpan framework has also been adapted for the teaching of Hebrew to immigrant children.

The Ulpan method is known throughout the world for its effectiveness. It is based on three main principles: the "direct method" of teaching Hebrew in Hebrew (a practice that grew out of pedagogic principles as well as the heterogenous nature of the classes); practice in the spoken language, centered at the beginners' stage around topics of everyday life; and a structured, graded syllabus. In its emphasis on communicative language, teaching the Ulpan has been a forerunner of modern methods of second language teaching.

FURTHER READING

Haramati, S.: *What is an Ulpan?* (New York: Department of Education and Culture of the Jewish Agency, 1967)
Weinberger, E.: *The Ulpan for Teaching Hebrew to Adults as a Second Language* (Jerusalem: Ministry of Education and Culture, 1979)

SHOSHANA BLUM-KULKA

Untermeyer, Louis (1885–1977) American anthologist and poet. Born in New York City,

Untermeyer was educated at public school 6, and Boy's High, which he left at 15 to work in the shipping room of his father's jewelry firm. In 1965 DeWitt Clinton awarded him the diploma that he had failed to earn in 1903. By 1923 he had become manager of the factory in Newark. His first book of verse had been published in 1910. By the time he was 57, he had edited, compiled, or written 95 books. Raised by a German governess, he translated 500 of Heine's lyrics, and wrote a biography, *Heinrich Heine: Paradox and Poet* (1937). His *Makers of the Modern World* (1954) presents the lives of 92 creative people. His *Lives of the Poets* (1959) covered 1,000 years of British and American literary history. He has compiled over 40 anthologies, served as poetry editor of several magazines, and written a number of children's books.

From 1961 to 1963, Untermeyer was consultant to the Library of Congress. He lectured at international conferences, as well as at many college campuses. He enjoyed the irony of having been appointed Phi Beta Kappa poet at Harvard in 1956, since he had been a high-school dropout.

The incisive critical introductions of his poetry anthologies made them useful in the classroom. When *Modern American Verse* first appeared in 1919, it was 170 pages; its eighth edition, *Modern American Poetry* has grown to 700 pages. Together with its companion volume, *Modern British Poetry*, first published in 1920, it has sold over a million copies, many as college textbooks.

Untermeyer's two autobiographies tell of his four marriages, and of his friendships with all the major literary figures of the twentieth century. His 50-year correspondence with Robert Frost was published in 1963 as *The Letters of Robert Frost to Louis Untermeyer*.

BIBLIOGRAPHY

From Another World (New York: Harcourt, 1939); *Bygones* (New York: Harcourt, 1965)

RUTH ROSENBERG

Urbach, Ephraim (b.1912) Rabbinic scholar. Urbach was born in Wloclawek, Poland

and was educated at the Jewish Theological Seminary in Breslau, and at the universities of Breslau and Rome. He was ordained as rabbi in 1934. Soon thereafter he accepted the position of Senior Lecturer at the Jewish Theological Seminary but emigrated to Israel in 1938.

Until 1941 Urbach was a teacher at the Rehavia *Gymnasium* in Jerusalem. After four years service with the British Army he became the Director of Ma'aleh secondary school in Jerusalem and later a lecturer in Talmud and Midrash at the Hebrew University. In 1960 he became Professor Emeritus of the Department of Jewish Studies at that University.

Urbach has concentrated his studies on Mishnah and Talmud, and has written some of the leading works on aspects of this field. His studies cover practically every branch of research into the Talmud and rabbinic literature, and also the *Aggadah*. His *Ba'alei hatosafot* (1955; The Tosafists, writings and methods), deals with the history of the Tosafists and their work, and analyzes their contribution to the development of the *halakhah*. In his major work *Hazal: pirkei emunot vede'ot* (1969; *The Sages, their Concepts and Beliefs*, 1975; revised and enlarged, 1979) Urbach summarizes rabbinic views on major theological issues. Based on an exhaustive study of the sources, this work examines the religious and social thought of the mishnaic and talmudic sages. Among Urbach's numerous publications are *Sefer pitron torah* (1978) a collection of *midrashim* and interpretations, and *The Halakhah: its Sources and Development* (1986).

For his work Urbach was awarded the Israel prize for Jewish Studies in 1955 and the Bialik Prize in 1982. He also served as President of the Israel Academy of Sciences and Humanities from 1980 to 1986.

JOHN MATTHEW

Uri, Aviva (b.1927) Israeli artist. Born in Safed, in 1956 Uri won the Dizengoff prize, and in 1957 had the first one-woman exhibition at the Tel Aviv Museum; she participated in the Venice Biennale in 1960. Her drawings were a direct reaction against the mainstream oil painting of Lyrical Abstraction which domin-

ated in Tel Aviv during the late 1940s and early 1950s, after the foundation of the New Horizons group. (Yossef ZARITSKY, Lea Nickel, Streichman, and Steimatzky). Yet like them, her subjective calligraphy is based on forms derived from nature and landscape. At the same time Aviva Uri's art opened up a new expressive alternative in the abstract mainstream in Israel. Amongst the artists she influenced are Gershuni and Raffi Lavie (who in his turn influenced the young generation of artists emerging in Tel Aviv during the 1970s and 1980s). Her medium is minimal: pencil or charcoal on paper, as are her subjects, minimized energetic statements, marked by a personal shorthand, yet with sensitive linear variety and richness. Although her art is influenced by Japanese calligraphy, it is not a direct derivation but is transmitted through Western artists such as Hartung.

Uri appears to be returning to several major themes, one of which is the bird which, in her early work, is the symbol of life, freedom, and vitality and, later, in *Requiem to a Bird*, it symbolizes a victim (1975–6). There is also the abstract simplification of parallel horizontal lines, simplification of landscapes and the Judean mountain terraces.

Her compositions reduce elements to their basic shapes and components: upper, lower, uplifting force, gravity, black and white.

FURTHER READING
Tal, M.: Three Women Artists. *Ariel* 21 (1967–8)

NEDIRA YAKIR BUNYARD

Uris, Leon (b.1924) American novelist. Born in Baltimore, Maryland, Uris has gained a reputation as a popular novelist. He served in the US Marine Corps in the Pacific during the Second World War. He drew upon his experiences during the war when he wrote his first novel, *Battle Cry*, published in 1953. His most successful novel, written on a Jewish theme, is *Exodus*, published in 1958. He has written several other novels on Jewish themes, including *Mila 18* (1961) and *QBVII* (1970), the former about the heroic resistance in the Warsaw Ghetto during the Nazi occupation during the Second World War, and the latter about the trial of an American novelist in Queen's Bench 7 for libeling a Polish surgeon by saying that he performed sterilizations of Jews in a Nazi concentration camp. He has also written several novels on non-Jewish themes. In addition to writing novels, several works of nonfiction, and journal articles, Uris worked for a newspaper shortly after the Second World War and during the Sinai Campaign. He also wrote several screen plays, including the highly successful one for his own novel, *Battle Cry*.

The great popularity of *Exodus* and of the film based on it has been attributed in part to the "positive, heroic Jewish types" in it (Liptzen, 1966). However, the book's blatant sentimentality also was instrumental in causing it to be so popular.

Uris has been criticized for shallow characterization, superficiality of theme, and lack of attention to details of plotting. Still, his strong storylines help his works stay extremely popular.

Other works include *Exodus Revisited*, nonfiction, with photographs by Dimitrius Harassiadis (1959), and *The Haj* (1984).

FURTHER READING

Liptzin, S.: *The Jew in American Literature* (New York: Bloch, 1968)
Peckham, S.: Leon Uris. *Publisher's Weekly* (29 March 1976) 6–7

RICHARD TUERK

Ury, Lesser (1861–1931)   German painter. Born in Poland, Ury arrived in Berlin with his family at the age of 12. He studied in Brussels and Düsseldorf and spent periods of time in Paris, the village of Volluvet in Belgium and in Munich, before finally settling in Berlin in 1887. His early work was impressionist in style, but towards the end of the century he was inspired by themes from the Bible. His best known works are Berlin street scenes for which he used his favorite medium, pastel, saving oils for interiors. He became recognized after an exhibition of his work in Berlin in 1916. His works were shown in the Berlin Secession in 1922 and in the following year the Nationalgalerie in Berlin acquired three of his paintings. A Memorial Exhibition was held at this same gallery in 1931. He was an excellent etcher and lithographer. In his centenary year the Bezalel National Museum, Jerusalem, held a major retrospective exhibition; the Galerie Pels–Leusden in Berlin have given him three one-man shows since his death.

FURTHER READING

Schwarz, K.: *Lesser Ury* (Berlin: Fritz Burlitt Verlag, 1920)

MURIEL EMANUEL

V

Vajda, Georges (1908–1981) Judaic scholar and Orientalist. Vajda studied Oriental languages under B. Heller at the Jewish Theological Seminary in his native Budapest, before coming to Paris in 1928, where he completed his studies and taught Bible and Jewish theology at the Séminaire Israélite from 1936 to 1960. Pursuing Islamic studies with L. Massignon, he presented a doctoral thesis on *Les Zindiqs en pays d'Islam* (1933). Specializing in Judeo-Arabic literature, his articles in this area began to appear from 1932 in the *Revue des Études Juives*, of which he was later the editor for nearly half a century. In 1937 he began teaching at the École Pratique des Hautes Études and in 1940 he was appointed director of the oriental section of the Institut de Recherches et d'Histoire des Textes, a position he held until his retirement in 1978. In 1970 he became the first professor of post-biblical Jewish literature at the Sorbonne, being responsible at the same time for the Arabic and Hebrew section at the Bibliothèque Nationale. His mastery of Oriental languages, scrupulous scholarship, and elegant style were completely to renew Jewish studies in France. He wrote several erudite monographs on Jewish philosophers of Arabic expression. Besides the new light he shed on well-known authors such as Sa'adyah Ga'on and Bahya Ibn Paqudah (1947), his intellectual curiosity is best illustrated by the interest he held in a number of secondary figures such as Judah Ibn Malka (1951), Isaac Albalag (1960), Abraham bar Hiyya, Joseph Ibn Zaddiq and the philosophical school of Kairuan, the object of a second thesis presented at the Sorbonne in 1945. Vajda was the first to have devoted an analytical study to the work of the Karaite scholar al-Qirqisâni. In his *Introduction à la Pensée Juive du Moyen Age*, he emphasized the neglected area of *kabbalah*. Subsequently he became interested in the relationship between philosophy and *kabbalah* in the mediaeval period, collaborating in this domain with Gershom SCHOLEM, some of whose works he translated or edited in French. Noteworthy in this area are his *Recherches sur la Philosophie et la Kabbale dans la Pensée Juive du Moyen Age* (1962) and *Le Commentaire d'Ezra de Gérone sur le Cantique des Cantiques* (1969).

BIBLIOGRAPHY
Transmission du Savoir en Islam (London: Variorum, 1983); G. E. Weil, ed.: *Mélanges Georges Vajda* (Hildesheim: Gerstenberg, 1982)

FURTHER READING
Fenton, P.: *Une Bibliographie des Écrits de G. Vajda* (Paris, 1989)

PAUL B. FENTON

Vas, István (b.1910) Hungarian poet, writer, and translator. Born in Budapest into a middle-class Jewish family, after finishing his secondary education he went to Vienna to study commerce. It was there that he became acquainted with Marxism, but apart from a short period of rebellious radicalism Vas wrote in a fairly traditional, though urbane manner. First a contributor to Kassák's review *Munka* (Work), in the 1930s Vas started printing poetry in *Nyugat* and became known as a distinguished member of

771

the "third (Nyugat) generation". His resolute anti-Fascism and Socialist sympathies made him welcome the sweeping social changes after 1945, but his allegiance to the ideals of European Humanism was expressed in the line written only a few years later: "I am looking back at the old and the new, and I am both of them". In another poem "Nicolaus Cusanus sírja" (The grave of Nicholas Cusanus) he calls himself "the point of intersection of contradictions". This skeptical attitude earned him official disapproval during the years of Stalinism and in the early 1950s most of his output consisted of translations of English and French poets. Since 1956 he has been recognized as one of the leading poets of his generation whose elegiac, meditative, alternatively sensual and metaphysical tone does not lessen his sensitivity to the problems of post-industrial society. He was awarded the Kossuth Prize twice, in 1962 and 1985.

Vas is also an essayist and a consummate translator of Shakespeare, Donne, and T. S. Eliot, but in recent years he has attracted most attention with his autobiographical reminiscences. The two volumes of *Nehéz szerelem* (1964, 1967; Difficult love) describe his emotional and intellectual development as a young man, including his rebellion against the business-oriented environment of his parents, while *Mért víjjog a saskeselyű?* (2 vols 1981; Why does the vulture screech?) takes the story further, up to the outbreak of the Second World War. It is in the latter that Vas defines his attitude to Jewishness: while not denying his Jewish roots (his grandfather was a provincial rabbi), he stresses his strong attachment to Hungarian culture and tradition and he evokes the hopes of his youth that the victory of Socialism will somehow solve the problem of anti-Semitism. In the 1930s Vas became a convert to Catholicism. This step, however, did not affect his poetic preoccupations or his position in society, and when, in 1944, with the German occupation of Hungary the Nuremberg Laws became applicable there, he wrote more in sorrow than bitterness: "Under my patch [that is, the yellow star] I am wearing / The large, yellow shame of the whole country" ("Április"). In his later poetry biblical themes appear frequently, from both the Old and New Testament, Jesus remaining as much in the center of the poet's attention as the prophets of Judea. The contemplation of beauty, however, is a constant theme of Vas and some of his most accomplished poems are odes to and rhapsodies about, the delights of the sensual world. His poems have been translated into English, some of them printed in *Lines Review* 59 (1976) and in *Modern Hungarian Poetry* (1977), as well as various issues of the *New Hungarian Quarterly*.

FURTHER READING

Fenyő, I.: *Vas István* (Budapest: Akadémiai Kiadó, 1977)
Gömöri, G.: István Vas at sixty. *Books Abroad* 45 (1971) 46–49

GEORGE GÖMÖRI

Verbitsky, Bernardo (1902–1979) Argentine novelist, University lecturer in literature, and journalist. Born in Buenos Aires of Russian immigrant parents, Verbitsky wrote 73 volumes of prose fiction and essays, beginning with *Es difícil empezar a vivir* (Beginning to live is hard) and including *Calles de tango* which was successfully filmed as *A Date with Life*, and the widely acclaimed *Villa miseria también es América* (All South America is a shanty town). His last novel *Hermana y sombra* (Sister and shadow) like his first, describes the struggle with poverty of an immigrant Russian Jewish family in Buenos Aires during the period of the First World War, and the problems of cultural assimilation.

The penultimate novel *Etiquetas a los hombres* (Labeling people) is the one which most explicitly deals with the problem of Jewish identity. Throughout the book characters are called upon to take sides on issues which they feel should not be conflicting, such as being both Argentine or Russian and a Jew, sympathizing with the Left and with Israel, respecting the rights of both Palestinians and Jews. Verbitsky challenges the concept of mutually exclusive categories through a series of impassioned confrontations. Issues such as the Six Day War are discussed against the background of the Holocaust of the Second World War, the continuing conflict in the Middle East, the threat of nuclear war and the problem of poverty in the Third World. The book is closer to inspired journalism than fiction, and has lost some of its topical flavor, though not its documentary value.

The basic issue, which conditions how all the others are approached, is that of "Why is it so difficult to be Jewish?" Various characters discuss what it means to them to be Jewish and how they integrate this into their lives. The specific problems of being a Jew in Argentina or Russia are explored, as well as the many different ways of being Jewish in Israel. This in turn raises many questions about Israel's survival and how best this could be secured. The protagonist concludes: "It is as difficult for Israel to be a state as it is for a Jew simply to be a human being". He also declares "If I could make an eleventh commandment, it would be: Do not put labels on people". Intolerance, war and torture happen because people forget that war is fratricide, that crimes against a sector of the population, such as the Jews, are crimes against humanity.

The central problem is timeless and does not only concern Jews. It raises the question of whether people belong where they were born or where their ancestors came from; whether their duty is to remain within an inimical society, or to seek a future elsewhere. Verbitsky provides no clear-cut solution but shows individuals struggling to find the answer most appropriate to their own socio-political context.

BIBLIOGRAPHY

Hermana y sombra (Buenos Aires: Planeta Argentina, 1977); *A Pesar de todo* (Caracas: Monte Avila, 1978)

ANN DUNCAN

Vermes, Geza (b.1924)

British historian. Born in Hungary, Vermes studied for a time at the University of Budapest, before moving to the University of Louvain, where he became *Licencié en Histoire et Langues Orientales* (1952) and *Docteur en Théologie* (1953). Between 1955 and 1957 he was in Paris, attached as a research worker to the CNRS. He then took up a post as Lecturer (later Senior Lecturer) in Divinity at the University of Newcastle-upon-Tyne, England. In 1965 he succeeded Cecil Roth as Reader in Jewish Studies at the University of Oxford. Twice President of the British Association for Jewish Studies (1975 and 1988), First President of the European Association for Jewish Studies (1981–4), Governor of the Oxford Centre for Postgraduate Hebrew Studies (from 1972), Vermes's contribution to his chosen discipline was recognized by his election in 1985 to a Fellowship of the British Academy.

Vermes's academic reputation was established by a series of pioneering studies of the Dead Sea Scrolls (notably *Les manuscrits du désert de Juda*, 1953). He identified the Qumran community as Essene and placed the "Teacher of Righteousness", the founder of the community, in the time of the High Priest Jonathan (152–43 BCE), whom he proposed as the "Wicked Priest" of the Scrolls. Vermes's early theories on the history of the Dead Sea Sect have stood well the test of time. In 1962 Penguin Books brought out his *Dead Sea Scrolls in English* which rapidly became the standard English rendering of the texts.

In the mid 1950s Vermes's attention turned increasingly to early Jewish Bible-exegesis (*midrash*), which he became convinced represented "the most basic and vital expression of the post-biblical [Jewish] mind", and had a central role to play in our understanding of early Judaism. Along with Renée Bloch he outlined a tradition-historical approach to the study of *midrash*, which involves tracing how the exegesis of a given Biblical passage or theme (e.g. the "Binding of Isaac" in Genesis 22) developed in early Jewish literature. *Scripture and Tradition in Judaism*, Vermes's most substantial early work outlining and demonstrating his approach to *aggadah*, caused little stir when it first appeared in 1961. In retrospect it can be seen as a turning-point in the modern study of *midrash*.

In his analysis of aggadic themes, Vermes from time to time quoted the New Testament as a source for the study of early Judaism. Implicit in this use was a view of the origins of Christianity which he began increasingly to draw out in the late 1960s. His interest in the New Testament culminated with the publication in 1973 of

Geza Vermes

Jesus the Jew: A Historian's Reading of the Gospels. In this work he tried to put Jesus into the context of the Judaism of his day, by suggesting that broadly speaking he was a Galilean *hasid* [holy man] of the type of Haninah ben Dosa.

In 1964 Vermes was invited, together with other scholars, to participate in the revision of Emil Schürer's classic *Geschichte des jüdischen Volkes im Zeitalter Jesu Christi.* The first volume of the revised Schürer appeared in 1973, and the task was brought to a successful conclusion with the publication of volume iii/2 in 1987. The New Schürer presents a monumental synthesis of current knowledge of Judaism in the late Second Temple period and will be the standard handbook on its subject for the foreseeable future.

Vermes's reputation has grown steadily over the years, and he is now widely regarded as a pivotal figure in the study of early Judaism. He has shown an ability to anticipate and to in-

fluence significant trends within his field. Possessed of a strong historical imagination, he formulates questions in direct, concrete terms, uncluttered by dogma or methodology. His answers to those questions are often couched in a simple but elegant style which masks deep learning and subtlety. At Oxford he has proved a successful teacher, and attracts students from all over the world to study with him. He has nurtured and influenced a generation of younger scholars who, in a variety of ways, carry forward his interests in early Judaism. He has received an honorary doctorate from Edinburgh University and, in 1989, became Professor of Jewish Studies at the University of Oxford.

BIBLIOGRAPHY
Post-Biblical Jewish Studies (1975); *The Dead Sea Scrolls: Qumran in Perspective* (London: Collins, 1977; rev. Philadelphia: Fortress Press, 1981); *The Gospel of Jesus the Jew* (Newcastle-upon-Tyne: University of Newcastle-upon-Tyne, 1981); *Jesus and the World of Judaism* (London: SCM, 1983)

PHILIP S. ALEXANDER

Vidal-Naquet, Pierre (b.1930) French historian, essayist and political activist. Director of Studies at the École des Hautes Études en Sciences Sociales, as well as being director of the Centre de Recherches comparées sur les Sociétés anciennes, Vidal-Naquet is one of France's leading ancient historians as well as a central figure in the intellectual and political battle against "revisionist" historians.

Born in Paris into a highly assimilated Jewish family with origins in the Provençal region near Carpentras, Vidal-Naquet grew up in an environment where religious life was minimal and Jewish influences almost totally absent. He first set foot in a synagogue in 1940 to attend a special memorial service for the dead in the War. For Vidal-Naquet at this time, Jewishness was a burden, Jewish identity an obstacle. His reactions concerning France's defeat in 1940 were purely patriotic, not at all Jewish. Though aware of anti-Jewish propaganda, the reality and immensity of the threat of Nazism only became fully apparent when his family hastily left Paris for the safer regions in the south.

Together with his cousins, he wrote a text, *Voyage de réfugiés*, which describes the spectacle and débâcle of defeat and retreat. Vidal-Naquet has stated that those surreal days served as the basis for his future vocation as an historian.

The events of the Second World War profoundly marked Vidal-Naquet's life. Barely escaping deportation, losing his parents in May, 1944, his psyche recognized the necessity for people of conscience to speak out against tyranny. In the late 1940s, this awareness tempted him to flirt with Marxism, only to reject it. He wrote against the wars in Indochina and Algeria.

During the 1960s, Vidal-Naquet emerged as one of France's leading intellectual figures who pressed for a revival of classical studies in the *lycée* and university curricula. Despite his passion for the classics, he was likewise motivated by his political activities and social conscience. His activity as Positivist historian led him to criticize the Algerian War as well as to lead the fight against revisionists such as Robert Faurisson. Vidal-Naquet is one of France's leading anti-revisionist thinkers who has championed numerous crusades against "historians" who have sought to promulgate the theory that the Holocaust did not happen but is the fabrication of a grand Jewish conspiracy.

Since 1964 Vidal-Naquet has been director of a series of history and social science publications, *Textes à appui*, at Les Éditions Maspero/La Découverte. He has also been instrumental in the formation of a committee of French Jewish and non-Jewish intellectuals who are seeking to find a negotiated solution to the Arab–Israeli conflict.

His own publications include *Mythe et Tragédie en Grèce ancienne* (1972), *Mythe et Tragédie, II* (1982), *Les Juifs, la mémoire et le présent* (1982) and *Les Assassins de la mémoire, "Un Eichmann de papier" et autres essais sur le revisionnisme* (1987).

SIMON SIBELMAN

Viertel, Berthold (1885–1953) Director, poet, dramatist. Viertel's colorful personality is captured in Christopher Isherwood's novel *Prater Violet* (1946), where he is portrayed as a flamboyant, creative figure, struggling with the English language, preparing a film, but only reluctantly making it. He never lost his enthusiasm for encouraging brilliant, independent minds to work alongside him.

He had studied philosophy in Vienna but graduated in the theater, and moved in literary circles, writing poetry – on which he believed his reputation rested – and contributing to its journals. In 1923 he co-founded the experimental theater group, *Die Truppe*, an expressionist reaction to the star-ridden commercial theater but it quickly collapsed and, in 1928, he turned to the cinema to clear his debts.

He began directing in Germany and in Hollywood, working on Murnau's *Four Devils* (1929) and *City Girl* (1930) as well as directing a few unspectacular films of his own. But he was unhappy and sought a career in Europe. Briefly and unwisely, he returned to Germany in 1933, but he was soon in England where he made three films: *The Little Sister* (1934), *The Passing of the Third Floor Back* (1935) and *Rhodes of Africa* (1936). The first provided the source-material for Isherwood's novel as well as the later *Christopher and his Kind* (1977). They are all experimental in a way which does not quite succeed. Viertel was active in the Free German League of Culture but returned to the USA when his residency permit was not renewed where he and his wife, the actress Salka Steuermann, now a successful Hollywood scriptwriter, became a center of émigré social and cultural life. He continued to produce plays and was involved with the Jewish Club of 1933. After the war he returned as a guest theater producer in Berlin and Vienna, where he had started his career.

Other films include: *Ein Puppenheim* (1922), *Die Arbenteur eines Zehnmarkscheines* (1924).

FURTHER READING

Ginsberg, E., ed.: *Berthold Viertel, Dichtungen und Dokumente: Gedichte, Prosa, Autobiographische Fragmente* (München: Kösel–Verlag, 1956)

Viertel, S.: *The Kindness of Strangers* (New York: Holt, Rinehart and Winston, 1969)

Viertels Welt: Der Regisseur, Lyriker, Essayist Berthold Viertel. *Ausfrisse* 4 (1988)

KEVIN GOUGH-YATES

Vigée, Claude (b.1921)   French essayist and poet. He was born into an old Alsatian family in the town of Bischwiller, and found his life radically altered by the German invasion of France. Initially he was active in the French Jewish Resistance and Underground, but in 1942 he was forced to flee to Spain, and then in 1943 to the USA. Vigée remained in the USA for the remainder of the war, studying at Ohio State University from which he received his Ph.D. in 1945. In the post-war years, Vigée taught at a number of American institutions, notably Wellesley College and Brandeis University. His efforts to promote French studies in general and French poetry in particular earned him the Palmes académiques in 1960 and then in 1965 the Ordre National du Mérite.

Vigée's first collection of poetry, *La Lutte avec l'ange* (1950), sounded the keynote for the thematic content of his work until 1963: the struggle for authentic Jewish identity. Vigée's status as both poet and Jew has resulted in a painful quest for complete identity and meaningful roots. These notions persist in his next two collections. *L'Été indien* (1957), and *Canaan d'exil* (1962). The theme of alienation arises again in two collections of essays, *Les artistes de la faim* (1960) and *Révolte et louages* (1962). In the latter collection, Vigée examines the lives of other "exiles" searching for an absolute.

In 1962 Vigée decided to make *aliyah* and since 1963 has been teaching at the Hebrew University in Jerusalem where he is Professor of French Literature. His move to Israel also incited a shift in the thematic direction of his work. Alienation evolved into a sense of being at one with a land, a people, and oneself, as evidenced in two collections *Le Poème du retour* (1962) and *Moison de Canaan* (1967). Vigée did not seek to abnegate his life in the Diaspora but rather attempted to integrate his heritage as a Jew with those traditions from Western civilization, a point he emphasized in "Civilisation française et genre hébraïque" (1967).

For Vigée, poetry became the quintessential expression of his Jewish condition. He views himself in the timeless tradition of the psalm-writers and storytellers of the past. In some ways this is a difficult path for Vigée to follow as the exalted feelings are often restrained by the classical confines of the French language he continues to use as his means of expression. Such obstacles, however, have not dulled his vision or the vitality of his language as demonstrated in his *Délivrance du souffle* (1977).

SIMON SIBELMAN

Viterbo, Carlo Alberto (1889–1974) Italian journalist, lawyer, and Zionist leader. Born in Florence, he was brought up in a perfectly assimilated and integrated atmosphere, and his education and cultural formation were within mainstream Italian culture. He came to Judaism at the age of 18 through the influence of his friend A. Pacifici and of Rabbi Margulies. He was a brilliant lawyer and dedicated himself enthusiastically both to the Italian Zionist movement, of which he was president in 1931, and to the Jewish Press.

After Italy's conquest of Ethiopia in 1936, Viterbo was sent by the Unione delle Comunità Israelitiche Italiane (The Union of Italian Jewish Communities) to Ethiopia, in order to make contact with the Fallasha Jews. In 1936–7 he visited Addis Ababa and penetrated the Godar. He learnt Amharic and gained a profound knowledge of the customs and rites of the Beta Israel. On his return to Italy, Viterbo wrote a detailed account of his experiences which remained incomplete and unpublished. Some fragments were published in Jewish periodicals of the time, such as *Annuario di Studi Ebraici*.

Viterbo was determinedly anti-Fascist and in 1940 he was imprisoned in Rome and then interned for 13 months in Sforzacosta concentration camp near Macerata, accused of being "a Jew, an anti-Fascist, and a Zionist". After the liberation of Rome by the Allies in 1944, Viterbo resumed his work on behalf of Italian Jewry with renewed effort. He relaunched the weekly *Israel* of which he was the chief editor; its publication ceased on his death.

He persevered in his study of Hebrew and published grammars including *Una via verso l'ebraico* (1968). His most important work was published after his death: "Relazione al Ministero dell'Africa Italiana dell'opera svolta in

A.O.I. in rappresenza dell'Unione delle Comunità Israelitiche Italiane", in *Israel, "Un decennio" 1974–1984: saggi sull'ebraismo italiano*, ed. F. Del Canuto, Rome (1984).

GABRIELLA MOSCATI-STEINDLER

Vriesland, Victor Emanuel van (1892–1974) Dutch poet and literary critic. Born in Haarlem into a wealthy family, van Vriesland had no regular education. He did not finish the *gymnasium*, but studied French literature in Dijon for a few years. He was, however, an ardent reader and was personally acquainted with many Dutch authors of his time. He became editor of a number of Dutch literary journals like *De Nieuwe Gids* and *Forum*. In 1931 he became literary editor of the important Dutch newspaper *Nieuwe Rotterdamsche Courant*. In the meantime much of his fortune was lost in the crash of 1929 and he was forced to make a living out of literature. In 1938 he became editor of the leftist weekly *De Groene Amsterdammer*.

Van Vriesland published poetry in *Drievoudig Verweer* (1949), a novel, *Het afscheid van de wereld in drie dagen* (1926) and critical essays which were collected in *Onderzoek en Vertoog* (2 vols, 1958). He also made a compilation of Dutch poems: *Spiegel van de Nederlandsche poëzie door alle eeuwen* (1939). His novel has not met with much success and interest in his cerebral poetry was limited to a small group of admirers. His importance lies mainly in his journalistic work and his gift for conversing on literary topics.

Although van Vriesland was the prototype of an assimilated Jew, he flirted with Zionism in his youth. At that time he held radical views about the impossibility of creating Jewish art in a non-Jewish world.

LUDY GIEBELS

W

Wald, Herman (1906–70) South African sculptor. Born in Cluj, Hungary, scion of six generations of rabbis, he showed an early interest in representational art. Owing to the Jewish proscription against graven images, his father discouraged him, but became reconciled with his art career after he had sculpted a triple-life-size bust of Herzl in his mother's pantry.

Studying art at the Academy of Fine Arts, Budapest, Wald supplemented his small bursary by singing in the Great Budapest Synagogue. He went to Vienna in 1930 and to Berlin in 1931. With Hitler's rise to power in 1933, he left for Paris and later London, where he was befriended and his work recognized by Jacob EPSTEIN. He taught sculpture at the Working Man's College.

He arrived in South Africa in 1937, and in 1940 joined the South African defense force, continuing to sculpt while in the army. His work *Engineers Laying Nose of Bridge* is in Johannesburg's War Museum.

His art, though universal, displays a deep Jewish influence. Some of his best work was entirely Jewish in concept. After the Second World War the influence of the Holocaust became apparent in his sculpture, and in 1946 he sculpted the *Kria* monument which, in 1957, was placed in the grounds of the Witwatersrand Jewish Aged Home in Sandringham, Johannesburg.

He received several commissions for work in synagogues among which was his sculpture *Wings of the Shechinah* (1967) which surrounds the ark in the Berea Synagogue, Johannesburg.

From 1957 he sculpted predominantly biblical subjects and in 1959 held an exhibition, *The Bible in Sculpture*, in Johannesburg. Several of his smaller works portray hasidic figures, often in dance or song.

One of his most important commissions was the monument to martyred European Jewry in the Westpark Jewish cemetery Johannesburg, 1956. Six gigantic fists emerging from its flat base, each holding a shofar, symbolize the protest of the six million. In the center is a sculpted flame combining the Hebrew letters of the commandment, "Thou shalt not kill". Wald was buried alongside this monument.

JOCELYN HELLIG

Walkowitz, Abraham (1878–1965) American painter. Born in Tumen, Siberia, Abraham Walkowitz was the son of a lay rabbi and cantor. Pogroms forced Walkowtiz's mother to emigrate with her children to the USA in 1889. They settled on the Lower East Side of New York; Walkowitz studied art at Cooper Union and the Educational Alliance. From 1898 to 1900 he studied at the National Academy of Design. His early work consisted of portraits of Lower East Side characters which were published in 1946 as *Faces from the Ghetto*.

In Paris in 1906–7 Walkowitz met, among others, Matisse, Picasso, and Isadora Duncan, all of whom were to exercise considerable influence on his art. For several years following his return to New York, he painted groups of figures at leisure in the style of Matisse, utilizing an agitated brushstroke and bright color. Between 1912 and 1917, as an important member of the circle of artists around Alfred Stieglitz and his gallery 291, Walkowitz produced his most avant-garde paintings and drawings: cityscapes in which the buildings of New York are rendered with networks of angular, Cubist facets, and jumbled patterns to convey the dynamism and energy of the city. Mesmerized by Isadora Duncan, Walkowitz painted and drew the dancer in motion throughout his entire artistic career, producing some 5,000 drawings of her.

With the closing of 291 in 1917, Walkowitz lost the support of Stieglitz, and with it, the creative energy of his early years. In the 1930s he worked on the WPA project and in 1945 he painted a mural for the Porter Library of the Kansas State Teachers College in Pittsburgh, Kansas.

Exhibitions of Walkowitz's work were held in 1949 at the Jewish Museum, New York and the following year at the Wadsworth Atheneum, Hartford, Connecticut. In 1982 the Long Beach Museum of Art in Long Beach, California organized an exhibiton featuring his figurative work.

FURTHER READING

Smith, K.: *Abraham Walkowitz Figuration 1895–1945* (Long Beach: Long Beach Museum of Art, 1982) [exhibition catalog].

Sewin, M.: *Abraham Walkowitz, 1878–1965*, (Salt Lake City: Museum of Fine Arts, 1975) [exhibition catalog]

KRISTIE A. JAYNE

Wallant, Edward Lewis (1926–1962)

American novelist. Wallant was born and raised in New Haven, Connecticut. He served in the US Navy and then studied commercial art at Pratt Institute. In 1950 he joined the art department of a New York advertising agency, and worked successfully in this field until 1962, when he won a Guggenheim Fellowship. He spent three months traveling in Europe and returned to devote himself full-time to writing. In December of that year, he died suddenly.

Only a handful of Wallant's stories were published in his lifetime, and two of his novels were published posthumously. In his first book, *The Human Season* (1960), winner of the Jewish Book Council Fiction Award, a widower denies the pain of loss and subsequent loneliness, along with most of his other emotions, but eventually reopens himself to human feeling, even at the risk of further pain. The hero of *The Pawnbroker* (1961) is a Holocaust survivor, who has hardened himself against remembering, but finds that hardness separating him from human contact until a clerk in his pawnshop, appropriately named Jesus, sacrifices himself to save the protagonist's life. The novel uses flashbacks to present the hero's memories and was made into a successful film by Sidney Lumet.

The two posthumously published novels offer variations on the same themes. The heroes of *The Tenants of Moonbloom* (1963), and *The Children at the Gate* (1965), a rent collector and a hospital orderly, respectively, take on the suffering of others as their own personal responsibility. Once the rent collector, Moonbloom, opens himself up to the pain of his tenants' lives, he embarks on a quixotic campaign to improve their physical surroundings. The orderly, Sammy Kahan, pushes his manic style of compassion to the limit and finally dies in a symbolic crucifixion. Although most of Wallant's novels focus on Jewish characters, he was fascinated with figures who, like Jesus, sacrifice themselves to spare others from suffering.

FURTHER READING

Galloway, D.: *Edward Lewis Wallant* (New York: Twayne, 1979)

Mesher, D.: Edward Wallant. In *Dictionary of Literary Biography* vol. 28 (Detroit: Gale Research Co., 1984)

MICHAEL SHAPIRO

Wallenstein, Meir (b.1904) Judaic scholar.

Born in Jerusalem, Wallenstein was educated at *heder, yeshivah,* and at the Mizrahi teachers' seminary in Jerusalem. He was a schoolteacher in Palestine until, in 1929, he decided to come to Britain in pursuit of a university education. In 1935 he gained an MA and then a Ph.D. at the University of Manchester where, in 1940, he was appointed assistant in Semitic languages and literature, and by 1961 he had risen to assistant professor in medieval and modern Hebrew. It was largely due to Wallenstein's knowledge and enthusiasm that modern Hebrew became recognized as a subject for the general BA, and that in 1945 medieval and modern Hebrew were recognized as a main subject for a BA Honours degree. Manchester was the first university in Britain to do so.

In his teaching and research Wallenstein paid special attention to the *piyyut* and to the Hebrew poetry written in medieval Spain. Wallenstein was amongst the earliest scholars to study the Dead Sea Scrolls discovered in 1947. From 1931 and until he left Manchester in 1970 he served as the president of Tarbut, the society for Hebrew speakers in Manchester. In 1944, together with Professor E. Robertson, he founded and edited *Melilah*, an annual devoted to research in Jewish studies, which was published by the Manchester University Press and continued to appear until 1955. While still in Manchester, Wallenstein was elected advisory member to the Academy of the Hebrew Language in Jerusalem. After his retirement from Manchester he became Visiting Professor for medieval manuscripts at Bar-Ilan University. His published books, articles, and reviews number over a hundred.

BIBLIOGRAPHY

Hymns from the Judean Scrolls (Manchester: Manchester University Press, 1950); *The Nezer and the Submission in Suffering from the Dead Sea Scrolls* (Leiden: Brill, 1956)

BATYA RABIN

Wassermann, Jakob (1873–1934)

Wassermann, Jakob (1873–1934) German novelist and essayist. Born in Würzburg into a Jewish family whose forebears had lived for four centuries in Franconia, Wassermann was sent, at the age of 16, after a notably unhappy childhood, to work for an uncle in Vienna with a view to a career in business. Evidently unsuited to business Wassermann rapidly spent a small inheritance on a carefree life in Munich. Then followed a period of restlessness, dissoluteness, and poverty. Finally, he returned to Munich and began to write for newspapers. His first poems and short stories were published in *Simplicissimus* in 1896. The success of his first novel *Die Juden von Zirndorf* (1897; *The Jews of Zirndorf*, 1933), marked the beginning of a literary career which was to make him one of the most widely read European novelists of the interwar years, although he bitterly regretted that his books were more popular in France, England, and the USA than in his native Germany.

The Jews of Zirndorf has as its central theme the eternal Jewish longing for spiritual redemption. The emphasis placed in all Wassermann's works on the need for metaphysical salvation is a function of the author's lifelong indifference to political Zionism. In 1908 Wassermann published his version of the history of Caspar Hauser (*Caspar Hauser*, 1928). Although it is a story without explicitly Jewish content, Wassermann saw much of his own experience as a Jew in Germany in the life of the young Caspar Hauser, who was unjustly despoiled of the inherent rights enjoyed by his fellow citizens.

Between 1900 and 1934 Wasserman produced a new work almost every year. In addition to the novels which form the basis of his reputation, he wrote five plays, several biographical studies, and a memorial tribute to his friend, the poet Hofmannsthal. His autobiography, *Mein Weg als Deutscher und Jude* (*My life as German and Jew*, 1933; 1934), describes his sorrow at the failure of Jewish Emancipation in Germany, which he attributed to the German unwillingness to consider Jews as individuals, and the consequent paralyzing effect of this rejection on the Jews.

All his life Wassermann circled with increasing exhaustion and despair around the problem of social injustice. In countless guises, often without full artistic control of his material, he reworked the themes of erotic slavery and personal debasement, and the indifference of individuals to the suffering of others. He did, however, exhibit an abiding belief in the redemptive power of human warmth and personal sacrifice.

FURTHER READING

Blankenagel, J. C.: *The Writings of Jakob Wassermann*. (Boston: Christopher Publishing House, 1942)

Garland, H., and Garland, M.: *The Oxford Companion to German Literature* (Oxford: Clarendon Press, 1976)

DAFNA CLIFFORD

Waten, Judah (1911–1985) Australian novelist, critic, and essayist. He was born in Odessa and emigrated to Perth in 1914. Waten was a contributor to the more important literary journals and was included in anthologies and annual collections of the best short stories of the year. Nevertheless, because of his socialist predilections, and membership of the Communist party, he was not always regarded as a member of the "inner coterie" of Australian novelists, until later in his life when his output and quality and changing Australian social attitudes, breached the barriers against him. English reviewers regarded him as a challenge to established Australian writers with his second book.

In the 1940s he was a prominent member of the Jewish Council to Combat Fascism and anti-Semitism. In the 1970s he became a member of the prestigious Literature Board of the Australia Council. He was a regular reviewer and critical writer for Australian national literary supplements and literary journals.

He wrote in English all his life, yet was heavily influenced by his Yiddish-speaking background. He moved to Melbourne in the 1920s where he became involved with a group of rising Jewish writers and painters with strong socialist views. He felt keenly his parents' economic deprivation and their sense of being without roots in their new homeland, and expressed this feeling in his early work, along with sharply expressed anti-capitalist views. His short stories were regarded as more successful than his novels in their social commentary because of their more modest targets and their sensitivity. His later work moved away a little from the pessimistic attitude of his earlier writings.

Although half of Waten's output was on Jewish themes he considered himself to be preeminently an Australian writer. Current assessments of Waten's work support this contention, indicating that his "ethnic" attitudes

Judah Waten

highlight the immigrant element in much of native Australian writing, thus placing him in the forefront of that writing.

His first novel, *The Unbending* (1954), was written on a Commonwealth Literary Fellowship, and this portrait of a Jewish family, combined with a partisan account of the 1916 anti-conscription struggles, was most controversial in the light of parliamentary attacks on the Commonwealth Literary Fund. In his *Distant Land* (1964), a novel about a Jewish immigrant couple from Poland who are trying to adapt to a new life, Waten became less ideologically militant than in his *Alien Son* (1952). This anthology of his published short stories has a dominant and recurring theme of migrant (Jewish) life in Australia.

Shares in Murder (1957) was an unusual departure for Waten. It is a murder mystery, with a lean dialogue and strong characterization, set in Australia. Other novels are *Time of Conflict* (1961), *Season of Youth* (1966), *So Far no Further* (1971), *Love and Rebellion* (1978), *Scenes of Revolutionary Life* (1982), which contains a passage from his unpublished novel, *Hunger*, written when he was 18, and an autobiographical record of his trips to Russia, *From Odessa to Odessa* (1969).

His novels have been translated into at least ten languages including Russian and Chinese (*Alien Son*).

FURTHER READING

Blainey, G.: Judah Waten. *Overland* 100 (1985) 47–50

Indyk, I.: The mainstream and the source, points of view on ethnic writing in Australia. *Ethnos* 56 (1986)

Martin, D.: Three realists in search of reality. *Meanjin* 18 no. 3 (1959)

ALAN D. CROWN

Weber, Max (1881–1961) American painter and sculptor. Max Weber emigrated to the USA from Russia with his family in 1891. He studied at Pratt Institute in Brooklyn, New York, from 1898 to 1900. In Paris between 1905 and 1908, he studied at the Académie Julian, the Académie Colarossi, the Académie de la Grande Chaumière, and in the studio of Matisse.

In 1911, two years after his return to the USA, Weber had an important one-man exhibition at Alfred Stieglitz's 291 Gallery in New York. The paintings of nudes he exhibited combined Matisse's bold line and color with Cézanne's proto-cubist structures. Weber's abstract paintings of 1915–8 fully embrace Cubism. Figures and/or motifs extracted from the urban environment are fragmented and placed in a shallow picture space. Weber often incorporated bits of decorative motifs, which, combined with bright colors he favored, created brilliant, calligraphic canvases.

All of Weber's paintings, prints, and sculptures after 1919 are representational. Beginning in the late 1930s, his interests turned increasingly to Jewish themes, painting such subjects as the Sabbath and figures studying the Torah. In the 1950s he reintroduced Cubist distortion, investing his late work with an expressive fervor.

Through the 1920s Weber supported himself by teaching. The Museum of Modern Art, New York, held a retrospective of his work in 1930, but he had no real financial success until the 1940s, when he exhibited annually at the Paul Rosenberg Gallery in New York. Retrospectives of his work were organized by the Whitney Museum of American Art in 1949 and by Pratt Institute, Brooklyn, New York, and the Newark Museum in New Jersey in 1959. Significant posthumous exhibitions include those at the Art Galleries of the University of California at Santa Barbara in 1968 and at the Jewish Museum, New York, in 1982.

FURTHER READING

North, P.: *Max Weber: American Modern* (New York: The Jewish Museum, 1982) [exhibition catalog]

Werner, A. *Max Weber* (New York: Harry N. Abrams, 1975)

KRISTIE A. JAYNE

Weidman, Jerome (b.1913) American novelist, short-story writer, playwright, and essayist. A prolific and disciplined writer for half a century, Weidman has written more than a dozen novels, several plays, 200 short stories, and some travel essays. His shrewd, witty works often depict ambitious men who claw their way up from immigrant poverty to material success and power. Some of them try to reform the establishment, but more often his protagonists become obsessed with their rise to the top of the heap, losing their humanistic values as they beat the environmental odds which have been stacked against them.

Among his eight plays, *Fiorello!* and *I Can Get It For You Wholesale* garnered the greatest success. In his novels, Weidman's translation of moral sell-outs into lively stories have won him a large popular following. He is a skilled teller of tales, producing gripping plot lines, intriguing characters, and slick, punchy dialogue in fictions which often have a didactic edge. Those men who achieve success through hustling and betrayal are often betrayed themselves, or at least experience their success to be inexplicably empty.

Weidman often draws directly on Jewish themes, values, and language patterns, and he frequently depicts the conflict between the Jewish and American cultures. For example, the protagonist of *The Center of the Action* (1969), a novel about the publishing world, is torn between his lust for American-style success, on the one hand, and his feelings of gratitude and loyalty to his benefactor, on the other. These feelings are complicated by the fact that his benefactor is, like him, descended from Eastern European Jews, whereas the man he sells out to is a supercilious, assimilated Jew of German origins. As in most Weidman novels, however, loyalty loses and betrayal is the name of the game. Some of the stories in *My Father Sits in Dark* (1961) and his autobiographical novel *Fourth Street East* (1970) feature more domestic accounts of the cultural dislocation experienced by American Jewish immigrants and their children.

SYLVIA FISHMAN

Weigl, Karl (1881–1949) Austrian composer, later naturalized American. Karl Weigl was one of many assimilated Jews who held a prominent role in Viennese musical life at the beginning of this century. In 1902 he graduated from the Vienna Music Academy where he studied composition with Alexander von Zemlinsky and musicology with Guido ADLER, also assimilated Jews. Weigl went on to complete a doctorate at the University of Vienna in 1903 with a dissertation on the life of E. A. Förster. He was a rehearsal conductor at the Vienna Hofoper under Gustav MAHLER from 1904–6. Weigl also taught for many years at the New Vienna Conservatory, being made Professor of Theory in 1930.

Weigl's music was highly regarded by contemporary Viennese luminaries: the composers Richard Strauss, Mahler, and Arnold SCHOENBERG, and the conductors Bruno Walter and Furtwängler. By the mid-1930s, however, the taint of Jewish ancestry caused his compositions to be blacklisted from performance, in spite of their previous esteem.

Sensing the tenor of the times, Weigl left Vienna for New York in 1938. He taught theory and composition for the New York Philharmonic Society's Committee on Training and Scholarships, and in the 1940s held successive faculty positions at Hartt School of Music, Brooklyn College, and the New England Conservatory of Music. In 1943 Weigl became an American citizen.

Stylistically, Weigl's music reflects the Viennese tradition in which he was raised. His output includes a wide variety of orchestral and chamber music works, in addition to numerous art songs in the vein of Wolf and Mahler.

ORLY LEAH KRASNER

Weil, Simone (1909–1943) French philosopher and religious thinker. On her father's side a descendant of a pious Alsatian–Jewish family, Weil grew up in a notably emancipated and agnostic Parisian home. She was educated at the lycée Henri IV, and the École Normale Supérieure where she showed early signs of intellectual brilliance, graduating with a thesis on Descartes. During her schooldays under the influence of the philosopher Alain, her passionate interest in politics led to her involvement in radical leftist activities, and to the nickname, the Red Virgin. She did not, however, join the Communist Party and became increasingly critical of the USSR. From adolescence she had shown an interest in Roman Catholicism which intensified during the 1930s, leading to thoughts about conversion to Christianity.

A year (1934–5) as a manual worker in a factory and participation in the Spanish Civil War were Weil's important experiences in the 1930s. During these years she produced the main body of her literary work, devoted mainly to social, political, and theological considerations.

She continued writing almost ceaselessly during the early years of the Second World War, in Marseilles, in New York where she had moved with her parents, and finally in London, where she joined De Gaulle's Free French Forces. She died in a sanatorium at Ashford, Kent, in August 1943, having starved herself to death, through compassion for those dying under the Nazi occupation.

Weil's main importance, acknowledged by writers and thinkers such as T. S. Eliot and Martin Buber, lies in her religious thought, expressed with pungent style. Though inclined towards Catholicism, Weil defined herself as standing "on the threshold of the Church", never actually undergoing conversion. If she acknowledged her Jewishness as a matter of course, her attitude towards it was hostile, for she saw it as a rigid and cruel religion. Rather ironically, one of the priests she consulted about her readiness to become a Christian said: "I found in her, not in her heart which I found very open to charity (in the evangelical sense of love) but in her spirit, something crude, rigid, and intransigent for which she reproached the Jewish people".

BIBLIOGRAPHY
Gravity and Grace, trans. E.; Cranford (London: Routledge & Kegan Paul, 1952); *Waiting for God* (New York: Capricorn Books, 1951); *Selected Essays* trans. R. Rees (London: Oxford University Press, 1962)

FURTHER READING
Pétrement, S.: *Simone Weil*, trans. R. Rosenthal (London: Mowbrays, 1977)
Perrin, J. B., and Thibou, G.: *Simone Weil as we Knew Her*, (London: Routledge & Kegan Paul, 1953)

YORAM BRONOWSKI

Weiler, Moses Cyrus (b.1907) South African rabbi. He was born in Riga, Latvia, and after his initial education in Latvia, studied in Palestine where he matriculated in 1926, and the USA where he studied for the rabbinate at the Hebrew Union College, Cincinnati.

He arrived in South Africa in 1933 where he was chiefly responsible for the founding of the progressive (reform) movement. Johannesburg's Temple Israel was opened in 1936 and he served as its rabbi, and later also as chief minister of the South African movement, until his *aliyah* to Israel in 1958.

His Talmudic scholarship and deep love of Zion, his forceful personality, persuasive oratory, and organizational ability, combined to mold progressive Judaism in South Africa. Unique in expression, it is very moderate in practice and has always been pro-Zionist.

He was concerned about gender and racial equality in South Africa and the M. C. Weiler School in the black township of Alexandra, Johannesburg, is a testimony to his care for the underprivileged. He encouraged the Sisterhood of the South African progressive movement to sustain its black schoolchildren with additional books and equipment.

After settling in Israel, he became a senior lecturer in rabbinics at the Hebrew Union College in Jerusalem. He is an honorary life vicepresident of the World Union of Progressive Judaism and an executive of the Jewish National Fund.

Two of his sons were killed in Israel – Adam in the War of Attrition 1970, and Gideon in the Yom Kippur War in 1973. His pro-Zionism, even in grief, was positive in that he established funds and scholarships in their honor.

JOCELYN HELLIG

Weill, Alexandre (1811–1899) French historian and philosopher. The eccentric self-proclaimed prophet of the Faubourg Saint-Honoré, the Parisian district where he lived and whence flowed a stream of books and pamphlets for 50 years, was born in a small village (Schirhof) near Strasbourg, the son of a cattle dealer well versed in Hebrew and the Bible, and the grandson, on his mother's side, of a rabbi who is said to have been a friend of Robespierre. Alexandre was given an Orthodox education of Torah, Talmud, and Hebrew, which he could read, it seems, at the age of three. When he was 13 he took to the road, sampling various *yeshivot* in Alsace-Lorraine and Frankfurt in search of teachers worthy of teaching him. Disappointed, and tempted of what the outside world had to offer, he abandoned his rabbinical studies together with his childhood faith and eventually made for Paris (1838) where he settled down to educating himself. Irreverent, witty, iconoclastic, a man of prodigious vitality and erudition, and a fair share of arrogance, "le petit Weill" soon became a well-know figure, frequenting the giants of the day: Hugo, Balzac, Baudelaire, Nerval, and especially Heinrich HEINE, who prefaced one of his books and to whom he sung Hebrew melodies. If the claim that Weill initiated Hugo into the *kabbalah* is now largely discredited, it is possible that he played the general role of Hebrew specialist or at least contributed to creating in the outside world a certain image of the prophetic-messianic side of Judaism, the other side of the Rothschild coin. His sociopolitical commitment is disconcerting in its swing from Utopian socialism (he contributed over a hundred articles to the Fourierist *la Phalange* and *La Démocratie pacifique*, 1841–7) to staunch conservatism (collaboration on the royalist-Catholic *Gazette de France*, 1848–51). At the same time he stood as independent Republican in the 1848 elections. The apparent instability is not without its logic, at least in terms of Weill's temperament, a mixture of libertarian critique of tyranny, whether of the right or the left, and a yearning for law and order. Disenchanted with politics, he returned to the Bible, previously studied as a sacred text and now examined in a philosophical light, as a guide to the perplexed. Weill's Judaism, central to his philosophical and moral thought, remains perplexing in its contradictions. It even contains fashionable anti-Semitic elements, notably a virulent hostility towards the Talmud, regarded as a barrier to Jewish Emancipation, and to the Rothschilds personifying the wrong sort of emancipation. He believed that in its uncorrupted form, Mosaic law and Prophetic teachings, Judaism could have fused with Christianity. If Weill was one of the first "Jewish Jews" to question the legitimacy of Jewish cultural survival, he was also one of the rare men to do battle, his last, with Drumont's anti-Semitic *La France Juive* (1886).

BIBLIOGRAPHY

De l'état des juifs en Europe. *La Revue Indépendante* 16 (1844); *Mes romans* (Paris: Cohen Frères, 1886) [with Heine's preface of 1847]; *Épîtres cinglantes à M. Drumont* (Paris: Dentu, 1888)

FURTHER READING

Friedemann, J.: *Alexandre Weill: écrivain contestataire el historien engagé (1811–1899)* (Strasbourg and Paris: Istra, 1980)

NELLY WILSON

Weill, Kurt (1900–1950) German composer (later naturalized American). Born in Dessau, the son of a cantor, his early musical influences included both nineteenth-century German synagogue music and the more traditional east European cantorial music, together with experience gained through participation in the secular musical life of the Dessau Court.

He studied briefly with Engelbert Humperdinck but principally with Busoni. Early compositions include such concert works as *Symphony No. 1* (1921), and *Concerto for Violin and Wind Orchestra* (1924), but he went on to write mainly for theater, partly because he believed that music should serve a purpose and reach a wide audience. He wrote three one-act operas, two, *Der Protagonist* (1925) and *Der Zar lässt sich photographieren* (1927), in collaboration with playwright Georg Kaiser, and one, *Royal Palace* (1926), with Iwan GOLL. These works begin to show such characteristics as his use of music to portray different levels of reality, jazz, popular song, and satire.

In 1926 he married Lotte Lenya and in 1927 began his collaboration with Brecht with *Mahagonny Songspiel*, followed by *Die Dreigroschenoper* (1928), a play with songs and musical interludes, based on John Gay's *The Beggars' Opera*, which fulfilled the political and artistic aims of Brecht and Weill. This was followed by the less successful *Happy End* (1929) and *Aufstieg und Fall der Stadt Mahagonny*, based on the earlier *Mahagonny Songspiel*. This, a complete opera, sung throughout, was a savage critique of capitalist society. Its first performance, in Leipzig in 1930, was greeted by riots in a theater packed with Nazi sympathizers.

In 1933 Weill fled to exile in Paris, where he composed various works including *Die Sieben Todesünden der Kleinbürger* (1933) with Brecht. In

Kurt Weill

1935 he was invited to the USA by Meyer Weisgal to work on a Zionist musical. *The Eternal Road*. He lived there until his death in 1950, having become a committed Zionist and a patriotic American, and wrote many songs and musicals, including *Knickerbocker Holiday* (1938), *Lady in the Dark* (1941), and *Lost in the Stars* (1949) but his music changed to become consciously American, lacking the satirical bite of his European compositions. Nevertheless, he continued to write for wide audiences, rather than for an educated elite, in keeping with his earlier artistic and political ideals.

FURTHER READING

Jarman, D.: *Kurt Weill: An Illustrated Biography* (London: Orbis, 1982)
Sanders, R.: *The Days Grow Short* (London: Weidenfeld & Nicholson, 1980)

ANDREA BARON

Weinberg, Elbert (b.1928) American sculptor. Born in Hartford, Connecticut, Elbert Weinberg studied painting for a year at the Hartford Art School in 1945 before turning to sculpture. Between 1948 and 1951 he studied sculpture at the Rhode Island School of Design.

Twice the recipient of the Prix de Rome (1951 and 1953), he spent several years in Europe. Later, he studied with José Rivera at Yale University, where he received the Silver Medal Award for Achievement in the Arts in 1959.

Weinberg has worked in bronze, wood, and marble. His sculpture displays an Expressionist pathos appropriate to the themes he has explored: Old and New testament subjects, the Holocaust, and mythological motifs. Other, more pedestrian subjects, for example animals, are given a transcendent symbolism.

Weinberg has received numerous commissions for sculptures. In 1959 he produced a piece entitled *Processions* for the Jewish Museum, New York, and in 1975 Temple Beth-El in West Hartford, Connecticut, commissioned him to create *Procession No. 2*. He has created several Holocaust memorials as well. In 1979–80 the Jewish Federation of Delaware commissioned him to create one for Freedom Plaza in Wilmington, Delaware. It comprises three fifteen-foot concrete columns on which are etched the names of several of the concentration camps along with the bronze figures of a man, woman, and mother and child, representing the victims of the Holocaust. In 1982 the Jewish Community Center of West Hartford, Connecticut, commissioned Weinberg to create a similar memorial to the Holocaust.

Weinberg has participated in numerous group exhibitions of sculpture. Since 1959 he has had several one-man exhibitions at the Grace Borgenicht Gallery in New York. His sculpture is found in many distinguished public collections including The Museum of Modern Art, New York, The Brooklyn Museum, Brooklyn, New York, and the Whitney Museum of American Art, New York.

FURTHER READING

Hecht, A.: *Elbert Weinberg* (New York: Grace Borgenicht Gallery, 1986) [Exhibition catalog]

KRISTIE A. JAYNE

Weinberg, Jacob (1879–1958) Composer, music critic, and pianist. Born in Russia, Weinberg became an active member of the Society for Jewish Folk Music founded by Yoel ENGEL.

In 1923 he emigrated to Palestine, where he was active as chamber music pianist, music critic and composer. His opera, *The Pioneers* (1924), to his own libretto, was the first Hebrew national opera composed in Palestine and based on modern Jewish history and Zionist ideology. Contrasting the idealized presentation of the life in a pioneer kibbutz community with life in the Polish Diaspora, the opera combines quotes of folk- and popular songs, synagogue cantillation, and Russian orientalism and symbols. Due to the difficulties of performing new art music in Palestine in the 1920s Weinberg emigrated to the United States in 1927. There he soon assimilated into the Jewish community in New York. *The Pioneers* was produced in 1934 and won a composition prize. In the United States Weinberg was very prolific. He preserved the Jewish spirit of hasidic dance tunes and prayer modes in his numerous compositions in small forms of piano solo and for solo instruments and piano, like the *Improvisation on a Jewish Folk Song* (1950) and *Berceuse Palestinienne* (1929). In larger forms he composed two oratorios (*Isaiah* and *The Life of Moses*) and a piano concerto, which reflects the strong influence of Ernest BLOCH's style.

FURTHER READING

Appleton, L., ed.: *Four American Jewish Composers – Their Life and Works* (New York: 1962)

JEHOASH HIRSHBERG

Weinberger, Jaromír (1896–1967) Czech–

American composer. Weinberger studied in Prague and later (1916) went to Leipzig to study composition with Reger. In 1922 he made his first visit to the USA and taught composition for a short time at the Ithaca Conservatory, New York. On his return to Czechoslovakia he was employed by the National Theater in Bratislava. In 1927 his opera, the work for which he is best known – *Shvanda the Bagpiper* – received its first performance in Prague, achieving great success; it was shortly performed all over the world and remains one of the most popular of all Czech operas. The appeal of the work arises from its happy combination of Czech and Slovak folk elements, a rich and subtle use of the orchestra, and great melodic invention. From the early 1930s Weinberger gave all his attention to composing. *Valdštejn* (1937), an opera based on Schiller's *Wallenstein*, was produced in Vienna. He left Europe in the face of Nazi persecution and in 1939 settled in the USA, first living in New York and later in St Petersburg, Florida, where, depressed at the lack of interest in his works, he took his own life.

Works of Jewish interest include: *Hatikvah* for voice and pianoforte (1919); *Neima Ivrit* (Hebrew Song) for orchestra (1936); *Psalm cl* for soprano, tenor, and organ (1940); and *Ecclesiastes* (Kohelet) for soprano, baritone, chorus, organ, and bells (1946).

FURTHER READING

Lee, A.: *Jaromir Weinberger – A Critic's Notebook* (Boston: 1943, repr. 1972)

SYDNEY FIXMAN

Weiner, Lazare (1897–1982) American

composer, conductor, and pianist. He was born in Cherkass, near Kiev in Russia, and died in New York City. He began his studies at the State Conservatory in Kiev but left at the age of 17 to emigrate to the USA and continue his studies with Frederick Jocoby and Joseph Schillinger. In 1923 he became the first conductor of the "Freiheit Gezangsverein", which led to a long association with similar choruses, especially the Workmen's Circle Chorus, which he conducted for many years.

All his life Lazare Weiner had a great love for the Yiddish language, and many of his works are settings of Yiddish poetry or translations of poems into the Yiddish language. There are larger works, such as *To Thee America* (1942) on a text by A. Leyeles; *Legend of Toil* (1934) on a poem by I. Goichberg; besides these larger works, there are many songs on Yiddish texts. Some of these are original; others are arrangements of traditional melodies. Weiner had a very recognizable style in these shorter vocal works, combining simple diatonic tunes with harmonies reminiscent of Debussy and the late Romantic Russian masters. In 1950 he wrote a cantata called *The Golem* (Prologue) on a poem by Leivik for tenor, bass chorus, and orchestra. In 1956 Weiner took up the same subject and this time wrote an opera, *The Golem*, with a libretto by Ray Smolover. There are some secular works, such as a string quartet and some piano pieces, but he is best known for his many liturgical works. His synagogue music demonstrates a strong feeling for the eastern European traditional melodic style combined with a complex harmonic background. His complete Friday Eve and Sabbath Morning Services, including a *Hasidic Service*, are frequently used in most Temples of North America, and his love of the liturgy was made manifest to the many students who attended his classes at the Sacred School of Music of the Hebrew Union College, where he taught until his death.

SAMUEL H. ADLER

Weinfeld, Yocheved Israeli artist, active since the 1970s. So far Weinfeld is the only female Israeli artist to explore female sexuality in her art. Her sexuality is the core of her unique individuality, defining her womanhood, but at the same time constituting her source of anxiety. Weinfeld's art is imbued with ironic statements, such as the contradiction between woman's labor and image. In photographic images in which parts of her body are sewn together she juxtaposes the act of sewing with the cliché of feminine beauty, in a destructive act, rather than an act of mending. With iconic irony, materials associated with the menstrual cycle, cotton wool, pubic hair, and pads are pasted up in a collagistic manner, like documented specimens.

In a public performance of the *Shulhan 'arukh*, passages relating to the obligations imposed on Jewish woman concerning the menstrual cycle, ritual cleansing and so on, were read while Weinfeld acted out those religious obligations.

In an interview in 1976 Weinfeld expressed an exorcizing attitude to her work, a desire to externalize that which intrinsically frightens and disgusts her. Her art can be seen as linked stylistically to the international tendency during the 1970s towards aggressive, at times self-

mutilating, attitudes, and expressed in gestures of bodily destruction and mutilation.

NEDIRA YAKIR BUNYARD

Weingreen, Jacob (b.1908) Hebrew grammarian and Old Testament Scholar. Weingreen was born in Manchester, England. In 1937 he became Professor of Hebrew at the University of Dublin, a post he held for 41 years until 1978. In 1946 he was Director of Education of the Displaced Persons' Camp, Bergen-Belsen, but returned to Dublin where he was elected a Fellow at Trinity College, Dublin. In 1969 he was elected to the Council of the World Union of Jewish Studies in Jerusalem.

Weingreen is perhaps best known for *A Practical Grammar for Classical Hebrew*, a textbook first published in 1939 and used ever since in classrooms around the world. He is also the author of "Hebrew Grammar" in the *Encyclopedia Judaica Year Book* (1979) and "The Jews, Early History" in *Encyclopaedia Britannica* (1964).

Aside from his publications on Hebrew grammar and syntax and his studies of biblical language, Weingreen has undertaken extensive research into the Old Testament in *Themes of Old Testament Stories* (1977), *English Versions of the Old Testament* (1972), and *The Concepts of Retaliation and Compensation in Biblical Law* (1976). He has also written on biblical interpretation, including an article on the history of biblical interpretation in *The Interpreter's Dictionary of the Bible*.

Jacob Weingreen is a past President of the British Association of Jewish Studies.

JOHN MATTHEW

Weininger, Otto (1880–1903) Austrian philosopher. Born in Vienna, Weininger studied at the university there, gaining his doctorate in 1902. Having converted to Protestantism, Weininger proceeded to expand his doctoral thesis on bisexuality, which resulted in the publication in 1903 of *Geschlecht und Charakter* (*Sex and Character*, 1906). Weininger committed suicide a few months after the publication, at which point he and his book became a *cause célèbre* for a large section of Vienna's avant-garde. A posthumously published collection of Weininger's essays, *Über die letzten Dinge* (1903; On the ultimate questions), went through almost as many editions as his magnum opus. Among Weininger's admirers were Karl KRAUS, Stefan ZWEIG, Arnold SCHOENBERG, and Ludwig WITTGENSTEIN.

Weininger's main reputation today is as a pathological phenomenon – a misogynist, anti-Semitic Jewish intellectual, whose suicide was the logical outcome of his Jewish self-hatred. This image arises from the statements in *Sex and Character* concerning Woman and the Jew. His work should be understood in the context of the then current debate on the nature of the sexes. According to Weininger everyone was, to some extent, bisexual, due to what he believed to be the existence of male and female plasma in everyone. On the basis of this theory, Weininger went on to develop ideal types of Man and Woman, with Man representing the intellectual and moral principle, and Woman representing sensuality and the earth-bound side of human nature. Man was all, the genius – Woman nothing. Yet, as everyone was a bit of both, it was unclear to what extent political or social conclusions could be drawn from this. The only true emancipation for women was not political emancipation but rather the emancipation from Woman, that side of her nature dominated by sex. Men must help women attain this, and Weininger thus recommends sexual abstinence as the solution to humanity's problems.

Weininger also devoted a chapter in his book to developing another polarity, between the Aryan and the Jew, who was in effect an expression of nihilism. The description of what is Jewish is extremely negative, but there are many ironies in Weininger's picture. Anti-Semitism, because it is a collectivist view, is "Jewish", while the Jew who overcomes his Jewish self is even greater than the Aryan genius, for he becomes the founder of religion, the religious genius. Weininger is, in this respect, not so much the classic self-hater, as the ultimate eulogist of the assimilation.

FURTHER READING

Kohn, H.: Eros and sorrow. *Leo Baeck Institute Yearbook* (1961)

Le Rider, J.: *Le cas Otto Weininger: racines de l'antiféminisme et de l'antisemitisme* (Paris: Puf, 1982)

STEVEN BELLER

Weinreich, Max (1894–1969) Yiddish scholar. Born into a German-speaking family in Goldingen, Latvia, Weinreich started publishing Yiddish articles in 1907, studied in Vilna from 1908, and attended the University of St Petersburg's Faculty of Philology and History from 1913 to 1917. He pursued his studies in Berlin and Marburg, where he completed his 1923 doctoral thesis on the history of Yiddish Studies. Inspired by the eastern European Yiddishist movement, Weinreich became one of its first leaders who was able to draw upon a rigorous west European academic training. He resettled in Vilna in 1923, where he taught at the Yiddish Teachers' Seminary, and became the principal co-founder of the Yivo. Because of the coinciding of the Fifth International Congress of Linguists in Brussels with Hitler's invasion of Poland, Weinreich was able to escape to New York where he assumed leadership of the American branch of the Yivo, which became its international headquarters following the Holocaust. Weinreich became the Professor of Yiddish par excellence, and trained a number of leading scholars, the most talented of whom was his son, Uriel WEINREICH.

Max Weinreich is considered the century's leading Yiddish scholar. Beyond meticulous scholarly work on a multitude of aspects of Yiddish language and literature, Weinreich, more than anyone else, constructed the theoretical systems which enabled the modern intellectual world to view the history and structure of Yiddish in a new way which has won general acceptance. Drawing upon advances in sociology, linguistics, and psychology, Weinreich saw in Yiddish a microcosm of the language and culture-forming process. Elaborating on Ber BOROKHOV's ideas, Weinreich proposed the three-way distinction between the components of

Yiddish (the German component, the Hebrew and Aramaic component, the Slavic component) which are out-and-out Yiddish, irrespective of origin, versus the determinants – those parts of German, Hebrew and Aramaic, and Slavic, that could have become Yiddish, whether they did or didn't, in view of the historical coincidence of proximity in time and place. Both component and determinant are distinguished in Weinreich's system from the actual stock languages – German, Hebrew and Aramaic, and Slavic. In a stroke, Weinreich imposed order where popular misconception and prejudice had reigned, and came up with a paradigm that has proved invaluable to the study of other languages, especially other Jewish languages.

Weinreich's first major work was *Shtaplen* (1923; Rungs), which comprised four distinct studies: a survey of the extant research literature in Yiddish Studies, a study of sixteenth-century Yiddish scholarship, a critical edition of a seventeenth-century historical poem, and finally, a dialect monograph on Courland Yiddish. All four became classic models for further works. His *Bilder fun der yidisher literatur-geshikhte* (1928; Pictures from the literary history of Yiddish) was likewise highly influential. Over the decades he published hundreds of papers and articles, most of which remain essential points of departure for students of the history of Yiddish. His magnum opus is the four-volume *Geshikhte fun der yidisher shprakh* (1973; History of the Yiddish language), of which a partial English translation appeared in 1980.

FURTHER READING

Katz, D.: The theory of Yiddish and the Max Weinreich heritage. *Jewish Frontier* 49, no. 4 (1982) 15–24

King, R. D.: *The Weinreich Legacy. The Fifth Annual Avrom-Nokhem Stencl Lecture in Yiddish Studies* (Oxford: Oxford Centre for Postgraduate Hebrew Studies, 1988)

DOVID KATZ

Weinreich, Uriel (1926–1967) American linguistic theoretician and Yiddish scholar. Son

of Max WEINREICH, Uriel Weinreich spent his youth steeped in the Yiddish cultural environment of the "capital of Yiddish" – Vilna, where he was born. He settled in New York with his parents in 1940, and graduated from Columbia University. After serving in the US Army, he returned to Columbia, completing his doctorate, *Research Problems in Bilingualism, with Special Reference to Switzerland* in 1951. In book form (*Languages in Contact*, 1953), it has become a classic of modern linguistics. His 1954 paper, "Is a Structural Dialectology possible?", published in *Word* (which he co-edited), catapulted him to the front ranks of American theoretical linguistics.

Throughout his short life, Uriel Weinreich profoundly impressed peers and readers with prolific output and the consistently first-rate quality of his work. In addition to his many publications in general and Yiddish linguistics, he embarked on large-scale projects. The greatest of these is the *Language and Culture Atlas of Ashkenazic Jewry*, an ambitious blueprint for recording the language and folklore of all of Ashkenazic Jewry – western as well as eastern European – and mapping the results to recover the internal linguistic and cultural differentiation. The project made use of a large scale questionnaire designed with the principles of structural linguistics in mind, a program for interviewing informants throughout the world, and the latest computer technology. The Atlas still awaits publication. His *English–Yiddish Yiddish–English Dictionary* appeared posthumously in 1968, and has since become the most widely used Yiddish dictionary. He had dedicated much of his energy during a tragic illness to ensure its completion. He was not yet 41 when he died.

FURTHER READING

King, R. D.: *The Weinreich Legacy. The Fifth Annual Avrom-Nokhem Stencl Lecture in Yiddish Studies* (Oxford: Oxford Centre for Postgraduate Hebrew Studies, 1988).

Malkiel, Y.: Uriel Weinreich, Jakob Jud's last student. *Romance Philology* 22 (1968) 128–32

DOVID KATZ

Weisgall, Hugo (b.1912) American composer, conductor, and educator. Born in Ivancice, Czechoslavakia he emigrated to the USA in 1920, settling in Baltimore where he attended the Peabody Conservatory (1928–31) and Johns Hopkins University (1929–35, 1937–44); from the latter institution, he received a doctorate in Germanics. He attended the Curtis Institute (1934–9), where he studied composition and conducting. He studied composition privately with Roger Sessions (1933–40).

Weisgall's outstanding ability as a linguist enabled him to rise quickly while serving in the US Army from a private to assistant military attaché to the Czech government-in-exile in London. In 1945 he was assigned as military attaché to the Czech government, then joined the Diplomatic Service as cultural attaché to the American Embassy in Prague, Czechoslavakia.

During his matriculation at Johns Hopkins, Weisgall served as musical director of Har Sinai Temple in Baltimore and, after returning from his army and diplomatic service, he resumed his conducting career, founding and directing the Baltimore Chamber Music Society and the Hilltop Musical Company. For 23 years he taught at Queens College, retiring in 1983 as Distinguished Professor of Music. Hugo Weisgall continues as Chairman of the Faculty of the Cantors Institute of the Jewish Theological Seminary in New York, and he lectures extensively on the topic of Jewish Music.

Weisgall has received a host of honors including membership in the National Institute of Arts and Letters, three Guggenheim fellowships and numorous grants.

The New Grove Dictionary of Music and Musicians (1980) has described Hugo Weisgall as "perhaps America's most important composer of opera". He tried his hand very early in his compositional career with a one-act opera, *Night* (1932), and a second one, *Lilith* (1934). Both of these have been withdrawn, but in 1959 his opera *Six Characters in Search of an Author* was produced by the New York City Opera and acclaimed as "the most significant American opera of the past thirty-five years".

Even though Weisgall has written works for all media, his interest has been concentrated mainly in the musical theater and concerned with music for the voice. He has written eight operas and has been commissioned by the San Francisco Opera for another one, *Esther*. His music is a true synthesis of the intense chromaticism of the second Viennese school with the clear structures, textures and lyricism of neoclassicism.

SAMUEL H. ADLER

Weiss, Ernst (1884–1940) Novelist. Born into a Jewish middle-class family in Brünn (Brno), he wished to become a "good mediocre citizen" and therefore decided to be a doctor. He finished his studies in 1911, practiced in Vienna, and served in 1914–18 as a regimental physician on the Eastern front. Only in 1920, after having worked for two years in a Prague hospital, did he finally realize the decision taken many years before, to be a writer. He moved to Berlin where he lived until 1933; then, to be near his sick mother he returned to Prague and, in 1934, went to Paris.

From Weiss's first novel *Die Galeere* (1914; The gallery), the basic theme of his novels remains man's probation in a hostile world, with the decision arrived at always against him. Weiss varies the ideas from the continued resigned existence of the protagonist to his absolute destruction; in *Tiere in Ketten* (1918; Animals in chains), one of the outstanding novels of literary Expressionism, and in *Boetius von Orlamünde* (1928), a further notion is added: that of the blessed existence of animals in their unawareness of death. In *Die Feuerprobe* (1928; Trial by fire), enlarged and partly changed in 1929, Weiss tried to probe the depth of man's mind and soul where the thoughts about murder and crime take root. In his dramas as well as in his numerous short stories and essays, Weiss followed the same line of thought and reasoning.

In the novels of his last creative period, 1930–9, the fate of the protagonist is ruled by his emotional ties with his father, which, in each case, determines the fate of the son and prevent him from forming lasting emotional ties with others. The supremacy of this motif in Weiss's novels must be attributed to the impact Franz KAFKA's personal fate left on Weiss, just as the readiness of these protagonists to accept "punishment" and "judgment" for their emotional insufficiency points to Kafka. Also the recurrent use of key words like "accused", "witness", and "trial" in *Georg Letham, Arzt und Mörder* (1931; Georg Letham, physician and murderer), *Der arme Verschwender* (1936; The poor squanderer) and *Der Verführer* (1938; The tempter), evoke Kafka, all the more as there is nothing in Weiss's personal life to explain his choice of motif. According to Kafka's diaries he met Weiss first in 1913 and the friendship between them progressed quickly; the disruption of this equivocal relationship – again Kafka's letters and diaries leave no doubt as to the strain and pleasure this friendship afforded him – a few years later deeply affected Weiss. Nevertheless Weiss' cycle of lyrics *Der Gegengott* (The anti-God), written in 1916/17, is dedicated to Kafka.

In four of Weiss' five later novels the protagonist is a physician, as also in the last one, *Ich–der Augenzeuge* (*The Eyewitness*, 1977), sent in September 1938 to the American Guild for German Cultural Freedom, and published in 1963. In this first psychological novel about Hitler, Weiss attempted to expose the source of individual and collective guilt, and responsibility for the events in Germany after 1933.

Weiss, being a Czech citizen, had tried to join the Czech army in 1939, but was rejected for medical reasons; he had neither the physical nor the emotional strength to join those of his friends who fled from Paris. On the day the German army entered Paris he committed suicide.

BIBLIOGRAPHY

The Eyewitness, trans. E. McKee (Boston: Houghton Mifflin, 1977) [introduction by R. Binion)

MARGARITA PAZI

Weiss, Isaac Hirsch (1815–1905) Talmudist and historian of rabbinic literature.

Born in Moravia, he received a traditional Talmudic education and pursued secular studies. Stung by economic reverses, he moved to Vienna in 1859 where he worked as a Hebrew proofreader until receiving an appointment to the faculty of Adolph Jellinek's "Beit Ha-Midrash" academy of Jewish studies, a post he held from 1864 until his death. In 1880, along with his colleague Meir Friedman, he founded *Beit Talmud*, a monthly journal devoted to scholarship in rabbinic literature. Weiss established a towering reputation in the research of this literature. He published critical editions of two tanaitic *midrashim*: *Sifra* (1862) and *Mekhilta* (1865), accompanied by introductions and commentaries which reflected his historical–critical methodologies. His greatest scholarly achievement, *Dor dor vedorshav*, appeared in five volumes from 1871 to 1891. As indicated by its German title, *Zur Geschichte der Jüdischen Tradition*, the work traces the history of the oral/rabbinic law from its beginnings to the end of the fifteenth century. Weiss argued the thesis that the rabbinic legal tradition experienced stages of development and change. The oral law, which predates the written Torah and is its indispensable commentary, changes through the activity of scholars and sages who expand and interpret it so that it suits the needs of the times. This position evoked harsh criticism from traditionalists, among them Isaac Halevy, whose six-volume *Dorot rishonism* (1897–1939), aimed especially against Weiss, denies a historical development of the oral law. Scholars have subsequently modified many of Weiss's findings and have noted apologetic tendencies in some of his conclusions. Nonetheless, his work set the pattern for future research and remains unmatched in its comprehensive scope.

FURTHER READING

Ginzberg, L.: Isaac Hirsch Weiss. In *Students, Scholars and Saints* (Philadelphia: The Jewish Publication Society of America, 1928)

MARK WASHOFSKY

Weiss, Peter (1916–1982) Playwright, poet, artist, and filmmaker of German birth. His father was a Jew who converted to the Lutheran faith. Weiss left Germany in 1934 and had his first exhibition of paintings in England in 1935. From 1936 to 1938 he studied at the Art Academy in Prague. In 1939 he settled in Sweden, adopting Swedish citizenship in 1945. His first literary works (1946–7) were prose poems written in Swedish. In the 1950s he returned to his mother tongue in his writings but worked mainly on Swedish avant-garde film documentaries, publishing a book, *Avantgarde Film* in 1956.

In the early 1960s he caused a stir with the publication of his surreal autobiographical works *Abschied von den Eltern* (1961; *Leavetaking*, 1966) and *Fluchtpunkt* (1962; Vanishing point). In *Leavetaking* the author returns home after the death of his father and relives his early life and his sense of confinement within the family home, recalling his discovery that his father was a Jew and his understanding of the reasons for the persecution he had suffered. In *Vanishing Point* he examines more fully his attitude to the Holocaust, dividing the world into victims and executioners, oppressors and oppressed, but feeling within himself the potential to be both victim and executioner.

His best-known work, *Die Verfolgung und Ermordung Jean Paul Marats dargestellt durch die Schauspielergruppe des Hospizes zu Charenton unter Anleitung des Herrn de Sade* (The persecution and assassination of Jean Paul Marat, as performed by the inmates of the Asylum of Charenton under the direction of the Marquis de Sade), is a play in rhyming verse, combining elements of cabaret, side show, and Theater of Cruelty, with flagellations, deformities, and perversions, which marked the turning point in Weiss's work. The "debate" between Marat and de Sade reflects Weiss's own undecided state of mind. After this, however, his work is that of a committed Marxist, in which the Jewish question is only part of a larger "human question", the result of a system – capitalism – where the weak are oppressed by the strong, whether it be for reasons of race, religion, or social or economic status, a view explicitly expressed by the central character in his 1969 play *Trotskiy i exil* (Trotsky in exile).

In 1964, the year in which the Marat/Sade

was first performed, Weiss wrote *Die Ermittlung* (*The Trial*, 1966), "an oratorio in 11 cantos", based on the records of the Auschwitz trial in Frankfurt. Only once, however, are the Jews, the victims of the horrors so clearly portrayed in the play, actually named, and blame is laid not only on the Nazis but on what is seen as the direct cause of the tragedy, capitalism.

In the 1970s Weiss worked mainly on *Die Ästhetik des Widerstands*, (1975–81; *The Esthetics of Resistance*, 1983), an anti-Fascist historical novel. His last work, premiered in Stockholm in 1982, was *The New Trial*, an updated version of Kafka's *The Trial*, in which he enumerated the crimes of multi-national combines.

The first major retrospective of his paintings was held in Zurich in 1979. Besides illustrating his own works, such as *The Shadow of the Coachman's Body*, with surreal collages inspired by Max Ernst and James Ensor, he illustrated works by other authors.

He received several literary awards, including the Charles Veillon Prize in 1963 and the Heinrich Mann Prize in 1966.

BIBLIOGRAPHY
Bodies and Shadows (New York: Delacorte Press, 1969)

FURTHER READING
Hoffmann, R.: *Peter Weiss: Malerei, Zeichnungen, Collagen* (East Berlin: Henschelverlag, 1984)
Vance, K. A.: *The Theme of Alienation in the Prose of Peter Weiss* (Las Vegas: Peter Lang, 1981)

CATHERINE PHILLIPS

Weizmann, Chaim (1874–1952) Zionist leader. Born in Motol, Russia, to a typical Pale of Settlement *shtetl* family, Weizmann was influenced by the populist *Hibbat Zion* movement. A letter written by him at the age of 11 showed a developing flair for leadership, and foreshadowed the future importance of England to the Zionist movement:

> For why should we look to the Kings of England for compassion that they should take pity upon us and give us a resting place? In vain, all have denied: The Jews must die, but England will nevertheless have mercy upon us. In conclusion, to Zion: Jews – to Zion let us go. (*Letters* vol. 1)

Weizmann studied science in Pinsk, Darmstadt, and Berlin. He completed his doctorate in chemistry at Fribourg University in Switzerland in 1898 and was appointed lecturer in chemistry at Manchester University in 1904. As a research chemist, he registered some one hundred patents under the name Charles Weizmann.

As a propagandist and speaker for the Zionist movement, Weizmann promulgated the view of AHAD HA'AM, that Jewish culture, representing the totality of historical, religious, and linguistic experience, was fully realizable only in a national homeland. In contradistinction to Herzl's agenda of settling the land through diplomatic maneuvering and the development of agriculture through wealthy patronage, Weizmann formed a "Democratic Fraction" within the Zionist movement, emphasizing the importance of the populist contribution. Influenced by his training as a chemist, Weizmann called this "synthetic Zionism", a blend of diplomacy with "dunam by dunam" colonization, and education of the people. He sought the development of a university in Palestine as well as the use of Hebrew as the language of instruction at the Technion.

As a research chemist during the First World War, Weizmann developed a new process for the production of acetone, essential to make cordite, a naval explosive. As a result of his contribution to the war effort, he influenced British policy regarding the disposition of Palestine, and the value of a Jewish presence there in its fight against the Ottoman Empire. The 1917 Balfour Declaration was the first acknowledgment by a world power of its interest in a Jewish return to Palestine.

This triumph propelled Weizmann to a position of leadership in the World Zionist Organization, of which he was elected president in 1920. He continued to fight for cultural and economic development, organizing the Jewish agency in 1929. When the State of Israel was established in 1948, Weizmann was its logical and sentimental choice for first president. He lived and was buried at Rehovot at the Weizmann Institute for Science. Weizmann completed his autobiography, *Trial and Error*, in 1949.

BIBLIOGRAPHY
The Letters and Papers of Chaim Weizmann, ed. M. Weisgal et al., vols 1–3, series A (London: Oxford University Press, 1968–72); vols 4–7, series A (Jerusalem: Israel Universities Press, 1973–5)

FURTHER READING
Reinharz, J.: *Chaim Weizmann: The Making of a Zionist Leader* (Oxford: Oxford University Press, 1985)
Weisgal, M., and Carmichael, J., eds: *Chaim Weizmann: A Biography by Several Hands* (New York: Atheneum, 1963)

JANE SHAPIRO

Werfel, Franz (1890–1945) Austrian novelist, poet, essayist, and framatist. Werfel was born in Prague, studied at the university there, and became a publisher's editor. After serving in the Austrian army, he settled in Vienna and married Alma Mahler-Gropius. In 1938 he emigrated and lived in Switzerland and France before going on to the USA. His death occurred at Beverly Hills, California, but his final resting place is in Vienna.

Werfel began his prolific literary career as one of the foremost poets of Expressionism (*Der Welfreund*, 1911; *Wir sind*, 1913; *Einander*, 1915). Love, friendship, and a passionate cosmic brotherhood are the main themes of his early poems, but Werfel continued to write poetry until the end of his life. The most successful of his earlier novels were *Verdi, Roman der Oper* (1924; *Verdi: A Novel of the Opera*, 1925) and *Die vierzig Tage des Musa Dagh* (1933; *The Forty Days of Musa Dagh*, 1934), the latter dealing memorably with the persecution of the Armenians by the Turks. That Werfel was, despite the timelessness of his religious quest and his humanistic orientation, very much of his time is indicated by such works as the novel *Barbara oder Die Frömmigkeit* (1929; *The Pure in Heart*, 1931), which asserts the primacy of individual religiosity and integrity over a flawed reality and dubious political activism. Man's fall and salvation is the theme of such plays as *Spiegelmensch* (1920) and *Paulus unter den Juden* (1926; *Paul Among the Jews*, 1928). In 1935 Werfel collaborated with Kurt WEILL and Max

REINHARDT on the biblical–historical pageant *Der Weg der Verheissung (The Eternal Road,* 1936), which was performed in New York as an antidote to Hitlerism.

Werfel's novel *Das Lied von Bernadette* (1941; *The Song of Bernadette,* 1942), the story of the shrine at Lourdes, became an international bestseller. Among Werfel's later plays is the "comedy of a tragedy" *Jacobowsky und der Oberst* (1944; *Jacobowsky and the Colonel,* 1944), the inspiring story of strange bedfellows on the flight from Nazi domination. The posthumously published *Der Stern der Ungeborenen* (1946; *The Star of the Unborn,* 1946) is a bit of philosophical science fiction. In later life Werfel came intellectually and emotionally close to Catholicism, but he never converted.

BIBLIOGRAPHY

Paul Among the Jews, trans. P. Levertoff (London: Diocesan House, 1928); *The Forty Days,* trans. G. Dunlop (London: Jarrolds, 1934); *The Eternal Road,* trans. L. Lewisohn (London: Jarrolds, 1937); *Verdi: A Novel of the Opera,* trans. H. Jessiman (London: Jarrolds, 1944); *The Song of Bernadette,* trans. L. Lewisohn (London: Pan Books, 1950)

FURTHER READING

Foltin, L. B.: *Franz Werfel* (Stuttgart: Metzler, 1972)
Steiman, L. B.: *Franz Werfel: The Faith of an Exile* (Canada: Wilfrid Laurier, 1985)
Zahn, L.: *Franz Werfel* (Berlin: Colloquium, 1966)

HARRY ZOHN

Arnold Wesker

Wesker, Arnold (b.1932) British dramatist. Born in Stepney, London, Wesker left school at 16. After working at various jobs he completed two years of national service in the Royal Air Force. This experience was to be utilized in Wesker's fifth play, *Chips With Everything* (produced London 1962). After his national service and a variety of jobs in Norfolk, Wesker worked as a chef in Paris during 1956, which provided material for his first play *The Kitchen* (produced London 1959). On his return to England Wesker entered the London School of Film Technique and, in 1957, met Lindsay Anderson who promoted *The Kitchen* and *Chicken Soup With Bar-* ley (produced London 1958) at the Royal Court Theater. It was with the production of this play in London that Wesker gained national recognition. This play takes as its subject matter the disintegration of a politically conscious family based in London's Jewish East End. It moves from the idealistic opposition to Fascism in October 1936 to the disillusionment, 20 years later, with the British Welfare State and Russian Stalinism. Focusing on a working-class Jewish family, this play also records the breakup of the close-knit Jewish community in London's East End and its resulting estrangement from the mass-produced values of modern industrial society.

It was Wesker's stark Naturalism and strident – even didactic – Socialism which particularly characterized his controversial early dramas. *Chicken Soup With Barley* proved to be the first part of a trilogy of plays, "The Wesker Trilogy", which included *Roots* (produced London 1959) and *I'm Talking About Jerusalem* (produced London 1960), and which received much critical acclaim. *Roots*, set in Norfolk in 1959, continues the theme of estrangement from the first part of the trilogy; *I'm Talking About Jerusalem* situates two Jewish characters from *Chicken Soup With Barley* in a Norfolk commune which is inspired by the ideals of William Morris. In this, the last part of the trilogy, Wesker showed, perhaps a little too obviously, that such laudable ideals are impossible to maintain in a society dominated by values which oppose such individual initiatives.

The controversial social realism of "The Wesker Trilogy" achieved an important symbolic dimension with the production of *Chips With Everything* in 1962. Other plays of this period such as *Their Very Own Garden City* (produced Brussels 1965) also explored the by now familiar Wesker theme of the failed revolutionary. In contrast, *The Four Seasons* (produced London 1965), eschewed any social context and doggedly explored the arena of private pain which began to interest Wesker increasingly in the mid 1960s. With the production of *The Old Ones* (produced London 1972), Wesker's phase of experimental drama was rewarded with a powerful play which examined the themes of toughness and survival in old age. Most of the characters in *The Old Ones* are Jewish, and the play also revolves around the building of a *sukkah*, as well as other Jewish sources and symbols. *The Wedding Feast* (produced Stockholm 1974) returns successfully to the Norfolk of Wesker's earlier plays and situates a paternalistic Jewish businessman against this background. Once again, Wesker contrasts the idealism of his characters with the harsh realities that surround them. This theme is given its most comprehensive treatment in Wesker's *The Merchant* (produced New York 1977) which is an impressive reworking of Shakespeare's *The Merchant of Venice* in a quasi-realistic historical setting.

In all, Wesker has written 19 plays and remains a controversial dramatist. One of his plays, *The Journalists* (London: Writers and Readers Cooperative, 1975), has not been professionally produced in England and most of his plays have generated intense critical debate. He has also published *Fears of Fragmentation* (London: Cape, 1970) and *The Journalists: a Triptych* (London: Cape, 1979) which refer to some of the controversies which have surrounded his plays. Other works include four volumes of short stories, some of which have been dramatized. Wesker was the artistic director of Center 42 which aimed to utilize trade-union support to popularize the arts in Britain. His latest work includes *Distinctions* (London: Cape, 1985) an anthology of his uncollected articles, many of which refer to his Jewishness which remains a central concern in both his life and drama.

FURTHER READING

Leeming, G.: *Wesker: The Playwright* (London: Methuen, 1983)

BRYAN CHEYETTE

Wessely, Naphtali Hartwig [Herz; Hirsch]

(1725–1805) Hebrew poet and scholar. Wessely was born in Hamburg to a well-to-do family which had fled from Poland in 1648. He lived in Copenhagen, Amsterdam, and Berlin and received a religious education, combined with modern studies. His first books were valuable contributions to the study of Hebrew grammar and philology, especially *Gan na'ul* (1765; A locked garden) which furthered the revival of the Hebrew language. He also contributed to Moses MENDELSSOHN's *Bi'ur* (translation of the Bible into German, with commentary) and, with Mendelssohn, served as one of the founding fathers of *Hame'assef*, the pioneering journal of the HASKALAH, devoted to Jewish cultural and educational reform and the revival of Hebrew.

Wessely's major contribution rested in two major works, the first being *Shirei tif'eret* (1789; Songs of glory), a five-volume rhymed epic, in part didactic, in part commentary, in addition to being a virtuoso poetic exercise, which described Moses and the Exodus in the popular pseudo-Classical style of the day. In its time this poem, influenced by Klopstock's *Messias*, achieved great popularity, running to a number of editions. Nevertheless it ultimately suffered the same fate as Klopstock's epic about which Lessing had said, "Everyone praises Klopstock and nobody reads him". However, Wessely's *Shirei tif'eret* exerted a direct influence on the writing of Judah Loeb GORDON.

The second of Wessely's major works, *Divrei shalom ve'emet* (1782; Words of peace and truth), came about as a result of Joseph II's Edict of Tolerance (1782) which ordered a reform of Jewish education and promised certain civil rights. Despite his own religious Orthodoxy and the oppsition of the ultra-Orthodox, Wessely set out the need for Jewish educational reform and proposed a course of Jewish study which would combine the religious and the secular, also advocating the study of the Bible in German. In his proposed synthesis – later to be echoed by Gordon – between the good Jew and the enlightened person, and in his educational ideals, Wessely summarized the entire program of the *Haskalah*, presenting what amounted to its manifesto, and began an important chapter in the history of the German *Haskalah* movement.

GLENDA ABRAMSON

West, Nathanael [Nathan Weinstein] (1903–1940) American writer. He grew up in New York City in a home in which Americanization was all-important. Because his German–Jewish parents spoke German at home, refusing to speak Yiddish or Russian (although they came from Lithuania), and identified with the assimilationist German–Jewish middle class, Nathan learned English as quickly as he learned how to become an American. He went to PS 81 and PS 186, and De Witt Clinton High School, where he was an ordinary student. He also went to Camp Paradox summers, a middle-class Jewish camp where he was dubbed "Pep", presumably because he was awkward and spoke slowly.

Although Nathan did not graduate from High School he was admitted to Tufts University, on a forged transcript, as Nathaniel Weinstein. A year later, in 1922, forced to withdraw, he succeeded in gaining admission to Brown University, again on a fraudulent transcript. At Brown, where he was known as a "Joe College" dude, he was refused admittance to a prestigious Christian fraternity, because he was Jewish. In June 1924, he wrote a piece which told the story of a flea named Saint Puce, born under Christ's armpit, who fed on his body, and died at the moment of Jesus's death. This story was later expanded into the central metaphor of *The Dream Life of Balso Snell*, which he wrote from 1924 to 1930.

In 1926–7, just before going to Paris for his "bohemian" trip, Weinstein changed his name legally to Nathanael West. *The Dream Life of Balso Snell* (1931) is a satirical attack on literary games and on the perversion of art in a mass culture. As Norman Podhoretz saw it *Balso Snell* was a "brilliantly insane surrealist fantasy that tries very hard to mock Western Culture out of existence". It was a brilliant, though uncontrolled, first novel, unfortunately both anti-Semitic and anti-Christian. The point is that, searching for something real to cling to, he ended by mocking every possible false dream.

Miss Lonelyhearts (1933), one of West's two best novels, is cynical and violent, as it contends that the myths of love and compassion are irrelevant to the real world.

In West's novel *A Cool Million: The Dismantling of Lemuel Pitkin* (1934), a satirical attack on the American Horatio Alger myth, the honest, industrious Lemuel is consistently victimized in the midst of a huge nightmare, the American Dream. Lemuel of course, can be seen as a betrayed hero or a schlemiel. Only in *The Day of the Locust* (1939) did West succeed in forging the parts together to make another first class novel. It combines amorality, apocalypse, and artificiality within the framework of movie-mad Hollywood. West caught the emptiness of Hollywood and made it frighteningly real.

According to I. J. Kapstein, West's close friend from Brown University days, West got even with American democracy, with the world that made him a Jew even though he was indifferent to his religion (however, most of his close friends were Jewish), and with Christianity, calling it a stupid illusion having nothing to do with the reality of human nature and the hard truths of life. In short, writing for West was a means to an end, the achievement to acceptance, the dream life of Nathanael West come true. It is inconceivable for West to have written as he did had he not been Jewish.

On 22 December 1940 West and his new bride, Eileen McKenny, were killed in an automobile crash near El Centro, California. As Jay Martin put it, his novels reflect his era but are also permanent and true explorations into the Siberia of the human spirit.

FURTHER READING

Hyman, S. E.: *Nathanael West* (St Paul: University of Minnesota, 1962).

Light, J. F.: *Nathanael West* (Evanston: Northwestern University, 1961).

Martin, J.: *Nathanael West* (New York: Farrar, Straus, 1970).

Walden, D.: Nathanael West. In *20th Century American Jewish Fiction Writers*. (Detroit; Gale Research Co., 1984) 323–31 [vol. 28 in the *Dictionary of Literary Biography* series]

DANIEL WALDEN

Whitman [Bashein]**, Ruth** (b.1922) American poet and translator. Born in New York, Whitman received her BA from Radcliffe College and her MA from Harvard University. Married three times, Whitman is the name of her first husband from whom she was divorced in 1958. The mother of three children, Whitman has had a wide range of editorial and teaching positions, including lecturer in poetry at Radcliffe College and at Harvard University. The winner of numerous awards, including the Poetry Society of America's di Castagnola Award for her manuscript-in-progress of *The Marriage Wig, and Other Poems* (1968) and the Kovner Award from the Jewish Book Council of America, she lists her religious affiliation in *Contemporary Authors* as "secular Jewish".

Her first collection of poetry, *Blood and Milk Poems* (1963) appeared just before three volumes of her translations, including a joint translation of Isaac Bashevis SINGER's *Short Friday* (1966) and *The Seance* (1968). In addition to joint translation of *Selected Poems* of Alain Bosquet (1963), she was editor and translator of a bilingual edition of *An Anthology of Modern Yiddish Poetry*

(1966). *The Marriage Wig*, the second volume of her own poetry, was followed by her translation of *The Selected Poems of Jacob Glatstein* [sic] (1972) to whose memory she dedicates one of her most moving poems "Lament for a Yiddish poet". Subsequent books include *The Passion of Lizzie Borden* (1973), *Tamsen Donner: A Woman's Journey* (1975), and a novella in prose and poetry, *The Testing of Hannah Senesh* (1986). In addition Whitman has contributed to and edited a number of works on teaching the writing of poetry and on being a woman artist.

Notable among her poems are several sequences in the voices of historical figures, "The Passion of Lizzie Borden", and the book-length "Tamsen Donner" which attempts to re-create the journal of that woman, a poet, who, with her husband, children, and several other families, embarked on an ill-fated trip from Illinois to California in 1846. Caught in the Sierra mountains by a series of fierce blizzards, much of the party perished and those surviving resorted to cannibalism. The trip is remembered as an example of the sometimes tragic struggles of American pioneers, and Whitman's sure words bring the reality of their courage into the present day. Tamsen's hunger makes her feel "filled with light, a music that the saints sought and called God" as Whitman in her own voice characterizes the quality engendered by "Yom Kippur: Fasting": "You are a harp for whatever wind / God wants to play".

FURTHER READING

Damashek, R.: Ruth Whitman. In *Contemporary Poets*, (4th edn, London and Chicago: St James Press, 1985) 923–4

Poetry Magazine (May 1964), (March 1970)

ELIZABETH KLEIN

Wieniawski, Henryk (1835–1880) Violinist and composer. Born in Lublin, Poland, Wieniawski was accepted in 1843 as a student at the Paris Conservatoire where, in 1846, he was awarded the First Prize. After a period (from 1848) in St Petersburg, where he gave a number of concerts, he returned to the Conservatoire in 1849 to concentrate on harmony.

In 1851 he began to travel as a performer, though he continued to compose and by 1853 had completed and published some 14 works, including his first violin concerto. His fame grew rapidly and he appeared in Paris with Anton RUBINSTEIN in 1858, and in 1859 in London. In 1860 he composed his famous *Légende*, opus 17. The same year he settled in St Petersburg where he was appointed violinist to the Czar, remaining there until 1872. During this period he composed his finest work, the second violin concerto in D minor, opus 22. In 1872 he started to travel again, beginning with a tour of North America. In 1875–7 he took an appointment as Professor of Violin at the Brussels Conservatory. Thereafter, in spite of ill-health, he continued his concert tours, returning finally to Moscow, where he died.

SYDNEY FIXMAN

Wiesel, Elie (b.1928) American novelist, essayist, and intellectual. Born in Sighet, Romania, his early education consisted of secular and religious studies. In 1944 he and his family were deported to Auschwitz, where his mother and youngest sister died. His father died in Buchenwald whence Wiesel was liberated. In 1946 he arrived in France where he continued his education, eventually adopting French as his literary language. Wiesel became an American citizen in 1963, and in 1976 was appointed Andrew Mellon Professor of Humanities at Boston University.

Following a brief career as a journalist (1948–54), Wiesel published his first book dealing with his experience in the *univers concentrationnaire*, *Un di Velt Hot Geshvign* (1956), which later appeared in a shorter French edition, *La Nuit* (1958; *Night*, 1960). These publications marked his debut as spokesman for the millions of murdered Jews and for the silent survivors. Wiesel depicts the particularity of the Jewish tragedy as being paradigmatic of the universal human experience. Four themes dominate his literature: being a witness; the realities and ramifications of silence; the symbolic revolt of laughter; and the necessity to establish dialogue. These themes are tightly woven together

with biblical and hasidic lore as Wiesel's protagonists seek to establish a meaningful post-Auschwitz mode of existence. He demonstrates this in works such as *Le Mendiant de Jérusalem* (1968; *A Beggar in Jerusalem*, 1970) and *Le Cinquième fils* (1983; *The Fifth Son*, 1985). Wiesel's writings have likewise focused attention on the plight of Soviet Jewry, notably in *Les Juifs du silence* (1966; *The Jews of Silence*, 1966) and *Le Testament d'un poète juif assassiné* (1981; *The Testament*, 1981).

Recipient of major Jewish, literary, and humanitarian awards, Wiesel is also a Commander of the Légion d'Honneur, holder of the United States Congressional Gold Medal, and was honored with a Medal of Liberty for his contributions to American life. In 1986 he was awarded the Nobel Peace Prize.

Other works in English include: *Souls on Fire* (1972), *The Oath* (1973), and *A Jew Today* (1979).

FURTHER READING

Brown, R. M.: *Elie Wiesel: Messenger to All Humanity*, (Notre Dame: University of Notre Dame Press, 1983)

Fine, E. S.: *Legacy of Night: The Literary Universe of Elie Wiesel* (Albany: State University of New York Press, 1982)

SIMON SIBELMAN

Winder, Ludwig (1889–1946) Czech-born novelist. Winder excelled in the convincing presentation of the coherence of human reaction and the unsurmountable influence of ethnic and social heritage. Born in Schaffa, Moravia, he grew up in small Moravian towns and therefore his experience of being a Jew was quite different from that of his later friends of the "Prague circle".

The aggressive reactions of the Jewish characters in Winder's first novel, *Die rasende Rotationsmaschine* (1917; The raving rotating apparatus), the compulsive rejection of the Orthodox Jewish surroundings in *Die jüdische Orgel* (1922; The Jewish organ), and the revolt against social ostracism in *Hugo: Tragödie eines Knaben* (1924; Hugo: the tragedy of a boy), represent the catharsis of the author's own childhood trauma.

In 1914, after a journalistic apprenticeship in Vienna, Winder joined the staff of the *Deutsche Zeitung Bohemia* in Prague where he held the position of literary editor until 1938. A keen observer of the events of his day, Winder also had a sharp perception of the interpenetration of individual reactions to historical events and his novels show an insight into the actuality of the sociopolitical development of the ČSR which was rare among German and Czech novelists. *Die nachgeholten Freuden* (1927; The recouped pleasures), and *Dr Muff* (1931) attain almost documentary value in their presentation of the problems caused by the political–historical upheaval in the early 1920s in the ČSR. *Der Thronfolger* (1937; The heir to the throne) again stresses the correlation of hereditary influences in Ferdinand d'Este and the decadence and shallowness of those institutions which ruled the monarchy. The English title of the novel written in England, *One Man's Answer* (1944; Die Pflicht), reflects its contents: the reaction of one man, a factory worker in occupied Prague, whose patriotism enables him to counteract all that until then had been most important to him, and to risk his own life and the lives of his wife and friends by sabotaging orders received from the Germans. In his unpublished last work, *Der Kammerdiener* (The lackey), Winder illustrates his conception of the danger that threatens those who let themselves be used by their "betters". The postulate uttered by the "new man" in this manuscript shows that the disbelief in a God who is willing to help, obvious in Winder's early novels, had turned into a belief in the holiness of human dignity.

MARGARITA PAZI

Wise, Isaac Mayer (1819–1900) American rabbi and religious leader. Born in Bohemia, Wise attended various *yeshivot* and received a spasmodic secular education. He developed a familiarity with rabbinic texts and an eagerness to absorb fresh knowledge, though not a disciplined approach to scholarship.

In 1846, after serving the Jewish congregation of Radnitz (near Pilsen) for three years, Wise emigrated to the USA and became rabbi of Congregation Beth El, Albany, New York. He immediately grasped the opportunity and the challenge presented by the New World to its burgeoning Jewish community: English-speaking rabbis needed to be trained, a religious literature provided, and a national organization established to settle religious problems and provide a uniform prayerbook; and these were problems the Jews could attack without government restriction. On the subject of Reform, Wise was ambivalent although he certainly favored reforms, which excited the suspicions of the Orthodox.

In 1850 Wise was forcibly ejected from his pulpit in Albany, but he was a fighter and immediately formed a congregation of his own. In 1854 he was appointed to Congregation B'nai Jeshurun, Cincinnati, where he remained for the rest of his life.

Immediately Wise started a weekly, *The Israelite*, to which he soon added a German supplement, *Die Deborah*. Then he pursued his grand design for American Jewry – synod, seminary, uniform prayerbook. These early efforts came to grief and involved Wise in violent controversies, especially with colleagues who thought him ready to betray the cause of reform. The Civil War put a stop to activity in this field, but Wise was persistent and, in 1873, saw the establishment in Cincinnati of the Union of American Hebrew Congregations. Hebrew Union College opened in 1875, with Wise as president. Almost single-handed he nurtured it through pinched early years, and in 1883 presided over the first ordination of rabbis. When, in 1889 the Central Conference of American Rabbis was established, Wise was elected president and held office until his death.

Wise wrote voluminously: history, theology, Bible exegesis, reminiscences, as well as opinions on events of the day, flowed readily from his pen. None of his books seems to have made any impact, save his prayer book, *Minhag America*. It is as builder of institutions that his influence has survived.

SEFTON D. TEMKIN

Wise, Stephen Samuel (1874–1949) American Rabbi and Zionist leader. Born in Budapest, Wise emigrated to the USA when he was less than two years old. He graduated from Columbia University at 18, was ordained in 1893, and served as rabbi of Congregation B'nai Jeshurun in New York. In 1900 he became rabbi of Temple Beth Israel in Portland, Oregon. In 1902 Wise received a Ph.D. from Columbia University for his edition of Solomon ibn Gabirol's *Improvement of the Moral Qualities*. As early as the late 1890s Wise began a Zionist career, advocating its ideology and organizing Zionists. Meeting Theodor HERZL at the second Zionist Congress in Basel in 1898, he agreed to serve as American secretary of the Zionist movement. Later he acted as an important intermediary to President Woodrow Wilson and Colonel Edward House in formulating the text of the Balfour Declaration. Though he worked with Chaim WEIZMANN, David BEN-GURION, and Abba Hillel Silver, he often disagreed with them on particular issues. Wise was among the first to point out the dangers of Nazism. In 1936 he organized the World Jewish Congress, and served as its president until 1949. In addition to his dedication to Zionism, Wise was an important rabbinic figure in American Jewish life. In 1907 he founded the Free Synagogue of New York which was based on freedom of the pulpit and free pews to all without fixed dues. In 1922 he established the Jewish Institute of Religion which provided training of rabbis from all branches of Judaism. In terms of social reform, Wise was a co-founder of the National Association for the Advancement of Colored People in 1909, and the American Civil Liberties Union in 1920. He was also active in such organizations as the Child Labor Committee, the Old Age Pension League, the Religion and Labor Foundation and the League to Enforce Peace. Wise's views are contained in *Free Synagogue Pulpit: Sermons and Addresses* (1908–32); *Child Versus Parent* (1922); *As I See It* (1944); and *Challenging Years* (1949).

FURTHER READING

Voss, C. H.: *Rabbi and Minister: The Friendship of Stephen S. Wise and John Haynes Holmes* (1964)

DAN COHN-SHERBOK

Wiseman, Adele (b.1928) Canadian novelist. Born in Winnipeg to Ukrainian immigrants, Wiseman earned a BA from the University of Manitoba. Subsequently she took various jobs in Canada and abroad while establishing herself as a writer.

Wiseman's work manifests profound identification with her Jewish roots. "My consciousness is Jewish", she declared in an interview. "I think I am a flower in somebody else's garden. I am a different flower and my selfhood and my 'otherness' I sing about...". The theme of her novels, *The Sacrifice* (1956) for which she received a Governor General's Award, and *Crackpot* (1974), focuses on Jewish immigration to Canada between the two world wars. Wiseman depicts the hardships of integration into the new reality in the larger context of Jewish tradition and culture. Her vision of the Canadian Jew is determined by the sense of complexity and distinctness of Jewish experience in history.

The Sacrifice draws upon the story of the *Akedah*, (the Binding of Isaac). Unlike the biblical patriarch, Abraham, the novel's protagonist, loses his sons. Despite the tragedy, the hope for redemption is signaled in the message of faith and love that Abraham communicates to his grandson, Moses.

Crackpot presents the kabbalistic vision of *Tikkun 'olam* – mending the world – through a seemingly incongruous character of Hoda, a Jewish prostitute. Thanks to her deep sense of identity, Hoda is capable, despite her own deprivation and suffering, of mending the shattered psyche of a Holocaust survivor. Thus, in a sense, she personifies the history of Jewish survival and regeneration. Wiseman's critical portrayals of the Canadian Jewish community tend to satirize its snobbery and materialism.

Other works include Wiseman's parents' life-story, *Old Woman at Play* (1978), and the play *The Lovebound*, set on a Jewish refugee ship in 1939.

FURTHER READING

Belkin, R.: The consciousness of a Jewish artist. *Journal of Canadian Fiction* 31/32 (1981) [interview with Wiseman]

Greenstein, M.: Vision and movement in *The Sacrifice*. *Canadian Literature* 80 (1979)

RACHEL FELDHAY BRENNER

Wissenschaft des Judentums [Science of Judaism] The movement for the scientific study of Jewish literature and history which developed in central Europe in the first half of the nineteenth century. Previously the Jewish past had been understood through the uncritical exposition of sacred texts. Diverse factors then encouraged a new approach: the *Haskalah* movement had encouraged Jews to think of themselves as part of European society; in Germany there was a new concern for the scientific study of history; some Jews felt that the recovery of the riches of the Jewish past would undermine both Gentile opposition to Jewish Emancipation and Jewish rejection of their own heritage, and that proof that Judaism had been susceptible to change in the past would weaken opposition to change in the present.

The beginnings of the movement can be traced to 1819 when a group of Berlin students founded the *Verein für Cultur und Wissenschaft der Juden*. The society was a failure, but one of its founders, Leopold ZUNZ, is considered the outstanding figure in the movement. In 1822 the Prussian government forbade as an unlawful innovation preaching in German in the synagogues. In his *Gottesdienstliche Vortraege der Juden* (1832) – a history of the Jewish sermon – Zunz showed that, though it had fallen into disuse, the vernacular sermon was an ancient Jewish institution. To do this required the patient sifting of literature deriving from many ages, until then treated as an undifferentiated mass. The outstanding worker in the field of bibliography was Moritz STEINSCHNEIDER. Attached to the Royal Library in Berlin, he produced scholarly catalogs of the Judaica collections in the major European libraries, the essential groundwork for literary and historical studies.

This emphasis gave the movement a detailed and specialist character, which, together with its pride in objectivity and detachment, limited its popular appeal. An exception was Heinrich GRAETZ, who, in addition to many learned monographs, produced an 11-volume *History of the Jews* (1853–75). This achieved wide popularity and was translated into several languages.

One outcome was the establishment, first at Breslau in 1854, of seminaries at which rabbis would be trained on modern academic lines. Another was the publication of learned periodicals, notably *Monatsschrift für Geschichte und Wissenschaft des Judentums* (1851), *Revue des Études Juives* (1888), and *Jewish Quarterly Review* (1890). Also established were societies for furthering scholarly research, especially in the field of Jewish history. Most of the interest came from the German *Kulturgebiet*. Eastern Europe remained the stronghold of religious Orthodoxy, which tended to regard *Wissenschaft* as heretical. Few Jewish scholars entered the field of Bible criticism.

Since the Second World War there has been a tendency to make light of the *Wissenschaft des Judentums*. Its focus was restrained by the concerns of the rabbinical seminaries which fostered it; it did not prove capable of attacking the external or internal problems of the Jewish communities where it took shape; and from the very country whose culture provided the paradigm, forces emerged which destroyed its established centres. Yet in fact the work has continued and even expanded. Established in Vilna in 1925, the Yiddish Institute for Scientific Research (Yivo) had the primary concern of elevating the Yiddish language intellectually and socially. This embraced the whole history and culture of the large Yiddish-speaking communities. When Yivo was re-established in New York in 1940 the work continued, though without the exclusive reliance on Yiddish. Judaic studies have a natural place in the universities of the State of Israel, and departments of Judaic Studies have been established at many universities in the USA and elsewhere.

FURTHER READING

Baron, S. W.: The modern age. In *Great Ideas and Ages of the Jewish People*, ed. L. W. Schwarz (New York: Random House, 1956) 379–84

Dawidowicz, L.: Max Weinreich (1894–1969): The Scholarship of Yiddish. *American Jewish Year Book* 70 (1969) 59–78

Elbogen, I.: *A Century of Jewish Life* (Philadelphia: The Jewish Publication Society of America, 1944)

Ettinger, S.: The modern period. In *History of the Jewish People*, ed. H. Ben-Sasson (London: Weidenfeld & Nicolson; Cambridge: Harvard University Press, 1976)

Katz, J.: *Out of the Ghetto* (New York: Schocken, 1978)

SEFTON D. TEMKIN

Wittels, Fritz (1880–1950) Austrian, later American psychoanalyst and psychiatrist. Born in Vienna, Wittels received his medical degree from the University of Vienna in 1904. He is best known as Freud's first biographer, writing *Sigmund Freud: His Personality, His Teachings, and His School* in 1924. Although his association with Freud's circle was short (1907–10), it was intense and unusually provocative. Indeed, he was the circle's *enfant terrible*.

During his brief tenure, Wittels advocated a freedom of sexual expression that neither Freud nor many of his supporters could long tolerate. His *Die Sexuelle Not* (1907) was a passionate entreaty for uninhibited sexual gratification. Carl Jung, in a review, wrote, "I have not read a book on the problem of sexuality that so harshly and mercilessly tears to pieces our present-day morality". But Wittels always maintained that his purpose was creative, not destructive. The next year he argued that the satisfaction of sexual needs would precipitate man's "supreme achievements". Although he recalled his delight "to hurl the importance of sex into the teeth of society", he also recognized, in this vision, the psychoanalytic task of mankind's ethical renewal: "Some of us believed that psychoanalysis would change the surface of the earth . . . [and introduce] a golden age in which there would be no room for neuroses any more. We felt like great men . . . Some people have a mission in their life".

If not for a small and obscure book he wrote in 1904, Wittels would have contributed little to our knowledge of the way Jewish self-consciousness imbued the nascent psychoanalytic movement. When he wrote *Der Taufjude* (The convert Jew), Wittels was already under the spell of Freud's writings, especially *The Interpretation of Dreams* (1900). *Der Taufjude* is more a confession than the polemic he clearly meant the book to be. He expressed the bitterness of being a victim of discrimination and insult (anti-Semitism had become popular and potent in Vienna). He desired his freedom and understood the "irresistible compulsion" to convert. But he fought off the temptation, concluding that conversion, besides prolonging racial discrimination and injustice, was timorous and morally bankrupt. Wittels instead encouraged Jews to stand up for themselves.

The essay becomes forceful, if not exuberant,

in declaring a new social purpose for Jews. Because they are the victims of widespread intolerance, a measure of society's growing inflexibility and obsolescence, Jews are "one of the few groups which, in the process of securing their own interests, must swing the sword of the ideal to secure at once the rudimentary conditions of a decent life". Wittels urged Jews to assume the "lofty passion of the oppressed". Since Jews ultimately and immediately "yearn for final redemption", they must accept "the struggle for justice" – the title of his final chapter – as their "life purpose".

The germ of Wittels' psychoanalytic crusade to "change the surface of the earth" is found in *Der Taufjude*. Though empty of anything specifically Jewish, his belief in the revolutionary significance of Jews appears to have propelled his quest in the movement to tap and unleash mankind's creative energy.

FURTHER READING

Klein, D. B.: *Jewish Origins of the Psychoanalytic Movement* (Chicago: University of Chicago Press, 1985)

Nunberg, H., and Federn, E., eds: *Minutes of the Vienna Psychoanalytic Society* vol. 2, trans. M. Nunberg (New York: International Universities Press, 1967)

DENNIS B. KLEIN

Wittgenstein, Ludwig (1889–1951) Austrian, later English philosopher. Born in Vienna, Wittgenstein was the son of one of the foremost industrialists of the Habsburg Monarchy, Karl Wittgenstein, also a great patron of modern Viennese culture. Wittgenstein was given a technical training at Linz, Berlin, and Manchester. In 1911 he began to study philosophy at Cambridge, where he made a great impact on Bertrand Russell. His researches on the nature of logic resulted eventually in the *Tractatus logico-philosophicus* (1921). By the time of publication, Wittgenstein had given up professional philosophy and become a teacher. After discouraging experiences in the Austrian country-side, he returned to philosophical questions, and to Cambridge, his new work culminating in *Philosophical Investigations* (1953).

Wittgenstein is one of the most important thinkers of this century. He has the rare distinction of having "founded" two schools of philosophy. The *Tractatus* asserted the primacy of the sentence over the word, and the impossibility of talking sense about the unverifiable. This work was taken up by the Vienna Circle of philosophers, and was the basis of logical positivism. His later work, which in many ways refuted his earlier ideas, became one of the most important sources of the analytical and linguistic philosophy which has dominated post-war philosophy in the English-speaking world.

Wittgenstein was not brought up in the Jewish religion, and the fact of his Jewish descent was obscure for a long time. However, anecdotal material, and remarks he made in recently discovered notes, now collected and published in *Culture and Value* (1980), show that Wittgenstein was conscious of his Jewish background, and felt himself to be Jewish. Although his father was Protestant and his mother Catholic, both were of (at least partly) Jewish descent, and the family preserved what they saw as their Jewish tradition of "esthetic idealism" (Janik & Toulmin, 1973). Wittgenstein made no public comment on his Jewish descent until 1937, when he made a "confession" to a number of friends in Cambridge. He had, however, made private notes as early as 1931, in which he saw himself as a Jewish thinker, and as such different in his ways of thought from Western thinkers. Accepting an argument of Otto WEININGER, Wittgenstein saw Jews as only talented, reproductive, not geniuses unless they became religious geniuses. According to Rhees (Rhees, 1984), however, Wittgenstein thought that there was nothing wrong in that, but that he must accept the Jewish traits in his character. Wittgenstein, in the 1930s at the latest, saw himself as thinking in a Jewish way.

FURTHER READING

Janik, A., and Toulmin, S.: *Wittgenstein's Vienna* (New York: Touchstone, 1973)
Rhees, R., ed.: *Recollections of Wittgenstein* (Oxford: Blackwell, 1984)

STEVEN BELLER

Wolfskehl, Karl (1869–1948) German poet. Born in Darmstadt and claiming descent from one of the oldest and most prominent German–Jewish banking families whose history in German lands could be documented back over 1,000 years, Wolfskehl studied German and comparative philology at the university in Giessen. Influenced decisively by his reading of Nietzsche, he came under the spell of the dynamic and influential German poet, Stefan George, and was admitted to the inner ring of the *George-Kreis* (George circle), the group of poets, writers, and intellectuals (some of whom were anti-Semitic) who dedicated themselves enthusiastically and unswervingly to George's neo-classical esthetic and cultural goals. He collaborated closely with George, although later turned to Expressionism. Wolfskehl first sought refuge during the Nazi period in Italy, but soon settled in New Zealand, after a short stay in Australia.

Ostensibly by chance, Wolfskehl attended the first Zionist Congress in Basel in 1897, and this positive experience, together with his proud Jewish background, enabled him to participate in the activities of the *George-Kreis,* some of which were German-nationalist and conservative in nature, without renouncing his Jewish roots. Wolfskehl imbued his poetry with a religious–mystical ambience and applied George's principles of poetic composition to biblical drama in his *Saul.* In some of his poetry he incorporated images and language derived from the psalms. At the same time, Wolfskehl contributed his poetry to Zionist publications and continued to do so after the rise of Nazism. He was a regular contributor to the Schocken Almanachs in the 1930s, donating his German translations of medieval Hebrew poetry, as well as his own poems to these volumes. In prose pieces like "Das jüdische Geheimnis", (The Jewish secret), he claimed that the mystery of Jewish existence was inexplicable.

Wolfskehl's best known volume of poetry is *Die Stimme spricht* (1934; The voice speaks) which contains many Jewish motifs. Also, his posthumously published cycle of Job poems expresses his late somber vision of Jewish survival.

MARK H. GELBER

Wolfson, Harry Austryn (1887–1974) American historian of philosophy and theology.

Born in Belorussia, and with an early *yeshivah* education, he moved to the USA in 1903. He spent 66 years of his life at Harvard University, first as a student and in 1925 as Professor of Hebrew Literature and Philosophy. He published an enormous amount of scholarship in book and article form, dealing with the structure and growth of philosophical systems from Plato to Spinoza, with particular reference to the medieval period. His *Crescas' Critique of Aristotle* (1929) is a monumental example of scholarship which draws upon a vast range of published and unpublished medieval material. *The Philosophy of Spinoza* (1934) linked Spinoza to his predecessors as the last of the medievals and the first of the modern philosophers. In *Philo: Foundations of Religious Philosophy in Judaism, Christianity and Islam* (1947) he attributed to Philo the origin of many of the leading notions and arguments in later medieval and modern philosophy. He also wrote extensively on the philosophy of Islam and the Church Fathers, and on the history of religious philosophy. He organized the publication of the *Corpus Commentariorum Averrois in Aristotelem* (Speculum 6, 1931, pp.412–27; Speculum 38, 1963, 88–104) which is in many ways characteristic of his approach to texts. This project is designed to produce comparative editions of the original texts by Averroës and their Hebrew, Latin, and English translations, with analysis of the contextual notes of contemporary interpreters and references back to the original Greek in Aristotle. Wolfson called his approach "hypothetico-deductive", by which he meant the careful testing of interpretations by reference to the whole body of texts which bear upon the passage in question, and the breadth of knowledge which he was able to bring to bear is frequently breathtaking. While his particular view of the structure of philosophy is not generally shared today, his scholarly contributions have encouraged much new research and provided a paradigm of excellence in the study of medieval philosophy and religion.

FURTHER READING

Schwartz, L.: *Wolfson of Harvard* (1977)

——: A bibliographical essay. *Harry Austryn Wolfson Jubilee Volume* 1 (1965) 1–46

Twersky, I.: Harry Austryn Wolfson 1877–1974. *American Jewish Year Book* 76 (1976) 99–111

OLIVER LEAMAN

Wolpe, David (b.1912)   South African Yiddish writer. Born in Keidan, Lithuania, he founded a Hebrew journal, *Ha-nesher* (The Eagle), at the age of 16. Writing poetry throughout, in 1930 he went to Palestine, returning to Lithuania in 1936 where he joined the army. In 1942 he was confined to the Kovno ghetto and in 1944 was sent to Dachau where his poetic writing "kept his heart alive". With the liberation of the camps he was sent to Bavaria where he met his wife, also a Holocaust survivor.

They emigrated to South Africa in 1951 where he continued to write in Yiddish. Although he speaks seven languages, Yiddish is "in his soul". He not only writes in it but "lives in it". Much of his work appeared under various pseudonyms and over the years his poetry has appeared in several countries and his elegies and verses of protest have been praised. He was the editor of the journal *Dorem Afrike* (South Africa) for 16 years until 1970.

In 1978 his substantial modernist anthology *A volkn un a veg* (A cloud and a way) was published. The pain and celebration in these poems were adjudged as being "as authentic as the Yiddish which enlivens them". The book won him international recognition as a poet and he was awarded the Itzik Manger Prize for Yiddish literature in Jerusalem in 1983.

In 1984 he published *A vort in zayn tsayt* (A word in its time), which is a collection of stories essays and critiques of public figures from Shakespeare to SHOLEM ALEICHEM, and covers some 40 years of creativity. A collection of short stories, *Heymen, khaloymes, koshmarn* (Homes, dreams, nightmares) was published in 1987.

As a survivor who believes that creative writing should express moral responsibility, one of the central themes in his writing is the Holocaust, and while the ghetto and camps are behind him, the "icy wind of loneliness and ruin" persists, creating a tension between pain and life-affirming hope which allows him to state, "forget all doubts, God's cosmos is eternally filled with song and stars".

JOCELYN HELLIG

Wolpe, Stefan (1902–1972)   American composer. He was born in Berlin and died in New York City. Wolpe studied music at the Berlin Hochschule and after graduating, be became associated with choral and theatrical groups in Berlin, promoting social causes and composing songs on revolutionary themes. At the same time, he studied with Ferruccio Busoni and Hermann Scherchen during the 1920s. Further, he had artistic contact with Paul Klee and artists around the Bauhaus school (Schlemmer, Tworkov, de Kooning) for the rest of his life. During 1933–4 he studied with Anton Webern. At the onset of the Hitler era in 1933 he went to Vienna, and after one year moved to Palestine where he taught music theory at the Jerusalem conservatory. In 1938 he emigrated to New York, where he devoted himself mainly to teaching and composing. Among his students were Elmer Bernstein, Ezra Laderman, Ralph Shapey, David Tudor, and Morton Feldman.

Wolpe's style, though broadly based, is a very personal and clearly definable and identifiable one. His early compositions, rather than being directly influenced by the giants of his time, developed parallel concerns: developing variations, asymmetrical meters and rhythms, nontriadic harmonies, and the generation of material from small intervallic relationships. During his stay in Jerusalem he became greatly involved with his Jewish heritage, and the music of that period reflects some traits of Semitic music, such as certain rhythmic impulses and melodic turns. The early style culminates in the ballet suite, *Man from Midian* (1942), and from then on is further refined and developed, later on using very sophisticated and intricate serial procedures.

He was an extremely prolific composer, having written operas, orchestral music, chamber and incidental music, and a symphony.

SAMUEL H. ADLER

Wouk, Herman (b.1915)   American novelist. Born of immigrant Russian–Jewish parents in New York, Wouk attended Columbia University, graduating BA 1934, where he edited the humor magazine and wrote variety shows. From 1935 to 1941 he was a radio comic writer,

working principally for Fred Allen. In 1942 he enlisted in the US Navy, serving in the South Pacific. He married Betty Sarah Brown in 1945. They had three sons. Wouk taught at Yeshiva University (1953–7) and was a trustee of the College of the Virgin Islands (1962–9).

Following the publication of *Aurora Dawn* (1947) and *The City Boy* (1948) Wouk established himself as a best-selling novelist with *The Caine Mutiny* (1951), which won a Pulitzer Prize. This success was followed by *Marjorie Morningstar* (1955), a novel which heralded the arrival of the American–Jewish literary renaissance and the appearance of that ubiquitous Jewish heroine, the Jewish American Princess.

After the death of a son, Wouk published *This is My God* (1959) a simplistic yet endearing account of his personal faith in Judaism. Subsequently four more novels, *Youngblood Hawke* (1962) *The Winds of War* (1971) *War and Remembrance* (1978), and *Inside, Outside* (1985), all of them sprawling but nonetheless highly engaging narratives, have become bestsellers. Less successful were three plays and the novel *Don't Stop the Carnival* (1965). *Inside, Outside* is more a schmaltzy memoir of a one-time Jewish gagwriter than an accomplished work of fiction. It typifies the best and the worst of Wouk's writing.

BIBLIOGRAPHY
The "Caine" Mutiny Court Martial (London: Jonathan Cape, 1954); *Slattery's Hurricane* (London: New English Library, 1956)

FURTHER READING
Geismar, M.: *American Moderns from Rebellion to Conformity* (New York: Hill & Wang, 1958)
Hyman, E. S.: Some questions about Herman Wouk. *Standards: A Chronicle of Books for Our Time* (New York: Horizon Press, 1966)

JOSEPH COHEN

Wyner, Yehudi (b.1929)   American composer, pianist, conductor, and educator. He was born in Calgary, Canada, but moved to the USA at an early age. Wyner was educated at the Juilliard School of Music, graduating with a Diploma in Piano in 1946; he then entered Yale University, receiving an AB in 1950 and the degrees of Bachelor of Music and Master of Music in 1953; in 1952 he was awarded an MA from Harvard University, where his composition teachers were Walter Piston and Randall Thompson. Wyner has won many awards, including the Prix de Rome at the American Academy in Rome (1953–6), two Guggenheim Fellowships (1959, 1976), The Brandeis Creative Arts Award (1963), and numerous grants.

Yehudi Wyner has taught on the faculty of Yale University (1963–78), was chairman in 1969, Dean of Music and Professor at SUNY College at Purchase (1978–82); he has been visiting professor at Hebrew Union College, Hofstra College, Cornell University, Tanglewood, and Brandeis University. He has also been extremely active as a performer, especially as the keyboard artist of the Bach Aria Group since 1968, and as a conductor–musical director of the Turnan Opera, guest conductor of the Boston Symphony Chamber Players, and many others.

He has had a lifelong interest in liturgical music. The son of Lazare WEINER, he was introduced early to Jewish music and has written some outstanding compositions for the synagogue including *Friday Evening Service* (1963); *Passover Offering* for flute, clarinet, trombone, and cello (1959); *Torah Service* with instruments (1966); *Liturgical Fragments* for the High holydays (1970); *Dances of Atonement* and *Wedding Music* (1976); and *Tanz and Maissele* for chamber group (1981).

Besides these works with Jewish interest, Yehudi Wyner has an impressive list of secular works, including works for chamber ensembles and for voice, and Incidental Music for Robert Lowell's play, *The Old Glory*.

SAMUEL H. ADLER

Y

Yadin, Yigael (1917–1984) Israeli archaeologist, general, and politician. Born and brought up in Jerusalem, son of the famous archaeologist E. L. SUKENIK, Yadin studied archaeology and Semitic languages at the Hebrew University 1935–45. He joined the *Haganah* at an early age and adopted the personal code name Yadin which later became his surname. Yadin played a decisive role in 1947–8 as Chief Operations Officer in the War of Independence and served as Chief of Staff in 1949–52, when he laid the foundations which transformed the Israel Defence Army into a modern army. He joined the Hebrew University in 1953 and was appointed Professor of Archaeology in 1963. From 1977 to 1981 he pursued a political career, during which he was member of the Knesset and Deputy Prime Minister, and after which he returned to his university post. Yadin was the most important Israeli archaeologist of the first generation of native-born Israelis. He followed his father's footsteps in studying the Dead Sea Scrolls and, together with N. Avigad, was the first to publish the *Genesis Apocryphon* (1956), the *Ben Sira Scroll from Masada* (1965) and the *Temple Scroll* (1977). His broad scope of studies included the archaeology of warfare in the biblical period and numerous problems in the archaeology of Palestine, as well as Islamic epigraphy. His most important achievements as archaeologist are his large-scale excavations at Hazor (1955–8, 1968–9), the Cave of Letters in the Judean Desert (1961–2), Masada (1963–5), soundings at Megiddo (1960–61), and Beth Shean (1983). These expeditions yielded very important discoveries (for example the documents from the period of Bar Kokhba from the Cave of Letters), and were decisive in forming Israeli archaeology. Yadin was a brilliant scholar, best when on his own, and a captivating lecturer.

BIBLIOGRAPHY

Greenfield, J.: Bibliography of Yigael Yadin (to 1980). *Journal of Jewish Studies* 33 (1982), 11–16

FURTHER READING

Israel Explorations Journal 34 (1984), 73–6 (obituary)
Astor, D., Barnett, R. D., Kane, J., and Vermes, G.: The Yigael Yadin Memorial Lecture. *Bulletin of the Anglo-Israel Archaeological Society* (1984–5) 9–23

DAN BARAG

Yaoz-Kest, Itamar (b.1934) Israeli poet and fiction writer. Born in Szarvas, Hungary, Yaoz-Kest spent 1944–5 in the concentration camp of Bergen-Belsen. In 1951 he emigrated to Israel. He studied Hebrew literature and Bible at the University. Since 1958 he has been the editor of the Eked publishing house.

His first poem in Hebrew appeared when he was 18 – a year and a half after his arrival in Israel. His first collection of poems: *Malakh lelo kenafayim* (Angel without wings) was published in 1959. In 1961 he published *Nof be'ashan – pirkei Bergen Belsen* (Vista of smoke, Bergen-Belsen chapters), and since then several other collections of his poems have appeared. Yaoz-Kest translates poetry, mainly from Hungarian; *Mivhar hashirah hayehudit behungaria vetoledoteiha* (A selection of Jewish poetry in Hungary and its history) appeared in 1959. Among his fiction is *Hamehager habaytah* (Emigrating home) – a sequence of four novels published between the years 1970–77. He also publishes essays on literature and art.

The autobiographical element in Yaoz-Kest's writing is very strong. He views himself as a son of a generation for which the basic experiences of childhood and youth have been the Second World War and the mass exodus to Israel. The thematic cycle of his poems and fiction is destruction, displacement, and the biographical–spiritual heritage. His writing is symbolic and surrealistic, mingled with realistic accounts of traumatic autobiographical experiences.

Yaoz-Kest's works in English translation are published in Frank, B. trans., *Modern Hebrew Poetry*, Iowa City, 1980, pp.134–140.

FURTHER READING

Dov, V.: Ashes and roots. *Hebrew Book Review* (Spring 1967) 12–14

RIVKA MAOZ

Avraham B. Yehoshua

Yehoshua, Avraham B. (b.1936) Hebrew novelist, playwright, and social critic. Born and educated in Jerusalem, Yehoshua is a fifth generation Jerusalemite on the side of his father, himself an author of stories about the Old City. His mother's family stems from North Africa. Yehoshua lives in Haifa, where he has taught and served as Dean of Students at Haifa University.

Yehoshua is one of the most widely read of Israeli authors. Beginning with his story "Mot ha-zaken" (1957; The death of the old man) and through the 1960s and early 1970s, Yehoshua wrote suspenseful allegorical tales reminiscent of the existentialist dimension of Franz KAFKA and S. Y. AGNON but often with a tense political–cultural level of engagedness. In several stories such as "Sheloshah yamim vayeled" (1965; "Three days and a child", 1970), sexual tension may be seen as a metaphor for the frustrations of an unhealthy society directed inward, very much as in stories by Amos Oz. In the stories "Massa ha'erev shel yatir" (1959; "An evening in Yatir vil-

lage", 1965) and "Mul haye'arot", (1963; "Facing the forests", 1970), the intentional derailing of a train and the burning down of a Jewish National Fund Forest, respectively, suggest a radical, violent indictment of the presuppositions of the Zionist state. In the latter story the more realistic descriptions of character and scenery prefigure Yehoshua's movement from the skeletally allegorical to more authentic portraiture. A similarly well-wrought blend of realism and expressionistic allegory characterizes his stories "Shetikah holekhet venimshekhet shel meshorer" (1966; "A poet's continuing silence", 1970) and "Tehillat kayitz 1970" ("Early in the summer of 1970", 1973). In many of the stories an "old man" type, reminiscent of the protagonist of Yehoshua's first story, is subjected to scathing pressure and criticism due to his cultural stagnation and senescence. The bizarre behavior of the collective "sons" in these stories presents the "fathers" in a tragic but culpable light.

Yehoshua's extremely well-received novel of the 1973 Yom Kippur War, *Hame'ahev* (1977; *The Lover*, 1978) completes Yehoshua's movement towards realism, with due consideration of the Faulknerian ordering of his narrative voices.

The theme of a husband who seeks a lover for his wife, then loses him in the commotion of the war, then searches for him in grotesque ways that bare the pain of a traumatized society indeed fall shy of the realistic epic. Yet Yehoshua's balance of the real and the grotesque seemed equal to the task of mirroring Israeli society at its nadir. Worthy of mention, too, is Yehoshua's most real and engaging description of the Arab boy, Na'im, a character that has already assumed an almost classical and visionary status in Israeli letters.

Yehoshua's more complex later novel, *Gerushim me'uharim* (1982; *A Late Divorce*, 1984), continues to study familial and societal pathologies in a symbolic, collective psychological, vein. A comparative study of Yehoshua's cultural criticism, as in his *Bizekhut hanormaliyut* (1980; *Between Right and Right*, 1981), suggests that in his fiction Yehoshua portrays some of the "neurotic" deviancies attendant upon flirtation with the Diaspora and with *yeridah* (emigration–abandonment). Yehoshua, as an avowed heir to the "Canaanite" ideology, has advocated "Israelism" as a healthy substitute for "Jewishness" in Israel. Yehoshua's plays, *Laylah bemai* (1969; *A Night in May*, 1974), *Tippulim aharonim* (1972) and *Hafatzim* (1986; *Objects*, 1986) stage some of the above themes with suspenseful dialogue and immediacy. Yehoshua's centrality to Israel's cultural scene can be culled from Joseph Yerushalmi's *A. B. Yehoshua: Bibliography, 1953–1979* (1980) with well over a thousand entries.

In *Molkho* (1987; *Five Seasons*, 1988) a middle-aged man loses his wife to cancer; he experiences the disorientation of unresolved grief, awkward courting situations, sexual dysfunction, and apathy, and a combined personal and quasi-ideological dilemma symbolized by his trip to Germany.

FURTHER READING

Ben-Ezer, E., ed.: *Unease in Zion* (New York: Quadrangle, 1974)

Elon, A.: *The Israelis, Founders and Sons* (New York: Bantam, 1972)

Fuchs, E.: *Israeli Mythologies: Women in Contemporary Hebrew Fiction* (Albany, NY: SUNY Press, 1987)

Moragh, G.: Reality and symbol in the fiction of A. B. Yehoshua, *Prooftexts* 2, no. 2 (1982) pp.179–96

——: Facing the wilderness: God and country in the fiction of A. B. Yehoshoa. *Prooftexts* 8, no. 3 (1988) 311–33

Nash, S.: Israeli fathers and sons revisited. *Conservative Judaism Magazine* 38 (Summer 1986) pp.28–37

STANLEY NASH

Yellin, David (1864–1942)

Hebrew scholar, educator, and lexicographer. Born in Jerusalem, Yellin was known as *'ish yerushalayim* (a man of Jerusalem), a fitting term for one who lived almost all his life in his birthplace. After being educated in a traditional *heder* and in the *yeshivah* of Etz Hayyim in the Old City of Jerusalem, Yellin traveled with his mother to London to seek financial help to continue his studies there. The quest was unsuccessful and he returned soon after to attend the ALLIANCE ISRAÉLITE UNIVERSELLE school in Jerusalem, where he became, at 17, a teacher of Hebrew language.

In the 1880s, Yellin and Eliezer BEN-YEHUDA were the only teachers in Palestine to teach "Hebrew in Hebrew". While Ben-Yehuda had conceived the idea, Yellin developed the pedagogical systems. Yellin continued to pursue his educational activities, becoming, in 1926 a professor at the Hebrew University. He was also deeply involved in political and public activities, and was elected the first Jewish Deputy Mayor of Jerusalem. Active in the development of scholarly institutions in Jerusalem, he was one of the founders of its first public library, and, together with Ben-Yehuda and his father-in-law, Yehiel Michal Pines, of the *Va'ad halashon ha'ivrit* (Hebrew Language Academy).

Yellin published his first article when he was 14 years old, and continued writing articles for *Hamagid* and *Hamelitz*, while at the same time editing his own newspaper, *Har Zion*. Later he published textbooks, and studies of Hebrew grammar and the Hebrew Bible. His major work is *Torat hashirah hasefaradit* (1940; A study of Hebrew poetry in Spain), and his other writings include *Toledot hitpathut hadikduk ha'ivri* (1945) on the history of the development of Hebrew grammar, and commentaries on the books of Job and Isaiah.

DEBORAH SCHECHTERMAN

Yezierska, Anzia (1883–1970) American short-story writer and novelist. Anzia Yezierska arrived in New York, via steerage, from a Russian–Polish village near Warsaw, in 1898. She wrote out of the pain and dislocation of the immigrant experience. Her stories are distinguished by their intensity, rather than by their artistic form, and they capture the powerful conflict of values which confronted Jewish immigrants and their children. She portrayed with vivid, graphic realism the colorful characters who inhabited New York's teeming, poverty-stricken immigrant neighborhoods, and illustrates both the new American dreams they cherished – and the manifold internal and external obstacles which kept them from achieving those dreams.

Yezierska's first book, *Hungry Hearts,* was published in 1920, and the book brought her not only critical approval but a Hollywood contract. Her first novel, *Salome of the Tenements,* received similar acclaim. She became something of a celebrity as the immigrant woman who had become an "overnight success", leaping from sweatshop rags to riches. However, as she described later in the semi-autobiographical, semi-fictional novel, *Red Ribbon on a White Horse,* (1950), she found the glamorous world of Hollywood both amoral and sterile. Although the Lower East Side was for Yezierska a world of pain and frustration, it was also the wellspring of her art. On her visits to Hollywood she found herself almost paralyzed, and she chose to spend most of her time in New York.

Yezierska excelled in particular in her portrayals of women in conflict. She wrote convincingly of the mutual cruelties between immigrants who try to retain older mores and the love of their children in a strange new land – and of the children who yearn and struggle toward American opportunities.

BIBLIOGRAPHY
Children of Loneliness (London: Cassell & Co., 1923); *Bread Givers* (London: William Heinemann, 1925); *Arrogant Beggar* (London: William Heinemann 1927); *All I Could Never Be* (New York: Brewer, Warren & Putnam, 1932)

SYLVIA FISHMAN

Yiddish Yiddish, the traditional language of Ashkenazic Jewry, has been spoken by more Jews than any other language. Ashkenaz was the Jewish name for the unique Jewish civilization established in Germanic-speaking lands some thousand years ago. Over the centuries the name has come to signify the culture, rather than the territory of the Ashkenazim. Yiddish came into being around a thousand years ago, when Jewish settlers on Ashkenazic territory (by the Rhine at its west, and – if current research is proven correct – most importantly, by the Danube at its east), fused the remnants of their two previous classical languages, Hebrew and Aramaic, along with a trickle of Romance, with the medieval German city dialects with which they were in daily contact. The vocabulary and morphology derive mostly from these medieval German dialects, but their cultural and linguistic evolution, in a constant state of fusion with the other components, are quintessentially Yiddish.

Old, Middle, and New Yiddish

Old Yiddish Yiddish may be divided, for orientation, into three periods – old, middle, and new. During the Old Yiddish period (from unknown beginnings to *c.*1350), the specific Jewish civilization of Ashkenaz was established, and its language, Yiddish, crystallized via highly specific "fusion formulas" by which Germanic on the one hand, and Hebrew and Aramaic on the other, could combine. Speakers were concentrated on German-speaking soil but national Jewish tragedies, including the Crusades (starting 1096) and the Black Death (1348), led to migration in most directions, a trend strengthened by the search for better economic conditions in eastern Europe. Very few

811

written monuments survive, among them proper names from 1096 and a sentence dated 1272.

Middle Yiddish The Middle Yiddish period (*c*.1350–*c*.1600) was characterized by extensive geolinguistic expansion. By the sixteenth century, the speech territory of Yiddish was one of the largest in the history of Europe, stretching from Holland in the northwest and Italy in the southwest deep into Russia in the east. Many manuscripts feature Yiddish reworkings of epic European knightly romances (for example, *King Arthur*) or adaptations of the epic poem genre to Jewish themes (for example, *Queen Esther*). From the 1530s and 1540s, Yiddish printing became a major enterprise for authors and publishers who sought to satisfy the needs of Yiddish speakers everywhere. A special typefont, known as *mashkit*, was used for Yiddish, contrasting both with square Hebrew letters and the rabbinic cursive known as Rashi type. Elijah Levita's *Bovo d'Antona* (Isny 1541), in ottava rima, is thought to be the greatest Yiddish literary work of the period. The language used in most works is now referred to as the *Old Literary Language* (or *Standard Yiddish I*), a watered-down and frequently colorless literary language based upon Western Yiddish. During the Middle Yiddish period, settlement in the Slavic and Baltic lands was so intense as to give rise to a new branch of Ashkenaz: Eastern Ashkenaz in contradistinction to Western Ashkenaz in central Europe.

Early New Yiddish Early New Yiddish (*c*.1600–*c*.1750) saw a vast demographic increase in the number and concentration of Yiddish speakers in eastern Europe. Still, inertia kept the Old Literary Language alive in Yiddish books, although eastern elements began to make their appearance. In Yiddish literature, the western appetite for courtly romances was replaced by a new eastern-based traditionalist genre of ethical and homiletic works. Among the best known were the *Tsene-rene* by Yankev ben Yitskhok Ashkenazi (the lost first edition probably appeared in the 1590s), a homiletic reworking of the Pentateuch, and such ethical treatises as Moyshe Henekh Altshuler's *Brantshpigl* (Krakow, 1597) and Yitskhok ben Elyokum's *Lev tov*

(Prague, 1620). Amsterdam became one of the leading publishing centers during the Early New Yiddish period. In the late 1670s two complete Yiddish Bible editions, by the competing translators Yekusiel Blitz and Yosef Witzenhausen, were published in Amsterdam.

New Yiddish The New Yiddish period (after *c*.1750) has been the most cataclysmic of all. Western Yiddish declined rapidly as the vernacular of Western Ashkenazim, who were increasingly assimilating to German culture and becoming "German Jews". The decline, hastened by Moses MENDELSSOHN's campaign against the language, was symbolized by the replacement of Yiddish by German in Yiddish letters. At the same time, Eastern Yiddish underwent uncanny demographic, cultural, and social growth. By the early nineteenth century, the *New Literary Language* (or *Standard Yiddish II = Modern Standard Yiddish*) arose. It is based upon the living dialects of eastern Europe. The old western-based written language swiftly disappeared, and its special typeface was replaced by square Hebrew characters (first with full Hebrew pointing, then with vowel marking only). The hasidic movement, the eastern Enlightenment movement, and the various other nineteenth-century tendencies and philosophies all used Yiddish to reach the east European masses, and all imbued it with new societal functions which brought Yiddish into the modern age in a few decades. From the mid-nineteenth century, Eastern Yiddish rose, by virtue of first rate authors, to the status of a major European language which has produced a world ranking literature. The classical authors of modern Yiddish literature are satirist MENDELE MOKHER SEFARIM (Moykher Sforim), affectionately known as *der zeyde* ("the grandfather") of modern Yiddish literature; humorist SHOLEM ALEICHEM, and romanticist I. L. PERETZ. An array of poets and prosaists have won international acclaim. The West has come to appreciate Yiddish literature in good measure through *Fiddler on the Roof*, based on Sholem Aleichem's *Tevye der milkhiker* (Tevye the milkman) and the works of Nobel laureate Isaac Bashevis SINGER.

Linguistically, New Yiddish is characterized by the acquisition and rooting of a prominent Slavic component. The morphological and lexical contours of the modern standard language were implicitly finalized by Mendele. Yiddish spelling was codified by Zalmen REYZEN in 1920.

The semantics of Yiddish

Because of its evolution in an exclusively Jewish civilization, Yiddish comprises a semantic structure interlinked with Jewish life and culture. The register for traditional Judaism, known as *yidishkayt*, is vast. A common example is the word for "God". The general term for the universal God is *got* (from German). God as he relates to Jews is *der reboyne sheloylem* (from Hebrew). A more reflective notion inheres in *der reboyne dealme* (from Aramaic). Loving diminutives derived from Slavic pave the way for such constructions as *gotenyu* ("dear God") and *tatenyu ziser* ("sweet little father") which facilitate one-to-one spiritual communication, with none of the cornyness or childishness conveyed by the English equivalents. Good-hearted colloquial use has *der eybershter* ("the highest one"). The Jewish versus general dichotomy produces such non-synonyms as Germanic *zind* "sin (in general)" versus Hebraic *aveyre* "transgression of Jewish law"; but their opposite, *mitsve*, from the Hebrew, has come to mean "good deed" in the universal sense. The embeddedness of Jewish tradition is also evident from the huge number of common expressions drawing on Jewish experience, for example *shtark vi Shimshn Hagiber* "strong as Samson" = "very strong", *klug vi Shloyme Hameylekh* "clever as Solomon" = "very clever", *lang vi der goles* "long as the Diaspora" = "very long".

The Talmudic vocabulary that thrives in spoken as well as written Yiddish has made precise logical nuance another prominent register (for example *aderabe* "to the contrary; of course", *avade* "definitely", *avade un avade* "most definitely", *kal vekhoymer* "a fortiori"), *dafke* "necessarily".

Yiddish enjoys unusual semantic wealth by virtue of several factors. First is the multicomponent structure which facilitates differentiation of nuance between what are "dictionary synonyms" in the donor languages. Thus, Germanic-derived *shtolts* "(healthy) pride" contrasts with Hebrew-derived *gayve* "(excessive) pride". Slavic-derived *tate* "father" and *mame* "mother" are much more intimate than their Germanic-derived counterparts *foter* and *muter*. Second is an extensively developed internal structure of diminutivization. Thus, personal forenames evoke warmth and love – *Shloyme* (masculine) gives diminutive *Shloymale, Shloymke, Shloymkale; Toybe* (feminine) gives *Taybl, Taybale, Taybke, Taybkale*. Diminutives in other contexts, for example with names of professions, express derision – *shrayber* "writer" gives *shrayberl* "talentless scribbler". Finally, Yiddish uses idiomaticity to a greater extent than most European languages. Such phrases as *klapn kop on vant* "knock your head against the wall", "*svet helfn vi a toytn bankes*", literally "it will do as much good as drawing blood with cupping glasses from a dead man" = "utterly useless", *vi got in Pariz*, literally "like for God in Paris" = "have a really good time"; and *a nekhtiker tog*, literally "yesterday's day" = "Impossible!" are characteristic of Yiddish conversation.

Another highly developed feature is the psychoadverbial insert, a phrase inserted into the middle of a sentence which serves to divulge the speaker's (or writer's) true feelings toward something or somebody without making that person or thing the overt topic of the sentence. Among the best known are *in a mazldiker sho* "in a lucky hour" = "hopefully" providing moral support; *kholile* "God forbid" = "hopefully not" instilling fear; *kin aynhore* "no evil eye" = "knock on wood" expressing pride; *lehavdl* "to be distinguished" = "shouldn't be mentioned in the same breath" signifying disdain to one of the two things compared; and *nebakh* "alas" evoking sympathy.

Yiddish today

The Nazi Holocaust decimated the Yiddish-speaking population of eastern Europe. Yiddish today is spoken by three major groups: middle and older generation eastern European-born émigrés (rapidly declining demographically), a number of leading hasidic groups (rapidly increasing demographically), and Jewish and non-Jewish youthful enthusiasts in small groups in a number of countries (gradually increasing).

FURTHER READING

Katz, D.: *Grammar of the Yiddish Language* (London: Duckworth, 1987)

Katz, D., ed.: *Origins of the Yiddish Language* (Oxford: Pergamon, 1987)

Kerler, D. B.: *The Eighteenth-Century Origins of Modern Literary Yiddish* (Oxford, D.Phil. Thesis, 1988. Published version forthcoming)

Samuel, M.: *In Praise of Yiddish* (New York: Cowles, 1971)

Weinreich, M.: *History of the Yiddish Language* (Chicago and London: University of Chicago Press, 1980)

DOVID KATZ

Yiddish humor The notion of "Yiddish humor" may refer either to the body of humor literature and folklore produced in Yiddish, or to the structure of the humor embedded in the language itself. The specificities of this latter category are a characteristic feature of Ashkenazic Jewish culture and have, to some degree, made their way into western languages, especially English, as spoken by Ashkenazim.

The rise–fall intonation (steep rise followed by slight fall, both concurrent with the final syllable of a word or phrase) supplies ready-made satire. It is frequently bolstered by an upward surge of the head and eyebrows. Typical cases are *Dos heyst a dokter*!, "This you call a doctor!" and *A fayner man*!, "Some nice fellow he is!". A more subtle variation reduces or omits the intonation, relying upon context, for example, *A groyser ekspert*! – "What an expert!".

Yiddish revels in self-deprecating humor, bordering on thinly-veiled self-psychoanalysis, in which the full extent of human foolishness or failure is unmasked by the perpetrator during nonchalant conversation. Thus, *Ikh hob es azoy gut gemakht az keyner hot nit gevolt koyfn*, "I made it so well that nobody wanted to buy any"; *Hob ikh em arayngezogt un gevizn ver iz der balebos: hot er mikh far groys shrek aroysgevorfn*, "So I told him off and showed him who is boss; out of great trepidation he threw me out"; and *Di khaverte hot mikh ibergelozt far a tsveytn hob ikh mit ir geendikt*, "My girlfriend left me for somebody else so I broke it off with her". This category is generally accompanied by a circular swoop of the index finger.

Devices for deflecting attack via humor include facetious agreement with the attacker, such as *Nu, avade bin ikh meshuge: ver vil den zayn normal?*, "Well, yes, of course I'm crazy; who would want to be normal?; *Yo, ikh bin dokh der shlekhter*, "Yes, after all I'm the bad one"; and *den* "then" and *dokh* "after all" have evolved a special function as "facetious agreement" markers. When interrogative, the arm is stretched out with the open hand facing up. When declarative, the hand faces outward.

Pros and cons of an argument are weighed up by subjecting each option to satiric attack to point up its weakness. This tack serves to invest initial attitudes to ideas and things with humor-laden skepticism, for example *Andekt Amerike*, "Discovered America!" = "That's actually been said before"; or *A khokhme!*, "A bit of wisdom" = "It's not really all that clever."

A favorite device entails enhancement or debasement of the importance of an issue. A person who has sought to dismiss a big issue by pretending it is a little issue may be debunked by *Eyn kleynikayt!* "one little thing" = "Some little thing!", which claims (with humor alongside the serious point being made) that it is big after all. A big issue is reduced to a minor problem by *A groyse mayse!*, "a big story" = "Big deal!".

In addition to devices per se, Yiddish boasts an armory of vocabulary that inherently evokes humor. Examples include *kapatsitet* "big-shot", *khevreman* "tough guy to deal with", *makharayke* "mechanical gadget, gizmo", *onshikenish* "pain in the neck" (literally "something sent onto one"). A large number of vocabulary items have humorous alternates, for instance *khasene* "wedding" vs. *khaslere* "(undesirable) wedding"; *ibertsien zikh* "move (house)" versus *iberpeklen zikh* "pick up all one's packages and move onward", *miese(r)* "ugly-looking person" versus *mieskayt* – the same but humorous.

FURTHER READING

Ausubel, N.: *A Treasury of Jewish Humor* (Garden City: Doubleday, 1951)

Freud, S.: *Jokes and their Relation to the Unconscious*, trans. J. Strachey (Harmondsworth: Penguin Books, 1983), vol. 6 of *The Pelican Freud Library*

Weinreich, U.: Notes on the rise-fall intonation contour. In M. Halle et al., eds. *For Roman Jakobson. Essays on the Occasion of his Sixtieth Birthday* (The Hague: Mouton, 1956) 633–43

DOVID KATZ

Yiddish Studies Yiddish Studies were initiated in the early sixteenth century. Pioneered by Christian humanist-inspired scholars of Hebrew and Aramaic, the early students of the language also included writers of business manuals for non-Jews, students of the German under-world language (Rotwelsch), and, anti-Semites seeking to "expose Jewish secrets". Philological remarks in the works of rabbis from the fourteenth century, and in the sixteenth-century grammatical treatises of Elijah Levita, more or less exhaust the limited extent of known early Jewish intellectual interest, although a large number of pedagogic works, including glosses and dictionaries, were compiled.

The mid-eighteenth century marks the onset of a new sophistication. Wilhelm Christian Just Chrysander published two influential books in 1750. One was a Yiddish grammar.

The nineteenth-century rise of modern comparative linguistics in Germany set the stage for modern inquiry into the origins and structure of Yiddish. The Romanian linguist Lazar Sainéan (1859–1934) and the Austrian philologist Alfred Landau (1850–1935) both demonstrated the kinship of the Germanic component of Yiddish with medieval (rather than modern) German, and the Hebrew poet Avrom Dov-Ber Mikhalishker LEBENSOHN, compared the Semitic component of Yiddish with various stages of Hebrew.

For all its advances, the approach of the "Germanists" (scholars who viewed Yiddish Studies as a satellite of Germanic linguistics) was severely limiting. At the 1908 Chernowitz Conference 23-year-old Matisyohu MIESES delivered the first scientific paper on Yiddish in which the language was studied through its own eyes, and those of the culture in which it arose. Several years later, the "Yiddishist" approach to Yiddish was formalized in the brilliant writings of Ber BOROKHOV who founded, in 1913, the "Yiddishist" school of Yiddish Studies, conceived as a self-contained science of Yiddish centered upon the language per se, rather than German, Hebrew, Slavic, or any other extraneous structure.

Following Borokhov's premature death in 1917, a number of talented young researchers, including Solomon A. BIRNBAUM, Zelig-Hirsh Kalmanovitsh (c.1885–1944), Zalmen REYZEN Nokhem SHTIF, and Max WEINREICH began to produce weighty works on the history and structure of Yiddish language and literature. Like Borokhov, Birnbaum and Weinreich were not native speakers of Yiddish. In 1925, on the initiative of Shtif and Weinreich, the Yivo, a Yiddish language academy, was established in Vilna. It is an acronym from its Yiddish name – *Yidisher visnshaftlekher institut* – and was known in English as the Yiddish Scientific Institute until its later name change, in the USA, to the Yivo Institute for Jewish Research. In the USSR special Yiddish academic units were established in Kharkov and Kiev. During the 1920s and 1930s both the Vilna and Soviet-based institutes published a prodigious number of high quality academic volumes, all of which appeared in Yiddish.

Bearing in mind that studies in Yiddish have not generally enjoyed government funding, the achievements of the field are phenomenal. Academic success can be traced in part to the Yiddishists' motivation by the linguistic nationalism characteristic of the emerging smaller European states as well as the movement for the rights of minority languages generally. Yiddish scholars have sought to trace and to analyze the history and structure of Yiddish, and its literature and folklore, as essential components of modern Jewish scholarship and contemporary Jewish culture.

Following the Nazi destruction of eastern European Jewry in its native homeland during the Second World War, Yiddish Studies, devastated, began to be re-established, first in the USA, then in Israel, and finally in Europe. The most striking growth has occurred since the late 1960s. Permanent programs in Yiddish have been endowed at a number of leading institutions, including Columbia University (New York), Hebrew University (Jerusalem), and the University of Oxford. The most frequently encountered frameworks for present-day study of Yiddish are foreign language programs; Judaic studies; general linguistics; comparative literature and any of the foregoing in the context of departments of Hebrew, German, or Slavic.

FURTHER READING

Althaus, H. P.: Yiddish. In T. A. Sebeok, ed., *Current Trends in Linguistics. Volume 9: Linguistics in Western Europe* (The Hague: Mouton, 1972) 1345–82

Katz, D.: On Yiddish, in Yiddish and for Yiddish: 500 years of Yiddish scholarship. In M. H. Gelber, ed., *Identity and Ethos. A Festschrift for Sol Liptzin on the Occasion of his 85th Birthday* (New York: Peter Lang, 1986) 23–36

DOVID KATZ

Yivo   See under YIDDISH STUDIES.

Yizhar, S. [Yizhar Smilanski] (b.1916) Israeli novelist. Yizhar was born in Rehovot, Israel. After studying at the Teachers' Seminary in Jerusalem, he worked in various high schools as teacher and principal and has lectured at a number of universities. From 1948 he served as a Mapai member of parliament and in 1965, when the party split, he joined David BEN-GURION's faction, Rafi. He retired from the Knesset in 1967.

Yizhar was born into the quintessential Second *Aliyah* family. His father, Ze'ev Smilanski, was one of its pioneers and theoreticians; his great-uncle, Moshe Smilanski, was among the founders of Rehovot and Hadera, as well as an essayist and writer, as was Moshe's brother, Meyer Smilanski (M. Siko).

Yizhar's preferred fictional genre is the short story and his one deviation from this form is the monumental novel (1,143 pages long) *Yemei Tziklag* (1958; The days of Ziklag). The rural, southern Israel landscape of Yizhar's youth finds expression in his narratives where the main vistas depicted are fields and deserts. The novel, too, is set in the south, during the Israeli

War of Independence. It occurs on the New Year (*Rosh hashanah*) and comprises the interactions between a group of battle-weary soldiers who are tired of war and object to fighting, but cannot find a way out. Their dialogues and monologues are interspersed with battle and juxtaposed with esthetically wrought scenic descriptions. The young soldiers are helpless: they fight a war they wish to stop but cannot, they seek a path that will free them from the world of their elders, but cannot find it. *The Days of Ziklag,* like Yizhar's short stories, may be categorized as "a tale of the collective" as the central characters are structured collectively and not as individuals. Yizhar's "collective protagonist" is typically characterized by indecision, fluctuating between the ethical and the intellectual, wishing to dissociate from the present, and full of regret.

Yizhar is said to be influenced by the work of A. N. Gnessin. This influence is very much in evidence in Yizhar's first story "Efrayim hozer le'aspeset" (1938; Ephraim returns to Aspeset), though even there Yizhar's own voice comes through. His narratives are replete with inner monologues, cumulative use of epithet, rather convoluted syntax combined with often extremely detailed descriptions of objects. These elements are joined to express the moment, and Yizhar's stories are more an interweaving of highlighted, fractured, yet full-blown experiences, than plot-constructed tales. The central concern of Yizhar's "collective" writing is, paradoxically, the conflict of the individual, or, more precisely, the individual's feelings, coming into contact with society's demands and mass mores. His work also addresses the cultural and ideological crisis in modern Israel.

Yizhar's published writing includes the short story collections: *Befátei Negev* (1945); *Hahorshah bagiv'ah* (1947); *Sippur Hirbet Hiz'ah* (1949); *Shishah sippurei kayitz* (1959); and *Arba'ah sippurim* (1959). Yizhar's work in English translation: *Midnight Convoy, and Other Stories* (Institute for the Translation of Hebrew Literature, 1969); "The Runaway", *The Bantam Book of Hebrew Stories*, ed. E. Spicehandler (1967); "The Prisoner", *Modern Hebrew Literature*, ed. R. Alter (1975) and *Israeli Short Stories*, ed. J. Blocker (1962); "Hauling the

Water-Tank", in *Jerusalem Quarterly* 12 (Summer 1979).

ZILLA JANE GOODMAN

Yushkevich, Semyon (1869–1927)

Russian–Jewish prose writer and dramatist. He was born and spent the major part of his life, until 1920, in Odessa, which was almost the sole fabric and background for all his work. In 1920 he emigrated to Paris, where he died. He was the most glorified Russian–Jewish writer of the pre-revolutionary era (both in the Jewish and in the non-Jewish environments). "An assimilated chronicler of disintegration" (according to a critical definition), he depicted the destruction of the traditional family and of social structures, and the products of this destruction: the Jewish upper bourgeoisie and the Jewish proletariat, prostitutes, petty thieves, and monstrous villains. These depictions often aroused the indignation of Jewish readers and theater audiences and even gave rise to accusations of anti-Semitism. The realistic manner of Yushkevich's writing harmonized (sometimes alternated) with the modernist (in the spirit of Maeterlinck or the Russian symbolists). In the 1900s he was close to Maxim Gorky, in terms not only of artistic interests but also Social-Democratic convictions. Yushkevich's main prose works include the following: the narrative tales "Raspad"; (1895–7; Disintegration, published in 1902), "Ita Gaine" (1901), "Nashi sestry" (1903; Our sisters), "Evrei" (1904; Jews), "Ulitsa" (1908; Street, published in 1911); the novel *Leon Drei* (vols 1–3, 1908–19); and the narrative tale "Epizody" (1921; Episodes). His principal dramatic works include *V gorode* (1905; In the city), *Korol* (1905; The king), *Dengi* (Money; staged in 1907), *Golod* (1906; Hunger), *Miserere* (1909), *Komediia braka* (1909; Comedy of marriage), *Mendel Spivak* (1914), *Chelovek vozdukha* (1915: A Person of the air), and *Povest o gospodine Sonkine* (1916; The tale of Mr Sonkin). Yushkevich's plays were staged in the best theaters of Russia, including the Moscow Art Theater.

FURTHER READING

Lvov-Rogachevsky, V.: *A History of Russian Jewish Literature* (Ann Arbor, Mich.: Ardis, 1979)

SHIMON MARKISH

Z

Zach, Nathan (b.1930) Poet, essayist, editor, and theater consultant. Zach has been one of the central, seminal figures in Israeli literature since the mid 1950s. Though surpassed by Yehuda AMICHAI in both productivity and popularity, Zach, more than any other poet, articulated, both in verse and in essay, the new poetics which mark Israeli poetry. In opposition to the poetics of Natan ALTERMAN and Avraham SHLONSKI which embodied the norms of Russian and French Symbolism, and was associated with the ideals of the pre-state *Yishuv*, Zach espoused a more open poetics derived from English, American, and German models and insisted upon the poet's freedom from all ideology.

Zach emigrated to Palestine early enough (1935) to have received the standard Hebrew education and acquire conversational speech patterns which are exploited in his poetry; he also read widely in both Anglo-Saxon and German modern literatures. Throughout his career he has lived in both the academic and literary worlds. A graduate of the Hebrew University, he pursued his doctoral studies and taught at the University of Essex (1968–79), and is Professor of World Literature at the Haifa University. At the same time, his literary productivity, particularly during his years in Israel, has been steady and amazingly varied. Though his first volume of poems, *Shirim rishonim* (First poems) appeared in 1955, it was his second volume, *Shirim shonim* (Various poems) which, together with his 1959 essay attacking Alterman's poetry, has had the greatest impact on Hebrew poetry. *Shirim shonim* both established a stan-

dard for the new type of poetry and set expectations for future Zach poems which the poet could not always meet, hence the critics' disappointment with some of his later poems which appeared in *Kol hehalav vehadevash* (1964; All the milk and honey), *Bimkom halom* (1966; A dream instead), *Tzefonit mizrahit* (1979; North easterly), and *Antimehikon* (1984; Hard to remember). Zach has also published a monograph on poetics (1966); a play, *The Dancing School* (1985); translations of plays and poems from English and German. As one of the editors of such journals as *Yokhani*, *Zemanim*, and *Akhshav*, Zach was influential in shaping the poetic taste of Israel after the 1950s. He was instrumental in focusing attention on such earlier modern Hebrew poets as Yàakov Steinberg, David Vogel, and Hayyim Lensky.

Although he is well known for his varied literary activities and individualistic political stances, Zach's enduring achievement lies in his individual lyric poems and the poetic idiom in which they are conveyed. Zach's style is distinctively marked by its attempt to avoid literary allusiveness, traditional prosodic forms, and direct expression of sentiments. This seemingly sparse, non-literary, almost prosaic medium, however, is carefully constructed from an array of subtle linguistic effects which exploit the intrinsic aspects of the Hebrew language or Israeli conversational Hebrew, often treated ironically or playfully. Though posing as antimetaphorical or anti-allusive, Zach is a strikingly literary poet; and though he attempts to avoid sentimentality, he is drawn to the perennial topics of the romantic poet: loneliness, lost love, the transience of experience. His "anti-romantic" poetry generates powerful emotional effects by creating dramatic situations. And though his poetry is often difficult to understand fully and is not metered, more than a few of his poems have been set to music.

Zach's poetry has elicited some of the best articles devoted to Israeli poetry, notably those published in the periodical *Siman Keriah*. A book-length monograph on his poetry has been published by Miri Baruch (*Haromantikan hamar*, 1979; The bitter romantic). A selection of his poems was translated into English (1982) as *The Static Element* by Peter Everwine and Shulamit Yasny.

ARNOLD J. BAND

Zadoc-Kahn [Zadoc Kahn] (1839–1905) Chief Rabbi of France and scholar. Zadoc-Kahn held the office of Chief Rabbi of Paris (from 1869) and subsequently of France (from 1889) at a critical stage both in the history of the Jewish community and in Franco-Jewish relations. He was tireless in his efforts to unite the divided faithful and to win back the assimilated, alienated young through educational activities. He directed and contributed to the translation of the Bible (1899–1906), and was one of the founders of *La Société Juive* and *La Revue des Études Juives* (1880). Leaving the past to the eminent contributors of the review, he devoted his eloquence to demonstrating in sermons and press articles that Judaism was a living faith, relevant to modern life, and in accord with French aspirations. This last point was severely tested in the age of the Dreyfus Affair. It is now known that Zadoc-Kahn was active behind the scenes, even encouraging his reluctant notables to speak out on anti-Semitism and secretly supporting heretics brave enough to do so, helping Zionists and immigrants, welcoming them as revitalizing forces. In public his freedom of speech and action was limited. However, oratorical skill often allowed him to turn a homily to the Czar, for example, into a utopian discourse, voicing criticism of the present by depicting the desired future.

NELLY WILSON

Zamenhof, Ludwik Lazar (1859–1917) Founder of the Esperanto language. Zamenhof was born in Bialystok, Poland, son of a language teacher, and he trained as an ophthalmologist, which profession he practiced in Warsaw. In his youth he had tried to write a Yiddish grammar, but he is said to have had, even then, the idea of an artificial international language, to improve the relations between nations. He also nurtured the idea of an international religion of peace, which he called "Hillelism", after the first-century Jewish thinker, Hillel, and his admonition "do not do to another person what you would not want to be done to you" (Babylonian Talmud, Sabbath).

In 1887 Zamenhof published an outline of his "Lingvo internacia", under the pseudonym "Doktoro Esperanto" – Dr Hopeful – which became the name of his new language. It was based upon the principal European languages, but with a simple and absolutely regular grammar, and with word-formation rules that made it possible to derive all words needed from a relatively small number of basic words. It had thus a practically unlimited possible vocabulary, and yet was easy to handle.

At one time Zamenhof appears to have thought of making Esperanto the common language of Jews from all countries who would settle in Palestine, but around 1880 Eliezer BEN-YEHUDA had already furthered the revival of HEBREW.

In 1905 the first Esperanto congress took place in France, attended by adherents from many countries. The regular congresses from then until the First World War not only raised the enthusiasm of the participants, but developed a kind of religious atmosphere.

Since then several other international languages have been proposed, most of them revisions of Esperanto, but Esperanto was the only one which survived, and still has a large number of adherents. In recent years, with the ever-growing contact between nations and the needs of multinational organizations, translations between different languages have become a problem, both technically and because of the large number of translators needed. This raised the idea of simplifying the procedure by first translating into Esperanto, and then from Esperanto to the individual languages of participant nationalitites. Information on this is to be found in the American-based quarterly "Language Problems and Language Planning" (University of Texas Press, Austin).

FURTHER READING

Gishron, J.: *Lingvo kaj religio, studio pri la frua esperantismo kun speciala atento al L. L. Zamenhof* [Language and religion, study of early esperantism, with special attention to L. L. Zamenhof] (Jerusalem: Eldonejo Sivron, 1986)

CHAIM RABIN

Zangwill, Israel (1864–1926)   British novelist and dramatist. Born in Whitechapel, London, Zangwill attended primary school in Bristol before his return to London where he attended the East London Jews' Free School. He continued his education at London University. During the 1880s Zangwill began to publish humorous short stories, and to edit an annual called *Purim*. After resigning his teaching position in 1888, he was to write a weekly column "Morour and Charousoth" for *The Jewish Standard* for the next three years. He also published his first novel *The Premier and the Painter: A Fantastic Romance* (1888) in collaboration with Louis Cowen. In 1889 Zangwill published his important article "English Judaism: A Criticism and Classification" in the *Jewish Quarterly Review* which led Judge Mayer Sulzberger, a founder of the Jewish Publication Society of America, to commission Zangwill to write a Jewish novel of general interest. By 1890, in fact, Zangwill was widely known as an English comic writer. He was the editor of *Ariel*, a journal of new humor, and this was to result in the publication of *The Batchelor's Club* (1891) which established Zangwill as a nationally known figure in England. With the publication of *Children of the Ghetto: A Study of a Peculiar People* (1892) under the patronage of Judge Sulzberger, Zangwill also became known as a Jewish novelist of considerable influence in both England and the USA.

In England *Children of the Ghetto* became a bestseller. It was the first British Jewish novel to depict the "ghetto" of the eastern European immigrant in London's East End. By the 1880s, with the increasing influx of Jewish immigrants into England and the resultant heightening of anti-Semitism, Zangwill's novel was of topical interest. He described it in an interview as a "conspectus of the whole life of the Jews of London", and was at pains to undercut the anti-Semitic imagery associated with Jewish "aliens" in England at the time. The novel, however, was not just an apology for Anglo-Jewry in the tradition of Grace AGUILAR's fiction. Zangwill's early satire's on Anglo-Jewry such as the pamphlet *Motsa kleis* (1880) and his column in *The Jewish Standard* meant that he was able, for the most part, to avoid the sentimentality associated with the apologetic Jewish novel in England. In this respect he was strongly influenced by such unapologetic writers as Amy LEVY which is especially apparent in the second half of *Children of the Ghetto*.

Although Zangwill continued to publish new humor in the 1890s he also published fiction of Jewish interest, such as *Ghetto Tragedies* (1893), a collection of short stories, and *The King of Schnorrers: Grotesques and Fantasies* (1894), a successful comic Jewish novella. Other novels published in this period, such as *The Master* (1895), about an immigrant child from Canada who becomes a famous artist and *The Mantle of Elijah* (1900) about the Boer War, have little Jewish interest. In fact, like many subsequent British Jewish writers, Zangwill pointedly demarcated his Jewish and non-Jewish fiction and this duality was most successfully articulated in his *Dreamers of the Ghetto* (1898). This work, perhaps his best, is a series of stories based on the lives of historical figures most of whom were torn between a Jewish and a non-Jewish world. As a number of critics have noted, much of *Children of the Ghetto* is concerned with this ambivalence, and Zangwill himself was divided throughout his life between a belief in the Jewish "ghetto" as the repository of Jewish spiritual values, and an ambivalent shift away from the Jewish world and Judaism.

With the successful dramatization of *Children of the Ghetto* (produced New York and London 1899), Zangwill began to write plays for both the American and English stage. The peak of his success as a playwright came with *The Melt-*

Sir Bernard Partridge Israel Zangwill. *National Portrait Gallery, London*

After 1908, Zangwill devoted most of his time and energy to unfruitful ITO activities.

Zangwill participated fully in the major debates of his day and was a well-known supporter of women's suffrage. He published nine plays in all and thirteen novels and volumes of short stories. He also published *Without Prejudice* (1894) a collection of his monthly column for the *Pall Mall Magazine* and *The Voice of Jerusalem* (1920), which is Zangwill's most important collection of articles on the Jewish question. Zangwill also published travel literature, poetry, and translations: *Selected Religious Poems of Solomon ibn Gabirol* (1923). In his day, Zangwill was an internationally known author and spokesman for world Jewry. In recent years there has been an increasing critical and historical interest in Zangwill in Europe, Israel, and the USA. Largely forgotten since the Second World War, he now looks set to regain his rightful place within Jewish historiography and English literary history.

FURTHER READING

Cesarani, D. ed.: *The Making of Modern Anglo-Jewry* (Oxford: Basil Blackwell, 1989)

Israel Zangwill: prophet of the ghetto. *Judaism* 13 no. 4 (1964)

Wohlgelernter, M. *Israel Zangwill: A Study (*New York: Columbia University Press, 1964)

BRYAN CHEYETTE

ing Pot (produced Washington, DC, 1908) whose first night included President Roosevelt in the audience. *The Melting Pot* takes as its theme the belief in the USA as "God's Crucible, the great melting-pot, where all the races of Europe are melting and re-forming". The melting away of Jewish particularism was further articulated in another play by Zangwill, *The Next Religion* (produced London, 1912), and in various essays written throughout Zangwill's life. However, at the same time as Zangwill was expressing his melting-pot theory, he published *Ghetto comedies* (1907), mainly about Anglo-Jewry. Since meeting Theodor HERZL in 1895, Zangwill was also considered one of the most prominent Zionists in England. But the rejection of Herzl's "Uganda Plan" at the seventh Zionist congress led Zangwill to found the Jewish Territorial Organization (ITO) in 1905.

Zaritsky, Yosef (1891–1985) Israeli painter. Zaritsky was a prominent figure in the development of Israeli painting, participating in most of the seminal movements in Israeli modernism by virtue of his stylistic versatility and considerable longevity. He was born in the Ukraine and studied art in Kiev, where his early association with the Suprematist movement prepared the way for his later experiments with abstraction.

In 1923 he emigrated to Palestine, where he became involved with the younger generation of artists then rebelling against the academic discipline and ideological priorities of the Bezalel School. As a leading member of the Jewish Artists Association during the 1920s, he exhibited at group shows at The Citadel, producing watercolors of Safed, Tiberias, and Jerusalem in which the landscape motifs are woven into semi-abstract compositions. Although these and later works were intensely concerned with the feel of the Israeli landscape (and the pulsations of light and shade which he felt to be its essence), Zaritsky rejected any attempt to define the "Israelness" or Jewishness of his work, preferring to see it as part of the international modern movement. In the 1930s he was involved with the Palestine Artists Group, (most of whom were influenced by Parisian abstraction at that time), producing oil paintings which he saw as being in dialogue with the work of Braque and Matisse.

In 1948 Zaritsky formed the "New Horizons" group (together with Marcel JANCO, who left shortly after), and during the 1950s the group evolved the collective style which came to be called "lyrical abstraction". Zaritsky's own work in this style has a gentle, delicate quality which seems to come more from within the artist than from the landscapes which inspired him. He was still painting in his nineties; fragile, loosely organized works which, at their best, are filled with trembling light.

FURTHER READING

Tribute to Zaritsky (Jerusalem: The Israel Museum, 1981) [exhibition catalog]

LAURA JACOBUS

Zeitlin, Solomon (b.1892) Scholar of post-biblical literature. Solomon Zeitlin was born in Russia to a family of devout Hasidim. His early studies were of a traditional nature. He was taught Talmud in Dvinsk by Rabbi Joseph Rozin (the Rogochover) and Rabbi Meir Simha.

In 1908 Zeitlin went to study at the Academy of Baron David Günzberg in St Petersburg. Here Zeitlin studied various courses in Oriental Studies and his roommate was Zalman (Rubashov) Shazar, third President of the State of Israel. Amongst his teachers at this academy were Simon DUBNOW and Judah Loeb Katznelson. In 1912 Zeitlin went to study at the École Rabbinique in Paris. While in Paris, he also took courses at the Sorbonne where one of his fellow students was Isaac Halevi Herzog, later Chief Rabbi of Israel. In the summer of 1914, Zeitlin went to Berlin, but with the outbreak of the First World War, his stay in this city became difficult, so he made his way to the USA via Denmark.

In the USA Zeitlin enrolled at Dropsie College, Philadelphia where he earned a Ph.D. in 1917 for *Megillat Ta'anit as a Source for Jewish Chronology and History in the Hellenistic and Roman Periods*. Together with a number of other distinguished American Jewish academics, Zeitlin founded the American Academy of Jewish Research in 1919. He joined the Rabbi Isaac Elchanan Theological Seminary (later to become Yeshiva University) as Professor of History, and in 1921 he became Professor of Rabbinics at Dropsie College. He held both posts until 1935 when he relinquished the post at Yeshiva University.

The main area of Zeitlin's scholarly activity was the period of the Second Commonwealth. He was particularly keen to clarify the historical background of talmudic discussion and legislation. Zeitlin soon extended his work to the literature of the Inter-Testamental period and the beginnings of Christianity. In 1942 he produced a book entitled *Who Crucified Christ?* – a book that presented a new approach to that question. He also argued that the Christ passage in Josephus was an interpolation by Eusebius (*Jewish Quarterly Review*, 1928). Zeitlin's accurate and correct use of the sources was his chief method of teaching and research.

With the discovery of the Dead Sea Scrolls in 1947, Zeitlin became the chief opponent to dating the scrolls to the Inter-Testamental period, arguing that they belonged to the medieval period.

In 1962 the first volume of his work entitled *The Rise and Fall of the Judaean State* appeared, followed by the second volume in 1967. This was a very ambitious project incorporating the political, religious, cultural, and economic development of the Second Jewish Commonwealth.

Solomon Zeitlin wrote over four hundred articles, reviews and books. In 1940 he became joint editor of the *Jewish Quarterly Review*.

FURTHER READING

Hoening, S.: *Solomon Zeitlin: Scholar Laureate; an Annotated Bibliography 1915–70, with Appreciations of his Writings* (1971)

DEBRA JANE ROSEN

Zelda See MISHKOVSKY, ZELDA.

Zephira, Bracha (b.1913)   Israeli singer. Zephira made a unique contribution to the emergence of the modern Israeli national school of composition. Born in Jerusalem to a poor Yemenite family, she was orphaned at the age of three and raised by volunteer foster families. of various ethnic groups. A musically alert child, she absorbed many of the traditional tunes she heard around her. Her talent for singing was revealed at her boarding school and she was sent for a brief period of study in Berlin. There she met the pianist Nahum Nardi, a brilliant performer and improviser, with whom she began to perform in Israel and in concert tours of Europe. This was the beginning of the exposure of western audiences to traditional eastern music, previously heard only in its own context. In 1939 Zephira severed her ties with Nardi and turned to several of the composers who had recently immigrated from Europe, and for whom she served as a welcome mediation between their purely western training and the Jewish ethnic traditions, which they could not approach directly. Paul BEN-HAIM, Oeden PARTOS, Marc LAVRY and others made transcriptions of her songs and provided her with arrangements for voice and various chamber and orchestral ensembles. Her special synthesis of east and west reached its climax with her performances with the Philharmonic orchestra. To complement the repertory she had learnt in childhood she approached members of several communities and registered their songs through her sharp musical memory. She also composed her own songs in traditional, oriental style. Her work was not that of an ethnomusicologist but of an ideologist, regarding a synthesis of east and west as the first step in the formation of a new national school of Israeli music. The special quality of her deep alto voice and her color-

ful, theatrical performances made her extremely popular with the audiences in the 1930s and 1940s. Zephira's songs were published in her autobiography, *Kolot Rabim* (Many voices).

JEHOASH HIRSHBERG

Zionism   The warm affection and concern that Jews in the Diaspora feel for the state of Israel is commonly called Zionism. Similarly, for the Jews living in Israel, the term connotes the bond that links them to Jewry abroad. The great majority of Jews today experience Zionism in this sense, as an essential ingredient of being Jewish. For the majority in Israel and the Diaspora who are not Orthodox, Jewish identity is in large part formed by the belief that the state of Israel is the Jewish state, in the sense of belonging to the Jewish people and not only to its own citizens.

Israel came into existence as the result of a different sort of Zionism from that which its existence now inspires. The ideology of Zionism, its forms of expression and its colloquial meanings, have undergone significant changes of essence and nuance since the Zionist movement was launched by Theodor HERZL nearly a century ago.

The term "Zionism", is derived from the name of a place, Zion, the site of the holy sanctuary in ancient Jerusalem. In a spiritual sense the term could aptly be used to connote the love of the land of Israel that has been built into Judaism since its ancient origins. However, the term was coined only a century ago to refer to the secular ideology of a political movement dedicated to the establishment of a Jewish state in Palestine. In this way the term came to be used primarily in relation to the *state* of Israel rather than the *land* of Israel.

The essential core of the Zionist movement was its undertaking to restore the Jewish people to national independence in its ancient homeland. Zionism forced a radical break with the spirit of religious messianism, in effect transmuting it from a religious doctrine to an instrument of secular politics. The Zionist movement harnessed Jewish yearning for the holy land, which had originated in religious belief but survived as a residual emotion among many who had abandoned the religious faith.

Conditions conducive to the rise of Jewish nationalism occurred in eastern Europe in the last two decades of the nineteenth century. Educated Jews who had been exposed to the Hebrew Enlightenment and had held high hopes for liberalization in Russia were appalled by the virulence of anti-Semitic outbreaks in 1881 and after. As pogroms spread throughout the Pale, the "enlighteners" concluded that there was no real prospect of Jewish Emancipation there. At the same time, the Jews were influenced by nationalist ferment that was rife throughout Europe. The nation rather than the individual was increasingly regarded as the proper subject of self-determination.

The most common Jewish response to anti-Semitism in Russia, Poland, and Romania was emigration to the west. Over two and a half million Jews from eastern Europe crossed the Atlantic in the three decades following the pogroms of 1881. Those who remained were for the most part attracted to Socialism. The nationalism of the socialist majority as well as the non-socialists was expressed in the form of Jewish cultural nationalism based on the Yiddish language, and rooted in the territories where they lived. Only a tiny minority of rebels saw Palestine as the land of future national reconstruction.

Leon PINSKER's *Autoemancipation* was the first Zionist tract to elicit a significant response. Pinsker's analysis pointed to the peculiar "ghost" status of the Jews as an alien minority in all the lands of their dispersion, as the cause of their persecution. He concluded that the dignity of the Jewish people in the modern world could be sustained only if it became a normal independent nation in its own territory. For Pinsker it was of little consequence where political independence might be established. However, the reception of his pamphlet quickly convinced him that only Palestine could inspire the emotional drive that might move the Jews to undertake their own emancipation.

The first aliyah: practical Zionism

Stimulated by Pinsker's pamphlet, the movement of *Hovevei Zion* (Lovers of Zion), spread branches throughout eastern Europe and beyond. *Hovevei Zion* encouraged direct settlement in Palestine as a means to personal Jewish fulfillment and national renewal. In response, the wave of immigration known as the first *aliyah* brought some 24,000 Zionist settlers to Palestine by the end of the century, doubling the Jewish population of the land.

The first *aliyah* lacked a clear political conception of the national challenge, nor did the new settlers have the means to establish a firm Jewish economic base in the country. Just as the Orthodox old *Yishuv* was dependent upon charity, so the new settlers became totally dependent on Baron Edmund de Rothschild of France to ward off bankruptcy and penury.

The first *aliyah* did make a crucial contribution to the revival of the Hebrew language, one of the most important Zionist aims, and it also attracted attention to Palestine and its possibilities. However, the economic failure of the settlers caused much skepticism about the efficacy of "practical" Zionism, as their approach was dubbed.

Zionism and western Europe

The political solution   Just when the Jews of eastern Europe were concluding that emancipation there was a forlorn illusion, in western Europe the fragile sensibility of many emancipated Jews met anti-Semitism in an altered constitution. The individual, rather than corporate Jewry, now often felt the scourge that the Zionists defined as "homelessness". The majority of Jews in the enlightened west still believed in the beneficence of universal liberalism as a guarantor for Jewish dignity. A minority, often those most assimilated and most privileged, like Theodor Herzl and his closest disciple, Max NORDAU, became convinced that anti-Semitism was ineradicable in Christian society.

In the western milieu in which liberal vistas afforded political consciousness and access, Herzl was able to coin a robust political formulation of Jewish nationalism. His seminal work, *The Jewish State*, published in 1896 in the aftermath of the Dreyfus Affair, analyzed anti-Semitism along the same lines as had Pinsker, whose work was unknown to Herzl. What Herzl added, apart from his charismatic leadership,

Settlers in Gedera, a settlement founded by BILU pioneers in 1884

was the all-important conviction that through political action a Jewish state was attainable. To this end Herzl, in 1897, established the World Zionist Organization as the political instrument of the movement. Zionism, under Herzl's inspiration, thus evolved from a political myth to a political program.

Herzl was not impressed by the haphazard efforts of the practical Zionists in Palestine. He believed that only a Jewish state recognized by the powers, displaying the flag of legal independence, would attract mass Jewish immigration to the land. Like Pinsker, Herzl did not at first see Palestine as the essential base for the Jewish state, but the Russian Jews soon convinced him that Palestine alone could muster the support of the people for the cause.

The religious problem Both the practical Zionists and the political Zionists came under fierce criticism from AHAD HA'AM, the pre-eminent Zionist thinker. Ahad Ha'am saw the crisis of Judaism as the central Jewish problem. For him the crisis of Jewry was derivative. Unlike Pinsker and Herzl, who began with the problem of

anti-Semitism, Ahad Ha'am saw the breakdown of traditional Jewish religious society in the modern world as the crux of the matter. He foresaw that Jews would continue to live in the Diaspora, which he did not negate. In his view, Jewish survival would depend on the modernization and regeneration of Jewish civilization. To this end he thought that a corps of elite pioneers, steeped in Jewish and Hebrew knowledge, should be settled in Palestine, where they would establish a spiritual center for world Jewry. From this center there would radiate cultural creativity to nourish and inspire the whole people and enable it to recapture its vitality.

From practical Zionism to Labor Zionism Throughout its history the Zionist movement was divided into many competing schools of thought as to the appropriate strategy for acquiring Jewish independence, and also as to the character of the future state to be built. Practical Zionism elicited cultural Zionism, which was in turn challenged by political Zionism. The "territorialists" doubted the importance of

825

Palestine. Another sectarian doctrine was that of the religious Zionists, who broke ranks with the anti-Zionist Orthodox mainstream, and organized to fight secularism from within the Zionist movement. Early in the twentieth century the socialist Zionists, drawing on the theories of Ber BOROKHOV, Nahman Syrkin, and others, elaborated a sophisticated version of practical Zionism, combining it with cultural and political Zionism in a synthesis prescribed by Chaim WEIZMANN. Known as labor Zionism, this was supported by Weizmann in the diplomatic arena, and led by David BEN-GURION in Palestine. It eventually became dominant in the movement, but not before it had generated considerable controversy within the socialist fold, and aroused the opposition of the revisionists led by Ze'ev Jabotinsky, who claimed to be the true heirs of Herzlian Zionism.

Anti-Zionism and assimilationism While engaged in intense internal debates the Zionists contended with the anti-Zionist convictions that were held by the majority of the people, at least until the Nazi regime came to power in Germany. The largest anti-Zionist organization, representing the majority of Polish Jewry, was the socialist *Bund*, which advocated Jewish national autonomy in Poland within a framework of socialist revolution. The Orthodox religious leadership, and in the west also the Reform movement, were both, from their differing perspectives, vehemently opposed to secularist Zionism. Above all, in the west, the leading antagonist of the Zionist program was the option of assimilation, honored in practice if not always in theory by the great majority. Assimilationist theory was most strongly adhered to by the upper-middle-class Jews of England who bitterly contested the Zionist diplomacy which, in 1917, procured the Balfour Declaration from the British government.

The Balfour Declaration, the Peel Commission, and the question of partition

Chaim Weizmann obtained this British promise of support for Zionism during the First World War, at a time when the British government considered that an alliance with the Jews might advance Britain's war aims and also its imperial interests in the Middle East. Weizmann persuaded Balfour in part by exaggerating the importance of Zionist influence within Jewry. Even after the Balfour Declaration gave its promise of British protection for Zionist development in Palestine, and after the British Mandate to govern Palestine in the Zionist interest was installed, Jewish immigration remained a mere trickle.

Arab opposition to the British incursion and to Jewish immigration under the British umbrella was constant, erupting in sporadic violence which culminated in an Arab general strike and rebellion in 1936–9. These years proved to be a historic turning point for Zionism. The Peel Commission, dispatched from London to investigate the situation in Palestine, concluded in its report in 1937 that the Zionist Mandate was unworkable, and it recommended partition of the country between Jews and Arabs.

The Zionist movement was deeply divided on the question of partition, but gradually came round to the view shared by Weizmann and Ben-Gurion that recognition of the principle of Jewish statehood by a great power such as Britain was intrinsically so valuable that it should not be rejected, even if it was held conditional on partition of the country. In the meantime, although Britain reversed its judgment on partition, the Zionists began to focus on statehood as a practical goal.

Hitherto Arab opposition had not been the primary concern of the Zionists, not because they underestimated the issue, but because they were more preoccupied by their failure to persuade Jewry that its future lay in Palestine. After 1937, since it appeared that Britain would no longer operate the Mandate in the Zionist interest, a struggle for the succession to British rule, which would inevitably involve a struggle with the Arabs, became the strategic goal of the Zionists. At the same time, with the rise of Hitler and the dire threat he posed to the Jews in Europe, Jewry was increasingly persuaded that a Jewish state was essential to save Jewish life. Between 1936 and 1948 a majority of Jews in the west became committed to supporting Zionism in the interest of rescue. It was as though Jewry remained skeptical about the validity of the Zionist ideology, while accepting its conclusions.

The birth of the State of Israel

In this period too, the center of gravity of the Zionist network of influence and authority shifted from the Diaspora to the *Yishuv*. The Jews of Palestine now began to harness institutional and communal sinews of power to embark on a self-serving struggle for independence, without detriment to their Zionist commitment on behalf of Jewry at large. The *Yishuv* now felt itself to be a vibrant new nation. Those who had transplanted themselves to Palestine with the aim of becoming a majority there were unwilling to contemplate a future status as a community under the rule of another people.

The national struggle of the *Yishuv* involved a transfer of authority within the movement from Weizmann to Ben-Gurion and from London to New York. American Jewry became the most powerful ally of the *Yishuv* in the aftermath of the Second World War, while the USA replaced Britain as the political center of Zionist support.

Ben-Gurion, the dominant leader of the *Yishuv*, piloted the people to statehood against heavy odds, despite dire contention between the majority and the dissident organizations, *Irgun* and *Lehi*. In the years 1936–48 the *Yishuv* effected a transition from Jewish powerlessness to Jewish sovereignty. The final triumph of Zionism in May 1948 resulted from Ben-Gurion's achievement in stamping his personal authority on the *Yishuv*, thereby making that revolutionary transition possible.

Zionism in the aftermath of statehood

Israel opened its gates to the survivors of the Holocaust, who were but a tragic remnant of those designated by Zionism for the task of national reconstruction. Mass immigration of Jews from the Middle East, displaced by the national struggle of the Jews and Arabs, brought to the country a population that had not been significantly involved in the Zionist drama. Israel thus forged a new nation made up of refugees rather than of idealistic Zionists choosing nationalist adventure. Nevertheless, the ideology of Zionism, in which the Diaspora was deemed to be exile, became state ideology.

In the west, where the liberal ethos continued to command confidence and where assimilation was the prevailing practice of secularist Jews, Zionist ideology had little appeal as a theory of the Jewish fate and future. But Zionism, in its new guise as shaped by the fact of Jewish statehood, became a focus of the assimilated Jewish identity. The common bond with Israel, linking Jewish communities throughout the world, in effect helped to maintain the identity of secularist Jews.

Most Orthodox Jews reconciled Zionism with religious obligation. While increasingly accepting and supporting Israel, the Orthodox continued to survive in order to be Jewish. For the secularist majority, the community of belongers rather than believers, Zionism generated a new way of being Jewish in order to survive.

FURTHER READING

Avineri, S.: *The Making of Modern Zionism* (London: Weidenfeld & Nicolson, 1981)

Avishai, B.: *The Tragedy of Zionism: Revolution and Democracy in the Land of Israel* (New York: Farrar, Straus, Giroux; London: Faber, 1985)

Gorny, Y.: *Zionism and the Arabs 1882–1948: A Study of Ideology* (Oxford: Clarendon Press, 1987)

Halpern, B.: *The Idea of the Jewish State* (2nd edn, Cambridge: Harvard University Press, 1969)

Hertzberg, A.: *The Zionist Idea: A Historical Analysis and Reader* (New York: Meridian Books, 1959)

Laqueur, W.: *A History of Zionism* (London: Weidenfeld & Nicolson, 1972)

Lucas, N.: *The Modern History of Israel* (London: Weidenfeld & Nicolson; New York: Praeger, 1975)

Vital, D.: *The Origins of Zionism* (Oxford: Clarendon Press, 1975)

———: *Zionism: The Formative Years* (Oxford: Clarendon Press, 1982)

———: *Zionism: The Crucial Phase* (Oxford: Clarendon Press, 1987)

NOAH LUCAS

Zorach, William (1887–1966) American sculptor. Born in Eurburg, Lithuania, Zorach came to the USA with his family in 1891, settling in Cleveland, Ohio. He received his first formal art training at the Cleveland Museum School of Art where he studied from 1902 until 1905. In 1907 he went to New York where he studied at the Art Students' League and the

National Academy of Design. Between 1910 and 1912 Zorach worked in Paris and in the south of France. In 1912 four of his paintings were exhibited in Paris at the annual Salon d'Automne. He returned to the USA. Throughout his early training period, Zorach was a painter who absorbed the predominant art trends of the early twentieth century, working first in a Fauvist style and then experimenting with Cubism. It was not until 1917 that he turned to sculpture, first creating carved reliefs and then moving to human and animal forms carved fully in the round. While Zorach rarely used Jewish subject matter in his early years, his method of direct carving was a skill in which Jewish craftsmen from Lithuania excelled American–Jewish sculptors such as Zorach and Chaim Gross applied the skill that had for centuries been used to decorate synagogues in eastern Europe to the carving of secular sculpture. Like many of his contemporaries, Zorach was also aware of African and other primitive arts fashioned in the direct carving method. The symmetry and frontality of many of Zorach's early sculptures reveal further influence of folk and ethnic arts that appealed to many serious artists of the period.

Angered and frustrated by the events of the Holocaust, Zorach, like a number of his fellow American–Jewish artists, later turned to Jewish subject matter as an expression of his outrage. His first works on Jewish themes such as *Head of a Prophet* (1946; Art Institute of Chicago) and *Adam* (*c*.1948; F. M. Hall Collection, University of Nebraska) were fairly representational and based on a close observation of nature. In 1949 Zorach was commissioned to submit a design for a Holocaust memorial on Riverside Drive in New York. His solution to the problem was a menorah-topped monolith with a Jewish mother and her young daughter on one side and a Jewish man on the other. The project was never realized, due to lack of adequate funding. Two heads carved in granite, *Man of Judah* (1950: Washington, DC, National Gallery of Art) and *Head of Moses* (1956; New York, Columbia University) reveal his interest in pursuing Jewish themes in the decade following the Second World War. In 1951 Zorach carved a full-sized figure of *Eve* (Hirshhorn Museum and Sculp-

ture Garden, Washington, DC). In these projects of the 1950s Zorach tended to distort and exaggerate forms in order to heighten the expressive quality of the works.

FURTHER READING

Baur, J. I.: *William Zorach* (New York: Frederick A. Praeger, 1959) [exhibition catalog]

Wingert, P. S.: *The Sculpture of William Zorach* (New York and Chicago: Pitman Publishing Corporation, 1938)

BARBARA GILBERT

Zukofsky, Louis (1904–1978) American poet and intellectual. Born in a poor Jewish neighborhood in New York City, Louis Zukofsky was to become one of the most original – although not the most well known – American poets of the twentieth century. His first language was Yiddish, and some of his early poetic efforts, such as "Poem Beginning 'The'" from *55 Poems* (1941), examine the tension between his Jewish heritage and his modern education. He wrote widely, on subjects ranging from politics to home life. His masterpiece "A", a poem in 24 complex sections published periodically throughout his career, found its material in the incidents and interests of different periods of his life. He also wrote challenging prose: his erudite *Bottom: On Shakespeare* takes Shakespeare as its starting point to consider epistemological questions of love.

His life was, in comparison with his more flamboyant friends, Ezra Pound and William Carlos Williams, quiet and studious, spent teaching and writing. His only brief alliance with any poetical movement was with Objectivism in the early 1930s. In 1939 he married composer Celia Thaew, with whom he collaborated on many projects, and with whom he raised one child, Paul. The intimacy and joy of domesticity is above all else the main concern of Zukofsky's poetry.

BIBLIOGRAPHY

All The Collected Shorter Poems, 1923–1964 (London: Jonathan Cape, 1967); *Prepositions: Collected Critical*

Essays of Louis Zukofsky (London: Rapp & Carroll, 1967)

FURTHER READING

Ahearn, B.: *Zukofsky's "A": An Introduction* (Berkeley: University of California, 1983)

Paideuma 7 (1978) [a Zukofsky memorial issue]

CHERYL WANKO

Zunz, Leopold (1794–1886)   German literary historian and scholar. Zunz was born in Detmold and educated at first by his father, then at the Samson School in Wolfenbüttel (where he was encouraged by the School's director, the noted pedagogue S. M. Ehrenburg); and later at the Wolfenbüttler *Gymnasium* where he was the first Jewish pupil. In 1815 he took up mathematical, philosophical, historical, and philological studies at the University of Berlin. Amongst his teachers were the famed classical and philological scholars Boeckh and F. A. Wolf. In 1819 Zunz was one of the founders of the short-lived *Verein für Kultur und Wissenschaft der Juden* and edited its journal *Zeitschrift für die Wissenschaft des Judentums* (1823). In later life he supported himself through teaching, journalism, and preaching; although he also received at times a modest stipend from the Berlin Jewish community, Zunz had frequently to live in near poverty. He was politically active on the liberal wing of German politics and attached exalted, almost messianic hopes to the revolution of 1848. As an active democrat he was chosen a member of the electoral council for the deputy to the Prussian and German national assemblies. He also spoke in honor of the victims of the March 1848 uprising in Berlin.

Zunz was the founder of the WISSENSCHAFT DES JUDENTUMS, one of the most influential movements in Jewish scholarship in modern times. In an essay, *Etwas über die rabbinische Literatur* (1818), Zunz published what became the manifesto of the movement. In this work he outlined what he saw as the task of the modern Jewish historian. It was, to some extent, influenced by his philological studies under Boeckh and Wolf, but the transfer to the Jewish world of scholarly techniques familiar in the Gentile world was a pioneering and fruitful endeavor. Zunz argued that Jewish literature in its entirety must be studied in a disinterested spirit, that is without reference to apologetics or matters of religious reform, not be limited to the religious tradition alone but also extended to include the natural sciences, mythology, music, jurisprudence, medicine, printing, and so on. Moreover, these manifestations of Jewish culture must not be studied in isolation from general culture but in the awareness of their interrelationship and shared influences with cognate Gentile manifestations. This approach would reveal Jewish and Hebrew literature as part of the culture of humanity. It is noteworthy that Zunz made no distinction between religious and secular writings – they were all treated indifferently as historical sources. However, historical research of this character would also testify to the past vitality of Jewish culture and thus contribute to the recognition of Jewish rights in modern society, a cause to which Zunz was ardently devoted. (Note, for example, his vigorous protest when Frederick William IV in 1841 jeopardized Jewish emancipation in Germany by attempting to give Jews the status of a separate corporation in Prussia, to be excluded from political life.) He also hoped to see Jewish studies included in the Prussian academic curriculum, but this was thwarted by the government.

Zunz's own writings concentrated on the history of liturgical and synagogal poetry and the evolution of the sermon. These writings included *Die gottesdienstlichen Vorträge der Juden* (1832) which dealt with the development of homiletic literature, based on the Midrash, the *Aggadah*, the Oral Law, and the prayer-book; *Die synagogale Poesie des Mittelalters* (1855), a study of poetry incorporated in the synagogue service and the context of this poetry; *Der Ritus des synagogalen Gottesdienstes* (1859), a conspectus of liturgical literature over two millenia; and a *Literaturgeschichte der synagogalen Poesie* (1865). He also edited and published Nachman KROCHMAL's *More nevukhei hazeman* (1851).

Zunz had no confidence in the future of Judaism. But his own work undermined this expectation and though he exercised no direct influence on any disciple, the work of such scho-lars as Heinrich GRAETZ, Moritz STEINSCHNEID-ER, Zecharias FRÄNKEL, Abraham GEIGER, and David Kaufmann is inconceivable without Zunz's stimulus.

BIBLIOGRAPHY

Gesammelte Schriften, 3 vols (Berlin: 1875–6)

FURTHER READING

Wallach, L.: *Liberty and Letters – The Thoughts of Leopold Zunz* (London: East & West Library, 1959)
Wieseltier, L.: "Etwas über die rabbinische Literatur" – Leopold Zunz and the inception of modern Jewish historiography. *History and Theory* 20 no. 2 (1981)

LIONEL KOCHAN

Zweig, Arnold (1887–1968) German writer. Born in Glogau in Lower Silesia, Zweig studied literature, history, and philosophy in Breslau, Tübingen, Munich, and Göttingen and embarked upon a career as a writer. His earliest writings reflect an interest in Jewish themes, and his early novella, "Aufzeichnungen über eine Familie Klopfer", (Notes on the Klopfer family) which is set in Palestine, indicates his early enthusiasm for Zionism. His play *Ein Ritualmord in Ungarn,* (1915; A blood libel in Hungary) presented a dramatic version of the famous Tisza Eszlar blood libel affair. The pro-Zionist expressions at the end are voiced by the figures Rabbi Akiba and the Ba'al Shem Tov in heaven. Owing to German censorship in the early days of the First World War, the play could not be produced until 1918. Under a new title, *Die Sending Semaels* (Semael's mission), it won the Kleist prize.

The impact of Martin BUBER on Arnold Zweig was decisive in terms of solidifying his commitment to Zionist tenets, as was his encounter with east European Jewry on the eastern Front, while he served in the German army during the First World War. Zweig became a contributor to Buber's *Der Jude* and for a short time, editor of the *Jüdische Rundschau* (Berlin), the German Zionist movement's newspaper. From his Zionist perspective, he wrote numerous essays, which also advocated Socialism. For example, he published in *Der Jude* a series of articles on German anti-Semitism in 1921–2, entitled "Der heutige deutsche Antisemitismus" (Contemporary German anti-Semitism), in which he viewed the gravity of contemporary German anti-Semitism as less pressing than the problems of building a Jewish society in Palestine and saving Russian Jewry. In *Das ostjüdische Antlitz* (1920; The eastern Jewish countenance), illustrated handsomely by the German Zionist artist Herman Struck, Zweig evidenced his strong romantic fascination for facets of east European Jewish life. In *Das Neue Kanaan* (1925; The new Canaan) he argued that the Jewish society in Palestine must be Socialist in order to ensure the traditional Jewish standards of social justice. He appreciated the contribution of the Orthodox Jewish segment in guaranteeing Jewish survival, and he felt that the Orthodox, as well as the native Arab population, would have to be taken fully into account by the Socialist Zionist vanguard.

In the 1920s, Zweig immersed himself in the work of Sigmund Freud and in *Caliban oder Politik und Leidenschaft* (1927; Caliban or politics and passion), he utilized Freudian teachings to devise a psychological interpretation of anti-Semitism. The publication of this work also inaugurated Zweig's well-known, 12-year-long correspondence with Freud, to whom he became very close, especially during the 1930s.

Zweig's most enduring book, *Der Streit um den Sergeanten Grischa* (1927; The case of Sergeant Grischa) is an anti-war novel, which depicts a Russian prisoner of war who is executed by the Germans after his innocence is irrefutably established. The complex issue of the rights of the individual over the collective whole, and the bureaucratic machinery of modern societies and institutions is thus placed in focus.

Immediately following the Nazi takeover, Zweig found refuge for a short time in France. Shortly thereafter, he attempted to realize his Zionist principles by moving to Palestine, and eventually he made his home in Haifa. Zweig found that the reality of the situation in the *Yishuv*, together with personal limitations, was more problematical than he ever anticipated. By 1937 he devised plans for leaving the *Yishuv* permanently. Zweig was embittered about the fact that he could not join the mainstream Hebrew culture in Jewish Palestine, since he despaired of ever mastering Hebrew. Also, his financial situation was somewhat precarious, and the struggling community in Palestine could offer only very meager assistance. Still, the outbreak of the war and other factors prevented him from departing until 1948. During the years in Haifa, Zweig gravitated further to the left politically, and he associated with communist endeavors in the *Yishuv*. He continued to write German fiction during this period.

Zweig's departure from Haifa only two months after the founding of the State of Israel, during the difficult War of Independence, was criticized severely in Zionist circles, but he had already distanced himself considerably from the particular course taken by the movement. In fact, in accordance with his communist perspective, he had begun to see Zionism as a tool of American imperialism in the 1940s. After a short stay in Prague, he was welcomed in East Berlin, where he found the recognition and prestige he had long sought. He was officially received with numerous honors, titles, and prizes by the new communist state, the German Democratic Republic. He was entrusted with the founding of the German Academy of Arts in East Berlin and became its first president (1950–3). One last controversy figured in his life, concerning his refusal to sign his name to a public condemnation of Israel by communist intellectuals in wake of the Six Day War in 1967.

FURTHER READING

Sol Liptzin, *Germany's Stepchildren* (Philadelphia: Jewish Publication Society, 1944) 281–4

MARK H. GELBER

Zweig, Stefan (1881–1942) Austrian biographer, novelist, dramatist, essayist, and poet. Zweig was born in Vienna, the son of a prosperous Jewish industrialist, and grew up in what he later described the "world of security". By the time he took a degree at the University of Vienna he was well launched on a literary career and had become a world traveler. His

Stefan Zweig

international outlook and his mission as a cultural mediator were shaped by his friendship with the Belgian poet Emile Verhaeren and the French writer and humanitarian Romain Rolland. While working at the Austrian War Archives during the First World War, Zweig was able to go to Zurich for the premiere of his pacifist play, *Jeremias* (1917; *Jeremiah*, 1922), the most important of his dramatic works.

In 1919 Zweig settled in Salzburg, and his impressive mountain home there became a shrine to his central idea, the intellectual unification of Europe, and the mecca of a cultural elite, many of whom Zweig numbered among his friends. His bibliophile pursuits promoted this most fecund period of his creativity. Zweig's move to England in 1934 marked the beginning of years of insecurity, globe-trotting, and mounting despair. Profoundly depressed by the fate of Europe, his spiritual homeland, Zweig committed suicide, together with his second wife, in Petropolis, Brazil.

Zweig the storyteller is noted for his vivid

style and psychological penetration of his characters. His work in the novella form ranges from *Die Liebe der Erika Ewald* (1904) to *Schachnovelle* (1942; *The Royal Game*, 1944). His only completed novel is *Ungeduld des Herzens* (1939; *Beware of Pity*, 1939). Rejecting any kind of nationalism, Zweig affirmed the value of the Jewish spirit in the Diaspora and spurned Zionism, but his legend *Der begrabene Leuchter* (1937; *The Buried Candelabrum*, 1937) has rightly been called "as sad an affirmation of Jewishness as ever was penned in our century" (Solomon Liptzin, *Germany's Stepchildren*, 1944).

Zweig's writings have appeared in 30 languages. He is particularly noted for his biographical esssays and *vies romancées* devoted to Marie Antoinettte, Fouché, Erasmus, Magellan, Amerigo Vespucci, Balzac, Freud, and many others. His collected poems (*Die gesammelten Gedichte*) appeared in 1924. Zweig's remarkably self-effacing autobiography *Die Welt von gestern* (1944; *The World of Yesterday*, 1943) is a brilliant and poignant evocation of European life and culture in the first half of this century.

BIBLIOGRAPHY

Jeremiah (London: G. Allen & Unwin, 1929); *The World of Yesterday* (London: Cassell & Co., 1943); *The Buried Candelabrum* (Oxford: East & West Library, 1944)

FURTHER READING

Arens, H., ed.: *Stefan Zweig: A Tribute to His Life and Work* (London: W. H. Allen, 1950)

Prater, D. A. *European of Yesterday* (Oxford: Clarendon Press, 1972)

Zweig, F. M.: *Stefan Zweig* (New York: Crowell, 1946)

HARRY ZOHN

Index

Index by Mary Norris